BUSINESS ETHICS

BUSINESS ETHICS
People, Profits, and the Planet

Kevin Gibson

Marquette University

Boston   Burr Ridge, IL   Dubuque, IA   Madison, WI   New York   San Francisco   St. Louis
Bangkok   Bogotá   Caracas   Kuala Lumpur   Lisbon   London   Madrid   Mexico City
Milan   Montreal   New Delhi   Santiago   Seoul   Singapore   Sydney   Taipei   Toronto

The McGraw·Hill Companies

Mc Graw Hill Higher Education

Published by McGraw-Hill, an imprint of The McGraw-Hill Companies, Inc., 1221 Avenue of the Americas, New York, NY 10020. Copyright © 2006. All rights reserved. No part of this publication may be reproduced or distributed in any form or by any means, or stored in a database or retrieval system, without the prior written consent of The McGraw-Hill Companies, Inc., including, but not limited to, in any network or other electronic storage or transmission, or broadcast for distance learning.

This book is printed on acid-free paper.

2 3 4 5 6 7 8 9 0 DOC/DOC 0 9 8 7 6

ISBN-13: 978-0-07-299872-6
ISBN-10: 0-07-299872-5

Editor in Chief: Emily Barrosse
Publisher: Lyn Uhl
Sponsoring Editor: Jon-David Hague
Signing Representative: Suzanne Earth
Marketing Manager: Zina Craft
Editorial Assistant: Allison Rona
Project Manager: Holly Paulsen
Manuscript Editor: Jennifer Gordon
Design Manager: Violeta Diaz
Text Designer: Amy Evans McClure
Cover Designer: Violeta Diaz
Illustrator: ElectraGraphics
Photo Research: Brian Pecko
Production Supervisor: Rich DeVitto
Media Project Manager: Ron Nelms

Composition: 10/13 Electra by ElectraGraphics, Inc.
Printing: 45# New Era Matte, R. R. Donnelley & Sons/Crawfordsville, IN

Cover: TS Lowry. *Industrial Landscape (Ashton-under-Lyne)*, 1952. Reproduced by courtesy of The Lowry Estate. Image courtesy The Lowry.

Credits: The credits section for this book begins on page 665 and is considered an extension of the copyright page.

Library of Congress Cataloging-in-Publication Data

Business ethics : people, profits, and the planet / [edited by] Kevin Gibson.
    p. cm.
  ISBN 0-07-299872-5 (alk. paper)
  1. Business ethics. 2. Social responsibility of business. 3. Corporations—Moral and ethical aspects. 4. International business enterprises—Moral and ethical aspects. 5. Corporations—Environmental aspects. 6. International business enterprises—Environmental aspects. 7. Executives—Professional ethics. 8. Corporate profits—Moral and ethical aspects. 9. Globalization—Moral and ethical aspects. 10. Globalization—Environmental aspects. I. Gibson, Kevin

HF5387.B87266 2005
174'.4—dc22

2005049609

www.mhhe.com

To Elizabeth, *sine qua non*

ABOUT THE AUTHOR

KEVIN GIBSON is an Associate Professor of Management and Associate Professor of Philosophy at Marquette University in Milwaukee, Wisconsin. He is Director of Marquette's Center for Ethics Studies. Among the things he has been paid to do are potato harvesting, bus driving, operating a spotlight at an ice show, leading an infantry platoon, corporate consulting, mediating divorce settlements, teaching, pea sorting, instructing rock climbing, bussing tables, and working on the railroad. He attributes this to the absence of a trust fund. He was a summer scholar at the Center for Advanced Study in the Behavioral Sciences at Stanford and has a master's degree in not-for-profit administration from Harvard University. His doctorate is from the Center for Values and Social Policy at the University of Colorado, Boulder. He has published extensively and is a five-time winner of the Marquette University Executive MBA Excellence in Teaching Award.

PREFACE

Business Ethics: People, Profits, and the Planet has a significantly distinct approach from the structure of standard anthologies in the area. It is based on my experience in teaching classes composed of a range of students—from people earning associate degrees to working managers to executive MBAs. It presents students with current and classic material in an interesting and coherent way; it allows instructors to survey material or concentrate on particular issues in substantial depth, and it is designed to allow students to integrate the vast resources available on the World Wide Web.

The text first looks at the forces that shape the way we do business, examining the conceptual frameworks that allow us to analyze business dealings in moral terms. It considers business relations with stakeholders, including employees, consumers, and the community at large. There is a deliberate emphasis on the global impact of business on individuals, nations, and the environment; diversity and intercultural issues; and insights raised by women and people with other cultural perspectives. The initial conceptual investigation allows readers to analyze a wide range of individual topics; for example, notions of autonomy or moral responsibility may be applied

to topics such as drug testing and consumer protection, among many others. This basis facilitates making connections and examining particular issues in a systematic way. *Business Ethics* is a primary text that can be used without supplementation, however, it can easily be complemented by information in the public domain, particularly the Internet.

I am convinced that it makes good pedagogical sense to broadly establish the context of moral decisions in business and the real-world dynamics that operate. Take, for example, the case of the space shuttle *Challenger* explosion. It could be, and often is, taken as a simple whistle-blowing case. But that ignores some of the other important features of the case. For instance, it took place in a context of a market economy where the manufacturer's contract was up for renewal. The ones making the immediate decisions were middle managers, even as there were larger institutional forces such as loyalty and obedience involved. There was a psychological push to conform with the team, and responsibility was seemingly abdicated at the leadership level. So, although it is interesting to look at the individuals making decisions in the heat of the moment, I have found it much more rewarding as a teacher to show how fertile and interesting the analysis can be when posed against a wider backdrop.

Several features make this book particularly useful as a text:

- A collection of accessible readings drawn from the best of current literature in business ethics, including gender issues, environmental concerns, and serious consideration of the potential effects of globalization. A number of seminal readings are anthologized here for the first time, including views of business from non-Western cultures, readings about objections to globalization from both wings of the political spectrum, and critical assessments about the way we in business and society make choices about the environment and animal welfare.
- Cases that invite students to do individual Web-based research. They are deliberately concise and do not bias the reader or reach a particular conclusion.

    Cases have often been used as moral tales—effectively, lessons in what we should not do. However, ethics in the real world is often more nuanced and multi-layered. The cases provide the essential facts and could be used as they stand. They also may be used as a springboard for discussion and research. For example, in the Malden Mills case, a company owner supported his workers after a devastating fire and was lionized for his actions. We can take those facts at face value, but enterprising students may find through their research that the fire occurred after the owner ignored multiple warnings from the fire department or that the firm subsequently faced bankruptcy. Most of the cases are drawn from discussions within the text (see "Cases Referenced to Readings" table of contents), but they can, of course, be used independently. The presentation of the cases gives readers an opportunity to find out how the story ends or to disagree with authors who cite the case to make a given point. Moreover, a number of cases are open-ended; for instance, the facts about World-Com and Enron are still being revealed.

- Students can be guided in their research by using the Web site associated with the text: www.mhhe.com/gibson1e. Through the Web site students are able to bring the latest information into their discussions. Teachers with Internet access in class can log onto the Web site during class time and use the links that connect to immediate video downloads. So, for example, if students are interested in the shuttle *Columbia* disaster, the instructor can follow the site links to downloads from NASA and CNN; or in the section on marketing, there is a link to the PBS *Frontline* series including the program *Merchants of Cool*—all of which can be played in real time.

- I actively embrace the potential of the Web as a pedagogical tool. Students learn in a variety of ways and through a variety of media. For instance, in talking about corporate responsibility, in the past I have used the *Exxon Valdez* case about an apparently negligent oil spill in Alaska. Several years ago I would use a made for TV movie called *Dead Ahead* to bring the story to life. However, it has a particular point of view and is pedagogically limited. Yet, today students standardly have access to the Web, and they invariably present new and interesting information including video and archived material based on very elementary Web searches. Although there is a concern that this could promote plagiarism, I have not had this problem because it is treated as research, and students have to show the source. They also have to learn that they cannot take all information at face value just because it appears on a Web site. In the last few years I have integrated Web-based research by students into the course, and it has been very successful.

This text capitalizes on the almost inexhaustible wealth of information available: Any case or resource mentioned in the readings has been given a link on www.mhhe.com/gibson1e. Thus, for example, in the David Messick and Max Bazerman reading, they use the ferry *Herald of Free Enterprise* wreck as a central discussion point. With this text, students may take the material as presented, or they could use the link on the Web site to find out more about the case and investigate the various ethical issues involved.

The text is designed to appeal to instructors of business ethics in either philosophy or business faculties. I am fortunate to have served joint appointments both at Marquette University and previously at the University of Colorado, Boulder. There are clear differences in the interests and emphases of these faculty, but at the same time I believe that we can learn a lot from each other. I have provided instructors with comprehensive teaching materials, which should go a long way toward assisting members of both disciplines to bridge the conceptual and language gaps. Thus, for example, I have found that it is difficult to discuss the practical aspects of business dealings without some reference to the business terminology of "negative externalities"—essentially, costs passed on to unknowing third parties. Philosophers, too, have concepts such as the "doctrine of double effect"—outcomes morally acceptable if they are foreseen but unintended—that can be vitally important in framing issues in business practice. For instance, a company may not mean harm to individual workers due to layoffs caused by its desire for greater profits. Integrating the language of business and philosophy is both neces-

sary and useful and allows us richer and more sophisticated discussions. Thus, the text itself draws from a number of sources and disciplines that enhance our understanding.

The textbook is designed for a 12- or 16-week term; instructors have sufficient material to do justice to topics by looking at them generally as well as the flexibility to examine the topics in much more depth. A number of the readings are deliberately short and straightforward to give teachers the option of presenting material in ways that are not intimidating to students; other readings provide subtler and richer analyses. Teachers using the supplementary instructional material along with the text will be able to individualize their courses so that they survey vital material but still concentrate on their own areas of special interest.

Part One, "The Moral Landscape of Business," moves from general considerations and abstract theory, to more immediate and practical concerns. It begins with a serious consideration of the nature and morality of free market capitalism and work. Specific readings present ethical theories, including a feminist viewpoint, a discussion of the relationship of theory to practice, and the problems and concerns that surround implementing good behavior in a business setting. An important addition to the standard curriculum is an examination of the ways in which organizations may influence individual moral decisions. My experience is that uninformed students tend to make intuitive responses, with little ability to supplement them if only given the general outlines of ethical theory. By putting individual topics in a systematic context, students have more resources to draw on when studying, say, how disputes are managed or how there is a very natural tendency to obey authority figures in an organizational setting. These lessons have a very immediate and practical application for students by helping them frame the concepts used in discussions.

Part Two deals with the ways in which we attempt to encourage or constrain the behavior of business and individuals, including another important but often-neglected dimension of business ethics: the notion of collective responsibility and role morality. This leads to a discussion of the clash between organizational and individual values and the ways in which business and law have tried to regulate conduct.

Part Three examines business in its dealings with stakeholder groups—especially employees, consumers, and the community. By grouping issues in this way, readers can see the thematic unity across topics. Hence we can take a concept like corporate paternalism, say, and apply it in a variety of settings—ranging from protecting consumers from their own poor choices or preventing workers from smoking to less obvious cases such as a firm's selective philanthropy.

The last part widens the lens of the inquiry to give a truly global perspective. I introduce non-Western views about the nature of business and issues involved in multinational dealings, including the hot topics of overseas outsourcing and sweatshops. The readings also go to the heart of the globalization debate—one that has forged an odd alliance between environmentalists and those dedicated to maintaining national sovereignty. Finally, because we all share the same planet and business has the ability to shape the environment for better or worse, we must look at the way that business considers the environment and animals. Would we be better off if the battlefield at Gettysburg were run by Disney, or if the beef industry were severely curtailed? If we do not use free market forces to make these decisions, what other means is there to decide them?

A central theme reflected throughout the text is the clear message that we are all personally responsible for our moral decisions, and we cannot abdicate or delegate that responsibility just because we are in business. The text is crafted to cause students—the professional decision-makers of the future—to pause while they integrate the moral dimension into their reasoning process. It is a relatively modest goal but one with monumental implications in today's world.

ACKNOWLEDGMENTS

This text has come about through the conscious and unconscious support and encouragement of a large number of people. Jon-David Hague, my editor at McGraw-Hill, championed the project from the very start. It would not have come about without the constant love of my wife, Elizabeth Lentini, and our children, Anna and Alex. Keith Murnighan and Max Bazerman saw potential where I saw doubt. Dale Jamieson and N. Ann Davis trained me to be a philosopher, and Jackie Colby helped me stick with it. My students taught me as much as I ever taught them, and I am grateful to them for that. I have had consistent support from my colleagues at Marquette University, especially from Bill Starr and James South. I have benefited from knowing my friends at the Milwaukee JCC.

I am grateful to Marquette University for giving me sabbatical support and for backing from the Ethics in Business Research Fund. I have had valuable research assistance from Arun Iyer and David Leichter.

I am following some very majestic footsteps in this field; Tom Donaldson was an early helper, and Pat Werhane has been an enthusiast ever since I met her. Norm Bowie, Peter French, and Daryl Koehn have guided me along the way. I am consistently surprised and delighted to have colleagues and friends in the field who are generous with their time and energy.

There are many writers represented in the text, and I am pleased to be able to promote their work. I gladly admit that it is easier to edit than to write. My writing has always benefited from helpful comments from reviewers, particularly:

David Haslett, University of Delaware

John Frederick Humphrey, Xavier University of Louisiana

Jeff Leon, University of Texas at Austin

Mark C. E. Peterson, University of Wisconsin Colleges

Michael Svoboda, Pennsylvania State University

I am happy to acknowledge the very significant contribution they have made to this text. Many others have helped in the long haul of turning a nifty idea into a practical classroom resource, especially Allison Rona, Holly Paulsen, Jennifer Gordon, Zina Craft, and Suzanne Earth.

I would also like to thank many others who probably do not know how much they contributed, if only by being decent and kind.

CONTENTS

Introduction   1

PART ONE ◆ **THE MORAL LANDSCAPE OF BUSINESS**   5

Chapter 1 ◆ **The Market System and Its Critics**   9

Elements of the Market System ◆ Rogene A. Buchholz and Sandra B. Rosenthal   13

The Invisible Hand ◆ Adam Smith   25

What Is Capitalism? ◆ Ayn Rand   27

An Egalitarian Theory of Justice ◆ John Rawls   33

Socialist Democracy ◆ Carl Cohen   39

The Right to Eat and the Duty to Work ◆ Trudy Govier   43

How Do Managers Think about Market Economies and Morality? ◆ Peter Ulrich
and Ulrich Thielemann   52

Chapter 2 ◆ **The Theoretical Backdrop of Business Ethics**   61

Thinking Ethically: A Framework for Moral Decision Making ◆ Manuel Velasquez,
Claire Andre, Thomas Shanks, S. J., and Michael J. Meyer   64

*Judging the Morality of Business Practices: The Influence of Personal Moral
Philosophies* ◆ Donelson R. Forsyth   67

Utilitarianism ◆ John Stuart Mill   76

The Ethics of Duty ◆ Immanuel Kant   83

Ethics as Virtues ◆ Aristotle   87

A Role for Virtue Ethics in the Analysis of Business Practice ◆ Daryl Koehn   91

*The Seven Habits of Highly Effective People: Restoring the Character
Ethic* ◆ Stephen R. Covey   97

Making Sense of Human Rights ◆ James W. Nickel   100

The Idea of a Female Ethic ◆ Jean Grimshaw   109

Feminist Morality and Competitive Reality: A Role for an Ethic of Care? ◆ Jeanne M. Liedtka   117

How Good a Person Do I Have to Be? ◆ Claudia Mills   133

Ethics Without the Sermon ◆ Laura L. Nash   137

Chapter 3 ◆ **Leadership, Values, and the Force of the Institution**   146

Managerial Ethical Leadership: Examples Do Matter ◆ Patrick E. Murphy and Georges Enderle   148

Ethical Leadership and the Psychology of Decision Making ◆ David M. Messick and Max H. Bazerman   158

Linking Groupthink to Unethical Behavior in Organizations ◆ Ronald R. Sims   172

Moral Mazes: Bureaucracy and Managerial Work ◆ Robert Jackall   184

Adapting Kohlberg to Enhance the Assessment of Managers' Moral Reasoning ◆ James Weber   193

Chapter 4 ◆ **The Moral Place of Corporations**   203

The Social Responsibility of Business Is to Increase Its Profits ◆ Milton Friedman   206

A Stakeholder Theory of the Modern Corporation: Kantian Capitalism ◆ R. Edward Freeman   211

PART TWO ◆ **MAKING BUSINESS MORAL**   223

Chapter 5 ◆ **Role Morality and Personal Responsibility**   225

Collective Responsibility ◆ Joel Feinberg   228

The Moral Responsibility of Corporate Executives for Disasters ◆ John D. Bishop   236

Workers as Agents and Corporate Responsibility ◆ Peter A. French   243

Contrasting Role Morality and Professional Morality ◆ Kevin Gibson   250

My View on the Pinto Affair ◆ Lee Iacocca   260

Chapter 6 ◆ **Conflicts Between Individual and Corporate Morality**   262

Changing Unethical Organizational Behavior ◆ Richard P. Nielsen   264

Some Paradoxes of Whistleblowing ◆ Michael Davis   276

Persons of the Year: 2002 ◆ *Time* Magazine, Richard Lacayo and Amanda Ripley   287

Just Pucker and Blow? An Analysis of Corporate Whistleblowers, the Duty of Care, the Duty of Loyalty, and the Sarbanes-Oxley Act ◆ Leonard M. Baynes   290

Chapter 7 ◆ **Encouraging Morality in Business**   304

Creating Ethical Corporate Structures ◆ Patrick E. Murphy   306

What Can We Learn from the U.S. Federal Sentencing Guidelines for Organizational Ethics? ◆ Dove Izraeli and Mark S. Schwartz   313

Breach of Trust: Leadership in a Market Economy ◆ Roger Leeds   325

PART THREE ◆ BUSINESS RELATIONS WITH STAKEHOLDERS — 333

Chapter 8 ◆ Employee Issues — 335

Work and Family: Should Parents Feel Guilty? ◆ Lynn Sharp Paine — 338

Rights in the Workplace: A Nozickian Argument ◆ Ian Maitland — 349

Discrimination, Harassment, and the Glass Ceiling: Women Executives as Change Agents ◆ Myrtle P. Bell, Mary E. McLaughlin, and Jennifer M. Sequeira — 353

Workplace Discrimination, Good Cause, and Color Blindness ◆ D. W. Haslett — 367

Diversity Dilemmas at Work ◆ Meg A. Bond and Jean L. Pyle — 378

Drug Testing and the Right to Privacy: Arguing the Ethics of Workplace Drug Testing ◆ Michael Cranford — 392

Chapter 9 ◆ Business and Consumers — 403

Risk Analysis and the Value of Life ◆ Claudia Mills and Douglas MacLean — 407

Paternalism in the Marketplace: Should a Salesman Be His Buyer's Keeper? ◆ James M. Ebejer and Michael J. Morden — 412

Barbie Banished from the Small Screen: The Proposed European Ban on Children's Television Advertising ◆ Janice Kang Choi — 415

The Doctrine of Double Effect, Deadly Drugs, and Business Ethics ◆ Lawrence Masek — 424

Consumer Protection—or Overprotection? ◆ Metta Winter — 431

Business on Trial: The Civil Jury and Corporate Responsibility ◆ Valerie P. Hans — 434

Chapter 10 ◆ Business and the Community — 443

Corporate Social Responsibility in the 21st Century: A View from the World's Most Successful Firms ◆ Jamie Snider, Ronald Paul Hill, and Diane Martin — 445

The Ethics of Corporate Social Responsibility and Philanthropic Ventures ◆ Myrna Wulfson — 453

Toledo: Failing to Deliver ◆ David E. Buchholz — 463

PART FOUR ◆ BUSINESS AND THE WORLD — 467

Chapter 11 ◆ Business from Other Perspectives — 469

What Can Eastern Philosophy Teach Us about Business Ethics? ◆ Daryl Koehn — 471

Business Ethics in Islamic Context ◆ Tanri Abeng — 480

Guiding Principles of Jewish Business Ethics ◆ Ronald M. Green — 484

Chapter 12 ◆ Doing Business Abroad — 492

The Price of International Business Morality: Twenty Years under the Foreign Corrupt Practices Act ◆ Jack G. Kaikati, George M. Sullivan, John M. Virgo, T. R. Carr, and Katherine S. Virgo — 495

Values in Tension: Ethics Away from Home ◆ Thomas Donaldson — 503

Ethical Dilemmas for Multinational Enterprise: A Philosophical
   Overview ◆ Richard T. De George   513

The Moral Responsibility of Multinational Corporations to Be Socially
   Responsible ◆ Patricia H. Werhane   518

Chapter 13 ◆ **The Ethics of Globalization**   524

The Lexus and the Olive Tree ◆ Thomas L. Friedman   527

Labor Standards in the Global Economy: Issues for Investors ◆ Pietra Rivoli   535

One World: One Economy ◆ Peter Singer   546

Chapter 14 ◆ **Business and the Environment**   561

People or Penguins: The Case for Optimal Pollution ◆ William F. Baxter   566

Cannibals with Forks: The Triple Bottom Line of 21st Century
   Business ◆ John Elkington   571

At the Monument to General Meade, or On the Difference Between Beliefs
   and Benefits ◆ Mark Sagoff   583

Sacrifice to Slaughter ◆ Jeremy Rifkin   595

Defending the Use of Animals by Business: Animal Liberation and Environmental
   Ethics ◆ Eric Katz   599

Shades of Green: Business, Ethics, and the Environment ◆ R. Edward Freeman,
   Jessica Pierce, and Richard Dodd   607

CASES   619

The Bhopal Disaster   620

Dow Corning and Breast Implants   621

DuPont and Benlate   622

Enron—from Pipelines to Pipedreams   624

The Exxon Valdez   627

The Ford Explorer and Firestone Tires   629

The Ford Pinto   630

Genetically Modified Foods   632

HealthSouth   634

The Herald of Free Enterprise   636

H.B. Fuller and Substance Abuse in Latin America   637

Hooters Restaurant   639

Johnson & Johnson and the Tylenol Poisonings   640

Johnson Controls   642

Love Canal   644

Malden Mills 645

McDonald's and the McLibel Case 647

McDonald's and the Stella Liebeck Scalding 648

Merck and River Blindness 650

NASA and the Challenger *Shuttle Disaster* 651

NASA and the Columbia *Shuttle Disaster* 653

Nike 655

Shell Oil in Nigeria 657

Turkish Airlines DC-10 Crash 658

WorldCom 660

Credits 665

ALTERNATIVE CONTENTS

CASES REFERENCED TO READINGS

The Bhopal Disaster   620
  De George   513
  Donaldson   503
  Elkington   571
  Freeman   211
  Friedman, M.   206
  Friedman, T.   527
  Werhane   518
Dow Corning and Breast Implants   621
  Hans   434
  Katz   599
  Murphy   306
DuPont and Benlate   622
  Feinberg   228
  Freeman et al.   607
  Hans   434
  Katz   599
  Masek   424
Enron   624
  Baynes   290
  Buchholz, R., and Rosenthal   13
  Davis   276
  Elkington   571

Grimshaw   109
Izraeli and Schwartz   313
Jackall   184
Koehn—virtues   91
Lacayo and Ripley, Time
  Persons   287
Leeds   325
Messick and Bazerman   158
Murphy   306
Murphy and Enderle   148
Nielsen   264
Sims   172
Ulrich and Thielemann   52
Weber   193
The Exxon Valdez   627
  Baxter   566
  Bishop   236
  Ebejer and Morden   412
  Elkington   571
  Feinberg   228
  Freeman   211
  Freeman et al.   607
  Friedman, M.   206

French 243
Izraeli and Schwartz 313
Mills and MacLean 407
Murphy and Enderle 148
The Ford Explorer and Firestone
Tires 629
Forsyth 67
Green 484
Hans 434
Iacocca 260
Mills and MacLean 407
The Ford Pinto 630
Bishop 236
Buchholz, R., and Rosenthal 13
Ebejer and Morden 412
Green 484
Hans 434
Iacocca 260
Mills and MacLean 407
Murphy and Enderle 148
Genetically Modified Foods 632
Elkington 571
Feinberg 228
Freeman 211
Freeman et al. 607
Friedman, M. 206
Friedman, T. 527
Katz 599
Masek 424
Nickel 100
Singer 546
Winter 431
HealthSouth 634
Baynes 290
Buchholz, R., and Rosenthal 13
Elkington 571
Jackall 184
Leeds 325
Messick and Bazerman 158

Murphy 306
Murphy and Enderle 148
Sims 172
Ulrich and Thielemann 52
Weber 193
The *Herald of Free Enterprise* 636
Bishop 236
Feinberg 228
Messick and Bazerman 158
H.B. Fuller and Substance Abuse
in Latin America 637
Abeng 480
De George 513
Donaldson 503
Ebejer and Morden 412
Elkington 571
Feinberg 228
Freeman 211
Friedman, M. 206
Koehn—virtues 91
Leeds 325
Murphy and Enderle 148
Werhane 518
Hooters Restaurant 639
Bell et al. 353
Haslett 367
Johnson & Johnson and the Tylenol
Poisonings 640
Covey 97
Feinberg 228
Forsyth 67
Freeman 211
Friedman, M. 206
Murphy 306
Murphy and Enderle 148
Weber 193
Johnson Controls 642
Bond and Pyle 378
De George 513

Donaldson   503
Feinberg   228
Freeman   211
Friedman, M.   206
Grimshaw   109
Haslett   367
Love Canal   *644*
   Baxter   566
   Ebejer and Morden   412
   Elkington   571
   Feinberg   228
   Freeman et al.   607
   Mills and MacLean   407
Malden Mills   *645*
   Covey   97
   Elkington   571
   Forsyth   67
   Freeman   211
   Friedman, M.   206
   Grimshaw   109
   Liedtka   117
   Mills   133
   Murphy and Enderle   148
   Rivoli   535
   Weber   193
   Wulfson   453
McDonald's and the McLibel Case   *647*
   Baxter   566
   Choi   415
   Donaldson   503
   Friedman, T.   527
   Rifkin   595
   Singer   546
   Winter   431
McDonald's and the Stella Liebeck
Scalding   *648*
   Ebejer and Morden   412
   Green   484
   Hans   434

Merck and River Blindness   *650*
   De George   513
   Donaldson   503
   Forsyth   67
   Freeman   211
   Friedman, M.   206
   Murphy and Enderle   148
   Liedtka   117
   Werhane   518
   Wulfson   453
NASA and the *Challenger* Shuttle
Disaster   *651*
   Baynes   290
   Bishop   236
   Davis   276
   Forsyth   67
   French   243
   Gibson   250
   Green   484
   Grimshaw   109
   Lacayo and Ripley, Time
      Persons   287
   Messick and Bazerman   158
   Murphy   306
   Nielsen   264
   Sims   172
   Ulrich and Thielemann   52
   Weber   193
NASA and the *Columbia* Shuttle
Disaster   *653*
   Bishop   236
   Davis   276
   Forsyth   67
   French   243
   Gibson   250
   Grimshaw   109
   Lacayo and Ripley, Time
      Persons   287
   Messick and Bazerman   158

Murphy   306
Nielsen   264
Sims   172
Ulrich and Thielemann   52
Weber   193
Nike   655
Abeng   480
Buchholz, R., and Rosenthal, S.   13
De George   513
Donaldson   503
Freeman   211
Friedman, M.   206
Friedman, T.   527
Koehn—Eastern   471
Rivoli   535
Singer   546
Werhane   518
Shell Oil in Nigeria   657
De George   513
Donaldson   503
Elkington   571
Freeman   211
Friedman, M.   206
Friedman, T.   527
Nickel   100

Rivoli   535
Singer   546
Werhane   518
Turkish Airlines DC-10 Crash   658
Bishop   236
Feinberg   228
French   243
WorldCom   660
Baynes   290
Buchholz, R., and Rosenthal   13
Davis   276
Forsyth   67
Gibson   250
Izraeli and Schwartz   313
Jackall   184
Lacayo and Ripley, Time
    Persons   287
Leeds   325
Messick and Bazerman   158
Murphy   306
Murphy and Enderle   148
Nielsen   264
Sims   172
Ulrich and Thielemann   52

AUTHORS REFERENCED TO CASES

Abeng   480
H.B. Fuller   637
Nike   655
Baxter   566
Exxon Valdez   627
Love Canal   644
McDonald's and McLibel   647
Baynes   290
Enron   624

HealthSouth   634
NASA *and the* Challenger   651
NASA *and the* Columbia   653
WorldCom   660
Bell et al.   353
Hooters   639
Bishop   236
The Herald of Free Enterprise   636
The Ford Pinto   630

NASA and the Challenger   651
NASA and the Columbia   653
Turkish Airlines   658
Bond and Pyle   378
Johnson Controls   642
Buchholz, R., and Rosenthal   13
Enron   624
Ford Pinto   630
HealthSouth   634
Nike   655
WorldCom   660
Choi   415
Malden Mills   645
McDonald's and McLibel   647
Covey   97
Johnson & Johnson   640
Malden Mills   645
Davis   276
Enron   624
NASA and the Challenger   651
NASA and the Columbia   653
WorldCom   660
De George   513
Bhopal   620
H.B. Fuller   637
Johnson Controls   642
Merck   650
Nike   655
Shell   657
Donaldson   503
Bhopal   620
H.B. Fuller   637
Johnson Controls   642
McDonald's and McLibel   647
Nike   655
Shell   657
Ebejer and Morden   412
Exxon Valdez   627

Ford Pinto   630
H.B. Fuller   637
Love Canal   644
McDonald's and Stella Liebeck   648
Merck   650
Elkington   571
Bhopal   620
Enron   624
Exxon Valdez   627
Genetically Modified Foods   632
HealthSouth   634
H.B. Fuller   637
Love Canal   644
Malden Mills   645
Shell   657
Feinberg   228
DuPont   622
Exxon Valdez   627
Genetically modified foods   632
H.B. Fuller   637
Herald of Free Enterprise   636
Johnson & Johnson   640
Johnson Controls   642
Love Canal   644
Turkish Airlines   658
Forsyth   67
Ford Explorer   629
Johnson & Johnson   640
Malden Mills   645
Merck   650
NASA and the Challenger   651
NASA and the Columbia   653
Freeman   211
Bhopal   620
Exxon Valdez   627
Genetically Modified Foods   632
H.B. Fuller   637
Johnson & Johnson   640

Johnson Controls   642
Malden Mills   645
Merck   650
Nike   655
Shell   657
Freeman et al.   607
DuPont   622
Exxon Valdez   627
Genetically Modified Foods   632
Love Canal   644
French   243
Exxon Valdez   627
NASA and the Challenger   651
NASA and the Columbia   653
Turkish Airlines   658
Friedman, M.   206
Bhopal   620
Exxon Valdez   627
Genetically Modified Foods   632
H.B. Fuller   637
Johnson & Johnson   640
Johnson Controls   642
Malden Mills   645
Merck   650
Nike   655
Shell   657
Friedman, T.   527
Genetically Modified Foods   632
McDonald's and McLibel   647
Nike   655
Shell   657
Gibson   250
NASA and the Challenger   651
NASA and the Columbia   653
WorldCom   660
Green   484
Ford Explorer   629
Ford Pinto   630

McDonald's and Stella Liebeck   648
NASA and the Columbia   653
Grimshaw   109
Enron   624
Johnson Controls   642
Malden Mills   645
WorldCom   660
Hans   434
Dow Corning   621
DuPont   622
Ford Explorer   629
Ford Pinto   630
McDonald's and Stella Liebeck   648
Haslett   367
Hooters   639
Johnson Controls   642
Iacocca   260
Ford Explorer   629
Ford Pinto   630
Izraeli and Schwartz   313
Enron   624
Exxon Valdez   627
WorldCom   660
Jackall   184
Enron   624
HealthSouth   634
WorldCom   660
Katz   599
Dow Corning   621
DuPont   622
Genetically Modified Foods   632
Koehn—Eastern   471
Nike   655
Koehn—Virtues   91
Enron   624
H.B. Fuller   637
Lacayo and Ripley, *Time* Persons   287
Enron   624

NASA *and the* Challenger   651
NASA *and the* Columbia   653
WorldCom   660
Leeds   325
  Enron   624
  H.B. Fuller   637
  HealthSouth   634
  WorldCom   660
Liedtka   117
  Malden Mills   645
  Merck   650
Masek   424
  DuPont   622
  Genetically Modified Foods   632
Messick and Bazerman   158
  Enron   624
  HealthSouth   634
  Herald of Free Enterprise   636
  NASA *and the* Challenger   651
  NASA *and the* Columbia   653
  WorldCom   660
Mills   133
  Malden Mills   645
  Merck   650
Mills and MacLean   407
  Exxon Valdez   627
  Ford Explorer   629
  Ford Pinto   630
  Love Canal   644
Murphy   306
  Dow Corning   621
  Enron   624
  HealthSouth   634
  Johnson & Johnson   640
  NASA *and the* Challenger   651
  NASA *and the* Columbia   653
  WorldCom   660
Murphy and Enderle   148
  Enron   624

Exxon Valdez   627
Ford Pinto   630
HealthSouth   634
H.B. Fuller   637
Johnson & Johnson   640
Malden Mills   645
Merck   650
WorldCom   660
Nickel   100
  Genetically Modified Foods   632
  Shell   657
Nielsen   264
  Enron   624
  NASA *and the* Challenger   651
  NASA *and the* Columbia   653
  WorldCom   660
Rifkin   595
  McDonald's and McLibel   647
Rivoli   535
  Malden Mills   645
  Nike   655
  Shell   657
Sims   172
  Enron   624
  HealthSouth   634
  NASA *and the* Challenger   651
  NASA *and the* Columbia   653
  WorldCom   660
Singer   546
  Genetically Modified Foods   632
  McDonald's and McLibel   647
  Nike   655
  Shell   657
Ulrich and Thielemann   52
  Enron   624
  HealthSouth   634
  NASA *and the* Challenger   651
  NASA *and the* Columbia   653
  WorldCom   660

Weber   *193*
   Enron   624
   HealthSouth   634
   Johnson & Johnson   640
   Malden Mills   645
   NASA and the Challenger   *651*
   NASA and the Columbia   *653*
   WorldCom   660
Werhane   *518*
   Bhopal   620

H.B. Fuller   637
   Merck   650
   Nike   655
   Shell   657
Winter   *431*
   Genetically Modified Foods   632
   McDonald's and McLibel   647
Wulfson   *453*
   Malden Mills   645
   Merck   650

INTRODUCTION

Doing well is the result of doing good. That's what capitalism is all about.
ADNAN KASHOGGI

Corporation, *n. An ingenious device for obtaining individual profit without individual responsibility.*
AMBROSE (GWINNETT) BIERCE, The Devil's Dictionary

The public tends to have mixed views about business. In general we realize that it is the economic engine that fuels our standard of living. Yet corporations are routinely portrayed in movies and literature as faceless predatory enterprises that care only about acquisition and profit. We tend to treat business like fire: thankful for its comfort and utility when it is under control but fearful that it could easily hurt us. Business, though, is a human artifact, chartered by society and subject to rules that people put in place. Business executives typically have discretionary authority, and individuals have the choice to align themselves with a company or to leave.

Many of us will spend proportionally more time at work than doing anything else in our lives, yet we rarely reflect on the nature of business and how it affects us and the world in which we live.

This text is about business ethics: how the concepts of good and bad, right and wrong, justice and fairness apply to business dealings. It explores basic assumptions we have about the relations among business, society, and the individual. The cornerstone of the text is that it is people who make decisions, and many of those decisions will be value laden. What this amounts to is that values are embedded in the very nature of business itself. A current adage suggests that people are in business to "add value." Here we will consider whether value may mean more than increasing profits.

As individuals, we have various kinds of personal values. Some are trivial preferences, whereas others matter more, but even those we would be willing to change for sufficient reason or compensation. But there are other values—core values—that are part of our identity. These are the ones for which we are prepared to stand up and be counted. They may literally matter more than life itself. For example, in the Second World War, thousands were prepared to sacrifice themselves for a cause in which they believed. An economic analysis alone cannot explain why people act in this way.

Warren Bennis famously said, "Managers do things right; Leaders do the right thing."[1] Authority in the workplace will get you just so far; to influence people in a significant way you have to present a vision that will inspire people to believe that what you say is important enough to move them to action. To do so, one has to use the language of values. Significant decisions, both in our personal and work lives, are rarely ascetic and neutral; rather, they reflect our largely unconscious belief systems and working assumptions about the world, and they are intimately interlaced with our values.

ETHICS AND THE LAW

One approach to business ethics is to look to the law and consider the two to be equivalent. The law provides a useful threshold of what a business should do, and certainly keeping within the law is a reasonable first step. However, there may be times when doing what is ethical means going over and above the legal requirements. For example, a firm may not have to inform employees about an impending plant closure, but it may be the ethical thing to do. Furthermore, the law is typically a reactive instrument, in that it deals with issues that have arisen and then need adjudication. From lawsuit to settled judgment after appeal is likely to take many years. This will not help us when we have immediate issues to deal with, and the law has not been settled.

Law also deals with discrete cases with a given fact pattern. If the circumstances are different, a law that applied in one case will not govern another. If there are novel or difficult circumstances, a lawyer is likely to give an opinion but

cannot absolutely guarantee what the final court judgment will be.

The American Institute of Certified Public Accountants is facing much the same issue in the wake of a number of scandals during the late 1990s. Accounting used to be a rule-governed process, where professionals could look to the appropriate provision in the code and apply it to the situation at hand—almost like an algorithm for behavior. Today there is a move in accounting to look more to the principles that support the rules. If people have to justify their actions, this approach means they have to refer to a guiding policy rather than admitting, say, that there was no rule prohibiting an action, and so they judged it acceptable.

Thus, while the law is a reasonable benchmark for ethical behavior, it does not provide answers to all the issues we face. Ethics often deals with the notorious gray area where there are no easy answers, and the options are not always good or bad but various shades of more or less morally justifiable. However, this does not mean that it is impossible to draw lines and make decisions—only that we should realize that it may be a difficult and time-consuming task. Charting an ethical course is likely to be much easier before a crisis hits than in the heat of the moment when video cameras are recording our actions.

From a legal point of view, our duties to others are quite limited; consider the sort of society that would result from only fulfilling these minimal requirements:

> A physician is under no duty to answer the call of one who is dying and might be saved, nor is anyone required to play the part of Florence Nightingale and bind up the wounds of a stranger who is bleeding to death, or to prevent a neighbor's child from hammering on a dangerous explosive . . . or cry a warning to one who is walking into the jaws of a dangerous machine. The remedy in such

---

[1] W. Bennis and J. Goldsmith, *Learning to Lead* (Reading, MA: Addison-Wesley, 1997), p. 4.

cases is left to the "higher law" and the "voice of conscience" which, in a wicked world, would seem to be singularly ineffective either to prevent harm or to compensate the victim.[2]

The question we have to face is whether the profit motive necessarily means that business ought to do any more than it needs to do in order to achieve legal compliance.

DOING GOOD AND DOING WELL

Some commentators have claimed that doing good will lead to market success. Unfortunately, while there is some anecdotal evidence in support of this idea, it is not an empirical fact and not obviously true. If it could be scientifically demonstrated, then business ethics would amount to little more than strategy. However, the lack of evidence does not, by itself, deny the proposition, and there are many in business—such as the pharmaceutical giant Merck—who take it as a fundamental axiom of profitable business. There are also those who believe that doing good is a sound bet in strategic terms. Consider two companies: one that skirts the law and engages in sharp practice while the other makes less money in the short term because it is honest in all its dealings. The argument is that once a company becomes transparent to its stakeholders, then its key asset and stock in trade is its reputation; once its credibility in the market is tarnished, it will inevitably fare badly.

We should also recognize the moral imperative: There may be times when we do the right thing, whatever the consequences. Perhaps a business issues safety gear to its workers or warns them of a layoff because it is simply the right way

to treat people. We will encounter a number of examples where business leaders have put aside the legal and strategic arguments and acted solely on the basis of morality.

THE STRUCTURE OF THE TEXT

In the book, we move progressively from the conceptual backdrop of business and ethics to individual moral positions. We look at the forces that, for better and worse, influence us at work and examine the relationship between the individual and business—for example, how much of our own moral authority do we give up to be a good team player? We then expand the range of concerns, from stakeholders—such as consumers, employees, and the community—to the wider issues about business in multinational and global terms, eventually examining the impact of business on the environment.

The text need not be read in this sequence, though; there are a variety of ways readers might choose to select and order the topics. There are representative readings from a wide range of views; some give an overview of topics whereas others go into more detail.

The cases are designed to be read in conjunction with the text, and many of them are mentioned in the readings. They are deliberately presented as short narratives sufficient to tell the story but also to let readers do their own research and derive their own lessons from the episodes. So, for example, in the *Herald of Free Enterprise* case, a ferry capsized causing almost 200 deaths because the bow door was left open when it pulled away from the dock. One interpretation is that it was the fault of the bosun, whose job included monitoring the door. Yet, it could also be argued that the firm had been cutting back on the number of employees. There is a big difference if we describe the bosun's action as "taking

---

[2] W. Prosser, *Handbook of the Law of Torts* (St. Paul, MN: West Publishing, 1971), pp. 340–41.

a nap" or as "fell asleep exhausted after a hard double shift." The authors of individual readings often use the cases to illustrate their points; the cases give additional background but at the same time encourage students to critically assess the writers' conclusions.

The readings are not an exhaustive survey of every topic that may be encountered in business, and some of the viewpoints and conclusions may be supplemented by using outside resources, including the World Wide Web. Thus, at the time of writing there have been very few indictments in the Enron, HealthSouth, or WorldCom scandals, and evidence that comes to light in a public trial may be illuminating in our moral assessment of those cases. Furthermore, there are examples used in the text—such as the European Union's proposed ban on advertising to children that was narrowly defeated since the article was published. The controversy has generated considerable press debate, though, which is a useful supplement to the text. Another instance is the Malden Mills case, where the owner was hailed as a moral hero and given a number of awards for rebuilding the plant after it burned down instead of taking the insurance money and putting people out of work. The mill had to declare bankruptcy a few years later, and many drew the conclusion that doing good does not pay. However, the firm has recently emerged from Chapter 11 with a string of government contracts. The point is that the subject matter is fluid, and some of our findings are best considered provisional until all the facts are known.

This book concentrates on the ethics of traditional for-profit businesses. Typically they exist in an environment that encourages survival, growth, and profit. Many of the same pressures exist for not-for-profit organizations, although instead of profit they look for greater efficiency: that is, increasing the amount of output for a given input. Essentially, the same kind of analysis and considerations apply. The book may also be used as an ethics text using applied examples.

It is worth bearing in mind that philosophical insights are not always instant or obvious; often they come months or years after a class, or when people are confronted with a situation that enables them to make connections that were previously too abstract or theoretical.

PART ONE

THE MORAL LANDSCAPE OF BUSINESS

W E GENERALLY BELIEVE that we are autonomous individuals, capable of exercising free will and making clear decisions. However, we do not live isolated lives; rather, we are part of various communities—work, school, home, religious organizations, and social groups. Our actions take place in a context; they have a history, a set of assumptions, and considerations. So, although we do make our own decisions, it is worthwhile to examine some background ideas that we have about the nature of the world and its causal relations.

For example, a manager may believe that there is nothing wrong with firing a worker who is not sufficiently productive. Behind that decision, though, are a number of working assumptions about, for instance, the nature of business and society, the responsibility of a business for its workers and their welfare, a company's obligation to encourage and train poor performers, and the social welfare programs that are in place. The manager is also likely to have views about what constitutes morality and the sorts of justifications that might be appropriate; for example, is she infringing on the rights of the employee or failing to respect him as a person through her actions? Is she behaving as her personal heroes would?

Thus, when we come to analyze the ethics of business, it is useful to consider the foundational ideas that frame the discussion. For example, within capitalism there has been a traditional view that corporations should properly be regarded as profit-generating vehicles whose main duty is to the investors who own them. While certainly a valid position, it is not obviously true, and it has been recently challenged by commentators who feel that a business should be responsible to all those who may be helped or harmed by its actions. To use an old adage, it is probably better to step back from time to time to sharpen an axe when cutting a tree. In the same way, in looking at the way that business acts, it is productive to initially examine our own views about nature and the role of the business enterprise. Much the same can be said in terms of our individual approach to issues of values; people do not always agree on what constitutes right and wrong, and so we ought to look at the basis of our individual beliefs before examining particular topics and cases.

Our moral decisions are also subject to a number of bedrock assumptions and psychological and institutional pressures of which we may be unaware. Magicians' card tricks often take advantage of choices we believe to be free but in fact turn out to be both unconscious and predictable. Although we cannot avoid our human nature and certain features of the way we think, we can design mechanisms to preserve our moral independence and clarity.

◆ ACTIVE AWARENESS

We should be aware of the assumptions and forces that often shape our decisions. Making them explicit will allow for discussion and justification at an abstract level; this may lead to a way of resolving issues on a more principled basis.

It may also be appropriate to institute a form of moral checks and balances so that an appointed person may be allowed to voice an opposing viewpoint without fear of reprisals. Similarly, firms could encourage peer discussion and review. Another approach would be to make some value-laden decisions more concrete by using flow-charts or decision trees so that the critical junctures are overt and can be openly discussed.

These measures may not bring unanimity to ethical issues in business, and they may not make difficult decisions easy. However, the experience of a number of successful executives suggests that having moral clarity at this fundamental level is extremely useful when dealing with urgent, complex, and novel ethical situations.

◆ OVERVIEW

Chapter 1 gives the range of social and political views that help to shape business practice and attitudes working executives hold about the nature of business and the role of individual managers. Chapter 2 presents a range of classical ethical theories that emphasize outcomes, duty and respect, rights, and character. It also questions whether there are different gender perspectives on morality and how they might be integrated into business dealings. The chapter also includes a short discussion about how good we need to be: Is it sufficient to be decent, or do we have to be moral heroes?

Chapter 3 examines the forces that may shape our behavior in the workplace. Most leaders are also followers, and being a follower may mean that our values are somewhat altered, for better or worse, by those in charge.

Chapter 4, the final chapter in Part One, presents a stark contrast of views about the fundamental nature of the corporation and management responsibility in a capitalist system; these views will resonate in various ways throughout the book. Either a corporation is essentially a morally neutral money-making vehicle for its owners, or it is a mechanism for increasing the overall welfare of everyone by acting as a benign citizen of the community and planet. Clearly, managers who adopt one approach are going to act very differently than those who adopt the other. Both have significant ethical implications for all who have an interest in the life of the corporation.

1

THE MARKET SYSTEM
AND ITS CRITICS

We must first recognize that business does not exist in isolation from the rest of society. Businesses are chartered under state and federal regulations, and there are certain expectations about business behavior. These, in turn, are based on assumptions about human society and human nature. So, for example, America has systems in place that offer something of a safety net to those who are let go by a private business, and health care is often available to those unable to afford it. These assumptions are not universal—they vary from nation to nation—and they are not necessarily self-evident. Therefore, a good starting place is to examine some of the foundational issues that support the structure of business, as it currently exists.

THE MARKET SYSTEM

The dominant economic system in the world today is capitalist. Capitalism in its ideal form involves a free market, where goods and services are offered without any centralized distribution and in response to consumer demand. Thus, the government does not order that there should be a set number of shoes or SUVs manufactured this year, nor where they should go. Consumers signal their choices by their willingness to pay and manufacturers respond: If people decide that a low carbohydrate diet is what they want, they will buy those food products and shun others, and soon the shelves will be full of what people want. In general, where individuals spend their money is considered a reasonable gauge of what they value: If consumers are willing to pay more for recycled goods or dolphin-friendly tuna, then it is a fair assumption that personal values are reflected in purchasing choice.

The market is said to work best when the consumer has

- sufficient readily available knowledge
- no impediments to open competition, such as taxes or outside regulation
- few transaction costs (the costs associated with doing a deal, not the price of the goods)

Profit as a Motive
Under this system, a firm will increase its bottom line when it provides quality goods to the market

9

at a low price. This will beat competition and spur the development of more efficient production, leading to a higher quality of life for the consumer. The incentive for development is that the firm that judges best what the market wants is rewarded by greater profits. People invest in a for-profit venture because they seek a return on their money, and under capitalism they are free to put their money wherever they find the greatest yields.

Rewards as a Motive

Individuals seeking their own best interests is considered to be beneficial. The demands that individuals make on the market in an uncoordinated way likely lead to producers offering goods and services that improve the overall welfare. Hence, a supermarket that offers a wide range of fruits and vegetables is likely to prosper, and so the firm does well by offering consumers maximum choice. Consumers and firms both act for their own best interest, yet the result benefits them both. This is the operation of the so-called invisible hand that guides the market indirectly, without outside intervention.

Just as firms look to profits, consumers want to get as much for their money as they can, and employees seek to exchange their work for the maximum reward available in the market. Some people are willing to trade monetary rewards for factors such as job satisfaction and security. Nevertheless, there is an exchange between a firm trying to hire employees at the lowest possible cost and employees looking for the best deal. This may lead to companies giving extra benefits to hire and retain desirable workers or to paying low wages in anticipation of high turnover.

The Market Requires Growth

The capitalist system encourages consumption beyond what is minimally necessary to sustain people and maintain the environment. Growth may lead to a higher quality of life for everyone. If production is highly efficient, then it may become cheaper for people to replace goods than fix them, which encourages production but also puts a burden on the vast, but finite, resources of the planet. Consider, for example, that it is easier to replace a lightbulb or CD player than to get them fixed. The broken goods are generally thrown out and dumped in a landfill.

The Market Recognizes and Rewards Merit

Under capitalism, the market reveals personal values: Fairness is a function of what we choose to reward, in the sense that if we choose to spend money on a teenage singing idol, then she is worth exactly the market she can generate. A golf celebrity may be worth $30 million in an endorsement deal if a company believes his association will bring in more than $30 million in additional profit. A company employee has to add value to warrant keeping his job: He has to justify his position by showing that what he does adds to the bottom line. There is a market for those with the most talent, and deadwood is let go.

MODIFIED CAPITALISM

Capitalism in present-day America and Europe may be modified in many ways and for a number of reasons; these reasons are explained in the following.

Government Regulation

The government regulates business in a wide variety of ways. The rationale for regulation is often that, as a matter of policy, we as a society have decided that economic concerns may have to be overridden.

Health and Safety For example, there are regulations that govern health and safety in the workplace. A strictly economic approach might suggest that workers in riskier jobs are paid a premium, and there will be a point at which the firm finds it is willing to pay more for safety equipment rather than pay "danger money." But the market mechanism to establish the point where a firm prefers paying for safety to paying compensation typically looks to economic decisions made after someone has been injured or killed. Regulation is preemptive in that it sets a standard ahead of time, and people do not have to be hurt in order to determine a firm's priorities.

Paternalistic Policy Sometimes we determine that the kind of society we want will take priority over business opportunities and even personal decisions. For example, we may restrict children from working more than a few hours a week, even if they or their parents want them to. We may also restrict the market on moral grounds by simply prohibiting certain practices — for example, by saying that it is just wrong to set up a market for human kidneys.

Stewardship Government also takes a stewardship role for business in general. Without reporting regulations, it might be difficult for investors to get trustworthy information and adequate transparency. Again, the market could be self-regulating, in that investors who get hurt by fraudulent companies would then be willing to pay more (or get a lower yield) to make sure that they were dealing with an honest company. However, as a society we have made a political decision to enforce standards rather than let them emerge through market mechanisms.

The Environment Regulations restrict economically viable development when ecological preservation and maintenance are seen as more important than generating a short-term return.

Rights Regulation may act to balance the power of an individual against a company. A company could use its resources to exploit individuals in ways that might compromise their rights. For example, a company might demand access to an individual's personal medical file. There might be good business reasons for this — the person might be a candidate for a highly stressful position where lives are at risk, for example — but there is potential for the information to be abused, and thus outside regulation might be in order.

Government Spending

The government itself is a significant provider of goods and services; it also buys tremendous amounts. Depending on the way it is measured, government spending accounts for roughly 20 percent of gross domestic product. Federal spending skews the free market in a number of ways; for example, it may be in the government's interest to preserve domestic manufacture of defense equipment rather than buying it cheaper from overseas; or safety of pharmaceuticals may matter more to a government agency than reducing cost. In a pure capitalist system, the government would probably not be such a major player in the market.

Communitarian Concerns

Libertarians hold individual choice to be paramount; they advocate the liberty to do as they choose. However, other views stress that in society we are necessarily part of a community that involves other people and that we are responsible for one another in some measure.

Socialists generally believe that in a just society we would pool our benefits and burdens, so that people are not hurt or promoted for reasons they have done nothing to deserve. For example, they would want decent universal elementary education as a right and suggest that allowing the rich a private education track gives them an unfair advantage. They would maintain that we accept restrictions on personal choice for the common good—as in the realm of security or health—and would say that there is nothing sacrosanct about individual wealth maximization.

In fact, there are always a number of people who do not do well in a market system, either because they have physical or mental challenges or because there is no demand for their skills. The policy question is whether those with means should be required to support those in need compulsorily through taxation or whether individuals left to their own devices will support others through voluntary donations. Western societies have generally chosen to build support through centralized taxation.

VIEWS OF MANAGERS

We might imagine that managers would hold virtually identical views of the nature of business and its place in the world; however, this is not so.

A central and persistent issue is whether a business is an independent enterprise, separate from the rest of life, with its own set of rules. By this view, business is thought of as predatory, profit as the dominant value, and all decisions as strategic. The contrasting view sees business as an extension of human activity and hence subject to the same moral constraints that govern other behaviors; it cannot be compartmentalized from everything else we do. This view suggests that there may be times when business should act morally by forgoing profit or taking on social responsibilities.

Of course, many businesses may mix these views, and sometimes their actions do not follow from their rhetoric. Still, it is worthwhile at the outset to look at the foundational assumptions and the rational frameworks built on those assumptions, giving us some background on the tensions that arise among business, government, and the individual.

Elements of the Market System

Rogene A. Buchholz and Sandra B. Rosenthal

We live under a capitalist economic market system. While that may seem like stating the obvious, we should recognize that it is a system: a group of independent but interrelated elements composing a unified whole. Here Buchholz and Rosenthal list 10 key elements of capitalism. Each of the individual elements has an important bearing on the conduct of businesses and individuals. For example, capitalism is grounded in ideas of private property, yet taxation and regulation may work against those ideas. Moreover, businesses are motivated to survive, grow, and make profits but doing so may put a strain on our environmental resources. Therefore, it is worthwhile for us to examine the assumptions that businesses operate under in some detail. We should not take them as self-evidently true without first subjecting them to critical scrutiny.

The market is believed to be, according to classical economic theory, the principle means by which modern Western societies organize themselves to provide goods and services people need to live and enhance their economic welfare. The market system is usually considered to be an economic system where economic wealth is created and where economic growth is promoted based upon private ownership of the means of production. The role of the corporation in this kind of system is to produce goods and services people need and want to materially enhance their lives, pay dividends to shareholders who in theory are the owners of the corporation, provide employment for people who choose to work for corporations, pay taxes to the government, and perform other economic functions that are considered to be appropriate for such an entity in the market system. In this manner, the corporation creates wealth and distributes it throughout society so people can buy the goods and services the corporation produces.

Every society has to make decisions about what to produce as far as goods and services are concerned, and in what quantities the goods and services shall be produced. Decisions also have to be made about how the goods and services that are produced shall be distributed in the society. In a market-oriented society, these decisions are made by individuals acting in their own self-interest, so it is held, and the market aggregates these individual decisions into a collective demand schedule that faces corporations. These productive mechanisms then have to meet the preferences of individual consumers who express their values by the decisions they make about the purchase of products and services that are available in the marketplace.

Thus, business organizations do not function in a vacuum but instead are part of a larger system where business activity is connected to the society as a whole and is made to serve its economic purposes. Business activity is guided by a so-called invisible hand to do what society wants done as far as production of goods and services is concerned. A corporation cannot just do as it pleases; it must be sensitive to consumer tastes and preferences so that it produces something people are willing to buy, and it must try to better the competition to make a product that can be sold at a price people are willing to pay. In this way the business can make a profit and continue in operation.

In a socialistic society, these decisions are made by a planning agency, or perhaps one should say a government bureaucracy, based on some scientific or quasi-scientific assessment of the needs of people as weighed against other needs of the society for military goods and services. The demand schedule that faces productive organizations is put together through a bureaucratic mechanism rather than a free market, and factories are given quotas to meet as far as production of goods and services is concerned. While consumers still have a choice to make relative to the purchase of the available goods and services, these choices do not affect the kinds of goods and services that are available nor the quantities that are produced. The distribution principle is from each according to one's ability and to each according to one's needs, and prices set by the bureaucracy are supposedly consistent with this principle. . . .

ELEMENTS OF THE MARKET SYSTEM

The Exchange Process

At the heart of a market system is an exchange process where goods and services are traded between the parties to a particular transaction. In a strictly barter type of situation where money is not used, goods and services are exchanged directly for other goods and services. Where money is present, it serves as an intermediate store of value in that goods and services are exchanged for money and then the same money can be used to purchase other goods and services immediately or some time in the future. Money has little or no value in and of itself, but it is valued for what it represents and what it can purchase. The use of money greatly facilitates exchange over a barter type of economy and greatly increases the number of exchange transactions that are possible.

Thus, in the market system, all kinds of exchanges between people and institutions are continually taking place. People exchange their labor for wages and salaries, and in turn exchange this money for goods in a retail establishment or for services they cannot or do not wish to provide for themselves. Investors exchange money for new stock or bond issues in a corporation, which exchanges this money for purchases of raw materials or new plant and equipment. Farmers exchange their produce for money, which may be used to buy new farm machinery or seed for the next planting.

Decisions as to whether or not to exchange one thing for another are made by individuals and institutions acting in their own self-interest as defined by them and based on the particular value they attach to the entities being exchanged. That is, people decide whether or not the item they want is of sufficient value to warrant the sacrifice of something they already have that is of value to them. Exchanges will not normally take place unless there is an increase of value to both parties of the exchange. The exchange process is usually a positive sum game as both parties believe themselves to be better off as a result of the exchange.

Based on these individual decisions in the market, then, resources are allocated according to the preferences of individuals for one kind of merchandise over another, one job over another, the stock of one corporation over another, and so forth across the entire range of choices the market offers. Thus, the values assigned to particular goods and services and the decisions that result with respect to the allocation of resources for the production and distribution of these goods and services are made through an exchange process.

Private Goods and Services

The nature of the goods and services that are exchanged is a second element of the market system. These goods and services are private in the sense they can be purchased and used by individual persons or institutions. They become the private property of the persons who obtain them and are of such a nature that they do not have to be shared with anyone else. The goods and services exchanged in the market are thus divisible into individual units and can be totally consumed and enjoyed by the people or institutions that obtain the property rights to these goods and services.

Thus, one can buy a house, a car, or a piece of furniture, and these items become one's property to enjoy and use entirely in one's own self-interest. People can also contract for or purchase services and have a legal right to expect that the services will be provided. The legal system supports this concept of property rights and enables people to enforce these rights if necessary to protect their property from unwanted encroachment by others. This social arrangement provides a degree of security for people regarding their own property and forces them, in turn, to respect the property rights of others. Thus, property rights can be assigned to the goods and services traded in the market because of their divisibility into individual units that can be privately owned and consumed.

Common Economic Value System

The value of all these entities that are exchanged in the market system is able to be expressed in common units that stem from an underlying economic value system. The worth of an individual's labor, the worth of a particular product or service, and the worth of a share of stock can all be expressed in economic terms. This is not to suggest that the fundamental value of everything is economic in nature. One person might value a particular piece of residential property because of the view it commands of the surrounding countryside, thus making the aesthetic value of the property of primary concern. Another person might desire a particular art object because of its religious value in reminding that person of certain events that are important in the history of the religion to which he or she belongs. But, in order for exchange to take place where money is involved, these other values eventually have to be translated into economic values.

This economic value system thus serves as a common denominator in that the worth of everything can be expressed in a common unit of exchange, such as dollars and cents in our society. The terms on which an object can be acquired in the marketplace reflect the collectivization of subjective evaluations of the worth of that object to many different people. This fact facilitates the exchange process and makes it possible for individuals to assess trade-offs much more easily than if such a common denominator were not available. People can make an informal benefit-cost analysis when making a decision in the marketplace by comparing the benefits a good or service will provide with the costs involved in acquiring the product or service. People enter a store, for example, with money they have earned or will earn and assess the price of the goods available by comparing the benefits these goods will provide to the real costs (the effort involved in earning the money) of obtaining them. Since both sides of this benefit-cost equation are expressed in the same units, this assessment can be made rather easily.

This common value system allows a society to allocate its resources according to the collective preferences of its members. All the diverse values that people hold in relation to private goods and services are aggregated through the market system into a collective demand schedule. If a particular product is not valued very highly by great numbers of people, aggregate demand for that product will not be very high and its price will have to be low in order for it to be sold, if it can be sold at all. Thus, not many resources will be used for its production and it may eventually disappear from the market altogether.

Depending on general economic conditions, if a particular job is valued very highly by society and the people who can perform the job are scarce relative to demand, the wage or salary paid to perform the job will have to be high to attract people to perform the job. Resources are thus allocated according to the values of society as expressed through the exchange process. Resources will go where the price, wage and salary, and return on investment are highest, all other things being equal, and are thus allocated to their most productive use where they can be combined to produce the greatest wealth for society in comparison with other alternatives.

Self-Interest

People are free in a market economy, according to traditional theory, to use their property, choose their occupation, and strive for economic gain in any way they choose, subject, of course, to limitations that may be necessary to protect the right of all people to do the same thing. Society may also place limitations on the use of property and choice of occupation because of moral standards or because of other reasons that are believed to be important enough to override market forces. The selling of drugs, for example, is illegal, even though there is a huge market for them in most countries. The same is true for other uses of property for purposes that are not seen as contributing to the welfare or real wealth of society. A strict libertarian approach to the use of property, however, would oppose these latter types of restrictions.

The pursuit of self-interest is assumed to be a universal principle of human behavior, with a powerful advantage, as far as motivation is concerned, over other forms of human behavior. The pursuit of one's own interest is believed to elicit far more energy and creativity from human beings than would the pursuit of someone else's interests, especially under coercive conditions. Not only is it difficult to determine what the interests of other people are, in most cases; it is also difficult to find a way to sustain a high level of motivation if much of the effort one expends goes for the benefit of other people.

The definition of self-interest in a market economy is not provided by government for all its citizens but by each individual participating in the exchange process. If the self-interest of an individual were defined by someone else, the concept would have no meaning. Thus, self-interest is an individual concept. Yet, within a market system, the definition of self-interest is not completely arbitrary, depending on the whims of each individual. The existence of a common underlying economic value system makes the definition of self-interest take on a certain economic rationality.

If one is engaged in some aspect of the productive process, economic rationality dictates that self-interest consists of maximizing one's return on his or her investment. Entrepreneurs are expected to maximize profits, investors to maximize their returns in the stock market, and sellers of labor are expected to obtain the most advantageous terms for themselves. On the consumption end of the process, consumers are expected to maximize satisfaction to themselves through their purchases of goods and services in the marketplace. If one were to seek the lowest return on investment or the least satisfaction from goods and services, this would not be viewed as rational behavior under normal circumstances, and one might be a candidate for a mental health clinic if such an irrational pursuit of self-interest persisted.

The Invisible Hand

Resources are allocated in a market system by an invisible hand, which is something of a mythological concept, but one that is a crucial element of a market system. There is no supreme authority in government such as a planning commission that makes decisions for the society as a whole about what goods and services get produced and in what quantities, and allocates resources accordingly. These decisions are made by the individuals who participate in the marketplace and express their preferences as based on their self-interest. These preferences are aggregated by the market and, if strong enough relative to particular goods and services, elicit a response from the productive mechanism of society to supply the goods and services desired.

The invisible hand consists of the forces of supply and demand that result from the aggregation of individual decisions by producers and consumers in the marketplace. Resources are allocated to their most productive use as defined by these individuals collectively. According to Adam Smith, society as a whole benefits more from this kind of a resource allocation process than if someone were to consciously try to determine the best interests of society. Pursuit of one's own selfish ends, without outside interference, is believed to result in the greatest good for the greatest number of people. Thus, the market system is given a utilitarian justification as far as ethics is concerned. . . .

Economic Roles

The marketplace requires certain roles to be performed in order for it to function. All of these roles have an economic character to them. People can be producers who take raw materials and give them utility by producing something that will sell on the market, consumers who buy these goods and services for their use, investors who provide capital for the producers, or employees who work for producers and receive wages or salaries in exchange for their contributions to the production process. All of these roles are vital to the functioning of a market system. They are called economic roles because people are thought to be pursuing their economic self-interest in performing them. There are other important roles to be performed in society, of course, but economic roles are by and large dominant in a society organized around free market principles, where people spend most of their time pursuing economic interests.

Consumer Sovereignty

The most important economic role in a market system, however, is supposedly performed by the consumer. At least in theory, consumers, through their choices in the marketplace, guide the productive apparatus of society and collectively decide what goods and services get produced and in what quantities. When there is enough demand for a product, resources will be allocated for its production. If there is not enough demand, the product will not be produced and resources will go elsewhere.

Consumer sovereignty is not to be confused with consumer choice. In any society, consumers always have a choice to purchase or not purchase the products that confront them in the marketplace. Consumer choice exists in a totally planned economy. But consumer sovereignty implies that the range of products with which consumers are confronted is also a function of their decisions, and not the decisions of a central planning authority. Thus, consumers are ultimately sovereign over the entire system.

There are those who would argue that consumer sovereignty in today's marketplace is a fiction, that consumers are manipulated by advertising, packaging, promotional devices, and other sales techniques to buy a particular product. Sometimes this manipulation is said to be so subtle that the consumer is unaware of the factors influencing his or her decision. Thus, the demand function itself, so it is maintained, has come under control of corporations and consumer sovereignty is a myth. Producers are sovereign over the system, and consumers are made to respond to the producers' decisions about what to produce.[1]

While there may be some truth to these views, they do not constitute the whole truth. It is hard to believe that consumers are totally manipulated by these techniques. They still have to make choices among competing products, and the producers selling these products are all trying to manipulate the consumers. In the final analysis, the individual consumer is still responsible for his or her decision, and undoubtedly many factors besides the particular sales techniques employed by a company influence the purchase decision. In the absence of a central authority making production decisions for the entire society, it is safe to assume that some degree of consumer sovereignty exists. As long as there are competing products or acceptable substitutes, some products may not sell well enough to justify continued production. Thus, they disappear from the marketplace, not because producers desire to remove them, but because consumers have decided not to buy them in sufficient quantities.

Profits as Reward

The reason products disappear when they do not sell is because there is no profit to be made. Profits are the lifeblood of a business organization, and without profits, a business organization normally cannot survive. Profits are a reward to the business organization or entrepreneur for the risks that have been taken in producing a good or service for the market. If the management of a business organization guesses incorrectly and produces something people do not want and cannot be persuaded to buy, the market is a stern taskmaster, as no rewards will be received for this effort. Thus, the product will be removed from the market.

Profits are also a reward for combining resources efficiently to be able to meet or beat the competition in producing a product for which there is a demand. Some entrepreneurs may be able to pay lower wages or employ a more efficient technology or have some other competitive advantage. Thus, a lower price can be charged and high-cost producers are driven from the market. This effort is rewarded with increased profits as society benefits from having its resources used more efficiently.

Business as the Major Institution

The major institutional actor in the market system is the business organization that is driven by the profit motive to produce goods and services to meet consumer demand. This is not to suggest that business is the only institution that is producing something useful for society. Hospitals provide medical services and governments produce a wide range of goods and services for citizens. But these other institutions are not driven by the profit motive as business is and cannot offer the full range of goods and services that business can when functioning in a market economy. The business organization is the primary productive institution in a market economy, and most of the decisions about the allocation of society's resources for the production of private goods and services are made by the business institution.

Operating Principles

The primary operating principles that are used to measure performance in a market system are concepts such as efficiency, productivity, and growth. These are basic concepts to the operation of a market system and are given a specific economic meaning in order to judge performance. There are quantitative measures for these concepts, and while they may be imprecise in many respects, these measures at least provide some idea as to how well the market system is functioning. If economic growth is declining or negative, for example, the economy is judged to be functioning poorly, and policy measures are taken to try and correct this deficiency. These principles are thus crucial to the operation of a market system, and good performance along these dimensions of efficiency, productivity, and growth helps a great deal to make market outcomes acceptable to society. . . .

. . . The traditional view of ethics and business subsumes ethics under marketplace performance and does not necessitate any conscious ethical considerations of business's responsibilities to society other than successful economic performance. Ethics is totally captured by the notion of economizing, which can be promoted by the development of scientific principles related to an efficient combination of resources. . . .

PROBLEMS WITH THE MARKET

There are many problems with this approach to ethical behavior in relation to markets. For one thing, markets are not perfectly competitive and do not function as economic theory would have us believe. There are many problems with competition in the real world that have to be dealt with in order to keep the system going. Market systems also enshrine property rights at the expense of human rights to safety and health and equal opportunity, for example, problems that are dealt with by legislation and regulation. Finally, there is difficulty with the way externalities such as pollution and other environmental problems are treated in a market system.

Competition

The ideal form of competition is pure competition, where the industry is not concentrated, where there are insignificant barriers to entry, and no product differentiations exist. In this kind of competitive system, the firm has no other choice but to meet the competition, since buyers and sellers are so small that they have no influence over the market, thus ensuring that the forces of supply and demand alone determine market outcomes. In this kind of context, competition will cause resources to be allocated in the most efficient manner, thus minimizing the cost of products and benefiting the consumer.

In practice, completely unregulated markets tend toward concentration, as competition in any industry is never perfectly balanced. If the object is to win out over competitors, as is true in a market system, the natural expectation is that eventually one or a few firms will come to dominate their industries because they were better competitors or were lucky enough to be in the right place at the right time with the right products. Thus, most industries in today's economy are oligopolistic, containing a few large firms that recognize the impact of their actions on rivals and therefore on the market as a whole. In an oligopolistic system, firms deal with each other more or less directly and take into account the effect of their actions on each other. What they do depends very much on how their rivals are expected to react. Oligopolistic firms adjust prices in response to changing market conditions or to changes introduced by rivals in the industry.

Modern large corporations are not simply passive responders to the impersonal forces of supply and demand over which they have no control. These large firms do have some degree of economic power and some influence in the marketplace. Economic power can be understood as the ability to control markets by the reduction of competition through concentration. Thus, markets may fall if the dominant firms in an industry are allowed to engage in collusive actions to maintain prices or interfere with the workings of supply and demand and the price mechanism in some other fashion. For these reasons, the society saw fit to establish antitrust laws to deal with this problem of concentration.

The purpose of these antitrust laws is to limit the economic power of large corporations that can control markets by reducing competition through concentration. The role of government is to maintain something called a "workable competition" on the theory that resources are allocated more efficiently and prices are lower in a competitive system than one dominated by large corporations. Workable competition refers to a system where there is reasonably free entry into most markets, no more than moderate concentration, and an ample number of buyers and sellers in most markets. The government accomplishes this goal by enforcing policies that deal with the size of corporations and the structure of the industries in which they function.

The competitive process is thus not a natural mechanistic process that maintains itself indefinitely. It is not some mechanistic process that automatically holds the economic power of atomic corporations in check through forces that are beyond the control of any economic actor. Rather, competition is something that the community strives to maintain because it is a community-held value, one that the community views as essential for the enhancement of its welfare. The

realization of this value is an achievement of society, not a naturally given fact embedded in a certain kind of economic system.

Furthermore, competitive behavior tends to sink to the lowest common denominator in an unregulated market system. If the object is again to win in terms of market share or profits or some other economic indicator, there is always likely to be one or more competitors that will engage in predatory or anticompetitive practices to destroy the competition in an effort to emerge as the sole victor. If these unethical practices do allow the perpetrator to succeed, these practices will have to be engaged in by all competitors if they are to stay in business and compete successfully.

For example, suppose a competitor begins to mislead the public in its advertising as to the health benefits its product provides and gains a larger market share as a result of this strategy because the public believes its claims and has no way of sorting out the truth regarding its advertising. Then all competitors will have to engage in the same kind of misleading advertising to stay competitive, and will have to tout the health benefits of their products and most likely exaggerate these claims to counter the effects of the advertising being done by their competitors. The conduct of the companies involved will then sink to the lowest common denominator, as ethical behavior is not necessarily rewarded in an unregulated market system.

Thus, the government passes regulations related to truth in advertising and food labeling to deal with this situation. The antitrust laws also deal with corporate conduct in addition to structure and promote fair competition by making certain forms of anticompetitive practices such as price fixing and price discrimination illegal. These practices, if allowed to continue, could eventually destroy the system and destroy trust in the fairness of competition.

The business community itself has a common interest in keeping the competitive game going.

No matter how strongly various members of this community may object to specific legislative and regulatory requirements and decisions by the courts, they all hold the common value of maintaining a competitive system and doing what is necessary to keep the game going. They have no interest in letting the game degenerate into a free-for-all where anything goes and the system eventually is destroyed. Determining what is necessary to keep the game going is an ongoing, experimental enterprise involving the entire society.

Property Rights

The market system is also based on the assumption that property rights override all other rights, and that people's right to use their property in their best interests takes precedence over other human rights related to safe workplaces, equal opportunity, safe products, and other such human concerns. The owners of capital or their representatives should be able to hire whom they please, produce products that have whatever level of safety they deem appropriate, and provide for the safety and health of their work force in whatever ways they please. If these concerns are consistent with earning profits, then they are likely to be given consideration. If they are not, human rights are subservient to property rights, and any interference by some external force to see that human rights are respected interferes with an efficient allocation of resources.

The market is based on a libertarian view of justice in that people should be free to use their property to advance their own interests, and concerns for social justice are of no importance. Thus, if the market system produces vast inequalities in income and wealth, these are considered appropriate if they are the result of an efficient use of property. This view of the market is consistent with the utilitarian justification given by Adam Smith, for a utilitarian view of ethics is indifferent concerning the way in which the good

is distributed. . . . The total good produced is what is important, not how it is distributed.

This emphasis on property rights causes problems when other groups in society begin to assert their rights, such as rights to be treated equally in the workplace with respect to hiring and promotion decisions, rights of consumers to safe products, rights of workers to hazard-free workplaces, and rights of employees to know when managers are considering closing of plants, to name only a few. Thus, over the past several years, these human rights, as they are called, have taken precedence over property rights, and there have been continual clashes over these rights that are difficult to resolve. There are also continual debates in our society over the scope and extent of entitlement programs that redistribute wealth in our society.

Externalities

Finally, when it comes to externalities such as environmental problems, the market does not respond very well if left to its own devices. The term *externality* is often used to refer to this condition and generally means that a third party who is not involved in the exchange is unintentionally harmed. The consenting parties to the transaction are able to damage the third party without compensating it; thus, the exchange does not adequately reflect the true costs to society. If a river is polluted and the fish are unsafe to eat and the water unsafe to swim in because of transactions between producers and consumers who have an interest in the lowest prices possible and want to dump environmental costs onto someone else, third parties who may not have been involved in any transactions with the producers have to pay the costs in that they may not be able to fish in the river anymore and swimming may be prohibited because it is unsafe.

There is no way the value of the environment or any of its components can be determined through a market process, since there is nothing to be exchanged. People cannot take a piece of dirty air, for example, and exchange it for a piece of clean air on the market, at least given the current state of technology. Some might want to argue that certain environmental goods could be provided through marketplace transactions. Suppose, for example, the market offered a consumer a choice of two automobiles in a dealer's showroom that are identical in all respects, even as to gas mileage. The only difference is that one car has pollution-control equipment to reduce emissions of pollutants from the exhaust while the other car has no such equipment. The car with the pollution-control equipment sells for $500 more than the other.

If a person values clean air, it could be argued that he or she would choose the more expensive car to reduce air pollution. However, such a decision would be totally irrational from a strictly economic point of view. The impact that one car out of all the millions on the road will have on air pollution is infinitesimal—it cannot even be measured. Thus, there is no relationship in this kind of decision between costs and benefits—one would, in effect, be getting nothing for one's money unless one could assume that many other people would make the same decision. Such actions, however, assume a common value for clean air that doesn't exist. Thus, the market never offers consumers this kind of choice. Automobile manufacturers know that pollution-control equipment won't sell in an unregulated market.

Moreover, there is another side to the coin. If enough people in a given area did buy the more expensive car so that the air was significantly cleaner, there would be a powerful incentive for others to be free riders. Again, the impact of any one car would not alter the character of the air over a region. One would be tempted to buy the polluting car for a cheaper price and be a free rider by enjoying the same amount of clean air

as everyone else and not paying a cent for its provision. Thus, there is kind of a double-whammy effect on the ability of a market mechanism to respond to environmental concerns that renders it ineffective as far as externalities are concerned.

Some call this inability of market systems to respond to environmental pollution and degradation as market failure, but to use this term is not entirely accurate. Market systems were not designed to factor in environmental costs and it is not fair to blame the system for not doing something for which it was not designed. Property rights are not appropriately assigned as regards the environment, and nature often lacks a discrete owner to look after its interests. The rights of nature can be violated by market exchanges, and as a common property resource, nature can be overused and degraded as it is subject to the tragedy of the commons.

Environmental degradation and pollution are external to normal market processes and are not taken into account in the price mechanism unless these costs are determined by some other process and imposed on the market system. The market system by itself cannot determine the value of the environment and determine the price of clean air or the value of preserving a particular piece of wilderness area in its natural state. These decisions have to be made through some other process and imposed on the market system in order for these values to be internalized and reflect themselves in market decisions. The ecological functions of environmental entities have no value as far as the market is concerned. It is only their economic utility or instrumental value that is of importance in a market economy.

Market systems evolved to serve human needs and wants; they are not constructed to protect the environment. The environment is treated as a source of raw materials to be used in the production process and as a bottomless sink in which to dispose of waste materials. The environment has no value in and of itself, but it is only worth something as it can be used to serve some human purpose such as enhancing living standards through the creation of more and more economic wealth. Market systems are limited in their scope and cannot be used to determine the value of the environment or any of its components.

A tree in the Amazon rainforest, for example, has no value as far as its ecological function is concerned. It only has value in Western market societies as it is cut down to be used for lumber, or left standing because it may be economically beneficial as far as providing nuts and fruits is concerned. Or perhaps, economic decision makers can be convinced that the tree has value because it is a rare species that may eventually have some kind of medicinal value in providing a cure for disease. But its ecological value in terms of providing the world with a carbon sink and contributing to the diversity of plant life in that part of the world has no economic value. From a strictly economic point of view, the tree has no value in its natural state and must be cut down and made into something useful or left standing as long as it is seen as productive in some other sense.

The same is true of wetlands, which cover vast areas of some parts of the world, both along coastal areas and inland. These wetlands perform valuable ecological functions that we are only now beginning to understand, yet from an economic point of view they only have value because they contain resources that can be exploited or because they can be filled in to provide land area for residential or commercial development. Most people probably consider wetland areas as wasteland and fail to appreciate the valuable ecological functions they perform in terms of providing a habitat for fish and other forms of wildlife and acting as water reservoirs to prevent flooding, just to mention a few.

THE MARKET AS A SOCIAL PROCESS

Our traditional understanding of the market system and how it works, as described on the previous pages, is based on the assumption of the atomic individual acting in its own interests, and an assumption that the market acts in a mechanical fashion to provide for people's needs and wants. The market is based on an individualistic conception of human beings, as people are expected to act as individual or atomic units in expressing their preferences in the marketplace, preferences which are then aggregated into demand schedules facing corporations. The marketplace is seen as nothing more than some mechanical process that performs this coordination function through the forces of supply and demand so that business organizations know what to produce and in what quantities. Competition is seen as some sort of mechanical regulator that puts constraints on individual egos and prevents business organizations from attaining a monopoly position in which competition could not perform its proper function.

The market system, however, is a social system and not only an economic system, as many people spend the greater part of their lives working for corporations or some other economic entity and spend another major portion of their lives in stores shopping for goods and services. The market provides the context in which much of our social life takes place, and provides the means for many of our social interactions. These social relations are based upon economics as we spend a great deal of time producing and consuming economic wealth and playing the roles of producers and consumers, or employees and investors in corporate entities. Other roles such as parents and citizens are not given an economic value, and are not seen to be as important as our economic activities when viewed in a market context. But such a view is a distortion of their true importance in society as a whole.

When market societies came into existence, they replaced the traditional social systems that had been in place and had served to prescribe roles and functions of people. Economic activity had always been subordinated to the social system and was merely a part of a larger social reality that provided for social interactions and gave people a sense of identity and belonging. But market systems and the market principle took over, so to speak, and became social systems in and of themselves, and other aspects of social life became subordinated to market duties and roles. The market itself became the principal manner in which society organized itself, and the roles of producer and consumer along with other economic roles became the primary roles in society.[2]

Other parts of the social world such as family, church, and the like have had to adapt themselves to economic life, which is the primary driving force in our society. Most of the important decisions we have to make are economic in nature. The primary wealth of our society is economic. And the dominant roles we play are eco-nomic in nature. All of which is to say that the economy and the way in which we provide ourselves with goods and services have become the dominant concern for the majority of the population in a market-oriented society. The market organizes our activities and provides us with a motivation to do what the market requires.

The emergence of laissez-faire capitalism thus turned human and social relations around and altered the relationship of humans with nature. Whereas in earlier times economic relations were embedded in and secondary to their broader social context, market systems actually embedded social relations into the economic system. The evolution of market-oriented societies occurred through the transformation of nature, humans, and capital, the so-called factors of production, into fictitious economic commodities that can be bought and sold on the market. While such a fictionalizing as economic elements of things that are fundamentally social ushered in a period of production of goods and services never before experienced, it also set loose forces that caused social, political, and environmental dislocation of an unparalleled nature.[3] ◆ ◆ ◆

◆ Endnotes

1. See, for example, John Kenneth Galbraith, *The New Industrial State* (Boston: Houghton Mifflin, 1967).
2. See Karl Polanyi, *The Great Transformation* (Boston: Beacon Press, 1944).
3. Robert H. Hogner, "We Are All Social: On the Place of Social Issues in Management," in *Contemporary Issues in Business and Society in the United States and Abroad*, Karen Paul, ed. (Lewiston, NY: Edwin Mellen Press, 1991), p. 8.

◆ Suggested Readings

Ayres, Clarence E. *The Theory of Economic Progress.* Chapel Hill: University of North Carolina Press, 1944.

Block, Walter, et al., eds. *Morality of the Market.* Vancouver, British Columbia, Canada: The Fraser Institute, 1985.

Etzioni, Amitai. *The Moral Dimension.* New York: The Free Press, 1988.

Gauthier, David P., ed. *Morality and Rational Self-Interest.* Englewood Cliffs, NJ: Prentice-Hall, 1970.

Goudzwaard, Bob. *Capitalism and Progress*. Grand Rapids, MI: William B. Eerdmans Publishing Co., 1979.

Kornai, Thomas S. *The Road to a Free Economy*. New York: W. W. Norton, 1990.

Mirowski, Phillip. *Against Mechanism*. Totowa, NJ: Rowman and Littlefield, 1988.

Polanyi, Karl. *The Great Transformation*. Boston: Beacon Press, 1944.

Reddy, William H. *The Rise of Market Culture*. Cambridge: Cambridge University Press, 1987.

Steidlmeier, Paul. *People and Profits: The Ethics of Capitalism*. Englewood Cliffs, NJ: Prentice Hall, 1992.

Zohar, Danah. *The Quantum Self*. New York: Quill/William Morrow, 1990.

The Invisible Hand

Adam Smith

In this short extract from The Wealth of Nations *(1776), Adam Smith lays out three key concepts that are often taken as axiomatic for contemporary capitalism. They are the division of labor, self-interest as the prime human motivation, and the invisible hand. The invisible hand is a metaphor that Smith uses to argue that individuals acting independently for themselves actually lead to mutual benefit. When reading the extract we should be willing to question his account of human psychology and examine whether the empirical evidence supports his conclusion: Are we, in fact, better off (however we define the term) as a result of widespread self-interest?*

Of the Principle Which Gives Occasion to the Division of Labour

This division of labour, from which so many advantages are derived, is not originally the effect of any human wisdom, which foresees and intends that general opulence to which it gives occasion. It is the necessary, though very slow and gradual consequence of a certain propensity in human nature which has in view no such extensive utility; the propensity to truck, barter, and exchange one thing for another.

Whether this propensity be one of those original principles in human nature of which no further account can be given; or whether, as seems more probable, it be the necessary consequence of the faculties of reason and speech, it belongs not to our present subject to inquire. It is common to all men, and to be found in no other race of animals, which seem to know neither this nor any other species of contracts. . . . [M]an has almost constant occasion for the help of his brethren, and it is in vain for him to expect it from their benevolence only. He will be more likely to prevail if he can interest their self-love in his favour, and show them that it is for their own advantage to do for him what he requires of them. Whoever offers to another a bargain of any kind, proposes to do this. Give me that which I want, and you shall have this which you want, is the meaning of every such offer; and it is in this manner that we obtain from one another the far greater part of those good offices which we stand in need of. It is not from the benevolence of the butcher, the brewer, or the baker that we expect our dinner, but from their regard to their own interest. We address ourselves, not to their humanity but to their self-love, and never talk to them of our own necessities but of their advantages. Nobody but a beggar chooses to depend chiefly upon the benevolence of his fellow-citizens. Even a beggar does not depend upon it entirely. The charity of well-disposed people, indeed, supplies him with the whole fund of his subsistence. But though this principle ultimately provides him with all the necessaries of life which he has occasion for, it neither does nor can provide him with them as he has occasion for them. The greater part of his occasional wants are supplied in the same manner as those of other people, by treaty, by barter, and by purchase. With the money which one man gives him he purchases food. The old clothes which another bestows upon him he exchanges for other old clothes which suit him better, or for lodging, or for food, or for money, with which he can buy either food, clothes, or lodging, as he has occasion. . . .

But the annual revenue of every society is always precisely equal to the exchangeable value of the whole annual produce of its industry, or rather is precisely the same thing with that exchangeable value. As every individual, therefore, endeavours as much as he can both to employ his capital in the support of domestic industry, and so to direct that industry that its produce may be of the greatest value; every individual necessarily labours to render the annual revenue of the society as great as he can. He generally, indeed, neither intends to promote the public interest, nor knows how much he is promoting it. By preferring the support of domestic to that of foreign industry, he intends only his own security; and by directing that industry in such a manner as its produce may be of the greatest value, he intends only his own gain, and he is in this, as in many other cases, led by an invisible hand to promote an end which was no part of his intention. Nor is it always the worse for the society that it was no part of it. By pursuing his own interest he frequently promotes that of the society more effectually than when he really intends to promote it. I have never known much good done by those who affected to trade for the public good. It is an affectation, indeed, not very common among merchants, and very few words need be employed in dissuading them from it.

What is the species of domestic industry which his capital can employ, and of which the produce is likely to be of the greatest value, every individual, it is evident, can, in his local situation, judge much better than any statesman or lawgiver can do for him. The statesman who should attempt to direct private people in what manner they ought to employ their capitals would not only load himself with a most unnecessary attention, but assume an authority which could safely be trusted, not only to no single person, but to no council or senate whatever, and which would nowhere be so dangerous as in the hands of a man who had folly and presumption enough to fancy himself fit to exercise it.

To give the monopoly of the home market to the produce of domestic industry, in any particular art or manufacture, is in some measure to direct private people in what manner they ought to employ their capitals, and must, in almost all cases, be either a useless or a hurtful regulation. If the produce of domestic can be brought there as cheap as that of foreign industry, the regulation is evidently useless. If it cannot, it must generally be hurtful. It is the maxim of every prudent master of a family never to attempt to make at home what it will cost him more to make than to buy. The tailor does not attempt to make his own shoes, but buys them of the shoemaker. The shoemaker does not attempt to make his own clothes, but employs a tailor. The farmer attempts to make neither the one nor the other, but employs those different artificers. All of them find it for their interest to employ their whole industry in a way in which they have some advantage over their neighbours, and to purchase with a part of its produce, or what is the same thing, with the price of a part of it, whatever else they have occasion for. ◆ ◆ ◆

What Is Capitalism?*

Ayn Rand

Rand (1905–1982) grew up in Russia and witnessed the Russian revolution firsthand. She immigrated to America where she became a writer famous for her views promoting individual triumph over collectivism. Ayn Rand's work is still enormously influential and has a considerable following. Her point of view is reflected in many discussions about topics in business ethics.

In this passage she defines the notion of objectivism. Rand believes there are values external to individuals, and the free market rewards those who discover them. Basic to her view is the paramount nature of personal property rights and voluntary choice. She rejects what she terms "tribalism," where members of a community are obliged to take care of others, or appeals to "the common good." She feels that capitalism has an unrivaled record of human achievement fueled by individuals seeking their own interests.

A social system is a set of moral-political-economic principles embodied in a society's laws, institutions, and government, which determine the relationships, the terms of association, among the men living in a given geographical area. It is obvious that these terms and relationships depend on an identification of man's nature, that they would be different if they pertain to a society of rational beings or to a colony of ants. It is obvious that they will be radically different if men deal with one another as free, independent individuals, on the premise that every

*Original footnotes have been omitted.

man is an end in himself—or as members of a pack, each regarding the others as the means to *his* ends and to the ends of "the pack as a whole."

There are only two fundamental questions (or two aspects of the same question) that determine the nature of any social system: Does a social system recognize individual rights?—and: Does a social system ban physical force from human relationships? The answer to the second question is the practical implementation of the answer to the first.

Is man a sovereign individual who owns his person, his mind, his life, his work and its products—or is he the property of the tribe (the state, the society, the collective) that may dispose of him in any way it pleases, that may dictate his convictions, prescribe the course of his life, control his work and expropriate his products? Does man have the *right* to exist for his own sake—or is he born in bondage, as an indentured servant who must keep buying his life by serving the tribe but can never acquire it free and clear?

This is the first question to answer. The rest is consequences and practical implementations. The basic issue is only: Is man free?

In mankind's history, capitalism is the only system that answers: Yes.

Capitalism is a social system based on the recognition of individual rights, including property rights, in which all property is privately owned.

The recognition of individual rights entails the banishment of physical force from human relationships: basically, rights can be violated only by means of force. In a capitalist society, no man or group may *initiate* the use of physical force against others. The only function of the government, in such a society, is the task of protecting man's rights, i.e., the task of protecting him from physical force; the government acts as the agent of man's right of self-defense, and may use force only in retaliation and only against those who initiate its use; thus the government is the means

of placing the retaliatory use of force under *objective control.*

It is the basic, metaphysical fact of man's nature—the connection between his survival and his use of reason—that capitalism recognizes and protects.

In a capitalist society, all human relationships are *voluntary.* Men are free to cooperate or not, to deal with one another or not, as their own individual judgments, convictions, and interests dictate. They can deal with one another only in terms of and by means of reason, i.e., by means of discussion, persuasion, and *contractual* agreement, by voluntary choice to mutual benefit. The right to agree with others is not a problem in any society; it is *the right to disagree* that is crucial. It is the institution of private property that protects and implements the right to disagree— and thus keeps the road open to man's most valuable attribute (valuable personally, socially, and *objectively*): the creative mind.

This is the cardinal difference between capitalism and collectivism. . . .

The "practical" justification of capitalism does not lie in the collectivist claim that it effects "the best allocation of national resources." Man is *not* a "national resource" and neither is his mind—and without the creative power of man's intelligence, raw materials remain just so many useless raw materials.

The *moral* justification of capitalism does not lie in the altruist claim that it represents the best way to achieve "the common good." It is true that capitalism does—if that catch-phrase has any meaning—but this is merely a secondary consequence. The moral justification of capitalism lies in the fact that it is the only system consonant with man's rational nature, that it protects man's survival *qua* man, and that its ruling principle is: *justice.*

Every social system is based, explicitly or implicitly, on some theory of ethics. The tribal notion of "the common good" has served as the moral justification of most social systems—and of all tyrannies—in history. The degree of a society's enslavement or freedom corresponded to the degree to which that tribal slogan was invoked or ignored.

"The common good" (or "the public interest") is an undefined and undefinable concept: there is no such entity as "the tribe" or "the public"; the tribe (or the public or society) is only a number of individual men. Nothing can be good for the tribe as such; "good" and "value" pertain *only* to a living organism—to an individual living organism—not to a disembodied aggregate of relationships.

"The common good" is a meaningless concept, unless taken literally, in which case its only possible meaning is: the sum of the good of *all* the individual men involved. But in that case, the concept is meaningless as a moral criterion: it leaves open the question of what *is* the good of individual men and how does one determine it?

It is not, however, in its literal meaning that that concept is generally used. It is accepted precisely for its elastic, undefinable, mystical character which serves, not as a moral guide, but as an escape from morality. Since the good is not applicable to the disembodied, it becomes a moral blank check for those who attempt to embody it. . . .

There are, in essence, three schools of thought on the nature of the good: the intrinsic, the subjective, and the objective. The *intrinsic* theory holds that the good is inherent in certain things or actions as such, regardless of their context and consequences, regardless of any benefit or injury they may cause to the actors and subjects involved. It is a theory that divorces the concept of "good" from beneficiaries, and the concept of "value" from valuer and purpose—claiming that the good is good in, by, and of itself.

The *subjectivist* theory holds that the good bears no relation to the facts of reality, that it is the product of a man's consciousness, created by his feelings, desires, "intuitions," or whims, and that it is merely an "arbitrary postulate" or an "emotional commitment."

The intrinsic theory holds that the good resides in some sort of reality, independent of man's consciousness; the subjectivist theory holds that the good resides in man's consciousness, independent of reality.

The *objective* theory holds that the good is neither an attribute of "things in themselves" nor of man's emotional states, but *an evaluation* of the facts of reality by man's consciousness according to a rational standard of value. (Rational, in this context, means: derived from the facts of reality and validated by a process of reason.) The objective theory holds that *the good is an aspect of reality in relation to man*—and that it must be discovered, not invented, by man. Fundamental to an objective theory of values is the question: Of value to whom and for what? An objective theory does not permit context-dropping or "concept-stealing"; it does not permit the separation of "value" from "purpose," of the good from beneficiaries, and of man's actions from reason.

Of all the social systems in mankind's history, *capitalism is the only system based on an objective theory of values.*

The intrinsic theory and the subjectivist theory (or a mixture of both) are the necessary base of every dictatorship, tyranny, or variant of the absolute state. Whether they are held consciously or subconsciously—in the explicit form of a philosopher's treatise or in the implicit chaos of its echoes in an average man's feelings—these theories make it possible for a man to believe that the good is independent of man's mind and can be achieved by physical force.

If a man believes that the good is intrinsic in certain actions, he will not hesitate to force others to perform them. If he believes that the human benefit or injury caused by such actions is of no significance, he will regard a sea of blood as of no significance. If he believes that the beneficiaries of such actions are irrelevant (or interchangeable), he will regard wholesale slaughter as his moral duty in the service of a "higher" good. It is the intrinsic theory of values that produces a Robespierre, a Lenin, a Stalin, or a Hitler. It is not an accident that Eichmann was a Kantian.

If a man believes that the good is a matter of arbitrary, subjective choice, the issue of good or evil becomes, for him, an issue of: *my* feelings or *theirs?* No bridge, understanding, or communication is possible to him. Reason is the only means of communication among men, and an objectively perceivable reality is their only common frame of reference; when these are invalidated (i.e., held to be irrelevant) in the field of morality, force becomes men's only way of dealing with one another. If the subjectivist wants to pursue some social ideal of his own, he feels morally entitled to force men "for their own good," since he *feels* that he is right and that there is nothing to oppose him but their misguided feelings.

Thus, in practice, the proponents of the intrinsic and the subjectivist schools meet and blend. (They blend in terms of their psychoepistemology as well: by what means do the moralists of the intrinsic school discover their transcendental "good," if not by means of special, non-rational intuitions and revelations, i.e., by means of their feelings?) It is doubtful whether anyone can hold either of these theories as an actual, if mistaken, conviction. But both serve as a rationalization of power-lust and of rule by brute force, unleashing the potential dictator and disarming his victims.

The objective theory of values is the only moral theory incompatible with rule by force. Capitalism is the only system based implicitly on an objective theory of values—and the historic tragedy is that this has never been made explicit.

If one knows that the good is *objective*—i.e., determined by the nature of reality, but to be discovered by man's mind—one knows that an attempt to achieve the good by physical force is a monstrous contradiction which negates morality at its root by destroying man's capacity to recognize the good, i.e., his capacity to value. Force invalidates and paralyzes a man's judgment, demanding that he act against it, thus rendering him morally impotent. A value which one is forced to accept at the price of surrendering one's mind, is not a value to anyone; the forcibly mindless can neither judge nor choose nor value. An attempt to achieve the good by force is like an attempt to provide a man with a picture gallery at the price of cutting out his eyes. Values cannot exist (cannot be valued) outside the full context of a man's life, needs, goals, and *knowledge*.

The objective view of values permeates the entire structure of a capitalist society. . . .

The free market represents the *social* application of an objective theory of values. Since values are to be discovered by man's mind, men must be free to discover them—to think, to study, to translate their knowledge into physical form, to offer their products for trade, to judge them, and to choose, be it material goods or ideas, a loaf of bread or a philosophical treatise. Since values are established contextually, every man must judge for himself, in the context of his own knowledge, goals, and interests. Since values are determined by the nature of reality, it is reality that serves as men's ultimate arbiter: if a man's judgment is right, the rewards are his; if it is wrong, he is his only victim.

It is in regard to a free market that the distinction between an intrinsic, subjective, and objective view of values is particularly important to understand. The market value of a product is *not* an intrinsic value, not a "value in itself" hanging in a vacuum. A free market never loses sight of the question: Of value *to whom?* And, within the broad field of objectivity, the market value of a product does not reflect its *philosophically objective* value, but only its *socially objective* value. . . .

Just as the number of its adherents is not a proof of an idea's truth or falsehood, of an art work's merit or demerit, of a product's efficacy or inefficacy—so the free-market value of goods or services does not necessarily represent their philosophically objective value, but only their *socially objective* value, i.e., the sum of the individual judgments of all the men involved in trade at a given time, the sum of what *they* valued, each in the context of his own life.

Thus, a manufacturer of lipstick may well make a greater fortune than a manufacturer of microscopes—even though it can be rationally demonstrated that microscopes are scientifically more valuable than lipstick. But—valuable *to whom?*

A microscope is of no value to a little stenographer struggling to make a living; a lipstick is; a lipstick, to her, may mean the difference between self-confidence and self-doubt, between glamour and drudgery.

This does not mean, however, that the values ruling a free market are *subjective*. If the stenographer spends all her money on cosmetics and has none left to pay for the use of a microscope (for a visit to the doctor) *when she needs it*, she learns a better method of budgeting her income; the free market serves as her teacher: she has no way to penalize others for her mistakes. If she budgets rationally, the microscope is always available to serve her own specific needs *and no more*, as far as she is concerned: she is not taxed to support an entire hospital, a research laboratory, or a space ship's journey to the moon. Within her own productive power, she does pay a part of the cost of scientific achievements, *when and as she needs them*. She has no "social duty," her own life is her only responsibility—and the only thing that a capitalist system requires of

her is the thing that *nature* requires: rationality, i.e., that she live and act to the best of her own judgment.

Within every category of goods and services offered on a free market, it is the purveyor of the best product at the cheapest price who wins the greatest financial rewards *in that field*—not automatically nor immediately nor by fiat, but by virtue of the free market, which teaches every participant to look for the *objective* best within the category of his own competence, and penalizes those who act on irrational considerations.

Now observe that a free market does not level men down to some common denominator—that the intellectual criteria of the majority do not rule a free market or a free society—and that the exceptional men, the innovators, the intellectual giants, are not held down by the majority. In fact, it is the members of this exceptional minority who lift the whole of a free society to the level of their own achievements, while rising further and ever further.

A free market is a *continuous process* that cannot be held still, an upward process that demands the best (the most rational) of every man and rewards him accordingly. While the majority have barely assimilated the value of the automobile, the creative minority introduces the airplane. The majority learn by demonstration, the minority is free to demonstrate. The "philosophically objective" value of a new product serves as the teacher for those who are willing to exercise their rational faculty, each to the extent of his ability. Those who are unwilling remain unrewarded—as well as those who aspire to more than their ability produces. The stagnant, the irrational, the subjectivist have no power to stop their betters.

(The small minority of adults who are *unable* rather than unwilling to work, have to rely on voluntary charity; misfortune is not a claim to slave labor; there is no such thing as the *right* to consume, control, and destroy those without whom one would be unable to survive. As to depressions and mass unemployment, they are not caused by the free market, but by government interference into the economy.)

The mental parasites—the imitators who attempt to cater to what they think is the public's known taste—are constantly being beaten by the innovators whose products raise the public's knowledge and taste to ever higher levels. It is in this sense that the free market is ruled, not by the consumers, but by the producers. The most successful ones are those who discover new fields of production, fields which had not been known to exist.

A given product may not be appreciated at once, particularly if it is too radical an innovation; but, barring irrelevant accidents, it wins in the long run. It is in this sense that the free market is not ruled by the intellectual criteria of the majority, which prevail only at and for any given moment; the free market is ruled by those who are able to see and plan long-range—and the better the mind, the longer the range.

The economic value of a man's work is determined, on a free market, by a single principle: by the voluntary consent of those who are willing to trade him their work or products in return. This is the moral meaning of the law of supply and demand; it represents the total rejection of two vicious doctrines: the tribal premise and altruism. It represents the recognition of the fact that man is not the property nor the servant of the tribe, that *a man works in order to support his own life*—as, by his nature, he must—that he has to be guided by his own rational self-interest, and if he wants to trade with others, he cannot expect sacrificial victims, i.e., he cannot expect to receive values without trading commensurate values in return. The sole criterion of what is commensurate, in this context, is the free, voluntary, uncoerced judgment of the traders.

The tribal mentalities attack this principle from two seemingly opposite sides: they claim that the free market is "unfair" both to the genius and to the average man. The first objection is usually expressed by a question such as: "Why should Elvis Presley make more money than Einstein?" The answer is: Because men work in order to support and enjoy their own lives—and if many men find value in Elvis Presley, they are entitled to spend their money on their own pleasure. Presley's fortune is not taken from those who do not care for his work (I am one of them) nor from Einstein—nor does he stand in Einstein's way—nor does Einstein lack proper recognition and support in a free society, on an appropriate intellectual level.

As to the second objection, the claim that a man of average ability suffers an "unfair" disadvantage on a free market—

> . . . When you live in a rational society, where men are free to trade, you receive an incalculable bonus: the material value of your work is determined not only by your effort, but by the effort of the best productive minds who exist in the world around you. . . .
>
> . . . The man who does no more than physical labor, consumes the material value-equivalent of his own contribution to the process of production, and leaves no further value, neither for himself nor others. But the man who produces an idea in any field of rational endeavor—the man who discovers new knowledge—is the permanent benefactor of humanity. . . . It is only the value of an idea that can be shared with unlimited numbers of men, making all sharers richer at no one's sacrifice or loss, raising the productive capacity of whatever labor they perform. . . .

In proportion to the mental energy he spent, the man who creates a new invention receives but a small percentage of his value in terms of material payment, no matter what fortune he makes, no matter what millions he earns. But the man who works as a janitor in the factory producing that invention, receives an enormous payment in proportion to the mental effort that his job requires of *him*. And the same is true of all men between, on all levels of ambition and ability.

The man at the top of the intellectual pyramid contributes the most to all those below him, but gets nothing except his material payment, receiving no intellectual bonus from others to add to the value of his time. The man at the bottom who, left to himself, would starve in his hopeless ineptitude, contributes nothing to those above him, but receives the bonus of all of their brains. Such is the nature of the "competition" between the strong and the weak of the intellect. Such is the pattern of "exploitation" for which you have damned the strong. (*Atlas Shrugged*)

And such is the relationship of capitalism to man's mind and to man's survival.

The magnificent progress achieved by capitalism in a brief span of time—the spectacular improvement in the conditions of man's existence on earth—is a matter of historical record. It is not to be hidden, evaded, or explained away by all the propaganda of capitalism's enemies. But what needs special emphasis is the fact that this progress was achieved by *non-sacrificial* means. . . .

America's abundance was not created by public sacrifices to "the common good," but by the productive genius of free men who pursued their own personal interests and the making of their own private fortunes. They did not starve the people to pay for America's industrialization. They gave the people better jobs, higher wages, and cheaper goods with every new machine they invented, with every scientific discovery or technological advance—and thus the whole country was moving forward and profiting, not suffering, every step of the way. ◆ ◆ ◆

An Egalitarian Theory of Justice

John Rawls

Rawls engages in a thought experiment where he asks us to imagine that we know the basic facts about human nature but not our place in the world. Under this "veil of ignorance," we are to design the general principles for a society. So, for example, we have an equal chance of being men or women, we cannot choose our racial heritage, and we have no say in our intellectual or physical abilities. Given these restrictions, Rawls believes that we will create a society that gives maximum opportunities to all.

We should note two things before reading the passage. First, this discussion is admittedly at a fairly abstract level. This means that refuting Rawls's claims needs to be done at the same level of principle, not on grounds, say, that such an initial contractual episode is unlikely to happen. Second, we should be careful to examine Rawls's conclusions closely. For example, he does not believe in absolute equality but in equality of opportunity. He is willing to allow differences to emerge, under certain conditions. The challenge for those who disagree with him is to pin down exactly the problems in his argument: Are his assumptions incorrect, or is there a flaw in the implications that he draws from them? Although not included in this passage, we might speculate about the nature of a society that would be based on his fundamental principles.

THE ROLE OF JUSTICE

Justice is the first virtue of social institutions, as truth is of systems of thought. A theory however elegant and economical must be rejected or revised if it is untrue; likewise laws and institutions no matter how efficient and well-arranged must be reformed or abolished if they are unjust. Each person possesses an inviolability founded on justice that even the welfare of society as a whole cannot override. For this reason justice denies that the loss of freedom for some is made right by a greater good shared by others. It does not allow that the sacrifices imposed on a few are outweighed by the larger sum of advantages enjoyed by many. Therefore in a just society the liberties of equal citizenship are taken as settled; the rights secured by justice are not subject to political bargaining or to the calculus of social interests. The only thing that permits us to acquiesce in an erroneous theory is the lack of a better one; analogously, an injustice is tolerable only when it is necessary to avoid an even greater injustice. Being first virtues of human activities, truth and justice are uncompromising.

These propositions seem to express our intuitive conviction of the primacy of justice. No doubt they are expressed too strongly. In any event I wish to inquire whether these contentions or others similar to them are sound, and if so how they can be accounted for. To this end it is necessary to work out a theory of justice in the light of which these assertions can be interpreted and assessed. I shall begin by considering the role of the principles of justice. Let us assume, to fix ideas, that a society is a more or less self-sufficient association of persons who in their relations to one another recognize certain rules of conduct as binding and who for the most part act in accordance with them. Suppose further that these rules specify a system of cooperation designed to advance the good of those taking part in it. Then, although a society is a cooperative venture for mutual advantage, it is typically marked by a conflict as well as by an identity of interests. There is an identity of interests since social cooperation makes possible a better life for all than any would have if each were to live solely by his own efforts. There is a conflict of interests since persons are not indifferent as to how the greater benefits produced by their collaboration are distributed, for in order to pursue their ends they each prefer a larger to a lesser share. A set of principles is required for choosing among the various social arrangements which determine this division of advantages and for underwriting an agreement on the proper distributive shares. These principles are the principles of social justice: they provide a way of assigning rights and duties in the basic institutions of society and they define the appropriate distribution of the benefits and burdens of social cooperation. . . .

In justice as fairness the original position of equality corresponds to the state of nature in the traditional theory of the social contract. This original position is not, of course, thought of as an actual historical state of affairs, much less as a primitive condition of culture. It is understood as a purely hypothetical situation characterized so as to lead to a certain conception of justice.[1] Among the essential features of this situation is that no one knows his place in society, his class position or social status, nor does any one know his fortune in the distribution of natural assets and abilities, his intelligence, strength, and the like. I shall even assume that the parties do not know their conceptions of the good or their special psychological propensities. The principles of justice are chosen behind a veil of ignorance. This ensures that no one is advantaged or disadvantaged in the choice of principles by the outcome of natural chance or the contingency of social circumstances. Since all are similarly situated and no one is able to design principles to favor his particular condition, the principles of justice are the result of a fair agreement or bargain. For given the circumstances of the original position, the symmetry of everyone's relations to each other, this initial situation is fair between individuals as moral persons, that is, as rational beings with their own ends and capable, I shall assume, of a sense of justice. The original position is, one might say, the appropriate initial status quo, and thus the fundamental agreements reached in it are fair. This explains the propriety of the name "justice as fairness": it conveys the idea that the principles of justice are agreed to in an initial situation that is fair. . . .

. . . The aim of the contract approach is to establish that taken together they impose significant bounds on acceptable principles of justice. . . .

. . . The idea here is simply to make vivid to ourselves the restrictions that it seems reasonable to impose on arguments for principles of justice, and therefore on these principles themselves. Thus it seems reasonable and generally acceptable that no one should be advantaged or disadvantaged by natural fortune or social circumstances in the choice of principles. It also seems widely agreed that it should be impossible to tailor principles to the circumstances of one's own case. We should insure further that particular inclinations and aspirations, and persons' conceptions of their good do not affect the principles adopted. The aim is to rule out those principles that it would be rational to propose for acceptance, however little the chance of success, only if one knew certain things that are irrelevant from the standpoint of justice. For example, if a man knew that he was wealthy, he might find it rational to advance the principle that various taxes for welfare measures be counted unjust; if he knew that he was poor, he would most likely propose the contrary principle. To represent the desired restrictions one imagines a situation in which everyone is deprived of this sort of information. One excludes the knowledge of those contingencies which sets men at odds and allows them to be guided by their prejudices. In this manner the veil of ignorance is arrived at in a natural way. This concept should cause no difficulty if we keep in mind the constraints on arguments that it is meant to express. At any time we can enter the original position, so to speak, simply by following a certain procedure, namely, by arguing for principles of justice in accordance with these restrictions. . . .

TWO PRINCIPLES OF JUSTICE

I shall now state in a provisional form the two principles of justice that I believe would be chosen in the original position. In this section I wish to make only the most general comments, and therefore the first formulation of these principles is tentative. As we go on I shall run through several formulations and approximate step by step the final statement to be given much later. I believe that doing this allows the exposition to proceed in a natural way.

The first statement of the two principles reads as follows.

> First: each person is to have an equal right to the most extensive basic liberty compatible with a similar liberty for others.
> Second: social and economic inequalities are to be arranged so that they are both (a) reasonably expected to be to everyone's advantage, and (b) attached to positions and offices open to all. . . .

By way of general comment, these principles primarily apply, as I have said, to the basic structure of society. They are to govern the assignment of rights and duties and to regulate the distribution of social and economic advantages. As their formulation suggests, these principles presuppose that the social structure can be divided into two more or less distinct parts, the first principle applying to the one, the second to the other. They distinguish between those aspects of the social system that define and secure the equal liberties of citizenship and those that specify and establish social and economic inequalities. The basic liberties of citizens are, roughly speaking, political liberty (the right to vote and to be eligible for public office) together with freedom of speech and assembly; liberty of conscience and freedom of thought; freedom of the person along with the right to hold (personal) property; and freedom from arbitrary arrest and seizure as defined by the concept of the rule of law. These liberties are all required to be equal by the first principle, since citizens of a just society are to have the same basic rights.

The second principle applies, in the first approximation, to the distribution of income and wealth and to the design of organizations that make use of differences in authority and responsibility, or chains of command. While the distribution of wealth and income need not be equal, it must be to everyone's advantage, and at the same time, positions of authority and offices of command must be accessible to all. One applies the second principle by holding positions open, and then, subject to this constraint, arranges social and economic inequalities so that everyone benefits.

These principles are to be arranged in a serial order with the first principle prior to the second. This ordering means that a departure from the institutions of equal liberty required by the first principle cannot be justified by, or compensated for, by greater social and economic advantages. The distribution of wealth and income, and the hierarchies of authority, must be consistent with both the liberties of equal citizenship and equality of opportunity.

It is clear that these principles are rather specific in their content, and their acceptance rests on certain assumptions that I must eventually try to explain and justify. A theory of justice depends upon a theory of society in ways that will become evident as we proceed. For the present, it should be observed that the two principles (and this holds for all formulations) are a special case of a more general conception of justice that can be expressed as follows.

> All social values—liberty and opportunity, income and wealth, and the bases of self-respect—are to be distributed equally unless an unequal distribution of any, or all, of these values is to everyone's advantage.

Injustice, then, is simply inequalities that are not to the benefit of all. Of course, this conception is extremely vague and requires interpretation.

As a first step, suppose that the basic structure of society distributes certain primary goods, that is, things that every rational man is presumed to want. These goods normally have a use whatever a person's rational plan of life. For simplicity, assume that the chief primary goods at the disposition of society are rights and liberties, powers and opportunities, income and wealth. . . . These are the social primary goods. Other primary goods such as health and vigor, intelligence and imagination, are natural goods; although their possession is influenced by the basic structure, they are not so directly under its control. Imagine, then, a hypothetical initial arrangement in which all the social primary goods are equally distributed: everyone has similar rights and duties, and income and wealth are evenly shared. This state of affairs provides a benchmark for judging improvements. If certain inequalities of wealth and organizational powers would make everyone better off than in this hypothetical starting situation, then they accord with the general conception.

Now it is possible, at least theoretically, that by giving up some of their fundamental liberties men are sufficiently compensated by the resulting social and economic gains. The general conception of justice imposes no restrictions on what sort of inequalities are permissible; it only requires that everyone's position be improved. . . .

Now the second principle insists that each person benefit from permissible inequalities in the basic structure. This means that it must be reasonable for each relevant representative man defined by this structure, when he views it as a going concern, to prefer his prospects with the inequality to his prospects without it. One is not allowed to justify differences in income or organizational powers on the ground that the disadvantages of those in one position are outweighed by the greater advantages of those in another. Much less can infringements of liberty be counterbalanced in this way. Applied to the basic structure, the principle of utility would have us maximize the sum of expectations of representative men (weighted by the number of persons they represent, on the classical view); and this would permit us to compensate for the losses of some by the gains of others. Instead, the two principles require that everyone benefit from economic and social inequalities. It is obvious, however, that there are indefinitely many ways in which all may be advantaged when the initial arrangement of equality is taken as a benchmark. . . .

THE TENDENCY TO EQUALITY

I wish to conclude this discussion of the two principles by explaining the sense in which they express an egalitarian conception of justice. Also I should like to forestall the objection to the principle of fair opportunity that it leads to a callous meritocratic society. In order to prepare the way for doing this, I note several aspects of the conception of justice that I have set out.

First we may observe that the difference principle gives some weight to the considerations singled out by the principle of redress. This is the principle that undeserved inequalities call for redress; and since inequalities of birth and natural endowment are undeserved, these inequalities are to be somehow compensated for.[2] Thus the principle holds that in order to treat all persons equally, to provide genuine equality of opportunity, society must give more attention to those with fewer native assets and to those born into the less favorable social positions. The idea is to redress the bias of contingencies in the direction of equality. In pursuit of this principle greater resources might be spent on the education of the less rather than the more intelligent, at least over a certain time of life, say the earlier years of school.

Now the principle of redress has not to my knowledge been proposed as the sole criterion of justice, as the single aim of the social order. It is plausible as most such principles are only as a prima facie principle, one that is to be weighed in the balance with others. For example, we are to weigh it against the principle to improve the average standard of life, or to advance the common good.[3] But whatever other principles we hold, the claims of redress are to be taken into account. It is thought to represent one of the elements in our conception of justice. Now the difference principle is not of course the principle of redress. It does not require society to try to even out handicaps as if all were expected to compete on a fair basis in the same race. But the difference principle would allocate resources in education, say, so as to improve the long-term expectation of the least favored. If this end is attained by giving more attention to the better endowed, it is permissible; otherwise not. And in making this decision, the value of education should not be assessed solely in terms of economic efficiency and social welfare. Equally if not more important is the role of education in enabling a person to enjoy the culture of his society and to take part in its affairs, and in this way to provide for each individual a secure sense of his own worth.

Thus although the difference principle is not the same as that of redress, it does achieve some of the intent of the latter principle. It transforms the aims of the basic structure so that the total scheme of institutions no longer emphasizes social efficiency and technocratic values. We see then that the difference principle represents, in effect, an agreement to regard the distribution of natural talents as a common asset and to share in the benefits of this distribution whatever it turns out to be. . . .

. . . The natural distribution is neither just nor unjust; nor is it unjust that persons are born into society at some particular position. These are simply natural facts. What is just and unjust is the way that institutions deal with these facts. Aristocratic and caste societies are unjust because they make these contingencies the ascriptive basis for belonging to more or less enclosed and privileged social classes. The basic structure of these societies incorporates the arbitrariness found in nature. But there is no necessity for men to resign themselves to these contingencies. The social system is not an unchangeable order beyond human control but a pattern of human action. In justice as fairness men agree to share one another's fate. In designing institutions they undertake to avail themselves of the accidents of nature and social circumstance only when doing so is for the common benefit. The two principles are a fair way of meeting the arbitrariness of fortune; and while no doubt imperfect in other ways, the institutions which satisfy these principles are just. . . .

There is a natural inclination to object that those better situated deserve their greater advantages whether or not they are to the benefit of others. At this point it is necessary to be clear about the notion of desert. It is perfectly true that given a just system of cooperation as a scheme of public rules and the expectations set up by it, those who, with the prospect of improving their condition, have done what the system announces that it will reward are entitled to their advantages. In this sense the more fortunate have a claim to their better situation; their claims are legitimate expectations established by social institutions, and the community is obligated to meet them. But this sense of desert presupposes the existence of the cooperative scheme; it is irrelevant to the question whether in the first place the scheme is to be designed in accordance with the difference principle or some other criterion. . . . ◆ ◆ ◆

◆ Notes

1. Kant is clear that the original agreement is hypothetical. See *The Metaphysics of Morals*, pt. I (*Rechtslehre*), especially §§47, 52; and pt. II of the essay "Concerning the Common Saying: This May Be True in Theory but It Does Not Apply in Practice," in *Kant's Political Writings*, ed. Hans Reiss and trans. by H. B. Nisbet (Cambridge, The University Press, 1970), pp. 73–87. See George Vlachos, *La Pensée politique de Kant* (Paris, Presses Universitaires de France, 1962), pp. 326–335; and J. G. Murphy, *Kant: The Philosophy of Right* (London, Macmillan, 1970), pp. 109–112, 133–136, for a further discussion.

2. See Herbert Spiegelberg, "A Defense of Human Equality," *Philosophical Review*, vol. 53 (1944), pp. 101, 113–123; and D. D. Raphael, "Justice and Liberty," *Proceedings of the Aristotelian Society*, vol. 51 (1950–1951), pp. 187f.

3. See, for example, Spiegelberg, pp. 120f.

Socialist Democracy

Carl Cohen

Before considering socialism as such, think about car insurance: At present, insurers divide drivers into classes by age, gender, and driving record. Those in the low-risk categories get lower premiums. This means that a young male driver, however safe, is lumped in a risk group with others who may statistically be at higher risk to make a claim. Is that fair? A socialist system pools the benefits and burdens of an entire community. In the insurance example, all drivers might pay a uniform premium based on the driving population as a whole rather than groupings decided by the insurance companies. Similarly, health insurance would not penalize those unlucky enough to be born with medical issues. Why should we punish people for problems they did not create or deserve?

In this extract, Cohen suggests arguments that a socialist might offer for extending this view of fairness into the economic and political realm. He points out that at present society protects the individual's political rights (freedom of speech and assembly, for example), but under socialism there would be protection of an individual's economic rights (freedom from unemployment and hunger) as well. Cohen examines some of the central claims underpinning capitalism and suggests that they are not as self-evidently true as they first appear to be. He also notes that we currently have forms of socialism in society, and we can extend that insight by recognizing that many European countries have ruling parties that are avowedly socialist, at least in name.

Every democracy, socialist or not, will seek to protect citizens' political rights—but only socialist democracies protect citizens' *economic* rights. Freedom of speech and assembly are priceless; are not freedom from unemployment and hunger equally so? We think so. The same collective action needed to defend the citizens against aggression from without is needed to organize production rationally and to distribute wealth justly within our own borders. In the economic sphere as much as any other, cooperation and foresight are central. The public ownership of industry is the only way to achieve them.

THE UNFAIRNESS OF PRIVATE OWNERSHIP

History confirms this. The private ownership of productive industry has always resulted in deprivation for most, luxury for a few. The owners of factories and mines are forced, by competition, to exploit both workers and resources. Where private interests have been the foundation of the system, they have always been advanced at the expense of public interests. Why not build a power project in the heart of the Hudson River valley or on the seashores of Maine? It is not a concern for beauty but for bookkeeping that pays off. Drill for oil wherever it can be found—in the last of the forests, on the beaches, on the lawn of the state capitol. Business is business. The great redwoods of California, each hundreds of years old and a monument to nature's grandeur, fall by the thousands; the forests are clear-cut, left as ugly, muddy hillsides. The drive for profit is the sharpest of all saws.

The system of private ownership encourages, even demands, selfishness at every turn. Let buyers, employees, the general public beware! Cornering the market in computing equipment, controlling access to the telephone system, delaying the marketing of steers in order to raise the price of beef, steadily increasing the price of gasoline when petroleum is in short supply—all such maneuvers are within the rules of the capitalist game. Sharp play and toughness yield riches; generosity yields bankruptcy; and no one may refuse to play.

To limit the injustices done in the name of private enterprise, some have tried to adjust the rules of the game. It does not work. Fair business practice codes, antitrust legislation, minimum-wage laws, and the like, do restrain some of the excesses of the capitalists. But such changes are no more than cosmetics, mitigating but not eliminating the real evil. Injustice flows not merely from the excesses of capitalism but from the essence of the system of private ownership itself.

Changing the rules cannot eliminate exploitation and gross inequality; only changing the entire game can. If everyone is to be free from economic need, everyone must have the right to participate in planning production and controlling distribution. That can be only when industrial production and distribution is entirely in public hands. Just as those who are not represented in parliament will suffer politically, those not represented in economic decision making

will surely suffer in the market. The very argument that justifies democracy in the political sphere justifies democracy in the economic sphere as well. Economic injustice in a private enterprise system is not an accident but a necessary outcome. To eliminate that injustice we must end the disproportion in the powers of its elements, just as the disproportionate powers of political elements were finally ended by giving the vote to all citizens. The case for socialism is the case for economic democracy.

THE INHUMANITY OF THE MARKET

Socialism is simply economic good sense. The long-term fruits of capitalism have become too bitter: cycles of boom and bust, unemployment and welfare, personal dissatisfaction and business failure. Inflation steals from everyone (except those who can raise prices and rents quickly); depression demoralizes everyone. Disorder and distress are widespread. Our land itself is abused, our water poisoned, and our air fouled. When everything is left "up for grabs," the grabbing will be vicious and the outcome chaotic. There can be no intelligent planning for future needs, no rational distribution of products or materials in short supply, no reasonable deployment of human energies, in an economy in which the fundamental rule is dog-eat-dog. Legislation designed to blunt the fangs can do no more than reduce the depth of a serious wound.

Capitalism relies upon the so-called "market economy." The prices asked or offered for raw materials and finished products it leaves entirely to private parties, individuals or business firms, who enter a supposedly open market. This free market, it is argued, will be self-regulating; supply and demand will rationalize prices, fairness and productivity will be ensured by competition, enterprise encouraged by the hope of profit.

None of this actually works in the way capitalist mythology depicts it. The system relies upon the wisdom and power of economic fairies that never did exist. Nothing in the market is dependable, since everything within it fluctuates in response to unpredictable and uncontrollable factors: the tastes of buyers, the moods of sellers, the special circumstances of either, accidents causing short supply, or fashions transforming reasonable supply into glut.

Rationality and fairness through competition? No claim could be more fraudulent. In a capitalist market prices depend largely upon the relative strengths (or weaknesses) of the traders. If I own all the orchards, and am therefore the seller of all the cherries in the market, you, dear buyer, will pay my price or eat no cherries. Steel, timber, farm machinery are for sale in the market. Go, dear friend, and bargain with the sellers. Anyone tempted to believe capitalist propaganda about the give and take in the market should put it to the test. Reflect upon your own recent experiences as a shopper: You were told the price of the item you looked at—a TV set or a can of beans—and you paid that price or left without. That is how the market works for ordinary folks. Giant firms, manufacturers or chain retailers, may bargain with suppliers on occasion—but even then the stronger get the better deals. Those who control resources and money control the market, manipulating it in their own interests. Those who enter the market (either as buyer or seller) with great needs but little power are squeezed and exploited. The weak get twisted, the strong do the twisting. That's free enterprise.

Fairness? Markets do not know the meaning of the word. All's fair in war—and market competition is perpetual war, through guile and threat, on a thousand fronts. Rewards go to the aggressive; the keys to victory are accumulation, possession, control. And rules for fair dealing? They will be evaded, broken surreptitiously, even ignored—just like the rules of war—when it profits the combatants.

Private enterprise is worse than unfair. It is nofair; it does not recognize justice as any concern for *homo economicus*. The only things that count, for it, are the things that can be counted. Such a system is by its nature, explicitly *inhumane*. To render it humane it is necessary to transform it into an instrument for humans. Socialism makes human concerns the fundamental concerns in the design, manufacture, and distribution of material goods. Only thus can an economic system achieve justice. What should appear in that holiest of capitalist places, "the bottom line"? A record of increased human satisfactions? Or a record of profit?

THE CRUELTY OF CAPITALISM

"Ah, but that callous system you attack," replies the capitalist, "is the most wonderfully productive in all the world. We do not, it is true, share everything and share alike—but by rewarding personal ambition and intellect, we encourage and tap the productivity of all. Capitalist societies may not be perfectly equitable, but they are rich—and that, in the end, is what we all want."

The true colors of the beast begin to show. Riches, material acquisition, is for it—but not for us—the paramount objective. Socialists think of human life in broader and deeper terms. For us money and goods are servants, not masters. General human well-being, we say, is the mark of a good society. Material wealth is only our tool.

Even on their own ground, however—measuring everything by prosperity—the case for capitalism fails. That private ownership leads to greater productivity is also myth. Enormous growth there has been, of course, in all modern economies; but that growth came with invention and discovery, with technological advance, with mass production and automation. It comes in capitalist countries *and* socialist countries, when relatively primitive methods of production are replaced by more efficient systems. Human intelligence, not capitalism, should get credit for that. There is no reason to believe that human intelligence must be less energetic, or less inventive, when put to common service than when serving private ends.

The ironic consequence of that private service is *deprivation*, the hidden *lack* of that very prosperity capitalism claims. In a system of private ownership the factories and mines must produce at a profit or not at all. Most steel foundries—under capitalism—operate well below capacity most of the time. Produce too much steel and the price will drop; what profit, after all, is there in that? Houses and apartments are needed by tens of millions of Americans; we have the capacity to build that housing, but it goes largely unused. Carpenters and masons wait impatiently in union halls for work; lumber yards and designers lay off workers; contractors and salesmen search desperately for buyers who can afford loans at high interest rates; banks wait cautiously for safe borrowers. The entire system permits even needed construction only when a profit is to be made. If there is no money in it, those in need of housing will simply wait. You cannot make a buck by being a nice guy. What does get built is outrageously expensive, affordable only by the rich. Building slows to a crawl while housing needs soar. The human need for housing plays second fiddle to the demand for profit, and the building industry floats like a chip on the waves of a capricious economic ocean.

So it is with every industry. Production within the plant may be organized and efficient in the highest degree—but the "free market" to which skills and products are brought is madness itself. Again and again capitalism carries itself, now with unbridled enthusiasm, now with unrelieved desperation, to the brink of dissolution. "Business cycles"—the euphemistic name for the manic booms and depressing busts of the capitalist market—are the inevitable consequence of stupid inaction, leaving to pure chance and private avarice the control of our essential common business. The resulting human misery has been incalculable. After a chain of depressions through the nineteenth and early twentieth centuries, capitalism produced the super depression of the 1930s—a slough of despair, fathomless in depth and a decade in length. It was cut short, at last, only by the productive impetus of a terrible war. . . .

SOCIAL PLANNING

Two practical principles . . . comprise the substance of democratic socialism. Public ownership is the first, the foundation of socialism. Planning production and distribution for the common good is the second, and the fruit of socialism. When all members of the community have equal voice in the management of the economy, the elected representatives of those voices will naturally seek to deploy productive powers rationally. The community, then fully in command of its own affairs, will deliberate carefully in choosing its economic goals and in devising the means to attain them. It will make plans.

All intelligent humans plan. Preparing for the future is the mark of rational beings. Capitalists plan thoughtfully for their own advancement, plan cautiously for the security of their families, plan assiduously for the growth of their businesses. Yet they bitterly attack us for advocating the same foresight in the larger community! In matters close to them they do not cease to think ahead. But they insist that the community as a whole should entrust its future to an "invisible hand" that is somehow to ensure social health and prosperity. Sophisticated in private affairs, their handling of public affairs is simply immature, primitive.

Critics of socialism (it should be noted in fairness) often do recognize the need to plan in some particular sphere of the economy. Doing so, of course, such critics implicitly abandon their devotion to "free" markets. They plan the supplies of oil or gas, the road system, the storage of grain, and the money supply. But if the use of careful planning is appropriate in any single sphere of the economy, it is no less appropriate for the economy as a whole. Capitalists who plan, but are infuriated by planning, are blinded by an ideology from which they cannot free their own minds. . . . ◆ ◆ ◆

The Right to Eat and the Duty to Work

Trudy Govier

There is a lot of discussion in business ethics about layoffs and downsizing. We need to recognize that these debates go on against the backdrop of a system that allows benefits to the unemployed and a safety net (of sorts) of welfare payments for those who cannot or will not work. Govier (writing from Canada) asks what responsibility society has for the welfare of its members. Any affirmative answer will have implications for business, in that government will restrict the free market and impose duties beyond furthering our own self-interest. Benefits have to be paid for, of course, and often this takes the form of taxation on business, which provides an incentive for seeking cheaper labor overseas.

Govier identifies three positions: (1) Individualist, where there is no right to state welfare benefits; (2) Permissive, where there is an unconditional right to benefits; and (3) Puritan, where benefits are made conditional, perhaps on one's willingness to work.

No matter which position you sympathize with, it is useful to have it in mind when reading selections about outsourcing, reductions in force, or layoffs. What happens to those left behind, and should they have been shrewd enough to save or retrain? Does our current system send the wrong incentive signals to people or businesses? Does (and should) the community as a whole mitigate the sometimes harmful effects of business decisions?

Although the topic of welfare is not one with which philosophers have often concerned themselves, it is a topic which gives rise to many complex and fascinating questions—some in the area of political philosophy, some in the area of ethics, and some of a more practical kind. The variety of issues related to the subject of welfare makes it particularly necessary to be clear just which issue one is examining in a discussion of welfare. In a recent book on the subject, Nicholas Rescher asks:

> In what respects and to what extent is society, working through the instrumentality of the state, responsible for the welfare of its members? What demands for the promotion of his welfare can an individual reasonably make upon his society? These are questions to which no answer can be given in terms of some *a priori* approach with reference to universal ultimates. Whatever answer can appropriately be given will depend, in the final analysis, on what the society decides it should be.[1]

Rescher raises this question only to avoid it. His response to his own question is that a society has all and only those responsibilities for its members that it thinks it has. Although this claim is trivially true as regards legal responsibilities, it is inadequate from a moral perspective. If one imagines the case of an affluent society which leaves the blind, the disabled, and the needy to die of starvation, the incompleteness of Rescher's account becomes obvious. In this imagined case one is naturally led to raise the question as to whether those in power ought to supply those in need with the necessities of life. Though the needy have no legal right to welfare benefits of any kind, one might very well say that they ought to have such a right. It is this claim which I propose to discuss here.[2]

I shall approach this issue by examining three positions which may be adopted in response to it. These are:

1. *The Individualist Position:* Even in an affluent society, one ought not to have any legal right to state-supplied welfare benefits.
2. *The Permissive Position:* In a society with sufficient resources, one ought to have an unconditional legal right to receive state-supplied welfare benefits. (That is, one's right to receive such benefits ought not to

depend on one's behaviour; it should be guaranteed).
3. *The Puritan Position:* In a society with sufficient resources one ought to have a legal right to state-supplied welfare benefits; this right ought to be conditional, however, on one's willingness to work. . . .

THE INDIVIDUALIST VIEW

It might be maintained that a person in need has no legitimate moral claim on those around him and that the hypothetical inattentive society which left its blind citizens to beg or starve cannot rightly be censured for doing so. This view, which is dramatically at odds with most of contemporary social thinking, lives on in the writings of Ayn Rand and her followers.[3] The Individualist sets a high value on uncoerced personal choice. He sees each person as a responsible agent who is able to make his own decisions and to plan his own life. He insists that with the freedom to make decisions goes responsibility for the consequences of those decisions. A person has every right, for example, to spend ten years of his life studying Sanskrit—but if, as a result of this choice, he is unemployable, he ought not to expect others to labour on his behalf. No one has a proper claim on the labour of another, or on the income ensuing from that labour, unless he can repay the labourer in a way acceptable to that labourer himself. Government welfare schemes provide benefits from funds gained largely by taxing earned income. One cannot 'opt out' of such schemes. To the Individualist, this means that a person is forced to work part of his time for others.

Suppose that a man works forty hours and earns two hundred dollars. Under modern-day taxation, it may well be that he can spend only two-thirds of that money as he chooses. The rest is taken by government and goes to support programmes which the working individual may not himself endorse. The beneficiaries of such programmes—those beneficiaries who do not work themselves—are as though they have slaves working for them. Backed by the force which government authorities can command, they are able to exist on the earnings of others. Those who support them do not do so voluntarily, out of charity; they do so on government command.

> Someone across the street is unemployed. Should you be taxed extra to pay for his expenses? Not at all. You have not injured him, you are not responsible for the fact that he is unemployed (unless you are a senator or bureaucrat who agitated for further curtailing of business which legislation passed, with the result that your neighbour was laid off by the curtailed business). You may voluntarily wish to help him out, or better still, try to get him a job to put him on his feet again; but since you have initiated no aggressive act against him, and neither purposefully nor accidentally injured him in any way, you should not be legally penalized for the fact of his unemployment.[4]

The Individualist need not lack concern for those in need. He may give generously to charity; he might give more generously still, if his whole income were his to use, as he would like it to be. He may also believe that, as a matter of empirical fact, existing government programmes do not actually help the poor. They support a cumbersome bureaucracy and they use financial resources which, if untaxed, might be used by those with initiative to pursue job-creating endeavours. The thrust of the Individualist's position is that each person owns his own body and his own labour; thus each person is taken to have a virtually unconditional right to the income which that labour can earn him in a free market place.[5] For anyone to preempt part of a worker's earnings without that worker's voluntary consent is tantamount to robbery. And the fact that the government is the intermediary through which

this deed is committed does not change its moral status one iota.

On an Individualist's view, those in need should be cared for by charities or through other schemes to which contributions are voluntary. Many people may wish to insure themselves against unforeseen calamities and they should be free to do so. But there is no justification for non-optional government schemes financed by taxpayers' money. . . .

. . . An Individualist account is also implied by some of the remarks made by Robert Nozick in his recent article, "Distributive Justice".[6] Nozick contrasts *historical* accounts of the justice of property holdings with *patterned* accounts of distributive justice. In the former, people are taken to be entitled to holdings in virtue of sequences of transaction which have actually occurred. In the latter, attempts are made to define a formula for distributing goods: 'to each according to his——'. Of these patterned theories and their attendant practices Nozick says

> Whether it is done through taxation on wages or on wages over a certain amount, or through seizure of profits, or through there being a big social pot so that it's not clear what's coming from where and what's going where, patterned principles of distributive justice involve appropriating the actions of other persons. Seizing the results of someone's labour is equivalent to seizing hours from him and directing him to carry on various activities. If people force you to do certain work, or unrewarded work, for a certain period of time, they decide what you are to do and what purposes your work is to serve apart from your decisions.[7]

. . .

THE PERMISSIVE VIEW

Directly contrary to the Individualist view of welfare is what I have termed the Permissive view. According to this view, in a society which has

sufficient resources so that everyone could be supplied with the necessities of life, every individual
ought to be given the legal right to social security,
and this right ought not to be conditional in any
way upon an individual's behaviour. *Ex hypothesi*
the society which we are discussing has sufficient
goods to provide everyone with food, clothing,
shelter and other necessities. Someone who does
without these basic goods is scarcely living at all,
and a society which takes no steps to change this
state of affairs implies by its inaction that the life
of such a person is without value. It does not execute him; but it may allow him to die. It does not
put him in prison; but it may leave him with a life
of lower quality than that of some prison inmates.
A society which can rectify these circumstances
and does not can justly be accused of imposing
upon the needy either death or lifelong deprivation. And those characteristics which make a person needy—whether they be illness, old age,
insanity, feeblemindedness, inability to find paid
work, or even poor moral character—are insufficient to make him deserve the fate to which an
inactive society would in effect condemn him.
One would not be executed for inability or failure to find paid work; neither should one be allowed to die for this misfortune or failing.

A person who cannot or does not find his own
means of social security does not thereby forfeit
his status as a human being. If other human beings, with physical, mental and moral qualities
different from his, are regarded as having the
right to life and to the means of life, then so too
should he be regarded. A society which does not
accept the responsibility for supplying such a
person with the basic necessities of life is, in effect, endorsing a difference between its members
which is without moral justification. . . .

The adoption of a Permissive view of welfare
would have significant practical implications. If
there were a legal right, unconditional upon behaviour, to a specified level of state-supplied ben-

efits, then state investigation of the prospective
welfare recipient could be kept to a minimum.
Why he is in need, whether he can work, whether
he is willing to work, and what he does while receiving welfare benefits are on this view quite irrelevant to his right to receive those benefits. A
welfare recipient is a person who claims from his
society that to which he is legally entitled under
a morally based welfare scheme. The fact that he
makes this claim licenses no special state or societal interference with his behaviour. If the Permissive view of welfare were widely believed,
then there would be no social stigma attached to
being on welfare. There is such a stigma, and
many long-term welfare recipients are considerably demoralized by their dependent status.[8]
These facts suggest that the Permissive view of
welfare is not widely held in our society.

THE PURITAN VIEW

This view of welfare rather naturally emerges
when we consider that no one can have a right to
something without someone else's, or some
group of other persons', having responsibilities
correlative to this right. In the case in which the
right in question is a legal right to social security,
the correlative responsibilities may be rather extensive. They have been deemed responsibilities
of 'the state'. The state will require resources and
funds to meet these responsibilities, and these do
not emerge from the sky miraculously, or zip into
existence as a consequence of virtually effortless
acts of will. They are taken by the state from its
citizens, often in the form of taxation on earned
income. The funds given to the welfare recipient
and many of the goods which he purchases with
these funds are produced by other members of
society, many of whom give a considerable portion of their time and their energy to this end. If
a state has the moral responsibility to ensure the
social security of its citizens then all the citizens

of that state have the responsibility to provide state agencies with the means to carry out their duties. This responsibility, in our present contingent circumstances, seems to generate an obligation to *work*.

A person who works helps to produce the goods which all use in daily living and, when paid, contributes through taxation to government endeavours. The person who does not work, even though able to work, does not make his contribution to social efforts towards obtaining the means of life. He is not entitled to a share of the goods produced by others if he chooses not to take part in their labours. Unless he can show that there is a moral justification for his not making the sacrifice of time and energy which others make, he has no legitimate claim to welfare benefits. If he is disabled or unable to obtain work, he cannot work; hence he has no need to justify his failure to work. But if he does choose not to work, he would have to justify his choice by saying 'others should sacrifice their time and energy for me; I have no need to sacrifice time and energy for them'. This principle, a version of what Rawls refers to as a free-rider's principle, simply will not stand up to criticism.[9] To deliberately avoid working and benefit from the labours of others is morally indefensible.

Within a welfare system erected on these principles, the right to welfare is conditional upon one's satisfactorily accounting for his failure to obtain the necessities of life by his own efforts. Someone who is severely disabled mentally or physically, or who for some other reason cannot work, is morally entitled to receive welfare benefits. Someone who chooses not to work is not. The Puritan view of welfare is a kind of compromise between the Individualist view and the Permissive view. . . .

The Puritan view of welfare, based as it is on the inter-relation between welfare and work, provides a rationale for two connected principles which those establishing welfare schemes in Canada and in the United States seem to endorse. First of all, those on welfare should never receive a higher income than the working poor. Secondly, a welfare scheme should, in some way or other, incorporate incentives to work. These principles, which presuppose that it is better to work than not to work, emerge rather naturally from the contingency which is at the basis of the Puritan view: the goods essential for social security are products of the labour of some members of society. If we wish to have a continued supply of such goods, we must encourage those who work to produce them. . . .

APPRAISAL OF POLICIES: SOCIAL CONSEQUENCES AND SOCIAL JUSTICE

In approaching the appraisal of prospective welfare policies under these two aspects I am, of course, making some assumptions about the moral appraisal of suggested social policies. Although these cannot possibly be justified here, it may be helpful to articulate them, at least in a rough way.

Appraisal of social policies is in part teleological. To the extent that a policy, P, increases the total human welfare more than does an alternative policy, P', P is a better social policy than P'. Or, if P leaves the total human welfare as it is, while P' diminishes it, then to that extent, P is a better social policy than P'. Even this skeletal formulation of the teleological aspect of appraisal reveals why appraisal cannot be entirely teleological. We consider total consequences—effects upon the total of 'human well-being' in a society. But this total is a summation of consequences on different individuals. It includes no judgements as to how far we allow one individual's well-being to decrease while another's increases, under the same policy. Judgements relating to the latter problems are judgements about social justice.

In appraising social policies we have to weigh up considerations of total well-being against considerations of justice. Just how this is to be done, precisely, I would not pretend to know. However, the absence of precise methods does not mean that we should relinquish attempts at appraisal: some problems are already with us, and thought which is necessarily tentative and imprecise is still preferable to no thought at all.

Consequences of Welfare Schemes

First, let us consider the consequences of non-scheme advocated by the Individualist. He would have us abolish all non-optional government programmes which have as their goal the improvement of anyone's personal welfare. This rejection extends to health schemes, pension plans and education, as well as to welfare and unemployment insurance. So following the Individualist would lead to very sweeping changes.

The Individualist will claim (as do [John] Hospers and Ayn Rand) that on the whole his non-scheme will bring beneficial consequences. He will admit, as he must, that there are people who would suffer tremendously if welfare and other social security programmes were simply terminated. Some would even die as a result. We cannot assume that spontaneously developing charities would cover every case of dire need. Nevertheless the Individualist wants to point to benefits which would accrue to businessmen and to working people and their families if taxation were drastically cut. It is his claim that consumption would rise, hence production would rise, job opportunities would be extended, and there would be an economic boom, if people could only spend all their earned income as they wished. This boom would benefit both rich and poor.

There are significant omissions which are necessary in order to render the Individualist's optimism plausible. Either workers and businessmen would have insurance of various kinds, or they would be insecure in their prosperity. If they did have insurance to cover health problems, old age and possible job loss, then they would pay for it; hence they would not be spending their whole earned income on consumer goods. Those who run the insurance schemes could, of course, put this money back into the economy—but government schemes already do this. The economic boom under Individualism would not be as loud as originally expected. Furthermore the goal of increased consumption–increased productivity must be questioned from an ecological viewpoint: many necessary materials are available only in limited quantities.

Finally, a word about charity. It is not to be expected that those who are at the mercy of charities will benefit from this state, either materially or psychologically. Those who prosper will be able to choose between giving a great deal to charity and suffering from the very real insecurity and guilt which would accompany the existence of starvation and grim poverty outside their padlocked doors. It is to be hoped that they would opt for the first alternative. But, if they did, this might be every bit as expensive for them as government-supported benefit schemes are now. If they did not give generously to charity, violence might result. However one looks at it, the consequences of Individualism are unlikely to be good. . . .

. . . The rationale underlying the Puritan scheme makes the degradation of welfare recipients a natural consequence of welfare institutions. Work is valued and only he who works is thought to contribute to society. Welfare recipients are regarded as parasites and spongers—so when they are treated as such, this is only what we should have expected. Being on welfare in a society which thinks and acts in this fashion can be psychologically debilitating. Welfare recipients who are demoralized by their downgraded status and relative lack of personal freedom can be expected to be made less capable of self-sufficiency. To the extent that this is so, welfare systems erected on Puritan principles may defeat their own purposes.

In fairness, it must be noted here that bureaucratic checks and controls are not a feature only of Puritan welfare systems. To a limited extent, Permissive systems would have to incorporate them too. Within those systems, welfare benefits would be given only to those whose income was inadequate to meet basic needs. However, there would be no checks on 'willingness to work', and there would be no need for welfare workers to evaluate the merits of the daily activities of recipients. If a Permissive guaranteed income system were administered through income tax returns, everyone receiving the basic income and those not needing it paying it back in taxes, then the special status of welfare recipients would fade. They would no longer be singled out as a special group within the population. It is to be expected that living solely on government-supplied benefits would be psychologically easier in that type of situation.

Thus it can be argued that for the recipients of welfare, a Permissive scheme has more advantages than a Puritan one. This is not a very surprising conclusion. The Puritan scheme is relatively disadvantageous to recipients, and Puritans would acknowledge this point; they will argue that the overall consequences of Permissive schemes are negative in that these schemes benefit some at too great a cost to others. (Remember, we are not yet concerned with the *justice* of welfare policies, but solely with their consequences as regards *total* human well-being within the society in question.) The concern which most people have regarding the Permissive scheme relates to its costs and its dangers to the 'work ethic'. It is commonly thought that people work only because they have to work to survive in a tolerable style. If a guaranteed income scheme were adopted by the government, this incentive to work would disappear. No one would be faced with the choice between a nasty and boring job and starvation. Who would do the nasty and boring jobs then? Many of them are not eliminable and they have to be done somehow, by someone. Puritans fear that a great many people — even some with relatively pleasant jobs — might simply cease to work if they could receive non-stigmatized government money to live on. If this were to happen, the permissive society would simply grind to a halt.

In addressing these anxieties about the consequences of Permissive welfare schemes, we must recall that welfare benefits are set to ensure only that those who do not work have a bearable existence, with an income sufficient for basic needs, and that they have this income regardless of why they fail to work. Welfare benefits will not finance luxury living for a family of five! If jobs are adequately paid so that workers receive more than the minimum welfare income in an earned salary, then there will still be a financial incentive to take jobs. What guaranteed income schemes will do is to raise the salary floor. This change will benefit the many non-unionized workers in service and clerical occupations.

Furthermore it is unlikely that people work solely due to (i) the desire for money and the things it can buy and (ii) belief in the Puritan work ethic. There are many other reasons for working, some of which would persist in a society which had adopted a Permissive welfare system. Most people are happier when their time is structured in some way, when they are active outside their own homes, when they feel themselves part of an endeavour whose purposes transcend their particular egoistic ones. Women often choose to work outside the home for these reasons as much as for financial ones. With these and other factors operating I cannot see that the adoption of a Permissive welfare scheme would be followed by a level of slothfulness which would jeopardize human well-being. . . .

In summary, we can appraise Individualism, Puritanism and Permissivism with respect to their anticipated consequences, as follows: Individualism is unacceptable; Puritanism is tolerable, but has some undesirable consequences for welfare recipients; Permissivism appears to be the winner. Worries about bad effects which Permissive welfare schemes might have due to high costs and (alleged) reduced work-incentives appear to be without solid basis.

Social Justice under Proposed Welfare Schemes

We must now try to consider the merits of Individualism, Puritanism and Permissivism with regard to their impact on the distribution of the goods necessary for well-being. Nozick has argued against the whole conception of a distributive justice on the grounds that it presupposes that goods are like manna from heaven: we simply get them and then have a problem—to whom to give them. According to Nozick we know where things come from and we do not have the problem of to whom to give them. There is not really a problem of distributive justice, for there is no central distributor giving out manna from heaven! It is necessary to counter Nozick on this point since his reaction to the (purported) problems of distributive justice would undercut much of what follows.

There is a level at which Nozick's point is obviously valid. If A discovers a cure for cancer, then it is A and not B or C who is responsible for this discovery. On Nozick's view this is taken to imply that A should reap any monetary profits which are forthcoming; other people will benefit from the cure itself. Now although it cannot be doubted that A is a bright and hardworking person, neither can it be denied that A and

his circumstances are the product of many cooperative endeavours: schools and laboratories, for instance. Because this is so, I find Nozick's claim that 'we know where things come from' unconvincing at a deeper level. Since achievements like A's presuppose extensive social cooperation, it is morally permissible to regard even the monetary profits accruing from them as shareable by the 'owner' and society at large.

Laws support existing income levels in many ways. Governments specify taxation so as to further determine net income. Property ownership is a legal matter. In all these ways people's incomes and possibilities for obtaining income are affected by deliberate state action. It is always possible to raise questions about the moral desirability of actual conventional arrangements. Should university professors earn less than lawyers? More than waitresses? Why? Why not? Anyone who gives an account of distributive justice is trying to specify principles which will make it possible to answer questions such as these, and nothing in Nozick's argument suffices to show that the questions are meaningless or unimportant. . . .

The Individualist attempts to justify extreme variations in income, with some people below the level where they can fulfil their basic needs, with reference to the fact of people's actual accomplishments. This approach to the question is open to the same objections as those which have already been raised against Nozick's non-manna-from-heaven argument, and I shall not repeat them here. Let us move on to the Puritan account. It is because goods emerge from human efforts that the Puritan advances his view of welfare. He stresses the unfairness of a system which would permit some people to take advantage of others. A Permissive welfare system would do this, as it makes no attempt to distinguish between those who choose not to work and those who cannot work. No one should be able to take advantage of another under the auspices of a government institution. The Puritan scheme seeks to eliminate this possibility, and for that reason, Puritans would allege, it is a more just scheme than the Permissive one.

Permissivists can best reply to this contention by acknowledging that any instance of free-riding would be an instance where those working were done an injustice, but by showing that any justice which the Puritan preserves by eliminating free-riding is outweighed by *injustice* perpetrated elsewhere. Consider the children of the Puritan's free-riders. They will suffer greatly for the 'sins' of their parents. Within the institution of the family, the Puritan cannot suitably hurt the guilty without cruelly depriving the innocent. There is a sense, too, in which Puritanism does injustice to the many people on welfare who are not free-riders. It perpetuates the opinion that they are non-contributors to society and this doctrine, which is over-simplified if not downright false, has a harmful effect upon welfare recipients.

Social justice is not simply a matter of the distribution of goods, or the income with which goods are to be purchased. It is also a matter of the protection of rights. Western societies claim to give their citizens equal rights in political and legal contexts; they also claim to endorse the larger conception of a right to life. Now it is possible to interpret these rights in a limited and formulistic way, so that the duties correlative to them are minimal. On the limited, or negative, interpretation, to say that A has a right to life is simply to say that others have a duty not to interfere with A's attempts to keep himself alive. This interpretation of the right to life is compatible with Individualism as well as with Puritanism. But it is an inadequate interpretation of the right to life and of other rights. A right to vote is meaningless if one is starving and unable to get to the polls; a right to equality before the law is meaningless if one cannot afford to hire a lawyer. And so on.

Even a Permissive welfare scheme will go only a very small way towards protecting people's rights. It will amount to a meaningful acknowledgement of a right to life, by ensuring income adequate to purchase food, clothing and shelter—at the very least. These minimum necessities are presupposed by all other rights a society may endorse in that their possession is a precondition of being able to exercise these other rights. Because it protects the rights of all within a society better than do Puritanism and Individualism, the Permissive view can rightly claim superiority over the others with regard to justice. ◆ ◆ ◆

◆ Notes

1. Nicholas Rescher, *Welfare: Social Issues in Philosophical Perspective*, p. 114.
2. One might wish to discuss moral questions concerning welfare in the context of natural rights doctrines. Indeed, Article 22 of the United Nations Declaration of Human Rights states, 'Everyone, as a member of society, has the right to social security and is entitled, through national effort and international cooperation and in accordance with the organization and resources of each State, to the economic, social and cultural rights indispensable for his dignity and the free development of his personality'. I make no attempt to defend the right to welfare as a natural right. Granting that rights imply responsibilities or duties and that 'ought' implies 'can', it would only be intelligible to regard the right to social security as a natural right if all states were able to ensure the minimum well-being of their citizens. This is not the case. And a natural right is one which is by definition supposed to belong to all human beings simply in virtue of their status as

human beings. The analysis given here in the permissive view is compatible with the claim that all human beings have a *prima facie* natural right to social security. It is not, however, compatible with the claim that all human beings have a natural right to social security if this right is regarded as one which is so absolute as to be inviolable under any and all conditions.

3. See, for example, Ayn Rand's *Atlas Shrugged*, *The Virtue of Selfishness*, and *Capitalism: The Unknown Ideal*.

4. John Hospers, *Libertarianism: A Political Philosophy for Tomorrow*, p. 67.

5. I say virtually unconditional, because an Individualist such as John Hospers sees a legitimate moral role for government in preventing the use of force by some citizens against others. Since this is the case, I presume that he would also regard as legitimate such taxation as was necessary to support this function. Presumably that taxation would be seen as consented to by all, on the grounds that all 'really want' government protection.

6. In *Philosophy and Public Affairs*, Fall 1973.

7. Nozick, 'Distributive Justice', p. 68.

8. See *The Real Poverty Report*, pp. 167–87.

9. See *A Theory of Justice*, pp. 124, 136. Rawls defines the free-rider as one who relies on the principle 'everyone is to act justly except for myself, if I choose not to', and says that his position is a version of egoism which is eliminated as a morally acceptable principle by formal constraints. This conclusion regarding the tenability of egoism is one which I accept and which is taken for granted in the present context.

How Do Managers Think about Market Economies and Morality?*

Peter Ulrich and Ulrich Thielemann

A common assumption is that there is unanimity among managers about their mission. They are, after all, typically trained to believe the paramount virtue in business is to maximize returns, and therefore we might expect that they tend to compromise the ethical in favor of the profitable. Ulrich and Thielemann tested the proposition and found the situation to be far more subtle. Managers tend to fall into four major categories that enable them to square their beliefs about the market with their personal ethics; Ulrich and Thieleman label these manager categories Metaphysical Economists, Conventionalists, Idealists, and Reformers. The authors then use subcategories to illustrate the range of views and provide statistics to show the distribution of the various types.

---

*Original footnotes have been omitted.

WHAT IS THE FUNDAMENTAL PROBLEM OF BUSINESS ETHICS?

. . . We . . . formulate the *fundamental problem of business ethics* as follows:

> How do managers reconcile the requirements of achieving and preserving managerial success with the ethical demands of which they as responsible persons are, or ought to be, aware?

Thus in our view, the systematic starting question for any fruitful empirical research into business ethics is not simply *whether* or *to what extent* managers are "ethical," but *what kind of thinking pattern* they have personally evolved for themselves in order to be able to legitimize their activities within the field of tension between ethics and economic success both before themselves and before others. . . .

Our empirical study was conceived in keeping with the research design. . . . It was then conducted in accordance with the methodological guidelines of interpretative (qualitative) social research. Of the 75 persons originally addressed, 60 executives from private companies of all sizes agreed to be interviewed. They were chiefly top managers, and both sexes were represented. . . .

A TYPOLOGY OF BUSINESS-ETHICAL THINKING PATTERNS

. . . Two fundamental dimensions of business-ethical ways of thinking were found to be particularly helpful with regard to the classification and assessment of qualitatively diverging replies. Each of these dimensions has two manifestations.

Dimension 1: Degree of Problem and Conflict Awareness

Depending on which of the two manifestations is prevalent, business ethics is either perceived as a problem and an actual challenge or not.

- *Either* it is assumed that as a rule, there is *harmony* between the pursuit of managerial success and ethical aspects. In this case, we speak of harmonists. It must then be asked what kind of guarantor is capable of providing such assumed harmony and how this authority is capable of legitimizing the corporate policy pursued.
- *Or* it is assumed, conversely, that the relationship between ethics and the pursuit of success is characterized by *conflict* (conflict perceivers). In this case, harmonization remains to be attained, and it must be asked how this is possible and who would assume responsibility for it.

Dimension 2: The Way in Which the Economy Is Perceived

It largely depends on this dimension how a state of harmony or conflict is justified.

- *Either* the economy is perceived as a relatively autonomous *system* which mainly follows its own functional logic. In this case it is ultimately the anonymous market mechanisms that determine what happens in the economy. Individual economic subjects are largely confined to adapting themselves to the market system's competitive conditions: if they want to participate in the economic "game" of holding their own in the marketplace, then they have to stick to its rules. It must then be asked whether the morality of the economic game is assumed to be intrinsic to "free markets" as such or to be established by the market's political framework.
- *Or* else the economy is perceived as a sphere of life like any other, as a normal part of the *world we live in*, which is basically not determined by anonymous system imperatives but by the prevailing economic *culture* (for the differentiation between lifeworld and system

Dim. 2 \ Dim. 1	System-Oriented 44%	Culture-Oriented 56%
Harmonists 88%	*Metaphysical Economists* 34%	*Conventionalists* 54%
Conflict Perceivers 12%	*Reformers* 10%	*Idealists* 2%

Figure 1 ◆ BASIC TYPES OF BUSINESS-ETHICAL CONCEPTS

as sociologically fundamental categories. In the view of culture-oriented managers, the economy is neither ascribed to a special "ethic-free" functional logic, nor is any particular ethics of the economic system called for: solely the application of the general yardsticks of moral action is required. In this case, the question is whether these moral yardsticks are to be attributed to a conventional or postconventional awareness of ethics.

From a "theoretical" perspective, four basic types of business-ethical thinking can now be derived from the two-dimensional matrix resulting from a "crossing" of the two dimensions and their respective two aspects (Figure 1).

In order to provide a first survey, Figure 1 also indicates the frequency of the thinking patterns subsumed in the four groups which we call basic types. This frequency, however, merely refers to the distribution of the *dominant* (primary) orientation in each case. Above and beyond this it turned out that virtually all interviewees' business-ethical concepts were also characterized by *additional* (secondary) orientations. . . . The basic types and the more tangible thinking patterns (real types) assigned to them will be outlined very briefly below. . . . A tabular

survey of the various types, as well as a brief characterization in a systematic cross-comparison, is provided by Figure 2.

The Economistic Arrangement As a rule, *Metaphysical Economists* assume that there is harmony between ethics and economic success; at the same time, they perceive the marketplace as an anonymous system. Yet they evidently do not regard this as an ethical problem: they place more confidence in the "rationality" of the economic system than in human beings' practical reason. Not responsibly acting people, but the structural interrelations of anonymous market occurrences themselves ensure that the economy takes its proper course. If single moral snags occasionally occur in economic activities nonetheless, then a strict metaphysical economist will, on principle, consider them a symptom of the fact that the influence of the market forces is too slight rather than too strong. Like any other metaphysics, his *market metaphysics* are not at all easy to refute along empirical lines.

The belief in a market-inherent moral reason has deep roots in the history of thought of the occidental market society. Originally, it is religious in nature. This is the belief in the "prestabilized harmony" (Leibniz) of the world and market order given by a superhuman agency, i.e. God. Its "invisible hand" guarantees that what we should do in terms of ethics will "automatically" grow from what we want to do in economic terms. In this fashion, individual economic subjects are *relieved* of any direct normative-ethical demands. In Adam Smith this "invisible hand" can still easily be identified as the "wisdom of God." Thus Smith, who stood on the threshold of modernity, is likely to have been the first and last economist for whom the market's power to harmonize interests was still more or less explicitly based on *metaphysics*. "Modern" versions of market harmonism, however, have long been oblivious of their own metaphysical roots—otherwise, such views could hardly be held *today*, particularly in their more distinctive forms of more or less "blind" *market worship*.

According to our study, the economistic belief in the market's "self-healing powers" can be found among two variants of executives who differ with regard to strictness. In the case of the *Metaphysical Manager*, as we call this type (17% of our sample), the market's impersonal and "superhuman" intrinsic morality is, as it were, spontaneously translated into the "appropriate" practice of management. Ultimately, the Metaphysical Manager is convinced that an enterprise is not moved by human beings, but by the "will of the market." Executives are only tools of the market and, when all is said and done, possess no power at all—at least to the extent to which they seek to boost their companies' permanent profitability stakes by banning any "non-corporate interests." Consequently, they cannot be held responsible for any ethical deplorable states of affairs: if you don't have power, you can't exercise it, and ethics doesn't as much as come into it. One of the managers interviewed expressed this as follows: *"only a human being can act ethically or unethically, but a company . . . ? Even if the person who runs a company is unethical, this does not mean that the company is unethical, too."* The market tells the executive what's what, and that's how it should be.

The lasting assurance of a company's existence and success requires far-sighted *long-term* investments, not merely a "speculative" maximization of short-term profits. Only this will ensure that management action will indeed be determined by the literally "suprapersonal" (anonymous) will of the market rather than by the "arbitrary" will of the managers themselves. Thus the business-ethical principle applies according to which *long-term profit is ethically good*. Then, however, the "invisible hand" of the market will ensure that *"everyone will do well if the company does well"*.

In such conditions, the proper way to run an enterprise must be inferred from the company's success in the market alone, especially for reasons of *ethical* responsibility—or as Milton Friedman famously put it: "The *social* responsibility of business is to increase its profits" (and nothing else). It verges on the "unethical" to have subjective value judgments interfere with market-intrinsic ethics, whereas it is "ethical" to follow the signals of the market and thus to "discover" ethically appropriate courses of action. As a consequence—and this is the key point of this thinking pattern—entrepreneurs and managers have to abstain as far as possible from any personal moral sentiments and value judgements and listen to the "objective" verdict of the market instead.

In contrast to the Metaphysical Manager, the *Instrumentalist* (again 17%, but recorded as an additional orientation with another 35%), is perfectly ready to admit ethical considerations as an element of management. Indeed, he even calls for them since he does not necessarily regard them as a departure from the virtuous path of managerial profit seeking. This is why his reconciliation concept appears to be more moderate than the rigoristic concept of the Metaphysical Manager, who must refrain from any personal and thus from any moral commitment within the economy precisely for ethical reasons. The Instrumentalist, however, casts himself in a more active role in this respect: he "discovers" and realizes the strategic potential of "ethics" as an investment. Thus the economistic principle of legitimation is apparently inverted: *ethics is long-term profit*. Or, in the words of a manager we interviewed: *"Ethics may even be a key success factor—if you handle it right."*

Thus the Instrumentalist's primary incentive to act "ethically" is not an inner conviction.

Type	Economism		Conventionalism	
	The Metaphysical Manager	*The Instrumentalist*	*The Paternalist*	*The Personalist*
Way of Reconciliation	Impersonal market control	Sound and clever profit seeking	Ethical authority and consideration of entrepreneurs	Social responsibility of executives
Resulting Action	Relief of management from demand of ethical reflection	Use of ethics as a management instrument	Charismatic leadership ("model" behaviour, "set examples")	Ethics as an "*accompanying factor*" of management
Justification	Long-term economy = ethics; neutralization of entrepreneurial power by the market	Ethics = long-term economy; this is regarded as a sign of harmony between success and ethics	Superior ethical competence of management	Power implies responsibility
Subject Responsible	Invisible hand of the market	Ultimately, invisible hand of the market	Entrepreneur as paterfamilias	Entrepreneur/ manager as decision-maker
Symptomatic Expression	"*There is no ethical or unethical management.*" "*Everyone will do well if the company does well.*"	"*Ethics can be a key success factor —if you handle it right.*"	"*Management must instil ethics from above.*"	"*I plead for an absolutely liberal business policy which must, however, be placed under managerial self-control.*"
Criticisms	• The metaphysics of the market • Rigorism	• Reduction of ethics to "good management" • Overlooks conflicts between the economy and ethics (harmonious world)	• Elitism • Low awareness of economic system • Fiction of corporate community represented by the entrepreneur	• Monological concept of responsibility • Low awareness of economic system
Incidence – dominant: – additional: – total:	17% 7% 24%	17% 35% 52%	13% 15% 28%	38% 22% 60%
Alternative tendency	Personalism (60%) Legalism (40%)	Personalism (70%)	Not ascertainable	Instrumentalism (26%)

Figure 2 ◆ TYPES OF BUSINESS-ETHICAL THINKING

		Idealism	Reformism	
The Cultural Harmonist	*The Legalist*	*The Idealist*	*The Framework Reformer*	*The New Entrepreneur*
Commitment to social conventions	Legally enacted law	Change in social awareness and values	Politics of economic order	A two-level business-ethical concept
Accomplish the "*social commission*"	Compliance with applicable legislation	Renunciation of "*unethical success*", appeal to individuals	1st level: "business as usual" 2nd level: co-responsibility re politics of economic order	1st level: search for profitable ways of ethical management 2nd level: co-responsibility re politics of economic order
The company is "*part of society*"	Legitimacy = legality	"*Egoism*" and "*materialism*" can only be curbed through individual self-discipline.	"*Companies only develop this to the desired extent under government pressure.*"	Syntheses of ethics and success as entrepreneurial challenge *and* as a mission to remodel the economic order
Members of the cultural community	Legislative (state)	Committed persons	Governmental politics shaping the economic order	"*Enlightened managers*" as members of the public sphere
"*The company is bound up with society and its principles*"	"*We always subject ourselves to the laws of the country in which we operate.*"	"*The free market economy would be wonderful if there were ideal people.*"	"*I have nothing against a strict legislative environ-ment if I can still usefully operate inside it.*"	"*It is an entrepre-neurial challenge to deal with ethical demands in a spirit of innovation.*"
• Outdated supposition of a "closed society" • Rigid code of values	• Uncritical legal positivism • Business-ethical passivity • Cannot be generalized	• Lack of an institutional perspective • Ethics of renunciation	• Understanding of business ethics "cut in half" • Partial economism (within the economic framework)	• None
3% 7% 10%	0% 12% 12%	2% 38% 40%	2% 20% 22%	8% 5% 13%
Instrumentalism (67%)	Does not apply	Resignation	Economism	None

Rather, he acts in this manner because (and insofar as) such a course of action will pay off in the long run. He therefore avails himself of ethics as a management *instrument* for, say, the motivation of his staff or in order to ensure that his corporate policy gains acceptance among the general public. He does not attempt to conceal the instrumental character of such management methods but actually emphasizes his economic motivation. Nevertheless, instrumentalism in this sense of the term must be conceived of as a business-*ethical* concept. Indeed, the fact that calculations with regard to long-term corporation profitability involve "ethics" is seen as a *sign* of basic harmony between the pursuit of economic success and ethical demands. Here, too, it is assumed that an "invisible hand" is at work in the market which provides the executives' profit-oriented action with an ethically appropriate sense of direction.

This signal character of market success is strongly reminiscent of the connection elaborated by Max Weber . . . between the specifically religious motives of Protestantism, particularly of Calvinism and Puritanism, and the "Spirit of Capitalism". The (Calvinist) entrepreneur subjects himself to the methodical discipline of "ceaseless work", striving for professional and market success because this is the only way in which he is able to overcome the unendurable uncertainty of whether God will grant him His Divine mercy, of whether he may be hopeful of "salvation" in the hereafter. He considers professional success as an unfailing "*sign* of being chosen"—not, however, as a high-handed "*means* of attaining salvation". It is therefore not human intentions and motives that he discerns "at work on all that occurs in life", but a mighty and omniscient God; and if this God "shows one of his people a profitable chance, then He will do so by intention", namely the intention of assuring him that he is in a state of grace.

In our view the parallels with the two versions of economism, which like "Protestant ethics" ad-

vocate a *revelation theory of the market*, are evident. Indeed we suspect that the historical roots of economism are religious in nature and lie in the Protestantism from which Max Weber saw the "spirit of capitalism" emerge. It would appear that those "modern" managers who believe in economism still rely on the "signs and tokens" of success even if their secularized consciousness has long discarded any religious motives.

The Conventionalist Arrangement *Conventionalists*, too, perceive a basic harmony in the relationship between ethical demands and the pursuit of economic success. Their reconciliation concept contrasts with the economistic one—at least on the surface—in that management ethics is not guaranteed by an anonymous system logic intrinsic to the market. Instead, it makes use of the general standards that have been handed down and also apply to daily life in general. Systemic constraints of profitability do not play any systematic role in Conventionalists' arguments—neither a harmonizing nor a problematic role. This is not because Conventionalists simply negate or repress these economic constraints, but because they perceive them in completely different categories. Should it still come to a concrete conflict between ethics and economic success, Conventionalists will not apprehend this as a structural antagonism between moral obligation and systemic constraint but, in terms of individual ethics, as a conflict between moral obligation and egoistic predilection or economic self-interest. Thus conventionalists are not overly bothered by free-rider problems, as they do not perceive the systemic character of the modern economy. Rather, they see the key to a guaranteed harmony between ethics and the market in the *character* of individual executives or—in the case of less elitist versions of conventionalism—in the cultural standards of the community of economic agents.

There is a variety of conventionalistic thinking patterns (real types) which differ from each other in their distinctive concepts of the cultural "locus" of ethics. Since these distinctions do not play any particular part in this text, they will only be indicated in brief.

For the thoroughly value-conservative *Paternalist* (13%), the company still retains something of an—internally hierarchic—*oikos* economy, whose fortunes he controls with a strict and considerate hand. He does not doubt his authority, which in his overall view of things is a matter of course. His sense of responsibility is thus linked with a self-conception of elitist tendencies and therefore remains uncritical in this respect.

The *Personalist* (with 38% the most frequent dominant orientation) is more strongly aware of his power, of the danger of its egoistic misuse, and thus of the fact that such power requires legitimation. Yet he primarily perceives this business-ethical challenge in terms of limiting such powers *himself* rather than of subjecting them to social control; as for the rest, he pleads for *"absolutely liberal business policies"*. His individually ethical or elitist approach is also evident in that he prefers to put the stress on managers' personal ethics rather than on business ethics in general. The notion of ordo-political support for any business-ethical commitment is alien to him (despite the real economic constraints and all the opportunities of free-riding) since he resolutely adheres to the idea of the separability of "private" economy from public politics.

By contrast, the *Cultural Harmonist's* (3%) thinking pattern is based on the idea that the company *"is bound up with society and its principles"*. He conceives of society as a more or less conflict-free unit held together by a generally recognized value system. As a consequence, ethical demands to be made on management are best satisfied by an adherence to *"the well-known basic ethical standards"*.

Conversely, the *legalist* (not found as a dominant orientation but recorded as a secondary one with no less than 12%) does not think of ethics as directly guaranteed by the culture of society, but by the constitutional state in the form of applicable laws (legal standards). He considers the legality of management to be the necessary, and at the same time sufficient condition for the legitimacy of management.

The Idealistic Arrangement In a marked contrast to both Conventionalists and Metaphysical Economists, the *Idealist* regards the pursuit of profit as highly problematic in ethical terms. The Idealist is distinctively aware of conflict, but not particularly system-conscious in his perception of the economy. He is critical of contemporary culture rather than of the actual market system. In his view, then, social or ecological issues he deplores are not the consequence of any anonymous market forces, but rather the result of the *"egoism"* and *"materialism"* which all too many economic subjects have fallen prey to. He regards the dominating cultural attitudes and codes of values as the actual problem, unlike the Cultural Harmonist, who regards them as the solution. Precisely for this reason, the Idealist hopes for a profound change in cultural consciousness.

Since the Idealist thinks in terms of individual ethics rather than systemic categories, his champion way of assuming responsibility is the individual's renunciation of her *"egoistic"* predilections. In the face of the real factual constraints of the economic system, however, this means that the Idealist—provided she does not "drop out"—is permanently exposed to tough ethical dilemmas between idealistic commitment and opportunism. This may explain the heroic pathos that is apt to accompany his comments (*"holding your ground in this conflict is part of the job"*). For the Idealist, this conflict between ethical demands and the pursuit of market success is ultimately insoluble: his business-ethical commitment is literally *at the expense* of the company's success. In this manner, however, his business ethics is characterized by a spirit of renunciation. It could be described as a "red-figure ethics" which does not do justice to the problem of the economic *impossability* of measures justified by ethical reasons. Such kind of business ethics can therefore hardly be considered sound management.

The Reform-Oriented Arrangement The point of departure of the *Reformers'* business-ethical reconciliation concept is the plain but reasonable view that ethics and success are neither locked in inevitable conflict, nor do they automatically enjoy a harmonious relationship. Rather, reformers recognize the opportunity that ethics may well be a *basis* of successful enterprise. Whether and in what conditions this is the case is regarded as an empirical question that can only be answered by means of a sober and differentiated analysis of the concrete problems to be solved.

Reformers are aware of ethical conflicts and functional constraints. They are critical of existing system constraints because they regard the *Idealists'* demands to do heroic battle *against* the signals of the market as exorbitant. In their view, the crucial prerequisite to put the manager's ethical responsibility into practice is a change in the ordo-political framework of markets, i.e., in the general rules and incentives for successful economic activities. Of course, these rules of the game have to be determined in a societally responsible and competition-neutral way.

One type of Reformer, the mere *Framework Reformer* (2%), sees the systematic locus of business ethics in an arrangement of the market's general conditions and rules alone, but not in any ethical considerations within these rules. Within a reasonable market's framework, "business as usual" has to take place. Thus the Framework Reformer pleads for ethical considerations on the level of the political framework of markets exactly *in order to* keep business activities free from ethical claims.

The other type of Reformer, whom we call the *New Entrepreneur* (8%), applies a managerial thinking pattern that is both more extensive and more differentiated. He has learnt to think in terms of two institutional levels at once. On the *first level* he discerns considerable creative scope for the attainment of business success which—like any other scope of action—can and should be exhausted in an ethically responsible manner. The New Entrepreneur thus considers it a *"managerial challenge to deal with the new ethical demands in a spirit of innovation".* Therefore, he takes the trouble to look for *syntheses of ethics and success* that are apt to be unconventional. . . . ◆ ◆ ◆

2

THE THEORETICAL BACKDROP OF BUSINESS ETHICS

Morality deals with human values—notions of what is right or wrong, good or bad, fair or unfair, just or unjust. The practice of studying morality is generally termed *ethics*.

Normative ethics tells us how we should act: what the appropriate norms or standards are and the elements we should consider in establishing principles for our behavior. There are several well-established ethical frameworks that have a direct bearing on how managers should make decisions in the workplace.

Consider an example: A company uses minimum-wage laborers to sort recycling. The workers wear gloves but sometimes get pricked by used hypodermic needles in the trash. Gloves that are heavy enough to resist being punctured also make it virtually impossible to sort the material. How should the company react? What is its responsibility to the workers and investors?

Ethical dilemmas do not often lend themselves to simple solutions. Asking what the law is in this case probably will not tell us the right thing to do. The issues are often gray rather than black or white, and we may not find an ideal so-lution. Nevertheless, we should be able to justify our decisions on a principled basis. One way to start discussion is to look to fundamental guiding principles; once those are established, the road to a solution may become more evident.

The problems in business rarely arise with fanfare in a clear and obvious way. More typically, they develop incrementally over time and do not get noticed until there is a crisis. Additionally, there usually is not time to reflect calmly on what steps to take in the face of a crisis. Therefore, it is incumbent on us to have a moral backdrop that we can refer to in difficult times.

One approach to thinking about this is to consider language. We all speak without much conscious reference to the underlying grammar. Yet there are sometimes difficult or novel cases where it is useful to have a reference work that will tell us the right usage. Similarly, in most cases we act without thinking too much about following specific behavioral principles. Nevertheless, there are certain occasions when it might be beneficial to look to a basic level of principle.

For instance, one ethical approach stresses our duty to respect the humanity of those we employ. If we could agree in the recycling case that we must treat the workers differently from their mechanical equivalents and not just as human capital, then we would have formed a common basis for discussion that will be much more productive than any intuitive gainsaying.

The areas covered in this chapter include utilitarianism, which assesses morality in terms of outcomes; deontology, which stresses duties; rights (here articulated in the U.N. Declaration of Human Rights); and virtue theory, which looks to character. Virtue theory has had a resurgence recently and has become integrated into popular management texts.

In the past decade a number of theorists have contended that established moral theories may be missing some special insights afforded by the way women approach ethics. This is important for at least two reasons: First is the insights themselves, which often stress developing care and compassion in our dealings with one another. Second, the way that business is structured and some of its assumptions may reflect a male template. That is, business has become what it is today largely based on a masculine view of how the world works, and perhaps a different lens will show us how it could work in ways that are more inclusive and considerate of one another.

Further, we should critically assess four of the core concepts presented by ethical theorists: ethical relativism, impartiality, sympathy, and moral sufficiency.

ETHICAL RELATIVISM

Many people believe that ethics is a question of individual choice and preference; we may not agree with others, but we have no right to impose our views on them. This view suggests there are no universal or absolute values on which people can agree. However, we should not take disagreement over values to suggest there are none. As Thomas Beauchamp has pointed out, the fact that people follow different religions does not lead them to believe that religion should be abandoned altogether. Humans live in societies and at a basic level maintain contracts to coexist. From this we can say that there is at least one level of agreement. The question, then, is not so much whether values are absolute or relative but, rather, How much do we agree on, and how much do we differ? Clearly there are cultural and historical differences on values, yet if we look at the level of principle we find that most, if not all, societies have concepts of care, respect, justice, and compensation, among others. These concepts may be manifested in different ways in different cultures, of course. The Forsyth reading deals with the ways managers approach ethical relativism and shows that it need not defeat the moral enterprise.

IMPARTIALITY

Most classical ethical theories suggest that we should treat one another as equals where everyone counts for one and none for more than one, to use Jeremy Bentham's famous phrase. By a strict interpretation, this means that we should consider the welfare of someone we do not know in Saharan Africa absolutely equally with our own or that of those we love and hold dear. The goal of utilitarianism, for example, to maximize the happiness of the maximum number, relies on us caring about everyone else in a significant way. While this may be a worthwhile moral ideal, in practice many people do favor themselves or people they know more than those they do not. Impartiality may result in a business manager being required to care as much about the welfare of customers or the local community as she does about the return to investors.

SYMPATHY

One way of understanding sympathy is as the imaginative ability to put yourself in someone else's shoes. In ethical theory we are often asked to care about the rest of humanity, often to the extent that we love our neighbor as ourselves, a high aspiration. In business terms, this may amount to a company being concerned with the welfare of individuals who may never be paying customers or considering others' objections to business operations that seem completely outrageous.

MORAL SUFFICIENCY

What separates the morally decent act from the morally heroic? If we are required, for example, to produce the maximum good for the maximum number, is there a place that one can stop on the grounds that we have done as much as could be reasonably expected? Alternatively, is there an imperative to do as much good as possible without regard for our own life plans?

THE ETHICAL CHALLENGE FOR BUSINESS

Business is often in the position of being able to bring about great benefit or great harm, which imposes a significant responsibility on managers and executives to the rest of society. Business-people are constantly facing a series of moral challenges; for instance, should we adopt a minimal standard such as just following the law, or do we set a higher standard? Furthermore, we have to determine what counts as decent behavior that we would demand from everyone and distinguish it from discretionary heroic behavior. What does it take to be a good person who is engaged in business? and how should we weigh the intention of an act against its outcomes? A manager will necessarily have to balance the demands of the workplace with demands of moral considerations. Sometimes they will be complementary, but often they will compete; and then people in business will have to rely on their discretionary judgment. Moral theory provides us with a way of framing our intuitions and applying general principles that can guide our decisions.

Thinking Ethically
A Framework for Moral Decision Making

Manuel Velasquez, Claire Andre, Thomas Shanks, S. J., and Michael J. Meyer

This reading provides a brief overview of the various ethical approaches that we could use when examining a moral issue in business. We can see how an issue might be decided very differently depending on the way we look at it and the approach we adopt. The article shows us that there is a way to reason to a conclusion rather than merely gainsaying one another's intuitions, and this will give us an analytical framework to shape our discussion when we examine particular topics.

Moral issues greet us each morning in the newspaper, confront us in the memos on our desks, nag us from our children's soccer fields, and bid us good night on the evening news. We are bombarded daily with questions about the justice of our foreign policy, the morality of medical technologies that can prolong our lives, the rights of the homeless, the fairness of our children's teachers to the diverse students in their classrooms.

Dealing with these moral issues is often perplexing. How, exactly, should we think through an ethical issue? What questions should we ask? What factors should we consider?

The first step in analyzing moral issues is obvious but not always easy: Get the facts. Some moral issues create controversies simply because we do not bother to check the facts. This first step, although obvious, is also among the most important and the most frequently overlooked.

But having the facts is not enough. Facts by themselves only tell us what *is*; they do not tell us what *ought* to be. In addition to getting the facts, resolving an ethical issue also requires an appeal to values. Philosophers have developed five different approaches to values to deal with moral issues.

THE UTILITARIAN APPROACH

Utilitarianism was conceived in the 19th century by Jeremy Bentham and John Stuart Mill to help legislators determine which laws were morally best. Both Bentham and Mill suggested that ethical actions are those that provide the greatest balance of good over evil.

To analyze an issue using the utilitarian approach, we first identify the various courses of action available to us. Second, we ask who will be affected by each action and what benefits or harms will be derived from each. And third, we choose the action that will produce the greatest benefits and the least harm. The ethical action is the one that provides the greatest good for the greatest number.

THE RIGHTS APPROACH

The second important approach to ethics has its roots in the philosophy of the 18th-century thinker Immanuel Kant and others like him, who focused on the individual's right to choose for herself or himself. According to these philosophers, what makes human beings different from mere things is that people have dignity based on their ability to choose freely what they will do with their lives, and they have a fundamental moral right to have these choices respected. People are not objects to be manipulated; it is a violation of human dignity to use people in ways they do not freely choose.

Of course, many different, but related, rights exist besides this basic one. These other rights (an incomplete list below) can be thought of as different aspects of the basic right to be treated as we choose.

- *The right to the truth*: We have a right to be told the truth and to be informed about matters that significantly affect our choices.
- *The right of privacy*: We have the right to do, believe, and say whatever we choose in our personal lives so long as we do not violate the rights of others.
- *The right not to be injured*: We have the right not to be harmed or injured unless we freely and knowingly do something to deserve punishment or we freely and knowingly choose to risk such injuries.
- *The right to what is agreed*: We have a right to what has been promised by those with whom we have freely entered into a contract or agreement.

In deciding whether an action is moral or immoral using this second approach, then, we must ask, Does the action respect the moral rights of everyone? Actions are wrong to the extent that they violate the rights of individuals; the more serious the violation, the more wrongful the action.

THE FAIRNESS OR JUSTICE APPROACH

The fairness or justice approach to ethics has its roots in the teachings of the ancient Greek philosopher Aristotle, who said that "equals should be treated equally and unequals unequally." The basic moral question in this approach is: How fair is an action? Does it treat everyone in the same way, or does it show favoritism and discrimination?

Favoritism gives benefits to some people without a justifiable reason for singling them out; discrimination imposes burdens on people who are no different from those on whom burdens are not imposed. Both favoritism and discrimination are unjust and wrong.

THE COMMON-GOOD APPROACH

This approach to ethics presents a vision of society as a community whose members are joined in the shared pursuit of values and goals they hold in common. This community comprises individuals whose own good is inextricably bound to the good of the whole.

The common good is a notion that originated more than 2,000 years ago in the writings of Plato, Aristotle, and Cicero. More recently, contemporary ethicist John Rawls defined the common good as "certain general conditions that are . . . equally to everyone's advantage."

In this approach, we focus on ensuring that the social policies, social systems, institutions, and environments on which we depend are beneficial to all. Examples of goods common to all include affordable health care, effective public safety, peace among nations, a just legal system, and an unpolluted environment.

Appeals to the common good urge us to view ourselves as members of the same community, reflecting on broad questions concerning the kind of society we want to become and how we are to achieve that society. While respecting and valuing the freedom of individuals to pursue their own goals, the common-good approach challenges us also to recognize and further those goals we share in common.

THE VIRTUE APPROACH

The virtue approach to ethics assumes that there are certain ideals toward which we should strive, which provide for the full development of our humanity. These ideals are discovered through thoughtful reflection on what kind of people we have the potential to become.

Virtues are attitudes or character traits that enable us to be and to act in ways that develop our highest potential. They enable us to pursue the ideals we have adopted.

Honesty, courage, compassion, generosity, fidelity, integrity, fairness, self-control, and prudence are all examples of virtues.

Virtues are like habits; that is, once acquired, they become characteristic of a person. Moreover, a person who has developed virtues will be naturally disposed to act in ways consistent with moral principles. The virtuous person is the ethical person.

In dealing with an ethical problem using the virtue approach, we might ask, What kind of person should I be? What will promote the de-velopment of character within myself and my community?

ETHICAL PROBLEM SOLVING

These five approaches suggest that once we have ascertained the facts, we should ask ourselves five questions when trying to resolve a moral issue:

- ◆ What benefits and what harms will each course of action produce, and which alternative will lead to the best overall consequences?
- ◆ What moral rights do the affected parties have, and which course of action best respects those rights?
- ◆ Which course of action treats everyone the same, except where there is a morally justifiable reason not to, and does not show favoritism or discrimination?
- ◆ Which course of action advances the common good?
- ◆ Which course of action develops moral virtues?

This method, of course, does not provide an automatic solution to moral problems. It is not meant to. The method is merely meant to help identify most of the important ethical considerations. In the end, we must deliberate on moral issues for ourselves, keeping a careful eye on both the facts and on the ethical considerations involved. ◆ ◆ ◆

Judging the Morality of Business Practices
The Influence of Personal Moral Philosophies

Donelson R. Forsyth

A problem for many who examine ethics is how to deal with relativism: the notion that standards may be context or subject dependent. This would make ethics an issue of preference or taste: I think that it is wrong, but what they think is up to them, and I have no right to criticize. When it comes down to it, though, very few people are complete relativists. It would be unusual to find someone who rationally, sincerely, and seriously believes it is not wrong to lie, steal, or break contracts (which would undermine cooperative living), assault, rape, or murder. The debate then turns around what the core or foundational beliefs are and the degree of moral relativism that is acceptable. Here Forsyth gives two scales for us to consider: how absolute we believe moral rules are and the level of care we should extend to others.

Ethical issues in business are intimately tied to more general moral values held by members of the community-at-large. Certain untoward practices—such as routine violations of employees' rights, deceiving consumers through misleading advertising, illegal price-fixing, insider trading, and the sale of merchandise that is known to be defective—may be unique to the business world, but individuals' reactions to such practices ultimately depend upon the same psychological and interpersonal processes that determine judgments of any morally evaluable action. Because appraisals of business practices are, at core, only a special case of general moral decision making, we approach the study of moral judgments of business practices by examining: (1) contrasting personal moral philosophies and their relationship to classical ethical philosophies; (2) the influence of personal moral philosophies on moral judgments; and (3) the implications of this psychological analysis of moral judgment for ethical debates over business practices.

FOUR MORAL PHILOSOPHIES

Most would morally condemn a company that deliberately violates government regulations designed to protect employees from harm, a business that knowingly sells faulty products that cause severe injury to uninformed consumers, or an unscrupulous executive who steals money from the pension fund, but this consensus is lost when the discussion turns to less clear-cut issues. This disagreement, however, is not unique to questions of business ethics. As early as 1898 Sharp complained that his studies of moral judgment were hindered by the lack of agreement among his subjects concerning what was moral and what was not. Although he speculated that people might be too incompetent or careless when they make moral judgments, he eventually concluded that disagreements concerning morality surface because people adopt different personal ethical systems.

The behavioral sciences offer a number of theoretical models that examine the nature of these divergences in moral judgment, including cognitive-developmentalism (Kohlberg, 1983), social learning theory (Bandura, 1990), and psychoanalytic theory (Freud, 1927). The current approach, however, assumes that individuals' moral beliefs, attitudes, and values comprise an integrated conceptual system or personal moral philosophy. Moreover, although the number of personal moral philosophies is unlimited, most can be contrasted in terms of relativism and idealism. At one end of the relativism dimension, highly relativistic individuals espouse a personal moral philosophy based on skepticism. They generally feel that moral actions depend upon the nature of the situation and the individuals involved, and when judging others they weigh the circumstances more than the ethical principle that was violated. People who are low in relativism, in contrast, argue that morality requires acting in ways that are consistent with moral principles, norms, or laws. The second distinction, idealism, describes the individual's concern for the welfare of others. Highly idealistic individuals feel that harming others is always avoidable, and they would rather not choose between the lesser of two evils which will lead to negative consequences for other people. Those who are less idealistic, in contrast, do not emphasize such ideals, for they assume that harm will sometimes be necessary to produce good (Forsyth, 1980; Schlenker and Forsyth, 1977).

These two dimensions, relativism and idealism, parallel distinctions made by both moral philosophers and psychologists (Boyce and Jensen, 1978; Waterman, 1988). Philosophers have traditionally contrasted moral theories based on principles (deontological models) and models that stress the consequences of actions (teleological models) (Forsyth, 1981a). Piaget (1983) believed that younger children tend to stress the consequences of an action—to the point of overlooking good intentions—whereas older children are able to take into consideration ethical rules when making judgments. Gilligan (1982, p. 65), in her analyses of sex differences in moral thought, notes that females "hope that in morality lies a way of solving conflicts so that no one will be hurt" (concern for positive consequences), while males' moralities tend to stress the rational application of principles. Similarly Derry (1989) argues that first-level managers' moral dilemmas are often caused by their desire to meet the demands of their role as well as protect the human needs and welfare of others, and that often role-responsibilities overshadow one's concern for others' welfare (cf., Kelley, 1989).

This model of personal moral philosophies, rather than assuming individuals are either rule-oriented or consequence-oriented, assumes individuals can range from high to low in their emphasis on principles and in their emphasis on consequences. The model thus identifies the four distinct personal moral philosophies shown in Table 1: situationism (relativistic and idealistic), subjectivism (relativistic but not idealistic), absolutism (not relativistic but idealistic), and exceptionism (neither relativistic nor idealistic).

Situationism

Individuals who eschew universal moral principles (high relativism) but still insist that one should produce positive consequences that benefit all involved (high idealism) are termed situationists. Because these individuals favor the close inspection of potential benefits their outlook is most similar to philosophic approaches based on ethical skepticism. For example, Fletcher in his *situation ethics* (1966) argues that an action, to

Table 1 ◆ A TAXONOMY OF PERSONAL MORAL PHILOSOPHIES

Ideology	Dimensions	Approach to Moral Judgment
Situationists	High relativism High idealism	Reject moral rules; ask if the action yielded the best possible outcome in the given situation.
Subjectivists	High relativism Low idealism	Reject moral rules; base moral judgments on personal feelings about the action and the setting.
Absolutists	Low relativism High idealism	Feel actions are moral provided they yield positive consequences through conformity to moral rules.
Exceptionists	Low relativism Low idealism	Feel conformity to moral rules is desirable, but exceptions to these rules are often permissible.

be moral, must be appropriate given the particular context; not necessarily good or right, but "fitting." *Utilitarianism* similarly maintains that one must act in ways that will generate the greatest good for the greatest number of people, and James's (1891/1973) *value pluralism* suggests that the consequences of an action determine its moral value.

Subjectivism

Subjectivists, like situationists, reject moral rules (high relativism); they are not, however, particularly positive about the possibility of achieving positive outcomes for everyone concerned. Because such individuals described their moral decisions as subjective, individualistic judgments that cannot be made on the basis of moral absolutes or the extent to which the action benefits others their viewpoint parallels an *egoistic* moral philosophy. This position maintains that no moral judgments can be considered valid except in reference to one's own behavior. The only moral conclusion possible is that all people should act to promote their own self-interest, rather than focus on producing positive outcomes for others in general. This teleological outlook admits that consequences must be considered when formulating moral judgments, but unlike the more idealistic situational ethics it does not insist that one strive to produce positive outcomes. Indeed, because each person must de-

termine the weights and values of the outcome obtained, individuals will differ dramatically in their moral conclusions.

Absolutism

Absolutists believe that one should strive to produce positive consequences (high idealism) but at the same time maintain strict adherence to general moral principles (low relativism). These individuals condemn certain actions, because (a) they harm people and (b) they violate fundamental moral absolutes. Such an outlook corresponds closely to a system of ethics known as *deontology*. To deontologists, acts are to be judged through their comparison with some exceptionless, universal moral rule. Immanuel Kant, generally regarded as the foremost proponent of the deontological position, prescribed that one must make certain that all actions adhere to categorical imperatives: exceptionless universal moral principles that can be derived through reason rather than empirical evaluation. Kant, for example, proposed that "to be truthful in all declarations is . . . a sacred unconditional command of reason and is not to be limited by any expediency" and that "all practical principles of justice must contain strict truths . . . since exceptions destroy the universality, on account of which alone they bear the name principles" (1873/1973, p. 258). In support of his position Kant maintained that a principle such as "Keep your promises only when it works to your advantage" negates the concept of a promise and therefore cannot qualify as a categorical imperative. The maxim "Always keep your promises," in contrast, does not generate any inconsistencies and therefore qualifies as a moral absolute.

Exceptionism

Exceptionists agree with the absolutist's appreciation of moral absolutes but they are not idealistic: they do not believe that harm can be avoided, that innocent people can always be protected, or that risking others' welfare is always wrong. They are, therefore, deontological, for they prefer to rely on moral principles as guidelines for action. At the same time, however, they are utilitarian in that they pragmatically admit that judgments should be made by balancing the positive consequences of an action against the negative consequences of an action. Their outlook thus corresponds most closely to a moral philosophy based on *rule-utilitarianism*: moral principles are useful because they provide a framework for making choices and acting in ways that will tend to produce the best consequences for all concerned. Following principles, however, will sometimes cause one to act in ways that will cause harm to innocent people, and in such instances exceptions are allowable.

Applications in Business Settings

The theoretically predicted differences among these four ethical types become clearer when their outlooks on various ethical issues that occur in business settings are contrasted. Consider, for example, a businesswoman reviewing an advertising campaign that describes the product somewhat inaccurately. The situationist is most concerned with the benefits to be obtained, both for the company and for the consumer. If she feels that the product is a good one and that, in the long run, the buyer will be benefitted, then

she will likely overlook any small inaccuracies in the ad copy. The subjectivist, in contrast, will most likely be fundamentally concerned with maximizing the company's profits, and will probably be perplexed if ethical issues are even raised. The absolutist will likely object to inaccuracies if she labels them as *lies*; if, however, they are described as mere puffery and the benefits of a successful campaign are made clear to her, then even the absolutist may be willing to overlook the inaccuracies. The exceptionist, too, is likely to overlook inaccuracies. Although she would agree that "truth in advertizing" is essential, she would likely point out that the need to make a profit and competitors' deceptive advertisements justify an exception in this case.

A businessman's decision to retain or let go a veteran employee who violates a company rule (e.g., personal long-distance phone calls, use of company credit card for personal purchases, pilfering, freelancing) provides a second example. The situationist would prefer to gather background information about the incident before making a decision, for he would wonder if circumstances justified or at least mitigated punishment for the employee's behavior. The subjectivist, in contrast, would be more likely to consider the practical consequences of the action for the company, but would also act on the basis of personal feelings. If, for example, the individual was a friend or relative, then the incident would probably be overlooked. The absolutist, in contrast, would likely react the most negatively provided the rule was stated publicly and clearly in company guidelines. He might regret the harm done to the individual, but he would feel that following company policy takes precedent over individual outcomes. Lastly, an exceptionist would be willing to overlook the untoward action if practical concerns weighed against termination. If the employee managed an important account, could make financial restitution to the company, or was very difficult to replace, then an exceptionist would not take action.

PERSONAL MORAL PHILOSOPHY AND MORAL JUDGMENT

Do these individual differences in personal moral philosophy influence other aspects of morality, including moral cognition, action, and effect? Although Hartshorne and May (1928), in their early studies of morality, concluded that moral behavior was more the product of the situation than the person, more recent models of moral phenomena advocate a transactional view of personality and behavior. Haan (1978; 1986; Haan et al., 1985), for example, argues that individuals' moral behavior varies because interpersonal demands vary across situations. Haan feels that moral action is "informed and influenced by variations in contexts" and by individuals' "own strategies of problem solving" when they confront a moral dilemma (Haan, 1986, p. 1282). Kurtines, by asking individuals to predict how they would behave in various social roles, found that individuals' use of principled moral reasoning varied across these role-settings (1984; 1986). Similarly, the approach described here assumes that the individual differences in personal moral philosophies influence behavior, but that the magnitude of this influence depends upon a number of situational factors.

Measuring Personal Moral Philosophy

The Ethics Position Questionnaire (EPQ) assesses personal moral philosophy by asking individuals to indicate their acceptance of items that vary in terms of relativism and idealism. The relativism scale includes items like "Different types of moralities cannot be compared as to 'rightness'" and "What is ethical varies from one situation to another." The idealism scale, in contrast,

measures one's perspective on positive and negative consequences with such items as "A person should make certain that their actions never intentionally harm another even to a small degree" and "If an action could harm an innocent other then it should not be done" (Forsyth, 1980). Overall, high scorers on the idealism subscale of the EPQ more strongly endorse items that reflect a fundamental concern for the welfare of others, whereas those who receive high scores on the relativism subscale of the EPQ tend to espouse a personal moral philosophy based on rejection of moral universals (Forsyth et al., 1988).

Moral Attitudes

Relative to the other three types, absolutists tend to be more conservative in their position on contemporary moral issues and practices. Leary et al. (1986), for example, found that scores on the Machiavellianism Scale correlated positively with relativism, but they correlated negatively with idealism. When Forsyth (1980) examined the relationship between one's moral philosophy and personal opinion on such issues as the artificial creation of human life, mercy killings, marijuana use, capital punishment, homosexuality, and abortion he found that absolutists, and male absolutists in particular, were relatively negative in their appraisals of test-tube babies, euthanasia, marijuana use, homosexuality, and abortion. This critical attitude was also noted in a follow-up study that focused specifically on sexual practices, including premarital sex, extramarital sex, and homosexuality (Singh and Forsyth, 1989). Although not yet examined empirically, these findings suggest that absolutists would be the most negative toward illegal business practices, such as bait-and-switch advertising, employee exploitation, inadequate waste management strategies, the sale of off-standard products, job or wage discrimination, kickbacks, or misuse of authority for personal gain. They would also be more likely to object to legal, but ethically questionable, behavior. Absolutists might, for example, react harshly to co-workers who adopt alternative lifestyles, are sexually promiscuous in the work place, or adopt nontraditional sexual preferences. They may prefer to work for a company that sells trucks rather than IUDs.

Moral Judgment

The negativity of the absolutists in their moral attitude corresponds to an overall negativity when formulating moral judgments. When judging actions that led to positive and negative consequences, absolutists were significantly harsher in their appraisals, whereas situationists based their judgments on both negative and positive consequence data. Absolutists also attributed more responsibility to people who produced negative consequences, evaluated specific consequences less favorably, and condemned the morality of the person being appraised more often than other judges. Exceptionists were the most positive (Forsyth, 1978). Similarly, when evaluating the morality of sixteen ethically controversial psychological studies, absolutists were more negative than all other types (Forsyth and Pope, 1984). They apparently focused on the potential harm for subjects created by researchers.

In many cases, however, situational and cognitive factors mediate the strength of the personal moral philosophy-judgment relationship. Forsyth (1981b), for example, found that absolutists were more negative than exceptionists, but only when the individual was clearly responsible for his action and the consequences of the action were extremely negative. In a related study, Forsyth (1985) asked individuals to appraise the morality of someone who, by either violating or conforming to a moral principle (such as "tell the truth," "do not steal," or "keep your promises"), produced positive or negative consequences for innocent others. As predicted, idealistic subjects (both absolutists and situationists) more strongly

condemned individuals who caused extremely negative consequences, whereas the relativistic subjectivists and situationists were more lenient when judging individuals who violated a moral norm. In terms of information integration, an averaging model with differential weights accounted for idealists' (situationists and absolutists) judgments since conformity to moral principles was discounted when the consequences were extremely negative or positive. Subjectivists' judgments conformed to an averaging model of information integration since mildly positive consequences lowered moral judgments of conforming actions, and exceptionists combined information in a strictly linear, additive fashion; the more positive the consequences or the greater the conformity of the action to a moral norm, the more positive the moral judgment.

Moral Behavior

The analysis of individual differences in moral and immoral behavior has traditionally stymied researchers, but the taking of personal moral philosophies into account yields some insight into this empirical puzzle. Forsyth and Berger (1982), in a study of cheating, found that 36% of the college students they studied cheated on a test when left alone with the answer key, but cheating was not related to either idealism or relativism. These researchers also tested resistance to moral temptation in a second study by adding a confederate who urged subjects to take answers from the answer key. Cheating increased to 83% in this study, but once again propensity to cheat wasn't linked to personal moral philosophy.

These studies suggest that personal moral philosophy does not influence moral behavior in most settings. A more circumspect approach, however, proposes that features of the social setting may possibly enhance—or reduce—the causal impact of moral values on behavior. For example, because absolutists and exceptionists emphasize the importance of moral rules, individuals who subscribe to these two types of personal moral philosophies may be more reluctant to engage in immoral behavior when moral rules are made salient by situational factors. Similarly, since the idealistic ideologies—situationism and absolutism—stress the need to achieve positive, humanitarian consequences, then individuals who accept these ideals might be more likely to engage in immoral action if such actions are the means to help others.

This revised approach was supported in a study of lying (Forsyth and Nye, 1990). Situationists, absolutists, subjectivists, and exceptionists were placed in a situation in which they were asked to tell a deliberate lie to another person. In making this request, the researcher emphasized that the information was simply a form of feedback (nonsalient moral norm) or that the information was a lie (salient moral norm). In addition, one half of the subjects were told that they would receive a bonus of three dollars by giving the information (either lie or feedback), while the remaining subjects were told that the information would probably have positive consequences for the person being misled (i.e., it was for "his own good").

As anticipated, the two situational variables—the salience of moral norms and the consequences of action—had a strong impact on moral action. While only 50.0% of the subjects agreed to lie when they were offered $3 and were told that they would be lying rather giving feedback, this percentage increased to 76.2% across the other three conditions. In addition, idealism influenced moral behavior, but in a surprising fashion. Although high idealists espouse a philosophy that condemns harming others, they were more likely to lie than the low idealists. Fully 91.66% of the situationists and absolutists (high idealists) agreed to tell the lie, while only 70.83% of the subjectivists and exceptionists (low idealists) complied with the experimenter's request. In fact, situationists and absolutists usually lied no matter what the consequences or salience of moral norms. Exceptionists, in contrast, were less likely to lie if offered money to lie and subjectivists were less likely to lie if they stood to gain from the lie and the action was labeled a lie.

This study supports the commonsense notion that people who espouse lofty moral values may tend to behave the most immorally. Although both situationists and absolutists strongly endorse such beliefs as "One should never psychologically or physically harm another person" and "It is never necessary to sacrifice the welfare of others," both groups were willing to tell a total stranger a lie. While these findings are not too damaging for situationists since these individuals believe that lying is permissible in some settings, absolutists staunchly maintain that lying violates fundamental moral principles, and are quite harsh when judging others who have broken this moral absolute. Yet, when they themselves were tempted to lie, they were more likely to succumb. Although additional research is needed to further explore the moral thought of absolutists, the current research attests to a "hypocrisy effect" that may be obscuring the link between moral values and moral behaviors: People who say they are the most morally upright may be most likely to fall prey to temptation (Forsyth and Nye, 1990).

Reactions to One's Own Moral Transgressions

Klass (1978), after reviewing a number of previous studies of individuals' feelings of guilt, shame, and self-esteem after breaking moral norms, concludes that "the same overt action seems to make some people feel better and others feel worse, and for still others, has no effects" (p. 766). The personal moral philosophy model accounts for these divergences by suggesting that individuals who emphasize obedience to moral norms (low relativists) but nonetheless find themselves acting contrary to a salient moral norm should display much more negative post-transgression reactions than other subjects. In contrast, idealistic individuals who achieve positive consequences for others should display more positive affective reactions following their transgression.

In the study of cheating mentioned earlier, these predictions were partially confirmed. The more absolutists cheated the more negatively they rated themselves, and exceptionists rated themselves more positively the more they cheated (Forsyth and Berger, 1982, Study 1). In a second study, absolutists who were prodded into cheating on a test rated themselves as more negative, weak, unlikable, and dirty than individuals in all the other personal moral philosophy categories (Forsyth and Berger, 1982, Study 2). Similarly, Forsyth and Nye (1990), in their study of lying, found that when subjects were lying to secure positive consequences for themselves, no differences due to personal moral values were obtained. When lying was motivated by a desire to help another person, situationists rated themselves very positively, especially in comparison to the absolutists.

Personal moral philosophies also tempered self-evaluations in a study of reactions to failure and success when working for personal profit or for a charity. Given high idealists' desire to achieve positive outcomes for others, they should feel more positive following charitable actions rather than for themselves. Relativists, in contrast, should not feel as positive about themselves after they help others than would nonrelativists. In a preliminary test of this prediction subjects assigned to the self-interest condition were informed that any money they earned during the study should be considered their salary. Subjects in the charity condition were told that any money they earned would be donated to the State Charity Foundations, and they were given a booklet describing this organization. After completing their work subjects were told their performance was a success (they were paid) or a failure (they

were not paid), at which time they completed measures of affect, morality, and self-esteem.

Overall subjects' self-ratings were more positive when they succeeded rather than failed. Differences due to personal moral philosophy, however, were obtained after failure. Once again absolutists demonstrated an hypocrisy effect, for they felt more moral when they failed in a charitable action than when they failed while trying to secure personal gain. Exceptionists, in contrast, rated themselves as particularly moral when they failed when working for personal gain. Lastly, low relativists' self-esteem scores were more positive when they failed rather than succeeded, irrespective of the nature (selfless vs. selfish) of the action (Forsyth and Matney, 1990).

THE WIDER IMPLICATIONS

In sum, predictions derived from the personal moral philosophy model have shown that individuals who differ in relativism and idealism divaricate when making moral judgments, in attitudes toward many contemporary moral issues, when attributing responsibility after wrongdoing, . . . and in resistance to moral temptations. Researchers have also reported theoretically predicted correlations between idealism, relativism, and other individual difference variables, including machiavellianism, an ethic of responsibility, and an ethic of caring. These studies, however, also suggest that the impact of relativism and idealism on moral judgment and behavior depends on the nature of the social situation. Consistent with an interactional approach to personality-behavior relationships, idealism and relativism are maximally influential when factors in the situation heighten the salience of these personal moral values. . . .

Resolving Moral Controversies
Given that individuals seem to adopt a variety of different personal moral philosophies, perfect

consensus regarding any given business practice can never be expected. Indeed, given that disagreement is the rule not the exception, then why bother to search for solutions to ethical dilemmas? The current approach suggests that problems of ethics can be addressed most profitably through open, reasoned discussion of ethical questions from each of four perspectives: situationism, subjectivism, absolutism, and exceptionism. Although a common ground on any given question cannot always be located, the discussion itself sparks greater understanding of the problems and is, of itself, progress. Individuals in the business community must operate within the limits that society places upon them; so long as these limits are violated, ethical and value conflicts will continue to disrupt our economic system, and endanger both the reputation and the effectiveness of business. However, if the relative importance of the many factors that influence moral judgments can be enumerated, clarified, and weighed through research and informed discussion, business ethicists will be able to deal effectively with problems that confront them. While the concept of individual differences in personal moral philosophy suggests that we will probably never reach the ideal of complete agreement, at least we can aim for a fuller understanding of our own and others' reactions to various types of business practices. ◆ ◆ ◆

◆ References

Bandura, A.: 1990, 'Selective Activation and Disengagement of Moral Control', *Journal of Social Issues* **46** (1), pp. 27–46.

Boyce, W. D. and Jensen, L. C.: 1978, *Moral Reasoning: A Psychological–Philosophical Integration* (U. of Nebraska Press, Lincoln).

Derry, R.: 1989, 'An Empirical Study of Moral Reasoning among Managers', *Journal of Business Ethics* **8**, pp. 855–862.

Fletcher, J.: 1966, *Situation Ethics* (Westminster Press, Philadelphia).

Forsyth, D. R.: 1978, *Moral Attribution and the Evaluation of Action*, unpublished doctoral dissertation (University of Florida, Gainesville, FL).

Forsyth, D. R.: 1980, 'A Taxonomy of Ethical Ideologies', *Journal of Personality and Social Psychology* **39**, pp. 175–184.

Forsyth, D. R.: 1981a, 'A Psychological Perspective on Ethical Uncertainties in Behavioral Research', in A. J. Kimmel (ed.), *New Directions for Methodology of Social and Behavioral Science: Ethics of Human Subject Research*, No. 10 (Jossey-Bass, San Francisco).

Forsyth, D. R.: 1981b, 'Moral Judgment: The Influence of Ethical Ideology', *Personality and Social Psychology Bulletin* **7**, pp. 218–223.

Forsyth, D. R.: 1985, 'Individual Differences in Information Integration during Moral Judgment', *Journal of Personality and Social Psychology* **49**, pp. 264–272.

Forsyth, D. R. and Berger, R. E.: 1982, 'The Effects of Ethical Ideology on Moral Behavior', *Journal of Social Psychology* **117**, pp. 53–56.

Forsyth, D. R. and Matney, L.: 1990, 'The Emotional Consequences of Selfish and Selfless Actions', paper presented at the Second Annual Convention (June 1990) of the American Psychological Society, Dallas, TX.

Forsyth, D. R. and Nye, J. L.: 1990, 'Personal Moral Philosophies and Moral Choice', *Journal of Research in Personality* **24**, pp. 398–414.

Forsyth, D. R., Nye, J. L. and Kelly, K.: 1988, 'Idealism Relativism, and the Ethic of Caring', *Journal of Psychology* **122**, pp. 243–248.

Forsyth, D. R. and Pope, W. R.: 1984, 'Ethical Ideology and Judgments of Social Psychological Research', *Journal of Personality and Social Psychology* **46**, pp. 1365–1375.

Freud, S.: 1927, 'The Psychopathology of Everyday Life' (Hogarth Press, London).

Gilligan, C.: 1982, *In a Different Voice* (Harvard University Press, Cambridge, MA).

Haan, N.: 1978, 'Two Moralities in Action Context', *Journal of Personality and Social Psychology* **36**, pp. 286–305.

Haan, N.: 1986, 'Systematic Variability in the Quality of Moral Action, as Defined in Two Formulations', *Journal of Personality and Social Psychology* **50**, pp. 1271–1284.

Haan, N., Aerts, E. and Copper, B.: 1985, *On Moral Grounds: The Search for Practical Morality* (New York University Press, New York).

Hartshorne, H. and May, M. A.: 1928, *Studies in the Nature of Character* (MacMillan, New York).

James, W.: 1891/1973, 'The Moral Philosopher and the Moral Life', in P. E. Davis (ed.), *Introduction to Moral Philosophy* (Columbus, OH).

Kant, I.: 1873/1973, 'Critique of Pure Reason and Other Works on the Theory of Ethics'. T. K. Abbott (trans), in P. E. Davis (ed.), *Introduction to Moral Philosophy* (Columbus, OH).

Kelley, M.: 1989, 'Commentary on "An Empirical Study of Moral Reasoning among Managers"', *Journal of Business Ethics* **8**, pp. 863–864.

Klass, E. T.: 1978, 'Psychological Effects of Immoral Actions: The Experimental Evidence', *Psychological Bulletin* **85**, pp. 756–771.

Kohlberg, L.: 1983, *Essays in Moral Development*, Vol. 2 (Harper & Row, New York).

Kurtines, W. M.: 1984, 'Moral Behavior as Rule Governed Behavior: A Psychosocial Role-Theoretical Approach to Moral Behavior and Development', in W. Kurtines and J. L. Gewirtz (eds.), *Morality, Moral Behavior, and Moral Development: Basic Issues in Theory and Research* (Wiley, New York).

Kurtines, W. M.: 1986, 'Moral Behavior as Rule Governed Behavior: Person and Situation Effects on Moral Decision Making', *Journal of Personality and Social Psychology* **50**, pp. 784–791.

Leary, M. R., Knight, P. D. and Barnes, B. D.: 1986, 'Ethical Ideologies of the Machiavellian', *Personality and Social Psychology Bulletin* **12**, pp. 75–80.

Schlenker, B. R. and Forsyth, D. R.: 1977, 'On the Ethics of Psychological Research', *Journal of Experimental Social Psychology* **13**, pp. 369–396.

Sharp, F. C.: 1898, 'An Objective Study of Some Moral Judgments', *American Journal of Psychology* **9**, pp. 198–234.

Singh, B. and Forsyth, D. R.: 1989, 'Sexual Attitudes and Moral Values: The Importance of Idealism and Relativism', *Bulletin of the Psychonomic Society* **27**, pp. 160–162.

Waterman, A. S.: 1988, 'On the Uses of Psychological Theory and Research in the Process of Ethical Inquiry', *Psychological Bulletin* **103**, pp. 283–298.

Utilitarianism

John Stuart Mill

The motto "the greatest good for the greatest number" derives from the ethical theory of utilitarianism, one of a family of "consequentialist" theories that judge morality on the basis of outcomes. Utilitarianism looks to the good that an act produces and that could be thought of as pleasure, happiness, or the degree of personal satisfaction a person obtains. It has been readily used in business, where it is echoed in the economic notion of cost/benefit analysis.

Here we see an early articulation of the theory by John Stuart Mill. As you read, question why utilitarianism demands the greatest good for all affected by an action: Do we have to be completely impartial and put ourselves in everyone else's shoes, or can we prefer our personal plans and lives? Mill was a strong believer in individual rights, but how do you think he would weigh majority interests against minority rights? How would a utilitarian deal with an oil company's demand to drill in the rain forest and move indigenous tribes from their traditional homelands? Furthermore, how should we match intention and outcomes in our moral assessments? Is it truly a case of "all's well that ends well"?

CHAPTER II: WHAT UTILITARIANISM IS

. . .

The creed which accepts as the foundation of morals *utility*, or the *greatest happiness principle,* holds that actions are right in proportion as they tend to promote happiness, wrong as they tend to produce the reverse of happiness. By 'happiness' is intended pleasure, and the absence of pain; by 'unhappiness,' pain, and the privation of pleasure. To give a clear view of the moral standard set up by the theory, much more requires to be said; in particular, what things it includes in the ideas of pain and pleasure; and to what extent this is left an open question. But these supplementary explanations do not affect the theory of life on which this theory of morality is grounded—namely, that pleasure, and freedom from pain, are the only things desirable as ends; and that all desirable things (which are as numerous in the utilitarian as in any other scheme) are desirable either for the pleasure inherent in themselves, or as means to the promotion of pleasure and the prevention of pain. . . .

If I am asked what I mean by difference of quality in pleasures, or what makes one pleasure more valuable than another merely as a pleasure, except its being greater in amount, there is but one possible answer. Of two pleasures, if there be one to which all or almost all who have experi-

ence of both give a decided preference, irrespective of any feeling of moral obligation to prefer it, that is the more desirable pleasure. If one of the two is, by those who are competently acquainted with both, placed so far above the other that they prefer it, even though knowing it to be attended with a greater amount of discontent, and would not resign it for any quantity of the other pleasure which their nature is capable of, we are justified in ascribing to the preferred enjoyment a superiority in quality, so far outweighing quantity as to render it, in comparison, of small account.

Now it is an unquestionable fact that those who are equally acquainted with, and equally capable of appreciating and enjoying, both, do give a most marked preference to the manner of existence which employs their higher faculties. . . . Whoever supposes that this preference takes place at a sacrifice of happiness—that the superior being, in anything like equal circumstances, is not happier than the inferior—confounds the two very different ideas, of *happiness* and *content*. It is indisputable that the being whose capacities of enjoyment are low, has the greatest chance of having them fully satisfied; and a highly endowed being will always feel that any happiness which he can look for, as the world is constituted, is imperfect. But he can learn to bear its imperfections, if they are at all bearable; and they will not make him envy the being who is indeed unconscious of the imperfections, but only because he feels not at all the good which those imperfections qualify. It is better to be a human being dissatisfied than a pig satisfied; better to be Socrates dissatisfied than a fool satisfied. And if the fool, or the pig, are of a different opinion, it is because they only know their own side of the question. The other party to the comparison knows both sides. . . .

I must again repeat, what the assailants of utilitarianism seldom have the justice to acknowledge, that the happiness which forms the utilitarian standard of what is right in conduct, is not the agent's own happiness, but that of all concerned. As between his own happiness and that of others, utilitarianism requires him to be as strictly impartial as a disinterested and benevolent spectator. In the golden rule of Jesus of Nazareth, we read the complete spirit of the ethics of utility. To do as you would be done by, and to love your neighbor as yourself, constitute the ideal perfection of utilitarian morality. As the means of making the nearest approach to this ideal, utility would enjoin, first, that laws and social arrangements should place the happiness, or (as speaking practically it may be called) the interest, of every individual, as nearly as possible in harmony with the interest of the whole; and secondly, that education and opinion, which have so vast a power over human character, should so use that power as to establish in the mind of every individual an indissoluble association between his own happiness and the good of the whole—especially between his own happiness and the practice of such modes of conduct, negative and positive, as regard for the universal happiness prescribes; so that not only he may be unable to conceive the possibility of happiness to himself, consistently with conduct opposed to the general good, but also that a direct impulse to promote the general good may be in every individual one of the habitual motives of action, and the sentiments connected therewith may fill

a large and prominent place in every human being's sentient existence. . . .

The objectors to utilitarianism cannot always be charged with representing it in a discreditable light. On the contrary, those among them who entertain anything like a just idea of its disinterested character sometimes find fault with its standard as being too high for humanity. They say it is exacting too much to require that people shall always act from the inducement of promoting the general interests of society. But this is to mistake the very meaning of a standard of morals, and confound the rule of action with the motive of it. It is the business of ethics to tell us what are our duties, or by what test we may know them; but no system of ethics requires that the sole motive of all we do shall be a feeling of duty; on the contrary, ninety-nine hundredths of all our actions are done from other motives, and rightly so done, if the rule of duty does not condemn them. It is the more unjust to utilitarianism that this particular misapprehension should be made a ground of objection to it, inasmuch as utilitarian moralists have gone beyond almost all others in affirming that the motive has nothing to do with the morality of the action, though much with the worth of the agent. He who saves a fellow creature from drowning does what is morally right, whether his motive be duty, or the hope of being paid for his trouble; he who betrays the friend that trusts him, is guilty of a crime, even if his object be to serve another friend to whom he is under greater obligations. But to speak only of actions done from the motive of duty, and in direct obedience to principle: it is a misapprehension of the utilitarian mode of thought, to conceive it as implying that people should fix their minds upon so wide a generality as the world, or society at large. The great majority of good actions are intended not for the benefit of the world, but for that of individuals, of which the good of the world is made up; and the thoughts of the most virtuous man need not on these occasions travel beyond the particular persons concerned, except so far as is necessary to assure himself that in benefiting them he is not violating the rights, that is, the legitimate and authorized expectations, of anyone else. The multiplication of happiness is, according to the utilitarian ethics, the object of virtue: the occasions on which any person (except one in a thousand) has it in his power to do this on an extended scale, in other words to be a public benefactor, are but exceptional, and on these occasions alone is he called on to consider public utility; in every other case, private utility, the interest or happiness of some few persons, is all he has to attend to. Those alone the influence of whose actions extends to society in general, need concern themselves habitually about so large an object. In the case of abstinences indeed—of things which people forbear to do from moral considerations, though the consequences in the particular case might be beneficial—it would be unworthy of an intelligent agent not to be consciously aware that the action is of a class which, if practiced generally, would be generally injurious, and that this is the ground of the obligation to abstain from it. The amount of regard for the public interest implied in this recognition is no greater than is demanded by every system of morals, for they all enjoin to abstain from whatever is manifestly pernicious to society. . . .

. . . [U]tility is often summarily stigmatized as an immoral doctrine by giving it the name of *expediency*, and taking advantage of the popular use of that term to contrast it with *principle*. But the *expedient*, in the sense in which it is opposed to the *right*, generally means that which is expedient for the particular interest of the agent himself; . . . as when a minister sacrifices the interests of his country to keep himself in place. When it means anything better than this, it means that which is expedient for some immediate object, some temporary purpose, but which violates a rule whose observance is expedient in a much higher degree. . . .

. . . There is no difficulty in proving any ethical standard whatever to work ill, if we suppose universal idiocy to be conjoined with it; but on any hypothesis short of that, mankind must by this time have acquired positive beliefs as to the effects of some actions on their happiness; and the beliefs which have thus come down are the rules of morality for the multitude, and for the philosopher until he has succeeded in finding better. That philosophers might easily do this, even now, on many subjects; that the received code of ethics is by no means of divine right; and that mankind have still much to learn as to the effects of actions on the general happiness, I admit, or rather, earnestly maintain. The corollaries from the principle of utility, like the precepts of every practical art, admit of indefinite improvement, and, in a progressive state of the human mind, their improvement is perpetually going on. But to consider the rules of morality as improvable, is one thing; to pass over the intermediate generalizations entirely, and endeavor to test each individual action directly by the first principle, is another. . . .

. . . We are told that a utilitarian will be apt to make his own particular case an exception to moral rules, and when under temptation will see a utility in the breach of a rule greater than he will see in its observance. . . . There is no ethical creed which does not temper the rigidity of its laws by giving a certain latitude, under the moral responsibility of the agent, for accommodation to peculiarities of circumstances; and under every creed, at the opening thus made, self-deception and dishonest casuistry get in. There exists no moral system under which there do not arise unequivocal cases of conflicting obligation. These are the real difficulties, the knotty points both in the theory of ethics, and in the conscientious guidance of personal conduct. They are overcome practically, with greater or with less success, according to the intellect and virtue of the individual; but it can hardly be pretended that anyone will be the less qualified for dealing with them, from possessing an ultimate standard to which conflicting rights and duties can be referred. . . .

CHAPTER IV: OF WHAT SORT OF PROOF THE PRINCIPLE OF UTILITY IS SUSCEPTIBLE

. . . The utilitarian doctrine is that happiness is desirable, and the only thing desirable, as an end; all other things being only desirable as means to that end. . . .

But does the utilitarian doctrine deny that people desire virtue, or maintain that virtue is not a thing to be desired? The very reverse. It maintains not only that virtue is to be desired, but that it is to be desired disinterestedly, for itself. Whatever may be the opinion of utilitarian moralists as to the original conditions by which virtue is made virtue; however they may believe (as they do) that actions and dispositions are only virtuous because they promote another end than virtue: yet this being granted, and it having been decided, from considerations of this description, what *is* virtuous, they not only place virtue at the very head of the things which are good as means to the ultimate end, but they also recognize as a psychological fact the possibility of its being, to the individual, a good in itself, without looking to any end beyond it; and hold that the mind is not in a right state, not in a state conformable to utility, not in the state most conducive to the general happiness, unless it does love virtue in this manner—as a thing desirable in itself, even although, in the individual instance, it should not produce those other desirable consequences

which it tends to produce, and on account of which it is held to be virtue. This opinion is not, in the smallest degree, a departure from the happiness principle. The ingredients of happiness are very various, and each of them is desirable in itself, and not merely when considered as swelling an aggregate. The principle of utility does not mean that any given pleasure, as music, for instance, or any given exemption from pain, as for example health, is to be looked upon as means to a collective something termed happiness, and to be desired on that account. They are desired and desirable in and for themselves; besides being means, they are a part of the end. Virtue, according to the utilitarian doctrine, is not naturally and originally part of the end, but it is capable of becoming so; and in those who love it disinterestedly it has become so, and is desired and cherished, not as a means to happiness, but as a part of their happiness.

To illustrate this farther, we may remember that virtue is not the only thing, originally a means, and which if it were not a means to anything else, would be and remain indifferent, but which by association with what it is a means to, comes to be desired for itself, and that too with the utmost intensity. What, for example, shall we say of the love of money? There is nothing originally more desirable about money than about any heap of glittering pebbles. Its worth is solely that of the things which it will buy; the desires for other things than itself, which it is a means of gratifying. Yet the love of money is not only one of the strongest moving forces of human life, but money is, in many cases, desired in and for itself; the desire to possess it is often stronger than the desire to use it, and goes on increasing when all the desires which point to ends beyond it, to be compassed by it, are falling off. It may, then, be said truly, that money is desired not for the sake of an end, but as part of the end. From being a means to happiness, it has come to be itself a principal ingredient of the individual's conception of happiness. The same may be said of the majority of the great objects of human life—power, for example, or fame; except that to each of these there is a certain amount of immediate pleasure annexed, which has at least the semblance of being naturally inherent in them; a thing which cannot be said of money. Still, however, the strongest natural attraction, both of power and of fame, is the immense aid they give to the attainment of our other wishes; and it is the strong association thus generated between them and all our objects of desire, which gives to the direct desire of them the intensity it often assumes, so as in some characters to surpass in strength all other desires. In these cases the means have become a part of the end, and a more important part of it than any of the things which they are means to. What was once desired as an instrument for the attainment of happiness, has come to be desired for its own sake. In being desired for its own sake it is, however, desired as *part* of happiness. The person is made, or thinks he would be made, happy by its mere possession; and is made unhappy by failure to obtain it. The desire of it is not a different thing from the desire of happiness, any more than the love of music, or the desire of health. They are included in happiness. They are some of the elements of which the desire of happiness is made up. Happiness is not an abstract idea, but a concrete whole; and these are some of its parts. And the utilitarian standard sanctions and approves their being so. Life would be a poor thing, very ill provided with sources of happiness, if there were not this provision of nature, by which things originally indifferent, but conducive to, or otherwise associated with, the satisfaction of our primitive desires, become in themselves sources of pleasure more valuable than the primitive pleasures, both in permanency, in the space of human existence that they are capable of covering, and even in intensity. . . .

CHAPTER V: ON THE CONNECTION BETWEEN JUSTICE AND UTILITY

. . .

To recapitulate: the idea of justice supposes two things—a rule of conduct and a sentiment which sanctions the rule. The first must be supposed common to all mankind and intended for their good. The other (the sentiment) is a desire that punishment may be suffered by those who infringe the rule. There is involved, in addition, the conception of some definite person who suffers by the infringement; whose rights (to use the expression appropriated to the case) are violated by it. And the sentiment of justice appears to me to be the animal desire to repel or retaliate a hurt or damage to oneself, or to those with whom one sympathizes, widened so as to include all persons, by the human capacity of enlarged sympathy and the human conception of intelligent self-interest. From the latter elements, the feeling derives its morality; from the former, its peculiar impressiveness and energy of self-assertion. . . .

. . . An examination of our own minds, I think, will show that these two things include all that we mean when we speak of violation of a right. When we call anything a person's right, we mean that he has a valid claim on society to protect him in the possession of it, either by the force of law, or by that of education and opinion. If he has what we consider a sufficient claim, on whatever account, to have something guaranteed to him by society, we say that he has a right to it. If we desire to prove that anything does not belong to him by right, we think this done as soon as it is admitted that society ought not to take measures for securing it to him, but should leave him to chance, or to his own exertions. Thus a person is said to have a right to what he can earn in fair professional competition, because society ought not to allow any other person to hinder him from endeavoring to earn in that manner as much as he can. But he has not a right to three hundred a year, though he may happen to be earning it; because society is not called on to provide that he shall earn that sum. . . .

To have a right, then, is, I conceive, to have something which society ought to defend me in the possession of. . . .

That first of judicial virtues, impartiality, is an obligation of justice, partly for the reason last mentioned, as being a necessary condition of the fulfilment of the other obligations of justice. But this is not the only source of the exalted rank, among human obligations, of those maxims of equality and impartiality which, both in popular estimation and in that of the most enlightened, are included among the precepts of justice. In one point of view, they may be considered as corollaries from the principles already laid down. If it is a duty to do to each according to his deserts, returning good for good as well as repressing evil by evil, it necessarily follows that we should treat all equally well (when no higher duty forbids) who have deserved equally well of *us*, and that society should treat all equally well who have deserved equally well of *it*, that is, who have deserved equally well absolutely. This is the highest abstract standard of social and distributive justice; towards which all institutions, and the efforts of all virtuous citizens, should be made in the utmost possible degree to converge. But this great moral duty rests upon a still deeper foundation, being a direct emanation from the first principle of morals, and not a mere logical corollary from secondary or derivative doctrines. It is involved in the very meaning of utility, or the greatest happiness principle. That principle is a mere form of words without rational signification, unless one person's happiness, supposed equal in degree (with the proper allowance made for kind), is counted for exactly as much as another's. Those conditions being supplied, Bentham's dictum,

"everybody to count for one, nobody for more than one," might be written under the principle of utility as an explanatory commentary. The equal claim of everybody to happiness in the estimation of the moralist and of the legislator, involves an equal claim to all the means of happiness, except in so far as the inevitable conditions of human life, and the general interest, in which that of every individual is included, set limits to the maxim; and those limits ought to be strictly construed. As every other maxim of justice, so this is by no means applied or held applicable universally; on the contrary, as I have already remarked, it bends to every person's ideas of social expediency. . . . All persons are deemed to have a *right* to equality of treatment, except when some recognized social expediency requires the reverse. And hence all social inequalities which have ceased to be considered expedient, assume the character not of simple inexpediency, but of injustice, and appear so tyrannical, that people are apt to wonder how they ever could have been tolerated; forgetful that they themselves perhaps tolerate other inequalities under an equally mistaken notion of expediency, the correction of which would make that which they approve seem quite as monstrous as what they have at last learnt to condemn. The entire history of social improvement has been a series of transitions, by which one custom or institution after another, from being a supposed primary necessity of social existence, has passed into the rank of a universally stigmatized injustice and tyranny. So it has been with the distinctions of slaves and freemen, nobles and serfs, patricians and plebeians; and so it will be, and in part already is, with the aristocracies of color, race, and sex.

It appears from what has been said that justice is a name for certain moral requirements which, regarded collectively, stand higher in the scale of social utility, and are therefore of more paramount obligation, than any others; though particular cases may occur in which some other social duty is so important, as to overrule any one of the general maxims of justice. Thus, to save a life, it may not only be allowable but a duty to steal or take by force the necessary food or medicine, or to kidnap and compel to officiate the only qualified medical practitioner. . . .

The considerations which have now been adduced resolve, I conceive, the only real difficulty in the utilitarian theory of morals. It has always been evident that all cases of justice are also cases of expediency: the difference is in the peculiar sentiment which attaches to the former, as contradistinguished from the latter. . . . Justice remains the appropriate name for certain social utilities which are vastly more important, and therefore more absolute and imperative, than any others are as a class. . . . ◆ ◆ ◆

The Ethics of Duty

Immanuel Kant

There is a significant movement in business ethics called Kantian capitalism, which supports the view that a guiding principle should be that humans have intrinsic worth and are worthy of respect. This means that a business has to treat its workers not just as human capital but by reference to the Golden Rule: Do unto others as you would have them do unto you. This view may be held independently of considerations such as maximizing profits or gaining a competitive edge because we treat people well merely because it is the right thing to do, as opposed to achieving some reward. This selection from Immanuel Kant gives us the theoretical foundation for these claims.

There is no possibility of thinking of anything at all in the world, or even out of it, which can be regarded as good without qualification, except a *good will*. Intelligence, wit, judgment, and whatever talents of the mind one might want to name are doubtless in many respects good and desirable, as are such qualities of temperament as courage, resolution, perseverance. But they can also become extremely bad and harmful if the will, which is to make use of these gifts of nature and which in its special constitution is called character, is not good. . . . The sight of a being who is not graced by any touch of a pure and good will but who yet enjoys an uninterrupted prosperity can never delight a rational and impartial spectator. Thus a good will seems to constitute the indispensable condition of being even worthy of happiness.

Some qualities are even conducive to this good will itself and can facilitate its work. . . . Moderation in emotions and passions, self-control, and calm deliberation are not only good in many respects but even seem to constitute part of the intrinsic worth of a person. But they are far from being rightly called good without qualification (however unconditionally they were commended by the ancients). For without the principles of a good will, they can become extremely bad; the coolness of a villain makes him not only much more dangerous but also immediately more abominable in our eyes than he would have been regarded by us without it.

A good will is good not because of what it effects or accomplishes, nor because of its fitness to attain some proposed end; it is good only through its willing, i.e., it is good in itself. When it is considered in itself, then it is to be esteemed very much higher than anything which it might ever bring about merely in order to favor some inclination, or even the sum total of all inclinations. Even if, by some especially unfortunate fate or by the niggardly provision of stepmotherly nature, this will should be wholly lacking in the power to accomplish its purpose; if with the greatest effort it should yet achieve nothing, and only the good will should remain (not, to be sure, as a mere wish but as the summoning of all the means in our power), yet would it, like a jewel, still shine by its own light as something which has its full value in itself. Its usefulness or fruitlessness can neither augment nor diminish this value. . . .

The concept of a will estimable in itself and good without regard to any further end must now be developed. This concept already dwells in the natural sound understanding and needs not so much to be taught as merely to be elucidated. It always holds first place in estimating the total worth of our actions and constitutes the condition of all the rest. Therefore, we shall take up the concept of *duty*, which includes that of a good will, though with certain subjective restrictions and hindrances, which far from hiding a good will or rendering it unrecognizable, rather bring it out by contrast and make it shine forth more brightly.

I here omit all actions already recognized as contrary to duty, even though they may be useful for this or that end; for in the case of these the question does not arise at all as to whether they might be done from duty, since they even conflict with duty. I also set aside those actions which are really in accordance with duty, yet to which men have no immediate inclination, but perform them because they are impelled thereto by some other inclination. For in this [second] case to decide whether the action which is in accord with duty has been done from duty or from some selfish purpose is easy. This difference is far more difficult to note in the [third] case where the action accords with duty and the subject has in addition an immediate inclination to do the action. For example, that a dealer should not overcharge an inexperienced purchaser certainly accords with duty; and where there is much commerce, the prudent merchant does not overcharge but keeps to a fixed price for everyone in general, so that a child may buy from him just as well as everyone else may. Thus customers are honestly served, but this is not nearly enough for making us believe that the merchant has acted this way from duty and from principles of honesty; his own advantage required him to do it. He cannot, however, be assumed to have in addition [as in the third case] an immediate inclination toward his buyers, causing him, as it were, out of love to give no one as far as price is concerned any advantage over another. Hence the action was done neither from duty nor from immediate inclination, but merely for a selfish purpose.

On the other hand, to preserve one's life is a duty; and, furthermore, everyone has also an immediate inclination to do so. But on this account the often anxious care taken by most men for it has no intrinsic worth, and the maxim of their action has no moral content. They preserve their lives, to be sure, in accordance with duty, but not from duty. On the other hand, if adversity and hopeless sorrow have completely taken away the taste for life, if an unfortunate man, strong in soul and more indignant at his fate than despondent or dejected, wishes for death and yet preserves his life without loving it—not from inclination or fear, but from duty—then his maxim indeed has a moral content.

To be beneficent where one can is a duty; and besides this, there are many persons who are so sympathetically constituted that, without any further motive of vanity or self-interest, they find an inner pleasure in spreading joy around them and can rejoice in the satisfaction of others as their own work. But I maintain that in such a case an action of this kind, however dutiful and amiable it may be, has nevertheless no true moral worth. It is on a level with such actions as arise from other inclinations, e.g., the inclination for honor, which if fortunately directed to what is in fact beneficial and accords with duty and is thus honorable, deserves praise and encouragement, but not esteem; for its maxim lacks the moral content of an action done not from inclination but from duty. . . .

The second proposition[1] is this: An action done from duty has its moral worth, not in the purpose that is to be attained by it, but in the maxim according to which the action is determined. . . .

The third proposition, which follows from the other two, can be expressed thus: Duty is the necessity of an action done out of respect for the law. I can indeed have an inclination for an object as the effect of my proposed action; but I can never have respect for such an object, just because it is merely an effect and is not an activity of the will. . . .

Thus the moral worth of an action does not lie in the effect expected from it nor in any prin-

ciple of action that needs to borrow its motive from this expected effect. For all these effects (agreeableness of one's condition and even the furtherance of other people's happiness) could have been brought about also through other causes and would not have required the will of a rational being, in which the highest and unconditioned good can alone be found. . . .

But what sort of law can that be the thought of which must determine the will without reference to any expected effect, so that the will can be called absolutely good without qualification? Since I have deprived the will of every impulse that might arise for it from obeying any particular law, there is nothing left to serve the will as principle except the universal conformity of its actions to law as such, i.e., I should never act except in such a way that I can also will that my maxim should become a universal law. Here mere conformity to law as such (without having as its basis any law determining particular actions) serves the will as principle and must so serve it if duty is not to be a vain delusion and a chimerical concept. The ordinary reason of mankind in its practical judgments agrees completely with this, and always has in view the aforementioned principle.

For example, take this question. When I am in distress, may I make a promise with the intention of not keeping it? I readily distinguish here the two meanings which the question may have; whether making a false promise conforms with prudence or with duty. Doubtless the former can often be the case. Indeed I clearly see that escape from some present difficulty by means of such a promise is not enough. In addition I must carefully consider whether from this lie there may later arise far greater inconvenience for me than from what I now try to escape. Furthermore, the consequences of my false promise are not easy to foresee, even with all my supposed cunning; loss of confidence in me might prove to be far more disadvantageous than the misfortune which I now try to avoid. The more prudent way might be to act according to a universal maxim and to make it a habit not to promise anything without intending to keep it. But that such a maxim is, nevertheless, always based on nothing but a fear of consequences becomes clear to me at once. To be truthful from duty is, however, quite different from being truthful from fear of disadvantageous consequences; in the first case the concept of the action itself contains a law for me, while in the second I must first look around elsewhere to see what are the results for me that might be connected with the action. For to deviate from the principle of duty is quite certainly bad; but to abandon my maxim of prudence can often be very advantageous for me, though to abide by it is certainly safer. The most direct and infallible way, however, to answer the question as to whether a lying promise accords with duty is to ask myself whether I would really be content if my maxim (of extricating myself from difficulty by means of a false promise) were to hold as a universal law for myself as well as for others, and could I really say to myself that everyone may promise falsely when he finds himself in a difficulty from which he can find no other way to extricate himself. Then I immediately become aware that I can indeed will the lie but can not at all will a universal law to lie. For by such a law there would really be no promises at all, since in vain would my willing future actions be professed to other people who would not believe what I professed, or if they over-hastily did believe, then they would pay me back in like coin. Therefore, my maxim would necessarily destroy itself just as soon as it was made a universal law.[2] . . .

The will is thought of as a faculty of determining itself to action in accordance with the representation of certain laws, and such a faculty can be found only in rational beings. Now what serves the will as the objective ground of its self-determination is an end; and if this end is given by reason alone, then it must be equally valid for all rational beings. On the other hand, what contains merely the ground of the possibility of the action, whose effect is an end, is called the means. The subjective ground of desire is the incentive; the objective ground of volition is the motive. Hence there arises the distinction between subjective ends, which rest on incentives, and objective ends, which depend on motives valid for every rational being. . . .

Now I say that man, and in general every rational being, exists as an end in himself and not merely as a means to be arbitrarily used by this or that will. He must in all his actions, whether directed to himself or to other rational beings, always be regarded at the same time as an end. All the objects of inclinations have only a conditioned value; for if there were not these inclinations and the needs founded on them, then their object would be without value. But the inclinations themselves, being sources of needs, are so far from having an absolute value such as to render them desirable for their own sake that the universal wish of every rational being must be, rather, to be wholly free from them. Accordingly, the value of any object obtainable by our action is always conditioned. Beings whose existence depends not on our will but on nature have, nevertheless, if they are not rational beings, only a relative value as means and are therefore called things. On the other hand, rational beings are called persons inasmuch as their nature already marks them out as ends in themselves, i.e., as something which is not to be used merely as means and hence there is imposed thereby a limit on all arbitrary use of such beings, which are thus objects of respect. Persons are, therefore, not merely subjective ends, whose existence as an effect of our actions has a value for us; but such beings are objective ends, i.e., exist as ends in themselves. Such an end is one for which there can be substituted no other end to which such beings should serve merely as means, for otherwise nothing at all of absolute value would be found anywhere. . . .

If then there is to be a supreme practical principle and, as far as the human will is concerned, a categorical imperative, then it must be such that from the conception of what is necessarily an end for everyone because this end is an end in itself it constitutes an objective principle of the will and can hence serve as a practical law. The ground of such a principle is this: rational nature exists as an end in itself. In this way man necessarily thinks of his own existence; thus far is it a subjective principle of human actions. But in this way also does every other rational being think of his existence on the same rational ground that holds also for me; hence it is at the same time an objective principle, from which, as a supreme practical ground, all laws of the will must be able to be derived. The practical imperative will therefore be the following: Act in such a way that you treat humanity, whether in your own person or in the person of another, always at the same time as an end and never simply as a means.[3] . . . ◆ ◆ ◆

◆ Notes

1. The first proposition of morality says that an action must be done from duty in order to have any moral worth. It is implicit in the preceding examples but was never explicitly stated.

2. This means that when you tell a lie, you merely take exception to the general rule that says everyone should always tell the truth and believe that what you are saying is true. When you lie, you do not thereby will that everyone else lie and not believe that what you are saying is true, because in such a case your lie would never work to get you what you want.

3. This oft-quoted version of the categorical imperative is usually referred to as the formula of the end in itself.

Ethics as Virtues

Aristotle

This reading is two short extracts from Book I, Chapter 7 and Book II, Chapters 1, 2, 6, and 9 from the Nicomachean Ethics. *The section is designed to be read in conjunction with Daryl Koehn's article on virtue ethics and business practice.*

Virtue ethics are end directed (teleological) in the sense that there is a purpose to human action. We should fulfill our lives by developing our potential, by becoming happy (eudaimonia) not in the sense of being amused but by living a full and rewarding life.

Another element to look for in the reading is Aristotle's description of a virtue as an active characteristic that is developed by practice: For Aristotle, we develop virtues by practicing them in much the same way as we learn to play a musical instrument.

As you read these sections, think about what characteristics of a job would be necessary for you to be truly fulfilled at work.

BOOK ONE

Chapter 7

But no doubt people will say, 'To call happiness the highest good is a truism. We want a more distinct account of what it is.' We might arrive at this if we could grasp what is meant by the 'function' of a human being. If we take a flautist or a sculptor or any craftsman—in fact any class of men at all who have some special job or profession—we find that his special talent and excellence comes out in that job, and this is his function. The same thing will be true of man simply as man—that is of course if 'man' does have a function. But is it likely that joiners and shoemakers have certain functions or specialized activities, while man as such has none but has been left by Nature a functionless being? Seeing that eye and hand and foot and every one of our members has some obvious function, must we not believe that in like manner a human being has a function over and above these particular functions? Then what exactly is it? The mere act of living is not peculiar to man—we find it even in the vegetable kingdom—and what we are looking for is something peculiar to him. We must therefore exclude from our definition the life that manifests itself in mere nurture and growth. A step higher should come the life that is confined to experiencing sensations. But that we see is shared by horses, cows and the brute creation as a whole. We are left, then, with a life concerning which we can make two statements. First, it belongs to

the rational part of man. Secondly, it finds expression in actions. The rational part may be either active or passive: passive in so far as it follows the dictates of reason, active in so far as it possesses and exercises the power of reasoning. A similar distinction can be drawn within the rational life; that is to say, the reasonable element in it may be active or passive. Let us take it that what we are concerned with here is the reasoning power in action, for it will be generally allowed that when we speak of 'reasoning' we really mean *exercising* our reasoning faculties. (This seems the more correct use of the word.) Now let us assume for the moment the truth of the following propositions. (*a*) The function of a man is the exercise of his noncorporeal faculties or 'soul' in accordance with, or at least not divorced from, a rational principle. (*b*) The function of an individual and of a *good* individual in the same class—a harp player, for example, and a good harp player, and so through the classes—is generically the same, except that we must add superiority in accomplishment to the function, the function of the harp player being merely to play on the harp, while the function of the good harp player is to play on it well. (*c*) The function of man is a certain form of life, namely an activity of the soul exercised in combination with a rational principle or reasonable ground of action. (*d*) The function of a good man is to exert such activity well. (*e*) A function is performed well when performed in accordance with the excellence proper to it.—If these assumptions are granted, we conclude that the good for man is 'an activity of soul in accordance with goodness' or (on the supposition that there may be more than one form of goodness) 'in accordance with the best and most complete form of goodness.'

Happiness is more than momentary bliss.

There is another condition of happiness; it cannot be achieved in less than a complete lifetime. One swallow does not make a summer; neither does one fine day. And one day, or indeed any brief period of felicity, does not make a man entirely and perfectly happy. . . .

BOOK TWO

This book is the first of a series (II–V) dealing with the moral virtues. But first we have to ask what moral virtue or goodness is. It is a confirmed disposition to act rightly, the disposition being itself formed by a continuous series of right actions.

Chapter 1

Virtue, then, is of two kinds, intellectual and moral. Of these the intellectual is in the main indebted to teaching for its production and growth, and this calls for time and experience. Moral goodness, on the other hand, is the child of habit, from which it has got its very name, ethics being derived from *ethos*, 'habit', by a slight alteration in the quantity of the *e*. This is an indication that none of the moral virtues is implanted in us by nature, since nothing that nature creates can be taught by habit to change the direction of its development. For instance a stone, the natural tendency of which is to fall down, could never, however often you threw it up in the air, be trained to go in that direction. No more can you train fire to burn downwards. Nothing in fact, if the law of its being is to behave in one way, can be habituated to behave in another. The moral virtues, then, are produced in us neither *by* Nature nor *against* Nature. Na-

ture, indeed, prepares in us the ground for their reception, but their complete formation is the product of habit. . . .

Chapter II

Since the branch of philosophy on which we are at present engaged differs from the others in not being a subject of merely intellectual interest—I mean we are not concerned to know what goodness essentially is, but how we are to become good men, for this alone gives the study its practical value—we must apply our minds to the solution of the problems of conduct. For, as I remarked, it is our actions that determine our dispositions. . . .

Let us begin with the following observation. It is in the nature of moral qualities that they can be destroyed by deficiency on the one hand and excess on the other. We can see this in the instances of bodily health and strength.[1] Physical strength is destroyed by too much and also by too little exercise. Similarly health is ruined by eating and drinking either too much or too little, while it is produced, increased and preserved by taking the right quantity of drink and victuals. Well, it is the same with temperance, courage, and the other virtues. The man who shuns and fears everything and can stand up to nothing becomes a coward. The man who is afraid of nothing at all, but marches up to every danger, becomes foolhardy. In the same way the man who indulges in every pleasure without refraining from a single one becomes incontinent. If, on the other hand, a man behaves like the Boor in comedy and turns his back on every pleasure, he will find his sensibilities becoming blunted. So also temperance and courage are destroyed both by excess and deficiency, and they are kept alive by observance of the mean.

Our virtues are employed in the same kinds of action as established them.

Let us go back to our statement that the virtues are produced and fostered as a result, and by the agency, of actions of the same quality as effect their destruction. It is also true that after the virtues have been formed they find expression in actions of that kind. We may see this in a concrete instance—bodily strength. It results from taking plenty of nourishment and going in for hard training, and it is the strong man who is best fitted to cope with such conditions. So with the virtues. It is by refraining from pleasures that we become temperate, and it is when we have become temperate that we are most able to abstain from pleasures. Or take courage. It is by habituating ourselves to make light of alarming situations and to confront them that we become brave, and it is when we have become brave that we shall be most able to face an alarming situation. . . .

. . . By 'goodness' I mean goodness of moral character, since it is moral goodness that deals with feelings and actions, and it is in them that we find excess, deficiency and a mean. It is possible, for example, to experience fear, boldness, desire, anger, pity, and pleasures and pains generally, too much or too little or to the right amount. If we feel them too much or too little, we are wrong. But to have these feelings at the right times on the right occasions towards the right people for the right motive and in the right way is to have them in the right measure, that is somewhere between the extremes; and this is what characterizes goodness. The same may be said of the mean and extremes in actions. Now it is in the field of actions and feelings that goodness operates; in them we find excess, deficiency and, between them, the mean, the first two being wrong, the mean right and praised as such.[2] Goodness, then, is a mean condition in the sense that it aims at and hits the mean.

Consider, too, that it is possible to go wrong in more ways than one. (In Pythagorean terminology evil is a form of the Unlimited, good of the Limited.) But there is only one way of being

right. That is why going wrong is easy, and going right difficult; it is easy to miss the bull's eye and difficult to hit it. Here, then, is another explanation of why the too much and the too little are connected with evil and the mean with good. As the poet says,

Goodness is one, evil is multiform.

. . .

But choice of a mean is not possible in every action or every feeling. The very names of some have an immediate connotation of evil. Such are malice, shamelessness, envy among feelings, and among actions adultery, theft, murder. All these and more like them have a bad name as being evil in themselves; it is not merely the excess or deficiency of them that we censure. In their case, then, it is impossible to act rightly; whatever we do is wrong. Nor do circumstances make any difference in the rightness or wrongness of them. When a man commits adultery there is no point in asking whether it is with the right woman or at the right time or in the right way, for to do anything like that is simply wrong. It would amount to claiming that there is a mean and excess and defect in unjust or cowardly or intemperate actions. If such a thing were possible, we should find ourselves with a mean quantity of excess, a mean of deficiency, an excess of excess and a deficiency of deficiency. But just as in temperance and justice there can be no mean or excess or deficiency, because the mean in a sense *is* an extreme, so there can be no mean or excess or deficiency in those vicious actions—however done, they are wrong. Putting the matter into general language, we may say that there is no mean in the extremes, and no extreme in the mean, to be observed by anybody. . . .

Chapter IX

I have said enough to show that moral excellence is a mean, and I have shown in what sense it is so. It is, namely, a mean between two forms of badness, one of excess and the other of defect, and is so described because it aims at hitting the mean point in feelings and in actions. This makes virtue hard of achievement, because finding the middle point is never easy. It is not everybody, for instance, who can find the centre of a circle—that calls for a geometrician. Thus, too, it is easy to fly into a passion—anybody can do that—but to be angry with the right person and to the right extent and at the right time and with the right object and in the right way—that is not easy, and it is not everyone who can do it. This is equally true of giving or spending money. Hence we infer that to do these things properly is rare, laudable and fine. ◆ ◆ ◆

◆ Notes

1. If we are to illustrate the material, it must be by concrete images.

2. Being right or successful and being praised are both indicative of excellence.

A Role for Virtue Ethics in the Analysis of Business Practice

Daryl Koehn

Does it matter more what you do or who you are? Who is your business hero? Koehn believes that virtue ethics has distinct advantages when addressing issues in business ethics. It puts corporate activity in the context of society and the political climate. It allows us to judge behavior over time rather than by snapshot assessments. Virtue ethics also promotes the idea of role models. In reading the selection, consider whether one ethical approach is superior and whether it would ever be appropriate to mix and match them in our analysis of business.

THE RELATION OF VIRTUE ETHICS TO OTHER ETHICS

Given that every action is performed by an agent and has an outcome, every ethic in some fashion must treat of outcome, act and actor. This observation has led some to conclude that the various ethics are best seen as differing according to where they put their primary focus. Thus virtue ethics is sometimes described as emphasizing the character traits of the agent, while utilitarianism concentrates on outcomes and deontological ethics on the act itself. However, this description of virtue ethics is somewhat misleading because outcome and act are central to the workings of a virtue ethics such as Aristotle's.[1] For Aristotle, character development is an inevitable outcome of the act. Consequently, outcomes are every bit as important in Aristotle's ethics as they are in John Stuart Mill's. The crucial difference lies in how outcomes are conceived. Aristotle, who views every act as inevitably developing a character who performs an act well or poorly, will not treat an outcome in isolation from past and future outcomes. An outcome is not just a consequence of an act but a consequence for one or more agents engaged in a series of actions. Act utilitarians, by contrast, will often focus on outcomes of one act in isolation from the outcome of other acts.[2]

Similarly, Aristotle cares every bit as much as a deontologist about the act itself. His system places tremendous weight upon the act because life itself is an *energeia* or activity of performing various acts. A good life is a happy life and a life will not be happy unless virtue is put into practice through a whole life. This is why Aristotle insists that the sleeping man is not happy, even if this man possesses some virtues.[3]

Rather than seeing virtue ethics as stressing the agent, it is, I think, more accurate and revealing to say that for the virtue ethicist no true description of what an act is can be given without considering (1) what thought processes are or are not reflected in a proposed or performed act; and (2) what further consequences that act has for that particular agent's ability to appropriately think through and then perform future acts. While Kant can judge suicide immoral on the ground that suicide is an irrational, self-contradictory act which would destroy the very self who is supposedly better off dead, a virtue ethicist will not consent to this context-free description of suicide. Aristotle, for example, distinguishes suicides from passion from other suicides[4] presumably because he wants to leave open the possibility that some

suicides in some situations may be perfectly rational—e.g., if one is a Jew on the way to the concentration camps who has exhausted every avenue of escape and who foresees a future in which all self-directed action is impossible in a state which denies that the Jew is a self and gives the Jew no voice in state policies. Killing oneself under this circumstance can be seen as a free act of self-preservation rather than an act of self-destruction in a state which would deny the status of self to the agent in question.

In other words, what suicide is—the morally relevant description of the act—cannot be stated apart from looking at the particular reasoning of the particular agent about particular circumstances now prevailing or likely to obtain in the future. Judging the Jew's act without considering all of these particulars would be a failure of equity. The good judge always judges with equity in a virtue ethic.[5] Since equity is not a virtue for Kant and does not enter into cost/benefit calculations of utilitarianism, the virtue ethicist's concept of the act being judged will always differ from that of other ethicists.

Given the need to analyze all of these particulars, a virtue ethicist will deny that there is or can be a mechanical algorithm for making a decision. Thus, while I would like to believe that we ethicists could take the insights of virtue ethics and readily combine them with modern decision theory to get a richer account of human behavior, I am not optimistic that we can do so. Decision theory (or at least that variant dominant in economic analysis) offers a single, rather mechanical, view of practical reasoning. Agents are seen as making expected value calculations (i.e., assigning various probabilities to different outcomes.) While these agents can be distinguished according to whether their assigned values reveal them to be risk-averse, risk-neutral or risk-loving, their process of reasoning is formally identical. Agents differ primarily in their attitude toward risk.

For Aristotle, by contrast, practical reasoning assumes different forms depending upon whether the agent is virtuous or vicious. He insists, for example, that the vicious man does not deliberately choose.[6] To our modern ears, this claim sounds odd. Surely Iago deliberately chooses the destruction of Othello just as certainly as Saddam Hussein chooses to bomb the Shiite Muslims. However, Aristotle is loathe to call such acts deliberately chosen because they do not fulfill the human mind's capacity to render what is implicit in an act explicit.[7] The ability to think through the meaning of a proposed act (e.g., genocide) is uniquely human, and it is this uniquely human capacity which the virtuous person exhibits in full. While Saddam Hussein has cunning, can figure out means to an end and can assign risk probabilities to various outcomes, such reasoning should not be confused with the qualitatively different sort of reasoning Hannah Arendt or Dietrich Bonhoeffer engaged in when they considered what man is, what a community is, how an act relates past to future and then decided on the basis of their insights to resist the Nazis. Mere cunning takes the end as given; deliberative choice, by contrast, explores and articulates the end at the same time as it considers how and whether the end should be pursued.[8] To put the same point more contentiously, from a virtue ethicist's perspective, utilitarian thinking is merely "logistical" (i.e., cunning) and, as such, resembles the thinking of evil men.

There is also a major difference between how virtue ethics and other systems conceive of an ethically good action. Suppose for a moment that a CEO is considering whether the company for which she works should give money to a public charity. From the utilitarian perspective, the CEO will have acted well if she considers whether this act of corporate giving or corporative giving as a rule promotes the greatest happiness of those affected by the act. For the virtue

ethicist, however, the CEO will behave well if and only if she is brutally honest with herself about her desires and her options in the case at hand. She must consider not only the effects of corporate charity but also the relative merits of other possible alternatives to corporate giving (e.g., private giving by employees; higher taxes paid to the government who then doles out money to various groups; payment of these funds into an employee health fund or pension fund instead, etc.) Furthermore, she must also ask herself whether her arguments are being made in good faith.[9] For example, if she finds many reasons for corporate charity, she must also reflect on whether she is perhaps secretly favoring this course because she knows her husband wants to go to gala charity benefits and to get his picture in the papers. In other words, truly good and noble behavior requires looking at one's motives for thinking some argument is compelling, not merely in simply lining up reasons pro and con for a particular course of action. What one finds compelling is not merely a matter of greater number of arguments but of one's psychological profile. Therefore, for the virtue ethicist, this profile must always be under scrutiny at the same time as one is evaluating reasons for an action.

I am not here arguing that virtue ethics has the right view of choice and other ethical systems the wrong view. Rather I am maintaining that there are profound differences in how the various ethical systems understand concepts as basic and central to ethics as practical reasoning and the truly good act and that their views may be mutually exclusive. It would seem, for example, that practical reasoning either is or is not identical with calculative reasoning/cunning. Taking virtue ethics seriously will probably mean that one ultimately has to choose one system over the other. I have trouble seeing how one is going to combine bits and pieces of the various theories into a satisfying whole.

VIRTUE ETHICS' DISTINCTIVE CONTRIBUTION TO UNDERSTANDING BUSINESS

Of course, if we do ultimately have to choose between theories, we have all the more reason to struggle as hard as we can to understand what is distinctive about each theory. Virtue ethics can add to the understanding and regulation of business behavior in at least six ways.

First, virtue ethics focuses on the conformity between right thinking and desire.[10] In this respect, it differs from a deontological ethic which always run the risk of developing schizophrenic agents who are compelled to do what duty dictates irrespective of whether they want to perform that act. The virtuous agent simply is the person habituated to desire to do what is good and noble. Indeed, having such a desire is for Aristotle both a requirement and sure sign of virtue. Virtue ethics has the merit of not demanding of people a divided attitude which is hard to maintain and perhaps even unhealthy (Recall that "health" is related to wholeness).[11]

Second, virtue ethics treats virtue as a manifest, perceptible feature of action. Virtuous acts are *kala k'agathos.* That is, they are noble (*kala*) as well as good (*agathos*) with *kala* meaning something like "visibly fine." For the virtue ethicist, it is possible to identify people within a corporation who are acting virtuously and therefore one can establish some persons as role models. These role models can then be appealed to when inculcating virtue. No such role models are possible within, say, a Kantian deontological system since, as Kant repeatedly insists, one cannot know another's motives and consequently cannot tell whether a given act is in fact done from good will.[12]

Third, virtue ethics conceives of human activity as continuous. Past actions, by molding character, become the cause of future actions. Virtue ethics are useful therefore for thinking about the lifecycle of a business. One will not simply focus on whether a particular act of a firm is right or wrong but will consider instead which past decisions of which people have led to a crisis and reorganization. The virtue ethicist will not merely want to evaluate whether Salomon Bros. acted wrongly in using customers' accounts to purchase government securities in excess of Salomon's legal allotment but will also want to look at what features of the environment at the firm led to the recruiting and retention of traders who would treat customers in this fashion and who felt justified in buying as many bonds as they could. For the virtue ethicist, the issue is less whether one can universalize a maxim to buy more bonds than the law allows than what features of Salomon's practices led to a general pattern of contempt for persons—e.g., throwing phones at passerbys on the trading floors, promising employees no layoffs only to fire them the next day, making sexually derogatory remarks, and so forth.[13] Only when one has thought about this whole pattern of behavior will one have a full and rich understanding of what, if anything, is wrong with the traders' bond purchases and will one know how to respond to their action.

Fourth, virtue ethics stresses the importance of individuals being able to make contributions of value to a society or communal enterprise. For Aristotle, people can be fully just only insofar as they participate in exchange.[14] The just person must be able to offer some act or service which will make others want to interact with him. Only when people are able to so interact does one have a healthy, thriving community. Deontological systems, by contrast, can lead to a passive citizenry because deontologists have tended to unpack the notion of justice in terms of agents' rights rather than their responsibilities to act. Rights are something a citizen, human being or rational being has or holds; one does not have to *do* anything with them. (Think, for example, of property rights).[15] On the contrary, the onus to act is usually placed on other people to do something for the rights bearer. If you have a welfare right to a job, then the just employer has to provide you with a job. It is, of course, very easy for an agent to assert some welfare right and to then point the finger at persons who allegedly have violated that right. Much energy is expended in lawsuits and in assigning blame rather than in getting on with the business of producing the wealth necessary to fund many of these supposed rights—e.g., the right to health care, the right to a job, etc.

Fifth, virtue ethics preserves a role for excellence and helps counter the leveling tendency of deontological ethics. The Kantian deontologist O'Nora O'Neill argues, for example, that competitions in which the winner intends to win are immoral because winner and loser are not treated with equal respect.[16] Virtue ethics, by contrast, celebrates the human capacity to develop a noble soul in and through friendly competition. One can interpret Aristotle's virtues as the habitual traits necessary to both produce and enable an agent to take a stand against others (courage) and to stick with the stand even when tempted by pleasure to deviate from it (temperance). A thriving agent intent upon excellence must also have the willingness to give up material assets for important causes (liberality). Self-confidence and esteem (Aristotle's "proper pride") are also necessary to attempt difficult projects and deeds to be accomplished with a sense of perspective (Aristotle's virtue of "wit"). Anyone in search of excellence will do well to consider each of Aristotle's virtues and their relation to a competitive agent's or firm's ability to

formulate challenging plans and to sensibly execute them in a world of demanding exchange partners.

Finally, virtue ethics stresses that people become what they are within a community. The community's political regime and laws dictate the education, the freedoms, the opportunities and, in general, the conditions for actions. It is for this reason that Aristotle defines ethics as part of the larger study of politics.[17] By placing individuals and corporations within this larger context, virtue ethics invites us to consider how the larger environment affects people's self-perceptions, choices, and actions. Even if one argues that individuals bear responsibility for their voluntary actions, what qualifies as voluntary may very well differ from regime to regime. Actions must therefore be considered against the larger political backdrop. Thus, while I personally think it is a category mistake to think of business as a game, I know that the idea of corporate gamesmanship has not arisen in a vacuum. Virtue ethics suggests that, if we want to critique this position, we should consider what aspects of American democracy (e.g., our general laissez-faire view of property) encourages or reinforces such behavior, behavior to which many people become habituated at a relatively young age. The ethicist who is concerned to have a practical effect on others cannot afford to overlook the larger political dimension.

In conclusion, taking virtue ethics seriously does not merely give us additional insights into business practice. It can play a far more serious role in business ethics by inviting us to re-evaluate and revise the notions of choice, act, and outcome implicit in other ethical systems by highlighting problems with or limitations of these other concepts and by offering an alternative understanding of them. ◆ ◆ ◆

◆ Notes

1. In the ensuing discussion, I refer only to Aristotelian ethics. While there is some dispute as to what qualifies as a virtue ethics, Aristotle's system surely does if any do.

2. This contrast may be a bit overstated but it does seem to me that utilitarians take a much more narrow view of outcomes of an act than do Aristotelians precisely because the latter see actions as forming a continuous fabric of life. Thus, while Mill worries that indulging in a bestial pleasure (sexual intercourse) in preference to a higher pleasure (listening to opera) over time may destroy the capacity to enjoy "nobler feelings," he does not claim that this indulgence will destroy the capacity to do a good act (e.g., to respect another's liberty by allowing this person to eat or not eat pork). Aristotle, by contrast, sees the pursuit of pleasure as such (be the pleasure "higher" or "lower") as corrupting the capacity to perform any and all virtuous actions (e.g., just, temperate, courageous, truthful, magnanimous, etc.) because the life of pleasure and life of virtue are two very different, mutually exclusive types of lives. Compare John Stuart Mill, *Utilitarianism* in *The Utilitarians* (Garden City, NY: Anchor Books, 1973), pp. 408–11 with Aristotle, *Nicomachean Ethics* 1095b15–1096a10.

3. *NE* 1095b30–1096a1.

4. *NE* 1138a5–18.

5. "Justice and equity are therefore the same thing, and both are good, though equity is the better." *NE* 1137b10–13.

6. *NE* 1152a8–15. For an excellent discussion of the senses in which the vicious person does and does not choose, see Nancy Sherman, *The Fabric of Character: Aristotle's Theory of Virtue* (Oxford: Clarendon Press, 1989), pp. 107–17.

7. For Aristotle, the notion of fulfillment or *entelechy* is crucial. Choice is an activity of the soul; and soul is for Aristotle the first *entelechy* of a natural body which has organs. Aristotle, *De Anima* 412b4. Insofar as mind or *nous* is part of soul, it is part of a fulfillment.

8. ". . . Aristotle says, 'We deliberate not about ends, but about what contributes to ends (*ta pros ta tele*).' This will include deliberation about the constituents and specifications of an end and about the means towards an antecedently fixed end." Sherman, p. 71.

9. For Aristotle, truth-telling is a virtue. It is striking that the truth Aristotle emphasizes as most important is truthfulness about one's own merits, a truthfulness which would seem to require knowledge of one's own motives. Such knowledge would be necessary to correct for, say, one's propensity to boast or to rule out certain considerations because one finds them unpleasant or an impediment to one's getting one's own way. The truthful person corrects such propensities; vicious persons do not. *NE* 1127b10–30.

10. "The function (*ergon*) of the practical [intelligence] is truth having correspondence to right desire." *NE* 1139a30–32.

11. Leon Kass, *Toward a More Natural Science* (New York: Macmillan, 1985), pp. 164–77.

12. "In actual fact it is absolutely impossible for experience to establish with complete certainty a single case in which the maxim of an action, in other respects right, has rested solely on moral grounds and on the thought of one's duty." Immanuel Kant, *Groundwork of the Metaphysic of Morals* trans. with notes by H. J. Paton (New York: Harper & Row, 1964), p. 74.

13. Lewis discusses the general atmosphere at Salomon Brothers in Michael Lewis, *Liar's Poker* (New York: W. W. Norton and Co., 1989).

14. For support for and explication of this claim, see Daryl Koehn, "Toward an Ethic of Exchange," *Business Ethics Quarterly* July 1992, vol. 2, no. 3, pp. 341–56.

15. It should be noted that deontologists have invoked duties as well as rights when describing justice. But even here they have tended to emphasize what a rational agent ought *not* do rather than what such an agent is ethically bound to do. Hence the literature is dominated by discussions of Kant's duty not to commit suicide; the duty not to make a lying promise; the duty not to tell a lie; etc.

16. "If winning is not the over-riding aim in [games and sports], if they are played for their own sake, the activity is consistently universalizable. But to play competitively with the fundamental intention of winning is to adopt an intention that makes of one's own case a necessary exception." O'Nora O'Neill, *Constructions of Reason: Explorations of Kant's Practical Philosophy* (Cambridge: Cambridge University Press, 1989), pp. 102–3.

17. *NE* 1094a25–1094b10.

The Seven Habits of Highly Effective People
Restoring the Character Ethic

Stephen R. Covey

This is a very short extract from a hugely popular business book (over 28 million copies in print). Covey is promoting what he calls the Character Ethic, which is based on unchanging principles. He says that we develop a good character by developing good habits based on these principles. Note the similarity to Aristotelian virtue theory and his belief in moral education.

THE PRINCIPLE-CENTERED PARADIGM

The Character Ethic is based on the fundamental idea that there are *principles* that govern human effectiveness—natural laws in the human dimension that are just as real, just as unchanging and unarguably "there" as laws such as gravity are in the physical dimension. . . .

The principles I am referring to are not esoteric, mysterious, or "religious" ideas. There is not one principle taught in this book that is unique to any specific faith or religion, including my own. These principles are a part of most every major enduring religion, as well as enduring social philosophies and ethical systems. They are self-evident and can easily be validated by any individual. It's almost as if these principles or natural laws are part of the human condition, part of the human consciousness, part of the human conscience. They seem to exist in all human beings, regardless of social conditioning and loyalty to them, even though they might be submerged or numbed by such conditions or disloyalty.

I am referring, for example, to the principle of *fairness*, out of which our whole concept of equity and justice is developed. Little children seem to have an innate sense of the idea of fairness even apart from opposite conditioning experiences. There are vast differences in how fairness is defined and achieved, but there is almost universal awareness of the idea.

Other examples would include *integrity* and *honesty*. They create the foundation of trust which is essential to cooperation and long-term personal and interpersonal growth.

Another principle is *human dignity*. The basic concept in the United States Declaration of Independence bespeaks this value or principle. "We hold these truths to be self-evident: that all men are created equal and endowed by their Creator with certain inalienable rights, that among these are life, liberty and the pursuit of happiness."

Another principle is *service*, or the idea of making a contribution. Another is *quality* or *excellence*.

There is the principle of *potential*, the idea that we are embryonic and can grow and develop and release more and more potential, develop more and more talents. Highly related to *potential* is the principle of *growth*—the process of releasing potential and developing talents, with the accompanying need for principles such as *patience, nurturance,* and *encouragement.*

Principles are not *practices*. A practice is a specific activity or action. A practice that works in one circumstance will not necessarily work in another, as parents who have tried to raise a second child exactly like they did the first can readily attest.

While practices are situationally specific, principles are deep, fundamental truths that have universal application. They apply to individuals, to marriages, to families, to private and public organizations of every kind. When these truths are internalized into habits, they empower people to create a wide variety of practices to deal with different situations.

Principles are not *values*. A gang of thieves can share values, but they are in violation of the fundamental principles we're talking about.

Principles are the territory. Values are maps. When we value correct principles, we have truth—a knowledge of things as they are.

Principles are guidelines for human conduct that are proven to have enduring, permanent value. They're fundamental. They're essentially unarguable because they are self-evident. One way to quickly grasp the self-evident nature of principles is to simply consider the absurdity of attempting to live an effective life based on their opposites. I doubt that anyone would seriously consider unfairness, deceit, baseness, uselessness, mediocrity, or degeneration to be a solid foundation for lasting happiness and success. Although people may argue about how these principles are defined or manifested or achieved, there seems to be an innate consciousness and awareness that they exist.

The more closely our maps or paradigms are aligned with these principles or natural laws, the more accurate and functional they will be. Correct maps will infinitely impact our personal and interpersonal effectiveness far more than any amount of effort expended on changing our attitudes and behaviors. . . .

We are what we repeatedly do.
Excellence, then, is not an act, but a habit.

Aristotle

Our character, basically, is a composite of our habits. "Sow a thought, reap an action; sow an action, reap a habit; sow a habit, reap a character; sow a character, reap a destiny," the maxim goes.

Habits are powerful factors in our lives. Because they are consistent, often unconscious patterns, they constantly, daily, express our character and produce our effectiveness . . . or ineffectiveness.

As Horace Mann, the great educator, once said, "Habits are like a cable. We weave a strand of it everyday and soon it cannot be broken." I personally do not agree with the last part of his expression. I know they can be broken. Habits can be learned and unlearned. But I also know it isn't a quick fix. It involves a process and a tremendous commitment.

Those of us who watched the lunar voyage of Apollo 11 were transfixed as we saw the first men walk on the moon and return to earth. Superlatives such as "fantastic" and "incredible" were inadequate to describe those eventful days. But to get there, those astronauts literally had to break out of the tremendous gravity pull of the earth. More energy was spent in the first few minutes of lift-off, in the first few miles of travel, than was used over the next several days to travel half a million miles.

Habits, too, have tremendous gravity pull—more than most people realize or would admit. Breaking deeply imbedded habitual tendencies such as procrastination, impatience, criticalness, or selfishness that violate basic principles of human effectiveness involves more than a little willpower and a few minor changes in our lives. "Lift off" takes a tremendous effort, but once we break out of the gravity pull, our freedom takes on a whole new dimension.

Like any natural force, gravity pull can work with us or against us. The gravity pull of some of our habits may currently be keeping us from going where we want to go. But it is also gravity pull that keeps our world together, that keeps the planets in their orbits and our universe in order. It is a powerful force, and if we use it effectively, we can use the gravity pull of habit to create the cohesiveness and order necessary to establish effectiveness in our lives. . . .

Achieving *unity*—oneness—with ourselves, with our loved ones, with our friends and working associates, is the highest and best and most delicious fruit of the Seven Habits. Most of us have tasted this fruit of true unity from time to time in the past, as we have also tasted the bitter, lonely fruit of disunity—and we know how precious and fragile unity is.

Obviously building a character of total integrity and living the life of love and service that creates such unity isn't easy. It isn't a quick fix.

But it's possible. It begins with the desire to center our lives on correct principles, to break out of the paradigms created by other centers and the comfort zones of unworthy habits.

Sometimes we make mistakes, we feel awkward. But if we start with the Daily Private Victory and work from the inside out, the results will surely come. As we plant the seed and patiently weed and nourish it, we begin to feel the excitement of real growth and eventually taste the incomparably delicious fruits of a congruent, effective life.

. . . , I quote Emerson: "That which we persist in doing becomes easier—not that the nature of the task has changed, but our ability to do has increased."

By centering our lives on correct principles and creating a balanced focus between doing and increasing our ability to do, we become empowered in the task of creating effective, useful, and peaceful lives . . . for ourselves, and for our posterity. ◆ ◆ ◆

Making Sense of Human Rights

James W. Nickel

Talking about rights can be difficult because people often have differing views on whether a right is possessed by virtue of being human or merely created by a legal code; there is also confusion about whether rights refer to protections (such as immunity from confession in the right to remain silent) or to claims that have to be fulfilled (the right to a living wage). In this selection, Nickel examines the implications of the U.N. Declaration of Human Rights, which the United States endorsed with 56 other countries in 1948. The Declaration is clear in its definitions of rights and stating where they apply. It is widely cited in international law and gives us a shared basis for discussing the topic.

Human rights, as conceived in twentieth-century human rights documents such as the Universal Declaration, have a number of salient characteristics. First, lest we miss the obvious, these are *rights*. The exact import of this status is unclear — and will be one of my subjects of inquiry — but the word at least suggests that these are definite and high-priority norms whose pursuit is mandatory.

Second, these rights are alleged to be *universal*, to be held by people simply as people. This view implies that characteristics such as race, sex, religion, social position, and nationality are irrelevant to whether one has human rights. It also implies that these rights are applicable all around the world. One of the distinctive features of human rights today is that they are international rights. Compliance with such rights has come to be seen as a legitimate object of international concern and action.

Third, human rights are held to *exist independently* of recognition or implementation in the customs or legal systems of particular countries. These rights may not be *effective* rights until legally implemented, but they exist as standards of argument and criticism independently of legal implementation.

Fourth, human rights are held to be *important norms*. Although they are not all absolute and exceptionless, they are strong enough as normative considerations to prevail in conflicts with contrary national norms and to justify international action on their behalf. The rights described in the Declaration are not ranked in terms of priority; their relative weights are left unstated. It is not claimed that some of them are absolute. Thus the rights of the Declaration are what philosophers call prima facie rights.

Fifth, these rights *imply duties* for both individuals and governments. These duties, like the rights with which they are linked, are alleged to exist independently of acceptance, recognition, or implementation. Governments and people everywhere are obligated not to violate a person's rights, although a person's own government may have the main responsibility to take positive measures to protect and uphold that person's rights.[1]

Finally, these rights *establish minimal standards* of decent social and governmental practice. Not all problems deriving from inhumanity or selfishness and stupidity are human rights problems. For example, a government that failed to provide national parks for its citizens might be criticized for being cheap or insufficiently concerned with recreational opportunities, but that would not be a matter of human rights.

Although human rights are viewed as setting minimal standards, contemporary rights declarations tend to posit rights that are numerous and specific rather than few and general. The Universal Declaration replaces Locke's three generic rights—to life, liberty, and property—with nearly two dozen specific rights. Among the civil and political rights asserted are rights to freedom from discrimination; to life, liberty, and security of the person; to freedom of religion; to freedom of thought and expression; to freedom of assembly and association; to freedom from torture and cruel punishments; to equality before the law; to freedom from arbitrary arrest; to a fair trial; to protections of privacy; and to freedom of movement. The Declaration's social and economic rights include rights to marry and found a family, to freedom from forced marriage, to education, to the availability of a job, to an adequate standard of living, to rest and leisure, and to security during illness, disability, and old age.

The Universal Declaration states that these rights are rooted in the dignity and worth of human beings and in the requirements of domestic and international peace and security. In promulgating the Universal Declaration as a "common standard of achievement," the United Nations did not purport to describe rights already recognized everywhere or to enact these rights within international law. Instead, it attempted to set forth the norms that exist within enlightened moralities. Although the goal of many of the participants was to enact these rights in both domestic and international legal systems, they were held to exist not as legal rights but as universal moral rights. . . .

ECONOMIC RIGHTS

When economic rights are mentioned in the United States, liberals think of welfare rights and conservatives think of the rights of entrepreneurs. Each side is likely to deny the status of human right to what the other side takes as its paradigm. This polarity obviously makes meaningful dialogue between left and right on economic issues very difficult—in part because the broad and simplistic categories used in the debate tend to hide any common ground that might exist. This chapter offers a framework for economic rights that may facilitate more meaningful discussions of these issues. Questions about the affordability of welfare rights in less developed countries are also addressed.

One of the most important ways in which the list of human rights in the Universal Declaration of Human Rights differs from earlier lists is that it includes rights to economic benefits and services. The idea that all people have rights to provision for their physical needs has received widespread acceptance in this century. After World War II, liberals, democratic socialists, and communists all insisted that a concern for economic justice and progress should be part of the agenda of the United Nations Organization. The parties to the UN Charter (1945) committed themselves to promoting "higher standards of living, full employment, and conditions of economic and social progress and development." The Universal Declaration of Human Rights and the subsequent International Covenant on Social, Economic, and Cultural Rights asserted rights to an adequate standard of living, health services, education, support during disability and old age, employment and protection against unemployment, and limited working hours.[2]

These rights to government-provided benefits were often rejected by conservatives who believed that the only genuine economic rights were rights to protections of property and the liberties involved in acquiring, holding, using, and transferring it. Advocates of this view often claimed that it made no sense to speak of human rights to supplies of economic goods.[3]

. . . [S]ome economic rights, including some welfare rights, are important moral or human rights. . . . [I] suggest that a plausible theory of economic rights requires two parts: one dealing with the production-related rights that conservatives emphasize and another dealing with the consumption-related rights, including welfare rights, that welfare-state liberals emphasize. I contend that a theory of economic rights cannot be plausible if it focuses entirely on the requirements of efficient production or—on the other side—entirely on the needs of those unable to provide for themselves.

An exclusive focus on production and property rights fails because not everyone can be productive and acquire property. There are always some people who because of age or disability are unable to engage effectively in production. An exclusive focus on welfare rights fails because not everyone can live on a supply that comes from others. Most people will need and want to provide for the physical needs of themselves and others by engaging in productive work. . . .

HUMAN RIGHTS AND ECONOMIC RIGHTS

To claim that any right is a human right is to assert that people have this right as persons rather than as citizens of a particular country, that this right exists and is valid as a weighty standard of moral criticism independently of its recognition or enforcement in particular countries, and that efforts to gain recognition for this right around the world are appropriate. The purpose of including economic rights among human rights is to identify areas within the economic sphere where powerful moral considerations provide fairly clear guidance for individual actions and social and political institutions. In these areas, basing economic decisions entirely on considerations of economic efficiency or personal gain is

inappropriate. If common areas of this sort can be identified in all contemporary economic systems, we can formulate a set of international economic rights. When effectively implemented, economic rights also help to constitute a country's economic system.

Civil and political rights often have implications not only for political and legal practices but also for economic activities and arrangements. Rights against violence, torture, and murder, for example, restrain what one can do not only to gain or keep political office but also to gain possession of land or to obtain laborers. Many familiar rights not normally classified as economic rights have implications for what is permissible or required in the economic area. For example, the right to freedom of assembly would protect meetings to discuss plans for a new labor union, and a right to education is partly justified on the grounds that it contributes to the productivity necessary to satisfy human needs. But some rights are always primarily focused on economic matters, and my concern here will be with these.

PRODUCTION-RELATED RIGHTS

Production-related rights are directly concerned with people's access to production or with their roles, safety, and fair treatment in productive activities.

Rights to Liberty, Health, and Safety for People Engaged in Production

Workplaces have often been scenes of danger, cruelty, coercion, and unfair exploitation, and specific rights of workers have often been formulated in response to these conditions. For example, the International Covenant on Economic, Social, and Cultural Rights includes a right against discrimination, a right to free choice of employment, a right to education, a right to fair wages and equal pay for equal work, a right to safe and healthy working conditions, a right to reasonable limitations of working hours, and a right to form trade unions and engage in strikes. Because their justifications are fairly obvious, these sorts of economic rights tend to be among the least controversial. This is not to say, however, that there is no controversy about the proper scope of these rights, the role of consent in making risky jobs permissible, the methods of implementation, or the levels of enforcement.

Rights Needed for Effective Production

Economic systems worldwide are as varied as political and legal systems, and economic rights should be formulated broadly enough to accommodate some of this variation. Just as due process rights allow some choice of methods for determining criminal guilt, economic rights should allow some choices among economic institutions. They should be stated in terms that would allow different kinds of economic systems to implement them in different ways. It may be helpful to begin by identifying, in broad terms, the activities and institutions required for production, some threats to them, and social and political means for responding to these threats. To find or make commodities with which to provision society, people must be able to

1. learn how to find or produce goods;
2. move in search of goods or the means to produce them;
3. plan and make arrangements for production, including arrangements for tools, materials, working groups, and labor supply (these arrangements may involve contracting, sharing, buying, borrowing, and renting);
4. engage individually or cooperatively in productive activities and associate with others for the purpose of doing so;
5. control the use and sale of resources and goods;
6. store resources and products to hedge against scarcity and famine; and
7. trade, sell, and ship goods.

All these are activities that people have usually managed to carry out to some degree; when survival is at stake, conditions do not have to be especially favorable for these activities to be possible. One reason human rights exist in this area is that the ability to obtain the material necessities of life is part of each person's claim to life. Further, reasonable and workable economic arrangements are important from the perspective of human rights because of the role that national economies play in providing the resources and supporting the institutions needed to implement human rights.

Human actions or omissions can endanger practices essential to production in many ways. Such threats can come from both individuals and governments. They include theft and fraud; violations of agreements; conflicting claims to labor, resources, tools, and products; wasteful use of resources; and ignorance of effective production techniques. Threats from governments include all of the foregoing plus the use of government powers to enrich officials and their families, disruptive taxation and appropriations, and—from foreign governments—threats to capture or control rich territories and to divert their resources.

When implemented, production-related rights provide not only social guarantees for the availability of freedoms and benefits but also a fixed structure within which economic transactions—and thus markets—can arise. Economic rights prescribe who has the power and liberty to use, or sell, or give various items and thereby make possible actions central to economic activity. Production-related rights not only restrain and supplement market processes but also help to constitute those processes.

Property. Any economic system requires arrangements to assign the control and use of holdings and to protect these holdings against unauthorized appropriations. As Hobbes argued, a legally enforced system of property that includes protections against theft and methods for dealing with competing claims to goods is needed to make possible the productivity that civilization requires.[4] Some workable system of property arrangements is thus of great importance; to create and maintain it, both collective action and systems of rights are clearly necessary. Property rights of individuals or collectivities, along with associated rights to buy, sell, and contract, serve not only to distribute power and benefits but also to structure the economic system by specifying which parties have the power and liberty to sell or give away various items. . . .

Private Productive Property. The focus of controversies about property is ownership of major means of production—land, factories, and equipment. A system of private ownership of land, factories, raw materials, and other goods used in production uses government power to confer on particular parties authority over the use and disposition of some of these resources or goods and to make others comply with that authority.[5] Private property serves to decentralize power by transferring a substantial measure of control over the use of productive resources from government to individuals or corporations.

When governments assign the control of productive resources to private owners, they typically enforce that control against unauthorized takeovers. It is clearly misleading to think of people with insufficient food as being "left alone" by a system of property. Such people are not left alone but rather are confronted by a system of property protections that prevents them from taking or using things needed for survival.[6]

There are many advantages to having a substantial private sector within a mixed national economy; it is not hard to make a case on utilitarian grounds for permitting regulated private ownership of productive resources. But I doubt whether a strong case can be made on grounds of basic liberty or fairness for a universal human right to own productive resources.

The claim to life, with its requirement that people have opportunities to obtain the necessities of life, does not necessarily require a right to ownership of productive property: socialist economies generally enable people to obtain the necessities of life. A country with a socialist economy may not reach the level of prosperity that some capitalist countries enjoy, but such a level is not necessary to satisfy basic rights. The right to life concerns results, not institutional specifics. The Universal Declaration sets out a right to "a standard of living adequate to . . . health and well-being" but does not specify the economic arrangements to make this possible. The Universal Declaration and its progeny prescribe neither capitalism nor socialism; they rather prescribe standards for what the economic system should do for people and not do *to* them.

Many believe that the liberty principle supports a human right to own productive property. One might claim that freedoms to acquire, hold, and dispose of productive property are extremely valuable both intrinsically or instrumentally. The importance of these freedoms is presupposed by Nozick's claim that socialism is incompatible with freedom, that socialist societies would have to forbid capitalist acts between consenting adults.[7] It is certainly true that some forms of individual acquisition, ownership, and disposition of productive resources are generally prohibited by noncapitalist societies; the result is that individuals lack some freedoms they would have under capitalism. But merely pointing out this fact does not settle the matter, for one may have freedoms in noncapitalist societies that one lacks under capitalism. Private property gives individuals or corporations authority over resources, which can and typically will limit the freedom of nonowners to the resource. In the case of land, nonowners are likely to be denied the liberty to enter, use, and occupy privately owned property. Nonowners are also likely to be denied the right to participate in decisions about the use of privately owned resources, even if these decisions affect them directly. Further, if most resources needed for production are privately owned, opportunities for self-employment are thereby restricted, and one may have to find employment with a property owner in order to have a means of life. This need for employment often gives employers power to restrict people's freedom.[8]

Capitalism and socialism, like all other forms of economic organization, allocate control over resources to some parties and hence reduce the liberty of others to use and benefit from those resources. The freedoms conferred by capitalism are not, in comparison with other alternatives, so obviously more important, or the restraints imposed so much less significant, that capitalism alone is compatible with people's claim to liberty. . . .

An argument for a right to hold private productive property might also appeal to considerations of fairness, asserting that it is unfair to have people invest their energies in inventing or building a new productive resource only to have ownership of that resource taken over by a collectivity. However, this alleged unfairness can be avoided by a system that gives such people forms of compensation other than ownership of the product. Innovators might be given income, prizes, or other personal property as compensation for a valuable contribution. This argument and others that appeal to the fact that one has mixed one's labor with a product do not succeed in establishing an individual right to productive property.

The Right to Employment

In an urbanized and heavily populated world, most people cannot rely for subsistence on self-organized production that uses their own property. They must rather rely on employment in productive enterprises run by individuals, corporations, or government agencies. Claims to economic resources and rewards, which might once have been made as claims to land reform, are now often made as claims to employment. In most societies today there are sizable numbers of people who lack both access to productive resources and opportunities for employment. The economic systems of many countries persistently consign a significant percentage of the work force to unemployment.

Unemployment and underemployment are difficult problems for all societies, including socialist ones, but programs that help to deal with these problems are available. Large-scale work programs for young people that combine work experience and job training can be created. Tax and other incentives to hire more people can be given to industries. Economic policies designed to run the economy at a faster rate can be adopted. The most ambitious solution is for government to become the employer of last resort, guaranteeing a job to every person who is able to work, wants a job, and has been unable to find one. . . .

A guarantee of employment is a guarantee of the availability of remunerative productive activity. What is at stake is the opportunity to participate in production and to share in its benefits. In a pre-agricultural society, the right to employment might cover permission to participate in hunting or gathering and to share in the resulting meals. As society and technology get more complicated, it becomes increasingly difficult for individuals to engage in production alone; modern production is apt to require cooperation within a large-scale enterprise. Hence in a modern society the main focus is on jobs that pay enough for a decent standard of living. A right to employment is not the same thing as a right to public assistance or to a minimum income. The availability of public assistance removes from the person who is unable to find a job the threat of starvation or of having to depend on friends or relatives for subsistence, but it does not generally provide the same financial and social benefits or support for self-respect that most jobs do. The assumption of those who emphasize the right to employment, socialists included, is that it is good for individuals and for society if people generally earn their own living through work. For this reason, employment is a production-related right rather than a consumption-related one. . . .

CONSUMPTION-RELATED RIGHTS

Economic rights are consumption-related if they serve to make possible the acquisition, use, and consumption of goods. The kinds of activities that may need protection here include shopping, purchasing, renting, borrowing, contracting, storing, using, sharing, giving, receiving, inhabiting, eating, and drinking. Those who dislike the images associated with the word "consumption" may prefer to think of these rights as use-related.

It is easy to think of ways in which these activities can be threatened. Supplies for consumption may be inadequate, or systems of distribution may be corrupt or otherwise inadequate, or people may lack money or other means to acquire needed goods. Knowledge of how to use available goods may also be lacking. Members of minority

groups may be excluded from markets or sources of credit by systems of caste or discrimination.

One important role of welfare rights, in my opinion, is to ameliorate the disruptive effects of many modernizing economic activities and thus to make the imposition of desirable economic changes morally tolerable. In the absence of effective welfare rights, well-meant programs for economic development can be fatal to people whose subsistence depends on traditional economic arrangements if they cannot find a place within the new system.[9] An assurance of provision for the dislocated helps make morally tolerable the often disruptive adjustments that are needed to adapt production to social and technological changes. This is an important way in which production-related and consumption-related rights intertwine.

The International Covenant on Economic, Social, and Cultural Rights does not mention consumers, but it does formulate a number of norms in response to the threats mentioned. First, it roundly condemns discrimination in economic and other areas. Second, in article 11, it recognizes the importance of education not only in regard to production but also in regard to "disseminating knowledge of the principles of nutrition." Third, the same article addresses supplies of food by committing its signatories to improving "methods of production, conservation and distribution of food" and to "developing or reforming agrarian systems." And fourth, it responds to inadequate purchasing power by formulating a right of everyone to an adequate standard of living, as well as rights to social security, medical services, and education.

The Right to Adequate Nutrition

Consumption-related rights include welfare rights, that is, rights to the availability of goods needed for survival and a decent life. Although the human rights movement has declared a number of welfare rights, my focus here will be on just one, the right to adequate nutrition. I choose this right as my example because it is arguably the most important welfare right and because examination of it will raise issues about welfare rights generally.

Reflection on the idea of a right to adequate nutrition leads many people to ask whom it is addressed to and what it requires; they wonder whether it obligates them personally to feed the needy. The answer to these questions is that this right, like most others, has both individuals and governments as its addressees. Individuals have negative duties not to deprive people of needed food or of the liberty and means to grow or buy it. They have positive duties to make a contribution to society, to provide food for their children and other family members, and perhaps to engage in charitable endeavors to supply food to those in need.

Governments have the same negative duties as individuals, but their positive duties are stronger. They must provide protections against violations of the negative duties described above, arrange a system of food production and distribution that provides an adequate supply of food in all parts of the country, and ensure that all people have the ability to draw from this supply enough food to provide adequate nutrition. This ability can be conferred by remunerative employment, by income grants, price subsidies, or direct distributions of food.

A right to adequate nutrition does not require that governments nationalize and collectivize agriculture or that they become the main suppliers of food. It does require that governments regulate agricultural and economic systems so that enough food for all is grown or imported and so that all people can get what they need. The right to adequate nutrition both grounds and limits other economic rights. Where weather is a large variable in a country's ability to feed itself, stored

food reserves may be necessary to prevent famine from crop failures or soaring prices. In the area of distribution, implementation of this right will require that food, or the money to buy it, be distributed in a manner that enables everyone to get the food they need. Most people, of course, will get their food, or the means to buy it, through work. But programs to provide food to those unable to find or perform remunerative work will also be needed; these might include meal programs for children and the elderly, food stamps, or guarantees of a minimum income.

One might think that the right to adequate nutrition could be rendered unnecessary if a right to employment or a right to a decent income were implemented. But a right to employment would not help people unable to work, and a right to a decent income, while solving the problem of purchasing power, would not necessarily solve problems of food production and distribution. Effective production often must be facilitated by land reform, water projects, and programs of agricultural research, development, and education. The right to adequate nutrition has both negative and positive elements. As with other economic rights, measures to implement it are likely to include noninvasion, protection, facilitation, and provision.

The Claim to Food and Its Basis. The first step in justifying a right to adequate nutrition is to show the great importance of what is at stake. This step is simple, as food is essential to people's ability to live, function, and flourish: without it, interests in life, health, and liberty are endangered and severe pain and death are inevitable. The connection is direct and obvious (something that is not always true with other rights), and thus there is no doubt that food is a basic good. When a good of such importance is at stake, people have a moral claim on others to refrain from depriving them of it and to render assistance when any are unable to obtain or protect the good by their own efforts.

Threats and the Necessity of a Right to Food.
The next step is to show that a political guarantee of the availability of food is necessary. Some very important goods, such as air, do not require social or political provision. But food is not like air; without one's own efforts and the help of others, it will often not be available. A number of threats to the production and consumption of food have already been identified, including inadequate supplies, inadequate purchasing power, and disruptions of traditional food systems by changing economic patterns. A political guarantee of adequate nutrition will have to cover more than the liberties to seek and consume food; even when these liberties are protected some people — the very young, the very old, the disabled, or the handicapped — will often have insufficient income to buy their own food.[10] . . .

Even where there is a socially recognized moral duty to support family members and hungry neighbors, such a duty is often ignored, and social pressure often provides inadequate support for compliance. Duties of charity always give donors some discretion concerning their gifts — if not discretion about when or to whom they will give, then at least about how much they will give. Charity is likely to be ineffective in providing for people who do not happen to be in the vicinity of a suitable donor. Many of those who are unable to get food for themselves have no families, or no family members who are willing and able to fulfill their moral duties of support.

Systems of charity tend to provide only spotty coverage; their capacities are generally insufficient to provide for everyone in need.

Because of these inadequacies of charitable and family support systems, there are strong reasons for developing government relief or welfare to supplement family support and charitable giving. Early measures of this sort involved poorhouses and other forms of public relief. When the welfare state emerged — with an income tax and other mechanisms to support it — it became possible for government to ensure adequate nutrition for all.

Feasibility.
Government guarantees of adequate nutrition are clearly feasible in the developed countries; in fact, such guarantees are in force — with varying degrees of effectiveness and comprehensiveness — in all the developed countries. Feasibility in less developed countries is another matter. . . .

OVERVIEW

My argument here has been that an adequate conception of economic life requires us to recognize two kinds of economic rights: production-related rights and consumption-related rights. Based on this argument, neither an account of property rights nor a theory of welfare rights alone can provide an adequate normative framework for economic policy. A more complex framework is needed, and this framework is already implicit in contemporary human rights documents. ◆ ◆ ◆

◆ Notes

1. On whether governments other than one's own must uphold one's human rights, see James W. Nickel, "Human Rights and the Rights of Aliens," in Peter G. Brown and Henry Shue, eds., *The* *Border That Joins* (Totowa, N.J.: Rowman & Littlefield, 1983), 31–45.

2. Philosophical discussions of welfare rights include Peter G. Brown, Conrad Johnson, and Paul

Vernier, eds., *Income Support: Conceptual and Policy Issues* (Totowa, N.J.: Rowman & Littlefield, 1981); Nicholas Rescher, *Welfare: The Social Issues in Philosophical Perspective* (Pittsburgh: University of Pittsburgh Press, 1972); and Carl Wellman, *Welfare Rights* (Totowa, N.J.: Rowman & Littlefield, 1982).

3. See, for example, Maurice Cranston, *What Are Human Rights?* (New York: Taplinger, 1973), 47–50, 65–72; Robert Nozick, *Anarchy, State, and Utopia* (New York: Basic Books, 1974), 26–42, 149–182.

4. Thomas Hobbes, *Leviathan* (1651), chap. 13. See also H. L. A. Hart, *The Concept of Law* (Oxford: Oxford University Press, 1961), 184–195.

5. On the concept of property and its moral status, see Lawrence C. Becker and Kenneth Kipnis, eds., *Property: Cases, Concepts, Critiques* (Englewood Cliffs, N.J.: Prentice-Hall, 1984); Lawrence C. Becker, *Property Rights* (London: Routledge & Kegan Paul, 1977); Adolf A. Berle, Jr., and Gardiner Means, *The Modern Corporation and Private Property* (New York: Harcourt Brace & World, 1968); Thomas C. Grey, "The Disintegra-tion of Property," in *NOMOS XXII: Property* (New York: New York University Press, 1980), 69–85; Virginia Held, *Property, Profits, and Economic Justice* (Belmont, Calif.: Wadsworth, 1980); Charles A. Reich, "The New Property," *Yale Law Journal* 73 (1964): 733–787.

6. James Sterba, *The Demands of Justice* (Notre Dame, Ind.: Notre Dame University Press, 1980). See also introduction to Held, *Property, Profits, and Economic Justice*, 1–20.

7. Nozick, *Anarchy, State, and Utopia*, 163.

8. On these points, see Cheyney C. Ryan, "Yours, Mine, and Ours: Property Rights and Individual Liberty," *Ethics* 87 (1977): 126–141; David Miller, "Constraints on Freedom," *Ethics* 94 (1983): 66–86; and Jeffrey H. Reiman, "The Fallacy of Libertarian Capitalism," *Ethics* 92 (1981): 85–95.

9. See Henry Shue, *Basic Rights* (Princeton, N.J.: Princeton University Press, 1980), 35–64.

10. For a study of famines arguing that absolute shortages of food are seldom their cause, see Amartya Sen, *Poverty and Famines: An Essay on Entitlement and Deprivation* (Oxford: Clarendon Press, 1981).

The Idea of a Female Ethic

Jean Grimshaw

Grimshaw examines the proposition that ethics is gendered; that is, the standards and criteria of morality are different for women and men. This claim takes several forms. One is that women have a different nature than men, and there are special feminine virtues such as selflessness. Other forms suggest that the social practices of women create a different set of concerns and priorities. Grimshaw sees problems with both views but feels that the distinction between public and private spheres, because it often dictates gendered roles, has shaped reality for many people. Thus, the particular experiences of women may offer critiques of the male-dominated public sphere. She concludes that if the activities and concerns traditionally associated with women were given equal value, then the moral and social priorities of society would be radically different from the priorities we have now.

Questions about gender have scarcely been central to mainstream moral philosophy this century. But the idea that virtue is in some way *gendered*, that the standards and criteria of morality are different for women and men, is one that has been central to the ethical thinking of a great many philosophers. It is to the eighteenth century that we can trace the beginnings of those ideas of a 'female ethic', of 'feminine' nature and specifically female forms of virtue, which have formed the essential background to a great deal of feminist thinking about ethics. The eighteenth century, in industrializing societies, saw the emergence of the concern about questions of femininity and female consciousness that was importantly related to changes in the social situation of women. Increasingly, for middle class women, the home was no longer also the workplace. The only route to security (of a sort) for a woman was a marriage in which she was wholly economically dependent, and for the unmarried woman, the prospects were bleak indeed. At the same time, however, as women were becoming increasingly dependent on men in practical and material terms, the eighteenth century saw the beginnings of an idealization of family life and the married state that remained influential throughout the nineteenth century. A sentimental vision of the subordinate but virtuous and idealized wife and mother, whose specifically female virtues both defined and underpinned the 'private' sphere of domestic life, came to dominate a great deal of eighteenth and nineteenth-century thought.

The idea that virtue is gendered is central, for example, to the philosophy of Rousseau. In *Emile*, Rousseau argued that those characteristics which would be faults in men are virtues in women. Rousseau's account of female virtues is closely related to his idealized vision of the rural family and simplicity of life which alone could counteract the evil manners of the city, and it is only, he thought, as wives and mothers that women can become virtuous. But their virtue is also premised on their dependence and subordination within marriage; for a woman to be independent, according to Rousseau, or for her to pursue goals whose aim was not the welfare of her family, was for her to lose those qualities which would make her estimable and desirable.

It was above all Rousseau's notion of virtue as 'gendered' that Mary Wollstonecraft attacked in her *Vindication of the Rights of Woman*. Virtue, she argued, should mean the same thing for a woman as for a man, and she was a bitter critic of the forms of 'femininity' to which women were required to aspire, and which, she thought, undermined their strength and dignity as human beings. Since the time of Wollstonecraft, there has always been an important strand in feminist thinking which has viewed with great suspicion, or rejected entirely, the idea that there are specifically female virtues. There are very good reasons for this suspicion. The idealization of female virtue, which perhaps reached its apogee in the effusions of many nineteenth-century male Victorian writers such as Ruskin, has usually been premised on female subordination. The 'virtues' to which it was thought that women should aspire often reflect this subordination—a classic example is the 'virtue' of selflessness, which was stressed by a great number of Victorian writers.

Despite this well-founded ambivalence about the idea of 'female virtue', however, many women in the nineteenth century, including a large number who were concerned with the question of women's emancipation, remained attracted to the idea, not merely that there were specifically female virtues, but sometimes that women were morally superior to men, and to the belief that society could be morally transformed through the influence of women. What many women envisaged was, as it were, an *extension* throughout society of the 'female values' of the private sphere of home and family. But, unlike many male writers, they used the idea of female virtue as a reason for women's entry into the 'public' sphere rather than as a reason for their being restricted to the 'private' one. And in a context where any sort of female independence was so immensely difficult to achieve, it is easy to see the attraction of any view which sought to re-evaluate and affirm those strengths and virtues conventionally seen as 'feminine'.

The context of contemporary feminist thought is of course very different. Most of the formal barriers to the entry of women into spheres other than the domestic have been removed, and a constant theme of feminist writing in the last twenty years has been a critique of women's restriction to the domestic role or the 'private' sphere. Despite this, however, the idea of 'a female ethic' has remained very important within feminist thinking. A number of concerns underlie the continued interest within feminism in the idea of a 'female ethic'. Perhaps most important is concern about the violent and destructive consequences to human life and to the planet of those fields of activity which have been largely male-dominated, such as war, politics, and capitalist economic domination. The view that the frequently destructive nature of these things is at least in part *due* to the fact that they are male-dominated is not of course new; it was common enough in many arguments for female suffrage at the beginning of the twentieth century. In some contemporary feminist thinking this has been linked to a view that many forms of aggression and destruction are closely linked to the nature of 'masculinity' and the male psyche.

Such beliefs about the nature of masculinity and about the destructive nature of male spheres of activity are sometimes linked to 'essentialist' beliefs about male and female nature. Thus, for example, in the very influential work of Mary Daly, all the havoc wreaked on human life and the planet tends to be seen as an undifferentiated result of the unchanging nature of the male psyche, and of the ways in which women themselves have been 'colonized' by male domination and brutality. And contrasted with this havoc, in Daly's work, is a vision of an uncorrupted female psyche which might rise like a phoenix from the ashes of male-dominated culture and save the world. Not all versions of essentialism are quite as extreme or vivid as that of Daly: but it is not uncommon (among some supporters of the peace movement for example) to find the belief that women are 'naturally' less aggressive, more gentle and nurturing, more co-operative, than men.

Such essentialist views of male and female nature are of course a problem if one believes that the 'nature' of men and women is not something that is monolithic or unchanging, but is, rather, socially and historically constructed. And a great deal of feminist thinking has rejected any form of essentialism. But if one rejects the idea that any differences between male and female values and priorities can be ascribed to a fundamental male and female 'nature', the question then arises as to whether the idea of a 'female ethic' can be spelled out in a way that avoids essentialist assumptions. The attempt to do this is related to a second major concern of feminist thinking. This concern can be explained as follows. Women themselves have constantly tended to be devalued or inferiorized (frequently at the same time as being idealized). But this devaluation has not simply been of women themselves—their nature, abilities and characteristics. The 'spheres' of activity with which they have particularly been associated have also been devalued. Again, paradoxically, they have also been idealized. Thus home, family, the domestic virtues, and women's role in the physical and emotional care of others have constantly been praised to the skies and seen as the bedrock of social life. At the same time, these things are commonly seen as a mere 'backdrop' to the more 'important' spheres of male activity, to which no self-respecting man could allow himself to be restricted; and as generating values which must always take second place if they conflict with values or priorities from elsewhere.

The second sort of approach to the idea of a 'female ethic' results, then, both from a critique of essentialism, and from an attempt to see whether an alternative approach to questions about moral reasoning and ethical priorities can be derived from a consideration of those spheres of life and activity which have been regarded as paradigmatically female. Two things, in particular, have been suggested. The first is that there *are* in fact common or typical differences in the ways in which women and men think or reason about moral issues. This view of course, is not new. It has normally been expressed, however, in terms of a *deficiency* on the part of women; women are incapable of reason, of acting on principles; they are emotional, intuitive, too personal, and so forth. Perhaps, however, we might recognize *difference* without ascribing *deficiency*; and maybe a consideration of female moral reasoning can highlight the problems in the male forms of reasoning which have been seen as the norm?

The second important suggestion can be summarized as follows. It starts from the assumption that specific social practices generate their own vision of what is 'good' or what is to be espe-

cially valued, their own concerns and priorities, and their own criteria for what is to be seen as a 'virtue'. Perhaps, then, the social practices, especially those of mothering and caring for others, which have traditionally been regarded as female, can be seen as generating ethical priorities and conceptions of 'virtue' which should not only not be devalued but which can also provide a corrective to the more destructive values and priorities of those spheres of activity which have been dominated by men.

In her influential book *In a Different Voice: Psychological Theory and Women's Development* (1982) Carol Gilligan argued that those who have suggested that women typically reason differently from men about moral issues are right; what is wrong is their assumption of the inferiority or deficiency of female moral reasoning. The starting point for Gilligan's work was an examination of the work of Lawrence Kohlberg on moral development in children. Kohlberg attempted to identify 'stages' in moral development, which could be analysed by a consideration of the responses children gave to questions about how they would resolve a moral dilemma. The 'highest' stage, the stage at which, in fact, Kohlberg wanted to say that a specifically *moral* framework of reasoning was being used, was that at which moral dilemmas were resolved by an appeal to rules and principles, a logical decision about priorities, in the light of the prior acceptance of such rules or principles.

A much quoted example of Kohlberg's method, discussed in detail by Gilligan, is the case of two eleven-year-old children, 'Jake' and 'Amy'. Jake and Amy were asked to respond to the following dilemma; a man called Heinz has a wife who is dying, but he cannot afford the drug she needs. Should he steal the drug in order to save his wife's life? Jake is clear that Heinz *should* steal the drug; and his answer revolves around a resolution of the rules governing life and property. Amy, however, responded very differently. She suggested that Heinz should go and talk to the druggist and see if they could not find some solution to the problem. Whereas Jake sees the situation as needing mediation through systems of logic or law, Amy, Gilligan suggests, sees a need for mediation through communication in relationships.

It is clear that Kohlberg's understanding of morality is based on the tradition that derives from Kant and moves through the work of such contemporary philosophers as John Rawls and R. M. Hare. The emphasis in this tradition is indeed on rules and principles, and Gilligan is by no means the only critic to suggest that any such understanding of morality will be bound to misrepresent women's moral reasoning and set up a typically male pattern of moral reasoning as a standard against which to judge women to be deficient. Nel Noddings, for example, in her book *Caring: A Feminine Approach to Ethics and Moral Education* (1984), argues that a morality based on rules or principles is in itself inadequate, and that it does not capture what is distinctive or typical about female moral thinking. She points out how, in a great deal of moral philosophy, it has been supposed that the moral task is, as it were, to abstract the 'local detail' from a situation and see it as falling under a rule or principle. Beyond that, it is a question of deciding or choosing, in a case of conflict, how to order or rank one's principles in a hierarchy. And to rank as a *moral* one, a principle must be universalizable; that is to say, of the form 'Whenever X, then do Y'. Noddings argues that the posing of moral dilemmas in such a way misrepresents the nature of moral decision-making. Posing moral issues in the 'desert-island dilemma' form, in which only the 'bare bones' of a situation are described, usually serves to conceal rather than to reveal the sorts of questions to which only situational and contextual knowledge can provide an answer,

and which are essential to moral judgment in the specific context.

But Noddings wants to argue, like Gilligan, not merely that this sort of account of morality is inadequate in general, but that women are less likely than men even to attempt to justify their moral decisions in this sort of way. Both of them argue that women do not tend to appeal to rules and principles in the same sort of way as men; that they are more likely to appeal to concrete and detailed knowledge of the situation, and to consider the dilemma in terms of the relationships involved.

Gilligan and Noddings suggest, therefore, that there are, as a matter of fact, differences in the ways in which women and men reason about moral issues. But such views of difference always pose great difficulties. The nature of the evidence involved is inevitably problematic; it would not be difficult to find two eleven-year-old children who reacted quite differently to Heinz's dilemma; and appeals to 'common experience' of how women and men reason about moral issues can always be challenged by pointing to exceptions or by appealing to different experience.

The question, however, is not just one of empirical difficulty. Even if there *were* some common or typical differences between women and men, there is always a problem about how such differences are to be described. For one thing, it is questionable whether the sort of description of moral decision-making given by Kohlberg and others really does adequately represent its nature. Furthermore, the view that women do not act on principle, that they are intuitive and more influenced by 'personal' considerations, has so often been used in contexts where women have been seen as deficient that it is as well to be suspicious of any distinction between women and men which seems to depend on this difference. It might, for example, be the case, not so much that women and men *reason differently* about moral issues, but that their ethical priorities differ, as that what is regarded as an important principle by women (such as maintaining relationships) is commonly seen by men as a *failure* of principle.

At best then, I think that the view that women 'reason differently' over moral issues is difficult to spell out clearly or substantiate; at worst, it runs the risk of recapitulating old and oppressive dichotomies. But perhaps there is some truth in the view that women's ethical *priorities* may commonly differ from those of men? Again, it is not easy to see how this could be very clearly established, or what sort of evidence would settle the question; but if it is correct to argue that ethical priorities will emerge from life experiences and from the ways these are socially articulated, then maybe one might assume that, given that the life experiences of women are commonly very different from those of men, their ethical priorities will differ too? Given, for instance, the experience of women in pregnancy, childbirth and the rearing of children, might there be, for example, some difference in the way they will view the 'waste' of those lives in war. (This is not an idea that is unique to contemporary feminism: it was, for example, suggested by Olive Schreiner in her book *Woman and Labour,* which was published in 1911.)

There have been a number of attempts in recent feminist philosophy to suggest that the practices in which women engage, in particular the practices of childcare and the physical and emotional maintenance of other human beings, might be seen as generating social priorities and conceptions of virtue which are different from those which inform other aspects of social life. Sara Ruddick, for example, in an article entitled 'Maternal thinking' (1980) argues that the task of mothering generates a conception of virtue which might provide a resource for a critique of those values and priorities which underpin much contemporary social life—including those of militarism. Ruddick does not want to argue that

women can simply enter the public realm 'as mothers' (as some suffragist arguments earlier in the twentieth century suggested) and transform it. She argues, nevertheless, that women's experience as mothers is central to their ethical life, and to the ways in which they might articulate a critique of dominant values and social mores. Rather similarly, Caroline Whitbeck has argued that the practices of caring for others, which have motherhood at their centre, provide an ethical model of the 'mutual realization of people' which is very different from the competitive and individualistic norms of much social life.

There are, however, great problems in the idea that female practices can generate an autonomous or coherent set of 'alternative' values. Female practices are always socially situated and inflected by things such as class, race, material poverty or well-being, which have divided women and which they do not all share. Furthermore, practices such as childbirth and the education and rearing of children have been the focus of constant ideological concern and struggle; they have not just been developed by women in isolation from other aspects of the culture. The history of childcare this century, for example, has constantly been shaped by the (frequently contradictory) interventions both of 'experts' in childcare (who have often been male) and by the state. Norms of motherhood have also been used in ways that have reinforced classist and racist assumptions about the 'pathology' of working-class or black families. They have been used, too, by women themselves, in the service of such things as devotion to Hitler's 'Fatherland' or the bitter opposition to feminism and equal rights in the USA. For all these reasons, if there is any usefulness at all in the idea of a 'female ethic', I do not think it can consist in appealing to a supposedly autonomous realm of female values which can provide a simple corrective or alternative to the values of male-dominated spheres of activity.

Nevertheless, it is true that a great deal of the political theory and philosophy of the last two hundred years *has* operated with a distinction between the 'public' and 'private' spheres, and that the 'private' sphere has been seen as the sphere of women. But that which is opposed to the 'world' of the home, of domestic virtue and female self-sacrifice, is not just the 'world' of war, or even of politics, it is also that of the 'market'. The concept of 'the market' defines a realm of 'public' existence which is contrasted with a private realm of domesticity and personal relations. The structure of individuality presupposed by the concept of the market is one which requires an instrumental rationality directed towards the abstract goal of production and profit, and a pervasive self-interest. The concept of 'the market' precludes altruistic behaviour, or the taking of the well-being of another as the goal of one's activity.

The morality which might seem most appropriate to the marketplace is that of utilitarianism, which, in its classic forms, proposed a conception of happiness as distinct from the various activities which lead to this, of instrumental reason, and of an abstract individuality, as in the 'felicific calculus' of Bentham, for example, whereby all subjects of pain or happiness are to be counted as equal and treated impersonally. But, as Ross Poole has argued, in 'Morality, masculinity and the market' (1985), utilitarianism was not really able to provide an adequate morality, mainly because it could never provide convincing reasons why individuals should submit to a duty or obligation that was not in their interests in the short term. It is Kantianism, he suggests, that provides a morality that is more adequate to the market. Others have to figure in one's scheme of things not just as means to an end, but as agents, and the 'individual' required by the market must be assumed to be equipped with a form of rationality that is not purely instrumental, and to be prepared to adhere to obligations and constraints

that are experienced as duty rather than inclination. The sphere of the market, however, is contrasted with the 'private' sphere of domestic and familial relations. Although of course men participate in this private sphere, it is the sphere in which female identity is found, and this identity is constructed out of care and nurturance and service for others. Since these others are known and particular, the 'morality' of this sphere cannot be universal or impersonal; it is always 'infected' by excess, partiality and particularity.

The first important thing to note about this contrast between the public sphere of the market and the private sphere of domestic relations is that it does not, and never has, corresponded in any simple way to reality. Thus working-class women have worked outside the home since the earliest days of the Industrial Revolution, and the exclusive association of women with the domestic and private sphere has all but disappeared. Secondly, it is important to note that the morality of the marketplace and of the private sphere exist in a state of tension with each other. The marketplace could not exist without a sphere of domestic and familial relations which 'supported' its own activities; yet the goals of the marketplace may on occasion be incompatible with the demands of the private sphere. The 'proper' complementarity between them can only exist if the private sphere is subordinate to the public sphere, and that subordinacy has often been expressed by the dominance of men in the household as well as in public life. The practical subordinacy of the private sphere is mirrored by the ways in which, in much moral and political philosophy and social thought, the immediate and personal morality of the private sphere is seen as 'inferior' to that which governs the exigencies of public life.

Furthermore, although, ideologically, the public and private spheres are seen as separate and distinct, in practice the private sphere is often governed by constraints and requirements deriving from the public sphere. A clear example of this is the ways in which views on how to bring up children and on what the task of motherhood entailed have so often been derived from broader social imperatives, such as the need to create a 'fit' race for the task of ruling an empire, or the need to create a disciplined and docile industrial workforce.

The distinction between the public and the private has nevertheless helped to shape reality, and to form the experiences of people's lives. It is still commonly true, for example, that the tasks of the physical and emotional maintenance of other people largely devolve upon women, who often bear this responsibility as well as that of labour outside the home. And the differences between male and female experience which follow from these things allow us to understand both why there may well often be differences between women and men in their perception of moral issues or moral priorities, and why these differences can never be summed up in the form of generalizations about women and men. Women and men commonly participate both in domestic and familial relations and in the world of labour and the marketplace. And the constraints and obligations experienced by individuals in their daily lives may lead to acute tensions and contradictions which may be both practically and morally experienced. (A classic example of this would be the woman who faces an acute conflict between the 'impersonal' demands of her situation at work, as well as her own needs for activity outside the home, and the needs or demands of those such as children or aged parents whose care cannot easily be fitted into the requirements of the workplace.)

If ethical concerns and priorities arise from different forms of social life, then those which have emerged from a social system in which women have so often been subordinate to men must be suspect. Supposedly 'female' values are not only the subject of little agreement among women; they are also deeply mired in conceptions of 'the feminine' which depend on the sort of polarization between 'masculine' and 'feminine' which has itself been so closely related to the subordination of women. There is no autonomous realm of female values, or of female activities which can generate 'alternative' values to those of the public sphere; and any conception of a 'female ethic' which depends on these ideas cannot, I think, be a viable one.

But to say this is not necessarily to say that the lives and experiences of women cannot provide a source for a critique of the male-dominated public sphere. Experiences and perspectives which are articulated by gender cannot be sharply demarcated from those which are also articulated along other dimensions, such as race and class; and there is clearly no consensus among women as to how a critique of the priorities of the 'public' world might be developed. Nevertheless taking seriously the experiences and perspectives of women—in childbirth and childcare for example—whilst not immediately generating any consensus about how things might be changed, generates crucial forms of questioning of social and moral priorities. It is often remarked, for example, that if men had the same sort of responsibility for children that women have, of if women had the same sorts of power as men to determine such things as priorities in work, or health care, or town planning, or the organization of domestic labour, many aspects of social life might be very different.

We cannot know in advance exactly what sorts of changes in moral and social priorities might result from radical changes in such things as the sexual division of labour or transformed social provision for the care of others; or from the elimination of the many forms of oppression from which women and men alike suffer. No appeal to current forms of social life can provide a blueprint. Nor should women be seen (as they are in some forms of feminist thinking) as 'naturally' likely to espouse different moral or social priorities from men. Insofar as there are (or might be) differences in female ethical concerns, these can only emerge from, and will need to be painfully constructed out of, changes in social relationships and modes of living; and there is every reason to suppose that the process will be conflictual. But there is every reason, too, to suppose that in a world in which the activities and concerns which have traditionally been regarded as primarily female were given equal value and status, moral and social priorities would be very different from those of the world in which we live now. ◆ ◆ ◆

Feminist Morality and Competitive Reality
A Role for an Ethic of Care?

Jeanne M. Liedtka

The language in the emergent ethics of care approach has recently appeared on the business scene. Liedtka examines the way it is used in business, suspecting that the rhetoric cloaks traditional bottom-line thinking. However, she then moves on to examine what caring properly means and whether it might open up new possibilities for morality in the corporate environment.

INTRODUCTION

The skit proved to be among the most memorable in the history of *Saturday Night Live.* In it, Lily Tomlin portrayed Ernestine, a Bell System telephone operator. Gleefully, she danced around a well-equipped computer control center flipping switches and chortling, "There goes Peoria!" as she plunged each city into a communications blackout. The scene closed with the corporate motto: "We don't care because we don't have to—we're your phone company."

How times have changed. No one, it seems these days, cares so much about us as our myriad of phone companies. AT&T is, after all, "our" phone company. Sprint reminds us that the "big guys" can't really care about us the way they do. MCI even cares about our "family and friends." Why? Because they have to—because the new realities of their marketplace award competitive advantage to those whose customers feel cared for.

Nor is this phenomenon limited to the telecommunications industry. A language of care and relationship-building has appeared with prominence in the business lexicon, across industries and geography. Corporate CEOs speak of "nurturing" their employees; in autonomous work teams and strategic alliances across the globe, individuals are "empowered" to build networks of collaborative relationships; everywhere, caring for the customer has become the new corporate mantra.

Ironically, after decades of work by ethicists striving to humanize the work of market mechanisms, the market itself may be offering us an opportunity to use it to drive organizations to care. As Thomas White (1992) has pointed out, many forces seem to be driving business practice into ever-closer alignment with much of the thinking underlying Carol Gilligan's (1982) notions of an "ethic of care" and its attention to relationships and connectedness as central. The avowed willingness to care for customers, at least, seems to be all around us. And can employee caring for customers be sustained if they are not cared for by their organization, in turn? Yet, can organizations care?

A decade of writing in feminist morality has focussed on the concept of an ethic of care; it seems timely to ask what relevance this body of work has for today's business context. Is the idea of creating organizations that "care" just another management fad that subverts the essential integrity of concepts of ethical caring? Conversely, are these concepts capable of beginning an important dialogue that may help us to see new possibilities for simultaneously enhancing both the effectiveness and the moral quality of organizations in the future? In this paper, I propose to address four questions that I see as central to these issues:

1. Is it possible for organizations to "care," in the sense of the term as used by scholars in the ethics area over the past decade?
2. What are the particular advantages such caring organizations might possess in the marketplace?
3. How might we translate these concepts into the kinds of attributes that would distinguish a caring organization in practice?

4. What are the problematic issues and unresolved questions associated with the concept of caring organizations?

By drawing upon both the academic literature and practitioner discussions of each of these issues in turn, I hope to initiate a conversation that I believe holds promise for bridging the gap between philosophical theorizing and business practice.

Placing Care in Context

The ethic of care focuses on the self as connected to others, with an emphasis on the caregiver's responsibility to the "other" to maintain that connection (Gilligan, 1982). It takes as its distinctive elements an attention to particular others in actual contexts (Held, 1993), a focus on the needs versus the interests of those particular others (Tronto, 1993a), and a commitment to dialogue as the primary means of moral deliberation (Benhabib, 1992). Care is "not a system of principles, but a mode of responsiveness" (Cole and Coultrap-McQuin, 1992).

Care is often compared with the stereotypical masculine ethic of justice. While the latter focuses on defining the self as separate and uses rights to protect boundaries between the self and other, care moves from its view of the connected self to an emphasis on relationships and the responsibilities that they entail. Gilligan's metaphor of the web to represent feminine thinking has been juxtaposed against the use of hierarchy to represent masculine thinking (White, 1992).

The ethic of care, while it departs from the focus on personal liberty and social contract which underlie the justice tradition, has both theoretical precedents and linkages. Tronto (1993b) situates it within the contextual ethics tradition of Aristotle, Adam Smith, and Alasdair MacIntyre; Benhabib (1992) links it with the discourse ethics of Habermas. Kittay and Meyers (1987) note:

> The interest in alternatives to a deductive, calculative approach to moral decision-making, with

its strong emphasis on individual autonomy, may be traced back to Aristotle and Hume and finds expression in a number of contemporary moral philosophers who stress the importance of virtue, rather than justice, in moral life. . . . For Aristotle, moral judgement springs from a moral character attuned to circumstantial and contextual features. It is not a product of an abstract concept of the Good. Moreover, Aristotle stresses the social embeddedness of the human being, a political animal by nature. In a related vein, Hume's ethics are grounded in emotion and personal concern. Hume argued that reason itself could not move us to act morally, but that our ethical life is guided by moral sentiments. Again, attention to relationships is prominent in this view. Alasdair MacIntyre and Bernard Williams are among the contemporary moral philosophers who call for a return to the notions of virtue, of moral character, and of a personal point of view to counteract the excessive formalism, the calculative ratiocination, and the impersonal perspective of the dominant moral traditions of Kant, on the one hand, and utilitarianism, on the other. (p. 8)

Other linkages exist as well. Though care theorists depart from Kant's focus on universalism, disagreeing with his belief that all rational individuals would construe morality the same way, they share what Rawls attributes to Kant—his premise of a socially constructed view of morality. Similarly, an ethic of care is clearly consistent with the 2nd formulation of the Categorical Imperative to always treat persons as ends, and not merely means. Interpreting this within an ethic of care, however, would require that we recognize and treat each person as a concrete, rather than a generalized other (Benhabib, 1992), and give attention to the particular self-defined ends that each aspires too. Care also has obvious linkages with Kant's duties of benevolence and mutual aid. Where Kant made these imperfect duties, care would render them obligatory, within bounds.

Since the publication, in 1982, of Gilligan's seminal work explicating the ethic of care, *In a Different Voice*, much care-related writing within the philosophy field has focussed on elaborating upon, analyzing, and evaluating the differences between the perspectives of Kohlberg, based on a Rawlsian theory of justice, and those of care. It is not my intention here either to explore this issue in detail, to argue for the superiority of a care ethic, or to trace its place in philosophical tradition. Instead, my interest is in considering specifically whether and how the inclusion of an ethic of care might contribute to enhancing both the effectiveness and the moral quality of the institutions in which we lead our work lives.

In this regard, the literature in business ethics has, until very recently, devoted little attention to any discussion of the ethic of care (White, 1992). This is surprising given the potential relevance of a relationship-based ethic to business, viewed (by some at least) as a relationship-based activity. It is also surprising, given the significant impact that stakeholder theory (Freeman, 1984) has had in this same literature, and the powerful linkages between stakeholder theory and the ethic of care (Wicks, Gilbert, and Freeman, 1994).

The Ethic of Care and Stakeholder Theory

Stakeholder theory, like the ethic of care, is built upon a recognition of interdependence. As Wicks, Gilbert, and Freeman (1994) note:

> The corporation is constituted by the network of relationships which it is involved in with employees, customers, suppliers, communities, businesses and other groups who interact with and give meaning and definition to the corporation. (p. 12)

Thus, for stakeholder theorists, the interdependence is between groups; for care theorists, it is between and among the individuals who comprise those groups. Care theorists might, in fact, be uncomfortable with the categorization of individuals into groups defined by others. Instead, they would look toward self-defined and possibly multiple identities that narrowly defined, mutually exclusive definitions of stakeholders might ignore. Despite these differences, both views stand in stark contrast to a view of business as a series of one-time arms-length transactions, a topic which we will shortly pursue at greater length.

Within this view of business as a web of ongoing connections, care and stakeholder theories act as activity-framing, rather than decision-making, theories. Both offer a perspective and guiding ethos for the moral agent, situated within the ongoing daily activities which characterize the operation of business. Neither theory offers a set of abstract principles to be used as decision heuristics in resolving particular moral dilemmas, arguing that the complexity of concrete circumstances makes a priori solutions impossible. Both theories need an ethic of justice to deal with competing claims and inadequate resources.

Both care and stakeholder theories see dialogue-based processes, rather than individual deliberation, as the foundation for the living of a moral life (Benhabib, 1992; Wicks et al, 1994). In stakeholder theory, these processes are driven by a consideration of the impact of actions on the projects of stakeholder groups. In the ethic of care, the focus is the concrete needs of particular individuals. Within care, in particular, it is the conduct of daily life, lived for the most part with long intervals in between the kind of moral dilemmas that have dominated business ethics discussions, that is the focus. In doing so, it places less emphasis on the exercise of free will and choice, and more on recognizing the moral demands ever-present imposed upon us (Scaltsas, 1992). Though this lack of interest in prescribing moral solutions has raised questions as to the adequacy of care as a moral theory (Koehn, 1995), it suits well the realities of corporate life, which is often about that which is required, rather than that which is chosen.

Thus, though care may not, in the absence of considerations of justice, provide a fully self-sufficient theory for moral business conduct (a point to which we will later return), its apparent saliency makes it a candidate worthy of careful attention. In addition, in empirical studies of ethical work climate (Victor and Cullen, 1988), caring has emerged as one of the dominant dimensions of such climates. From both normative and descriptive viewpoints, then, the role of caring in the business context warrants serious attention.

CAN ORGANIZATIONS CARE?

Now we turn to the question of whether the expressions of care prevalent in today's business lexicon are consistent with the notion of ethical caring. Furthermore, is it even possible to take Gilligan's essentially individual level theory and extend it to the level of an organization, without subverting it in the process? Only by exploring the particulars of feminist theorists' arguments in detail can these questions be answered.

Defining Care

Central to our inquiry is Noddings' (1984) distinction between "caring for" and "caring about." Ethical caring, she argues, only applies to those persons that we care for. She uses the term, "aesthetical caring" for objects and things that we care about, and is concerned about the extent to which our caring for things subverts our caring for people, by encouraging us to use them instrumentally to achieve other ends. The caring about versus caring for distinction is also made in relation to human beings. If it is people that we care about, versus for, Noddings views this as representing only a "verbal commitment to the possibility of care" (p. 18). We cannot, she argues, care "for" those who are beyond our reach. Caring represents a personal investment that must always remain at the level of "I"; caring at the more abstract level of "We" is an illusion. This quality of particularity is essential—caring lives in the relationship between me, an individual, and you, another individual. Without this particularity the caring connection is lost and we must re-label the new process: no longer "caring", it becomes "problem-solving", in Nodding's terminology. . . .

Tronto (1993a) acknowledges Noddings' distinction between caring for and caring about and uses it to lay out four stages in the caring process. Rather than excluding caring about persons from ethical caring, she views it as a precondition (necessary, but insufficient) for fully realized care. Care begins with "caring about" (stage 1), identifying a need as one that ought to be met. Care progresses to "taking care of" (stage 2), assuming the responsibility for meeting the need. It moves to "care-giving", directly meeting the need (analogous to Noddings' "caring for"), in stage 3. The process culminates with care receiving in stage 4, as the recipient of care responds. Here, too, the personal nature of care ultimately remains fundamental—as it must, for as long as we care "about" the other, they remain generalized rather than concrete. As Benhabib (1992) points out, it is only in the process of personally engaging with the particular other that we gain the specialized knowledge of their context, history, and needs that permits us to fully care for them on their terms, rather than ours.

The Practice of Care

In describing care as a practice, Tronto (1993a) emphasizes its concern with both thought and action, directed towards some end, and dependent upon the resources of time, skill, and material goods. Along with other scholars (Held, 1993; Ruddick, 1989), Noddings has used the relationship between a mother and her child to illustrate, at its deepest level, her notion of what it means to care. Thus, the essence of caring becomes a focus on acceptance of the other, both in his or her current state, and as one capable of growth. Nurturing the development of the one cared for is the critical activity in caring relationships. Contrary to a stereotypical view of caring

as fostering dependence, it's aim is the opposite—to care means to respect the other's autonomy and to work to enhance the cared-for's ability to make his or her own choices well. This recognition of the importance of the need, for all humans, to realize their capacities goes back to Aristotle. As Herman (1993) has noted in her exploration of Kant's duties for benevolence and mutual aid, the focus here, as there, is not on pursuing one's ends for them, it is on enhancing their capability to pursue their own ends. If, as Flanagan (1982) states, the "motor of cognitive development is contradiction, caring may well be comprised more of "tough love" than of indulgence. Anthropologist and biographer Mary Catherine Bateson observes (1990):

> The best care-taker offers a combination of challenge and support. . . . To be nurturant is not always to concur and comfort, to stroke and flatter and appease; often, it requires offering a caring version of the truth, grounded in reality. Self-care should include the cold shower as well as the scented tub. Real caring requires setting priorities and limits. Even the hard choices of triage have their own tenderness. (p. 155)

Another aspect of developing an enhanced ability to choose well, is the recognition that choices are made within the context of a "community of mutual aid" (Herman, 1993). Learning to care is essential to my ability to take my place in the community. The community, in insisting that its members develop a capacity to care, helps both the individuals and the larger community in the process. The existence of a transcending mutual purpose that seeks to accommodate and respect, yet, of necessity sometimes bound, the personal projects of individuals within the community's goals, is critical. Without this combination of shared purpose and personal project, caring risks becoming the process of self-sacrifice and denial of self that some feminists fear (Scaltsas, 1992), seeing in it a continuation of women's history of accepting oppression in the name of caring. Self-care, Gilligan argues, is a precondition for giving morally mature care to others. Similarly, bereft of a strong regard for particularity, communities can smother difference and subjugate those in need of care.

In caring, the focus on the other is complete — that is, I focus on them within the context of their world view, and not mine. Caring always involves "feeling with" — receiving the other, rather than projecting one's own view onto the other. Thus, the development process evolves out of the aspirations and capabilities of the cared for, rather than being driven by the needs and goals of the care-giver. This quality, more than any other, plays upon the mother/child imagery so central to work in feminist morality.

Thus, in order for an organization to "care" in the sense that feminist ethicists have used the term, such caring would need to be:

a. focused entirely on persons, not "quality," "profits," or any of the other kinds of ideas that much of today's "care-talk" seems to revolve around,
b. undertaken as an end in and of itself, and not merely a means toward achieving quality, profits, etc.,
c. essentially personal, in that it ultimately involves particular individuals engrossed, at a subjective level, in caring for other particular individuals.
d. growth-enhancing for the cared-for, in that it moves them towards the use and development of their full capacities, within the context of their self-defined needs and aspirations.

Care in the Business Context: The Market Mechanism at Work

The above conditions make clear that much of the potential "caring" that organizations engage in constitutes "problem-solving" in Noddings' vocabulary. It is impersonal, instrumental, and object-focussed. Organizations often use their resources, including employees and suppliers, as means to solve problems in pursuit of the only end of significance — profits. In this view, organizations ordinarily represent a defined set of solutions in search of an appropriate set of problems. To the extent that customers come attached to these problems, firms are forced to engage them in a process in which customers come to believe that the firm's solutions will solve their problems. The term "caring for customers" has been used to describe this process. In this same vein, firms contract with employees and suppliers who have problems of their own, for which they also have solutions. In neither case are the needs of the "other" of interest to the firm, except in so far as they represent a potential source of profitability. This is the market mechanism at work, and it is difficult not to agree with Noddings that "caring" has little role in its functioning. Nor would caring's inclusion appear to offer much in enhancing its effectiveness, if we leave its basic assumptions of arms-length transactions among independent entities pursuing their own projects intact. Relationships here have relevance only so long as they are profitable, in a literal sense. In such a system, caring is likely to foreclose options, make the dissolution of unprofitable relationships more difficult, and increase costs.

The underlying premise here is that of the abstract other — one customer is as good as another, any employee is replaceable, each represents only today's point of intersection between supply and demand — tomorrow may well bring a different set. . . . The predominance of this view of business, and the self-sustaining loop of short-term-oriented, narrowly self-interested behavior that it fosters, accounts for the persistence of non-caring organizations.

Business as Relationships: An Alternative View

. . . Recent research (Collins and Porras, 1994) asserts that visionary companies, those with a strong set of non-financial values and a long-term perspective, both outperform and outlast their less visionary counterparts. Consider the words of George Merck, son of the founder of Merck & Co. and former chairman (Business Enterprise Trust, 1991):

> We try never to forget that medicine is for the people, it is not for the profits. The profits follow, and if we have remembered that, they have never failed to appear. The better we have remembered it, the larger they have been. (p. 3)

If such views, echoed by other corporate leaders over time, support an alternative conception of business as based on on-going relationships where outcomes other than only profits can be important, how might ethical caring be different in practice than the market mechanisms described above? What does it mean to care for these others—whether they be customers, employees, suppliers, or other stakeholders?

To say that I care about my customers or my employees would place them as particular others and the capabilities that they represent at the center of my attention, and to work with them to realize those capabilities. The customer, for instance, is seen here as having a set of needs and possibilities to which, as a care-giver, I must attend. It is these needs, rather than the organization's pre-packaged solutions, that drive my response in a process that is part of an on-going relationship, rather than a transaction.

From Individual to Organizational Caring

Does, then, an assembly of appropriately caring individuals constitute a "caring" organization? Considerable precedent exists, of course, for such anthropomorphizing—we speak of organizations that have values, that learn, that reward. Yet, it would certainly be possible for a subgroup of caring individuals to exist within an organization that worked to subvert their efforts. Thus, I would argue that a caring organization, in addition to being composed of individuals who met the conditions, would need to actively support their efforts through its goals, systems, strategies, and values. This is important for three reasons: (1) it is the organization which determines the reach of each individual, as it defines their roles, responsibilities, and decision-making scope, (2) it is the organization that must provide the resources that allow individual care-givers to successfully care within their reach, (3) it is the organization that must create the system in which care is self-sustaining, in which the reward systems support care-givers and discourage the rogues.

Individual caring is only sustainable, in the long term, within caring systems (Kahn, 1993): "To be cared for is essential for the capacity to be caring" (Gaylin, 1976). The personal investment required to care is substantial and the risks of "burnout" are ever-present, as countless studies of the traditional care-giving professions have demonstrated. In reviewing these studies, however, researchers (Scott, Aiken, Mechanic, and Moravcsik, 1995) found burnout not to be associated with the direct care-giving activities themselves (e.g., caring for AIDS and cancer patients). Instead, it was linked to the organizational context, in the form of lack of influence in decision-making, dealing with bureaucratic inconveniences, and the lack of opportunities for creativity. Avoiding burnout, these authors argue, requires decentralized decision-making, adequate resources, opportunities for development, and a collaborative environment. Caring, then, though a particular relationship between individuals, is situated within the context of a community, derives its shared focus from the needs of that community, and is only sustainable with the support of that community; care becomes self-reinforcing within that context. Thus, both because it derives its meaning within the context of community, and because of the personal investment required to care, organizations that support individual caring, that create self-reinforcing systems of caring, are essential if caring is to persist at all.

MARKET-BASED ADVANTAGES OF CARE

If the idea of a caring organization exists as a possibility, albeit unrealized in much of today's "care-talk", what kinds of enhanced competitive advantages might these organizations enjoy? Let me begin to address this question by playing out in more detail (in an obviously oversimplified way) the distinctions that we have already raised between the attitudes and behaviors embedded in the transactional focus of the market mechanisms versus the relationship-based processes of care (see table).

Under what situations might these two very different types of organizations enjoy competitive advantage? Addressing this question requires that we move from discussions of philosophy to business strategy.

Sources of Competitive Advantage

The strategy literature, within the past decade, has shifted dramatically, away from a focus on firms' assets and industry structure as a source of competitive advantage towards a belief that competitive advantage lies with the extent to which an organization is able to build a set of capabilities that allows it serve its customers uniquely well within the demands of their marketplace (Rumelt, Schendel, and Teece, 1991). Building on Day's (1994) definition, these capa-

bilities consist of "complex bundles of skills and accumulated knowledge, exercised through organizational processes, and within organizational contexts, that enable firms to coordinate activities and make use of their assets." Stalk, Evans, and Shulman (1992) argue that four principles underlie capability-based competition:

1. The building blocks of corporate strategy are not products and markets but business processes.
2. Competitive success depends upon transforming a company's key processes into strategic capabilities that consistently provide superior value to customers.
3. Companies create these capabilities by making strategic investments in a support infrastructure that links together and transcends traditional functions.
4. Capability-based strategies, because they cross functions, must be championed by senior leadership.

Furthermore, Day (1994) argues that the strategic value of any particular capabilities set is determined by three "tests":

1. Whether it makes a disproportionate contribution to the provision of customer value
2. Whether it can be readily matched by rivals
3. Whether it speeds the firm's adaptation to environmental change

Taken together, a number of themes emerge as common across these perspectives. Perhaps the most obvious is the central role of the customer and the focus on creating value for that customer. This is a very different focus than that of product/market selection, the key strategic task that had long dominated the strategy field. In the past, the customer was a generalized other, the replaceable element—it was the product that had salience and permanence. In the new thinking,

Role	Business as Market Transaction	Business as Caring Relationship
Customer	Ancillary: Process is driven by organization's need to sell its solutions to some identified set of problems. These come with customers attached.	Primary: Process is driven by the organization's desire to attend carefully to customer's self-defined needs and aspirations and facilitate their achievement.
Employees	Expendable/Replaceable: Their labor is purchased at market rates in order to produce and sell organization's solutions.	Primary: Developing members of a community of mutual purpose and linchpin that creates the organizational capability set and connects it with customer needs.
Suppliers	Interchangeable: Interested in selling their solutions as input into the production of next downstream product. As their customers, our firm is ancillary to their purpose.	Primary: As partners in the process of attending to the end user in the value chain that we share, they attend to us and make possible our customer focus.
Organization and Senior Management	Primary: To plan, supervise, control, and monitor the processes of production and selling to ensure quality and efficiency.	Supporting: To create a caring context and systems which provide resources and decentralized authority that enables employees to care for customers.
Shareholders	Primary: As owners of the business, their interests, in the form of profits earned, dominate decision-making.	Supporting: As members of the workplace community, they provide capital that facilitates the process of meeting the needs of other stakeholders. Their needs are met as the project succeeds.

today's product is no more than a temporary attempt to create value for a particular customer. Since "value" is obviously in the eye of the beholder, success belongs to those who can move with the customer as his or her needs, and therefore definition of value, changes. Thus, it is the relationship with the customer that has permanence, and today's product which is temporary.

A second theme that emerges concerns the centrality of employees to this process of value creation. If competitive advantage lies in maintaining relationships with customers, then it is the employees who deal directly with these customers who ultimately determine the firm's success or failure. The rest of the organization, including senior management, exists to support and respond to, rather than control and monitor, these front-line workers. In fact, control by senior managers, far removed from customer contact, would appear to increase the risk of losing touch with changing customer needs. In addition, if the source of advantage lies in "bundles of skills and accumulated knowledge," these too reside in employees—not the traditional asset categories of property, plant, and equipment. Rather than

viewing these knowledgeable workers as replaceable, sustaining advantage requires that they remain as members of the firm's community—not competitors'. It also requires that flexibility and adaptability be encouraged, so that the need for new capabilities can be anticipated.

The final theme that emerges is a concern that traditional structural categories, like function and hierarchy, can impede, rather than facilitate, success. What is called for are pathways—infrastructure—that encourage coordination and cooperation across units and companies, that support, link, and create processes. This stands in contrast to the scalar chain of command and turf protection mentalities prevalent today.

The Capabilities Created by Transaction vs. Care Orientations

Returning to our question of a role for an ethic of care, we need to ask what kinds of different capabilities the market transaction-based and the caring relationship-based firms might possess, and what implications these might have for competitive success.

Our transactions-oriented firm ought, I argue, to excel at the creation of standardized products and services for identified needs—producing them efficiently and consistently, and marketing them aggressively. To the extent that they know their customer well, their products will be perceived as a good value, and their employees and suppliers will comply with the "day's work for a day's pay" contract that they have created with them. Their chief vulnerability lies with changes in their marketplace. Though they may "know" their customer today, they do not have a ready mechanism for learning should that customer change. The employees who deal with that customer are: (1) likely focussed on getting the job done as specified, rather than attending to customer voices and (2) even having heard a change in the voices, are far removed from the centers of influence, in terms of decision-making. Mistakes in this carefully orchestrated system are expensive, and so middle managers are risk-averse, as well. If competitors respond more quickly to the changes, customers will merely take their transactions elsewhere, having little to lose by doing so.

Contrast this with the different set of capabilities potential in a care-based organization. Because of its shared purpose around and attention to customers' self-defined needs, both current and future, and empowered employee and supplier community, its strengths would lie in its responsiveness and flexibility. Those who dealt with customers would have ownership of that relationship and the resources and decision-making scope to respond quickly. Rather than being constrained by the narrow limits of organizationally-defined roles, employees would be more likely to adopt the "supra-role" citizenship behaviors (Schnake, 1991) conducive to smooth organization functioning. The vulnerability here would appear to be the potential, from a senior management perspective, of a system "out of control."

If we believe the enormous volume of business writing today, in both practitioner and aca-

demic circles, the world of business is no longer characterized by stability and predictability. If this is true, we can assert that the most successful organizations of the future will be flatter, quicker, and more intelligent at every level (Pinchot and Pinchot, 1993; Quinn, 1992). They will need to listen, to inquire, and to experiment. They will be collaborative enterprises (Gray, 1989), which value the diversity of their workforce, and who work in partnership with their suppliers and in the communities in which they reside. They will need to have a strong sense of purpose and employees who care. As Bartlett and Ghoshal have argued:

> Traditionally, top-level managers have tried to engage employees intellectually through the persuasive logic of strategic analyses. But clinically framed and contractually based relationships do not inspire the extraordinary effort and sustained commitment required to deliver consistently superior performance. For that, companies need employees who care, who have a strong emotional link with the organization. (p. 81)

Few topics in the practitioner literature have so captured the interest of managers as Peter Senge's (1990) concept of learning organizations. In a world of constant change, the ability to learn may prove to be the only source of competitive advantage in the long-term (Senge, 1990). Senge defines learning as increases in the capacity for effective action, and the similarities between Senge's description of the properties of learning organizations and those we have attributed to organizations centered on an ethic of care are striking. Learning, he asserts, occurs within communities that share a sense of purpose that connects each member to each other, and to the community at large. Learning organizations are characterized by an ability to maintain an open dialogue among members, that seeks first to understand, rather than evaluate, the perspectives of each. Finally, a learning organization looks to the whole of a process, rather than its pieces. Learning organizations exhibit the kind of "constructed knowing" (Belensky, Clinchy, Goldberger, and Tarule, 1986) that connects reason and emotion, intuition and rationality, and that thrives on complexity and ambiguity, rather than simplicity and certainty. Care-based organizations would seem ideally suited for such processes.

The degree of improvement in the moral quality of such organizations, relative to transaction-based firms, would also be substantial. Employees, customers, and suppliers would be treated as ends in themselves, and not merely means to a far greater extent than the instrumentalism of today's market allows. The development of their capacities as community members would occupy a more central role. Embedded within the web of support, trust, and open inquiry, the climate in the workplace would be attentive to the dignity of all, and more welcoming of difference. Such an environment, as Benhabib (1992) has noted, would enhance not only our ability to see the other's perspective, but our commitment to act on that knowledge, to use it to care, as well.

Yet, the challenges of transforming today's organizations into caring organizations are staggering. One has to be troubled that, amid all of the talk about the organization of the future, it remains questionable whether much is really changing within organizations today. Far from becoming more caring, many organizations appear to be moving in quite the opposite way. Hamel and Prahalad (1994), leading thinkers in the strategy field, have argued that the organizational appetite for cost-cutting and downsizing constitutes a business version of anorexia:

> . . . the United States and Britain have produced an entire generation of denominator managers. They can downsize, declutter, delayer, and divest better than any managers in the world. . . . One of the inevitable results of downsizing is plummeting employee morale. Employees have a hard time squaring all the talk about the importance of

human capital with seemingly indiscriminate cutting. . . . And no wonder so few first-level and mid-level employees bring their full emotional and intellectual energies to the task of restructuring. . . . Downsizing belatedly attempts to correct the mistakes of the past; it is not about creating the markets of the future. The simple point is that getting smaller is not enough. Downsizing, the equivalent of corporate anorexia, can make a company thinner; it doesn't necessarily make it healthier. (pp. 9–11)

Creating these new organizations requires more than coining new words to describe them—it requires new organizational structures, systems and processes, and new managerial skills and mindsets. Caring, in its ethical sense, cannot be grafted onto business as usual. Caring is difficult in today's traditional rule-based hierarchies because they are not designed to foster care.

THE ATTRIBUTES OF CARING ORGANIZATIONS

If the idea of a caring organization exists as a possibility, and if that organization might possess significant market-based advantage, it is important to explore what an organization designed to care would look like in practice. Unfortunately, there has been little attention given to this subject in the literature.

The Architecture of Care

Perhaps the clearest point emerging from the discussions to-date concern what caring organizations would not look like. They are not bureaucracies. Scholars have argued for decades that personal and professional values are difficult to honor in a bureaucratic environment; Ferguson (1984) has argued persuasively that bureaucracy is antithetical to the ability to care. The rules in a bureaucracy become, over time, the ends rather than the means. Thus, caring, even for the customer or client, is subordinated to perpetuation of the organization in its current state. All behavior takes on a political motive, as the superior becomes internalized as the only "other" worthy of concern. Similarly, the divorcing of planning from performing tasks puts even those we deal with directly "out of our reach," since reach is determined as much by sphere of influence as it is by proximity. Finally, Ferguson asserts that openness, which is central to caring, is impossible to sustain in a bureaucracy, as it threatens the status quo that the structure lives to protect.

If caring organizations cannot be bureaucracies, how could they structured? Because the concept of reach, so fundamental to caring, is partially a function of decision-making scope, the architecture of the organization would need to be highly decentralized to give each individual the "reach" necessary to carry out the caring work on a daily basis, in an autonomous way. It would entail the creation of a web, or network, of connections, where the focus was on the relationships between individuals, rather than the position of "boxes" in a hierarchy.

This would need to be coupled with the provision of the resources necessary to enable successful care-taking—whether those be information, expertise, or budget. Thus, the infrastructure to support care would be as important as the organizational structure. Advances in information technology add importantly to the ability of those who deal with customers to provide individualized care. The image of the front-line service person, equipped with all of the expertise that the firm has to offer available online to better serve the customer, fits well the image of a caring organization.

De-Alienating the Workforce
The relationship of the individual to the organization would be characterized by engagement and focus. Iannello (1992) has reported on similar efforts at "de-alienating the workforce," by

putting "meaning and values back in jobs." Engagement, based on Kahn's work (1990), is itself the product of meaningful work, a safe environment and the availability of resources. A focus on meaningful work cycles us back to individual decision-making autonomy, coupled with purposefulness. The concept of purposefulness is increasingly prominent in the management literature and occurs when the goals and values of the organization arise from, and are shared with, the individuals in the firm (Senge, 1990; Solomon, 1992). A purposeful firm strategy focuses on excellence in meeting its goals, not beating the competition (Solomon, 1992), and is consistent with such influential theories as Deming's "Quality Principles" and Prahalad and Hamel's "Strategic Intent." In this world, organizational members at every level need to be strategic thinkers, who understand the organization's purpose and its capabilities, as they respond to ever-changing opportunities to better meet customers' needs. Members must also collectively be given a voice in the setting of strategic direction (Iannello, 1992).

A safe environment offers support and the opportunity to fully involve one's self without fear of consequences (Kahn, 1990). Because a willingness to care places the care-giver at risk (for rejection and for burn-out), a sense of safety is critical to a willingness to be engaged. Similarly, there must be clear boundaries around each individual's and each organization's responsibility to care. Such focus is necessary to avoid overwhelming the care-giver with responsibilities that exceed his or her emotional, intellectual, and physical capacity to care. This is where the creation of trusted collaborative networks can be essential in supporting and extending the capacity of individual care-givers (Handy, 1994).

Internal organizational processes would be characterized by communication, constructive conflict, shared expertise, and continual redefinition and renewal. Communication would reflect the kind of balance between inquiry and advocacy that Senge (1990) describes. Belensky et al (1986) draw a similar distinction between didactic and "real" talk. The first goal of communication in inquiry or "real" talk mode is to achieve an understanding of the assumptions and values underlying the position of the "other," rather than the selling of one's own solution. Questions would be as valued as answers; listening as important as speaking.

Tension will be ever-present. There will always be conflict among stakeholders and more needs than can be met; the caring organization will not be free of conflict. On the contrary, it will acknowledge and work with conflict, rather than suppressing and ignoring it, by using dissent constructively to forge solutions that better serve the needs of the cared-for. Pascal (1990) argues for a dialectical, rather than a trade-off, approach to decision-making, asserting that contention, properly handled through dialogue rather than debate, enhances creativity and personal growth.

Expertise will be shared and individuals will be teachers of some things and learners of others simultaneously, as individuals are constantly stretched to develop their talents. Contrary to the image of sentimentality often attached to the notion of care, "tough love," as noted previously, may be a more apt description. Caring organizations will need to be as tough-minded and results-oriented as any other organization. It will be their methods and aspirations that distinguish them, not their lack of attention to outcomes. The values of mutual respect, honesty, and patience will be its foundation.

QUESTIONS CONCERNING THE CARING PERSPECTIVE

In the decade since the ethic of care was introduced, a significant volume of literature critical of the adequacy of care as a moral theory has been produced. The most visible concerns raised in the literature relate to questions about the use of the mother/child dyad, so prevalent in feminist moral writings, as a model for non-familial relationships, issues around freedom and fairness that a more rights-focused perspective offers, and the question of how one sets the boundaries of care. I address each in turn.

Concerns about Matriarchy

The "mothering" image of caring that is so powerful also raises significant concerns. One of these relates to the issue of power. Is the power differential between parent and child one that we want to embrace as a model for relationships at work? Do we want to replace patriarchy with matriarchy? Held (1993) is not disturbed by these concerns. In proposing her "post-patriarchal" model, she notes that disparity in power is a given in our society and cannot be avoided. Yet, traditional notions of power are useless in the mothering context. Mothers, she argues, do not "wield" power. Instead, "the power of a mothering person is to empower others—to foster transformational growth" through influence (p. 209). Iannello (1992) agrees, also advocating a shift in our thinking from power to empowerment. She observes that our current societal context associates power with domination. Yet, power also implies the ability, strength, and energy to get things done. Using the latter conception of power, she argues, allows us to differentiate between power as controlling others and empowerment as controlling oneself.

Ferguson (1984) believes otherwise, asserting that both the presence of inequality and "natural love" inherent in mothering make it unsuitable for generalization outside the bounds of the family. Instead, she offers the model of citizenship, and uses the town meeting with its decentralization, public decision-making, and openness to conflicting views as a guide for care-based organizations. Her view is strikingly similar to that contained in Charles Handy's (1994) recent call for "federated structures," which contain local and separate activities served by a common center. Such structures, he believes, led by the center and managed by the parts, "combine the benefits of scale and autonomy, while retaining a sense of meaning that connects people to purpose."

Questions of Justice

But how are concerns related to fairness and equality addressed within a care-based ethic? Again, Held (1993) argues that our definitions need reframing. Equality no longer corresponds with equal rights or equal treatment; rather, it requires that we view each member as worthy of equal respect and consideration, and respond to the unique needs they bring with them. In a similar vein, Ferguson asserts that freedom is essential. But rather than viewing freedom as "an arena of privacy surrounding each individual, (where) community is a secondary arrangement among already autonomous beings; freedom must be located in relations among others . . . caring for others by caring for their freedom."

Thus, the issues of freedom, fairness, and power, these theorists argue, can be reconciled within the framework of a care-based organization. Gilligan, in fact, believes that rights are an essential, though not dominant, component of caring. Without rights, "the injunction to care is paralyzing, rights allow us to appropriately value self-interest . . . to act responsively towards self and others and thus to sustain connection." (p. 149). Despite the attention given in the literature to characterizations of care versus justice, a majority of feminist philosophers would embed care within an ethic of justice. As Tronto (1993a) explains, "the point is not to undermine current moral premises, but to show that they are incomplete." We need justice, she argues, to determine which needs should be met, given limited capacity and resources. . . .

Setting the Boundaries of Care

If we accept a premise of care as theoretically embedded within justice, however complex this may prove to be to practice, the issue of how we set the boundaries of care still requires serious attention. Without such attention it is difficult to make an operationally meaningful translation to the business environment, which remains a competitive one, as Daryl Koehn has noted (1995). Do we, for instance, need to care about competitors? Do all customers or employees have an equal claim on our care-giving resources? What are the defenses against the "rogues" inevitable in such environments? A host of questions like these must be answered before we can implement concepts of care in organizational life.

Though it is beyond the scope of this paper to seriously address these boundary issues, some general guidelines could be offered, based on our discussions to-date. Clearly, one's responsibility to care, in its fullest sense that incorporates all four of Tronto's stages, is bounded by one's reach. Reach, in turn, is determined by one's resources of time, skill, and goods, as well as by actual contact. The focus of care is also upon needs, rather than interests. Self-care is also important, so that I do not have a responsibility to give care where to do so would be of significant harm to me. Thus, the business organization, conceived of as a "community of mutual care," would have a responsibility to care for those in proximity to them who have needs that they are especially well-suited, by their capability base, to fulfill, where giving such care does not act against their own needs. Such care should be growth-enhancing for its recipients. The circle of care, as drawn here, would place competitors within the justice realm, employees within the realm of care. It would place small towns in which they had facilities in the realm of care, it would place large cities in which they did not in the realm of justice. It would place potential customers who could be profitably served in the realm of care. Since to give away products on a significant scale would be harmful, it would place potential customers who could not pay in the realm of justice. An exception here would be in an instance where the organization was uniquely suited to meet an important need, and could do so without harming itself. Merck's donation of the cure for river blindness would fall into this category, and be seen as an appropriate act of responsible caring, not extraordinary largesse. Caring's dual focus on the needs and development of the cared for would also bound the types of products and services offered, I believe. It would be difficult to argue that a caring organization could produce cigarettes, or market expensive sneakers aggressively to poor teenagers.

The Question of Organizational Size

A final question, not discussed in the literature but critical to arguing for the relevance of care to businesses on a large scale, is the question of size. How large could a caring organization be? Iannello's work on consensus-based organizations (1992) suggests that they must remain small enough for the collective, as a group, to participate together in strategic decision-making. Hierarchy impedes care; yet, hierarchy is the only well-developed model that we have today to organize large institutions. Can we create new organizational forms that combine the necessary decentralized reach, with an ability to marshall a collective voice in strategic decisions, and achieve the advantages of economies of scale on a centralized basis? Addressing this issue, in particular, requires an interdisciplinary approach that spans the fields of ethics, organizational theory, and strategy.

CONCLUSION

The above discussion makes clear, I hope, the extent to which the potential inherent in organizations centered around an ethic of care is significant, for reasons relating to both the marketplace and the moral realm. I have endeavored here to begin a conversation. Many questions remain to be answered; much work remains to be done. Fieldwork directed at examining these ideas within the context of practicing organizations is essential. To return to the question posed at this paper's outset, the concept of a caring organization does offer new possibilities for simultaneously enhancing both the effectiveness and the moral quality of organizations. The realization of that possibility will require enormous change in the way today's organizations operate—changes that we, as scholars, can help to initiate and foster. The current business environment offers unprecedented opportunities to do so.   ◆ ◆ ◆

◆ Bibliography

Bartlett, C. and S. Ghoshal (1994). "Changing the Role of Top Management: Beyond Strategy to Purpose," *Harvard Business Review*, November/December; pp. 79–88.

Bateson, M. (1990). *Composing a Life.* New York: Penguin Books.

Belensky, M., Clinchy, G., Goldberger, N. and J. Tarule (1986). *Women's Ways of Knowing.* New York: Basic Books.

Benhabib, S. (1992). *Situating the Self: Gender, Community, and Postmodernism in Contemporary Ethics.* New York: Routledge.

Business Enterprise Trust (1991). Merck & Co., Inc. (A). Stanford, CA: Business Enterprise Trust.

Cole, E. and S. Coultrap-McQuin (1992). *Explorations in Feminist Ethics.* Bloomington: Indiana University Press.

Collins, J. and J. Porras (1994). *Built to Last*. New York: Harper Business.

Day, G. (1994). "The Capabilities of Market-Driven Organizations," *Journal of Marketing*, 58 (October), pp. 37–52.

Ferguson, K. (1984). *The Feminist Case Against Bureaucracy*. Philadelphia: Temple University Press.

Flanagan, O. (1982). "Virtue, Sex, and Gender: Some Philosophical Reflections on the Moral Psychology Debate," *Ethics*, April, pp. 499–512.

Freeman, R. E. (1984). *Strategic Management: A Stakeholder Approach*. Boston: Pitman.

Gaylin, W. (1976). *Caring*. New York: Knopf.

Gilligan, C. (1982). *In a Different Voice*. Cambridge, MA: Harvard University Press.

Gary, B. (1989). *Collaborating: Finding Common Ground for Multiparty Problems*. San Francisco: Jossey-Bass.

Held, V. (1993). *Feminist Morality: Transforming Culture, Society, and Politics*. Chicago: University of Chicago Press.

Hamel, G. and C. Prahalad (1994). *Competing for the Future*. Boston: Harvard Business School Press.

Handy, C. (1994). *The Age of Paradox*. Boston: Harvard Business School Press.

Herman, B. (1993). *The Practice of Moral Judgment*. Cambridge, MA: Harvard University Press.

Iannello, K. (1992). *Decisions Without Hierarchy*. New York: Routledge.

Kahn, W. (1990). "Psychological Conditions of Personal Engagement and Disengagement at Work," *Academy of Management Journal*, 33(4): pp. 692–724.

Kahn, W. (1993). "Caring for the Caregivers: Patterns of Organizational Caregiving," *Administrative Science Quarterly*, 38: pp. 539–563.

Kittay, E. and D. Meyers (1987). *Women and Moral Theory*. Totowa, NJ: Rowman & Littlefield.

Koehn, D. (1995). "How Relevant Are Female Ethics of Trust and Care to Business Ethics?" presented at the 1995 Annual Meeting of the Society for Business Ethics, Vancouver, B.C.

Larrabee, M. (1993). *An Ethic of Care: Feminist and Interdisciplinary Perspectives*. New York: Routledge.

Lyons, N. (1983). "Two Perspectives: On Self, Relationships, and Morality," *Harvard Educational Review*, 53(2): pp. 125–145.

Noddings, N. (1984). *Caring: A Feminine Approach to Ethics and Moral Education*. Berkeley, CA: University of California Press.

Pascal, R. (1990). *Managing on the Edge*. New York: Simon and Schuster.

Pinchot, G. and E. Pinchot (1993). *The End of Bureaucracy and the Rise of the Intelligent Organization*. San Francisco: Berrett-Koehler Publishers.

Quinn, J. (1992). *Intelligent Enterprise*. New York: The Free Press.

Ruddick, S. (1989). *Maternal Thinking*. Boston: Beacon Press.

Rumelt, R., Schendel, D. and D. Teece (1991). "Strategic Management and Economics," *Strategic Management Journal*, 12 (Winter), pp. 5–30.

Scaltsas, P. (1992). "Do Feminist Ethics Counter Feminist Aims?" in E. Cole and S. Coultrap-McQuin, Eds., *Explorations in Feminist Ethics*. Bloomington: Indiana University Press, pp. 15–26.

Schnake, M. (1991). "Organizational Citizenship: A Review, Proposed Model, and Research Agenda," *Human Relations*, 44(7): 735–759.

Scott, R., Aiken, L., Mechanic, D. and S. Moravcsik (1995). "Organizational Aspects of Caring," *Milbank Quarterly*, 73(1): 77–95.

Senge, P. (1990). *The Fifth Discipline*. New York: Doubleday.

Solomon, R. (1992). *Ethics and Excellence*. New York: Oxford University Press.

Stalk, G., Evans, P. and L. Shulman (1992). "Competing on Capabilities: The New Rules of Corporate Strategy," *Harvard Business Review*, 70 (March/April), pp. 57–69.

Tronto, J. (1993a). *Moral Boundaries: A Political Argument for an Ethic of Care*. New York: Routledge.

Tronto, J. (1993b). "Beyond Gender Differences to a Theory of Care," in M. Larrabee, Ed., *An Ethic of*

Care: Feminist and Interdisciplinary Perspectives. New York: Routledge, pp. 240–257.

Victor, B. and J. Cullen (1988). "The Organizational Bases of Ethical Work Climates," *Administrative Science Quarterly*, 33: 101–125.

West, C. (1993). *Race Matters.* New York: Vintage Books.

Wicks, A., Gilbert, D., and R. E. Freeman (1994). "A Feminist Reinterpretation of the Stakeholder Concept," *Business Ethics Quarterly* 4(4): 475–498.

White, T. (1992). "Business, Ethics, and Carol Gilligan's 'Two Voices'," *Business Ethics Quarterly* 2(1): 51–59.

How Good a Person Do I Have to Be?

Claudia Mills

Mills wants to know if there are acceptable limits on how morally good we expect someone to be. She gives more to charity than the average person in her socioeconomic group, but then she has recently indulged herself with a nice sound system. How can she justify that in the face of suffering in the world that she could help relieve? She notes the demands of some utilitarians, such as Singer, that we give a set percentage of our income. She concludes that there is more to living a life than just doing charitable works and that we have a right to fulfill some of our life ambitions even if it means that we allow some suffering to continue. We can generalize the discussion to ask whether we can morally do less than we might to prevent suffering and distress.

How good a person am I? This is a question most of us care about being able to answer, and most of us, I suspect, know what we would like the answer to be. I, for one, would like to think that I'm a pretty good person, not saintly, but as good as most and better than some of my colleagues and friends. I'd like to be able to pat myself on the back, but also to point a finger at others; I want the requirements of morality to be lenient enough so I'll score high, but tough enough so my high score still means something. It would be nice if it turned out that however good I am is just about exactly how good a person ought to be. Contemporary moral philosophers have given a great deal of attention to these questions. What kind of a moral report card would the rest of us get from them?

BEING A GOOD PERSON

If my household's gross income last year was $40,000 and I gave away $2,000 to charity, am I (a) a splendid person, (b) a good person, (c) an okay person, or (d) a bad person? A 1984 Rockefeller Brothers Fund survey reports that the average family with an income in that range donated $1,060, but while that lets me know that my hypothetical level of giving is somewhat higher than average, it doesn't tell me whether it is enough to satisfy the demands of morality. When I think of friends who probably gave less, I feel like leaving my income tax return casually lying around so they can see what a good person I am. But when I think about the amount of human suffering to be alleviated in the world, my contribution suddenly seems much less generous.

Most of us tend to decide what we owe others in part by seeing what's left over after we've secured a moderately comfortable—but not extravagant—standard of living for ourselves. We feel we shouldn't be faulted for aspiring to a middle-class lifestyle; the wealthy, on the other hand, have a good deal to apologize for. Not surprisingly, surveys show that 95 percent of Americans consider themselves middle or working class. The rich—those who ought to be "soaked" to provide benefits for the rest of us— are invariably those who have $10,000 a year more than we have.

I confess that I recently bought a $1,500 stereo system. That sum of money, as the United Nations International Children's Emergency Fund reminds me, can purchase a lot of vials of penicillin at twenty-five cents each. "But," I hasten to explain, "this is the first nice stereo I've ever bought in my whole entire life. And I know for a fact that many of my friends have stereos worth five times as much. *That's* selfish, in a world where millions of people go to bed every night hungry." Of course, someone who sold her stereo to raise money for the homeless will view me much as I view my stereophile colleagues. The difference between their lifestyle and mine is far less than the difference between my lifestyle and that of starving children sleeping on the streets in Calcutta. True enough. But a St. Francis who gives all that he has to the poor is just that: a saint. I'm not expected to be morally magnificent, but only morally decent, a middling sort of person, who does my share and then goes home to listen to *Don Giovanni* on my compact disc player. To do more is to qualify for moral extra credit.

Some philosophers define the boundaries of what we have a right to keep for ourselves more narrowly, however. Utilitarians are notorious for denying the whole category of moral extra credit. In their view, not to do a good thing is just the same morally as doing a bad thing, so every time we pass up an opportunity for a good deed, we not only forgo canonization but also invite moral criticism. Peter Singer, for one, argues that "if it is in our power to prevent something very bad happening, without thereby sacrificing anything of comparable moral significance, we ought to do it." The trouble is that, given how many very bad things are happening in the world and how very bad they are, little else is of comparable moral significance, which means we may be called on morally to give up a *lot*. Singer gives a partial list: "color television, stylish clothes, expensive dinners, a sophisticated stereo system, overseas holidays, a (second?) car, a large house, private schools for our children . . ."

Nor are utilitarians the only ones who saddle the rest of us with burdensome obligations. Rights theorists are likely to think that if somebody has a right, somebody else has a duty, and the somebody else, as often as not, turns out to be us. Henry Shue, writing in *Basic Rights*, maintains that "One is required to sacrifice, as necessary, anything but one's basic rights in order to honor the basic rights of others." It sounds suspiciously like that involves sacrificing our stereos.

These arguments suggest, moreover, that we not only ought to *have* less but also we ought to *do* more. It's true that a poet earning $10,000 a year can give only so much before cutting into her own basic needs. But maybe she should consider a new career on Wall Street. Maybe the moral high road doesn't involve earning as little as you can, but earning as much as you can, so as to have more to give away. Philosophers who would make the rest of us feel guilty for not giving more may be at fault themselves for remaining in a nonlucrative profession when they could be more gainfully, if less happily, employed elsewhere. Whoever said you had a right to do just what you please?

Well, a number of philosophers have said, not that we have a right to do whatever we please, but that it's important to be able to make certain key choices that give meaning and coherence to our lives. In a famous argument against utilitarianism, Bernard Williams rejects the view that one is required to abandon one's own deepest commitments whenever they fail to advance the greatest good of the greatest number. To require someone to surrender his chosen life's work or his passionate creative pursuits would be "to alienate him in a real sense from his actions and the source of his actions in his own convictions. . . . It is thus, in the most literal sense, an attack on his integrity." Moreover, the project of going around all day making other people happy can only get off the ground if there are at least some "first-order projects," if at least somebody is *being* happy. After the revolution somebody has to be left to do the *living*.

One problem here is that, while we want some selfishness to turn out to be justified, we don't want *all* selfishness to turn out to be justified. The challenge, according to Shelly Kagan, philosopher at the University of Illinois at Chicago Circle, is a complex one: We want to explain why "it is sometimes permissible to refuse to perform an optimal act. But all those unwilling to embrace egoism must at the same time avoid arguments that rule out the possibility of there being any moral requirements at all. Thus the explanation must also account for the fact that sometimes a given optimal act *is* required by morality." If we try to establish some protected zone of self-interest, we will have trouble showing that this zone can ever be legitimately encroached on. And if we argue that reasons of self-interest sometimes outweigh moral reasons, then we will have to say that moral sacrifice is sometimes actually *unjustified*. But certainly we want it to be permissible, even if not required, for the moral saint to go the extra mile. Kagan concludes that it is difficult to set principled limits to what morality may demand of us.

In any case, some cold comfort may be derived from the fact that almost without exception philosophers who call for moral sacrifices fail to practice what they preach. They themselves are not rushing off to sign up with Mother Teresa. Some of them drive very nice cars. And insofar as they propose any specific guidelines for moral behavior, these tend to be calculated to reassure. Singer advocates (at minimum) giving "a round percentage of one's income like, say, 10 percent—more than a token donation, yet not so high as to be beyond all but saints." *That* isn't too bad, we might think. Shue points out that worldwide poverty could be reduced significantly with relatively modest sacrifices by affluent nations: "The affluent are expected not to enjoy less, but only to acquire more at a somewhat slower rate than they would if they maximized their own interests, narrowly construed." One feels uneasy, however, at Kagan's challenge: Why this much and no more?

BEING A SAINTLY PERSON

Despite our fond wishes otherwise, it may turn out that morality is indeed uncomfortably demanding. Its bare minimum may look a lot like our maximum: Maybe Mother Teresa herself should be doing more than she is. But those of us who don't want, frankly, to be a whole lot more moral than we are, may want to reply instead: All right, morality demands a lot. But do we have to do *everything* it demands?

Susan Wolf, a philosopher at The Johns Hopkins University, suggests that being as morally good as we can be isn't in fact an admirable goal. Glad that she and her loved ones are not "moral saints," Wolf argues that "moral perfection . . . does not constitute a model of personal well-being toward which it would be particularly rational or good or desirable for a human being to strive." In a moral saint, she argues, the moral virtues (all present and all to an extreme degree) "are apt to crowd out the nonmoral virtues, as well as many of the interests and personal characteristics that we generally think contribute to a healthy, well-rounded, richly developed character." Someone who devotes all his time to raising money for Oxfam "necessarily is not reading Victorian novels, playing the oboe, or improving his backhand." Thus his is "a life strangely barren." Nor can the moral saint, it would seem, encourage in himself otherwise delightful characteristics that go "against the moral grain," such as a cynical or sarcastic wit. A moral saint, Wolf observes, "will have to be very very nice." Nice, and dreary company.

Wolf cautions, however, that "the fact that models of moral saints are unattractive does not necessarily mean that they are unsuitable ideals. Perhaps they are unattractive because they make us feel uncomfortable — they highlight our own weaknesses, vices, and flaws. If so, the fault lies not in the characters of the saints, but in those of our own unsaintly selves." But she notes that some of the qualities the moral saint necessarily lacks are *good* qualities, qualities we *ought* to admire, "virtues, albeit nonmoral virtues, in the unsaintly characters who have them."

Thus, Wolf concludes that "moral ideas do not, and need not, make the best personal ideals. . . . we have sound, compelling, and not particularly selfish reasons to choose not to devote ourselves univocally to realizing [our] unlimited potential to be morally good." In Wolf's view, we need not be defensive about the fact that our lives are not as morally good as they might be, because "a person may be *perfectly wonderful* without being *perfectly moral*." It is not always better to be morally better.

CONCLUSION

If Wolf is right, we can concede that morality is indeed demanding, but we can devote our lives at least in part to pursuits other than making ourselves maximally moral. Her view is not a rationalization of selfishness, however, not the view that if God hadn't meant for us to grab as much as we could, he wouldn't have given us two hands to grab it with. Instead, it is a call for a broader and more diverse ideal of human excellence, for taking the opportunity to cultivate in ourselves a rich array of both moral and nonmoral excellences.

There is little immediate danger, of course, that most of us will knock ourselves out to be too good. Whatever the optimal balance between moral and nonmoral excellences (and Wolf leaves it open how this balance should be struck), most of us err on the side of selfishness pure and simple. Nothing Wolf says gives any reason *not* to adopt, say, a policy of tithing.

But perhaps we have reason not to become overly obsessed with moral report cards. What's tiresome is not so much being good, but harping on goodness from morning to night. We could all probably stand to be a lot better morally than we are, and a lot better nonmorally as well, but maybe a first start toward progress would be simply to do more and to talk less.   ◆ ◆ ◆

◆ **References**

Sources quoted in the article are Peter Singer, *Practical Ethics* (Cambridge: Cambridge University Press, 1979); Henry Shue, *Basic Rights* (Princeton, N.J.: Princeton University Press, 1980); Bernard Williams, "A Critique of Utilitarianism," in J. J. C. Smart and Bernard Williams, *Utilitarianism: For and Against* (Cambridge: Cambridge University Press, 1973); Shelly Kagan, "Does Consequentialism Demand Too Much?" *Philosophy & Public Affairs* 13, no. 3 (Summer 1984); and Susan Wolf, "Moral Saints," *Journal of Philosophy* 79, no. 8 (August 1982).

Ethics Without the Sermon

Laura L. Nash

This article originally appeared in the Harvard Business Review. *Nash gives a 12-point checklist to managers that will help them assess whether their actions are ethical. The piece deliberately aims at people in business and keeps theory to a minimum. It is significant because although we want to provide simple and straightforward ways of assessing the morality of business action, we run the risk of omitting important considerations or dismissing some of the sophisticated analysis that difficult issues demand. How useful is such a checklist, and what would you add or subtract from it?*

SIDESTEPPING TRIASSIC REPTILES

Philosophy has been sorting out issues of fairness, injury, empathy, self-sacrifice, and so on for more than 2,000 years. In seeking to examine the ethics of business, therefore, business logically assumes it will be best served by a "consultant" in philosophy who is already familiar with the formal discipline of ethics.

As the philosopher begins to speak, however, a difficulty immediately arises; corporate executives and philosophers approach problems in radically different ways. The academician ponders the intangible, savors the paradoxical, and embraces the peculiar; he or she speaks in a special language of categorical imperatives and deontological viewpoints that must be taken into consideration before a statement about honesty is agreed to have any meaning.

Like some Triassic reptile, the theoretical view of ethics lumbers along in the far past of Sunday School and Philosophy 1, while the reality of practical business concerns is constantly measuring a wide range of competing claims on time and resources against the unrelenting and objective marketplace.

Not surprisingly, the two groups are somewhat hostile. The jokes of the liberal intelligentsia are rampant and weary: *"Ethics and Business*—the shortest book in the world." "Business and ethics—a subject confined to the preface of business books." Accusations from the corporate cadre are delivered with an assurance that rests more on an intuition of social climate than on a certainty of fact: "You do-gooders are ruining America's ability to compete in the world." Of course, the cancer reports on —— [choose from a long list] were terribly exaggerated."

What is needed is a process of ethical inquiry that is immediately comprehensible to a group of executives and not predisposed to the utopian, and sometimes anticapitalistic, bias marking much of the work in applied business philosophy today. So I suggest, as a preliminary solution, a set of twelve questions that draw on traditional philosophical frameworks but that avoid the level of abstraction normally associated with formal moral reasoning.

I offer the questions as a first step in a very new discipline. As such, they form a tentative model that will certainly undergo modifications after its parts are given some exercise. The Exhibit . . . poses the twelve questions. . . .

THE TWELVE QUESTIONS

1. *Have you defined the problem accurately?*

How one assembles the facts weights an issue before the moral examination ever begins, and a definition is rarely accurate if it articulates one's loyalties rather than the facts. The importance of factual neutrality is readily seen, for example, in assessing the moral implications of producing a chemical agent for use in warfare. Depending on one's loyalties, the decision to make the substance can be described as serving one's country, developing products, or killing babies. All of the above may be factual statements, but none is neutral or accurate if viewed in isolation.

EXHIBIT: TWELVE QUESTIONS FOR EXAMINING THE ETHICS OF A BUSINESS DECISION

1. Have you defined the problem accurately?
2. How would you define the problem if you stood on the other side of the fence?
3. How did this situation occur in the first place?
4. To whom and to what do you give your loyalty as a person and as a member of the corporation?
5. What is your intention in making this decision?
6. How does this intention compare with the probable results?
7. Whom could your decision or action injure?
8. Can you discuss the problem with the affected parties before you make your decision?
9. Are you confident that your position will be as valid over a long period of time as it seems now?
10. Could you disclose without qualm your decision or action to your boss, your CEO, the board of directors, your family, society as a whole?
11. What is the symbolic potential of your action if understood? if misunderstood?
12. Under what conditions would you allow exceptions to your stand?

Similarly, the recent controversy over marketing U.S.-made cigarettes in Third World countries rarely noted that the incidence of lung cancer in underdeveloped nations is quite low (from one-tenth to one-twentieth the rate for U.S. males) due primarily to the lower life expectancies and earlier predominance of other diseases in these nations. Such a fact does not decide the ethical complexities of this marketing problem, but it does add a crucial perspective in the assignment of moral priorities by defining precisely the injury that tobacco exports may cause.

Extensive fact gathering may also help defuse the emotionalism of an issue. For instance, local statistics on lung cancer incidence reveal that the U.S. tobacco industry is not now "exporting death," as has been charged. Moreover, the substantial and immediate economic benefits attached to tobacco may be providing food and health care in these countries. Nevertheless, as life expectancy and the standards of living rise, a higher incidence of cigarette-related diseases appears likely to develop in these nations. Therefore, cultivation of the nicotine habit may be deemed detrimental to the long-term welfare of these nations.

According to one supposedly infallible truth of modernism, technology is so complex that its results will never be fully comprehensible or predictable. Part of the executive's frustration in responding to Question 1 is the real possibility that the "experts" will find no grounds for agreement about the facts.

As a first step, however, defining fully the factual implications of a decision determines to a large degree the quality of one's subsequent moral position. Pericles' definition of true courage rejected the Spartans' blind obedience in war in preference to the courage of the Athenian citizen who, he said, was able to make a decision to proceed in full knowledge of the probable danger. A truly moral decision is an informed decision. A decision that is based on blind or convenient ignorance is hardly defensible.

One simple test of the initial definition is the question:

2. How would you define the problem if you stood on the other side of the fence?

The contemplated construction of a plant for Division X is touted at the finance committee meeting as an absolute necessity for expansion at a cost saving of at least 25%. With plans drawn up for an energy-efficient building and an option already secured on a 99-year lease in a new industrial park in Chippewa County, the committee is likely to feel comfortable in approving the request for funds in a matter of minutes.

The facts of the matter are that the company will expand in an appropriate market, allocate its resources sensibly, create new jobs, increase Chippewa County's tax base, and most likely increase its returns to the shareholders. To the residents of Chippewa County, however, the plant may mean the destruction of a customary recreation spot, the onset of severe traffic jams, and the erection of an architectural eyesore. These are also facts of the situation, and certainly more immediate to the county than utilitarian justifications of profit performance and rights of ownership from an impersonal corporation whose headquarters are 1,000 miles from Chippewa County and whose executives have plenty of acreage for their own recreation.

The purpose of articulating the other side, whose needs are understandably less proximate than operational considerations, is to allow some mechanism whereby calculations of self-interest (or even of a project's ultimate general beneficence) can be interrupted by a compelling empathy for those who might suffer immediate injury or mere annoyance as a result of a corporation's decisions. Such empathy is a necessary prerequisite for shouldering voluntarily some responsibility for the social consequences of corporate operations, and it may be the only solution to today's overly litigious and anarchic world.

There is a power in self-examination: with an exploration of the likely consequences of a proposal, taken from the viewpoint of those who do not immediately benefit, comes a discomfort or an embarrassment that rises in proportion to the degree of the likely injury and its articulation. Like Socrates as gadfly, who stung his fellow citizens into a critical examination of their conduct when they became complacent, the discomfort of the alternative definition is meant to prompt a disinclination to choose the expedient over the most responsible course of action. . . .

In the example of Division X's new plant, it was a simple matter to define the alternate facts; the process rested largely on an assumption that certain values were commonly shared (no one likes a traffic jam, landscaping pleases more than an unadorned building, and so forth). But the alternative definition often underscores an inherent disparity in values or language. To some, the employment of illegal aliens is a criminal act (fact #1); to others, it is a solution to the 60% unemployment rate of a neighboring country (fact #2). One country's bribe is another country's redistribution of sales commissions.

When there are cultural or linguistic disparities, it is easy to get the facts wrong or to invoke a pluralistic tolerance as an excuse to act in one's own self-interest: "That's the way they do things over there. Who are we to question their beliefs?" This kind of reasoning can be both factually inaccurate (many generalizations about bribery rest on hearsay and do not represent the complexities of a culture) and philosophically inconsistent (there are plenty of beliefs, such as those of the environmentalist, which the same generalizers do not hesitate to question).

3. How did this situation occur in the first place?

Lex Motor Company, a subsidiary of Lex Service Group, Ltd., had been losing share at a 20% rate in a declining market; and Depot B's performance was the worst of all. Two nearby Lex depots could easily absorb B's business, and closing it down seemed the only sound financial decision. Lex's chairman, Trevor Chinn, hesitated to approve the closure, however, on the grounds that putting 100 people out of work was not right when the corporation itself was not really jeopardized by B's existence. Moreover, seven department managers, who were all within five years of retirement and had had 25 or more years of service at Lex, were scheduled to be made redundant.

The values statement provided no automatic solution, for it placed value on both employees' security and shareholders' interest. Should they close Depot B? At first Chinn thought not: Why should the little guys suffer disproportionately when the company was not performing well? Why not close a more recently acquired business where employee service was not so large a factor? Or why not wait out the short term and reduce head count through natural attrition?

As important as deciding the ethics of the situation was the inquiry into its history. Indeed, the history gave a clue to solving the dilemma: Lex's traditional emphasis on employee security *and* high financial performance had led to a precipitate series of acquisitions and subsequent divestitures when the company had failed to meet its overall objectives. After each rationalization, the people serving the longest had been retained and placed at Depot B, so that . . . the facility had more managers than it needed and a very high proportion of long-service employees.

So the very factors that had created the performance problems were making the closure decision difficult, and the very solution that Lex was inclined to favor again would exacerbate the situation further!

In deciding the ethics of a situation it is important to distinguish the symptoms from the disease. Great profit pressures with no sensitivity to the cycles in a particular industry, for example, may force division managers to be ruthless with employees, to short-weight customers, or even to fiddle with cash flow reports in order to meet headquarters' performance criteria.

Dealing with the immediate case of lying, quality discrepancy, or strained labor relations — when the problem is finally discovered — is only a temporary solution. A full examination of how the situation occurred and what the traditional solutions have been may reveal a more serious discrepancy of values and pressures, and this will illuminate the real significance and ethics of the problem. It will also reveal recurring patterns of events that in isolation appear trivial but that as a whole point up a serious situation.

Such a mechanism is particularly important because very few executives are outright scoundrels. Rather, violations of corporate and social values usually occur inadvertently because no one recognizes that a problem exists until it becomes a crisis. This tendency toward initial trivialization seems to be the biggest ethical problem in business today. Articulating answers to my first three questions is a way of reversing that process.

4. To whom and what do you give your loyalties as a person and as a member of the corporation?

Every executive faces conflicts of loyalty. The most familiar occasions pit private conscience and sense of duty against corporate policy, but equally frequent are the situations in which one's close colleagues demand participation (tacit or explicit) in an operation or a decision that runs counter to company policy. To whom or what is the greater loyalty—to one's corporation? superior? family? society? self? race? sex?

The good news about conflicts of loyalty is that their identification is a workable way of smoking out the ethics of a situation and of discovering the absolute values inherent in it. As one executive in a discussion of a Harvard case study put it, "My corporate brain says this action is O.K., but my noncorporate brain keeps flashing these warning lights."

The bad news about conflicts of loyalty is that there are few automatic answers for placing priorities on them. "To thine own self be true" is a murky quagmire when the self takes on a variety of roles, as it does so often in this complex modern world.

Supposedly, today's young managers are giving more weight to individual than to corporate identity, and some older executives see this tendency as being ultimately subversive. At the same time, most of them believe individual integrity is essential to a company's reputation.

The U.S. securities industry, for example, is one of the most rigorous industries in America in its requirements of honesty and disclosure. Yet in the end, all its systematic precautions prove inadequate unless the people involved also have a strong sense of integrity that puts loyalty to these principles above personal gain.

A system, however, must permit the time and foster the motivation to allow personal integrity to surface in a particular situation. An examination of loyalties is one way to bring this about. Such an examination may strengthen reputations but also may result in blowing the whistle (freedom of thought carries with it the risk of revolution). But a sorting out of loyalties can also bridge the gulf between policy and implementation or among various interest groups whose affiliations may mask a common devotion to an aspect of a problem—a devotion on which consensus can be built.

How does one probe into one's own loyalties and their implications? A useful method is simply to play various roles out loud, to call on one's loyalty to family and community (for example) by asking, "What will I say when my child asks me why I did that?" If the answer is "That's the way the world works," then your loyalties are clear and moral passivity inevitable. But if the question presents real problems, you have begun a demodulation of signals from your conscience that can only enhance corporate responsibility.

5. What is your intention in making this decision?

6. How does this intention compare with the likely results?

These two questions are asked together because their content often bears close resemblance and, by most calculations, both color the ethics of a situation.

Corporation Buglebloom decides to build a new plant in an underdeveloped minority-populated district where the city has been trying with little success to encourage industrial development. The media approve and Buglebloom adds another star to its good reputation. Is Buglebloom a civic leader and a supporter of minorities or a canny investor about to take advantage of the disadvantaged? The possibilities of Buglebloom's intentions are endless and probably unfathomable to the public; Buglebloom may be both canny investor and friend of minority groups.

I argue that despite their complexity and elusiveness, a company's intentions *do* matter. The "purity" of Buglebloom's motives (purely profit-seeking or purely altruistic) will have wide-reaching effects inside and outside the corporation—on attitudes toward minority employees in other parts of the company, on the wages paid at the new plant, and on the number of other investors in the same area—that will legitimize a certain ethos in the corporation and the community.

Sociologist Max Weber called this an "ethics of attitude" and contrasted it with an "ethics of absolute ends." An ethics of attitude sets a standard to ensure a certain action. A firm policy at headquarters of not cheating customers, for example, may also deter salespeople from succumbing to a tendency to lie by omission or purchasers from continuing to patronize a high-priced supplier when the costs are automatically passed on in the selling price. . . .

The goodness of intent pales somewhat before results that perpetrate great injury or simply do little good. Common sense demands that the "responsible" corporation try to align the two more closely, to identify the probable consequences and also the limitations of knowledge that might lead to more harm than good. Two things to remember in comparing intention and results are that knowledge of the future is always inadequate and that overconfidence often precedes a disastrous mistake.

These two precepts, cribbed from ancient Greece, may help the corporation keep the disparities between intent and result a fearsome reality to consider continuously. The next two questions explore two ways of reducing the moral risks of being wrong.

7. *Whom could your decision or action injure?*

The question presses whether injury is intentional or not. Given the limits of knowledge about a new product or policy, who and how many will come into contact with it? Could its inadequate disposal affect an entire community? two employees? yourself? How might your product be used if it happened to be acquired by a terrorist radical group or a terrorist military police force? Has your distribution system or disposal plan ensured against such injury? Could it ever?

If not, there may be a compelling moral justification for stopping production. In an integrated society where business and government share certain values, possible injury is an even more important consideration than potential benefit. In policymaking, a much likelier ground for agreement than benefit is avoidance of injury through those "universal nos"—such as no mass death, no totalitarianism, no hunger or malnutrition, no harm to children.

To exclude *at the outset* any policy or decision that might have such results is to reshape the way modern business examines its own morality. So often business formulates questions of injury only after the fact in the form of liability suits.

8. *Can you engage the affected parties in a discussion of the problem before you make your decision?*

If the calculus of injury is one way of responding to limitations of knowledge about the probable results of a particular business decision, the participation of affected parties is one of the best ways of informing that consideration. Civil rights groups often complain that corporations fail to invite participation from local leaders during the planning stages of community development projects and charitable programs. The corporate foundation that builds a tennis complex for disadvantaged youth is throwing away precious resources if most children in the neighborhood suffer from chronic malnutrition. . . .

The issue of participation affects everyone. (How many executives feel that someone else should decide what is in *their* best interest?) And yet it is a principle often forgotten because of the pressure of time or the inconvenience of calling people together and facing predictably hostile questions.

9. *Are you confident that your position will be as valid over a long period of time as it seems now?*

As anyone knows who has had to consider long-range plans and short-term budgets simultaneously, a difference in time frame can change the meaning of a problem as much as spring and autumn change the colors of a tree. The ethical coloring of a business decision is no exception to this generational aspect of decision making. Time alters circumstances, and few corporate value systems are immune to shifts in financial status, external political pressure, and personnel. (One survey now places the average U.S. CEO's tenure in office at five years.) . . .

Ideally, a company's articulation of its values should anticipate changes of fortune. As the hearings for the passage of the Foreign Corrupt Practices Act of 1977 demonstrated, doing what you can get away with today may not be a secure moral standard, but short-term discomfort for long-term sainthood may require irrational courage or a rational reasoning system or, more likely, both. These twelve questions attempt to elicit a rational system. Courage, of course, depends on personal integrity.

Another aspect of the ethical time frame stretches beyond the boundaries of Question 9 but deserves special attention, and that is the timing of the ethical inquiry. When and where will it be made? . . .

10. *Could you disclose without qualm your decision or action to your boss, your CEO, the board of directors, your family, or society as a whole?*

The old question, "Would you want your decision to appear on the front page of *The New York Times?*" still holds. A corporation may maintain that there's really no problem, but a survey of how many "trivial" actions it is reluctant to disclose might be interesting. Disclosure is a way of sounding those submarine depths of conscience and of searching out loyalties.

It is also a way of keeping a corporate character cohesive. The Lex Group, for example, was once faced with a very sticky problem concerning a small but profitable site with unpleasant (though in no way illegal) working conditions, where two men with 30 years' service worked. I wrote up the case for a Lex senior managers' meeting on the promise to disguise it heavily because the executive who supervised the plant was convinced that, if the chairman and the personnel director knew the plant's true location, they would close it down immediately.

At the meeting, however, as everyone became involved in the discussion and the chairman himself showed sensitivity to the dilemma, the executive disclosed the location and spoke of his own feelings about the situation. The level of mutual confidence was apparent to all, and by other reports it was the most open discussion the group had ever had.

The meeting also fostered understanding of the company's values and their implementation. When the discussion finally flagged, the chairman spoke up. Basing his views on a full knowledge of the group's understanding of the problem, he set the company's priorities. "Jobs over fancy conditions, health over jobs," Chinn said, "but we always *must disclose.*" The group decided to keep the plant open, at least for the time being. . . .

11. *What is the symbolic potential of your action if understood? if misunderstood?*

Jones Inc., a diversified multinational corporation with assets of $5 billion, has a paper manufacturing operation that happens to be the only major industry in Stirville, and the factory has been polluting the river on which it is located. Local and national conservation groups have filed suit against Jones Inc. for past damages, and the company is defending itself. Meanwhile, the corporation has adopted plans for a new waste-efficient plant. The legal battle is extended and local resentment against Jones Inc. gets bitter.

As a settlement is being reached, Jones Inc. announces that, as a civic-minded gesture, it will make 400 acres of Stirville woodland it owns available to the residents for conservation and recreation purposes. Jones's intention is to offer a peace pipe to the people of Stirville, and the company sees the gift as a symbol of its own belief in conservation and a way of signaling that value to Stirville residents and national conservation groups. Should Jones Inc. give the land away? Is the symbolism significant?

If the symbolic value of the land is understood as Jones Inc. intends, the gift may patch up the company's relations with Stirville and stave off further disaffection with potential employees as the new plant is being built. It may also signal to employees throughout the corporation that Jones Inc. places a premium on conservation efforts and community relations.

If the symbolic value is misunderstood, however, or if completion of the plant is delayed and the old one has to be put back in use—or if another Jones operation is discovered to be polluting another community and becomes a target of the press—the gift could be interpreted as nothing more than a cheap effort to pay off the people of Stirville and hasten settlement of the lawsuit.

The Greek root of our word *symbol* means both signal and contract. A business decision—

whether it is the use of an expense account or a corporate donation—has a symbolic value in signaling what is acceptable behavior within the corporate culture and in making a tacit contract with employees and the community about the rules of the game. How the symbol is actually perceived (or misperceived) is as important as how you intend it to be perceived.

12. *Under what conditions would you allow exceptions to your stand?*

If we accept the idea that every business decision has an important symbolic value and a contractual nature, then the need for consistency is obvious. At the same time, it is also important to ask under what conditions the rules of the game may be changed. What conflicting principles, circumstances, or time constraints would provide a morally acceptable basis for making an exception to one's normal institutional ethos? For instance, how does the cost of the strategy to develop managers from minority groups over the long term fit in with short-term hurdle rates? Also to be considered is what would mitigate a clear case of employee dishonesty.

Questions of consistency—if you would do X, would you also do Y?—are yet another way of eliciting the ethics of the company and of oneself, and can be a final test of the strength, idealism, or practicality of those values. A last example from the experience of Lex illustrates this point and gives temporary credence to the platitude that good ethics is good business. An article in the Sunday paper about a company that had run a series of racy ads, with pictures of half-dressed women and promises of free merchandise to promote the sale of a very mundane product, sparked an extended examination at Lex of its policies on corporate inducements.

One area of concern was holiday giving. What was the acceptable limit for a gift—a bottle of whiskey? a case? Did it matter only that the company did not *intend* the gift to be an induce-ment, or did the mere possibility of inducement taint the gift? Was the cut-off point absolute? The group could agree on no halfway point for allow-ing some gifts and not others, so a new value was added to the formal statement that prohibited the offering or receiving of inducements.

The next holiday season Chinn sent a letter to friends and colleagues who had received gifts of appreciation in the past. In it he explained that, as a result of Lex's concern with "the very complex area of business ethics," management had decided that the company would no longer send any gifts, nor would it be appropriate for its employees to receive any. Although the letter did not explain Lex's reasoning behind the decision, apparently there was a large untapped consen-sus about such gift giving: by return mail Chinn received at least twenty letters from directors, general managers, and chairmen of companies with which Lex had done business congratu-lating him for his decision, agreeing with the new policy, and thanking him for his holiday wishes. . . . ◆ ◆ ◆

LEADERSHIP, VALUES, AND THE FORCE OF THE INSTITUTION

Individuals have to make their own moral decisions and are ultimately accountable for what they do. We may explain or excuse what we do in various ways, but there is no one who has sufficient moral authority to override our individual morality. Although we can make mistakes or adopt someone else's values as our own, ultimately we have to take personal responsibility. At the same time, there may be forces that shape our decisions—some explicit, such as orders, and others that may be much more subtle and unconscious.

In this chapter we move from systemic influences that create a backdrop for our actions to the way in which institutions such as businesses may act as a force that encourages us to be more or less moral in our decisions. Once we are aware of these influences, we can consciously try to create a mental space where we can consider dilemmas in a fresh light away from institutional pressures. An effective tool is to pose contrary views to a decision from alternate perspectives or to ask whether a decision could be justified in retrospect.

In the case of orders, we have to decide whether they come from a legitimate authority and are morally sound. Although people may try to abdicate responsibility by saying they were just following orders, there is a long tradition in military and civil justice of holding people accountable based on the fact that they should have been aware of the situation and the particular consequences of their actions. Nevertheless, there is clear empirical evidence that effective leadership, obedience to authority figures, abdicating choice to others, or simply ignoring the value dimension of decisions often influences our morality.

Patrick Murphy and Georges Enderle look at the way in which four successful business executives created a moral environment in their businesses. They are examples of strong individuals who helped shape a culture that promotes ethical awareness and they illustrate that these forces may act for good as well as ill.

David Messick and Max Bazerman bring a psychological perspective to management decision making. They show how managers tend to create their own view of the world and see business situations from their personal perspective. They also show us a number of ways in which we fail to make purely rational choices. For example, they explain that we all have a "confirmation bias." When we examine our decisions, we tend to seek information that will confirm what we already think. Moreover, when things start to go wrong we have a natural tendency to attribute it to poor judgment on the part of others but bad luck if it happens to us. Loan officers, for example, paradoxically tend to give additional money to people with bad loans, rationalizing that their original loan decision could not have been incorrect but rather the individual has been unlucky. Messick and Bazerman apply the discussion to cases where they believe individuals may have put more emphasis on the morality of the situation if they had the luxury of a clear and unbiased perspective.

The Ronald Sims reading demonstrates the effects of groupthink. Humans are naturally social, and we want to please others by conforming; it is uncomfortable to be the odd man out or not part of the team. Robert Jackall, a sociologist, examined the workings of a company and found that many pressures to be a team player align with the culture of the institution. Although these forces are not necessarily pernicious in themselves, we can see that any group that is focused solely on achieving a mission may make moral compromises along the way. Without a devil's advocate or some sort of check-and-balance mechanism, it is remarkably easy for individuals to shelve their personal moral responsibility and go along with everyone else.

James Weber reinforces these findings. He first presents Lawrence Kohlberg's framework of moral development. Kohlberg says that we move through a series of stages from thinking of morality as simply being punished for bad deeds and rewarded for good deeds to eventually considering whether our acts conform to universal ethical principles. Kohlberg's standard tool for seeing where we are on his six-stage scale involved using a fairly abstract case that asks whether an impoverished man should steal drugs from a pharmacy for his dying wife. Weber's critical finding is to show that if we alter the story so that it resembles a familiar situation, or if it is put in an organizational setting, we find that most people routinely drop a stage or two. This means that if we think we have seen this sort of case before or if it happens in a structured institution like a corporation, we are much less likely to give it significant reflective consideration than if we think about it as an abstract intellectual exercise. Clearly, this implies that just by virtue of our psychological makeup it will be difficult to engage in serious moral thinking in the pressure of the workplace.

These insights do not necessarily mean we should not censure bad behavior. However, they do go a long way in showing us that we should not rush to judgment without recognizing that forces at work in an institution will either promote or detract from an individual's personal moral sensitivity.

We might still question, however, whether the explanation of outside influence is a valid excuse. For example, the heady atmosphere of success and invulnerability that pervaded HealthSouth led to a strong sense of corporate identity and teamwork, but the same dynamics encouraged widespread fraud and wrongdoing. When the demagogue Senator Joseph McCarthy's witch hunt was racking America for communists in the 1950s, he was finally stopped when a single lawyer had the courage to ask, "Have you no sense of decency?" That question acted as a catalyst for the public to realize that they had been tolerating proceedings that were fundamentally immoral. Similarly, perhaps we should individually aspire to be the person who has the moral courage to recognize and call to account corporate wrongdoing despite the various forces aligned against us.

Managerial Ethical Leadership
Examples Do Matter

Patrick E. Murphy and Georges Enderle

It is often said that in an ethical company, the tone and direction comes from the top; we cannot expect the workforce to be ethical when the senior managers are abusing their privileges by padding expenses or misusing company resources. Moreover, the CEO and others must clearly articulate that ethics matters in the firm and is a central feature of the way it does business. Murphy and Enderle look at four exemplars of strong ethical leadership in business and isolate five factors they have in common. Look for the practical steps that these individuals have taken to align what they say and what they do, and contrast their behavior with CEOs involved in recent corporate scandals.

INTRODUCTION

As in other spheres of human activities, examples of managerial ethical leadership may contain extraordinarily rich experiences. They are vital not only for business practice, but also for reflecting on it from descriptive-analytical and normative-ethical points of view. Theoretical concepts always are, to some extent, generalized ones and therefore cannot fully grasp the uniqueness of persons and companies, their situations and developments. When examples are presented in a simplified manner, they normally express and illustrate only preframed ideas, concepts, or theories. However, if examples, taken from real life situations, contain highly complex characteristics shaped by the historical, bibliographical and social context, they cannot be adequately captured by theoretical frameworks. Rather, their unique richness has a great heuristic potential and often puts preframed mental

artifacts into question. With regard to the practice of ethical leadership, examples may be inspirational; they may open new horizons and show what is possible, based on accomplishments already realized.

Of course, real life examples also have their limits, since by their uniqueness they cannot "prove" the validity of a theory. We do not claim that these exemplary ways of ethical conduct are the only method to study or promote such behavior. Contingent on many contextual factors, they do not allow for general conclusions. For reasons of limited space and information, we present only a few outstanding examples of managerial ethical leadership. Other, more comprehensive, presentations can be found in the literature cited below.

As a corollary of the importance of examples, we should briefly add a methodological implication. The best method to understand, and learn from, these examples is likely the narrative approach, i.e., to tell stories and provide histories of those persons and companies (see e.g., Williams and Houck, 1992; also De George, 1993: 109). By narration, the uniqueness and particularities of examples can be effectively communicated.

In order to select the individuals for examination here we applied three criteria: The first is that they have achieved the Chief Executive Officer (CEO) status. This is commonly viewed as "the" leadership position in major corporations. Although Boards of Directors have become a more important force in setting the direction for companies during recent years, the CEO still holds the dominant position in most firms and serves as a role model for many managers throughout the organization. Furthermore, many other executives no doubt have exhibited leadership qualities. However, the unquestioned leader within most firms is the person occupying the CEO's chair. By applying this positional criterion, we do not imply that leadership as an interactive process is necessarily linked to the CEO status. There are numerous leaders without that status and CEOs who do not excel in interactive leadership. Thus the CEO criterion used here implies the positional as well as the interactional dimension of leadership.

The second criterion says that these managers must have written or spoken about ethics multiple times. This "paper trail" allows one to evaluate their thinking and positions on ethical matters from these documents. Once again, using this benchmark excludes many ethical executives who lead exclusively by example or by communicating only with their internal audience.

A third criterion is that the persons discussed here are all retired from their respective positions. In essence, their business careers are over and the book is closed on their tenure as a CEO. It is then easier to evaluate their record since there will probably not be decisions or events that will transpire which will significantly change how they

are judged. Of course, an accomplished career does not imply that its interpretation will forever remain unchanged.

Using these three criteria, four former CEOs were selected. They are James Burke of Johnson & Johnson, Sir Adrian Cadbury of Cadbury Schweppes, Max De Pree of Herman Miller and J. Irwin Miller of Cummins Engine. Undoubtedly, many other individuals would qualify for inclusion and have been discussed elsewhere.[1] They are obviously too numerous to mention here. However, these four men seem to personify the values that one commonly associates with ethical leaders.

ASSUMPTIONS

At the outset we should also mention some important assumptions implied in these cases. First, there is no doubt that each of these persons has a keen understanding and extraordinary skills of business and leadership, not just in terms explicitly regarding the ethical dimension of these activities. Unquestionably they are "good business leaders" and deservedly gained this public reputation. Consequently, by emphasizing the relevance of ethical values in decision making, they don't claim that "purely business" considerations were less important; on the contrary, precisely from an ethical angle, these aspects have to be taken very seriously.[2]

Second, in the real life decision making situations it is impossible to separate "ethical issues" from "business and other issues;" however, it is crucial to distinguish between them. Otherwise, by not perceiving potential and actual conflicts between the ethical and other perspectives, one would necessarily avoid them and could not bring them to deliberate resolution. For instance, decisions about worker participation or downsizing include economic, financial, legal, ethical and other dimensions. Each should be clearly identified although they all relate to the same concrete decision making situation at stake.

Third, the business leaders selected for our investigation are deeply convinced that "good business" and "good ethics" can be reconciled, even if it is sometimes very demanding and requires paying a price. They are all proponents of the position that ethics pays in the long run, but can be financially costly in the short term.

Fourth, they do not see the business world as a sphere where economic (and other) mechanisms fully determine the decision making of each agent. Rather, according to their understanding, these agents, particularly business leaders, have the freedom to choose among more than one option for making decisions and taking actions. This is a necessary condition for ethical responsibility in leadership (see Enderle, 1987: 659–660) and for virtuous behavior (see Pincoffs, 1992).

Fifth, to assume that these examples represent decisions and actions exclusively of individuals would be erroneous. In each case the relationship between leader and company is intrinsically intertwined, as many business scholars also emphasize (for instance, Schein, 1992: xii, 374). Corporate culture, public trust in a firm, issues of participation and distributive justice within a corporation, etc.,—all these concepts relate to the collective entity of a company and cannot be broken up in single parts of individuals, although leaders may play an important role to build up (or to dismantle) such collective realities.[3]

Finally, in their view, the meaning of "ethics" and "ethical" is taken very literally. Because the main question of ethics is "What ought we do?" the main answer is doing, i.e., making decisions and taking actions, not talking about the right answers. These leaders are convinced that "actions speak louder than words." Talking about ethics without firm will and appropriate strategies for implementation is dangerous and a contradiction in terms.

JAMES BURKE

James Burke was born in 1925 and was educated at Holy Cross and the Harvard Business School. His undergraduate school is a Catholic, Jesuit college and the education he received at Harvard also had an impact on his moral development. In Burke's words: ". . . the thing that amazed me, and was totally unexpected, is that in everything we did, we were reminded of the moral values—the importance of the moral values of our decision making" (Smith and Tedlow, 1989a: 3, and 1989b). Burke began his career at Procter & Gamble in 1949 and moved to Johnson & Johnson (J&J) in 1953 after pursuing some of his personal business interests. After a year at the company, he quit out of frustration in not being able to set up a new products division. A few days later he was called by a J&J executive and offered both an opportunity to head up the new products division and a 50% salary increase. During the next decade, James Burke held a series of marketing and management positions while climbing the corporate ladder.

After he was named as the Chairman and CEO designate in 1975, Burke decided to call together the J&J top management team to a series of Credo challenge meetings. The Credo was 30 years old by then and Burke wanted to make sure that it had not lost its meaning and significance to the firm. What resulted from these meetings was a reaffirmation of the ideals set out in the original Credo and a slight rewording of the document (see Nash, 1988, and Horton, 1986: 27–29). This action of challenging the status quo and calling into question the moral foundation of the firm seemed to set the tone for Burke's tenure as CEO.

Under Burke's guidance, Johnson & Johnson experienced a period of substantial sales growth. The major product contributing to this growth was Tylenol, and James Burke was viewed as the person most responsible for it. In late September of 1982 two individuals died after taking Extra Strength Tylenol. It was determined that the capsules were poisoned with cyanide. This event was a major setback for Burke personally and the company. After a thorough examination of their plants, J&J was certain that the cyanide was injected at some point in the distribution chain rather than at the point of manufacture.[4]

The response to this crisis by J&J and Burke in particular was one of openness and candor. They fielded thousands of calls from reporters and set up an 800 number to accept calls from consumers. One little known aspect of the Tylenol story is that the FBI personnel who were involved "felt adamantly that a national recall of the product would constitute an overreaction at that time" (Smith and Tedlow, 1989b: 3). Despite this government position and comments by experts that Tylenol was in effect a dead product/brand, Burke and the J&J management team believed that the brand could be revived. They found in consumer surveys that there was much goodwill toward the brand and company. The company pulled 31 million bottles of Extra Strength Tylenol from the shelves in early October, 1982 and set in motion a plan for reintroduction. They also worked with the federal government and state agencies to develop tamper proof packaging.

In 1986 a second round of poisonings occurred. Burke responded by setting up a series of three press conferences where he discussed the company's position regarding this situation. The final resolution was that the capsules were permanently withdrawn from the market because, despite the tamper proof packaging, J&J could not assure consumers that the product would be safe. In this crisis and the previous one, Burke was obsessed with preserving the high level of trust in J&J's products. He saw that trust was tied closely to ethics when he made the following statement while being interviewed by *Fortune*:

"Every relationship that works is based on trust, and you don't develop trust without moral behavior" (Guzzardi, 1990: 120). Furthermore, he felt as CEO that he must maintain the history of trust compiled over the years by his predecessors. Burke said:

> All of the previous managements who built this corporation handed us on a silver platter the most powerful tool you could possibly have— institutional trust. Everybody who puts something into this organization that builds that trust is enhancing the long term value of the business. I think that these values were here. We traded off them. We articulated them through the Credo. We spent a lot of time getting people to understand what we meant in the Credo. We got challenged by a very dramatic event of unparalleled proportions. Not only did we face up to the challenge, but we demonstrated that all of that hundred years of trust works to help solve problems, no matter how serious they may be. (Smith and Tedlow, 1989b: 6)

Burke's leadership qualities were recognized by many sources after his and the firm's reaction to these crises. Some of these publications are among the most widely recognized and respected. They include *The New York Times* (which commended Burke's leadership by saying that "he has left little doubt about who is calling the shots at the company") and *Fortune* (J&J ranked No. 1 in *Fortune*'s most admired corporations in corporate citizenship, in no small part because of Jim Burke's leadership). Burke retired from J&J in April, 1989. He summed up his feelings about ethics and leadership and the role of business school fostering it during an interview for a Harvard Business School case. He stated: "But as long as you have—as I believe we do—a very strong, thoughtful business leadership, and as long as you have business schools that address this subject— and all of the ethical values that we've talked about—I think we'll find a way to deal with it" (Smith and Tedlow, 1989b: 13).

ADRIAN CADBURY

George Adrian Hayhurst Cadbury was born in 1929 and educated at Eton and King's College at Cambridge University. He was the fourth generation of his Quaker family to head Cadbury Schweppes—the maker of chocolate products and beverages. He became CEO in 1969 and aggressively pushed the firm into international markets including the United States. His management style emphasized decentralized decision making.

This move into the international arena forced the company to adapt to the culture of different countries. Cadbury Schweppes has a tradition of strong worker participation and they try to involve people in their subsidiary companies in decision making. He pushed all top executives to spend time traveling to various plant locations and building personal relationships within the firm. According to Cadbury, "In the end, the glue that holds the company together is personal contact and a belief that the company stands for something worthwhile and to spread the shared values" (in Blodgett, 1983: 141).

Two characteristics of Cadbury Schweppes that he emphasized were fairness and openness. The firm has developed a reputation for fairness in the normally hostile British labor environment and provided complete information to various power groups. This fairness extends beyond employee issues to acquisitions and divestment. The company will only acquire a firm if it can function better as part of the company (Pastin and Harrison, 1987: 54–58). Similarly, the firm spun off its UK Food Group when the subsidiary argued that it could operate better as a separate company. Sir Adrian strongly advocates openness: "But I believe in the principle that you should manage in an open way: tell people what is going on and listen to what they have to offer, particularly when it concerns matters which af-

fect them very directly" (Blodgett, 1983: 137). He also included openness as one of the eight guiding characteristics of the firm (Cadbury, 1984).

In an article that could be labeled a primer on ethical management, Cadbury (1987) outlined his philosophical position on a number of ethical issues facing business. He offered many sage words in this treatise and attributed the ethical values that pervade his firm to his grandfather. According to Cadbury the ethical standards of a company are judged by its actions rather than statements of good intentions. In making management decisions, Cadbury uses a two-step process: first to determine what our personal rules of conduct are and second to think through who else will be affected by the decision and how we should weight their interest in it.

To deal with one of the most difficult ethical issues facing managers in the international arena (how far to go in buying business?), Cadbury uses two simple rules of thumb. Is the payment on the face of the invoice? Would it embarrass the recipient to have the gift mentioned in the company newspaper? The first test makes certain that all payments are recorded and "on the books." The second, which is a version of *The Wall Street Journal* test, is aimed at distinguishing bribes from gifts. The logic behind these rules is that openness and ethics go together. He indicates that openness is the "best way to disarm outside suspicion of companies' motives and actions" (Cadbury, 1987).

Cadbury retired from his position at Cadbury Schweppes in 1990, but his influence on ethical management practices in the UK continued. He has been involved in Business in the Community to encourage the formation of new enterprises with a sense of social responsibility. Most recently, he headed the influential Cadbury Commission which reported on corporate governance and methods for placing outside directors on Boards to insure that they can provide an independent voice regarding management decisions (Cadbury, et al., 1992 and 1992a).

MAX DE PREE

Max De Pree was born in 1924 and received his education at Wheaton and Hope College. He served in a number of positions at Herman Miller, the office furniture manufacturer. The company was founded by D. J. De Pree, the father of Max, and has a very progressive reputation in a number of areas. One was worker participation. The firm adopted the Scanlon Plan in 1950 which provides extra pay for workers when their unit's goals are met. In 1988 the plan was revitalized to create a new, deeper covenant between customers, management, and employees (File, 1989). Another noteworthy characteristic of Herman Miller is that the CEO's salary is limited to 20 times the amount made by an average factory worker. This decision was made after De Pree consulted with his friend, Peter Drucker. This amount is drastically lower than the 117 times that a typical Fortune 500 CEO earns (Mitchell, 1992).

Max De Pree has written two inspirational books that provide his views on leadership. The first, *Leadership Is an Art*, talked at length about the covenant model of leadership that builds upon the principles of worker participation. De Pree believes that while a contract is legally binding and outlines responsibilities, a covenant is an emotional bond creating a mutual trust built on shared goals and values. He defines integrity as "a fine sense of one's obligations" and listed it as the first characteristic of future leaders (De Pree, 1989).

In his second book, De Pree included a chapter entitled: Where do ethics and leadership intersect? His answer was that they intersect all the time and that a sacred relationship exists between leaders and followers. Performance by effective leaders according to De Pree is based on trust, vision, competence and fidelity. This intersection was based on three points (De Pree, 1992).

1. Ethical leadership withers without justice. Here De Pree touches upon fair distribution of results and the CEO compensation is used as an example. Leaders should be indebted to those who follow and communications must be scrutinized with justice in mind.
2. A second connection between ethics and leadership is "celibacy" (leaving room for God and others in one's life). This involves assuming stewardship of limited resources and exercising personal restraint so that meaningful relationships in life such as leaders' families and the families of the ones they lead receive their due.
3. Ethics and leadership intersect in the common good. Leaders should subsume their needs to those of their followers and they must learn how to make a commitment to the common good. Finally, leaders should know how to bear, rather than inflict, pain.

Max De Pree retired as CEO of Herman Miller in 1988 and is recognized for his outstanding leadership qualities. His books have allowed readers to gain insight into his leadership which is very much of a "hands on" approach and is based on the precepts noted above. The concluding comments on the ethics and leadership chapter summarize well his position: "A leader's commitments and beliefs are part and parcel of the same thing. A true leader cannot commit herself without beliefs. But in composing voice and touch, action must follow closely a solid sense of one's ethics" (De Pree, 1992: 139).

J. ERWIN MILLER

Joseph Irwin Miller was born in 1909. He holds two degrees from Yale and an M.A. from Oxford as a Rhodes Scholar. He assumed the CEO role at Cummins Engine in 1951 and served in this capacity until 1977. Miller is viewed as one of the pioneers of modern management with strong ethical underpinning. His many accomplishments while CEO at Cummins include service as the first lay President of the National Council of Churches of Christ (1960–63), the civil rights March on Washington in the 1960s, and hiring noted architects to design buildings in Columbus, Indiana (Cummins' hometown). He has long been a proponent of business' responsibility to solve the social problems of the country and believes that business must provide leadership to make this happen (Patterson, 1968). He has advocated that business become a "revolutionary instrument for social reform" to help reverse discrimination, combat poverty and pollution and ultimately to refashion society.

Miller has written and spoken extensively on the subject of business ethics. One of the most interesting selections appeared in the Harvard Divinity Bulletin where Miller set out his views on how religious commitments shape corporate decisions (Miller, 1984). He stressed the importance of the group rather than the individual in arriving at decisions. Rank should not be emphasized as much as those who have multiple responsibilities should help, train and offer judgment. The importance of managers themselves demonstrating commitment and trust first before expecting it of their employees is key.

In an interview Miller spelled out some of his operating principles regarding ethics in business (Freudberg, 1986). He indicated that ethical practice is only long-term planning and the unwillingness to deviate from or to compromise long-term objectives for short-term gain. The way that employees learn about the values of the corporation is from the example of top executives rather than sermonizing them or espousing corporate platitudes on ethics. He said: "All of the corporate standards of ethics don't mean anything unless the persons in the corporation perceive the top people to abide by them when the going is really tough" (Freudberg, 1986). Responsible behavior in Miller's mind is behaving the way you would if you could look back from some distant point in your future. He offered pithy words of advice for employees faced with an ethical dilemma: "When in doubt, either don't do it or call home" (Freudberg, 1986: 201).

Miller has also spoken to business schools on the importance of including some discussion of ethics within the classroom setting. He offered several bits of advice. First, a priority in selecting students for enrollment in business schools should be character and maturity. Second, students should also be selected on the basis of their innate selflessness, capacity to commit and natural inclination to work with and for each other. A third aspect deals with the importance of the example set by instructors and other students. Fourth, the contents of any course in ethics should allow students an opportunity to reflect and discuss the importance of personal and organizational moral standards in decision making. Finally, the ethical aim of business schools might well be to discover and to lead American business into new forms of enterprise and to greater long run effectiveness (Miller, 1989).

SUMMARY OBSERVATIONS

Reviewing these four examples, it may strike observers, especially from non-English cultures, how naturally and fearlessly these business leaders express themselves in "ethical" terms. This seems to be part of a broader culture, where the society recognizes excellence also in "ethical" terms. In fact, these individuals and their companies have been praised for their stand on ethics. For example, *Business Ethics* magazine gave its 1989 awards for excellence in ethics to

Herman Miller and Johnson & Johnson. Both James Burke and J. Irwin Miller have been enshrined in *Fortune*'s National Business Hall of Fame. Herman Miller's (ultimately De Pree's) view on CEO compensation has been praised by *The Wall Street Journal*. The policies of Cadbury Schweppes have received recognition not only in Europe, but also throughout the world for its fairness in dealing with employees.

Certainly the usage of ethical terms is culture-dependent and needs careful interpretation. Although, in each culture, business activities and leadership are assessed in terms of good and bad, right and wrong, the forms of expressing those judgments may vary widely. Therefore, it seems to be wise to account for that culture-boundedness when we try to more deeply understand these examples of leadership by putting them into a broader, international context. Not being able to do it here, we would like, at least, to point to this fundamental aspect and signal the crucial importance to be aware of the cultural dependence of moral languages. If, for instance, there is a strong reluctance among business leaders to use ethical terms—as it is the case in many European countries and in Japan—the "paper trail," mentioned as a second criterion for selecting the examples of this paper, would have to be interpreted in this light. In order to grasp more precisely the contents of what these leaders label "ethical," we would have to analyze in detail how their understandings of "ethical" terms are interpreted (and perhaps modified) by their deeds and, furthermore, how far they may pass the test of broader ethical reasoning.

We conclude with a few observations, which are structured in line with the criteria of managerial ethical leadership discussed in Enderle (1987) and implied in Schein's characterization of "The Learning Leader as Culture Manager" (Schein, 1992: 374–392). The first common theme that seems to run through the professional and personal lives of these four men is a strong commitment "to perceive and interpret reality" in the context of openness and honesty. Burke faced the Tylenol crisis with openness and candor. Cadbury provided information to various power groups and fought for openness in management to disarm outside suspicion. De Pree holds that a sacred relationship exists between leaders and followers, which implies mutual openness and trust. For Miller it was paramount to perceive and understand the business challenges in society as realistically as possible. All showed "a high degree of objectivity about themselves and their own organization" (Schein, 1992, 387).

Second, all four leaders were able "to create reality" by reaffirming the ideals of their respective firms. Burke did it by challenging J&J's Credo and overcoming the later crises. Cadbury accomplished it by improving corporate governance in his company and in Britain. De Pree was able to create this reality by achieving the covenant model of leadership. Finally, Miller's career consisted of many attempts at making business an important instrument of social reform.

Third, these persons seem to have an uncommon concern for how their decisions affect others. They realize the enormity of managerial decisions such as plant closings, acquisitions and divestment on the lives of others. De Pree mentions in his chapter that decisions affect families rather than just individuals. Burke wrestled with the impact of the Tylenol recall on the various stakeholders of J&J and ultimately decided that customer safety should take precedence over the others. Miller raised this concern for others in his writings on both management and business school education. Furthermore, this characteristic enhanced their respective firm's ability to create worker participation, customer commitment, community involvement, and other desired stakeholder actions.

Fourth, looking at the personalities of these leaders, they incorporate an unusually high degree of "motivation" and "emotional strength" (Schein, 1992: 387–388). One could characterize them in terms of Aristotelian virtue ethics (see Pincoffs, 1992). These virtues are in evidence in their decisions and writings. For example, James Burke displayed great courage or fortitude in the Tylenol decision. Moreover, Cadbury and De Pree are strong advocates for justice or fairness in their treatment of all employees. The innovative personnel policies at these firms stem from the inherent sense of justice that the company owes its workers. Miller advocates temperance in many of his thoughts regarding the ethical policies that he instilled in his firm.

Finally, these personalities distinguish themselves by strong religious values. Their moral commitment appears rooted in religious conviction that brings a sense of unconditional obligation to others. They come from different religious denominations: Burke is Catholic, Cadbury Quaker, De Pree Dutch Reformed, and Miller Presbyterian. They all mention religious beliefs in their writings. For example, De Pree's "covenantal relationships" and "celibacy" notions have their foundations in religious teachings. Furthermore, Miller's service as Council of Churches and on the Board of a seminary probably represents the strongest formal commitment

of the four. However, all of them seem to be religious individuals and the way they treat other human beings transcends their positions and viewpoints. Ethics for them, then, appears to be grounded in a religious tradition and their sense of managerial responsibility was shaped and influenced by it.

Examples are instructive in any endeavor and such is the case in managerial ethical leadership too. Ethical principles and rules indicate only minimal requirements for decision making or action and cannot comprehend the full richness of the lives of leaders and companies. Being ethical means doing more than fulfilling moral minima, rather it involves striving also for ideals which includes moral imagination and moral courage (see De George, 1993: 107–111; 184–192). Actual examples of such managerial ethical leadership prove that such high standards are attainable because they have already been realized. They provide a wide range of ideas about how ethics and leadership in business are intrinsically intertwined. At the same time, their claim is not doctrinaire for the future. The next generation of leaders operate in a different time and some of the qualities mentioned above may be of greater or lesser importance in the future. It is up to them, as successful leaders, to make difficult decisions without compromising their ethical beliefs.   ◆ ◆ ◆

◆ Notes

1. See Tuleja, 1985; Freudberg, 1986: Part Five; Horton, 1986. More general reflections in Burns, 1978: chapter 2 on "The Structure of Moral Leadership."
2. This first assumption—to take "purely business" considerations seriously without mentioning them explicitly—holds for many other situations under investigation, e.g. Kaufmann et al., 1986; ASFOR, 1989. This assumption is not necessarily

"a personalistic reduction of the fundamental problem of business ethics" as Ulrich and Thielemann (1993) claim.
3. This assumption nicely fits in to the three-level conception of business ethics, discussed in Enderle, 1993a, and 1993b.
4. For a more complete analysis of the Tylenol poisoning story and its aftermath, see Moore, 1982, and Waldholz and Kneale, 1982: 1.

◆ Bibliography

ASFOR (Associazione per la formazione alla direzione aziendale). 1989. Il manager di fronte ai problemi etici. Milano: ASFOR.

Becker, L. C. (ed.), Becker, C. B. (associate ed.). 1992. *Encyclopedia of Ethics.* New York/London: Garland Publishing.

Blodgett, T. B. 1983. "Cadbury Schweppes: More than Chocolate and Tonic." *Harvard Business Review,* 64(1): 134–144.

Burns, J. M. 1978. *Leadership.* New York: Harper & Row.

Cadbury, A. 1984. *Cadbury Schweppes: The Character of the Company.* London: Cadbury Schweppes.

Cadbury, A. 1987. "Ethical Managers Make Their Own Rules." *Harvard Business Review,* 68(5): 69–73.

Cadbury, A. et al. 1992. *Financial Aspects of Corporate Governance.* London: Gee and Company.

Cadbury, A. 1992a. "Calling Firms to Account Without Stifling the Spirit of Enterprise." *The Times,* May 28, 1992.

De George, R. T. 1993. *Competing with Integrity in International Business.* New York/Oxford: Oxford University Press.

De Pree, M. 1989. *Leadership Is an Art.* New York: Dell Trade Paperback.

De Pree, M. 1992. *Leadership Jazz.* New York: Currency Doubleday.

Enderle, G. 1987. "Some Perspectives of Managerial Ethical Leadership." *Journal of Business Ethics,* 6: 657–663.

Enderle, G. 1993a. *Handlungsorientierte Wirtschaftsethik.* Grundlagen und Anwendungen. [Action-oriented Business Ethics. Foundations and Applications.] Bern: Haupt.

Enderle, [[sic]] G. 1993b. "What Is Business Ethics?" In Dunfee, T., Nagayasu, Y. (Eds.) 1993. *Business Ethics: Japan in a Global Economy.* Dordrecht/Boston/London: Kluwer Academic Publishers, 133–150.

File, K. M. 1989. "The 1989 Business Ethics Awards." *Business Ethics,* November/December: 20–25.

Freudberg, D. 1986. *The Corporate Conscience: Money, Power, and Responsible Business.* New York: AMACOM.

Guzzardi, W. 1990. "The National Business Hall of Fame." *Fortune,* March 17.

Horton, T. R. 1986. *What Works for Me: 16 CEOs Talk about Their Careers and Commitments.* New York: Random House.

Kaufmann, F.-X., Kerber, W., Zulehner, P. 1986. *Religion und Ethos bei Führungskräften.* München: Kindt.

Miller, J. I. 1984. "How Religious Commitments Shape Corporate Decisions." *Harvard Divinity Bulletin,* February–March: 4–7.

Miller, J. I. 1989. Business Ethics Seminar, Indiana University, Bloomington, Indiana, October 24, 1989.

Mitchell, J. 1992. "Herman Miller Links Worker-CEO Pay." *The Wall Street Journal,* May 7, B1 and B8.

Moore, T. 1982. "The Fight to Save Tylenol: The Inside Story of Johnson & Johnson's Struggle to Revive Its Most Important Product." *Fortune,* November 29.

Nash, L. N. 1988. "Johnson & Johnson Credo." In Keogh, J. (Ed.) *Corporate Ethics: A Prime Business Asset.* New York: The Business Roundtable, 93–104.

Pastin, M., Harrison, J. "Social Responsibility in the Hollow Corporation." *Business and Society Review,* Fall: 54–58.

Patterson, W. D. 1968. "J. Irwin Miller: The Revolutionary Role of Business." *Saturday Review,* January 13.

Pincoffs, E. L. 1992. "Virtues." In Becker et al. 1992, vol. II, 1283–1288.

Schein, E. H. 1992. *Organizational Culture and Leadership.* San Francisco: Jossey-Bass Publishers.

Smith, W. K., Tedlow, R. 1989a. "James Burke: A Career in American Business (A)." Harvard Business School Case 9-389-177.

Smith, W. K., Tedlow, R. 1989b. "James Burke: A Career in American Business (B)." Harvard Business School Case 9-390-030.

Tuleja, T. 1985. *Beyond the Bottom Line: How Business Leaders Are Turning Principles into Profits.* New York: Facts on File.

Ulrich, P., Thielemann, U. 1993. "Business-Ethical Thinking Patterns of Managers—An Empirical Study." *Journal of Business Ethics*, 12: 879–898.

Waldholz, M., Kneale, D. 1982. "Tylenol's Maker Tries to Retain Good Image in Wake of Tragedy." *The Wall Street Journal*, October 8.

Williams, O. F., Houck, J. W. (Eds.) 1992. *A Virtuous Life in Business. Stories of Courage and Integrity in the Corporate World.* Lanham, MD: Rowman & Littlefield Publishers.

Ethical Leadership and the Psychology of Decision Making

David M. Messick and Max H. Bazerman

Some of the readings imply that we are always capable of making rational, dispassionate ethical choices, unaffected by the pressures and influences exerted in an organizational setting. Messick and Bazerman cite evidence that we are much worse at making decisions than we might imagine.

Management is all about decision making. Some decisions have value implications; they may lead to results that hurt people or are otherwise unjust or unfair. Therefore, managers should strive to make the best moral decisions they can. However, most decisions are made in difficult circumstances; there is either too much information or not enough, there are time constraints, and there are other institutional influences. The result is that we develop mental shortcuts and tend to abbreviate the process; we could not cope otherwise. But in doing so, we may also shortchange a full and rational exploration of the moral issues. Messick and Bazerman show that we develop functional theories about the world, ourselves, and other people that help us make rapid decisions. They point out, however, that these valuable skills may lead us to make seriously flawed ethical choices. For example, we often select only evidence that supports our confident view of a situation, while ignoring other equally valid facts that go against our beliefs. They give a number of examples, including the wreck of the Herald of Free Enterprise *passenger ferry, which sank after leaving port with its bow doors open to the sea. In fact, though, these dynamics do not apply just to dramatic cases but to most of our everyday interactions as well.*

Executives today face many difficult, potentially explosive situations in which they must make decisions that can help or harm their firms, themselves, and others. How can they improve the ethical quality of their decisions? How can they ensure that their decisions will not backfire? The authors discuss three types of theories—theories about the world, theories about other people, and theories about ourselves—that will help executives understand how they make the judgments on which they base their decisions. By understanding those theories, they can learn how to make better, more ethical decisions.

Changes in today's business environment pose vexing ethical challenges to executives. We propose that unethical business decisions may stem not from the traditionally assumed trade-off between ethics and profits or from a callous disregard of other people's interests or welfare, but from psychological tendencies that foster poor decision making, both from an ethical and a rational perspective. Identifying and confronting these tendencies, we suggest, will increase both the ethicality and success of executive decision making.

Executives today work in a moral mine field. At any moment, a seemingly innocuous decision can explode and harm not only the decision maker but also everyone in the neighborhood. We cannot forecast the ethical landscape in coming years, nor do we think that it is our role to provide moral guidance to executives. Rather, we offer advice, based on contemporary research on the psychology of decision making, to help executives identify morally hazardous situations and improve the ethical quality of their decisions.

Psychologists have discovered systematic weaknesses in how people make decisions and process information; these new discoveries and theories are the foundation for this paper. These discoveries involve insights into errors that people make when they estimate risks and likelihoods, as well

as biases in the way they seek information to improve their estimates. There are new theories about how easily our preferences can be influenced by the consequences we consider and the manner in which we consider them. Social psychologists have new information about how people divide the world into "us" and "them" that sheds new light on how discrimination operates. Finally, there has been important new research into the dimensions along which people think that they are different from other people, which helps explain why people might engage in practices that they would condemn in others.[1]

We focus on three types of theories that executives use in making decisions—theories about the world, theories about other people, and theories about ourselves. Theories about the world refer to the beliefs we hold about how the world works, the nature of the causal network in which we live, and the ways in which our decisions influence the world. Important aspects of our theories about the world involve our beliefs about the probabilistic (or deterministic) texture of the world and our perceptions of causation.

Theories about other people are our organized beliefs about how "we" are different from "they." Interestingly, "they" may be competitors, employees, regulators, or foreigners, and whoever is "we" today may be "them" tomorrow. Our beliefs about others influence the ways in which we make judgments and decisions about other people, and these influences are often unconscious.

Finally, we all correctly believe that we are unique individuals. However, theories about ourselves lead us to unrealistic beliefs about ourselves that may cause us to underestimate our exposure to risk, take more than our fair share of the credit for success (or too little for failure), or be too confident that our theory of the world is the correct one. If most of the executives in an organization think that they are in the upper 10 percent of the talent distribution, there is the potential for pervasive disappointment.

Our discussion of these three theories focuses on the ways they are likely to be incorrect. Our message, however, is not that executives are poor decision makers. We focus on problem areas because they are the danger zones where errors may arise. They are the places where improvements may be achieved, areas in which executives would like to change their decision making if only they better understood their existing decision processes.

THEORIES ABOUT THE WORLD

Successful executives must have accurate knowledge of their world. If they lack this knowledge, they must know how to obtain it. One typical challenge is how to assess the risk of a proposed strategy or policy, which involves delineating the policy's consequences and assessing the likelihood of various possibilities. If an executive does a poor assessment of a policy's consequences, the policy may backfire and cause financial as well as moral embarrassment to the firm and the decision maker. There are three components to our theories of the world: the consideration of possible consequences, the judgment of risk, and the perception of causes.

The Cascade of Consequences

A principle in ecology that Hardin has called the First Law of Ecology is, simply stated, "You can never do just one thing."[2] Major decisions have a spectrum of consequences, not just one, and especially not just the intended consequence. Everyday experience as well as psychological research suggests that, in making complex choices, people often simplify the decision by ignoring possible outcomes or consequences that would otherwise complicate the choice. In other words, there is a tendency to reduce the set of possible

consequences or outcomes to make the decision manageable. In extreme cases, all but one aspect of a decision will be suppressed, and the choice will be made solely on the basis of the one privileged feature. The folly of ignoring a decision's possible consequences should be obvious to experienced decision makers, but there are several less obvious ways in which decision errors can create moral hazards. The tendency to ignore the full set of consequences in decision making leads to the following five biases: ignoring low-probability events, limiting the search for stakeholders, ignoring the possibility that the public will "find out," discounting the future, and undervaluing collective outcomes.

◆ *Ignoring Low-Probability Events.* If a new product has the potential for great acceptance but a possible drawback, perhaps for only a few people, there is a tendency to underestimate the importance of the risk. In the case of DES (diethylstilbestrol), a synthetic estrogen prescribed for women with problem pregnancies, there was some early indication that the drug was associated with a higher than normal rate of problems not only in pregnant women but also in their daughters. The importance of this information was insufficiently appreciated. Worrisome risks may be ignored if they threaten to impede large gains.

◆ *Limiting the Search for Stakeholders.* DES's most disastrous effects did not befall the consumers of the drug, namely, the women who took it; the catastrophe struck their daughters. When there is a tendency to restrict the analysis of a policy's consequences to one or two groups of visible stakeholders, the decision may be blindsided by unanticipated consequences to an altogether different group. A careful analysis of the interests of the stakeholders (those persons or groups whose welfare may be affected by the decision under consideration) is essential to reasonably anticipating potential problems. A basic tenet of moral theories is to treat people with respect, which can be done only if the interests of all concerned people are honestly considered. Assessing others' interests would have required research, for instance, on the longterm effects of DES.

◆ *Ignoring the Possibility that the Public Will "Find Out."* The stakeholder who should always be considered is the public in general. Executives should ask, "What would the reaction be if this decision and the reasons for it were made public?" If they fear this reaction, they should reconsider the decision. One reason for the test is to alert executives that if the decision is made, they will have to conceal it to avoid adverse public response. The need to hide the decision, and the risk that the decision and its concealment might be disclosed, become other consequences to face. The outrage provoked by the revelation that a crippling disease, asbestosis, was caused by asbestos exposure was partly due to the fact that Johns Manville had known about and hidden this relationship for years while employees and customers were continuously exposed to this hazard. A decision or policy that must be hidden from public view has the additional risk that the secret might be revealed. Damage to self-respect and institutional respect of those who must implement and maintain the concealment should also be considered a consequence.

◆ *Discounting the Future.* The consequences that we face tomorrow are more compelling than those we must address next week or next year. The consequences of decisions cascade not only over people and groups, but also over time. Figuring out how to address the entire temporal stream of outcomes is one of the most challenging tasks executives face. Policy A will earn more money this year than Policy B, but a year from now, if we get there, Policy B will probably leave us stronger than Policy A. Theories of the world that fail to cope with the temporal distribution of consequences will not only leave executives puzzled about why they are not doing better; they will also expose executives to accusations that they squandered the future to exploit the present. The tendency to discount the future partly explains the decaying urban infrastructure, the U.S. budget deficit, the collapse of fisheries, global warming, and environmental destruction. While there is much debate about the destructiveness of these issues, in each instance, the key decision makers have clearly underweighed the future in making the appropriate balanced decisions.

◆ *Undervaluing Collective Outcomes.* Accurate theories of the world must also be sensitive to the collective consequences of decisions. When E. F. Hutton's managers decided to earn money by kiting checks, not only did they put the reputation of their own firm in jeopardy, they also endangered the reputation of the entire securities industry. When a chemical firm decides to discharge waste into a public lake, it pollutes two collective resources, the lake and the reputation of the chemical industry in general. There is a tendency to treat these collective costs as externalities and to ignore them in decision making. To do so, however, is to ignore a broad class of stakeholders whose response could be, "If they voluntarily ignore the collective interests, then it is in the collective interest to regulate their activity."

Ethical decisions must be based on accurate theories about the world. That means, at a minimum, examining the full spectrum of a decision's consequences. Our perspective suggests that a set of biases reduces the effectiveness of the search for all possible consequences. It is interesting to evaluate the infamous Pinto decision from this consequential perspective. Ford executives knew that the car had a fire risk, but the cost they associated with it was small. Their deliberations gave no consideration to their customers' interests. They made no effort to ask car buyers if they were willing to pay an extra $10 to shield the gas tank. The Pinto decision proved a colossal embarrassment to Ford; when the documents were released, the effort to conceal the decision failed, and public opinion, fueled by Ralph Nader's book *Unsafe at Any Speed,* ran deeply and strongly against Ford.[3] The public felt that there was a collective interest in automobile safety and that Ford and, by association, the other auto manufacturers, were indifferent to that concern. From the public's perspective, it would be stupid to permit unethical firms to police themselves.

Judgment of Risk

Theories of the world will be inaccurate if they systematically fail to account for the full spectrum of consequences associated with decisions. And they will be inaccurate if they systematically err in assessing the probabilities associated with the consequences. Let's first consider these two scenarios:

◆ A tough-minded executive wants to know if the company's current promotion practices have caused any specific case of demonstrated discrimination against a minority employee. He explains that he is not interested in vague possibilities of discrimination but is concerned that the firm not do anything that "really" causes discrimination.

◆ Edmund Muskie, a candidate in the 1972 U.S. presidential election, borrowed the words of President Harry Truman when he stated that what this country needed was a "one-armed" economist. When asked why, he responded that he was tired of economists who said "on the one hand . . . , but on the other hand. . . ."

Denying Uncertainty. These decision makers are grasping for certainty in an uncertain world. They want to know what will or did happen, not what may or might have happen(ed). They illustrate the general principle that people find it easier to act as if the world were certain and deterministic rather than uncertain and often unpredictable. The executive in the first scenario wants to know about "real" discrimination, not the possibility of discrimination. Muskie expressed frustration with incessantly hearing about "the other hand." What people want to hear is not what might happen, but what will happen. When executives act as if the world is more certain than it is, they expose themselves to poor outcomes, for both themselves and others. It is simply foolish to ignore risk on one's own behalf, but it is unethical to do so on behalf of others.

There are some good reasons why people underestimate the importance of chance. One is that they misperceive chance events. When the market goes up on five consecutive days, people find a reason or cause that makes the world seem deterministic (for example, a favorable economic report was published). If the market goes up four days and then down on the fifth, people say a "correction" was due. Statistical market analyses suggest that changes in indices such as the Dow Jones index are basically random. Yet each morning, we are offered an "explanation" in the financial pages of why the market went up or down.

One implication of the belief in a deterministic world is the view that evidence should and can be perfect. The fact that there is a strong statistical relationship between smoking and bad health, for instance, is insufficient to convince tobacco company executives that cigarettes are harmful, because the standard of proof they want the evidence to meet is that of perfection. Any deviation from this standard is used strategically as evidence that smoking is not harmful.

We believe in a deterministic world in some cases because we exaggerate the extent to which we can control it. This illusion of control shows up in many contexts, but it seems maximal in complex situations that play out in the future. The tendency appears in experimental contexts in which people prefer to bet on the outcome of a flip of a coin that has not yet been tossed rather than on one that has already been thrown but whose outcome is unknown to the bettor.[4] The illusory sense that a bet may influence the outcome is more acute for future than for past events. . . .

One common response to the assertion that executives underestimate the importance of random events is that they have learned through experience how to process information about uncertainty. However, experience may not be a good teacher. In situations in which our expectations or predictions were wrong, we often misremember what our expectations, in fact, were. We commonly tend to adjust our memories of what we thought would happen to what we later came to know did happen. This phenomenon, called the "hindsight bias," insulates us from our errors.[5]

We fail to appreciate the role of chance if we assume that every event that occurred was, in principle, predictable. The response "I should have known . . ." implies the belief that some future outcome was inherently knowable, a belief incompatible with the fact that essentially random events determine many outcomes. If every effort has been made to forecast the result of a future event, and the result is very different from

predictions, it may be ill-advised to blame ourselves or our employees for the failure. This, of course, assumes that we made every effort to collect and appropriately process all the information relevant to the prediction.

Risk Trade-offs. Uncertainty and risk are facts of executive life. Many risky decisions concern ethical dilemmas involving jobs, safety, environmental risks, and organizational existence. How risky is it to build one more nuclear power plant? How risky is it to expose assembly line employees to the chemicals for making animal flea collars? At some point, our decisions are reduced to basic questions like: What level of risk is acceptable? How much is safety worth?

One unhelpful answer to the second question is "any price." That answer implies that we should devote all our efforts to highway improvement, cures for cancer, reducing product risks, and so on, to the exclusion of productivity. Throughout our lives, dealing with risk requires trading off benefits and costs; however, this is not a process that people find easy. It is much simpler, but completely unrealistic, to say "any price." The illusion that a riskless world can be created is a myth that is consistent with a theory of the world that minimizes the role of chance.

If we deal irrationally or superficially with risk, costly inconsistencies can occur in the ways we make risk trade-offs. Experts point out the U.S. laws are less tolerant of carcinogens in food than in drinking water or air. In the United Kingdom, 2,500 times more money per life saved is spent on safety measures in the pharmaceutical industry than in agriculture. Similarly, U.S. society spends about $140,000 in highway construction to save one life and $5 million to save a person from death due to radiation exposure.

A special premium seems to get attached to situations in which all risk can be eliminated. Consider the following two scenarios:

Scenario A. There is a 20 percent chance that the chemicals in your company's plant might be causing ten cancer-related illnesses per year. Your company must decide whether to purchase a multimillion-dollar filtration system that would reduce this probability to a 10 percent chance.

Scenario B. There is a 10 percent chance that the chemicals in your company's plant might be causing ten cancer-related illnesses per year. Your company must decide whether to purchase a multimillion-dollar filtration system that would entirely eliminate this risk.

Evidence suggests that executives would be more likely to purchase the filtration system in scenario B than in scenario A.[6] It appears to be more valuable to eliminate the entire risk than to make an equivalent reduction from one uncertain level to another. Rationally, all reductions in a risk of 10 percent should have the same value for the decision maker. The "preference for certainty" suggests that a firm might be willing to spend more money to achieve a smaller risk reduction if that smaller reduction totally eliminated the risk. Were this the case, not only would the firm's decision be wasteful, it would be unethical because it failed to accomplish the greatest good with the budget allocated for it.

Perceptions of risk are often faulty, frequently resulting in public and private decision makers' misdirected risk-reduction efforts. Is it not a breech of ethics if incoherent policies save fewer lives at greater costs than other possible policies? Failure to explicitly deal with risk trade-offs may have created precisely such a situation.

Risk Framing. Whether a glass is half-full or half-empty is a matter of risk framing. When the glass is described as half-full, it appears more attractive than when described as half-empty. Similarly, a medical therapy seems more desirable when described in terms of its cure rate than its failure rate. This finding probably occurs because the cure rate induces people to think of the cure (a good thing), whereas an equivalent description in terms of failures induces people to think of failures (not a good thing).

A less obvious effect has been found with regard to the framing of risks. Consider this example:

A large car manufacturer has recently been hit with a number of economic difficulties. It appears that it needs to close three plants and lay off 6,000 employees. The vice president of production, who has been exploring alternative ways to avoid the crisis, has developed two plans.

Plan A will save one of the three plants and 2,000 jobs.

Plan B has a one-third probability of saving all three plants and all 6,000 jobs, but has a two-thirds probability of saving no plants and no jobs.

Which plan would you select? There are a number of things to consider in evaluating these options. For example, how will each action affect the union? How will each plan influence the motivation and morale of the retained employees? What is the firm's obligation to its shareholders? While all these questions are important, another important factor influences how executives respond to them. Reconsider the problem, replacing the choices provided above with the following choices.

Plan C will result in the loss of two of the three plants and 4,000 jobs.

Plan D has a two-thirds probability of resulting in the loss of all three plants and all 6,000 jobs, but has a one-third probability of losing no plants and no jobs.

Now which plan would you select? Close examination of the two sets of alternative plans finds the two sets of options to be objectively the same. For example, saving one of three plants and 2,000 of 6,000 jobs (plan A) offers the same objective outcome as losing two of three plants and 4,000 of 6,000 jobs (plan C). Likewise, plans B and D are objectively identical. Informal empirical investigation, however, demonstrates that most individuals choose plan A in the first set (more than 80 percent) and plan D in the second set (more than 80 percent).[7] While the two sets of choices are objectively the same, changing the description of the outcomes from jobs and plants saved to jobs and plants lost is sufficient to shift the prototypic choice from risk-averse to risk-seeking behavior.

This shift is consistent with research showing that individuals treat risks concerning perceived gains (e.g., saving jobs and plants—plans A and B) differently from risks concerning perceived losses (e.g., losing jobs and plants—plans C and D). The way in which the problem is "framed" or presented can dramatically change how executives respond. If the problem is framed in terms of losing jobs and plants, executives tend to take the risk to avoid any loss. The negative value placed on the loss of three plants and 6,000 jobs is usually perceived as not being three times as bad as losing one plant and 2,000 jobs. In contrast, if the problem is framed in terms of saving jobs and plants (plans A and B), executives tend to avoid the risk and take the sure "gain." They typically view the gain placed on saving three plants and 6,000 jobs as not being three times as great as saving one plant and 2,000 jobs.

This typical pattern of responses is consistent with a general tendency to be risk averse with gains and risk seeking with losses.[8] This tendency has the potential for creating ethical havoc. When thinking about layoffs, for instance, most employees surely focus on their potential job loss. If executives adopt a risk-prone attitude in such situations—that is, if they are willing to risk all to attempt to avoid any losses—they may be seen as reckless and immoral by the very people whose jobs they are trying to preserve. If different stakeholders have different frames, the potential for moral disagreement is great.

Perception of Causes

The final aspect of executives' theories of the world, perhaps the most important, is the beliefs that executives and other people cherish about the causal texture of the world, about why things happen or don't happen. Everyone holds beliefs about business successes and failures. As we mentioned earlier, every morning we're given a reason for why the stock market rose, fell, or stayed the same, thus reinforcing the theory that the world is deterministic. Moreover, judging causal responsibility is often a precursor to judging moral accountability and to blaming or praising a person, organization, or policy for an outcome. However, even under the best of circumstances, causation is usually complex, and ambiguity about causation is often at the heart of disputes about responsibility, blame, and punishment.

Consider, for example, the *Herald of Free Enterprise*, a ferry that carried automobiles from the Belgian port of Zeebrugge to Dover, England. Several years ago, it sank in a placid sea a few minutes after leaving Zeebrugge; 180 persons drowned. An investigation determined that the boat sank because the bow doors, through which the cars enter, had been left open, allowing water to pour into the vessel. The assistant bosun, who was responsible for closing the bow doors, had, tragically, taken a nap.

There were no alarm lights to warn the captain that the doors were open. The captain had requested such lights, but the company had denied his request; it felt warning lights were unnecessary because the first mate monitored the closing. On this occasion, the first mate failed to monitor the bow-door closing because he was needed elsewhere on board due to a chronic manpower shortage. Furthermore, the monitoring system was a "negative" check system, which means that signals were sent only if problems were detected. The lack of a signal was construed as an indication that all was well; the captain did not have to wait for a "positive" signal from the boat deck. Finally, there was the question of why water entered the ship since the bow doors are normally several meters above sea level. The answer was that the ship had taken on ballast to enable it to take cars onto the upper car deck. The captain had not pumped out the ballast before departing because he needed to make up twenty minutes to get back on schedule. Thus the ship left harbor at full throttle, creating a bow wave, with the ship's bow unusually low in the water.

What caused the *Herald of Free Enterprise* to capsize? Who is to blame? We have many candidates for blame: the assistant bosun, the first mate, the captain, the person who refused to provide warning lights, the person who instituted the negative check system, and the owners of the line for failing to provide adequate crew for the boat.

Focus on People. A central issue in this case is the tendency of most people to blame a person. This principle is at the heart of the slogan of the National Rifle Association, a U.S. lobbying organization for gun manufacturers and users: "Guns don't kill people, people do." "Human error" becomes the cause assigned to many accidents involving complex technologies (such as ferries). We tend to blame people because it is easy to imagine them having done something to "undo" or prevent the accident. If the assistant bosun had not fallen asleep, if the first mate had stayed on the car deck to supervise the bow-door closing, if the captain had not left the harbor at full speed before pumping the ballast, and so on.

It is less easy to imagine changing the ship's equipment and procedures, and these appear less salient as a cause of the disaster. The absence of warning lights allowed the ship to depart with the bow doors open. The negative check system invited a nonmessage to be misconstrued as an "all clear" signal. The point is that human "errors" occur within systems that may vary widely in the degree to which they are "error proof." Our theories about the world usually involve people as the causal agents, rather than environments either that influence people for good or bad or that can compensate for human weaknesses such as drowsiness. From an engineering viewpoint, what is easier to change—warning lights or periodic drowsiness?

Different Events. Theories about causes often lead people to disagree, because, as McGill has pointed out, they are explaining different events.[9] When Sears introduced a commission-based sales system at its automotive repair shops, there was an increase in consumer complaints, usually accusing the shop of performing unnecessary, expensive work. Sears acknowledged that there had been some "isolated abuses" but denied that the problem was widespread. In subsequent public discussions, some of the controversy confused two phenomena. The first is why a particular employee would recommend and perform unnecessary work. The question, "Why did Jack do this?" may lead to determining how Jack is different from Bill and other employees who did not recommend unnecessary work. These causes answer the question, "Why did Jack do this, while others did not?" Are there changes in Jack's situation that can explain his misconduct? "Why did Jack do this now, when he did not do it earlier?" is another way to construe this question.

The second question is why Sears had more complaints in the new system. The fact that there was a change raises an important issue: different systems may produce different levels of unethical conduct. If we focus only on Jack, or if we never change the system, we fail to see that the system itself can be a cause of problems. In many cases, something like the method of compensation appears in the background. If an employee behaves dishonestly, we tend to contrast him or her with honest workers, rather than ask if there is something encouraging dishonesty. When we change situations, we can sometimes see that an organization's features can have a causal impact on human actions, analogous to what happens when a community is exposed to a carcinogenic agent. The overall cancer rate in the community will increase, but it may be difficult to ever determine whether any specific individual's cancer was caused by the toxin. There may be convincing proof that the agent is a cause of cancer in the community generally, but not of any particular cancer.

Sins of Omission. We have no problem judging that the assistant bosun bears some responsibility for the passenger deaths on the *Herald of Free Enterprise*, even though his contribution to the disaster was a failure to act. In many other situations, in which expectations and duties are not as well defined as they were with the *Herald*, a failure to take an action is used to shield persons from causal and, hence, moral responsibility. Is a public health official who decides not to authorize mandatory vaccinations responsible for the deaths of those who succumb to the disease?[10] Is the executive who fails to disclose his knowledge of a colleague's incompetence responsible for the harm that the colleague causes the firm? Many people would answer these questions in the negative, largely because they perceive that the immediate cause of the deaths or harm is the virus or incompetence. But since the actions of the public health official and the executive could have prevented the harm, their actions are logically in the same category as those of the assistant bosun. It is an old adage that evil prevails when good people fail to act, but we rarely hold the "good" people responsible for the evil.

THEORIES ABOUT OTHER PEOPLE

An executive's social world is changing at least as fast as his or her physical world. The internationalization of manufacturing and marketing exposes executives to very different cultures and people, and they need to be tolerant of different customs, practices, and styles. More women are entering the work force. In the United States, both the African American and Latino populations are growing faster than the Anglo population, a demographic fact reflected in labor markets. Also, the United States, like many other nations, prohibits employment discrimination on the basis of religion, race, gender, age, and other types of social or personal information. This combination of factors—the increasing social diversity of the business world and the inappropriateness of using such social information in making decisions—creates many ethical hazards that executives must avoid. Incorrect theories about social groups—about women, ethnic minorities, or other nationalities—increase executives' danger markedly. In this section, we discuss how executives, like other people, are likely to harbor erroneous theories about other groups.[11]

Ethnocentrism

The characteristics of our nation, group, or culture appear to us to be normal and ordinary, while others appear foreign, strange, and curious. Implicit in this perception is the assumption that what is normal is good and what is foreign, different, and unusual is less good. This perception that "our" way is normal and preferred and that other ways are somehow inferior has been called ethnocentrism. In the ethnocentric view, the world revolves around our group, and our values and beliefs become the standard against which to judge the rest of the world.

Everyone is ethnocentric to some degree. We probably cannot escape the sense that our native tongue is "natural" while other languages are artificial, that our food is normal while others are exotic, or that our religion is the true one while others are misguided. The fact that ethnocentrism is basic and automatic also makes it dangerous. We do not have to harbor hostile views of members of other groups in order to subtly discriminate. We must merely believe that our own group is superior, a belief that is often actively and officially encouraged by the groups in question and that most of us find all too easy to maintain.

The consequences of ethnocentrism are pervasive. We may describe the same actions of "us" and "them" in words that are descriptively equivalent but evaluatively biased. We are loyal, hard-working, and proud; they are clannish, driven, and arrogant. We are fun loving; they are childish. . . .

. . . Consider the charge of pervasive racial discrimination in mortgage lending. There is evidence that a higher proportion of minority applicants than white applicants are rejected. This difference in rejection rates remains after accounting for the effects of differences in income, employment stability, credit history, and other indicators of credit worthiness. Yet mortgage bankers vigorously deny that they are harder on minority applicants than on white ones.

Much research indicates that the way ethnocentrism often works is not by denigrating "them" but by rendering special aid to "us." This has been called the "in-group favoritism" hypothesis.[12] In mortgage lending, this hypothesis suggests that the difference in approval rates for whites and minorities may not reflect the fact that qualified minority applicants are denied, but that unqualified

white applicants are given loans. This difference has important implications for banks that want to understand and correct the disparity. Establishing a review procedure for rejected minority loans would not be an advisable policy if the in-group favoritism hypothesis is correct, because there may be few, if any, qualified minorities who are rejected. Looking only at rejected minority loans would uncover no evidence of racial discrimination. To find where the discriminatory action lies, the bank needs to examine the marginally unqualified applicants. The in-group favoritism hypothesis predicts that, of this group, more white than minority applicants will be approved.

Stereotypes

In addition to the "theory" that "our" group is better than others, we often have specific beliefs about particular groups, which constitute implicit theories about people in these groups. We have stereotypes about different nationalities, sexes, racial groups, and occupations. To the extent that we rely on stereotypes rather than information about individuals, we risk making unfair, incorrect, and possibly illegal judgments. The issue here is not the extent to which stereotypes are accurate; the issue is whether people will be judged and evaluated on the basis of their individual qualities or on the basis of their group membership. The fact that women are generally smaller and weaker than men is irrelevant to the question of whether a particular woman is strong enough to perform a physically demanding job.

Like ethnocentrism, stereotypes are dangerous because we are often unaware of their influence. We tend to think that our beliefs about groups are accurate, and we can often draw on experience to support these beliefs. Experience, however, can be a misleading guide. Think about the people whom you consider to be the most effective leaders in your company. What qualities do they have that make them effective?

For a purely historical reason, there is a good chance that the people who come to mind as effective leaders are men. For that reason, many of the qualities you associate with effective leadership may be masculine. Consequently, you may find it difficult to imagine a woman who could be an effective leader.

It is instructive to review the origins of the common belief that business leaders are masculine. First, there is the fact that twenty to thirty years ago, almost all businesspeople were men. Thus successful businesspeople today—those who have been in business twenty or thirty years—are also men. If we form our impressions of what it takes to succeed by abstracting the qualities of the successful people we know, a perfectly reasonable process, our impressions will have a distinctly masculine aura. It is not that we have evidence that women do not succeed; rather, we have little evidence about women at all. If you are asked to imagine people in your company who are notorious failures, the people you conjure up would probably also be men. The stereotypical failure is probably also a man. . . .

Many decisions that executives make involve promotion, hiring, firing, or other types of personnel allocations. These decisions are stereotypical when they use considerations about the group rather than information about the person. "Women can't handle this kind of stress" is a stereotypical statement about women, not an assessment of a particular individual. Executives should be especially alert for inappropriate theories about others when the criteria for evaluation and the qualifications under discussion are vague. Ethnocentric or stereotypical theories are unlikely to have a large impact if rules state that the person with the best sales record will be promoted. The criteria and qualifications are clear and quantified. However, vague criteria such as sociability, leadership skill, or insight make evaluation susceptible to stereotyping.

One of the most effective strategies for combating ethnocentrism and stereotypes is to have explicit corporate policies that discourage them, such as adopting and publishing equal opportunity principles and constantly reminding employees that group-based judgments and comments are unacceptable. Executives must be the ethical leaders of their organizations.

THEORIES ABOUT OURSELVES

Low self-esteem is not generally associated with successful executives. Executives need confidence, intelligence, and moral strength to make difficult, possibly unpopular decisions. However, when these traits are not tempered with modesty, openness, and an accurate appraisal of talents, ethical problems can arise. In other words, if executives' theories about themselves are seriously flawed, they are courting disaster. Research has identified several ways in which peoples' theories of themselves tend to be flawed.[13] We discuss three: the illusion of superiority, self-serving fairness biases, and overconfidence.

Illusion of Superiority

People tend to view themselves positively. When this tendency becomes extreme, it can lead to illusions that, while gratifying, distort reality and bias decision making. . . .

Illusion of Favorability. This illusion is based on an unrealistically positive view of the self, in both absolute and relative terms. For instance, people highlight their positive characteristics and discount their negatives. In relative terms, they believe that they are more honest, ethical, capable, intelligent, courteous, insightful, and fair than others. People give themselves more responsibility for their successes and take less responsibility for their failures than they extend to others. People edit and filter information about themselves to maintain a positive image, just as totalitarian governments control information about themselves. . . .

[This] may also characterize peoples' attitudes about the organizations to which they belong. The result is a kind of organizational ethnocentrism. . . . [E]xecutives may feel that the damage their firms cause society is not as harmful as that created by other organizations. Such a pattern of beliefs can create a barrier to societal improvement when each organization underestimates the damages that it causes. Often, however, firms and their executives genuinely believe that they are being fair and just in their positions (and that others are biased, an illustration of the illusion of favorability).

Self-Serving Fairness Biases

Most executives want to act in a just manner and believe they are fair people. Since they are also interested in performance and success, they often face a conflict between fairness and the desired outcome. They may want a spacious office, a large share of a bonus pool, or the lion's share of the market. Furthermore, they may believe that achieving these outcomes is fair because they deserve them. Different parties, when judging a fair allocation among them, will often make different judgments about what is fair, and those judgments will usually serve the party's interest. These judgments often reflect disagreements about deservedness based on contributions to the collective effort. It is likely that if you asked each division in your organization to estimate the percentage of the company's worth that is created by the division, the sum of the estimates would greatly exceed 100 percent. (Research has . . . shown this to be true with married couples. The researchers who did the study reported that they had to ask the questions carefully because spouses would often be amazed, and then angry, about the estimates that their mates gave to questions like, "What percentage of the time do you clean up the kitchen?"[14])

One important reason for these self-serving views about fairness is that people are more aware of their contributions to collective activities than others are likely to be; they have more information about their own efforts than others have or than they have about others. Executives may recall disproportionately more instances of their division helping the corporation, of their corporation helping the community, and of their industry helping society.

Furthermore, executives, like other people, credit themselves for their efforts, whereas they are more likely to credit others only for their achievements. They also credit themselves for the temptations that they resisted but judge others strictly by their actions, not by their lack of action. An executive who is offered a substantial bonus to misrepresent the financial well-being of her firm may feel proud of her honesty when she declines, but others may either not know of the temptation or, if they do, believe that she merely followed the rules. While she may feel that the firm owes her gratitude, the firm may not share that feeling. . . .

Overconfidence

Most people are erroneously confident in their knowledge. In situations in which people are asked factual questions and then asked to judge the probability that their answers are true, the probability judgments far exceed the actual accuracy measures of the proportion of correct answers.[15] For instance, when asked, "Which city is farther north, Rome or New York?," most respondents choose New York and indicate a probability of about 90 percent that it is true. In fact, it is not true; Rome is slightly north of New York. Research has indicated that when people (including executives) respond to a large group of two-option questions for which they claim to be

75 percent certain, their answers tend to be correct only 60 percent of the time.[16] For confidence judgments of 100 percent, it is not uncommon for subjects to be correct only 85 percent of the time. Other research found that subjects who assign odds of 1,000:1 to their answers are correct only 90 to 96 percent of the time.[17] Overconfidence has been identified among members of the armed forces, executives, business students, and C.I.A. agents.[18]

The danger of overconfidence is, of course, that policies based on erroneous information may fail and harm others as well as the executive who established the policy. Overconfidence, as part of our theories about ourselves, coupled with flawed theories about the world or about other people, poses serious threats to rational and ethical decision making.

To the degree to which people are overconfident in their (conservative) risk assessments— in their beliefs about the availability of scarce resources or the character of people unlike themselves—they will fail to seek additional information to update their knowledge. One cost of overconfidence is a reluctance to learn more about a situation or problem before acting.

Even if people acknowledge the need for additional information, research has shown that their process for gaining that information may be biased to confirm prior beliefs and hypotheses.[19] . . .

. . . You need to ask questions that, if answered positively, would disconfirm your rule. This is a less comfortable mode of acquiring information, partly because it may appear that you are not confident in your belief. . . .

IMPROVING ETHICAL DECISION MAKING

. . . Sometimes executives cannot escape making decisions and judgments on subjective, intuitive bases. But they can take steps to prevent some of the biases from distorting judgment. To combat overconfidence, for instance, it is effective to say to yourself, "Stop and think of the ways in which you could be wrong." Similarly, to avoid minimizing risk, you can ask, "What are the relevant things that I don't know?" Often, a devil's advocate, who is given the role of scrutinizing a decision for false assumptions and optimistic projections, can play this role. A major difference between President Kennedy's Bay of Pigs fiasco and his skillful handling of the Cuban missile crisis was his encouragement of dissenting opinions and inclusion of people whose political orientations disagreed with his own.[20] . . .

The topic of executive ethics has been dominated by the assumption that executives are constantly faced with an explicit trade-off between ethics and profits. We argue, in contrast, that unethical behavior in organizations is more commonly affected by psychological tendencies that create undesirable behavior from both ethical and rational perspectives. Identifying and confronting these psychological tendencies will increase the success of executives and organizations.   ◆ ◆ ◆

◆ References

1. For the research on which we based this article, see: M.H. Bazerman, *Judgment in Managerial Decision Making* (New York: John Wiley, 1994); R.M. Dawes, *Rational Choice in an Uncertain World* (San Diego, California: Harcourt Brace Jovanovich, 1988); T. Gilovich, *How We Know What Isn't So* (New York: Free Press, 1991); and S. Plous, *The Psychology of Judgment and Decision Making* (New York: McGraw Hill, 1993). A forthcoming book will explore these and other topics in greater detail. See: D.M. Messick and A. Tenbrunsel, [*Codes of Conduct:*] *Behavioral Research* [*into*] *Business Ethics* (New York: Russell Sage Foundation, [1997]).

2. G. Hardin, *Filters Against Folly* (New York: Penguin, 1985).

3. R. Nader, *Unsafe at Any Speed* (New York: Grossmans Publishers, 1965).

4. M. Rothbart and M. Snyder, "Confidence in the Prediction and Postdiction of an Uncertain Outcome," *Canadian Journal of Behavioral Science* 2 (1970): 38–43.

5. B. Fischhoff, "Hindsight: Thinking Backward," *Psychology Today* 8 (1975): 71–76.

6. D. Kahneman and A. Tversky, "Prospect Theory: An Analysis of Decision under Risk," *Econometrica* 47 (1979): 263–291.

7. Bazerman (1994); and Kahneman and Tversky (1979).

8. Kahneman and Tversky (1979).

9. A.L. McGill, "Context Effects in the Judgment of Causation," *Journal of Personality and Social Psychology* 57 (1989): 189–200.

10. I. Ritov and J. Baron, "Reluctance to Vaccinate: Omission Bias and Ambiguity," *Journal of Behavioral Decision Making* 3 (1990): 263–277.

11. For further details on many of these issues, interested readers may consult: S. Worcheland and W.G. Austin, *Psychology of Intergroup Relations* (Chicago: Nelson-Hill, 1986).

12. M.B. Brewer, "In-Group Bias in the Minimal Intergroup Situation: A Cognitive-Motivational Analysis," *Psychological Bulletin* 86 (1979): 307–324.

13. For example, see: S.E. Taylor, *Positive Illusions* (New York: Basic Books, 1989).

14. M. Ross and F. Sicoly, "Egocentric Biases in Availability and Attribution," *Journal of Personality and Social Psychology* 37 (1979): 322–336.

15. S. Lichtenstein, B. Fischhoff, and L.D. Phillips, "Calibration of Probabilities," in D. Kahneman, P. Slovic, and A. Tversky, eds., *Judgment under Uncertainty: Heuristics and Biases* (Cambridge: Cambridge University Press, 1982), pp. 306–334.

16. B. Fischhoff, P. Slovic, and S. Lichtenstein, "Knowing with Certainty: The Appropriateness of Extreme Confidence," *Journal of Experimental Psychology: Human Perception and Performance* 3 (1977): 552–564.

17. Ibid.

18. R.M. Cambridge and R.C. Shreckengost, "Are You Sure? The Subjective Probability Assessment Test" (Langley, Virginia: Office of Training, Central Intelligence Agency, unpublished manuscript, 1980).

19. P.C. Wason, "On the Failure to Eliminate Hypotheses in a Conceptual Task," *Quarterly Journal of Experimental Psychology* 12 (1960): 129–140.

20. I.L. Janis, *Groupthink: Psychological Studies of Policy Decisions and Fiascoes* (Boston: Houghton Mifflin, 1982).

Linking Groupthink to Unethical Behavior in Organizations

Ronald R. Sims

One view of morality is that we are isolated individuals who make decisions independently of one another. However, evidence suggests that there are certain dynamics that lead to us doing acts that we would never do if left to make our own choices. An archetype of these dynamics is groupthink, where we effectively abdicate our own moral responsibility and go along with others. We get swept along with the crowd, especially when there is strong affiliation to the group, and we do not have the opportunity to sit back and reflect on the situation. The nature of organizations and groups also means that they can take on attitudes and behaviors while paradoxically no particular individual may be accountable for what goes on.

It has been said of the Enron fiasco that 16 key executives could not have perpetrated a $60 million fraud by themselves. Consider, when you read the article by Sims, what might have caused many of the employees to go along with actions against their best judgment and think about whether you have ever been influenced by these kinds of forces.

GROUPTHINK: A PRECURSOR TO UNETHICAL BEHAVIOR

What guides the behavior of managers and employees as they cope with ethical dilemmas? Or keeping in line with the main focus of this paper, what results in the unethical behavior of some groups in organizations? Trevino (1986) has developed a model that suggests that individuals' (and groups') standards of right and wrong are not the sole determinant of their decisions. Instead, these beliefs interact with other individual characteristics (such as locus of control) and situational forces (such as an organization's rewards and punishments and its culture). All of these factors shape individual and group decisions and behavior that results from them. Trevino's model shows how people can choose to engage in acts they consider unethical when the culture of an organization and its prevailing reward structure overwhelm personal belief systems.

As evidenced in Trevino's (1986) work, organizational culture is a key component when looking at ethical behavior. It is the contention of this paper that the literature on "groupthink" (Janis, 1972) may help explain why some organizations develop cultures in which some individuals and groups knowingly commit unethical acts, or ignore them even though they believe the activities to be wrong. The presence or absence of ethical behavior in organizational members' actions is both influenced by the prevailing culture (ethical climate) and, in turn, partially determines the culture's view of ethical issues. The organizational culture may promote the assumption of responsibility for actions taken by individuals and groups, thereby increasing the probability that both will behave in an ethical manner. Alternatively, the culture may diffuse responsibility for the consequences of unethical behavior thereby making such behavior more likely. In addition, there is the increased potential for groupthink, a precursor to organizational counternorms and unethical behavior.

According to Janis, *groupthink* is "a mode of thinking that people engage in when they are deeply involved in a cohesive in-group, when the members' striving for unanimity override their motivation to realistically appraise alternative courses of action" (Janis, 1972). During groupthink small groups develop shared illusions and related norms that interfere with critical thinking and reality testing. Bales' (1950) studies of groups whose members did not previously know one another supports Janis' concept of groupthink. For the purposes of this paper, groupthink occurs when a group places a higher priority on organizational counternorms that lead to organizational benefits, thus, encouraging and supporting unethical behavior. In addition, these counternorms are shaped and maintained by key organizational actors and the organization's reward system.

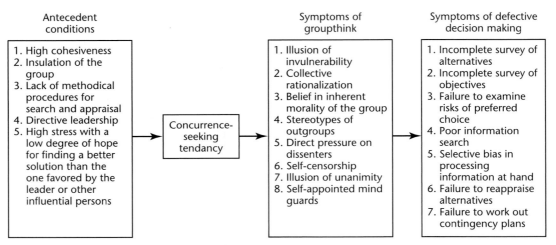

Figure 1 ◆ ANALYSIS OF GROUPTHINK, BASED ON COMPARISONS OF HIGH- AND LOW-QUALITY DECISIONS BY POLICY-MAKING GROUPS.

Source: Decision Making: A Psychological Analysis of Conflict, Choice, and Commitment by Irving L. Janis and Leon Mann. Copyright © 1977 by The Free Press.

From his analysis of good and bad decisions made by such groups, Janis argues that antecedent conditions lead to a concurrence-seeking tendency (*groupthink*) in small decision-making groups as depicted in Figure 1 (Janis and Mann, 1977).

Antecedents to groupthink are high cohesiveness and the insularity of the decision-making group, lack of methodological procedures for searching for appraising information, it may be led in a highly directive manner, and it may operate under conditions of high stress combined with low hope for finding a better solution than the one favored by the leader or other influential people. Particularly under stress, members of the group develop a number of cognitive defenses that result in a collective pattern of avoidance. These defenses include (1) misjudging relevant warnings, (2) inventing new arguments to support a chosen policy, (3) failing to explore ominous implications of ambiguous events, (4) forgetting information that would enable a challenging

event to be interpreted correctly, and (5) misperceiving signs of the onset of actual danger.

Table 1 lists the major symptoms of a group caught in groupthink (Janis, 1972). Evidence of most of these symptoms appear in the unedited transcripts of the deliberations of the people involved in the Watergate cover-up (Van Fleet, 1991) and records on discrimination violations, horizontal or vertical price-fixing, and intentional securities fraud.

The flaws in the groupthink decision-making process often result in the kinds of ethical decision-making defects and outcome variables listed in Figure 2. Groupthink occurs in organizations that knowingly commit unethical acts when the group is cohesive, a leader promotes solutions or ideas even if they are unethical, and the group has no internal rules or control mechanisms to continually prescribe ethical behavior.

Just like entering an organization, employees entering a group are provided opportunities to become schooled in and committed to the group's

TABLE 1 ◆ SYMPTOMS OF GROUPTHINK

Symptoms	Potential Hazards
Illusion of invulnerability, shared by all or most members of the group	Excessive optimism Extreme risk taking
Collective efforts to rationalize the group's course of action	Warnings are ignored
Unwillingness to reconsider assumptions	Group members recommit themselves to past policy decisions without considering alternatives
Unquestioned belief in the group's inherent morality	Members are inclined to ignore the ethical and moral consequences of their decisions
Stereotyped views of those not in the group as "colored by naivete and impractical ideals"	No attempt will be made to understand others' ethical concerns Group members may underestimate others' potential to contribute relevant information to goal accomplishment
Suppression of dissent within the group, by direct pressure on "disloyal" members Self-censorship of views that deviate from the group's apparent consensus Shared illusion of unanimity Emergence of self-appointed mindguards	Group members hesitate to express any arguments against any of the group's stereotypes, illusions, or commitments Group members falsely assume that silence means consent Group members are insulated from adverse information that might shatter their shared complacency about the effectiveness and morality of their decisions

Source: Adapted from Janis, I. J.: 1972, *Victims of Groupthink* (Boston: Houghton Mifflin, 1972)

goals, objectives, and ways of conducting business. Such commitment is the relative strength of an individual's identification with and involvement in a particular group. It usually includes the following factors that lead to the group characteristics in Figure 2: (1) group cohesiveness—a strong belief in the group's goals and values; (2) a willingness to exert considerable effort on behalf of the group; (3) a strong desire to continue as a group member; (4) excessive and almost blind loyalty to the group; (5) arrogance and overconfidence; (6) a bottom-line mentality; (7) insulation from ethical opinion and control; and (8) leader promotion of unethical solutions (that is, any behaviors that ensure that the group wins). This kind of commitment to the group then is not simply loyalty to a group. Rather, it is an ongoing process through which group members express their concern for the group and its continued success and well-being even to the extent of committing unethical actions.

A major factor contributing to the groups' defective decision making is that for each member of the cohesive group one particular incentive looms large: the approval or disapproval of his or her fellow group members and their leader. Notice in Figure 2 the six defects in the decision making of groups affected by groupthink. The group is likely to perceive few ethical alternatives and to ignore potential problems with the preferred alternative. The group may reject any opinion that does not support the preferred alternative, and it is unlikely to reconsider an alternative previously dismissed by the group, even in light of new evidence. Decisions made through such a process are not always unethical, but there is a higher probability of the occurrence of unethical behavior.

Groupthink can occur in decision making within almost any organization, as may have been the case at Beech-Nut, E. F. Hutton, and more recently at Salomon Brothers. The experiences provide examples of how even the most reputable of companies can suffer from an ethical breakdown through groupthink and subsequent poor judgment.

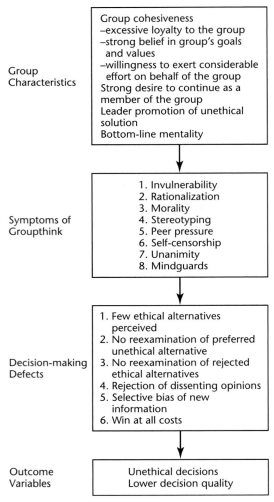

Group Characteristics

Group cohesiveness
–excessive loyalty to the group
–strong belief in group's goals and values
–willingness to exert considerable effort on behalf of the group
Strong desire to continue as a member of the group
Leader promotion of unethical solution
Bottom-line mentality

Symptoms of Groupthink

1. Invulnerability
2. Rationalization
3. Morality
4. Stereotyping
5. Peer pressure
6. Self-censorship
7. Unanimity
8. Mindguards

Decision-making Defects

1. Few ethical alternatives perceived
2. No reexamination of preferred unethical alternative
3. No reexamination of rejected ethical alternatives
4. Rejection of dissenting opinions
5. Selective bias of new information
6. Win at all costs

Outcome Variables

Unethical decisions
Lower decision quality

Figure 2 ◆ GROUPTHINK AND UNETHICAL DECISION-MAKING PROCESS

Source: Adapted from Gregory Moorhead, "Groupthink: Hypothesis in Need of Testing," Group & Organization Studies, Vol. 7, No. 4 (December 1982), pp. 429–444.

Beech-Nut. The admission by Beech-Nut, the second largest baby-food producer in the United States, that it sold millions of jars of "phony" apple juice shocked many company employees as well as industry executives. Since 1891, purity, high quality, and natural ingredients had served as the foundation of its corporate culture and had

been a consistent marketing theme. What had caused Beech-Nut to stray from its heritage and reputation?

The answer to this question is complex. However, underlying the company's ethical failure were strong financial pressures. Beech-Nut was losing money and the use of the cheap, adulterated concentrate saved millions of dollars. Beech-Nut employees seemed to use two arguments to justify their actions: (1) They believed that many other companies were selling fake juice, and (2) they were convinced that their adulterated juice was perfectly safe to consume. In addition, some employees took refuge in the fact that no conclusive test existed to determine natural from artificial ingredients. Although with regard to this latter point, Beech-Nut seems to have shifted the burden of proof around. Other juicemakers have been known to cut off suppliers if the supplier cannot demonstrate that their product is genuine. At Beech-Nut, senior management apparently told R&D that *they* would have to prove that an inexpensive supplier's product was adulterated before the company would switch to another supplier. Beech-Nut compounded their problems when government investigations began by "stonewalling" rather than cooperating, apparently in order to gain time to unload a $3.5 million inventory of tainted apple juice products. Thus while at first Beech-Nut appears to have been the innocent victim of unscrupulous suppliers, the company by its later actions changed a civil matter into criminal charges (Welles, 1988).

Strong pressures also characterize the process surrounding the unethical decision of E. F. Hutton's "check kiting."

E. F. Hutton. In 1985 the E. F. Hutton Group Inc., one of the nation's largest brokerage firms, pleaded guilty to two thousand counts of wire and mail fraud, paid a fine of almost $3 million, and put over $9 million into funds to pay back defrauded banks and investors. The court case focused the nation's attention on banks' overdraft policies, but it also provided an example of how groupthink can cause trouble for even the mightiest institutions.

Hutton's crime involved a form of "check kiting." A money manager at a Hutton branch office would write a check on an account in bank A for more money than Hutton had in that account. Because of the time lag in the check-collection system, these overdrafts sometimes went undetected, and Hutton could deposit funds to cover the overdraft in bank A's account on the following day. Even if the bank noticed the overdraft, it was unlikely to complain, because Hutton was such an important customer and because certain kinds of overdrafts are fairly routine.

In any case, the Hutton manager would deposit the check from bank A into an account in bank B, where the money would start earning interest immediately. In effect, the scheme allowed Hutton to earn a day's interest on bank A's account without having to pay anything for it. A day's interest may not sound like much, but Hutton was getting as much as $250 million in free loans every day, and a day's interest on such a sum is substantial (Goleman, 1988; *ASA Banking Journal*, 1987; Seneker, 1986).

More recently, wrongdoings by Salomon Brothers in the Treasury auction scandal provides another example of how groupthink can be linked to unethical behavior.

*Salomon Brothers. A Chronology:
How It All Unfolded*

Dec. 1990—Salomon submits bids in the names of customers who hadn't authorized them at an $8.57 billion auction of four-year notes. The bids enable the firm to buy 46% of the securities, breaching Treasury rules that bar individual bidders from buying more than 35% at any single sale.

Feb. 1991—Through unauthorized customer bids, Salomon buys 57% of securities sold at an auction of $9.04 billion of five-year Treasury notes.

Feb.—As a "practical joke" against a Salomon employee, a managing director persuades an unidentified customer to submit a bogus bid for $1 billion at the $11.01 billion auction of 30-year Treasury bonds. The plan goes awry, and the bid is actually submitted.

April—In a $9.06 billion auction of five-year notes, Salomon exceeds the bidding limit with a 35% bid for its own account, in addition to a $2.5 billion bid for a customer and the repurchase of $600 million of that bid at the auction price.

Late April—Paul Mozer, managing director in charge of government bond trading, informs Salomon Chairman John Gutfreund, President Thomas Strauss and Vice Chairman John Meriwether about the illegal bidding in February. No immediate action is taken.

May 22—In the Treasury's $12.26 billion auction of two-year notes, Salomon effectively buys at least 44% of the issue. The firm bids $2 billion for a customer and repurchases $500 million from the customer at the auction price, in addition to "inadvertently" failing to disclose its own position of $497 million. Government investigators allege that Salomon may have controlled as much as 85% of the issue. Dealers charge that Salomon forced up prices to squeeze its competitors.

June—SEC and Justice Department issue subpoenas to Salomon and certain clients.

July—Salomon reviews its government bond operations and launches "full" investigation.

Aug. 9—Salomon first discloses that it violated bidding rules in December, February and May and suspends Mr. Mozer, his top aide, Thomas Murphy, trader Christopher Fitzmaurice and clerk Henry Epstein.

Aug. 14—Salomon discloses that Messrs. Gutfreund, Strauss and Meriwether knew of the violations in April and releases details of additional violations.

Aug. 16—Messrs. Gutfreund and Strauss announce that they will resign at Aug. 18 board meeting. Warren E. Buffet is named interim chairman.

Aug. 18— The Treasury Department bars Salomon from participating in government securities auctions for customers' accounts, but allows the firm to continue bidding for its own accounts. Deryck C. Maughan, former head of Salomon's Tokyo operations, is named chief operating officer in charge of day-to-day operations. Salomon board accepts resignations of Messrs. Gutfreund, Strauss and Meriwether and fires Messrs. Moser and Murphy (Siconolfi and Cohen, p. A4).

Mr. Gutfreund, a one-time bond trader, kept this tough-guy image to the end. After formally offering to resign, Mr. Gutfreund told top executives at a closed door meeting: "I'm not apologizing for anything to anybody. Apologies don't mean (expletive). What happened, happened." (Siconolfi and Cohen, 1991, p. A4) The same arrogance that enabled Mr. Gutfreund to build Salomon into the dominant force in the $2.3 trillion Treasury securities market also led to his becoming ensnared in a government trap that became his and other key company executives undoing.

Collusion and price fixing in the $2.3 trillion Treasury securities market have been routine for more than a decade, according to traders and top Wall Street executives (Siconolfi, *et al.*, 1991). The most prevalent and potential damaging practice has been the sharing of confidential information among an elite group of bond dealers about their bids at auctions of Treasury securities. Current and former traders at several prominent Wall Street investment banks say they regularly have shared secrets about the size and price of their bids at these multibillion-dollar government auctions.

Mr. Buffet, the interim chairman, conceded that Salomon's freewheeling, aggressive style probably contributed to its current difficulties. He said that style would be toned down. "There were aspects of the culture that could have contributed to that," Mr. Buffet said. "(It is) what some might call macho, some might call cavalier."

Everyone knows that selling jars of "phony" apple juice is unethical. In addition, everyone who has a checking account knows that bouncing checks is wrong, and you do not have to be a financial wizard to know that writing bad checks is illegal. And finally, everyone now knows that illegal bidding in Treasury auctions is wrong. So how could some of the country's most sophisticated executives and money managers become involved in such unethical behavior? The answer in all likelihood may well be groupthink. That is groupthink that may be fostered by what Wolfe (1988) refers to as the *bottom-line mentality*. This line of thinking supports financial success as the only value to be considered. It promotes short-term solutions that are immediately financially sound, despite the fact that they cause problems for others within the organization or the organization as a whole. It promotes an unrealistic belief in some organizational groups that everything boils down to a monetary game. As a result, such rules on ethical conduct are merely barriers, impediments along the way to bottom-line financial success.

Beech-Nut's employees were under a lot of financial pressures and instead of cooperating with government investigators they compounded their problems by "stonewalling" rather than cooperating. Hutton's employees were under a lot of pressure to make money, and the company no doubt paid more attention to profit figures than to how those figures were achieved. The practice may even have started accidentally, but once it got going, the money managers apparently wrote unnecessary checks solely to profit from the check-kiting scheme as the money passed from bank to bank.

Company employees evidently had the necessary company loyalty and commitment to enable groupthink to come into play. Most important, once it became clear that high-level executives were not going to stop the scheme, employees became very good at ignoring any information that might lead them to conclude that the practice was illegal. An internal Hutton memo recommended that "if an office is overdrafting their ledger balance consistently, it is probably best not to request an account analysis" (Goleman, 1985). Executives at Salomon showed group characteristics found in groupthink experiences; for example, they exhibited excessive or blind loyalty, a bottom-line mentality, arrogance and overconfidence, and a promotion of unethical solutions by its leaders. In addition, like Beech-Nut and E. F. Hutton, Salomon Brothers also showed clear symptoms of groupthink, decision-making defects, and outcome variables depicted in Figure 2. In each organization individuals were willing to take the approach of, "let's all close our eyes to this problem."

In a sense, individuals and groups in Beech-Nut, E. F. Hutton, and Salomon Brothers committed unethical acts because of an overabundance of characteristics that didn't allow them to operate ethically in a large, freewheeling organization. The values of organization members in all three organizations were important. That is, groupthink and the ensuing unethical behavior may have been precipitated by arrogance. Arrogance is the illegitimate child of confidence and pride found in groups experiencing groupthink. Arrogance is the idea that not only can you never make a mistake, but no one else can ever be right.

In Beech-Nut, E. F. Hutton, and Salomon Brothers this arrogance was an insurmountable roadblock to ethical behavior. The flipside of arrogance is the ability to shine, to star, while working within the limits of ethical policies and guidelines. Another reason why groupthink may have occurred in these organizations is that they lacked the value of ethical commitment. That is,

a willingness to commit to a goal that's bigger than they are—to keep acting ethically, even when there is a threat of failure, until they finally come up with ethical business decisions.

A third reason for the unethical acts committed by Beech-Nut, E. F. Hutton, and Salomon Brothers has to do with another human value—loyalty. It's something valued in all organizations. No one wants to work with anyone who has no concern for anyone or anything else. Loyalty counts in organizations; however, it should not be an unwillingness to question the unethical behavior of a group or organization. Groupthink occurs when arrogance, overcommitment and loyalty help a group to shine above the ethical interests of an organization.

When groupthink occurs, organizations like Beech-Nut, E. F. Hutton, and Salomon Brothers are more likely to strive for unanimity, ignore the voices of dissenters and conscience, and make decisions which result in unethical behavior. But by ignoring voices of caution and conscience and working with a bottom-line mentality for short-term profit, all three companies' managers ended up severely damaging their company's reputation. To decrease the likelihood of unethical behavior, organizations must do a better job of promoting positive and ethical cultures, and reduce the probability of groupthink by programming conflict into decisions.

PROGRAMMING CONFLICT THROUGH DEVIL'S ADVOCATE AND DIALECTIC METHODS

Programmed conflict through the devil's advocate and dialectic methods can raise different opinions regardless of the personal feelings of the managers (Cosier and Schwenk, 1990) or members of groups into decisions. The usefulness of the devil's advocate technique was illustrated by Janis when discussing famous fiascos such as Watergate and Vietnam. Janis recommends that everyone in the group assume the role of a devil's advocate and present a critique of the proposed course of action. This avoids the tendency of agreement interfering with problem solving while still serving as a precaution for the occurrence of unethical behavior. Potential unethical behaviors are identified and considered before the decision is final.

The conflict generated by the devil's advocate may cause groups to avoid false assumptions and closely adhere to guidelines for ethical analysis in decisions. The devil's advocate raises questions that force an in-depth review of the group's decision making process. The devil's advocate is assigned to identify potential pitfalls or unethical behavior with a proposed course of action. A formal presentation to the key decision makers by the devil's advocate raises potential concerns. Evidence needed to address the critique is gathered and the final decision is made and ensuing behavior monitored. The devil's advocate decision program (Cosier and Schwenk, 1990) is summarized in Figure 3.

Cosier and Schwenk (1990) suggest that it is a good idea to rotate people assigned to devil's advocate roles. This avoids any one person or group being identified as the critic on all group decisions. The devil's advocate role can assist organizations like Beech-Nut, E. F. Hutton, and Salomon Brothers avoid costly mistakes by hearing viewpoints that identify pitfalls instead of foster agreement.

While the devil's advocate technique lacks what Cosier and Schwenk (1990) call an "argument" between advocates of two conflicting positions, the dialectic method can program conflict into a group's decisions while offsetting potentially unethical behavior. The dialectic method calls for structuring a debate between

1. A proposed course of action is generated.

2. A devil's advocate (individual or group) is assigned to criticize the proposal.

3. The critique is presented to key decision makers.

4. Any additional information relevant to the issues is gathered.

5. The decision to adopt, modify, or discontinue the proposed course of action is taken.

6. The decision is monitored.

Figure 3 ◆ A DEVIL'S ADVOCATE DECISION PROGRAM

Source: Cosier, R. A. and Schwenk, C. R.: 1990, 'Agreement and Thinking Alike: Ingredients for Poor Decisions', *Academy of Management Executive* 4(1), pp. 69–74.

conflicting views regardless of members' personal feelings. The benefits of the dialectic method are in the presentation and debate of the assumptions underlying proposed courses of action. False or misleading assumptions become apparent and can head off unethical decisions that are based on these poor assumptions. The dialectic method shown in Figure 4 can help promote ethical decisions and counteract groupthink.

Programming conflict into the group decision-making process allows dissent and can decrease the likelihood of groupthink and unethical behavior. Such conflict requires organizations to ensure that decisions are challenged, criticized, and alternative ideas are generated. Programmed conflict also insures that a comprehensive decision framework becomes a part of the group decision-making process.

1. A proposed course of action is generated.

2. Assumptions underlying the proposal are identified.

3. A conflicting counterproposal is generated based on different assumptions.

4. Advocates of each position present and debate the merits of their proposals before key decision makers.

5. The decision to adopt either position, or some other position, e.g., a compromise, is taken.

6. The decision is monitored.

Figure 4 ◆ THE DIALECTIC DECISION METHOD

Source: Cosier, R. A. and Schwenk, C. R.: 1990, 'Agreement and Thinking Alike: Ingredients for Poor Decisions', *Academy of Management Executive* 4(1), pp. 69–74.

CONCLUSION

It has not been the intent of this article to suggest that groupthink is an easy phenomenon to overcome, especially since there is some evidence that the symptoms of groupthink presented in this paper thrive in the sort of climate outlined in the following critique of corporate directors in the United States (Baum, 1986):

> Many directors simply don't rock the boat. "No one likes to be the skunk at the garden party," says (management consultant) Victor Palmieri. . . . "One does not make friends and influence people in the boardroom or elsewhere by raising hard questions that create embarrassment or discomfort for management (p. 60).

In short, policy- and decision-making groups can become so cohesive that strong-willed executives are able to gain unanimous support for poor decisions. Still, organizations committed to ethical

behavior in their organizations must work toward the reduction and prevention of groupthink. However, they must first understand what is meant by groupthink and that there is, indeed, a link between groupthink and unethical behavior. Specifically, the ultimate result of groupthink is that group members become isolated from the world around them. They read positive signs as a reaffirmation of their goals and intentions; they read negative signs as an indication that there are individuals who do not understand what they are doing and that these individuals should be ignored (and perhaps even punished). During this entire process, it is common to find the group changing to a belief that its ideals are humanitarian and based on high-minded principles. As a result, no attempt is made by the members to challenge or question the ethics of the group's behavior. A second common observation is high *esprit de corps* and amiability among the members. This often leads them to believe that those who question their approach or intentions are acting irrationally.

Quite often groupthink is only recognized after a group has made a disastrous decision. When this occurs, the members are apt to ask, "How could we have been so blind? Why didn't anyone call attention to our errors?" Unfortunately, at the time the group was making its decision(s), it is unlikely that any criticism or questioning of its actions would have been given serious consideration. Laboratory studies using college students as subjects validate portions of Janis's groupthink concept. Specifically, it has been found that:

◆ Groups with a moderate amount of cohesiveness produce better decisions than low- or high-cohesive groups.
◆ Highly cohesive groups victimized by groupthink make the poorest decisions, despite high confidence in those decisions (Callaway and Esser, 1984; Leana, 1985).

How can organizations like Beech-Nut, E. F. Hutton, and Salomon Brothers overcome or deal with groupthink effectively? Hodgetts suggests a number of useful rules that can be employed:

> First, the organization and its managers must encourage open airing of objections and doubts. Second, one or more outsiders should be invited into the group to challenge the views of its members. Finally, after reaching a preliminary decision, the group should hold a "second chance" meeting at which every member expresses, as vividly as possible, all his or her doubts and the group thinks through the entire issue again before making a final decision (p. 1, 3, 4).

Janis (1972) offers the following prescriptions for helping managers reduce the probability of groupthink:

A. *Leader Prescriptions*
  1. Assign everyone the role of critical evaluation.
  2. Be impartial, do not state preferences.
  3. Assign the devil's advocate role to at least one group member.
  4. Use outside experts to challenge the group.
B. *Organizational Prescriptions*
  1. Do not automatically opt for a "strong" culture. Explore methods to provide for diversity and dissent, such as grievance or complaint mechanisms or other internal review procedures.
  2. Set up several independent groups to study the same issue.
  3. Train all employees in ethics (these programs should explain the underlying ethical, legal (Drake and Drake, 1988), groupthink-prevention techniques, and devil's advocate and dialectic methods.
  4. Establish programs to clarify and communicate values.
C. *Individual Prescriptions*
  1. Be a critical thinker.
  2. Discuss the group's deliberations with a trusted outsider and report back to the group.
D. *Process Prescriptions*
  1. Periodically break the group into subgroups to discuss the issues.
  2. Take time to study external factors.
  3. Hold second-chance meetings to rethink issues before making a commitment.
  4. Periodically rotate new members into groups and old members out.

Note that all the suggestions encourage group members to evaluate alternatives critically and discourage the single-minded pursuit of unanimity, which is a key component of groupthink. By making use of the above prescriptions organizations can give employees the confidence to be on the lookout for groupthink and act with the understanding that what they are doing is considered correct and will be supported by top management and the entire organization.

[Maier and Maier (1973) suggest] that organizations should realize that the actions of leaders in groups often can "make or break" the decisions made in that group. Therefore, organizations should ensure that group leaders are trained to develop the following skills:

1. Learn to state the problem or issue the group is dealing with in a nondefensive, objective manner.
2. Supply essential facts and clarify any constraints on solutions.
3. Draw out all group members. Prevent domination by one person and protect members from being attacked or severely criticized.
4. Wait out pauses. Don't make suggestions and/or ask leading questions.
5. Ask stimulating questions that move the discussion forward.
6. Summarize and clarify at several points to mark progress.

Notice that these skills are not vague attitudes, but specific behaviors. Thus, they are subject to training and practice. There is good evidence that this quality training can be accomplished through role-playing, and that it can help counteract groupthink.

Organizations must also ensure that they do not support financial success as the only value to be considered. Such an attitude will not promote a bottom-line mentality and an unrealistic belief that everything boils down to a monetary game. By not emphasizing short-term revenues above long-term consequences, organizations will create a climate in which individuals and groups understand that unethical behavior is unacceptable. In addition, organizations must be willing to take a stand when there is a financial cost to any group's decision. This stand will discourage ethical shortcuts by its members.

In order for values to provide the ethical "rules of the road" employees organizations must ensure that they are stated, shared, and understood by everyone in an organization. Formal programs to clarify and communicate important ethical values can help accomplish this objective in organizations and counteract groupthink. In addition, organizations should pay proper attention to employee recruitment, selection, and orientation.

The values of prospective employees should be examined and discussed, and the results used in making selection decisions. A person's first encounters with an organization and its members also "say" a lot about key beliefs and values. Every attempt should be made to teach them "the ethical way we do things here." Organizations also should develop appropriate training and development opportunities to establish and maintain skills in programmed conflict methods. In addition, values can and should be emphasized along with other important individual attributes.

Finally, organizations can make use of progressive rewards to encourage ethical behavior by individuals and groups. Rewards in the form of monetary compensation, employee benefits, and special recognition can reinforce individual values, counteract groupthink, and maintain enthusiasm in support of ethical organizational values. Organizations can find creative ways to reward employees for displaying ethical values that are considered essential to organizational success.

In conclusion, organizations can take a number of steps to reduce the probability of groupthink. They can develop strong norms of critical appraisal. Group leaders can abstain from pushing their own views and using their influence, and instead encourage genuine debate. Groups can attempt to avoid isolation by involving more than one group in the decision-making process. Finally, an important key to counteract groupthink is to program conflict into the decision-making situation (Cosier and Schwenk, 1990; Janis, 1989). The specific impacts of groupthink on the behavior of employees covered in this paper are illustrative rather than exhaustive. The paper has simply tried to familiarize the reader with some of the important ones and with the related issues. Remember, ethical behavior foundations are first established when an organization commits itself to success that results from ethical behavior by its members. ◆ ◆ ◆

◆ References

ASA *Banking Journal*: 1987, 'A Violation of Business Ethics or Outright Fraud?' (July), 30–34.

Bales, R.: 1950, *Interaction Process Analysis* (Addison-Wesley, Reading, Mass.).

Baum, L.: 1986, 'The Job Nobody Wants', *BusinessWeek* (September 8), p. 60.

Callaway, M. R. and J. K. Esser: 1984, 'Groupthink: Effects of Cohesiveness and Problem-Solving

Procedures on Group Decision Making', *Social Behavior and Personality* **12**(2), 157–164.

Cosier, R. A. and C. R. Schwenk: 1990, 'Agreement and Thinking Alike: Ingredients for Poor Decisions', *Academy of Management Executive* 4(1), 69–74.

Drake, B. H. and E. Drake: 1988, 'Ethical and Legal Aspects of Managing Corporate Cultures', *California Management Review* (Winter), 120–121.

Goleman, D.: 1985, 'Following the Leader', *Science* (October), **85**, 18.

Hodgetts, R. M.: 1990, *Modern Human Relations At Work* (4th ed.) (Dryden Press, Hinsdale, IL).

Janis, I. L.: 1972, *Victims of Groupthink* (Houghton Mifflin, Boston).

Janis, I. L.: 1989, *Crucial Decisions: Leadership in Policy Making and Crisis Management* (Free Press, New York).

Janis, I. L. and L. Mann: 1977, *Decision Making: A Psychological Analysis of Conflict, Choice, and Commitment* (Free Press, New York).

Leana, C. R.: 1985, 'A Partial Test of Janis's Groupthink Model: Effects of Group Cohesiveness and Leader Behavior on Defective Decision Making', *Journal of Management* (Spring), 5–17.

Maier, R. and B. Maier: 1973, *Comparative Psychology* (Brooks/Cole, Monterey, CA).

Moorehead, G.: 1982, 'Groupthink: Hypothesis in Need of Testing', *Group and Organization Studies* (December), 434.

Seneker, H.: 1986, 'Nice Timing', *Forbes* (January 27), 102.

Siconolfi, M. and L. P. Cohen: 1991, 'Sullied Solly: How Salomon's Hubris and a U.S. Trap Led to Leaders' Downfall', *Wall Street Journal* (August 19), A1, A4.

Siconolfi, M., M. R. Sesit and C. Mitchell: 1991, 'Collusion, Price Fixing Have Long Been Rife in Treasury Market', *Wall Street Journal* (August 19), A1.

Trevino, L. K.: 1986, 'Ethical Decision Making in Organizations: A Person-Situation Interactionist Model', *Academy of Management Review* **11**(3), 601–17.

Van Fleet, D. D.: 1991, *Behavior in Organizations* (Houghton Mifflin, Dallas).

Welles, C.: 1988, 'What Led Beech-Nut Down the Road to Disgrace', *BusinessWeek* (February 22), 124–128.

Wolfe, D.: 1988, 'Is There Integrity in the Bottomline: Managing Obstacles to Executive Integrity', in S. Srivastva (ed.), *Executive Integrity: The Search for High Human Values in Organization Life* (Jossey-Bass, San Francisco), pp. 140–171.

Moral Mazes

Bureaucracy and Managerial Work

Robert Jackall

Jackall, a sociologist, studied organizations to see how institutional structure influenced moral consciousness. He describes the moral rules-in-use by which managers guide their behavior at work. He explicitly avoids normative ethics (such as, What should we do?) and just reports his observations.

In this extract, Jackall discusses the effect of the promotion of teamwork. He notes the pervasive sports metaphors and the characteristics they encourage. Jackall concludes that succeeding in the organization means curbing one's impulses and repackaging one's image.

Although Jackall does not make judgment on what we should do, it is clear from this reading that if people act in the way he describes there will be moral implications. His managers appear as moral chameleons, who are ready to adjust both their thinking and appearance and do whatever is needed in order to be successful players in the organization. This suggests that the organization (or ambitious individuals in the organization) will exert a tremendous influence on managers to be morally pliant. Thus, consequences such as moral abdication (through rationalized excuses) or groupthink ought not to surprise us. The question becomes how much we blame people for what they do within the organizational bureaucracy: Are they off the hook because they are subject to external influences or because they are just playing the game?

It is . . . crucial to be perceived as a team player. This multifaceted notion has its metaphorical basis in team sports, principally football, a game that parallels managerial work in its specialization, segmentation, strategy, hierarchy, and the possibility of sudden bursts of spectacular individual effort made possible by the group. Of all major sports, football resonates most deeply with managers' preferred image of what they do and lends a myriad of phrases to managerial argot. For instance:

Football Phrases	*Metaphorical Meaning for Managers*
Players	Anyone who has a stake in and is therefore involved in a decision
Carrying the ball	Responsible for an assignment
Taking the ball and running with it	Showing initiative and drive
Fumbling the ball	Messing up in an assignment
Passing the ball	Getting rid of a responsibility
Punt	Employ a defensive strategy while waiting for things to sort out
Sidelined	Getting taken out of the game; benched
Run the clock down	Wear out an opponent by stalling
Huddle	A quick meeting
Reverse or Reversing fields	Changing one's story or public rationale for an action; changing strategies
Going over the top	Achieving one's commitments
Running interference or Blocking	A patron using personal influence to knock down opposition to a client's ideas or plans
Broken field run	A virtuoso individual performance
Getting blindsided	Being unexpectedly undercut by another in public
Quarterback	The boss

Cooperative teamwork can, of course, produce enormous accomplishments and every corporation that I have studied has stories of great victories achieved through team play, all cast into dramatic form. Alchemy managers recall both staff and line personnel working side by side to contain the damage done by an accidental explosion at a plant; managers in the Consumer Division of Weft Corporation remember how they frantically turned their whole cloth finishing operation around to get the jump on competitors in producing a printed fabric suddenly desirable to New York designers; and managers and workers alike in a now defunct book publishing firm recall fondly how the entire company was mobilized for the herculean task of producing one million copies of the Warren Commission report in three days. Managers often point, too, to the coordination and cooperation achieved through team play in the space program, sentiments voiced before the string of Challenger disasters. These images of the possibilities of cooperative effort, of coordinating people and resources to meet a crisis or great challenge, seem to legitimate for managers their actual day-to-day experiences with the ethos of team play.

The main dimensions of team play are as follows.

1. One must appear to be interchangeable with other managers near one's level. Corporations discourage narrow specialization more strongly as one goes higher. They also discourage the expression of moral or political qualms. One might object, for example, to working with chemicals used in nuclear power, or working on weapons systems, and most corporations today would honor such objections. Publicly stating them, however, would end any realistic aspirations for higher posts because one's usefulness to the organization depends on versatility. As one manager in Alchemy Inc. comments: "Well,

we'd go along with his request but we'd always wonder about the guy. And in the back of our minds, we'd be thinking that he'll soon object to working in the soda ash division because he doesn't like glass." Strong convictions of any sort are suspect. One manager says:

> If you meet a guy who hates red-haired persons, well, you're going to wonder about whether that person has other weird perceptions as well. You've got to have a degree of interchangeability in business. To me, a person can have any beliefs they want, as long as they leave them at home.

Similarly, one's spouse's public viewpoints or activities could reduce others' perceptions of a manager's versatility or indeed ability. In reference to another manager whose wife was known to be active in environmental action groups, lobbying in fact for legislation on chemical waste disposal, one Alchemy manager says: "If a guy can't even manage his own wife, how can he be expected to manage other people?" Interchangeability means then not just generalized skills but a flexibility of perspective that will permit rapid adjustment to internal and external exigencies.

2. Another important meaning of team play is putting in long hours at the office. The norms here are set, of course, by higher-ups and vary from corporation to corporation. The story is told in Covenant Corporation about how the CEO was distressed, upon first taking power, to find no one at work when he reached corporate headquarters at his accustomed hour of 6:30 A.M. He remedied the loneliness of the situation by leaving notes on the desks of all his top executives saying, "Call me when you get in." Since he usually stays in the office well into the evening, he had effectively lengthened the work day for everyone by several hours. Higher level managers in all the corporations I studied commonly spend twelve to fourteen hours a day at the office. This requires a great deal of sheer physical

energy and stamina, even though much of this time is spent not in actual work as such, but in social rituals—like reading and discussing articles in *The New York Times*, *The Wall Street Journal*, *Harvard Business Review*, and *Forbes*; having informal conversations; casually polling the opinions of participants in upcoming meetings; or popping in and out of other managers' offices with jokes, cartoons, or amusing or enraging journalistic articles. These kinds of readily observable rituals forge the social bonds—what might be called the professional intimacy—that make real managerial work, that is, group work of various sorts, possible. One must participate in the rituals to be considered effective in the work. Managers who do not put in the time at the office or who do not engage in the endless round of face-to-face encounters that make up daily managerial life and that provide the opportunity to prove one's trustworthiness will find themselves "sidelined" or off the team altogether. For this reason, executives do not like to take extended business trips and many break up their vacations into one-week segments rather than risk being away from the office for too long. The public reason for such attentiveness to one's duties is, of course, one's devotion to the organization. The real reason is a fear that prolonged absence from one's everyday interactional milieux will cause or tempt others to forget that one exists.

3. Team playing means being seen as an effective group member, sticking to one's assigned position. The good team player is not a prima donna. This holds true even when one is considered a rising star. For example, a top executive of Weft Corporation says:

> Who gets ahead? They are people who are good team players. Most are not prima donnas. Prima donnas are very disruptive in this company. Even if a person is a prima donna, he usually tries hard not to look like one. The success of the operating

divisions depends on the close cooperation of a number of people—in sales and merchandising and in the South. So that the person who is to really succeed here has to be a team player first and foremost.

Striking, distinctive characteristics of any sort, in fact, are dangerous in the corporate world. One of the most damaging things, for instance, that can be said about a manager is that he is brilliant. This almost invariably signals a judgment that the person has publicly asserted his intelligence and is perceived as a threat to others. What good is a wizard who makes his colleagues and his customers uncomfortable? Equally damaging is the judgment that a person cannot get along with others—he is "too pushy," that is, he exhibits too much "persistence in getting to the right answers," is "always asking why," and does not know "when to back off." Or he is "too abrasive," or "too opinionated," unable "to bend with the group." Or he is a "wildman" or a "maverick," that is, someone who is "outspoken." Or he may be too aloof, too distant, "too professional." A manager who has "ice water in his veins" or is thought to be a "cold fish" might impress others with his tough pragmatism, but he will win few alliances and in time his social standing and effectiveness will be eroded. Women, in particular, face a troublesome dilemma here. If a female executive's public face presents a warm, engaging femininity that distinguishes her from the minions of female clerical workers adopting the "corporate clone" look and practicing the new techniques of self-assertiveness, she runs the risk of being seen by her male colleagues as a "cookie" or a "fluff-head" and dismissed as inconsequential. If she, on the other hand, assumes a public severity in her demeanor, especially if she seems ambitious, she may be labeled a "calculating bitch," a difficult label to shake. Moreover, an effective group member looks to others in making decisions, recognizes that one must always think defensively to protect one's boss and one's associates, and knows that he must "keep his nose clean" and stay out of trouble because "people who have made big mistakes are very damaging to the team approach."

4. Team play also means, as one manager in the chemical company puts it, "aligning oneself with the dominant ideology of the moment" or, as another says, "bowing to whichever god currently holds sway." Such ideologies or gods may be thought of as official definitions of reality. . . . [B]ureaucracies allow their employees a diverse range of private motives for action in return for assent to common rules and official versions of reality, that is, explanations or accounts that serve or at least do not injure the organization itself. Organizations always try, of course, to mobilize employees' belief in manufactured realities; such efforts always meet with some success particularly at the middle levels among individuals who still labor under the notion that success depends on sincerity. However, the belief of insiders in abstract goals is not a prerequisite for personal success; belief in and subordination to individuals who articulate organizational goals is. One must, however, to be successful in a bureaucratic work situation, be able to act, at a moment's notice, as if official reality is the only reality. The contexts for understanding this meaning of team play are the complicated levels of conflict within corporations and the probationary state of mind endemic to managerial work. The knowledgeable practitioners of corporate politics, whether patrons or leaders of cliques and networks, value nothing more highly than at least the appearance of unanimity of opinion among their clients and allies, especially during times of turmoil. They invoke the vocabulary of team play to bring their own people into line as well as to cast suspicion on others who pose some threat to them. If one examines the way team play is defined, invoked, and experi-

enced at different levels of a hierarchy, one can see its use as an ideology. For instance, a top official at Alchemy Inc. states:

> Now I would define a team player as someone who sinks his personal ambition to the good of the company; someone who agrees to the consensus on a decision even though he might see things differently.

Another highly ranking executive in Covenant Corporation says:

> Team play means the sacrifice of one's individual feelings for the sake of the unified effort. It doesn't mean that you don't express your own views but your objective is not your own advancement. Rather you're working for the correct solution to some problem.

Some managers at the upper-middle and middle levels echo and reinforce these official sentiments. An upper-middle level manager in the chemical company says:

> Well, I strongly believe in [team play]. I've seen enough to know that you have to work together; there has to be a common understanding. Sometimes you don't like the assignment you might get but you've got to look at it like a football . . . team. The management has to assign the roles. . . . Management . . . wants a team that works well together. This means an understanding of what has to be done and having the access to the resources to do it the right way, the best way. And not having people who are going to say—I don't want to do that.

Many other managers, however, see the pronouncements of their superiors and some of their peers with a skeptical eye. An upper-middle level executive in the chemical company demonstrates the accepted rhetoric of team play:

> Team play—it's each individual on a team doing his job to the best of his ability and the combination of each person with each other leading to an

objective. It means fulfilling your assignment on a project to the best of your ability to the end that the objective is met in a timely and efficient manner. That's team play.

He goes on to discuss what he considers the real meaning of the ideology, shifting back and forth between the perspective of subordinate and boss:

> Now what it really means is going with the flow and not making waves. If you disagree with something, bowing to the majority without voicing your disagreement. You can indict a person by saying that he's not a team player. That doesn't mean he won't follow directions. It's because he voices an objection, because he argues with you before doing something, especially if he's right. That's when we really get mad—when the other guy is right. If he's wrong, we can be condescending and adopt the "you poor stupid bastard" tone. . . .

The skillful boss uses ideologies such as team play adroitly, counting on subordinates to get the message and do what he wants. The same executive continues:

> Another meaning of team play is its use as a club. You use it to push people into corners without seeming to. If I say to you, do this and you say that you don't really want to, but I insist, well, you've put the guy in an uncomfortable position and yourself too. But if you do it skillfully, the guy is not going to go away boxed. So, on the other hand, you can't force them to do something, but you also can't manipulate them to do it; people resent this. What you do is to appeal to something like teamwork and they choose to do it because they know how important and valued it is in the organization. The boss has the extra vote but he has to cast it with some skill.

A team player is a manager who does not "force his boss to go to the whip," but, rather, amiably chooses the direction his boss points out. Managers who choose otherwise or who evince stubbornness are said to "have made a decision," a phrase almost always used to describe a choice that will shorten a career.

A middle-level manager in Alchemy Inc. puts a sharp edge on the same sentiment:

> Someone who is talking about team play is out to squash dissent. It's the most effective way to tell people who have different perspectives to shut up. You say that you want a team effort. . . . You can and you have to learn to keep your mouth shut. My boss is like that. Everyone likes him because he is like that. It's hurt me because I have spoken out. It might be that someone has formed the opinion that I have interesting things to say, but more likely, it gives you a troublemaker label and that's one that is truly hard to get rid of. The troublemaker is often a creative person but truly creative people don't get ahead; to get ahead you have to be dependable and a team player. You have to be steady. . . . When I hear the word, I immediately think it's an effort to crush dissent. . . . [Bosses] say they don't want a yes man, but, in fact, most bosses don't want to hear the truth. And this is particularly true if it disagrees with what they want to do.

Younger managers learn quickly that, whatever the public protestations to the contrary, bosses generally want pliable and agreeable subordinates, especially during periods of crisis. Clique leaders want dependable, loyal allies. Those who regularly raise objections to what a boss or a clique leader really desires run the risk of being considered problems themselves and of being labeled "outspoken," or "nonconstructive," or "doomsayers," "naysayers," or "crepehangers."

Organizations vary in this respect and some tolerate, and indeed encourage, high degrees of dissent and controversy within particular work groups or within given strata of managers, that is, between peers or managers of different rank who consider themselves colleagues. Moreover, generally speaking, dissent on points of demonstrable fact is acceptable provided that one corrects others, even superiors, tactfully and does not make others look foolish in public. However, when interpretive judgments or plain desires are involved, or when an issue spills out of smaller groups into the larger political structures of an organization, or when higher authorities get involved, a new dynamic takes over. What are "frank perspectives" in a strictly collegial context can get interpreted in the political or hierarchical arenas as "downbeat negativism" or even "disloyalty." Wise and ambitious managers know that public faces of cheerful cooperativeness, which of course they generally require from their own subordinates, put superiors and important allies at ease. And, of course, the ability to put others at ease is an important skill in a world where one must be continually on guard against the eruption of usually suppressed conflict.

5. Team players display a happy, upbeat, can-do approach to their work and to the organization. A vice-president in the Metals Division of Covenant Corporation states:

> Your degree of happiness is important. If someone is always pissing and moaning then that affects your evaluation of them. . . . If you're not happy in what you do, you can generate a synergism of apathy. If everybody talks about failure, you're going to fail. Happy people are nicer to be around. It's important to be an up person. And to keep an up perspective. I mean, how do you like it when you ask a guy how things are and he says: "Well, I have a corn on my toe and I don't feel well and so on and on"? He's telling you more than you want to know. And that attitude will poison everyone around him. I always start looking for a positive result. . . . You have to feel that way. People don't want to parade in unison into a vale of doom.

A world geared toward pragmatic accomplishments places a great premium on the appearance of buoyant optimism. Looking on the bright side of things, always "try[ing] to see the glass as half full rather than half empty," is felt to be a prereq-

uisite for any action at all, let alone managerial work that involves imparting energy, enthusiasm, and direction to others, indeed a sense of social cohesiveness.

In a word, a team player is alert to the social cues that he receives from his bosses, his peers, and the intricate pattern of social networks, coteries, and cliques that crisscross the organization. Depending on the vocabulary of his company, a team player "fits in," "gets along with others," is "a good old country boy," "knows how to schmooze." He is a "role player" who plays his part without complaint. He does not threaten others by appearing brilliant, or with his personality, his ability, or his personal values. He masks his ambition and his aggressiveness with blandness. He recognizes trouble and stays clear of it. He protects his boss and his associates from blunders. When he disagrees with others, he does so tactfully, preferably in private, and then in ways that never call others' judgments into question. Even in dark times, he keeps a sunny disposition and learns always to find the bright side of bleak news. In short, he makes other managers feel *comfortable*, the crucial virtue in an uncertain world, and establishes with others the easy predictable familiarity that comes from sharing taken for granted frameworks about how the world works.

Top corporate executives are rarely described as "team players" and middle managers are rarely described as "leaders." Such terms, however, depend less on personal attributes than on social position in the organization. All but the topmost person in a hierarchical organization is a subordinate to others and must, to some extent, cultivate the virtues of team play. Otherwise he will never reach a position where subordinates come to think of him as a leader.

Moreover, to keep rising, managers must have the proper style to differentiate themselves from other managers and to push themselves into the organizational limelight. One of the top executives in the chemical company says:

> Now I'll admit that the majority of the work is done at G-13 or around that level, say G-12, G-13, and G-14. That's where the real *work* work is done. Beyond that level is more management, more planning, more promotion, more accountability oriented. There's less day-to-day work involved. Now at the G-13 or G-14 levels, the same kind of skills are needed as later on, but higher up a different set of skills become *predominant.* It's *style.* You have to remember that a firm gets very narrow after a certain point and, when you get right down to it, if you have an ability and others have the same ability, what is going to make the difference? Not intellectual ability. It's going to be *style* . . . that differentiates one person from the next.

He goes on to discuss the principal constituents of style.

> [It's] being able to talk with and interrelate with people, all kinds of people. Being able to make a good case for something. Being able to sell something. Being able to put things well; being articulate. [It's] presentation ability in particular.

Other managers emphasize the crucial importance of presentational ability. A middle-level product manager at Weft Corporation explains:

> Persons who can present themselves well, who can sell themselves the best are the kind of people who get ahead. It's an image type thing. Not just doing the job right but being able to capitalize on it in certain ways. Some people are gifted at doing that. They handle themselves very well. They may not be take-charge people but they give you the impression that they are. They dress properly and dress is very important. And how they handle themselves at a meeting is extremely important. This is especially true at pressure-cooker-type meetings which is what divisional meetings are. People get up and review their numbers. It's a stagelike atmosphere. People have to justify their numbers. And everybody knows why things fall

apart sometimes, but some people are able to explain things better and highlight the good points in ways that impress other people. It's having a certain grace, charm, adroitness, and humor. . . . I think what's important is to portray yourself as very decisive, as being able to think on your feet. There are some people who will go after you and the important thing is not to get flustered. Most people work at this self-presentation. They rehearse their slides before they have to give a talk. . . . Or they'll rehearse their speech again and again and stay up going over the numbers.

A general manager at Alchemy emphasizes the importance of seeming to be in command:

> [Style] is being able to talk easily and make presentations. To become credible easily and quickly. You can advance quickly even without technical experience if you have style. You get a lot of points for style. You've got to be able to articulate problems, plans, and strategies without seeming to have to refer to all sorts of memos and so on. The key in public performances and presentations is in knowing how to talk forcefully without referring to notes and memoranda. To be able to map out plans quickly and surely.

An upper-middle executive in the chemical company points out how certain occupational specialties in management offer more opportunities than others to make presentations. The ability to seize these chances, using the requisite skills, can propel a manager's career in a hurry:

> Sales people and business people [are] constantly being exposed to management, making presentations to the Operating Committee. If they are articulate, well-dressed, articulate their program well, they make an indelible impression. I've seen many guys who on the basis of *one presentation* have been promoted beyond their abilities. And if they're telling the top guys good news in the bargain, well, that just helps them. I'm always astonished by this emphasis on appearances. I mean . . . *if they like the way you look*, you have a good

chance to impress them. . . . When the top guys see a guy and say: "Hey, he's great," the myth about the guy is perpetuated. If they say to a plant manager that some guy is great, the plant manager is not going to say that he can't find his ass in a rainstorm. And suddenly the guy is on the fast track.

Having the right style also means mirroring the kind of image that top bosses have of themselves, "mak[ing] the people most responsible for [one's] fate *comfortable.*" Without such a clear meshing of styles, and this is a central meaning of the notion of comfort, managers have little chance of being taken into the higher circles of an organization. A top Alchemy executive states:

> When you get to the very top—and this is an observable thing—your style cannot be in conflict with the style of the guys on top. If there is a conflict, you're not going to last very long.

The style that most large corporations want their up-and-coming managers to project both within the organization and in other public arenas is that of "the young, professional, conservative person" who "knows what is going on in the world" and who is "broad as a person" with interests that transcend the work milieu. When top corporate circles mesh with high intellectual, artistic, political, and civic social circles of metropolitan areas—this is particularly true of Weft Corporation and Images Inc.—breadth, here measured by social poise and conversational ability, becomes crucial. A top official of Weft explains:

> We want someone with breadth, with some interests outside the business, someone who is broad as a person. And this can be in anything—the arts, sports, or both, in local politics, in Toastmasters, in Little League, in the eleemosynary organizations. Why? Because they're bigger people and they can do the job better in the long run if they have bigger interests, broader interests. We'd like to think that they represent [Weft Corporation]

well when they're in public—that when someone asks them what they do and they say that they work for [Weft Corporation] the person has a good impression of the company through them. And you can sense what kind of people will create that kind of impression.

In short, managers with the right style possess a subtle, almost indefinable sophistication and polish, essentially a *savoir faire,* marked especially by an urbane, witty, graceful, engaging, and friendly demeanor. They are men and women of discriminating taste, of ostensibly balanced judgment, marked with an open-minded tolerance towards others' foibles and idiosyncrasies, at least in public, and with an ability to direct social interaction and conversation into well-grooved and accepted channels. They are able to frame issues with a graceful flair, subtly but forcefully dramatizing themselves in the process. Finally, men and women with the right style know how to assess and adjust themselves with poised ease and an air of quiet decisiveness to the nuances, exigencies, and shifting moralities of social situations.

Some observers have interpreted such conformity, team playing, continual affability, and emphasis on social finesse as evidence of the decline of the individualism of the old Protestant ethic.[1] To the extent that commentators take the public faces that managers wear at face value, and I include here the predictable trappings of upper-middle-class affluence that mark managers' lifestyles, these writers miss the main point. Managers up and down the corporate ladder adopt their public faces quite consciously; they are, in fact, the masks behind which the real struggles and moral issues of the corporation can be found.

Karl Mannheim's conception of self-rationalization[2] or self-streamlining, that is, the systematic application of functional rationality to the self to attain certain individual ends, is useful in understanding one of the central social psychological processes of organizational life. In a world where appearances—in the broadest sense—mean everything, the wise and ambitious manager learns to cultivate assiduously the proper, prescribed modes of appearing. He dispassionately takes stock of himself, treating himself as an object, as a commodity. He analyzes his strengths and weaknesses and decides what he needs to change in order to survive and flourish in his organization. And then he systematically undertakes a program to reconstruct his image, his publicly avowed attitudes or ideas, or what-

ever else in his self-presentation that might need adjustment. As I have suggested, this means sharply curbing one's impulses, indeed spontaneity of any sort, and carefully calculating instead both the appropriate modes of packaging oneself and the social consequences of one's every action. Such self-regulation requires simultaneously great discipline and "flexibility," since one must continually adjust oneself to meet the ever-changing demands of different career stages and, of more immediate consequence, the expectations of crucial social circles in ever-changing organizational milieux. . . . ◆ ◆ ◆

◆ Notes

1. This viewpoint is put forth most completely in William H. Whyte, *The Organization Man* (New York: Simon and Schuster, 1956); and in David Riesman, in collaboration with Reuel Denney and Nathan Glazer, *The Lonely Crowd: A Study*

   of the Changing American Character (New Haven, Conn.: Yale University Press, 1950).

2. Karl Mannheim, *Man and Society in An Age of Reconstruction* (London: Paul [Kegan], Trench, Trubner & Co. Ltd., 1940), p. 55.

Adapting Kohlberg to Enhance the Assessment of Managers' Moral Reasoning

James Weber

Lawrence Kohlberg, a psychologist, suggested that we operate at various levels of moral development. We start by simply responding to outside stimuli—punishment and reward—and may eventually be motivated by an internal desire to act in accordance with universal moral principles. In this article we will look at a brief overview of Kohlberg's views. Then we will look at Weber's findings, which suggest that although we may respond to an abstract hypothetical situation (say, whether a man should steal medicine for his critically ill wife) at a fairly sophisticated level of reasoning, people are generally less reflective when they think they have seen the situation before or if it happens in an institutional context. One lesson from the reading is that we should be aware that our practical moral decisions might be less well considered than our classroom responses.

Current research has found that managers often face moral and ethical conflicts in the workplace (Toffler, 1986; Waters, Bird & Chant, 1986). Yet little empirical research has sought to understand the reasoning process managers use to resolve these conflicts. An enhanced understanding of managers' moral reasoning could lead to a greater awareness of the influences upon managerial decision making when faced with ethical dilemmas (e.g., individual values, organizational culture), a greater predictability of managerial and organizational ethical behavior, and the construction of organizational guides and incentives to aid managers toward ethical action.

One of the major impediments toward a better understanding of managers' reasoning lies in the lack of available and appropriate methods to assess managers' decision-making processes when confronted with ethical or moral dilemmas (Cavanagh & Fritzsche, 1985; Frederick, 1987). One possible method, developed by Lawrence Kohlberg and his associates, was recently presented in *The Measurement of Moral Judgment* (Colby & Kohlberg, 1987). This method is based upon a theoretical foundation found in Kohlberg's earlier works (1981, 1984). In their effort to understand an individual's moral development and the corresponding articulation of different types of moral reasoning, Kohlberg and others constructed a series of stages of moral reasoning. In addition, they developed an instrument and scoring method to measure an individual's reasoning, the Moral Judgment Interview and Standard Issue Scoring respectively.

While this work provides a basis for the assessment of managers' moral decision making,

Kohlberg's objective was to assess the development of an individual's moral reasoning from childhood to adulthood. Thus the instrument used in Kohlbergian research possesses characteristics essential for the study of moral development (e.g., dilemmas which can be understood by individuals from age 6 to 30). However, due to its developmental nature, the method contains characteristics which are unnecessary and may hinder the assessment of managers' moral decision-making processes.

Thus, in order to better understand managers' reasoning when confronted with an ethical or moral dilemma, the Kohlberg method must be modified. The modification presented in this paper emphasizes four points which will enhance the method of measuring managers' moral reasoning: (1) a mixture of less familiar moral dilemmas with more familiar dilemmas from a business organization context, (2) followup interview questions which probe managers' moral reasoning by focusing upon key organizational values, (3) the flexibility of utilizing either an oral or written interview method, and (4) a simpler, yet reliable, system for scoring the managers' responses and identifying their stage of moral reasoning. This paper will then empirically test this newly adapted method for measuring managers' moral reasoning.

KOHLBERG'S STAGES OF MORAL REASONING

Kohlbergian research is based upon earlier work by Piaget and the expanded notions contained in Kohlberg's own theory of moral development

(1981, 1984). This stream of research concentrates upon the reasons given why certain actions are perceived as morally just or preferred. These reasons, for Kohlberg, are the indicators of the stage of moral maturity. As Kohlbergian research bears out, when one looks at the reasons people give for their moral judgments or moral actions, significant differences in their moral outlook become apparent. These differences are captured in Kohlberg's "Stages of Moral Development."

Kohlberg identifies three levels of moral development through which individuals progress: preconventional, conventional, and postconventional, with two stages within each level. The second stage within each level represents a more advanced and organized form of the first stage. A brief description of these six stages of moral reasoning is presented next (for a more detailed discussion, see Colby & Kohlberg, 1987).

Preconventional Level

At this level, a person responds to notions of "right" or "wrong," especially when expressed in terms of consequences of action (punishment, rewards, exchange of favors), or in terms of imposition of physical power by those enunciating the rules. At stage 1 (Punishment and Obedience Orientation) the physical consequences of action determine its goodness or badness. Avoidance of punishment and unquestioning deference to power are valued in their own right. Right action is defined in stage 2 (Instrumental Relativist Orientation) as that which satisfies one's own needs. Elements of fairness and equal sharing are always interpreted in terms of the physical or pragmatic consequences to the decision maker.

Conventional Level

At this level, maintaining the expectations of the individual's family, group or nation is perceived as valuable. Stage 3 ("Good Boy-Nice Girl" Orientation) emphasizes behavior that pleases or helps others and is approved by them. There is much conformity to stereotypical images of what is majority or "natural" behavior. At stage 4 (Law and Order Orientation) the individual takes the perspective of a generalized member of society. This perspective is based on a conception of the social system as a consistent set of societal, legal, or religious codes and procedures that apply impartially to all members in a society.

Postconventional Level

At this level, there is a clear effort to define moral values and principles which have validity and application apart from the authority of the groups and persons holding these principles. Generally with utilitarian overtones, stage 5 (Social-Contract Legalistic Orientation) defines right action in terms of general individual rights and in terms of standards which have been critically examined and agreed upon by the whole society. Rather than rigidly maintaining laws in terms of stage 4 law and order, stage 5 emphasizes the possibility of changing law in terms of rational considerations of social utility. At stage 6 (Universal Ethical Principle Orientation) right is defined by the decision of conscience in accord with self-chosen ethical principles appealing to logical comprehensiveness, universality, and consistency.

Over the past twenty years numerous criticisms have been lodged against Kohlberg's stage theory (Gilligan, 1982; Rest, 1982; Sullivan, 1974). Kohlberg and his associates have responded to their major critics (see Kohlberg, Levine & Hewer, 1983), addressing issues of stage sequencing, subjectivity in the scoring method, gender and cultural bias, and others. In general, Kohlberg's stage theory has been clarified or redefined to withstand these challenges and is widely used and accepted in the field of moral development. . . .

MORAL JUDGMENT INTERVIEW

The operationalization of Kohlberg's theory and stages of moral development is found in the Moral Judgment Interview. In the interview a subject is presented with a situation involving a value conflict. For example, in the often-used Heinz dilemma (Should Heinz steal a drug to save his dying wife if the only druggist able to provide the drug insists on a high price that Heinz cannot afford to pay?), the conflict is between the value of preserving life and the value of upholding the law. Life and law are the standard issues in the dilemma. Once the dilemma is presented, the subject is asked a series of probe questions designed to elicit information on the subjects' conceptions of these two issues.

The Moral Judgment Interview [see box] is designed to "elicit a subject's (1) own construction of moral reasoning, (2) moral frame of reference or assumptions about right and wrong, and (3) the way these beliefs and assumptions are used to make and justify moral decisions" (Colby & Kohlberg, 1987:61). Questions are explicitly prescriptive so as to draw out normative judgments about what one should do, rather than descriptive or predictive judgments about what one would do.

Adaptation 1: Moral Dilemmas

In the various versions of the Moral Judgment Interview instrument only less familiar dilemmas (or, as Kohlberg describes them, hypothetical dilemmas) are used. There are a number of advantages, perceived by Kohlberg and his associates, in using the hypothetical situations. First, hypothetical situations can be easily understood by all subjects. Since much of the Kohlbergian research is developmental, subjects can range from young children through adults. Second, Kohlberg is seeking to measure the highest stage of the subject's moral reasoning. Colby and Kohlberg argue that "people do not always use

their highest stage of moral reasoning. We have attempted to minimize the gap between competence and performance by using hypothetical dilemmas" (1987:5). Third, the dilemmas used by Kohlberg and others have been found to be universally understood. Cross-cultural research has repeatedly found that subjects ranging from primitive tribespeople to Western urban adults can understand and respond to the hypothetical dilemmas (Snarey, 1985).

While accepting the advantages inherent in hypothetical, less familiar moral dilemmas, there may be specific advantages in not exclusively using these dilemmas when assessing the moral reasoning of managers. The bases for using less familiar dilemmas are less relevant to the assessment of managerial moral reasoning. Specifically, the concern for subjects of all ages achieving an understanding of the dilemma is not critical for research assessing the moral reasoning of adult managers. In addition, there may be advantages in constructing realistic, if not commonplace, dilemmas set in the context of a business organization.

Straughan (1985) argues that hypothetical dilemmas necessarily lack the first-hand immediacy which is an essential ingredient of genuine moral experience. Moreover, by placing the moral dilemma into a corporate context, the familiarity of the dilemma for the manager should be enhanced. Freeman and Giebink (1979) found a significant impact exhibited by the "situational familiarity-remoteness" condition. The subjects in their study achieved higher stages of reasoning for the remote dilemmas than for the more familiar dilemmas. The authors conclude that "the kind of dilemma presented affects the level of moral judgment rendered" (1979:46). In assessing managers' moral reasoning, Weber (1990) found significantly higher moral stage responses for the less familiar dilemma than for the more familiar dilemmas placed in a business context.

MORAL JUDGMENT INTERVIEW (ADAPTED)

Instructions

(The following instructions were read by the interviewer to the subjects during the oral Moral Judgment Interview, and provided as the first page of the Moral Judgment Interview for those completing the written interview.)

The Moral Judgment Interview consists of several stories that we believe present some challenging issues. Some of you might choose one solution to the stories, others of you may choose another. We are primarily interested in the explanations or reasons you give for your decisions. Try to justify and explain your statements as fully as possible. Very short answers are of no help to us so be sure to elaborate fully. Use the backside of the paper provided to complete your answers if necessary. Keep in mind that we are more interested in your answers to the why questions than to the what questions. Even if you give a long description of what you think is right or what you think should be done, it is of no help if you do not explain why you think it is right or why you think it should be done. Answer each question the best you can. Please do not compare an answer to prior answers.

OK, please begin the Moral Judgment Interview by reading the first story. . . .

Heinz

In Europe, a woman was near death from a special kind of cancer. There was one drug that the doctors thought might save her. It was a form of radium that a druggist in the same town had recently discovered.

The drug was expensive to make, but the druggist was charging ten times what the drug cost him to make. He paid $400 for the radium and charged $4,000 for a small dose of the drug.

The sick woman's husband, Heinz, went to everyone he knew to borrow the money and tried every legal means, but he could only get together about $2,000, which was half of what it cost.

He told the druggist that his wife was dying, and asked him to sell it cheaper or let him pay later. But the druggist said, "No, I discovered the drug and I'm going to make money from it." So having tried every legal means, Heinz gets desperate and considers breaking into the man's store to steal the drug for his wife.

1. Should Heinz steal the drug? _____ (Yes or No) Why, or why not?
2. Does it make a difference whether or not he loves his wife?
3. Suppose the person dying is not his wife but a stranger. Should Heinz steal the drug for the stranger?
4. Suppose the only chance Heinz had to acquire the money is to steal funds from his employer. Should Heinz steal his employer's money to purchase the drug?
5. Is it important for people to do everything they can to save another's life? Explain.
6. It is against the law for Heinz to steal. Does that make it morally wrong?
7. In general, should people try to do everything they can to obey the law?

Evelyn

Evelyn worked for an automotive steel casting company. She was part of a small group asked to investigate the cause of an operating problem that had developed in the wheel castings of a new luxury automobile and to make recommendations for its improvement. The problem did not directly create an unsafe condition, but it did lead to irritating sounds. The Vice President of Engineering told the group that he was certain that the problem was due to tensile stress in the castings.

Evelyn and a lab technician conducted tests and found conclusive evidence that the problem was not tensile stress. As Evelyn began work on other possible explanations of the problem, she was told that the problem has been solved. A report prepared by Evelyn's boss strongly supported the tensile stress hypothesis. All of the data points from Evelyn's experiments have been changed to fit the curves, and some of the points which were far from where the theory would predict have been omitted. The report "proved" that tensile stress was responsible for the problem.

(continued)

MORAL JUDGMENT INTERVIEW (ADAPTED) *(continued)*

1. Should Evelyn contradict her boss's report? _____ (Yes or No) Why, or why not?
2. Should the potential conflict with Evelyn's boss have any impact on Evelyn's actions? Why, or why not?
3. If the report supporting the tensile stress hypothesis was issued by the lab technician working on the project, should Evelyn contradict the report?
4. Is it important that people do everything they can to have the truth known? Explain.
5. Suppose the problem with the brake involved more than irritating sounds. Would it make a difference if the brake problem caused uneven brake applications and skids which could lead to possible human injury?
6. The data in the boss's report are false. Does it make it morally wrong if Evelyn fails to contradict the report?
7. Should people do everything they can to work within the corporate organization and support their superiors?

Roger

Roger worked for a small auditing firm and conducted an annual audit of a machinery manufacturer. During the audit he discovered that the firm had received a large loan from the local savings and loan association. It is illegal for a savings and loan association to make a loan to a manufacturing firm; they are restricted by law to mortgages based upon residential real estate.

Roger took his working papers and a xerox copy of the ledger showing the loan to his boss, the partner in charge of the auditing office. His boss listened to Roger, and then told Roger: "I will take care of this privately. We simply cannot afford to lose a client of this status. You put the papers you have through the shredder."

1. Should Roger shred his papers? _____ (Yes or No) Why, or why not?

2. Does the illegality of the loan and Roger's duty as an auditor make a difference in Roger's decision to shred his papers?
3. If Roger had been advised by one of his peers to shred his papers, should Roger shred his papers?
4. Is it important for people to do everything they can to follow their conscience? Explain.
5. Shredding papers is against the AICPA Code and covers up an illegally made loan. Is Roger also morally wrong if he shreds his papers?
6. What if Roger's career was threatened if he refused to shred his papers?
7. Should people do everything they can to further their own careers?

Abbreviated Scoring Guide [Moral Stage Assignment and Typical Concerns Expressed]

1. Harm to self
2. Personal needs
   Personal satisfaction
3. Consequences to immediate group
   Personal relationships with others
   How others will perceive me
4. Professional responsibilities
   Commitment to a code, oath or principle
   Duties to a larger societal group
   Social harmony
   Society's laws
5. Personally held values about justice, fairness, rights
   A moral law above society's laws
   A "social contract" that protects everyone's rights
   Greatest good for the greatest number affected
6. Universal principles of justice, fairness
   Universal laws governing behavior, superseding society's laws

The familiarity embodied in realistic dilemmas set in a corporate context might better elicit from the managers their actual type of moral reasoning, rather than measure the highest form of moral reasoning as sought by traditional Kohlbergian research. This brings us to the first important adaptation of Kohlberg's method: the use of a combination of less familiar and more familiar moral dilemmas, the latter set in an organizational context, to elicit from the managers their stage of moral reasoning.

Research in the field of ethical and moral issues provides a focus for the type of issues commonly faced by corporate managers and a basis for the issues presented in the "realistic" moral dilemmas. Barbara Toffler (1986) reported that 66 percent of her subjects encountered ethical dilemmas when managing organizational processes or company personnel. Corporate managers interviewed by Toffler indicated that they more frequently perceived ethical issues within the "micro" (internal) corporate environment, rather than the "macro" (external) corporate environment. In a survey of 33 corporate managers, Waters, Bird and Chant (1986) reported that employee issues were the most common ethical dilemmas faced by managers (36% of the 193 ethical issues reported). LaRue Hosmer (1987) identified numerous personal ethical issues: prejudice in hiring, discovery of corporate illegality, test results falsification, unsafe working conditions, and knowledge of corporate bribery. These issues provided a pool of ethical issues for developing "business environment" moral dilemmas.

As shown . . . , the dilemmas entitled "Evelyn" and "Roger" present moral dilemmas set in a business organization context. These dilemmas embody ethical conflicts recognized as commonplace by managers. In general, the dilemmas pit the values of honesty and professional integrity against the organizational values of corporate loyalty and obedience to your superior. In the empirical investigation which field-tested these dilemmas, managers expressed little difficulty in understanding the relevance of these conflicting issues in the workplace, as well as noting the probability of these conflicts arising at work.

Adaptation 2: Probe Questions

The followup probe questions for each dilemma were constructed from the criteria established by Kohlberg and his associates. These questions are shown in [the interview]. Contained within the series of probe questions is an emphasis upon key organizational values, as well as references to the attributes inherent to Kohlberg's stages of moral reasoning. The intent was to seek to understand managers' moral reasoning within the context of the organizational values which might influence the managers' reasoning process. For example, in the Roger dilemma the subject is asked about the influence of a professional code of conduct (question 2), job security (question 6), and the importance of career development (question 7).

Thus, a critical adaptation of Kohlberg's Moral Judgment Interview instrument is: the inclusion of key organizational values into the followup probe questions. This modification results in an analytical tool more germane to a sample of managers who may be influenced by the values of the business organization that employs them. . . .

Sample

Two groups of 37 corporate managers were selected for the study. The managers were chosen from a larger set of data acquired for a different research purpose. The subjects used in the study were selected on the basis of creating two groups of managers with nearly identical demographic characteristics. The managerial demographic variables considered were age, gender, ethnic origin, and years of corporate work experience. The size of the organization employing the manager and the industry membership of the employing organization were also considered. The average subject in the sample was 40.3 years of age, with 20 years of corporate work experience. They were predominantly male (84.1%) and white (96.3%). Sixty-seven percent of the managers worked in the manufacturing industry, with thirty percent employed by financial services firms. Sixty-five percent of the managers worked for firms having over 1,000 employees. Preliminary tests showed no significant differences in the managers' reasoning due to any of the managerial or organizational characteristics.

Method

... Three moral dilemmas and followup questions for each dilemma were formulated and presented during an oral interview. ... The first dilemma, Heinz, was taken from Colby and Kohlberg (1987). The remaining two dilemmas were drawn from current business ethics research (Hosmer, 1987) and were constructed from the criteria established by Kohlberg and his associates. ...

Results and Discussion

The findings from the empirical investigation are shown in Tables 1 through 3. The findings are presented and discussed in relation to the adaptation presented earlier in this paper.

The first adaptation recommended the use of a combination of less familiar and more familiar moral dilemmas. The Heinz dilemma provided a less familiar situation; whereas the Evelyn and Roger dilemmas dealt with business practices that were considered by managers to be familiar problems in the workplace. ... As shown in Table 1, there is a significant difference between the managers' stages of moral reasoning when comparing differences in the type of moral dilemma (for all t-test comparisons p = .000). The average stage score is higher for the Heinz dilemma than for the Evelyn dilemma or the Roger dilemma. These findings appear to confirm the earlier results reported by Freeman and Giebink (1979) and Weber (1990). The more remote the situation contained in the dilemma, the higher the stage of moral reasoning; and, conversely, the more familiar the situation, the lower the stage of moral reasoning. Thus, if the

Table 1 ◆ MORAL REASONING BY DILEMMA

Stage Score	Heinz	Evelyn	Roger
6	0	0	0
5	15 (20.3%)	4 (5.4%)	4 (5.4%)
4	31 (41.9%)	6 (8.1%)	36 (48.6%)
3	28 (37.8%)	54 (73.0%)	21 (28.4%)
2	0	9 (12.2%)	13 (17.6%)
1	0	1 (1.3%)	0
n =	74	74	74
mean =	3.82	3.04	3.42

t-test comparing Heinz and Evelyn = 9.53, p = .000
t-test comparing Heinz and Roger = 5.28, p = .000
t-test comparing Evelyn and Roger = –4.43, p = .000

Table 2 ◆ INFLUENCE OF ORGANIZATIONAL VALUES ON MORAL REASONING

Stage Score	Evelyn Dilemma		Roger Dilemma	
	Org'l Loyalty	Honesty	Prof. Norm	Job Security
6	0	0	0	0
5	11	3	9	5
4	11	5	33	24
3	45	59	22	22
2	7	5	10	23
1	0	2	0	0
n =	74	74	74	74
mean =	3.35	3.03	3.55	3.15

t-test comparing Org'l loyalty and Honesty = 4.34, p = .000
t-test comparing Prof. norm and Job security = 6.69, p = .000

research objective is to assess the actual stage of managerial moral reasoning when confronted with an ethical dilemma, the adaptation of Kohlberg's Moral Judgment Interview to include dilemmas set in the business context appears to be warranted.

The inclusion of key organizational values into the followup probe questions is the focus of the second adaptation to the Moral Judgment Interview. In the empirical investigation various followup probe questions containing references to organizational values were developed to assess

Table 3 ◆ COMPARISON OF MORAL REASONING BY INTERVIEW METHOD

Stage Score	Heinz		Evelyn		Roger	
	Oral	Written	Oral	Written	Oral	Written
6	0	0	0	0	0	0
5	7	8	4	0	1	3
4	17	14	4	2	18	18
3	13	15	25	29	11	10
2	0	0	4	5	7	6
1	0	0	0	1	0	0
n =	37	37	37	37	37	37
mean =	3.84	3.81	3.21	2.86	3.35	3.48

t-test comparing Heinz oral and written = 0.15, p = .878
t-test comparing Evelyn oral and written = 2.25, p = .028
t-test comparing Roger oral and written = –0.69, p = .495
t-test comparing overall global score oral and written = 1.03, p = .292

differences in managerial responses. Table 2 shows that the managers' moral stage response to the organizational loyalty and honesty questions for the Evelyn dilemma were significantly different (t = 4.34, p = .000). A similar observation can be made regarding the managerial responses to the professional norm and job security questions attached to the Roger dilemma (t = 6.69, p = .000). It appears from these findings that particular organizational values embodied in followup probe questions might influence managers' moral responses. . . .

The results are shown in Table 3 and indicate that there is little difference between the two groups of managers' stages of moral reasoning. The average stage score for the managers is nearly identical for the Heinz dilemma (t = 0.69, p = .495). There is, however, statistical differences when comparing the managers' responses to the Evelyn dilemma (t = 2.25, p = .028). . . .

CONCLUSIONS

. . .

As shown in Table 1, the context of the dilemma appears to exert a critical influence upon the managers as they develop a response to the ethical conflict. Confirming earlier work by Freeman and Giebink (1979) and Weber (1990), managers' moral reasoning was higher for the less familiar (Heinz) dilemma, yet regressed when the managers consider their response to the dilemmas often found in the workplace (Evelyn and Roger dilemmas). . . .

Various organizational values also appear to influence managers' moral reasoning. Thus, great care should be exercised in considering the impact of these values through the use of carefully worded followup probe questions during the interview. As shown in both the Evelyn and Roger dilemmas, some organizational values appear to be associated with particular stages of moral reasoning, as indicated by the managers' responses to specific followup probe questions. . . .

. . . Heightened understanding of managers' ethical decision-making processes could lead to greater predictability of managerial and organizational ethical behavior. In addition, based upon an improved understanding of managerial moral reasoning, organizational guides and incentives may be constructed to aid managers toward ethical action. ◆ ◆ ◆

◆ *References*

Cavanagh, G. F., & Fritzsche, D. J. 1985. "Using Vignettes in Business Ethics Research." In L. E. Preston (Ed.) *Research in Corporate Social Performance and Policy:* 279–293. Greenwich, CT: JAI Press.

Colby, A. & Kohlberg, L. 1987. *The Measurement of Moral Judgment, Volume I: Theoretical Foundations and Research Validations.* Cambridge, MA: Cambridge University Press.

Frederick, W. C. 1987. "Introduction: The Empirical Dimension of Business Ethics and Values." In W. C. Frederick (Ed.) *Research in Corporate Social Performance and Policy:* vii–xi. Greenwich, CT: JAI Press.

Freeman, S. J. M. and Giebink, J. W. 1979. "Moral Judgment as a Function of Age, Sex, and Stimulus." *The Journal of Psychology,* 102: 43–47.

Gilligan, C. 1982. *In a Different Voice.* Cambridge, MA: Harvard University Press.

Hosmer, L. T. 1987. *The Ethics of Management.* Homewood, IL: Irwin.

Kohlberg, L. 1981. *Essays in Moral Development, Volume I: The Philosophy of Moral Development.* New York: Harper & Row.

Kohlberg, L. 1984. *Essays in Moral Development, Volume II: The Psychology of Moral Development.* New York: Harper & Row.

Kohlberg, L., Levine, C. & Hewer, A. 1983. *Moral Stages: A Current Formulation and a Response to Critics.* New York: Karger.

Rest, J. R. 1982. "Morality." In J. H. Flavell & E. M. Markman (Eds.) *Handbook of Child Psychology, Volume III: Cognitive Development:* 556–629. New York: John Wiley & Sons.

Snarey, J. R. 1985. "Cross-cultural Universality of Social-moral Development: A Critical Review of Kohlbergian Research," *Psychological Bulletin,* 97 (2): 202–232.

Straughan, R. 1985. "Why Act on Kohlberg's Moral Judgments?" In S. Modgil & C. Modgil (Eds.) *Lawrence Kohlberg: Consensus and Controversy:* 149–161. Philadelphia: Falmer Press.

Sullivan, E. V. 1974. "Moral Development Research: A Case Study of Scientific Cultural Bias." *Human Development,* 17: 81–106.

Toffler, B. L. 1986. *Tough Choices: Managers Talk Ethics.* New York: John Wiley & Sons.

Waters, J. A., Bird, F. & Chant, P. D. 1986. "Everyday Moral Issues Experienced by Managers." *Journal of Business Ethics,* 5: 373–384.

Weber, J. 1990. "Managers' Moral Reasoning: Assessing Their Responses to Three Moral Dilemmas." *Human Relations,* 43: 687–702.

4

THE MORAL PLACE
OF CORPORATIONS

This short chapter highlights a central difference in the way people view corporations. It is a critical distinction in terms of whether we should expect corporations to have moral responsibilities to society and to the environment.

The first position, articulated here by Milton Friedman, suggests that a corporation is essentially amoral; that is, it is morally neutral, responds only to outside stimuli such as consumer demand, and has no responsibilities other than obeying the law and generating financial return to investors. From this perspective, business has a compartmentalized "two hats" morality: A worker comes in, takes off his or her personal hat, and puts on that of the company. While at work, the paramount duty is to maximize returns to the company's owners—the investors. If the firm spews out noxious fumes that kill off songbirds, the only real restraint is the law; if the gas emissions are legal, then the managers should not take the initiative to lessen the pollution if doing so would cost the firm money. Concerned employees are welcome to take their paychecks and, after work, in a private capacity, lobby for any law they choose through the political process, which

will, in turn, restrict the company. Also, the firm is not there to make paternalistic decisions for consumers: If the company can save money by using saturated fat in foods, it should defer that decision to the customers. If the public is indifferent, the company should do whatever it needs to do to increase profits, but if customers object, signaled by a refusal to buy the product, then the firm should react to regain market share. It is not the place of the company to spontaneously undertake civic good works or to enhance its products unless there is a clear-cut indication that those acts will lead to increased profits. Under Friedman's view, the greatest service of business is to provide goods and services in a profitable manner. Because of a free and competitive market, this means giving consumers high quality goods at the lowest possible price, leading to an overall increase in the standard of living. This view closely mirrors the theoretical work of libertarians like Ayn Rand.

The second position is represented by R. Edward Freeman, who contends that we should reconsider how we traditionally think of corporations. He feels they should be thought of as vehicles for enhancing the welfare of all those who have a stake in the company. The language of stakeholder analysis is prevalent in business today. Taking Freeman's approach, a company executive cannot favor one group of stakeholders over another. He or she has to balance the concern of maximizing returns to investors with making sure that the interests of consumers, suppliers, communities, employees, and the environment are also addressed. Echoing Rawls's philosophical position, Freeman believes a manager should be impartial to the various stakeholders. There is no more priority, for example, given to an investor than a consumer: They should all benefit from the firm's existence.

We can also chart an intermediate position. In this case, a firm is essentially a moneymaking vehicle, as with Friedman. However, strategically, to remain profitable it has to consider the interests of a wide range of stakeholders. The corporation cares about satisfying consumers and environmental groups not because it values their interests as such, but it recognizes that they may have the power to influence the firm's profitability. So, for example, if it does not take environmentalists' interests into account, it may be faced with a campaign aimed at dissuading customers from buying its products. Therefore, it is good management practice to take a wide perspective on issues and determine which groups may be able to help or hurt the firm. Typically, this is a long-term strategy, which might be called benign self-interest, meaning the incentive to care about others and promote social institutions springs from a belief that doing so will ultimately benefit the firm. It may invest in community welfare programs, for example, with the understanding that these improvements will make a more attractive place to live for their workers, thus reducing employee attrition. At the same time, though, the motivation for doing so is to retain profits.

We might consider whether actions undertaken for profit count as fully moral; it would be easy to dismiss them as merely prudential (self-interested). But works that are not purely altruistic (doing good for its own sake) may still promote human welfare. We might temper the claim along the following lines:

- Businesses are designed to make profit.
- They have a choice whether to enhance the world or not.
- The world is a better place if businesses underwrite social projects.
- If businesses are going to operate, then it is better if they include social projects.

Thus a major department store might promote college scholarships. They could be doing so out of a feeling that this is an appropriate social function, or they could be justifying it internally by treating it like goodwill advertising. Either way, though, the business has a choice about what it wants to support, and in this case there is a beneficial outcome to some students. This result may not satisfy deontological moralists, who believe that the purity of intention is the main ethical criterion.

Another way of considering the moral role of business is to ask the question, Will a firm do well by doing good? If the answer were a simple and quantifiably demonstrable yes, then business ethics would be much easier. However, in the absence of such evidence, the proposition could still be correct. Moreover, the truth of the claim ultimately may not matter if the participants in a practice believe in its truth. To make an analogy, a man may act like a saint in order to earn a place in heaven after death. The truth of the existence of heaven (and the conditions for entry) will not change the fact that he had a belief that made a radical difference in his everyday behavior. Similarly, if all businesses operated as if it were true that doing good works would promote their profits, it would likely become self-verifying.

Using the law as the gauge of morally appropriate behavior has some clear disadvantages. First, the law is largely a reactive instrument; that is, laws are often passed after some problem or issue has arisen, and thus there is a significant time lapse before new and emergent cases are settled. During that time, firms could cause harm until they are actively prevented. The dietary supplement Ephedra, for instance, was sold up to the point that it was banned, even though there was considerable evidence available to the manufacturers that it was potentially lethal to people with cardiovascular disease. However, despite some dramatic examples, the view that businesses relentlessly chase profit to the exclusion of all other considerations goes against a body of evidence from the public statements that companies make and from their support of socially responsible causes. The characterization that businesses only do what they have to do to satisfy the law turns out to be a misleading generalization.

If a firm were genuinely cutthroat in its pursuit of profit, then it may do well in the short term. Over the long term, however, reputation for fairness and honest dealing may win out. There is evidence that supports both approaches. Perhaps the question we should ask is, Should a business consider its success in any other terms than short-term monetary returns to shareholders? Another way of thinking about business is to recall the law of the jungle. We tend to think of it as a justification for predatory and competitive behavior, but the original context shows us that even life in the jungle is essentially a cooperative affair:

> Now this is the Law of the Jungle—as old and as
> true as the sky;
> And the Wolf that shall keep it may prosper, but
> the Wolf that shall break it must die.
> As the creeper that girdles the tree-trunk the Law
> runneth forward and back—
> For the strength of the Pack is the Wolf, and the
> strength of the Wolf is the Pack.[1]

---

[1]Rudyard Kipling's *The Law of the Jungle*.

The Social Responsibility of Business Is to Increase Its Profits

Milton Friedman

In this selection, Milton Friedman presents us with a challenge: Business is a narrow activity that is clearly profit driven and amoral (not his term). It is essentially neutral and devoid of moral content because it responds to and reflects consumer demand: The market will be the ultimate arbiter of values. Thus, for example, a manager should not decide to lower profitability by frying a burger in healthier but more expensive fat; that is a consumer-driven choice, which will be tested in the marketplace. The only responsibility of business is to increase profits "so long as it stays within the rules of the game, which is to say, engages in open and free competition without deception or fraud." Why, then, should we demand any more from a business than that? Answering that question will motivate many of the writers in the remainder of this text.

In Friedman's view, corporate officers are agents of the owners, and their moral concerns are separate from their work duties. As long as they follow ethical norms of business and stay within the law, then they are doing all that is required. They should not step beyond their bounds and meddle in social policy or try to improve society unless it is off the company clock on private time. Their training and expertise makes them good at making profitable business decisions but not necessarily competent as benign social engineers. Publicly held businesses are designed to make money for their owners, and in Friedman's view they may engage in "social responsibilities" such as charitable donations or community clean-up projects only as long as they benefit the company in terms of goodwill or increased sales.

When I hear businessmen speak eloquently about the "social responsibilities of business in a free-enterprise system," I am reminded of the wonderful line about the Frenchman who discovered at the age of 70 that he had been speaking prose all his life. The businessmen believe that they are defending free enterprise when they declaim that business is not concerned "merely" with profit but also with promoting desirable "social" ends; that business has a "social conscience" and takes seriously its responsibilities for providing employment, eliminating discrimination, avoiding pollution and whatever else may be the catchwords of the contemporary crop of reformers. In fact they are—or would be if they or anyone else took them seriously—preaching pure and unadulterated socialism. Businessmen who talk this way are unwitting puppets of the intellectual forces that have been undermining the basis of a free society these past decades.

The discussions of the "social responsibilities of business" are notable for their analytical looseness and lack of rigor. What does it mean to say that "business" has responsibilities? Only people can have responsibilities. A corporation is an artificial person and in this sense may have artificial responsibilities, but "business" as a whole cannot be said to have responsibilities, even in this vague sense. The first step toward clarity to examining the doctrine of the social responsibility of business is to ask precisely what it implies for whom.

Presumably, the individuals who are to be responsible are businessmen, which means individual proprietors or corporate executives. Most of the discussion of social responsibility is directed at corporations, so in what follows I shall mostly neglect the individual proprietors and speak of corporate executives.

In a free-enterprise, private-property system, a corporate executive is an employee of the owners of the business. He has direct responsibility to his employers. That responsibility is to conduct the business in accordance with their desires, which generally will be to make as much money as possible while conforming to the basic rules of the society, both those embodied in law and those embodied in ethical custom. Of course, in some cases his employers may have a different objective. A group of persons might establish a corporation for an eleemosynary purpose—for example, a hospital or a school. The manager of such a corporation will not have money profit as his objectives but the rendering of certain services.

In either case, the key point is that, in his capacity as a corporate executive, the manager is the agent of the individuals who own the corporation or establish the eleemosynary institution, and his primary responsibility is to them.

Needless to say, this does not mean that it is easy to judge how well he is performing his task. But at least the criterion of performance is straightforward, and the persons among whom a voluntary contractual arrangement exists are clearly defined.

Of course, the corporate executive is also a person in his own right. As a person, he may have many other responsibilities that he recognizes or assumes voluntarily—to his family, his conscience, his feelings of charity, his church, his clubs, his city, his country. He may feel impelled by these responsibilities to devote part of his income to causes he regards as worthy, to refuse to work for particular corporations, even to leave his job, for example, to join his country's armed forces. If we wish, we may refer to some of these responsibilities as "social responsibilities." But in these respects he is acting as a principal, not an agent; he is spending his own money or time or energy, not the money of his employers or the time or energy he has contracted to devote to their purposes. If these are "social responsibilities," they are the social responsibilities of individuals, not of business.

What does it mean to say that the corporate executive has a "social responsibility" in his capacity as businessman? If this statement is not pure rhetoric, it must mean that he is to act in some way that is not in the interest of his employers. For example, that he is to refrain from increasing the price of the product in order to contribute to the social objective of preventing inflation, even though a price increase would be in the best interests of the corporation. Or that he is to make expenditures on reducing pollution beyond the amount that is in the best interests of the corporation or that is required by law in order to contribute to the social objective of improving the environment. Or that, at the expense of corporate profits, he is to hire "hard-core" unemployed instead of better qualified available workmen to contribute to the social objective of reducing poverty.

In each of these cases, the corporate executive would be spending someone else's money for a general social interest. Insofar as his actions in accord with his "social responsibility" reduce returns to stockholders, he is spending their money. Insofar as his actions raise the price to customers, he is spending customers' money. Insofar as his actions lower the wages of some employees, he is spending their money.

The stockholders or the customers or the employees could separately spend their own money on the particular action if they wished to do so. The executive is exercising a distinct "social responsibility," rather than serving as an agent of the stockholders or the customers or the employees, only if he spends the money in a different way than they would have spent it.

But if he does this, he is in effect imposing taxes, on the one hand, and deciding how the tax proceeds shall be spent, on the other.

This process raises political questions on two levels: principle and consequences. On the level of political principle, the imposition of taxes and the expenditure of tax proceeds are governmental functions. We have established elaborate constitutional, parliamentary and judicial provisions to control these functions, to assure that taxes are imposed so far as possible in accordance with the preferences and desires of the public—after all, "taxation without representation" was one of the battle cries of the American Revolution. We have a system of checks and balances to separate the legislative function of imposing taxes and enacting expenditures from the executive function of collecting taxes and administering expenditure programs and from the judicial function of mediating disputes and interpreting the law.

Here the businessman—self-selected or appointed directly or indirectly by stockholders—is to be simultaneously legislator, executive and jurist. He is to decide whom to tax by how much and for what purpose, and he is to spend the proceeds—all this guided only by general exhortations from on high to restrain inflation, improve the environment, fight poverty and so on and on.

The whole justification for permitting the corporate executive to be selected by the stockholders is that the executive is an agent serving the interests of his principal. This justification disappears when the corporate executive imposes taxes and spends the proceeds for "social" purposes. He becomes in effect a public employee, a civil servant, even though he remains in name an employee of a private enterprise. On grounds of political principle, it is intolerable that such civil servants—insofar as their actions in the name of social responsibility are real and not just window dressing—should be selected as they are now. If they are to be civil servants, then they must be elected through a political process. If they are to impose taxes and make expenditures to foster "social" objectives, then political machinery must be set up to make the assessment of taxes and to determine through a political process the objectives to be served.

This is the basic reason why the doctrine of "social responsibility" involves the acceptance of the socialist view that political mechanisms, not market mechanisms, are the appropriate way to determine the allocation of scarce resources to alternative uses.

On the grounds of consequences, can the corporate executive in fact discharge his alleged "social responsibilities"? On the one hand, suppose he could get away with spending the stockholders' or customers' or employees' money. How is he to know how to spend it? He is told that he must contribute to fighting inflation. How is he to know what action of his will contribute to that end? He is presumably an expert in running his company—in producing a product or selling it or financing it. But nothing about his selection makes him an expert on inflation. Will his holding down the price of his product reduce inflationary pressure? Or, by leaving more spending power in the hands of his customers, simply divert it elsewhere? Or, by forcing him to produce less because of the lower price, will it simply contribute to shortages? Even if he could answer these questions, how much cost is he justified in imposing on his stockholders, customers, and employees for this social purpose? What is his appropriate share and what is the appropriate share of others?

And, whether he wants to or not, can he get away with spending his stockholders', customers' or employees' money? Will not the stockholders fire him? (Either the present ones or those who take over when his actions in the name of social responsibility have reduced the corporation's profits and the price of its stock.) His customers and his employees can desert him for other producers and employers less scrupulous in exercising their social responsibilities.

This facet of "social responsibility" doctrine is brought into sharp relief when the doctrine is used to justify wage restraint by trade unions. The conflict of interest is naked and clear when union officials are asked to subordinate the interest of their members to some more general purpose. If union officials try to enforce wage restraint, the consequence is likely to be wildcat strikes, rank-and-file revolts and the emergence of strong competitors for their jobs. We thus have the ironic phenomenon that union leaders—at least in the U.S.—have objected to Government interference with the market far more consistently and courageously than have business leaders.

The difficulty of exercising "social responsibility" illustrates, of course, the great virtue of private competitive enterprise—it forces people to be responsible for their own actions and makes it difficult for them to "exploit" other people for either selfish or unselfish purposes. They can do good—but only at their own expense.

Many a reader who has followed the argument this far may be tempted to remonstrate that it is all well and good to speak of Government's having the responsibility to impose taxes and determine expenditures for such "social" purposes as controlling pollution or training the hard-core unemployed, but that the problems are too urgent to wait on the slow course of political processes, that the exercise of social responsibility by businessmen is a quicker and surer way to solve pressing current problems.

Aside from the question of fact—I share Adam Smith's skepticism about the benefits that can be expected from "those who affect to trade for the public good"—this argument must be rejected on the grounds of principle. What it amounts to is an assertion that those who favor the taxes and expenditures in question have failed to persuade a majority of their fellow citizens to be of like mind and that they are seeking to attain by undemocratic procedures what they cannot attain by democratic procedures. In a free society it is hard for "evil" people to do "evil," especially since one man's good is another's evil.

I have, for simplicity, concentrated on the special case of the corporate executive, except only for the brief digression on trade unions. But precisely the same argument applies to the newer phenomenon of calling upon stockholders to require corporations to exercise social responsibility (the recent G.M. crusade for example). In most of these cases, what is in effect involved is some stockholders trying to get other stockholders (or customers or employees) to contribute against their will to "social" causes favored by the activists. Insofar as they succeed, they are again imposing taxes and spending the proceeds.

The situation of the individual proprietor is somewhat different. If he acts to reduce the returns of his enterprise in order to exercise his "social responsibility," he is spending his own money, not someone else's. If he wishes to spend his money on such purposes, that is his right, and I cannot see that there is any objection to his doing so. In the process, he, too, may impose costs on employees and customers. However, because he is far less likely than a large corporation or union to have monopolistic power, any such side effects will tend to be minor.

Of course, in practice the doctrine of social responsibility is frequently a cloak for actions that are justified on other grounds rather than a reason for those actions.

To illustrate, it may well be in the long-run interest of a corporation that is a major employer in a small community to devote resources to providing amenities to that community or to improving its government. That may make it easier to attract desirable employees, it may reduce the wage bill or lessen losses from pilferage and sabotage or have other worthwhile effects. Or it may be that, given the laws about the deductibility of corporate charitable contributions, the stockholders can contribute more to charities they favor by having the corporation make the gift than by doing it themselves, since they can in that way contribute an amount that would otherwise have been paid as corporate taxes.

In each of these—and many similar—cases, there is a strong temptation to rationalize these actions as an exercise of "social responsibility." In the present climate of opinion, with its widespread aversion to "capitalism," "profits," and the "soulless corporation" and so on, this is one way for a corporation to generate goodwill as a by-product of expenditures that are entirely justified in its own self-interest.

It would be inconsistent of me to call on corporate executives to refrain from this hypocritical window-dressing because it harms the foundations of a free society. That would be to call on them to exercise a "social responsibility"! If our institutions, and the attitudes of the public make it in their self-interest to cloak their actions in this way, I cannot summon much indignation to renounce them. At the same time, I can express admiration for those individual proprietors or owners of closely held corporations or stockholders of more broadly held corporations who disdain such tactics as approaching fraud.

Whether blameworthy or not, the use of the cloak of social responsibility, and the nonsense spoken in its name by influential and prestigious businessmen, does clearly harm the foundations of a free society. I have been impressed time and again by the schizophrenic character of many businessmen. They are capable of being extremely farsighted and clearheaded in matters that are internal to their businesses. They are incredibly short-sighted and muddle-headed in matters that are outside their businesses but affect the possible survival of business in general. This short-sightedness is strikingly exemplified in the calls from many businessmen for wage and price guidelines or controls or income policies. There is nothing that could do more in a brief period to destroy a market system and replace it by a centrally controlled system than effective governmental control of prices and wages.

The short-sightedness is also exemplified in speeches by businessmen on social responsibility. This may gain them kudos in the short run. But it helps to strengthen the already too prevalent view that the pursuit of profits is wicked and immoral and must be curbed and controlled by external forces. Once this view is adopted, the external forces that curb the market will not be the social consciences, however highly developed, of the pontificating executives; it will be the iron fist of Government bureaucrats. Here, as with price and wage controls, businessmen seem to me to reveal a suicidal impulse.

The political principle that underlies the market mechanism is unanimity. In an ideal free market resting on private property, no individual can coerce any other, all cooperation is voluntary, all parties to such cooperation benefit or they need not participate. There are no values, no "social" responsibilities in any sense other than the shared values and responsibilities of individuals. Society is a collection of individuals and of the various groups they voluntarily form.

The political principle that underlies the political mechanism is conformity. The individual must serve a more general social interest— whether that be determined by a church or a dictator or a majority. The individual may have a vote and say in what is to be done, but if he is overruled, he must conform. It is appropriate for some to require others to contribute to a general social purpose whether they wish to or not.

Unfortunately, unanimity is not always feasible. There are some respects in which conformity appears unavoidable, so I do not see how one can avoid the use of the political mechanism altogether.

But the doctrine of "social responsibility" taken seriously would extend the scope of the political mechanism to every human activity. It does not differ in philosophy from the most explicitly collectivist doctrine. It differs only by professing to believe that collectivist ends can be attained without collectivist means. That is why, in my book *Capitalism and Freedom*, I have called it a "fundamentally subversive doctrine" in a free society, and I have said that in such a society, "there is one and only one social responsibility of business—to use its resources and engage in activities designed to increase its profits so long as it stays within the rules of the game, which is to say, engages in open and free competition without deception or fraud." ◆ ◆ ◆

A Stakeholder Theory
of the Modern Corporation
Kantian Capitalism

R. Edward Freeman

One way of thinking about a corporation is as a boat, on an ocean, that casts its nets over the side and then hauls in the catch. A corporation is a profitmaking vehicle dedicated to maximizing returns to its owners: the shareholders. It can pull profit from a community but has no other obligation than engaging in free and open competition with other companies. A corporation, like the fishing boat, can move to follow greater profitability at will.

Freeman wants to overthrow this view entirely. His conception of the corporation is as a member of a community—one that has duties and responsibilities to act as a good citizen. A stakeholder is anyone who has a stake or interest in the company, essentially anyone who may be helped or hurt by corporate action. Under the stakeholder view, a company has to be responsible to many stakeholders, including shareholders, workers, consumers, suppliers, and the community at large. A manager's prime duty is not to maximize returns to shareholders but to balance the interests of all stakeholders. In the article he presents six ground rules to create stakeholder management.

INTRODUCTION

Corporations have ceased to be merely legal devices through which the private business transactions of individuals may be carried on. Though still much used for this purpose, the corporate form has acquired a larger significance. The corporation has, in fact, become both a method of property tenure and a means of organizing economic life. Grown to tremendous proportions, there may be said to have evolved a "corporate system"—which has attracted to itself a combination of attributes and powers, and has attained a degree of prominence entitling it to be dealt with as a major social institution.[1]

Despite these prophetic words of Berle and Means (1932), scholars and managers alike continue to hold sacred the view that managers bear a special relationship to the stockholders in the firm. Since stockholders own shares in the firm, they have certain rights and privileges, which must be granted to them by management, as well as by others. Sanctions, in the form of "the law of corporations," and other protective mechanisms in the form of social custom, accepted management practice, myth, and ritual, are thought to reinforce the assumption of the primacy of the stockholder.

The purpose of this paper is to pose several challenges to this assumption, from within the framework of managerial capitalism, and to suggest the bare bones of an alternative theory, *a stakeholder theory of the modern corporation.* I do not seek the demise of the modern corporation, either intellectually or in fact. Rather, I seek its transformation. In the words of Neurath, we shall attempt to "rebuild the ship, plank by plank, while it remains afloat."[2]

My thesis is that I can revitalize the concept of managerial capitalism by replacing the notion that managers have a duty to stockholders with the concept that managers bear a fiduciary relationship to stakeholders. Stakeholders are those groups who have a stake in or claim on the firm. Specifically I include suppliers, customers, employees, stockholders, and the local community, as well as management in its role as agent for these groups. I argue that the legal, economic, political, and moral challenges to the currently received theory of the firm, as a nexus of contracts among the owners of the factors of production and customers, require us to revise this concept. That is, each of these stakeholder groups has a right not to be treated as a means to some end, and therefore must participate in determining the future direction of the firm in which they have a stake.

The crux of my argument is that we must reconceptualize the firm around the following question: For whose benefit and at whose expense should the firm be managed? I shall set forth such a reconceptualization in the form of a *stakeholder theory of the firm.* I shall then critically examine the stakeholder view and its implications for the future of the capitalist system.

THE ATTACK ON MANAGERIAL CAPITALISM

The Legal Argument

The basic idea of managerial capitalism is that in return for controlling the firm, management vigorously pursues the interests of stockholders. Central to the managerial view of the firm is the idea that management can pursue market trans-actions with suppliers and customers in an un-constrained manner.

The law of corporations gives a less clearcut answer to the question: In whose interest and for whose benefit should the modern corporation be governed? While it says that the corporations should be run primarily in the interests of the stockholders in the firm, it says further that the corporation exists "in contemplation of the law" and has personality as a "legal person," limited liability for its actions, and immortality, since its existence transcends that of its members. There-fore, directors and other officers of the firm have a fiduciary obligation to stockholders in the sense that the "affairs of the corporation" must be con-ducted in the interest of the stockholders. And stockholders can theoretically bring suit against those directors and managers for doing other-wise. But since the corporation is a legal person, existing in contemplation of the law, managers of the corporation are constrained by law.

Until recently, this was no constraint at all. In this century, however, the law has evolved to ef-fectively constrain the pursuit of stockholder in-terests at the expense of other claimants on the firm. It has, in effect, required that the claims of customers, suppliers, local communities, and employees be taken into consideration, though in general they are subordinated to the claims of stockholders.

For instance, the doctrine of "privity of con-tract," as articulated in *Winterbottom v. Wright* in 1842, has been eroded by recent developments in products liability law. Indeed, *Greenman v. Yuba Power* gives the manufacturer strict liability for damage caused by its products, even though the seller has exercised all possible care in the preparation and sale of the product and the con-sumer has not bought the product from nor en-tered into any contractual arrangement with the manufacturer. Caveat emptor has been replaced, in large part, with caveat venditor.[3] The Con-sumer Product Safety Commission has the power to enact product recalls, and in 1980 one U.S. automobile company recalled more cars than it built. Some industries are required to pro-vide information to customers about a product's ingredients, whether or not the customers want and are willing to pay for this information.[4]

The same argument is applicable to manage-ment's dealings with employees. The National Labor Relations Act gave employees the right to unionize and to bargain in good faith. It set up the National Labor Relations Board to enforce these rights with management. The Equal Pay Act of 1963 and Title VII of the Civil Rights Act of 1964 constrain management from discrimina-tion in hiring practices; these have been followed with the Age Discrimination in Employment Act of 1967.[5] The emergence of a body of adminis-trative case law arising from labor-management disputes and the historic settling of discrimina-tion claims with large employers such as AT&T have caused the emergence of a body of practice in the corporation that is consistent with the le-gal guarantee of the rights of the employees. The law has protected the due process rights of those employees who enter into collective bargaining agreements with management. As of the present, however, only 30 percent of the labor force are participating in such agreements; this has prompted one labor law scholar to propose a statutory law prohibiting dismissals of the 70 per-cent of the work force not protected.[6]

The law has also protected the interests of lo-cal communities. The Clean Air Act and Clean Water Act have constrained management from "spoiling the commons." In an historic case, *Marsh v. Alabama*, the Supreme Court ruled that a company-owned town was subject to the provisions of the U.S. Constitution, thereby guaranteeing the rights of local citizens and negating the "property rights" of the firm. Some states and municipalities have gone further and passed laws preventing firms from moving plants or limiting when and how plants can be closed. In sum, there is much current legal activity in this area to constrain management's pursuit of stockholders' interests at the expense of the local communities in which the firm operates.

I have argued that the result of such changes in the legal system can be viewed as giving some rights to those groups that have a claim on the firm, for example, customers, suppliers, employees, local communities, stockholders, and management. It raises the question, at the core of a theory of the firm: In whose interest and for whose benefit should the firm be managed? The answer proposed by managerial capitalism is clearly "the stockholders," but I have argued that the law has been progressively circumscribing this answer.

The Economic Argument

In its pure ideological form managerial capitalism seeks to maximize the interests of stockholders. In its perennial criticism of government regulation, management espouses the "invisible hand" doctrine. It contends that it creates the greatest good for the greatest number, and therefore government need not intervene. However, we know that externalities, moral hazards, and monopoly power exist in fact, whether or not they exist in theory. Further, some of the legal apparatus mentioned above has evolved to deal with just these issues.

The problem of the "tragedy of the commons" or the free-rider problem pervades the concept of public goods such as water and air. No one has an incentive to incur the cost of clean-up or the cost of nonpollution, since the marginal gain of one firm's action is small. Every firm reasons this way, and the result is pollution of water and air. Since the industrial revolution, firms have sought to internalize the benefits and externalize the costs of their actions. The cost must be borne by all, through taxation and regu-

lation; hence we have the emergence of the environmental regulations of the 1970s.

Similarly, moral hazards arise when the purchaser of a good or service can pass along the cost of that good. There is no incentive to economize, on the part of either the producer or the consumer, and there is excessive use of the resources involved. The institutionalized practice of third-party payment in health care is a prime example.

Finally, we see the avoidance of competitive behavior on the part of firms, each seeking to monopolize a small portion of the market and not compete with one another. In a number of industries, oligopolies have emerged, and while there is questionable evidence that oligopolies are not the most efficient corporate form in some industries, suffice it to say that the potential for abuse of market power has again led to regulation of managerial activity. In the classic case, AT&T, arguably one of the great technological and managerial achievements of the century, was broken up into eight separate companies to prevent its abuse of monopoly power.

Externalities, moral hazards, and monopoly power have led to more external control on managerial capitalism. There are de facto constraints, due to these economic facts of life, on the ability of management to act in the interests of stockholders.

A STAKEHOLDER THEORY OF THE FIRM

The Stakeholder Concept
Corporations have stakeholders, that is, groups and individuals who benefit from or are harmed by, and whose rights are violated or respected by, corporate actions. The concept of stakeholders is a generalization of the notion of stockholders, who themselves have some special claim on the firm. Just as stockholders have a right to demand

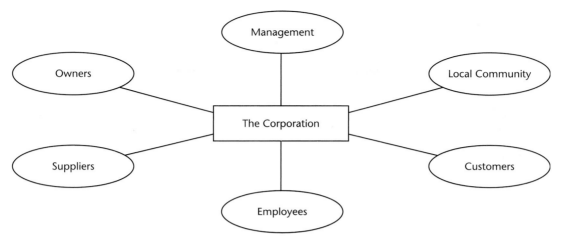

Figure 1 ◆ A STAKEHOLDER MODEL OF THE CORPORATION

certain actions by management, so do other stakeholders have a right to make claims. The exact nature of these claims is a difficult question that I shall address, but the logic is identical to that of the stockholder theory. Stakes require action of a certain sort, and conflicting stakes require methods of resolution.

Freeman and Reed (1983)[7] distinguish two senses of *stakeholder*. The "narrow definition" includes those groups who are vital to the survival and success of the corporation. The "wide definition" includes any group or individual who can affect or is affected by the corporation. I shall begin with a modest aim: to articulate a stakeholder theory using the narrow definition.

Stakeholders in the Modern Corporation

Figure 1 depicts the stakeholders in a typical large corporation. The stakes of each are reciprocal, since each can affect the other in terms of harms and benefits as well as rights and duties. The stakes of each are not univocal and would vary by particular corporation. I merely set forth some general notions that seem to be common to many large firms.

Owners have financial stake in the corporation in the form of stocks, bonds, and so on, and they expect some kind of financial return from them. Either they have given money directly to the firm, or they have some historical claim made through a series of morally justified exchanges. The firm affects their livelihood or, if a substantial portion of their retirement income is in stocks or bonds, their ability to care for themselves when they can no longer work. Of course, the stakes of owners will differ by type of owner, preferences for money, moral preferences, and so on, as well as by type of firm. The owners of AT&T are quite different from the owners of Ford Motor Company, with stock of the former company being widely dispersed among 3 million stockholders and that of the latter being held by a small family group as well as by a large group of public stockholders.

Employees have their jobs and usually their livelihood at stake; they often have specialized skills for which there is usually no perfectly elastic market. In return for their labor, they expect security, wages, benefits, and meaningful work. In return for their loyalty, the corporation is expected to provide for them and carry them through difficult times. Employees are expected to follow the instructions of management most of the time, to speak favorably about the company, and to be responsible citizens in the local communities in which the company operates. Where they are used as means to an end, they must participate in decisions affecting such use. The evidence that such policies and values as described here lead to productive company-employee relationships is compelling. It is equally compelling to realize that the opportunities for "bad faith" on the part of both management and employees are enormous. "Mock participation" in quality circles, singing the company song, and wearing the company uniform solely to please management all lead to distrust and unproductive work.

Suppliers, interpreted in a stakeholder sense, are vital to the success of the firm, for raw materials will determine the final product's quality and price. In turn the firm is a customer of the supplier and is therefore vital to the success and survival of the supplier. When the firm treats the supplier as a valued member of the stakeholder network, rather than simply as a source of materials, the supplier will respond when the firm is in need. Chrysler traditionally had very close ties to its suppliers, even to the extent that led some to suspect the transfer of illegal payments. And when Chrysler was on the brink of disaster, the suppliers responded with price cuts, accepting late payments, financing, and so on. Supplier and company can rise and fall together. Of course, again, the particular supplier relationships will depend on a number of variables such as the number of suppliers and whether the supplies are finished goods or raw materials.

Customers exchange resources for the products of the firm and in return receive the benefits of the products. Customers provide the lifeblood of the firm in the form of revenue. Given the level of reinvestment of earnings in large corporations, customers indirectly pay for the development of new products and services. Peters and Waterman (1982)[8] have argued that being close to the customer leads to success with other stakeholders and that a distinguishing characteristic of some companies that have performed well is their emphasis on the customer. By paying attention to customers' needs, management automatically addresses the needs of suppliers and owners. Moreover, it seems that the ethic of customer service carries over to the community. Almost without fail the "excellent companies" in Peters and Waterman's study have good reputations in the community. I would argue that Peters and Waterman have found multiple applications of Kant's dictum, "Treat persons as ends unto themselves," and it should come as no surprise that persons respond to such respectful treatment, be they customers, suppliers, owners, employees, or members of the local community. The real surprise is the novelty of the application of Kant's rule in a theory of good management practice.

The local community grants the firm the right to build facilities and, in turn, it benefits from the tax base and economic and social contributions of the firm. In return for the provision of local services, the firm is expected to be a good citizen, as is any person, either "natural or artificial." The firm cannot expose the community to unreasonable hazards in the form of pollution, toxic waste, and so on. If for some reason the firm must leave a community, it is expected to work with local leaders to make the transition as smoothly as possible. Of course, the firm does not have perfect knowledge, but when it discovers some danger or runs afoul of new competition, it is expected to inform the local community and to work with the community to overcome any problem. When the firm mismanages its relationship with the local community, it is in the same position as a citizen who commits a crime. It has violated the implicit social contract with the community and should expect to be distrusted and ostracized. It should not be surprised when punitive measures are invoked.

I have not included "competitors" as stakeholders in the narrow sense, since strictly speaking they are not necessary for the survival and success of the firm; the stakeholder theory works equally well in monopoly contexts. However, competitors and government would be the first to be included in an extension of this basic theory. It is simply not true that the interests of competitors in an industry are always in conflict. There is no reason why trade associations and other multi-organizational groups cannot band together to solve common problems that have little to do with how to restrain trade. Implementation of stakeholder management principles, in the long run, mitigates the need for industrial policy and an increasing role for government intervention and regulation.

The Role of Management

Management plays a special role, for it too has a stake in the modern corporation. On the one hand, management's stake is like that of employees, with some kind of explicit or implicit employment contract. But, on the other hand, management has a duty of safeguarding the welfare of the abstract entity that is the corporation. In short, management, especially top management, must look after the health of the corporation, and this involves balancing the multiple claims of conflicting stakeholders. Owners want higher financial returns, while customers want more money spent on research and development. Employees want higher wages and better benefits, while the local community wants better parks and day-care facilities.

The task of management in today's corporation is akin to that of King Solomon. The stakeholder theory does not give primacy to one stakeholder group over another, though there will surely be times when one group will benefit at the expense of others. In general, however, management must keep the relationships among stakeholders in balance. When these relationships become imbalanced, the survival of the firm is in jeopardy.

When wages are too high and product quality is too low, customers leave, suppliers suffer, and owners sell their stocks and bonds, depressing the stock price and making it difficult to raise new capital at favorable rates. Note, however, that the reason for paying returns to owners is not that they "own" the firm, but that their support is necessary for the survival of the firm, and that they have a legitimate claim on the firm. Similar reasoning applies in turn to each stakeholder group.

A stakeholder theory of the firm must redefine the purpose of the firm. The stockholder theory claims that the purpose of the firm is to maximize the welfare of the stockholders, perhaps subject to some moral or social constraints, either because such maximization leads to the greatest good or because of property rights. The purpose of the firm is quite different in my view.

"The stakeholder theory" can be unpacked into a number of stakeholder theories, each of which has a "normative core," inextricably linked to the way that corporations should be governed and the way that managers should act. So, attempts to more fully define, or more carefully define, a stakeholder theory are misguided. Following Donaldson and Preston, I want to insist that the normative, descriptive, instrumental, and metaphorical (my addition to their framework) uses of 'stakeholder' are tied together in particular political constructions to yield a number of possible "stakeholder theories." "Stakeholder theory" is thus a genre of stories about how we could live. Let met be more specific.

A "normative core" of a theory is a set of sentences that includes among others, sentences like:

1. Corporations ought to be governed . . .
2. Managers ought to act to . . .

where we need arguments or further narratives which include business and moral terms to fill in the blanks. This normative core is not always

Exhibit 1 ◆ A REASONABLE PLURALISM

	A. *Corporations ought to be governed . . .*	*B.* *Managers ought to act . . .*	*C.* *The background disciplines of "value creation" are . . .*
Doctrine of Fair Contracts	. . . in accordance with the six principles.	. . . in the interests of stakeholders.	—business theories —theories that explain stakeholder behavior
Feminist Standpoint Theory	. . . in accordance with the principles of caring/connection and relationships.	. . . to maintain and care for relationships and networks of stakeholders.	—business theories —feminist theory —social science understanding of networks
Ecological Principles	. . . in accordance with the principle of caring for the earth.	. . . to care for the earth.	—business theories —ecology —other

reducible to a fundamental ground like the theory of property, but certain normative cores are consistent with modern understandings of property. Certain elaborations of the theory of private property plus the other institutions of political liberalism give rise to particular normative cores. But there are other institutions, other political conceptions of how society ought to be structured, so that there are different possible normative cores.

So, one normative core of a stakeholder theory might be a feminist standpoint one, rethinking how we would restructure "value-creating activity" along principles of caring and connection.[9] Another would be an ecological (or several ecological) normative cores. Mark Starik has argued that the very idea of a stakeholder theory of the *firm* ignores certain ecological necessities.[10] Exhibit 1 is suggestive of how these theories could be developed.

In the next section I shall sketch the normative core based on pragmatic liberalism. But, any normative core must address the questions in columns A or B, or explain why these questions may be irrelevant, as in the ecological view. In addition, each "theory," and I use the word hesitantly, must place the normative core within a more full-fledged account of how we could un-

derstand value-creating activity differently (column C). The only way to get on with this task is to see the stakeholder idea as a metaphor. The attempt to prescribe one and only one "normative core" and construct "a stakeholder theory" is at best a disguised attempt to smuggle a normative core past the unsophisticated noses of other unsuspecting academics who are just happy to see the end of the stockholder orthodoxy.

If we begin with the view that we can understand value-creation activity as a contractual process among those parties affected, and if for simplicity's sake we initially designate those parties as financiers, customers, suppliers, employees, and communities, then we can construct a normative core that reflects the liberal notions of autonomy, solidarity, and fairness as articulated by John Rawls, Richard Rorty, and others.[11] Notice that building these moral notions into the foundations of how we understand value creation and contracting requires that we eschew separating the "business" part of the process from the "ethical" part, and that we start with the presumption of equality among the contractors, rather than the presumption in favor of financier rights.

The normative core for this redesigned contractual theory will capture the liberal idea of fairness if it ensures a basic equality among stakeholders in terms of their moral rights as these are realized in the firm, and if it recognizes that inequalities among stakeholders are justified if they raise the level of the least well-off stakeholder. The liberal ideal of autonomy is captured by the realization that each stakeholder must be free to enter agreements that create value for themselves, and solidarity is realized by the recognition of the mutuality of stakeholder interests.

One way to understand fairness in this context is to claim *a la* Rawls that a contract is fair if parties to the contract would agree to it in ignorance of their actual stakes. Thus, a contract is like a fair bet, if each party is willing to turn the tables and accept the other side. What would a fair contract among corporate stakeholders look like? If we can articulate this ideal, a sort of corporate constitution, we could then ask whether actual corporations measure up to this standard, and we also begin to design corporate structures which are consistent with this Doctrine of Fair Contracts.

Imagine if you will, representative stakeholders trying to decide on "the rules of the game." Each is rational in a straightforward sense, looking out for its own self-interest. At least *ex ante*, stakeholders are the relevant parties since they will be materially affected. Stakeholders know how economic activity is organized and could be organized. They know general facts about the way the corporate world works. They know that in the real world there are or could be transaction costs, externalities, and positive costs of contracting. Suppose they are uncertain about what other social institutions exist, but they know the range of those institutions. They do not know if government exists to pick up the tab for any externalities, or if they will exist in the nightwatchman state of libertarian theory. They know success and failure stories of businesses around the world. In short, they are behind a Rawls-like veil of ignorance, and they do not know what stake each will have when the veil is lifted. What groundrules would they choose to guide them?

The first groundrule is "The Principle of Entry and Exit." Any contract that is the corporation must have clearly defined entry, exit, and renegotiation conditions, or at least it must have methods or processes for so defining these conditions. The logic is straightforward: each stakeholder must be able to determine when an agreement exists and has a chance of fulfillment. This is not to imply that contracts cannot contain contingent claims or other methods for resolving uncertainty, but rather that it must contain methods for determining whether or not it is valid.

The second groundrule I shall call "The Principle of Governance," and it says that the procedure for changing the rules of the game must be agreed upon by unanimous consent. Think about the consequences of a majority of stakeholders systematically "selling out" a minority. Each stakeholder, in ignorance of its actual role, would seek to avoid such a situation. In reality this principle translates into each stakeholder never giving up its right to participate in the governance of the corporation, or perhaps into the existence of stakeholder governing boards.

The third groundrule I shall call "The Principle of Externalities," and it says that if a contract between A and B imposes a cost on C, then C has the option to become a party to the contract, and the terms are renegotiated. Once again the rationality of this condition is clear. Each stakeholder will want insurance that it does not become C.

The fourth groundrule is "The Principle of Contracting Costs," and it says that all parties to the contract must share in the cost of contracting. Once again the logic is straightforward. Any one stakeholder can get stuck.

A fifth groundrule is "The Agency Principle" that says that any agent must serve the interests of all stakeholders. It must adjudicate conflicts within the bounds of the other principals. Once again the logic is clear. Agents for any one group would have a privileged place.

A sixth and final groundrule we might call, "The Principle of Limited Immortality." The corporation shall be managed as if it can continue to serve the interests of stakeholders through time. Stakeholders are uncertain about the future but, subject to exit conditions, they realize that the continued existence of the corporation is in their interest. Therefore, it would be rational to hire managers who are fiduciaries to their interest and the interest of the collective. If it turns out the "collective interest" is the empty set, then this principle simply collapses into the Agency Principle.

Thus, the Doctrine of Fair Contracts consists of these six groundrules or principles:

1. The Principle of Entry and Exit
2. The Principle of Governance
3. The Principle of Externalities
4. The Principle of Contracting Costs
5. The Agency Principle
6. The Principle of Limited Immortality

Think of these groundrules as a doctrine which would guide actual stakeholders in devising a corporate constitution or charter. Think of management as having the duty to act in accordance with some specific constitution or charter.

Obviously, if the Doctrine of Fair Contracts and its accompanying background narratives are to effect real change, there must be requisite changes in the enabling laws of the land. I propose the following three principles to serve as constitutive elements of attempts to reform the law of corporations.

The Stakeholder Enabling Principle
Corporations shall be managed in the interests of its stakeholders, defined as employers, financiers, customers, employees, and communities.

The Principle of Director Responsibility
Directors of the corporation shall have a duty of care to use reasonable judgment to define and direct the affairs of the corporation in accordance with the Stakeholder Enabling Principle.

The Principle of Stakeholder Recourse
Stakeholders may bring an action against the directors for failure to perform the required duty of care.

Obviously, there is more work to be done to spell out these principles in terms of model legislation. As they stand, they try to capture the intuitions that drive the liberal ideals. It is equally plain that corporate constitutions which meet a test like the doctrine of fair contracts are meant to enable directors and executives to manage the corporation in conjunction with these same liberal ideals. ◆ ◆ ◆

◆ Notes

1. Cf. A. Berle and G. Means, *The Modern Corporation and Private Property* (New York: Commerce Clearing House, 1932), 1. For a reassessment of Berle and Means' argument after 50 years, see *Journal of Law and Economics* 26 (June 1983), especially G. Stigler and C. Friedland, "The Literature of Economics: The Case of Berle and Means," 237–68; D. North, "Comment on Stigler and Friedland," 269–72; and G. Means, "Corporate Power in the Marketplace," 467–85.

2. The metaphor of rebuilding the ship while afloat is attributed to Neurath by W. Quine, *Word and Object* (Cambridge: Harvard University Press, 1960), and W. Quine and J. Ullian, *The Web of*

Belief (New York: Random House, 1978). The point is that to keep the ship afloat during repairs we must replace a plank with one that will do a better job. Our argument is that stakeholder capitalism can so replace the current version of managerial capitalism.

3. See R. Charan and E. Freeman, "Planning for the Business Environment of the 1980s," *The Journal of Business Strategy* 1 (1980): 9–19, especially p. 15 for a brief account of the major developments in products liability law.

4. See S. Breyer, *Regulation and Its Reform* (Cambridge: Harvard University Press, 1983), 133, for an analysis of food additives.

5. See I. Millstein and S. Katsh, *The Limits of Corporate Power* (New York: Macmillan, 1981), Chapter 4.

6. Cf. C. Summers, "Protecting All Employees Against Unjust Dismissal," *Harvard Business Review* 58 (1980): 136, for a careful statement of the argument.

7. See E. Freeman and D. Reed, "Stockholders and Stakeholders: A New Perspective on Corporate Governance," in C. Huizinga, ed., *Corporate Governance: A Definitive Exploration of the Issues* (Los Angeles: UCLA Extension Press, 1983).

8. See T. Peters and R. Waterman, *In Search of Excellence* (New York: Harper and Row, 1982).

9. See, for instance, A. Wicks, D. Gilbert, and E. Freeman, "A Feminist Reinterpretation of the Stakeholder Concept," *Business Ethics Quarterly*, Vol. 4, No. 4, October 1994; and E. Freeman and J. Liedtka, "Corporate Social Responsibility: A Critical Approach," *Business Horizons*, Vol. 34, No. 4, July–August 1991, pp. 92–98.

10. At the Toronto workshop Mark Starik sketched how a theory would look if we took the environment to be a stakeholder. This fruitful line of work is one example of my main point about pluralism.

11. J. Rawls, *Political Liberalism*, New York: Columbia University Press, 1993; and R. Rorty, "The Priority of Democracy to Philosophy" in *Reading Rorty: Critical Responses to Philosophy and the Mirror of Nature (and Beyond)*, ed. Alan R. Malachowski, Cambridge, MA: Blackwell, 1990.

PART TWO

MAKING BUSINESS MORAL

I N THE CASE OF THE *Exxon Valdez* oil spill, the company ended up paying billions of dollars for the apparent mistake of a single individual: the ship's captain. When the shuttle *Challenger* blew up shortly after takeoff, the inquiry focused primarily on the actions of middle managers and largely ignored the role of senior management and the corporate culture. Writing in his autobiography, the executive in charge of the Ford Pinto acknowledged that the company put it on the road with a known design flaw but described it as a "legal and public relations problem." This section deals with the way moral responsibility is shared within corporations and the possible means that we have to promote desired behaviors in business.

One view of business is that employees should entirely adopt and adapt to the company's values as part of the employment contract. Others feel that there are compromises they are not willing to make, whatever the consequences. An element in framing these discussions is the extent to which the individual should be held accountable for doing the corporation's bidding and, conversely, the extent to which the corporation should be accountable for rogue workers who do wrong while on the company payroll.

Chapter 5 looks closely at what it means to be morally responsible, both as an individual and as part of a group. At times we might consider that leadership is accepting responsibility for whatever transpires "on your watch." To be more than an empty phrase, though, we might expect someone who accepts the blame to step down or pay reparations. Pontius Pilate notoriously washed his hands after condemning Jesus, who he considered a just man, believing his washing absolved him of responsibility. But very often we find we are part of an organization that has been involved with acts of which we do not approve, even in a tangential way. This might make us complicit through association, because we are part of the overall group. Perhaps we cannot abdicate responsibility or shield ourselves from future accountability merely by declaring that we were not directly involved in the original act.

Yet, it is unrealistic to think that we can be fully and continually aware of everything that goes on in a company; much of the time we have to trust the company to do the right thing. Corporate codes and policies may go a long way in providing guidelines for employees in this regard. One view outlined by a butler reflecting on his years of service is that the most important moral stage is when first joining the company or institution; the individual makes a conscious decision at that time to affiliate with an organization and adopt many of its values as personal ones. After this initial decision, going against an employer will inevitably involve an element of disloyalty.

At some point employees might be moved to act by a clash of values with the company, even to the point where they will go outside the usual corporate structure to announce wrongdoing to the world at large. It is worth examining these cases in some detail because they represent dramatic tipping points where loyalty to the company is overridden by a duty to the common good. Whistle-blowing still carries the schoolyard stigma of being a tattletale even though society at large considers it heroic. Chapter 6 examines these issues and the recent legislative attempts to promote and protect whistle-blowing.

Corporations can certainly influence individual behavior, and they often shape it through overt policies. Chapter 7 looks at political attempts to steer corporations away from the behavior that resulted in a series of scandals in the late 1990s. High executives now have to hold themselves personally accountable for acts by their staffs, and there are new criminal penalties for managers involved in corporate crime. These reforms have been met with mixed reactions, and it is probably still too early to judge their effectiveness. The open question remains: If codes and laws are insufficient to buttress moral action in business, are there other alternatives?

ROLE MORALITY
AND PERSONAL RESPONSIBILITY

When we work for an organization, we typically give up some degree of control over our lives. We cannot just do what we want, when we want, in the way we want. Some jobs are much more restrictive than others—employees may have to wear uniforms, for example. In many cases the firm has a code of conduct that prohibits certain behaviors and permits others. Personal discretion in making business choices is often limited. For example, many customer service agents follow a company script when dealing with the general public.

If we give up so much, to what extent are we a mere voice box for a corporation? If a company dictates our behavior, what differentiates us from cyborgs? Ultimately, we have the choice to quit our job or speak out against the company as a whistle-blower. But most of the time we are in the awkward position of balancing—and sometimes compromising—our own values with those of the company. We may feel that it would be right to accept a late payment from someone who has just been laid off or to reject a returned television at the electronics store when it has obviously been used as a free rental for a weekend;

yet we do not always have the discretion to substitute our own judgment for company policy. When we take off our individual hat and put on the company's, we are agents of the employer and may have to adopt that morality; we may find ourselves acting in ways that we might not in our everyday lives.

This dynamic cuts both ways. A company may have a rogue employee who contravenes the code of conduct and causes harm. Even if there is a clear paper trail and evidence that shows the individual broke company policy, very often the company remains responsible for the acts of its employees. The law may treat a company as a *persona ficta*—a fictitious person—for some purposes such as signing contracts, and similarly we may find it useful to consider a company as a collective entity. This may be especially true if there is a strong corporate culture that inculcates people into a particular set of behaviors. These companies may not even have a written set of procedures, but it becomes clear to employees that there is a company way of doing things, and those who adopt them will prosper, but those who do not will not last long in that environment.

So, when something happens for good or ill, who is morally responsible? Take the case of the *Exxon Valdez*, where the captain left a supertanker in the charge of an unqualified sailor while he retired to his cabin. The tanker ran aground on a reef, spilling millions of gallons of crude oil into an ecologically pristine area. There are a number of ways of looking at the issue. Among the candidates for blame are

- The helmsman who may have made a mistake
- The captain who was in charge of the tanker
- The division of Exxon that hired a known alcoholic as captain
- Exxon as a corporation
- Any and all employees of Exxon, including local service stations
- Consumers who value cheap gas over extra protections for transport, including double-hulled ships

Does it make sense for us to assign collective blame? That is, even though the law treats corporations as if they were individuals, is a corporation a moral actor in the same way a person is? If we said, Exxon is responsible for the wreck, would that be meaningful or just shorthand for the claim that someone or many people at Exxon are responsible? That is, does it function as a collective noun that represents every member of the company? And if that is the case, how do we divide the responsibility? In the case of a very large organization, the degree of individual responsibility may turn out to be very little indeed. Moreover, should we taint everyone in an organization for the faults of a few?

Additionally, we have another issue if we cannot find a paper trail or there is no one person to whom we can assign blame. We can certainly imagine that a company has a set of understandings—say, "shift the goods no matter what it takes"—where everyone knows what is expected, but there is no written policy or no individual who can be held accountable. Will the moral responsibility just evaporate in that case?

Responsibility is an elusive term in English. Consider the following uses:

a. The captain of the *Titanic* was a responsible person.
b. The captain of the *Titanic* was a responsible seaman.
c. The captain of the *Titanic* was responsible for the loss of the ship.
d. The captain of the *Titanic* was responsible for his actions on the night the ship was lost.
e. The captain of the *Titanic* was not responsible for the loss of the ship.
f. The captain of the *Titanic* was held responsible for the loss of the ship.
g. The White Star line, owner of the *Titanic*, was held responsible for the loss of the ship.[1]

In (a), Captain Smith's personal qualities are referred to; no doubt he paid his debts on time and kept his word. Use (b) focuses on his professional standing, and indeed he was a highly qualified and experienced sailor. There are two different elements operating in (c). There may have been things he did not do that contributed to the tragedy—for example, he ignored warnings about icebergs and refused to slow the ship. It also speaks to a doctrine that suggests that the captain of a ship is ultimately responsible for everything that happens on board, whether or not he is directly aware of all that is going on. In (d), the focus again is on personal responsibility, but here it is in the sense that Smith had not been drinking that night and so retained his

[1]This list is drawn from examples used by H. L. A. Hart, "Varieties of Responsibility," *Law Quarterly Review* 83 (1967). See also K. Gibson, "Going Beyond Intuitions," *Teaching Business Ethics* 6(2002).

capacity for autonomous and rational thought. Use (e) suggests that the captain was not the one who caused the accident, and so it is perfectly consistent with (c) where he is the one who is held accountable even though it could have been the failure of the lookout that led to the collision. The usage in (f) is more legalistic; there could have been policies in place at the time that would apportion the blame based on the current admiralty regulations. An inquiry was held after the tragedy, and that assessment of the facts put the captain at fault. Plausibly, the shipyard might have made the ship from unusually brittle metal that could not withstand a collision at sea that might not have destroyed other ships. A finding that held the shipyard legally responsible would not be inconsistent with (c): Liners, especially brittle ones, should avoid icebergs. Finally, the captain did go down with the ship, and thus if we are more interested in compensation than assigning blame, we look to the parent company or its insurers (g).

The writers in this chapter isolate what it means to be morally responsible in an organizational setting. Joel Feinberg looks at some of the various ways that we delineate collective responsibility. John Bishop takes on the "captain of the ship" view: If a disaster happens to a company, to what extent should an executive be held accountable? He points out that executives are very often isolated from bad news and so may sincerely claim that they had no knowledge of a problem. Yet, the same could also be said of many of the positive things that occur that lead to CEOs getting bonuses, and in that case they are only too happy to take responsibility. In Japan, it is not unusual for the president of a company to resign after a tragic incident and to offer personal apologies. We might ask what cultural differences lead to U.S. executives acting defensively and often laying the blame on middle management.

Peter French recounts a discussion with a customer service representative and makes a compelling case that he was talking to the company rather than to an individual. The lesson he draws from the encounter is that corporations can be very powerful moral actors, in addition to the individuals who make up the organization. Kevin Gibson looks at the purported difference between role morality and professional morality by referring to four examples. A professional is assumed to have greater autonomy and more loyalty to the professional code than to an individual employer. He concludes that two additional elements need to be considered to provide a more complete analysis of behavior in role. The first is to look at the discretionary power that an individual has, because even a judge who seems to be a professional may be forced to follow mandatory sentencing guidelines despite personal misgivings. Second, the way that a situation is presented is crucial. Sometimes incidents in the workplace are portrayed so that they no longer come under rigid guidelines or are written off as not morally considerable but just doing business. Postmodernist writers have effectively shown that we all create stories to make sense of our world. The way a situation is described makes a tremendous difference, and there may not be a single objective truth. In the case of the shipwreck of the *Herald of Free Enterprise*, for example, one writer describes the sailor who should have checked the watertight doors as taking a nap whereas others concentrate on the fact that the owners had cut back on staffing and many of the crew were exhausted from working double shifts.

The chapter concludes with a very short extract from Lee Iaccoca's autobiography where he describes his role in the Pinto affair, which allows readers to draw their own conclusions about the narrative he chooses and how appropriate it is in the context of executive responsibility.

Collective Responsibility

Joel Feinberg

Should you be held responsible for something you did not do? Feinberg specializes in the philosophy of law. In this piece he traces what is meant by personal and collective responsibility. He examines the question of whether an individual shares responsibility by virtue of belonging to an organization, even if he or she was not involved in any questionable activity. He also looks at the notion of "strict liability" where a corporation is held responsible for any harm that results from its goods or services, regardless of fault. Thus, a company might be penalized for an injury caused by someone misusing their product or failing to read the instructions. Although he is generally talking about the law in this selection, there are clear implications for individual moral responsibility in institutional settings. If things have gone badly for your company, do they inevitably taint you, or can you shield yourself or totally abdicate responsibility?

When we state that a person is responsible for some harm, we sometimes mean to ascribe to him *liability* to certain responsive attitudes, judgments, or actions. Some responsive actions require authority; of these some are punitive, and others force compensation of a harmed victim. In the typical case of individual liability to unfavorable responses from others, three preconditions must be satisfied. First, it must be true that the responsible individual did the harmful thing in question, or at least that his action or omission made a substantial causal contribution to it. Second, the causally contributory conduct must have been in some way *faulty*. Finally, if the harmful outcome was truly "his fault," the requisite causal connection must have been directly between the faulty aspect of his conduct and the outcome. It is not sufficient to have caused harm

and to have been at fault if the fault was irrelevant to the causing. We can use the expression "contributory fault" to refer compendiously to these three conditions. Thus, in the standard case of responsibility for harm, there can be no liability without contributory fault.

Certain familiar deviations from the standard case, however, give rise to confusion and misgiving. . . . The cases I have in mind can be discussed under three headings.

STRICT LIABILITY

What is called "strict liability" in the law is simply any liability for which the contributory fault condition is weakened or absent. This is the most general category; vicarious and collective liability are among its more interesting subspecies. For the most part, contractual liability has always tended to be "strict." Since this is liability that one imposes on oneself voluntarily, there is rarely any doubt expressed about its propriety. And no doubt can be expressed about its utility. Manufacturers brag about their warrantees and unconditional guarantees; and private bargainers quite often find it to their mutual advantage when one promises that, "if anything goes wrong, I'll bear the loss, no matter whose fault it is." In the law of torts, certain classes of persons are put on warning that, if they engage in certain ultra-hazardous activities, then they must be prepared to compensate any innocent parties who may incidentally be harmed, no matter how carefully and faultlessly the activities are carried out. There is always a risk of harm to others when one starts fires even on his own land, or keeps wild animals, or engages in blasting with high explosives. The law, of course, permits such activities, but it assigns the risk in advance to those who engage in them. This may seem to be a hard arrangement, since even if a construction company, for example, takes every reasonable precaution before dynamiting, it nevertheless can be found liable, if through some freakish chance a person at a great distance is injured by a flying rock set in motion by the blast, and can be forced to compensate the injured party for his losses. That the company was faultlessly careful in its operations is no defense. Still, this rule is by no means an arbitrary harassment, and its rigors are easily mitigated. The prospective responsibility imposed on blasters by law applies even to events beyond their control, but, *knowing this in advance* (an all-important consideration), they will be more careful than ever; and, further, they can guard against disastrous expenses by adjusting their prices and figuring compensation costs among their normal business costs.

Strict liability in the criminal law is much less likely to accord with reasonable standards of justice than in contracts and torts; but even penalties and punishments may, in certain circumstances, dispense with the requirement of fault, provided that prior assignments of risks are clear and that some degree of prior control is possible. Perhaps the best known strict liability statutes in the criminal law are those creating "public welfare offenses." Here the rationale for disregarding actual fault is similar, in part, to that supporting strict liability for ultra-hazardous activities in torts. All milk producers, for example, are put on notice by one statute that, if any of their marketed product is found to be adulterated, they will be subject to stiff penalty. The producers have the power and authority to regulate their own facilities, procedures, and employees. The law in effect tells them that, since there is such a paramount public interest in pure foods, they must give the public an unconditional guarantee of the purity of their product. If the guarantee fails, no questions will be asked about fault; the fine will be imposed automatically. Then it will be up to the company to exercise its control by locating and eliminating the fault. If this arrangement seems unfair, the company can be reminded that the risk is well known and is in fact the price producers pay for the privilege of serving the public for their own profit—a price they presumably have been quite willing to pay. Moreover, it really does protect the public by providing incentive to vigilant safety measures; and the penalties, in any case, are only fines. No perfectly innocent persons are sent to prison. . . .

In all the examples of plausibly just strict liability, the liable party must have had some control over his own destiny—some choice whether to take the risk assigned him by the law and some power to diminish the risk by his own care. When liability may be imposed even without such control, however, then it can "fall from the sky," like a plague, and land senselessly on complete strangers. Strict liability, when rational, is never totally unconditional or random.

VICARIOUS LIABILITY

Much, but by no means all, strict liability is also vicarious liability. There can be strict liability when *no one* is at fault, or where the question of contributory fault cannot be settled. There is vicarious liability, on the other hand, when the contributory fault, or some element of it, is properly ascribed to one party (or group of parties), but the liability is ascribed to a different party (or parties). In such cases we say that the latter party is responsible for the harmful consequences of a faulty action or omission of the former party. The person who did or caused the harm is not the one who is called upon to answer for it.

One familiar and surely unobjectionable type of vicarious liability is that which derives from the process of *authorization*. One party, called a "principal," authorizes another party, called the "agent," to act, within a certain range, for him. "He that acteth for another," wrote Hobbes, is said to bear his person, or act in his name."[1] Acting in another's name is quite another thing than merely acting in his interests (also called "acting for him") or merely substituting for him, as an understudy, for example, replaces an indisposed actor (also called "acting in place of him"). An agent acts "for" or "in place of" his principal in a different sense. The agent is often given the right to act, speak, sign contracts, make appointments, or the like, and these acts are as binding on the principal as if he had done them himself. The relation of authorization, as Hanna Pitkin points out,[2] is lopsided: the rights go to the agent, and the responsibilities to the principal.

The relation of authorization can take two very different forms, depending on the degree of discretion granted to the agent, and there is a continuum of combinations between the extremes. On the one hand, there is the agent who is the mere "mouthpiece" of his principal. He is a "tool" in much the same sense as is a typewriter or telephone: he simply transmits the instructions of his principal. Thus messengers, delegates, spokesmen, typists, and amanuenses are sometimes called agents. . . . The principal acts *through* his agent much as he might act through some mechanical medium. On the other hand, an agent may be some sort of expert hired to exercise his professional judgment on behalf of, and in the name of, the principal. He may be given, within some limited area of expertise, complete independence to act as he deems best, binding his principal to all the beneficial or detrimental consequences. This is the role played by trustees and some other investment managers, some lawyers, buyers, and ghost-writers. . . .

It is often said that the very actions of agents themselves, and not merely their normative consequences, are directly ascribable to their principals, through "a kind of fiction";[3] but this, I submit, is a dangerously misleading way of talking. If A has B's power of attorney, he may have the right to sign B's signature; and if he signs it on a contract or a check, the pecuniary consequences may be exactly as they would be had B himself signed his name. The results are *as if B* had himself acted; but it is nevertheless true that *he* did not act—A acted for him. . . .

Another form of vicarious liability is the responsibility of employers ("masters") to compensate victims of the negligence or even, in some cases, the deliberate wrongdoing of their employees ("servants"), even when the employee is acting without, or in direct defiance of, the explicit orders of his boss, and the boss committed no negligence in hiring the employee in the first place, or in supervising, instructing, or outfitting him. Here, indeed, "the sins of the servant are visited upon the master." If my dog bites you, the biting is imputed to him, the liability to me.[4] Similarly, if the driver of my delivery truck, while doing his job, puts a dent in your fender or a crease in your skull, the liability to enforced compensation is mine, not his. (*His* liability is to *me*; he is now subject to being fired.) The rationale of this universal but once highly controverted practice is clear enough. If an accident victim has only a truck driver to sue, he may end up paying most of his disastrous medical expenses himself. The employer, having a "deeper pocket," is a more competent compensator; and, moreover, since he has *control* over the selection of employees for dangerous work, the rule will make him more careful in his assignment of tasks. It may be unfair to him to make him pay for an accident that was not his fault, but it would impose an even greater hardship and injustice to put the burden mainly on the shoulders of the equally faultless accident victim. And, again, there are means open to employers of anticipating and redistributing losses caused by their employees' negligence.

Still another form of vicarious liability derives from the relation of *suretyship.* A bonding company may insure an employer against the dishonesty of a new employee for a fee that may be paid by either employer or employee. If the employee commits embezzlement and makes his escape, the fault, guilt, agency, and causation all belong to the employee, but the liability to make good the losses is the innocent surety's. Similarly, the guarantor of another's debt pays if the other fails; and the poster of bail forfeits, if the bailed prisoner fails to make appearance.

Vicarious liability through authorization, hierarchy, mastership, and suretyship can thus be rational, in the sense that they rest on intellectually respectable, if not always convincing, rationales. Most of what has passed as vicarious criminal liability in human history is otherwise. Holmes traced the origin of both civil and criminal liability to certain animistic conceptions common to the Hebrews, Greeks, Romans, and Germans, and apparently to all human cultures at a certain stage in their development. The instrument of harm, whether it were a tool, a weapon, a tree, an ox, a slave, or a child, was regarded as the immediate and "natural" object of vengeance. It was "noxal," that is, accursed, and had to be forfeited to the victim, or his family, to be torn apart and annihilated. Later the principle of composition was adopted, and the owner of the noxal instrument could buy off its victim as an alternative to forfeiture. Nevertheless, in the early centuries of all major legal systems, inanimate objects and animals were "punished"; and the related practices of blood feud, noxal surrender, and substitute sacrifice flourished. . . .

COLLECTIVE LIABILITY

. . .

Collective liability, as I shall use the term, is the vicarious liability of an organized group (either a loosely organized, impermanent collection or a corporate institution) for the actions of its constituent members. When the whole group as such is held responsible for the actions of one or some of its members, then, from the point of view of any given "responsible" individual, *his* liability in most cases will be vicarious.

Under certain circumstances, collective liability is a natural and prudent way of arranging the affairs of an organization, which the members might well be expected to undertake themselves, quite voluntarily. This expectation applies only to those organizations (usually small ones) where there is already a high degree of *de facto* solidarity. Collective responsibility not only expresses the solidarity but also strengthens it; thus it is a good thing to whatever extent the preexistent solidarity was a good thing. Where prior solidarity is absent, collective liability arrangements may seek their justification through the desperate prior *need* for solidarity.

When does a group have "solidarity"? Three intertwined conditions, I think, must be satisfied to some degree. There has to be first of all, a large *community of interest* among all the members, not merely a specific overlap of shared specialized interests, of the sort that unite the members of a corporation's board of directors, for example, no matter how strong. A community of interest exists between two parties to the extent that each party's integrated set of interests contains as one of its components the integrated interest-set of the other. Obviously, this will be difficult to arrange in large and diverse groups. A husband, for example, might have as his main interests (whose fulfillment as a harmonious set constitutes his *well-being*) his health, his material possessions, his professional reputation, his professional achievement, *and* the well-being (also defined in terms of an integrated set of interests) of his wife and his children. His interests would thus include or contain the interests of several other people. If those other persons' interests, in a precisely similar way, were to embrace his, then there would be between them a perfect community of interest. Secondly, such "community" is often associated with bonds of sentiment directed toward common objects, or of reciprocal affection between the parties. (R. B. Perry defined "love" as an interest in the interests of someone else). Thirdly, solidarity is ordinarily a function of the degree to which the parties share a common lot, the extent to which their goods and harms are necessarily collective and indivisible. When a father is jailed, his whole family shares the disgrace and the loss of his provisions. There is no hurting one member without hurting them all; and because of the way their interests are related, the successes and satisfactions of one radiate their benefits to the others.

Individuals normally pool their liabilities when they share a common cooperative purpose, and each recognizes in the others complementary abilities of a useful or necessary kind. Thus salesmen combine with administrators to become business partners, pooling their talents and

sharing their risks. Joint authorships are often cases of mutual ghost-writing, where each party stands answerable for the joint product of their several labors. Athletic team members must all win or all lose together: victory is not the prize of individual merit alone, nor is defeat linked to "contributory fault." Similarly, in underground conspiracies and desperate dangerous undertakings, the spirit of "all for one and one for all" is not merely a useful device; it is imposed by the very nature of the enterprise. What makes collective liability natural in such cases is that parties who are largely of one mind to begin with are led (or forced) by circumstances to act in concert and share the risk of common failure or the fruits of an indivisible success. . . .

Collective-responsibility arrangements are most likely to offend our modern sensibilities when the liabilities are to criminal punishment. Yet there was a time when primitive conditions required that the policing function be imposed on local groups themselves through a system of *compulsory universal suretyship.* Among the early Anglo-Saxons, the perfectly trustworthy man was he who did not stray from the village where his many kin resided, for they were his sureties who could guarantee his good conduct. In contrast, the stranger far from his kindred had nothing to restrain him, and since his death would excite no blood feud, he had no legal protection against the assaults of others.[5] With the development of Christian feudalism, the ancient system of kindred liability broke down, for churchmen without kin or local tie began to appear among suspicious villagers, and "as time went on, many men who for one reason or another moved away from their original environments and sought their fortunes elsewhere . . . could not depend on ties of kindred to make them law-worthy and reputable."[6] Hence a new system of compulsory suretyship, based on neighborhood rather than kin was developed. Everyone was *made* "law-worthy and reputable" by being assigned to a neighborhood group every member of which was an insurer of his conduct. If an offender was not produced by his surety group to answer criminal charges, a fine was levied on each member of the group, and sometimes liability to make compensation as well. . . .

. . . In olden times a man could not wonder for long whether he was his neighbor's keeper, for the voice of authority would instruct him unmistakably that he'd damn well better be. Today we prefer not to become involved in the control of crime, with the result that those who are charged with the control of crime become more and more involved with us.

In summary, collective criminal liability imposed on groups as a mandatory self-policing device is reasonable only when there is a very high degree of antecedent group solidarity and where efficient professional policing is unfeasible. Furthermore, justice requires that the system be part of the expected background of the group's way of life and that those held vicariously liable have some reasonable degree of *control* over those for whom they are made sureties. It is because these conditions are hardly ever satisfied in modern life, and not because individual liability is an eternal law of reason, that collective criminal responsibility is no longer an acceptable form of social organization.

So much for collective responsibility as a form of *liability without fault.* People often have other models in mind, however, when they speak of "collective responsibility."

LIABILITY WITH NONCONTRIBUTORY FAULT

Various faults can exist in the absence of any causal linkage to harm, where that absence is only a lucky accident reflecting no credit on the person who is at fault. Where every member of a group shares the same fault, but only one member's fault leads to any harm, and that not because it was more of a fault than that of the others, but only because of independent fortuities many outsiders will be inclined to ascribe collective liability to the whole group. Other outsiders may deny the propriety of holding even a faulty or guilty person liable for harm that was not "his fault"; but for a group member himself to take this public stand would be an unattractive piece of self-righteousness. It would be more appropriate for him to grieve, and voluntarily make what amends he can, than to insist stubbornly on the noncontributory character of his fault, which was a matter of pure lucky chance. . . .

CONTRIBUTORY GROUP FAULT: COLLECTIVE AND DISTRIBUTIVE

Sometimes we attribute liability to a whole group because of the contributory fault of each and every member. Group responsibility, so conceived, is simply the sum of all the individual responsibility. Since each individual is coresponsible for the harm in question, no one's responsibility is vicarious. Nevertheless, problems are raised by three kinds of situations: first, where large numbers of people are independently at fault without any concert or communication between them; second, where the harm is caused by a joint undertaking of numerous persons acting cooperatively; and, third, where the harm is to be ascribed to some feature of the common culture consciously endorsed and participated in by every member of the group. . . .

. . . [A] kind of case exemplifying group fault distributable to each member is that where the members are all privy to a crime or tort as conspirators or accomplices or joint tortfeasors. In complicated crimes, *complicity* is ascribed unavoidably to persons whose degree of participation in the crime is unequal. The common law, therefore, divides guilty felons into four categories, namely, "perpetrators," "abettors," "inciters" (all three of these are "accomplices"), and "criminal protectors," so that one may be guilty of a given crime either as its principal perpetrator (and even perpetration is a matter of degree, abettors counting as "principals in the second degree") or as accessories, that is, inciters or protectors. Thus one can be guilty, as an accessory, even of crimes that one is not competent to perpetrate. A woman, for example, may be found guilty of rape, as an abettor or inciter to the man, who must, of course, be the principal perpetrator of the crime on some other woman.

Suppose C and D play a bank robbery, present their plan to a respected friend A, receive his encouragement, borrow weapons from B for the purpose, hire E as getaway driver, and then execute the plan. Pursued by the police, they are forced to leave their escape route and take refuge at the farm of E's kindly uncle F. F congratulates them, entertains them hospitably, and sends them on their way with his blessing. F's neighbor G learns of all that has happened, disapproves, but does nothing. Another neighbor, H, learns of it but is bribed into silence. On these facts A, B, C, D, E, and F are all guilty of the bank robbery—C and D as perpetrators, A and B as inciters,[7] E as an abettor, and F as a protector. G is guilty of the misdemeanor called "misprision of felony," and H of the misdemeanor called "compounding a felony." On the other hand, if J, an old acquaintance of C and D, sees them about to enter the bank, notices suspicious bulges in their pockets, surmises that they are up to no good, yet does nothing out of simple reluctance to "get involved," he is not legally guilty. Yet he is certainly subject to blame; and, as moralists, we might decide this marginal case differently than the lawyers and brand him a kind of "moral accessory" before the fact, "morally guilty," though to a

lesser degree than the others. We can afford to have stricter standards of culpability than the lawyers, since no formal punishment will follow as a result of *our* verdicts and we do not have to worry about procedural complexities.

Part of the problem of determining degrees of responsibility of individuals in joint undertakings, where the responsibility is not vicarious, is assessing the extent of each individual's *contribution* to the undertaking. This involves assessment of various incommensurable dimensions of contribution—degrees of initiative, difficulty or causal crucialness of assigned subtasks, degrees of authority, percentage of derived profit, and so on. Although these matters cannot be settled in any mathematical way, rough and ready answers suggest themselves to common sense, and the legal categories of complicity have proved quite workable. The more difficult problems require estimates of *voluntariness*. . . .

CONTRIBUTORY GROUP FAULT: COLLECTIVE BUT NOT DISTRIBUTIVE

There are some harms that are ascribable to group faults but not to the fault of every, or even *any*, individual member. Consider the case of the Jesse James train robbery. One armed man holds up an entire car full of passengers. If the passengers had risen up as one man and rushed at the robber, one or two of them, perhaps, would have been shot; but collectively they would have overwhelmed him, disarmed him, and saved their property. Yet they all meekly submitted. How responsible were they for their own losses? Not very. In a situation like this, only *heroes* could be expected to lead the self-sacrificial charge, so no individual in the group was at fault for not resisting. The whole group, however, had it within its power to resist successfully. Shall we say, then, that the group was collectively but not distributively at fault? Can the responsibility of a group be more than the sum of the responsibility of its members? There is surely a point in affirming so. There was, after all, a flaw in the way the group of passengers was organized (or unorganized) that made the robbery possible. And the train robbery situation is a model for a thousand crises in the history of our corporate lives. No individual person can be blamed for not being a hero or a saint (what a strange "fault" that would be!), but a whole people can be blamed for not producing a hero when the times require it, especially when the failure can be charged to some discernible element in the group's "way of life" that militates against heroism.

One would think that, where group fault is nondistributive, group liability must be so too, lest it fall vicariously on individual members who are faultless. But, for all overt unfavorable responses, group liability is inevitably distributive: what harms the group as a whole necessarily harms its members. Hence if the conditions of justifiable collective liability—group solidarity, prior notice, opportunity for control, and so on—are not satisfied, group liability would seem unjustified.

An exception, however, is suggested by the case where an institutional group persists through changes of membership and faultless members must answer for harms caused, or commitments made, by an earlier generation of members. Commitments made in the name of an organized group may persist even after the composition of the group and its "will" change. When, nevertheless, the group reneges on a promise, the fault may be that of no individual member, yet the liability for breach of contract, falling on the group as a whole, will distribute burdens quite unavoidably on faultless members. . . . ◆ ◆ ◆

◆ Notes

1. *Leviathan*, ed. Michael Oakeshott (Oxford: Basil Blackwell, 1946), Part 1, Ch. 16, 105.
2. *The Concept of Representation* (Berkeley and Los Angeles: University of California Press, 1967), 19.
3. The limits of "fictitious attribution" (the phrase is from Hobbes) are clearly marked out by A. Phillips Griffiths in "How Can One Person Represent Another?", *Proceedings of the Aristotelian Society*, Supp. 34 (1960), 187–224, and by Pitkin, op. cit., 49–54.
4. W. D. Falk, "Intention, Motive and Responsibility," *Proceedings of the Aristotelian Society*, Supp. 19 (1945), 249.
5. L. T. Hobhouse, *Morals in Evolution* (London: Chapman & Hall, 1951), 81.
6. S. B. Chrimes, *English Constitutional History* (London: Oxford University Press, 1953), 77.
7. "An inciter . . . is one who, with *mens rea*, aids, counsels, commands, procures, or encourages another to commit a crime, or with *mens rea*, supplies him with the weapons, tools, or information needed for his criminal purpose." Rollin M. Perkins, *Criminal Law* (Brooklyn: The Foundation Press, 1957), 558.

The Moral Responsibility of Corporate Executives for Disasters

John D. Bishop

Popular legend has it that the captain of a sinking ship is duty-bound to go down with the ship; it is a fine and noble thing to do. Furthermore, the captain of a ship or the pilot of an airplane are in charge of every aspect of their commands and may be held responsible whether or not they are aware of a problem. Should the same dynamic apply to a corporation?

Bishop reports that in some cases of disaster, corporate executives have claimed ignorance of the facts and argue that they would have acted differently if they had known what was going on. He examines some of the dynamics that may prevent information from reaching the executives and then argues that they have a positive duty to be aware of potential problems in the company. He concludes that even if they honestly say that they did not know, they nevertheless bear some measure of responsibility for the outcome.

I. INTRODUCTION

When large corporations are criticised for causing disasters, the senior executives of those corporations usually protest their personal innocence, and deny that they should bear any moral responsibility for the tragedy. They often protest that they were not given information which could have warned them of impending problems even though they made honest efforts to obtain such information. Subsequent investigations have sometimes revealed that others in the corporation (often engineers) knew of safety problems, but that this information failed to reach decision making executives. Examples of this phenomenon include the cargo door problem on the DC-10, and the explosion of the Challenger—both tragedies involving loss of life.

This denial of moral responsibility intuitively conflicts with the high remuneration that CEOs and other executives receive in return for being responsible for corporations. In particular, it conflicts with the bonus remuneration which they receive if the corporation performs well. If they benefit when the corporation flourishes, should they not accept responsibility when things go horribly wrong?

The denial also conflicts with the current trend in our society of holding senior executives more socially responsible (Brooks, 1989). To note a single example, a U.S. District Judge recently insisted that the CEO of Pennwalt Corp. should personally attend his court to enter a guilty plea on a toxic spill charge. Note that the judge was not making a legal point, (corporate lawyers could have just as easily entered the plea), but a point about social responsibility (Globe and Mail, 1989).

This paper will analyse to what extent we can or should hold executives morally responsible for disasters. In particular, it will examine the case in which knowledge indicating impending problems is available to someone in the corporation, but has failed to reach decision making executives.

To help clarify the issues that the rest of the paper will deal with, the next section will eliminate some cases in which executives clearly are not responsible. Section III will elaborate on the reasons executives give for denying responsibility; in particular this paper concentrates on the case in which executives claim that they did not have and could not be expected to have had information vital to preventing the disaster. The reasons why apparently powerful executives cannot get information from their own corporation needs to be examined carefully (Section IV) before moving on in the final two sections to analysing to what extent we are justified in holding executives morally responsible.

It perhaps should be made clear at the outset that moral responsibility, or the lack of it, does not have direct implications for legal liability. The legal aspects of this problem are complicated, especially when the tragedy is in one country, and the corporate head office is in another. Legal issues are not dealt with in this paper.

II. LIMITS ON EXECUTIVE RESPONSIBILITY

It is commonplace in discussing morality that people should not be held responsible for events over which they have no influence or control. In this section, several types of events over which executives have no influence are eliminated from discussion. Executives cannot be held responsible for acts of God, nor, in their role as executives, for actions which are not performed on behalf of the corporation. Events not excluded in this section are not necessarily the moral responsibility of executives, but they are the actions which will be the basis of discussion in the rest of this article.

It can be accepted that executives are not responsible for obvious "acts of God". This does not mean that they should not be held accountable for the results of a natural event, for they may well be in a position to determine the outcome even when the event itself is inevitable. For example, suppose an earthquake causes a factory to collapse, killing several workers. Obviously, we cannot hold the executives of the company which owns the factory responsible for the earthquake itself; earthquakes are natural events which are beyond human control. However, we might hold the executives responsible for the factory being built in an earthquake zone, or we might hold them responsible for the use of money saving construction methods which caused the building to collapse. In these cases, we would consider the executives at least partly responsible for the workers' deaths. The fact that a person has no influence or control over an event does not necessarily exempt him or her from responsibility for the consequences of that event. What we hold him or her responsible for are the actions which determined those consequences.

Corporate executives, in their role as executives, should also not be held responsible for events which are not the result of the corporation's activities. The concepts of the "executive's role" and of the "corporation's activities" both need explaining.

Executives, because they are people, have moral responsibilities, as citizens, neighbours, parents, etc. Such responsibilities, while not being denied, will not be discussed in this paper. The purpose of the present discussion is limited to the moral responsibility of executives in their role as executives. However, this should not be taken to mean that the moral principles that apply to persons acting in the role of executives are any different from those which apply in the rest of their lives. Although it is sometimes argued that the morality of professional activities differs from the morality of everyday life (Carr, 1968), that is a position which cannot be applied to executives without the most careful examination (Callahan, 1988-A; Gillespie, 1983; Nagel, 1978). . . .

"Corporate activities" can . . . refer to the actions of the corporation's employees which are done in their capacity as employees. Presumably, executives are in a position to influence such actions on the part of employees, and it is their responsibility for such actions that the rest of this paper will be concerned with. Executives may, for social reasons, be in a position to influence employee behaviour off the job, but the use of such influence does not concern us here. We will confine our examination to events which result from the actions of employees while on the job. To hold the executives responsible for such events (if we decide to do so) is to hold them responsible for the actions of others, but it is assumed that executives have some influence or control over the actions of employees. The question we need to discuss is to what extent the executive has such influence and control, and whether it extends only to actions the executive directly instigates, or to all actions and omissions of employees as employees. . . .

III. WHY EXECUTIVES MAY NOT BE MORALLY RESPONSIBLE

When things go horribly wrong, executives sometimes deny responsibility on the grounds that they did not know, and could not be expected to know, the information they needed to prevent the disaster. They maintain this even when some of the corporation's employees knew, or ought to have known, the relevant information.

Consider the case of DC-10 Ship 29, which crashed near Paris on March 3, 1974 when its cargo doors flew off. All 346 people aboard were killed. Subsequent investigations revealed that McDonnell-Douglas, the manufacturer of the aircraft, was aware of the cargo door problem, and that Ship 29 had been returned to the corporation for FAA ordered corrections to the door locking mechanism. These corrections were never made, though stamped inspection sheets indicated they had been. John Brizendine, President of the Douglas division of McDonnell-Douglas, denied all knowledge of this failure to fix the doors (French, 1981), though it is clear that at least some people in the company must have known. Since there is no reason to question Brizendine's honesty, we will assume that the information that could have prevented the disaster failed to reach him. (We will also assume that he would have acted on the information if he had received it.)

As a second example, consider the explosion of the Challenger space shuttle, again with loss of life. Engineers at Morton Thiokol, which manufactured the solid rocket booster, had repeatedly expressed concerns, in written memos and verbally, about possible failure of O-ring seals on cold weather launches (Grossman, 1988). These concerns failed to reach decision making management at NASA, who maintain that they would have stopped the launch had they been aware of the engineers' opinion (Callahan, 1988-B). Again, vital information that could have prevented disaster failed to reach executives responsible for the final decision.

I do not want to raise the issue of the honesty of the executives when they claim they did not know. It has transpired in some cases that executives knew more than they were willing to admit—such was the case in the Dalkon shield tragedy (Mintz, 1985), or the knowledge of tobacco executives about early cancer studies (White, 1988). However, it is clear that executives often do not know, and are not told even if others in the corporation have the information. The immorality of lying, and of being able to stop a disaster and not doing so, are beyond doubt; the responsibility (if any) of executives when they actually are not told is more problematic, and is the central topic of this paper. It will be assumed that in the cases cited (the DC-10 cargo door problem and the Challenger disaster), executives were in fact in the dark about impending problems.

IV. NEGATIVE INFORMATION BLOCKAGE

Can executives be taken seriously when they claim that they cannot be expected to know about impending tragedy? After all, they have the authority to demand that information be given to them. And it is their job to know what is going on in their corporation. If someone in the company has or can get the information (which is the most interesting case), then why cannot the executives simply send a memo to all employees saying such information is to be sent directly to their attention? This question needs to be examined carefully if we are to determine whether executives are responsible when disaster strikes, or whether we should accept the claim that they did not know and could not have known the information needed to prevent the tragedy.

The problem with getting information to executives is a well-known phenomenon in corporate and other hierarchical organizations which I will call "negative information blockage". In brief, information regarding the riskiness of a corporation's plans is stifled at source or by intervening management, even when senior executives have demanded that such information be sent on to them. . . .

The notion of negative information requires the distinction between a corporation's objectives and its constraints. The objectives (or goals—I will use the two words interchangeably) of a corporation are what its senior executives are perceived as wanting to achieve. These objectives are, of course, the executive's, but it is convenient to refer to them as the corporation's. These goals may or may not be what the executives think they want to achieve, or what they say they want to achieve; corporate mission statements may not be honest or may not be believed. The actual goals of the executives (or the corporation) can only be identified by examining what sorts of behaviour the executives reward, as will be discussed below. . . .

Within a corporation, goals and constraints are treated very differently. Rewards are given for employee behaviour which appears to help the company achieve its goals. Observing legal, moral, and safety constraints is seldom rewarded; it tends to be assumed that employees will observe such constraints without reward. Instead, employees in companies which enforce constraints are usually punished when violation of the constraint is discovered; they are not usually rewarded just for observing constraints. Complete failure of a corporation to enforce legal, moral, or safety constraints raises obvious moral problems; this discussion will be centered on the more interesting case in which constraints are enforced by the corporation (i.e., by the executives), but ignored by some of the employees. Why they are ignored, even under the threat of punishment, has to do with the different ways in which executives encourage employees to pursue goals, and discourage them from violating constraints.

In general, employee behaviour which enhances corporate goals is rewarded, observing constraints is not. Hindering objectives is almost always punished. Constraints are constraints on the pursuit of the company's goals, and hence observing them can threaten an employee's rewards. In fact, observing constraints and asking one's management to do so as well may impede the company's goals to the point where the behaviour itself is punished. Surely this encourages violation of constraints.

There are other pressures on employees to put rewards for pursuing goals before the observance of constraints. Violation of constraints is only punished if one is caught; hence there is an element of gamble involved. The time factor also plays a major role; rewards are usually immediate, while discovery of violated constraints may be months or years away, by which time the employee has had his promotion and is safely elsewhere.

To complicate matters further, corporations are hierarchical. If an employee does resist temptation and observes constraints at the risk of losing rewards, his manager, or his manager's manager, may not. If getting a company to observe a constraint requires escalating concerns to the senior executive level (and this is the case we are concerned with in this article), then a single failure to resist temptation may block the concern from reaching the executives. This is the phenomenon of negative information blockage.

Since negative information blockage is inherent in the nature of goals, constraints, rewards and punishments, then to what extent can executives be held responsible for getting information past the blockage? The next section will consider two possible views on this topic.

V. EXECUTIVE RESPONSIBILITY AND NEGATIVE INFORMATION BLOCKAGE

The first of the two views is that executives are responsible for doing whatever they can to prevent negative information blockage. They have a moral duty to structure the corporation to ensure that risks of disaster are discovered and made known to themselves (and then, of course, to act on the information.) They have a moral responsibility to do as much as they can to prevent tragedy.

What exactly executives can do I will not discuss in detail; a few examples will suffice. They can offer rewards for information brought to them; they can keep an "open door" policy so junior employees can go around the blockages; they can set a personal example of concern for moral, legal, and safety constraints. These ideas are generally discussed in business ethics literature under the topic of whistle-blowing, since whistle-blowing is often the result of frustration with negative information blockage. (See, for example, Callahan, 1988-C.) . . . [W]e can summarize the first view of corporate executive responsibility by suggesting they should do whatever is reasonably possible to prevent knowledge of potential disasters from being blocked before it reaches them.

The second view is that executives, especially CEOs, are responsible for preventing tragedy, excepting only those cases, such as acts of God, which were discussed above in Section II. This view is radically different from the first; just how different can be seen if we consider how executives would be judged in the event of a tragedy. On the first view, the impartial spectator making moral judgements would inquire what steps the executives had taken prior to the tragedy to make sure information on the impending disaster had been conveyed to them. And, of course, they would ask whether the executives had acted on anything they knew. On the second view, the impartial spectator would hold the executive morally responsible for the failure to acquire sufficient information to prevent the tragedy, regardless of whether or not steps had been taken to circumvent negative information blockage. This view is essentially holding that since the tragedy happened, the steps taken were obviously not sufficient, and hence the executives are morally culpable.

It should be noted that on the second view, we are holding executives morally responsible even though they did not know the disaster might happen, and even though they may have taken some steps to acquire the knowledge. We are holding them morally responsible for the result, not the effort. The first view holds them responsible only for the effort.

There are many cases in life where people are held responsible for results rather than effort; it is one of the painful lessons we learn as children. For example, on examinations, students, especially in such subjects as medicine and engineering, are quite rightly marked on results, not the amount of effort they put into studying. And executives themselves do not hesitate to hold employees responsible for getting results.

Demanding results on the job, not just effort, is acceptable because it is necessary. When an engineer designs a bridge, it is important to society that it does not collapse. It is important to society that doctors are competent, not just that they are doing their best. We are often justified in holding people responsible for doing their job well.

If people fail in their jobs, they may or may not be held legally liable depending on the circumstances, but in any case their careers suffer, and they may lose their jobs. The fact that they are held responsible is reflected in the impact on their professional standing when they succeed or fail. To distinguish this type of responsibility from legal and moral responsibility, I will refer to it as professional responsibility.

The case of professional responsibility that best parallels the situation of executives is that of cabinet ministers in a parliamentary system. When things go wrong in an area of ministerial responsibility, the minister is held accountable and is expected to resign. They are not supposed to argue that they tried, that they have not been negligent, or that they are not legally liable. Thus Lord Carrington resigned when Argentina invaded the Falklands; he did not stay on protesting that it was not his fault (though it probably was not). The questions we must now deal with are: should we

apply professional responsibility to executives? And secondly, how does professional responsibility relate to moral responsibility?

VI. PROFESSIONAL RESPONSIBILITY

The concept of professional responsibility applies when the outcome of a professional activity is of great concern to a person or people other than the person doing the activity. It especially applies if the outcome is of concern over and above any contract the professional has with some other person, or if the outcome is of great concern to bystanders. Let me illustrate these points with an example.

When I buy a pair of shoes and find them faulty, I take them back to the shoe store and generally will be satisfied if I am given back my money. The responsibility is limited to reversing the contract. When I go to a doctor for an operation, I am not interested in hearing that he or she will refund me the cost of the operation if it goes wrong, especially if I die. We can say in this case that the doctor has a professional responsibility which goes beyond the "contract." It goes beyond because the consequences of failure go beyond the contract. Similarly, if an engineer designs a bridge that collapses, then refunding the money he or she received for the design hardly helps those who were on the bridge when it collapsed. It helps so little that that course of action is seldom pursued. The engineer, in this case, has a professional responsibility.

Liability laws generally reflect the fact that responsibility can extend far beyond reversing the original contract, but this discussion is not an attempt to define legal liability. The point is that professional responsibility arises when the consequences of failure have effects on other people (customers or bystanders) which exceed the confines of the initial contract.

Clearly, this applies to executives. If they fail to create a corporate culture which overcomes negative information blockage and disaster results, it often involves the death of their customers (or of their customers' customers, as in the case of the DC-10s). It is clear that we are justified in holding executives professionally responsible when tragedy happens. In other words, we hold them professionally responsible for failing to obtain the information needed to prevent the disaster, whether or not they tried to.

But is holding executives professionally responsible different from holding them morally responsible? In the cases we have been examining, there is a close connection between the two.

Executives and everyone else have a moral responsibility to ensure that their activities do not result in the deaths of others if that result can be prevented. Executives, therefore, have a moral responsibility to do their best to obtain the information needed to prevent disasters. They have a professional responsibility, as we have seen, not just to do their best, but to actually succeed in preventing avoidable disasters. The latter grows out of the former in the sense that executives have a professional responsibility to succeed in fulfilling their moral responsibilities. (Of course, they also have professional responsibilities with other origins as well). Thus, although normally a person only has a moral responsibility for trying to avoid immoral results, in this case (and in others) a person has a professional responsibility to succeed in fulfilling the underlying moral responsibility.

This conclusion has a major implication for judging executives; namely, when tragedy happens, we are justified in holding them responsible based on moral values. If they object that they did not have the information necessary to prevent the disaster and that they had made an honest effort to obtain that information, then we can accept that as individuals they have fulfilled their moral obligations. (We are assuming honesty.) But as professional executives, they have failed to fulfil their professional obligation to carry out moral requirements. We are still justified in holding them responsible based on moral considerations. ◆ ◆ ◆

◆ References

Brooks, L. J.: 1989, 'Corporate Ethical Performance: Trends, Forecasts, and Outlooks', *Journal of Business Ethics* 8, No. 1, pp. 31–8.

Callahan, J. C.: 1988-A, *Ethical Issues in Professional Life* (Oxford University Press, Oxford), pp. 49–50.

Callahan, J. C.: 1988-B, *Ethical Issues in Professional Life* (Oxford University Press, Oxford), p. 342.

Callahan, J. C.: 1988-C, *Ethical Issues in Professional Life* (Oxford University Press, Oxford), pp. 337–39.

Carr, A. Z.: 1968, 'Is Business Bluffing Ethical?', *Ethical Issues in Professional Life*, C. Callahan, ed. (Oxford University Press, Oxford), pp. 69–72.

French, Peter A.: 1981, 'What Is Hamlet to McDonnell-Douglas, McDonnell-Douglas to Hamlet: DC-10', *Business and Professional Ethics* 2, Spring.

Gillespie, Norman Chase: 1983, 'The Business of Ethics', *Ethical Issues in Professional Life*, J. C. Callahan, ed. (Oxford University Press, Oxford), pp. 72–6.

Globe and Mail: 1989, 'Polluting firm's chairman hauled into court by U.S. judge', Associated Press, Globe and Mail, August 10, 1989, p. B10.

Grossman, Brian A.: 1988, *Corporate Loyalty: A Trust Betrayed* (Penguin Books, Markham Ont.), pp. 177–79.

Mintz, Morton: 1985, *At Any Cost: Corporate Greed, Women, and the Dalkon Shield* (Random House, Inc., New York).

Nagel, Thomas: 1978, 'Ruthlessness in Public Life', *Ethical Issues in Professional Life*, J. C. Callahan, ed. (Oxford University Press, Oxford), pp. 76–83.

White, Larry C.: 1988, *Merchants of Death: The American Tobacco Industry* (Beech Tree/Morrow, New York).

Workers as Agents and Corporate Responsibility

Peter A. French

French contends that corporations may be moral actors in their own right; they cannot be reduced to their human members alone. In that sense, it makes sense to say, for example, that Exxon is blameworthy for spilling oil in Alaska. He thinks that corporate activity is more than shorthand for all the individual moral actors involved: There was a culture or intentionality that allowed things to happen, and the actions of the allegedly intoxicated captain in charge of their tanker ought not to be viewed as holding sole responsibility. This is an especially useful way of looking at moral responsibility if there is no paper trail that puts a particular person at fault.

French uses an example of his encounter with a customer service agent to show that individual humans may abdicate their moral agency while working in a company role. In his conversation, the woman chose to stick to a corporate script, which French feels makes her an instrument of the corporate will. Reflecting on his exchange, French believes it is more correct to say that he was dealing with the corporation than with the individual person. If French is correct, the moral analysis has to include some nonhuman moral agents that may operate at a fairly primitive level of moral reasoning—reacting to simple punishment and reward—and yet these agents may have significant potential to affect our lives for better or worse.

The Exxon Corporation was responsible for the worst oil spill in American history when the *Exxon Valdez* ran aground on Bligh's Reef dumping 11 million gallons of crude oil into the waters of Prince William Sound, Alaska. Let us suppose that statement is true. It and its variants have been written and spoken untold times since that fateful day, March 24, 1989. And, at least to some degree, Exxon, the corporation, acknowledged its responsibility, took blame for the accident, and volunteered to clean up the mess. But many ethical theorists will tell us that the responsibility ascription targeting Exxon and Exxon's own acceptance of blame are really just ways of holding the captain of the *Exxon Valdez* responsible for the terrible pollution of Prince William Sound and its effects on the animals and humans living there. Or they might maintain that all of those corporate responsibility claims really reduce to nothing more than the ascription of responsibility for the spill to some managerial team at Exxon, that is, its transportation division, or to the chairman of Exxon or to its president (both of whom were criminally indicted).

Who would deny, except him, his lawyer, (and perhaps his mother), that the captain of the *Exxon Valdez* bears moral responsibility, in some measure, for the disaster? After all, he was, by his own admission, not on the bridge and was either drunk or hungover or sleeping in his cabin while his ship, in the hands of a junior officer, was traversing through the passage in Prince William Sound. A blood alcohol test, administered more than ten hours after the spill, still showed the captain to be legally drunk. But is there no one with whom the captain should share responsibility for the spill? What of those folks in Exxon's transportation division? Suppose that each of them conscientiously acted on corporate policies, especially those concerned with profitability, and none had any personal reasons to vary from that course, that is, they weren't being bribed to do so, they didn't harbor deep-seated hatreds for the Prince William Sound area, nor did they despise sea otters ever since traumatic childhood encounters with the creatures while on an outing to the zoo. They were just doing the jobs they were hired to do. Would it make sense to say that the transportation division's management team or its individual employees were responsible for the Alaskan oil spill?

If certain conditions can be shown to have existed, it might make sense to say that some of the managers, perhaps all in that division, were responsible. For example, suppose the transportation division had received reports that the single-hulled tankers Exxon uses are dangerous in Alaskan waters, that the Japanese fleet used multi-hulled vessels because of the high risk of puncture, and that certain officers of Exxon tankers were often drunk when they left port. Suppose they had records indicating that the captain assigned to the *Exxon Valdez* had a record of drunken-driving arrests and was known to frequent the bars in the port just before his ship was scheduled to depart. Suppose that they chose to ignore such reports and let the operations go on as in the past on the *Exxon Valdez*. After all, they hadn't had a disaster in the Prince William Sound area, and the captain's record at sea was spotless. It would cost a great deal of money and time to redesign the tankers, and recent directives from the top management at Exxon had mandated the implementation of as many cost-cutting measures as possible. A spill such as the one that occurred was thought to be likely to happen only once in 241 years. Perhaps they decided that Exxon's interest in getting its crude oil to its refineries as expediently and cheaply as possible should override all other issues.

Sorting out corporate and individual responsibility quickly becomes complicated in cases of this sort. The simplest thing to do, if your ethics comes from the seventeenth century, is to pin all of the responsibility, at least the moral variety on individual human beings; if not on the captain of the tanker, then on the senior executives of Exxon. But that solution is grossly unfair and flies in the face of the standard principles of responsibility that have marked Western ethics since Aristotle. Exxon's chairman may not even have known of the specific issues in the transportation division reports or the dangers of single-hulled tankers in the Alaskan waters out of Valdez. He might not have known of the captain's drinking habits. To hold him morally to account in this case is to regard as irrelevant the fact that he did not act with intention or with knowledge concerning the events of March 24, 1989, in Prince William Sound. It is difficult to say what he specifically *did*, let alone what he intentionally did, that resulted in the disaster. To hold him responsible would amount to making moral responsibility in corporate cases a strict liability ethical offense for such senior executives. That seems hardly just, though it is exactly the sort of approach that would be taken by someone who had abandoned the attempt to understand the corporate actor and the human person in our social world in order to preserve some antiquated theory.

As noted above, it has been relatively standard, since at least the time of Aristotle, to say that for something to be responsible for what it does it must have acted intentionally. It must be an actor. If, as I would have it, corporations, in and of themselves, are going to be susceptible to ethics (like holding Exxon morally responsible for the pollution of Prince William Sound), they must be intentional actors in a way that cannot be eliminated by merely and systematically reducing what they do to the actions of individual human beings, like the captain, the members of a certain managerial team, or the chief executive officer of the corporation.

The condition that requires that corporate actions cannot be simply reduced to individual human actions allows us to distinguish between corporate actors and other kinds of collectivities. It may be said, for example, that a rioting mob was responsible for destroying the stores on Crenshaw Boulevard in Los Angeles. Such an ascription of responsibility can usually be distributed to those who comprised the mob. That is another way of saying that the mob is not a moral entity. The mob is, for moral purposes, only an aggregate of human persons, each of whom may or may not be held individually responsible for the damage, or some of it, on Crenshaw Boulevard.

An important reason for not holding the mob itself responsible is that a mob has no established way of making rational decisions, of planning or partial planning with respect to its goals, of setting goals in the first place, of assigning tasks, and so on.[1] The people in the mob could each have been on Crenshaw Boulevard for purely personal reasons. Some may have been shopping, some out for a walk, some doing business, some just hanging out. Something happened and, bang, the destruction ensued. There was no organization, it was just a mob. If you were a member of it, then you were probably responsible for some of the damage. So you may need a good excuse or an alibi if someone challenges your behavior. (You were just there looking for a good deal on a VCR. The store window broke. You have no idea how. And this four head, stereo VCR just fell into your hands. Well, if you left it there someone would have stolen it, so you took it to your house to protect it from theft and with the intention of returning it. You decided to hook it up to see if it really worked, as there would be little point in returning it if it were broken.)

Morally, you, as a member of the mob, might be thought to share in the responsibility for all of the damage on Crenshaw Boulevard. The mob itself, however, cannot bear moral blame. It goes out of existence when its members cease behaving in a riotous fashion and disperse.

Corporations are not like mobs in a variety of fairly obvious ways. In the first place, corporations will usually remain the same entity even though the group of principals and agents associated with them changes. The list of a corporation's stockholders, executives, board members, and employees is typically in a state of flux. Stock, for example, is bought and sold, employees die, resign, are fired, hired, and so on. Yet the corporation goes on, and it makes sense to talk of it as the same corporation regardless of such changes in principals and agents.

Imagine that we have two lists. One is the list of all principals and agents for IBM as of noon on Monday, May 17, 1993. The other is the list of principals and agents of IBM as of 4:00 p.m. on that same day. Let's say, though it would be highly improbable in the constantly changing world of the corporation, that the names on both lists are identical except that "Rebecca Martinez" appears on the first list as a stockholder and not on the second. Ms. Martinez sold her shares in IBM that afternoon in order to make another investment. Would it be right to say that the name "IBM Corporation" does not at 4:00 p.m. denote the same corporate actor it did at noon on May 17, 1993? Do we have two different corporations? Surely not. "IBM" refers to the same corporation whether or not Rebecca Martinez is one of its principals. And that would be true even if at 3:45 p.m. on that day the entire senior management of IBM resigned their positions and took up similar ones at Coca Cola. Coca Cola would not have become IBM. The identity of a corporation is not dependent on particular humans being in specific positions in the corporation.

Being a discrete and persisting entity, however, is not enough to make IBM or Coca Cola or any other corporation a member of the moral community, a proper target of ethical scrutiny. A corporation will, in and for itself, have to evidence the functional capacities of an actor. The primary one of those is that it must be able to act intentionally.

If a corporation, Mazda for example, is an intentional actor, then some events must be describable in a way that will support the truth of sentences that say that what Mazda did was intended by it and not just by its agents. Let's see how a case might be made. Start with events and the descriptions of events. A certain event may be described in a number of ways, all of which are there. In some descriptions it may not be an intentional action; in others, it is. . . .

Now suppose we witness someone moving a pen across a piece of paper. We might be able to describe that event as just the physical movement of a human hand or as nothing more than certain muscular contractions. It can also be described as someone, Kim S., signing the letter to me about the property taxes on my leased car. The event will be an intentional action only if those physical movements can truthfully be described as done to bring about some state of affairs or done to realize certain plans or goals, to achieve certain interests, and so on. . . .

So, you perform *intentional* actions and plain actions. Something you do is one of your actions only if it can be truthfully described in some way as one of your intentional actions. The same event described one way may be an intentional action, but when described in another way may only be an action. . . . Perhaps it was an accident, but then it couldn't have been a mistake. Mistakes are actions. To make a mistake you must be intending to do something that you fail to do. J. L. Austin tells the story of a girl, Miss Plimsoll, who buys a book in which to keep daily accounts of her life and then carefully letters across its cover in permanent ink "DAIRY." She made a mistake. It wasn't accidental. Accidents just happen to you.

When Kim S. signed the letter to me, she probably intended to affix her signature to that document, but we could imagine a situation in which she signed the letter mistakenly thinking she was signing something else, possibly a personal letter to her friend Rachel R. Though she intended to sign the letter to Ms. R., still, she intentionally wrote her signature, and signing that paper was signing the letter to me, so signing the letter to me was one of her actions, though not one of her intentional actions. . . . There are more levels of descriptions to be considered. Kim S.'s signing the letter to me was Mazda dunning me for a property tax payment. That is, the sentence, "Mazda dunned me for the property tax payment on the leased car," is a true description of the event that could otherwise be described as "Kim S. signing the letter to me." Her signing is Mazda dunning. But Mazda duns me whether Kim signed the letter to me intentionally or mistakenly thought she was signing another letter, one to Rachel R., that was also on her desk. Mazda acted when Kim S. signed the letter, even if signing that particular letter was not what she thought she was doing when she did it. In effect, by her signing the letter, Mazda opened a conversation with me, and a not very pleasant one, at that. For all intents and purposes, Kim S. then was irrelevant to this encounter between a human person and a corporate actor.

As we have seen, the same event can be described in a number of different and nonequivalent ways. Though a number of different descriptions may be true of the same event, some may not be substituted without a significant change in meaning. At various levels of description the same event also may be identified as an intentional action, and at each such level there must be an intentional actor performing it. So we can ask whether, when, and how the physical movement of Kim S.'s hand that was her signing a letter to me reveals the existence of a corporate actor acting intentionally and not just a human person acting, whether or not intentionally. Is there a level of descriptions of that event at which we can truthfully say that Mazda acted with the intention of dunning me for the unpaid tax? I think there is, but it will have to be a level at which the event is described as Mazda being committed to charging me for the property tax payment. That is what Mazda intends, what it plans.

A corporation's doing something usually involves or includes human persons doing things and those humans usually can be described as having reasons and plans with respect to their behavior in their corporate positions. I realize that you've likely had enough of my encounter with Mazda and Kim S., but there is just a bit more to the matter that is revealing. At the bottom of the letter she invited me to call her on a toll-free number if I had any questions. I had questions, the first of which was, "What's this about another property tax bill on the leased car? I promptly paid three of these already this year and I can prove it." Her first response was, as you would expect, "Sir, I'll bring it up on the computer, but I doubt we've made a mistake." "I'm sure you have. In fact, last year I only got two bills for such taxes. You hit me for three this year and now want a fourth. What are you trying to do?" "I'm just doing my job, sir. Oh, here it is. Yes, you did not pay the assessment from the county school district." "There is no county school district in this county. You've obviously screwed up. What

are you going to do, pocket the money?" "Sir, we at Mazda have this bill here from your county school district. We've paid it, and according to your lease agreement, you are to reimburse us." "But this is wrong. I'm telling you, we have independent school districts here, not a county district, and if you will kindly check your records for the past years, you'll see that I have never been billed for such a tax before. Besides which, I have no record of ever having received a bill from you for this tax before or I would have complained months ago." We went on to talk about the dependability of the U.S. mails and actually drifted into some rather congenial conversation, though she staunchly stuck to her guns about the tax payment being overdue.

During this telephone call I had conversations with two different types of entities, a corporation and a human person. The conversation with the human took the least amount of time and accomplished little or nothing because Kim S. is a consummate corporate agent. From her perspective, however, there might have been an interesting moral conflict. At some point during our exchange, she might have been tempted to tell me that she would see that the whole matter was canceled and that all records of that tax bill were deleted from Mazda's computer system. Somehow she braced herself against that temptation and carried out her corporate duties. Though she had it in her control or power to manipulate the situation to my benefit, she acted to further Mazda's interests.

Suppose the call had not been from me but from Rachel R., her lifelong friend, and the conversation, in substance if not demeanor, went along the same lines. The temptation to use her control over the corporation's interests in the case to benefit her friend might have weighed more heavily on Kim S. than it did in my case. Would she have acted in the same manner? Should she have? The difference between human persons and corporate agents is especially clear in such circumstances. "Come on, do it for a friend."

Coleman rather nicely captures the situation when he writes:

> Analytically it is clear that any person in such a situation has two sets of resources: his own, that is, his as a personal actor; and those of the corporate actor for whom he is an agent. Any employee of a firm traveling on the firm's business at its expense has two kinds of money, which he could, if he desired, physically separate into two pockets. In one pocket would be his own money, which he could spend however he desires. In the other pocket would be the firm's money, which he may use only for expenses that are incurred in pursuit of the firm's business. Because the agent has physical control of expenditures, a common occurrence is the use of the corporate actor's resources by the agent in his own interests. Numerous devices have been employed in social organizations to prevent this appropriation from occurring.[2]

At first, at least, I suspect that Kim S. was personally indifferent to me and the communication with me which she had initiated. Admittedly, I may have given her some personal reasons to pursue the matter with more than usual vigor during our phone conversation.

How do we determine when actions performed by a human being, such as Kim S., are also the intentional actions of a corporate actor, such as Mazda? The answer has to do with the way corporations are run. Every corporation has an established way by which it makes decisions and converts them into corporate intentional actions. . . . I have called this the Corporation's Internal Decision Structure or CID structure. CID structures have two elements crucial to our understanding of how acting corporations emerge at certain levels of the description of events: (1) an organizational flow chart that delineates stations and levels within the corporation; and (2) rules that reveal how to recognize decisions that are corporate ones and not simply personal decisions of the humans who occupy the positions identified on the flow chart. These rules are typically embedded, whether explicitly or implicitly, in statements of corporate policy. Its CID structure is an organization of personnel (agents) for the exercise of the corporation's power with respect to its ventures and interests and, as such, its primary function is to draw various levels and positions within the corporation into rational decision making, ratification, and action processes.

When operative, a CID structure subordinates and synthesizes the intentions and actions of various human persons (and even the behavior of machines) into a corporate action. Because the workings and elements of CID structures are relatively easy to detect, they can be called epistemically transparent. Anyone with access to these structures can discover everything about how they work, so CID structures can be confidently used as the basis from which to transform the description of certain events. Described in one way, an event may be the actions or the mere behavior of humans (those who occupy various stations on the organizational chart). But seen "through" the CID structure, it is a corporate act. The corporate character of the event is exposed. . . .

To see how this works think of the CID structure of a corporation as containing two sorts of rules: organizational rules and policy and procedure rules. These rules make descriptions of events possible that would not be possible if those rules did not exist. These rules play a role similar to the role rules play in our descriptions of sporting events. A person may toss a round ball into a hoop on a gymnasium wall, but without the rules of basketball the activity is not describable as sinking a jump shot and scoring two points. In basketball, there are also two types of rules: those that define positions—the dimensions of the court, the number of players per side, and so forth—and those that allow certain activities of the players and forbid others. These include rules that permit attempting to shoot the ball into the basket in some ways and not others, that forbid certain ways of stopping an opponent from scoring, and such.

The organizational chart of a corporation distinguishes players and clarifies their rank and maps out the interwoven lines of responsibility within the corporation. The organizational chart could tell us, for example, that anyone holding the title executive vice president for finance administration, stands in a superior position to anyone holding the title, director of the property tax collections department, and to anyone holding the title treasurer. These "players" report to the executive vice president. He ratifies their actions, and so on. The organizational chart maps the interdependent and dependent relationships, line and staff, that produce corporate decisions and actions. The organizational chart provides what might be called the grammar of corporate decision making. The policy and procedure rules provide its logic.

Policy and procedure rules are, in effect, recognition rules. That is, they are rules that yield conclusive and affirmative grounds for describing a decision or an act as having been made or performed for corporate reasons. Recognition rules in a CID structure may address either procedural or policy matters. Some of the procedural rules are already embedded in the organizational chart. For example, by looking at the chart, we should be able to see that certain kinds of decisions are to be reached collectively at certain levels, but that they must be ratified at higher levels.

A corporate decision, and subsequently an action, is recognized, however, not only by how it is made, but by the policy that is reflected in it. Every corporation creates a general set of policies (as well as an image) that are easily accessible to both its agents and those with whom it interacts. When an action performed by someone in the employ of a corporation is an implementation of its corporate policy, then it is proper to describe the act as done for corporate reasons or for corporate purposes to advance corporate plans, and so as an intentional action of the corporation.

Corporate plans and purposes might differ from those that motivate the human persons who occupy corporate positions and whose bodily movements are necessary for the corporation to act. Using its CID structure, we can, however, describe the behavior of those humans as corporate actions done with a corporate intention, to execute a corporate plan or as part of such a plan. That should expose to the light of ethics the corporate intentional actor that otherwise lurks in the shadows controlling much of what has become contemporary society. ◆ ◆ ◆

◆ Notes

1. See Larry May, *The Morality of Groups* (Notre Dame: Notre Dame Press, 1987).

2. James Coleman, *Foundations of Social Theory* (Cambridge, MA: Harvard/Belknap Press, 1990), p. 198.

Contrasting Role Morality and Professional Morality

Kevin Gibson

In this article Gibson uses four case studies to examine role morality and professional morality. Many readings, such as the Milton Friedman selection, suggest that you have one set of morality at home, but when you arrive at the factory or office you take off your personal hat and put on your employee hat, including the moral attitudes it incorporates, even if they are at odds with your own. Professional morality is sometimes seen as distinct, because lawyers, doctors, and accountants often claim more autonomy in their work lives. Their moral yardstick is often a code of conduct generated by a professional organization. "Business" is not a profession as such, but managers often belong to professional groups and aspire to professional status. The article concludes that the real issue is the way behavior is described, the power of the individual within the institution, and whether such behavior is endorsed by society.

The notion of role morality suggests individuals may adopt a different morality depending on the roles they undertake. Effectively, we wear two "moral hats"—one for work and one for everywhere else. Investigating role morality is important, since the mentality of role morality may allow agents to believe they can abdicate moral responsibility when acting in a role. This is particularly significant in the literature dealing with professional morality where professionals, because of their special status, may find themselves morally at odds with their best moral judgments; so, for example, lawyers may feel compelled to vigorously cross-examine a fragile witness for the opposing side, or doctors may feel compelled to make heroic efforts to save a dying patient. . . . Here I tell four stories and draw out some distinctions. I conclude that role morality is a genuine and useful moral distinction. However, I suggest the purported distinction between role morality and professional morality is over-determined.

Therefore, alleged conflicts between the demands of role and profession (such as the different pressures on Pinto designers as employees and as engineers) are not conflicts between different kinds of demands, but rather the sort of conflicts arising from divergent roles that most workers will encounter regularly in their working lives. Finally, I suggest we should stress moral awareness at a fairly abstract level for all employees and reinforce the moral primacy of individual choice.

1. STEVENS THE BUTLER

At the end of his three decades of service at Darlington Hall, Stevens the butler reflects on his career. His employer, an English nobleman, was a Nazi sympathizer prior to the Second World War. Stevens once unquestioningly dismissed two maids who were Jewish at the behest of his employer.

It occurs to me in recalling these words that, of course, many of Lord Darlington's ideas will seem today rather odd—even, at times, unattractive . . . Let us establish this quite clearly: a butler's duty is to provide good service. It is not to meddle in the great affairs of the nation. The fact is, such great affairs will always be beyond the understanding of those such as you and I, and those of us who wish to make our mark must realize that we best do so by concentrating on what *is* within our realm; that is to say, by devoting our attention to providing the best possible service to those great gentlemen in whose hands the destiny of civilization truly lies. I refer to that strand of opinion in the profession which suggested that any butler with serious aspirations should make it his business to be forever reappraising his employer—scrutinizing the latter's motives, analysing the implications of his views. Only in this way, so the argument ran, could one be sure one's skills were being employed to a desirable end . . . It is, in practice, simply not possible to adopt such a critical attitude towards an employer and at the same time provide good service . . . *if a butler is to be of any worth to anything or anybody in life, there must surely come a time when he ceases his searching; a time when he must say to himself: 'This employer embodies all that I find noble and admirable. I will hereafter devote myself to serving him.' This is loyalty **intelligently** bestowed.* What is there 'undignified' in this? One is simply accepting an inescapable truth: that the likes of you and I will never be in a position to comprehend the great affairs of today's world, and our best course will always be to put our trust in an employer we judge to be wise and honorable, and to devote our energies to the task of serving him to the best of our ability . . . It is hardly my fault if his lordship's life and work have turned out today to look, at best, a sad waste—and it is quite illogical that I should feel any regret or shame on my own account [emphasis added].[1]

Stevens has been the loyal and unquestioning servant of his employer; he has been the quintessential "good soldier." When challenged about his personal role, he claims there is and ought to be no day-to-day questioning of his employer's actions, and, by extension, his own when acting under instructions. He suggests there is an initial mutual probationary episode, but after that an employee should commit wholesale to the employer. One can draw an analogy with marriage: in order for the relationship to work, it has to be based on acceptance, followed by total trust and commitment. . . .

2. THE CUSTOMER SERVICE AGENT

Anna is a customer service agent at a local bank. The bank has a policy of penalizing customers for overdrawn or returned cheques. Typically, customers are assessed a $20 fee for each cheque drawn on insufficient funds. If more than one cheque arrives on a given day, they are not processed according to their time of arrival, but rather in descending dollar amounts and are all posted to that day's transactions. Handling them this way means that if cheques for $20, $25, $50 and $100 arrive on the same day and there is $95 in the account, the bank will process the largest cheque first, putting the account into the red, and then charge fees on all four. If they processed them in the order of arrival, the customer would most likely only have to pay fees on the $100 cheque. Moreover, customers are treated differently depending on their account status and history with the bank. Anna has the discretion to waive the penalty altogether for customers with a preferred status.

It is not unusual for Anna to deal with angry and embarrassed customers: she has training in telephone techniques but cannot alter the bank policy. Few customers are in a position to question exactly when their cheques arrived, and if they do she acknowledges that the largest was processed first, intimating (but not insisting) it must have arrived earliest. Anna realizes the bank's policy maximizes profits, but she feels some qualms about what they do and her role in it. She presumes, correctly, that those most hurt by the policy are those least able to afford it, and it offends her personal sense of justice that the more affluent customers are treated preferentially. Yet, in her own words, this is "not the hill I have chosen to die on." When a customer calls, she essentially reads from a script. She cannot alter bank policy. Although she introduces herself, for the sake of our argument, the customer might as well be talking to the bank itself. If Anna were to meet the customer socially she would probably "speak her own mind," although it would not be surprising if she were judicious in commenting on the policies of her employer. So, if she went to a party where someone told her about the outrageous behaviour of the bank over his slight chequing balance miscalculation, she could: voice her own opinion; politely listen and avoid further conversation on the topic; advocate (literally "give voice to") the bank's position; or ask whether he would like her to respond either as a sympathetic individual or as a bank employee (the "two hats"). In a similar vein, if she wrote to the customer explaining bank policy and signed the letter, she would be signing in her role of bank agent, not as a morally independent individual.

Still, Anna retains her moral autonomy in that she has a moral life at work independent of the bank—after all she feels qualms about what she is doing—and she does have a choice in going along with the demands of the role. Her allegiance is conditional. We can certainly imagine there may come a time when she is sufficiently at odds with the corporate policy to resign.

3. CELESTE THE DOCTOR

Celeste is a doctor who works primarily at a women's health clinic. Recently, she has encouraged a number of her patients to undergo a newly approved test for genetic disposition to breast cancer. Certain types of cancer tend to occur among blood relations. Therefore, Celeste has actively encouraged patients with positive results to share their findings with their relatives so that they, too, may be tested and increase the chances of detecting cancer in its early stages.

Celeste has a middle-aged patient, Noel, who has just tested positive, although she has no symptoms of any active cancer. In discussing the results with her, Celeste has strongly encouraged Noel to let her daughters and sister know about the test. Noel has refused point blank to do so. Celeste realizes there could be many reasons for her reluctance, including Noel's sense of guilt, her feeling that she will unnecessarily promote anxiety among her relatives, not wishing to draw attention to herself, or simple embarrassment. Celeste has a very strong desire to let the women know they are at risk. She analogizes that if she had a patient with AIDS, she could let those at risk know because she has a moral and legal duty to prevent harm. In this case, though, she is not faced with preventing harm, but more the promotion of benefit and assistance, and, as such, she is constrained from informing third parties about Noel's test result by her professional code.

4. DELLA THE JUDGE

Della, a judge at the state level, is accustomed to sentencing criminals using state guidelines and her own assessment of any particular case. Recently, the state has enacted a so-called "three strikes" law mandating long prison terms for criminals found guilty of a third offense. Her latest case involves Harold, convicted twice before. He was detected shoplifting a single Kit Kat candy bar from a convenience store. He readily confessed to the local police and claimed it was the result of thoughtlessness while waiting impatiently in a long queue to pay for petrol (which he did). Because of the state mandate, Della is now in the position of sentencing Harold to prison for no less than ten years for stealing an item worth less than fifty cents. She has severe doubts about the justice of what she is about to do, but feels her hands are tied by the state legislature.

SIMILARITIES

All four individuals are employed by others and acting in a role for which they are paid. As a result of taking on that role they are facing a moral quandary. Even Stevens the butler, who thinks himself utterly committed, has misgivings about his calling.

First, I think it is significant that this is not a black and white issue. Writers such as Friedman and Carr appear to assume we can cleanly switch between moralities.

> If an executive allows himself to be torn between a decision based on business considerations and one based on his private ethical code, he exposes himself to a grave psychological strain . . . the decisions of the successful business strategist are usually as impersonal as those of a surgeon performing an operation—concentrating on objective and technique and subordinating personal feelings.[2]

At the other pole, some like Andy Gustafson have claimed individuals ought to have only one pervasive morality (a moral integrity) and that role morality is a seriously misleading concept.[3] Both claims are too simple, and (I suspect) the truth is that most of us are confronted with role demands and are willing to make compromises. It would be very rare for someone who works for another either to be completely morally aligned with his or her job, or to be the complete moral chameleon that Carr recommends.

Second, given the lack of alignment, the cases all show there may be tensions between our everyday moral intuitions and the demands of the workplace. The tensions may be of greater or lesser degree. We may acknowledge that the acts in a role are, in fact, less than fully moral, and that we should not be doing them. It is possible that isolating and identifying an act as governed by role morality or professional morality is a hallmark of a departure from our everyday notions of right and wrong.

Third, the individuals involved have autonomous choice. That is, they are free to act differently from the way indicated by the role. Anna could use her limited discretion to wipe out the penalties imposed on someone she feels has been treated unfairly; Celeste could inform Noel's sister without getting consent. Naturally, these acts are liable to lead to sanctions. Nevertheless, it is important to see that the individuals could argue their case, act independently of the role, or resign. They are in the roles because they have voluntarily consented to be, and the constraints on them are largely financial and reputational (for example, Anna would find it hard to get a similar job if she had chosen to go against bank policy).

Fourth, all the actors may claim a significant degree of moral immunity because they were acting in a role. Stevens may never have independently been a Nazi sympathizer, Anna would not deliberately penalize the poor, Celeste would do more to protect women if she could, and Della would not imprison someone over a candy bar if it were up to her alone. But in each case, the major moral actor is the institution or profession, not the individual. The people in these cases are acting as conduits for the moral stance of the institution to which they have, for whatever reason, pledged their allegiance.

DIFFERENCES

The most startling difference in these cases is that two individuals are direct employees and their role acts are a direct function of the manifested values of the employer. They are acting essentially as mouthpieces and do their bidding. In contrast, the "professionals," who nominally have more discretion in their work, are constrained by outside authorities. The judge, who is literally employed to use her judgment, is reduced to sentencing by algorithm. The doctor's actions are governed by a professional code of conduct to which members of the profession subscribe: indeed, it is a characteristic of a profession that there is just such a code.

In the case of the butler and the bank agent, it seems clear the employer is the one who benefits from having a functionary carry out their instructions at arm's length. In the somewhat archaic legal jargon, these are master/servant relationships, and the "servants" are paid to do what they are told. This is not so clear-cut in the case of the professional.

PROFESSIONAL MORALITY EXAMINED

In cases of professional morality, the claim that acts involved in a role benefit an employer is circuitous. Instead of a master/servant relationship, the professional is beholden to a set of rules established by a professional body or association. Members of the profession draft those rules. Significantly, though, the rules are not to benefit the profession itself. The essential nature of a profession is to provide service to individuals, but more importantly, to society as a whole.[4] Professional codes may occasionally override individual interests but this may be justified on the basis of the overall good.[5]

A profession may be formed around a set of skills, proficiencies, techniques, or competencies involved in a line of work. Also, professions . . . involve training and certification. Professional roles are largely the products of public policy and culture; they perform a public function and hence are underwritten on a societal level. The propriety of actions in a professional context can ultimately be justified in terms of whether the role-agent acts in accordance with social policy. This policy element also distinguishes professional roles from other social roles; we would think of doctors, teachers and firefighters as acting in roles, but not thieves or chess players since they are not engaged in a sanctioned social function. The status of "professional" also gives special powers. Thus police officers are given the power of arrest and the powers that arise from special immunities. They are allowed, in the United States at least, to stop cars on the highway more readily than common citizens. Similarly, teachers are in a power relationship with their students, so that they have a distinct ability to punish and reward them.

Professional role moralities arise as a measure to prevent agents acting in a role from abusing the societally mandated power that they have—a situation described as "betraying the public trust." Police officers may overstep the bounds of professional conduct by using excess violence, for example, or a teacher may exploit his or her position by, say, giving unwarranted bad grades to a student that he or she dislikes.

THE MORALITY OF PROFESSIONAL ACTS

. . .

Professionals . . . are guided by a supervenient set of obligations, outlined in a code of conduct which over-arches particular positions or employers. Still, we should not treat them as simple calculations that require slavish adherence. More often, they are crafted in such a way as to allow for interpretation based on governing principles.[6] As John Stuart Mill noted:

> It is not the fault of any creed, but of the complicated nature of human affairs, that rules of conduct cannot be so framed as to require exceptions, and that hardly any kind of action can safely be

laid down as either always obligatory or always condemnable . . . There exists no moral system under which there do not arise unequivocal cases of conflicting obligation. These are the real difficulties, the knotty points both in the theory of ethics and in the conscientious guidance of personal conduct. *They are overcome practically, with greater or less success, according to the intellect and virtue of the individual* [emphasis added].[7]

Professional morality involves more than following a code. David Luban has suggested that role morality is not mere authorization for treating role-governed behaviour as completely determined and without the need for any further deliberation. Instead, he views role morality as an abbreviated form of more sophisticated arguments comprising four elements, each of which needs to be appraised. These are (a) the institution, (b) the role, (c) the role obligation, and (d) the role act. Instead of a general appeal to a role, a professional will have to make a cumulative assessment of each factor before proceeding in any given case.

Consider Luban's own example in which a local boss in a remote village of an undeveloped country orders the murder of a man. A logistics officer of Oxfam, the famine relief agency, overhears the order, but also needs the co-operation of the boss to procure trucks desperately needed to deliver relief supplies. The boss realizes that he has been overheard, and tells the officer that if the intended victim is warned, Oxfam will not get the trucks it needs. Thus there seems to be a case for an institutional excuse, in that the officer may say that her job (providing famine relief) is more important than an individual life. The fourfold analysis, however, demands a more detailed way of examining issues than just pitting the life of the potential victim against those suffering from the famine. Luban suggests that it is, in fact, inappropriate for the officer to claim she is saving many lives; actually, she is acting in an institutional role that may save lives, and hence

the dilemma is strictly "saving one life or doing my job (which is a necessary but not a sufficient condition of saving many lives."[8]

The fourfold analysis takes the institutional excuse to have the following form: the agent

a. justifies the institution by demonstrating its moral goodness
b. justifies the role by appealing to the structure of the institution
c. justifies the role obligations by showing that they are essential to the role
d. justifies the role act by showing that the obligations require it.

Extrapolating this analysis to, say, Celeste's case, she would balance patient confidentiality and the overall benefit of confidence in the medical profession against the immediate potential benefit to the female relatives. In rough terms, the immediate (beneficent) act would be precluded by the necessity to retain the rule of confidentiality.

Key, though, to this analysis is premise (c). This is the assumption that the general rule of confidentiality is good and cannot allow exceptions. We should note at least three elements here: (i) that this is an empirical claim; (ii) that it is essentially self-verifying; and (iii) it is promoted by the profession itself. Questioning these, we first see it is not self-evidently true that occasional, well-reasoned and well-justified exceptions to a rule (such as confidentiality) are unacceptable, and that a concern that breaking the watertight seal would lead to general abuse is over-determined. Indeed, there are a number of exceptions granted under the law. If a doctor is presented with evidence of child abuse he or she is obliged to report it, even against the wishes of the child, for example; or if a patient with AIDS announces he is about to deliberately infect an unwitting partner, the doctor may reveal that information based on the principle of avoiding harm. In this case, the move from justified avoidance of harm to justified doing good is, at least, arguably reasonable.

The second element is that claims about confidentiality (and other constraints on professional behaviour) are largely self-verifying. Thus, if all lawyers work on the baseline assumption that every discussion with their clients is necessarily privileged and confidential, there will be no control group against which we can judge the efficacy of their behaviour. We just don't know what would happen to the adversarial system if there were a basis upon which a client's confidences could be revealed at the lawyer's discretion. The very lack of cases of professional censure when professionals have gone against the code to act in morally heroic ways indicates that we might (at least) open these assumptions to debate.

The third element is troubling in that professions are wells of expertise, and thus many claims about professional behaviour will have to be assessed by members of the profession itself. So, for example, risk-acceptability issues in nuclear engineering may be appropriately assessed only by a nuclear engineer, which makes independent oversight difficult.[9] Similarly, the proliferation of technology means that technical rather than moral experts will be likely to make judgments about what constitutes appropriate applications or restraint on behaviour. (For example, ethical issues in cloning appear to be driven largely by the scientific community).

The tensions that arise in working life are rarely as discrete as those given in the examples: the most likely case is one, like the Pinto, where demands in the workplace come into conflict with professional codes.[10] In effect, there will be multi-layered, conflicting and crosscutting demands of differing moralities—the individual's own values, those imposed by the employer, and the constraints of professional codes. . . .

The distinction of professional codes from other forms of role morality is, in fact, one of *degree* rather than *kind*. Let us return to the bank agent: in most forms of institutionalized business, there will be a set of policies which function in precisely the same way as a professional code. It will specify the minimally acceptable standards and give goals to which one can aspire. Typically, it will present cases of appropriate behaviour and suggest the principles behind the rules.[11] In that sense, Anna is acting under a code. Business does not have professional organizations that formulate a given code, to be sure, but it is a type of behaviour mandated and regulated by society. There are lobbying groups and business organizations of banks (apart from professional organizations of practice, such as accountancy or economics), and these organizations generate standards of operation in a manner similar to that in which professional organizations do.[12] The bank is endowed with special authority (like assignment of creditworthiness) that correlates to the specific authority of professionals. Thus, if we were to examine Anna's actions under Luban's analysis, we would see that there is an institutional under-girding to what she does, and the defense of her actions would ultimately refer to the beneficial role of banking in a capitalist society.

A business is not automatically or necessarily a profession.[13] Yet the purported special status of professions is less meaningful than it originally appears. For the sake of my argument, I need only propose that the operation of business is sufficiently like a profession that we should treat all actions in a role as subject to the same moral analysis. The claim to uniqueness in professions is based, in part, on the fact that the professional is loyal to the profession rather than any particular employer. This is not as compelling as it first seems. What it does show is that some people will have continuing and determined role-identities that survive different forms of employment, whereas others will take on different roles depending on their assignment. However, the tensions involved in role morality will be of a similar type in both continuing and assigned roles.

Looking at examples through this lens shows that the defense of professional acts on the basis of profession tends to collapse into an appraisal of role morality in more general terms. The sort of detailed examination proposed by Luban is entirely appropriate, but misplaced when he suggests tensions of role morality are somehow significantly different when applied to professions alone.

We should take moral tensions caused by acting in role (widely understood) as having similar status, so that the moral qualms felt by the bank agent and the doctor are similar in type. Often an individual will take on multiple roles within an organization, all of which should be subject to similar scrutiny. Thus, one may assess acts appearing unfair or unjust by looking at the utility of the role and the institution undergirding that role. The key element is that the individuals feel morally constrained by their roles, and the issue can be complicated if the individual has multiple roles. In all cases, the person has to make a personal interpretation of what is morally correct. This can be influenced by professional or employer guidelines, but ultimately the decision is the responsibility of the individual. Generally, role morality implies that we can abdicate some degree of moral responsibility. In cases where, say, some immoral action has occurred, there is no significant difference in the claim that the individual was compelled to do it either because of employer demands—as in the notorious case of engineers fudging results when designing an aircraft brake,[14] or because of a professional code—like the Lake Pleasant case where lawyers refused to disclose the whereabouts of a body to the grieving parent.

Consider the examples once again: Stevens would not normally be thought of as a professional (despite his use of the term). Yet, his belief that a capable individual should not be constantly questioning his employer but rather should select and then commit is very similar to the way in which many professionals, such as lawyers, do treat their work. They may have some concerns about the adversarial system while at law school, but, in effect, they 'buy into' the system once they begin to practice and subsequently zealously attorn for their clients, defending their actions largely on the professional code. . . .

Some roles may be more inclusive than others, and that may dictate the way in which individuals are able to compartmentalize their actions. It may be easier to excuse oneself, for example, by saying that the actions were only appropriate in role, at work. The butler, while willing to follow orders, may only be willing to follow orders insofar as they apply to him as a butler. In matters of managing the household he might well feel bound by his employer's instructions even if they are to perform distasteful acts such as firing Jewish maids, but his being a butler does not necessarily mean that he would obey if told to go and rob a bank or shoot somebody. The limitations within which he can be given orders, and within which his having the role of butler might provide excuse for an action he or others find distasteful, are set by what it is to be a butler.

Still, it is a peculiar feature of work roles that they can figure so largely in an individual's identity. In *The Remains of the Day*, Stevens' aspiration is always to comport himself with the dignity of his office, and he prides himself on overcoming his fallible self to become more like the ideal butler.[15] Moreover, he believes that by doing so he is ultimately serving humanity at large, which gives a moral dimension to his work.[16] He believes what he is doing is so important that his personal satisfaction (and his personal life) are secondary. In that sense, although he might not go outside actions understood to be in his job description, he has, in fact, tailored his life to his job.

An individual's belief that his or her role involves submission or delegation of control may be a significant factor, too. In his famous experiments on obedience to authority, Stanley Milgram set up subjects to administer apparent electric shocks to a "victim" who was actually an actor. The question at hand was how far naive individuals would blindly follow orders. Milgram recounts the case of a teacher at a major divinity school who refused to inflict punishment. When he was debriefed, the teacher revealed that he did not feel the experimenter had the right to give him orders, and that he felt that ultimate authority lies with God. Milgram notes, somewhat wryly, that this subject did not justify his actions in terms of autonomy, but instead he was looking for "good" authority rather than "bad," with the clear implication that if the teacher believed the authority issuing the orders was legitimate he would have had no qualms in hurting an innocent person.[17] Adapting this insight to our present case, we can speculate that Stevens may not have shot someone on behalf of his employer, but we can certainly imagine him being an unwitting collaborator in an occupied country who gives the address of the Jews to the Nazis. It seems that the act of abdicating personal responsibility in role, which he clearly does, is at least as morally significant as the particular functions that he carries out in his duties.

A closely related issue is the question of what constitutes a proper description of an act carried out in a role. Acting in a role in an institutional context can have a considerable effect on the appropriate description of an act. Della the judge might be thought of as keeping a hardened criminal off the streets, or, alternatively as depriving a family of its breadwinner. In effect, the discussion of role morality is based on making different descriptions of the act available.[18] Moral perplexity may arise from the novelty of a case, where there are no clear analogies to settled issues, or because there are no clear guiding principles. However, in the cases I have posed above, there are a number of principles available to the agents, and the descriptions involved are very much dependent on the level of principle that the agent has chosen to work from. In Stevens' case, he has reconciled himself to unreflective obedience on the basis that such action is the best function he can fulfil to further the development of civilization: Under Luban's terminology, he has given paramount importance to the role rather than the role acts. Similarly, Della would describe her actions not merely by the effect of having someone locked up, but more in terms of the workings of the legal institutions. Although we have a range of descriptions available in any case, these are not strictly dilemmas, but rather pose a choice about the level of principle at work. This choice, as Luban indicates, ought not to be intuitive but instead should come about though deliberate reflection on the part of the actor.

In all these cases, then, the most appropriate approach is, ironically, indicated by Stevens the butler when he pronounces that loyalty has to be given *intelligently*.[19] There will be a degree of tension and compromise when acting in a role, and so we need to engage in something like Luban's examination of the fourfold root. Clearly, this cannot be done in an urgent moment, but requires adequate time and research to find reflective equilibrium. It also demands a fairly sophisticated level of understanding of the nature of institutions within society. The emerging tensions arise because of the competing justifications of correct action in context. The label of "profession" has no special moral significance for this discussion, other than that it portrays one set of moral demands among a constellation that individuals encounter at work. . . .

Lastly, it is important to revisit the potential harm involved in traditional analyses of agent behaviour and professional behaviour, in that role morality fosters excuses for actions that individuals would not endorse out of a role. The simple truth is that, ultimately, individuals are responsible for their actions whatever the pressures, circumstances or heuristics at work.[20] Professional

codes and bosses' demands alike do not, by themselves, make difficult decisions easy or immoral actions moral. Slavish obedience to a code is not morally distinct from unthinking obedience to authority. People are faced with awkward moral problems and these often entail either a compromise or a lesser-of-two-evils solution. The solution is likely to be found in developing a wider understanding of role actions in an overall societal context. This would apply to all workers in an institutional environment, whatever their status or profession. ◆ ◆ ◆

◆ Notes

1. K. Ishiguro (1989) *The Remains of the Day* (New York, Vintage), 199–201. Emphasis added.
2. A. Carr (1968) *Business as a Game* (New York, Signet), p. 151.
3. A. Gustafson (2000) In support of ethical holism, *Business Ethics Quarterly* 10, 2, 441–450.
4. See, for example, the *Concise Oxford English Dictionary*.
5. See, for example, claims by Michael Bayles (1981) in his book *Professional Ethics* (Belmont, CA, Wadsworth).
6. This is reflected in the demands of the 1991 Federal Sentencing Guidelines. See, for example, Robert J. Rafalko (1994) Remaking the corporation: the 1991 U.S. Sentencing Guidelines, *Journal of Business Ethics*, 13.
7. J. S. Mill (1863) *Utilitarianism* (New York, Signet Meriden Press) 277.
8. D. Luban (1988) *Lawyers and Justice* (New Jersey, Princeton University Press).
9. This is based on my personal experience of consulting with nuclear engineers.
10. See, for example, Richard T. De George (1981) Ethical responsibilities of engineers in large organizations: the Pinto case, *Business and Professional Ethics Journal*, 1, Fall.
11. This sort of code is demanded under the 1991 Federal Sentencing Guidelines, see note 6 above.
12. For example, a code promoted by the American Banker's Association, Washington, DC. http://www.aba.com/about+aba/aba_privprinpublic.htm
13. For a detailed discussion on this topic, see Alan Goldman (1980) *The Moral Foundations of Professional Ethics* (Totowa, New Jersey, Rowman and Littlefield).
14. K. Vandivier (1972) Why should my conscience bother me? The aircraft brake scandal, in R. Heilbroner et al (eds.) *In the Name of Profit* (New York, Doubleday).
15. *Remains of the Day*, 228.
16. *Remains of the Day*, 116.
17. Stanley Milgram (1974) *Obedience to Authority* (New York, Harper and Row) 41.
18. This point is brought up in Julius Kovesi (1967) *Moral Notions* (New York, Humanities Press), especially section IV.
19. Clearly, intelligent does not always mean correct (e.g., the actions of university professors and administrators).
20. See, for a similar view, K. Gibson (2000) Excuses, excuses: moral slippage in the workplace, *Business Horizons* 43, 6, 65–72.

My View on the Pinto Affair

Lee Iaccoca

Iaccoca was the chief executive in charge of the Ford Motor Company Pinto project. The Pinto was a small car with a rear-mounted gas tank that was liable to burst into flames when the vehicle was struck from behind. A large number were produced, and it was a very popular model. It met all federal regulations at the time it was made.

At the same time, Ford was actively lobbying against more stringent safety measures. In Canada there were tougher regulations that required additional modifications, and those models did not have the same problems. The moral issue arises because executives at Ford were aware of the danger and knew that it could be fixed by a relatively inexpensive part. However, they chose not to recall the Pinto, largely based on an economic analysis that balanced the cost of the recall against paying for lawsuits and compensation. This is an abstract from Iaccoca's best-selling autobiography where he discusses the Pinto in less than two pages. He feels that it was not a moral problem so much as a public relations and legal problem. He also blames himself for stonewalling. Several of the readings so far have made claims about the responsibility of individuals within the corporation, particularly those in executive positions, even if they were not fully aware of what was going on. The reading and individual research should give us an opportunity to assess responsibility in a real case.

I can't talk about bad cars without a few words on the Ford Pinto. We brought out the Pinto in 1971. We needed a subcompact, and this was the best one you could buy for under $2,000. A lot of people must have agreed—we sold over four hundred thousand Pintos in the first year alone. This made the car a great success and put it in the category of the Falcon and the Mustang.

Unhappily, the Pinto was involved in a number of accidents where the car burst into flames after a rear-end collision. There were lawsuits—hundreds of them. In 1978, in a major trial in Indiana, the Ford Motor Company was charged with reckless homicide. Ford was acquitted, but the damage to the company was incalculable.

There were two problems with the Pinto. First, the fuel tank was located behind the axle, so if the car got hit hard enough from behind, there was the possibility of a fire.

The Pinto was not the only car with this problem. In those days, *all* small cars had the fuel tank behind the axle. And all small cars were occasionally involved in fires.

But the Pinto also had a filler neck on the fuel tank that sometimes, in a collision, was ripped out on impact. When that happened, raw gas spilled out and frequently ignited.

We resisted making any changes, and that hurt us badly. Even Joan Claybrook, the tough director of the National Highway Traffic Safety Administration and a Nader protégé, said to me one day: "It's a shame you can't do something about the Pinto. It's really no worse than any other small car. You don't have an engineering problem as much as you have a legal and public-relations problem."

Whose fault was it? One obvious answer is that it was the fault of Ford's management—including me. There are plenty of people who would say that the legal and PR pressures involved in such a situation excuse management's stonewalling in the hope the problem will go away. It seems to me, though, that it is fair to hold management to a high standard, and to insist that they do what duty and common sense require, no matter what the pressures.

But there's absolutely no truth to the charge that we tried to save a few bucks and knowingly made a dangerous car. The auto industry has often been arrogant, but it's not that callous. The guys who built the Pinto had kids in college who were driving that car. Believe me, nobody sits down and thinks: "I'm deliberately going to make this car unsafe."

In the end, we voluntarily recalled almost a million and a half Pintos. This was in June 1978, the month before I was fired. ◆ ◆ ◆

CONFLICTS
BETWEEN INDIVIDUAL
AND CORPORATE MORALITY

In the last chapter we saw how individuals may have to tailor their behavior in the workplace to meet the demands of an employer. Generally we do not object to some compromises; however, there may come a time when individuals will refuse to do what an employer demands and may quit if asked to do something that goes against their fundamental beliefs. In some cases workers feel so strongly about an issue that they are compelled to publicly denounce their employers. Whistle-blowing typically involves an employee going outside the formal organizational structure in order to prevent harm.

Consider the following case: you pass a professor's office and see through a partly open door that he has his arms around a young female student. She is sobbing. Do you have a duty to intervene? Of course, it will depend on what is actually going on. It could be that he is sexually harassing her, but it might just as easily be that her father has died and she is being comforted. In the absence of real knowledge, a natural response is to ignore the situation and get on with your life. But what would it take to move you sufficiently to get involved? Perhaps the young

woman bursts out of the office yelling, "It's over, leave me alone!" Should you approach her? How much moral responsibility should we put on the apparent victim? Would it be proper for you to pursue the case even if she did not want to?

There are typically reporting mechanisms within colleges that would allow you to report what you have seen. Most witnesses to wrongdoing report it to the appropriate authority and then feel they have done as much as anyone could reasonably be asked to do. Yet if the matter seems to rest there, should they do more? Clearly, two factors will make a difference:

- The available evidence
- The degree of potential harm

In the NASA *Challenger* case, an engineer named Roger Boisjoly said that he was 100 percent certain that if the shuttle launched, a fatal accident would result. If someone has that degree of confidence and the issue involves human life, perhaps he should have stopped at nothing to prevent takeoff. On the other hand, if we were talking about possible fraud, what amount would it take to justify reporting your suspicions to the general public? Thousands of dollars? Millions? Thousands of millions? Paraphrasing the words of a judge in the HealthSouth case, "The perpetrators meant no harm, and nobody got killed." Nevertheless, the investments of thousands of institutions and individuals were wiped out, and many retirement nest eggs were decimated by the fraud.

Most of the time we are dealing with uncertainty, especially if the concerns are dealt with in the meantime. For instance, if you are a nuclear engineer and say publicly that a valve needs to be replaced in order to prevent a meltdown, your credibility will be undermined if nothing is done and subsequently there is no meltdown. But if you find that management has quietly replaced the valve, you are put in the position of having to argue that if they had not done so, there would have been a problem, which is extraordinarily difficult to prove.

Most data are subject to a degree of interpretation and expert analysis. In the Enron case, Sherron Watkins felt there was something wrong with the partnership agreements that appeared to turn debts into assets, but the documents were innovative and complicated hedging arrangements that would be very difficult for a nonspecialist to understand. She confronted her boss with her suspicions, and he assured her nothing was amiss. At that point, it might have been reasonable for her to stop her investigation.

The other constant in whistle-blowing cases is that the individual's motives are often questioned, and the company typically takes reprisal action. The whistle-blower should expect to be treated more as a snitch than a savior. Generally, the company describes the person as a disgruntled employee or as having a self-promoting agenda.

All of these factors tend to discourage appropriate whistle-blowing; it is so much easier to keep walking past the door, pretending to have seen nothing. At the same time, whistle-blowers are often like people who stop at the scene of a car accident: They probably did not ask to be involved but see that they have a compelling moral duty; other consequences become secondary.

The readings in this chapter are important because they discuss cases where traditionally loyal employees find themselves in a position where they feel they have to speak out for the public good. We should ask if they are doing the moral minimum or going beyond it. What workplace conditions would move us to act similarly?

Richard Nielsen's reading surveys a range of possible actions for someone who discovers a moral wrong in the organization and specifically asks when we should work within the group as opposed to going outside it. Michael Davis's reading challenges the typical idea of whistle-blowing. He concludes that very often whistle-blowers are, in fact, complicit in some wrong and go public in order to distance themselves from their involvement. The *Time* magazine extract profiles three women—Sherron Watkins, Coleen Rowley, and Cynthia Cooper—as its "Persons of the Year" for blowing the whistle and gives us some insight into their common experiences. Finally, Leonard Baynes's reading examines the conflicts of loyalty that come into play for whistle-blowers and some of the protections afforded by the recent Sarbanes-Oxley legislation.

Changing Unethical Organizational Behavior

Richard P. Nielsen

At the end of the day, individuals have to make their own conclusions about what is right and wrong. These values may clash with those of the company, and there may come a time when it is appropriate to speak out publicly about practices that you condemn.

Nielsen describes a number of dilemmas that an individual may encounter in a business organization and reviews intervention strategies that may be appropriate. He identifies two approaches called "being as an individual" and "being as part of a group." An individual may choose to work against others and the organization or act as a leader working with others to alter the way things are done. He gives a number of cases and suggests which approach (or blend) would be most effective in each scenario.

"To be, or not to be: that is the question:
Whether 'tis nobler in the mind to suffer
The slings and arrows of outrageous fortune,
Or to take arms against a sea of troubles,
And by opposing end them?"

William Shakespeare, *Hamlet*

What are the implications of Hamlet's question in the context of organizational ethics? What does it mean to be ethical in an organizational context? Should one suffer the slings and arrows of unethical organizational behavior? Should one try to take arms against unethical behaviors and by opposing, end them?

The consequences of addressing organizational ethics issues can be unpleasant. One can be punished or fired; one's career can suffer, or one can be disliked, considered an outsider. It

may take courage to oppose unethical and lead ethical organizational behavior.

How can one address organizational ethics issues? Paul Tillich, in his book *The Courage to Be*, recognized, as Hamlet did, that dire consequences can result from standing up to and opposing unethical behavior. Tillich identified two approaches: *being* as an individual and *being* as a part of a group.[1]

In an organizational context, these two approaches can be interpreted as follows: (1) Being as an individual can mean intervening to end unethical organizational behaviors by working against others and the organizations performing the unethical behaviors; and (2) being as a part can mean leading an ethical organizational change by working with others and the organization. These approaches are not mutually exclusive; rather, depending on the individual, the organization, the relationships, and the situation, one or both of these approaches may be appropriate for addressing ethical issues.

BEING AS AN INDIVIDUAL

According to Tillich, the courage to be as an individual is the courage to follow one's conscience and defy unethical and/or unreasonable authority. It can even mean staging a revolutionary attack on that authority. Such an act can entail great risk and require great courage. As Tillich explains, "The anxiety conquered in the courage to be . . . in the productive process is considerable, because the threat of being excluded from such a participation by unemployment or the loss of an economic basis is what, above all, fate means today. . . ."[2]

According to David Ewing, retired executive editor of the *Harvard Business Review*, this type of anxiety is not without foundation.

> "There is very little protection in industry for employees who object to carrying out immoral, unethical or illegal orders from their superiors. If the employee doesn't like what he or she is asked to do, the remedy is to pack up and leave. This remedy seems to presuppose an ideal economy, where there is another company down the street with openings for jobs just like the one the employee left."[3]

How can one *be* as an individual, intervening against unethical organizational behavior? Intervention strategies an individual can use to change unethical behavior include: (1) secretly blowing the whistle within the organization; (2) quietly blowing the whistle, informing a responsible higher-level manager; (3) secretly threatening the offender with blowing the whistle; (4) secretly threatening a responsible manager with blowing the whistle outside the organization; (5) publicly threatening a responsible manager with blowing the whistle; (6) sabotaging the implementation of the unethical behavior; (7) quietly refraining from implementing an unethical order or policy; (8) publicly blowing the whistle within the organization; (9) conscientiously objecting to an unethical policy or refusing to implement the policy; (10) indicating uncertainty about or refusing to support a cover-up in the event that the individual and/or organization gets caught; (11) secretly blowing the whistle outside the organization; or (12) publicly blowing the whistle outside the organization. Cases of each strategy are considered below.

Cases

1. *Secretly blowing the whistle within the organization.* A purchasing manager for General Electric secretly wrote a letter to an upper-level manager about his boss, who was soliciting and accepting bribes from subcontractors. The boss was investigated and eventually fired. He was also sentenced to six months' imprisonment for taking $100,000 in bribes, in exchange for which he granted favorable treatment on defense contracts.[4]

2. *Quietly blowing the whistle to a responsible higher-level manager.* When Evelyn Grant was first hired by the company with which she is now a personnel manager, her job included administering a battery of tests that, in part, determined which employees were promoted to supervisory positions. Grant explained:

> "There have been cases where people will do something wrong because they think they have no choice. Their boss tells them to do it, and so they do it, knowing it's wrong. They don't realize there are ways around the boss. . . . When I went over his [the chief psychologist's] data and analysis, I found errors in assumptions as well as actual errors of computation. . . . I had two choices: I could do nothing or I could report my findings to my supervisor. If I did nothing, the only persons

probably hurt were the ones who 'failed' the test. To report my findings, on the other hand, could hurt several people, possibly myself."

She quietly spoke to her boss, who quietly arranged for a meeting to discuss the discrepancies with the chief psychologist. The chief psychologist did not show up for the meeting; however, the test battery was dropped.[5]

3. *Secretly threatening the offender with blowing the whistle.* A salesman for a Boston-area insurance company attended a weekly sales meeting during which the sales manager instructed the salespeople, both verbally and in writing, to use a sales technique that the salesman considered unethical. The salesman anonymously wrote the sales manager a letter threatening to send a copy of the unethical sales instructions to the Massachusetts insurance commissioner and the *Boston Globe* newspaper unless the sales manager retracted his instructions at the next sales meeting. The sales manager did retract the instructions. The salesman still works for the insurance company.[6]

4. *Secretly threatening a responsible manager with blowing the whistle outside the organization.* A recently hired manager with a San Francisco Real Estate Development Company found that the construction company his firm had contracted with was systematically not giving minorities opportunities to learn construction management. This new manager wrote an anonymous letter to a higher-level real estate manager threatening to blow the whistle to the press and local government about the contractor unless the company corrected the situation. The real estate manager intervened, and the contractor began to hire minorities for foremen-training positions.[7]

5. *Publicly threatening a responsible manager with blowing the whistle.* A woman in the business office of a large Boston-area university observed that one middle-level male manager was sexually harassing several women in the office. She tried to reason with the office manager to do something about the offensive behavior, but the manager would not do anything. She then told the manager and several other people in the office that if the manager did not do something about the behavior, she would blow the whistle to the personnel office. The manager then told the offender that if he did not stop the harassment, the personnel office would be brought in. He did stop the behavior, but he and several other employees refused to talk to the woman who initiated the actions. She eventually left the university.[8]

6. *Sabotaging the implementation of the unethical behavior.* A program manager for a Boston-area local social welfare organization was told by her superior to replace a significant percentage of her clients who received disability benefits with refugee Soviet Jews. She wanted to help both the refugees and her current clients; however, she thought it was unethical to drop current clients, in part because she believed such an action could result in unnecessary deaths. Previously, a person who had lost benefits because of what the program manager considered unethical "bumping" had committed suicide: He had not wanted to force his family to sell their home in order to pay for the medical care he needed and qualify for poverty programs. After her attempts to reason with her boss failed, she instituted a paperwork chain with a partially funded federal agency that prevented her own agency from dropping clients for nine months, after which time they would be eligible for a different funding program. Her old clients received benefits and the new refugees also received benefits. In discussions with her boss, she blamed the federal agency for making it impossible to drop people quickly. Her boss, a political appointee who did not understand the system, also blamed the federal agency office.[9]

7. *Publicly blowing the whistle within the organization.* John W. Young, a chief of NASA's astronaut office, wrote a 12-page internal memorandum to 97 people after the Challenger explosion that killed seven crew members. The memo listed a large number of safety-related problems that Young said had endangered crews since October 1984. According to Young, "If the management system is not big enough to stop the space shuttle program whenever necessary to make flight safety corrections, it will not survive and neither will our three space shuttles or their flight crews." The memo was instrumental in the decision to broaden safety investigations throughout the total NASA system.[10]

8. *Quietly refraining from implementing an unethical order/policy.* Frank Ladwig was a top salesman and branch manager with a large computer company for more than 40 years. At times, he had trouble balancing his responsibilities. For instance, he was trained to sell solutions to customer problems, yet he had order and revenue quotas that sometimes made it difficult for him to concentrate on solving problems. He was responsible for signing and keeping important customers with annual revenues of between $250,000 and $500,000 and for aggressively and conscientiously representing new products that had required large R&D investments. He was required to sell the full line of products and services, and sometimes he had sales quotas for products that he believed were not a good match for the customer or appeared to perform marginally. Ladwig would quietly not sell those products, concentrating on selling the products he believed in. He would quietly explain the characteristics of the questionable products to his knowledgeable customers and get their reactions, rather than making an all-out sales effort. When he was asked by his sales manager why a certain product was not moving, he explained what the customers objected to and why. However, Ladwig thought that a salesman or manager with an average or poor performance record would have a difficult time getting away with this type of solution to an ethical dilemma.[11]

9. *Conscientiously objecting to an unethical policy or refusing to implement it.* Francis O'Brien was a research director for the pharmaceutical company Searle & Co. O'Brien conscientiously objected to what he believed were exaggerated claims for the Searle Copper 7 intrauterine contraceptive. When reasoning with upper-level management failed, O'Brien wrote them the following:

> "Their continued use, in my opinion, is both misleading and a thinly disguised attempt to make claims which are not FDA approved. . . . Because of personal reasons I do not consent to have my name used in any press release or in connection with any press release. In addition, I will not participate in any press conferences."

O'Brien left the company ten years later. Currently, several lawsuits are pending against Searle, charging that its IUD caused infection and sterility.[12]

10. *Indicating uncertainty about or refusing to support a cover-up in the event that the individual and/or organization gets caught.* In the Boston office of Bear Stearns, four brokers informally work together as a group. One of the brokers had been successfully trading on insider information, and he invited the other three to do the same. One of the three told the others that such trading was not worth the risk of getting caught, and if an investigation ever occurred, he was not sure he would be able to participate in a cover-up. The other two brokers decided not to trade on the insider information, and the first broker stopped at least that type of insider trading.[13]

11. *Secretly blowing the whistle outside the corporation.* William Schwartzkopf of the Commonwealth Electric Company secretly and

anonymously wrote a letter to the Justice Department alleging large-scale, long-time bid rigging among many of the largest U.S. electrical contractors. The secret letter accused the contractors of raising bids and conspiring to divide billions of dollars of contracts. Companies in the industry have already paid more than $20 million in fines to the government in part as a result of this letter, and they face millions of dollars more in losses when the victims sue.[14]

12. *Publicly blowing the whistle outside the organization.* A. Earnest Fitzgerald, a former high-level manager in the U.S. Air Force and Lockheed CEO, revealed to Congress and the press that the Air Force and Lockheed systematically practiced a strategy of underbidding in order to gain Air Force contracts for Lockheed, which then billed the Air Force and received payments for cost overruns on the contracts. Fitzgerald was fired for his trouble, but eventually received his job back. The underbidding/cost overruns, on at least the C-5/A cargo plane, were stopped.[15]

Limitations of Intervention

The intervention strategies described above can be very effective, but they also have some important limitations.

1. *The individual can be wrong about the organization's actions.* Lower-level employees commonly do not have as much or as good information about ethical situations and issues as higher-level managers. Similarly, they may not be as experienced as higher-level managers in dealing with specific ethical issues. The quality of experience and information an individual has can influence the quality of his or her ethical judgments. To the extent that this is true in any given situation, the use of intervention may or may not be warranted. In Case 8, for example, if Frank Ladwig had had limited computer experience, he could have been wrong about some of the products he thought would not produce the promised results.

2. *Relationships can be damaged.* Suppose that instead of identifying with the individuals who want an organization to change its ethical behavior, we look at these situations from another perspective. How do we feel when we are forced to change our behavior? Further, how would we feel if we were forced by a subordinate to change, even though we thought that we had the position, quality of information, and/or quality of experience to make the correct decisions? Relationships would probably be, at the least, strained, particularly if we made an ethical decision and were nevertheless forced to change. If we are wrong, it may be that we do not recognize it at the time. If we know we are wrong, we still may not like being forced to change. However, it is possible that the individual forcing us to change may justify his or her behavior to us, and our relationship may actually be strengthened.

3. *The organization can be hurt unnecessarily.* If an individual is wrong in believing that the organization is unethical, the organization can be hurt unnecessarily by his or her actions. Even if the individual is right, the organization can still be unnecessarily hurt by intervention strategies.

4. *Intervention strategies can encourage "might makes right" climates.* If we want "wrong" people, who might be more powerful now or in the future than we are, to exercise self-restraint, then we may need to exercise self-restraint even when we are "right." A problem with using force is that the other side may use more powerful or effective force now or later. Many people have been punished for trying to act ethically both when they were right and when they were wrong. By using force, one may also contribute to the belief that the only way to get things done in a particular organization is through force. People who are wrong can and do use force, and win. Do we want to build an organization culture in which force

plays an important role? Gandhi's response to "an eye for an eye" was that if we all followed that principle, eventually everyone would be blind.

BEING AS A PART

While the intervention strategies discussed above can be very effective, they can also be destructive. Therefore, it may be appropriate to consider the advantages of leading an ethical change effort (being as a part) as well as intervening against unethical behaviors (being as an individual).

Tillich maintains that the courage to be as a part is the courage to affirm one's own being through participation with others. He writes,

> "The self affirms itself as participant in the power of a group, of a movement. . . . Self-affirmation within a group includes the courage to accept guilt and its consequences as public guilt, whether one is oneself responsible or whether somebody else is. It is a problem of the group which has to be expiated for the sake of the group, and the methods of punishment and satisfaction . . . are accepted by the individual. . . . In every human community, there are outstanding members, the bearers of the traditions and leaders of the future. They must have sufficient distance in order to judge and to change. They must take responsibility and ask questions. This unavoidably produces individual doubt and personal guilt. Nevertheless, the predominant pattern is the courage to be a part in all members of the . . . group. . . . The difference between the genuine Stoic and the neocollectivist is that the latter is bound in the first place to the collective and in the second place to the universe, while the Stoic was first of all related to the universal Logos and secondly to possible human groups. . . . The democratic-conformist type of the courage to be as a part was in an outspoken way tied up with the idea of progress. The courage to be as a part in the progress of the group to which one belongs. . . ."[16]

Leading Ethical Change

A good cross-cultural conceptualization of leadership is offered by Yoshino and Lifson: "The essence of leadership is the influential increment over and above mechanical compliance with routine directives of the organization."[17] This definition permits comparisons between and facilitates an understanding of different leadership styles through its use of a single variable: created incremental performance. Of course, different types of leadership may be more or less effective in different types of situations; yet, it is helpful to understand the "essence" of leadership in its many different cultural forms as the creation of incremental change beyond the routine.

For example, Yoshino and Lifson compare generalizations (actually overgeneralizations) about Japanese and American leadership styles:

> "In the United States, a leader is often thought of as one who blazes new trails, a virtuoso whose example inspires awe, respect, and emulation. If any individual characterizes this pattern, it is surely John Wayne, whose image reached epic proportions in his own lifetime as an embodiment of something uniquely American. A Japanese leader, rather than being an authority, is more of a communications channel, a mediator, a facilitator, and most of all, a symbol and embodiment of group unity. Consensus building is necessary to decision making, and this requires patience and an ability to use carefully cultivated relationships to get all to agree for the good of the unit. A John Wayne in this situation might succeed temporarily by virtue of charisma, but eventually the inability to build strong emotion-laden relationships and use these as a tool of motivation and consensus building would prove fatal."[18]

A charismatic, "John Wayne type" leader can inspire and/or frighten people into diverting from the routine. A consensus-building, Japanese-style leader can get people to agree to divert from the routine. In both cases, the leader creates incremental behavior change beyond the routine. How does leadership (being as a part) in its various cultural forms differ from the various intervention (being as an individual) strategies and cases discussed above? Some case data may be revealing.

Cases

1. *Roger Boisjoly and the Challenger launch.*[19] In January 1985, after the postflight hardware inspection of Flight 52C, Roger Boisjoly strongly suspected that unusually low temperatures had compromised the performance effectiveness of the O-ring seals on two field joints. Such a performance compromise could cause an explosion. In March 1985, laboratory tests confirmed that low temperatures did negatively affect the ability of the O-rings to perform this sealing function. In June 1985, the postflight inspection of Flight 51B revealed serious erosion of both primary and backup seals that, had it continued, could have caused an explosion.

These events convinced Boisjoly that a serious and very dangerous problem existed with the O-rings. Instead of acting as an individual against his supervisors and the organization, for example, by blowing the whistle to the press, he tried to lead a change to stop the launching of flights with unsafe O-rings. He worked with his immediate supervisor, the director of engineering, and the organization in leading this change. He wrote a draft of a memo to Bob Lund, vice-president of engineering, which he first showed and discussed with his immediate supervisor to "maintain good relationships." Boisjoly and others developed potential win-win solutions, such as investigating remedies to fix the O-rings and refraining from launching flights at too-low temperatures. He effectively established a team to study the matter, and participated in a teleconference with 130 technical experts.

On the day before the Challenger launch, Boisjoly and other team members were successful in leading company executives to reverse their tentative recommendation to launch because the overnight temperatures were predicted to be too low. The company recommendation was to launch only when temperatures were above 53 degrees. To this point, Boisjoly was very effective in leading a change toward what he and other engineering and management people believed was a safe and ethical decision.

However, according to testimony from Boisjoly and others to Congress, the top managers of Morton Thiokol, under pressure from NASA, reversed their earlier recommendation not to launch. The next day, Challenger was launched and exploded, causing the deaths of all the crew members. While Boisjoly was very effective in leading a change within his own organization, he was not able to counteract subsequent pressure from the customer, NASA.

2. *Dan Phillips and Genco, Inc.*[20] Dan Phillips was a paper products group division manager for Genco, whose upper-level management adopted a strategy whereby several mills, including the Elkhorn Mill, would either have to reduce costs or close down. Phillips was concerned that cost cutting at Elkhorn would prevent the mill from meeting government pollution-control requirements, and that closing the mill could seriously hurt the local community. If he reduced costs, he would not meet pollution-control requirements; if he did not reduce costs, the mill would close and the community would suffer.

Phillips did not secretly or publicly blow the whistle, nor did he sabotage, conscientiously object, quietly refrain from implementing the plan, or quit; however, he did lead a change in the organization's ethical behavior. He asked research and development people in his division to investigate how the plant could both become more cost efficient and create less pollution. He then asked operations people in his division to estimate how long it would take to put such a new plant design on line, and how much it would cost. He asked cost accounting and financial people within his division to estimate when such a new operation would achieve a breakeven payback. Once he found a plan that would work, he negotiated a win-win solution with upper-level management: in exchange for not closing the plant and increasing its investment in his division, the organization would over time benefit from lower costs and higher profitability. Phillips thus worked with others and the organization to lead an inquiry and adopt an alternative ethical and cost-effective plan.

3. *Lotus and Brazilian Software Importing.*[21] Lotus, a software manufacturer, found that in spite of restrictions on the importing of much of its software to Brazil, many people there were buying and using Lotus software. On further investigation, the company discovered that Brazilian businessmen, in alliance with a Brazilian general, were violating the law by buying Lotus software in Cambridge, Massachusetts and bringing it into Brazil.

Instead of blowing the whistle on the illegal behavior, sabotaging it, or leaving Brazil, Lotus negotiated a solution: In exchange for the Brazilians' agreement to stop illegal importing, Lotus helped set them up as legitimate licensed manufacturers and distributors of Lotus products in Brazil. Instead of working against them and the Lotus salespeople supplying them, the Lotus managers worked with these people to develop an ethical, legal, and economically sound solution to the importing problem.

And in at least a limited sense, the importers may have been transformed into ethical managers and business people. This case may remind you of the legendary "Old West," where government officials sometimes negotiated win-win solutions with "outlaw gunfighters," who agreed to become somewhat more ethical as appointed sheriffs. The gunfighters needed to make a liv-ing, and many were not interested in or qualified for such other professions as farming or shopkeeping. In some cases, ethical behavior may take place before ethical beliefs are assumed.

4. *Insurance company office/sales manager and discrimination.*[22] The sales-office manager of a very large Boston-area insurance company tried to hire female salespeople several times, but his boss refused to permit the hires. The manager could have acted against his boss and the organization by secretly threatening to blow the whistle or actually blowing the whistle, publicly or secretly. Instead, he decided to try to lead a change in the implicit hiring policy of the organization.

The manager asked his boss why he was not permitted to hire a woman. He learned that his boss did not believe women made good salespeople and had never worked with a female salesperson. He found that reasoning with his boss about the capabilities of women and the ethics and legality of refusing to hire women was ineffective.

He inquired within the company about whether being a woman could be an advantage in any insurance sales areas. He negotiated with his boss a six-month experiment whereby he hired on a trial basis one woman to sell life insurance to married women who contributed large portions of their salaries to their home mortgages. The woman he hired was not only very successful in selling this type of life insurance, but became one of the office's top salespeople. After this experience, the boss reversed his policy of not hiring female salespeople.

Limitations to Leading Ethical Organizational Change

In the four cases described above, the individuals did not attack the organization or people within the organization, nor did they intervene against individuals and/or the organization to stop an unethical practice. Instead, they worked with people in the organization to build a more ethical organization. As a result of their leadership, the organizations used more ethical behaviors. The strategy of leading an organization toward more ethical behavior, however, does have some limitations. These are described below.

1. In some organizational situations, ethical win-win solutions or compromises may not be possible. For example, in 1975 a pharmaceutical company in Raritan, New Jersey decided to enter a new market with a new product.[23] Grace Pierce, who was then in charge of medical testing of new products, refused to test a new diarrhea drug product on infants and elderly consumers because it contained high levels of saccharin, which was feared by many at the time to be a carcinogen. When Pierce was transferred, she resigned. The drug was tested on infant and elderly consumers. In this case, Pierce may have been faced with an either-or situation that left her little room to lead a change in organizational behavior.

Similarly, Errol Marshall, with Hydraulic Parts and Components, Inc.,[24] helped negotiate the sale of a subcontract to sell heavy equipment to the U.S. Navy while giving $70,000 in kickbacks to two materials managers of Brown & Root, Inc., the project's prime contractor. According to Marshall, the prime contractor "demanded the kickbacks. . . . It was cut and dried. We would not get the business otherwise." While Marshall was not charged with any crime, one of the upper-level Brown & Root managers, William Callan, was convicted . . . of extorting kickbacks, and another manager, Frank DiDomenico, pleaded guilty to extorting kickbacks from Hydraulic Parts & Components, Inc. Marshall has left the company. In this case, it seems that Marshall had no win-win alternative to paying the bribe. In some situations it may not be possible to lead a win-win ethical change.

2. Some people do not understand how leadership can be applied to situations that involve organizational ethics issues. Also, some people—particularly those in analytical or technical professions, which may not offer much opportunity for gaining leadership experience—may not know how to lead very well in any situation. Some people may be good leaders in the course of their normal work lives, but do not try to lead or do not lead very well when ethical issues are involved. Some people avoid discussing ethical, religious, and political issues at work.

For example, John Geary was a salesman for U.S. Steel when the company decided to enter a new market with what he and others considered an unsafe new product.[25] As a leading salesman for U.S. Steel, Geary normally was very good at leading the way toward changes that satisfied customer and organizational needs. A good salesman frequently needs to coordinate and spearhead modifications in operations, engineering, logistics, product design, financing, and billing/payment that are necessary for a company to maintain good customer relationships and sales. Apparently, however, he did not try to lead the organization in developing a win-win solution, such as soliciting current orders for a later delivery of a corrected product. He tried only reasoning against selling the unsafe product and protested its sale to several groups of upper-level engineers and managers. He noted that he believed the product had a failure rate of 3.6% and was therefore both unsafe and potentially damaging to U.S. Steel's longer-term strategy of entering higher technology/profit margin businesses. According to Geary, even though many upper-level managers, engineers, and salesmen understood and believed him, "the only desire of everyone associated with the project was to satisfy the instructions of Henry Wallace [the sales vice-president]. No one was about to buck this man for fear of his job."[26] The sales vice-president fired Geary, apparently because he continued to protest against sale of the product.

Similarly, William Schwartzkopf of Commonwealth Electric Co.[27] did not think he could either ethically reason against or lead an end to the large-scale, long-time bid rigging between his own company and many of the largest U.S. electrical contractors. Even though he was an attorney and had extensive experience in leading organizational changes, he did not try to lead his company toward an ethical solution. He waited until he retired from the company, then wrote a secret letter to the Justice Department accusing the contractors of raising bids and conspiring to divide billions of dollars of contracts among themselves.

Many people—both experienced and inexperienced in leadership—do not try to lead their companies toward developing solutions to ethical problems. Often, they do not understand that it is possible to lead such a change; therefore, they do not try to do so—even though, as the cases here show, many succeed when they do try.

3. Some organizational environments—in both consensus-building and authoritarian types of cultures—discourage leadership that is nonconforming. For example, as Robert E. Wood, former CEO of the giant international retailer Sears, Roebuck, has observed, "We stress the advantages of the free enterprise system, we complain about the totalitarian state, but in our individual organizations we have created more or less a totalitarian system in industry, particularly in large industry."[28] Similarly, Charles W. Summers, in a *Harvard Business Review* article, observes, "Corporate executives may argue that . . . they recognize and protect . . . against arbitrary termination through their own internal procedures. The simple fact is that most companies have not recognized and protected that right."[29]

David Ewing concludes that "It [the pressure to obey unethical and illegal orders] is probably most dangerous, however, as a low-level infection. When it slowly bleeds the individual conscience dry and metastasizes insidiously, it is most difficult to defend against. There are no spectacular firings or purges in the ranks. There are no

epic blunders. Under constant and insistent pressure, employees simply give in and conform. They become good 'organization people.' "[30]

Similar pressures can exist in participative, consensus-building types of cultures. For examples, as mentioned above, Yoshino and Lifson write, "A Japanese leader, rather than being an authority, is more of a communications channel, a mediator, a facilitator, and most of all, a symbol and embodiment of group unity. Consensus building is necessary to decision making, and this requires patience and an ability to use carefully cultivated relationships to get all to agree for the good of the unit."[31]

The importance of the group and the position of the group leaders as a symbol of the group are revealed in the very popular true story, "Tale of the Forty-Seven Ronin." The tale is about 47 warriors whose lord is unjustly killed. The Ronin spend years sacrificing everything, including their families, in order to kill the person responsible for their leader's death. Then all those who survive the assault killed themselves.

Just as authoritarian top-down organizational cultures can produce unethical behaviors, so can participative, consensus-building cultures. The Japanese novelist Shusaku Endo, in his *The Sea and Poison*, describes the true story of such a problem.[32] It concerns an experiment cooperatively performed by the Japanese Army, a medical hospital, and a consensus-building team of doctors on American prisoners of war. The purpose of the experiment was to determine scientifically how much blood people can lose before they die.

Endo describes the reasoning and feelings of one of the doctors as he looked back at this behavior:

> "'At the time nothing could be done. . . . If I were caught in the same way, I might, I might just do the same thing again. . . . We feel that getting on good terms ourselves with the Western Command medical people, with whom Second [section] is so

cosy, wouldn't be a bad idea at all. Therefore we feel there's no need to ill-temperedly refuse their friendly proposal and hurt their feelings. . . . Five doctors from Kando's section most likely will be glad to get the chance. . . . For me the pangs of conscience . . . were from childhood equivalent to the fear of disapproval in the eyes of others—fear of the punishment which society would bring to bear. . . . To put it quite bluntly, I am able to remain quite undisturbed in the face of someone else's terrible suffering and death. . . . I am not writing about these experiences as one driven to do so by his conscience . . . all these memories are distasteful to me. But looking upon them as distasteful and suffering because of them are two different matters. Then why do I bother writing? Because I'm strangely ill at ease. I, who fear only the eyes of others and the punishment of society, and whose fears disappear when I am secure from these, am now disturbed. . . . I have no conscience, I suppose. Not just me, though. None of them feel anything at all about what they did here.' The only emotion in his heart was a sense of having fallen as low as one can fall."[33]

WHAT TO DO AND HOW TO BE

In light of the discussion of the two approaches to addressing organizational ethics issues and their limitations, what should we do as individuals and members of organizations? To some extent that depends on the circumstances and our own abilities. If we know how to lead, if there's time for it, if the key people in authority are reasonable, and if a win-win solution is possible, one should probably try leading an organizational change.

If, on the other hand, one does not know how to lead, time is limited, the authority figures are unreasonable, a culture of strong conformity exists, and the situation is not likely to produce a win-win outcome, then the chances of success with a leadership approach are much lower. This may leave one with only the choice of using one of the intervention strategies discussed above. If an individual wishes to remain an effective member of the organization, then one of the more secretive strategies may be safer.

But what about the more common, middle range of problems? Here there is no easy prescription. The more win-win potential the situation has, the more time there is, the more leadership skills one has, and the more reasonable the authority figures and organizational cultures are, the more likely a leadership approach is to succeed. If the opposite conditions exist, then forcing change in the organization is the likely alternative.

To a large extent, the choice depends on an individual's courage. In my opinion, in all but the most extreme and unusual circumstances, one should first try to lead a change toward ethical behavior. If that does not succeed, then mustering the courage to act against others and the organization may be necessary. For example, the course of action that might have saved the Challenger crew was for Boisjoly or someone else to act against Morton Thiokol, its top managers, and NASA by blowing the whistle to the press.

If there is an implicitly characteristic American ontology, perhaps it is some version of William James' 1907 *Pragmatism*, which, for better or worse, sees through a lens of interactions the ontologies of being as an individual and being as a part. James explains our situation as follows:

"What we were discussing was the idea of a world growing not integrally but piecemeal by the contributions of its several parts. Take the hypothesis seriously and as a live one. Suppose that the world's author put the case to you before creation, saying: 'If I am going to make a world not certain to be saved, a world the perfection of which shall be conditioned merely, the condition being that each several agent does its own 'level best.' I offer you the chance of taking part in such a world. Its safety, you see, is unwarranted. It is a real adventure, with real danger, yet it may win through. It is a social scheme of co-operative work genuinely to be done. Will you join the procession? Will you trust yourself and trust the other agents enough to face the risk? . . . Then it is perfectly possible to accept sincerely a drastic kind of a universe from which the element of 'seriousness' is not to be expelled. Who so does so is, it seems to me, a genuine pragmatist. He is willing to live on a scheme of uncertified possibilities which he trusts; willing to pay with his own person, if need be, for the realization of the ideals which he frames. What now actually are the other forces which he trusts to co-operate with him, in a universe of such a type? They are at least his fellow men, in the stage of being which our actual universe has reached."[34]

In conclusion, there are realistic ethics leadership and intervention action strategies. We can act effectively concerning organizational ethics issues. Depending upon the circumstances including our own courage, we can choose to act and be ethical both as individuals and as leaders. Being as a part and leading ethical change is the more constructive approach generally. However, being as an individual intervening against others and organizations can sometimes be the only short or medium term effective approach. ◆ ◆ ◆

◆ Endnotes

1. Paul Tillich, *The Courage to Be*. New Haven, CT: Yale University Press, 1950.
2. See Endnote 1, page 159.
3. David Ewing, *Freedom Inside the Organization*. New York: McGraw-Hill, 1977.
4. The person blowing the whistle in this case wishes to remain anonymous. See also Elizabeth Neuffer, "GE Managers Sentenced for Bribery," *The Boston Globe*, July 26, 1988, p. 67.
5. Barbara Ley Toffler, *Tough Choices: Managers Talk Ethics*. New York: John Wiley, 1986, pp. 153–169.
6. Richard P. Nielsen, "What Can Managers Do About Unethical Management?" *Journal of Business Ethics*, 6, 1987, 153–161. See also Nielsen's "Limitations of Ethical Reasoning as an Action Strategy," *Journal of Business Ethics*, 7, 1988, pp. 725–733, and "Arendt's Action Philosophy and the Manager as Eichmann, Richard III, Faust or Institution Citizen," *California Management Review*, 26, 3, Spring 1984, pp. 191–201.
7. The person involved wishes to remain anonymous.
8. The person involved wishes to remain anonymous.
9. See Endnote 6.
10. R. Reinhold, "Astronauts Chief Says NASA Risked Life for Schedule," *The New York Times*, 36, 1986, p. 1.
11. Personal conversation and letter with Frank Ladwig, 1986. See also Frank Ladwig and Associates' *Advanced Consultative Selling for Professionals*. Stonington, CT.
12. W. G. Glaberson, "Did Searle Lose Its Eyes to a Health Hazard?" *Business Week*, October 14, 1985, pp. 120–122.
13. The person involved wishes to remain anonymous.
14. Andy Pasztor, "Electrical Contractors Reel Under Charges that They Rigged Bids," *The Wall Street Journal*, November 29, 1985, pp. 1, 14.
15. A. Ernest Fitzgerald, *The High Priests of Waste*. New York: McGraw-Hill, 1977.
16. See Endnote 1, pp. 89, 93.
17. M. Y. Yoshino and T. B. Lifson, *The Invisible Link: Japan's Saga Shosha and the Organization of Trade*. Cambridge, MA: MIT Press, 1986.
18. See Endnote 17, p. 178.
19. Roger Boisjoly, address given at Massachusetts Institute of Technology on January 7, 1987. Reprinted in *Books and Religion*, March/April 1987, 3–4, 12–13. See also Caroline Whitbeck, "Moral Responsibility and the Working Engineer," *Books and Religion*, March/April 1987, 3, 22–23.
20. Personal conversation with Ray Bauer, Harvard Business School, 1975. See also R. Ackerman and

Ray Bauer, *Corporate Social Responsiveness.* Reston, VA: Reston Publishing, 1976.

21. The person involved wishes to remain anonymous.

22. The person involved wishes to remain anonymous.

23. David Ewing, *Do It My Way or You're Fired.* New York: John Wiley, 1983.

24. E. T. Pound, "Investigators Detect Pattern of Kickbacks for Defense Business," *The Wall Street Journal,* November 14, 1985, pp. 1, 25.

25. See Endnote 23. See also Geary vs. U.S. Steel Corporation, 319 A. 2nd 174, Supreme Court of Pa.

26. See Endnote 23, p. 86.

27. See Endnote 14.

28. See Endnote 3, p. 21.

29. C. W. Summers, "Protecting All Employees Against Unjust Dismissal," *Harvard Business Review,* 58, 1980, pp. 132–139.

30. See Endnote 3, pp. 216–217.

31. See Endnote 17, p. 187.

32. Shusaku Endo, *The Sea and Poison.* New York: Taplinger Publishing Company, 1972. See also Y. Yasuda, *Old Tales of Japan.* Tokyo: Charles Tuttle Company, 1947.

33. See Endnote 32.

34. William James, *Pragmatism: A New Name for Some Old Ways of Thinking.* New York: Longmans, Green and Co., 1907, pp. 290, 297–298.

Some Paradoxes of Whistleblowing

Michael Davis

Are whistle-blowers moral heroes? Do they risk all for the sake of telling the truth? Whistle-blowing is central to any discussion of business ethics because it represents the clash of personal and organizational values.

Davis examines what he describes as the standard analysis of whistle-blowing to prevent serious harm: An individual is morally permitted to speak out after going through the regular channels without success but is absolutely required to do so when the person has convincing evidence and a good chance of preventing the harm.

Davis does not think that this analysis properly describes most cases of whistle-blowing. He uses the case of the Challenger *and the whistle-blower Roger Boisjoly to illustrate his claim. Davis believes that it is often more accurate to think of whistle-blowing in terms of complicity, where the person has been involved in some moral wrong and now feels compelled to speak out.*

INTRODUCTION

By "paradox" I mean an apparent—and, in this case, real—inconsistency between theory (our systematic understanding of whistleblowing) and the facts (what we actually know, or think we know, about whistleblowing). What concerns me is not a few anomalies, the exceptions that test a rule, but a flood of exceptions that seems to swamp the rule.

This paper has four parts. The first states the standard theory of whistleblowing. The second argues that the standard theory is paradoxical, that it is inconsistent with what we know about whistleblowers. The third part sketches what seems to me a less paradoxical theory of whistleblowing. The fourth tests the new theory against one classic case of whistleblowing, Roger Boisjoly's testimony before the presidential commission investigating the *Challenger* disaster ("the Rogers Commission"). I use that case because the chief facts are both uncontroversial enough and well-known enough to make detailed exposition unnecessary. For the same reason, I also use that case to illustrate various claims about whistleblowing throughout the paper.

JUSTIFICATION AND WHISTLEBLOWING

The standard theory is not about whistleblowing, as such, but about justified whistleblowing—and rightly so. Whether this or that is, or is not, whistleblowing is a question for lexicographers. For the rest of us, mere moral agents, the question is—when, if ever, is whistleblowing justified? . . .

Generally, we do not *need* to justify an act unless we have reason to think it wrong (whether morally wrong or wrong in some other way). So, for example, I do not need to justify eating fruit for lunch today, though I would if I were allergic to fruit or had been keeping a fast. We also do not need a justification if we believe the act in question wrong. We do not need a justification because, insofar as an act is wrong, justification is impossible. The point of justification is to show to be right an act the rightness of which has been put in (reasonable) doubt. Insofar as we believe the act wrong, we can only condemn or excuse it. To condemn it is simply to declare it wrong. To excuse it is to show that, while the act was wrong, the doer had good reason to do it, could not help doing it, or for some other reason

should not suffer the response otherwise reserved for such a wrongdoer.

Most acts, though permitted or required by morality, need no justification. There is no reason to think them wrong. Their justification is too plain for words. Why then is whistleblowing so problematic that we need *theories* of its justification? What reason do we have to think whistleblowing might be morally wrong?

Whistleblowing always involves revealing information that would not ordinarily be revealed. But there is nothing morally problematic about that; after all, revealing information not ordinarily revealed is one function of science. Whistleblowing always involves, in addition, an actual (or at least declared) intention to prevent something bad that would otherwise occur. There is nothing morally problematic in that either. That may well be the chief use of information.

What seems to make whistleblowing morally problematic is its organizational context. A mere individual cannot blow the whistle (in any interesting sense); only a member of an organization, whether a current or a former member, can do so. Indeed, he can only blow the whistle on his own organization (or some part of it). So, for example, a police officer who makes public information about a burglary ring, though a member of an organization, does not blow the whistle on the burglary ring (in any interesting sense). He simply alerts the public. Even if he came by the information working undercover in the ring, his revelation could not be whistleblowing. While secret agents, spies, and other infiltrators need a moral justification for what they do, the justification they need differs from that which whistleblowers need. Infiltrators gain their information under false pretenses. They need a justification for that deception.[1] Whistleblowers generally do not gain their information under false pretenses.

What if, instead of being a police officer, the revealer of information about the burglary ring were an ordinary member of the ring? Would such an informer be a (justified) whistleblower? I think not. The burglary ring is a criminal organization. The whistleblower's organization never is, though it may occasionally engage in criminal activity (knowingly or inadvertently). So, even a burglar who, having a change of heart, volunteers information about his ring to the police or the newspaper, does not need to justify his act in the way the whistleblower does. Helping to destroy a criminal organization by revealing its secrets is morally much less problematic than whistleblowing.

What then is morally problematic about the whistleblower's organizational context? The whistleblower cannot blow the whistle using just any information obtained in virtue of membership in the organization. A clerk in Accounts who, happening upon evidence of serious wrongdoing while visiting a friend in Quality Control, is not a whistleblower just because she passes the information to a friend at the *Tribune*. She is more like a self-appointed spy. She seems to differ from the whistleblower, or at least from clear cases of the whistleblower, precisely in her relation to the information in question. To be a whistleblower is to reveal information with which one is *entrusted*.

But it is more than that. The whistleblower does not reveal the information to save his own skin (for example, to avoid perjury under oath).[2] He has no excuse for revealing what his organization does not want revealed. Instead, he claims to be doing what he should be doing. If he cannot honestly make that claim—if, that is, he does not have that intention—his revelation is not whistleblowing (and so, not justified as whistleblowing), but something analogous, much as pulling a child from the water is not a rescue, even if it saves the child's life, when the "rescuer" merely believes herself to be salvaging old clothes. What makes whistleblowing morally problematic, if anything does, is this high-minded but unexcused

misuse of one's position in a generally law-abiding, morally decent organization, an organization that *prima facie* deserves the whistleblower's loyalty (as a burglary ring does not).[3]

The whistleblower must reveal information the organization does not want revealed. But, in any actual organization, "what the organization wants" will be contested, with various individuals or groups asking to be taken as speaking for the organization. Who, for example, did what Thiokol wanted the night before the *Challenger* exploded? In retrospect, it is obvious that the three vice presidents, Lund, Kilminster, and Mason, did not do what Thiokol wanted—or, at least, what it would have wanted. At the time, however, they had authority to speak for the company—the conglomerate Morton-Thiokol headquartered in Chicago—while the protesting engineers, including Boisjoly, did not. Yet, even before the explosion, was it obvious that the three were doing what the company wanted? To be a whistleblower, one must, I think, at least temporarily lose an argument about what the organization wants. The whistleblower is disloyal only in a sense—the sense the winners of the internal argument get to dictate. What can justify such disloyalty?

THE STANDARD THEORY

According to the theory now more or less standard,[4] such disloyalty is morally permissible when:

S1. The organization to which the would-be whistleblower belongs will, through its product or policy, do serious and considerable harm to the public (whether to users of its product, to innocent bystanders, or to the public at large);

S2. The would-be whistleblower has identified that threat of harm, reported it to her immediate superior, making clear both the threat itself and the objection to it, and concluded that the superior will do nothing effective; and

S3. The would-be whistleblower has exhausted other internal procedures within the organization (for example, by going up the organizational ladder as far as allowed)—or at least made use of as many internal procedures as the danger to others and her own safety make reasonable.

Whistleblowing is morally required (according to the standard theory) when, in addition:

S4. The would-be whistleblower has (or has accessible) evidence that would convince a reasonable, impartial observer that her view of the threat is correct; and

S5. The would-be whistleblower has good reason to believe that revealing the threat will (probably) prevent the harm at reasonable cost (all things considered).

Why is whistleblowing morally required when these five conditions are met? According to the standard theory, whistleblowing is morally required, when it is required at all, because "people have a moral obligation to prevent serious harm to others if they can do so with little cost to themselves."[5] In other words, whistleblowing meeting all five conditions is a form of "minimally decent Samaritanism" (a doing of what morality requires) rather than "good Samaritanism" (going well beyond the moral minimum).[6]

A number of writers have pointed out that the relation between the first three conditions and the full five does not seem to be that between the morally permissible and the morally required.[7] If, for example, the whistleblower lacks evidence that would convince a reasonable, impartial observer of the threat in question (S4), her whistleblowing could not prevent harm. Since it could not prevent harm, her whistleblowing would not

be even morally permissible: what could make morally permissible an attempt to help a stranger when the attempt will probably fail and the cost be high both to the would-be Samaritan and to those to whom she owes a competing obligation? The most that can be said for blowing the whistle where only conditions S1–S3 are met seems to be that the whistleblower has an excuse when (without negligence) she acts on inadequate evidence. So, for many writers, the standard view is that S1–S5 state sufficient conditions for morally *required* whistleblowing even though S1–S3 do not state sufficient conditions for morally permissible whistleblowing but (at best) for morally *excusable* whistleblowing.

The standard theory is not a definition of whistleblowing or even of justified whistleblowing. The theory purports to state sufficient conditions, not necessary conditions (a "when" but *not* an "only when"). But these sufficient conditions are supposed to identify the central cases of morally justified whistleblowing. Since a theory that did only that would be quite useful, we cannot object to the theory merely because it is incomplete in this way. Incomplete only in this way, the theory would be about as useful as theories of practical ethics ever are.

THREE PARADOXES

That's the standard theory—where are the paradoxes? The first paradox I want to call attention to concerns a commonplace of the whistleblowing literature. Whistleblowers are not minimally decent Samaritans. If they are Samaritans at all, they are good Samaritans. They always act at considerable risk to career, and generally, at considerable risk to their financial security and personal relations.[8]

In this respect, as in many others, Roger Boisjoly is typical. Boisjoly blew the whistle on his employer, Thiokol; he volunteered information, in public testimony before the Rogers Commission, that Thiokol did not want him to volunteer. As often happens, both his employer and many who relied on it for employment reacted hostilely. Boisjoly had to say goodbye to the company town, to old friends and neighbors, and to building rockets; he had to start a new career at an age when most people are preparing for retirement.

Since whistleblowing is generally costly to the whistleblower in some large way as this, the standard theory's minimally decent Samaritanism provides *no* justification for the central cases of whistleblowing.[9] That is the first paradox, what we might call "the paradox of burden."

The second paradox concerns the prevention of "harm." On the standard theory, the would-be whistleblower must seek to prevent "serious and considerable harm" in order for the whistleblowing to be even morally permissible. There seems to be a good deal of play in the term "harm." The harm in question can be physical (such as death or disease), financial (such as loss of or damage to property), and perhaps even psychological (such as fear or mental illness). But there is a limit to how much the standard theory can stretch "harm." Beyond that limit are "harms" like injustice, deception, and waste. As morally important as injustice, deception, and waste can be, they do not seem to constitute the "serious and considerable harm" that can require someone to become even a minimally decent Samaritan.

Yet, many cases of whistleblowing, perhaps most, are not about preventing serious and considerable physical, financial, or psychological harm. For example, when Boisjoly spoke up the evening before the *Challenger* exploded, the lives of seven astronauts sat in the balance. Speaking up then was about preventing serious and considerable physical, financial, and psychological harm—but it was not whistleblowing. Boisjoly was then serving his employer, not be-

traying a trust (even on the employer's understanding of that trust); he was calling his superiors' attention to what he thought they should take into account in their decision and not publicly revealing confidential information. The whistleblowing came after the explosion, in testimony before the Rogers Commission. By then, the seven astronauts were beyond help, the shuttle program was suspended, and any further threat of physical, financial, or psychological harm to the "public" was—after discounting for time—negligible. Boisjoly had little reason to believe his testimony would make a significant difference in the booster's redesign, in safety procedures in the shuttle program, or even in reawakening concern for safety among NASA employees and contractors. The *Challenger*'s explosion was much more likely to do that than anything Boisjoly could do. What Boisjoly could do in his testimony, what I think he tried to do, was prevent falsification of the record.[10]

Falsification of the record is, of course, harm in a sense, especially a record as historically important as that which the Rogers Commission was to produce. But falsification is harm only in a sense that almost empties "harm" of its distinctive meaning, leaving it more or less equivalent to "moral wrong." The proponents of the standard theory mean more by "harm" than that. De George, for example, explicitly says that a threat justifying whistleblowing must be to "life or health."[11] The standard theory is strikingly more narrow in its grounds of justification than many examples of justified whistleblowing suggest it should be. That is the second paradox, the "paradox of missing harm."

The third paradox is related to the second. Insofar as whistleblowers are understood as people out to prevent harm, not just to prevent moral wrong, their chances of success are not good. Whistleblowers generally do not prevent much harm. In this too, Boisjoly is typical. As he has said many times, the situation at Thiokol is now much as it was before the disaster. Insofar as we can identify cause and effect, even now we have little reason to believe that—whatever his actual intention—Boisjoly's testimony actually prevented any harm (beyond the moral harm of falsification). So, if whistleblowers must have, as the standard theory says (S5), (beyond the moral wrong of falsification) "good reason to believe that revealing the threat will (probably) prevent the harm," then the history of whistleblowing virtually rules out the moral justification of whistleblowing. That is certainly paradoxical in a theory purporting to state sufficient conditions for the central cases of justified whistleblowing. Let us call this "the paradox of failure."

A COMPLICITY THEORY

As I look down the roll of whistleblowers, I do not see anyone who, like the clerk from Accounts, just happened upon key documents in a cover-up.[12] Few, if any, whistleblowers are mere third-parties like the good Samaritan. They are generally deeply involved in the activity they reveal. This involvement suggests that we might better understand what justifies (most) whistleblowing if we understand the whistleblower's obligation to derive from *complicity* in wrongdoing rather than from the ability to prevent harm.

Any complicity theory of justified whistleblowing has two obvious advantages over the standard theory. One is that (moral) complicity itself presupposes (moral) wrongdoing, not harm. So, a complicity justification automatically avoids the paradox of missing harm, fitting the facts of whistleblowing better than a theory which, like the standard one, emphasizes prevention of harm.

That is one obvious advantage of a complicity theory. The second advantage is that complicity invokes a more demanding obligation

than the ability to prevent harm does. We are morally obliged to avoid doing moral wrongs. When, despite our best efforts, we nonetheless find ourselves engaged in some wrong, we have an obligation to do what we reasonably can to set things right. If, for example, I cause a traffic accident, I have a moral (and legal) obligation to call help, stay at the scene until help arrives, and render first aid (if I know how), even at substantial cost to myself and those to whom I owe my time, and even with little likelihood that anything I do will help much. Just as a complicity theory avoids the paradox of missing harm, it also avoids the paradox of burden.

What about the third paradox, the paradox of failure? I shall come to that, but only after remedying one disadvantage of the complicity theory. That disadvantage is obvious—we do not yet have such a theory, not even a sketch. Here, then, is the place to offer a sketch of such a theory.

Complicity Theory

You are morally required to reveal what you know to the public (or to a suitable agent or representative of it)[13] when:

C1. what you will reveal derives from your work for an organization;

C2. you are a voluntary member of that organization;

C3. you believe that the organization, though legitimate, is engaged in serious moral wrongdoing;

C4. you believe that your work for that organization will contribute (more or less directly) to the wrong if (but *not* only if) you do not publicly reveal what you know;

C5. you are justified in beliefs C3 and C4; and

C6. beliefs C3 and C4 are true.

The complicity theory differs from the standard theory in several ways worth pointing out here. The first is that, according to C1, what the whistleblower reveals must derive from his work for the organization. This condition distinguishes the whistleblower from the spy (and the clerk in Accounts). The spy seeks out information in order to reveal it; the whistleblower learns it as a proper part of doing the job the organization has assigned him. The standard theory, in contrast, has nothing to say about how the whistleblower comes to know of the threat she reveals (S2). For the standard theory, spies are just another kind of whistleblower.

A second way in which the complicity theory differs from the standard theory is that the complicity theory (C2) explicitly requires the whistleblower to be a *voluntary* participant in the organization in question. Whistleblowing is not—according to the complicity theory—an activity in which slaves, prisoners, or other involuntary participants in an organization engage. In this way, the complicity theory makes explicit something implicit in the standard theory. The whistleblowers of the standard theory are generally "employees." Employees are voluntary participants in the organization employing them.

What explains this difference in explicitness? For the Samaritanism of the standard theory, the voluntariness of employment is extrinsic. What is crucial is the ability to prevent harm. For the complicity theory, however, the voluntariness is crucial. The obligations deriving from complicity seem to vary with the voluntariness of our participation in the wrongdoing. Consider, for example, a teller who helps a gang rob her bank because they have threatened to kill her if she does not; she does not have the same obligation to break off her association with the gang as someone who has freely joined it. The voluntariness of employment means that the would-be whistleblower's complicity will be more like that of one of the gang than like that of the conscripted teller.[14]

A third way in which the complicity theory differs from the standard theory is that the complicity theory (C3) requires moral wrong, not harm, for justification. The wrong need not be a new event (as a harm must be if it is to be *prevented*). It might, for example, consist in no more than silence about facts necessary to correct a serious injustice.

The complicity theory (C3) does, however, follow the standard theory in requiring that the predicate of whistleblowing be "serious." Under the complicity theory, minor wrongdoing can no more justify whistleblowing than can minor harm under the standard theory.[15] While organizational loyalty cannot forbid whistleblowing, it does forbid "tattling," that is, revealing minor wrongdoing.

A fourth way in which the complicity theory differs from the standard theory, the most important, is that the complicity theory (C4) requires that the whistleblower believe that her work will have contributed to the wrong in question if she does nothing, but it does *not* require that she believe that her revelation will prevent (or undo) the wrong. The complicity theory does not require any belief about what the whistleblowing can accomplish (beyond ending complicity in the wrong in question). The whistleblower reveals what she knows in order to prevent complicity in the wrong, not to prevent the wrong as such. She can prevent complicity (if there is any to prevent) simply by publicly revealing what she knows. The revelation itself breaks the bond of complicity, the secret partnership in wrongdoing, that makes her an accomplice in her organization's wrongdoing.[16] The complicity theory thus avoids the third paradox, the paradox of failure, just as it avoided the other two.

The fifth difference between the complicity theory and the standard theory is closely related to the fourth. Because publicly revealing what one knows breaks the bond of complicity, the complicity theory does not require the whistleblower to have enough evidence to convince others of the wrong in question. Convincing others, or just being able to convince them, is not, as such, an element in the justification of whistleblowing.

The complicity theory does, however, require (C5) that the whistleblower be (epistemically) justified in believing both that his organization is engaged in wrongdoing and that he will contribute to that wrong unless he blows the whistle. Such (epistemic) justification may require substantial physical evidence (as the standard theory says) or just a good sense of how things work. The complicity theory does not share the standard theory's substantial evidential demand (S4).

In one respect, however, the complicity theory clearly requires more of the whistleblower than the standard theory does. The complicity theory's C6—combined with C5—requires not only that the whistleblower be *justified* in her beliefs about the organization's wrongdoing and her part in it, but also that she be *right* about them. If she is wrong about either the wrongdoing or her complicity, her revelation will not be justified whistleblowing. This consequence of C6 is, I think, not as surprising as it may seem. If the would-be whistleblower is wrong only about her own complicity, her revelation of actual wrongdoing will, being otherwise justified, merely fail to be justified *as whistleblowing* (much as a failed rescue, though justified as an attempt, cannot be justified as a rescue). If, however, she is wrong about the wrongdoing itself, her situation is more serious. Her belief that wrong is being done, though fully justified on the evidence available to her, cannot justify her disloyalty. All her justified belief can do is *excuse* her disloyalty. Insofar as she acted with good intentions and while exercising reasonable care, she is a victim of bad luck.

Such bad luck will leave her with an obligation to apologize, to correct the record (for example, by publicly recanting the charges she publicly made), and otherwise to set things right.

The complicity theory says nothing on at least one matter about which the standard theory says much—going through channels before publicly revealing what one knows. But the two theories do not differ as much as this difference in emphasis suggests. If going through channels would suffice to prevent (or undo) the wrong, then it cannot be true (as C4 and C6 together require) that the would-be whistleblower's work will contribute to the wrong if she does not publicly reveal what she knows. Where, however, going through channels would *not* prevent (or undo) the wrong, there is no need to go through channels. Condition C4's if-clause will be satisfied. For the complicity theory, going through channels is a way of finding out what the organization will do, not an independent requirement of justification. That, I think, is also how the standard theory understands it.[17]

A last difference between the two theories worth mention here is that the complicity theory is only a theory of morally required whistleblowing while the standard theory claims as well to define circumstances when whistleblowing is morally permissible but not morally required. This difference is another advantage that the complicity theory has over the standard theory. The standard theory, as we saw, has trouble making good on its claim to explain how whistleblowing can be morally permissible without being morally required.

TESTING THE THEORY

Let us now test the theory against Boisjoly's testimony before the Rogers Commission. Recall that under the standard theory any justification of that testimony seemed to fail for at least three reasons: First, Boisjoly could not testify without substantial cost to himself and Thiokol (to whom he owed loyalty). Second, there was no serious and substantial harm his testimony could prevent. And, third, he had little reason to believe that, even if he could identify a serious and considerable harm to prevent, his testimony had a significant chance of preventing it.

Since few doubt that Boisjoly's testimony before the Rogers Commission constitutes justified whistleblowing, if anything does, we should welcome a theory that—unlike the standard one—justifies that testimony as whistleblowing. The complicity theory sketched above does that:

C1. Boisjoly's testimony consisted almost entirely of information derived from his work on booster rockets at Thiokol.

C2. Boisjoly was a voluntary member of Thiokol.

C3. Boisjoly believed Thiokol, a legitimate organization, was attempting to mislead its client, the government, about the causes of a deadly accident. Attempting to do that certainly seems a serious moral wrong.

C4. On the evening before the *Challenger* exploded, Boisjoly gave up objecting to the launch once his superiors, including the three Thiokol vice presidents, had made it clear that they were no longer willing to listen to him. He also had a part in preparing those superiors to testify intelligently before the Rogers Commission concerning the booster's fatal field joint. Boisjoly believed that Thiokol would use his failure to offer his own interpretation of his retreat into silence the night before the launch, and the knowledge that he had imparted to his superiors, to contribute to the attempt to mislead Thiokol's client.

C5. The evidence justifying beliefs C3 and C4 consisted of comments of various officers of Thiokol, what Boisjoly had seen at Thiokol over the years, and what he learned about the rocket business over a long career. I find this evidence sufficient to justify his belief both that his organization was engaged in wrongdoing and that his work was implicated.

C6. Here we reach a paradox of *knowledge*. Since belief is knowledge if, but only if, it is *both* justified *and* true, we cannot *show* that we know anything. All we can show is that a belief is now justified and that we have no reason to expect anything to turn up later to prove it false. The evidence now available still justifies Boisjoly's belief both about what Thiokol was attempting and about what would have been his part in the attempt. Since new evidence is unlikely, his testimony seems to satisfy C6 just as it satisfied the complicity theory's other five conditions.

Since the complicity theory explains why Boisjoly's testimony before the Rogers Commission was morally required whistleblowing, it has passed its first test, a test the standard theory failed. ◆ ◆ ◆

◆ **Notes**

1. This is, I think, one (but not the only) reason to reject the forgotten—but perceptive—definition of "whistleblowing" in Frederick Elliston, John Keenan, Paula Lockhart, and Jane van Schaick, *Whistleblowing Research: Methodological and Moral Issues* (New York: Praeger, 1984), p. 15: "An act of whistleblowing occurs when: (1) an individual performs an action or series of actions intended to make information public; (2) the information is made a matter of public record; (3) the information is about possible or actual, nontrivial wrongdoing in an organization; and

(4) the individual who performs the action is a member or former member of the organization." While this definition confounds whistleblowers with spies, informers, and the like and is designed for research on whistleblowing rather than for developing a justification, its wrong-based approach makes it closer to the complicity theory offered below than to the standard theory. (Though the book has four authors, they credit the whole of the first chapter, including this definition, to someone else, Deborah Johnson.)

2. I do not mean that, for some purpose, for example, a whistleblower protection act; it might not be convenient to include among whistleblowers those who reveal information unwillingly. What I mean is that, for purposes of developing a general theory of justified whistleblowing, such cases are uninteresting. Avoiding contempt of court or Congress generally provides sufficient justification for testifying about serious wrongdoing, and avoiding perjury, a sufficient justification for telling the truth, which is a stronger justification than either the standard theory or the alternative I shall offer.

3. There is, of course, a problem about organizational loyalty, especially when the organization is a business and it understands its employees as instruments rather than members. While justifying whistleblowing is easier the less loyalty one owes the organization in question, we will learn more if we focus on the harder cases, those where we admit significant obligations of loyalty. So, that is what I do here.

4. Throughout this paper, I take the standard theory to be Richard T. De George's version in *Business Ethics*, 3rd. Edition (New York: Macmillan, 1990), pp. 200–214 (amended only insofar as necessary to include non-businesses as well as businesses). Why treat De George's theory as standard? There are two reasons: first, it seems the most commonly cited; and second, people offering alternatives generally treat it as the one to be replaced. The only obvious competitor, Norman Bowie's account, is distinguishable from De George's on no point relevant here. See

Bowie's *Business Ethics* (Englewood Cliffs, NJ: Prentice-Hall, 1982), p. 143.

5. De George, *op. cit.* Specifically, p. 214, De George says something more daring: "It is not implausible to claim both that we are morally obliged to prevent harm to others at little expense to ourselves, and that we are morally obliged to prevent great harm to a great many others, even at considerable expense to ourselves." De George (quite rightly) considers the opportunity to prevent great harm (as distinct from serious harm) so rare that he can safely ignore it.

6. There is now a significant literature on the responsibilities of the minimally decent Samaritan. See, for example: Peter Singer, "Famine, Affluence, and Morality," *Philosophy and Public Affairs*, Vol. 7, No. 2 (1972): 229–243; Alan Gewirth, *Reason and Morality* (Chicago: University of Chicago Press, 1978), pp. 217–230; Patricia Smith, "The Duty to Rescue and the Slippery Slope Problem," *Social Theory and Practice*, Vol. 16, No. 1 (1990): 19–41; John M. Whelan, "Charity and the Duty to Rescue," *Social Theory and Practice*, Vol. 17, No. 3 (1991): 441–456; and David Copp, "Responsibility for Collective Inaction," *Journal of Social Philosophy*, Vol. 22, No. 2 (1991): 71–80.

7. See, for example, David Theo Goldberg, "Tuning In to Whistle Blowing," *Business and Professional Ethics Journal*, Vol. 7, No. 2 (1988): 85–94.

8. For an explanation of why whistleblowing is inevitably a high risk undertaking, see my "Avoiding the Tragedy of Whistleblowing," *Business and Professional Ethics Journal*, Vol. 8, No. 4 (1989): 3–19.

9. Indeed, I am tempted to go further and claim that, where an informant takes little or no risk, we are unlikely to describe her as a whistleblower at all. So, for example, I would say that using an internal or external "hot-line" is whistleblowing only when it is risky. We are, in other words, likely to consider using a hot-line as disloyalty (that is, as "going out of channels") only if the organization (or some part of it) is likely to respond with considerable hostility to its use.

10. After I presented this paper in Klamath Falls, Boisjoly told me that, though his motive for

testifying as he did was (as I surmised) to prevent falsification of the record, part of his reason for wanting to prevent that was that he wanted to do what he could to prevent the managers responsible for the disaster from having any part in redesigning the boosters. This *secondary* motive is, of course, consistent with the complicity theory.

11. De George, p. 210: "The notion of *serious* harm might be expanded to include serious financial harm, and kinds of harm other than death and serious threats to health and body. But as we noted earlier, we shall restrict ourselves here to products and practices that produce or threaten serious harm or danger to life and health."

12. See Myron Peretz Glazer and Penina Migdal Glazer, *The Whistleblowers: Exposing Corruption in Government and Industry* (New York: Basic Books, 1989) for a good list of whistleblowers (with detailed description of each); for an older list (with descriptions), see Alan F. Westin, *Whistleblowing! Loyalty and Dissent in the Corporation* (New York: McGraw-Hill, 1981).

13. The problems with "public" in any definition of "whistleblowing" are well known (perhaps even notorious). I simply ignore them here. For our purposes, the public to whom the whistleblower reveals information is that individual or group to whom she must reveal it in order to end her complicity. Who the public is will vary with circumstances.

14. Do I claim that slaves, prisoners, inmates in mental hospital, or students in a school cannot blow the whistle—or, at least, cannot do so justifiably? Well, not exactly. That the usual lists of whistleblowers include no involuntary participants in wrongdoing is, I think, important evidence for the claim that involuntary participants cannot blow the whistle. But, since how we *have* used a

word does not determine how we *can* use it (especially a word like "whistleblowing" where usage is still evolving), that evidence is hardly decisive. What I think is clear is that involuntary participants will not have the same obligation of loyalty as the typical whistleblower; hence, any theory justifying their "going public" will have a somewhat different structure than the theory developed here. What about *voluntary* participants who are not employees, such as unpaid volunteers in a political campaign? While the complicity theory clearly counts them as capable of justified whistleblowing, the standard theory must make some special provision.

15. If the revelation seems likely to prevent harm as well, or to undo some injustice as well, that will, of course, strengthen the justification, making that much better a justification already good enough. But, according to the complicity theory, such good consequences are not necessary for justification.

16. We are, of course, assuming the standard case of whistleblowing where complicity involves only information. We can imagine more complicated cases where, in addition to information, there are benefits from the wrongdoing (say, a bonus derived from past wrongdoing). In such complex cases, revealing information (including the bonus) may not be all that is morally required but, even so, it will, I think, end the complicity relevant to whistleblowing. That, however, is a matter about which I am still thinking.

17. Compare De George, p. 211: "By reporting one's concern to one's immediate superior or other appropriate person, one preserves and observes the regular practices of firms, which on the whole promote their order and efficiency; this fulfills one's obligation of minimizing harm, and it *precludes precipitous whistle blowing*." (Italics mine.)

Persons of the Year: 2002

Time Magazine, Richard Lacayo and Amanda Ripley

Every year, Time *magazine selects a "person of the year": the individual or group of individuals who have had the biggest effect on the year's news. Past winners have included presidents and prominent figures such as Nelson Mandela and Amazon.com founder Jeffrey Bezos. In 2002 the winners were Cynthia Cooper of WorldCom, Coleen Rowley of the FBI, and Sherron Watkins of Enron—collectively, "the whistle-blowers." The article gives a brief description of their actions and extols their courage and conviction in speaking out. Are their actions consistent with the descriptions of whistle-blowers in other articles in this section? Were they involved in the wrongdoing? Did they prevent harm? Do you believe that* Time *accurately reflects the common perception of the nature of whistle-blowing and the acclaim it deserves?*

This was the year when the grief started to lift and the worries came in.

During the first weeks of 2002, two dark moods entered the room, two anxieties that rattled down everybody's nerve paths, even on good days, and etched their particulars into the general disposition. To begin with, after Sept. 11, the passage of time drew off the worst of the pain, but every month or so there came a new disturbance—an orange alert, a dance-club bombing in Bali, a surface-to-air missile fired at a passenger jet—that showed us the beast still at our door.

In the confrontation with Iraq, in the contested effort to build a homeland defense, we all struggled to regain something like the more secure world we thought we lived in before the towers fell. But every step of the way we wondered—was this the way back? What exactly did we need to be doing differently?

And all the while there was the black comedy of corporate fraud. Who knew that the swashbuckling economy of the '90s had produced so many buccaneers? You could laugh about the CEOs in handcuffs and the stock analysts who turned out to be fishier than storefront palm readers, but after a while the laughs came hard. Martha Stewart was dented and scuffed. Tyco was looted by its own executives. Enron and WorldCom turned out to be Twin Towers of false promises. They fell. Their stockholders and employees went down with them. So did a large measure of public faith in big corporations. Each new offense seemed to make the same point: with communism vanquished, capitalism was left with no real enemies but its own worst impulses. It can be undone by its own overreaching players. It can be bitten to pieces by its own alpha dogs.

Day after day, one set of misgivings twined around the other, keeping spooked investors away from the stock market, giving the whole year its undeniable saw-toothed edge. Were we headed for a world where all the towers would fall? All the more reason to figure out quickly, before the next blow to the system, how to repair the fail-safe operations—in the boardrooms we trusted with our money, at the government agencies we trust with ourselves—that failed.

This is where three women of ordinary demeanor but exceptional guts and sense come into the picture. Sherron Watkins is the Enron vice president who wrote a letter to chairman Kenneth Lay in the summer of 2001 warning him that the company's methods of accounting were improper. In January, when a congressional subcommittee investigating Enron's collapse released that letter, Watkins became a reluctant public figure, and the Year of the Whistle-Blower began. Coleen Rowley is the FBI staff attorney who caused a sensation in May with a memo to FBI Director Robert Mueller about how the bureau brushed off pleas from her Minneapolis, Minn., field office that Zacarias Moussaoui, who is now indicted as a Sept. 11 co-conspirator, was a man who must be investigated. One month later Cynthia Cooper exploded the bubble that was WorldCom when she informed its board that the company had covered up $3.8 billion in losses through the prestidigitations of phony bookkeeping.

These women were for the 12 months just ending what New York City fire fighters were in 2001: heroes at the scene, anointed by circumstance. They were people who did right just by doing their jobs rightly—which means ferociously, with eyes open and with the bravery the rest of us always hope we have and may never know if we do. Their lives may not have been at stake, but Watkins, Rowley and Cooper put pretty much everything else on the line. Their jobs, their health, their privacy, their sanity—they risked all of them to bring us badly needed word of trouble inside crucial institutions. Democratic capitalism requires that people trust in the integrity of public and private institutions alike. As whistle-blowers, these three became fail-safe systems that did not fail. For believing—really believing—that the truth is one thing that must not be moved off the books, and for stepping in

to make sure that it wasn't, they have been chosen by *Time* as its Persons of the Year for 2002.

WHO ARE THESE WOMEN?

For starters, they aren't people looking to hog the limelight. All initially tried to keep their criticisms in-house, to speak truth to power but not to Barbara Walters. They became public figures only because their memos were leaked. One reason you still don't know much about them is that none have given an on-the-record media interview until now. In early December *Time* brought all three together in a Minneapolis hotel room. Very quickly it became clear that none of them are rebels in the usual sense. The truest of true believers is more like it, ever faithful to the idea that where they worked was a place that served the wider world in some important way. But sometimes it's the keepers of the flame who feel most compelled to set their imperfect temple to the torch. When headquarters didn't live up to its mission, they took it to heart. At Enron the company handed out note pads with inspiring quotes. One was from Martin Luther King Jr.: "Our lives begin to end the day we become silent about things that matter." Watkins saw that quote every day. Didn't anybody else?

What more do they have in common? All three grew up in small towns in the middle of the country, in families that at times lived paycheck to paycheck. In a twist that will delight psychologists, they are all firstborns. More unusually, all three are married but serve as the chief breadwinners in their families. Cooper and Rowley have husbands who are full-time, stay-at-home dads. For every one of them, the decision to confront the higher-ups meant jeopardizing a paycheck their families truly depended on.

The joint interview in Minneapolis was the first time the three had met. But in no time they recognized how much they knew one another's experience. During the ordeals of this year, it energized them to know that there were two other women out there fighting the same kind of battles. In preparation for their meeting in Minneapolis, WorldCom's Cooper read through the testimony that Enron's Watkins gave before Congress. "I actually broke out in a cold sweat," Cooper says. In Minneapolis, when FBI lawyer Rowley heard Cooper talk about a need for regular people to step up and do the right thing, she stood up and applauded. And what to make of the fact that all are women? There has been talk that their gender is not a coincidence; that women, as outsiders, have less at stake in their organizations and so might be more willing to expose weaknesses. They don't think so. As it happens, studies have shown that women are actually a bit less likely than men to be whistle-blowers. And a point worth mentioning—all three hate the term whistle-blower. Too much like "tattletale," says Cooper.

But if the term unnerves them a bit, that may be because whistle-blowers don't have an easy time. Almost all say they would not do it again. If they aren't fired, they're cornered: isolated and made irrelevant. Eventually many suffer from alcoholism or depression.

With these three, that hasn't happened, though Watkins left her job at Enron after a few months when she wasn't given much to do. But ask them if they have been thanked sincerely by anyone at the top of their organization, and they burst out laughing. Some of their colleagues hate them, especially the ones who believe that their outfits would have quietly righted all wrongs if only they had been given time. "There is a price to be paid," says Cooper. "There have been times that I could not stop crying."

Watkins, Rowley and Cooper have kick-started conversations essential to the clean operation of American life, conversations that will continue for years. It may still be true that no one could have prevented the attacks of Sept. 11, but the past year has shown that the FBI and the CIA overlooked vital clues and held back data from each other. No matter how many new missile systems the Pentagon deploys or which new airport screening systems are adopted, if we can't trust the institutions charged with tracking terrorists to do the job, homeland defense will be an empty phrase. The Coleen Rowleys of the federal workforce will be the ones who will let us know what's going on.

As for corporate America, accounting scams of the kind practiced at Enron and WorldCom will continually need to be exposed and corrected before yet another phalanx of high-level operators gets the wrong idea and a thousand Enrons bloom. And the people best positioned to call them on it will be sitting in offices like the ones that Watkins and Cooper occupied. The new Sarbanes-Oxley Act, which requires CEOs and CFOs to vouch for the accuracy of their companies' books, is just one sign of what Cooper calls "a corporate-governance revolution across the country."

These were ordinary people who did not wait for higher authorities to do what needed to be done. Literature's great statement on unwelcome truth telling is Ibsen's play *An Enemy of the People.* Something said by one of his characters reminds us of what we admire about our Dynamic Trio. "A community is like a ship," he observes. "Everyone ought to be prepared to take the helm." When the time came, these women saw the ship in citizenship. And they stepped up to that wheel. ◆ ◆ ◆

Just Pucker and Blow?

An Analysis of Corporate Whistleblowers, the Duty of Care, the Duty of Loyalty, and the Sarbanes-Oxley Act

Leonard M. Baynes

Whistle-blowing is popularly lionized and privately scorned. Often the whistle-blower is thought of as a tattletale rather than a moral exemplar. In the wake of a number of corporate scandals, the government has sought to promote and protect legitimate whistle-blowing in the securities industry. Here Baynes lays out the duty of loyalty that an employee may have and why individuals may go against it. He gives principled reasons for and against whistle-blowing so we may understand that it is not merely individual mavericks on a mission.

Baynes first looks at the whistle-blowing case of Sherron Watkins at Enron. He then moves to examine the general fiduciary obligations of corporate insiders who want to blow the whistle. He outlines the protections for whistle-blowers against retaliation in the Sarbanes-Oxley Act of 2002 and then notes five areas where the act may be inadequate in shielding corporate whistle-blowers.

"You know how to whistle, don't you, Steve? You just put your lips together—and blow."

Lauren Becall to Humphrey Bogart
in *To Have and Have Not*

INTRODUCTION

In the past year, we have seen a number of corporate scandals involving major business entities such as Enron, Adelphia, Worldcom, Arthur Andersen, Tyco, and Martha Stewart. The *New York Daily News* described this bad behavior by corporate executives in a caption entitled "These Little Piggies Went to Market." *Newsweek* magazine in a headline called these executives the "Bad Boys Club." Well-known financial journalist Lou Dobbs called the bad boy executives "CEO Hogs." In addition, we have seen scenes of the Adelphia senior executives being carted off to jail in handcuffs like common criminals doing the so-called "perp walk." This corrupt conduct has involved various instances of fraud, ranging from using generally unacceptable accounting principles (like using partnerships to hide corporate losses and treating ordinary expenses as capital expenses to increase corporate profits), to providing exorbitant loans to senior executives. Insider trading also has been alleged. These scandals have led investors to be fearful of investing in the stock market. They also have caused major corporations difficulty in attracting CEOs, as well as prompted soul searching over the direction of our capitalist system, the decision to become a corporate executive, and whether the United States has a two-tiered moral system—one for bosses and one for the rest.

In the midst of this new anti-corporate environment, corporate whistleblowers recently have received a lot of favorable press. For instance, Sherron Watkins has been described as the whistleblower who exposed the Enron fraud, although even she admits that she was not the first person at Enron to complain about its shady accounting practices. In many respects, Ms. Watkins was the prototypical, yet atypical, corporate whistleblower. This article will examine the fiduciary obligations of corporate insiders who want to blow the whistle. It will compare the executives' contemporaneous (and often conflicting) duties of care and loyalty. It will show how the Sarbanes-Oxley Act of 2002 (the "Act") attempts to address these issues by providing some protection against retaliation. Finally, this article will highlight the various considerations that the Act failed to address, but that the Securities and Exchange Commission (SEC) should take into account when promulgating its rules of implementation.

THE ULTIMATE WHISTLEBLOWER, SHERRON WATKINS

Ms. Watkins was a Vice-President at Enron Corp. She earned a master's degree in professional accounting from the University of Texas at Austin. In 1982, she began her career as an auditor with the accounting firm Arthur Andersen, spending eight years at its Houston and New York offices. In 1983, she became a certified public accountant. Enron Vice-President Andrew Fastow hired Ms. Watkins to manage Enron's partnership with the California Public Employee Retirement System. From June to August 2001, Ms. Watkins worked directly for Mr. Fastow. During this time, Ms. Watkins learned that Enron was engaging in accounting improprieties with certain affiliated entities. She believed that Enron was using its own stock to generate gains and losses on its income statement. Ms. Watkins testified before the House Subcommittee on Oversight and Investigations that she failed to receive satisfactory explanations regarding these accounting transactions from Enron executives. Ms. Watkins admitted that she was troubled by the accounting practices but was uncomfortable reporting them to either Mr. Fastow or former Enron President Jeff Skilling, fearing termination if she approached them directly.[1] On August 15, 2001, Ms. Watkins sent to Kenneth Lay, the CEO of Enron, a seven-page anonymous letter. In the letter, Ms. Watkins asked, "Has Enron become a risky place to work?" She also more specifically described the accounting improprieties and stated that "to the layman on the street [it will look like] we are hiding losses in a related company and will compensate that company with Enron stock in the future." She shared her prescient fears that Enron might "implode in a wave of accounting scandals." On August 22, 2001, Ms. Watkins met with Mr. Lay and outlined her concerns about the accounting improprieties, and requested a transfer from working for Mr. Fastow. In late August she was reassigned to the human resources group. Ms. Watkins reported that Mr. Lay assured her that he would investigate the irregularities. Ms. Watkins never reported her concerns to the SEC, the Department of Treasury, or any other governmental official.

Upon Ms. Watkins's disclosure, Mr. Lay passed Ms. Watkins's letter to Enron's general counsel, James V. Derrick, who hired Enron's attorneys, Vinson & Elkins, to investigate, even though the law firm was involved in some of the transactions that Ms. Watkins criticized.[2] The Vinson & Elkins report indicates that Mr. Derrick acknowledged the "downside of hiring Vinson & Elkins because it had been involved." Mr. Derrick concluded that that the decision to hire Vinson & Elkins was permissible because the investigation was to be a "preliminary one."[3] Vinson & Elkins (along with Arthur Andersen)[4] investigated Ms. Watkins's allegations, but used no independent accountant. This investigation reported only limited cosmetic problems and no illegal activities.[5] Vinson & Elkins' investigation, however, "was largely predetermined by the scope and nature of the investigation and the process employed."[6]

In October 2001, before Enron announced a huge third quarter loss, Arthur Andersen auditors, in a memo, warned Enron officials that its public explanation for the loss "was potentially misleading and illegal."[7] On October 16, 2001, Enron announced a $618 million third quarter loss. Two weeks later, the SEC announced that it was investigating Enron. In early November, Enron announced that, since 1997, it had overstated its earnings by $586 million. On December 2, 2001, Enron filed for bankruptcy. On January 23, 2002, Ken Lay resigned as CEO of Enron, stating "we need someone at the helm who can focus 100 percent of his efforts on reorganizing the company.[8]

AN ANALYSIS OF SHERRON WATKINS' ACTIONS

Ms. Watkins is the prototypical whistleblower because she had knowledge of damaging information and she disclosed it to her supervisor's supervisor. At the same time, she is very atypical for several reasons. First, as an accountant, she had the expertise to know that her corporation was possibly breaking the law and defrauding the public. Second, her disclosure in and of itself to the president of the corporation did not lead to the type of investigation that was necessary to stop any wrongdoing. Her actions did not cause the immediate collapse of the Enron financial giant. Third, even though she "ratted" out her

boss and may have engaged in insider trading herself,[9] her disclosure did not compromise her job security. In fact, Ms. Watkins has received a lot of positive press from her actions.[10] Many have called Ms. Watkins a hero and courageous. Ms. Watkins was even named *Time* magazine's "Person of the Week."[11] *Washington Post* reporter Paul Farhi noted that women like Sherron Watkins often are perceived to be insiders with "outsider values" and are more likely to blow the whistle than their male counterparts.[12] A movie deal also is reportedly in the works that will paint Ms. Watkins as a "feminist icon," like Erin Brockovich. After her disclosure, Ms. Watkins testified that Cindy Olson told her that Mr. Fastow wanted to terminate her employment and have her computer seized. Instead, she was moved to a different position and was advised to download all pertinent data from her computer. She thus retained a job and became a symbol for corporate whistleblowers. In fact, since the collapse of Enron, the number of e-mailed complaints received by the SEC increased from an average of 325 per day in 2001 to 763 e-mails received on February 5, 2002.

So whistleblowing now is viewed more favorably than it had been historically. At least, in the popular press, the whistleblower is portrayed as heroic. In Sophocles's *Antigone*, a messenger tells Creon that someone has given proper funeral rites to Polyneices' body and remarks "no[one] delights in the bearer of bad news."[13] As evidenced by this ancient Greek play, society has often blamed and disliked the bearer of bad news. Even in our more recent American history, whistleblowers have often been portrayed as liars,[14] sometimes vile or untrustworthy,[15] and sometimes, even racist.[16] Ms. Watkins is very lucky; the press and the business community probably were looking for at least one person that they could call a hero in this whole sordid affair, and she came closest to being one. Despite the recent positive press for Ms. Watkins, whistle-blowing is fraught with dangers and risks. Whistle-blowing sits at the vortex of a corporate officer's fiduciary duties of care and loyalty. The whistle-blower may be damned if she does "just pucker and blow," and damned if she does not.

OFFICERS AND OTHER SENIOR MANAGERS

Corporations specify the number and types of officers in their bylaws.[17] The board of directors appoints the officers.[18] The officers select the senior managers. Both corporate officers and senior managers can be removed from their positions at any time.[19] An officer in performing her duties shall act in good faith, with the care that a person in a like position would reasonably exercise under similar circumstances, and in a manner that the officer reasonably believes will be in the best interests of the corporation.[20] Non-officer senior managers are agents of the corporation and, as such, are governed by the law of agency. As agents, these senior managers also have fiduciary duties to the corporation.

The Duty of Loyalty

Corporate officers and senior executives have a duty of loyalty to the corporation. They must act in good faith and in a manner that they reasonably believe will be in the best interests of the corporation,[21] including safeguarding corporate information.[22] Many times, these duties are buttressed by corporate requirements that these individuals sign confidentiality agreements. In *Coady v. Harpo, Inc.*,[23] Elizabeth Coady, a former senior associate producer of *The Oprah Winfrey Show*, signed an agreement entitled "Business Ethics, Objectivity, and Confidentiality Policy."[24] The agreement required Ms. Coady to keep confidential, during her employment and thereafter, all information about Ms. Winfrey and her production

company. The Court found that the agreement was enforceable. In addition, a corporation may require senior executives to sign agreements granting to the corporation all ownership of their work product. These agreements strengthen the executive's fiduciary obligations to the corporation and specifically make the executive liable for conversion of property.[25] They clarify what property the corporation owns. If the senior executive uses any property of the corporation, without authority, she is liable to the corporation irrespective of whether the property was used in competition against the principal.[26] Providing confidential information to law enforcement authorities might constitute conversion. More specifically, New York makes it illegal to duplicate computer-stored information regardless of whether the information is available elsewhere.[27]

The confidentiality and assignment of property rights agreements often give the corporation protections above and beyond the basic common law or statutory fiduciary duties. In addition, these agreements may be tied into the agent's duty to obey the principal. "In every contract of service it is implied that the employee shall obey the lawful orders of the master. . . ."[28] The rationales for these kinds of confidentiality agreements and for imposing the duty of loyalty and obedience on senior executives are twofold. First, the duty is designed to protect the employer from economic exploitation by the employee. For example, in *Wexler v. Greenberg*,[29] the court stated that "[s]ociety as a whole greatly benefits from technological improvements. Without some means of post-employment protection to assure that valuable developments or improvements are exclusively those of the employer, the businessman could not afford to subsidize research or improve current methods." Second, the duty of loyalty is enmeshed in notions of morality and is designed to protect employers who may be vulnerable to exploitation from employees. For instance, the court in *Maryland Metals, Inc. v. Metzner*[30] stated that "[f]airness dictates that an employee not be permitted to exploit the trust of his employer so as to obtain an unfair advantage in competing with the employer in a matter concerning the latter's business." The nature of the corporation requires it to rely on the officers and managers to run the day-to-day business. These employees have access to a very precious commodity, that is, vital and privileged corporate information. In the more mundane duty of loyalty cases, the senior executive has access to important corporate information dealing with customer lists,[31] customer preferences,[32] customer pricing,[33] new opportunities,[34] and secret formulas.[35]

Even though these cases and examples generally deal with a senior executive stealing corporate opportunities, these principles still apply in the whistleblowing context. For example, the whistleblower may convert corporate proprietary information by taking corporate records and sharing them with the authorities. The whistleblower could disclose information that, at worst, could lead to civil or criminal liabilities for the corporation and its other senior officers and directors. At best, certain disclosures could lead to significant embarrassment or humiliation. In either case, deciding how to make such disclosures would usually be a decision of the board of directors and senior managers of the corporation. For example, if the disclosure might give rise to criminal or civil liability, the corporation under the best of circumstances would want to vest its decision with its attorneys in an effort to minimize its potential liability and maximize profits. If the whistleblower discloses the information, she may make it impossible for the corporation and other senior executives to obtain a good deal from prosecutors. If the information disclosed is not rooted in civil or criminal misconduct, but nevertheless is scandalous, the corporation may

want to refrain from disclosing such information. The whistleblower may cause a great deal of public relations harm by disclosing such information. Because of this knowledge, senior executives know where the corporation may be most vulnerable. The senior managers are in a position to inflict harm on the corporation in a way that strangers cannot.[36]

The Duty of Care

Corporate officers and senior executives have a duty of care to the corporation. They have an obligation to perform their duties with the care that a person in a like position would reasonably exercise under similar circumstances.[37] This duty has been analogized to the diligence, care, and skill that ordinarily prudent individuals would exercise in the management of their affairs. The classic example of a breach of the duty of care is demonstrated in *Francis v. United Jersey Bank*.[38] In *Francis*, Mrs. Pritchard and her sons were the shareholders and directors of a reinsurance brokerage business. When Mrs. Pritchard's husband died, she inherited forty-eight percent of the corporation's stock. Her two sons owned the remaining fifty-two percent. Before he died, Mrs. Pritchard's husband warned her that his son Charles would "take the shirt off my back. . . ." After her husband's death, Mrs. Pritchard became depressed and drank heavily. She paid no attention to the business, and she failed to review any of the corporation's financial reports. As a consequence of her failure to monitor, her sons misappropriated over twelve million dollars.

The court found that Mrs. Pritchard had breached her duty of care.[39] The *Francis* court explained that corporate executives are under a duty to obtain at least a rudimentary understanding of the business of the corporation. They are also under a continuing obligation to monitor and be informed about the corporation. More may be expected of senior corporate executives than of mere board members.[40] For instance, in *Bates v. Dresser*,[41] the Court found the bank president liable for the failure to detect and stop the bookkeeper's embezzlement. The Court, however, failed to find the bank's board members liable. The Court reasoned that the board members had no reason to suspect a problem, whereas the bank president had discovered several incidents that should have alerted him to the bookkeeper's dishonesty. Of course, the *Francis* court points out that these senior executives can absolve themselves from liability by objecting to any wrongdoing or resigning.[42] In fact, the duty may exceed merely resigning and objecting in cases where the corporation is in a precarious financial condition and an implied trust exists in which the corporation holds funds. In those cases, the duties imposed on senior executives might require them to use "all reasonable action to stop the continuing conversion."

In the case of whistleblowing, tension between the duty of loyalty and duty of care exists. The senior executive is required to disclose her objections to certain actions that she believes are illegal. But how is she supposed to do that? As a non-director officer, she could disclose her objections to her supervisor or her supervisor's supervisor like Sherron Watkins did at Enron. This objection may take the form of a "cover your ass" memo. But will this really stop wrongdoing? In some cases, such a memo may be insufficient to stop the wrongdoing, and the senior executive may have an obligation to report the matter to the authorities. She may, however, be in a bind because her contractual obligations and her duty of loyalty responsibilities may limit the type of information that she could give to the authorities. In addition, unless someone has real inside information allowing them to actually observe the wrongdoing and has the expertise to know that the wrongdoing is illegal, what safe harbor exists to protect the senior executive from mistakenly reporting wrongdoing? This conflict may place the senior executive in a dilemma, which the Act does not totally ease.

SARBANES-OXLEY ACT'S WHISTLEBLOWING PROTECTIONS

Prior to the Sarbanes-Oxley Act, the protections for private[43] corporate whistleblowers varied depending upon state law. Because of these varied protections, senior officers and managers had to worry about the fact that, in some states, they held their jobs at will. Therefore, they could be fired at any time for no reason. Forty-two states and the District of Columbia, however, now recognize a cause of action for retaliatory discharge.[44] These statutes and rulings protect at-will employees who "blow the whistle" on important public policy issues. Therefore, an employee who is terminated for refusing to violate the law or for reporting a violation of the law can bring an action for wrongful discharge against her employer. Upon successful litigation of her suit, the "wronged" employee can get damages[45] and reinstatement to her job. The interpretations of what constitutes protected whistleblowing varies depending on the state.[46] One of the goals of the Act was to afford a whistleblowing employee the same protection irrespective of her state of residence.[47] Most state claims for wrongful retaliation revolved around claims for wrongful discharge based on the employee's termination for refusing to violate a law, rule, or regulation or for reporting such violation.[48] The employee could, however, be fired if the reported behavior did not actually violate an existing law. For example, in *Bohatch v. Butler & Binion*,[49] a partner, Bohatch, reported to the law firm's managing partner that one of the partners was over billing a client. The next day, the accused partner told Ms. Bohatch that the same client was dissatisfied with her work. The law firm investigated the allegations, determined that the client was satisfied that the bills were reasonable, and terminated Ms. Bohatch. The court refused to recognize an anti-retaliation exception to the at-will nature of partnerships.[50] Most states seem to protect employees who report issues of safety or who are required to report safety violations.[51] Those employees who were merely reporting failures to follow company procedure were least protected. In addition, several states deny protection for those whistleblowers who make unfounded claims or who fail to sufficiently investigate their claims. These states merely require that the employee's allegation be made in "good faith."

The Sarbanes-Oxley Act prohibits any public company from discriminating against any employee who lawfully provides information or otherwise assists in an investigation of conduct that the employee "reasonably believes" constitutes a violation of the federal securities laws.[52] This provision was designed from the lessons learned from Sherron Watkins's testimony. As Senator Patrick Leahy stated, "'We learned from Sherron Watkins of Enron that these corporate insiders are the key witnesses that need to be encouraged to report fraud and help prove it in court.'"[53] The legislation protects an employee from retaliation by an employer for testifying before Congress or a federal regulatory agency, or giving evidence to law enforcement of possible securities fraud violations.[54] To secure this protection, the employee must have assisted in an investigation, which was conducted by Congress, a federal agency, the employee's supervisor, or anyone else authorized by the employer to conduct an investigation. Under the Act, within ninety days of the discriminatory act, the employee must file an administrative claim with the Secretary of Labor.[55] If the Secretary of Labor fails to issue a final decision within 180 days of filing of the complaint,[56] the employee can bring a private cause of action at law or equity for de novo review in federal district court.[57] Relief available under this statute shall include compensatory damages, such as reinstatement with the same level of seniority, back pay with interest, and any special damages, that is, litigation costs, expert witness fees, and reasonable attorney fees.[58] In addition, every public company is required to establish mechanisms to allow the employees to provide information anonymously to the corporation's board of directors.[59]

The Sarbanes-Oxley Act was designed to promote investor confidence by ensuring that the public receives more information about possible corporate fraud. Such disclosures would ensure that the markets have perfect information so that investors could make informed investment choices. Senator Leahy reported that the Act is designed to "include all good faith and reasonable reporting of fraud, and there should be no presumption that reporting is otherwise, absent specific evidence."[60] This reasonable person standard would include the usual standard used in a variety of contexts. In fact, Senator Leahy stated that the type of action taken by the corporation or the agency would be "strong indicia that it could support such a reasonable belief." In addition, Senator Leahy explained that the whistleblowing provision would exclude unlawful actions such as the "improper public disclosure of trade secret information."

Undoubtedly, the Sarbanes-Oxley Act provides an extra level of protection for employees. Despite this added protection and the increased prominence of whistleblowers, we must be cognizant that federal whistleblowers have low success rates in their suits before government agencies. *The Whistleblowers Survival Guide* reports that "the rate of success for winning a reprisal lawsuit on the merits in administrative hearings for federal whistleblower laws has risen to between 25 and 33 percent in recent years."[61] Under the Act, the corporate senior executive or employee is likely to confront some of the same dilemmas, which the Act does not quite address, and is likely to also have a low rate of success under its whistleblowing provisions. First, the statute only affords protection against retaliations based on securities fraud.[62] Whistleblowing of other kinds of wrongdoing remain unprotected under this Act. In these cases, the whistleblower then must rely on the vagaries of state law, which generally give preference to those allegations dealing with public safety. For example, a senior executive may overhear a high-ranking executive make disparaging remarks about a particular racial group and state that he would never hire or promote members of that group. The corporation employs very few members of this particular group and has none in senior management. The senior executive believes that the corporation is engaged in race discrimination. The senior executive has a fiduciary obligation to hold certain corporate information like employee demographics in confidence but has an obligation to resign or object from his position when confronting corporate wrongdoing. The Act provides protection only for those matters that involve security fraud. If this senior manager discloses, she would have to rely on the protections of the state laws.

Second, low-level employees are also relatively unprotected. They probably are unaware of these new protections. They may feel particularly oppressed by the many layers of management that may exist in some corporations. Some may be unsophisticated and may not know whether certain actions violate the law. Many of the wrongful or illegal activities that they observe may not rise to the level of securities fraud. For example, an employee at McDonald's may notice that large numbers of pre-packaged hamburgers disappear shortly after delivery. The disappearance may be the result of conversion by the store manager. The McDonald's employee might be in the best position to ascertain whether this wrongdoing is occurring, but she is unprotected by the Sarbanes-Oxley Act because this conversion does not involve securities fraud. She will have to rely on the vagaries of state law. In addition, many of these employees rely very heavily on their paychecks; a high turnover rate exists in these jobs. Students and those re-entering the workforce hold many of these jobs. These individuals may be particularly reluctant to "rock the boat" and report wrongdoing unless they are guaranteed that their job is protected. The Act does nothing to address this population of whistleblowers.

Third, for both senior executives and low-level employees, the Sarbanes-Oxley Act gives little guidance as to the circumstances under which an employee is to disclose allegations of wrongdoing to her supervisor as opposed to law enforcement authorities. Senior executives also have an obligation to use "reasonable efforts" to disclose to the principal information, which is "relevant to affairs entrusted to [the agent]" and which the principal would desire to have.[63] To some extent, this decision may be a judgment call by the whistleblowing employee. In some instances, however, the whistleblowing employee who reports wrongdoing to her supervisor might not be doing enough to stem the wrongdoing behavior. For instance, once she has made the report, the wrongdoing supervisor might exclude the employee from access to information that would allow her to continue to observe the wrongful behavior. In those cases, the reporting employee may have breached her duty of care to the corporation by using insufficient actions to stop the wrongdoing. In addition, her reports to her supervisor may give notice to the supervisor to claim that he had no knowledge. Conversely, if the whistleblowing employee reports the evidence of wrongdoing immediately to law enforcement authorities, she may be violating her duty of loyalty to the corporation especially if her allegations are unfounded. These senior-executives are subject to a duty not to use or to communicate confidential information acquired during their employment, "unless the information is a matter of general knowledge."[64] She has an obligation to protect certain proprietary and confidential corporate information. Also by going to the law enforcement authorities right away, she may be depriving the corporation of the opportunity to resolve the matter or, in the case of wrongdoing, get the best deal for the corporation. In addition, the employee who jumps the gun and goes to law enforcement authorities may be putting herself in a difficult political situation at her corporation. Even though the terms of her position and employment may remain the same, she will always, to her detriment, be remembered for making that report.

Fourth, the Sarbanes-Oxley Act gives no guidance concerning whether the whistleblowing employee should disclose the information to her direct supervisor or her supervisor's supervisor. Who is the principal of senior executives? Is it the corporation? Is it the board of directors? Is it the senior executive's boss? To some extent, this decision may be a judgment call by the whistleblowing employee. In some instances, however, the whistleblowing employee who reports wrongdoing to her direct supervisor might not be doing enough to prevent the wrongdoing behavior. For instance, as stated above, once she has made the report, the wrongdoing supervisor might also exclude the employee from access to information that would allow her to continue to observe the wrongful behavior. In those cases, the reporting employee may have breached her duty of care to the corporation by using insufficient actions to stem the wrongdoing. In addition, her reports to her supervisor may have put him on notice to claim that he had no knowledge. In those cases, she may be required to report the wrongdoing to a higher level of authority in the corporation. By immediately going to the supervisor's supervisor, however, she may be depriving her direct supervisor of the opportunity to resolve the matter,

which might be in the best interest of the corporation and the supervisor. In addition, the employee who "jumps the gun" and goes to her supervisor's supervisor may be putting herself in a difficult political situation at her corporation in that her direct supervisor may never trust her. If she discloses to her supervisor's supervisor, she may be perceived as a "rat fink," which may be a career-limiting move.

Fifth, the legislative history of the Sarbanes-Oxley Act states that the employee's actions have to be reasonable in making reports.[65] Employee actions will be deemed reasonable depending on the types of actions taken by the corporation or the investigating agency. In the context of suspected wrongdoing by others, the senior executives may be in a precarious position. Most cases may not be as clear-cut as the one involving Sherron Watkins. Because she was an accountant, she had a very good idea that Enron's accounting policies were illegal. For most other whistleblowers, they may have only a slight inkling that something might be amiss. In those circumstances, what are they supposed to do? Depending on the nature of the corporation, they may have an obligation to investigate further. We then may require the senior executives of major corporations to be "Nancy Drew, Girl Detective." With downsizing and more responsibilities, many of these employees already have many additional responsibilities. If, however, they fail to properly investigate their suspicions, they may violate their duty of care to the corporation. In addition, although Senator Leahy stated that the Act protects whistleblowers who report and disclose their reasonable suspicions,[66] the statutory language fails to explicitly provide such protection. Whistleblowers who report and disclose their reasonable suspicions are in a tough spot if their allegations turn out to be unfounded. The Sarbanes-Oxley Act's statutory protections will fail to protect the whistleblower's ensuing loss of credibility among her corporate peers.

Sixth, the Sarbanes-Oxley Act prohibits a corporation from "discharg[ing], demot[ing], suspend[ing], threaten[ing], harass[ing], or in any other manner discriminat[ing] against an employee in the terms and conditions of employment" because she blew the whistle.[67] Senator Leahy conceded, however, that "most corporate employers, with help from their lawyers, know exactly what they can do to a whistleblowing employee under the law."[68] The types of retaliation that can occur include: (1) "attacking the [whistleblower's] motives, credibility, [or] professional competence";[69] (2) "build[ing] a damaging record against [the whistleblower]"; (3) threatening the employee with "reprisals for whistleblowing"; (4) "reassign[ing]" the employee to an isolated work location; (5) "publicly humiliat[ing]" the employee; (6) "set[ting] . . . up [the whistleblower] for failure" by putting them in impossible assignments; (7) "prosecut[ing the employee] for unauthorized disclosures [of information]"; (8) "reorganiz[ing]" the company so that the whistleblower's job is eliminated; and (9) "blacklist[ing]" the whistleblower so she will be unable to work in the industry. Of course some methods on this list would clearly violate the Act. A deft supervisor, however, could "set up" the whistleblowing employee for failure. For instance, the employer may place the whistleblower in a job unsuitable to her skill level to ensure her failure. The employer could then document the employee's poor performance. The Act provides protections for whistleblowing employees except in cases where valid business reasons exist for their termination like inferior work performance. In addition, even if the employer refrains from discriminating against the whistleblowing employee in the terms and conditions of her employment, the employer is unlikely to give that employee any opportunities for advancement. By blowing the whistle, she may have "tapped out" her career trajectory. For instance, Sherron Watkins's present job and terms of employment are probably very secure, but can we really imagine her ever advancing from her present position at Enron? Her future supervisors will probably always worry that she is not a "team player" who may go over their heads when she suspects they are doing something wrong.

CONCLUSION

Despite the recent positive press concerning corporate whistleblowers, it is fraught with grave dangers. The whistleblower is under simultaneous duties of loyalty and care. By reporting suspicious activities, the whistleblower may violate her duty of loyalty to the corporation by misusing corporate proprietary information, but at the same time the failure to report such activities may be a violation of the duty of care. The Sarbanes-Oxley Act provides the whistleblower with some federal protection against retaliation but does not ease the tension between the whistleblower's duty of care and loyalty. In addition, there are several matters that the Act fails to address or provide sufficient protection, i.e., (1) non-securities fraud matters are not covered; (2) low-level employees may not be aware of the protections; (3) no guidance is given as to when to report wrongdoing to outside authorities or to a supervisor; (4) no guidance is given as to when the whistleblower should go over his or her supervisor's head to senior management; and (5) no protection is given to undercover retaliations that do not quite manifest themselves as a "discharge, demotion, suspension, threat, or other manner of discrimination." In promulgating its rules in implementing this matter, the SEC, to the extent possible, should take some of these limitations of the Act into account. As a consequence, the corporate whistleblower cannot just pucker and blow. She has to use a great deal of thought to whether and how she may want to blow the whistle. ◆ ◆ ◆

◆ Notes

1. *See The Financial Collapse of Enron—Part 3: Hearing Before the Subcomm. on Oversight and Investigations of the House Comm. on Energy and Commerce*, 107th Cong. (Feb. 14, 2002) (testimony of Sherron Watkins, Vice-President of Corporate Development, Enron Corp.), *available at* http://frwebgate.access.gpo.gov/cgi-bin/getdoc.cgi?dbname=107_house_hearings&docid=f:77991.wais [hereinafter *Watkins Testimony*].

2. Kurt Eichenwald, *Another Inquiry: Company Hobbled Investigation by Its Law Firm, Report Says*, N.Y. TIMES, Feb. 4, 2002, at A19.

3. *Id.*

4. Andersen may have also gotten into trouble because it allowed regional partners to overrule auditing experts, known as the Professional Standards Group (PSG). Andersen e-mails and memos show that Andersen's PSG vigorously objected to Enron's accounting practices, but they were overruled by regional Andersen partners who falsely wrote memos that the PSG approved of the transactions. Mike McNamee, *Out of Control: Internal Memos Detail How the Firm's Unusually Lax Controls Allowed Its Enron Team to Call the Shots*, BUS. WK., Apr. 8, 2002, at 32. A former Andersen employee said that local control over accounting issues was a selling point, and the effect was insidious because the "rainmakers were given the power to overrule the accounting nerds." *Id.* at 33.

5. Naftali Bendavid, *Enron's Law Firm Begins to Draw Fire*, CHIC. TRIB., Mar. 14, 2002, at 17; Samantha Miller & Gabrielle Cosgriff, *To Tell the Truth*, PEOPLE, Feb. 4, 2002, at 63. However, Joseph Dilg, managing partner of Vinson & Elkins, testified before Congress that "Vinson & Elkins did not advise Enron that there were no problems. Our written . . . reports pointed out significant issues. . . ." *The Financial Collapse of Enron: Hearing Before the House Subcomm. on Oversight and Investigation of the House Comm. on Energy and Commerce*, 107th Cong. (2002) (statement of Joseph C. Dilg, Managing Partner, Vinson & Elkins, L.L.P.). Rep. Christopher Shays, Republican from Connecticut, thought that Vinson & Elkins "became too cozy with Enron and did not provide reasonable scrutiny of its dealings." Bendavid, *supra*. Harry Reasoner, Senior Partner at Vinson & Elkins, charged that "Enron's primary counsel were their in-house legal staff. . . . [T]hey had 250 lawyers." *Id.* Mr. Reasoner does not discuss the fact that many of Enron's in-house lawyers started their careers at Vinson & Elkins. *See id.*

6. Eichenwald, *supra* note 2. Some of the problems with Vinson & Elkins' review might be due to the restrictions that Enron placed on Vinson & Elkins' investigation. The law firm was told not to review the underlying accounting issues, which went to the heart of Ms. Watkins's allegations. *Id.* Enron, however, was Vinson & Elkins' single largest accounting client and comprised seven percent of Vinson & Elkins' total revenue. Mike France et al., *One Big Client, One Big Hassle: Vinson & Elkins' Heavy Reliance on Enron is Now a Potential Liability for the Law Firm*, BUS. WK., Jan. 28, 2002, at 39. In addition, according to one undisclosed Enron employee, "[Enron] might not have been able to pull off many of the transactions . . . without Vinson & Elkins' opinion letters." *Id.*

7. Robert Schlesinger, *Enron Chief Executive Lay Resigns Anderson Memo Says Firm Was Warned in October* (sic), BOST. GLOBE, Jan. 24, 2002, at A2 (noting then-Andersen partner David Duncan wrote the warning memo). Arthur Andersen later fired Mr. Duncan because of his alleged role in destroying documents related to Enron. *Id.*

8. *Id.* (Lay stated that his decision was "reached in cooperation" with Enron's creditors committee and that he would remain a member of Enron's board of directors). *Id.*

9. In her testimony before the House of Representatives, Ms. Watkins acknowledged that she traded about $47,000 in Enron stock about the time that she was blowing her whistle. She claimed that she was selling the stock because she routinely diversified, and that the transactions in October

2001 were a "kneejerk reaction" to September 11th. *The Financial Collapse of Enron: Hearing Before the House Subcomm. on Oversight and Investigations of the House Comm. on Energy and Commerce*, 107th Cong. (2002) (testimony of Sherron Watkins, Vice-President of Corporate Development, Enron Corp.). For insider trading liability, an insider like Ms. Watkins must either refrain from trading or disclose any non-public information, neither of which she did.

10. Katie Fairbank, *You Know How to Whistle, Don't You?*, DALLAS MORN. NEWS, Feb. 27, 2002, at 1A; *Lauded by Lawmakers, Enron Whistle-Blower Escapes the Worst*, AGENCE FRANCE PRESSE, Feb. 15, 2002 [hereinafter *Lauded by Lawmakers*]. *But see* Julie Mason, *The Fall of Enron; Watkins' Own Ethics Questioned*, HOUS. CHRON., Feb. 15, 2002, at 21 (noting that Watkins, as a Certified Public Accountant, may have been obligated to report her concerns to state regulators or to the Securities and Exchange Commission). *But see* Curtis C. Verschoor, Ethics of Enron "Whistle-Blower" Questioned, 83 STRATEGIC FINANCE (May 1, 2002) (noting that since Ms. Watkins was not involved in the Andersen extrinsic audit, she was not subject to SEC Rule 10A requiring CPA reporting to the board of directors and the SEC of illegal client acts).

11. Frank Pellegrini, *Person of the Week: "Enron Whistleblower" Sherron Watkins*, Time.com (Jan. 18, 2002), *available at* http://www.time.com/time/pow/printout/0,8816,194927,00.html (noting she was not technically a whistleblower since she should have blown the whistle by writing to the Houston Chronicle long before August). The Article suggests that maybe her memo was a "cover your ass" memo. *See also* Dan Ackman, *Sherron Watkins Had Whistle, But Blew It*, Forbes.com (Feb. 14, 2002), *available at* http://www.forbes.com/2002/02/14/0214watkins.html (asserting that Ms. Watkins' actions actually provided cover for Lay and the Enron board because her warning allowed Lay to assert that he had no prior knowledge and needed to be warned).

12. Paul Farhi, *A Whistle That Can Pierce the Glass Ceiling*, WASH. POST, July 6, 2002, at C1 (noting that the most recent whistleblowers have been women, including Cynthia Cooper, the internal auditor at WorldCom, Coleen Rowley, the FBI lawyer who detailed mistakes in the September 11th investigation, and Sherron Watkins).

13. SOPHOCLES, ANTIGONE, *available at* http://classics.mit.edu/Sophocles/antigone.pl.txt (last visited Oct. 21, 2002).

14. Some thought that John Dean, who testified against former President Richard Nixon in the Watergate hearings, was initially lying, until the Watergate tapes were released. *See* Len Colodny, *Hidden History: The Day Nixon Lost His Presidency, The Nixon Era Times, available at* http://www.watergate.com/stories/watergate.asp (last visited Oct. 16, 2002) ("[T]he truth [was] never something that Dean ever [let] get in the way of his version of events.").

15. Many Americans had a very low opinion of Linda Tripp, who taped the telephone conversations of her friend Monica Lewinsky, which were used in the impeachment proceedings against former President Bill Clinton. *See* Keating Holland, *Poll: Most Americans Hold Unfavorable Views of Tripp, Lewinsky, available at* http://www.cnn.com/ALLPOLITICS/1998/07/02/poll (July 2, 1998) (finding 52% of Americans have an unfavorable opinion of Tripp).

16. Recently Eunice Stone reported that she overheard three American Muslim medical students making threats of terrorist acts in South Florida on September 13th at a Shoney's restaurant in Georgia. She followed the students into the parking lot and reported their license plates to the authorities. A region-wide terror alert was announced, and the three men were apprehended and detained for over seventeen hours. They were released when the authorities found no incriminating evidence. After this incident, people question whether the students were playing a hoax or whether Ms. Stone might have been stereotyping them because of their swarthy appearance. *See generally* Clarence Page, Editorial, *Muslim Students Victims*

of Paranoia, GRAND RAPIDS PRESS, Sept. 24, 2002, at A9; Robert Steinback, *Who, If Anybody, Erred in Alligator Alley Terror Scare*, MIAMI HER., Sept. 21, 2002, at 1.

17. MODEL BUS. CORP. ACT § 8.40(a) (1999); DEL. GEN. CORP. LAW § 142(a) (Aspen Supp. 2002).

18. MODEL BUS. CORP. ACT § 8.40(b) (1999); DEL. GEN. CORP. LAW § 142(b) (Aspen Supp. 2002).

19. MODEL BUS. CORP. ACT § 8.43(b) (1999). *See generally* Shapiro v. Stahl, 195 F. Supp. 822, 826 (M.D. Pa. 1961) (noting that agency relationships can be terminated at any time by mutual consent).

20. MODEL BUS. CORP. ACT § 8.42(a)(1)–(3) (1999).

21. *Id.*

22. *See id*; MODEL BUS. CORP. ACT § 8.42(d)(2) (1984).

23. 719 N.E.2d 244 (Ill. App. Ct. 1999).

24. *Id.* at 246.

25. RESTATEMENT OF AGENCY § 402 (1958).

26. Miller v. Dean Witter & Co., 314 N.Y.S.2d 380, 382 (N.Y. Civ. Ct. 1970).

27. N.Y. PENAL LAW § 156.30 (Consol. 2000).

28. Walker v. John Hancock Mut. Life Ins. Co., 80 N.J.L. 342, 344 (1911); *see also* Granite State Fire Ins. Co. v. Mitton, 98 F. Supp. 706, 710 (D. Colo. 1951), *aff'd*, 196 F.2d 988 (10th Cir. 1952).

29. 160 A.2d 430 (Pa. 1960) (involving the chemist of a soap manufacturer who stole a trade secret).

30. 382 A.2d 564 (Md. 1978).

31. *See, e.g.*, Town & Country House & Home Serv., Inc. v. Newbery, 147 N.E.2d 724 (N.Y. 1958) (involving customers' names taken by departing house cleaners).

32. *See, e.g.*, Corroon & Black-Rutters & Roberts, Inc. v. Hosch, 325 N.W.2d 883 (Wis. 1982) (involving customer lists, which contained detailed information on customer insurance policies).

33. *See, e.g.*, Ackerman v. Kimball Int'l, Inc. 634 N.E.2d 778 (Ind. Ct. App. 1994).

34. *See, e.g.*, Gen. Auto. Mfg. Co. v. Singer, 120 N.W.2d 659 (Wis. 1963) (concluding that a general manager made secret profits by turning over some business to competitors).

35. *See, e.g.*, PepsiCo, Inc. v. Redmond, No. 94-C6838, 1995 U.S. Dist. LEXIS 19437 (N.D. Ill. Jan. 26, 1995).

36. Terry A. O'Neill, *Employees' Duty of Loyalty and the Corporate Constituency Debate*, 25 CONN. L. REV. 681, 705 (1993).

37. MODEL BUS. CORP. ACT § 8.42(a)(1)–(3)(1984).

38. 432 A.2d 814 (N.J. 1981).

39. In this case, Mrs. Pritchard breached her duty of care to the creditors of the corporation because the corporation held funds in trust for creditors. *Id.* at 829.

40. This enhanced fiduciary duty for officers as opposed to directors is analogous to the enhanced duties that managing partners have in a partnership. *See generally* Meinhard v. Salmon, 164 N.E. 545, 463–65 (N.Y. 1928).

41. 251 U.S. 524 (1920).

42. *See generally* Francis v. United Jersey Bank, 432 A.2d 814 (N.J. 1981) (dealing with the responsibilities of the corporate director to address wrongdoing by other members of the board; this rule probably applies to officers and senior executives). *Cf. id.* at 823 (pointing out "the fulfillment of the duty of a director may call for more than mere objection and resignation. Sometimes a director may be required to seek the advice of counsel").

43. In contrast, government whistleblowers were afforded a variety of statutory protections under the Civil Service Reform Act, 5 U.S.C. § 2302(b), and the Whistleblower Protection Act, 5 U.S.C. § 1201, and its 1994 amendments. 140 CONG. REC. S14668–70, H11419–22 (Oct. 7, 1994).

44. TOM DEVINE, GOV'T ACCOUNTABILITY PROJECT, THE WHISTLEBLOWER'S SURVIVAL GUIDE: COURAGE WITHOUT MARTYRDOM 133–34 (1997).

45. *See* Jane P. Mallor, *Punitive Damages for Wrongful Discharge of At Will Employees*, 26 WM. & MARY L. REV. 449, 479–95 (1985) (discussing that several states allow punitive damages for such wrongful dismissals); *see also* Elletta Sangrey Callahan & Terry Morehead Dworkin, *The State of State Whistleblower Protection*, 38 AM. BUS. L.J. 99, 129–30 (2000) (noting that "[s]everal courts have considered the monetary relief available to whistleblowers who have statutory claims . . . [however,] [t]he majority of courts

have not allowed punitive damages under the relevant whistleblower act, particularly if the state is the defendant").

46. DEVINE, *supra* note 44 (noting that there might be additional federal protection tucked away in the confines of a variety of specialty statutes dealing with environmental protection, occupational health and safety, or labor regulations).

47. *See* CONG. REC. S7420 (July 26, 2002) (statement of Sen. Leahy).

48. *See* Callahan & Dworkin, *supra* note 45, at 105.

49. 977 S.W.2d 543 (Tex. 1998).

50. *See id.* at 546–47 (restating general rule that "a law firm can expel a partner to protect relationships both within the firm and with clients" and declining to carve out anti-retaliation exception).

51. *See* Callahan & Dworkin, *supra* note 45, at 105–07, 113–14, 118.

52. Sarbanes-Oxley Act of 2002 §806(a), Pub. L. No. 107-204, 116 Stat. 745, 802 (to be codified at 18 U.S.C. § 1514A(a)(1)).

53. *The Truth Is Out There,* LEGAL WK. GLOBAL, Aug. 20, 2002, *available at* http://www.legalweek.net/ViewItem.asp?id=10241.

54. *Sarbanes-Oxley Paves Way For Potential Whistleblowers, Too,* (CNNFN television broadcast, Aug. 5, 2002) (Interview of Peter Zlotnick, corporate attorney, Mintz Levin); Transcript # 080505cb.129.

55. Sarbanes-Oxley Act § 806(b)(1)(A) (to be codified at 18 U.S.C. § 1514A(b)(1)(A)).

56. *Id.* § 806(b)(1)(B) (to be codified at 18 U.S.C. § 1514A(b)(1)(B)).

57. *Id.* § 806(b)(1)–(2) (to be codified at 18 U.S.C. § 1514A(b)(1)–(2)).

58. *Id.* § 806(c) (to be codified at 18 U.S.C. § 1514A(c)).

59. *Id.* § 301(m)(4) (to be codified at 15 U.S.C. § 78f-(m)(4)).

60. LEGISLATIVE HISTORY OF TITLE VIII of H.R. 2673: THE SARBANES-OXLEY ACT OF 2002, 148 CONG. REC. S7420 (statement of Sen. Leahy).

61. Devine, *supra* note 44, at 116.

62. *See* Sarbanes-Oxley Act § 806(a)(1) to be codified at 18 U.S.C. § 1514A(a)(1)).

63. RESTATEMENT (SECOND) OF AGENCY § 381.

64. *Id.* § 395.

65. *See* LEGISLATIVE HISTORY OF TITLE VIII OF H.R. 2673: THE SARBANES-OXLEY ACT OF 2002, 148 CONG. REC. S7420 (statement of Sen. Leahy).

66. *See id.*

67. Sarbanes-Oxley Act § 806(a) (to be codified at § 1514A(a)).

68. LEGISLATIVE HISTORY OF TITLE VIII of H.R. 2673: THE SARBANES-OXLEY ACT OF 2002, 148 CONG. REC. S7420 (statement by Sen. Leahy).

69. Devine, *supra* note 44, at 28.

ENCOURAGING MORALITY
IN BUSINESS

There are two major ways that we can advance morality in business and promote positive behavior. Internally, we can strive for a corporate culture that gives clear ethical directives. Externally, we can demand a set of legal norms that set the moral tone for business dealings.

There is an adage stating that we cannot legislate morality. Although this is true to an extent, there are ways that individuals and corporations can be encouraged to act. They can be given incentives to do good, and they can be sanctioned if they fail to achieve the appropriate standards. This approach is behavioristic in that it conditions subjects to act in certain ways, as opposed to appealing to their free will. Some philosophers may suggest that acting without personal intentionality is not properly called moral. However, another view of moral development, drawn from Aristotle, could counter by saying that we have to train people to be moral, and this starts with obedience. For example, at one time seat belts were optional, but once they were required by law people complied, the behavior became habitual, and now it is so ingrained that it feels awkward not to wear them. Similarly, although we may have to be forced to do what is right initially, once we take on those behaviors as our own, they become intentional acts that we have chosen.

Externally, two significant laws have changed the way companies approach ethics. The first is the 1991 federal sentencing guidelines (FSGs). These provide incentives for companies to proactively set up programs that require employee compliance with the law and the corporate code of conduct. Now companies have a financial interest in creating meaningful ethics programs and structures within their organization. The net result is that it is no longer acceptable for a new employee to get the corporate code on joining the company and then allow it to sit on a shelf for the rest of her work life; the law requires at least an annual review of company policies and active training.

The other major change came about after a wave of scandals in the late 1990s. With enactment of the Sarbanes-Oxley Act in 2002, firms became more transparent to investors, preventing conflicts of interest by auditors and others; the act also made the highest-ranking corporate officers personally responsible for the reports they present to the public. Codes and laws cannot make bad people good and cannot stop all corporate wrongdoing. However, they are significantly valuable tools in building and maintaining ethical organizations.

Within a company, the culture can be established through a corporate code of conduct and ethics programs. However, these may be ineffective unless backed up by a company-wide commitment to ethical behavior. For example, in the Tylenol poisoning case, capsules tainted with poison randomly killed several purchasers. The murders started a national panic. The manufacturer, Johnson & Johnson, pulled the product and took a huge loss. The executives ex-

plained that the decision was, in fact, easy, because they were able to draw on the company's well-established credo, which simply articulates the core values of the company.

A finely crafted code can act as a compass point for managers faced with new or difficult decisions. The Patrick Murphy reading outlines several forms of guidance that a firm can promote internally. Dove Izraeli and Mark Schwartz believe that the FSGs have been a hugely successful American experiment from which other countries could learn. Roger Leeds examines the Sarbanes-Oxley Act. He contends that although it has some very useful provisions, we still need to rely on human relationships and trust to encourage a robust marketplace.

Creating Ethical Corporate Structures

Patrick E. Murphy

Having an ethical workplace may be intrinsically good, but it also has a direct effect on the bottom line by reducing losses and inefficiencies. How do companies promote ethical behavior in a proactive rather than reactive fashion? Murphy states that companies try to create and sustain an ethical culture. He identifies three approaches that are proven and workable: corporate credos, ethics programs, and codes of ethics. In the article, he describes the benefits and limitations of each with reference to examples of major corporations.

Employees are looking for guidance in dealing with ethical problems. This guidance may come from the CEO, upper management, or immediate supervisors.[1] We know that ethical business practices stem from an ethical corporate culture. Key questions are, How can this culture be created and sustained? What structural approaches encourage ethical decision making? If the goal is to make the company ethical, managers must introduce structural components that will enhance ethical sensitivity.

In this paper, I examine three promising and workable approaches to infusing ethical principles into businesses:

◆ corporate credos that define and give direction to corporate values;
◆ ethics programs where companywide efforts focus on ethical issues; and
◆ ethical codes that provide specific guidance to employees in functional business areas.

Below I review the virtues and limitations of each and provide examples of companies that successfully employ these approaches.

CORPORATE CREDOS

A corporate credo delineates a company's ethical responsibility to its stakeholders; it is probably the most general approach to managing corporate ethics. The credo is a succinct statement of the values permeating the firm. . . .

Any discussion of corporate credos would be incomplete without reference to Johnson & Johnson, whose credo is shown in Table 1. This document focuses on responsibilities to consumers, employees, communities, and stockholders. (. . . J&J president, David Clare, explains that responsibility to the stockholder is listed last because "if we do the other jobs properly, the stockholder will always be served.") The first version of this credo, instituted in 1945, was revised in 1947. Between 1975 and 1978, chairman James Burke held a series of meetings with J&J's 1,200 top managers; they were encouraged to "challenge" the credo. What emerged from the meetings was that the document in fact functioned as it was intended to function; a slightly reworded but substantially unchanged credo was introduced in 1979.

Table 1 ◆ JOHNSON & JOHNSON CREDO

We believe our first responsibility is to the doctors, nurses, and patients, to mothers and all others who use our products and services. In meeting their needs everything we do must be of high quality. We must constantly strive to reduce our costs in order to maintain reasonable prices. Customers' orders must be serviced promptly and accurately. Our suppliers and distributors must have an opportunity to make a fair profit.

We are responsible to our employees, the men and women who work with us throughout the world. Everyone must be considered as an individual. We must respect their dignity and recognize their merit. They must have a sense of security in their jobs. Compensation must be fair and adequate and working conditions clean, orderly, and safe. Employees must feel free to make suggestions and complaints. There must be equal opportunity for employment, development, and advancement for those qualified. We must provide competent management, and their actions must be just and ethical.

We are responsible to the communities in which we live and work and to the world community as well. We must be good citizens— support good works and charities and bear our fair share of taxes. We must encourage civic improvements and better health and education. We must maintain in good order the property we are privileged to use, protecting the environment and natural resources.

Our final responsibility is to our stockholders. Business must make a sound profit. We must experiment with new ideas. Research must be carried on, innovative programs developed and mistakes paid for. New equipment must be purchased, new facilities provided, and new products launched. Reserves must be created to provide for adverse times. When we operate according to these principles, the stockholders should realize a fair return.

Over the last two years, the company has begun to survey all employees about how well the company meets its responsibilities to the four principal constituencies. The survey asks employees from all fifty-three countries where J&J operates questions about every line in the credo. An office devoted to the credo survey tabulates the results, which are confidential. (Department and division managers receive only information pertaining to their units and composite numbers for the entire firm.) The interaction at meetings devoted to discussing these findings is reportedly very good.

Does J&J's credo work? Top management feels strongly that it does. The credo is often mentioned as an important contributing factor in the company's exemplary handling of the Tylenol crises several years ago. It would appear that the firm's commitment to the credo makes ethical business practice its highest priority. One might question whether the credo is adequate to deal with the multitude of ethical problems facing a multinational firm; possibly additional ethical guidelines could serve as reinforcement, especially in dealing with international business issues.

When should a company use a corporate credo to guide its ethical policies? They work best in firms with a cohesive corporate culture, where a spirit of frequent and unguarded communication exists. Generally, small, tightly knit companies find that a credo is sufficient. Among large firms, Johnson & Johnson is an exception. J&J managers consciously use the credo as an ethical guidepost; they find that the corporate culture reinforces the credo.

When is a credo insufficient? This approach does not offer enough guidance for most multinational companies facing complex ethical questions in different societies, for firms that have merged recently and are having trouble grafting disparate cultures, and for companies operating in industries with chronic ethical problems. A credo is like the Ten Commandments. Both set forth good general principles, but many people need the Bible, religious teachings, and guidelines provided by organized religion, as well. Similarly, many companies find that they need to offer more concrete guidance on ethical issues.

ETHICS PROGRAMS

Ethics programs provide more specific direction for dealing with potential ethical problems than general credos do. Two companies—Chemical Bank and Dow Corning—serve as examples. Although the thrust of the two programs is different, they both illustrate the usefulness of this approach.

Chemical Bank, the nation's fourth largest bank, has an extensive ethics education program. All new employees attend an orientation session at which they read and sign off on Chemical's code of ethics. . . . The training program features a videotaped message from the chairman emphasizing the bank's values and ethical standards. A second and more unusual aspect of the program provides in-depth training in ethical decision making for vice presidents.[2]

The "Decision Making and Corporate Values" course is a two-day seminar that occurs away from the bank. Its purpose, according to a bank official, is "to encourage Chemical's employees to weigh the ethical or value dimensions of the decisions they make and to provide them with the analytic tools to do that." This program began in 1983; more than 250 vice presidents have completed the course thus far. Each meeting is limited to twenty to twenty-five senior vice presidents from a cross-section of departments; this size makes for a seminarlike atmosphere. The bank instituted the program in response to the pressures associated with deregulation, technology, and increasing competition.

The chairman always introduces the seminar by highlighting his personal commitment to the program. Most of the two days is spent discussing case studies. The fictitious cases were developed following interviews with various Chemical managers who described ethically charged situations. The cases are really short stories about loan approval, branch closings, foreign loans, insider trading, and other issues.[3] They do not have "solutions" as such; instead, they pose questions for discussion, such as, Do you believe the individual violated the bank's code? Or, What should X do?

Program evaluations have yielded positive results. Participants said they later encountered dilemmas similar to the cases, and that they had developed a thinking process in the seminar that helped them work through other problems. This program, while it is exemplary, only reaches a small percentage of Chemical's 30,000 employees. Ideally, such a program would be disseminated more widely and would become more than a one-time event.

Dow Corning has a longstanding—and very different—ethics program. Its general code has been revised four times since its inception in 1976 and includes a seven-point values statement. The company started using face-to-face "ethical audits" at its plants worldwide more than a decade ago. The number of participants in these four-to-six-hour audits ranges from five to forty. Auditors meet with the manager in charge the evening before to ascertain the most pressing issues. The actual questions come from relevant sections in the corporate code and are adjusted for the audit location. At sales offices, for example, the auditors concentrate on issues such as kickbacks, unusual requests from customers, and special pricing terms; at manufacturing plants, conservation and environmental issues receive more attention. An ethical audit might include the following questions.

◆ Are there any examples of business that Dow Corning has lost because of our refusal to provide "gifts" or other incentives to government officials at our customers' facilities?

◆ Do any of our employees have ownership or financial interest in any of our distributors?

◆ Have our sales representatives been able to undertake business conduct discussions with distributors in a way that actually strengthens our ties with them?

◆ Has Dow Corning been forced to terminate any distributors because of their business conduct practices?

- Do you believe that our distributors are in regular contact with their competitors? If so, why?
- Which specific Dow Corning policies conflict with local practices?

John Swanson, manager of Corporate Internal and Management Communications, heads this effort; he believes the audit approach makes it "virtually impossible for employees to consciously make an unethical decision." According to Swanson, twenty to twenty-three meetings occur every year. The Business Conduct Committee members, who act as session leaders, then prepare a report for the Audit Committee of the board. He stresses the fact that there are no shortcuts to implementing this program—it requires time and extensive interaction with the people involved. Recently the audit was expanded; it now examines internal as well as external activities. (One audit found that some salespeople believed manufacturing personnel needed to be more honest when developing production schedules.) One might ask whether the commitment to ethics is constant over time or peaks during the audit sessions; Dow Corning may want to conduct surprise audits, or develop other monitoring mechanisms or a more detailed code.

When should a company consider developing an ethics program? Such programs are often appropriate when firms have far-flung operations that need periodic guidance, as is the case at Dow Corning. This type of program can deal specifically with international ethical issues and with peculiarities at various plant locations. Second, an ethics program is useful when managers confront similar ethical problems on a regular basis, as Chemical Bank executives do. Third, these programs are useful in organizations that use outside consultants or advertising agencies. If an independent contractor does not subscribe to a corporate credo, the firm may want to use an ethical audit or checklist to heighten the outside agency's sensitivity to ethical issues.

When do ethics programs come up lacking? If they are too issue centered, ethics programs may miss other, equally important problems. (Dow's program, for example, depends on the questions raised by the audit.) In addition, the scope of the program may limit its impact to only certain parts of the organization (e.g., Chemical Bank). Managers who want to permanently inculcate ethical considerations may be concerned that such programs are not perceived by some employees as being long term or ongoing. If the credo can be compared with the Ten Commandments, then ethics programs can be likened to weekly church services. Both can be uplifting, but once the session (service) is over, individuals may believe they can go back to business as usual.

TAILORED CORPORATE CODES

Codes of conduct, or ethical codes, are another structural mechanism companies use to signal their commitment to ethical principles. Ninety percent of Fortune 500 firms, and almost half of all other firms, have ethical codes. According to a recent survey, this mechanism is perceived as the most effective way to encourage ethical business behavior.[4] Codes commonly address issues such as conflict of interest, competitors, privacy, gift giving and receiving, and political contributions. However, many observers continue to believe that codes are really public relations documents, or motherhood and apple pie statements; these critics claim that codes belittle employees and fail to address practical managerial issues.[5]

Simply developing a code is not enough. It must be tailored to the firm's functional areas (e.g., marketing, finance, personnel) or to the major line of business in which the firm operates. The rationale for tailored codes is simple. Functional areas or divisions have differing cultures and needs. A consumer products division, for example, has a relatively distant relationship with customers, because it relies heavily on advertising to sell its products. A division producing industrial products, on the other hand, has fewer customers and uses a personal, sales-oriented approach. A code needs to reflect these differences. Unfortunately, very few ethics codes do so.

Several companies have exemplary codes tailored to functional or major business areas. I describe two of these below—the St. Paul Companies (specializing in commercial and personal insurance and related products) and International Business Machines (IBM).

The St. Paul Companies [has an] extensive corporate code. . . . All new employees get introduced to the code when they join the company, and management devotes biannual meetings to discussing the code's impact on day-to-day activities. In each of the five sections, the code offers specific guidance and examples for employees to follow. The statements below illustrate the kinds of issues, and the level of specificity, contained in the code.

◆ Insider Information. For example, if you know that the company is about to announce a rise in quarterly profits, or anything else that would affect the price of the company's stock, you cannot buy or sell the stock until the announcement has been made and published.
◆ Gifts and Entertainment. An inexpensive ballpoint pen, or an appointment diary, is a common gift and generally acceptable. But liquor, lavish entertainment, clothing, or travel should not be accepted.
◆ Contact with Legislators. If you are contacted by legislators on matters relating to the St. Paul, you should refer them to your governmental affairs or law department.

The "Employee Related Issues" section of the code is the most detailed; it directly addresses the company's relationship to the individual, and vice versa. This section spells out what employ-ees can expect in terms of compensation (it should be based on job performance and administered fairly), advancement (promotion is from within, where possible), assistance (this consists of training, job experience, or counseling) and communications (there should be regular feedback; concerns can be expressed without fear of recrimination). It also articulates the St. Paul Companies' expectation of employees regarding speaking up (when you know something that could be a problem), avoiding certain actions (where the public's confidence could be weakened), and charting your career course.

The company also delineates employee privacy issues. The code outlines how work-related information needed for hiring and promotion is collected. (Only information needed to make the particular decision is gathered; it is collected from the applicant/employee where possible. . . .) The St. Paul informs employees about what types of information are maintained. Finally, information in an individual's file is open to the employee's review.

The code covers other important personnel issues in depth, as well. It touches on equal opportunity by mentioning discrimination laws, but the emphasis is on the company recognition of past discrimination and its commitments to "make an affirmative effort to address this situation in all of its programs and practices." Data acquired from the St. Paul supports this point. . . . In addition, the code informs employees that the company will reimburse all documented business expenses. And it covers nepotism by stating that officers' and directors' relatives will not be hired; other employees' relatives can be employed, so long as they are placed in different departments.

Being an ethical company requires providing clear guidelines for employees. The St. Paul Companies' extensive discussion of personnel policies does just that. Employees may strongly disapprove of certain policies, but they are fully informed. The termination policy, for example, states that employment is voluntary and that individuals are free to resign at any time; the company, too, can terminate employees "at any time, with or without cause." Some people may consider that policy unfair or punitive, but at least the rules of the game are clear. One limitation of the code is that all sections are not uniformly strong. For example, the marketing section is only one paragraph long and contains few specifics.

The second illustration is of a code tailored to the company's major line of business. IBM's "Business Conduct Guidelines" were instituted in the 1960s. . . . New employees receive a copy and certify annually that they abide by the code. It has four parts; the most extensive section is entitled "Conducting IBM's Business." Since IBM is, at its core, a marketing and sales organization, this section pertains primarily to these issues.

Six subsections detail the type of activities IBM expects of its sales representatives. First, "Some General Standards" include the following directives, with commentaries: do not make misrepresentations to anyone, do not take advantage of IBM's size, treat everyone fairly (do not extend preferential treatment), and do not practice reciprocal dealing. Second, "Fairness in the Field" pertains to disparagement (sell IBM products on their merits, not by disparaging competitors' products or services). In addition, it prohibits premature disclosure of product information and of selling if a competitor already has a signed order. Third, "Relations with Other Organizations" cautions employees about firms that have multiple relationships with IBM (deal with only one relationship at a time, and do not collaborate with these firms).

The fourth and fifth sections address "Acquiring and Using Information for or about Others." The code spells out the limits to acquiring information (industrial espionage is wrong) and to using information (adverse information should not be retained). Employees must determine the confidentiality of information gathered from others. The final section outlines IBM's policy on "Bribes, Gifts, and Entertainment." The company allows customary business amenities but prohibits giving presents that are intended to "unduly influence" or "obligate" the recipient, as well as receiving gifts worth more than a nominal amount.

One might contend that it is easy for a large, profitable company like IBM to have an exemplary code. On the other hand, one could also argue that a real reason for the company's continued success is that its sales representatives do subscribe to these principles. Is this a perfect code? No. The gifts area could use more specificity and, even though the company spends millions of dollars a year on advertising, that subject is not addressed in any section of the code. Further, IBM's legal department administers the code, which may mean that problems are resolved more by legal than ethical interpretation.

When should a company use a tailored code of ethics? If a company has one dominant functional unit (like IBM), or if there is diversity among functional areas, divisions, or subsidiaries, then a tailored code might be advisable. It allows the firm to promulgate specific and appropriate standards. Tailored codes are especially useful to complex organizations because they represent permanent guidelines for managers and employees to consult.

When should they be avoided? If a firm's leaders believe specific guidelines may be too restrictive for their employees, then a tailored code is an unsatisfactory choice. Codes are not necessary in most small firms or in ones where a culture includes firmly entrenched ethical policies. If a credo is similar to the Ten Commandments, and programs are similar to religious services, then tailored [codes] can be considered similar to the Bible or to other formal religious teachings. They provide the most guidance, but many people do not take the time to read or reflect on them.

CONCLUSION

My research on ethics in management suggests several conclusions that the corporate manager may wish to keep in mind.

◆ *There Is No Single Ideal Approach to Corporate Ethics.* I would recommend that a small firm start with a credo, but that a larger firm consider a program or a tailored code. It is also possible to integrate these programs and produce a hybrid: in dealing with insider trading, for example, a firm could develop a training program, then follow it up with a strongly enforced tailored code.[6]

◆ *Top Management Must Be Committed.* Senior managers must champion the highest ethical postures for their companies, as James Burke of J&J does. This commitment was evident in all the companies described here; it came through loud and clear in the CEOs' letters, reports, and public statements.

◆ *Developing a Structure Is Not Sufficient by Itself.* The structure will not be useful unless it is supported by institutionalized managerial processes. The . . . seminars at Chemical Bank are examples of processes that support structures.

◆ *Raising the Ethical Consciousness of an Organization Is Not Easy.* All the companies mentioned here have spent countless hours—and substantial amounts of money—developing, discussing, revising, and communicating the ethical principles of the firm. And in fact there are no guarantees that it will work. McDonnell Douglas has an extensive ethics program, but some of its executives were implicated in a . . . defense contractor scandal.

In conclusion, let me add that managers in firms with active ethics structures—credos, programs, and tailored codes—are genuinely enthusiastic about them. They believe that ethics pay off. Their conviction should provide others with an encouraging example. ◆ ◆ ◆

◆ References

1. P. E. Murphy and M. G. Dunn, "Corporate Culture and Marketing Management Ethics" (Notre Dame, IN: University of Notre Dame, working paper, 1988).

2. A more detailed discussion of Chemical's comprehensive program, and of Johnson & Johnson's, appears in *Corporate Ethics: A Prime Business Asset* (New York: Business Roundtable, February 1988).

3. One of the case studies appears in "Would You Blow Whistle on Wayward Colleague?" *American Banker*, 17 June 1988, p. 16.

4. Touche Ross, *Ethics in American Business* (New York: Touche Ross & Co., January 1988).

5. [R. E. Berenbeim, *Corporate Ethics* (New York: The Conference Board, Research Report no. 900,] 1987), p. 17.

6. G. L. Tidwell, "Here's a Tip—Know the Rules of Insider Trading," *Sloan Management Review*, Summer 1987, pp. 93–99.

What Can We Learn from the U.S. Federal Sentencing Guidelines for Organizational Ethics?

Dove Izraeli and Mark S. Schwartz

The 1991 federal sentencing guidelines represent a sea change in the way corporations treat ethics in the workplace. Prior to their enactment, wrongdoing was akin to a speed trap on a highway. When there was an egregious breach of the law, the firm was taken to court and fined. The penalties often represented only a fraction of the cost of the offense; a firm might embezzle $100,000 from the government, for example, and only be fined $20,000. Among other failings, inappropriate sentencing did not act as a deterrent.

After the guidelines were introduced, firms were treated as corporate citizens, with an obligation to promote compliance with the law and their own code of conduct. Firms who ignored these requirements could face damages multiplied several times, whereas companies that showed active monitoring and compliance would have their fines substantially reduced. The guidelines have had a dramatic effect on making firms proactive rather than reactive in their ethical stance.

In this article, Izraeli and Schwartz give an overview of the guidelines and their effect on American business. After reading the selection, decide if you agree with their conclusion that this legal model could be usefully exported to other countries.

PART ONE—THE U.S. FEDERAL SENTENCING GUIDELINES

INTRODUCTION

In November, 1991, an innovative piece of legislation was enacted in the United States which had a profound effect on corporate America (Izraeli, 1997). The legislation, referred to as the U.S. Federal Sentencing Guidelines ("Guidelines"), used "the stick and the carrot" approach to create . . . incentives for thousands of corporations to create or modify their compliance (ethics) programs.

The Guidelines were developed by the United States Sentencing Commission, a new govern-mental body which came into existence in 1984. The Commission was charged with the responsibility for creating uniformity in the sentencing of offenders of federal laws. Following the promulgation of Guidelines in 1987 for sentencing individuals convicted of federal offenses, the Commission proceeded to create Guidelines for organizations which were to become law in 1991 (Kaplan [et al.], 1993, pp. 136–137). The Guidelines (discussed in greater detail below) consisted essentially of a manual for judges to consider when determining the appropriate sentence for corporations convicted of a federal crime. Judges were being asked for the first time to consider whether the convicted corporation had established an "effective compliance program" prior to the violation taking place, in other words, whether the corporation had taken appropriate steps to prevent and detect violations of the law.

According to Win Swinsen, the former Deputy General Counsel of the Sentencing Commission, one of the primary reasons for the enactment of sentencing guidelines for organizations was that the U.S. government lacked a clear corporate crime sentencing and enforcement policy. As a result, judges were having great difficulty in finding meaningful ways to sentence corporations. Empirical research conducted by the Sentencing Commission on corporate sentencing practices demonstrated that ". . . corporate sentencing was in disarray . . . nearly identical cases were treated differently." In addition, average fines were found to be ". . . less than the cost corporations had to pay to obey the law" (Sentencing Commission, 1995, p. 30).

To address these concerns, the Commission eventually came to accept the "carrot and stick" approach to corporate sentencing. This approach was based on three principal and related objectives: (1) to define a model for good corporate citizenship; (2) to use the model to make corporate sentencing fair by providing objective, defined criteria; and (3) to use the model to create incentives for companies to take crime-controlling actions. The final objective was designed to shift from the previous "speed trap" enforcement policy of the past (i.e., merely lie and wait for corporate offenders and then fine them), to a more interactive approach. By providing financial incentives, the government was inviting companies to undertake effective, crime-controlling actions which in turn would put less pressure on already limited government enforcement resources (Sentencing Guidelines, 1995, p. 34).

Since the enactment of the law, hundreds of corporations have been prosecuted under the Guidelines, some suffering fines and penalties in the tens and even hundreds of millions of dollars. Empirical evidence is now suggesting that the implementation of these programs is raising the level of legal and ethical behavior in corporations. Somewhat surprisingly, despite their impact and apparent success, the Guidelines appear to remain somewhat of a mystery to non-U.S. countries and corporations (Izraeli, 1995).

It may be the case that the time has arrived for countries other than the U.S. to consider the development of legislation similar to the Guidelines, using the Guidelines as a model or framework to follow. To make this argument, this paper will consist of two parts. Part one discusses the Guidelines in general, their purpose, impact, utilization by the U.S. courts, and effectiveness in achieving their objectives. Part two discusses why the time has arrived for other countries to consider the Guidelines due to foreign companies operating in the U.S., the development of a globalized business community, and a changing regulatory environment.

The paper will conclude by suggesting the potential benefits for other countries in adopting legislation similar to the Guidelines, the current limitations of the Guidelines and how they might be addressed, and finally an initial implementation strategy for countries to utilize in designing their own respective legislation.

(1) What Are the Guidelines?

According to the Guidelines, any organization is liable to sentencing, fines, and to periods of probation for federal offenses connected with antitrust, securities, bribery, fraud, money laundering, criminal business activities, extortion and embezzlement, conspiracy, and others. The preamble to the Guidelines states that the organization operates only through its agents, usually its managers, and is, therefore, liable for the offenses committed by them. Naturally, the managers are personally responsible and liable for their own behavior. The innovation of the Guidelines lies in the fact that the sentences imposed on the organization and its agents are designed to achieve the following objectives: (a) just punishment; (b) sufficient deterrence; and (c) encourage the development of internal mechanisms to prevent, identify and report on criminal behavior in organizations (i.e., through a "carrot and stick" approach).

To assist corporations in knowing exactly what constitutes an appropriate internal mechanism, the Guidelines list seven elements indicating what is considered an "effective compliance program." These elements include but are not limited to the following: (1) compliance standards and procedures (e.g., a code of conduct or ethics); (2) oversight by high-level personnel (e.g., a compliance or ethics officer); (3) due care when delegating authority; (4) effective communication of standards and procedures (e.g., training); (5) auditing/monitoring systems and reporting mechanisms (e.g., a "hotline"); (6) enforcement of disciplinary mechanisms; and (7) appropriate response after detection (Kaplan [et al.], 1993, pp. 138–142).

To achieve the objectives, the Guidelines provide the following measures: (1) the organization is required to remedy all damage that it has caused and to pay a fine based on the severity of the offense and the degree of guilt of the offender. Moreover, probation periods are set to ensure that the punishment is indeed implemented and that the organization has taken steps to reduce the probability that the offense will be repeated; (2) the Guidelines include a schedule of prison sentences for the agents of the organization and fines on the organization and its agents. The base level of prison sentences is up to three years and the fines are up to $72.5 million. All sentences are also liable to a probation period to ensure that remedial action has been taken or to continue investigations. The level of the sentence is liable to be increased substantially, depending upon the past behavior of the offender, so that the maximum fine may reach up to $290 million, or even higher in some instances (the "stick" approach); (3) an organization that proves it has developed an effective program for preventing offenses and has begun implementing the program prior to the offense is eligible to have its fines and punishments reduced by over 95% (the "carrot" approach).

(2) Impact of Guidelines

Although the Guidelines have been in existence for only half a decade, they have already had a significant impact on corporate America. As determined by a number of surveys, the primary impact has been the creation or enhancement of compliance or ethics programs by thousands of companies across the United States, and even outside of the U.S.

In some cases, the Guidelines have provided a model for the entire compliance or ethics program. For example, the Bank of Tokyo has made the Guidelines "the focal point of its overall compliance effort" (U.S. Sentencing Commission, 1995, p. 63). According to the bank, the Guidelines gave them ". . . a clear picture of what a compliance program should look like and a set of instructions on how to construct a program." The bank also found that ". . . virtually every compliance directive we received, regardless of the source, fit comfortably within the structure that is suggested by the [seven elements for compliance]" (U.S. Sentencing Commission, 1995, p. 65). In addition to the Tokyo Bank, other New York-area banks as well as a Canadian bank, the CIBC, ". . . have begun to use the guidelines as a foundation for their overall compliance efforts" (U.S. Sentencing Commission, 1995, p. 67).

Other companies, even if they already had some sort of compliance or ethics program in place before 1991, have indicated that the Guidelines were one of the factors which influenced the enhancement of already existing ethics programs. According to "A National Study of Compliance Practices" which involved 333 corporations representing various sizes and industries, 44 percent of the respondents stated that the Guidelines caused them to add vigor to their compliance programs, while 20 percent added compliance programs because of their awareness of the Guidelines (U.S. Sentencing Commission, 1995, p. 134). According to Andrew Apel, the author of the study, ". . . certainly, the guidelines are having a significant impact on what organizations are doing to prevent and detect violations of law" (U.S. Sentencing Commission, 1995, p. 129). Another study by the Council of Ethical Organizations of approximately 750,000 employees from 203 large U.S. companies also found that the Guidelines have had an influence on corporate ethics programs. The survey found that 38 percent of the companies significantly improved their ethics compliance environments following the enactment of the Guidelines (U.S. Sentencing Commission, 1995, p. 178).

Unfortunately, the studies did not break down the impact of the Guidelines on individual components of ethics programs. Despite this gap, one can assume that the Guidelines have had the greatest impact on four components: (1) ethics training; (2) ethics officers; (3) ethics offices; and (4) ethics hotlines. Each of these components can be related to one of the seven elements of an effective compliance program as stipulated by the Guidelines. It should be noted, however, that one component in particular, a code of ethics, has not come into existence merely as a result of the Guidelines. As several studies have indicated, the vast majority of large companies (93 percent) already had a code of ethics in place by 1990 (Center For Business Ethics, 1992).

(3) Utilization by Courts

The Guidelines have clearly had an impact on the establishment or enhancement of corporate ethics programs. One of the reasons for this achievement is that in case of an offense the size of the fine is conditional on the existence of a compliance or ethics program.

According to the U.S. Sentencing Commission Annual Report, in 1995, 111 organizational defendants were sentenced according to the Guidelines, with 83 cases subject to the Guidelines' fine provisions. This was an increase from 1994 which saw only 86 corporate Guidelines' sentencings. In 1994 the average fine was $420,000, with the average fraud fine about $1 million and the highest single fine $15.5 million (which involved an environmental fraud offense) (Kaplan, 1995, p. 1).

The Guidelines have had an even more significant impact on probation. Fifty-eight percent of companies sentenced during 1994 were placed on probation, with 20 percent of these being ordered to implement compliance programs. The Guidelines were to have less of an impact on compliance programs and corporate fines. Only four of the prosecutions during 1994 involved a direct consideration of the defendant's compliance program by the court. In one case, the fine was reduced on the basis of the company being held to have an effective compliance program (Kaplan, 1995, p. 1). This situation was to change dramatically in February, 1996. In what was the largest criminal fine in U.S. history, a Manhattan federal court sentenced Daiwa Bank to pay a fine of $340 million under the Guidelines. The case involved a bank employee who lost $1.1 billion in unauthorized trades. The two main reasons for the fine were the bank's "lack of a meaningful compliance program" and its "consequent failure to report the employee's wrong-doing" (Kaplan, 1996, p. 1).

Another development which has been noted due to the Guidelines is being referred to as "the shadow effect." Essentially, the Guidelines are also being considered by courts and government agencies in criminal cases other than those brought under the Guidelines. Companies such as National Medical Enterprises (involving kickbacks) (now Tenet Healthcare), Lucas Aerospace (involving falsifying test data), and C. R. Bard (involving fraud) were all ordered to adopt extensive compliance programs in addition to paying fines. Even civil cases such as Prudential Securities (involving fraud) or Grumman Corporation (involving kickbacks) were ordered to implement compliance programs, which were much more onerous than if conducted voluntarily (Kaplan, 1995, pp. 2–3).

(4) *Effectiveness of Guidelines*

It can be seen from the above discussion that the Guidelines have had an impact on the creation and implementation of ethics programs, and have actually been utilized by the courts in assessing fines and placing companies on probation. Despite this impact, one could ask a more fundamental question: "Have the Guidelines helped to achieve their ultimate purpose, the reduction of corporate crime and an improvement in ethical behavior?"

Although it may be some time before we can know the answer to this question with any degree of certainty, a study released by the Ethics Resource Center entitled, "Ethics in American Business: Policies, Programs and Perceptions" provides an initial indication that ethics programs are beneficial in improving organizational ethics. The survey examined employee attitudes and behavior in relation to the existence of three components of an ethics program: (1) codes of conduct, (2) the introduction of ethics into employee and management training, and (3) the establishment of ethics and compliance offices. Over 4,000 U.S. workers were surveyed representing different levels of responsibility, job functions, company size, and industries (Ethics Resource Center, 1994).

The survey indicates that ethics programs appear to improve ethical behavior. The results are summarized as follows:

Corporate ethics programs appear to have a distinctly positive impact on employee behavior and their opinions about the ethics of fellow employees, management, their companies and even themselves. The most positive effects were reported in companies which had all three program components—codes of conduct, ethics training, and ethics offices. Striking differences could be seen in the responses of employees in companies with comprehensive ethics programs and the responses of those in companies with no program elements or with only a code of conduct. Indeed, a code of conduct as the sole element of an ethics effort often seemed to have a negative effect on employee perceptions. Ethics initiatives appeared to increase employee awareness of misconduct, employee willingness to report misconduct, and the level of satisfaction with the outcome of their reporting (Ethics Resource Center, 1994, p. 6).

Another study by the Council of Ethical Organizations of 750,000 employees from large U.S. corporations found that, "Employees of companies that had implemented or fortified comprehensive ethics compliance programs in response to the guidelines . . . reported that they were less likely to violate laws and policies" (Sentencing Commission, 1995, p. 178).

There are a few cautionary notes to consider, however, regarding the noted above studies.

Although studies have shown that corporations have enhanced their ethics programs because of the Guidelines, and that companies with a comprehensive ethics program appear to have a higher level of ethical behavior, one cannot necessarily make the conclusion that the Guidelines are responsible for improved ethical behavior. . . . In any event, the evidence to date indicates that the Guidelines have had an influence on ethics programs which appear to lead to improved ethical behavior in organizations.

PART TWO—COULD OTHER COUNTRIES BENEFIT FROM ADOPTING LEGISLATION SIMILAR TO THE GUIDELINES?

There are numerous reasons to suggest why the time has arrived for countries around the world to consider adopting legislation similar to the Guidelines. These reasons include foreign companies operating in the U.S., the development of a globalized business environment, and a changing regulatory environment around the world.

(5) Foreign Companies Currently Operating in the U.S.

Most large corporations in the world currently conduct business in the U.S. Many of these companies will establish U.S. subsidiaries with branch offices or factories located in the U.S. or obtain U.S. supplied financing and list their shares on American stock exchanges. For these companies, there is a direct and immediate reason to create compliance or ethics programs, regardless whether their home country has created any legislative incentives to do so. Failure to create programs for the U.S. based operation can result in financial penalties which could otherwise be avoided. Daiwa Bank, as discussed above, is an excellent example of a company which suf-

fered by not having implemented an appropriate compliance or ethics program.

According to Jeff Kaplan, the Daiwa Bank lesson is especially important for foreign companies doing business in the U.S., ". . . [T]he entire disaster occurred not because the bank was greedy or malevolent, but simply because it failed to accord due weight to U.S. regulatory mandates" (Kaplan, 1996, p. 11). According to Lori Tansey, president of the International Business Ethics Institute, "Without question many foreign companies doing business in the United States fail to understand the requirements of United States law. Most are not aware of the sentencing guidelines or their implications" (Kaplan, 1996, p. 11). If this is the case, non-U.S. companies will continue to suffer by not taking into consideration the potential impact of the Guidelines.

For those countries with companies operating in the U.S., there is then a direct benefit to adopting legislation similar to the Guidelines. Non-U.S. corporations would have an automatic incentive to create compliance or ethics programs in their home country, and if the programs are applicable to operations in the U.S., these corporations would gain automatic protection from non-compliance when doing business in the U.S. Unfortunately for some non-U.S. companies, such as Daiwa Bank, they had to learn their lesson the hard way.

(6) Changing Business Environment: Globalization

One can point to the changing business environment around the world as a major motivator for countries to consider implementing legislation similar to the Guidelines. Clearly, the business world is becoming a smaller place. According to Lori Tansey, "the most significant development in today's business world is globalization" (Tansey, 1995, p. 1). Several world trading blocks have been established, such as NAFTA (North

American Free Trade Agreement) and the EU (European Union). International sales by U.S. multinationals were over $1 trillion in 1991 (Tansey, 1995, p. 1). Other evidence of globalization includes the growth of multinational corporations and international joint ventures. Changing technologies such as the internet, e-mail, fax, and video conferencing continue to make the world a smaller place where communication anywhere around the world is almost instantaneous. As the international corporate world becomes more closely interconnected, the obligations of multinational corporations to take measures to comply with worldwide legislation increase.

Another development over the years has been the increasing internationalization of ethical standards. According to DeGeorge, "the growth of multinationals and the closer integration of U.S. and non-U.S. firms makes all the more necessary the development of business ethics on an international scale" (DeGeorge, 1987, p. 209). Several initiatives have demonstrated the need to generate consensus around the world on the issue of ethical standards. For example, Getz (1990) has pointed to four international codes which multinational corporations are required to follow: (1) the International Chamber of Commerce (ICC); (2) the Organization for Economic Cooperation and Development (OECD); (3) the International Labour Organization (ILO); and (4) the United Nations Commission on Transnational Corporations (UN/CTC).

The Caux Principles, created by leaders from the Japanese, European, and U.S. business communities, emphasize the growing importance of international ethical standards:

The Caux Round Table believes that the world business community should play an important role in improving economic and social conditions. As a statement of aspirations, this document aims to express a world standard against which business behavior can be measured. [They] seek to begin a process that identifies shared values, reconciles differing values, and thereby develops a shared perspective on business behavior acceptable to and honored by all (Caux Round Table, 1994, p. 2).

In addition to international codes, organizations devoted to encouraging international standards of ethical conduct have emerged. Transparency International, based in Berlin, Germany, is an organization which was established to focus on grand corruption in international business transactions. One of the goals is ". . . practical change, in laws, institutions and policies, that will drastically reduce the incidence of corruption in the future" (Transparency International, 1996, p. 7). By the end of 1995, the organization had over fifty national chapters established or in progress around the world (Transparency International, 1996, p. 7).

These developments of globalized business and acceptable international business conduct serve to reinforce the impetus for countries around [the] world to both individually and collectively . . . work together in creating incentives for the corporations to establish compliance or ethics programs designed to reduce corporate crime and unethical activity. Developing legislation similar to the Guidelines would provide that incentive to the international corporate world.

(7) Changing Regulatory Environment: Other Countries

Is the United States the only country in the world to have developed legislation which creates incentives for corporations to adopt compliance or ethics programs? A survey of three political entities, Europe, Australia, and Canada, indicates that these areas of the world have already developed or are in the process of developing measures which in some respects even go beyond those of the U.S. Sentencing Guidelines.

Europe has already taken steps to create incentives for companies to establish compliance programs. The Commission of the European Union has mitigated the penalties for firms for a number of years when they have been found to have compliance programs with respect to competition law (Tansey, 1995, p. 1).

Australia may be the world leader, at least on paper, in terms of corporate compliance initiatives. Two pieces of legislation are particularly significant. The first is the Australian Trade Practices Act, enacted in 1986, which regulates such activities as antitrust or misleading advertising. According to the Act, "an effective compliance program can constitute a corporate defense" and is also a key factor in the assessment of the penalty. Not only sound policies and procedures must be adopted, but the corporation must also actively supervise and enforce these policies (Tansey, 1995, p. 2). Australia also took a major step in 1994 by amending its Criminal Code (assented to on March 15, 1995). One of the key provisions of the Code now states that a corporation can be criminally responsible if it is established that "a corporate culture existed within the body corporate that directed, encouraged, tolerated or led to non-compliance with the relevant provision" or by showing that "the body corporate failed to create and maintain a corporate culture that required compliance with the relevant provision." [Criminal Code Bill 1994, Part 2.5, Division 12, Section 12.3(2) (c and d)]. What is substantially different about this legislation is that it relates directly to liability, and not merely the sentencing of corporations as does the U.S. Sentencing Guidelines.

Canada is somewhat behind the U.S., Europe, and Australia, but is catching up quickly. The Canadian government is now beginning to recognize the importance and value of encouraging companies to develop compliance systems. A recent Consultation Draft Bulletin from the Canadian Competition Bureau, which regulates the Canadian Competition Act (e.g., bid-rigging, price discrimination, misleading advertising), looks remarkably similar to the U.S. Federal Sentencing Guidelines in recommending that companies establish an "effective compliance program" with respect to the Act. By doing so, the draft Bulletin suggests that companies may benefit in terms of alternative case resolutions, immunity and sentencing recommendations, and due diligence defences. The fact that the program relates not only to sentencing but to actual defences is an aspect which goes beyond the U.S. Guidelines. An "effective compliance program" is defined as including five components: (1) the involvement and support of senior management; (2) development of relevant policies and procedures; (3) on-going education of management and employees; (4) monitoring and audit mechanisms; and (5) disciplinary mechanisms (Schwartz, 1996, p. 7).

One of the most potentially significant developments in the Canadian legal context for corporate compliance and ethics to date are the recent proposals to amend the Canadian Criminal Code. A consultation paper has been issued which asks for comments on the following question: "Should corporate criminal liability be . . . based on 'corporate culture'?" (Schwartz, 1996, p. 7). The new Criminal Code section would read as follows: "A corporation commits an offense when there exists within the corporation an attitude, policy, or practice that directed, encouraged, tolerated or led to the offense, or that failed to require its representatives to comply with the law" (Department of Justice Canada, 1994, p. 27). Similar to the Australian Criminal Code, if the Canadian Criminal Code is amended to include such a provision, compliance programs would relate directly to liability, and not merely sentencing or potential defences to liability.

All of these countries have moved to some degree, and in some respects even beyond the U.S. Sentencing Guidelines. This worldwide trend combined with the increasing globalization of business serves as an impetus for other countries to consider the development of legislation similar to the Guidelines.

(8) Benefits of Adopting Guidelines

Would the Guidelines serve a purpose in the rest of the world? One does not have to look too far to find evidence of the extent and cost of corporate fraud and corruption around the world. A survey by KPMG found that "fraud is a significant problem for companies around the world" (KPMG, 1996, p. 4). The survey included a total of 18 countries representing North America, Asia, Europe, Australia, Africa, and the Middle East. The survey found that 52% of respondents stated that they had experienced fraud in the past year, with 48% believing that fraud is a major problem for their business today and over 50% believing that fraud will continue to increase (KPMG, 1996, p. 4). An Ethics Resource Center study found that 31% of the U.S. employees surveyed had observed misconduct at work in the last year which violated the law or company policy. Of those employees who did observe misconduct, fewer than half actually reported such misconduct to an appropriate person in the company (Ethics Resource Center, 1994, p. 23). One might speculate whether the same situation exists in other countries of the world, suggesting that worldwide corporate misconduct is even more pervasive than current surveys suggest.

There have been several estimates of the total cost of fraud. One commentator suggests that "white-collar crime is conservatively estimated to cost businesses well in excess of $100 billion per year" (Driscoll et al., 1995, p. 233). The KPMG survey suggests that ". . . fraud costs corporations worldwide billions of dollars each year" (KPMG, 1996, p. 10). A similar international study by Ernst and Young found that over one quarter of businesses surveyed had lost over $1 million (U.S.) in total due to fraud (Ernst and Young, 1996, p. 1).

Assuming that the Sentencing Guidelines create economic incentives for corporations to adopt measures to reduce corporate crime, fraud, corruption, and improve ethical behavior, then almost all stakeholders may benefit. Corporations benefit by reducing the extent of corporate crime and unethical activity, meaning the preservation of corporate assets, and to have illegal or unethical activity reported internally before reaching the court system or the media. Consumers benefit by not being forced to bear the costs of unethical activity by employees. Employees benefit by having the corporation provide the means through compliance and ethics programs by which employees are able to do what they know is right and legal, and not to feel pressured to act otherwise. Governments benefit by creating an economic incentive for corporations to self-regulate themselves, relieving much of the burden from enforcement agencies. Society is the net beneficiary of less corporate crime and unethical activity, as potentially hundreds of billions in economic benefits are generated as a result, leading to an overall increase in both the global standard of living and quality of life.

One of the advantages of the Guideline's approach is that motivation for adopting compliance or ethics programs is not necessarily an issue. Although U.S. courts may consider whether the company has adopted the program as mere window dressing, and is not really enforcing its standards, it really does not matter whether the company is complying only because of the Guidelines, or because it is the right thing to do. It may even be the case that even if companies adopt programs as a type of insurance policy, they may eventually come to see that there is an ethical justification for adopting such programs. What is evident is that it is easier to convince senior management to spend money to create a compliance or ethics program when there is an external economic incentive for doing so. Later, after seeing the program in effect, senior management would be in a position to see the intangible and the economic benefits of having such a program in place.

Another advantage of the Guidelines is that they only suggest a minimum framework for setting up an "effective compliance program." Companies can and probably should go beyond the seven elements listed. This approach would be easily transferable to other countries in the world. The flexibility of the approach would enable countries to develop their own recommended elements. For example, the Canadian government lists only five elements in their list of components of an "effective compliance program." What companies have found most helpful about the Guidelines, however, is that at least, they provide a definition of what constitutes an acceptable compliance program.

(9) Limitations of Guidelines

Despite the potential benefits for other countries of adopting something similar to the Guidelines, there are still a number of potential limitations to the Guidelines which must be recognized and addressed. One possible criticism of the Guidelines is that they really only create an incentive for companies to create legal compliance programs. In other words, although the Guidelines are often mentioned in conjunction with ethics programs, companies are really only being required to adopt measures which require employees to follow the law, and not necessarily engage in activity which goes "beyond the law." A secondary problem is that companies may end up creating codes of ethics which are essentially le-gal documents, which are more difficult to understand and less accepted by employees (Sentencing Commission, 1995, p. 177).

It is somewhat understandable that the Guidelines take this approach. To make a pronouncement that companies must create a program which leads to employees acting "beyond the law" or "ethically" and will be rewarded for doing so would not necessarily serve a purpose, and may no longer be functional. In addition, several companies are finding that although they might begin with a legal compliance approach, over time they shift the emphasis of their programs to an ethics, values, or integrity approach. For example, Levi Strauss and Co., which began with a lengthy code of ethics, has shifted to a one page statement of their values and principles (Raiborn and Payne, 1990, p. 883). Other companies are finding that a combined legal compliance and ethics approach is the best route to go. In any event, one can argue that a company with a legal or compliance program is better than one without any program.

Another potential limitation or weakness of the Guidelines is that they only relate to compliance with U.S. federal law, of a criminal nature. The Guidelines do not relate to state law or civil litigation. The Guidelines also only relate to sentencing (e.g., fines or probation), as opposed to possible defences to liability or actual liability itself. As observed above, other countries such as Australia and Canada may relate compliance or ethics initiatives directly to liability and to possible defences which can be raised. It has also been the case that U.S. state courts and courts considering civil litigation matters are also beginning to take direction from the Guidelines. All of this activity provides a certain degree of assurance that other countries, in adopting legislation similar to the Guidelines, have the ability to determine the range of activity which their legislation would cover. . . .

An argument may be raised that suggesting that other countries consider the development of legislation similar to the U.S. Guidelines is just a further continuation of the imposition of U.S. legal/ethical norms or standards upon other jurisdictions, or at least the emulation of such norms or standards. This may be one reason why it has been difficult for other countries in the world to adopt legislation similar to the U.S. Foreign Corrupt Practices Act. For many countries, there may be an automatic resistance to following any legislative model being used by the U.S. . . .

A further limitation to the Guidelines being adopted by other countries is that multinational corporations are going to be faced with a situation involving an even more pronounced conflict of laws or ethical norms. For example, if one of the requirements is to create a code of ethics, how would a company deal with the wide range of laws and ethical norms which exist throughout the world?

This limitation may be less problematic than it appears on its surface. Multinationals are already addressing such concerns by modifying their corporate codes of ethics to adjust to situational concerns. Although many like to argue that ethics vary across the world, others point out that there may be greater consensus on what activity is considered ethical or unethical than is currently accepted. For example, although certain countries of the world are known to be prone to extensive bribery, ". . . there is no country in the world where bribery is either legally or morally acceptable" (Heimann, 1994, p. 7).

(10) Implementation Strategy

The discussion above is designed to provide readers with a basic understanding of the Sentencing Guidelines, their purpose, impact, effectiveness, and arguments to support their adoption by other countries around the world. Clearly, the actual implementation strategy will depend on a number of factors to be considered by the respective governments. The following is a possible checklist of initial considerations in developing an implementation strategy:

◆ What is the current extent of corporate crime and unethical activity? Are we concerned about these levels and their impact on society?
◆ What type of political system is in effect? Is there sufficient political support and will for the adoption of this type of legislation? Which government department or departments are best suited to administer this type of legislation?
◆ How developed is our legal framework (e.g., legislation, court system)? If the legislation is adopted, will it be enforced (i.e., considered by the courts or administrative tribunals)?
◆ What are the current cultural and religious norms in effect? Should these norms be considered when making recommendations as to what constitutes an "effective compliance program"?

CONCLUSION

All of society stands to benefit from a reeducation in corporate crime and unethical activity. The U.S. Federal Sentencing Guidelines provide a model which to date appears to be successful in achieving this goal. Other countries around the world, including Australia, Europe, and Canada, have already adopted or are in the process of adopting similar legislation.

Hopefully the success of the Guidelines will encourage other countries to consider developing their own legislative incentives for corporations to abide by the law and engage in activities to promote the level of ethics in all organizations. ◆ ◆ ◆

◆ References

[Caux Round Table: 1994, 'The Caux Principles,' www.cauxroundtable.org.]

Center for Business Ethics: 1992, 'Instilling Ethical Values in Large Corporations', *The Journal of Business Ethics* 11, 863–867.

DeGeorge, R. T.: 1987, 'The Status of Business Ethics: Past and Future', *Journal of Business Ethics* 6, 201–211.

Department of Justice Canada and J. W. O'Reilly: 1994: 'Toward A New General Part of the Criminal Code of Canada: Details on Reform Options'.

Driscoll, D. M., W. M. Hoffman and E. S. Petry: 1995: *Ethical Edge* (MasterMedia Limited, New York).

Ernst and Young: 1996, 'Fraud: The Managed Risk' (May).

[Ethics Resource Center: 1994, 'Ethics in American Business Survey', www.ethics.org.]

Getz, K. A.: 1990, 'International Codes of Conduct: An Analysis of Ethical Reasoning', *Journal of Business Ethics* 9(7), 567–577.

Heimann, F. F.: 1994, 'Should Foreign Bribery be a Crime?' presented at the Conference on Bribery in International Trade, Milan, Italy (November 8).

Izraeli, D.: 1995, 'Impact of the U.S. Sentencing Guidelines on Organizations', 3rd International Jerusalem Conference on Ethics in the Public Service, June 25–29, 1995.

Izraeli, D.: 1997, 'Promoting Business Ethics Through Legislation', in Dove Izraeli and Noam Zohar (eds.), *Ethics and Social Responsibility—Israeli Studies* (Hebrew), Tel-Aviv, Tscherikover Publishers-Gomeh Scientific Publications.

Kaplan, J. M.: 1995, 'The Sentencing Guidelines: A 'Still Developing' Picture', *Ethikos* 9(1) (July/August).

Kaplan, J. M.: 1996, 'Why Daiwa Bank Will Pay $340 million under the Sentencing Guidelines', *Ethikos* 9(6) (May/June).

Kaplan, J. M., L. S. Dakin and M. R. Smolin: 1993, 'Living With the Organizational Sentencing Guidelines', *California Management Review* 36(1), 136–146.

KPMG: 1996, 'International Fraud Report' (April).

Raiborn, C. A. and D. Payne: 1990, 'Corporate Codes of Conduct: A Collective Conscience and Continuum,' *Journal of Business Ethics* 9, 879–889.

Schwartz, M.: 1996, 'Corporate Compliance and Ethical Decision Making in Canada', *Corporate Conduct Quarterly* 5(6), 6–7, 17.

Tansey, L.: 1995, 'Corporate Compliance Programs: International Implications', *Corporate Conduct Quarterly* 4(2).

Transparency International: 1996, Annual Report.

U.S. Sentencing Commission: 1995, 'Corporate Crime in America: Strengthening the "Good Citizen" Corporation,' Proceedings of the Second Symposium on Crime and Punishment in the United States, Washington, D.C. (September 7–8).

Breach of Trust
Leadership in a Market Economy

Roger Leeds

In the 1990s very few people questioned business practice in America: It was prosperous, and everyone seemed to be doing well. However, at the turn of the millennium investor confidence was shaken by a series of high-profile corporate scandals. The government response was to hastily enact legislation, the Sarbanes-Oxley Act of 2002, designed to make executives more accountable and the company dealings more transparent. Leeds gives a brief history of factors that led to the scandals and then goes through some of the main provisions of the act. But, as he asks, can we legislate morality? The wrongdoing of these scandals was apparently not deterred by the legislation in force at the time. Is it a question of closing loopholes? Or of altering the moral climate in business? If so, how can we promote executive integrity?

If leadership is about setting an example that others seek to emulate, who could argue with the proven track record of sustained economic success in the United States? During the boom years of the 1990s, it was hard to find fault with the country's economic performance. With the stock markets breaking records on a daily basis and the economy reveling in the longest period of uninterrupted growth in the post-war era, the United States could rightfully claim the mantle of undisputed global leader in creating and practicing a brand of capitalism that was the envy of much of the world. Although far from perfect, at the core of the US economic model was an elaborate network of institutions and individuals who presumably practiced the virtues of fairness and transparency while maintaining a so-called level playing field—precisely the qualities that serve as the foundation for competitive markets and sustainable economic growth. Largely because of these characteristics, corporate access to investment capital—the fuel that drives private sector performance in any economy—was broader and deeper by far in the United States than any other country.

Regardless of the country or culture, a prerequisite for market efficiency is public trust—trust in a system where investor decisions are based on reasonably accurate and complete corporate disclosure, where all participants have equal access to information, and where the laws and regulations governing market behavior are effective and enforced. These are the underpinnings that allow investors and regulators to make comparative assessments about risk, price, and performance of those seeking to raise capital in the marketplace. In a market economy, trust is embodied most prominently in an interconnected network of public and private institutions that conveniently fall into three categories: the main government agencies that set the rules of the game for corporate and financial market behavior and monitor their performance, such as the regulators of securities markets and banks; the private sector self-regulating bodies that set standards for acceptable conduct within specific professions, such as accounting, law and banking; and perhaps most importantly, the companies themselves, along with their independent directors, outside legal counsel and financial advisors. The model works at its best when the investing public, the suppliers of capital, has confidence in the competence and integrity of these institutions, as well as in the individuals in key leadership positions who set the standards defining how these institutions operate on a day-to-day basis. The overpowering strength of the US economy, especially during the 1990s, seemed to provide the ultimate validation that the model worked like a finely tuned machine and enjoyed a high level of public confidence.

The credibility of this premise, however, has been seriously damaged by the flood of revelations describing corporate misconduct that began when Enron declared bankruptcy in December 2001. Although the alarm was first sounded in the United States, where the scandals rapidly seemed to take on epidemic proportions, similar headlines exposing corporate chicanery soon began to appear regularly in country after country. The cumulative evidence began to suggest convincingly that this was not simply a story of one or two rogue corporations and their advisors circumventing the rules of the game, or a one-off breakdown by public institutions responsible for oversight and supervision of financial markets. Instead, there appeared to be a systemic erosion of governance standards and practices on all three levels of institutional responsibility: government agencies demonstrably failed to effectively monitor corporate and financial market behavior, the self-regulators were far more intent on protecting than monitoring the performance of their professional members, and corporate executives were enriching themselves at the expense of their shareholders, apparently with the acquiescence of their boards and outside financial and legal advisors. The eruption of scandal

raised serious and challenging questions about the effectiveness of the public and corporate governance practices that are at the heart of the model that drives market economies everywhere. These are the rules, standards, and enforcement mechanisms that define how corporate and financial managers disclose material information to investors and regulators, and how they are held accountable. Each revelation . . . provided a graphic reminder that effective governance is critical to the functioning of a market economy. Absent disclosure and accountability, as the scandals demonstrated, public confidence evaporates and the self-correcting magic of the marketplace is unable to function.

WHAT WENT WRONG?

Each corporate scandal demonstrated first and foremost a violation of an essential requirement for the functioning of a market economy: public disclosure. In each incident, material information about the companies and the actions of their senior executives was purposefully withheld from shareholders, regulators, independent rating agencies, and others who are entitled to the information. As the evidence mounted in company after company, a severe crisis of public confidence erupted. This is the simple context that unleashed a torrent of criminal indictments, government investigations, and journalistic muckraking that has challenged a broad range of corporate financing practices that were once taken for granted—and considered legal. Although the intense public scrutiny understandably began in the United States, where wrongdoing by Enron, WorldCom, Tyco, and a growing number of other large companies was exposed, within a matter of months a similar pattern of corporate deception began to unfold in countries around the world. It was more than coincidental, for example, that the gigantic Dutch supermarket retailer, Royal Ahold, announced . . . that earnings had been overstated by more than US$500 million during the previous two years, notwithstanding a clean audit by one of the four large accounting firms, Deloitte & Touche. Or that the CEO of one of South Korea's largest chaebols, the huge private holding companies that dominate the country's economy, was indicted earlier in 2003 after revelations that profits had been fraudulently inflated to the tune of billions of dollars over a number of years. Clearly, the revelations in the United States triggered a global wake-up call as country after country began to uncover its own scandals.

Regardless of the specifics of each case, the belief that the problems are systemic has been reinforced by a growing recognition that virtually all stakeholders in the capital raising process appear to be complicit or directly involved: senior corporate executives involved in kickbacks, insider trading and other self-enrichment schemes at shareholder expense; accountants so closely entangled with their corporate clients that they appear to have lost sight of their public responsibilities to ensure full disclosure and validate the accuracy of financial reporting; outside corporate directors, allegedly independent, failing to diligently fulfill their fiduciary responsibility to shareholders by holding management accountable; investment bankers playing multiple roles, including creditor, underwriter, investment advisor, and sometimes investor in the deals they structure; stock analysts, purportedly conducting objective research, making recommendations on stocks that are underwritten and traded by the same investment bankers who decide their level of compensation; attorneys compensated by corporations to provide legal opinions on the legitimacy of financial transactions and then retained again by the same company to investigate whether the original opinions were appropriate; and politicians writing regulations to govern the

same companies, accounting firms, and investment banks that finance their campaigns. All self-righteously claim to be independent and objective. But the professional judgment of every one of these stakeholders could be clouded by their large financial interest in the outcome of the capital raising process, victimizing the one stakeholder left outside the loop: the public investor.

Some of the alleged corporate crimes are surprising in their audacious simplicity, such as the undisclosed use of corporate funds by senior executives to pay for the purchase of personal property. This is robbery, plain and simple. Others were technically legal, but demonstrated an egregious disrespect for shareholder interests. For example, the former Chairman of ABB, the Swiss-based industrial conglomerate, awarded himself an US$87 million tax-free, lump sum "pension" when he stepped down as the company's CEO, a detail he had neglected to mention to his Board or to disclose in documents filed with securities market regulators. But some violations were characterized by a sophistication that required the participation and complicity of a small army of highly trained professionals. Enron, for example, created more than 3,500 so-called Special Purpose Entities (SPEs) that frequently were structured for the explicit purpose of skirting regulatory oversight, hiding the extent of corporate indebtedness, and exaggerating earnings. Worse yet, according to recent federal indictments, the CFO and his cronies were receiving multimillion dollar kickbacks for their efforts, often with the assistance of both employees and outside advisors. As one former Enron executive explained in an April 2003 *Financial Times* article, "10 people alone could not pull off a US$60 billion hoax. You need lieutenants." The same could be said for most of the scandals.

How could such widespread abuse by so many continue undetected for so long? Some of the protective mechanisms that should have prevented such corporate malfeasance are embodied in a country's legal framework, as defined and enforced by public authorities; others are established within the private sector itself by specific industry groups, such as the New York Stock Exchange and the International Accounting Standards Board. But the first line of defense is in the firms themselves, where the senior executives and the members of the boards of directors define and practice the corporate governance standards. These are the individuals who set the behavioral tone for their legions of employees and ultimately they are responsible for how well a firm adheres to the spirit and letter of the law, as well as to industry-imposed professional standards. Their personal behavior ultimately defines the ethical culture for every company, and they inflict untold damage on investor confidence when they fail to recognize the enormity of this responsibility. As the CEO of one Dutch company explained in a March 2003 *Financial Times* piece, "Good corporate governance does not reside in rules but in the culture of a company, as defined by executive management and the board." Apparently, however, the effectiveness of this elaborate network of checks and balances does not work very well, and has led to a severe erosion of public confidence.

THE PUBLIC POLICY RESPONSE

In the six months after Enron's declaration of bankruptcy, barely a day passed without another headline revealing a new corporate scandal. Even though public outrage around the world was rapidly gaining momentum, attention predictably focused on the United States, where the presumed global leader was reeling from the exposed weaknesses in its brand of capitalism. Despite the shrill volume of indignant rhetoric, however, most pundits were initially skeptical that much would change in the United States,

where well funded and politically connected vested interests are highly influential. According to conventional wisdom, a massive lobbying campaign on Capitol Hill, backed by the deep-pocketed barons of Wall Street, corporate United States and an unabashedly pro-business president, would successfully derail proposals for legislative action. As the *Financial Times* reported in June 2002, "A wave of enthusiasm for overhauling the nation's corporate and accounting laws has ebbed, and the toughest proposals for change are all but dead." And a leading US Senator exclaimed with relief, "The feeding frenzy is pretty much over."

Less than a month after these prophetic pronouncements, a new federal law was in place that was as ambitious as any corporate reform legislation enacted since the 1930s. Astoundingly, the Senate voted unanimously in favor of the so-called Sarbanes-Oxley Act, and it passed by a lopsided 423 to 3 in the US House of Representatives. One week later, amidst great fanfare, US President George [W.] Bush declared a new era of corporate reform as he placed his signature on the legislation—less than eight months after Enron declared bankruptcy. The new law could hardly be labeled a global blueprint for corporate reform, but business leaders and government officials everywhere paid close attention to both the content of the legislation and the reactions of the various stakeholders. If the US system of public and corporate governance had once been considered the gold standard that other nations sought to emulate, perhaps the rapid and sweeping legislative response would also serve as a worthy example.

Although hastily patched together and far from perfect, the new law included a number of provisions designed to strengthen both public and private oversight of corporate behavior, and subject violators to far harsher penalties. For the first time, the CEOs and CFOs of all publicly listed companies must personally certify on an annual basis the accuracy of the financial statements released to regulators and the public. Equally significant, false representations now will be subject to criminal penalties, significantly upping the ante for those with a penchant for corporate corruption. The law also includes more stringent conflict of interest provisions to govern the behavior of stock analysts and tougher public disclosure requirements for off-balance sheet transactions. It even places the onus on attorneys to report to the public authorities "evidence of a material violation of securities law or a breach of fiduciary duty," and stipulates that violators will be banned from practicing before the Securities and Exchange Commission (SEC), a penalty that is tantamount to excommunication for securities lawyers. To bolster enforcement of the new law, Congress also provided the SEC with a massive budget increase, primarily to expand the professional staff.

Perhaps the most far-reaching reform instigated by the Act is the establishment of a new, five-member board, accountable to the SEC that will oversee the disgraced accounting profession. In effect, this measure puts an end to self-regulation of the industry and creates far more rigorous oversight by an independent board of distinguished experts who will have authority to set auditing rules, inspect accounting firms, and discipline auditors. Auditors, for example, will no longer be permitted to accept consulting assignments, nor will they be permitted to pass through the revolving door to be hired by the same firms that were their audit clients. These tough new provisions, not surprisingly, were met by howls of protest and a fierce lobbying campaign by business groups, the American Bar Association, and others who hoped to dilute the most onerous provisions.

Just as the epidemic of corporate scandal spread far beyond the United States, so did the reaction of many governments and multilateral organizations. In Germany, for example, the Finance Minister responded to a series of high profile domestic corporate scandals by proposing a special task force to combat accounting fraud and better protect investors in private pension funds. The European Union began to actively consider tighter standards for auditors of public companies, new codes of conduct for securities analysts, and a new set of rules for the structuring and trading of derivatives. And the quasi-official International Accounting Standards Board gained credibility and influence at the expense of the Financial Accounting Standards Board, pressuring the United States to conform to a new set of international accounting standards, rather than the other way around. Indeed, regulators around the globe, whether or not emulating the specific provisions of Sarbanes-Oxley, began to actively rethink the boundaries that separate permissible from illegal corporate behavior, and they kept a close eye on the reforms that were unfolding in the United States.

In developing countries too, governance issues have begun to resonate as never before. The International Finance Corporation (IFC), an affiliate of the World Bank, initiated a series of regional corporate governance roundtable meetings with high-level policy makers and business leaders in Latin America, Asia, and Eastern and Central Europe. The sessions were convened to promote and explain the OECD's recently published "Principles of Corporate Governance," a pioneering initiative to develop the core elements of internationally acceptable corporate governance standards and practices. Although the Preamble to the document appropriately recognizes that every country must adapt the Principles to their own legal and institutional circumstances, the document emphasizes that "common to all good corporate governance regimes is a high degree of priority placed on the interests of shareholders, who place their trust in corporations to use their investment funds wisely and effectively." This theme provided the basis for the regional corporate governance meetings, and as one IFC participant observed, "after years of trying to get policy makers and business leaders in developing countries to recognize the essential connection between corporate governance and access to capital markets, the unprecedented publicity triggered by the scandals in the United States and Europe has immeasurably elevated the attention paid to our agenda."

GOVERNANCE BEYOND GOVERNMENT

After an initial period of self-denial about the significance of the unfolding scandals, there has been a palpable shift in sentiment among even the most ardent defenders of free market orthodoxy, who hold that poorly performing companies should be accountable only to the merciless discipline of their shareholders. Many business leaders began to recognize that not only were individual reputations being destroyed, but the image and reputation of entire professions were being ridiculed and subjected to scathing indictments because their internal oversight and monitoring of corporate behavior had proven to be alarmingly negligent. Few would disagree with the assessment of the globally respected Peter Peterson, former US Secretary of Commerce and Chairman of one of the largest private equity firms, who observed that the public now puts the integrity of corporate CEOs about on par with used car dealers.

Goldman Sachs Chairman and CEO Henry Paulson reflected the extraordinary degree of reassessment that was going on in the international financial community when he conceded in a speech before the National Press Club in Washington, DC, . . . that his own investment banking industry had contributed to a "crisis of confidence" that "has been a drag on the economy and the performance of our capital markets." This astonishing mea culpa by the leader of a venerable financial institution with a long roster of blue chip corporate and government clients was symptomatic of a sobering recognition at the highest echelons of the business world that a sweeping review of internal governance procedures was warranted and underway. Around the globe, other prominent business leaders exhibited a similar awareness that issues of corporate disclosure and accountability were suddenly in the public domain. Almost overnight, it became difficult to identify a major corporation, investment bank, law practice, or accounting firm that had not begun a serious reassessment of how it governs itself, examining such fundamentals as enforcement of corporate codes of conduct, the roles and responsibilities of outside directors, standards of disclosure of financial information to shareholders and regulators, and guidelines for determining executive compensation.

A similar wave of reform was instigated within the associations and industry groups that are charged with defining and enforcing performance standards for their respective professions. In both the United States and Europe, for example, stock exchanges suddenly announced their intention to tighten disclosure requirements for listed companies and review the permissibility of certain financing practices that were considered commonplace and acceptable pre-Enron. The National Association of Securities Dealers in the United States has become more aggressive in policing the behavior of its thousands of member firms and their employees, and recently launched an international campaign to advise the securities industry in other countries. And in Japan, where managerial concern for shareholder interests has rarely been at the top of the corporate agenda, the most influential private business association initiated a major review of corporate governance guidelines for its members in response to a growing rash of scandals. Even major business schools in the United States and Europe are hopping on the bandwagon, offering high priced executive training programs on a range of corporate governance subjects.

Ultimately, however, it is the shareholders who have the most at stake, and the scandals have jolted them into a newfound awareness of their own responsibility. Throughout the 1990s, as stock markets soared inexorably higher and higher, they were perfectly content to "buy and hold," seldom questioning the optimism of corporate executives, stock analysts, independent rating agencies, and everyone else who preached that the United States had entered an era of endless prosperity. Now, due to the scandals, they know better. Stung by the consequences of their passivity, shareholders have begun to exercise their responsibilities more diligently. Last May in London, for example, the shareholders of GlaxoSmithKline, a gigantic international pharmaceutical company, took the unprecedented step of voting to reject the proposed exorbitant pay package of the CEO and other senior executives. In like manner, shareholders in TV Azteca, one of Mexico's largest television stations, resisted the controlling shareholder's attempt to use the company's resources to finance his unauthorized purchase of cellular phone licenses. And the *Financial Times* reported in August 2003 that in South Korea, the leader of one of the most influential shareholder lobby groups, the People's Solidarity for Participatory Democracy, proclaimed the necessity of "a major overhaul of accounting procedures in

Korea," as his organization filed a formal complaint with securities market regulators against the country's largest auditing firm.

The most powerful shareholders are the large institutional investors, such as pension funds, insurance firms, and mutual funds, and they too have belatedly begun to exert pressure on companies with their enormous voting power. The Chief Investment Officer of Calpers, one of the world's largest pension funds with more than US$130 billion of assets under management, noted that the scandals have had the beneficial effect of unleashing "a new age of corporate governance." In a startling display of shareholder activism that would have been unheard of a few years ago, he wrote a letter to 500 other large institutional investors who have substantial holdings in General Electric stock to encourage each of them to vote in favor of measures that will pressure management to align the executive stock option plan more closely with the company's performance. Nothing will do more to restore confidence in the integrity of financial markets than actions like this that demonstrate a higher level of vigilance and activism through the exercise of voting rights. It is the shareholders themselves, as the Calpers initiative demonstrates, that are the single most important safeguard against corporate abuse.

REASONS FOR OPTIMISM

One litmus test of leadership, whether embodied in a government, a company or an individual, is the capacity to respond effectively to crisis. By this measure there is cause for optimism that the corporate scandals are serving as a catalyst for constructive change around the world. Unquestionably, there is a higher level of public awareness about the importance of transparency, effective governance and integrity by those who participate in financial markets, and the severe consequences that result from lapses in vigilance and oversight. One World Bank governance specialist observed, for example, "I no longer need to explain what I mean by the term corporate governance. Wherever I go, it's become a household word." Ultimately, better-informed, more vigilant stakeholders will do as much to raise the level of integrity in the marketplace as any new law or regulation.

This extraordinary newfound level of public awareness, coupled with an equally potent sense of outrage, explains why governments have responded with alacrity to the scandals with something more than rhetoric. After a similar torrent of scandals was exposed following the 1929 stock market crash, more than three years passed before Congress enacted a set of reforms that dramatically changed the landscape of financial market regulation in the United States, setting a standard that many other countries followed. In contrast, the Sarbanes-Oxley Act became law less than eight months after Enron declared bankruptcy, creating a new benchmark that is being subjected to careful global scrutiny. Regardless of the country or culture, new laws are being passed to tighten oversight and enforcement of firms that raise capital in public securities markets. Although some may continue to argue that the self-correcting mechanisms of the market will suffice to punish corporate wrongdoers and restore the public's confidence in the integrity of corporate affairs,

that refrain has begun to ring hollow even for capitalism's strongest supporters.

Finally, the scandals have served as a sober reminder that a well functioning market economy must continuously strive to calibrate the balance between public and private governance responsibilities. Well-designed and enforced public policies can help strengthen the incentives, both positive and negative, that encourage appropriate behavior by those responsible for ensuring that the marketplace operates fairly and efficiently. But personal integrity and sound judgment cannot be legislated, particularly in an open, competitive market economy where the legal and ethical boundaries will never be completely clear. These qualities must be embedded in the individuals who go to work every day in the marketplace; they are the ones who must earn the public's confidence for the system to work effectively. These practitioners presumably rise to the pinnacle of their respective professions not only because of their technical competence and ability to manage others effectively, but also because of their integrity. Rather than tough new legislation, perhaps the ultimate good that will result from the scandals is a newfound recognition by corporate executives and their legions of financial and legal advisors that they have as profound a public responsibility as any civil servant. If this lesson is first learned and then practiced, the public's confidence and trust in the model so many sought to emulate will be restored.

PART THREE

BUSINESS RELATIONS WITH STAKEHOLDERS

THE CARMAKER CHRYSLER took over an aging plant in Kenosha, Wisconsin, and publicly stated to the United Auto Workers union that they would stay for at least five years. At the time, the state made about $5 million in state and local funds available to Chrysler to retrain workers. Within two years, Chrysler executives announced that they would no longer make cars at the factory and slashed the payroll from 5,500 to less than 1,000, saying that they had been overly optimistic in their projections. The announcement was met with a firestorm of bad press and a threatened lawsuit from the governor and the union over the broken promise. Eventually, the company created a $20 million trust fund to benefit the fired workers and the local area—an amount equivalent to a year's profits to Chrysler from its car sales in the state.

The Chrysler case shows us that businesses rarely have discrete dealings. A customer may not just purchase a vehicle but live in the community and even work at the factory. His sales tax dollars helped bring the corporation to town, and now he has an incentive to buy its products as part of the bailout package.

Stakeholder theory tells us that a firm may have both a moral and strategic interest in balancing the welfare of those who can potentially help or harm the business. As the Kenosha case shows us, the parties involved may have overlapping and intertwined interests. Even if Chrysler wanted to restrict its goals to maximizing investor returns, merely responding to the economic signals and ignoring other stakeholders by precipitously closing the plant appears to have been ill advised.

This section looks at the web of relationships that a firm has with its employees, consumers, and the community. As Meg Bond and Jean Pyle note in Chapter 8, legal compliance has not been an effective engine for social transformation in the past 50 years. Corporations may have the potential to be moral leaders of constructive change, but those goals often conflict with short-term economic efficiency. This means that even the best-intentioned business will have to develop policies that keep the firm profitable while satisfying the demands of morality. For example, a company may want to institute flexible work hours for single parents, but it may turn out to be too costly for the firm. A beach-themed restaurant might want to institute gender-blind hiring practices only to find that its customers much preferred young and sexually attractive women, whatever their serving competence, with the result that customers take their trade elsewhere.

Employees give up a number of rights under a work contract, and the firm may have the opportunity to exploit its position of power. It may value workers who do not smoke, or who are fit vegetarians, and currently may legally discriminate on those grounds. It has the power to demand confidential personal medical files. The moral issue is whether a firm should show restraint in its dealings with employees, especially if it has the law on its side.

Chapter 9 questions who knows what is best for consumers—the manufacturer, the government, or the consumer. It might be reasonable to let individuals decide whether to buy a home body-piercing kit or drugs over the Internet as long as they are aware of the risks. Nevertheless, we can draw an analogy with activities that might imperil others or impose a cost on third parties: We let people go skydiving without restriction but do not let them drive without a license. One of the key issues for a manufacturer is whether it is in the position of knowing more about the dangers of a product than a reasonable person could be assumed to know, and if so, should it have a continuing responsibility for the goods it puts on the market? Despite lurid anecdotes of accident victims winning the jackpot by suing rich companies, Valerie Hans shows us that juries tend to hold companies to much the same standard as they would an educated professional, and they still place a significant amount of responsibility on the individual.

Chapter 10 expands the scope of the discussion to examine whether business has a responsibility to the community. If we think of businesses as responsible—and relatively wealthy—citizens, then perhaps they should act with noblesse oblige—that is, an obligation to do good works because of their advantageous position. Another way of viewing this is that a business draws on the resources of a community and should rightfully repay it in some form. Some commentators would say that, fundamentally, all corporate philanthropy is strategic, aimed to benefit the company in one way or another. Yet, even if this is the case, is the world better off with corporate giving than without it?

EMPLOYEE ISSUES

In this chapter we will look at the relationship between an employer and employees. A privately held company typically seeks profit through maximizing efficiency. This may mean employing those most qualified and likely to add value and encouraging workers to be more productive. In short, a company will attempt to make its human capital as profitable as possible. However, employees are individuals with their own interests and biographies, and they merit respect in a way that a machine does not. Thus, there may be a tension between the demands of the marketplace and how a firm should treat its employees as human beings with personal dignity.

We spend more of our time proportionally at work than doing anything else. Over half the households in the United States are supported by two incomes, which usually means that arrangements have to be made for looking after school-age children. Moreover, of the 70 million families in the United States, currently less than a quarter are traditional nuclear families with a working father and a stay-at-home mom. Given the juggling of responsibilities in families where there is a single parent or both parents work, should firms be flexible in accommodating their needs—for instance, those who need to care for children or elderly relatives? Are companies working with a 50-year-old template of employees as heads of traditional families? Does that need to be changed to fit contemporary reality?

Firms have a significant amount of control over employees' lives, both in and out of the workplace. The employer may choose to hire on the basis of social habits, for example. The employer may legally discriminate against smokers, even though the practice is legal, and the employee may only smoke at home. Random and intrusive testing for drug use is a common practice that is usually defended on the grounds that someone who uses even so-called soft drugs will be less productive and could be a safety hazard; but alcohol and sleep deprivation may cause the same results.

However, the corporation is not completely free to do as it chooses. It is subject to a wealth of regulations governing the minimum that employees can be paid, conditions in the workplace, who can be fired at will, and the amount of information to which employers are entitled, among other things. Many firms see these regulations as unnecessary restrictions on free trade, which artificially inflate the cost of doing business.

Recall that one prevalent attitude is that businesses are morally neutral entities that merely respond to consumer demand. If that were the case, then customers unwilling to be served by African Americans, say, would wield power with the business; the moral onus would rest on the customers and not the business. In effect, the business could wash its hands of the apparent racism. However, others would say that the business should not condone or be complicit in immoral and unjust practices. The current social and political reality, though, is that businesses are required to conform to notions of justice and fairness instituted at a legislative level.

Under the American system of employment-at-will (EAW), an employer may fire a worker for good reasons, bad reasons, or no reasons at all. Traditionally, the law protects certain classes of workers because they were felt to have unequal bargaining power to protect their rights. Thus, the 1964 Civil Rights Act says that an employer may not discriminate on the basis of race, color, religion, national origin, and gender. Later restrictions preclude firing on the basis of marital status, age (if over 40), and disability; many states now protect jobs that are threatened on the basis of sexual preference. However, we should be clear that these laws do not mean that members of a protected class cannot be fired—only that they cannot be selectively fired on grounds that are held to be discriminatory. A firm can fire a black woman, but it will be held accountable if she can show that she was fired not because of business exigency but because of her race or gender alone. Other groups are unprotected, and hence employers may choose not to hire them or to fire them with impunity. So, for example, someone who is obese or has big ears can be fired without explanation or recourse.

Some businesses have chosen to embrace diversity and actively recruit and promote traditionally underrepresented groups in the workforce. There may be good business reasons to do so, given the changing demographics of the country

as a whole. On the other hand, some firms have a definite social agenda that they promote through their hiring practices. Opponents sometimes refer to this course of action as reverse discrimination, based on the notion that the practices are still discriminatory because the selection is not made on merit alone; rather, the target group is now typically white males.

The readings do not concentrate on the law itself but look at the moral arguments involved. Lynn Paine asks whether working parents should feel guilty about leaving their children in day care. She concludes that such feelings may be entirely appropriate but at the same time believes that employers should show more flexibility. Ian Maitland gives a traditional analysis that suggests that the market is an adequate vehicle for assigning worker rights: In a competitive labor market, firms will seek out the best workers by giving them additional privileges and benefits, but we should not confuse these with automatic entitlements that are not earned or negotiated.

The next three readings discuss discrimination and diversity. Myrtle Bell and her colleagues talk about the failure of antidiscrimination legislation to deal with three problems: the apparent glass ceiling that limits the upward mobility of women in the workforce, sexual harassment, and sexual discrimination. D. W. Haslett deals directly with the issue of racial discrimination and asks whether companies have a moral duty to go beyond the dictates of business success. Meg Bond and Jean Pyle consider the tension between nondiscrimination and affirmative action. Affirmative action means selectively promoting members of a group based on non-work-related factors, which seems to be evident discrimination. Bond and Pyle take a wide perspective on the issue by looking at the competing notions of America as either a melting pot or a multicultural society. They trace the history of affirmative action policy and conclude that lip service legal compliance may paradoxically lead to a backlash and probably will fail to bring about any significant change.

One general point is worth considering: We can legislate against discrimination, but does that get to the root of the issue? People may no longer make overt racist or sexist slurs and may act in a superficially nondiscriminatory fashion, yet old practices continue in a more subtle and institutionalized way; in effect, discrimination goes underground while it continues unabated. Employers may advertise more widely and actively recruit traditionally underrepresented groups, but if those employees do not make it into positions of power, perhaps discrimination has just put on a different mask.

The final reading in this section deals with drug testing, which in many ways is representative of the employer/employee relationship. Michael Cranford believes that personal autonomy and privacy rights are not compromised if the company is up-front about its expectations and has a legitimate interest in the information it seeks. Although initially this may not seem objectionable, it does require that employees can trust the company to restrict its investigation and be fair in assessing the results. Psychometric tests can reveal latent personality traits, and we may soon have the technology to determine some-

one's susceptibility to disease well before onset. The temptation for companies is to use any information they discover, of course. If an applicant has a disposition to develop Parkinson's disease in 15 years, this might eventually boost medical insurance rates for the company, and the conservative course would be to not hire the person. An additional concern is the security and accuracy of results. If someone has a false positive, are there assurances that the mistake can be corrected, or will he be tainted by the accusation?

Employers try to serve the interests of a number of different constituents while remaining profitable in a competitive environment. The view that they are merely neutral conduits for the demands of the market is probably too simplistic; inevitably, a company has to make value-laden decisions that affect both consumers and employees. If the company were just a moneymaking vehicle for its owners, many of these decisions would be clear and obvious. However, when we consider that businesses are dealing with real individuals with their own interests and concerns, the issues become much more difficult. The authors in this section provide arguments that balance business and individual well-being, and the question we should consider is whether there is a point where increased profits no longer justify further compromises of individual rights.

Work and Family
*Should Parents Feel Guilty?**

Lynn Sharp Paine

Many of the issues we have looked at so far deal with the interaction of the firm, the individual, and the state. At this point we will look at the tensions that arise because many individuals are part of a family and have family responsibilities outside the workplace. The demands of work, especially for career-minded couples, do not leave much time for family obligations. Paine's article deals with the fact that many parents feel guilty about leaving their children in the care of others while at work. She shows that many commentators think the guilt is either neurotic or misplaced because the children do not seem to suffer in emotional or cognitive development. However, Paine contends that guilt is a moral feeling that springs from failing to live up to ideals or from doing the wrong thing. She presents an ideal of parenting that includes parental modeling of loving relationships and moral education. Her view is that hired hands such as nannies or caregivers cannot substitute for parents, and so the guilt is a valid response. Once we acknowledge its legitimacy, we should be motivated to make fundamental changes in the template for working parents rather than just seeking mechanisms to cope with managing child-related activities.

Many working parents feel guilty about the time they spend away from their children. Until recently, judging from media coverage, career-minded women seemed to be the primary sufferers. It is increasingly clear, however, that fathers, too, feel conflict and guilt about their children's care. A recent Stanford University study found that among couples whose members both hold graduate business degrees, husbands have *more* anxiety about the children than their wives. Advertisers have discovered that parental guilt is a theme with sales potential, and entrepreneurs have discovered that it is a source of economic opportunity.

Employers are concerned about the effects of parental guilt on productivity. "Executive Guilt: Who's Taking Care of the Children?" appeared recently as a cover story for *Fortune* magazine. The article, which describes corporate responses to employees' child-care problems, quotes Dr. Lee Salk, professor of psychology and pediatrics at New York Hospital-Cornell Medical Center. Says Salk, "Guilt is what parents are coming to talk to me about."

What, exactly, do these parents feel guilty about? According to these articles and studies, many parents believe they are not giving their

---

*Original notes have been omitted.

children enough personal time and attention. Many who aspire to traditional careers in the professions and business, or to high levels of achievement in other fields, entrust their young children to caretakers for most of the child's waking hours. As a result, some parents carry with them a nagging sense of guilt. Even when their children appear to be developing normally and have the best child care money can buy, some parents feel they are not fulfilling their parental responsibilities.

Are such feelings appropriate? Is it reasonable for parents to feel guilty about their absences when their children are well cared for by others? The thrust of the popular literature on parental guilt is that absence-related guilt feelings are generally irrational and inappropriate. This view, I will argue, rests on failure to acknowledge the moral foundations of guilt feelings and on a very narrow conception of parents' obligations. On a different conception of parental obligations and values, a conception I will elaborate, absence-related guilt can be seen to be a morally fitting response to the situation of working parents.

My ultimate aim is practical. I want to know how parental guilt feelings are best dealt with. But to answer this practical question we must understand the basis of these feelings. If parental guilt is a neurosis with no rational basis, as suggested by some commentators, counseling or psychiatric treatment may be called for. But if, as I argue, guilt is a morally fitting response to the situation of working parents, efforts to address the situation, not simply the feelings, will be in order.

I. MORALITY AND GUILT FEELINGS

Concerned about employment opportunities for women, many popular writers have urged mothers to dismiss their feelings of guilt. Perhaps they fear that acknowledging the possible legitimacy of guilt will cause mothers to flee the workplace and justify employers in refusing to hire them. One approach to undermining the seriousness of guilt feelings is to redescribe them as nonmoral feelings—as unhappiness, regret, or anxiety, for example. Another is to explain them as vestiges, like the human appendix, which no longer serve any identifiable function but survive as a reminder of the past. Both approaches are ultimately unsatisfying because they neglect essential attributes of guilt feelings, attributes such as the self-criticism and sense of moral failure that are part of feeling guilty. The truth that these accounts fail to acknowledge is that guilt feelings are moral feelings. They cannot be understood apart from the unsatisfied moral imperative or unrealized moral ideal underlying them. . . .

Disregard for the moral basis of guilt feelings is also seen in other attempts to explain maternal guilt. One psychologist, for example, attributes mothers' guilt to "a mismatch between the current realities of family life and ideas about motherhood and children that suited the late-nineteenth and early-twentieth centuries." The author argues that today's mothers suffer guilt because they are not living up to the nineteenth-century ideal of exclusive attachment between mother and child.

This account of maternal guilt is unsatisfactory for many reasons. Besides leaving fathers' guilt untouched, its historical accuracy is questionable. Among the Victorian middle and upper classes, children were often looked after by relatives, nannies, wet nurses, and various domestics, while their mothers attended to the myriad aspects of household management and family and social life. But setting aside historical accuracy, the account fails to explain why the ideal of exclusive attachment should persist while other nineteenth-century ideals have been abandoned with changing circumstances. Moreover, if parents were only clinging wistfully to outmoded conceptions of parenthood, why would they describe themselves as feeling guilty rather than nostalgic or regretful?

The answer is found by noticing the moral imperative implicit in the governing ideal of parenthood. Parents feel guilty because they see themselves as failing to be the kind of parent they believe they *ought* to be, not simply the kind of parent they would *like* to be. Unlike nineteenth-century ideals of entertaining or landscaping which are also impractical in today's world, the purportedly nineteenth-century ideal of motherhood has a moral dimension which is ignored by the vestige theory of maternal guilt. Once we notice this dimension, we cannot simply discard the ideal as impractical and inconvenient. We must look more deeply at its foundations and its relationship to human well-being.

"Guilt" is a popular and perhaps overused word. No doubt, some parents mistakenly describe as "guilt," feelings that are more accurately described as "regret," or "sadness," arising from missing their children. Some parents may falsely report feeling guilty when, in fact, they are relieved to spend most of their time in a professional environment in the company of adults. Some reports of guilt may reflect simple hypocrisy driven by the desire to present oneself as a dutiful parent. Still, the existence of spurious claims does not eliminate the problem. Parents who feel guilty about not seeing enough of their children are expressing feelings of moral inadequacy. If these feelings are genuine, they cannot be resolved by redescriptions and explanations of the sort commonly found in the popular literature. Fashioning a suitable and effective response to parents' guilt feelings requires that we take them seriously and acknowledge their moral foundations.

II. RESOLVING FEELINGS OF GUILT

Guilt is not altogether a bad thing. A testament to our commitment to important values, guilt feelings have a positive role in moral life. They can lead to conduct that affirms important moral standards, restores human relationships, and improves the well-being of others. Guilt feelings aroused by the contemplation of forbidden conduct can sometimes deter it. But unresolved guilt can have a destructive effect on personality and on the ability to function effectively. Gnawing guilt can interfere with concentration and with the self-esteem and hope necessary to forge ahead with one's projects and daily activities. In extreme cases, it can lead to personality disorders involving obsessive behavior and even to madness. It is thus understandable that many people are concerned about parental guilt and would like to reduce its frequency.

The first step toward a fitting and effective resolution of parental guilt is to assess its moral appropriateness. The goal is not simply to eliminate guilt feelings—an objective which could probably be achieved in many cases through a program of belief or behavior modification—but to do so while acknowledging guilt's positive role in upholding morality. This more complex aim demands that morally appropriate guilt be resolved in a way that affirms the moral standards at stake. Affirmation may take many forms: an apology, a change in behavior, reparation or compensation for harm done, confession, acceptance of punishment. Even a symbolic affirmation may be fitting. The important point is that the suitability of a resolution depends on the nature of the moral deficiency in question.

Fashioning an effective resolution thus depends centrally on correct identification of the moral standards and factual beliefs behind the feelings. Failure to appreciate the full range of parents' moral concerns, is, I suggest, another problem with much of the mass-media advice and many employer-sponsored child-care programs intended to help parents. The prevailing assumption seems to be that parental guilt is driven by a moral principle of avoiding harm to children, where harm is thought of narrowly in terms of children's present interests in physical, intellectual, social, or emotional health, and is measured by the degree of departure from some standard of normalcy.

The assumption that parents' central concern is their children's interests in "normal" or "average" development along these discrete dimensions is implicit in much popular advice. One writer, for instance, instructs that, "Reality guilt is when you have neglected or abused your children. Neurotic guilt is the conflict you feel between what you want to do and what you feel you have to do." Other commentators reassure parents by pointing to studies showing "that children in quality daycare don't suffer any cognitive loss or feel any less attached to their parents." The same assumption influences the direction of child-care research, which tends to focus on finding out whether daycare is harmful to children's physical, cognitive, or socio-emotional development. Studies typically test hypotheses about the intellectual achievement and ability, or the emotional and social development of daycare children as compared to non-daycare children.

Assumptions about the moral norms behind guilt feelings affect our assessment of their appropriateness and shape our approach to resolving them. If we assume that parental guilt is based on concerns about children's physical, intellectual, and socio-emotional development, its appropriateness becomes an empirical question to be resolved, at the general level, by social scientists. On the evidence to date, a case can be made that the guilt feelings we are exploring here—absence-related guilt felt by parents whose children enjoy high-quality substitute care—are simply inappropriate. Research on the effects of daycare is inconclusive in many respects, and much debate centers on its effects, especially the effects of infant daycare. But, as yet, it does not appear that children cared for by parent substitutes suffer identifiable cognitive, physical, social, or emo-

tional deficiencies. Children looked after in quality daycare centers perform as well, and sometimes better, than non-daycare children on the chosen dimensions.

Within this moral framework, the central, perhaps the only, issue is the quality of substitute care. Guilt felt by parents whose care arrangements lead to sub-normal child development is seen as appropriate and suitably resolved by improving the quality and availability of substitute care. On the other hand, guilt feelings of parents whose children are developing normally along the defined dimensions are regarded as inappropriate and best dealt with through reasoning, counseling, or therapy. Such parents are advised to recognize how others—their parents, doctors, and children—"make them" feel guilty. They are exhorted to examine the scientific studies showing that daycare is not harmful and can actually enhance their children's social skills. Their guilt feelings come to be seen as psychological aberrations rather than morally appropriate feelings calling for an affirmation of their moral ideals.

Some parents may find this line of reasoning comforting. For a variety of reasons, others will find it interesting but unsatisfying. The evidence—the long-term evidence—is not really "in." We know little about the effects of child-rearing practices on adult development. Perhaps, the social, emotional, or cognitive harms will show up later. Many parents feel that parental obligation goes beyond protecting children from harm—that is, protecting them from falling below a minimal standard defined by statistical averages—and requires the positive promotion of each child's cognitive, physical, and social capabilities. Even those with a more minimal conception of parental obligation may continue to be concerned about the possibly harmful effects, not of daycare in general, but of the particular arrangements they have devised for their children.

Still other parents will find this line of reasoning largely irrelevant because it rests on a faulty assumption about the moral standard at issue. For these parents, guilt persists in the face of excellent substitute care not because of concerns about their children's cognitive, physical, or socio-economic health, but because they have a moral ideal of parenthood that calls for greater personal involvement with their children. Departures from this ideal are problematic not because of the effects typically measured in studies of substitute care, but because of the moral harm involved—moral harm to both children and their parents. On this alternative conception of the underlying moral imperative, I suggest, parental guilt feelings are a very appropriate response to a situation in which parents have little time to spend with their children. As I will explain, the persuasiveness of this suggestion depends on the strength of the case for the ideal.

III. MORALLY APPROPRIATE GUILT

Guilt feelings can fail to be appropriate in one of two ways. They may be inappropriate because based on a moral standard for which there is no reasonable justification. Or they may be inappropriate because based on mistaken factual beliefs about, among other things, the consequences of conduct, the availability of morally preferable alternatives, or the degree of fault. As we have seen, one line of reasoning about parental guilt treats it as inappropriate because based on false beliefs about the effects of substitute care.

Assessing the appropriateness of guilt feelings thus requires inquiry into both the relevant facts and the underlying moral standards. This assessment may sometimes be a straightforward, though not necessarily simple, matter of ascertaining the truth of critical beliefs and matching conduct against moral requirements, as the legal model of criminal guilt might suggest. But in other cases, perplexing problems attend our judgments about the moral standards to which

we hold ourselves. There is, for instance, the problem of conflicting obligations. Sometimes I have no choice but to violate some general moral obligation, even though, after careful consideration, I decide that I ought, all things considered, to take one course of action rather than another. Are my feelings of guilt appropriate if I have done the best I can?

A similar problem arises when I am forced by others to do something which is morally wrong. I may not be culpable, strictly speaking, but I have nevertheless done something which ought not be done. Should I feel guilty? The best response is that guilt is understandable even though perhaps inappropriate under the specific circumstances. My character is such that I have an aversion to doing things that generally I ought not do, and feel guilty when I do those things even for a good reason. A little extra guilt may be the price of a good character. Of course, if I have arranged things in a way that makes it likely that conflicts will arise, my feelings of culpability are more appropriate.

Problematic cases aside for the moment, feeling guilty is sometimes clearly appropriate: if, for example, I knowingly lie about my qualifications to gain an advantage in a job competition. My subsequent feelings of guilt are perfectly appropriate because, very simply, I did what I ought not to have done under the circumstances—namely, lie. The conclusion that guilt is appropriate is unproblematic in this case. The link between the breach of a morality and the feelings of guilt is straightforward. The general prohibition against lying is widely accepted and easily justifiable by almost any standard of moral justification. Even the most minimal morality contains a prohibition on lying. The case involves no factual questions and there appear to be no factors mitigating blameworthiness. My lie was not an act of desperation intended to secure the only available opportunity for a livelihood for my dependents. It was simply a means of capturing for myself an advantage over similarly situated competitors.

More difficult are questions about the appropriateness of guilt in cases involving standards that are not so widely accepted because they are thought to be supererogatory or simply different. For example, some people believe they are obligated to contribute a tenth of their income to charity and may feel guilty when their contributions fall below this standard. Others would regard such a standard as far too onerous. Some people are more inclined than others to impose moral requirements on themselves. It is very likely that these people will more frequently see themselves as falling short and thus carry a heavier burden of guilt than those who demand less of themselves.

This example resembles the case of parental guilt: both involve moral standards that are far from universally accepted. Unlike the principle of honesty or fidelity to promises, for example, the standards seem somewhat optional. . . .

. . . This case is problematic just because there is no consensus on the ideal underlying the feelings. . . . We must . . . examine the basis for the underlying moral ideal and decide whether it makes sense to hold oneself to such a standard.

IV. PARENTAL LOVE AND PARENTAL PRESENCE

Feelings of guilt associated with parental absence can be explained by a moral ideal of parenthood calling for attentive love and personal engagement with one's children. This ideal has a variety of closely related sources. As I will elaborate, it flows from parents' responsibilities for their children's moral education and their obligations as fiduciaries for their children's interests. It also has roots in the needs and interests of adults and the community. But it rests fundamentally on a judgment that deep personal commitments, relationships of love involving personal engagement with

other human beings, have intrinsic moral value. A life with such relationships, and the joys and hardships they entail, is morally better than a life without them.

Relationships of love offer the most thoroughgoing experience of sympathetic identification with another that we are likely to encounter. These relationships are enriching, enlarging, a source of unique joy. They are onerous, trying, and a source of unique pain. But they are our link with other human beings as ends in themselves and in this respect have intrinsic moral worth. The giving of oneself and the appreciation of the other at the core of these relationships are the sources of their moral value. Although parental love lacks the mutuality of love between friends or spouses, it is based, like other love relationships, on concern for the other for his own sake. The very absence of mutuality is perhaps a reason to see in parental love greater moral value than in relationships between equals.

Insofar as the ideal of parenthood outlined here depends upon the intrinsic moral value of personal relationships of love, there can be no substitute for some degree of personal interaction between parent and child. Parents cannot delegate to others the responsibility for providing love and attention as they delegate the responsibility for providing transportation, medical care, or music education. For the parent, the moral value of personal involvement lies not just in bringing about a certain result for the child but also from the giving of himself and actively caring for the child. Only through direct involvement can the parent enjoy this moral good.

Personal involvement also has instrumental moral value for parents. By testing and enhancing their capacity to care deeply and continuously for others, parenthood can propel adults into a new phase of their own moral development. Parents who take seriously their role as moral example and teacher are bound to experience moral growth through the reassessment of moral beliefs and commitments that goes with personal involvement in child care. Moreover, personal involvement enhances parents' performance as fiduciaries for their children. Without a substantial core of shared experience, it is doubtful that parents could know their children well enough to make intelligent decisions in their behalf.

These are compelling reasons to think that personally caring for one's children can be a source of great moral value for a parent. There are also reasons to think that the moral good for children is promoted by personal involvement with their parents. These reasons can be seen by looking more closely at some tasks of parenthood.

One of the central tasks of parenthood is to prepare children for life by nurturing the capacities and interests that will permit them to flourish when no longer dependent on their parents. A great deal has been made of the centrality of autonomous decision-making. In this connection, the ability to relate to others and moral behavior are equally important. The capacity to participate in intimate relationships of love later in life and the capacity to engage in moral thought and action appear to be closely linked, both causally and conceptually, with each other and with the experience of being loved by one's parents.

For children, the moral importance of parental love rests not only on its causal role in contributing to dispositions to be honest and responsible and to trust others, but also on its role as exemplar. A child's conception of what it is to love another has its earliest roots in the experience of being the recipient of parental love and an observer of the love between her parents. Besides being the child's first sustained love relationship, the parent-child relationship provides a uniquely intimate acquaintance with the vicissitudes of love and the meaning of personal commitment. The importance of parental love as an example—positive or negative—of what love requires may only surface in adulthood.

A parent's engagement with his child is not only an expression of love for the child, it is also an indication of how much the parent values intimate relationships. Parents' choices reflect their conception of the good and provide children with an example of how diverse goals and values—love, self, work, achievement, money, morality—can and should be integrated into a coherent life. In many cases, parents are the only adults to whom children can look for such an example, for they are the only adults children know well enough. Others—teachers, doctors, family members, friends—are seen only in their particular roles or seen too infrequently to provide useful examples of how life might be lived. It is not surprising that absence-related guilt seems to afflict career-oriented professionals whose work, while perhaps socially valuable, is also a source of self-gratification and for whom the giving up of work-related opportunities may require self-sacrifice. At the margin—after fulfilling legitimate material requirements—the decision to take on more work rather than to attend to one's children may reflect the choice of a lesser moral good over a greater one, and the choice of self-interest over the interests of others. For the parent who subscribes to the ideal of parenthood I have described, all-consuming work may be a source not only of absence-related guilt but of guilt related to the discrepancy between professed moral values and conduct.

A certain amount of parental presence is necessarily required for parental love to fulfill the functions outlined here. If parental love is to serve as an example of a relationship of love, it must be accessible to the child and the child must perceive it to be such a relationship. Parents' personal involvement is also important if parental love is to fulfill its causal role in strengthening moral dispositions and preparing children for participation in later love relationships. This is, quite simply, because what matters from the child's perspective is not only that she be loved, but that she also believe herself to be loved.

Unfortunately, a child can feel unloved and quite alone at the same time his parents see themselves as deeply loving. The discrepancy may arise because of the child's level of cognitive and emotional development. He may not be able to appreciate the depth of a parent's abstract love or impersonal expressions of concern: the trouble a parent may take, for instance, in finding a day-care provider. Children's limited knowledge of the world, their shorter time horizons, and their emerging conceptions of self—all affect their perceptions of their parents' love and concern. There is a risk that impersonally expressed concern for a child's well-being will be inadequate to support the child's belief that she is loved.

The importance of parental presence is not due exclusively to children's limited cognitive capacities, however. Most of us, children and adults alike, feel loved and valued by those who seek out our companionship, take our perspectives and problems seriously, give us a high priority in their scheme of things, and support us even in difficult times. Aristotle's idea that loving entails caring for another for that person's sake captures an important motivational element in genuine love: it must proceed from concern for the beloved and not from the lover's concern for herself. Our belief that we are loved depends on our perception of the lover's motives and on the presence of certain expressions of love. I will not believe you love me if your attentions appear to be a means to your own advantage. Nor will I believe you love me if you show insufficient interest in me as a person.

An example may be helpful. Suppose, while assuring me of his love, my husband regularly arranges to have his personal agent or substitute join me for dinner or evenings out, counsel me on problems, and perhaps occasionally even spend the night. At some point, no matter how carefully and efficiently he manages the coming and going of his substitutes, no matter how much I like them, and no matter how much he protests that he really loves me, I will begin to doubt him. I will begin to think his excuses of responsibilities at work are bogus or that he loves his work first and foremost. Or I may think his attentions to me spring from some source other than love of me.

These same difficulties are present when parents delegate to others too much of the responsibility for providing their children with loving care and attention. The child's understanding of his parents' reasons for delegating his care are very important. The child who realizes that the family's very livelihood depends on his parents' being away from home is quite likely to feel differently from the child who sees his parents' absence as selfish expressions of their desire for self-fulfillment. It is impossible to assess the effects of parental absence without including the motives and perceived motives of parents. The precise amount of personal attention required to sustain a child's trust in the parent's love is probably quite variable since it depends in part on the child's ability to comprehend and interpret the parents' conduct and motives as well as on the child's conceptual maturity. As the child's capacity for abstract thought matures, the amount of personal attention required could be expected to diminish. Nevertheless, as with adult love, there would appear to be some minimum amount of personal attention necessary for a parent to love his child in a way that the child recognizes as love.

As noted, delegating too much of the responsibility to give children love and attention may jeopardize their trust in their parents' love. But one might wonder why parents' love should matter so much if children believe they are loved by the nannies, daycare providers, and other caregivers hired by parents. The difficulty with all these parent surrogates is the very limited nature of their love and commitment. The employment relationship is a tenuous foundation for bonds of love. This is especially true given the low pay, high turn-over, and low morale characteristic in today's child-care and domestic labor markets. The more serious problem, however, stems from fundamentals of the employment relationship.

Except in extraordinary cases, the child's welfare occupies quite a different position in a parent's and an employee's scheme of priorities. Usually, no matter how much an employee loves her charges, her attachment is contingent on receipt of adequate compensation. Assisting the child—as teacher, nanny, babysitter—is a job and must be seen in that context. Employment mobility and the needs of the employee's own family limit the commitment most are willing to make. If fulfilling parental responsibilities requires a stable, constant and relatively permanent attachment, all non-family parent substitutes suffer a comparative disadvantage. The parents' affection for the child and the relative permanence of the parent/child attachment give parents a stake in the child's welfare much greater than the stake any employee could be expected to have. This differential, coupled with the other factors noted, may translate into less rigorous protection and promotion of the child's interests. While the caretaker may well be affectionate, she probably will not and should not be expected to demonstrate the level of personal commitment normally associated with a love relationship.

If the child does become attached to the parent substitute, the substitute's departure for a better job may be that much more problematic. The consequences for the child's self-esteem must be considered but also his developing conception of love hangs in the balance. What sort of love can be so easily withdrawn? The serious question is how much of the responsibility for giving children love and attention can be delegated to others without unacceptably distorting the love. It is perfectly possible to hire someone to give a child affection and attention within the confines of an employment relationship. The risk is that this form of limited love will provide an inadequate foundation for a conception of fully committed love, and that the parents' more permanent, but less involved, expressions of love will be inadequate, too. There may be no one the child perceives as fully committed and from whom he learns what it means to love.

Instrumental justifications for spending time with one's children must not obscure this basic value judgment: that relationships of love are intrinsically valuable as elements of a morally good and satisfying life. Acceptance of this judgment is perhaps the central, though not the only, reason many parents both want and feel they ought to spend more time with their children than their jobs and professional commitments permit.

V. CONCEPTIONS OF THE FAMILY

Guilt associated with parental absence rests centrally on parents' obligation to give their children love. But it is also linked to a conception of the family as the primary source of the individual's sense of self-worth and sense of morality. Within such a conception, parents have a special responsibility to show children they are valued for themselves and not just for the role they fulfill or for their achievements. In contrast, for example, to business firms in which individuals are valued primarily for their contribution to the firm's goals, the family is a place where ideally they are also valued for themselves and for their personal qualities. Parents communicate this sense of individual worth through the love and friendship they extend to their children and through their attitudes toward themselves and their roles in the family. To the extent that parents willingly delegate parental responsibilities to others, they reflect a view of themselves as replaceable functionaries rather than uniquely important members of the family unit.

No less important is the family's special responsibility for moral education. The fundamental moral capacities for trust and for caring, as well as the dispositions to respect certain basic principles of honesty and fidelity to one's word must be nurtured from the very beginnings of life. Given the existing structure of social institutions, there is no practical alternative to the family for this basic grounding in morality. The family is the only organization in which membership is sufficiently permanent to provide the constancy and consistency conducive to the development of these basic moral capacities and dispositions. Ideally, of course, morality will be reinforced by other social institutions. But it is doubtful that other institutions can make up for the family's failures in moral education.

In summary, the connections among parental love, parental involvement, and morality are multifaceted. Insofar as morality rests on willingness to care for others for their own sake, it rests on an attitude of love which receives its earliest nurturing through parental example. To the extent that morality involves dispositions to act in certain ways and not others, it is nurtured through the example, instruction, and consistent discipline provided by parents over the long term. Insofar as morality raises questions about how to live and what is valuable, parents can be children's greatest resource.

Parental involvement is essential if the family is to fulfill its role as the primary source of the individual's self-worth and sense of morality. Within this conception, the parent is both a source of love and a moral teacher, and as such, cannot be replaced. While these particular parental responsibilities are not delegable in the ways that many others are, they are not in principle inconsistent with parents' roles as breadwinners, household managers, overseers of children's education and health, or with parents' roles outside the family. But they depend on a personal commitment of time that may in practice conflict with the demands of other roles and responsibilities.

A managerial conception of parenthood which appears to be taking hold among some parents permits an easier reconciliation of these competing demands. Unlike the ideal outlined here, the managerial ideal is, in principle, consistent with the delegation of all parental responsibilities. The parental role becomes that of a manager who delegates, coordinates, and monitors performance. Inconsistent with commitment to the intrinsic value of love, the managerial conception also reflects an instrumental view of the individual. Good management dictates that every member of an organization be regarded as replaceable and that substitution of one individual for another not affect its functioning.

Managing children's activities is a very essential task of parenthood, but it is not the only one. If parents come to see themselves primarily as managers of their children's upbringing, not involved personally but only as higher-order supervisors, there is a danger that the distinctive competencies and roles of the family will be lost—that the family will come to be just another organization and the parent, just another functionary. Adopting the managerial conception of parenthood may lead to a reduction in the guilt experienced by parents who spend little time with their children, but it may also lead to morally diminished quality of life for children, parents, and society. To the extent that parental love provides the foundation for the moral community in which we live as adults, widespread adoption of the managerial conception of parenthood is a threat to that community.

If this argument is correct, employment practices incompatible with family life must be reassessed. We must recognize that the economic benefits yielded by these practices are won at considerable moral and social expense. Insofar as the operation of the economy depends on the moral fabric of the community, we must consider whether these practices may not be ultimately self-defeating, even from an economic point of view.

VI. PRACTICAL IMPLICATIONS: RESOLVING PARENTAL GUILT

I have outlined a case for the moral ideal of parenthood which I believe lies behind the guilt feelings reported by middle-class professionals. Many parents who are experiencing guilt may not have articulated for themselves these ideals and responsibilities, so pervasive is the view that guilt feelings are irrational and inappropriate. I have tried to show not only that these ideals are not irrational, but that there are strong arguments in their favor. There appear to be very good reasons to regard some parental responsibilities as non-delegable and to support parents who believe that they ought to spend more time with their children. Guilt-plagued parents should not be treated as neurotic or mistaken and sent for counseling to overcome their guilt. Instead, they should be encouraged to reorganize their lives to give expression to deeply held and important familial values and to speak up for patterns of employment that are compatible with fulfilling parental responsibilities as they see them.

From a social point of view, serious reconsideration must be given to the organization of work and to the usual child-care benefits offered by government and private employers. Birth leave, tax breaks through "cafeteria" benefit plans, full-time child-care services, employer-sponsored referral services, sick leave for children's illnesses—the usual benefits discussed—will do nothing to assuage the guilt aroused by regular day-to-day parental absences. That will be dealt with only by rather radical changes in patterns of work and career development. Opportunities for part-time work, self-directed work, job-sharing, and career breaks represent path-breaking steps in the right direction, but these practices must become more widely available and fully institutionalized as normal and acceptable if they are to make a significant contribution to the problem of parental guilt.

The nation's child-care policy must include support for daycare for the many families that need it. However, a policy that focuses only on daycare will not resolve the guilt problem discussed here. This problem will require public policy initiatives that encourage employers to accommodate variable work commitments as well as insurance and benefit plans that do not rigidly exclude part-time workers. It will require employers to take the lead in creating and permitting their employees to create new career patterns. Ultimately, however, such initiatives will succeed only if there is widespread recognition of the moral importance of the parent-child relationship and the value of parents' involvement with their children.

Given the various factors involved in each family situation, it is impossible to say, in general, just how much time it takes to satisfy the parental ideal I have described. However, there is no reason to think that being a good parent takes just the amount of time left over after work is finished or even after normal working hours as conventionally defined in today's business world. Ideological blinders and women's desires to enter the professional and managerial work force on a par with men have made the issue of time for children a taboo topic. Now that women's competence is no longer in question and now that men are taking on more parental responsibilities, we can perhaps give this matter the attention it deserves. ◆ ◆ ◆

Rights in the Workplace
A Nozickian Argument

Ian Maitland

There are costs associated with treating employees decently and well. Especially in the age of globalization, there are constant pressures for firms to economize and become more competitive. Maitland draws on the work of Robert Nozick to argue that some worker rights may be conditional on the economic climate and shows us that, once granted, they have to be paid for by someone—either the worker, the employer, or, ultimately, the consumer. In reading this selection, consider the cost of your clothes and ask yourself how much more you would have been prepared to pay for them to guarantee the rights of workers in the apparel industry.

There is a growing literature that attempts to define the substantive rights of workers in the workplace, a.k.a. the duties of employers toward their workers. Thus it has been proposed that employers have (at least *prima facie*) duties to provide workers with meaningful/fulfilling/self-actualizing work, some degree of control over work conditions, advance notice of plant closures or layoffs, due process before dismissal, etc. (See, for example, Goldman, 1980; Schwartz, 1984; Donaldson, 1982; Werhane, 1985).

The argument of this paper is that in a competitive labor market these standards are superfluous and, indeed, may interfere with workers' rights to freely choose their terms of employment. Furthermore, these supposed moral rights in the workplace may come at the expense of non-consenting third parties—like other workers or consumers.

NOZICK ON MEANINGFUL WORK

Since my argument basically extends Nozick's (1974, pp. 246 ff) discussion of meaningful work,

let us start with that. Assuming that workers wish to have meaningful work, how does and could capitalism respond? Nozick notes that if the productivity of workers *rises* when the work tasks are segmented so as to be more meaningful, then individual employers pursuing profits will reorganize the production process in such a way out of simple self-interest. Even if productivity were to remain the same, competition for labor will induce employers to reorganize work so as to make it more meaningful.

Accordingly, Nozick says, the only interesting case to consider is the one where meaningful work leads to reduced efficiency. Who will bear the cost of this lessened efficiency? One possibility is the employer. But the individual employer who unilaterally assumes this cost places himself at a competitive disadvantage and eventually—other things equal—will go out of business. On the other hand, if *all* employers recognize their workers' right to meaningful work (and if none cheats), then consumers will bear the cost of the industry's reduced efficiency. (Presumably, too, we would have to erect trade barriers to exclude the products of foreign producers who do not provide their workers with meaningful work, otherwise they would drive the domestic industry out of business).

What about the workers? If they want meaningful work, they will presumably be willing to give up something (some wages) to work at meaningfully segmented jobs:

> They work for lower wages, but they view their total work package (lower wages plus the satisfactions of meaningful work) as more desirable than less meaningful work at higher wages. They make a trade-off . . .

Nozick observes that many persons make just such trade-offs. Not everyone, he says, wants the same things or wants them as strongly. They choose their employment on the basis of the overall package of benefits it gives them.

THE MARKET
FOR MEANINGFUL WORK

Provided that the firm's lessened efficiency is compensated for by lower wages, then the employer should be indifferent between the two packages (meaningful work at lower wages or less meaningful work at higher wages). Indeed, if workers prize meaningful work highly, then they might be prepared to accept *lower* wages than are necessary simply to offset the firm's lower productivity. In that case, entrepreneurial employers seeking higher profits should be expected to offer more meaningful work: they will, by definition, reduce labor costs by an amount greater than the output lost because of less efficient (but more meaningful) production methods. In the process, they will earn higher profits than other firms (Frank, 1985, pp. 164–5).

In other words, there is a market for meaningful work. The employer who can find the combination of pay and meaningful work that matches workers' desires most closely will obtain a competitive advantage. Thus Goldman (1980, p. 274) is wrong when he claims that "profit maximization may . . . call . . . for reducing work to a series of simple menial tasks." On the contrary, profit maximization creates pressures on employers to offer workers meaningful work up to the point where workers would prefer higher pay to further increments of meaningfulness. Goldman's claim holds only if we assume that workers place no value at all on the intrinsic rewards of their work.

To "legislate" moral rights in the workplace to a certain level of meaningfulness, then, would interfere with workers' rights to determine what package of benefits they want.

EXTENDING THE LOGIC (1):
EMPLOYMENT AT WILL

In her discussion of employment at will (EAW), Werhane (1985, p. 91) says "[i]t is hard to imagine that rational people would agree in advance to being fired arbitrarily in an employment contract." According to her estimate, only 36% of the workforce is covered by laws or contracts which guarantee due process procedures with which to appeal dismissal. Werhane regards EAW as a denial of moral rights of employees in the workplace.

But, is it inconceivable that a rational worker would voluntarily accept employment under such conditions? Presumably, if the price is right, some workers will be willing to accept the greater insecurity of EAW. This may be particularly true, for example, of younger, footloose and fancy-free workers with marketable skills. It is also likely to be truer in a metropolitan area (with ample alternative employment opportunities) than a small town and when the economic outlook is good.

Likewise, some employers may value more highly the unrestricted freedom to hire and fire (smaller businesses, for example) and may be willing to pay higher wages for that flexibility. There may be other employers—larger ones in a position to absorb the administrative costs or ones with more stable businesses—who will find it advantageous to offer guarantees of due process in return for lower wages. Such guarantees are also more likely to be found where employees acquire firm-specific skills and so where continuity of employment is more important (Williamson, 1975).

According to this logic, wage rates should vary inversely with the extent of these guarantees, other things equal. In other words, workers purchase their greater security in the form of reduced wages. Or, put another way, some firms pay workers a premium to induce them to do without the guarantees.

If employers were generally to heed business ethicists and to institute workplace due process in cases of dismissals—and to take the increased costs or reduced efficiency out of workers' paychecks—then they would expose themselves to the pirating of their workers by other (less scrupulous?) employers who would give workers what they wanted instead of respecting their rights.

If, on the other hand, many of the workers not currently protected against unfair dismissal would in fact prefer guarantees of workplace due process—*and* would be willing to pay for it—then such guarantees would be an effective recruiting tool for an entrepreneurial employer. That is, employers are driven by their own self-interest to offer a package of benefits and rights that will attract and retain employees. If an employer earns a reputation for treating workers in a high-handed or inconsiderate way, then he (or she) will find it more difficult (or more expensive) to get new hires and will experience defections of workers to other employers.

In short, there is good reason for concluding that the prevalence of EAW does accurately reflect workers' preferences for wages over contrac-

tually guaranteed protections against unfair dismissal. (Of course, these preferences may derive, in part, from most workers' perceptions that their employers rarely abuse EAW anyway; if abuses were widespread, then you would expect the demand for contractual guarantees to increase).

EXTENDING THE LOGIC (2): PLANT CLOSURE/LAYOFF NOTIFICATION

Another putative workplace right is notice of impending layoffs or plant closures. The basis for such a right is obvious and does not need to be rehearsed here. In 1988 Congress passed plant-closing notification provisions that mandate 60-days' notice. Earlier drafts of the legislation had provided for 6 months' advance notification.

But the issue of interest here is employers' moral responsibilities in this matter. The basic argument is by now familiar: if employers have not universally provided guarantees of advance notice of layoffs, that reflects employers' and workers' choices. Some workers are willing to trade off job security for higher wages; some employers (e.g., in volatile businesses) prefer to pay higher wages in return for the flexibility to cut costs quickly. If employers have generally underestimated the latent demand of workers for greater security (say, as a result of the graying of the baby boomers), then that presents a profit opportunity for alert employers. At the same (or lower) cost to themselves, they should be able to put together an employment package that will attract new workers.

A morally binding workplace "right" to X days' notice of a layoff would preempt workers' and employers' freedom to arrive at an agreement that takes into account their own particular circumstances and preferences. In Nozick's aphorism, the "right" to advance notice may prohibit a capitalist act between consenting adults.

It would mean, for example, that workers and managers would be (morally) barred from agreeing to arrangements that might protect workers' jobs by enhancing a firm's chances of survival. This might be the case if, say, the confidence of creditors or investors would be strengthened by knowing that the firm would be free to close down its operations promptly if necessary.

Likewise, the increased expenses associated with a possible closure might deter firms from opening new plants in the first place—especially in marginal areas where jobs are most needed. In that case workers won't enjoy the rights due them in the workplace because there won't be any workplace. As McKenzie (1981, p. 122) has pointed out, "[r]estrictions on plant closings are restrictions on plant openings."

The effects of rights to notice of layoffs are not limited to the workers. If resources are diverted from viable segments of a (multiplant) firm in order to prolong the life of the plant beyond its useful economic life, then the solvency of the rest of the firm may be jeopardized (and so too the jobs of other workers).

If the obstacles to plant shutdowns are serious enough and if firms are prevented from moving to locations where costs are lower, then (as McKenzie, p. 120, points out) "Workers generally must pay higher prices for the goods they buy. Further, they will not then have the opportunity of having paying plants moving into their areas. . . ." And if such restrictions reduce the efficiency of the economy as a whole (by deterring investment, locking up resources in low-productivity, low-wage sectors of the economy), then all workers and consumers will be losers. Birch (1981, p. 7) has found that job creation is positively associated with plant closures: "The reality is that our most successful areas [at job creation] are those with the highest rates of innovation and failure, not the lowest." Europe has extensive laws and union agreements that make it prohibitively expensive to close plants, order layoffs or even fire malingerers and, not coincidentally, it has barely added a single job in the aggregate in the 1980's (as of 1987). Europe's persistent high unemployment is usually attributed to such "rigidities" in its labor market—what the London *Economist* picturesquely terms "Eurosclerosis."

It may be objected by some that workers' "rights claims cannot be overridden for the sake of economic or general welfare" (Werhane, 1985, p. 80; see also Goldman, p. 274). This is probably not the place to debate rights vs. utilities, but this discussion raises the question of whether workplace rights may sometimes violate the rights of third parties (other workers, consumers).

RESPECTING WORKERS' CHOICES

The argument of this paper has been that to set up a class of moral rights in the workplace may invade a worker's right to freely choose the terms and conditions that he (or she) judges are the best for him. The worker is stuck with these rights no matter whether he values them or not; they are inalienable in the sense that he may not trade them off for, say, higher wages. *We* might not be willing to make such a trade, but if we are to respect the worker's autonomy, then *his* preferences must be decisive.

Along the way the paper has tried to indicate how competition between employers in the labor market preserves the worker's freedom to choose the terms and conditions of his employment within constraints set by the economy. This competition means that employers' attempts to exploit workers (say, by denying them due process in the workplace without paying them the "market rate" for forgoing such protections) will be self-defeating because other would-be employers will find it profitable to bid workers away from them by offering more attractive terms. This point bears repeating because many of the accounts of rights in the workplace seem to assume pervasive market failure which leaves employers free to do pretty much what they want. Any persuasive account of such rights has to take into account the fact that employers' discretion to unilaterally determine terms and conditions of employment is drastically limited by the market. ◆ ◆ ◆

◆ References

Birch, David: 1981, 'Who creates jobs?', *Public Interest* (vol. 65), fall.

Donaldson, Thomas: 1982, *Corporations and Morality* (Prentice Hall, Englewood Cliffs, N.J.).

Frank, Robert: 1985, *Choosing the Right Pond* (Oxford University Press, New York).

Goldman, Alan: 1980, 'Business ethics: profits, utilities, and moral rights', *Philosophy and Public Affairs* 9, no. 3.

McKenzie, Robert: 1981, 'The case for plant closures', *Policy Review* 15, winter.

Nozick, Robert: 1974, *Anarchy, State and Utopia* (Basic Books, New York).

Schwartz, Adina: 1984, 'Autonomy in the workplace', in Tom Regan, ed., *Just Business* (Random House, N.Y.).

Werhane, Patricia H.: 1985, *Persons, Rights and Corporations* (Prentice Hall, N.Y.).

Williamson, Oliver E.: 1975, *Markets and Hierarchies* (Free Press, N.Y.).

Discrimination, Harassment, and the Glass Ceiling
Women Executives as Change Agents

Myrtle P. Bell, Mary E. McLaughlin, and Jennifer M. Sequeira

Dominant social groups tend to perpetuate their power by restricting entry into the group. At times, this can be unintentional—for example, when recruiters tend to unconsciously select people who resemble themselves instead of going strictly by credentials. These dynamics mean that there are often covert barriers to advancement.

Ideally, equals should be treated alike and only discriminated for or against on the basis of qualifications material to the position. Legislation has sought to protect certain groups that have been traditionally disadvantaged. Yet, Bell, McLaughlin, and Sequeira suggest that legal requirements and organizational change in the past 30 years have not been sufficient to eradicate sexism from corporations.

In this reading, the authors spell out what is meant by harassment, discrimination, and the glass ceiling, and they note the relevant legislation. They suggest that affirmative promotion of women will be the most effective means of bringing about widespread change.

Although sex discrimination is prohibited by law in the United States and various other regions, it continues to be a widespread problem for working women.[1] Title VII of the Civil Rights Act of 1964, amended in 1991 to include punitive damages, prohibits sex discrimination in the U.S. in all employment-related matters. Women in the U.S. have made considerable progress in organizations in the nearly 40 years since Title VII was passed and affirmative action for women was implemented. Nonetheless, women in the U.S. earn only about 76 cents to the dollar that men earn (Wall Street Journal, 1998), are more concentrated in lower earning industries and organizations than are men (Kim, 2000), and are under-represented in managerial and executive positions—positions of power, decision-making, and influence. Though comprising almost 50% of the U.S. workforce, women occupy only about 30% of all salaried manager positions, 20% of middle manager positions, and about 5% of executive level positions (Bose and Whaley, 2001; Fagenson and Jackson, 1993; Rice, 1994). These disparities in earnings, status, and position cannot be completely or largely explained by differences in the education, job tenure, or experience of working women, leaving much to be attributed to employment discrimination (Blau et al., 1998; Cain, 1986).

As in the U.S., discrimination against women is a continuing problem around the world (e.g., Can, 1995; Maatman, 2000; Muli, 1995; Korabik, 1993; Shaffer et al., 2000). Various countries provide prohibitions against discrimination. The Sex Discrimination Act of 1975 in the United Kingdom, the Canadian Human Rights Act, the Sex Discrimination Acts of 1984 and 1992 in Australia (Barak, 1997) and the Hong Kong Sex Discrimination Ordinance of 1996 (Shaffer et al., 2000) all prohibit discrimination on the basis of sex. These prohibitions provide criminal and/or individual penalties for such behavior (Maatman, 2000). Nonetheless, despite bans against sex discrimination, in most countries, as in the U.S., women's lower earnings, status, and occupation of managerial positions when compared with men's provide evidence of its continued existence (Roos and Gatta, 2001).

In this article, we discuss the relationships between discrimination, harassment, and the glass ceiling, arguing that many of the factors that preclude women from occupying executive and managerial positions also foster sexual harassment. We suggest that measures designed to increase representation of women in higher level positions will also reduce sexual harassment. We first define and discuss discrimination, harassment, and the glass ceiling, relationships between each, and relevant legislation. We next discuss the relationships between gender and sexual harassment, emphasizing the influence of gender inequality on sexual harassment. We then present recommendations for organizations seeking to reduce sexual harassment, emphasizing the role that women executives may play in such efforts and, importantly, the recursive effects of such efforts on increasing the numbers of women in higher level positions in organizations. Though much of the discussion focuses on U.S. women, because discrimination and harassment are issues for working women worldwide, we include available references to such issues in various regions outside of the U.S. In addition, our suggestions for addressing discrimination and harassment should be useful for organizations worldwide, particularly given the increasing recognition of the problems of discrimination and harassment for working women around the world (e.g., Maatman, 2000; Shaffer et al., 2000).

DISCRIMINATION, HARASSMENT, AND THE GLASS CEILING

We propose three forms of sex discrimination that affect women in organizations: overt discrimination,[2] sexual harassment, and the glass ceiling. Though by no means exhaustive of discriminatory acts, each has negative effects on women's status and therefore on women's ability to effect change regarding such discrimination. We discuss each form of discrimination, their shared antecedents, and a possible solution below.

Overt Discrimination

Overt discrimination is defined as the use of gender as a criterion for employment-related decisions. This type of discrimination was targeted by Title VII of the Civil Rights Act of 1964, which prohibited making decisions based on sex (as well as on race/ethnicity, national origin, and religion) in employment-related matters such as hiring, firing, and promotions. Overt discrimination includes, but is not limited to, such behaviors as refusing to hire women, paying them inequitably, or steering them to "women's jobs". Overt discrimination has long been a factor in women's employment experiences, yet its inclusion in Title VII is said to have been an "after-thought" perceived as certain to ensure its failure to pass.

Along with societal norms and perceptions of gender-appropriate occupations, overt dis-

crimination led to occupational sex-segregation. Occupational sex-segregation, in which at least 75% of workers in an occupation are male or female, has declined somewhat in the past three decades, however, most jobs remain fairly well sex-segregated (Bose and Whaley, 2001). In the U.S., women constitute the majority of nurses, flight attendants, and secretaries, in positions supportive of men, who comprise the majority of physicians, pilots, and executives, respectively (Roos and Gatta, 2001). Indeed, 7 of the 10 most common jobs for women are sex segregated (secretaries, cashiers, registered nurses, nursing aides/orderlies/assistants, elementary school teachers, and servers; Bose and Whaley, 2001). These jobs are characterized by low pay, low status, and short career ladders (Reskin, 1997).

Women's occupational sex-segregation, and the concomitant low status, short career ladders, and low pay, are common in other regions around the world (Kemp, 1994; Shaffer et al., 2000). In the U.S. and other countries, women who are low in organizational status, have low organizational power, and who earn significantly less than men are more frequent targets of sexual harassment (Fain and Anderton, 1987; Gruber, 1998; Gruber and Bjorn, 1982). Further, in these lower status positions, and many others that women occupy, women are considerably more likely to be supervised or managed by men than by women (Gutek and Morasch, 1982; Nieva and Gutek, 1981), which increases the risk that they will be harassed by their male superiors.

Sexual Harassment

Sexual harassment, a form of sex discrimination, is but one manifestation of the larger problem of employment-related discrimination against women. It now appears obvious that sexual harassment is a form of sex discrimination. However, its inclusion under Title VII was not the original intent of the act (Clarkson et al., 1995, p. 743). Early legal cases under Title VII questioned whether sexual harassment constituted sex discrimination (Lee and Greenlaw, 2000), often finding that it did not. Some cases ruled that supervisor sexual harassment resulted from individual proclivities over which organizations had little control (e.g., Corne v. Bausch & Lomb, In., 1975). However, in 1980, using Title VII, the U.S. Equal Employment Opportunity Commission (EEOC) published guidelines on sexual harassment. These guidelines clarified the illegality of harassment, describing two specific types as being unlawful sex discrimination: quid pro quo and hostile environment harassment.

In quid pro quo harassment, employment-related bribery or threat is used to obtain sexual compliance. The coercive nature of quid pro quo harassment requires that the harasser have some power over the target, thus most of such harassment is perpetrated by managers or supervisors. Hostile environment harassment occurs when sexual behaviors have "the purpose or effect of unreasonably interfering with an individual's work performance or creating an intimidating, hostile, or offensive" work environment (EEOC, 1980, p. 74677). This type of harassment may be perpetrated by managers, supervisors, peers, or subordinates (Paetzold and O'Leary-Kelly, 1996).

As is overt discrimination, sexual harassment is a persistent workplace problem for women worldwide. Numerous regions include prohibitions against such harassment (e.g., Canada, Israel, the United Kingdom, Australia; Barak, 1997), though with varying levels of stringency and application. Though specific prohibitions, terminology, and stringency vary worldwide, researchers have empirically identified three psychological dimensions of sexual harassment that persist across international boundaries: sexual coercion, gender harassment, and unwanted sexual attention (Fitzgerald et al., 1995; Gelfand et al., 1995). These dimensions have been confirmed in the U.S., Brazil, China, Canada, and other regions (e.g., Barak, 1997; Gelfand et al., 1995; Shaffer et al., 2000).

It is estimated that at least half of all U.S. women and about 15% of men will be sexually harassed at some point during their careers (Gutek, 1985; USMSPB, 1981, 1988). Although most sexual harassment targets do not file formal charges, more than 15,000 charges are filed with the U.S. EEOC each year (Buhler, 1999), an amount that has increased five-fold since the late 1980s. Most of those filing charges are women; 91% in 1992 and 86% in 2000 (EEOC, 2000). In contrast, most harassment perpetrators are men (Baugh, 1997; Keyton, 1996; O'Donohue, 1997, p. 2); clearly, sexual harassment is a gendered problem (Riger, 1991; Welsh, 1999). Indeed, reasons frequently suggested as explanations for the persistence and pervasiveness of sexual harassment are often gender-based, specifically, gender differences in perceptions of what constitutes harassment (e.g., Baugh, 1997; McKinney, 1992; Piotrkowski, 1998; Riger, 1991; Welsh, 1999) and gender differences in access to power and status (both a consequence and a cause of overt discrimination and harassment).

Sexual harassment may contribute to the perpetuation of occupational sex-segregation. Women may purposefully enter occupations typically dominated by women—occupations that have lower pay and fewer opportunities for advancement (Gutek and Koss, 1993; Kemp, 1994), in part to be safer from harassing co-workers. O'Farrell and Harlan (1982) found that women working in non-traditional, craft worker jobs experienced frequent harassment. Similarly, women who were blue-collar trade and transit workers in Mansfield et al's (1991) study, also jobs not traditionally held by women, were more likely to be harassed than were secretaries. In these cases, such sexual harassment may be deliberate and resentful behavior, designed to deter women from entering historically male jobs (Kemp, 1994; Martin, 1989; Miller, 1997; Tangri et al., 1982). The sometimes virulent harassment experienced by some women in male-dominated environments (e.g., Yoder and Aniakudo, 1996) makes the suggestion of intentional, purposeful creation of an inhospitable working environment appear credible.

The Glass Ceiling

The glass ceiling is the third form of discrimination that we discuss as affecting women in organizations and is an important factor in women's lack of access to power and status in organizations. The term "the glass ceiling" refers to invisible or artificial barriers that prevent women (and people of color) from advancing past a certain level (Federal Glass Ceiling Commission—FGCC, 1997; Morrison and von Glinow, 1990). As discussed above, women comprise about 30% of *all* managers, but less than 5% of executive managers in the U.S. At the lowest levels, women comprise a larger percentage of managers, making more obvious the disparities between women in high- and low-level managerial positions. The barriers that result in such disparities are often subtle, and include gender stereotypes, lack of opportunities for women to gain the job experiences necessary to advance, and lack of top management commitment to gender equity and equal employment initiatives. As with overt discrimination and sexual harassment, the glass ceiling exists in other regions of the world. According to Antal and Izraeli (1993), in industrialized nations overall, the number of women in the highest levels of management is about 6% (compared with about 5% in the U.S.). Of managerial women in China, Korabik (1992, p. 204) stated that "the higher the post, the fewer the women."

As an "invisible" barrier, the glass ceiling is difficult to eradicate through legislation. Informal networking and mentoring are frequently suggested as means of increasing the numbers of executive women (FGCC, 1997), yet these suggestions have had limited time to demonstrate effectiveness for women. Further, networking with and mentoring offered by executive men can be less fruitful and more problematic for junior women, who may be assumed to be sexually involved with their mentors. These problems can be particularly difficult for women of color (Thomas, 1989).

In sum, the relative lack of women managers and executives, the support roles many women workers provide to men workers, and occupational sex-segregation all facilitate sexual harassment. We propose that because overt discrimination, the glass ceiling, and sexual harassment are all forms of sex discrimination with (some) shared antecedents, measures to mitigate one will necessarily address the others. In the sections that follow, we discuss how having women in managerial and executive positions may be one particularly effective measure for reducing discrimination, for multiple reasons.

WOMEN EXECUTIVES AND HARASSMENT PREVENTION

In the previous sections we have discussed ways in which discrimination, the glass ceiling, and harassment affect women workers. Women who have attained executive positions have apparently achieved some measure of success against sex discrimination in matters of promotion and advancement. However, as evident by the existence of the glass ceiling, executive women are by no means discrimination free. Nonetheless, in the following sections, we propose that such executive women are uniquely positioned to address sexual harassment as illegal discrimination in their organizations in a variety of ways. From the perspective of the need for women executives in the battle against sexual harassment, we suggest that (1) women who work for male supervisors or managers report greater harassment and perceive their organizations as being more tolerant of harassment, (2) women rarely perpetrate harassment, (3) women view harassing behaviors differently from men and (4) women executives are more likely to have personal experience with sexual harassment than are men. Each is discussed below.

Supervisor Gender and Organizational Tolerance of Sexual Harassment

Research suggests that leader gender and behavior influence perceptions of organizational tolerance for sexual harassment and the actual existence of sexual harassment in an organization. For example, in Gutek's (1985) stratified random sample of workers in Los Angeles, women who had a male supervisor were more likely to report being harassed. Most of these women were harassed by male co-workers, who may have perceived that such behavior was tolerated (or condoned) by male supervisors. In Hulin et al's (1997) study, women who reported to a male supervisor viewed the organization as being more tolerant of harassment than did women who reported to a female supervisor. Finally, in her study of women office workers who worked in male-dominated environments, Piotrkowski (1998) found that women whose supervisors were men experienced more frequent sexual harassment than did women whose supervisors were women. Further, the most frequent hostile environment harassment was reported by women whose supervisors were men whom they perceived as being biased against women (Piotrkowski, 1998). Gruber (1997, p. 95) reporting several studies, summarized the relationship between leader behavior and harassment, noting that "organizations whose leaders were perceived as discouraging harassment had a lower incidence of harassment." For those perceived as encouraging harassment and bias the opposite was true.

Supervisor Gender and Harassment Perpetration

Supervisor gender itself is also a factor in sexual harassment, in a fairly simplistic way. Women infrequently perpetrate sexual harassment; EEOC estimates suggest that female to male harassment comprises about 9% of harassment while male to female harassment comprises 90% of harassment, with the remainder being same sex harassment (Keyton, 1996). Thus, it appears that merely employing women in managerial and executive positions would necessarily reduce sexual harassment to some extent—particularly sexual coercion.[3]

Gender Differences in Perceptions of Harassing Behaviors

In addition to differing in the experience and perpetration of sexual harassment, some gender differences exist in the determination of what behaviors constitute sexual harassment. These differences are less pronounced with sexual coercion; men and women view such behavior similarly and clearly, both perceiving it as harassment (Blakely et al., 1995; Burgess and Borgida, 1997; Williams et al., 1997). Sexual coercion occurs less frequently than does hostile environment harassment (Gruber and Bjorn, 1982; Munson et al., 2000; O'Hare and O'Donohue, 1998). Whether the more frequent, but less clear cut behaviors, such as sexual joking, making obscene comments, and persistent requests for dates are deemed harassment depends largely on the pervasiveness and persistence of the behavior and the gender of the perceiver. Specifically, women are more likely to interpret ambiguous behaviors as harassing than are men; in situations where the behavior is less clear cut, women are more likely to label those behaviors as being harassing than are men (e.g., Konrad and Gutek, 1986; Thacker and Gohmann, 1993; Wiener and Hurt, 2000). Thus, the types of behaviors that are more common are also the types of behaviors about which there are gender differences in perceptions of whether sexual harassment has occurred (see also Baugh, 1997). These differences may help to explain the persistence of sexual harassment (Baugh, 1997). Even though women are more likely than men to believe that certain behaviors do constitute harassment, they are unlikely to be in positions of power to influence *behaviors*, which contributes further to the persistence of sexual harassment. Further, as suggested by Dipboye (1985), women may not be treated fairly in organizations because the organizational culture may directly and indirectly communicate that they should not be. The absence of women in such positions may signal to potential harassers that women are not viewed as valuable members of the organization.

Women Executives and the Experience of Sexual Harassment

Despite being of higher level and status than most working women, as noted earlier, women executives remain far outnumbered by men executives and also experience sexual harassment. In addition to harassment from higher status executives and peers, women executives may also experience "contra-power" harassment, in which higher status women are harassed by lower status men (Benson, 1984; Grauerholz, 1989; McKinney, 1990, 1992). Galen et al. (1991) reported that 53% of the National Association of Female Executives in their survey had been sexually harassed. In a study of healthcare executives, twenty-nine percent of the women executives and five percent of the men executives reported having been harassed (Burda, 1996). Executive women in a 1992 survey by *Working Woman* were also harassed at a higher rate than non-executive women. *Working Woman* attributed this in part to the employment of such executive women in male-dominated companies (Sandoff, 1992). One respondent noted that "the higher up you climb, the worse the harassment gets," reflecting her belief that the harassment resulted from men's efforts to deter advancement of women (Sandoff, p. 48). Finally, in a sample of professional and managerial Canadian women, Burke and McKeen (1992) found that sexual harassment was a significant problem and resulted in lower organizational commitment and less job satisfaction. Clearly, sexual harassment is not limited to women of low occupational status, which may be beneficial in cessation efforts.

Women executives, as persons who are more likely to have experienced harassment than are men executives, may have a greater ability to empathize with harassment targets than would men. In addition, regardless of whether they have personally experienced harassment, executive women will be likely to perceive harassing behaviors similarly to other women, who, as discussed earlier, view such behaviors differently from men. As policy-makers, regardless of a genuine intent to maintain a harassment free environment, executive men may be perceptually disadvantaged with regard to sexual harassment. Specifically, due to their position as men, and a lifetime of unfamiliarity with sexual harassment or fear of assault, executive men may be less able to perceive sexually harassing behaviors as do women. Wells and Kracher (1993) have argued that life experiences and socialization make women likely to perceive sexual behaviors as offensive and possibly frightening; men may perceive the same behaviors as harmless or flattering. These differences in perception accentuate the need for women executives to battle in the war against sexual harassment.

INCREASING WOMEN EXECUTIVES: EQUITY AND POLICIES

We have discussed relationships between discrimination, harassment, and the glass ceiling, arguing that they are all factors that preclude women from occupying executive and managerial positions. Thus, we are in a double-bind with respect to executive women, discrimination, and harassment. More women are needed in executive positions to help curb sexual harassment. At the same time, sexual harassment (along with other forms of discrimination against women) may be preventing or limiting the advancement of women to executive positions. In the following sections, we provide suggestions for coping with this conundrum, drawn from the literatures on sexual harassment, discrimination, and gender equity. We begin with organizational support of gender equity, which is an important factor in reducing discrimination and harassment. Given the small percentage of women in positions of power and decision-making in organizations, such a commitment to gender equity would necessarily require the commitment of men in such positions. The high costs of sexual harassment, in the forms of withdrawal behaviors and intentions (Shaffer et al., 2000), physical and psychological effects on harassed employees (Hulin et al., 1997; Piotrkowski, 1998; Schneider et al., 1997), lowered job satisfaction (O'Farrell and Harlan, 1982; Piotrkowski, 1998), litigation costs, and damage awards if found liable, should result in executives of both genders and other stakeholders being wholeheartedly in support of efforts to curb harassment.

Organizational Support of Gender Equity

Grundmann et al. (1997, p. 177) have argued that efforts to prevent sexual harassment would include equal numbers of women and men in various levels of authority, and clearly communicated job roles with expected duties and limits. Gutek and Morasch (1982) indeed found that women working in gender-integrated settings with approximately equal numbers of men and women reported the lowest levels of harassment. We thus propose that concerted organizational efforts be made to reduce sex segregation and to employ women and men in various levels of authority, across the organization. Women would be employed in non-stereotyped positions, in decision-making, and policy-making positions, and earning pay comparable to men. Although overt efforts to employ women in male-dominated environments may initially increase levels of sexual harassment and backlash (see Burke and McKeen, 1996 for a discussion), over time, sexist barriers and hostile environments should be reduced. In their research on sexual harassment of women working in male-dominated fields, Mansfield et al. (1991) noted that the women who experienced the most harassment were working in more recently sex-integrated environments. We suggest that in organizations committed to gender equity, awareness of the potential for increased harassment would mean more concerted prevention efforts, including a strong harassment policy that reflects women's perspectives.

Sexual Harassment Policies

Strong sexual harassment policies have long been suggested as an important means of curbing sexual harassment (e.g., Dekker and Barling, 1998; Pryor et al., 1993). Stronger prohibitions and sanctions against harassment are associated with fewer reports of sexual harassment (Dekker and Barling, 1998; Pryor et al., 1993). Further, researchers have suggested that considering a feminist view of harassment in designing harassment policies is important (Maier, 1997; Riger, 1991). Despite large damage awards discussed in the media, most women who are harassed do not file lawsuits or even formally complain (Gutek and Koss, 1993; Sandoff, 1992). Baugh (1997) and Riger (1991) have argued that women's failure to complain reflects gender bias in policies, stemming from perceptual differences in the way women and men view harassment and from women's belief that their complaints will not be taken seriously. Riger has also suggested that informal grievance procedures for sexual harassment complaints may be more successful than formal ones, given women's relative lack of power. In addition, rather than punishment or retribution, many harassed women simply want the behavior to stop (Riger, 1991; Robertson et al., 1988). This suggests that in addition to formal grievance policies, organizations should include informal dispute resolutions that focus on harassment cessation for harassment targets who would be more comfortable with such measures.

WOMEN EXECUTIVES: AN UNTAPPED ADVANTAGE

Women Executives' Leadership Styles

A growing body of research indicates that women executives differ from men executives in many ways that enhance their management style and success (e.g., Rigg and Sparrow, 1994; Rosener, 1990; Stanford et al., 1995), which may translate into how they address issues of sexual harassment. A woman is more likely to lead an organization from the center of a network of interrelated teams, rather than from the top of a traditional command hierarchy as do most male leaders (Gilligan, 1982; Helgesen, 1990). As such "centralist" leaders, women executives are more likely to gain information directly about harassing or discriminatory behaviors, and can thus be more responsive (Smith, 2000, p. 38). As noted earlier, they may also be more likely to see such behaviors similarly to other women, rather than discounting or doubting them.

Another benefit of increased numbers of executive women may be higher satisfaction and retention of other managerial and professional women—those who would be future executives, shaping future policies. Burke and McKeen (1996) have reported that managerial and profes-

sional women working in organizations with predominantly men in higher level positions were less satisfied with their jobs and had greater intentions to quit than women in organizations with less skewed gender ratios in higher level positions. Burke and McKeen (1996) have also argued that the absence of women in executive positions may also result in the reluctance to create policies supportive of career goals of lower level managerial and professional women. We suggest that an under-representation of women may also result in reluctance or inability to create sexual harassment policies that meet the needs of women and men who are harassed. . . .

Feminist Perspective, Equity, and Effectiveness

Feminists and other researchers have long argued that viewing discrimination and its effects from a feminist rather than masculinist perspective would be beneficial in many ways. For example, Maier (1997, p. 943) has suggested that feminist alternatives be considered in organizations, rather than continuing to "take the prevailing masculinist managerial paradigm for granted." He also suggested that efforts toward gender equity would be beneficial for men as well as for women, given the prevailing (mis)perceptions and dysfunctionality inherent in masculinist assumptions. Maier (1997, p. 943) argued that these assumptions disadvantage women, parents (including men), and reduce overall organizational performance. He suggests that "feminist-based organizational transformation" would promote gender equity as well as more effective and ethical organizational behavior.

We suggest that women executives may increase organizational effectiveness in other areas as well. A climate of intolerance of sexual harassment is associated with a climate of tolerance for differences (e.g., in terms of race or ethnicity, culture, religion, or physical ability) and one that supports employee growth, participation, and empowerment through training, mentoring programs, and equitable pay for all employees. Such a climate is associated with a positive public image, and the concomitant attraction and retention of top talent (e.g., *Fortune*, 2000). In order to compete for human resources in today's tight labor market, men (as well as women) executives in other organizations will likely see the need to adopt similar policies that foster a healthy organizational climate. Policies and actions that promote gender equity may also be adopted in other organizations as the latest "management fashion" or trend (Abrahamson, 1996; DiMaggio and Powell, 1983; Weaver et al., 1999). Thus, women executives have the potential to make sweeping, progressive changes, both within and beyond their organizations.

CONCLUSION

In this manuscript, we have discussed three forms of sex discrimination: overt discrimination, sexual harassment, and the glass ceiling. We have argued that women in executive leadership roles are uniquely positioned to reduce sex discrimination, and that because all three have some common antecedents, steps to reduce one form will likely affect the others. We focused on the reduction of sexual harassment in particular, and argued that not only should simply increasing the numbers of women in executive positions decrease sexual harassment, but also that women executives use their positions of influence to increase gender equity and reduce sexual harassment. A particularly important contribution of our work is our explication of how women ex-

ecutives are especially motivated and qualified to reduce sexual harassment and increase gender equity, and the specific steps that they may take to do so. Given the beneficial consequences of such actions, and the imitative nature of organizations, they will likely "spillover" and be adopted in other organizations as well (e.g., Abrahamson, 1996).

There is a critical, immediate need for such actions. For over 20 years, employers have had EEOC guidelines on sexual harassment, which include clarification of what it is and steps to prevent it, along with litigation and numerous damage awards that serve as warning signals. Nonetheless, the rate of sexual harassment charges filed with the EEOC has grown. This rate of growth in charges filed *may* be a good sign, insofar as it reflects the targets' understanding of their rights and willingness to report incidences of harassment, perhaps as a consequence of training and information about sexual harassment provided by organizations. On the other hand, the sheer number of charges filed indicates that sexual harassment continues to be a problem, if not a growing problem. The persistence of sexual harassment despite efforts to curb it via methods used thus far (i.e., legislation and organizational policies) points to the critical need for innovative strategies. We believe that increasing representation of women at executive levels in organizations is just such a strategy, and one that will have comprehensive effects on all forms of sex discrimination and improve gender equity at all levels. This is no quick, easy solution, but one that is likely to have broad ranging positive effects on *all* employees, male as well as female, in the long run. ◆ ◆ ◆

◆ *Notes*

1. We acknowledge that the experience of sex discrimination and/or harassment is not limited to women; however, most discrimination and harassment involve women as targets. Thus, we focus our discussion on discrimination against and harassment of women.

2. We use the term overt discrimination to differentiate this type of discrimination from sexual harassment and the glass ceiling.
3. It could be argued that women do not perpetrate sexual harassment because they have not historically had the access to power and position that

men have had; however, as women are 30% of all managers, but are estimated to be 9% of all harassers, it appears that managerial women are less likely to perpetrate sexual harassment than are men.

◆ References

Abrahamson, E.: 1996, 'Management Fashion', *Academy of Management Review* **21**, 254–285.

Antal, A. and D. Izraeli: 1993, 'A Global Comparison of Women in Management: Women Managers in their Homelands and as Expatriates', in E. Fagenson (ed.), *Women in Management* (Sage Publications, Newbury Park, CA), pp. 52–96.

Barak, A.: 1997, 'Cross-cultural Perspectives on Sexual Harassment', in W. O'Donohue (ed.), *Sexual Harassment: Theory, Research, and Treatment* (Allyn and Bacon, Boston, MA), pp. 263–300.

Baugh, S. G.: 1997, 'On the Persistence of Sexual Harassment', *Journal of Business Ethics* **16**, 899–908.

Benson, K.: 1984, 'Comment on Crocker's "An Analysis of University Definitions of Sexual Harassment"', *Signs* **9**, 516–519.

Blakely, G. L., E. H. Blakely and R. H. Moorman: 1995, 'The Relationship between Gender, Personal Experience, and Perceptions of Sexual Harassment in the Workplace', *Employee Responsibilities and Rights Journal* **8**, 263–274.

Blau, F., M. Ferber and A. E. Winkler: 1998, *The Economics of Women, Men, and Work*, 3rd edition (Prentice-Hall, Upper Saddle River, NJ).

Bose, C. E. and R. B. Whaley: 2001, 'Sex Segregation in the U.S. Labor Force', in D. Vannoy (ed.), *Gender Mosaics: Social Perspectives (Original Readings)* (Roxbury Publishing, Los Angeles, CA), pp. 228–248.

Buhler, P. M.: 1999, 'The Manager's Role in Preventing Sexual Harassment', *Supervision* **60**(4), 16–18.

Burda, D.: 1996, 'ACHE Survey Response Spurs Expedited Sexual Harassment Policy', *Modern Healthcare* **26**(42), 2–3.

Burgess, D. and E. Borgida: 1997, 'Sexual Harassment: An Experimental Test of Sex-role Spillover Theory', *Personality and Social Psychology Bulletin* **21**, 63–75.

Burke, R. J. and C. A. McKeen: 1992, 'Social-sexual Behaviors at Work: Experiences of Managerial and Professional Women', *Women in Management Review* **7**(3), 22–30.

Burke, R. J. and C. A. McKeen: 1996, 'Do Women at the Top Make a Difference? Gender Proportions and the Experiences of Managerial and Professional Women', *Human Relations* **49**, 1093–1104.

Cain, G.: 1986, 'The Economic Analysis of Labor Market Discrimination: A Survey', in O. Ashenfelter and R. Layard (eds.), *Handbook of Labor Economics* (Elsevier Science Publishers, B. V., Amsterdam), pp. 693–785.

Can, T.: 1995, 'The Existence of Sexual Harassment in China', *Chinese Education and Society* **28**, 6–15.

Clarkson, K. W., R. L. Miller, G. A. Jentz and F. B. Cross: 1995, *West's Business Law: Text, Cases, Legal, Regulatory, and International Environment* (6th ed.) (West Publishing Co., St. Paul, MN).

Conte, A.: 1997, 'Legal Theories of Sexual Harassment', in W. O'Donohue (ed.) *Sexual Harassment: Theory, Research, and Treatment* (Allyn and Bacon, Boston, MA), pp. 50–83.

Corne v. Bausch & Lomb, Inc., 390 F. Supp. 161 (D. Arz. 1975), vacated, 562 F.2d 55 (9th Cir. 1977).

Dekker, I. and J. Barling: 1998, 'Personal and Organizational Predictors of Workplace Sexual Harassment of Women by Men'. *Journal of Occupational Health Psychology* **31**, 7–18.

Dimaggio, P. J. and W. W. Powell: 1983, 'The Iron Cage Revisited: Institutional Isomorphism and Collective Rationality in Organizational Fields', *American Sociological Review* **48**, 147–160.

Dipboye, R. L.: 1985, 'Some Neglected Variables in Research on Discrimination in Appraisals', *Academy of Management Review* **10**, 116–127.

Equal Employment Opportunity Commission: 1980, 'Guidelines on Discrimination Because of Sex', *Federal Register* **45**, 74676–74677.

Equal Employment Opportunity Commission: 2000, 'Sexual harassment charges EEOC & FEPAs Combined: FY 1992–FY 2000', [On-line]. Available: http://www.eeoc.gov/stats/harass.html.

Fain, T. C. and D. L. Anderton: 1987, 'Sexual Harassment: Organizational Context and Diffuse Status', *Sex Roles* **5**(6), 291–311.

Fagenson, E. A. and J. J. Jackson: 1993, 'The Status of Women Managers in the United States', *International Studies of Management and Organizations* **23**, 93–112.

Federal Glass Ceiling Commission: 1997, 'The Glass Ceiling', in D. Dunn (ed.), *Workplace/Women's Place: an Anthology* (Roxbury Publishing, Los Angeles, CA), pp. 226–233.

Fitzgerald, L. F., C. L. Hulin and R. Drasgow: 1995, 'The Antecedents and Consequences of Sexual Harassment in Organizations: An Integrated Model', in G. P. Keita and J. J. Hurrell, Jr. (eds.), *Job Stress in a Changing Workforce: Investigating Gender, Diversity, and Family Issues* (American Psychological Association, Washington, DC), pp. 55–73.

Fortune: July 10, 2000, 'America's 50 Best Companies for Minorities', pp. 190–200.

Galen, M. J., J. Weber and A. Cuneo: 1991, 'Out of the Shadows, the Thomas Hearings Force Business to Confront an Ugly Reality', *Business Week* (October 28), 30–31.

Gelfand, M. J., L. F. Fitzgerald and F. Drasgow: 1995, 'The Structure of Sexual Harassment: A Confirmatory Analysis Across Cultures and Settings', *Journal of Vocational Behavior* **47**, 164–177.

Gilligan, C.: 1982, *In a Different Voice* (Harvard University Press, Cambridge, MA).

Grauerholz, E.: 1989, 'Sexual Harassment of Women Professors by Students: Exploring the Dynamics of Power, Authority, and Gender in a University Setting', *Sex Roles* **21**, 789–801.

Gruber, J. E.: 1997, 'An Epidemiology of Sexual Harassment: Evidence from North America and Europe', in W. O'Donohue (ed.), *Sexual Harassment: Theory, Research, and Treatment* (Allyn and Bacon, Boston), pp. 84–98.

Gruber, J. E.: 1998, 'The Impact of Male Work Environments and Organizational Policies on Women's experiences of Sexual Harassment', *Gender and Society* **12**, 301–320.

Gruber, J. E. and L. Bjorn: 1982, 'Blue-collar Blues: The Sexual Harassment of Women Autoworkers', *Work and Occupations* **93**, 271–298.

Grundmann, E. O., W. O'Donohue and S. H. Peterson: 1997, 'The Prevention of Sexual Harassment', in W. O'Donohue (ed.), *Sexual Harassment: Theory, Research, and Treatment* (Allyn and Bacon: Boston), pp. 175–184.

Gutek, B. A.: 1985, *Sex and the Workplace* (Jossey-Bass, San Francisco).

Gutek, B. A., and M. P. Koss, 1993, 'Changed Women and Changed Organizations: Consequences of and Coping with Sexual Harassment', *Journal of Vocational Behavior* **42**, 28–48.

Gutek, B. A. and B. Morasch: 1982, 'Sex Ratios, Sex-role Spillover, and Sexual Harassment of Women at Work', *Journal of Social Issues* **38**, 55–74.

Helgesen, S.: 1990, *The Female Advantage: Women's Ways of Leading* (Doubleday, Garden City, NY).

Hulin, C. L., L. F. Fitzgerald and F. Drasgow: 1997, 'Organizational Influences on Sexual Harassment', in M. S. Stockdale (ed.), *Sexual Harassment in the Workplace*, Vol. 5 (Sage, Thousand Oaks, CA), pp. 127–150.

Kemp, A.: 1994, *Women's Work: Degraded and Devalued* (Prentice-Hall, Englewood Cliffs, NJ).

Keyton, J.: 1996, 'Sexual Harassment: A Multidisciplinary Synthesis and Critique', in B. R. Burleson (ed.), *Communication Yearbook*, Vol. 19 (Sage, Thousand Oaks, CA), pp. 92–155.

Kim, Marlene: 2000, 'Women Paid Low Wages: Who They Are and Where They Work', *Monthly Labor Review* **123**(9), 26–30.

Konrad, A. M. and A. Gutek: 1986, 'Impact of Work Experiences on Attitudes Toward Sexual Harassment', *Administrative Science Quarterly* **31**, 422–438.

Korabik, K.: 1992, 'Women Hold Up Half the Sky: The Status of Managerial Women in China', in W.

Wedley (ed.), *Advances in Chinese Industrial Studies*, Vol. 3 (JAI Press, Greenwich, CT), pp. 197–211.

Korabik, K.: 1993, 'Managerial Women in the People's Republic of China', *International Studies of Management and Organizations* 23(4), 47–64.

Lee, R. D., Jr. and P. S. Greenlaw: 2000, 'Employer Liability for Employee Sexual Harassment: A Judicial Policy-making Study', *Public Administration Review* 60(2), 123–133.

Maatman, G. L., Jr.: 2000, 'Harassment, Discrimination Laws Go Global', *National Underwriter* 104(37), 34–35.

Maier, M.: 1997, 'Gender Equity, Organizational Transformation, and Challenger', *Journal of Business Ethics* 16(9), 943–962.

Mansfield, P. K., P. B. Koch, J. Henderson, J. R. Vicary, M. Cohn and E. W. Young: 1991, 'The Job Climate for Women in Traditionally Male Blue-collar Occupations', *Sex Roles* 25, 63–79.

Martin, S.: 1989, 'Sexual Harassment: The Link Joining Gender Stratification, Sexuality, and Women's Economic Status', in J. Freeman (ed.), *Women: A Feminist Perspective*, 4th ed. (Mayfield Publishing, Mountain View, CA), pp. 57–75.

McKinney, K.: 1990, 'Sexual Harassment of University Faculty by Colleagues and Students', *Sex Roles* 23, 431–470.

McKinney, K.: 1992, 'Contrapower Sexual Harassment: The Effects of Student Sex and Type of Behavior on Faculty Perceptions', *Sex Roles* 27, 1–17.

Miller, L. L.: 1997, 'Not Just Weapons of the Weak: Gender Harassment as a Form of Protest for Army Men', *Social Psychology Quarterly* 60, 32–51.

Morrison, A. M. and M. A. von Glinow: 1990, 'Women and Minorities in Management', *American Psychologist* 45, 200–208.

Muli, K.: 1995, '"Help Me Balance the Load": Gender Discrimination in Kenya', in J. Peters and A. Wolper (ed.), *Women's Rights, Human Rights: International Feminist Perspectives* (Routledge, London), pp. 78–81.

Munson, L. J., C. Hulin and F. Drasgow: 2000, 'Longitudinal Analysis of Dispositional Influences and Sexual Harassment: Effects on Job and Psychological Outcomes', *Personnel Psychology* 53, 21–46.

Nieva, V. F. and B. A. Gutek: 1981, *Women and Work: A Psychological Perspective* (Praeger, New York).

O'Donohue, W.: 1997, 'Introduction', in W. O'Donohue (ed.), *Sexual Harassment: Theory, Research, and Treatment* (Allyn & Bacon, Needham Heights, MA), pp. 1–5

O'Farrell, B. and S. L. Harlan: 1982, 'Craftworkers and Clerks: The Effects of Male Coworker Hostility on Women's Satisfaction with Nontraditional Jobs', *Social Problems* 29, 252–264.

O'Hare, E. A. and W. O'Donohue: 1998, 'Sexual Harassment: Identifying Risk Factors', *Archives of Sexual Behavior* 27, 561–580.

O'Leary-Kelly, A. M., R. L. Paetzold and R. W. Griffin: 2000, 'Sexual Harassment as Aggressive Behavior: An Actor Based Perspective', *The Academy of Management Review* 25, 372–388.

Paetzold, R. L. and A. M. O'Leary-Kelly: 1996, 'The Implications of U.S. Supreme Court and Circuit Court Decisions for Hostile Environment Sexual Harassment Cases', in M. S. Stockdale (ed.) *Sexual Harassment in the Workplace*, Vol. 5 (Sage, Thousand Oaks, CA), pp. 85–104.

Piotrkowski, C. S.: 1998, 'Gender Harassment, Job Satisfaction, and Distress Among Employed White and Minority Women', *Journal of Occupational Health Psychology* 3, 33–43.

Pryor, J. B., E. R. DeSouza, J. Fitness, C. Hutz, M. Kumpf, K. Lubbert, O. Pesonen and M. Erber: 1997, 'Gender Differences in the Interpretation of Social-sexual Behavior: A Cross-cultural Perspective on Sexual Harassment', *Journal of Cross-Cultural Psychology* 28, 509–534.

Reskin, B.: 1997, 'Sex Segregation in the Workplace', in D. Dunn (ed.), *Workplace/Women's Place* (Roxbury Publishing, Los Angeles, CA), pp. 69–73.

Rice, F.: 1994, 'How to Make Diversity Pay', *Fortune*, August 8.

Riger, S.: 1991, 'Gender Dilemmas in Sexual Harassment Policies and Procedures', *American Psychologist* 46(5), 497–505.

Rigg, C. and J. Sparrow: 1994, 'Gender Diversity, and Working Styles', *Women in Management Review* 9(1), 9–16.

Robertson, C., C. E. Dyer and D. Campbell: 1988, 'Campus Harassment: Sexual Harassment Policies and Procedures at Institutions of Higher Learning', *Signs* **13**(4), 792–812.

Roos, P. A. and M. L. Gatta: 2001, 'The Gender Gap in Earnings', in G. Powell (ed.), *Handbook of Gender and Work* (Sage, Thousand Oaks, CA), pp. 95–123.

Rosener, J. B.: 1990, 'Ways Women Lead', *Harvard Business Review* **68**(6), 119–126.

Sandoff, R.: 1992, 'Sexual Harassment: The Inside Story (Working Woman Survey)', *Working Woman* (June), 47–78.

Schneider, K. T., S. Swan and L. F. Fitzgerald, 1997, 'Job-related and Psychological Effects of Sexual Harassment in the Workplace: Empirical Evidence from Two Organizations', *Journal of Applied Psychology* **82**, 401–415.

Shaffer, M. A., J. R. W. Joplin, M. P. Bell, T. Lau and C. Oguz: 2000, 'Gender Discrimination and Job-related Outcomes: A Cross-cultural Comparison of Working Women in the United States and China', *Journal of Vocational Behavior* **57**(4), 395–427.

Smith, S. M.: 2000, *Women at Work: Leadership for the Next Century* (Prentice-Hall, Upper Saddle River, NJ).

Stanford, J. H., B. R. Oates and D. Flores: 1995, 'Women's Leadership Styles: A Heuristic Analysis', *Women in Management Review* **10**(2), 9–16.

Tangri, S., M. Burt and I. Johnson: 1982, 'Sexual Harassment at Work: Three Explanatory Models', *Journal of Social Issues* **38**(4), 33–54.

Thacker, R. A. and S. F. Gohmann: 1993, 'Male/Female Differences in Perception and Effect of Hostile Environment Sexual Harassment: Reasonable Assumptions?', *Public Personnel Management* **22**, 461–471.

Thomas, D. A.: 1989, 'Mentoring and Irrationality: The Role of Racial Taboos', *Human Resource Management* **28**, 279–290.

U.S. Merit Systems Protection Board: 1981, *Sexual Harassment in the Federal Workplace: Is It a Problem?* (U.S. Government Printing Office, Washington, DC).

U.S. Merit Systems Protection Board: 1988, *Sexual Harassment in the Federal Workplace: An Update* (U.S. Government Printing Office, Washington, DC).

Wall Street Journal: 1998, 'Pay Gap between Men and Women Begins to Narrow Again After a Pause', June 10, B6A.

Weaver, G. R., L. K. Treviño and P. L. Cochran: 1999, 'Integrated and Decoupled Corporate Social Performance: Management Commitments, External Pressures, and Corporate Ethics Practices', *Academy of Management Journal* **42**, 539–552.

Wells, D. L. and B. J. Kracher: 1993, 'Justice, Sexual Harassment, and the Reasonable Victim Standard', *Journal of Business Ethics* **12**, 423–431.

Welsh, S.: 1999, 'Gender and Sexual Harassment', *Annual Review of Sociology* **25**, 169–190.

Wiener, R. and L. Hurt: 2000, 'How Do People Evaluate Social Sexual Conduct at Work? A Psycholegal Model', *Journal of Applied Psychology* **85**, 75–85.

Williams, C., R. Brown, P. Lees-Haley and J. Price: 1997, 'An Attributional (Causal Dimensional) Analysis of Perceptions of Sexual Harassment', *Journal of Applied Social Psychology* **25**, 1169–1183.

Yoder, J. D. and P. Aniakudo: 1996, 'When Pranks become Harassment: The Case of African American Women Firefighters', *Sex Roles* **35**, 253–270.

Workplace Discrimination, Good Cause, and Color Blindness

D. W. Haslett

One view is that business ought to be self-managing, without outside interference. On the issue of discrimination, we have government interference to benefit individual workers. It is not always clear what is meant by discrimination, though; typically it means to treat people differently on grounds that have nothing to do with their abilities at work. Although it certainly sounds immoral, the government only protects certain classes. A larger question is whether the government has a mandate to dictate morality at work.

The clash that arises in business is that companies are geared to make profit, and there may be cases where discrimination is the more profitable course of action. Moreover, any regulation that restricts a business from making its own decisions may lead to increased inefficiencies.

In this selection, Haslett takes us through a number of examples that serve to isolate the moral issue in each case; for instance, is it acceptable to fire an underemployed worker because the company has racist clients who refuse to do business with him? Haslett then proposes a general moral principle, stating that in most cases an employer should be color-blind. He briefly discusses affirmative action and makes a couple of exceptions where he thinks that it will be acceptable to take race into account.

The article concentrates on issues of color. When we consider the law, we see there are a number of protected classes (race, gender, age, religion, marital status, and so on). Do Haslett's conclusions apply to all these classes? Do you think compensation for past wrongs is appropriate? Do you agree that there is a significant difference between discrimination on the basis of color and, for example, obesity or having a big nose?

By general consensus, employers are morally obligated to not discriminate. But do we really know what unethical discrimination in the workplace is? If we try to explain exactly what it is, we may soon discover that we are not as clear about it as we had thought. Let us consider what we may call the *Bank Teller* case. In a small town in the year 1925, one of the town's two banks, State Trust, has a teller who is a black person. Although this teller's job performance is fine, the bigoted townspeople are expressing their disapproval of having a black person handling their money by taking their business to the town's other bank. This is causing a slow, but continuous loss of business for State Trust, which, although not threatening to the bank's existence, is nevertheless responsible for a serious, steady drain upon its profits. For the purpose of preventing any further drain upon profits, State Trust, with expressions of genuine regret, terminates the teller's employment. Does terminating his employment constitute unethical, workplace discrimination? Let us also consider affirmative action, in the form of preferential treatment for minorities and women. Is it, as its opponents claim, simply another form of unethical discrimination? If not, exactly why not? If questions such as these are to be answered adequately, we need an exact account of what unethical, workplace discrimination really is.

Since our concern is with morality, not law, we should suspend judgment about the legal status of any hypothetical cases we will consider, and concentrate only on their moral status independent of any law. For practical purposes, their legal status is important. But for theoretical purposes, their moral status is even more important since, ultimately, law should be guided by justifiable morality.

1. WORKPLACE DISCRIMINATION IN THE GENERIC SENSE

Not very long ago, the word "discrimination" had no moral connotations. "To discriminate" meant to differentiate, and "discrimination" meant differentiation. "Discrimination" is still used in a morally neutral sense, but this use is becoming obsolete; typically "to discriminate" means to differentiate among individuals in a way that is morally wrong. The difference between "differentiate" and "discriminate" is thus becoming analogous to the difference between "kill" and "murder." "Kill" remains morally neutral, while "murder" carries a negative moral connotation. We shall examine "discrimination" only as used in the sense in which it carries a negative moral connotation.

Let us begin by distinguishing the wrong of discrimination from other moral wrongs, such as theft. The wrong of theft consists of taking what belongs to someone else. The wrong of discrimination consists of treating people differently for no good reason. What constitutes a good reason

for differential treatment generally depends upon what the purpose of the differential treatment is. For determining if a good reason exists, the purpose of the differential treatment need not even be ethical. Consider, for example, an unscrupulous employer, Sam Swindler, whose purpose is to enrich himself by withholding for taxes more from the paychecks of his employees than he should. If Swindler does this only to his employees too uneducated to notice the scam, then the way in which he treats the uneducated employees is not discriminatory because, relative to Swindler's disreputable purpose, there is a perfectly good reason for this differential treatment. Thus, although Swindler's behavior is indeed unethical, it is not unethical discrimination. Instead, it is unethical because it is taking what belongs to others. But suppose that Swindler is not only a thief, but a bigot as well, and, as such, practices his withholding-tax scam only upon uneducated employees who are black, leaving uneducated, white employees alone. This does constitute unethical discrimination, not because it is an unethical scam, but because it treats people differently for no good reason. Thus, in this case, Swindler does not just one unethical thing, but two, stealing from employees and unethically discriminating against blacks.

But to say that discrimination consists of treating people differently for no good reason does not really tell us much about discrimination, since what constitutes a good reason for a difference in treatment varies from context to context. In certain contexts, such as that of choosing a spouse, mere personal preference is a good reason. In other contexts, differential treatment resulting from purely random choice may even be for good reason. These are contexts in which a choice must be made and each person is equally deserving, such as where a teacher calls on students to answer questions in class, and no student is any more deserving of being called on than any other. But let us focus specifically on the workplace, and ask what, in general, constitutes a good reason in this context, starting with the most serious action an employer can legitimately take against an employee, one that is often alleged to have been taken discriminatorily, firing the employee.

According to common law, just as an employee may quit working for an employer for any reason at all, an employer may fire an employee for any reason at all. As a Tennessee court put it, employers "may dismiss their employees at will . . . for good cause, for no cause, or even for cause morally wrong, without thereby being guilty of legal wrong."[1] If, for example, an employer does not like yellow shirts, or does not like big ears, and an employee occasionally wears yellow shirts, or has big ears, then, according to common law, the employer may legally fire the employee for that. But this common law standard is no longer law anywhere in the United States. It has been modified by the Civil Rights Act of 1964, which makes it illegal for an employer with fifteen or more employees "to discriminate against any individual . . . because of such individual's race, color, religion, sex, or national origin."[2] Additional legislation has made it illegal also to discriminate because of pregnancy, age, or disability. Because of this legislation, a person may no longer be fired for being black, or being female, since a person's race and gender are now legally protected properties, but a person may still be fired for wearing yellow shirts, or having big ears. In Montana, however, common-law has been superseded by a good-cause standard, according to which a person may not be fired except for good cause. "Good cause" means good reason. Thus a person may not be fired for wearing yellow shirts or having big ears in Montana, provided only that these reasons are not good reasons.

It would appear that something like the good-cause standard is also the standard for morality.

There are good reasons why this should be the standard. Morality should, of course, protect a person from being fired for such unreasonable causes as being black or being female. But it makes little sense for morality to protect a person from being fired for these unreasonable causes, while not protecting a person from being fired for such equally unreasonable causes as wearing yellow shirts or having big ears. For morality to protect people from being fired for some unreasonable causes but not others hardly seems coherent, and coherence is one requirement that a code of morality must meet to be justified. Thus, regardless of what standard for justifiable firing the law may incorporate, the good-cause standard is the one that morality should incorporate. To understand workplace discrimination, we must therefore try to develop a general account of what constitutes good cause in the workplace.

For firing an employee, inadequate job performance constitutes good cause. But a general account of good cause merely in terms of inadequate job performance will not do. Plant relocations, takeovers, recessions, and downsizing to maximize profits may all, under certain conditions, be good causes for firing certain employees, even though their job performances remain exemplary. Consider, for example, the case of *Viking Vehicle*, a company that, in 1910, manufactures both horse-drawn carriages and automobiles. Suppose that, to remain profitable, Viking must cut back its operations by eliminating either its carriage division or its automotive division, and that, while the performance of the workers in its carriage division is better than that of the workers in its automotive division, the highly technical skills of workers in each division cannot be transferred, cost-effectively, to those in the other division. If management concludes that the outlook for profits from Viking's automotive division is much brighter than the outlook for profits from its carriage division and, as a result, lays off the workers in its carriage division, this will be for good cause even though these workers have the better job performance. Consider also the case of *Jordan Michael,* in which an accounting firm must lay off either John Whiz, who performs his job as an accountant with distinction, or Jordan Michael, a world-famous, retired basketball player who performs his job as an accountant satisfactorily, but not with distinction. Suppose, however, that, since many people want to shake hands with the famous Jordan Michael, he brings in considerable new business and, for this reason, does more to add to the profits of the firm than Whiz. If, even though Whiz is the better accountant, the firm retains Michael instead, then, once again, this will be for good cause. When job performance and profitability conflict, it normally counts as good cause to give priority to profitability.

This suggests that good cause for firing an employee should be construed in terms of profit. Profit is a perfectly legitimate reason for being in business. Moreover, justifying termination decisions in terms of profit is more efficient than justifying them in terms of irrelevant factors like skin color or ear size, and, other things being equal, the more efficient businesses are, the more they contribute to the well-being of the community in general. Indeed, perhaps justifiability in terms of profit should count as good cause for any differential treatment by a workplace organization. We might, thus, try to characterize good cause in the workplace by saying that any person who is treated differently from any other person is treated differently for good cause if and only if the difference in treatment can be justified in terms of profit.

Yet this will not do. Many workplace organizations do not have profit as a purpose at all. The purpose of a governmental workplace organization is not profit, but the general welfare, and the purpose of a charitable organization is not profit, but helping others. In addition, even for a workplace organization which is a private business with profit as a purpose, profit may not qualify as its fundamental purpose. A fundamental purpose is a purpose, or combination of purposes, that, in the case of a conflict between it and other purposes, always has priority. Choosing what purpose, or combination of purposes, is to count as fundamental for a business is the prerogative of its owner. Profit will therefore not qualify as the business's fundamental purpose if its owner chooses, as fundamental, some other purpose, such as the owner's well-being, which may not always be best achieved by maximizing profits. Alternatively, an owner could choose, as fundamental, some purpose relating to the well-being of others. But being able to justify a difference in treatment in terms of profit normally is crucial if the organization is a privately owned business. For a privately owned business therefore, whether or not a difference in treatment can be justified in terms of profit is a legitimate rule of thumb for determining whether or not it can be justified in terms of the fundamental purpose of the business. A rule of thumb is, of course, subject to being overridden. Absent evidence to the contrary, however, it is reasonable to assume that the fundamental purpose of a privately owned business, although not necessarily equivalent to maximizing profits, nevertheless calls for maximizing profits. But good cause cannot, in general, be characterized in terms of profits since not all workplace organizations are privately owned businesses with profits as a purpose and, although the fundamental purpose of most privately owned businesses calls for maximizing profits, this need not be true of all privately owned businesses.

Perhaps then we should characterize good cause in terms of fundamental purpose, and say that any person who is treated differently from any other person by a workplace organization is treated differently for good cause if and only if the difference in treatment can be justified in terms of the fundamental purpose of the organization. But as we can see from the following variations of the famous *Johnson Controls* case, this is still not a complete account of good cause.[3] Suppose that any woman who does a certain job at Johnson Controls will be exposed to lead particles that will permanently damage her reproductive system in such a way that, if she goes on to have children, they are likely [to] be born with serious brain damage. Suppose also that, contrary to the real *Johnson Controls* case, exposure to the particles has no effect upon the male reproductive system. Is Johnson Controls morally obligated to prohibit women from doing this job unless they can prove they are unable to have children? Suppose that the lead particles do not damage the reproductive system of a woman, but damage that of a man in such a way that, whenever he has sex with a woman, he will transmit a poison that will slowly kill her. Is Johnson Controls morally obligated to prohibit men from doing this job, even men who swear to give up sex forever? If so, then it does not constitute unethical discrimination for the company to treat men differently from women in this way even if doing so cannot be justified in terms of the organization's fundamental purpose. To cover cases like this, we must revise our account of good cause to the following: Any person who is treated differently from any other person by a workplace organization is treated differently for good cause if and only if either the difference in treatment is morally obligatory, or it can be justified in terms of the fundamental purpose of the organization.

This account should be understood in terms of the following four provisos. First, although we are focusing here on what is good cause for differences in how a workplace organization treats employees and job candidates, this account should be understood as delineating also what is good cause for differences in how the organization treats customers, suppliers, clients, and anyone else. Second, to the extent that the superior contribution someone makes to the fundamental purpose of an organization is attributable to the violation of a moral or legal obligation by that person, it cannot be used to justify a difference in treatment. Thus a butcher cannot justify paying one his clerks more than the others if the superior contribution she makes to profits is attributable merely to the fact that she puts her thumb on the scales. Third, if a choice must be made between two or more individuals, such as two or more candidates for the same job, and there is no basis at all in terms of the organization's fundamental purpose for distinguishing between the individuals, then whatever choice is made counts as being for good cause. The final proviso is that this account of good cause calls for weak justification only. This means that, to justify a difference in treatment, a workplace organization need not show that the difference in treatment really is in fact the best means for realizing its fundamental purpose. All it needs to show is that believing the difference in treatment to be the best means is not unreasonable. . . .

Discrimination in the generic sense consists of treating people differently for no good reason or cause. Since we now have an account of good cause within the workplace, we have an account of workplace discrimination in the generic sense. Let us return to the *Bank Teller* case, which concerns a bank the fundamental purpose of which calls for maximizing profits. One of the bank's tellers is a black person and, even though he is doing a good job, the bigoted townspeople are taking their business elsewhere because he is black, thereby causing a slow, but steady drain upon the bank's profits. Since terminating this teller's employment can be justified in terms of the bank's fundamental purpose, it is, according to this account, for good cause, and since it is for good cause, terminating the teller's employment does not constitute discrimination in the generic sense.

2. THE VEIL-OF-IGNORANCE PRESUMPTION

According to this account so far, a workplace organization is discriminating in the generic sense if and only if it treats people differently without good cause. A difference in treatment is for good cause if it can be justified in terms of the organization's fundamental purpose. Perhaps there was a time when, to capture most people's moral intuitions about workplace discrimination, this account would have been sufficient. But this is no longer true. Let us consider, for example, the case of *Billy Bob*. Billy Bob is founder and sole owner of a small automobile repair business known as Billy Bob's Body Shop. He is also a white bigot who automatically turns down all black people who apply for openings at his business, no matter how good they may be at repairing automobiles. He justifies this exclusionary policy by proclaiming the fundamental purpose of his business to be "income for white people only," a purpose, he says, that, for him, has priority over even that of maximizing profits. Obviously no black person can contribute to this fundamental purpose as well as can any white person. Therefore, according to how good cause has been construed here so far, Billy Bob is acting for good cause in automatically turning down all black applicants, and thus is not discriminating. Yet most people will object that automatically turning down all black applicants is a paradigm of unethical workplace discrimination. Thus they will conclude that something very important must be missing from how good cause has been construed here so far. Something is indeed missing, something that would enable this account of good cause to accommodate cases such as *Billy Bob*.

One way to modify the account is by stipulating that an organization's purpose may not count as fundamental if, like Billy Bob's, it is a discriminatory purpose. But even if we could formulate a non-circular distinction between purposes that are discriminatory and ones that are not, the account would still fail to capture most people's moral intuitions, as shown by the case of *Unequal Pay*. This case involves a privately owned textile factory, Primary Textiles, the fundamental purpose of which calls for maximizing profits. Because of widespread, deeply-ingrained discrimination against black people throughout the entire society, Primary Textiles can get by with paying black people less than it pays white people for the same work, and does so. This difference in treatment can be justified in terms of profit since less pay for black people is more profitable than equal pay. Moreover, profit is not a discriminatory purpose. Therefore, even with an account of good cause modified to rule out all discriminatory purposes, less pay for black people in this case would be for good cause. In fact, however, it is another paradigmatic example of unethical discrimination. Thus modifying the account to rule out all discriminatory purposes would not solve the problem.

The most satisfactory solution is, instead, to modify the account of good cause so that it incorporates a veil-of-ignorance presumption somewhat like the well-known, veil-of-ignorance presumption that John Rawls imposes, hypothetically, upon parties deliberating about moral justification.[4] To avoid confusion with Rawls's veil of ignorance, let us refer to the veil-of-ignorance presumption to be incorporated into this account as the workplace veil. This veil is to be imposed, hypothetically, upon workplace organizations that are deliberating about whether their differences in treatment are for good cause. It differs from Rawls's veil in several important respects. In one respect, it is thinner than Rawls's veil. The people about whom knowledge is to be presumed hidden by Rawls's veil include everyone, while the people about whom knowledge is to be presumed hidden by the workplace veil include only individuals about whom a difference in treatment is at issue. Yet, in other respects, the workplace veil is thicker than Rawls's veil. . . . [W]ith Rawls's veil the knowledge is presumed hidden only during the time that the parties are deliberating about justification, while, with the workplace veil, the presumption is that the knowledge is hidden from everyone at all times, past, present, and future. . . . Not only is it to be presumed that certain knowledge is hidden from people at all times, but it is also to be presumed that, at all times, past, present, and future, the people behave in a way that is consistent with this knowledge being hidden from them.

Let us suppose that the only knowledge to be presumed hidden by the workplace veil is knowledge of a person's race. By adding this veil-of-ignorance presumption to our previous account of good cause, we get the following. Any person who is treated differently from any other person by a workplace organization is treated differently for good cause if and only if either the difference in treatment is morally obligatory or, presuming that it is not known what race either person is, the difference in treatment can be justified in terms of the organization's fundamental purpose. For purposes of justifying their differences in treatment, workplace organizations are, according to this account, to presume that, with respect to the race of those they are treating differently, the entire world is under a veil of ignorance. They are to presume that, to this extent, everyone is race blind or, as some prefer to put it, color blind. Many people argue that a color-blind requirement such as this will only serve to perpetuate racial injustice. Before we address that argument, let us see how this veil-of-ignorance presumption, or color-blind requirement, works.

Let us consider Billy Bob's business, the fundamental purpose of which is income for white people only. The veil-of-ignorance presumption does not require that Billy Bob actually be ignorant of what race those he hires are. This presumption requires only that he be able to justify his hiring decisions as if he were indeed ignorant of their race, even though he is not. Although his ignorance of their race is therefore merely hypothetical, it places powerful constraints upon what lines of justification are open to him. In particular, it is not open to Billy Bob to justify his hiring decisions by pointing out that, as called [for] by his fundamental purpose, the people he hires are in fact white. This line of justification is not open to him since, for purposes of justification, he must presume that he does not . . . know that they are white. Therefore, although this presumption does not rule out racially-biased purposes such as Billy Bob's directly, it does so indirectly. Because of the veil-of-ignorance presumption, justifying pay differences between white people and black people for the same work, as in the case of *Unequal Pay*, is impossible as well. A workplace organization must, in justifying differences in pay, presume that it pays its employees as if their race were not known. But if it pays its employees as if their race were not known, then it cannot possibly justify a difference in pay that can be put into effect only if their race is indeed known. A workplace organization cannot justify trying to do that which, for purposes of the justification, it must presume that it cannot do.

Let us consider again the *Bank Teller* case, in which bigoted townspeople are taking their business away from a bank because one of its tellers is black. Without any veil-of-ignorance presumption with respect to race, firing the teller is not, as we have seen, unethical discrimination, since firing the teller can indeed be justified in terms of the bank's fundamental purpose, which calls for maximizing profits. With a veil-of-ignorance presumption, however, we must conclude the opposite; that firing him is unethical discrimination. As we have seen, in justifying any differences in the way they treat people, workplace organizations are to presume that the races of the people are unknown not only to them, but to everyone else as well. This means that, in trying to justify its treating the black teller differently from white tellers whose work is no better, the bank must presume, hypothetically, that the townspeople are, and will remain, under a veil of ignorance with respect to the race of its tellers. If the townspeople do not, and never will, know that the black teller, whose work is exemplary, is black, there is no reason for the bank to believe that, because of him, people will, in the future, be taking their business elsewhere. Therefore, the bank cannot justify firing him on the grounds that his continued employment is likely to decrease future profits. . . .

Let us see what effect this veil-of-ignorance presumption has upon the moral status of affirmative action. The general idea of affirmative action is to benefit minorities and women by granting them a certain advantage over white males in the competition for positions. To simplify matters, let us focus only on affirmative action for the benefit of black people. Can such a practice be shown to be for good cause? The problem is that the veil-of-ignorance presumption, by precluding any knowledge of a person's race, seems to preclude justifying any racially-based differences in how black people are treated, even, as with affirmative action, differences designed to benefit black people. Yet justification may, for the following reasons, still be possible. As we have seen, the veil-of-ignorance presumption precludes workplace organizations from taking into consideration any differences in qualifications that would not have existed except for the fact that something was known that workplace organizations are

supposed to presume was not known. Consider two candidates for a job, one white and the other black, and suppose that the white candidate has a somewhat greater potential for contributing to profits. Ordinarily this would justify choosing the white candidate. But suppose also that the difference in their qualifications would not have existed except for the fact that the black candidate had been discriminated against at school, and elsewhere, because he was black. Knowledge of this candidate's race is knowledge that the workplace organization is supposed to presume was not known. Since, by hypothesis, there would have been no difference in the qualifications of the two candidates if the race of the black candidate had never, in fact, been known, the difference in their qualifications is, so to speak, tainted, and may not, therefore, be taken into consideration. . . . In general, differences in qualifications between people are tainted, and thus may not be taken into consideration, to the extent that the differences exist because, and only because, of prior discrimination that would never have occurred except for the fact that their race was known. Thus affirmative action, by bestowing upon black people a certain artificial advantage in the competition for positions, may be justified as a very rough attempt at neutralizing the advantage white people have from differences in qualifications that are tainted. It may be justified as a rough attempt at canceling out these tainted differences in qualifications so that, in effect, the tainted differences end up playing no role in workplace decisions.

It might be argued, however, that any attempt, by means of affirmative action, at neutralizing the tainted differences in qualifications is bound to be so extremely rough, and have so many practical disadvantages, such as that of stirring up resentment, that it is best that no attempt be made at all. Thus more remains to be said before concluding that affirmative action is in fact justified. But let us instead turn to several things about the veil-of-ignorance presumption that still need to be determined. The veil-of-ignorance presumption, as it stands so far, is a little too strong. It precludes certain differences in treatment that are indeed for good cause from counting as such. Consider the case of two people, one white and the other black, who are auditioning for the role of Hitler in a movie. Surely if, in this case, the white person is chosen because he is white, it should count as being for good cause. Yet, by precluding any comparison of the two applicants with respect to their race, the veil-of-ignorance presumption precludes such a choice from being for good cause. Similar problems arise if we add a person's gender or religion to the list of properties to be presumed hidden. We would then be precluded from, say, deliberately choosing only females to be attendants in women's restrooms, and deliberately choosing only Methodists to be ministers in Methodist churches. To avoid these problems, the veil-of-ignorance presumption needs to be qualified so that it allows properties that otherwise should be hidden to be taken into consideration in just the cases in which the properties really do constitute what, in law, are called bona fide occupational qualifications. We need to determine when a property that otherwise should be hidden is a bona fide occupational qualification or consideration, permitting workplace organizations to drop the veil-of-ignorance presumption with respect to that property.

For people of every race, differences in treatment within the workplace based on race tend to do more harm than good. After the damages wrought by centuries of vicious racism, the reasons are obvious. Differences in treatment based on race breed intense resentment that undermines fruitful interaction among those of different races, and may well lead to violence, all of which is detrimental to members of all races. Differences in treatment based on race also undermine equality of opportunity, preventing invaluable potential from ever being realized, thereby decreasing overall productivity, again to the detriment of members of all races. This does not mean that differences in treatment based on race are never likely to benefit any people at all from the preferred race. But except in cases in which race really is a bona fide consideration, such differences in treatment are, for any race, unlikely to benefit members of the race in general. For workplace organizations to act on preferences for one race over another results in resentment, hostility, and unrealized potential that generally make these differences in treatment counterproductive for the members in general of every race. . . .

. . . It is obvious that most members of every race would agree that it is reasonable for race to be taken into consideration in choosing an actor to play Hitler. The veil-of-ignorance presumption with respect to race may therefore be dropped to that extent. It is also obviously not the case that most members of every race would agree that it is reasonable for race to be taken into consideration in hiring people to work in Billy Bob's repair shop. Therefore, in the case of *Billy Bob*, the presumption may not be dropped.

The second thing we still need to determine about the veil-of-ignorance presumption is its scope. We need to determine what properties of a person should be on that list of properties to be presumed hidden by the veil. It would appear that this list should at least include all of the properties that the American Civil Rights Act of 1964 prohibits workplace organizations from using as bases for differences in treatment. After adding these properties to the list, our account of good cause in the workplace is as follows: Any person who is treated differently from any other person by a workplace organization is treated differently for good cause if and only if either the difference in treatment is morally obligatory or, presuming that it is not known what race, color, religion, gender, or national origin either person is, the difference in treatment can be justified in terms of the fundamental purpose of the organization. The presumption about what is not known may, in any given case, be dropped to the extent that most people of every relevant group would agree that dropping it is not unreasonable.

But what other properties, if any, should we add to the list of properties to be presumed hidden? To answer this question, let us begin by considering what the well-known economist, Milton Friedman, says about workplace discrimination. He argues that the problem of workplace discrimination against minority groups always solves itself, since prejudiced businesses that refuse to hire members of minority groups, even when they are the people most qualified, will only be hurting themselves. They will, he says, eventually lose out to businesses that are more efficient because they do hire the most qualified people regardless of minority-group membership. Friedman concludes that, as the more efficient, unprejudiced businesses thus take over the market from the less efficient, prejudiced businesses, workplace discrimination will die out on its own accord.[5]

Friedman's argument may be sound with respect to atypical, workplace discrimination, such as discrimination against people who wear yellow shirts or have big ears. But with respect to workplace discrimination that is part of a widespread and deeply ingrained pattern of discrimination, such as the pattern of discrimination that has existed in the United States against black people, the argument is problematic. In the case of workplace discrimination that is part of such a pattern, people will, as in the *Bank Teller* case, tend to do such things as boycott businesses that place minorities in important positions, and businesses will, as in the *Unequal Pay* case, be able to get by with such practices as paying their minority workers less than others for the same work. Perhaps a few unusually good-hearted businesses

will refuse to surrender to the boycotts, or refuse to pay minority workers less than others. But their refusal will decrease their profits. Thus the good-hearted businesses will tend to lose out to their less good-hearted, but more profitable, competitors. Instead of the good driving out the bad, as Friedman says, the bad will drive out the good. Far from dying out on its own accord, workplace discrimination that is part of a widespread and deeply ingrained pattern of discrimination tends to be self-perpetuating. Moreover, because of the resentment, hostility, and unrealized potential engendered by such discrimination, members of all relevant groups are better off without it. The list of personal properties to be presumed hidden should therefore include just those properties, such as race, that are bases for widespread and deeply ingrained patterns of discrimination. The discrimination referred to here is discrimination in the generic sense in which differences in treatment lack good cause even prior to any veil-of-ignorance presumption being added to the definition of "good cause."

Consider, for example, a pattern of discrimination that exists with respect to race. The pattern will be sustained by practices such as racially based differentials in pay, and boycotts against businesses that refuse to surrender to the pattern. As, however, we have learned from the cases of *Unequal Pay* and *Bank Teller*, once race is included on a list of properties to be presumed hidden, the practices can no longer be shown to be for good cause. Once the practices can no longer be shown to be for good cause, surrendering to them counts as unethical discrimination. Moreover, once race is put on a list of properties that are legally protected by legislation such as the Civil Rights Act of 1964, surrendering to the practices counts as illegal discrimination as well. If surrendering to the practices counts as unethical and illegal, then, over time, more and more businesses will refuse to surrender. As more and more businesses refuse to surrender to the practices, refusing to surrender will no longer tend to put a business at a competitive disadvantage. The practices, along with the vicious pattern of discrimination they help sustain, will then eventually die out.

In addition to race, color, religion, gender, and national origin, the properties that meet this criterion for being on the list of properties to be presumed hidden may well include age, disability status, and sexual orientation. . . .

It has been argued here that, for purposes of justifying differences in treatment, workplace organizations should presume the entire world is not only color-blind, but gender-blind, religion-blind, and blind to all other properties on the list of hidden properties. Many people, however, argue that a color-blind requirement will only serve to perpetuate racial injustice. The standard argument against a color-blind requirement is put forth well by Amy Gutmann.[6] She grants that "If we assume an ideal society, with no legacy of racial injustice to overcome, there is everything to be said for the color blind standard."[7] But, she goes on to argue, real societies are not ideal, and a color-blind requirement, along with precluding unethical uses of color in workplace decision-making, also precludes ethical uses that are beneficial. She claims there are two ways in which it is ethical and beneficial for workplace organizations to take a person's color into account. One way is by implementing reasonable preferential-treatment programs that make color a basis for overriding legitimate qualifications for a position. The other way is by using color itself as a legitimate qualification. Consider, she says, university admissions. Among the proper goals of a university, she points out, is to cultivate, in its students,

tolerance, appreciation, and respect for diverse life experiences. Universities often attempt to achieve this goal by admitting applicants from remote geographical areas. But, Gutmann says, for achieving this goal it is important to admit applicants of color from minority groups as well. It is therefore important for universities to include color among the legitimate qualifications that an applicant may have for admission. Each of these ways of taking a person's color into account can, she claims, help achieve racial justice throughout society sooner than would be possible otherwise, but each would be precluded by a color-blind requirement. Thus, Gutmann concludes, such a requirement cannot be justified.

It is true that neither way of taking a person's color into account in workplace decisions should be precluded *a priori*. But neither way is precluded *a priori* by the color-blind requirement set out here. This requirement does not preclude preferential treatment since it allows preferential treatment to be justified in principle as a rough attempt at neutralizing the advantages whites have from differences in qualifications that are tainted. This requirement does not preclude using color as a legitimate qualification for a position either. It allows color to be used as a legitimate qualification for a position whenever most people of every color would agree that doing so is not unreasonable. Thus the color-blind requirement set out here leaves limited room for both ways of taking color into account. Taking color into account any more than this is not likely to bring an end to racial injustice any sooner, but, through generating misunderstanding, resentment, and hostility, it is likely only to prolong it. ◆ ◆ ◆

◆ Notes

1. *Payne v. The Western & Atlantic Railroad Company et al.*, 81 Tenn 507 (1884), pp. 519 & 520. Also see Lawrence E. Blades, "Employment at Will versus Individual Freedom: On Limiting the Abusive Exercise of Employer Power," *Columbia Law Review* 67 (1967).

2. 42 U.S.C. Title VII, Section 2000e-2(a)(1)–(2).
3. See *International Union v. Johnson Controls, Inc.*, 111 S.Ct. 1196 (1991). Also see George J. Annas, "Fetal Protection and Employment Discrimination — The Johnson Controls Case," *New England Journal of Medicine* 325 (10) (5 September 1991); and Hugh M. Finneran, "Title VII and Restrictions on Employment of Fertile Women," *Labor Law Journal* 31 (4) (April 1980).
4. See John Rawls, *A Theory of Justice* (Cambridge, Mass.: Harvard University Press, 1971), sec. 24.
5. See Milton Friedman, *Capitalism and Freedom* (Chicago: University of Chicago Press, 1964), ch. VII.
6. See K. Anthony Appiah and Amy Gutmann, *Color Conscious* (Princeton, N.J.: Princeton University Press, 1996), pp. 118–138.
7. Ibid., p. 119.

Diversity Dilemmas at Work

Meg A. Bond and Jean L. Pyle

People are essentially equal but existentially unique. Modern societies, especially America, have citizens from a variety of ancestral backgrounds with varied cultural experiences. There is an inherent tension in thinking of America as simultaneously a multicultural society and a melting pot. Managers are also likely to confront the complexities of trying to reconcile the demands of equal opportunity, affirmative action, and diversity in the workplace.

When employers try to be color-blind, gender-blind, and so forth, they may overlook the special needs and identity of a group. An employer may stir up hostility and old biases by trying to treat everyone equally as well as by making special accommodations. For example, an employer may put in place a liberal policy allowing parents to have flexible time to deal with family emergencies. However noble this sounds, it is likely to be used more by women and equally likely that male supervisors will interpret their use of the leave as being less than fully committed to the firm.

Bond and Pyle highlight a number of problems with diversity policies and suggest some ways that they might be implemented to satisfy the spirit of the law as well as achieving legal compliance.

As more women and people of color have entered the U.S. workforce, the management of diversity in organizations has become both a focus of academic inquiry and central to the consulting industry. However, recent reports about the racism in several major corporations and about the ongoing harassment and discrimination against women make it clear that much racism and sexism still exist in the United States. There is also evidence that when the diversity among workers is addressed, it is approached passively — "responding chiefly to government mandates rather than responding proactively to create value for diversity in . . . organizations" (Miller, 1994, p. 1). Thus, even though an increasing number of organizations are articulating a value for diversity and developing diversity initiatives, the overall commitment is at best unstable and ambivalent.

This article addresses some critical dilemmas that have emerged as the workplace diversity movement has gained more visibility. We examine some underlying reasons why the incorporation and retention of diverse groups throughout the workforce are fraught with complexities that have constrained progress. To set a context and lay the groundwork for understanding how and why the dilemmas have arisen, we begin by examining the origins of the sudden shift to managing diversity from a focus on equal employment opportunity (EEO) legislation and affirmative action (AA). We then briefly describe the current status of diverse groups in the U.S. workforce. The United States has made surprisingly little progress toward promoting amicable, productive working relationships across differences given the changing demographics of the workforce and the changing demands on organizations. The lack of progress, alongside all the forces that make effective diversity management a clear imperative for the survival of today's organizations, compels us to look deeper.

We argue that current efforts to promote diversity in the workplace are complicated by countervailing forces rooted in economic and social trends, organizational traditions, and interpersonal dynamics. As a result, at least three central dilemmas feed the lack of resolve around workplace diversity. The majority of the article is devoted to examining these dilemmas. They involve the themes of (a) underlying assumptions regarding equality and difference, (b) backlash dynamics, and (c) the resistance of organizational cultures to incorporating diversity. We conclude by arguing that a multileveled, contextualist approach that attends to both policy-level and more informal interpersonal processes is necessary to manage the tensions inherent in these three dilemmas.

DIVERSITY POLICY TRENDS

Throughout the history of the United States, there have been alternating points of view about whether the United States will be a melting pot or a multicultural society. On one hand, the melting pot point of view assumes peoples of different races and ethnicities blend together or assimilate into a common culture. On the other hand, a multicultural society is one in which different ethnic groups retain their cultures and coexist in a smoothly functioning society (Triandis, 1995). Through most of this century, the prevailing point of view has been that the United States was a melting pot and that different ethnic groups and immigrants should assimilate to an "American" way of life. The worker of early managerial approaches such as Taylorism and Fordism was a homogeneous worker. Workers did not have diverse identities. Similarly, citizens were conceptualized as homogeneous, abstract individuals who have equal rights. In spite of realities to the contrary, political theory denied or ignored most differences, projecting a color-blind or difference-blind point of view (Skrentny, 1996).

However, the United States has always been diverse. There has been a strong current or undercurrent of multiculturalism throughout our history; in reality, workers and citizens have never been homogeneous. In spite of the melting pot ideology and the notion that people would assimilate, by the 1950s and early 1960s it was clear that all groups were not equally integrated into the workforce. Many women and minorities occupied low-wage jobs in an occupationally segregated labor force (Amott & Matthaei, 1996; Blau, Ferber, & Winkler, 1998; Jacobsen, 1994). White males occupied the preferred, higher-wage positions. Blacks and women became acutely aware of the pervasive racism, sexism, and discrimination they faced in education, in the workplace, as consumers, and in the community. They developed strategies for resistance designed to improve their status, which culminated in the Civil Rights movement, the women's movement, and much unrest in the 1960s. It was at this time that politicians began formulating approaches to redress inequalities through EEO and AA policies. . . .

. . . Affirmative action first surfaced in the United States in the 1935 National Labor Relations Act, specifying that an employer who was found to discriminate against an employee must take affirmative action to restore the victim to where the person would have been in the absence of discrimination. In spite of these earlier occurrences of affirmative action policies and practices, EEO and AA are widely thought to date from the 1960s in the United States because of the proliferation of policies that were established beginning in 1961. Policies ranged from those that encouraged more equal treatment to ones that mandated the adoption of goals and timetables. They typically addressed the situation of minorities first, then added gender.[1] . . .

Even though EEO and AA moved some women and minorities into the workforce (Badgett & Hartmann, 1995; National Council for Research on Women, 1996), the prevailing view of the worker as homogeneous remained unchanged. Employers continued to take an assimilationist view of employees (Loden & Rosener, 1991; Thomas, 1992). Loden and Rosener (1991) argue that most organizations and managers in the United States believe "members of all diverse groups want to become and should be more like the dominant group" (p. 28) and that, accordingly, organizations often counsel others to invest in training that will make them more like the dominant group (assertiveness training, public speaking, etc.). Thomas (1992) adds that because it has been assumed that women and minorities would assimilate to the dominant culture, organizations have not been challenged to undergo fundamental change in integrating them.

These policies have generated controversy and backlash from the late 1970s. EEO policies are passive policies that forbid discrimination, whereas AA policies are active ones that require employers to make efforts to balance their workforces. It is AA, an often misunderstood term, that has aroused the most controversy. In actuality, AA consists of policies, laws, executive orders, court-ordered practices, as well as voluntary practices that are designed to *promote* equity. To assert that it *requires* quotas or the hiring and promotion of unqualified candidates is erroneous (National Council for Research on Women, 1996; Simms, 1995). The attack on AA intensified in the years of Ronald Reagan's presidency such that federal enforcement of AA was virtually abandoned.

The shift from AA to "managing diversity" began in the late 1980s during the second term of President Reagan. During the Reagan years, there was a concerted effort to liberalize the economy—that is, to reduce the role of government in the economy and increase the role of the market—and to become more competitive internationally by curtailing production costs. A major component of the deliberate shift to so-called free markets was deregulation; other components involved reductions in federal government expenditures (particularly cutbacks in provision of social services) and efforts to curtail the already limited power of labor unions. The reduction in regulation involved diminished emphasis on monitoring and enforcing EEO and AA policies as well as decreased attention to worker health and safety concerns and environmental conditions.

It is within this context during the second half of the 1980s that several broad trends made managing diversity appear to be a strategic necessity for organizations seeking to maintain competitiveness (Arrendondo, 1996; Cox, 1993; Jackson & Alvarez, 1992). One major impetus was the publication of Workforce 2000 (Johnson & Packard, 1987) which projected that United States–born White males would be only 15% of the *net* new entrants to the labor force (entrants minus leavers) during the period from 1985 to 2000 (Arredondo, 1996; Jackson & Ruderman, 1995).[2] Also influential were other changes in the structure and the composition of the internal labor force: the movement of some women and minorities up from the lower levels of the hierarchies, the flattening of hierarchies with the elimination of layers of middle managers during the corporate restructuring of the 1980s, and the increasing age diversity of the workforce.

In addition, the ability to manage diversity was thought to lead to better decision making and increased productivity. Organizations that foster good working relationships between diverse people can theoretically draw more widely on the available labor force and more fully develop workers' capabilities. Studies have shown that employee morale is related to identity groups (gender, racio-ethnicity, nationality) and, in turn, is linked to work quality, productivity, absenteeism, and turnover, all of which affect profitability (Cox, 1993). In addition, creativity, innovation, and problem solving can potentially be enhanced by pooling perspectives of diverse people (Thomas, 1992). Therefore, if diversity management facilitates people working well together, it can reduce costs and increase productivity (Cox & Blake, 1991). Furthermore, organizations were seeking to compete more effectively in domestic and international markets that involved different ethnic or racial groups and recognizing the usefulness of having diverse employees on the front lines (Arredondo, 1996; Jackson & Ruderman, 1995). Given this wide range of incentives, many corpo-

rations have established diversity programs (see Jackson, LaFasto, Schultz, & Kelly, 1992; National Council for Research on Women, 1992). . . .

EMERGING DILEMMAS

As is evidenced by historical trends and the current status of women and people of color in the United States workforce, there remains a lack of clear resolve around fully supporting and promoting diversity in our current workforce. Underlying the lack of progress—in very quiet and generally unarticulated ways—lie three dilemmas. First, assumptions about the relationship of similarity and difference to equality can give rise to contradictory paradigms for approaching diversity. Second, initiatives on behalf of workplace diversity have triggered serious unintended consequences and backlash reactions at multiple levels of analysis. Third, diversity efforts have been hampered by limited changes in team cultures and organizational values. These dilemmas make progress toward achieving an effective and diverse workforce the particularly complex challenge that it is today.

Dilemma 1: False Dualisms

Assumptions about sameness, difference, and equality can give rise to seemingly contradictory paradigms for diversity work.

Policy makers rarely stop to reflect on the paradigmatic assumptions about sameness and difference underlying their EEO/AA or diversity initiatives, yet conflicts at this level can easily derail even the most earnest of organizational efforts. As previously described, the seemingly compatible policies of EEO/AA and managing diversity have actually been driven by very different economic and political priorities. The rationale behind EEO/AA emphasizes equity in terms of giving all people the same access to opportunities. Underlying the managing diversity movement are promises of increased efficiency when differences among employees are respected. In a sense, both purport to strive for fairness; however, the rationales and thereby the assumptions about what constitutes fairness are quite different. Similarly, when organizations adopt diversity programs (even when they include some elements of both AA and diversity management), they often do so without reconciling the guiding paradigms. As a result, approaches to diversity in the workplace can vary dramatically in terms of the assumptions made about the relative importance of sameness and difference among workers.

In the simplest form, sameness paradigms emphasize that all people should be treated the same and that inequity results when groups are treated differently. This perspective is akin to Ryan's (1981) fair play perspective, which stresses that all individuals should have the freedom to pursue opportunities. However, the perspective also assumes that there is no guarantee of success and that natural processes

> will insure that the ablest, most meritorious, ambitious, hardworking, and talented individuals will acquire the most, achieve the most, and become the leaders of society. The relative inequality that this implies is seen as not only tolerable, but as fair and just. (Ryan, 1981, p. 9)

In fact, by extension, equality of results is seen "as unjust, artificial, and incompatible with the more basic principle of equal opportunity" (Ryan, 1981, p. 9). This has been the dominant perspective in the United States almost from the beginning.

Difference paradigms emphasize the existence of diversity among people and the need to design strategies for equity that attend to those differences. From this worldview, inequality results from ignoring basic differences in power,

opportunities, and access to resources. Similarly, Ryan (1981) describes a fair shares conception of equality that "emphasizes the right of access to resources as a necessary condition for equal rights to life, liberty and happiness" and is "committed to the principle that all members of the society obtain a reasonable portion of the goods that society produces" (p. 9). This is an entirely different view of what constitutes fairness and justice; and, as Ryan very eloquently argues, "the conflict between Fair Play and Fair Shares is real, deep, and serious, and it cannot be easily resolved" (p. 9).

These differing paradigms have major implications for organizations seeking to foster workplace diversity. The sameness versus difference distinction gives rise to questions about whether diversity initiatives should strive for equality of access or move more toward equality of results. Many legal mandates operate from an emphasis on access and define equity as *identical* treatment. However, this denial of difference conflicts with most organizational development perspectives about how to actually manage a diverse group that emphasize the need to treat people differently based on their varied and unique cultural backgrounds (i.e., tailoring approaches to people based on their gender, race, culture, etc.). . . .

EEO and AA both primarily focus on equality of opportunity; however, as mentioned earlier, EEO does so in a more passive manner than does AA. The overarching rationales for establishing them were to prohibit discrimination (EEO legislation) or take steps to ensure and monitor movement toward parity (AA). By redressing differences created by historical inequities and by requiring employers to monitor progress, AA also begins to attend to equality of outcomes. Even though driven by pragmatics, diversity management efforts move in the direction of addressing equality of outcomes. Managing diversity is a major shift from EEO/AA in many ways. The worker is no longer considered homogeneous. In fact, it is quite the opposite. As the dimensions of managing diversity unfold, each worker becomes a combination of many diverse identities. Managing diversity is taken to mean valuing the uniqueness of each individual. Thus, rather than treating all people the same (a focus of EEO) or providing some preferential treatment for selected groups (AA in its special efforts to recruit, promote, and retain women and minorities), this approach moves toward treating individuals differently. This view assumes people will be integrated but not necessarily assimilated. . . .

In short, policy debates are often inappropriately framed as a choice between dualisms or dichotomies (i.e., sameness vs. difference, difference vs. equality, equal opportunity vs. equal outcomes, fair play vs. fair shares, . . .). In addition, there are some complex side effects of adopting a singular focus on either similarities or differences—effects that contradict the original intent of the stance.

. . . The intent of the equal opportunity and fair play perspectives is ostensibly to create an even playing field and move forward from there. However, adopting such a position based on the sameness of treatment is, in essence, rooted in an individualistic analysis. This stance, in effect, deemphasizes the importance of group membership and represents an individualizing of experience even when the original intent of a policy (e.g., AA) might have been to address prior inequities experienced by a class of people.

Emphasizing sameness of treatment is also an essentially acontextual perspective. It ignores the fact that the meaning of an individual's behavior can vary with race, gender, and power (e.g., jokes that might be considered harassing behavior by a woman when told by a male supervisor in her office would not necessarily constitute harassment when told by a lone woman coworker in an otherwise all-male shop). The interpretation of a person's behavior is affected by race and gender dynamics (e.g., the classic scenario in which the woman who leaves early to pick up children is seen as lacking commitment whereas the man who leaves for the same reason is considered heroic). The implications of a policy can clearly differ based on race and gender. For example, given common differences in African American and Anglo family structures, an African American man living in the north who comes from a close extended southern Black family may need more than 1 day off to travel to an uncle's funeral, whereas his White coworker might not even need the full day he would be allowed because attending a distant funeral is less likely. Another perhaps more classic example involves family leave policies, which generally have a greater impact on women because women tend to be the family caretakers. Thus, as Scott (1994) argues, if we ignore difference in the case of subordinated groups, it "leaves in place a faulty neutrality" (p. 362) and totally de-contextualizes our analysis of organizational behavior.

If sameness is equated with equality, we reinforce and recreate the problems associated with assuming a homogeneous worker, we run the risk of ignoring critical contextual determinants of organizational behavior, and we diminish our capacity to think creatively about how to build productive work teams. . . .

A focus on distinctiveness can . . . result in erroneous or misguided attributions about the sources of difference. Mednick (1989) argues that constructs used to describe the distinctiveness of women (whether fear of success, androgyny, or the notion of a different voice) attribute the uniqueness primarily to gender and thereby ignore the influence of "cultural, socioeconomic, structural, or contemporaneous situational factors that may affect behavior" (p. 1120). This emphasis on gender as the primary correlate of a particular behavior pattern or work outcome for women stands in direct contradiction to research that indicates that some previously assumed gender differences no longer emerge when researchers control for power and status (e.g., Crawford, 1995; Holloway, 1994; Lott, 1987; Unger, 1992). Similarly, it is important to avoid confounding cultural distinctiveness among racial groups with adaptive responses to oppression (Ogbu, 1993; Watts, 1992). A focus on intrinsic differences between women and men or between different racial groups leads us almost inevitably to individual-level change prescriptions and to ignoring sociopolitical analyses (Crawford, 1995; Mednick, 1989). Thereby, as Mednick (1989) argues, what might have begun as genuine efforts to appreciate uniqueness are transformed into support for "conservative policies that, in fact, could do little else but maintain the status quo" (p. 1122).

Summary. It is essential that we address the dilemma that emerges when diversity initiatives pay attention only to difference or only to similarity. The positions of same versus different or equality of opportunity versus equality of outcome are essentially extreme positions and can result in nonproductive debates if allowed to remain dualisms. Both focusing on and ignoring difference risk recreating it, and as Scott (1994) argues, "the antithesis itself hides the interdependence of the two terms, for equality is not the elimination of difference, and difference does not preclude equality" (p. 362). To counter the problems that emerge from a focus on sameness versus difference, we need to adopt a perspective that is founded on the belief that each group organizes and defines experience within its own set of cultural assumptions and experiences. However, we need to work from models that both acknowledge differences and refuse to accept them as full explanations for employment patterns, that is, adopt models that challenge dualistic thinking. We need conceptual approaches that

are ecologically based and that keep the discussion of distinctiveness rooted in awareness of social, political, and cultural forces such as racism and sexism that shape the unequal distribution of power and resources. In essence, managers, consultants, and researchers all need to work from models that consider sameness and difference simultaneously and contextually—that place differences in the context of similarities and similarities in the context of differences.

Dilemma 2: The Unanticipated Fallout

Diversity policies and programs have generated a set of reactions that work in opposite direction of the original policy intent.

Both the externally driven policies and the internally designed diversity management programs have generated fallout and side effects that are barriers to further progress toward a fully integrated and effective workforce. First, diversity policies have triggered an intense public debate about whose civil rights are at issue. Second, the use of EEO legislation and AA policies to address the problems of workplace inequities and discrimination has resulted in a conundrum of legislation to address still more inequities, additional guidelines and rulings to interpret the legislation, and more opportunities for litigation. Third, the more recent focus on managing diversity has generated direct reactivity to diversity programs. In a sense, we see all three of these phenomena as evidence of the disruption people feel as a result of the increased attention being paid to diversity in the workforce. They are each indicative of the fears and the potential for redistribution of resources associated with the deep economic and psychological changes that are facing us.

Questioning of Whose Civil Rights? AA policies have been controversial since the late 1970s and have recently been under widespread attack on many levels. As discussed earlier, much of the controversy is over the actual meaning of AA and perceptions of what constitutes fairness. Statements have become politically charged as campaigns reduce these issues to hyperbole and sound bites. Opponents often shape the debate in misleading ways that make people fear that AA involves quotas, hiring of less qualified candidates, and reverse discrimination. However, the National Council for Research on Women (1996) reports the results of a survey that shows that when people understand that AA does not specify quotas, they overwhelmingly support it. Plous (1996) reports the results of five public opinion polls in 1995 regarding AA. When surveys offer intermediate choices regarding AA (rather than a dichotomous choice between AA as it currently exists versus no AA at all), most people favor maintaining some form of AA.

Debates regarding EEO and AA policies increasingly focus on the question of whose civil rights, with each side indicating they believe that their rights have been infringed upon. A backlash has developed as some people who were denied positions (particularly males and/or Caucasians) assert that such policies result in reverse discrimination (i.e., the males or Whites argue they have been discriminated against because they feel women and minorities are given preference). Considerable press and political attention are given to such allegations. A 1995 Department of Labor study, however, disputes the notion of widespread reverse discrimination of Whites. It reports that only 100 of 3,000 discrimination cases filed involved reverse discrimination, and only six of these had claims that could be substantiated (Wilson, 1995). The Equal Employment Opportunity Commission (EEOC) reports that of 10,000 reverse discrimination cases filed during the period from 1987 to 1994, only 10% had merit (National Council for Research on Women, 1996).

This backlash is at least partially rooted in a comfort with what has been the status quo and a sense that changes in this situation are a violation of workers' rights. The reaction that changes are unfair is further fueled by the belief among White men that women and minorities do not experience discrimination in the form of unequal resource support and do have equal, if not better, chances of receiving organizationally based rewards (Fine et al., 1990; Kossek & Zonia, 1993). The backlash is like a homeostatic mechanism pulling against change—pulling back to a situation that is believed by those who benefit most from it (i.e., White males) to be stable. However, much evidence exists to suggest that the current situation is neither stable nor perceived by many women or people of color as fair. . . .

In another form, backlash has erupted among workers without children who increasingly resent what they perceive as special policies (i.e., family-friendly policies such as flexible scheduling, family leave, and child care assistance) tailored to employees with children. Although more than 20% of those surveyed in a study indicated that they had to accept added responsibilities to cover for parents with whom they worked (Williams, 1994), the starting assumption for the concerns is that the current arrangement is fair or neutral. However, workers with children can argue that the current workday structure itself (9 to 5) is a biased arrangement that is convenient only for the childless or those with a home-based partner or helper. In response, some organizations have established work-life programs. More recently, organizations are being encouraged to define *family* to encompass all of an employee's personal concerns for a more balanced life and to restructure jobs to accommodate these concerns (Shellenbarger, 1996).

Proliferating Legislation. Complications around EEO/AA–driven policies have arisen as new legislation is continually passed or existing legislation is interpreted to address additional potentially discriminatory situations. In the 1990s, new legislation has included the Americans With Disabilities

Act (1990), the Glass Ceiling Act (1991), and the Family and Medical Leave Act (1993). The number of different groups seeking legal redress under existing or new laws has grown. For example, people who are readily distracted by noise at work have sought protection under the Americans with Disabilities Act (ADA), requesting more isolation, new work assignments, or changes in managerial styles (Pollock & Lublin, 1997). As the number of laws rises, it becomes clear that it is impossible to write legislation to specifically address all situations. Meanwhile, as legislation increases, possibilities for litigation multiply. The increased litigation has resulted in conflicting rulings in the courts in different states and at different levels of the judicial system, adding further complexity to implementing "the law." . . .

Although EEO/AA laws were originally passed to enforce more equitable policies, the legal reactions to these policies have brought home the fact that every act of inequality cannot be legislated away. The proliferation of legislation has, at best, created a mass of laws that are difficult to navigate and, at worst, reduced the effort to absurdity. Rather than instilling a value for diversity, which ultimately is a desired outcome of EEO/AA policies, they risk being seen more as a hindrance (even by corporations that believe in AA) and/or as something to be maneuvered around. Ironically, the rise of the managing diversity movement itself, where the differences that are to be valued are much more widely defined than under the EEO/AA legislation of the 1960s and 1970s, may have contributed to this burgeoning legislative tangle.

Reactions to In-House Diversity Programs. The prevailing idea behind most in-house diversity programs is that support for diversity will be enhanced if understanding is increased and the sexism/racism of individual employees is confronted, challenged, and changed. Diversity initiatives range from short one-shot orientations or movies to extensive training and development that is integrated into other organizational development efforts.

Numerous unanticipated problems have ensued from both the one-shot and the more intense programs. First, many employees perceive their organization's interest in diversity as simply a superficial gesture that will not result in any fundamental change in the organizational culture. This can be particularly problematic when workshops on the value of diversity are also perceived as condescending and/or disconnected from the realities of everyday life at work. In addition, at times, employees see diversity training as a tool to support a strictly management agenda particularly when the initiatives lack inclusiveness and an understanding of the power differentials at work. In such cases, participants resist the diversity programs by not taking them seriously. Second, when workers feel unfairly accused or blamed for inequalities in the workplace or when discussion of differences results in the generation or reinforcement of stereotypes, what was designed to be a set of exercises in coming together can result in increased divisiveness and rising animosities. The increased resentment is obviously the opposite of what was originally intended. . . .

Summary. Any attempts to increase support for diversity must consider the variety of problems and backlashes that can result. From a macro perspective, much of the controversy and backlash can be understood as a recurring phenomenon that emerges in response to limited resources and societal power shifts. Whether instituting organization-wide EEO-type policies or mandating diversity training programs, organizations must also understand more micro level changes in the support systems that people need to enable them to adapt to dramatic shifts in expectations. Any efforts to address the diversity challenge need to incorporate an appreciation for the interplay between the meaning that increased diversity holds for the individual (e.g., threat versus opportunity), the capacity of the organization to provide support for change (both formally and informally), and the options or constraints provided by broader policy and legislative trends.

Dilemma 3: Culture Change
Efforts to support workforce diversity have been hampered by limited changes in organizational values.

In addition to the problems posed by diversity paradigms and various backlashes is the equally troublesome dilemma that organizational cultures have not changed dramatically enough to fully support diversity. EEO, AA, and internal diversity programs have simply not been the successful antidotes proponents had hoped for, partly because underlying community and organizational attitudes and values have not changed significantly. In fact, the hostility between groups in society at large is mirrored by workplace conflict involving such issues as race, gender, age, sexual orientation, class, and disability.

A study conducted by the Center for the New American Workplace (Miller, 1994) found that, whereas many organizations have implemented some sort of policy and/or training initiative to address the unique needs of different types of people, the initiatives often do not translate into changes in the quality of work life for employees. Just responding to legislative mandates clearly does not automatically lead to changes in organizational culture and values. . . .

Underground Racism and Sexism. As policies have made blatant discrimination illegal and unacceptable, biases are expressed in more subtle forms. Even though this may not be a conscious or deliberate change on the part of any particular individual or organization, it is, nonetheless, insidious. This more subtle form of racism, termed *aversive racism*, is being increasingly recognized (Dovidio & Gaertner, 1996; Gaertner & Dovidio, 1986). Aversive racism involves underlying racially biased attitudes and behaviors of people who claim that they are not prejudiced. Parallel to this, gender discrimination perpetuated by people who believe themselves not sexist could be termed aversive sexism. What is often expressed is a subtle racism and sexism communicated through eye contact, who is credited with good ideas and good work, how company celebrations are framed, where and when important decisions are made, and what stated points of view are actually acted on.

Research indicates that aversive racism works in some unexpected ways. First, it may not lead people to express more negative feelings about minorities or have lower expectations of minority group members. It may, rather, lead them to express fewer positive reactions. That is, there may be little direct expression of negative sentiments, but White men continue to receive more positive evaluations when all else is considered equal (Messick & Mackie, 1989). In addition, there is the observed difference between what people indicate as their values and what they are willing to do about them (Messick & Mackie, 1989). As a result, much of the discrimination felt by members of underrepresented groups is not the subject of formal complaints and is almost impossible to address through legal and policy-based mechanisms (cf. Bond & Pyle, in press). Organizational policies and diversity initiatives may inhibit direct expressions of hostility, but they leave underlying biases untouched. These more subtle forms of discriminatory behavior have serious consequences in the workplace as well as in society.

Many would hope that a younger generation has grown up with more awareness of diversity and thus would be more tolerant. However, studies reveal that even younger generations prefer to work with others like themselves. Contrary to the expectation that younger workers would have backgrounds equipping them to work with diverse peoples, workers younger than age 25 showed no greater preference for diversity. Employees having a greater tolerance for working with people different from themselves are people who have been exposed to different cultures in their home community or neighborhoods. Most people younger than 25 have not had such exposure (Families and Work Institute, 1993).

The subtle forms of discrimination are difficult to recognize and, therefore, to address. The move from the blatant to the more subtle expressions is a manifestation of the fact that underlying values cannot be mandated away. Furthermore, the less blatant nature of the biases renders the problem fairly inaccessible to additional policy efforts. Thus, what often emerges is a gap between the formally stated goals of diversity initiatives and the values actually adopted during day-to-day organizational life. Ultimately, the informal values that coalesce into an organizational culture will dictate what supports really exist for diverse groups of employees.

The Example of Family-Friendly Policies. Family-friendly policies are not as common as the popular press might lead one to expect. Even in those organizations that offer options for working at home, part-time schedules, flextime, or job sharing, the reality is that limited numbers of employees take advantage of them. Some organizations adopt such policies as public relations and recruitment tools, but the benefits are often not available to all employees. Options provided for top-level managers are less available to others in lower level jobs, particularly women in nontraditional work.

In addition, some policies are more token than real. The highly debated Family and Medical Leave Act of 1993 has provided employees in companies with 50 or more employees the option for a 3-month *unpaid* leave when needed for family care. Since its passage, few have made use of the option. An employee survey found that losing 3 months of income is simply not an option for most working families particularly when faced with a new and/or ill family member (McGonagle, Conner, Herringa, Veerkamp, & Groves, 1995). There is also evidence of widespread organizational noncompliance with the law. A year after it became law, 4 in 10 companies affected by the law were not adhering to it (O'Gara, 1995). . . .

In addition, family-friendly policies have actually had adverse effects for some women. Unwritten rules of the organization often punish women who make use of such policies (e.g., relegate them to a no-growth "mommy track"). The very existence of the policies can emphasize differences between women and men, which as discussed under Dilemma 1, can make it harder to overcome stereotypes. The use and impact of such policies is highly dependent on the supportiveness of individual supervisors and the overall organizational culture (Shinn, Wong, Simko, & Ortiz-Torres, 1989). For example, policies may allow a woman to rearrange her schedule to care for a sick child, but if her supervisor then judges her less committed, gives her a poor performance evaluation, and reassigns her important tasks to others, the policy is virtually useless. . . .

Empowerment, Teams, and Diversity. There are several current trends in organization development circles: employee empowerment, team development, and diversity management. Although theoretically more broad-based, empowerment and team building efforts generally focus on the individual and/or the small work group. Effective diversity efforts need to be operationalized as cutting across levels (individual, group, and organizational). When diversity initiatives are implemented in organizations that are also promoting empowerment and self-directed teams, there can be conflicting messages regarding what core ideology really underlies management priorities and thus what values actually guide the diversity initiative. . . .

Summary. Efforts to address diversity through policy and/or other formal means will be ineffective unless supported by deeper changes in attitudes, values, and the culture of the organization. Thus, to create organizations that are truly supportive of diversity, the more subtle forms of discrimination (aversive racism/sexism) must be addressed and reduced. All initiatives, whether they are designed to combat aversive discrimination or whether they are to implement EEO/AA or family-friendly policies, diversity programs, and/or teambuilding must be accompanied by changes in core organizational and community values. Within organizations, people's preferences are often taken as givens (particularly by economists). They are indeed difficult to change. However, to provide the backdrop for important changes in attitudes, we need to develop supports for communal attitudes, foster a sense of community responsibility, and challenge the rampant individualistic approaches to solving problems. We will need to address the organizational processes that maintain segregation and unequal access to resources. Although we must work to develop such basic attitudes within our current organizations, we also need to challenge the community and social processes that reinforce segregation and produce a workforce unprepared to face the expanding diversity.

CHALLENGES FOR THE FUTURE

. . .

Whereas managing diversity may in theory be an initiative that is seemingly less dramatic (or at least less imposed) than EEO or AA, it nonethe-

less also disrupts the status quo and creates anxiety about change. The emerging challenge for organizations is to find ways to creatively harness and maximize the benefits of diversity and also acknowledge the loss of comfort and sense of disruption that come from dealing with the unfamiliar. Thus, it is imperative that we pay more attention to the meaning (e.g., both real and anticipated impact) diversity initiatives have for all employees as well as to the types of organizational mechanisms that will integrate diversity into daily expectations and operations. Diversity-specific efforts need to be paralleled by general quality of work-life initiatives that also incorporate expectations for diverse representation and smooth working relationships across differences. The values that undergird both the diversity and more general organization development efforts need to be consciously institutionalized through integration into organizational practices ranging from job descriptions to performance expectations to organizational rituals and community celebrations.

In short, our analysis of the current dilemmas impeding progress towards a diverse workforce leads us to argue that effectively supporting diversity requires fundamental shifts in organizational processes. First, we need management practices and organizational models that understand that people exist in the context of profound and dynamic cultural, economic, social, and political forces. Second, organizations must understand that diversity initiatives signal shifts in power dynamics. They thereby require attention to individual fears and the creation of appropriate organizational supports alongside solid resolve to address inequities and to affirm support for integrated work groups. Third, we must recognize that all efforts toward creating an effective diverse workforce must be anchored in deeply rooted organizational values for diverse approaches and contributions. . . .   ◆ ◆ ◆

◆ Notes

1. Key workplace-related legislation during the 1960s and 1970s consisted of Executive Order 10925 in 1961 (which, under President Kennedy, encouraged federal contractors to hire more minorities); Equal Pay Act of 1963 (which addressed equal pay for men and women doing work requiring equal skill, effort, and responsibilities); Title VII of the Civil Rights Act in 1964 (which, under President Johnson, barred discrimination because of race, color, religion, sex, or national origin in hiring, firing, promotion, compensation, and other terms and conditions of employment); Executive Order 11246 in 1965 (which, under Johnson, required federal contractors to adopt goals and timetables to achieve proportional racial representation and placed affirmative action under the jurisdiction of the Department of Labor); Executive Order 11375 in 1967 (which, under Johnson, added *sex* to the categories protected by AA); Executive Order 11478 in 1969 (which, under President Nixon, imposed specific goals and timetables on federal contractors regarding African Americans); Revised Order #4 in 1971 (which, under Nixon, required federal contractors to establish AA programs for women); and EEO Act in 1972 (which, under Nixon, empowered EEOC to take legal action in federal courts to enforce Title VII of the Civil Rights Act). A detailed outline of all major legislation and cases is available from the National Council for Research on Women (1996).

2. Women, minorities, and immigrants would be 85%. Updated projections for the period from 1990 to 2005 confirmed that this trend would continue. White non-Hispanic males would comprise only 14.5% of the net increase in the workforce, whereas women would be 57% of the net increase and minorities would be 53.7%. Non-Hispanic White males would comprise only 38.2% of the workforce by the year 2005, down from 43.1% in 1990 (based on data in Fullerton, 1991). Given these projections, it became clear to many organizations that the ability to productively incorporate diverse workers would be essential for survival.

◆ References

Amott, T., & Matthaei, J. (1996). *Race, gender and work* (Rev. ed.). Boston: South End Press.

Arredondo, P. (1996). *Successful diversity management initiatives.* Thousand Oaks, CA: Sage.

Badgett, M. V. L., & Hartmann, H. (1995). The effectiveness of equal employment opportunity policies. In M. C. Simms (Ed.), *Economic perspectives on affirmative action* (pp. 55–91). Washington, DC: Joint Center for Political and Economic Studies.

Berman, P. (1996, April 14). Redefining fairness. *The New York Times,* pp. 16–17.

Blau, F. D., Ferber, M. A., Winkler, A. (1998). *The economics of women, men and work* (3rd ed.). Upper Saddle River, NJ: Prentice Hall.

Cox, T. (1993). *Cultural diversity in organizations. Theory, research and practice.* San Francisco: Berrett Koehler.

Cox, T., & Blake, S. (1991). Managing cultural diversity: Implications for organizational competitiveness. *Academy of Management Executive, 5,* 45–56.

Crawford, M. (1995). *Talking difference: On gender and language.* Thousand Oaks, CA: Sage.

Dovidio, J. F., & Gaertner, S. L. (1996). Affirmative action, unintentional racial biases, and intergroup relations. *Journal of Social Issues, 52*(4), 51–75.

Families and Work Institute. (1993). *The national study of the changing workforce.* New York: Author.

Fine, M. G., Johnson, F. L., & Ryan, M. S. (1990). Cultural diversity in the workplace. *Public Personnel Management, 19*(3), 305–319.

Fullerton, H. N. (1991). Labor force projections: The baby boom moves on. *Monthly Labor Review, 114*(11), 31–44.

Gaertner, S. L., & Dovidio, J. F. (1986). The aversive form of racism. In J. F. Dovidio & S. L. Gaertner (Eds.), *Prejudice, discrimination and racism* (pp. 61–89). Orlando, FL: Academic Press.

Holloway, W. (1994). Beyond sex differences: A project for feminist psychology. *Feminism and Psychology, 4,* 538–546.

Jackson, B. W., LaFasto, F., Schultz, H. G., & Kelly, D. (1992). Diversity. *Human Resource Management, 31*(1/2), 21–34.

Jackson, S. E. (Ed.) (1992). *Diversity in the workplace: Human resources initiatives.* New York: Guilford.

Jackson, S. E., & Alvarez, E. B. (1992). Working through diversity as a strategic imperative. In S. E. Jackson (Ed.), *Diversity in the workplace: Human resources initiatives* (pp. 13–35). New York: Guilford.

Jackson, S. E., & Ruderman, M. N. (1995). *Diversity in work teams.* Washington, DC: American Psychological Association.

Jacobsen, J. P. (1994). *The economics of gender.* Cambridge, MA: Blackwell.

Johnson, W. B., & Packard, A. H. (1987). *Workforce 2000: Work and workers for the 21st century.* Indianapolis: Hudson Institute.

Kossek, E., & Zonia, S. (1993). Assessing diversity climate: A field study of reactions to employer efforts to promote diversity. *Journal of Organizational Behavior, 14,* 61–81.

Loden, M., & Rosener, J. B. (1991). *Workforce America!* Burr Ridge, IL: Irwin.

Lott, B. (1987). *Feminist, masculine, androgynous or human.* Paper presented at the American Psychological Association, New York.

McGonagle, K. A., Conner, J., Heringa, S., Veerkamp, P., & Groves, R. (1995). *Commission on leave survey of employees on the impact of the family and medical leave act.* Ann Arbor, MI: Institute for Social Research.

Mednick, M. (1989). On the politics of psychological constructs: Stop the bandwagon—I want to get off. *American Psychologist, 44,* 1118–1123.

Messick, D., & Mackie, D. M. (1989). Intergroup relations. *Annual Review of Psychology, 40,* 45–81.

Miller, J. (1994). *Corporate responses to diversity: A benchmark study.* Report from the Center for the New American Workforce, Queens College.

National Council for Research on Women. (1996). Affirmative action: Beyond the glass ceiling and the sticky floor [special issue]. *Issues Quarterly, 1*(4).

O'Gara, J. (1995). *Making workplaces work: Quality work policies for small business.* Washington, DC: Business and Professional Women's Foundation.

Ogbu, J. U. (1993). Difference in cultural frame of reference. *International Journal of Behavior Development, 16*(3), 483–506.

Plous, S. (1996). Ten myths about affirmative action. *Journal of Social Issues, 52*(4), 25–31.

Pollock, E. J., & Lublin, J. S. (1997, May 1). Employers are wary of rules on mentally ill. *The Wall Street Journal,* p. B1.

Ryan, W. (1981). *Equality.* New York: Pantheon.

Scott, J. (1994). Deconstructing equality-versus-difference: or, the uses of poststructuralist theory for feminism. In A. C. Herman & A. J. Stewart (Eds.), *Theorizing feminism: Parallel Trends in the Humanities and Social Sciences.* Boulder: Westview.

Shellenbarger, S. (1996, May 15). Family-friendly jobs are the first step to efficient workplace. *The Wall Street Journal,* p. B1.

Shinn, M., Wong, N., Simko, P., & Ortiz-Torres, B. (1989). Promoting the well-being of working parents: Coping, social support, and flexible job schedules. *American Journal of Community Psychology, 17*(1), 31-56.

Simms, M. C. (1995). Introduction. In M. C. Simms (Ed.), *Economic perspectives on affirmative action* (pp. 1–6). Washington, DC: Joint Center for Political and Economic Studies.

Skrenty, J. D. (1996). *The ironies of affirmative action.* Chicago: University of Chicago Press.

Thomas, R. (1992). Managing diversity: A conceptual framework. In S. E. Jackson (Ed.), *Diversity in the workplace: Human resources initiatives* (pp. 13–35). New York: Guilford.

Triandis, H. C. (1995). A theoretical framework for the study of diversity. In M. M. Chemers, S. Oskamp, & M. A. Costanzo (Eds.), *Diversity in organizations* (pp. 11–36). Thousand Oaks, CA: Sage.

Unger, R. (1992). Will the real sex differences please stand up? *Feminism and Psychology, 2,* 231–238.

Watts, R. J. (1992). Elements of a psychology of human diversity. *Journal of Community Psychology, 20,* 116–130.

Williams, L. (1994, May 29). Childless workers demanding equity in corporate world. *The New York Times,* pp. 1, 11.

Wilson, R. (1995, May). *Affirmative action: Yesterday, today, and beyond.* Report. Washington, DC: American Council on Education.

Drug Testing and the Right to Privacy
Arguing the Ethics of Workplace Drug Testing

Michael Cranford

The issue of workplace testing for illegal drugs brings to the forefront the clash between worker privacy and the employer's right to know. Individuals will say that, as long as they perform adequately on the job, what they do in their personal lives is not the business of the employer, whether the behavior relates to their hobbies, their marital lives or personal relationships, their diet, or their use of prescription or illegal drugs.

The standard response is that employers do, in fact, have a vested interest in the whole life of the employee, both to aid productivity and to help control health insurance costs. Thus, it matters whether employees smoke tobacco or drink to excess when they are not at work.

The argument is also made that if employees have nothing to hide, then they have nothing to fear: Testing will result in no harm. This is again countered by statements that the results are beside the point; employers should not have the right to pry into every aspect of an individual's personal affairs.

There are strong arguments on both sides. Cranford is on the side of testing when there is suspicion of drug use, but only if safeguards are built in. Others worry that individual rights will be violated and that there is now an open door to blanket testing—testing that could reveal not only drug use but a wealth of other information at the same time.

Drug testing is becoming an increasingly accepted method for controlling the effects of substance abuse in the workplace. Since drug abuse has been correlated with a decline in corporate profitability and an increase in the occurrence of work-related accidents, employers are justifying drug testing on both legal and ethical grounds. Recent estimates indicate that the costs to employers of employee drug abuse can run as high as $60 billion per year.[1] Motorola, before implementing its drug testing program in 1991, determined that the cost of drug abuse to the company—in lost time, impaired productivity, and health-care and workers compensation claims—amounted to $190 million in 1988, or approximately 40% of the company's net profit for that year.[2] As these effects on the workplace are viewed in light of a much larger social problem—one which impacts health care and the criminal justice system, and incites drug-related acts of violence—advocates of drug testing argue that the workplace is an effective arena for engaging these broader concerns. The drug-free workplace is viewed as causally antecedent and even sufficient to the development of drug-free communities.

The possibility of using workplace drug interventions to effect social change may obscure the more fundamental question of whether or not drug testing is an ethical means of determining employee drug abuse. While admitting that drug testing could mitigate potential harms, some CEOs have elected not to follow the trend set by

Motorola and an estimated 67% of large companies,[3] and instead argue that drug testing surpasses the employer's legitimate sphere of control by dictating the behavior of employees on their own time and in the privacy of their own homes.[4] Recent arguments in favor of a more psychologically-sensitive definition of employee privacy place employer intrusions into this intimate sphere of self-disclosure on even less certain ethical grounds.[5] The ethical status of workplace drug testing can be expressed as a question of competing interests, between the employer's right to use testing to reduce drug-related harms and maximize profits, over against the employee's right to privacy, particularly with regard to drug use which occurs outside the workplace.

In this paper I will attempt to bring clarity to this debate and set the practice of workplace drug testing on more certain ethical grounds by advancing an argument which justifies workplace drug testing. I will begin by showing that an employee's right to privacy is violated when personal information is collected or used by the employer in a way which is irrelevant to the contractual relationship which exists between employer and employee. I will then demonstrate that drug testing is justified within the terms of the employment contract, and therefore does not amount to a violation of an employee's right to privacy. . . .

PRIVACY AND PERFORMANCE OF CONTRACT

Legal definitions of privacy inevitably rely on the 1890 *Harvard Law Review* article "The Right to Privacy" by Samuel Warren and Louis Brandeis. This article offered an understanding of privacy for which a constitutional basis was not recognized until the 1965 case *Griswold v. Connecticut* (381 U.S. 479). In both instances, privacy was understood as an individual's right "to be let alone," with the Griswold decision according citizens a "zone of privacy" around their persons which cannot be violated by governmental intrusion. This definition, utilized by the Court in numerous decisions since the 1965 ruling, will not be adequate for describing the employee's claim to privacy in an essentially social and cooperative setting like the workplace. In such a condition an absolute right "to be let alone" cannot be sustained, and it may well prove impossible for an employee to maintain a "zone of privacy" when the terms of employment entail certain physical demands. This is not to argue that a right to privacy does not exist in this setting; rather, we must conclude that the aforementioned conditions are not necessary components in such a right.[6]

A more useful definition begins with the idea of a person's right to control information about herself and the situations over which such a right may be legitimately extended. For example, information to the effect that an individual possesses a rare and debilitating disease is generally considered private, but a physician's coming to know that a patient has such a disease is not an invasion of privacy. One might also note that while eavesdropping on a conversation would normally constitute an invasion of privacy, coming to know the same information because the individual inadvertently let it slip in a casual conversation would not. These and other examples demonstrate that the right to privacy is not violated by the mere act of coming to know something private, but is instead contingent on the relationship between the knower and the person about whom the information is known.

George Brenkert formulates this understanding as follows: Privacy involves a relationship between a person A, some information X, and another individual Z. A's right of privacy is violated only when Z comes to possess information X and no relationship exists between A and Z that would justify Z's coming to know X.[7] Brenkert notes that what would justify Z coming to know X is a condition in which knowing X and having a certain access to A will enable Z to execute its role in the particular relationship with A. In such a case, Z is entitled to information X, and A's privacy is in no way violated by the fact that Z knows. Thus, a physician is justified in coming to know of a patient's disease (say, by running certain diagnostic tests), since knowing of the disease will enable her to give the patient medical treatment. One cannot be a physician to another unless one is entitled to certain information and access to that person. Conversely, one can yield one's right to privacy by disclosing information to another that the relationship would not normally mandate. To maintain a right to privacy in a situation where another would normally be entitled to the information to enable them to fulfill the terms of the relationship is, quite simply, to violate the terms of the relationship and make fulfillment of such terms impossible. In the case of our earlier example, to refuse a physician access to the relevant points of one's health status is to make a physician-patient relationship impossible. Similarly, to refuse an employer access to information regarding one's capability of fulfilling the terms of an employment contract is to violate an employer-employee relationship.

The argument advanced at this point is that drug testing involves access to and information about an employee that are justified under the terms of the implicit contractual agreement between employer and employee. An employer is therefore entitled to test employees for drug use. This statement relies on at least two important assumptions. First, a contractual model of employer-employee relations is assumed over against a common law, agent-principal model. It is not the case that employees relinquish all privacy rights in return for employment, as the common law relationship may imply, but rather that the terms of the contract, if it is valid, set reasonable boundaries for employee privacy rights con-

sistent with the terms and expectations of employment. The argument offered here is that drug testing does not violate those boundaries. I am also assuming that drug abuse has a measurable and significant impact on an employee's ability to honor the terms of the employment contract. Employers are entitled to know about employee drug abuse on the grounds that such knowledge is relevant to assessing an employee's capability to perform according to the terms of the agreement. Without arguing for the connection between drug abuse and employee performance at length, the reader's attention is directed to studies which, if not absolutely incontestable in their methodology, are nonetheless reasonably set forth.[8]

In support of this argument, I would first direct attention to other types of information about an employee that an employer is entitled to know, and in coming to know such information does not violate the employee's privacy. Employers are entitled to information about a current or prospective employee's work experience, education, and job skills—in short, information relevant for determining whether or not the employee is capable of fulfilling her part of the contract. More critically, the employer is not only entitled to such information, but is entitled to obtain such information through an investigatory process, both to confirm information the employee has voluntarily yielded about her qualifications, as well as to obtain such relevant information as may be lacking (i.e., inadvertently omitted or, perhaps, intentionally withheld).

Brenkert further adds that an employer is entitled to information which relates to elements of one's social and moral character:

> A person must be able not simply to perform a certain activity, or provide a service, but he must also be able to do it in an acceptable manner—i.e., in a manner which is approximately as efficient as others, in an honest manner, and in a manner

compatible with others who seek to provide the services for which they were hired.[9]

Again, the employer is entitled to know, in the case of potential employees, if they are capable of fulfilling their part of the contract, and, in the case of existing employees, if they are adhering to the terms and expectations implicit in the contract. While this latter case can often be confirmed by direct observation of the employee's actions at the work site, on occasion the employer is entitled to information regarding behavior which can be observed at the workplace but originates from outside of it (such as arriving at work late, or consuming large quantities of alcohol prior to arriving). As all of these actions may be in violation of the term of employment, the employer is entitled to know of them, and in coming to know of them does not violate the employee's privacy.

My point in offering these examples is to suggest that drug testing is a method of coming to know about an employee's ability to fulfill the terms of contract which is analogous to those listed. An exploratory process, in seeking to verify an employee's ability to do a certain job in connection with reasonable expectations for what that job entails, may also validly discover characteristics or tendencies that would keep the employee from performing to reasonable expectations. Drug testing is precisely this sort of process. As a part of the process of reviewing employee performance to determine whether or not they are fulfilling the terms and expectations of employment satisfactorily, drug testing may be validly included among other types of investigatory methods, including interviews with co-workers, skills and proficiency testing, and (in some professions) medical examinations. The fact that an employee may not want to submit to a drug test is entirely beside the point; the employee may just as likely prefer not to include a complete list of personal references, or prefer that the employer not review her relations with other employees. In all these cases, the employer is entitled to know the relevant information, and in coming to know these things does not violate the employee's privacy. The employee may withhold this information from the employer, but this action is tantamount to ending the employer-employee relationship. Such a relationship, under the terms of employment, includes not only each party's commitment to benefit the other in the specific way indicated, but also entitles each to determine if the other is capable of performance according to the terms of contract. In this way, each retains the free ability to terminate the relationship on the grounds of the other's nonperformance.

Of course, not just any purpose of obtaining information relevant to evaluating performance under the terms of contract can automatically be considered reasonable. For instance, an employer cannot spy on a prospective employee in her own home to determine if she will be a capable employee. I offer the following criteria as setting reasonable and ethical limits on obtaining relevant information (though note that the requirement of relevancy is in each case already assumed).

1. The process whereby an employer comes to know something about an employee (existing or prospective) must not be unnecessarily harmful or intrusive

The information may not result from investigatory processes which are themselves degrading or humiliating by virtue of their intrusiveness (e.g., strip searches, spying on an employee while they use the bathroom, interviewing a divorced spouse, or searching an employee's locker) or which may prove unhealthy (e.g., excessive use of x-rays, or torture). (Note: Degrading processes of securing information must be distinguished from processes of securing information which is itself degrading. The latter is not necessarily in violation of this or successive criteria.)

2. The process whereby an employer comes to know something about an employee must be efficient and specific

The information must result from an efficient and specific process—i.e., a process which is the most direct of competing methods (though without compromising point 1 above), and should result in information which corresponds to questions of performance under the terms of the employment contract, and should not result in information that does not so correspond. For example, detailed credit checks may help a bank decide whether a prospective employee is a capable manager of finances, but not directly (only inferentially), and it would also provide a great deal of information that the employer is not entitled to see. Consulting the employee's previous employer, on the other hand, may provide the relevant information directly and specifically.

3. The process whereby an employer comes to know something about an employee must be accurate, or if not itself precise, then capable of confirmation through further investigation

The information must result from a dependable source; if a source is not dependable and is incapable of being verified for accuracy, the employer is not justified in pursuing this avenue of discovery. Thus, the polygraph must be excluded, since it is occasionally inaccurate and may in such cases result in information that cannot be verified. In addition, disreputable sources of information, or sources that may have an interest in misrepresenting the information being sought, should not be used.

Having outlined these, I offer my argument in full: Drug testing is not only a method of coming to know about an employee's ability to fulfill the terms of contract which is analogous to those listed earlier, but which also is reasonable under the criteria listed above.

1. Drug testing is not harmful or intrusive

In the Supreme Court case *Samuel K. Skinner v. Railway Labor Executives' Association* (489 U.S. 602), the Court determined that both blood and urine tests were minimally intrusive.[10] While the Court acknowledged that the act of passing urine was itself intensely personal (ibid., p. 617), obtaining a urine sample in a medical environment and without the use of direct observation amounted to no more than a minimal intrusion (ibid., p. 626). The Court justified not only testing of urine but also testing of blood by focusing on the procedure of testing (i.e., "experience . . . teaches that the quantity of blood extracted is minimal," ibid., p. 625) and pointing out that since such tests are "commonplace and routine in everyday life," the tests posed "virtually no risk, trauma, or pain" (ibid., p. 625). The Court's findings on this case are compelling, and are consistent with my contention that drug testing is not unnecessarily harmful or intrusive. While such testing does amount to an imposition upon an employee (i.e., by requiring her to report to a physician and provide a urine sample) in a way that may not be commonplace for many employees, the Court ruled that since this takes place within an employment context (where limitations of movement are assumed), this interference is justifiable and does not unnecessarily infringe on privacy interests (ibid., pp. 624–625).

2. Drug testing is both efficient and specific

In fact, drug testing is the most efficient means of discovering employee drug abuse. In addition to providing direct access to the information in question, the results of drug testing do not include information that is irrelevant. The test targets a specific set of illegal substances. It can be argued (and has been) that drug testing is not efficient because it does not test for impairment—only for drug use. But this point ignores the fact that the test is justified on a correlation between drug abuse and employee productivity more generally; impairment is itself difficult or impossible to measure, since the effects of a given quantity of substance vary from individual to individual and from one incidence of use to another. The fact that impairment is an elusive quantity cannot diminish the validity of testing for drug abuse. This criticism also ignores the fact that the test is an effective means of deterring impairment, providing habitual users a certain expectation that their drug use will be discovered if it is not controlled.

3. Drug testing can be conducted in a way which guarantees a high degree of precision

It is well known that the standard (and relatively inexpensive) EMIT test has a measurable chance of falsely indicating drug use, and is also susceptible to cross-reactivity with other legal substances. But confirmatory testing, such as that performed using gas chromatography/mass spectrometry, can provide results at a high level of accuracy. This confirmatory testing, as well as a host of other stringent safeguards, is required of all laboratories certified by the National Institute on Drug Abuse.[11]

In summary, my contention is that an employer is entitled to drug test on the grounds that the information derived is relevant to confirm the employee's capacity to perform according to the terms of employment, and that such testing is a reasonable means of coming to know such information. Other points in favor of drug testing, which are not essential to my preceding argument but congruent with it, include the following two items.

First, drug testing is an opportunity for employer beneficence. Testing permits the employer to diagnose poor employee performance and require such individuals to participate in employer-sponsored counseling and rehabilitative measures. Employers are permitted to recognize that drug abuse is a disease with a broad social impact that is not addressed if employees who perform poorly as a result of drug abuse are merely terminated.[12] Second, a specific diagnosis of drug abuse in the case of poor employee performance might protect the employer from wrongful termination litigation, in the event that an employee refuses to seek help regarding their abuse. The results of drug testing might confirm to the court that the termination was effected on substantive and not arbitrary grounds.

DRUG TESTING AND QUESTIONS OF JUSTIFICATION

A number of arguments have been offered which suggest that drug testing is not justified under terms of contract, or is not a reasonable method by which an employer may come to know of employee drug abuse, and therefore amounts to a violation of employee privacy. These arguments include a rejection of productivity as a justification for testing, charges that testing is coercive, and that it amounts to an abuse of employee privacy by controlling behavior conducted outside the workplace. I will respond to each of these in turn.

First, some have charged that arguing from an employer's right to maximize productivity to a justification for drug testing is problematic. DesJardins and Duska point out that employers have a valid claim on some level of employee performance, such that a failure to perform to this level would give the employer a justification for firing or finding fault with the employee. But it is not clear that an employer has a valid claim on an optimal level of employee performance, and that is what drug testing is directed at achieving. As long as drug abuse does not reduce an employee's performance beyond a reasonable level, an employer cannot claim a right to the highest level of performance of which an employee is capable.[13]

DesJardins and Duska further point out the elusiveness of an optimal level of performance. Some employees perform below the norm in an unimpaired state, and other employees might conceivably perform above the norm in an impaired state. "If the relevant consideration is whether the employee is producing as expected (according to the normal demands of the position and contract) not whether he/she is producing as much as possible, then knowledge of drug use is irrelevant or unnecessary."[14] This is because the issue in question is not drug use *per se*, but employee productivity. Since drug use need not correlate to expectations for a given employee's productivity, testing for drug use is irrelevant. And since it is irrelevant to fulfillment of the employment contract, testing for drugs is unjustified and therefore stands in violation of an employee's privacy.

While I agree that it is problematic to state that an employer has a right to expect an optimal level of performance from an employee, I would argue that the employer does have a right to a workplace free from the deleterious effects of employee drug abuse.[15] Drug testing, properly understood, is not directed at effecting optimal performance, but rather performance which is free from the effects of drug abuse. Since the assessment which justifies drug testing is not based on the impact of drug abuse on a given employee's performance, but is correlated on the effects of drug abuse on workplace productivity more generally, drug testing does measure a relevant quantity.

It is also overly simplistic to state that employers need not test for drugs when they can terminate employees on the mere basis of a failure to perform. Employers are willing to tolerate temporary factors which may detract from employee performance; e.g., a death in the family, sickness, or occasional loss of sleep. But employers have a right to distinguish these self-correcting factors from factors which may be habitual, ongoing, and increasingly detrimental to productivity, such as drug abuse. Such insight might dramatically impact their course of action with regard to how they address the employee's failure to perform. It is therefore not the case, as DesJardins and Duska suggest, that "knowledge of the cause of the failure to perform is irrelevant."[16]

A more critical series of arguments against basing drug testing on an employer's right to maximize productivity has been leveled by Nicholas Caste. First, Caste attacks what he identifies as "the productivity argument":

> The productivity argument essentially states that since the employer has purchased the employee's time, the employer has a proprietary right to ensure that the time purchased is used as efficiently as possible. . . . the employer must be concerned with "contract enforcement" and must attempt somehow to motivate the employee to attain maximal production capacity. In the case of drug testing, the abuse of drugs by employees is seen as diminishing their productive capacity and is thus subject to the control of the employer.[17]

From this argument, Caste states, one can infer that any manipulation is acceptable as long as it is maximizing productivity, and he defines manipulation as an attempt to produce a response without regard for that individual's good, as he or she perceives it.[18] Caste goes on to give two examples of hypothetical drugs which, assuming the productivity argument, an employer would be justified in requiring employees to take. The first drug increases employee productivity while also increasing pleasure and job satisfaction. The second drug increases productivity while inflicting painful side-effects on the employee. The fact that the productivity argument appears to sanction the use of both drugs, and in fact cannot morally distinguish between them, seems to argue for its invalidity. Since the productivity argument cannot distinguish between causing an employee pleasure or pain, by adopting its logic one would be forced to the morally unacceptable conclusion that an employee's best interests are irrelevant.

Caste points out that what is wrong with the second drug is not that it causes pain "but that it is manipulatively intrusive. It establishes areas of control to which the employer has no right."[19] He concludes that what is wrong with the productivity argument is that it is manipulative. And what is wrong with manipulation is not the effects it produces (which may, coincidentally, be in the subject's best interests) but rather that it undermines the subject's autonomy by not allowing their desires to be factored into the decision making process.[20] Since drug testing is justified by appeal to productivity arguments, it also is fundamentally manipulative and results in a morally unacceptable degree of employee control. Drug testing is therefore unethical, and should be rejected. . . .

The failure of Caste's argument becomes clear when we realize that, if he is correct, virtually every action required of an employee at a work site would qualify as manipulative—whether the action in question was in her best interests or not, and whether or not she desired to comply, since Caste defines manipulation as a function of restricting autonomy. Dress codes, starting times, and basic performance expectations all may be similarly justified by appeal to the productivity argument—but most of us are not prepared to count these things as manipulative or unjustified. Requirements of this sort are not instances of manipulation, but are justified expectations which honor a contractual agreement. Similarly, an employee who demands a paycheck of her employer is engaging in manipulation, according to Caste's definition—but this cannot be correct. In the contract, each party is apprised that the other has a right to benefit from the arrangement, and each has a commensurate

responsibility to uphold their part. Accountability to the terms of the contract does not amount to manipulation when the accountability in question is reasonable. In agreement with Caste's original criticism, it is not true that an employer has a right to ensure maximal productivity. But an employer does have the right to hold an employee accountable to the terms of the contract, which express reasonable expectations of productivity. From this it cannot be inferred, however, that just any activity to maximize (or even minimally ensure) productivity is justifiable, since the contractual model expressly allows that the employee has certain morally justified claims that cannot be bargained away in return for employment. Since the productivity argument, as Caste depicts it, is in fact not a justification for drug testing under a contractual model, it is not the case that drug testing must be rejected.

In a similar vein, some argue that any testing which involves coercion is inherently an invasion of employee privacy. Placing employees in a position where they must choose between maintaining their privacy or losing their jobs is fundamentally coercive. "For most employees, being given the choice between submitting to a drug test and risking one's job by refusing an employer's request is not much of a decision at all."[21] While Brenkert's arguments against the use of the polygraph are directed at that device's inability to distinguish the reason behind a positive reading (which may not, in many instances, indicate an intentional lie), his argument that the polygraph is coercive is pertinent to the question of drug testing as well.

Brenkert notes that if an employee

. . . did not take the test and cooperate during the test, his application for employment would either not be considered at all or would be considered to have a significant negative aspect to it. This is surely a more subtle form of coercion. And if this be the case, then one cannot say that the person has willingly allowed his reactions to the questions to be monitored. He has consented to do so, but he has consented under coercion. Had he a truly free choice, he would not have done so.[22]

Brenkert's point is surprising, in that his own understanding is that A's privacy is limited by what Z is entitled to know in order to execute its role with respect to A. If Z (here, the corporation) is entitled to know X (whether or not the employee abuses drugs) in order to determine if A (the employee) is capable of performing according to the terms of employment, then the employee has no right to privacy with respect to the information in question. While this does not authorize the corporation to obtain the information in just any manner, the mere fact that the employee would *prefer* that the employer not know cannot be sufficient to constitute a right to privacy in the face of the employer's legitimate entitlement. The employee can freely choose to withhold the information, but this is not so much invoking a right to privacy as it is rejecting the terms of contract.

If Brenkert's criticism of employer testing were valid, then potentially all demands made by the employer on the employee—from providing background information to arriving at work on time—would count as coercive, since in every case where the employee consents to the demand there is a strong possibility that she would not have consented if she was offered a truly free choice. But these demands are reasonable, and the employer is entitled to demand them under the terms of employment, just as the employee is entitled to profit by acceding to such demands.

The final argument considered here is the charge that drug testing is an attempt to "control the employee's actions in a time that has not actually been purchased."[23] Even if we assume that an employer has the right to maximize profitability by controlling the employee's behavior during normal work hours, the employer has no right to control what an employee does in her free time. To attempt to do so is a violation of employee rights. This argument also falls flat, however, when we realize that the demands of a standard employment contract inherently place limitations on an employee's free time. In a sense, the employment contract demands priority, requiring the employee to organize her free time around her employment schedule in a way that permits her to honor the contractual obligation. For instance, time traveling to and from work occurs during an employee's "free time," and is dependent on the employee's own personal resources, but is rightfully assumed within the terms of the contract. Time and money spent shopping for work attire also falls outside the normal time of employment, but is essential for honoring a mandatory dress code. These are not normally considered violations of an employee's private life, or unethical "controls" placed on an employee by an employer, but are justified, again, under the terms of contract. Drug testing is justified similarly.

RESERVATIONS AND POLICY RECOMMENDATIONS

. . .

It is the position adopted in this article that a corporation is entitled to drug test its employees to determine employee capacity to perform according to the terms of the employment contract. That drug testing is not, however, in the large majority of cases, directed at maximizing the employee's best interests, suggests that employers should avail themselves of their right to drug test within reasonable limits. In light of this conclusion, the following policy recommendations are directed at employers, with the goal of balanc-ing the employer's right to drug test with a more substantive regard for the dignity and privacy of employees.

1. Testing should focus on a specifically targeted group of employees

In the case of employers who are testing without regard for questions of safety, I would strongly urge that testing only be done when probable cause exists to suspect that an employee is using controlled substances. Probable cause might include uncharacteristic behavior, obvious symptoms of impairment, or a significantly diminished capacity to perform their duties. Utilizing probable cause minimizes the intrusive aspect of testing by yielding a higher percentage of test-positives (i.e., requiring probable cause before testing will inherently screen out the large majority of negatives). Even with this stipulation, a drug program may provide a reasonable deterrence factor at the workplace.

It should be noted that this qualification does not apply in cases of job applicants. Employers who insist on testing potential employees will typically do so under a general suspicion of drug use, and may in that case assume a condition of probable cause.

2. When testing is indicated, it should not be announced ahead of time

Regularly scheduled testing runs the risk of losing its effectiveness by providing an employee sufficient time to contrive a method of falsifying the sample. Drug testing, if it is to be used at all, should be used in a way which maximizes its effectiveness and accuracy.

3. Employees who test positive for drug abuse should be permitted the opportunity to resolve their abusive tendencies and return to work without penalty or stigma

Employees should only be terminated for an inability to resolve their abuse, once early detection and substantial warning have been made. Employers can mitigate the dehumanizing aspect of this technology by using it as an opportunity to assist abusive employees with their problems, and permitting them to return to their old positions if they can remedy their habitual tendencies. Toxicological testing should therefore be accompanied by a full range of employee assistance interventions.

◆ Notes

1. According to SAMHSA (Substance Abuse and Mental Health Services Administration), cited in Ira A. Lipman, 'Drug Testing is Vital in the Workplace', *U.S.A. Today Magazine* **123** (January 1995), 81.
2. Dawn Gunsch, 'Training Prepares Workers for Drug Testing', *Personnel Journal* **72** (May 1993), 52.
3. According to the U.S. Bureau of Labor Statistics, cited in Rob Brookler, 'Industry Standards in Workplace Drug Testing', *Personnel Journal* **71** (April 1992), 128.
4. See Lewis L. Maltby, 'Why Drug Testing is a Bad Idea', *Inc.* (June 1987), 152.
5. On this point see Michele Simms, 'Defining Privacy in Employee Health Screening Cases: Ethical Ramifications Concerning the Employee/ Employer Relationship', *Journal of Business Ethics* **13** (1994), 315–325.
6. DesJardins further argues that these conditions are not sufficient to constitute a right to privacy. In the example of subliminal advertising, if it was effective, one's right "to be let alone" would be violated, but without any clear violation of one's privacy (Joseph R. DesJardins, 'An Employee's Right to Privacy', in J. R. DesJardins and J. J. McCall (eds.), *Contemporary Issues in Business Ethics* [Wadsworth, Belmont, CA, 1985], p. 222).
7. George G. Brenkert, 'Privacy, Polygraphs, and Work', *Business and Professional Ethics Journal* **1** (1981), 23. In agreement see DesJardins, 'An

Employee's Right to Privacy', p. 222; Joseph DesJardins and Ronald Duska, 'Drug Testing in Employment', *Business and Professional Ethics Journal* **6** (1987), 3–4.

8. See for example U.S. Department of Health and Human Services, *Drugs in the Workplace: Research and Evaluation Data*, ed. S. W. Gust and J. M. Walsh (National Institute on Drug Abuse Monograph 91, 1989), and National Research Council/Institute of Medicine, *Under the Influence? Drugs and the American Work Force*, ed. J. Normand, R. O. Lempert and C. P. O'Brien (Committee on Drug Use in the Workplace, 1994). For example, a prospective study of preemployment drug testing in the U.S. Postal Service showed after 1.3 years of employment that employees who had tested positive for illicit drug use at the time they were hired were 60% more likely to be absent from work than employees who tested negative (*Drugs in the Workplace*, pp. 128–132; *Under the Influence*, p. 134).

9. Brenkert, 'Privacy, Polygraphs, and Work', 25.

10. While the legal opinion itself only summarizes and does not in and of itself justify a moral argument, it does in this case demonstrate a broad consensus and both rational and intuitive appeals to the matter at hand.

11. See Brookler, "Industry Standards in Workplace Drug Testing," 129.

12. *Contra* DesJardins and Duska, who state, "Of course, if the employer suspects drug use or abuse as the cause of the unsatisfactory performance, then she might choose to help the person with counseling or rehabilitation. However, this does not seem to be something morally required of the employer. Rather, in the case of unsatisfactory performance, the employer has a prima facie justification for dismissing or disciplining the employee" ('Drug Testing in Employment', 6–7).

13. DesJardins and Duska, 'Drug Testing in Employment', 5.

14. Ibid., 6.

15. Implicit in this statement is the assumption that employees do not have an absolute right to abuse drugs. This is a point I am neither able (for lack of space) nor interested in taking up at this point, but would instead appeal to a broad societal consensus on drug abuse, legislation against the use of illicit substances (and abuse of legal substances), and various negative social correlates to drug use. Thus, I am convinced that drug abuse can be distinguished from other legitimate (but potentially deleterious) behaviors, such as poor dietary habits.

16. Ibid.

17. Nicholas J. Caste, 'Drug Testing and Productivity', *Journal of Business Ethics* **11** (1992), 301.

18. Ibid., 302.

19. Ibid., 303.

20. As a side note, I should point out that Caste has gone wrong in assessing his own definition of manipulation (understood as an attempt to produce a response without regard for that individual's good, as they perceived it). What is wrong with manipulation is *not* that it undermines autonomy, since undermining autonomy is neither a necessary nor a sufficient component in manipulation as he defines it (i.e., I can undermine your autonomy in a way which is in complete accord with your good as you perceive it, and this would not qualify as manipulation). If the subject willingly embraces the act in question, and is in complete agreement with a policy mandating the action, it would still be manipulative under Caste's definition, since manipulation turns not on the effect, nor on the victim's will, but on the motivation of the agent behind the act.

21. DesJardins and Duska, 'Drug Testing in Employment', 16–17. This is also implied in DesJardins, 'An Employee's Right to Privacy', p. 226, but in neither case is the argument fully developed.

22. Brenkert, 'Privacy, Polygraphs, and Work', 28–29.

23. Caste, 'Drug Testing and Productivity', 303. See also Maltby, 'Why Drug Testing is a Bad Idea', 152.

◆ **9** ◆

BUSINESS AND CONSUMERS

Does business have any responsibility to its customers? Some believe that consumers are autonomous individuals who can make their own purchasing decisions in a free and open market and who should be prepared to live with the results. The Latin phrase for this is *caveat emptor*: let the buyer beware. If people are free to make a choice, are rational, and have adequate information, then when they enter a contract they take on responsibility for future consequences.

According to this view, if customers prefer, say, fancy rims on a car to optional side air bags, that is something they should be able to choose. If they are subsequently injured in a crash from the side, they cannot blame the carmaker for not providing adequate protection. One condition of this approach, however, is the assumption that the proper information is available to those who elect to use it. In the notorious case of the Ford Pinto, the company had information about problems with the design of the gas tank that was not readily available to the general public. Although a reasonable person might be expected to know something about engines and safety features, in this case specialized knowledge was suppressed; in short, potential buyers could not have had sufficient information to make a rational decision. In

all fairness, however, we should point out that once the charge was made in a national magazine, people still bought the Pinto in large numbers.

What is the salient information for a consumer, and what duty does a company have to provide it? Current government regulations force food manufacturers to list some, but not all, nutritional information. How much is enough, and what would be too much? Some firms use information to market their products. For example, an aerosol may carry the information "no CFCs" (the chlorofluorocarbons that damage the ozone); although this seems to be useful information in making a purchasing decision, in fact the law bans CFCs and no product has them. Are there problems with being overinformed as well as underinformed? Is it realistic to expect customers to check everything on the shelves, or should there be a level of trust and confidence between vendor and buyer that smoothes out transactions?

LIABILITY

At the opposite end of the scale from caveat emptor is the doctrine known as strict liability. This makes a producer completely liable for any and all consequences of its products or services, even when consumers misuse the product or use the product beyond its service life. For example, many commercial airplanes now being flown are over their projected work life. Should the original manufacturer be held liable if there were an incident that was not anticipated when the plane was made?

An intermediate position suggests that we can expect reasonable care on the part of a business when it designs and manufactures goods, but there are degrees of fault that can be determined if there is a problem. Thus a firm that makes lawn mowers might be held liable if the gas tank bursts into flames in hot weather due to poor design but should be immune from injury claims arising from a customer who tried to use it to trim his hedge while standing on a stepladder.

However, assigning fault is a costly enterprise. In the United States it typically takes the form of a jury trial, where lawyers for both sides present their cases in an adversarial contest. American law also allows for punitive damages, where not only may an injured party sue for compensation but a jury may choose to punish a company as well. Generally, we are wedded to the idea of assigning blame; it seems right that bad people and companies should be subject to a public trial and consequent punishment.

An alternative approach acknowledges that the cost of trials and awards gets passed on to consumers in general. People with this viewpoint would like to get rid of the very costly judicial middlemen: Pay people who have been injured while using a product, and then let the market decide what it values. Firms that make shoddy goods would have to pay out a lot, and this would be an economic incentive to make better, safer products. The worker's compensation system essentially operates in this way: Employees injured on the job are entitled to a standard level of compensation in return for giving up legal redress. A

classic objection is that such a system would be abused, but there again market forces would regulate fraud. Losing a finger might be worth, say, $1,000, but if people choose to chop off their fingers and claim injury, the compensation would be reduced to the point where the potential fraudsters would rather keep their fingers intact.

One of the purported benefits of strict liability is that it gives injured parties compensation while sending a general message to manufacturers about the standard of care that is expected. But should a manufacturer be forced to pay just because it has so-called deep pockets? In the case of the pesticide Benlate, the chemical company DuPont withdrew it from the market after the company was found liable for a wide range of injuries that were claimed to be associated with the pesticide's use. The company maintains that the product is safe and beneficial but that it cannot withstand the economic risks of constantly defending jury trials. Determining how risky a product is can be difficult and time-consuming, and sometimes problems will not come to light until it has been on the market for a long time or used by a wide population. Moreover, many of the cases are emotional and involve significant human distress while the disputes over causal relationships are often highly technical. It is not surprising, therefore, that a jury of untrained specialists will be swayed when shown catastrophic harm purportedly brought about by a firm with deep pockets.

In the case of Dow Corning, the company went bankrupt largely as a result of thousands of claims from women who contended that they had been harmed by dangerous breast implants. The current scientific evidence tends to show that there is no connection, and the silicone involved was safe. In court, scientists were asked if they could definitively rule out bad side effects, and generally they answered that there was no scientific evidence of a connection, but it could not be absolutely discounted as a possibility. Faced with a claimant exhibiting clear physical distress and experts who could not deny a causal link, juries often chose to award compensation.

PATERNALISM

Paternalism refers to a belief that an authority figure knows better than a particular individual what is in the individual's best interest. In the case of children, for example, a mother might demand that the child wears a helmet while cycling, over the child's objections. The parent might do this because she is more aware of the potential dangers than her child, and she cares about the youngster's welfare. A college advisor might tell a student to consider taking more advanced courses because he feels the student is capable of doing the work, and it will open up more opportunities for him in the future. An example of the government acting in this way would be the unhappy experiment of the 18th Amendment, which forbade the sale of alcohol in the United States.

The philosopher John Stuart Mill articulated his argument against paternalism in *On Liberty*, where he said the individual should be sovereign over his own self, and the odds are that outside interference, however benign, is likely to be done in the wrong way and end up badly. Most of us have probably experienced unwelcome advice that was well meant but led to distress. Mill felt that the only legitimate reason to interfere was in the case of imminent harm. Yet the advisor above might be genuinely doing good by offering good counsel. The difference seems to be that advice presents information and leaves the ultimate choice to the individual, whereas paternalism involves having control over another.

In business, the question is to what extent should a company act paternalistically. If there is evident customer demand for a burger with lots of red meat, bacon, cheese, and mayonnaise, is it the place of the company to warn consumers of the dangers of a high-fat diet? The company may have specialized knowledge that is difficult for the average consumer to access or understand. Does it have an obligation to interpret that information for the buying public even if that might deter sales? Would it be wrong, for example, to sell life insurance to an elderly man when there are no likely benefits to the person or his survivors? How much are businesses their brother's keeper?

The readings in this chapter explore these issues in some depth. The first, by Claudia Mills and Douglas MacLean, asks how much value we should put on a human life. The easy answer is to say that life is infinitely valuable, and we cannot put a price tag on it. Nevertheless, there are a number of ways that we do exactly that: We insure our lives for a chosen amount, and juries often put a figure on a life in wrongful death suits. We also signal our values by our behavior. We might say that a smoker or a rock climber demonstrates that he is ready to compromise the "infinite" value of his life. If we drive unsubstantial and poorly made cars, then we are at least making an implicit risk assessment about death and injury.

Manufacturers and the government face similar issues. The government could regulate, or producers could market, cars with 6 feet of foam padding around them and capable of traveling only at speeds less than 10 miles per hour. There would likely be protests against these cars, though, showing that we make compromises between convenience and safety. It is worth noting that we do so for aesthetic reasons as well. Airplane travel would be much safer if the seats faced the back, because a hard landing would be cushioned by the seat rather than passengers bending at the waist and hitting the tray table in front. Yet we like to look forward, and that is reflected in airplane design.

Mills and MacLean look at the varying numbers used by government agencies; The Consumer Product Safety Commission uses a $50,000 figure for the value of a human life, whereas the Occupational Safety and Health Administration estimates it at $12 million. This discrepancy leads to differing policy decisions and government inefficiency. In explaining the wide variance, the authors suggest that there are different ways to approach valuing a life, and there may be good reasons for individual departments to arrive at their numbers.

James Ebejer and Michael Morden examine the notion of paternalism with respect to advertising. They conclude that an advertiser should not actively lie but that it is not doing wrong by providing less than full disclosure. Their analysis relies on a number of assumptions, including the availability of information. One question to consider is whether the advent of the Internet would alter their findings.

Janice Kang Choi's reading discusses recent initiatives within the European Union to ban advertising that is directly aimed at children. Companies have found that children are especially susceptible to certain kinds of advertising and that they are able to exert tremendous pressure on their parents to buy them things. Consider, for example, that the sugary cereals in boxes with cartoon characters are most often found on the lower shelves in the supermarket. Different countries within the EU have varying attitudes, and the proposed legislation also has to answer the claim that the parents, not the manufacturers, have the primary moral responsibility in the purchasing decision. Choi concludes by looking at some of the newer ways of marketing to children, such as donations of classroom material and equipment replete with corporate logos.

Lawrence Masek brings the perspective of the doctrine of double effect to business ethics. The doctrine says that an act may be morally acceptable if there are foreseeable but unintended bad effects. Thus, a carmaker is aware that people may die using its product, but it does not intend to deliberately murder people by putting its vehicle on the road. In the same way, a chemical producer may recognize that in rare cases people may have a reaction to its product, but they are trying to benefit humanity in what they do, and collateral damage may be an acceptable price to pay. Masek believes that in an era of open information, there might be nothing wrong with putting a potentially lethal drug on the market and letting people make their own choice about the risks involved. We could extrapolate his findings to almost any goods, not just dangerous ones, because almost everything from aspirin to latex could potentially be associated with harm to humans.

The brief article by Metta Winter discusses the paternalistic way the government currently restricts manufacturers from promoting their products by using health information that is not yet definitive. She feels this is overly restrictive and may prevent consumers from making good choices.

The last article in the chapter discusses the empirical findings from jury trials. There is a lot of anecdotal speculation about the amounts awarded by so-called runaway juries against companies. Valerie Hans disputes many of the common understandings and concludes that it appears that juries expect companies to act in a reasonable and conscientious manner in much the same fashion that professionals are expected to treat clients.

Risk Analysis and the Value of Life

Claudia Mills and Douglas MacLean

An expense that both government and industry face is maximizing safety for both workers and consumers. While we might like to think that life has infinite value, realistically we take risks and make compromises—as do the manufacturers of cars, airplanes, and food products. At some point, we will not spend ever more money to preserve and protect life. The tension between rationally putting a price on human (or even nonhuman) life and our desire to put life beyond market concerns is a constant in the world of business and society.

In their analysis, Mills and MacLean draw on the inconsistency among different government agencies that are charged with protecting life. The amounts that they allocate vary enormously, which seems both inefficient and unfair. Mills and MacLean conclude that the diverse government agencies play a symbolic and expressive role that recognizes the value of individual's lives differently, and so agreeing on a single valuation for a life may not be as attractive as it first seems. After reading the article, consider how a business might place a price on risk when health and safety are concerned.

One of the chief mandates of government is to protect the lives of its citizens. It does this through providing military defense against foreign attack and criminal sanctions against domestic assault. But death comes not only through war and bloodshed, and in this century, government, via its regulatory agencies, has protected people as well against various more diffuse threats to life and health; death from any cause leaves its victims just as dead. We believe it falls within the jurisdiction of government to protect its citizens with equal vigilance against many threats to life.

But if we look at the mandates of different regulatory agencies that share the common goal of protecting life, we see that they pursue this goal with differing degrees of zeal. Some agencies must balance gains in safety or health against the costs of achieving them; others must act to reduce risks in whatever ways are technologically feasible. This leads to some startling differences in standards. A review of the cost effectiveness of some proposed lifesaving programs has shown that the median cost of saving a life was $50 thousand at the Consumer Product Safety Commission and $64 thousand at the National Highway Traffic Safety Commission, while the same median value was $2.6 million at the Environmental Protection Agency (EPA) and $12.1 million at the Occupational Safety and Health Administration (OSHA). Surely this comparison suggests that we are spending too much in some areas, too little in others, or both.

The estimated cost of saving a life should no doubt be brought more into line across different programs, not only for reasons of equity, but also for reasons of efficiency. We could save more lives for the same total regulatory budget if we allocated these funds differently. But which inequalities should we accept? How should other values weigh against the number of lives we could save? And what should the overall median value be anyway? How do we decide?

THE SOCIAL VALUE OF LIFE

Policy analysts have been trying to answer these questions for some years now. One of their practical goals is to bring more order and coherence to the piecemeal approach to health and safety regulation of the 1960s and early 1970s. The methods they have developed—different specific techniques for analyzing and comparing risks, costs, and benefits—are intended to help us think clearly and comprehensively about all these issues.

One way to do this is to calculate what risk-analysts call "the social value of life." They look at consumer choices that reveal preferences for safety, as opposed to other goods, and at social decisions to accept some level of risk when the cost of reducing it further would be too great. Measures such as these can be used to establish a systematic, consistent benchmark for deciding what we should spend on lifesaving policies.

A justification for being explicit and analytic about what we are willing to spend to save lives is that by allocating our risk budget more efficiently, we can reduce everyone's risk of early death. Equally important, since every dollar we spend on increased safety is a dollar diverted from enhancing our lives in other ways, we can make better comparisons between improving life's quality and increasing its longevity. Living longer, after all, is a poor substitute for living well.

But many find the prospect of setting a social value for life a chilling one. This may be partly because they fear entrusting such decisions to a technocratic elite that might abuse its powers. Even setting aside this fear, however, it seems unconscionably cold and calculating to tote up the dollar value of individual human lives in an accountant's ledger. If, for example, we decide to forgo certain safety measures in coal mines, because we have coolly estimated that their costs do not justify their benefits, this will almost certainly mean some miners' deaths will not be prevented. It means, that is, some real flesh-and-blood human beings will die in order to save what may amount to only a few pennies on a dollar. Likewise, if we decide certain pollution control measures in a larger power plant are not worth their cost, numerous deaths can be expected to result. Isn't this killing to save money?

The risk-analyst's response is that, like it or not, trade-offs between safety and other goods do have to be made. We could always spend more—perhaps a good deal more, to make the world safer—perhaps a little bit safer. At some point, as a society, we have to strike a balance. Risk analysis helps us do this in an orderly, rational way. According to Allan Gibbard, professor of philosophy at the University of Michigan, "'Killing to save money' is a tendentious way of describing the operation of a power plant with substantial pollution controls. . . . The phrase would allow us to dismiss a thousand man-years of sweat and toil as mere 'money' while underlining diffuse effects on health as 'killing.'" Impassioned rhetoric will not let us off the hook of making hard choices.

Furthermore, a sufficiently sophisticated risk analysis, one that in Gibbard's terms addresses "the expected total intrinsic reward" of our lives, will not ride roughshod over our actual feelings about safety and health, or anything else. Even if our feelings are not rational or consistent, they matter, Gibbard explains, because they are ours:

"They determine much in the way we experience our lives and the ways we experience each other." Frustrating them has costs of its own, to be counted in with all the rest: "A risk-cost-benefit analysis that takes into account all contributions to expected total intrinsic reward must count things other than lives saved, injuries and illnesses avoided, and resources diverted to do these things. It must count effects on the ways people who stand ready to carry out a policy experience their lives."

Suppose, for example, we could save more lives if we spent our budget for mine safety on preventing accidents rather than on heroic, extremely expensive rescue efforts for trapped miners. Nevertheless, Gibbard recognizes, it may be "dehumanizing to stand idly by when strenuous, expensive effort has a substantial chance of saving lives." An ideal risk analysis would count the benefits of saving more lives but also the costs of forfeiting some of the psychological rewards of human fellowship.

But can risk analysis take account of all our other values, throwing them in one gigantic hopper with the number of lives saved and the dollar costs of saving them? Is risk analysis just a neutral way of structuring our decisions, incorporating all our values, whatever they are, and giving them whatever weight we determine to be important? Or do some values resist treatment in this way?

Many people are uncomfortable with the suggestion that risk analysis should be a decision procedure for making choices that seem important both for their consequences and for the real and symbolic value that attaches to how they are made. For this reason, decisions about life and death are decisions we might especially resist consigning to the risk-analyst's decision machine.

Human life, we might say, has a sacred or priceless value. This is often taken to mean that life has infinite value, but this is not the correct interpretation of what it is for something to be held as sacred. Certainly we are not willing to spend infinite sums of money to save lives; we have other competing priorities. Indeed, many of the things we regard as priceless may have perfectly well-determined market values. To call something priceless may only mean it is not for sale, not that no one could afford it.

The mark of a sacred object lies less in how much we value it than in how we express that value. In every culture, sacred values are attended by special ceremonies and rituals. We might characterize rituals as irrational or nonrational behavior, actions in which the relationship between means and ends is deliberately inefficient. This aspect of rituals indicates their symbolic meaning and draws the attention of the community to objects, relationships, or roles that have a special place in the life of the group.

Our culture, too, has its own rituals for expressing the sacred value of life. These include saving crash victims, fliers lost at sea, or astronauts; retrieving the wounded or dead in battle; diverting resources used for making mines safer in order to mount rescue missions for trapped miners; or even supporting individual medical treatment rather than more public health measures. These defy economic sense—they are intended to defy economic sense. They are intended to show that life has a value that cannot be cashed out in purely economic terms.

We can conclude from this that the value of life is complex. It has at least two aspects that can conflict with each other. First, human life has intrinsic value: Saving lives or preventing early deaths is good, and the more lives saved the better. Risk analysis is an important tool for furthering this value. Second, human life has a sacred value, which must be expressed through rituals and other special actions. Setting acceptable levels of risk must be guided by both aspects of this value, even though they may have to be balanced and traded off against each other. We might reasonably choose to accept certain inefficiencies—to save fewer lives than we might otherwise save—in order to maintain the sacredness of human life. Risk-analysts insist that we are willing to accept some risks as a trade-off to improve life's quality; why should we not also accept some risks, some localized inefficiencies, in order to maintain the integrity of the value of human life?

For these reasons we might resist across-the-board applications of risk analysis. But Gibbard responds that a sensitive form of risk analysis can meet these objections. In the end, he argues, we can still look at the various rituals we engage in to show the sacred value of life and ask whether on balance they contribute, in the deepest sense, to the intrinsic reward of our lives. We can ask: Does the existence of this or that ritual—however passionately we are attached to it in the press of daily life—really make our lives more worth living? "In a cool hour," Gibbard maintains, "we should be willing to reflect on what we regard with reverence in normal life." This is the kind of detachment involved in relying on ideal risk-cost-benefit analysis, which tries to remain sensitive to all the values and procedures that contribute to intrinsically rewarding lives.

MUDDLING THROUGH

Can sacred values, personal commitments, and the important but subtle conventions and practices that characterize a culture be treated in this way? What would it mean to incorporate even these deepest values into some grand risk-cost-benefit analysis that aims at maximizing the intrinsic reward of our lives, in the broadest sense?

We might be skeptical that any formal system of analysis could ever capture all our values and concerns with the requisite sensitivity, since these depend so much on details of the concrete contexts in which they arise. Moreover, it is not

clear what the yardstick for measurement is to be. If all our values are to be compared and assessed on one single scale, what is that scale? Most risk-analysts have taken the common currency to be money, the amount we as individuals or as a society are willing to pay to satisfy our preferences and promote our values. But Gibbard rejects this standard, since, given the vast differentials in income, different amounts of money mean different things to people differently situated. His measure is the far broader notion of the intrinsic reward of a person's life. But is this too vague to be of any practical application?

We might be better off giving up the search for a sensitive, yet workable metric, consigning risk analysis to a more limited and less inclusive role. We might focus our attention on directly examining our values more closely, without presupposing that we can ever find a method that will make them orderly and systematic. Why should we, after all, think we would be better off allowing our judgments and intuitions to be corrected by some general analytic method?

CONCLUSION

What should we conclude from this about how systematic and coherent our government agencies should be in tackling risks to life and health?

Annette Baier, professor of philosophy at the University of Pittsburgh, gives one reason why it may make for more systematic and coherent policy not to aim at a standard across-the-board policy for preserving life. She suggests that our traditional approach has its own rationale that may make more sense and achieve better results than the alternative presented by risk analysis. Traditionally, we have divided the responsibility for facing various dangers not on the basis of what interests or rights are threatened, but instead by the source of the threat. Thus, the judicial system protects security of life, liberty, property, and contract—all against threats by individual offenders; the Environmental Protection Agency protects many of our vital interests and rights against threats to the environment— furthermore, not against all threats to the environment, only those "that come from thoughtless or ruthless human policies." Different public authorities, on Baier's view, "take on different public 'enemies,' each of which may threaten several vital interests." Should we worry that under this division of labor no one is thinking about *all* the threats to security of life, or coordinating all measures to protect it?

Baier thinks not: "To try to deal in one budget (the total lifesaving budget) with the threat to human life posed by a rise in terrorism, and to deal with the threat terrorism poses to liberty in a different budget (the total liberty-saving budget) would lead to less, not greater, coordination. Doubtless there are better ways to partition our public labor than we have yet devised, but . . . 'rationalizing,' if that amounts to identifying some abstract common goal in several areas and then adopting an efficient total plan to reach it, aiming at consistency in all the areas affected, may be one of those rational strategies that it is even more rational to restrict."

Thus, it would be a mistake for federal regulatory agencies to aim in a coordinated way at maximizing the overall efficiency of how government resources for lifesaving are expended. Regulatory agencies like EPA and OSHA are not invisible bureaucracies established to duplicate the work of the Office of Management and Budget and bring efficiency and coherence to regulatory policies. They are, rather, very public institutions that the public expects to vocalize the ideals of a society that cares deeply about the lives and health of its citizens.

Although we now realize how important it is to the nation and to its economy for these agencies to be cost-conscious, nevertheless, when the administrator of EPA appears at a press conference to announce a regulatory decision, people are not primarily concerned with knowing that the agency has found the ideal cost-benefit ratio. People want to know that things they value deeply—our health, the environment, and our natural resources—are being guarded and protected by the agency we have created to be the trustee of these values.

In sum, the actions of such agencies have symbolic and expressive significance. This may help us to understand the "rituals" that have been forced on some of these agencies, like the taboos against looking at cost-benefit analyses or establishing a social value of human life. It might help us to understand why modest inconsistencies in achieving our lifesaving goals may be less worrisome than certain efforts to correct them. If life is indeed sacred, we may not always choose to protect it in the most efficient way, but in a way that recognizes—and expresses—its special value. ◆ ◆ ◆

Paternalism in the Marketplace
Should a Salesman Be His Buyer's Keeper?

James M. Ebejer and Michael J. Morden

Which is preferable: an interlaced or noninterlaced computer monitor? Is it worthwhile to purchase extended warranties for appliances? If people do not realize that jumbo-size popcorn is the same as a regular tub, is it good business practice to exploit their ignorance? If people are willing to buy home piercing kits to put studs in themselves, should we be concerned if they get hurt?

As consumers we are faced with a significant number of choices. We could arm ourselves with research, but it would take much less time and effort if we trusted the salesperson to be acting in our interest. In this reading, Ebejer and Morden suggest that rather than being predatory, sellers have an active duty to assist buyers by finding out their needs and disclosing information about the goods or service.

We might agree that if there is an expectation of repeat business, reputation and service matter, and they should be developed. However, not everyone would agree that the seller has to disclose information the buyer does not ask for or give up a competitive advantage based on superior knowledge. To what extent are we responsible for others, especially if we are in a sales relationship? Do you think that developing technology, such as the readily available information on the World Wide Web, affects this argument?

The moral relationship between salespersons and their customers can range from *caveat emptor* to paternalism. We propose that between these extremes is a realistic professional ethic for sales that we will refer to as "limited paternalism."

At one extreme is *caveat emptor*—"let the buyer beware." We do not claim there is anything inherently immoral about such a position, only that it is no longer appropriate in our society. Games can be played by various rules, as long as all participants know those rules. When two old horse-traders tried to strike a bargain, it was understood that the seller could be assumed to misrepresent the condition of the animal and the buyer was warned to be on his guard. Perhaps this situation was not unfair since both partici-pants knew the rules, entered into the agreement voluntarily, and had the opportunity to examine the merchandise. However, the contemporary consumer frequently purchases goods or services which he cannot be expected to judge for himself. The workings of an insurance policy are as mysterious to us as those of a VCR. A salesperson, with her superior understanding, is in such a position to exploit our ignorance, that few of us would want to play the game if the rule of the marketplace were understood to be strictly "let the buyer beware."

At the other extreme is the practice of paternalism. A standard definition of paternalism is "the interference with a person's liberty of action justified by reasons referring exclusively to the welfare, good, happiness, needs, interests, or values of the person being coerced" (Dworkin, 1971). In other words, paternalism occurs when an individual, presumably in a position of superior knowledge, makes a decision for another person to protect this other from some type of harm. Paternalism implies that the first person deprives the second of liberty or autonomy. This infraction on liberty is thought justified because, in the mind of the first person, it is "for his own good." Recently, a merchant refused to sell tropical fish to a person because she felt he was not changing the water in his tank often enough. Although the merchant was infringing on the customer's liberty based on her superior knowledge, the interference was for his own good (and presumably the good of the fish). The merchant was being paternalistic.

Most of us expect paternalism in certain situations. If the service we are purchasing is an appendectomy, we typically allow the salesman (in this case the surgeon) a major role in deciding whether we need the service. We rely on the ethics of the profession to protect us from the possible exploitation. The old-fashioned physician considered such paternalism part of his role, but modern medicine emphasizes the patient's informed consent. The professionals use their superior knowledge to make the medical diagnosis, but they are expected to explain treatment options available to the patient so the latter can make the moral decision. Thus even in the most paternalistic of contexts we find that professionalism justifies only a limited paternalism.

This limited paternalism, which is typically an element in professionalism, applies when an individual in a position of superior knowledge has an active duty to explain the consequences of a decision. Here the "father-like" individual does not make the decision for the other. The only liberty that is violated is the freedom to be ignorant: the consumer is protected from an uninformed decision that could be detrimental to him.

To claim that a salesperson is professionally required to inform customers fully about a product or service, to disclose fully all relevant information without hiding crucial stipulations in small print, to ascertain that they are aware of their needs and the degree to which the product or service will satisfy them, is to impose upon the salesperson the positive duty of limited paternalism. According to this standard a salesperson is, to a limited degree, "his buyer's keeper."

Consider the following example: A woman takes her car to an auto repair shop and tells the mechanic she needs a new muffler and exhaust pipes because her car makes too much noise. While examining the car, the mechanic concludes that the excessive noise occurs because there is a hole in the tail pipe. The mechanic was told to replace the exhaust pipes and the muffler. He has three options: (1) replace the exhaust pipes and the muffler as requested by the car's owner and collect (say) $90.00; (2) talk to the owner, refuse to do as requested since all that is needed is a $20.00 tail pipe; (3) talk to the owner, explain the situation, and let her decide for herself if she really wants to spend $70.00 more than is necessary to fix the car.

When confronted with this situation, many repairmen or auto parts salespersons would choose the first option: collect as much money as possible. This is perfectly legal since the car's owner did authorize complete replacement. Some perhaps would act paternalistically by following the second option: replace the tail pipe for $20.00, but refuse to replace the longer exhaust pipe and the muffler because it is not necessary. But now he has infringed on the owner's right to decide for herself. Perhaps the owner wanted to be absolutely certain that her exhaust system was perfect and would not need work again soon. Maybe she is rich and does not mind spending the extra money. In any case, it is her car, her money, and her decision. Option number three is the best ethical choice and the standard required for professional responsibility: the mechanic has a duty to inform the owner of facts of which she might not be aware since she is not the expert. The choice should be left to the owner.

But consider a different situation: a customer in a store that specializes in stereo equipment is consulting a salesperson about the specifications, quality and prices of various amplifiers. The salesperson is considered an expert on all equipment available for sale in the show room. After some deliberation, the customer tentatively decides he would like to own a Super Max amplifier. But before making the purchase, he asks the salesperson one more question: "Is there anything else I should know about this particular model before giving you the cash?" Now, to the best of her knowledge, the salesperson has accurately communicated the advantages of the amplifier, told him the price—$400, and that this particular unit does meet his needs. However, she also knows that the same model is being sold at an appliance store across the street for only $350! Does our standard require that she tell the buyer about this possible savings? Clearly not. Although the salesperson was aware of the competitor's price, she did not withhold information that only an expert would know. Anyone could easily find out how much the amplifier sold for at the other stores. The knowledge was not part of the technical expertise that marks her as a pro-

fessional and which the buyer was presumably relying upon. However, if she held back information, relevant to the decision, which a non-expert could not be expected to know, then her behavior would be unethical by our standard.

Nearly all "hard sell" techniques are unethical according to this standard. Many salespersons intentionally keep information from potential buyers. They try to sell the most expensive product a customer will buy without regard to the needs of that person. Granted, some revenue may be lost in the short term from telling customers the bad as well as the good about a product or service, but profits will increase in the long run. Once a salesperson earns a reputation for being "honest"—i.e., ethical, interested in mutual exchange to mutual advantage rather than exploitation—he will have more satisfied customers, more referrals, and, eventually, greater income from an overall increase in sales. Even where the policy might not profit the salesperson in a specific case, it is a rule which if generally followed would produce the greatest good for the greatest number. Furthermore, it treats the customer the way we ourselves would want to be treated; it is a rule we would agree to even if we didn't know whether we were going to be the salesperson or the customer; finally, it bases sales ethics on widely accepted standards of professionalism. Clearly it is consistent with our ordinary ethical assumptions. ◆ ◆ ◆

◆ **Reference**

Gerald Dworkin: 1971, 'Paternalism', in *Morality and Law*, ed. Richard Wasserstrom (Belmont, CA), p. 108.

Barbie Banished from the Small Screen
The Proposed European Ban on Children's Television Advertising

Janice Kang Choi

We live in a sea of commercial promotion. Walking down the street, we are bombarded by stimuli that encourage us to consume. According to the National Institute on the Media and Family:

- ◆ *99 percent of American families have TV sets, with the average family owning 2.75 sets.*
- ◆ *American children, ages 2–17, watch television on average almost 25 hours per week or 3½ hours a day. Almost one in five watches more than 35 hours of TV each week.*
- ◆ *Television is the top after-school activity chosen by children ages 6 to 17.*
- ◆ *20 percent of 2- to 7-year-olds, 46 percent of 8- to 12-year-olds, and 56 percent of 13- to 17-year-olds have TVs in their bedrooms.*

These statistics suggest that children are at some risk from manipulative advertising. This presents a problem because in general we do not want to restrict free speech or a free market. At the same time, we want to protect a vulnerable population. The European Union is considering a ban on advertising, but as Choi points out, this may bring as many problems as it solves. She concludes that, paradoxically, an absolute ban might have negative consequences by encouraging advertising through other means such as corporate sponsorship in schools.

Advertisers, toymakers, and candy companies are in a cold sweat all over Europe. Sweden took the helm of the European Union ("EU") as President in January 2001, and is expected to press for an EU-wide ban on television advertising to children. Will the ban pass? Should the ban pass?

Calls for tighter restrictions on television advertising abound in Europe. Currently, alcohol, drugs, cars, and even fatty foods will soon come under scrutiny to determine whether commercials for such products should be banned.[1] Concerns run to fraud and the glamorization of dangerous activities. But the issue most hotly debated at present is the proposed ban on television advertising aimed at children.

. . . [I]f the ban does pass, it could send children out of the frying pan and into the fire. If marketers are barred from television, they may instead choose to infiltrate the classroom, where children are more likely to believe what they hear and are unable to choose not to listen. Thus, if a ban is enacted, regulation of children's advertising should also govern corporate sponsorship of schools. . . .

I. THE ROOTS OF EUROPEAN POLICY

On October 3, 1989, the EU issued the Directive "Television without Frontiers." Article 16 pertains specifically to television advertising aimed at children:

> Television advertising shall not cause moral or physical detriment to minors, and shall therefore comply with the following criteria for their protection:
>   a. it shall not directly exhort minors to buy a product or a service by exploiting their inexperience or credulity;
>   b. it shall not directly encourage minors to persuade their parents or others to purchase the goods or services being advertised;
>   c. it shall not exploit the special trust minors place in parents, teachers, or other persons;
>   d. it shall not unreasonably show minors in dangerous situations.[2]

Generally, the idea behind this Directive was to provide the regulatory framework necessary for freedom of broadcasting; in regards to children, the Directive sought to limit the potentially harmful effects of unregulated broadcasting. Article 16 of "Television without Frontiers" had four objectives: (1) safeguard diversity of information and opinion by ensuring freedom of broadcast, (2) protect children from moral, mental or physical detriment, (3) maintain broadcasters' commitment to provide educational and entertaining programming, and (4) preserve program quality.[3]

Looking at the European Commission's (hereinafter "EC" or "Commission") discussions at the proposal stage of this directive, the Commission appeared in favor of rather heavy-handed regulation of advertising to children. At this early stage, the Commission "sought to limit broadcast advertising to prevent advertisers from displacing the informational, educational, cultural, and entertainment functions of television." The Commission called upon special standards to govern advertising to children in order to prevent advertisements to unduly influence youth. Further, the Commission urged "systematic consumer education" to equip children to understand and critically evaluate advertisements. . . .

The . . . suggestions reflected several European nations' existing regulations. Greece, for example, had already had such a law prohibiting the advertisement of toy weapons on the books for two years. Greece had even gone a step further to ban all toy commercials between the hours of 7 and 10 p.m. Naturally, European toy manufacturers were swift to decry this measure as Greece's protectionist attempt to block toy manufacturers, the vast majority of whom were not Greek. In 1994, Toy Industries of Europe ("TIE") lodged a complaint against Greece, arguing that the ban infringed the Treaty of Rome, which provides for the free movement of goods and services between member states of the EU. TIE claimed Greece's ban conflicted with the whole purpose of the EU, which was to promote a single market and remove barriers to trade.[4] . . .

TIE did not prevail. Five years later in August of 1999, the majority of the outgoing EC voted to dismiss these complaints, claiming ban was "proportionate" and not an excessive measure to prevent exposure of children to commercial pressure.[5] . . .

The issue remains alive and well in the minds of the EU's ruling body. The EC launched a continent-wide study of television advertising aimed at children in January 2000. According to EC official Aviva Silver, the purpose of the study is to inform any necessary revisions to the current EU rules.[6]

II. CURRENT REGULATIONS

Currently, the EU member states oversee the advertising industry in different ways. The United Kingdom's advertising industry engages in rather vigorous self-regulation. The Advertising Standards Authority is the largest, most active and best-financed self-regulatory system in the world. It is aided by quasi-governmental agencies which serve as various checkpoints for advertising.[7] First, the guidelines disseminated by Britain's Independent Television Commission ("ITC") states that advertisements must not (a) harm children, (b) take advantage of their credulity, (c) lead children to believe they will be inferior without the product, or (d) exhort children to pester parents.[8] Second, the Broadcast Advertising Clearance Center checks for concealed red flags in the commercials before they are aired. Third, individual television companies scrutinize the ads before airing. Apparently, the system works—in 1998, less than 0.5% of complaints to the ITC concerned children's advertising.[9]

In other European countries, the regulation of the advertising industry is a mixed picture. The Scandinavian countries established the consumer ombudsman to replace self-regulation nearly twenty years ago. The ombudsman receives complaints and resolves or litigates them.[10] In Germany, advertising law authorizes private causes of action to control misleading advertising, much like the United States' Lanham Act.[11] Italy, in contrast to Germany, seeks to protect competitors—not consumers—by its advertising law and thus favors self-regulation. France and Belgium follow the German model much more closely than Italian advertising law.[12] . . .

Sweden and Norway's regulations are the most draconian: a 24-hour ban on advertisements aimed at children under twelve as well as an absolute ban on all advertisements during and immediately before and after children's programs. Now Sweden wants to spread its mission of protecting children to all of Europe. According to Ann-Christin Nykvist, the Swedish Under-Secretary for Culture, the push for an all-Europe ban is motivated by a belief in the ban's popularity among parents in other countries. Further-

more, Sweden believes the more liberal rules in other European countries violate the "Television Without Frontiers" Directive, particularly where it calls for advertising to be "readily recognizable as such." . . .

III. ARGUMENTS FOR A EUROPE-WIDE BAN

The most obvious argument opposing children's advertising is a moral one. Swedish consumer ombudsman Edling depicts advertising aimed at children as exploitation of very small consumers. Since children lack experience and maturity, it is unethical to direct commercially-biased messages at them.[13] Research at Texas A & M University supports Edling's view, showing that young children tend to trust advertising messages much more than adults; only at the age of eleven or twelve does a child start to build up doubts and defenses in response to advertising.[14] Another study demonstrated that nine-year-olds, after watching a commercial, ignored their established product preferences and opted for the advertised product.[15]

Current European lobbyists such as the Advertising Association argue that Sweden's ban is anti-competitive because by denying children the opportunity to see television commercials, the ban favors products already in the market. Seeking to defuse that argument, supporters of the ban claim that if the ban were EU-wide, it would level the playing field. Another blow to the protectionist argument is that if Greece's ban was aimed to curtail outside competition, Greece has cut off its nose to spite its face. Since the enactment of the ban, Greek toymakers' inventory turnover has decreased 40%.[16] Even worse, Greek television producers can no longer afford to produce original programs and have been forced to import cheap children's programming from overseas.[17] . . .

The ban on tobacco advertising has become increasingly draconian in both Europe and the

United States; a ban on advertising to children may follow suit.[18] What brought down the tobacco industry's advertising is precisely what is proposed here: an EU Directive against certain types of advertising. Although initially many sniffed at the tobacco ban as unlikely, five years later the ban was enacted.[19] Ironically, advertisers of tobacco defended themselves by pointing to the advertising's ineffectiveness; but authorities were not convinced and proceeded to ban tobacco advertising.[20] An Adviser to TIE recalls that tobacco advertising fell victim to the domino effect. One EU member after another enacted restrictions on tobacco advertising where previously there were none.[21] Therefore, advertisers targeting children should best beware.

Television is acknowledged as one of the most powerful and popular forms of media for children. Supporters of the ban cite statistics such as an online poll in which 59% of British children would choose television over any other medium.[22] Advertisers, fully aware of this, may thus choose television as their primary medium to reach young children.[23] . . .

Pester power is particularly dangerous in the hands of advertisers. The European Director of Marketing for advertising giant Saatchi and Saatchi openly exulted in children's susceptibility to advertising and pester power: "Quite often we can exploit [children's affinity for advertising] and get them actually pestering their parents for products."[24] Pester power can bring about woeful results. The manager of Birmingham's Consumer Credit Service describes family budgets devastated by overspending, driven by pressure from advertisements.[25] . . .

Marketer Miles Hanson attributes the potency of pester power to the culture of modern family life. The increasing rate of divorce, single parenthood and working women mean that even very young children have more and more direct input into family purchasing decisions. The oft-absent parent may feel guilty and therefore more indulgent of the child's whims. Moreover, the child has greater access to media and technology in the home since television and the Internet may serve as a substitute babysitter.[26]

Support for the ban also comes from various corners. Environmentalists dislike how advertisements make early consumers out of children because consumption often harms the environment. Those who encourage healthy diets for everyone would delight in the downfall of children's advertisers, most of whom peddle sweets and soda instead of vegetables and vitamins.[27] Consumers International, a watchdog organization based in London, conducted a study that found that 95% of commercials aimed at children on British television pushed foods that were high in fat, sugar or salt.[28] Regulatory bodies are also pitching in: the United Kingdom's nascent Food Standards Agency, established in 2000, is drawing up plans to implement new codes for food advertising aimed at children.[29]

IV. ARGUMENTS AGAINST A EUROPE-WIDE BAN

Organizations, ranging from advertising industry groups to the Tories in British Parliament, find a ban on children's television quixotic in today's day and age. With the explosion of commerce, children should know about choices that exist in the marketplace; thus, a ban on advertising to youth would be irresponsible treatment of children within a modern free society. Advertising is a fact of life . . . which children should be prepared for, not shielded from. Raising children without any exposure to advertising could backfire, resulting in a generation gullible about advertising and willing to believe whatever they are told.[30] Moreover, opponents of the ban argue, children are savvier than the ban gives them credit for.[31]

A University of Michigan study bolsters the view of the modern child as more sophisticated than previous generations. Now, children's exposure to social interaction is widely varied at a young age due to the rise of day care and the increasing rarity of nuclear families. The study shows that by the age of five or six children have a substantial understanding of the concept of deception, which is at the heart of most concerns about advertising. England's University of Exeter also studied children's understanding of advertising, focusing on whether they realize the difference between advertisements and television programs. Sixty-six four- to eight-year-olds watched two kinds of commercials: one in which a face cream was praised because it made users beautiful and one in which a face cream was touted as giving users hideous spots. While the four- and five-year-olds could not see anything wrong with the second commercial, eight-year-olds were much the wiser and condemned the second as unrealistic and out of line with advertising principles.[32]

The ban could curtail consumer choice and choke off the quality children's programming funded by advertising. Children's advertising within the EU produces a net income of 240 million euros a year to member states; of this income, 95% is used to fund home production or television rights for children's programs.[33] . . . Children's television programming in Greece dwindled down to nothing after the ban because the ban left Greek television producers without a vital source of funding.[34] After the ban took force in 1993, Greek television stations lost approximately 45 million dollars in revenue. Thus, Greek broadcasters could only afford cheap, poor-quality cartoons from overseas.[35] . . .

Taking a more principled tack, some allege that a Europe-wide ban would be curbing freedom of speech—namely, freedom of commercial speech.[36] But Sweden defends its acts as necessary in this area. Swedish Under-Secretary for Culture Nykvist maintains that Sweden is traditionally a country with liberal laws governing censorship; however, the laws must be strict when advertisements prey upon vulnerable children to make them consumers at an early age.[37] Nonetheless, proponents of this view characterize commercial speech as the "voice of the free enterprise system and the foundation of an independent media."[38] . . . Detractors of the ban also claim that an EU-wide advertising restriction would impair the free movement of goods and services within a single market, thus defeating one of the original objectives of the EU.[39]

Some dismiss Sweden's moral stance on the ban as rubbish. True, Sweden is generally known to be a socially regulated society and a welfare state with a wide reach—but this ban is overstepping its bounds.[40] Rupert Howell of the Institute of Practitioners in Advertising tags Sweden's ban as pure hypocrisy. Sweden may be on high moral ground regarding children's advertising on television, but Sweden has refused to back a European ban on exporting hard-core pornography.[41] Even the Swedish government's own research has failed to find substantial evidence that advertising affects children's material values, nutrition and eating habits.[42]

Marketers also contend that children will see advertisements anyway, in shop windows, on the Internet, etc.[43] Where would the ban draw the line? Would it also target any sort of marketing directed at children? The BBC's Teletubbies is one of the most successful properties with a very extensive marketing program including a vast array of merchandising and licensed tie-ins.[44] Would the ban bar the production of a Tinky-Winky doll as well?

Television advertising may just be a scapegoat; last year's hottest toys, the Furby and the yo-yo, were never advertised anywhere. Playground or peer pressure may be much more powerful than television advertising.[45] Furthermore, children have always wanted the toys other children have, regardless of advertising. Age-old neighbor envy and word of mouth are more likely culprits than television commercials.[46] . . .

As in all debates, the battle of statistics has been waged by both parties—both supporters and detractors of the ban have cited surveys and studies to bolster their respective positions. In this case, the same survey has been wielded by both sides of the debate, with the creator of the statistics championing the cause of those against the ban. Dr. Erling Bjurstrom of the Institute for Working Life in Sweden conducted a study used by the Swedish government to justify its ban. However, at a conference hosted by the UK Advertising Association, Dr. Bjurstrom claimed that his study had been misconstrued as demonstrating that all children under age 12 were incapable of understanding the nature of advertising. In fact, his findings were that children under age 12 might not understand it, but that did not establish that children could not distinguish between programming and advertisements. Furthermore, the study found that even some adults are unable to understand advertising.[47] . . .

Although supporters of the ban may charge avaricious and evilly-motivated marketers with the extraordinary rate of growth of advertising to children, studies have pointed the finger elsewhere. James McNeal of Texas A & M University has tracked spending on children's advertising as increasing 15 to 20 percent a year for the past six or seven years. McNeal attributes this to the growing spending power of children, due in part to parents giving children more pocket money and spending more on children. He also points to the rise of "filiarchy," or the growth of children's power within the family. Because this generation's parents are disenchanted with government, educational and religious institutions, they have a gloomy outlook on what society will bring their children. Therefore, the parents feel moved to give their children the best start they can in order to equip them for a hard world.[48] Hence, McNeal would probably conclude that parents are self-motivated to buy—not driven to buy by the whines or wheedling of children that is sparked by the greedy glut of television commercials aimed at children. Taking a similar approach, toy industry officials also place the burden of protecting children on parents. According to Sarah Mooney of toy giant Hasbro, blocking children from seeing commercials is no solution: "You can't keep children in a vacuum, you just have to learn to say no to them."[49] . . .

VI. SHOULD THE BAN PASS?

Considering the aggressive expansion of television advertising to children, it may be wise not to give advertisers who target children free rein over the airwaves. Television advertising to children is becoming more assertive and pervasive. The quantity of advertising aimed at children in the United Kingdom has grown 500% over the last ten years.[50] This increase is most likely due to the recent sharp increase in children's spending power and influence within the family as well as children's exposure to media.[51] Self-regulation—like the United Kingdom's various checkpoints and safeguards—seems a relatively good model for regulation of advertising to children, while an absolute ban could face enforcement problems and actually worsen the situation.

If an absolute ban passes, children may be even more at risk for exploitation by corporations. Although businesses may simply revise their marketing strategies to include point-of-purchase gimmicks and Internet advertising, they may also respond by getting creative and sneaky to avoid regulations, spawning even more insidious types of advertising to children. Toy advertisers could take a cue from tobacco, which has found a myriad of ways to maintain healthy sales and a high profile despite the ban.[52]

Corporate sponsorship within schools is one example of a worrisome marketing tactic. The focus of marketers may indeed be moving from the living room to the classroom. Cause-related marketing campaigns, such as retailers sponsoring Computers for Schools programs and cereal companies publishing books on nutrition for use in schools, are on the rise.[53] In fact, approximately 85% of Great Britain's 32,000 schools have experienced some form of commercial activity within the classroom. With the rise of expensive high technology, educators predict the trend will only continue.[54]

Other examples of corporate sponsorship within schools is Procter & Gamble's Sunny Delight, which is offering branded support of children's athletic activities by hosting an in-school three-on-three basketball program. News International and Walkers Crisps has organized a Books for Schools promotion in which consumers collect coupons from papers and snack bags in exchange for free books for the school; this promotion has the backing of the Department of Education. One of the most popular programs is JazzyBooks, which provides curricular material featuring advertisements on the cover and a few inside pages. JazzyBooks has earned the endorsement of the National Confederation of Parent Teacher Associations ("NCPTA") in Great Britain.[55] Another promotional campaign that has earned the stamp of approval from the NCPTA is The Primary Bag and the Secondary Bag. These are "goodie bags," stuffed with free samples pre-approved by the NCPTA and distributed to students ages five and above.[56]

These programs may sound benign; but when corporations sponsor curricular materials, a dangerous commercial message may be subtly woven into the educational message. Furthermore, children may mistake the appearance of a corporate logo on a book cover or on a hallway banner as the school's blanket endorsement of the product.

Although JazzyBooks may blur the line between commercialism and education, it is a tame version of the infiltration corporations can achieve by sponsoring educational materials.[57] Some U.S. businesses are introducing curricular materials that loudly smack of corporate propaganda. Exxon distributes to schools a video on the Valdez spill that downplays its ecological impact (and naturally fails to mention who exactly was responsible for the spill.) Chevron's civics or science lesson reminds students they will be able to vote soon and make "important decisions" about global warming—an event which Chevron dismisses as "incomplete science."[58]

Yet another cause for concern is schools selling access to students to be market research guinea pigs. London-based Youth Research Group treats the classroom as a market research laboratory and gives the schools free Internet access and software in exchange for use of the students as focus groups and survey subjects. Some 21,000 children have been subjected to the Group's practices, allowing the Group to sell its studies to everyone from television producers to clothing manufacturers.[59]

Corporate sponsorship of schools can be a symbiotic relationship that is beneficial to both parties. Money goes to the school and good public relations goes to the corporation; corporations also benefit from an opportunity to give back to the community—not to mention priceless credibility via association with trusted teachers. But when commercialism invades the school curriculum, corporations may dangerously twist the facts and deceive students.

The EU should be just as concerned about corporate sponsorship in schools as it is about television advertising directed at children. At least with television, children have the option of changing the channel or walking away. But within the classroom, children are even more captive to corporate pitches, especially if they come disguised as corporate-sponsored curricular materials. The EC has evidenced some concern about this, directing a study to be done on both "sponsoring at schools" and television advertising to children.[60] However, the EC has also come out in support of corporate sponsorship of schools. The EC recently issued a report stating that certain types of corporate advertising would "open schools to the economic world."[61] Such an argument can be a slippery slope and mere commissioned studies and reports are not enough. Individual schools and local governments should be vigilant about this form of advertising.

Although the EU should not permit advertisers to children to run amok on the potent marketing tool that is television, the EU should not implement an absolute ban all over Europe. To do so could simply divert a dangerous flow to the schoolyard. ◆ ◆ ◆

◆ *Notes*

1. *See* Brian Wheeler, *Image Guardians*, MARKETING WK., Sept. 30, 1999, at 29.
2. Daniel E. Frank, *Regulating Television Advertising in the European Community and the United States: Preventing Harm to Children*, 1992 U. CHI. LEGAL F. 399, 400 (1992).
3. *Id.* at 401.
4. *See AA Urges Brussels to Rethink Greek Ban on Toy Advertising*, MARKETING WK., Aug. 5, 1999, at 11.
5. *See [id].*
6. *See* Peter Ford, *Europe Puts Mute on Kid Ads*, THE CHRISTIAN SCI. MONITOR (Paris), Dec. 16, 1999, at 1.
7. *See* Ross D. Petty, *Advertising Law and Social Issues: The Global Perspective*, 17 SUFFOLK TRANSNAT'L L. REV. 309, 320 (1994).
8. *See* Allyson Stewart-Allen, *Rules for Reaching Euro Kids Are Changing*, MARKETING NEWS, June 7, 1999, at 10, *available in* LEXIS, News Library, Marketing News File.
9. *See* David McCall, *Plan to Ban Children's TV Ads is an Age-old Mistake*, MARKETING WK., Sept. 2, 1999, at 14.
10. *See* Petty, *supra* note 7, at 317.
11. *See id.* at 319.
12. *See id.*
13. *See [*Richard Tompkins, *Selling to a Captivated Market*, FIN. TIMES (London), April 20, 1999, at 14.]
14. *See id.*
15. *See* Nick Higham, *Industry Divided Over Prospect of Ban on Children's Advertising*, MARKETING WK., July 8, 1999, at 17.
16. *See* [Darran Gardner, *Toy Makers Vow to Fight If EU Bans Advertising*, THE SUNDAY HERALD (Glasgow), Aug. 22, 1999, at 6, *available in* LEXIS, News Library, Sunday Herald File.]
17. *See* David Cohen, *Toy Story*, NEW SCIENTIST, Oct. 30, 1999, at 38.
18. For more specific information on the terms of the tobacco advertising ban in Europe, EC Directive 98/43, passed in July 1998, see *UK Government: Tobacco Advertising to End by December*, M2 PRESSWIRE, June 17, 1999, at 1, *available in* LEXIS, News Library, M2PressWire File.
19. *See* Stefano Hatfield, *I'm Sindy, Buy Me*, THE TIMES (London), Aug. 13, 1999, at Features.
20. *See* John Morrish, *They Want Your Children*, THE INDEP. (London), Jan. 9, 2000, at 25.
21. *See* [Jeremy Slater, *EC Lets Stand Toy Ad Ban*, ADVERTISING AGE INT'L SUPP., Aug. 1, 1999, at 1.]
22. *See* Harriet Marsh, *Children's Choice*, MARKETING, July 15, 1999, at 27.
23. *See id.*
24. *See* Graham Keeley, *How TV Ads Pander to Tiny Pester Power*, WESTERN DAILY PRESS (Bristol), Oct. 1999, at 10, *available at* 1999 WL 246862172.
25. *See* Jenny Hudson, *Will Banning Toy Ads Stop "Pester Power"?*, SUNDAY MERCURY (Birmingham), Sept. 26, 1999, at 18, *available at* 1999 WL 2187357.
26. *See* Virginia Matthews, *Yielding to the Pressure of Pester Power*, FIN. TIMES (London), Aug. 17, 1999, at 8.
27. *See* Higham, *supra* note 15, at 17.

28. Consumers International has expressed much concern over other facets of children's advertising beyond nutrition. For example, it singles out three types of advertising to children as the most worrisome. First, it disparages cartoon or other fictitious characters as unfair advertising devices since they may prey upon children's affection and loyalty to such characters, thus blurring the line between programming and advertisements. It also warns that the all-too-fluid transition from show to commercial break, sponsorship of children's programs, and other similar ploys may likewise cause children to view advertisements with the same credulity as the scheduled programming.

The watchdog organization has released a raft of recommendations for the regulation of the advertising industry, whether via self-regulation or statutory, including:
   ◆ Independence and impartiality.
   ◆ Fully transparent decision-making process.
   ◆ Adequate consumer representation.
   ◆ A majority of non-industry interests in decision-making bodies.
   ◆ Pre-screening and monitoring of advertisements to ensure compliance with regulations.
   ◆ Openness to consumer complaints, with the burden of proof on the advertiser.
   ◆ Power to enforce decisions and demand appropriate redress.
   ◆ Cooperation at the international level.
   See A Spoonful of Sugar, at http://www.consumersinternational.org/campaigns/tvads (last visited Nov. 9, 2000).

29. *See* [Cordelia Brabbs, *Will Kids Be Cut Off from Ads?*, MARKETING, Nov. 30, 2000, at 22.]

30. *See* Pat Anderson, *Child's Play*, MARKETING WK., Sept. 9, 1999, at 47, *available at* 1999 WL 8313659.

31. *See* Higham, *supra* note 15, at 17.

32. *See* Cohen, *supra* note 17, at 38.

33. *See Sweden Seeks Extension to Child Advertising Bans*, NORDIC BUS. REP., June 14, 1999, at 1, *available at* 1999 WL 10322989.

34. *See* [Gardner, *supra* note 16, at 6.]

35. *See* Cohen, *supra* note 17, at 38.

36. *See* Tomkins, *supra* note 13, at 14.

37. *See* [Roger Harrabin, *A Commercial Break for Parents*, THE INDEP. (London), Sept. 8, 1998, at 19.]

38. Richard M. Corner, *Free Flow of Commercial Speech Essential to World Market*, LEGAL BACKGROUNDER, Aug. 20, 1999, at 31, *available in* LEXIS, News Library.

39. *See* Gardner, *supra* note 16, at 6.

40. *See* Conor Dignam, *Ethics Will Be Key in Battling EU-Led Children's Ad Ban*, MARKETING, Apr. 22, 1999, at 1.

41. *See* Jon Rees, *Swedes Seek European Toy Ads Ban*, SUNDAY BUS. (London), May 2, 1999, at 13, *available in* LEXIS, News Library.

42. *See* [Anna Griffiths, *Advertising a Threat to Our Children?*, CAMPAIGN, Aug. 27, 1999, at 30, *available at* WL 8349730.]

43. *See* McCall, *supra* note 9, at 14.

44. *See* Marsh, *supra* note 22, at 27.

45. *See* Higham, *supra* note 15, at 17.

46. *See* Hatfield, *supra* note 19, at Features.

47. *See* Brabbs, *supra* note 29, at 22.

48. *See* Tomkins, *supra* note 13, at 14.

49. Brabbs, *supra* note 29, at 22.

50. *See* Griffiths, *supra* note 42, at 30.

51. *See Pressure Grows to Curb Advertising to Children*, IRISH TIMES, Apr. 23, 1999, at 70.

52. *See* Oliver Swanton, *Does the Butt Stop Here?*, THE INDEP. (London), Oct. 17, 1999, at 1.

53. *See* Stewart-Allen, *supra* note 8, at 10.

54. *See* Keeley, *supra* note 24, at 10.

55. *See* Harriet Marsh, *Analysis: Useful Lessons in Targeting Pupils*, MARKETING, June 5, 1997, *available in* LEXIS, News Library. JazzyBooks may attribute the support of the NCPTA to its agreement to conform to the guidelines set out by the National Consumer Council for socially responsible firms targeting students via educational material. According to these guidelines, companies should make sure that:
   ◆ "Material offers educational value and is relevant to the curriculum.
   ◆ [Materials] give a balanced and objective view of the issue. This means acknowledging the existence of alternative views, distinguishing between factual statements and

opinions and making the sponsor's market interest clear.

◆ Material is only developed after consultation with teachers and after a test for its educational value using pupils in the target group.

◆ Material does not include sales and promotional messages. This means no explicit branding, no messages playing on children's fears or lack of experience, no purely promotional material and no claims of superiority, unless backed by documentary evidence. Use of slogans and logos should be limited to those necessary to identify the sponsor.

◆ The project does not include sponsored gifts, awards, voucher schemes and other promotional/marketing activities.

◆ No unsolicited marketing messages are sent to pupils.

◆ Materials avoid stereotypes. This means the project must be free from politically incorrect statements.

◆ All material and activities are fully labeled by the sponsor. This means identifying the target market and including a description of all pre-launch consultation and testing."

56. *See* Ken Gofton, *Building Up a Class Act*, Marketing, Sep. 9, 1993, at 1.

57. *See* Rob Gray, *Perils of Sending Brands to School*, Marketing, Apr. 22, 1999, at 1.

58. John F. Borowski, *Schools with a Slant*, N.Y. Times, Aug. 21, 1999, at A13, Col. 1.

59. *See* [James Geary, *Childhood's End?*, Time (Int'l Ed.), Aug. 2, 1999, at 36; *available in* LEXIS, News Library, Time File.]

60. *See* European Parliament, Committee on Economic and Monetary Affairs and Industrial Policy, *Resolution on the Communication from the Commission to the Council, the European Parliament and the Economic and Social Committee on the Follow-Up to the Green Paper on Commercial Communications in the Internal Market*, Official J., Apr. 14, 1999, at 130.

61. Geary, *supra* note 59, at 36.

The Doctrine of Double Effect, Deadly Drugs, and Business Ethics

Lawrence Masek

Business activity always has the potential of causing collateral damage—that is, it may cause harm that was foreseeable but never intended. A firm makes knives that could be used as weapons, or consumers may choose to abuse over-the-counter medicines. It is plausible that we could design goods to be completely foolproof, but that may make them very expensive and unwieldy. Alternatively, Masek argues, we could let the market decide on the level of acceptable risk. As long as consumers have the available information, he believes, consumers ought to shoulder the risks and not hold companies responsible for the harms they could foresee but did not intend.

A single action often leads to both good and bad effects. This simple fact creates many ethical dilemmas—especially in the business world. For example, should pharmaceutical companies market drugs that help many people but also have harmful side effects? Or should automobile manufacturers sell sport utility vehicles that survive crashes well but also roll over more easily than other automobiles? Before making moral evaluations of these situations, we must consider the good effects, as well as the bad. . . .

SUMMARY OF THE DOCTRINE OF DOUBLE EFFECT (DDE)

DDE applies when an act has more than one effect—including at least one bad effect. It permits such an act only if the act satisfies the following five criteria:[1]

1. The act itself is not immoral.
2. The agent does not positively will the bad effect.
3. The agent cannot obtain the good effect without the bad effect.
4. The good effect results at least as directly as does the bad effect.
5. The good effect is sufficiently good to offset the bad effect.

. . . This is more restrictive than deontology, which concerns (1) and (2), and consequentialism, which concerns only (5).

Unfortunately, DDE provides no precise way to decide if the good effect actually is sufficiently good to offset the bad effect. I claim that free markets often, but not always, provide the best way to compare the good and bad effects. This discussion constitutes the majority of my paper, but to overlook the first four criteria reduces DDE to consequentialism. . . .

APPLYING DDE TO BUSINESS DECISIONS

I use the fictional company Ethicorp and its drug Virilium, which provides men stamina and vigor, to apply DDE to some ethical dilemmas that confront businesses. To simplify, I will assume that Ethicorp is a publicly owned company, that its stockholders expect return on their investment, and that all managerial decisions are made by one person, the CEO. Clearly, this is an oversimplification, but the CEO represents the many people involved in business decisions.

The Proper Role of Profit in Business Decisions

Although some might consider profits irrelevant to ethical questions, any application of DDE to businesses must include profits among the effects of a decision. Stockholders rightfully expect a return on their investment, as T. J. Rodgers, CEO of Cypress Supercomputers explains:

> The retirement plan of thousands of other people also depend on Cypress stock—$1.2 billion worth of stock—owned directly by investors or through mutual funds, pension funds, 401k programs, and insurance companies. . . . Any choice I would make to jeopardize retirees and other investors from achieving their lifetime goals would be fundamentally wrong.[2]

Corporate profits affect real people, not just bottom lines of faceless corporations. Hence, they must be considered among the good effects of a business decision, although the profit motive can, and often does, lead to unethical acts.

The economist Milton Friedman recognizes the ethical problem when an executive puts society's interests before stockholders:

> The stockholders or customers or employees could separately spend their own money on the particular action if they wished to do so. . . . But if

[the executive] does this, he is in effect imposing taxes, on the one hand, and deciding how the tax proceeds shall be spent, on the other.[3]

To see the strength in this argument, suppose that I entrust a housesitter to watch my house while I go on vacation. When I return, I find that she has donated some of my furniture to my favorite charity. Like most people, I would be incredulous that she used my property without consulting me first—although I might plan to give even more to the charity myself.

Is the housesitter who donates my furniture to charity analogous to the executive who sacrifices stockholders' profits to achieve good effects? If so, a corporation ought to consider nothing but return to stockholders, which would bring my paper to a screeching halt. Clearly, the housesitter's selling my furniture is stealing, so DDE forbids this act (assuming that stealing is immoral). If an executive's sacrificing stockholders' profits also constitutes stealing, then DDE would forbid that too—regardless of the good effects that result. Hence, DDE would forbid Ethicorp from warning its consumers of the dangerous side effects of Virilium if this would reduce profits.

This conclusion seems intuitively wrong, but in order to avoid it without abandoning DDE, I must show that an executive's sacrificing potential return to stockholders is not inherently immoral. Stealing occurs when the thief takes what *rightfully* belongs to another without the other's consent. I suggest that the potential profits that would result from a business's withholding information about the dangers of its products do not rightfully belong to stockholders. Hence, the analogy to the housesitter fails, because the housesitter takes what rightfully belongs to me. If I am correct, then sacrificing return to stockholders in order to provide important information to consumers satisfies the first criterion of DDE.

However, we still must count loss of profits as a bad effect of a business decision. Remember

that DDE allows the act only if there is no way to achieve the good effect without the bad effect, so Friedman is correct that an executive should not sacrifice profits to achieve desirable ends that could be achieved through a democratic process. In my example of Ethicorp and Virilium, Ethicorp cannot warn consumers without sacrificing profits, so Ethicorp's warnings do pass the third criterion of DDE.

Ethicorp and the First Criterion of DDE

Suppose that before the FDA approves Virilium for sale, Ethicorp's own research department finds evidence that the drug causes severe nausea in a small percentage of men. The FDA asks for the research data, and Ethicorp has a chance to falsify it. The CEO feels great pressure to get the drug out on the market as soon as possible, and he knows that if the FDA receives the data, it will take at least six months longer to approve Virilium. The research department has assured the CEO that Virilium is no more dangerous than other drugs on the market, so she does not doubt that the FDA eventually will approve it. The problem is that Ethicorp will lose millions in foregone sales while it waits for the approval, and thousands of men will suffer from being unable to buy it.

Lying to the FDA will have the good effects of increasing profits and of helping many men and the bad effect of causing severe nausea in a few. Assume that the good effect does offset the bad effect and that Ethicorp cannot produce a drug that lacks the undesired side effect. The CEO neither positively wills for the some men to suffer nausea nor uses their suffering as a means to the good effects.

Lying to the FDA satisfies four of the criteria of DDE, but it fails the first, which says that the act itself cannot be immoral. Therefore, assuming that lying is immoral, the CEO may not lie to the FDA. Whether lying is immoral exceeds the scope of this paper, but the same analysis applies if the CEO must use another immoral activity, such as murder or adultery, in order to ensure that the FDA promptly approves Virilium.

Ethicorp and the Second and Fourth Criteria of DDE

Now suppose that the date is December 1999 and that Ethicorp needs to complete the last small step of installing new software to prevent the Year 2000 bug. Ethicorp again is waiting on the FDA to approve Virilium when its own research department finds evidence that the drug causes severe nausea in a few men. Also, suppose that the risk is a bit more severe and that the FDA might not approve the drug if it has all the available information. Someone suggests to the CEO that instead of lying to the FDA, Ethicorp can delay installing the software so that the data about Virilium's causing nausea will be lost until after the FDA approves the drug. The CEO must decide if Ethicorp should postpone the software installation.

Postponing the installation has the good effects of increasing profits and of helping thousands of men, and it has the bad effects of preventing the FDA from making an informed decision and of leading to severe nausea in a few men. It is not immoral in itself, so it satisfies the first criterion—unlike the example where Ethicorp lies to the FDA.

However, it fails the second criterion, which says that the agent may not positively will the bad effect. Here, Ethicorp does will to prevent the FDA from making an informed decision. Postponing the installation also fails the fourth criterion, because the good effects of increasing profits and of helping thousands of men do not result as directly from the act as does the bad effect of preventing the FDA from making an informed decision. . . . I suspect that most businesses do not actually will bad effects or use them as means to good effects. Instead, they allow them in order to realize good effects, and

perhaps they allow more than most people would consider ethical.

DDE's prohibition against using immoral actions and of willing bad effects is unambiguous, but more difficult questions arise in deciding if the good effects offset the bad. But before discussing this question of proportionality (the fifth criterion of DDE), I turn to the requirement to consider alternatives.

Ethicorp and the Third Criterion of DDE [4]

Clearly, if Ethicorp discovers harmful side effects of Virilium, it should consider safer alternatives. With all other things equal, it would be immoral for Ethicorp to market a drug that causes nausea if it has an alternative that does not. Unfortunately, all things are not always equal. If Ethicorp discovers that its drug causes severe nausea and the researchers tell the CEO that they can develop a safer, and no more expensive, alternative during their lunch break, then for the CEO to market the unsafe drug would be immoral. More plausibly, the researchers tell the CEO that they might be able to develop a safer alternative if Ethicorp delays the release of Virilium for six months and spends millions of dollars on the research. Now Ethicorp must decide how much time and money to spend looking for an alternative.

The third criterion of DDE requires that the agent cannot achieve the good effect without the bad effect. . . . [T]he amount of time and resources the agent must devote to looking for alternatives is positively related to the seriousness of the bad effect and is negatively related to the urgency of achieving the good effect. In deciding how much effort to devote to the search for a safer drug, the CEO has no exact formula to compare the seriousness of causing nausea to the urgency of marketing the drug, which will increase profits and will help thousands of men. The resources it expends in the search for a safer alternative increase the cost of producing the drug, which will lead to an increase in the price of Virilium. Hence, the decision to look for alternatives has the obvious good effect of eliminating the severe nausea, but it also has the bad effects of reducing return to investors and/or of increasing the price so that many men will not be able to afford it.

Assume that the CEO truly does want to act ethically; she probably feels overwhelmed at the complexity of measuring the proportionality of the good and bad effects of her possible choices. I contend that the prices in a free market offer a useful, although sometimes imperfect, way to measure this proportionality.

The Virtues of the Free Market

The last section asked if Ethicorp should market Virilium if it has a safer alternative. I answer that when Ethicorp finds information that Virilium causes severe nausea in a few men, it should inform consumers of the risk and continue to sell the drug. The resources it devotes to searching for an alternative should reflect consumers' response to the new information. If it finds a safer and more expensive alternative, it should continue to sell Virilium and the alternative as long as it makes a profit on both. This is a good *economic* decision, but I need to explain why it also is the best *ethical* decision. Consider the following argument:

A. We should let a mentally competent person[5] judge the proportionality of the good and bad effects of decisions for himself, as long as he does not harm others or put them at risk against their wills.
B. Choosing to risk one's health or life to achieve another good does not reflect mental incompetence.

Therefore,

C. We should allow a mentally competent person to take such risks if he judges the risk to be proportionate to the good [A, B].

D. Producing a dangerous product is not immoral in itself.
E. Firms have a duty to inform others of potential harm resulting from their products.

Therefore,

F. Firms that discover dangerous side effects of their products ought to inform consumers of the risks, and to allow mentally competent consumers to use the products [C, D, E].

I can defend (A) with both a popular and a deontological principle of ethics. The Golden Rule tells me to do unto others as I would have them do unto me.[6] I certainly would not want someone to prevent me from risking my life and health in order to achieve another good. For example, I would not want someone to prevent me from drinking alcohol because it might cause liver cancer. Therefore, I should not force others to judge the proportionality of the good effect and the risk as I would. Similarly, Kant's categorical imperative instructs me to respect the autonomy of all other rational beings, and preventing another rational being from freely assuming risks would violate this.

Our experience confirms (B), which says that choosing to risk one's life and health in exchange for other goods does not indicate mental incompetence. As I have suggested, we do this every time we drink alcohol or drive a car. Also, people risk their lives even for very small benefits; consider how many people—especially cab drivers—drive recklessly in order to save a few minutes. However, my argument does not defend reckless driving, because this puts others at risk against their wills. Note that (B) concerns only *risking* one's health and life. Perhaps someone could prevent me from risking my own life if she has conclusive evidence that my death would result, but my second premise need not apply to this case, because risk implies uncertainty.

(C) follows from the first two premises and says that we should allow a mentally competent person to risk his own life and health if he considers the good to outweigh the risk. It does not prevent us from attempting to convince him that the risk is unwise.

The fourth premise, (D), says that producing a dangerous product is not immoral in itself. This seems uncontroversial to me. Here, I use "dangerous product" to refer to a product whose use entails the risk of a serious and undesirable side effect. That such production is not immoral in itself does not mean that businesses should not warn consumers of risks, and the fifth premise adds that firms have a duty to inform others of potential harm resulting from their products. To ignore this duty puts others at risk against their wills, which is immoral.

I conclude that when Ethicorp discovers that Virilium causes severe nausea in a few men, it ought to inform consumers of the risks and to allow consumers to decide for themselves whether or not the benefit outweighs the risk. Relying on the free market to measure the proportionality of the good and bad effects does not excuse Ethicorp from all moral responsibility. As I have explained, it must inform consumers of the risks of Virilium even if this reduces profits.

Many proponents of the free market base their arguments on the utilitarian ground that relying on the invisible hand of capitalism maximizes utility for society. This might be true, but I have relied instead on the need to respect the autonomy of others. Even if I consider a certain risk foolish, I should not prevent another mentally competent person from taking it (as long as he does not put others at risk against their wills), although I may try to dissuade him. By notifying consumers of the risks of Virilium and then allowing them to compare the good and bad effects for themselves, Ethicorp respects the autonomy of consumers.

Unfortunately, no clear formula specifies how Ethicorp should warn consumers and how many resources it should expend to do so. Each case varies. If Virilium causes mild headaches, then a simple warning label might suffice. But if it causes severe nausea, then Ethicorp must do more to ensure that consumers make an informed decision—such as directing pharmacists to sell the drug only after ensuring that consumers understand the risk. . . .

What If the Drug Has Potentially Deadly Side Effects?

Finally, suppose that Ethicorp finds that several older men use Virilium, engage in certain activities, and then suffer heart attacks. Now selling Virilium has the bad effect of leading to deaths, not just to severe nausea. Should Ethicorp sell it? . . .

. . . [M]y argument allows businesses to sell dangerous products—even potentially deadly ones—as long as they allow consumers to make informed decisions about the risks. . . . Even if the CEO of Ethicorp estimates that the bad effects of Virilium will outweigh the good, she should respect the autonomy of consumers.

Concluding Remarks

I deliberately have focused on examples where the defect in the product affects only the user. Comparing good and bad effects becomes more difficult in cases where the defect causes a risk to others, not just to the user. For example, if an automobile manufacturer finds that sport utility vehicles roll over more often than other automobiles, it must consider the risk to all drivers, whose risk tolerance might differ from those who buy the sport utility vehicles. The free market does not supplant the need for moral judgments; businesses must consider it a useful tool, not the last word.

Another problem with my arguments is that businesses will have an incentive to provide less than adequate information. Even if Ethicorp wants to act ethically, its desire to maximize profit might cloud its judgment about how much money to spend on informing consumers of the risks of Virilium. This problem extends beyond the business world; all agents might overestimate the good effects of actions when the good effects concern the agent and the bad effects affect others. DDE does not guarantee that people will judge the proportionality correctly.

In conclusion, DDE instructs businesses to ask themselves the following questions in order to decide if they should perform actions that involve both good and bad effects:

Is the act itself immoral?
Are we actually willing the bad effects to occur?
Can we obtain the good effects without the bad effects?
Do the bad effects result as directly from the act as do the good effects?
Are the good effects insufficient to offset the bad effects?

If the answer to any of these questions is "yes," then DDE judges the act unethical. I have focused on the problem of product safety, but my arguments provide a framework to address many other problems of business ethics as well. ◆ ◆ ◆

◆ Notes

1. Cf. *The New Catholic Encyclopedia*, Volume IV (Washington, D.C.: The Catholic University of America, 1967), p. 1021.
2. *Directors and Boards* 20 (1996): 13–17.
3. "The Social Responsibility of Business Is to Increase Its Profits," *New York Times Magazine*, September 13, 1970. Friedman also makes this argument in Chapter VIII of *Capitalism and Freedom* (Chicago: The University of Chicago Press, 1962).
4. This section supposes that Virilium might cause severe nausea; the next section that it might lead

to deaths. I reach the same conclusion in both sections.
5. I exclude mentally incompetent, including children and the insane, from the first premise. Clearly, we should not allow children or psychopathic killers to play with chainsaws. However, I ignore the difficult question of how to define mental incompetence.
6. Matthew 7:12.

Consumer Protection—or Overprotection?

Metta Winter

Winter discusses the work of Alan Mathios in this brief article. Mathios has been following consumer reaction to disclosures about nutrition: for example, whether people shift away from high-fat foods when they learn that they may contribute to heart disease. He concludes that the public makes reasoned decisions when given adequate information. At the same time, he feels that government regulation is overly restrictive by preventing manufacturers from using preliminary health findings (in contrast to conclusive evidence that is much harder to prove) in their advertising.

One of the hottest news stories going these days is the controversy over genetically engineered foods. Nearly two-thirds of the processed foods made in the United States contain genetically modified organisms (GMOs), yet the debate rages over whether they are safe to eat.

Food manufacturers are likely to tout the benefits of genetically engineered foods. As they seek to do so, governments soon are likely to be faced with a fundamental question: What degree of regulation should be imposed on the claims these firms make? Alan Mathios believes that food manufacturers should be able to promote truthfully the benefits of their bioengineered products and that government, as it attempts to monitor and prevent deceptive advertising, must be careful not to stifle the flow of this information.

For more than a decade Mathios, an associate professor of policy analysis and management, has been investigating how the regulation of nutrition information affects consumer knowledge and behavior. What he's found is surprising, and his findings may have lessons for the regulation of the marketing of biotechnology products.

Beginning in the 1950s there was strong scientific evidence linking the consumption of fat—especially saturated fat and cholesterol—to serum cholesterol levels and, in turn, to heart disease. In the 25 years between the early 1960s and the mid1980s, public health organizations, the government, and the press tried to get the word out to the American public. For example, in the early 1960s the American Heart Association began advising consumers that they could reduce their risk for heart disease by controlling the amount of saturated fat in their diet. The same ideas were explored extensively in radio, television, and print media.

In the 1970s the government began issuing documents putting forth dietary advice that made explicit the role of diet in several chronic diseases. By the early 1980s, publications such as the Dietary Guidelines for Americans and the Surgeon General's Report on Nutrition and Health recommended that Americans not only limit saturated fat consumption to reduce heart disease risk but also add more fiber to their diet as a means of lowering cancer risk.

Despite such educational efforts, the public didn't get it.

"In 1984 only 1.1 percent of individuals with less education than a high school diploma reported knowledge of the relationship between fiber and cancer, and only 15 percent of college grads did," says Mathios, referring to findings from research he conducted in collaboration with Federal Trade Commission (FTC) economist Pauline M. Ippolito on cereal advertising and labeling.

During the same 25-year period, federal regulations explicitly prohibited food manufacturers from making any claims that linked nutrients with disease risk. They were not even permitted to quote from the government's own official dietary advice either on their labels or in their advertising.

Then in 1985 the federal ban on making "truthful claims about well-established diet-disease relationships in advertising and labeling" was eased. What followed was a dramatic difference in both consumer knowledge and behavior. Just a year later, for example, 18 percent of people with less than a high school education knew that eating a high-fiber diet could reduce cancer risk. Mathios notes that before 1985 cereal manufacturers had been allowed to display the amount of fiber in their products on the package label, but that information apparently didn't affect consumer knowledge.

"So it clearly was very important that cereal manufacturers be permitted to explain the reasons consumers should care about fiber," he points out.

What's more, by 1985 manufacturers began making cereals with a higher fiber content, knowing they could advertise the health benefits of such products. In turn, more people began to buy them. Mathios estimates that the advertising prompted approximately 2 million more households to consume high-fiber cereals.

In additional studies, Mathios and Ippolito examined the impact of advertised health claims on how much consumers knew about the relationships between other nutrients and disease—including fat, saturated fat, and cholesterol—and how their buying habits changed. The researchers found the same pattern as in the cereal studies.

"When the ban on health claim advertising was lifted, there were quite dramatic changes in the ways consumers changed their diets," Mathios says. "The constant push of health claims in product advertising generated more interest by the media, and the information environment in general changed."

But can consumers trust food manufacturers as educators, given the assumption that they present only the virtues of their products? Mathios and Ippolito found that competition among producers tends to benefit consumers, who in the end get more complete nutrition information.

"In cereal advertising, one firm would tout the fiber and another would point out low sodium content," he says. "Then the media would write articles questioning the completeness of their claims, drawing increased attention to the health effects."

Too, Mathios credits manufacturer advertising for the wide range of "healthy" prepared foods—Lean Cuisine, Healthy Choice—that have flooded the market in the past 10 years. These products were created, in part, because they could be marketed in a specific way—as promoting good health and nutrition.

At times these studies haven't made Mathios and Ippolito popular at the Food and Drug Administration (FDA), which oversees what can be written on product labels. Their stand on how the government decides which health claims manufacturers are allowed to make is even more controversial.

Current law says that only claims backed by scientific consensus can be publicized. Mathios disagrees. For 25 years, he points out, consumers were denied information about the link between saturated fat and heart disease. Is this, he asks, the best way to protect consumers? Hardly. Mathios would prefer that food manufacturers be allowed to use preliminary scientific evidence in their advertising as long as the science is done well and the claim is qualified so that it is consistent with the level of certainty of the science.

Mathios notes that savvy consumers regularly incorporate new scientific findings into behavior as they learn from print and other media about new findings by nutritionists—for instance, that trans fatty acids may be bad for you. So why not allow that in advertising? The arguments used in favor of protecting free private speech often apply to commercial speech as well, he says. With respect to the latter, competition between manufacturers promoting truthful but necessarily incomplete information may lead to a more complete information environment.

In addition to limitations in advertising based on the requirement for scientific consensus, food manufacturers are restricted from making FDA-approved claims based on a number of criteria. For example, no health claims about the link between saturated fat and heart disease can be made on any product that contains more than 14 grams of fat per serving size. This includes cooking oils, which are entirely fat.

At first glance, this restriction may seem reasonable. But in recent research (published in the Agricultural and Resource Economics Review) on consumer purchases of cooking oils, Mathios found that such restrictions can have a deleterious effect. Before federal limitations on health claims, Wesson and other food manufacturers marketed canola oil with ad copy that explained to consumers who were concerned about heart disease the difference between saturated and polyunsaturated fats. It went on to point out that oils lowest in saturated fats, such as canola and

olive oils, were more "heart healthy"—as scientific studies continue to confirm today. But when the Nutrition Labeling and Education Act took effect in 1994, such advertising became illegal because of the disqualifying level of total fat in those oils. Mathios recently looked at scanner data from Wegman's Food Markets—a supermarket chain based in Rochester, N.Y.—and found that when such advertising disappeared, the amount of saturated fat in purchased cooking oils went up; that is, consumers bought oils higher in saturated fat than those purchased previously.

"So the question becomes," Mathios asks, "is it good consumer policy?" Mathios thinks the lessons learned from the regulation of diet-disease claims can be important as governments soon are likely to see the marketing of biotechnology products by food manufacturers and others. . . .

The fear among consumers is that bioengineered foods are unhealthy. But the real issue, Mathios says, is not absolutely do these foods have risks, but what are the risks relative to how we protect the food supply and the environment as a whole?

In the case of Bt crops, there are some clear environmental benefits. For example, corn that has been modified with a gene from the bacterium Bacillus thuringiensis (Bt), a natural pesticide, is more resistant to crop-destroying insects than other types of corn. This means that farmers spray less chemical pesticide into the environment. In September the Environmental Protection Agency released a preliminary report backing up its longstanding contention that Bt crops are not harmful to the environment.

Mathios expects that manufacturers of Bt crops will attempt to market this attribute to the public. Should the government constrain this advertising because there are potentially other environmental aspects of the product? Mathios thinks that in most cases firms should be permitted to make these claims, and he hopes that regulators will not seek to regulate health and environmental claims about genetically engineered products the way diet-disease claims are regulated.

"Instead of viewing biotechnology as fraught only with risks, health and environmental claims would, in the end, help consumers get a better sense of the trade-offs that we're really facing here," Mathios contends, "that there are benefits as well as risks." ◆ ◆ ◆

Business on Trial
The Civil Jury and Corporate Responsibility

Valerie P. Hans

Business often has to balance various stakeholder needs: creating a profit at the same time as satisfying government regulation and supplying customer needs. Where, exactly, is the line between corporate paternalism and individual responsibility? From what we read in the popular press, we might imagine that suing a corporation for an injury is like hitting the jackpot. However, Hans tells us that juries are wary of individuals who sue businesses and side with the corporation more often than we might think. Hans says that juries, which are, after all, made up of ordinary citizens, reflect an attitude that business ought to act with the care and forethought of a professional person, but other than that, there is no evidence that corporations are losing lawsuits consistently without good reason. This may imply, although she does not say so directly, that corporations are doing an adequate job in consumer safety and should not be more paternalistic than they presently are. Hans concludes that juries in civil cases may have an important function in defining the boundaries between individual and corporate responsibility.

At the beginning of the twentieth century, industrial accidents were causing about 2 million injuries and 35,000 deaths a year.[1] Because legal doctrines and practice favored businesses, most of those injured were never compensated. But the extent of the injuries increasingly challenged the wisdom of the day, which ascribed causal responsibility to the victims and deflected responsibility away from businesses.

Historian Arthur McEvoy argues that high-visibility cases of industrial injury were an important stimulus for legal change. McEvoy's compelling essay about an infamous industrial accident, the Triangle Shirtwaist Factory fire of 1911, describes a fire that broke out in a New York City garment factory, killing 146 workers, most of them young immigrant women. Although the company had committed numerous safety violations, including locked exit doors and fire escapes so inadequate that they collapsed as the women tried to flee, a jury acquitted the company's owners of all criminal charges. Just one survivor of the fire went to a civil trial, where the jury was unable to agree on a verdict and the court dismissed the case. Twenty-three wrongful death actions were settled for seventy-five dollars each.[2]

These legal outcomes, though harsh by today's standards, reflected prevailing assumptions about causality and responsibility in the workplace. As one of the Triangle Shirtwaist trial jurors observed: "I can't see that any one was responsible . . . it must have been an act of God. I think the factory was well managed, and was as good or better than many others. I think that the girls, who undoubtedly have not as much intelligence as others might have in other walks of life, were inclined to fly into a panic."[3]

Analyzing the jurors' reaction, McEvoy maintains that their explanation for the trial and the deaths of so many workers was embedded in a view of the world that placed overwhelming importance on individual responsibility. People were supposed to look after themselves, and if they made choices that had negative consequences, they were presumed to have accepted those consequences. The fact that the Triangle Shirtwaist factory workers were primarily immigrant women did not mean that their employer had greater responsibility for these vulnerable workers. Rather, it suggested that the limitations of the workers themselves had contributed to their deaths.[4] By the laws and the mores of the day, the Triangle victims were seen as having assumed the risks of their jobs; their panic in response to the fire was assigned a contributory role in their deaths. Nevertheless, McEvoy argues that the very public nature of the fire and subsequent investigations of the garment industry helped to shape new understandings of the causes of industrial accidents, ultimately changing who the public found responsible for these accidents.

During the course of the nineteenth and early twentieth centuries, then, the sheer number of business-related injuries tended to undermine the clarity of such doctrines as assumption of risk, contributory negligence, and the fellow-servant rule. Ultimately their importance and power diminished. Changes on the political front, including increasing calls to regulate the business community, also altered the legal landscape. Workers organized to protest unfair and dangerous conditions, and pressured legislatures to curb the worst excesses of industry. The Progressive Movement and the New Deal swept in new attitudes about the collective responsibilities of businesses and government for dealing with the problems of the citizenry. The advent of workers' compensation in the early decades of the twentieth century was especially significant. Both the workers and the business community obtained substantial benefits in the deal that created workers' compensation. By covering the medical expenses and lost wages of injured workers and following a preset schedule of payments for injuries, employers purchased freedom from most lawsuits. Workers' compensation also signaled the business community's acknowledgment of its own responsibility for workers injured on the job.

Although a general trend toward greater liability for business can be observed over the nineteenth and twentieth centuries, a dramatic acceleration began in the 1960s. A tort "revolution" generated novel theories of liability, which allowed business corporations to be held liable under a wider range of circumstances.[5] Product liability laws underwent substantial change. Companies were held to a standard of strict liability for defective products.[6] The idea of market-share liability, in which companies would pay a proportion of the claims for injuries stemming from a defective product according to their market share of the product rather than their demonstrated negligence toward specific plaintiffs, was proposed.[7] Criminal charges against corporations for wrongdoing in the course of business also increased.[8]

All these modifications enhanced the role of law in regulating business transactions and increased business presence in the courts. Large business corporations constitute a notable presence in the federal courts today.[9] Overall, studies of federal court filings show that business litigation has increased since the 1960s. Most of the public attention has been focused on cases in which individual plaintiffs sue business defendants. . . . However, there have also been some marked changes in the extent to which businesses use the courts to resolve disputes among themselves.[10] The Benlate cases, for example, often pitted small-business users of the product against [DuPont] the much larger manufacturer. Even though some types of business litigation have leveled off or even decreased somewhat since the mid-1980s, certain kinds of high-visibility cases involving businesses, such as product liability and class actions, continue to expand. And one study of federal litigation in the 1990s found that business disputes ranked first among the most intractable cases confronting the judiciary, comprising about a third of the cases that were three or more years old.[11]

Analysts have attempted to explain the increased presence of business corporations in the courtroom. Some commentators focus on why people now appear to be more willing to sue businesses over defective products, workplace and consumer injuries, and discrimination than they were in the past. Some trace this increased propensity to sue to a changed legal culture with the basic tenet that innocent victims of injury should receive compensation.[12] Others assert that standards of personal responsibility have eroded and that Americans are an overly litigious people who hobble businesses with lawsuits. Still other scholars focus on why businesses themselves are more apt to bring their disputes against other businesses into the courtroom. This greater

willingness to sue other businesses has been attributed to changes in business practices that encourage reliance on the law.[13] It has also been linked with the degree to which businesses face competition, instability, and uncertainty.[14] . . .

◆ "Juries face accidents up close, viewing them in the lurid setting of an individual tragedy already completed. . . . The only human reaction to the individual tragedy viewed close up, is unbounded generosity, which any large corporation or insurer can surely afford to underwrite."[15]

◆ "The presence of juries increases the lottery aspects of the tort system. Skillful plaintiffs' attorneys may select only the most appealing clients, and focus their efforts primarily on mobilizing the sympathy of the jury. . . . The resultant verdict may have little to do with the merits of the case, and everything to do with theater."[16]

◆ "Jury awards for punitive damages grab headlines as they've spiraled into the millions, not to mention billions of dollars. . . . Plaintiffs' attorneys trolling the waters in the hope of landing a big one, have cast their nets in an ever widening circle that promises to choke business and clog the courts. . . . Defendants with seemingly deep pockets (big companies, professionals, etc.) are paralyzed by the threat of huge jury awards and/or the likelihood of paying damages grossly out of proportion to their share of the blame."[17]

◆ "Is it any surprise that many commercial contracts these days have a clause where each party waives its right to a jury trial? Doesn't that tell you something? That they are not willing to trust twelve peers off the street with the complexity of their business transaction."[18]

Claims like these are leveled against the civil jury every day, in newspapers, board meetings, and coffee shops. Critics accuse the lay jurors of bringing their sympathies for the plaintiff and their biases against business into the courtroom, reaching into the deep pockets of corporations to reward plaintiffs even when the negligence of the corporations has not been proven. The failings of the civil jury in business cases are seen as a drain on American business competitiveness.

In spite of these serious charges against an important legal institution, until now there has been little empirical study of how juries operate in lawsuits with business litigants. It is time to take stock. Which of these charges against the civil jury in business cases have been supported, and which have been refuted, by the empirical findings of my research project? Let us address the three main charges against the civil jury in business cases: that it is pro-plaintiff, that it is anti-business, and that it is motivated by deep pockets.

THE MYTH OF THE PRO-PLAINTIFF JURY

The first claim, that juries are pro-plaintiff, cannot be supported. The studies that have contrasted judicial views and civil jury verdicts find substantial overlap between judge and jury, and when their decisions diverge, juries are no more likely to favor the plaintiff in civil litigation, including litigation with business defendants. My research and that of others also contradict the popular perception that jurors are uniformly sympathetic to plaintiffs who bring claims against businesses. A more accurate characterization is that jurors are often suspicious and ambivalent toward people who bring lawsuits against business corporations. Jurors and the public are deeply committed to an ethic of individual responsibility, and they worry that tort litigation could be fraying the social fabric that depends on a personally responsible citizenry. Even in my sample of cases, which had a higher-than-average

win rate, a substantial number of jurors described hostility toward the plaintiffs in their civil lawsuits. Jurors reported examining plaintiffs' claims with a critical eye, probing for ways in which plaintiffs were responsible for their own injuries and assessing the degree to which they could be overstating their injuries. Part of the jury's task, as they saw it, was to be vigilant about spotting frivolous lawsuits.

These attitudes are consistent with the general tendency among members of the public to question the general validity of lawsuits and to believe that the amount of litigation is out of control. The jurors' concerns about the legitimacy of plaintiff claims and their beliefs in a litigation explosion were linked to judgments that favor defendants, including business defendants, in civil lawsuits.

Although I conducted my research in only one jurisdiction, the critical stance toward the civil plaintiff is not merely a local phenomenon. The mistrustful attitudes about civil litigation that I uncovered are virtually identical to those found in national surveys and in polls in other jurisdictions. Across the country, Americans express deep concern about spiraling litigation and unjustified lawsuits. Media reporting and advertising campaigns by business and insurance are certainly part of the reason why Americans are convinced that there is a substantial amount of frivolous litigation. Yet jurors and other citizens respond to the news reports and advertisements because they resonate with their own concerns that expansive rules of civil liability might undermine our societal commitment to individual personal responsibility. . . .

THE MYTH OF THE ANTI-BUSINESS JURY

The second claim, that civil jurors are hostile to business, also does not find much support in a close empirical analysis. The jurors I interviewed did not display the widespread hostility to business litigants that is commonly asserted. Instead, jurors and the public supported business as a general rule, and worried about how excessive litigation might detrimentally affect the strength of the business community. Jurors expressed concern about the effect of an award on the business defendant, wondering whether it might lead to a loss of jobs or otherwise harm the company. Most business litigants in the cases that were part of this study were described in a neutral or positive light. In a minority of cases, jurors levied some harsh comments against particular business defendants, but to the extent that I could determine through interviews, their criticism seemed to be linked largely to trial evidence of business wrongdoing rather than to jurors' preexisting anti-business hostility. In fact, general attitudes toward business were only modestly related, at best, to judgments of business wrongdoing.

My study allowed me to move beyond a focus on whether jurors were hostile toward business to examine how their consideration of a business corporation compared to their treatment of an individual person. There was substantial overlap, whether we rely on jurors' own assessments or on experimental comparisons. Jurors appeared to adopt an individual template, regarding the business corporation as a "person" for the purposes of determining liability. As they decided whether a corporation should be held liable, they reasoned whether a similarly situated individual would be responsible. Indeed, many jurors stated that the presence of a corporation made little or no difference to their decision making. However, jurors did not appear to equate the business corporation with an ordinary, run-of-the-mill person. The analogy that better captures jurors' predominant view is that of a professional individual, such as a doctor or a scientific expert, who possesses a substantial degree of knowledge and resources.

The experiments and interviews showed that under some circumstances the behavior of a corporate litigant is evaluated differently than the actions of an individual litigant. Experiments that varied the identity of the defendant in mock trial simulations showed that business corporations are held to a higher standard of behavior. What might be viewed as accidental and excusable for an individual is seen as negligent for a corporation. Many members of the public, including jurors, endorsed the position that corporations, because of their greater knowledge, resources, and potential impact, should be held to a higher standard of responsibility than individuals. My research suggests that in particular kinds of cases, such as asbestos and product liability trials, a distinctive approach to corporate negligence is even more likely. Here the jurors reflect some of the same motivations that have led lawmakers over the past several decades to create a broad range of special rules of business responsibility. Taken as a whole, the findings indicate that the higher standards that jurors insist upon for business corporations are derived from specific expectations about what is necessary and desirable for business actors, rather than generally negative (or positive) views of the business community. My finding that citizens hold business litigants to higher standards converges with the results of independent studies carried out in California, North Carolina, and even Japan.

Attitudes toward business were not as strongly and reliably related to case judgments as were attitudes about the civil justice system. Nevertheless, there was a good deal of overlap between how participants in my project viewed the business community and how respondents in national surveys perceive business. One exception was that my study participants seemed to be more concerned about the power of big business than are national survey respondents. To the extent that such attitudes about the business community were sometimes related to case outcomes, I predict that in jurisdictions with more positive attitudes toward business, jurors would at times display a tendency to favor the defendant in business trials. However, as my research and that of many other psychologists document, the general attitudes that jurors possess are likely to play only a small role in their verdicts.

It is worth emphasizing again that my jury trial sample contained predominantly tort trials in which individual litigants sued business defendants, and I focused on personal injury tort cases in my line of experiments. In jurisdictions with different case mixes, or in types of trials that are not reflected here, juries could take different approaches that I was not able to observe.

Given that business-business litigation has increased over time, it would be instructive to examine in greater detail how jurors respond to such cases. Do jurors still attempt to fashion an individual template for the evaluation of corporate behavior when both parties are corporations and the issue is a business dispute that bears little relation to ordinary individual experience? Do they try to construct a David-and-Goliath scenario, pitting a larger and stronger corporation against a smaller one?

Another issue to be explored is whether the plaintiff-blaming phenomenon that is so evident in my work with tort cases also dominates contract cases. Some scholars have hypothesized that people do not derogate the individual who brings a contract claim with the same degree of fervor that they reserve for the tort plaintiff.[19] I looked at too few contract cases to make systematic comparisons, but the possibility is intriguing. If jurors do not come to a contract case with the same distrust of plaintiff claims, what other jury dynamics come into play? Similarly, do jurors hold to the same high expectations for business litigants when the behavior is a failure to comply with a contract instead of the infliction of personal injury?

THE MYTH OF THE ROBIN HOOD JURY

The findings . . . also cast doubt on the jury's identity as a modern-day Robin Hood. Most jurors stated that the business defendant's financial status had little impact on their decision making; some stated that it would be unfair to consider the defendant's finances. They were more concerned, they said, with assessing the defendant's negligence and the plaintiff's needs. By themselves, those reports might be subject to question, because they could be affected by the jurors' inability to discern the impact of finances on their own decision making, or to their desires to present themselves in a socially desirable light. Nonetheless, supporting the jurors' claims are the results of experimental tests of the independent effect of deep pockets on case judgments and awards. An experiment that I conducted, and subsequent research by other investigators, varied the financial resources of a defendant, but it made no difference in negligence or award judgments. Research projects in California, North Carolina, and Illinois have all looked for the predicted relationship between an increase in a defendant's financial wealth and awards to plaintiffs who sue them.[20] But all the projects thus far have failed to find the predicted deep-pockets effect. These research findings from the juror interviews and the experiments are contrary to expectations. However, the convergence across methods and studies increases my belief that a defendant's financial resources are not a major factor leading to high jury awards.

Why? One possibility is that the equity norms that would support higher awards against wealthier defendants are balanced in the jury room by equality norms that value equal treatment. Another is that what has appeared to be jurors' deep-pockets approach toward business defendants is better explained by their beliefs that for-profit businesses should cover the full costs of injuries associated with making their products. This approach overlaps with the cost internalization arguments of some tort theorists. A third possibility is that the ubiquity of insurance makes the actual net worth of a business defendant essentially irrelevant. . . .

In a country where it is now routinely expected that businesses are insured, does it make sense to withhold the details of insurance information from the jury, as current law requires? The experimental findings that mock jurors do not vary their awards after learning of a defendant's net worth suggest that informing jurors of insurance might have little or no impact. Net worth may not be critically important so long as a business defendant is presumed to hold liability insurance. How insurance information affects juries, and how it interacts with the norms of equity and equality, should be examined empirically. . . .

OTHER FUNCTIONS OF THE CIVIL JURY

. . . [T]he reality [is] that the evaluation of the central issues in most trials depends on basic human judgment, not on highly technical issues understood by only a few experts. Was a store negligent for leaving dangerous objects where children could get them? Should a car dealership be sanctioned for failing to address repeated problems with an owner's new car? Here the jury's ability to represent the community and its range of values arguably makes it superior to a single judge. The jury includes representatives of both constituencies—the business person and the consumer.

The strongest argument in favor of the jury's continuing role is that it incorporates into its verdicts in business and corporate cases the public's sense of the responsibility and role of the corporation in contemporary society. The range of views that jurors convey in their interviews indicates vigorous debate and difference of opinion about where individual responsibility ends and corporate responsibility begins. My research reveals that juries and their verdicts reflect societal tension over the appropriate level of business responsibility. Civil juries help to define, and redefine, this line between individual and corporate accountability. Indeed, in some cases in which juries resist expansive rules of business liability, the jury can be the corporation's best friend in the courtroom! Traditional and widely held beliefs about the importance of individual responsibility are challenged by the complexities of the modern social world. The continuing presence of the jury in civil litigation allows that debate to be crystallized in the evaluation of specific cases.

As our collective understanding of the line between individual and corporate responsibility shifts, expanding corporate responsibility in some domains and contracting it in others, the jury's verdicts embody that changing understanding. Noted Yale law professor Peter Schuck, commenting about the tort system and the jury, observed: "Tort liability, more than most areas of law, mirrors the economic, technological, ideological, and moral conditions that prevail in society at any given time. . . . The master ideas that drive tort doctrine—reasonableness, duty of care, and proximate cause—are as loose-jointed, context-sensitive, and openly relativistic as any principles to be found in law. . . . Legal principles, after all, are neither self-sustaining nor self-defining; their true significance only emerges as they are applied to actual disputes. The institution of the jury, as much as legal doctrine, infuses tort law with new life and meaning in the light of new configurations of social facts and values."[21] . . . ◆ ◆ ◆

◆ *Notes*

1. My summary is necessarily brief and paints with a broad brush. Several classic citations include more detailed analysis: Friedman, Lawrence M. (1985), *A history of American law*, 2d ed., New York: Simon and Schuster; Horwitz, Morton J. (1977), *The transformation of American law, 1780–1860*, Cambridge: Harvard University Press; and Hurst, James Willard (1956), *Law and the conditions of freedom in the nineteenth-century United States*, Madison: University of Wisconsin Press.

2. McEvoy, Arthur F. (1995), The Triangle Shirtwaist Factory fire of 1911: Social change, industrial accidents, and the evolution of common-sense causality. *Law & Social Inquiry*, 20, 621–651.

3. *Id.* at 637.

4. *Id.* at 637–638.

5. Priest, George L. (1991), The modern expansion of tort liability: Its sources, its effects, and its reform. *Journal of Economic Perspectives*, 5, 31–50. As Priest observes, before the 1960s "a ladder was a ladder, and a fall was a deviation from normal consumer use," and "no one thought to sue ladder manufacturers for injuries suffered from falls off ladders" (p. 38). By the 1990s, lawsuits alleging product defects against ladder manufacturers and others were common. See also Priest, George L. (1985), The invention of enterprise liability: A critical history of the intellectual foundations of modern tort law, *Journal of Legal Studies*, 14, 461–527.

6. E.g., Greenman v. Yuba Power Prod. Inc., 59 Cal.2d 57, 377 P.2d 897, 27 Cal. Rptr. 697 (1963); *Restatement (Second) of Torts*, section 402A (1964).

7. E.g., Sindell v. Abbott Laboratories, 26 Cal.3d 57, 607 P.2d 924 (1980), *cert. denied*, 449 U.S. 912 (1980).

8. Brickey, Kathleen F. (1984), *Corporate criminal liability: A treatise on the criminal liability of corporations, their officers and agents*, Wilmette, Ill.: Callaghan.

9. Dunworth, Terence, & Joel Rogers (1996), Corporations in court: Big business litigation in U.S. federal courts, 1971–1991, *Law & Social Inquiry*, 21, 497–592.

10. Professor Marc Galanter of the University of Wisconsin's School of Law analyzed trends in federal court statistics over time, from 1960 to 1986, and discovered dramatic increases in court filings for various types of commercial litigation, including contract litigation, intellectual property disputes, and bankruptcy cases. Galanter, Marc (1988), The life and times of the big six; or, the federal courts since the good old days, *Wisconsin Law Review*, 1988, 921–954. See also Galanter, Marc, & Joel Rogers (1991, April), *A transformation of American business disputing? Some preliminary observations*, working paper DPRP 10–3, Institute for Legal Studies, University of Wisconsin, Madison.

11. Business cases clog courts (1995, August 5), *National Law Journal*, p. A1 and section C. The complexity of the cases may be one reason why the cases do not proceed more swiftly through the courts. Another possibility is that large corporations have the financial resources to litigate vigorously, which prolongs litigation and makes cases more difficult to resolve.

12. Friedman, Lawrence (1985), *Total justice*, New York: Russell Sage Foundation.

13. For example, comparisons of manufacturers from the 1960s to the 1990s have revealed that manufacturers today are more likely to rely on new forms of contracts to regulate their dealings with other companies, such as contractors and suppliers, than they were in the 1960s, when companies depended more on general norms and customs of business than on the law. Compare the classic study of the minimal use of formal contracts by manufacturers in Macauley, Stewart (1963), Noncontractual relations in business: A preliminary study, *American Sociological Review*, 28, 55–67; with Esser, John P. (1996), Institutionalizing industry: The changing forms of contract, *Law & Social Inquiry*, 21, 593–629, showing the rise of "relational" contracting.

14. Galanter & Rogers, *supra* note 10. See also Kenworthy, Lane, Stewart Macauley, & Joel Rogers (1996), "The more things change . . . ": Business

litigation and governance in the American automobile industry, *Law & Social Inquiry, 21,* 631–678.

15. Huber, Peter (1988), *Liability: The legal revolution and its consequences,* New York: Basic Books. The quotation is from p. 185.

16. Angell, Marcia (1996), *Science on trial: The clash of medical evidence and the law in the breast implant case.* New York: Norton. The quotation is from p. 74.

17. Sensible solutions #3—Civil justice: Balance the scales, Material presented on the Web by the Mobil Corporation at http://www.mobil.com/this/news/opeds/sensible/ss3.html (downloaded June 17, 1997). It originally appeared in the *New York Times,* February 16, 1995, at A15.

18. Participant E-3: 47, pp. 112–113, in Lande, John (1995), *The diffusion of a process pluralist ideology of disputing: Factors affecting opinions of business lawyers and executives.* Ph.D. dissertation, University of Wisconsin, Madison. A summary of his findings is published in Lande, John (1998), Failing faith in litigation? A survey of business lawyers' and executives' opinions, *Harvard Negotiation Law Review, 3,* 1–70.

19. Engel, David (1984). The oven bird's song: Insiders, outsiders, and personal injuries in an American community, *Law & Society Review, 18,* 551–581.

20. The studies . . . include: the Los Angeles project, MacCoun, Robert J. (1996), Differential treatment of corporate defendants by juries: An examination of the "deep-pockets" hypothesis, *Law & Society Review, 30,* 121–161; the North Carolina project, Vidmar, Neil (1995), *Medical malpractice and the American jury: Confronting the myths about jury incompetence, deep pockets, and outrageous damage awards.* Ann Arbor: University of Michigan Press (the deep-pockets studies are described in chapter 18, pp. 203–220); and finally, the Illinois project, Diamond, Shari S., Michael J. Saks, & Stephan Landsman (1998), Juror judgments about liability and damages: Sources of variability and ways to increase consistency, *DePaul Law Review, 48,* 301–325.

21. Schuck, Peter H. (Ed.), *Tort law and the public interest: Competition, innovation, and consumer welfare,* New York: Norton. The quotation is from Schuck, Peter H., Introduction: The context of the controversy, at 18.

10

BUSINESS AND THE
COMMUNITY

Contemporary stakeholder theory suggests that businesses should act like good citizens in the community. What does this entail? To some degree, it means giving back to the community that hosts the company; this may take the form of monetary gifts, support for community enterprises, or projects to enhance the quality of life in the area.

The current term encompassing business and community relations is *corporate social responsibility* (CSR). Many companies boast of their dedication to benefiting society at large and their civic involvement. These activities may be philanthropic (the company gives outright gifts) or they may be strategic (an engineering firm sponsoring scholarships at a local university).

A firm that makes a commitment to CSR still faces a number of questions: What resources should be dedicated to the community? How should we define the appropriate community: locally, regionally, nationally, or internationally? How should the resources be accounted for? Is there any expectation of a return for the outlay? Under what conditions would the firm pull back from its commitment?

What prompts CSR? In the Malden Mills case, a textile mill burned to the ground, and the owner of the closely held company made a personal commitment to rebuild it for the good of the workers and the local area. He said it was an obligation he had to fulfill. When Merck, the pharmaceutical company, found that it had a cure for river blindness that the victims could not possibly afford, it made a commitment to supply the drug for free for as long as it was needed. The company explained its actions by referring to a corporate understanding that if they did the right thing regardless of profitability, they would find that profits followed.

Jamie Snider and her colleagues compare public statements available from the Web sites of the top 50 American and top 50 multinational firms. Snider found that there is a remarkable consistency in what they say. One of her key insights is that these corporations undertake CSR voluntarily; there is no apparent market compulsion through the action of competitors or any assurance of payback. She finds that companies do not feel the need to justify CSR, and, moreover, there is scant reference to how the programs will be funded.

Now, it might be said that this is an area where hypocrisy pays. If the company says the right

443

thing, it need not necessarily follow it up by action: The public face of the saint and hypocrite are identical. Still, absent any compulsion to make these statements, there seems no reason to post them at all if they are not backed up by some institutional commitment. Therefore, we should probably take the evidence at face value. Whatever a skeptic might say, there is a groundswell presumption that a successful company is committed to socially responsible action. "Triple bottom line" accounting suggests that a company should not confine its assessment of accomplishment to profit alone—that it should consider its effect on the social community and natural environment. Looked at in this way, perhaps a company is drawing on the assets of its host community and should rightfully contribute back to it.

Myrna Wulfson gives a comprehensive survey of the different kinds of corporate philanthropy in her article. She notes a very important background condition to CSR in America and other developed countries: The tax codes allow corporations to deduct charitable donations, which provides an enormous incentive for CSR activities. Some in-kind donations are also allowable. Thus if a computer software manufacturer gives schools products for free, it may take a deduction but may also oblige the school to use its products predominantly and hence encourage usage by the students in general.

Wulfson also looks at so-called cause-related giving, where a portion of a purchase is donated to a given cause. When we think about many of these programs, it is interesting to see that they are often associated with luxury goods: We buy premium ice cream, and the maker gives money toward rain forest preservation. This is economically inefficient, of course; if we want to preserve the rain forest we would be better off donating more directly, especially if we went without the treat. However, we might still justify the practice by saying that if people are inevitably going to eat ice cream, it is better that the company does a social good at the same time.

The final short article deals with the community's relationship with the company—specifically, when it gives the company economic incentives to relocate to the area. David Buchholz found that these programs were not very effective in promoting new business, and the companies did not seem to feel any reciprocal obligation in return for the benefits they received. This brings up a question about the nature of gifts in general: If they are freely given, no strings attached, should we be surprised if the recipient is not grateful or treats the gift as an entitlement? Furthermore, does it matter if the donor is wealthy—a solid multinational company such as Merck that is unlikely to founder in the near future—or a state like Ohio that pays for the incentive program at the cost of funding other resources?

A final question we might consider is whether CSR should be a core value for a company or whether it is mainly a function of being stable and rich enough to pay for these programs. Thus, if you were a member of a start-up company struggling to survive, would you make CSR a priority? Perhaps the real test of CSR will come in lean times when budgets are tight, and a wrong decision might cause a company to go under. Malden Mills went bankrupt after it was rebuilt, largely because of the debts incurred by supporting the workers while they were laid off. However, it has since successfully emerged from Chapter 11, and some commentators have attributed the company's ability to rebound to the loyalty of the employees and local community. In this case, CSR may not have been the most fiscally efficient course of action, but it appears to have contributed to preserving a viable community when the area might easily have been severely harmed by losing its economic anchor.

Corporate Social Responsibility in the 21st Century

A View from the World's Most Successful Firms

Jamie Snider, Ronald Paul Hill, and Diane Martin

What do the world's top firms say about their commitment to corporate social responsibility (CSR)? Snider and her colleagues looked at the Web pages of Forbes *magazine's top 50 U.S. and top 50 multinational firms to see what they announced publicly about CSR. They found a remarkable consistency in the content of the messages. When you read about these public statements, bear in mind that there is no compulsion for any company to make CSR claims. Why do you think they do so? Also consider the justifications (if any) that are given for CSR and whether there is any discussion of how the costs will be covered.*

CORPORATE SOCIAL RESPONSIBILITY

The Corporate Social Responsibility (CSR) construct describes the relationship between business and the larger society. An exact definition of CSR is elusive since beliefs and attitudes regarding the nature of this association fluctuate with the relevant issues of the day (Pinkston and [Carroll], 1996). As such, viewpoints have varied over time and occasionally are even oppositional. However, Milton Friedman contributed to the creation of a general CSR theory by asking questions such as "Should companies take responsibility for social issues?" (Kok et al., 2001, p. 286). He argued that the only social responsibility of business is to increase profits by legal means. Consequently, the use of organizational resources for the larger good, such as donating to charities, is detrimental to firms since it may decrease profitability or increase product prices or both (Pinkston and Carroll, 1996).

Critics of this perspective argue that business exists to serve the greater community as well as direct beneficiaries of the company's operations. Accordingly, CSR may be defined in general terms as "the obligation of the firm to use its resources in ways to benefit society, through committed participation as a member of society, taking into account the society at large and improving welfare of society at large independent of direct gains of the company" (Kok et al., 2001, p. 288). Consistent with this approach, Carroll (1999) identified four components of CSR: economic, legal, ethical, and discretionary or philanthropic. The economic component is business's fundamental responsibility to make a profit and grow. The legal component is their duty to obey the law and to play by "the rules of the game." The ethical component is their responsibility to respect the rights of others and to meet the obligations placed on them by society that ensure these rights. Finally, the discretionary component involves philanthropic activities that support the broader community.

A research paradigm that parallels this perspective is stakeholder theory, whereby business is deemed responsible on such dimensions to specific stakeholder groupings (Maignan and Ralston, 2002). Stakeholders are identified and categorized by their "interest, right, claim or ownership in an organization" (Coombs, 1998, p. 289). While there is some variance in the designation of appropriate clusters, customers, employees, suppliers, and the community are nearly always considered pertinent. Research with U.S. corporations and U.K. firms reveals that companies often report socially responsible behaviors in terms of such specific stakeholder groups (see Robertson and Nicholsom, 1996). Hence, stakeholder theory provides a useful framework to evaluate corporate social responsibility through social reporting activities.

CORPORATE SOCIAL REPORTING AND THE INTERNET

Corporate social reporting is a method of self-presentation and impression management conducted by companies to insure various stakeholders are satisfied with their public behaviors (see Hooghiemstra, 2000; Patten, 2002). Gray et al. (1996, p. 3) defines corporate social reporting as "the process of communicating the social and environmental effects of organizations' economic actions to particular interest groups within society and to society at large." While most companies historically used traditional mass media as the preferred communication channels, corporations increasingly have turned to the Internet because of its growing reach. A study reported by the United Nations reveals that in 1995 there were 16 million Internet users worldwide; in 2000 that number had climbed to 400 million (Hill and Dhanda, 2002). The number of Internet users is predicted to reach one billion by 2005. . . .

Numerous studies have examined aspects of companies' self-presentation of their corporate social responsibility on websites. These investigations focused primarily on the number of CSR statements, the stakeholder groups CSR messages were directed to, and the differences in types of CSR messages across companies/nations. For example, Esrock and Leichty (1998) used a sample of *Fortune* 500 firms and found that 82% addressed at least one corporate social responsibility issue. A more recent study by the same authors showed that over 85% of these websites contained information for two or more publics (Esrock and Leichty, 2000). Maignan and Ralston (2002) compared the corporate social responsibility and stakeholder issues from websites in the U.S. and Europe, revealing that countries differed significantly in the importance they attached to reporting socially responsible behaviors as well as the CSR issues they wished to emphasize.

RESEARCH PURPOSE

Research involving corporate social responsibility and social reporting on the Internet has focused on the groups addressed and the types of messages directed to them. However, there is a lack of scholarship examining the content of what firms are actually saying to these stakeholders. In light of recent interest in social responsibility as a result of corporate scandals, along with the rise of the World Wide Web as a social reporting tool, the following research question is posed:

What is the content of issues within stakeholder groups that leading firms are addressing on their websites regarding corporate social responsibility?

METHODOLOGY AND FINDINGS

Method

Analysis of the websites followed the tenets of grounded theory and qualitative content analysis. Glaser and Strauss (1967) designed the grounded theory method as a way to systematically collect and analyze data for the construction of a theoretical model. Such analyses focus on revealing patterns among the information rather than imposing a framework or concept from outside the discourse/meaning system of the messages under study. The data for this investigation included websites of "top firms" as defined by revenue rankings: the 2002 *Forbes* top 50 U.S. firms and the 2001 *Forbes* top 50 global (non-U.S.) firms. Both U.S. based and other multinational corporations were included to be consistent with previous research and because issues of social responsibility are being addressed around the world. In total 50 U.S. websites and 43 international websites were available for study. . . .

. . . [T]he analysis followed steps suggested by Hill (1994). First, the websites were scanned in their entirety for explicit or implicit statements regarding firms' moral, ethical, legal, or social responsibilities to all internal or external constituencies. Second, the information acquired was sorted and then categorized by stakeholder. Third, a search for similarities within the information was undertaken for each category, resulting in the discovery of a number of interrelated and expressive themes. This step involved the reading and rereading of all data points several times, organizing like information into separate groupings, and seeking appropriate identifying monikers. Fourth, the possibility of differences between U.S. and other global firms was explored among the themes and stakeholders.

The next section presents the findings that resulted from this data collection, which occurred during the spring and summer of 2002. Following brief explanations of particular themes within stakeholder groupings, statements from various websites that denote appropriate exemplars are provided. As with most qualitative investigations, these testimonials are representative of the range of responses discovered during the analysis rather than their frequency across websites (see Ozanne, Hill, and Wright, 1998).

Findings

The results of this study reveal that both sets of organizations concentrate their attention on a similar set of stakeholders and approximately the same CSR issues. The variation that occurs between U.S. and other global firms typically is in the specificity of their CSR messages with regard to their ultimate goals and objectives. When such differences exist, they are noted within the appropriate subcategories below.

General Value Statements. Many of the firms espouse an ethical framework that guides the accomplishment of their overall mission within society. This framework covers a broad spectrum of ethical issues and provides a context within which they define their relationships with internal and external publics. Such CSR messages often include a listing of core values and their descriptions. Both U.S. and other global firms act similarly in their use of general value statements.

JP Morgan Chase provides an excellent example of this genre of CSR messages among U.S. corporations. It includes a brief statement of core values followed by a generic definition of each.

Behaviors and principles that describe what we stand for—integrity and respect—and what we deliver—excellence and innovation.

Integrity—Striving at all times to do what's right and adhere to the highest ethical standards.

Respect—Valuing the perspectives and expertise of all to surface the best ideas and insights.

Excellence—Achieving high-quality results by continuous improvement and superb execution.

Innovation—Going beyond the commonplace to break new ground.

. . .

Environmental Policies. As an addendum to these general value statements, both U.S. and other global firms often establish comprehensive environmental policies. These CSR messages are developed for a variety of stakeholder groups, and they typically reveal a proactive concern for the larger ecology while serving the needs of their customers. Some are more broadly articulated with little specificity, while others are listed numerically and provide operational details.

In the next message, Coca-Cola demonstrates their general interest in the ecology and their efforts within the context of their own market domain. The statement provided is an exemplar of the more general form of environmental policies.

A large part of our relationship with the world around us is our relationship with the physical world. While we have always sought to be sensitive to the environment, we must use our significant resources and capabilities to provide active leadership on environmental issues, particularly those relevant to our business. We want the world we share to be clean and beautiful. We are always innovating to bring you different delicious beverages. This same spirit of innovation comes alive in our environmental programs. We're committed to preserving our environment, from the use of more than $2 billion a year in recycled content and suppliers, and neighborhood collection and beautification efforts.

The global firm Marubeni, on the other hand, presents a more detailed CSR message that exemplifies the operational form of environmental policies. Such messages often open with a general statement like the exemplar from Coca-Cola, followed by several action plans that are designed to preserve or improve the larger ecology:

1. International environmental guidelines and environmental laws and regulations related to the country concerned and local self-governing body etc. will be observed.
2. At the time new investment and business is commenced and new equipment introduced, the reduction of environmental impacts will be considered. This will be especially true for resource development projects where the preservation of the natural ecosystem and regional environment will be given great consideration and care.
3. In daily office work, green procurement, energy savings, resource savings, reduction of waste, and improvement of business efficiency will be carried out.
4. Efforts to create goods, services and social systems related to protection and/or improvement of the environment will be made.

Customers. The first stakeholder grouping that flows naturally from these CSR messages are organizations' consumers. On occasion, general value statements are adapted to or supplemented by ethical protocols that are focused specifically on the relationship between firms and their customers. More typical, however, are messages that describe how corporations provide value to their consumers through a partnership with them that is designed to understand and satisfy their needs. Both U.S. and the other global firms operate similarly in this regard. . . .

The delivered-value statements come in two basic varieties. The first is a general CSR message that describes a comprehensive policy to provide value through an explicit focus on customers' needs. The second is a more specific statement that gives operational details regarding how the organization delivers value through partnerships. An example of the former is from the global firm Fujitsu, and an exemplar of the latter is from the U.S.-based Home Depot.

> In all our business activities, we place paramount importance on "customer focus," seeking to maximize customer satisfaction by continuously looking at things from our customers' perspectives and anticipating their needs.

> At the Home Depot, our associates take great pride in providing the very best in customer service. Our stores offer a variety of services, including, free design and decorating consultations, truck and tool rental, home delivery, free potting, and many other services to accommodate our customers' home improvement needs. And our free in-store clinics help homeowners develop their do-it-yourself skills.

Employees. Current and prospective workers are another stakeholder grouping that is embraced by U.S. firms and other global organizations. Both sets of corporations provide CSR messages that concentrate on the importance of employee development and advancement for the good of the individual as well as the success of the organization. Additionally, they discuss the importance of diversity among their workforces and suppliers as another key to improving their ability to serve the marketplace. However, only U.S.-based firms extend the discussion of diversity to include a commitment to work-life balance as a way to attract and retain employees. This same set of firms also is more likely to discuss the issue of employee safety from a protection-from-injury perspective. . . .

While the global corporation Shell defines diversity as "all the ways in which we differ,"

most organizations concentrate on issues of gender and race. Within this context, the same guiding principle exists for diversity as for employee development—its inclusion advances the individual/group as well as the ability of the firm to compete effectively. The first CSR message below is a general statement by UBS (a global firm) that explicitly acknowledges the importance of a diverse workforce to serving an increasingly diverse customer base. The second CSR message broadens this philosophy to the incorporation of the same values in the U.S.-based Pepsi's selection of suppliers.

> A diverse workforce increases the ability to deal with diverse clients and reach out to new investors by providing innovative solutions and services of a superior quality and value. Diversity also forms an important part of developing a strong and compelling corporate culture in the workplace.

> The steadily increasing business with minority and women-owned firms has improved our company's supplier base. It has also helped to strengthen the suppliers' firms as well as the minority community infrastructure with regard to such benefits as employment, training, role-modeling, buying from other minority and woman-owned businesses, and supporting community organizations.
>
> When it comes to business, minority and majority goals are more alike than different. It's up to us to reaffirm those bonds and to act on them in ways that benefit us all.

One way in which U.S.-based firms manifest their promise to nurture a diverse workforce is through the creation of programs that help employees balance their commitment to work and family. . . .

U.S.-based organizations also focus more explicitly on safeguarding employees from harm at work than other global firms. Whether this emphasis is fostered by legal obligations or other considerations, such concerns primarily extend to job-related injuries and workplace violence, as the following exemplars from Phillips and UPS (respectively) demonstrate.

> Health, Environment & Safety protection is a line responsibility that extends to all levels of management. All employees and contractors are to perform their work in accordance with this policy.

> UPS is committed to a safe work environment and prohibits all types of workplace violence, including physical assaults, threatening comments, intimidation and the intentional destruction of any company property, employee property, or merchandise.

Stockholders. Regardless of their nation of origin, most organizations designate stockholders as an important stakeholder grouping. The concentration of the CSR messages directed to this target audience includes two categories. The first presents an explicit statement that firms intend to deal honestly and with integrity in all their communications to their owners. The second describes their level of commitment to building shareholder value through the generation and marketing of high-quality goods and services.

An example of the first type of message comes from the website of the global firm Credit Suisse. In the following statement, they emphasize the need to establish trust with their owners through clearly articulated and timely pronouncements.

> We believe investors should know they can depend on our reporting publications, and trust in us to clearly explain our company's performance, our strategy and the reasoning behind it. We are also committed to prompt disclosure of any facts which might affect your investment in our company.

Duke Energy, a U.S.-based corporation, presents the second type of shareholder CSR message. This exemplar reveals the organization's promise to advance the interests of their owners by serving the needs of the marketplace exceptionally well.

> At Duke Energy, creating shareholder value has always been an important goal. And we have delivered.
>
> By building superior capabilities in the production, delivery and sale of energy and energy-related products and services for our customers worldwide, we continue to fulfill the promise to our shareholders.

Competitors. The stakeholder group with the fewest number and variety of CSR messages is competitors. The available statements describe a pledge by organizations to go beyond the letter of the law and to meet the ethical demands of the countries in which they operate. As the following exemplar from the U.S.-based United Technologies Corporation indicates, the foundation of this assurance is to compete fairly based on the preeminence of firms' products.

> UTC will compete in the global marketplace on the basis of the merits of our products and services. Legal and ethical considerations dictate that marketing activities be conducted fairly and honestly. Marketing and selling practices should be based on the superiority of our product offerings. In making comparisons to competitors, care must be taken to avoid disparaging a competitor through inaccurate statements.

Society. Both U.S.-based and other global corporations segment this stakeholder grouping into three distinct categories—the local community, nation states in which firms operate, and the world in general. At the local level, organizations concentrate their discussions on community-based activities that support the places where employees work and live. With regard to particular countries, companies describe their attention to national interests in culture, sports, natural disasters, and other calamities. Worldwide concerns are more universal in their declarations, and tend to focus on human rights from the quality of life perspective advocated by the United Nations (UN). CSR messages at all three levels tend to include general statements of support as well as specific reports of accomplishments.

The global firm Fortis gives an apt illustration of a commitment to the local community, with an emphasis on particular areas of service. . . .

> The Fortis companies have deep roots in diverse communities around the world. Through participation in community-based programs such as sponsorships, donations, and employee volunteer programs, we work to fight illness and disease, promote education, aid and protect children, and prevent hunger and homelessness. We encourage our employees to give back to their communities and commend those who actively take time to assist and support those around them. Our commitment to serving local communities in America goes back over 100 years. That tradition continues today—each and every day. . . .

At the country level, the global corporation Nissan reveals their promise to invest time, talent, and treasure in support of national initiatives. One issue that dominated the pronouncements of some organizations doing business with the U.S. was the devastation that occurred on September 11, 2001. The following CSR message shows Nissan's empathy for the loss of life and their activities in support of survivors.

> All of us at Nissan are deeply affected by the tragic events of September 11, 2001. Our thoughts and prayers go out to everyone impacted by this tragedy and the events that have followed. . . .
>
> Nissan employees throughout the country are assisting in these efforts. We are especially proud of the Nissan employees and family members who are serving in the military or volunteer emergency services or otherwise supporting the recovery. . . .

While some CSR messages at the worldwide level explicitly recognize agreements such as the UN Universal Declaration of Human Rights,

many statements are couched in terms that are specific to the product categories in which firms market their goods and services. The exemplar below from Bristol-Myers Squibb presents such a message, with an emphasis on healthcare in general and the pharmaceutical industry in particular.

> The Bristol-Myers Squibb Foundation supports philanthropic initiatives that help extend and enhance human life. Funded by the Bristol-Myers Squibb Company, the Foundation's activities support a broad range of programs that address important health matters and social issues around the world. [Including:]
>
> The Women's Health Education Program, which supports novel approaches to educating women about their health and well-being, primarily through Better Health for Women: A Global Program.
>
> Donations of pharmaceutical products to people in need in developing countries and to victims of natural disasters and civil unrest throughout the world.

DISCUSSION AND CONCLUSIONS

. . .

Several common premises weave throughout these findings and are worthy of note. The first involves the role of social responsibility among global firms today. Our results indicate that the multinational organizations represented by this investigation act similarly in their development and dissemination of CSR messages. For the most part they concentrate their attention on the same stakeholder groups, advancing statements that often are interchangeable except for the company name and the product category. This perspective is consistent with recent scholarship on globalization, which suggests that corporations operating on a worldwide basis employ like market management strategies regardless of their nation of origin (Hill and Dhanda, 2002).

A second common premise is the interplay between the overall missions of organizations and their perceived corporate social responsibility. For example, fulfilling companies' ethical obligations to employees, even meeting diversity needs, are expressed in terms of the positive impact on their marketplace goals and objectives. The same principle can be applied to other constituencies, including customers, shareholders, and, to a lesser extent, even competitors. This duality is reminiscent of the old adage "What is good for General Motors is good for the country." The only CSR messages that challenge this perspective are those directed towards society, where statements are focused on the greater good without concern for the bottom line. However, none of these firms provides a description of the costs incurred as a consequence of socially responsible actions.

A third and final premise emphasizes the consistency with which organizations promote the ethical standards of their positions and behaviors across messages and stakeholders. From broad-based value statements to specific duties toward internal and external constituencies, these corporations express an unwavering commitment to a set of norms that drive their operations. Such pronouncements have a universal quality that defies national or cultural boundaries, which may be part of the "borderless" nature of the global firms included in this study. A central tenet that permeates these standards is an implied balance between serving their own needs, those of relevant publics, and their obligations to humankind. . . . ◆ ◆ ◆

◆ References

Carroll, A.: 1999, 'Corporate Social Responsibility: Evolution of a Definitional Construct', *Business and Society* **38**(3), 268–295.

Coombs, T.: 1998, 'The Internet as a Potential Equalizer: New Leverage for Confronting Social Irresponsibility', *Public Relations Review* **24**(3), 289–303.

Esrock, S. and G. Leichty: 1998, 'Social Responsibility and Corporate Web Pages: Self-presentation or Agenda Setting? *Public Relations Review* **24**(3), 305–319.

Esrock, S. and G. Leichty: 2000, 'Organization of Corporate Web Pages: Publics and Functions', *Public Relations Review* **26**(3), 327–344.

Forbes 500s: 2002, www.forbes.com.

Forbes International 500: 2001, www.forbes.com.

[Glaser, B. and A. Strauss: 1967, *The Discovery of Grounded Theory: Strategies for Qualitative Research* (Aldine, NY).]

Gray, R., D. Owen and C. Adams: 1996, *Accounting and Accountability: Changes and Challenges in Corporate Social and Environmental Reporting* (Prentice Hall, London).

Hill, R. P.: 1994, 'Bill Collectors and Consumers: A Troublesome Exchange Relationship', *Journal of Public Policy & Marketing* **13**(1), 20–35.

Hill, R. P. and K. Dhanda: 2002, 'Advertising, Technology, and the Digital Divide: A Global Perspective', *Advances in International Marketing: New Directions in International Advertising Research* **12**, 175–193.

Hooghiemstra, R.: 2000, 'Corporate Communication and Impression Management—New Perspectives Why Companies Engage in Corporate Social Reporting', *Journal of Business Ethics* **27**(1/2), 55–68.

Kok, P., T. V. D. Weile, R. McKenna and A. Brown: 2001, 'A Corporate Social Responsibility Audit within a Quality Management Framework', *Journal of Business Ethics* **31**(4), 285–297.

Maignan, I. and D. Ralston: 2002, 'Corporate Social Responsibility in Europe and the US: Insights from Businesses' Self Presentations', *Journal of International Business Studies* **33**(3), 497–514.

Ozanne, J. L., R. P. Hill and N. Wright: 1998, 'Juvenile Delinquents' Use of Consumption as Cultural

Resistance: Implications for Juvenile Reform Programs and Public Policy', *Journal of Public Policy & Marketing* **17**(2), 185–196.

Patten, D. M.: 2002, 'Give or Take on the Internet: An Examination of the Disclosure Practices of Insurance Firm Web Innovators', *Journal of Business Ethics* **36**(3), 247–259.

Pinkston, T. and A. Carroll: 1996, 'A Retrospective Examination of CSR Orientations: Have They Changed?' *Journal of Business Ethics* **15**(2), 199–207.

Robertson, D. C. and N. Nicholsom, 1996, 'Expressions of Corporate Social Responsibility in U.K. Firms', *Journal of Business Ethics* **15**(10), 1095–1106.

The Ethics of Corporate Social Responsibility and Philanthropic Ventures

Myrna Wulfson

Many buildings at universities and colleges are the result of donations by corporate benefactors. Much of the computer software used in American higher education has been donated by the manufacturers. And many students attend college through the generosity of a charitable donation from a corporation or foundation. Corporate giving, in fact, is all around us. If a corporation is in the business of making money, though, why would it then just give it away? Perhaps it is noblesse oblige—*a feeling that the wealthy and privileged have an obligation to help out the less fortunate. In that sense, corporations would be acting like benign and prosperous community members. Alternatively, they may be strategically giving away money in the belief that there will be some future payoff, such as improved public relations or developing new markets.*

Wulfson examines the history and development of corporate philanthropy and outlines the various approaches. She points out the recent striking success of cause-related marketing, now the largest portion of corporate giving, where a corporation, say, will donate 1 cent to cancer research for every item sold.

When you read the article, consider whether you think a corporation owes anything to the community and how such expenses could be justified to shareholders. Also consider motives: Does it matter why the corporation is doing good, as long as the community benefits?

He who dies rich, dies thus disgraced

Andrew Carnegie

Before Social Security, Medicare, and the United Way were helping the needy members of society, some business people reached out to their communities to provide assistance. In doing so they were attempting to counteract the critics who claimed that business leaders were uncaring and interested only in the bottom line. While this paper will look at what corporations have done in the past and what some are doing in the present, there is a need for more study of current practices to determine how social responsibility and philanthropic ventures can best meet the needs of the various constituencies.

In the early 1900's corporations were criticized for being too big, too powerful, and guilty of antisocial and anticompetitive practices. Antitrust laws, banking regulations, and consumer-protection laws were written to curb corporate power.

To improve their public image many business leaders gave donations to charitable institutions. Andrew Carnegie founded the Carnegie Corporation of New York to fund education, the Carnegie Endowment for International Peace, the Carnegie Foundation for the Endowment of Teaching, and the Carnegie Institution of Washington, which conducts scientific research. Over 2,500 libraries were built with $56 million of Carnegie's charitable funds. When he retired in 1899, Carnegie published *The Gospel of Wealth*, which outlined how large personal fortunes should be used to better society. At the time his ideas were the exception rather than the rule. He believed that businesses and wealthy individuals were the caretakers or stewards of their property, holding it in trust for the benefit of society as a whole. In *The Gospel of Wealth*, he stated:

> This, then, is held to be the duty of a man of wealth. First, to set an example of modest,

unostentatious living, shunning display or extravagance; to provide moderately for the legitimate wants of those dependent upon him; and after doing so, to consider all surplus revenues which come to him simply as trust funds, which he is called upon to administer, and strictly bound as a matter of duty to administer in the manner which, in his judgment, is best calculated to produce the most beneficial results for the community—the man of wealth thus becoming the sole agent and trustee for his poorer brethren, bringing to their service his superior wisdom, experience, and ability to administer—doing for them better than they would or could do for themselves. (657)

Others, like Henry Ford, founder of the Ford Foundation, created paternalistic programs to support the recreational and health needs of their employees. In 1913 J. D. Rockefeller donated $183 million to start the Rockefeller Foundation. "The point to emphasize is that these business leaders believed that business had a responsibility to society that went beyond or worked in parallel with their efforts to make profits." (Post 41)

With the creation of the Community Chest in the 1920's, the forerunner of today's United Way, charitable contributions moved from the individual philanthropist's contributions to charity to corporation donations. According to Post, Frederick et al., charitable giving is not the only form that corporation social responsibility takes. It also can be found in the stewardship principle, when corporate managers see themselves as stewards or trustees who act in the general public's interest and "recognize that business and society are intertwined and interdependent." (43) Business executives changed from contributing to charity or giving aid to the needy to the concept of stewardship, or acting as a public trustee and considering all corporation stakeholders when making business decisions.

In 1997 Ted Turner, founder of CNN, made one of the largest philanthropic donations to a specific cause when he donated $1 billion to the United Nations' Children's Fund. He then challenged wealthy business people to follow his lead to promote human welfare and goodwill. On September 16, 1999 Bill Gates created the $1 billion "Gates Millennium Scholarship" designed to create college scholarships for black, Hispanic and American Indian students.

In other words, a philanthropist believes he has a moral duty towards helping the less-fortunate in a society through charitable distribution of earnings while the steward (trustee) believes his primary mission involves an obligation to earn a profit.

CORPORATE SOCIAL RESPONSIBILITY

A business that makes nothing but money is a poor kind of business.

Henry Ford

Davis and Blomstrom define "corporate social responsibility" as the obligation of the internal corporate decision makers to "take action which protects and improves the welfare of society as a whole along with their own interests." (6) While corporate social responsibility does not negate earning a profit, it does require corporations to balance the benefits to be gained against the cost of achieving those benefits. "Corporate social responsibility means that a corporation should be held accountable for any of its actions that affect people, their communities, and their environment." (Post 37)

A. B. Carroll's Pyramid of Corporate Social Responsibility demonstrates the idea of conciliating the drive for profit with the public welfare. At the foundation of the pyramid are economic responsibilities. The organization must be profitable to survive. At the second level are the legal responsibilities of those involved in the organiza-

tion. The corporation must obey the law, which is the codification of what is right and wrong. At the third level, one finds the ethical responsibilities, which represent the obligations of each member of the corporation to do what is fair, just, and right. At the top of the pyramid are the philanthropic responsibilities that make the corporation a good corporate citizen, and which can only be reached after economic, legal, and ethical responsibilities have been achieved. (39–48)

J. Davidson in "The Case for Corporate Co-operation in Community Affairs" defines social responsibility as "an obligation that private enterprise owes to society in general, and subgroups of that society in particular." (294) The four categories of social responsibility include:

◆ Maintaining community relations through charitable activities and financial support;
◆ Contributing to humanistic efforts such as equality in the workplace;
◆ Expressing environmental obligations that affect air and water; and
◆ Giving a priority to consumers with fair pricing and safety issues.

Charitable giving by U.S. corporations increased . . . to $7.4 billion in 1995, indicating that companies were getting more serious about their social responsibility. According to Keith E. Ferrazzi, a national director at Deloitte & Touche Consulting Group in Chicago, companies have increased their philanthropic donations because they:

◆ have the need to polish the company image—which may have been tarnished by downsizing;
◆ feel the need to help fill the gap created by cutbacks in federal and state aid to nonprofit groups;
◆ sense that philanthropy is an important corporate responsibility. (Miller 21)

Many companies are increasing their noncash contributions. For example, in 1995, Mentor Graphics Corp., a software manufacturer, was identified as the nation's top corporate giver by *Corporation Giving Watch*, a publication serving nonprofit organizations. All but $200,000 of Mentor's $100.2 million in contributions in 1994 were in the form of computer software donated to colleges and universities. In 1995, AT&T announced it would provide free Internet access and voice-messaging service to 100,000 public and private schools during the next five years. (22)

Between 1995 and 1998 Microsoft donated more than $103 million in software, licenses and grants to educational institutions. Critics contend Microsoft's donations benefit Microsoft by allowing the company to get its foot in the door to market more packaged Microsoft products. Other corporations such as Oracle, Apple, and Intel also participate in college give-aways. (Guernsey A28)

While the courts have ruled that charitable contributions fall within the legal and fiduciary powers of the corporation's policymakers, some critics have argued that corporate managers have no right to give away company money that does not belong to them and any income earned by the company should be either reinvested in the company or distributed to the stockholders. . . .

In 1953 the New Jersey Supreme Court (A. P. Smith Mfg. Co. v. Barlow) set aside stockholder complaints and commended corporations for their contributions to the general social and economic welfare. In this case a New Jersey fire hydrant manufacturing corporation had decided to donate $1,500 to Princeton University. Several stockholders objected to this dissipation of their assets and sued. The President of Princeton University argued that a corporation had a right to be "socially responsible." It was also noted that "closer to the bottom line, such contributions benefited the corporation indirectly by improv-

ing public relations and gaining favorable publicity." (Morris 3)

In 1994, when Albert Dunlap was the head of Scott Paper Co., he decided to end the company's charitable giving program. He believed that the company had an obligation to its shareholders rather than to donations. (*Industry Week* 16) Where should the line be drawn between obligations to shareholders and society?

Contributions—Corporate

The Random House College Dictionary defines "philanthropy" as donations of money, property, or work to needy persons or to socially useful purposes. Does a company contribute to its community because it is ethical and morally correct or because of the positive tax-implications and publicity received by having its name in the public eye? Recognizing that today's students will become tomorrow's employees as well as consumers, many companies donate money and equipment to schools to help improve the quality of education as well as stimulate name recognition and brand-loyalty.

According to a 1998 survey by Gutterbock and Fries of the Center for Survey Research of the University of Virginia there are approximately 1.2 million non-profit organizations in [the] United States, including about 600,000 charities and religious institutions and more than 35,000 foundations. (AARP Survey 1) Business corporations are the source of financial contributions for corporate foundations and corporate giving programs. In most cases corporate foundation grants are made from the profits of a corporation and not from investment income. By law, corporations are allowed to receive a tax deduction for giving up to 10 percent of their pre-tax earnings. (Minnesota Corporate 1) . . .

Reynold Levy in his book *Give and Take* cites cases to illustrate how corporate contributions help a company. For example:

Since 1946, Dayton-Hudson Corporation has donated 5 percent of its pre-tax net income to charity, almost four times the amount of the average company that contributes cash to nonprofit. Such philanthropic activity advances sales and marketing objectives, raises employee morale, and its good works become more widely known because its employees are proud believers of the concept. (4) . . .

IBM Corporation is strongly identified with philanthropic efforts to advance public school reform and the use of technology as a learning tool. These efforts provide IBM brand recognition and "create a receptive environment for the sale of its products and services. These school children will become an important customer base to IBM in the future." (5)

. . .

Approximately a half-billion dollars a year are donated to nonprofit organizations for allowing their good names to be marketed on everything from nicotine patches to pain relievers. Pravachol, a cholesterol-lowering drug made by Bristol-Myers Squibb Company, featured the name and logo of the American Heart Association, which was paid $600,000 for its cooperation. Electrolux L.I.C. formed an alliance with the Asthma and Allergy Foundation as part of its campaign to convince consumers that a cleaner home is a healthier home. In an advertising campaign in 1997, SmithKline Beecham, P.I.C. makers of Nicoderm and the American Cancer Society were described as "partners in helping you quit." The Cancer Society, which claims it endorses no commercial products, received approximately $1 million for the use of its name and logo. (Abelson A1) . . .

The problem with these advertisements is that many consumers believe the use of a logo is considered an endorsement by the nonprofit organization. If an organization is not endorsing a product, why are they allowing their name to be used on that product? The American Cancer Society and the American Heart Association allow their names and logos to be used in advertisements for drugs or medical devices. Since these groups are seen by the public as experts in their field, it is feared that the public will treat these endorsements as support of specific products.

Mildred Cho, a researcher at the Stanford Center for Biomedical Ethics, believes that charities should ask themselves whether there really is a difference between allowing their names to be used in marketing and an all-out endorsement. "If the goal is to educate generally about smoking cessation or nutrition, you don't need to mention a specific product." (A22)

In 1991 because of the Boy Scouts of America's (BSA) refusal to admit gays as members or as troop leaders, the San Francisco United Way withdrew a contribution of $9,000, and the city's board of education banned BSA activities on school property during school hours. In 1992 Levi Strauss & Company decided to end its annual financial support ($40,000–$80,000) to the BSA because the organization's exclusion of homosexuals was "at odds" with the company's "core values." The company stated that it "could not fund any organization that discriminates on the basis of sexual orientation and religious beliefs." (Hochswender A12) Between 1990 and 1991 U.S. West gave $300,000 to the Boy Scouts of America in Colorado. In response to employees' questions regarding the BSA's admitting policies, which the company found to be "particularly troubling . . . in light of U.S. West's values around pluralism and diversity," the board of directors of U.S. West recommended that the foundation "review its giving practices, working to align its funding decisions with its own policies and with U.S. West's values." (Bettelheim 1A) The U.S. West foundation decided to continue to support BSA and released the following statement:

> There is no litmus test we can apply to every organization we fund on every issue. We do not have

to agree with everything an organization espouses in order to support the good it does overall (1A)

Sue Anderson, director of the Gay and Lesbian Community Center in Denver, noted:

> It is unfortunate they [U.S. West] claim to back gay and lesbian employees, but at the same time support an organization that actively works against them. It really sets a confusing standard. (1A)

. . .

Contributions—Foundations

A foundation's giving differs from a corporation's in that it is funded in a different manner and has a different philosophy. Under federal regulations, foundations must give away 5 percent of its assets a year.

The United Way, a national organization that funnels funding to charities through a payroll-deduction system, has been in existence since the 1920's. The United Way has been criticized for many of its activities including:

> Being coercive—Bonuses are offered for companies achieving 100 percent employee participation. Betty Beene, president of United Ways of Tristate (New York, New Jersey, and Connecticut) has discontinued the bonuses. She believes that "If participation is 100 percent, it means someone has been coerced." (Garland 39)

> Excessive salary and perks to executives—Between 1970 and 1992, William Aramony, president of United Way was paid $463,000 per year, flew first class on commercial airlines, spent $20,000 in one year for limousines, and used the Concorde for trans-Atlantic flights. (39) In September of 1994, Aramony and two other United Way officers, including the chief financial officer, were indicted by a federal grand jury for conspiracy, mail fraud, and tax fraud. On April 3, 1995 Aramony was found guilty of twenty-five counts of fraud, conspiracy, and money laundering. (Jennings 282)

The United Way still has not recovered. In 1998, donations fell 11 percent while overall charitable giving was up 9 percent. (282) . . .

On September 16, 1999 the Bill and Melinda Gates Foundation, financed with two large donations of Microsoft stock and having about $17 billion in assets, announced the formation of the "Gates Millennium Scholarship" which is open to all racial minorities and is aimed especially at blacks, Hispanics, and American Indians. It will help a minimum of 1,000 high school students a year, by providing enough money to cover tuition, room, board, and other expenses for college and graduate degrees pursued. (Verhovek, A1) The foundation has also committed $200 million for work in developing and distributing vaccines for malaria, AIDS, and other diseases. They have also pledged a similar amount of programs that will bring computers and Internet hookups to schools and libraries in poor areas in North America. Those who have criticized Mr. Gates believe the contributions were part of a public relations campaign by Microsoft, whose image has been battered by the massive antitrust court battles now underway in Washington, D.C.

STRATEGIC PHILANTHROPY

Philanthropy is almost the only virtue which is sufficiently appreciated by mankind.

Henry David Thoreau

Beginning in the 1980's many CEO's began linking their corporations to social causes strategically viewing these arrangements as a way to differentiate their products to consumers. The corporate movement involving charitable giving and reflecting the highly competitive environment of the 1990s has been termed "strategic philanthropy." It involves corporate giving that serves dual purposes: contributing needed funds to charitable causes while simultaneously bene-fiting the firm's financial bottom line and en-hancing business political legitimacy. (Hemphill 57) "Strategic giving" or "strategic philanthropy" has become a generally accepted Solomon-like solution to a problem that allows a corporation to satisfy altruistic impulses to contribute to char-itable causes while serving the bottom line. While pure philanthropy is concerned with as-sistance to education, arts and culture, health and social services, civic and community proj-ects; business-sponsored philanthropy benefits the corporation through cause-related marketing activities as public relations, good will, and polit-ical access. Strategic philanthropy combines pure philanthropy and business sponsorship with giving programs that are directly or indirectly linked to business goals and objectives. (Post 484)

Alan Sloan in his article "Can Need Trump Greed?" states that "a corporate image is bol-stered through the firm's identification with con-tributions aimed at the local communities in which it operates and its employees reside." An example of this policy is that of the Target stores. Stickers are placed on products informing con-sumers that 5 percent of its "pre-taxed annual profits" goes directly back into the Target stores communities across the nation.

A specific example of the growing importance of strategic philanthropy to market strategy is "cause related" marketing, which is a way to link business goals to charitable donations.

Cause-Related Marketing

Exxon's "Save The Tiger" Weekend was held on September 18 and 19, 1999, at The Bronx Zoo, in New York City. Though the event was sponsored by the Wildlife Conservation Society, National Fish and Wildlife Foundation, and Exxon, it was the Exxon name that appeared in the publicity for the event designed to celebrate the Zoo's Siberian tigers and to help save the last of Asia's wild tiger population. While such an event is a public relation writer's dream, are we the Ameri-can public paying indirectly for such corporate giving?

Cause-related marketing (CRM) was defined by Varadarajan and Menon as:

> the process of formulating and implementing marketing activities that are characterized by an offer from the firm to contribute a specified amount to a designated cause when customers en-gage in revenue-producing exchanges that satisfy organizational and individual objectives (60)

Cause-related marketing became big business in the 1980's and its popularity has increased in the 1990's. It involves a marketing and advertising campaign that promotes both the corporation and the cause or social issue. According to J. Mullen, "strategic charitable giving should be included in the public relations plan." One 1994 survey of 463 companies identified the most common charita-ble giving areas and found that monetary contri-butions are the most common methods of giving (95%); followed by in-kind (66%); and product do-nations (53%). (Mullen 45)

Many companies are attempting to fill the void created by government cutbacks by making contributions to nonprofit organizations. While companies realize they have a social responsibil-ity to their community they must also counter the negative publicity caused by downsizing, layoffs, and relocations. Varadarajan and Menon cau-tion that "firms walk a fine line between reaping increased sales, goodwill, and positive publicity and incurring negative publicity and charges of exploitation of causes." (69)

Cause-related marketing that involves linking a company's marketing strategy with that of a nonprofit organization or charity can be highly effective. The theory behind this approach joins a product or company to a core customer value, deepening relationships and building strong bonds of trust. The concept was introduced in 1981 by American Express. It was the first corporation to use cause-related marketing nationally in a campaign linking credit card usage with a corresponding company contribution. In 1983, it contributed $1.7 million of the restoration of the Statue of Liberty.

In a 1995 study conducted by Cone/Roper more than 84 percent of consumers believed that cause-related merchandising creates a positive image that is associated with a cause they care about, and 54 percent said they would pay more for a product that supports a cause they endorse. (Naughton 1) According to Mark Feldman, vice president of Cone Communications, a Boston-based marketing firm, "three-quarters of consumers say they'll switch brands to a company involved with a charitable cause, if price and quality are equal." (Lorge 72) . . .

Many companies have participated in such ventures:

> In July of 1995 Rubbermaid formed a "cause-related marketing partnership" with Habitat for Humanity. Rubbermaid assists a good cause by donating funds and products, conducting intensive marketing campaigns to build recognition and increase public support of the nonprofit agency.
>
> StirCrazy Enterprises located in Chicago donates 10 percent of their customers' checks to Children's Memorial Hospital. Customers receive a $2 coupon to be used towards a meal. The company believes that it is a good strategic alliance, raising awareness for both the charity and the restaurant. . . .
>
> BMW of North America, Buick, Ford, and Avon donate money for breast cancer research. Sears, Roebuck and Co., has started a company-wide initiative to raise at least $1 million over the next five years for Gilda's Club (for support and education of cancer patients and their friends and

families) with various promotions tied to sales of specific store items.

> American Express card donates 3 cents to Share Our Strength, an anti-hunger organization, to a total of up to $5 million.
>
> Liz Claiborne, Lady Foot Locker, and The Body Shop provide funds to combat domestic violence.
>
> American Airlines allows its frequent-flier customers to donate miles to provide transportation for seriously ill children to receive treatment.

A nonprofit organization must be cautious when accepting donations based on a cause-related marketing approach. The nonprofit organization may become involved in a superficial campaign or find itself linked to a company whose business practices go against the values of the nonprofit organization. For example, in 1997 Gifts In Kind International was accused of compromising its mission of serving non-profits by catering to its corporate contributors. Plagued with financial, personnel, and management problems, this nonprofit organization distributed $245 million worth of products to charities in 1996, a 40 percent increase from the previous year. As reported by the *Chronicles of Philanthropy*, interviews with charities found serious complaints with failure to fill requests and misleading description of goods, leading to accusations that Gifts In Kind was serving the company's desire to secure tax deductions rather than the needs of the charities' clients. (Moore 30)

LEGISLATION

The law is reason free from passion.
                    Aristotle: *Politics*, III, c.322 B.C.

On August 30, 1935 Congress began allowing corporations a tax deduction for charitable contributions. (Public Laws U.S. 1016) Since 1936, the federal government has encouraged corporate giving for educational, charitable, scientific, and religious purposes.

Reaganomics reduced government funding to non-profit organizations, thereby shifting the responsibility to corporations and foundations. In 1986 Congress passed the Tax Reform Act, designed to encourage greater financial investment by the private sector into social programs and issues. The current Internal Revenue Service rules permit corporations to deduct contributions from the company's before-tax income. In other words, a company with a before-tax income of $1 million might contribute up to $100,000 to nonprofit community organizations. There is nothing to prevent a corporation from giving more than 10 percent of its income for philanthropic purposes, but it would not be given a tax break above the 10 percent level. (Post 482) As noted earlier, foundations must give away 5 percent of its assets each year. . . .

Under current law shareholders have their right to request charitable contribution information from publicly traded companies, but nothing requires that the company release the information. "Although corporate foundations are required to list donations by recipients in their tax filings, which are available to the public, most corporate charitable contributions are donated directly to nonprofits, which have no legal requirements of public disclosure. . . .

CONCLUSION

One approach a corporation can use when arriving at an ethical decision concerning its philanthropic efforts would be to consider the utilitarian calculation, comparing the costs and benefits of a decision when deciding to make contributions to nonprofit causes.

We have seen that business exists to make a profit for its stockholders and that contributions to various causes affect profits. However, in today's business world the corporation must be aware of its public image. Corporations must decide if the long-term gains will justify making a contribution to a nonprofit cause. The long-term consequences of an action must be weighed when reaching a moral decision. Today one expects corporations to be good citizens, and therefore the utilitarian cost/benefit calculation should not be the only factor used when deciding how much and to whom one should contribute. . . .

It is impossible for a corporation to satisfy the needs of all its stakeholders in every situation. A corporation has a responsibility to its Board of Directors, stockholders, employees, and to society. Corporations have the resources, expertise, and obligation to meet their social responsibility through philanthropic ventures which in turn can:

◆ build product or service awareness;
◆ create a relationship with consumers;
◆ create consumer loyalty;
◆ enhance or polish the company image; and
◆ demonstrate corporate concern while raising money for a worthy community-cause. ◆ ◆ ◆

◆ *References*

AARP Survey Offers New Perspectives on Civic Involvement. March 29, 1998. http://ombwatch.org/html/aarpsur.html.

Abelson, Reed: 1999: 'Marketing Tied To Charities Draws Scrutiny From States', *New York Times* Vol. CXLVII . . . No. 51,511 (May 3).

Aug. 30, 1935, Cap. 829 Sec. 102(c); Vol. 49 Part I., Public Laws U.S. 1016; See IRS Code, Sec. 170.

Bettleheim, Adriel: 1991, 'Scout Aid May Be Cut', *Denver Post* (November 7).

Carnegie, Andrew: 1889, 'Wealth', *North American Review* 148, no. 391 (June 1889).

Carroll, A. B.: 1991, 'The Pyramid of Corporate Social Responsibility: Toward the Moral Management of Organizational Stakeholders', *Business Horizons* (July-August).

Davidson, J.: 1994, 'The Case for Corporate Cooperation Community Affairs', *Business and Society Review* 90.

Davis, K. and R. L. Blomstrom: 1975, *Business and Society: Environment and Responsibility*, 3rd ed. (McGraw-Hill, New York).

Garland, Susan: 1992, 'Keeping a Sharper Eye on Those who Pass the Hat', *Business Week* (March 16).

Guernsey, Lisa: 1999, 'Corporate Largesse: Philanthropy or Self-Interest?', *The Chronicle of Higher Education* 44(33) (April 24).

Hemphill, Thomas A.: 1999, 'Corporate Governance, Strategic Philanthropy, and Public Policy', *Business Horizons* (May-June), v. 32, I3, Foundations for the School of Business at Indiana University.

Hochswender, Woody: 1992, 'Boy Scouts Learn Levis Don't Fit', *New York Times* (June 5).

Jennings, Marianne M.: 1999, *Business Ethics*, 3rd ed. (West Educational Publishing Company, New York).

Levy, Reynold: 1999, *Give and Take—A Candid Account of Corporate Philanthropy* (Harvard Business School Press, Massachusetts).

Lorge, Sarah: 1998, 'Is Cause-Related Marketing Worth It?, *Sales & Marketing Management* 150(6), Bill Communications Inc. (June).

Miller, William H.: 1996, 'Citizenship That's Hard to Ignore', *Industry Week* 245(16), Penton Publishing, Inc. (September 2).

'Minnesota Corporate Philanthropy Overview', Minnesota Council on Foundations' Guide to Minnesota Foundations and Corporate Giving Programs 1997–1998, and the Minnesota Council of Nonprofits' Minnesota Grants Directory 1999. http://www.mncn.org/fund_cor.htm.

Moore, Jennifer and Grant Williams: 1997, 'Taking the Bad Along with the Good', *The Chronicles of Philanthropy* (March 20).

Morris, Jane Anne: 'America Needs A Law Prohibiting Corporate Donations', http://www.purfood.org/corpdon.html.

Mullen, Jennifer: 1997, 'Performance-based Corporate Philanthropy: How "Giving Smart" Can Further Corporate Goals', *Public Relations Quarterly* 42(2) (Summer).

Naughton, Julie: 1996, 'Conscience Makes Cash, Says CARE', *HFN The Weekly Newspaper for the Home Furnishing Network* 70(1), Capital Cities Media, Inc. (January 1).

Post, James E., William C. Frederick, Anne T. Lawrence, and James Weber: 1996, *Business and Society Corporate Strategy, Public Policy, Ethics*, 8th ed. (McGraw-Hill, Inc., New York).

Sloan, Allan: 1997, 'Can Need Trump Greed?', *Newsweek* (April 28).

Varadarajan, P. Rajan and Anil Menon: 1988, 'Cause-Related Marketing: A Coalignment of Market Strategy and Corporate Philanthropy', *Journal of Marketing* 52 (July).

Verhovek, Sam Howe: 1999, *New York Times* (September 16), Vol. CXLVIII, No. 51,647.

Toledo
Failing to Deliver

David E. Buchholz

Basic economic theory says a firm will seek to become maximally efficient. This may involve relocating a plant or closing it down altogether. What should a community do when faced with this prospect? One response is for the community to give the company incentives to stay, perhaps in the form of tax breaks. Or, if the company takes stakeholder theory seriously, then perhaps it should feel an obligation to the community and address community concerns as seriously as their own.

The experience of Toledo, Ohio, is instructive. Given the rising tide of corporations moving their operations overseas, we can learn how communities should confront potential closings. Do you believe that a financial incentive by a community involves a duty of reciprocity on the part of the company? From the reading, are both sides acting in good faith? Who do you think are the winners and losers from this sort of program?

The city of Toledo, Ohio got in the incentives game early.

In 1978, city officials gave Owens-Illinois $24 million, a generous sum in those days, to stay in town. Unfortunately, the firm was sold to a New York company several years later, and hundreds of the jobs that Toledo thought it had bought were cut.

A nearly identical break would be offered to Owens Corning in 1994 to keep *it* from moving. The city's development director, Holly Wiedman, said the break was worth it for P.R. reasons. "[Losing Owens Corning] would have been a black mark on Toledo that would have gotten more national publicity than we would have wanted." Company officials responded that the tax breaks *were* key to keeping the firm downtown, although, they said, it might have just moved somewhere else within Toledo without them.

Toledo, struggling to maintain its shrinking industrial base, was long an aggressive player in the incentives game. When the state authorized an Enterprise Zone program in 1983, Toledo was quick to take advantage.

Local officials touted the tax breaks as necessary and effective. "Due to the present cost of doing business," said Mayor Carty Finkbeiner, "Toledo must utilize any and all incentives available to keep business from leaving the city and to lure business from other states and outside areas."

But the results of the program were less than stellar. In 1996, the *Toledo Blade* delved into the jobs that had purportedly been created, reviewing every deal since 1983. They found that *over half* of the businesses were not in compliance or had not created the number of jobs they had promised.

General Motors, for instance, accepted $11.7 million in tax breaks for creating "over 400 new jobs" in ten years, according to the firm. But records showed that *all* of the "new" positions were filled by current plant employees or employees from other GM plants. Taken as a whole, only 62 percent of the jobs that were promised were actually delivered.

More astoundingly, *no company had ever been penalized for this*. Despite a state law mandating annual monitoring by the city, this provision was often ignored, and what "monitoring" was done was simply done through form letters.

County Auditor Larry Kaczala said that follow-up was not done because city officials did not *want* to know if their job predictions did not come true. "They just want the new jobs on their scorecard." But Bruce Gyde, a city administrator in charge of overseeing the program, disagreed. Anyway, he maintained, businesses should not be punished for non-compliance. "It is not pro-business if you start penalizing somebody because they guessed wrong."

Toledo, as it turned out, was not alone. The *Blade* later expanded its analysis, reviewing tens of thousands of records pertaining to the entire state's Enterprise Zone program, which had given away $300 million in 1995 alone. Ohio had a whopping 310 zones, on Governor Voinovich's theory that more zones would mean more jobs lured from other states.

The paper found that *no* major Ohio city routinely visited the subsidized companies to monitor their compliance. In Youngstown, for instance, a full sixty percent of companies had reneged on their job promises. The city eventually hired an auditor to look at the program, who reported that monitoring was "extremely weak." "I think the grade has to be pretty close to an F."

But the city's development director argued in response that the program should be regulated even *less*, not more. An earlier study, reviewing all of the state's economic development pro-grams during most of the 1980s, found that "retained" jobs had been overestimated by 51 percent, and new jobs had been overestimated by nearly 100 percent.[1]

The *Blade* reported that many of the full-time jobs claimed were part-time or seasonal, and that wages were overreported. More damning still, they found that the state was paying to shift jobs from within the state. Despite Voinovich's intent, every job that an EZ drew from a competing state was matched by *six* jobs relocated from another Ohio community. Tax breaks had gone, in fact, to over seven hundred companies that closed or reduced their facilities elsewhere in Ohio as a result of a subsidized move.

Back in Toledo, this was having grave ramifications. Twice as many jobs were lured *out* of Toledo than lured in by the Enterprise Zone program. The lesson that Toledo officials were learning, however, was that they were not being generous enough.

Perhaps the most dramatic case was Toledo's historic Jeep plant. In 1986, after Chrysler had taken over American Motors Corporation, it announced that it would close either the Toledo plant or one in Kenosha, Wisconsin. The whipsawing strategy worked, and the two states got into a bidding war over the plant. At one point, Wisconsin's governor publicly committed to offering the best incentive package.

But Chrysler was looking for concessions from more than just state and local governments. When the union local at the Toledo plant offered to renegotiate *its* contract in order to save its jobs, adding lucrative concessions to the public subsidies, the deal was sealed. In 1988, Chrysler closed the Kenosha plant, despite union claims that Lee Iacocca had privately promised to keep it open.

The victory would be short-lived. By the middle of the next decade, Chrysler announced that it would close and rebuild the plant, although the location was negotiable. Several states got the hint, and got in the hunt. Ohio and Toledo officials, however, desperate to keep the facilities, put together a successful $262 million package to keep the plant in Toledo.

The story was not all bright, however. For one thing, the new plant was actually *cutting* jobs, reducing employment from 5,600 to 4,900. Not only were governments subsidizing these job cuts, they were, unintentionally, creating more job losses.

As part of the package, the city agreed to pay for moving businesses and residences off the proposed site. Finding that it underestimated the cost of the relocations by $20 million, the city had to secure a federal loan to cover the difference. In August 1998, one of the targeted companies, Allied Healthcare Products, announced that it would close its plant and transfer the 160 jobs to its St. Louis location, rather than rebuild in Toledo.

State Senator Charles Horn, an outspoken critic of incentives, said that the Chrysler deal is a perfect example of wasted dollars and unintended consequences. "Governments at all levels have contributed over $280 million to cut almost 900 jobs in the Toledo area."

Horn is not alone in his criticism of the area's incentive policies. David Beckwith, a Toledo community organizer, argues that the evidence shows incentives to be bad policy. "When public officials look taxpayers in the eyes and say, 'We have to give tax breaks, and the tax breaks are working,' they are telling two lies in a row."[2]

◆ ◆ ◆

◆ Endnotes

1. Loh 1993. The study still assumes that all of the reported jobs were created or retained "because of" the incentives, a dubious notion.

2. The above narrative was based on Roe 9/1/96; Roe 12/8/96; Roe 12/9/96; Wilkinson and Roe 12/9/96; Rubenstein 1992; Snell 1997; Charles Horn, personal communication.

PART FOUR

BUSINESS
AND THE WORLD

T HIS TEXT IS BEING WRITTEN on a computer that has no single country of origin. There are dozens of components from various sources. It is sold by an American company, incorporates a Japanese microprocessor, and was assembled in Indonesia. If a buyer were to call a customer service representative, the call would likely be answered in India. Using the World Wide Web, we can bid on additional components from an Australian source against another buyer in France in real time. The nature of business is changing rapidly, and managers now confront a range of ethical issues that are made more immediate by the speed of commerce and the globally competitive open market.

Part Four expands our perspective to issues that arise from the internationalization of business. Initially we take a look at some of the working assumptions provided by distinct religious and philosophical approaches that emphasize specific aspects of business while downplaying others. So, for example, Americans may chide the Chinese for failing to respect human rights in the workplace, yet the concept of individual rights is largely rooted in Western political traditions that are not universally embraced. We may abhor sweatshop practices, but in order to effectively communicate our concerns, we may have to recognize the conceptual framework from which they arise and be prepared to critically assess them in the terminology of the host culture.

There are obvious differences between cultures; the readings discuss whether a company that applies or intervenes in a foreign country is being paternalistic or imposing cultural imperialism by enforcing standards we automatically assume to be superior. Alternatively, embracing local standards may mean that U.S. and other First World companies engage in profitable practices that they would never tolerate at home. Thus, managers need to carefully assess whether their domestic standards ought to apply to their overseas operations.

Globalization is sometimes used to refer to the spread of capitalism around the world, with the aim of global free markets. Some commentators see it as the path to democracy and prosperity, whereas others are concerned with the potential loss of national sovereignty and the effects of vastly increased consumption on the planet's ability to sustain our quality of life.

As the final reading warns, unless we make the right choices about the environment, many of our other ethical concerns will become insignificant. It is worthwhile, then, to examine the methods we use to value nature and animals and to see if they give us a realistic model for making business decisions.

Ultimately, our moral decisions are our own, and we are individually responsible for what we do. However, our collective personal choices, each made with the best of intentions and with minimal ecological impact, could potentially result in hurting the future of mankind unless we can incorporate the value of the environment into our decision making.

11

BUSINESS FROM OTHER PERSPECTIVES

A teacher in the United States once taught a business ethics class to visiting Japanese students. He asked what a company owner ought to do if one of his employees was diagnosed with cancer but had no health insurance. One of the students replied, "Invite him to commit suicide." The answer is jarring to Western sensibilities, but it demonstrates significant cultural differences — for example, cancer has different connotations in Japan, and the notion of suicide is less abhorrent there than it is in the West. As business becomes increasingly international, we need to consider the value of putting ourselves in other people's shoes so that we can communicate more effectively and be more sympathetic to their point of view.

So far we have examined business dealings from a Western secular perspective. It is tempting to think that capitalism embodies a set of values that supercede cultural or religious values and that globalization may bring about a homogenization of the ethics of business. In this chapter we will look at some other traditions that serve as a useful counterpoint to this view and show us that even within a market economy, the religious

and cultural backdrop may serve to emphasize particular values and minimize others.

The selection by Daryl Koehn draws from Eastern philosophy, which can differ radically from many of the belief systems with which we are acquainted. Still, when we consider the extent and potential for international business, we realize that we are likely to be dealing with people who hold a significantly different worldview from ours. Koehn reminds us that we should be cautious when making broad cultural generalizations and that is perhaps more appropriate to study the influence of individual thinkers. She focuses on two, Watsuji Tetsuro and Confucius. One of the main differences Koehn highlights is the lack of individual rights talk in the East and the dominance of it is in Western thinking.

The Islamic and Jewish viewpoints in this chapter give us insight into ways in which religious belief may guide how business ought to be conducted. This is not to say that business ethics in the United States does not also have a religious basis — indeed, it often does — but the views presented in this section may be less familiar to many students. Tanri Abeng's reading on Islam reflects a number of similarities with Western teaching, including the legitimacy of work and the duty to deal fairly. Among other issues, it stresses treating friend and stranger alike and the importance of charitable works by those who have prospered. Ronald Green emphasizes that his comments about Jewish law apply strictly to Torah-observant Jews. On the other hand, they demonstrate a style of reasoning from biblical text and its application to contemporary issues. He explores how the Jewish perspective assigns responsibility and imposes positive duties in the case of a horrific crash of a school bus.

The chapter does not attempt to be comprehensive or definitive but instead suggests that there may be profound benefits for people in business from studying other value systems.

What Can Eastern Philosophy Teach Us about Business Ethics?

Daryl Koehn

Most of the readings we have examined so far are from a Western perspective. Yet business today is conducted in a global context, and, of course, other cultures may not share our worldview. Koehn first looks at whether the notion of Asian culture is conceptually sound and then draws on the thinking of two great Eastern thinkers, Watsuji Tetsuro and Confucius, to illustrate how it might influence the business approach of those acquainted with their teaching. One focus of her article is the notion of individual rights. Do you think that cross-cultural discussions about business ethics can occur with widely differing views on fundamental ideas?

As Asian markets have grown, there has been a corresponding increase in interest among businesspeople and philosophers in so-called "Asian Values." Knowledge of the values and ethical systems of Asians is touted as necessary if Western businesses are to successfully negotiate the opening of markets in Japan, South Korea and China and to sell their products to the citizens of these countries. *Real politik* has played an important role as well in generating interest in Asian Values. With the increased wealth of these developing countries has come a greater say in international affairs.[1] Westerners now feel compelled to take note of Asians and to understand them as well as possible. Moreover, as Asian markets have become more lucrative, the power of Southeast Asian governments has increased simply by virtue of the fact that they control which businesses get access to their people and on what terms. The power of voice, coupled with this power to regulate access, has gotten the West's attention.

However, although it is now fashionable to allude to Asian Values,[2] it is far from clear what this term means. In the first part of this paper, I argue: (1) that it is dubious whether such values exist other than as a rhetorical category; (2) that we need to consider the ethics of using such a term; and (3) that we are better advised to speak of certain strands of ethical thinking articulated by particular thinkers within specific countries (e.g., Japan, South Korea, China, etc.). In the second part, I take up two such strands—the ethical views of the famous Japanese ethicist Watsuji Tetsuro and of Confucius. I argue that many of their ideas have profound implications for the conduct of business and the way in which we evaluate that conduct.

PART ONE: THE RHETORIC OF "ASIAN VALUES"

It is questionable whether Asian Values do exist or ever could do so. The term "Asia" refers to an enormous geographical area. China, Japan, India and the rest of the Southeast and East Asian countries fall under the rubric. The former U.S.S.R., too, historically has been considered part of Asia by Europeans. The same is true of what we now term the Mideast. The Greek historian Herodotus, for example, consistently treats Persia and Phoenicia as Asian empires.[3] As one would expect, given the vastness of Asia, the cultures therein vary tremendously, reflecting just about every world religion—Buddhism (in numerous varieties), Shintoism, Confucianism, Islam, Christianity, etc. While we can carve out a certain region of the globe and label it "Asia," it is very hard to ascertain what values all of these different cultures might share. . . .

Given the exceptionally diverse cultures of that region we in the West name "Asia"; and given the dynamism inherent in cultural values, we have good reason to doubt whether some monolithic static set of Asian Values exists now, ever has, or ever will. That is not to deny that some leaders in some countries in this region routinely invoke Asian Values. But the rhetorical purposes to which this invocation are being put need to be critically evaluated.

On the one hand, the appeal to Asian Values can be seen as a positive step by so-called Third World countries to exercise their autonomy. During the last twenty years, scholars and thinkers from the East have challenged the Western interpretation of the East. Nineteenth and early twentieth century scholarship, they argue, has consistently portrayed the peoples of the Orient (including both what the West calls the "Middle East" and "Far East") as completely alien, mysterious and backward.[4] This interpretation of the East has both reflected and supported colonial domination. The people of these other regions have not been allowed to describe themselves, their concerns, their values and their history in their own voices.[5] Instead, the Occident has presumed to tell them who they are. This Occidental strategy has worked to stifle any dissent or challenge to colonial power and has led to repression and genocide.

Colonial powers consistently have seen themselves as "enlightened" and other countries or tribes as "primitive." The "Enlightenment" has functioned as a very powerful searchlight, illuminating many important Western values—the inalienable dignity of the individual; the right of people to choose their own governments; the power of reason to enable human beings to master their environment. But the same searchlight used to delineate Western identity and norms of right conduct has cast a very long shadow over those people in other regions, people with sometimes different aspirations and values. By its very nature, this searchlight has been unable to illuminate its own blindspot, this huge shadow. A "heart of darkness" thus lies at the core of Western thinking about ethics and politics. Joseph Conrad's novel *Heart of Darkness* reveals how easy it was for those Western conquerors who did not and could not really see those they dominated to conclude that their victims should not exist. In this sense, the postscript of Conrad's conqueror Kurtz—"Exterminate the brutes"—might be seen as a succinct statement of colonial policy and colonial legacy.[6]

Asian leaders' insistence upon their distinctive Asian Values might thus be seen as a way of asserting the right of the peoples of the East to define themselves and their identity and thereby to shake off the yoke of Western oppression.[7] But the appeal to Asian Values has its own dark side. The problems with it are both formal and substantive. Viewed formally, the practice of opposing Asian to Western values is extremely polarizing. If the two systems of values are, as some claim, radically incommensurate,[8] the temptation will grow "to push away others as completely alien or to force one's own values onto the other."[9] In this polarizing atmosphere, it is unlikely that either group will initiate an effort to find common ground.[10]

Furthermore, the appeal to Asian Values works to strengthen the position of Asia's "strong men," serving as yet another weapon in the arsenal of fearmongers and tyrants. Talk of Asian Values spooks Westerners by raising the specter of a coming culture war with the booming nations (read: "threatening hordes") of the Far East.[11] It also diminishes the ability of the citizens in the Far East to hold their authoritarian rulers accountable. The supposition that there is a class of "Asian Values" to be articulated exclusively by Asians plays nicely into the hands of rulers who are only too happy to be able to make themselves immune to internal and external criticism by assuming the mantle of Defender of Unique Asian Values.

The more substantive issue centers on just what the content of these supposedly unique Asian Values are. It is said, for example, that Asians focus more on responsibilities while Westerners are obsessed with rights.[12] While it is true that neither Buddhism nor Confucianism conceptualizes human rights, the fact that they have not been mentioned in the past by these religions does not mean that the idea of rights in no way resonates with the peoples living in Asia. Confucius' injunction "Let the government not interfere, so that the people may thrive" sounds like a Western liberal value. Buddhism does not appear especially hostile to rights either. Given this religion's focus on human development, the Buddhist might very well accept that there are human rights but then try to connect them with human potentiality and "feelings and consciousness relative to injustice and inequality."[13] One can get some sense of what such a connection might look

like in the context of the Tibetan legal system. This legal system recognizes the individual's "right" to a fair trial, and the court employs procedures designed to insure a fair trial. The system differs from that of most Western countries in the way in which it thinks about punishment. In Tibet, the punishment is not designed to "fit the crime" so much as to suit the particular individual being punished. The punishment should be such as to bring the "criminal" to greater insight and a higher level of awareness.[14]

To summarize: The contrast between Asian and Western values is misleading because it seems very unlikely that there is some monolithic static set of Asian (or, for that matter, Western) values. Positing an incommensurable gap between the two prevents us from trying to ascertain where there might be common ground. While the assertion of Asian Values is often meant to gain a hearing for previously silenced voices, the polarizing strategy of opposing the values of the East to the West paradoxically may lead to a further silencing. After all, if these values are completely distinct and incommensurable, why bother listening to what the other has to say? There is nothing that can be learned from another whose values are so different from ours as to make it impossible for either of us to intelligibly compare our respective positions.

PART TWO: LEARNING FROM WATSUJI TETSURO AND CONFUCIUS

At one level, then, "Eastern ethics" has nothing to teach us about business ethics since such ethics may not even exist. If we take the expression "Eastern ethics" in a more limited sense, however, and think of it as applying to the ethics of particular individuals living within China or Japan or India, then business can learn something from Eastern ethics. While there may not be a single ethic of the Japanese or Chinese, individual thinkers such as Confucius and Watsuji Tetsuro have unquestionably both captured and influenced some dimensions of the ways in which their fellow citizens think about what is morally right. In the remainder of this paper, I draw upon these two thinkers to examine three larger themes:

1. the meaning of trust;
2. relations for life;
3. ethics beyond rights.

The Meaning of Trust

Since Watsuji speaks at length about trust, I will develop his idea of trust and show how it contrasts with some views dominant within the Anglo-American tradition. For Watsuji, human social relations are not grounded in trust. Rather trust is based in human being or *ningen sonzai*. Society cannot be the result of a voluntary decision by citizens to come together and to agree to show each other mutual good will. Trust exists because we are all always already related to each other in a variety of ways—as parents of children and children of parents; as spouses, clients, employees, supervisors, subordinates, etc. We move within these relations conforming to expectations we did not form. Even to deny these expectations is indirectly to confirm them. Over time such role expectations change as the result of individual rebellion, but they do not disappear. Another set of role expectations emerges to take the place of the prior set.

Trusting others is nothing other than living and acting within this social matrix. Sometimes people betray us, but betrayals do not destroy trust. There is no betrayal where there is no trust; and trust exists wherever there are human beings—i.e., activities in accordance with relations. In fact, most betrayals are parasitic upon trust. To take Watsuji's example: The pickpocket can operate only as long as people are not excessively guarded when shopping, going to movies or, more generally, moving within the public space. A theft does not destroy this trust. It might make the individual more cautious but that individual will still be trusting in most dimensions of his or her life. Our trust is never the result of some cost-benefit calculation. Nor is it something we repose in another on the strength of evidence. Anyone who is human trusts simply by virtue of being human.

Perhaps only among enemies at war has trust completely ceased to exist. When each side desires to exterminate the other, humanity is not present. Or maybe we should say it is present but in a very attenuated form. For even here there is a relation of sorts—the relation of enemy to enemy. To declare someone an enemy is to say he or she is not a friend. That means, though, that friendship is potentially applicable to the enemy in a way that it is not with respect to inanimate things. We do not go around saying of rocks or a bottle of distilled vinegar, "It is my enemy." So enemies have a relation and maybe even a modicum of trust.

This non-voluntaristic, non-contractarian, non-evidentiary notion of trust has several interesting implications for business practice: For example, trust is not something companies can or should market. Companies already have our trust, a point that gets driven home every time we read how easy the unscrupulous find it to con the rest of us. Instead of seeing themselves as winning our trust by compiling a good record of healthy products and safe working conditions, businesses should understand themselves as striving to be true to the trust they enjoy simply by virtue of being a human institution operating within the social matrix. Being true to this trust should be the guiding intention behind every action, not just an idea that comes into play when it is time to roll out a major marketing campaign or to negotiate with workers. There is no single moment when trust is reposed or withheld. It is always present as part of the structure of humanity. The issue is therefore less one of whether others will trust you than one of whether you will be true to human being.

Truth also takes on a different meaning within this scheme. Trust cannot be built up by speaking the truth—i.e., by making one's words and deeds correspond with the fact of the matter. Truth depends upon trust. A "true" friend is not one who gives us the facts. Rather true friends speak in the way our friendship with them merits. Similarly businesses will not earn our trust by pursuing a strategy of "truth in advertising." Instead businesspeople should speak in accordance with a consciousness of what it means to be a businessperson in society, a businessperson who is already trusted by customers, government officials, suppliers, etc. Truth should not emerge as the result of a strategic calculation but out of the businessperson's strong sense of himself or herself as a human being in that role which is but one among many.

Truth and trust have the same structure wherever they exist. Watsuji would thus agree in spirit with the powerful statement of Aaron Feuerstein, the CEO whose family rebuilt Malden Mills after a devastating fire: "God is one. There is no god of the family, god of the marketplace, god of the temple. God is one and is present everywhere." For Feuerstein, there never was a possibility of not rebuilding the family-owned business. He was a human being in a community of people who had built their lives around the mill. He thus spoke as a true CEO when he rejected out of hand suggestions that he rebuilt because doing so was a shrewd way of making money.

Relations Are for Life

Both Watsuji and Confucius reject the radical, atomistic understanding of human beings. To be human is always already to be in relation—

or, more precisely, in a matrix of inter-related highly determinate relations (e.g., parent-child; older-younger sibling; teacher-student; superior-subordinate, etc.). These relations are for life. Certain problems which plague Western thought simply do not arise in this alternative worldview. For example, if the person is an individual and if an individual is identified with the capacity for rational thought, then a comatose person suffering extensive brain damage may not be a person at all within this Western framework. This problem does not arise in a Watsujian or Confucian framework. The comatose daughter does not cease to be the daughter of the mother. She is and forever will be that mother's child. Should she die, she remains the mother's "dead daughter." Nor does the next daughter in line become the eldest daughter upon her sister's death. She, too, remains the second daughter for life.

Since relations are for life, the person of *jen* or humanity does not form new relations lightly. Friendships, for example, require both parties to show good will to each other as long as each is alive. The sense of obligation to the friend may extend beyond death. For example, the friend may feel it is necessary to help the child of a dead friend to get a college education. The Chinese were shocked and offended when Nixon declared himself a friend to China because America and China would each get something out of the relation.[15] This attitude of expediency is utterly foreign to the way the person of *jen* or person with a true heart (*makoto*) thinks about friendship. Showing good will, not getting advantage, is the mark of the true friend.

From the Watsujian and Confucian perspectives, commercial relations are longterm as well. An action or choice is not good simply because it has taken into account the interests of stockholders or many stakeholders. It goes without saying that the effect of one's actions on the larger social matrix of relations must always be considered. It is also necessary for the actor to consider the longterm effect of her actions on relations. Each generation of agents shows such regard; and that accounts for why many commercial relations in Japan and China (Taiwan, Hong Kong, etc.) go back many generations.

Businesses are not, therefore, selling products or marketing their reputation. They are establishing a relation or, in the catchy phrase of one modern author, developing a customer for life.[16] Customers in Japan historically have not been especially price-conscious;[17] they stick with those they know. Habits have changed somewhat as the Japanese travelled abroad and came to see how much more costly some items were in Japan than in America or Europe.[18] Yet customers still expect that those who sell them a product will stand behind that product for years and will prove solicitous in their service to the buyer. Some Japanese realtors will go into a home after the escrow has been closed and get the utilities turned on as part of the after-sales follow-up.[19] They understand the real relationship begins after the house has been purchased. Manufacturers will continue to buy from suppliers with whom they have done business in the past, even if these suppliers charge more than others. In China, too, people feel beholden to those who have helped them in the past. Favors are not accepted lightly because one will have to reciprocate.[20]

There are numerous problems with such a system. It is difficult to dump a distributor or supplier who fails to do a good job. These longterm relations may limit competition. Newcomers cannot simply buy marketshare by offering loss leaders in a system where customers remain exceptionally loyal to brandnames. On the other hand, there is an important lesson here for both businesspeople and business ethicists—namely, that business transactions do not occur in a void or in some separate discrete "economic" sphere completely cut off from the rest of social life. The

habits acquired in one sphere carry over into others. If we want our citizenry to know what it means to be a good parent and a true friend, then we need to think about the form and bases of our economic transactions as well. Encouraging people to respond only to price signals may develop a deeply-rooted worldview in which everything is valued using a standard of expediency alone.

Ethics Beyond Rights

A third important strand common to Watsuji and Confucius is their emphasis on what we owe to each other. It is tempting to say that their systems and, for that matter, the Japanese and Chinese cultures are duty-based while Western cultures are rights-based. This distinction, while nice and tidy, simplifies too much. If the ethics of the Japanese and Chinese have no idea of rights, they equally have no idea of duty. Duties are the correlatives of rights. There cannot be one without the other. Both duties and rights are enforceable claims. Citizens have the right to demand that elected officers fulfill their responsibilities— i.e., the duties of their office. If the officers fail to do so, the citizens have a right to impeach them, sue, vote them out of office, etc. But the duties Watsuji and Confucius are describing are not enforceable. Quite the contrary. As the noted Japanese legal theorist Kawashima Takeyoshi has observed, it is ethically "improper for the other party (beneficiary) of an obligation to demand or claim that the obligated person fulfill his obligation. An obligation is considered valueless, if, although it is fulfilled by the obligated person, he does not fulfill it in addition with a special friendliness or favor toward the other party.

"In other words, the actual value of social obligations depends upon the good will and favor of the obligated person, and there is no place for the existence of the notion of right. . . ."

So an obligation does not derive ethical value from the fact that a rational being would make this demand and want to enforce it. Whatever ethical worth it has comes from the agent's perception or intuitive understanding of her place in the whole of human relations. This understanding will lead her to act with *makoto* or a true-heartedness or *jen*—i.e., humanity. Acts of *makoto* or *jen* are ethically good. An act which honored another's "rights" but which was not done voluntarily or in the spirit of *jen* would not be ethically (or politically) good.

This point of view subordinates the law to moral considerations. Mere adherence to a statute (or, for that matter, a principle such as the categorical imperative) cannot be ethically good. Simple conformity does not exhibit *makoto* or *jen*. In addition, always obeying the law will lead one into a mechanical life. Laws by definition are general. They are not necessarily suited to the circumstances of the particular case or the specific relation. They may therefore be hostile to our true-hearted efforts to honor the requirements of particular human relations. It is better not to try to legislate too much. What laws do exist should be enforced in a spirit of equity or *jen*.

This more flexible approach can be dangerous. Those who enforce the law are given a tremendous amount of discretion. If the judges are people of *makoto*, then perhaps the decisions will prove just and appropriate. But such people are not always at the helm of the ship of state. If the judge hands down a bad decision, those affected by the decision have traditionally had few, if any, rights to which they can appeal in order to protest the decision.

The approach does have certain strengths, though, that are relevant to business practice. Managers and employees avoid asserting mutually incompatible rights. While there sometimes are strikes in Japan, these strikes usually occur after a settlement has been reached. They last for one day and are intended more as a PR device for making a statement than a mechanism of confrontation designed to force management's hand.[21] (Strikes also occur with some frequency in South Korea, a supposedly Confucian country. This difference may be due to the greater impact the rights-oriented United States has had on the Korean subcontinent where it has maintained a military presence since 1950; a presence on which the S. Koreans rely in order to preserve their democracy.)

Parties who are disagreeing are not so likely to get locked into a rigid position. Both sides must consider what it would mean to be true to the employee-manager relation. Doing so will almost certainly involve them in what Richard Nielsen has termed "double-loop" negotiations. In this form of negotiations, each side does not try to win and to enforce its will. Instead, they put their controlling values—the values behind their position—into play along with their demands. Each side has the opportunity to affect and mold the other side's values. The opportunity does not guarantee that these controlling values will be refined. But it at least opens the door to this possibility.

Finally, this more flexible approach changes what it means for a business to be socially responsible. In the West, we tend to say, "Business has a right to make a profit, but they must do so in a socially responsible way." This formulation makes it hard to assess social responsibility. How much profit does business have a right to make? And might not the largely unfettered pursuit by private institutions of maximum profit lead to the greatest social good? If so, then it would be better to just let business go its own way without interference by the government or any other social institution. In other words, having granted business the right to make a profit, the problem becomes one of fitting business back into society. The Watsujian and Confucian approaches, by contrast, treat business as just one of many institutions thoroughly embedded within the social matrix. It is not entitled to make absolute claims for itself. The question for the businessperson, as for every human being in the society, is: What is the good of the larger whole and how can I behave in such a way as to contribute to that whole? The first responsibility of an agent is to consider the whole. Only after having done so is the agent able to be true to the specific human relation in which he or she is operating.

On this second view, the business ethicist should be less concerned with whether multinational corporations or their local subsidiaries are honoring workers' rights to a safe environment or a living wage and more concerned with the larger questions of what contributions business is making to China or Japan. As Henry Rosemont, a Sinologist, has put it, we should be asking what a person of good will would wish for the Chinese at this point in their moral development (Rosemont). When we ask that question, we are driven to admit that it is not at all clear that the Chinese will be well-served if American and European countries sell them hundreds of thousands of cars. The Chinese already have severe pollution problems and do not have the road infrastructure to support a huge increase in automobile transportation. The loss of life may be huge just as it was in Nigeria when Western automobiles arrived before eye glasses. Focussing on the rights questions obscures these larger questions, questions which require Westerners to look at their own business practices and controlling values more closely instead of demonizing the Chinese or other developing countries in Asia.

CONCLUSION

Adopting the perspective of Watsuji or Confucius is certainly not a panacea for all that ails the West. However, taking this tradition seriously will help us to identify our own prejudices regarding business practice as well as to learn about some alternative conceptions of key business ideas such as trust. We may not want to accept these ideas but at least we will be in a better position to make an informed argument for why they should be rejected and to understand the criticisms some Chinese or Japanese businesspeople and philosophers may make regarding our own tradition. ◆ ◆ ◆

◆ Notes

1. APEC (Asia Pacific Economic Cooperation) is now the most important regional economic organization in the world, with its members constituting 53% of the world economy. Kiyohiko Fukushima, Book review of *Asia Pacific Fusion: Japan's Role in APEC* in *SAIS Review*, vol. 16, no. 2 (1996), pp. 205–207.

2. An internet search for the term "Asian values" yields over 400,000 hits as of February 25, 1997.

3. Herodotus, *The Persian Wars*, trans. A. D. Godley (Cambridge: Harvard University Press, 1975).

4. Xiaorong Li, "'Asian Values' and the Universality of Human Rights," Report from the Institute for Philosophy and Public Policy, vol. 16, no. 2, Spring 1996 at http://www.puaf.umd.edu/ipp/.

5. Edward Said, *Orientalism* (London: Routledge, Kegan and Paul, 1978). See also Koichi Iwabuchi, "Complicit Exoticism: Japan and Its Other" in *Continuum: The Australian Journal of Media & Culture*, vol. 8, no. 2 (1994) at http://kali.murdoch.edu.au/~continuum/8.2/Iwabuchi.html.

6. Lindqvist ends his book as follows: "Anywhere in the world where there exists a deeply concealed knowledge which, if brought out into the open, would make us conscious, splinter our world view and force us to question ourselves, you find the Heart of Darkness." Lindqvist quoted in Stein Tonnesson, "Orientalism, Occidentalism, and Knowing About Others," in *NIASnytt*, no. 2

(April, 1994) at http://nias.ku.dk./Nytt/Thematic/Orientalism/orientalism.html.

7. Amartya Sen suggests we think of Asian Values as whatever Asians would prefer if given the freedom to make their own choices. Sen quoted in Leslie Nurse, "Speaker Challenges Ideas of Asian Values" at http://www.cis.yale.edu/ydn/paper/9.28/9.28.95storyno.E.A.html.

8. This claim is enshrined in the 1993 Bangkok Declaration.

9. [Akio Kawato, "Beyond the Myth of Asian Values," first published in *Chuokoron*, December 1995 at http://ifrm.glocom.jp/DOC.]

10. Shinji Fukukawa, Chairman and CEO of DIHS, questions whether it is possible for Asia to share values with Europe and the United States: "The Western concept of respecting the notions of the public and a framework of systems may not be compatible with Asian ways of thinking centered on blood relations and connections developed through local contacts or professional contacts, as well as the respect for harmony. There is sufficient reason to believe that this could develop into conflicts between Asia, on the one hand, and Europe and the United States. . . ." Shinji Fukukawa, "The Need for Analysis on Values and Characteristics Shared by Asians" at http://www.dihs.co.jp/ACTIVITY/2FUKUKAWA_E.HTML. Fukukawa's claim is somewhat disingenuous given the huge amount of conflict already occurring *within* Asia. We are entitled to wonder about Asia's "respect for harmony" when we look at recent events. Even if some peoples of the East do share a high esteem for certain behaviors not considered especially praiseworthy in the West, major religious and economic differences contribute to substantial tensions in the Far East. One need only think of the border skirmishes involving North and South Korea, China's missile firings in the Taiwan strait and Taiwan's countering military maneuvers, the tension between Japan and South Korea regarding the Sea of Japan, the dispute between Thailand and Malaysia over fishing rights in the Gulf of Siam, and the ongoing war of words among China, Taiwan, Vietnam, and the Philippines concerning the oil-rich Spratly Islands.

11. [Thi Lam, "The Notion of 'Asian Values' Is a Myth" at http://www.viet.net/vietmag/507.] Fruin also refers to the "peril" posed by the Japanese and notes Americans' worries about Japanese economic strength. In 1990, up to 25% of Americans had unfriendly feelings toward the Japanese. W. Mark Fruin, *The Japanese Enterprise System* (Oxford: Clarendon Press, 1994), p. 1.

12. Stein Tonnesson, "Do Human Rights and Asian Values Go Together?" in *NIASnytt*, no. 4 (December 1996) at http://nias.ku.dk/Nytt/Thematic/human_rights/hasianvalk.html.

13. Kenneth Inada, "A Buddhist Response to the Nature of Human Rights," in *Journal of Buddhist Ethics* at http://www.gold.ac.uk/jbe/2/inada.1.html.

14. Rebecca Redwood French, *The Golden Yoke: The Legal Cosmology of Buddhist Tibet* (Ithaca, NY: Cornell University Press, 1995), pp. 318–319.

15. Huang Quanyu, Richard S. Andrulis, and Chen Tong, *A Guide to Successful Business Relations with the Chinese* (NY: The Haworth Press, 1994), pp. 119–120.

16. Carl Sewell and Paul B. Brown, *Customers for Life: How to Turn That One-Time Buyer into a Lifetime Customer* (NY: Doubleday Currency, 1990.

17. Boye Lafayette De Mente, *How to Do Business with the Japanese* (Lincolnwood, IL: NTC Publishing, 1994), p. 211.

18. Mente, p. 217.

19. Diana Rowland, *Japanese Business Etiquette* (NY: Warner Books, 1995), p. 112.

20. Chin-ning Chu, *The Asian Mind Game* (NY: Rawson Associates, 1991), p. 156.

21. Mente, p. 170.

Business Ethics in Islamic Context

Tanri Abeng

Business can be seen as an isolated activity with its own set of rules, or it can be seen as one social activity among many. The second view invites us to consider how beliefs may influence business dealings. Here we will look at some Islamic teachings to see how they could affect the way that people do business in Muslim cultures.

Abeng gives a personal speech about his feelings on business ethics in an Islamic context. He highlights a number of comments pertaining to business in the Koran and shows how they may influence business dealings. He concludes by promoting five habits that he feels are critical for a Muslim business leader.

THE ISLAMIC PERSPECTIVES

Business has always played a vital role in the economic and social life of all people throughout the ages. This is equally true, if not more so, of our contemporary world. As part and parcel of the contemporary world, Muslim cannot be an exception to this rule. Their religion (Islam) not only permits them, but also encourages them to do business. The prophet of Islam was himself a full-time businessman for a considerable period of time. However, contemporary Muslims find themselves confronted with serious dilemmas. Despite their active participation, they are not sure whether some of their business practices are valid or not. It is not the business per se that has confused them, but rather the brand new forms, institutions, methods and techniques of modern business.

Whether the problem is real or mere illusion, resulting perhaps from lack of knowledge, needs to be thoroughly investigated. The current dynamic business environment warrants the need for a clearly formulated theory of Islamic business ethics. Ideally, such a 'theory' should have the capability of serving as a touch-stone for ascertaining the validity of any business practices.

As a Muslim, I am convinced that rules and guidelines for all aspects of life, including business phenomena, are found in the Quran. I must confess, however, that my knowledge of Islamic sciences and the interpretation of the Quranic verses is less than marginal. I was fortunate to have met Dr. Alwi Shihab, professor in Islamic science and senior fellow at Harvard University, Center for the Study of World Religion.

There is no doubt, according to Dr. Shihab, about the fact that the legality of business is duly acknowledged by the Quran. The Quran has not stopped just at the pronouncement of its legality, but alluded to quite a number of explicit and implicit imperatives and prohibitions regarding business transactions. It also pointed out through unequivocal statements the importance of distribution of wealth in society. There as well as other relevant injunctions, would have to be taken into consideration in order to construct a 'theory' of business ethics based on an appropriate synthesis of all such injunctions.

Islam attaches utmost importance to all sort of productive work. Not only has the Quran elevated al-'Amal (productive work) to the level of a religious duty but it mentioned such a work consistently, in more than 50 verses, in conjunction with imaan (faith). The relationship between faith and work is similar to that of root and tree, one cannot exist without the other. The Quran, for instance, enjoins upon Muslims to resume their work after the congregational worship. Furthermore, it is human's duty to work harder and smarter (as khalifah or vicegerent on earth) in order to build this world and to utilize its natural resources in the best possible manner. Therefore, the Quran is very much against laziness and waste of time by either remaining idle or by engaging oneself in an unproductive activity.

Moreover, the Quran encourages humans to acquire skills and technology by calling it fadhl (grace) of God, and highly praises those who strive in order to earn for living. The ethics of Islam clearly counsels against begging, against being parasite living on the labors of others. The importance of business activity can also be seen from the Quranic extensive usage of business terminology. The Quran is not only replete with a variety of exhortations to the vocation of trade, but it encourages traders to undertake long trips and conduct business with the inhabitants of foreign lands. In fact, globalization of business and trade has already been envisaged over thousand years ago.

Besides its general appreciation for the vocation of business, the Quran often speaks about honesty and justice in trade. (See Quran 6:152; 17:35; 55:9). The Quran also presents Allah as the prototype of good conduct. The Muslims, therefore, are supposed to emulate Him throughout their lives, including, of course, their conduct in business. The attributes of Allah and the principles ordained by Him, as propounded by the Quran, cannot but influence both the thought and the behavior of the Muslim, molding them into a desired ethical shape. The knowledge of Allah's attribute and principles forms a vital prelude to the unique concept of business which the Quran has expounded.

Among others, the Quran calls for an equitable and fair distribution of wealth in the society. Besides its moral exhortations to al-infaq (voluntary charitable acts) and its condemnation of concentration and hoarding, the Quran has established, through its legal enactment, several institutions for the distribution of wealth; such as zakat (alms giving) and the law of inheritance. While the Quran seeks to eradicate absolute poverty (faqr) absolutely and ensures social security for every member of the society, the distributive system of the Quran eliminates the exploitative element from the realm of business. Thus it helps not only in maintaining the business activity on just and ethical lines, but also, in its growth and enhancement.

The approved business conduct in Islam is founded on two fundamental principles, namely freedom and justice. The Quran's emphasis on justice in general and maintenance of straight balance in particular is evident from its forceful and oft-repeated injunctions. The fundamental mission of all the prophets according to the Quran, was to keep the balance straight and to uphold justice. "The Quran commands Muslims to be fair even when dealing with those opposed to them," according to Hisham Altalib (Training Guide for Islamic Workers, 1992). And this is exactly stated, for example, in the Quran (4:135) commanding that "O you who believe! Stand out firmly for justice, as witnesses to Allah, even as against yourselves, or your parents or your kin, and whether it be against rich or poor, for Allah can protect both. . . ." See also the Quran 4:58 and 5:8.

Freedom in matters of business transactions envisages the right of owning property, the legality of trade, and the presence of mutual consent. Mutual consent, however, can exist only when there is volition, honesty and truthfulness overagainst coercion, fraud and lying. Nevertheless, constructive criticism should not be avoided;

and "the leader should strive," according to Altalib, . . . "to create an atmosphere of free thinking, healthy exchange of ideas, criticism, and mutual advice so that the followers feel very comfortable in discussing matters on interest to the group."

On the other hand, justice in matters of business transactions includes:

1. Fulfillment of promises (pacts and contracts — or verbal and written)
2. Exactness in weights and measures (specifications) in all business related items including work, wages and payment, and labor movement
3. Truthfulness, sincerity and honesty. While lying and cheating are condemned, the quality of truthfulness, sincerity and honesty is not only commended but commanded by the Quran (Quran 55:7–9 and 83:1–6)
4. Efficiency, i.e., jobs should be carried out without any lapse or omission, with best planning and to be the best of their efficiency and competency
5. Selection of merit. The Quranic standard of eligibility is the required merit and competency for the job (Quran 28:26)
6. Investigation and verification. They are essential because they constitute a prelude for the right and ethical conduct. The Quran commands to probe and verify any given statement or piece of information before making a decision or taking any action accordingly (Quran 17:36 and 49:6).

The Quran as well as the tradition of the Prophet Muhammad have prescribed certain manners and recommended certain others for the proper ethical conduct in business. Broadly speaking, such manners can be summarized under three headings:

1. Leniency. It constitutes the foundation and core of good manners. This quality of acts includes politeness, forgiveness, removal of hardship, and compensation
2. Service-motive. In all business activities, Muslim should intend, according to the Quran, to provide a needed service to his/her own community and the humanity at large
3. Consciousness of Allah. A Muslim is required to be mindful of Allah even when engrossed in business engagements. Business activity, therefore, must be compatible with the morality and the higher values prescribed by the Quran.

In summary, the moral laws of the Quran, including its business ethics, are not left totally to an individual's personal choice or discretion. The Quran has made it clear that the leaders (even the Prophet himself), should consult their companions. The Quran defines this as mutual consultation or shura (see the Quran 42:38 and 3:159).

Therefore, any business activity bereft of ethical content or when pursued an end in itself is condemned by the Quran (Quran 9:38; 30:7; 4:47; 42:20). Likewise, all business practices involve explicit or implicit harm and injustice to the contracting parties or to the public at large are disapproved by Islam. Muslims are exhorted to seek the felicity of the day of the hereafter (al-Akhiarh) through making a proper use of the bounties provided by Allah here on earth. Although the Quran has declared business as lawful, yet it is equally explicit in reminding the Muslims that their business engagements should not become a hindrance in the way of compliance with God's imperatives (Quran 24:37).

LEADERSHIP IN BUSINESS

The Prophet Muhammad told us that: "Every one of you is a shepherd and every one is responsible for what he is shepherd of" (as quoted by Altalib).

As a Muslim business leader, I try to manage on the premise that business exists and grows. So it must generate cash flow by making profits. One may ask how are the profits being made, and in the process whether or not the business should be ethical? . . . "To be ethical as a business because it may increase your profits is to do so for entirely the wrong reason. The ethical business must be ethical because it wants to be ethical." I tend to agree to this quotation. Business, after all, is people. The moral value of the individuals in business organization, and in particular the leadership which plays the crucial role in shaping corporate culture in turn dictates the behavior of the organization. . . .

[A] leader must have value system based on moral culture. This is where, I believe, the core influence of ethical conduct of any leader rests. The long term survival and growth of the business, in line with the approved business conduct in Islam, is founded on the principles of 'freedom' and 'justice.' Freedom which envisages, among others, the right of owning property, should be viewed in the context of organizational (business) long term objective to prosper and grow. In fact, the life of a business enterprise is manifested in its ability to accumulate assets or property. Assets, however, should not be limited to physical property such as building, equipment, monetary instruments, etc. but also—and in some instances more importantly—are capability, technological know-how and image which all together can be more valuable than all the physical assets combined.

The question is how does a business enterprise build up its assets base? This is where the second principle—justice—comes into the center stage. Based on the premise that successful business, in the long run, does not depend on the monolith structure seeking to maximize profits from each transaction (but a series of partnerships so arranged as to benefit all parties in the spirit of win-win situation), the moral value attached to the business conduct should, among others, be including but not limited to [fairness and a commitment to business integrity]. . . .

. . . More and more business leaders are faced with tough decisions. Management science alone, in its multiple disciplines, cannot cope up with the risk of making incorrect decisions. Judgment, therefore, plays increasingly important role in today's dynamic business environment. As a Muslim, however, I believe in Allah's final reward or punishment. But I have to do the right things, apply my accumulated knowledge and skill at hands—with honesty and sincerity with the conviction that final result is up to Him, and the One and the Only Almighty: Allah.

And for that, I agree with Dr. Histham Altalib that the five habits the Muslim leaders (including of course Muslim business leaders) should cultivate are:

1. Know where your time goes. Control it, rather than letting it control you, by making every second work.
2. Focus on concrete result. Concentrate on results rather than just the work itself. Look up from your work and look outward towards goals.
3. Build on strengths, not weaknesses. This includes not only your own, but those of other brothers/sisters. Acknowledge and accept your strengths and weaknesses and be able to accept the best in others without feeling that your position is threatened.
4. Concentrate on a few major areas where consistent hard work will produce outstanding results. Do this by setting and sticking to priorities.
5. Put your complete trust in Allah and aim high instead of limiting your goals to only the safe and easy things. As long as you are working for Him, be afraid of nothing. ◆ ◆ ◆

Guiding Principles of Jewish Business Ethics

Ronald M. Green

Would our business behavior change if we thought of it as an extension of our religious beliefs? Green gives an outline of six principles that would be obligatory for a "Torah-obedient" Jew. He uses the case of a school bus crash to illustrate the perspective that human life is sacred, which implies that we would have an affirmative duty to protect it whenever we could. He also suggests that Jewish tradition considers business activity and profit to be legitimate but at the same time stresses a strong obligation to go beyond the letter of the law to avoid misrepresentation and fraud. Although he recognizes that these principles are not universally binding, Green's article ought to make us question whether our business and religious lives are separable.

This discussion develops six of the most important guiding principles of classical Jewish business ethics and illustrates their application to a complex recent case of product liability. These principles are: (1) the legitimacy of business activity and profit; (2) the divine origin and ordination of wealth (and hence the limits and obligations of human ownership); (3) the preeminent position in decision making given to the protection and preservation (sanctity) of human life; (4) the protection of consumers from commercial harm; (5) the avoidance of fraud and misrepresentation in sales transactions; and (6) the moral requirement to go beyond the letter of the law. Although these Talmudic principles are clearly obligatory only for "Torah-obedient" Orthodox and Hasidic Jews, many Jews share a sensibility informed by them. Non-Jews, too, may be instructed by Jewish teachings about business ethics.

At 11 PM on Saturday May 14, 1988, 27 young people were killed on Interstate 71 when a church-owned school bus in which they were riding was hit by a pickup truck driven in the wrong direction by a 34-year-old man who was probably intoxicated. The pickup struck the school bus head on, causing the gas tank in the bus to rupture and catch fire. The 27 deaths were from smoke inhalation, the result of the fire. A number of other youngsters on the bus were injured. The pickup driver had one previous drunk-driving arrest and conviction. He survived the accident and was charged with 27 counts of murder. The driver of the bus, a church official, died in the collision.

At the time of the accident, the bus was headed back to Radcliffe, Kentucky, after an all-day excursion to Kings Island, an amusement park north of Cincinnati. The round trip distance from Radcliffe to Kings Island was 320 miles. The bus was typical of the nearly 350,000 school buses on the nation's roads. It was designed to carry students to and from schools, and not of the type commonly used by commercial passenger carriers for long distance, interstate travel. It had been manufactured early in 1977 by Ford Motor Company and Sheller Globe Corporation. Ford made the chassis and Sheller

Globe the body. The Meade County public schools owned the bus until 1987, when it was sold to the First Assembly of God in Radcliffe.

In April 1977, several months after the bus was manufactured, new federal regulations governing school bus safety went into effect. Among other things, they required that all school bus gasoline tanks be protected by a crash-resistant steel cage and that all fuel lines be of metal tubing rather than flexible hose. These regulations, however, applied only to buses manufactured after that date. In 1984 Congress passed the Motor Carrier Safety Act which imposed stricter design and performance standards on all private bus carriers, but at the time of the accident, the Department of Transportation had still not worked out the regulations needed to implement the act.

The bus's 60-gallon gasoline tank was located under the right side of the bus, just behind the main passenger entrance. It had been filled shortly before the accident. Following the collision, investigators found that the tank had been gashed in the front and pushed about two feet to the rear.

As the summer of 1988 began, it was clear that a long legal battle lay ahead to determine whether Ford or Sheller Globe, the only actors with pockets deep enough to make a difference, would bear financial responsibility for the damages caused by the accident.[1]

THE JEWISH TRADITION OF BUSINESS ETHICS

Hard cases for decision provide a useful "lens" to focus the distinctive teachings of a religious/ethical tradition. Because Jewish teaching about economic life and commercial activities was developed long before the large-scale manufacture of complex industrial products, there is no specific rabbinic opinion dealing with a case like that of the Kentucky school bus. Nevertheless,

Judaism has a long and rich history of reflection on issues in business ethics and business law. Of the 613 divine commandments identified by the Rabbis in the Bible, well over 100 deal with matters of economic life. The Talmud, Judaism's vast compendium of normative teaching, further develops these scriptural beginnings, as do subsequent codes of Jewish law (halakha), and collections of rabbinic opinions (responsa).

The vast majority of Jews today are not consciously familiar with this body of halakhic teaching. They enter as a direct influence on the business conduct only of those who identify themselves as "Torah-obedient," that is, members of the Orthodox and Ultraorthodox (or Hasidic) communities. Nevertheless, within this corpus of material one can find guiding principles that form a distinctive outlook on commercial life, some of which continue to influence Jewish culture as a whole. Even Reform, Conservative or Reconstructionist Jews, who usually shape their lives by contemporary secular ethical precepts and pay only occasional attention to the tradition, have been subtly influenced by some of these centuries-old teachings. In what follows I want to develop the most important of these principles and illustrate their application by applying them to the complex issues of responsibility raised by the school bus case.

GUIDING PRINCIPLES

1. The Legitimacy of Business Activity and Profit. It is important first to understand that Judaism permits and approves of business activity conducted within a framework of religious and ethical norms. There is no tradition in Judaism of asceticism or mistrust of material goods and commercial life, as has sometimes existed in Christianity. Classical Jewish teachers regarded economic activity as an indispensable aspect of worldly existence, and they recognized the importance and legitimacy of the profit motive. This is illustrated by a Talmudic teaching that prohibits one from engaging a physician who is free of charge (perhaps a relative of one's family) when complying with the biblical commandment to heal someone you have injured. Recognizing the power and legitimacy of financial incentives, the rabbis ruled that "a physician who heals for nothing is worth nothing."[2]

2. The Divine Origin and Ordination of Wealth. Nevertheless, just as strongly as they rejected asceticism, the rabbis also refused to accept the view that because commercial life is governed by its own internal dynamics that work to ensure optimal economic outcomes, it should be free of moral or legal regulation. The rabbis recognized the many ways that human greed and misconduct can corrupt the market system, and they identified human needs that cannot be met by market forces alone. As a result, they elaborated an extensive body of halakhic teaching that set limits on economic behavior. Since Jewish communities for most of their history functioned within other societies as self-governing legal entities, this body of teaching usually had the force of law.

Much of this rabbinic legislation lies outside the sphere of business ethics per se and pertains to the larger issue of social justice. The guiding principle here is the biblically-founded view that all wealth derives from and, in a sense, belongs to God, who apportions it to human beings as caretakers and stewards. The refrain, "The earth is the Lord's, and the fullness thereof" (Psalms 24:1) was taken literally by the Jewish tradition. . . . This way of thinking explains the biblical requirements for the distribution of the land's produce to the two landless groups: the priests and the poor. Later on, in rabbinic thinking, these biblical foundations led to an extensive body of Talmudic social welfare legislation that sought to put an economic "floor" under those not able to fend for themselves within the commercial sector: widows and orphans, the elderly and disabled, refugees from persecution, and those genuinely unable to find employment. . . .

Other Talmudic teachings set limits on competitive practices when these have the consequence of inordinately disadvantaging some members of the community. Although the free market was generally seen as an efficient and pragmatic mechanism, the rabbis were willing to impose a concept of just price and reasonable profit to protect consumers from exploitation. One expression of this was the Ona'ah requirement which imposed a limit of one sixth profit on the sale of vital commodities such as basic foodstuffs (chayei nefesh, literally "things on which life depends"). The rabbis derived this requirement from the biblical verse (Lev. 25:14) "When you sell to your neighbor or buy from your neighbor's hand you shall not oppress one another."[3] . . .

Finally, it is worth mentioning that the principle of the divine ownership and ordination of property has recently been applied by some commentators to the issue of business conduct as it affects the environment. The role of human beings as administrators and caretakers of the world was traditionally held to impose responsibilities on all of us to preserve and protect the natural environment.[4] Within rabbinic discussions this idea is allied with the teaching of Bal taschit, according to which individuals are not permitted to vandalize or destroy even their own property, because in doing so they eliminate a divinely intended source of value for others.[5]

3. The Sanctity of Human Life. Viewing all economic life within a framework of divine intentionality, the rabbis rejected the absolute autonomy of economic activity and elaborated a set of norms that set limits to the conduct of commercial activities. In this regard, no principle is more fundamental than the sanctity of human life and the primacy that Jewish ethics places on its protection and preservation. The rabbis not only prohibited activities that unnecessarily endangered human life, they were prepared to require persons to undertake a substantial degree of affirmative effort to prevent harm to others. These obligations are captured by the Pikuach nefesh and Lo ta'amod requirements.

Pikuach nefesh, literally the saving of a living soul, amounts to an interdict against any activity that puts someone's life or health in danger. This extends not just to others but to oneself. Hence, Pikuach nefesh forms the basis for rabbinic prohibitions on suicide or any activities that increase the danger to one's life. So seriously did the rabbis take this obligation that they permitted one to override any of the 613 commandments (except those against murder, idolatry, adultery and incest) if this is needed to prevent death or injury to a living person.[6]

The Lo ta'amod requirement was derived from the injunction in Leviticus 19:16, "You shall not stand idly by while your brother's blood is shed." Although usually applied to positive actions of assistance to others that helped prevent death, in some cases it was generalized into a requirement that one act to prevent even serious suffering. One of the most authoritative codes of Jewish law, Joseph Caro's 15th century Shulchan Arukh, describes this requirement:

> He who sees his neighbor drowning or being attacked by robbers or by wild animals and is able to save him himself, or to hire others to do so, and did not do so; or if he heard people plotting against his neighbor to do him harm or to inflict damage on him and did not inform his neighbor; or even one who is able to comfort his fellow man for his agony or sorrow and does not do so with words—whoever does all these and similar things is guilty of transgressing the biblical commandment "You shall not stand [idly by while your brother's blood is shed]" [Lev. 19:16].[7]

The rabbis did not hesitate to apply both these requirements to the sphere of property relations and commercial life. . . . In contemporary terms, both workplace and product safety regulations follow from this set of guiding principles. Recently, some scholars of Jewish ethics have also interpreted these concerns as reinforcing the environmental responsibility of business whenever polluting activities threaten human life or health.[8] It follows from Jewish principles that although workers and communities may tolerate a measure of environmental pollution if this is inseparable from needed economic activity, no one may impose or willingly accept pollution that represents a threat to life or health.

4. *Protecting Consumers from Harm.* The divine ordination of property and the importance Jewish teaching places on human life also lead to the conclusion that the principle of caveat emptor has a very qualified place in Jewish business ethics. Regardless of the opportunity for profit, one cannot sell even to a willing customer products that seriously harm or unnecessarily risk human life. Responsibility for products also extends beyond their time of sale.[9] This teaching is reinforced by a strong doctrine of implied warranty, which makes the seller responsible for the quality and safety of products even in the absence of written guarantees. The Talmudic teaching in this respect was that "the omission of the clause of guarantee by the seller is merely an error of the scribe."[10] The rabbis were realists, of course, and recognized that guarantees were not usually unlimited but varied with the nature and quality of the goods sold.

Beyond immediate threats to life, the rabbis generalized the seller's obligations to the customer by developing a category of proscribed behavior known as Lifnei ivver. This was based on the biblical injunction "You shall not put a stumbling block in the path of the blind" (Lev. 19:14). Lifnei ivver was originally understood to prohibit the giving of unwise business advice, but it was eventually extended to prohibit the sale of goods, which though legal, are physically or morally detrimental to the welfare of their buyer.[11] The rabbis interpreted Lifnei ivver as prohibiting the sale of guns to robbers or other violent individuals. . . . More recently, some rabbinic commentators have brought the requirements of Lifnei ivver and Pikuach nefesh to bear on questions raised by the sale and use of tobacco products.[12]

5. *Avoiding Fraud and Misrepresentation.* Judaism's rejection of the concept of "buyer beware" is further illustrated by its strong insistence on honesty in sales transactions. Fraud in sales practices was expressly prohibited by the Hin zedek imperative, the biblically imposed requirement to maintain "just balances, weights and measures" (Leviticus 19:36). This was taken to forbid lying in sales situations on the part of both sellers and buyers. Thus, a shopper was prohibited by the Hin zedek imperative from stating an intent to purchase an item merely to determine its price. . . .

Rabbinic teachings forbid not only active deception, but all forms of tacit misrepresentation and harmful failures to disclose. This was expressed in the requirement of Genevat da'at (literally the prohibition of the "stealing of another's mind"). In the Shulchan Arukh, Joseph Caro lists among the practices that violate Genevat da'at feeding a cow bran before selling her to make her look fat and sleek, painting old baskets to make them look new, or soaking meat in water to enhance its appearance.[13] In addition to prohibiting misrepresentations of this sort, Genevat da'at calls for active disclosure of relevant information whenever it is reasonable to suppose that nondisclosure would create a false impression. Again, the rabbis were realists. They applied this affirmative obligation more rigorously in retail situations, where buyers were presumed to lack expert knowledge about the goods or services involved, than they did in the context of wholesale transactions involving knowledgeable dealers.

6. *Going Beyond the Letter of the Law.* Finally, it is important to note that whatever the strict requirements of the law, Jewish teaching has a broad category of behavior known as Lifenim mi-shurat ha-din, literally the requirement that one conduct oneself beyond the strict letter of the law both as a claimant and defendant in matters of conflict. . . .

Since most of the requirements of Jewish religious ethics operated as enforced and actionable legal norms within the autonomous Jewish communities ruled by rabbinic courts of law (beth din), the category of Li-fenim mi-shurat ha-din describes behavior above and beyond the letter of the law. This involves at least two distinct categories of behavior. One includes recognizably supererogatory ethical behavior whose omission is not morally blameworthy but whose practice is commended (this is sometimes termed "saintly" conduct by Jewish sources). A second includes ethically appropriate behavior whose violation, though not legally punishable, is looked on askance and is thus regarded as subject to the disapproval of "Heaven." Using more familiar contemporary terms or concepts, this second category of Li-fenim mi-shurat ha-din points to the sphere of "business ethics" as opposed to business law. It is the normatively prescribed, though not legally enforceable, sphere of business conduct. In general, Li-fenim mi-shurat ha-din required greater punctiliousness in all commercial relationships, and took to higher levels the standards of honesty, avoidance of misrepresentation, and the protection of vulnerable consumers from harm.

THE SCHOOL BUS CASE IN JEWISH PERSPECTIVE

These principles by no means exhaust Jewish thinking about the ethical responsibilities of business. As I indicated, a substantial number of the commandments deal with economic matters, and these elicit an ever widening and never ending circle of Talmudic and rabbinic commentary. But these principles are basic to Jewish teaching and often form the first and last grounds of appeal in business decision making. Taken together, they also lead Jewish thinking to distinctive conclusions in some complex cases for decision, and their application to the case of the Kentucky school bus shows how this is so.

In terms of both American business law and some approaches to business ethics, many would argue that neither Ford nor Sheller Globe should have to bear legal responsibility for the damages caused by this accident. Although elements of American product liability law support the claim that manufacturers must be on watch for possible defects in their products and must strive to avoid harm even when existing standards permit sale of those products, there are also some legal and business theorists who argue that it is unfair and economically unwise to require individual firms to exceed legally established safety standards. These thinkers ask how manufacturers who must ethically exceed uniform legal standards can be expected to survive in a competitive environment where at least some less scrupulous competitors will exploit the situation to produce less costly products. Will not such requirements operate to penalize ethical business and promote the survival of the ethically "unfit"? Reasoning this way, those persuaded by Milton Friedman's well known article "The Social Responsibility of Business Is to Increase Its Profits" might make a strong argument that in this instance government bears the primary responsibility for the general welfare, that manufacturers should not be required to exceed existing norms, and that neither Ford nor Sheller Globe should be punished in any way, by civil or criminal penalties, for their conduct in this situation.

These conclusions might be reinforced by the ample moral blame that can be directed at others in this episode. Officials of the Meade County school district bear a large measure of responsibility for their failure to correct the deficiencies in the bus that became obvious following the enactment of more stringent safety requirements and during the district's long ownership of the vehicle. Sale of the bus to a church school with even fewer means to correct these problems was also culpable. The church's decision to use the bus for the kind of long-distance, high-speed transport for which it was not designed contributed to the tragedy. And of course, the criminal behavior of the driver of the pick-up was the immediate cause of the disaster. In ethical terms, this driver has the blood of these children on his hands. It can be argued that it is one further tragedy of this case that this individual lacks the means to pay any of the financial damages his conduct created. Nevertheless, this is not a reason for imposing the costs on Ford or Sheller Globe, however deep their pockets.

These conclusions are not unreasonable, although there are also competing lines of analysis available in U.S. business law and in the thinking of various business ethicists. What is noteworthy, however, is that Jewish thinking about business ethics seems to point in a markedly different direction, laying blame at the door of one or both of these manufacturers. We have seen, for example, how salient are the Pikuach Nefesh and Lo ta'amod requirements. Together these forbid any activity, in the commercial sphere or elsewhere, that unnecessarily risks human life, and they require active efforts to step in and prevent harm, even when it is caused by others.

There are obviously few aspects of school bus manufacture more critical than the protection of the fuel system and the prevention of fire, since this is one of the few ways that massive death or injury can occur in an accident. That stricter specifications went into effect in April 1977 suggests that Ford and/or Sheller Globe (whichever was responsible for the fuel system or final assembly) must have known about the debate surrounding this issue. Although one might understand that reasonable competitive considerations might have prevented them from introducing these innovations well before the law went into effect, or even that delays in implementation might have permitted the bus to leave their factory without the newer safeguards, there was clearly a period of time surrounding and following the bus's delivery when the manufacturers were aware that they had made a relatively unsafe product. Jewish teaching in the Pikuach nefesh and Lo ta'amod requirements seems to demand an active effort on their parts to see that the vehicle is recalled and its fuel system upgraded. Although a fair apportionment of costs suggests that the bus's new owners should pay the costs of this retrofit, under Jewish teaching the manufacturers would probably have to assume the expense of this program if this proved the only way of ensuring that the upgrade was done.

These conclusions are reinforced by Judaism's strong doctrine of implied warranty, and the doctrine of Lifnei ivver that prohibits the sale of goods, which though legal, are physically or morally detrimental to the welfare of their buyer. Although this doctrine was normally applied to products like guns or drugs whose existence is an invitation to misconduct in irresponsible hands, it seems to apply in this case as well. The core idea in Jewish thinking here is that others' irresponsible behavior does not exonerate those who sell a product reasonably subject to misuse. Thus, the undeniable responsibility of the church school in using this product in ways for which it was not intended does not free the manufacturers of blame. A product so poorly designed as to invite or accentuate injury when subject to reasonably expectable misuse certainly represents a modern exemplification of a "stumbling block in the path of the blind."

Jewish interdicts against fraud, misrepresentation, and failure to disclose in sales practices (the Hin zedek and Genevat da'at requirements) indicate that more was called for than was presumably forthcoming at every point in the sales history of this bus. Ford and/or Sheller Globe had, at a minimum, an obligation to inform Meade County officials of the impending changes in law and the options before them if they chose to purchase this already outdated vehicle. Later on, Meade County officials were required to highlight the relative deficiencies in this unit when they passed the bus on to the church. Jewish teaching's insistence on the seller's obligation to avoid activities that risk life indicates that neither the manufacturers nor school officials could acquit themselves of responsibility merely by exercising this duty to inform, however. They were also required to take active steps to prevent the reasonably foreseeable injury that use of this vehicle involved.

On a purely ethical plane, these conclusions are reinforced by the Li-fenim mi-shurat ha-din requirement. Even if it could be argued (as I think is not the case in religious Jewish law) that the manufacturers should go legally or financially unpunished in this episode, a sense of moral opprobrium would be attached by Jewish ethical thinking to behavior so violative of the requirement to protect and preserve human life. Using Jewish terms, their behavior might be subject to the "disapproval of Heaven."

CONCLUSION

Although this case discussion illustrates only some of the relevant principles of Jewish teaching, it gives us a glimpse into the distinctive attitudes and approaches of this tradition. At their best, religious ethical teachings instruct our secular moral sensibilities and point to higher levels of moral accomplishment. As this discussion suggests, I believe this is true with regard to the Jewish tradition of business ethics. If the principles outlined here were taken seriously, some of the most prevalent but questionable business practices current today would be disallowed. For example, in view of our knowledge about the addictive and harmful effects of tobacco, it is hard to believe that Jewish law would countenance the sale or export of these products. The same might be said of many other lines of trade (such as handguns, international arms sales, or the export of toxic wastes) that imperil human life. At the level of sales and advertising, classical Jewish teachings impose a level of honesty and disclosure considerably higher than current practice.

Today, these standards are clearly obligatory only for "Torah-obedient" Orthodox and Hasidic Jews. However most Jews, including those of Reform, Conservative, Reconstructionist or even entirely secular identity, share a sensibility informed by millennia of teaching and should find in these traditional norms a source of guidance and inspiration.

Non-Jews, too, may be instructed by Jewish teachings about business ethics. For one thing, there is the expectation of Jewish faith which holds that in at least the most fundamental matters touching on the protection of human life and the maintenance of civil order, we are all "children of Noah" and are held to a common moral-legal standard.[14] For another, throughout its history, Jewish faith has aspired to exemplify the highest moral standards and to convey these standards to other traditions of law and ethics. There is an enduring vision in this faith of Judaism as a "light to the nations" (Isaiah 49:6). The guiding principles we have looked at deserve to be understood and studied both by Jews and non-Jews as we seek to improve the ethical performance of business.

◆ Notes

1. This case is substantially based on Numan A. Williams and Howard M. Hammer's discussion of "The Case of the Kentucky School Bus," in *CPCU Journal* (December 1988), 196–206. Additional materials have been drawn from articles in *The New York Times* and *Wall Street Journal*, May 16, 17, 18 May and 5 and 9 July 1988.
2. Babylonian Talmud, Tractate Baba Kamma 85a.
3. For a discussion of rabbinic teachings with regard to just price and the limitation of competition, see Meir Tamari, *With All Your Possessions: Jewish Ethics and Economic Life* (New York: The Free Press, 1987), Ch. 5.
4. Midrash-Rabbah, Kohelet, 713.
5. Babylonian Talmud, Tractate Shabbat 105b.
6. Babylonian Talmud, Tractates Shabbat 150a; Yoma 84b.
7. Choshen Mishpat, Holkhot Shmirat Hanefesh, Section 425.
8. [Aaron Levine, *Economics and Jewish Law: Halakhic Perspectives* (New York: KTAV, 1987), p. 94.]
9. Babylonian Talmud, Tractate Baba Metzia 49b.
10. Babylonian Talmud, Tractate Baba Metzia 49b.
11. Levine, *Economics and Jewish Law*, pp. 8–9, 68; Tamari, *With All Your Possessions*, p. 47.
12. The evolving debate on this topic is apparent in the articles by Rabbi J. David Bleich, *Tradition* 14:4 (Summer 1977), 121–123 and *Tradition* 17:3 (Summer 1978), 140–142; and Fred Rosner, "Cigarette Smoking and Jewish Law," *Journal of Halachah and Contemporary Society* 4 (Fall 1982), 33–45.
13. Shulchan Arukh, Choshen Mishpat, Hilkhot G'neivah, section 358.
14. Babylonian Talmud, Tractate Sanhedrin 57a.

12

DOING BUSINESS ABROAD

Laws and moral standards vary country by country; some national regulations are more punitive to companies than others. If a firm does business in more than one country, it may have the option of selecting which standard should apply—the "home" rules or the "host" rules. Thus, if there are regulations in the United States that require extensive protective equipment to be supplied to workers who may be exposed to asbestos dust, the temptation may be to conform to the less restrictive and less costly local standards if a firm operates overseas.

Moreover, the local norms may put a multinational company at a competitive disadvantage if it maintains the rules that apply domestically. For example, if it is normal to bribe petty officials to expedite bureaucratic clearances in Asia, then refusing to do so on the grounds that the company does not sanction such behavior may lead to its products languishing on a loading dock while others' products are shipped expeditiously.

Multinational companies (MNCs) have come in for a great deal of criticism for taking advantage of lower standards overseas, which is sometimes viewed as exploiting poorer countries that have little negotiating leverage. MNCs may pay cents for services and labor that cost dollars in America. The moral issue here is whether there are threshold standards that should apply even if they are not demanded by the local laws. An apparel manufacturer might be able to get away with using child labor in the Third World, but we can always ask whether it should just because it could. Consumers have a role in these practices, too. For example, if purchasers demanded clothing with a "union made in the USA" label and were willing to pay a premium for it, then manufacturers would respond to the market. On the other hand, if customers are more interested in clothing that costs less than they are overseas conditions, they must bear some of the responsibility for the overseas practices.

America is unique in the world in legislating that companies avoid perceived corrupt practices overseas. The Foreign Corrupt Practices Act (FCPA) of 1977 requires U.S.-based companies to abide by domestic standards even if it puts them at a competitive disadvantage. The first reading by Jack Kaikati and his colleagues describes the history of the act and its subsequent amendment. They present some arguments in its defense—notably that American companies have benefited because they have a reputation for high moral standards and honest dealing.

These writers believe that with the growth of international business and trading organizations, the legislation could be a model for future transnational standards.

The reading by Thomas Donaldson directly confronts the home/host dilemma. His analysis is based on a strong notion of human rights. He believes there are some moral constants, such as consideration for worker health and safety, that should not be compromised for the sake of economic efficiency. At the same time, though, Donaldson thinks there are some valid cultural differences to which a company may adapt—hence the tension in values in his title. He is against what he terms "cultural imperialism": the notion that, independent of context, we have the right answer and should impose our values on others. The difficulty for managers arises when they try to distinguish practices that are different from those that are wrong. Donaldson thinks that corporate codes can provide useful guidance for overseas operations, but only if they are fairly specific.

A key feature of Donaldson's approach is a demand that managers employ what he calls "moral imagination." He describes this as the ability to think around a problem creatively without being biased to a solution that favors one side. In essence, this is the ability to try on the perspective of someone from another culture and see if there is some common ground. In many ways, it reflects the concepts used in win/win literature that suggest conflicts should be seen less as adversarial contests and more as opportunities for mutual problem solving. We should, however, recognize that this is not a case of "anything goes" for Donaldson: Every acceptable solution will have to respect what he contends are universal core values that cannot be compromised.

In Richard De George's reading we look at the way in which MNCs can impose their practices on a host country and the criticism that is leveled against them. He feels broad criticism is inappropriate and that we should look instead to specific cases. The argument that sweatshop workers are paid less than workers in the United States, for example, is practically meaningless if it does not compare equivalent industries and the relative cost of living. Like Donaldson, De George is not an absolutist but believes there are baseline standards and gray areas where standards may differ. One of his main concerns is what the duties of a MNC are when the host government lacks the background institutions required to provide monitoring or enforcement of threshold standards in areas such as security, health, and safety. If these foundations are absent, should the MNC intervene to create them, or if they are poorly implemented, should the MNC take over where the government leaves off? He looks in some depth at the case of the Bhopal gas leak. Bhopal is a city in India, roughly the size of Milwaukee. The U.S. multinational Union Carbide jointly developed a chemical plant near the center of the city but left operational control in the hands of the local managers. Poor maintenance and supervision led to a leak of deadly gas that killed between 3,000 and 6,000 people and left many others injured. De George uses the case to illustrate the problems of working where there are lax business norms. He emphasizes the point that the operation of a MNC does not absolve the host government of responsibility for establishing and enforcing business regulations.

But intervention overseas may be morally troubling. One person imposing her values on another may amount to a breach of autonomy, even if it is done with the best of intentions and even if the result is ultimately beneficial. Should we give the same respect to national sovereignty? This is especially difficult if we feel that our values are superior—for instance, if a MNC is working in a country run by a repressive military dictator. Before the state-sponsored racial discrimination system in South Africa known as apartheid was abandoned in 1990, companies struggled with how they should act. Some refused to do business there, while others believed that hope for progressive change lay in "constructive engagement"—the idea that you could exert some influence while doing business there but none if you merely shunned the country. Yet dealing with South Africa inevitably involved compromising some values. The Reverend Leon Sullivan came up with a set of principles outlining acceptable and unacceptable practices, and many companies publicly adopted them. A number of multinationals still publicly associate themselves with the principles as part of their corporate moral stance.

Patricia Werhane is concerned that if a multinational intervenes in the sovereignty of a nation, it may do so badly. Recall Milton Friedman's objections to social responsibility, where he points out that business executives have expertise in building profits—not politics or social engineering. There have been cases where corporations have ignored the local laws to the benefit of the general population, but there are also cases of concern, such as the United Fruit Company, which virtually ran parts of Central America in the 1950s with very mixed results. A corporation always has an incentive to maximize profits, whereas a political administration may have other priorities, and it is not clear that even the most benign intervention will be in a country's best interest. For instance, a company might think it a great service to provide free vaccinations or build roads, yet these actions may cause social unrest and destroy a traditional way of life in rural areas. Werhane suggests that intervention should be done very sparingly, and with great sensitivity, in order to preserve national sovereignty. This may mean that a company stands by while individual rights are quashed by a repressive government, or social conditions worsen, say, by lax pollution standards. She maintains this may be better overall than an imperialistic approach where we believe we know better than the indigenous leaders and run roughshod over the native culture. Werhane is not against assisting local agencies but feels that political direction needs to be set by the national authorities.

The readings are largely consistent. Yet we might consider the case of a young woman assigned by a multinational company to work in a society where women are not allowed to drive or be seen in public without a headscarf. The company will not allow her to take credit for her work in front of local clients although they reassure her that her work will be recognized and rewarded by U.S. standards. She feels uncomfortable in the society and discriminated against. Should the company not do business there, or should they avoid sending women? Perhaps the company should make a stand for social justice and actively promote and publicize their employment of women in professional positions. Further, it could actively lobby in the overseas political arena to get things changed. Our responses to this scenario are framed in large part by our understanding of core human values, the employer/employee relationship, and whether a company from overseas should intervene in national politics.

The Price of International Business Morality

Twenty Years under the Foreign Corrupt Practices Act

Jack G. Kaikati, George M. Sullivan, John M. Virgo,
T. R. Carr, and Katherine S. Virgo

The 1977 Foreign Corrupt Practices Act (FCPA) came into force largely in reaction to a number of high-profile cases, such as a U.S. airplane executive discovered carrying suitcases of money to his Japanese contacts. The Act was significantly amended in 1988. The authors describe the main provisions and changes. The FCPA holds American business to a domestic standard, a stricter standard than most other countries in the world. In contrast, many European countries allow companies to write off foreign bribes against their taxes. Also, the Act has not led to many prosecutions. The authors recognize that maintaining the standards of the FCPA may put American business at a competitive disadvantage but argue that it is an effective and useful piece of legislation that promotes moral behavior.

INTRODUCTION

Last year marked the 20th anniversary of the Foreign Corrupt Practices Act (FCPA) of 1977. The FCPA is the first and only statute prohibiting bribery and other corrupt business practices by U.S. citizens and companies conducting business overseas. The FCPA has been an important consideration for those planning to do business abroad. In reviewing the FCPA, it should be remembered why the 1977 Act was enacted. It was enacted with great fanfare and controversy. The Act is rooted in the Watergate scandal and the disclosure that, in the '70s, U.S. corporations engaged in widespread bribery of foreign government officials.

At the behest of Congress, the SEC conducted an investigation into American business practices abroad covering a period between 1974 and 1976. The SEC investigation culminated in an extensive report to Congress dealing with questionable payments to foreign officials (Securities and Exchange Commission, 1976). Over 400 corporations, including 117 of the top Fortune 500 admitted to making more than $300 million questionable or illegal payments. The scandals emanating from these revelations subsequently caused the resignation of many important foreign officials, especially in Japan, Italy, and the Netherlands. In response to discoveries of foreign corruption involving major U.S. corporations, Congress passed the FCPA which was signed by President Carter on December 20, 1977.

The objective of this paper is to provide an overview of the FCPA during the two decades of its existence. More specifically, the objectives of this paper are four-fold. First, the paper provides background information about the FCPA of 1977 and subsequent amendments in 1988. Second, the paper discusses the enforcement of the FCPA since its passage by examining the number of cases prosecuted under the FCPA and the respective penalties imposed. Third, the paper discusses the economic impact of the FCPA by addressing whether the FCPA places U.S. companies at a competitive disadvantage. The argument is that the FCPA is an insurmountable hurdle to U.S. companies attempting to do business in countries where corruption is a way of life and other foreign companies continue to pay bribes. Fourth, the paper provides public policy recommendations to expand the reach and scope of the FCPA. It covers efforts to criminalize bribery through multilateral organizations, such as the Organization for Economic Cooperation and Development (OECD), the World Trade Organization (WTO), and the Organization of American States (OAS). It also covers bilateral arrangements and efforts by non-governmental organizations such as Transparency International.

PROVISIONS AND SUBSEQUENT AMENDMENTS

The original 1977 FCPA had two sets of provisions designed to prevent corrupt payments: the accounting provisions and foreign payments provisions. The accounting provisions set forth strict accounting and record-keeping requirements.

More specifically, firms whose securities are registered with the Securities and Exchange Commission are required to keep detailed books, records and accounts that accurately reflect corporate payments and transactions. These firms are also required to institute and maintain internal accounting systems that would assure management's control over the company's assets. In essence, the accounting provisions are designed to prevent the concealment of foreign bribery. The foreign payments provisions, which are by far the better-known part of the FCPA, prohibit all American businesses and persons from making direct or indirect payments of bribes to foreign government officials in order to influence their official acts.

Since the FCPA was passed in 1977, it was subject to wide criticism for being overly burdensome and vague and that zealous compliance with its requirements reduced the ability of American corporations to compete effectively overseas. As a result of the discontent, several attempts have been made to amend it. Amendments were introduced in Congress in 1980, 1981, 1983, 1985, and 1987. The amendments passed by Congress in 1988 became part of the Omnibus Trade and Competitiveness Act of 1988, which was signed by President Reagan on August 23, 1988 (Fremantle and Katz, 1989).

The 1988 amendments made four significant changes in the 1977 FCPA, particularly in the foreign payments provisions. First, they altered the definition of "corrupt payments" by shifting the focus from the person to whom payment was made to the purpose for which the payment was made. The original FCPA permitted payments to government officials "whose duties are essentially ministerial or clerical." The 1988 amendments generally broadened the existing exception by permitting *any* payment to *any* foreign official if it was a "facilitating or expediting payment—the purpose of which was to expedite or to secure the performance of a routine governmental action." The statute defined "routine governmental action" in terms of a laundry list of petty bureaucratic tasks such as issuing permits and licenses and processing visas.

Second, the 1988 amendments deleted the "reason to know requirement." The original FCPA prohibited any payment to a third party "while knowing or having reason to know that all or a portion" of the payment would be used to bribe foreign officials. The 1988 amendments deleted "reason to know" and imposed liability for an illicit payment only if it was made with "knowledge" that all or a part of the payment would be used for bribery. What this means is that the "reason to know" standard with respect to payments to agents is being replaced by a standard that is much harder for a prosecutor to meet.

Third, the 1988 amendments added two affirmative defenses for U.S. companies thereby further enhancing the environment for bribing foreign officials and making prosecution of violations of the FCPA more difficult. The first affirmative defense is that the payment was lawful under the written laws and regulations of the foreign country. The second affirmative defense is that the payment was reasonable expenditure on behalf of a foreign official directly related to the promotion of products and services or the execution of a contract with a foreign government or agency.

Fourth, the so-called Eckhardt Amendment has been repealed. Under the Eckhardt Amendment, which was part of the original 1977 FCPA, an individual corporate employer or agent could be prosecuted for violating the foreign payments provisions only *after* the corporation had been found guilty of violating the FCPA. With the repeal of the Eckhardt Amendment, individual employees and agents are subject to criminal liability regardless of whether the corporation has been found guilty or even prosecuted. Thus, the

repeal of the Eckhardt Amendment opened the door for the "scapegoat" scenario. It would subject middle-level managers to prosecution but exempts senior-level executives who can show they have no knowledge of questionable payments. This change not only will create an adversarial working environment but also will require that employers involved in overseas transactions retain their own counsel where there is the potential for a violation of the FCPA.

Finally, in addition to modifying the FCPA requirements, the 1988 amendments increased the penalties for violation of the FCPA. The maximum corporate fine has been increased from $1 million to $2 million, while the maximum individual fine has been increased from $10,000 to $100,000. The possibility of imprisonment for up to five years remains unchanged. In order to maximize the effectiveness of the penalties, fines imposed on individuals may not be paid directly or indirectly by their companies. Therefore, companies are prevented from indemnifying their officers and employees against liability under the FCPA. The Department of Justice has primary responsibility for enforcing the antibribery provisions of the FCPA, while the Securities and Exchange Commission oversees compliance with the accounting and record-keeping provisions. . . .

ENFORCEMENT OF THE FCPA

The U.S. government has not enforced the FCPA aggressively for much of its history. Although the overall number of FCPA prosecutions has not been large, the Department of Justice has prosecuted a variety of schemes, companies, and individuals under the Act. Only about four dozen cases have been brought since the inception of the law. This averages less than three cases per year. While there are not many prosecutions under the FCPA, there have been several high profile cases in more than a dozen countries (Pendergast, 1995). . . .

. . . Illegal payments ranged from $22,000 to $9.9 million and represented varying percentages of up to 20 percent of the business obtained. In most cases, these illegal payments were paid into third-world country bank accounts.

Overall, seventeen companies have been charged under the FCPA. Typically corporate fines range from $10,000 to $3.45 million; however, in January 1995, Lockheed agreed to pay a record criminal fine of $21.8 million and entered a civil settlement for $3 million. Two Lockheed officials also pleaded guilty in connection with the violations, and one of them served a prison sentence. Additionally, thirty-three individuals have been charged under the FCPA. Individual fines ranged from $5,000 to $75,000. . . .

ECONOMIC IMPACT OF THE FCPA

Ever since the enactment of the FCPA in 1977, U.S. business executives have complained that enforced honesty was leaving them at a competitive disadvantage. Their European and Asian counterparts were not only beating them out of lucrative deals all over the world, but they were also deducting the bribes as business expenses. How much of this lost business was real and how much involved sour grapes, has never been clear.

There are two schools of thought pertaining to the economic impact of the FCPA. One school of thought tends to conclude that the FCPA has not hurt the competitive position of U.S. industry. Based on empirical data, one study (Graham, 1983) concluded that:

a. During the 1978–1980 period, the FCPA had no negative effect on export performance of American industry. No differences in U.S. markets shown were discovered in nations where the FCPA was reported to be

a trade disincentive both in terms of total trade with each country as well as for sales in individual product categories.

b. During the 1977 statute, U.S. trade with bribe-prone countries has actually outpaced our trade with non-bribe-prone ones.

The other school of thought believes that the FCPA is placing U.S. corporations at a competitive disadvantage in the international arena. For example, a report by the General Accounting Office in 1981 on the FCPA, documents the deterrent effect of the Act (Business Week, 1983). Recent studies and public proclamations from top U.S. officials tend to show that the FCPA is an impediment that has to be taken seriously. . . .

A study by a Harvard University economist confirms that the FCPA has weakened the competitive position of U.S. companies in the global marketplace (Hines, 1996). The study revealed that U.S. corporate direct investments and exports declined significantly in countries where corruption was prevalent in the five years after the FCPA was enacted. On the other hand, U.S. foreign competitors significantly increased their exports and direct investment in these "corrupt" countries during the same time period. Other studies have also concluded that the FCPA has had an adverse impact on foreign sales of U.S. companies (Greenberger 1995).

MAGNITUDE OF OVERSEAS BRIBERY

Some analysts suggest that bribery is so widespread in international business dealings that efforts to stamp it out will prove fruitless. The magnitude of overseas bribery and corruption is documented by multinational organizations. A study conducted by the International Monetary Fund (IMF) revealed that a direct (inverse) correlation exists between the level of corruption prevalent in a country and the level of investment as a percentage of Gross Domestic Product. For example, Singapore has a low level of corruption and high level of investment as a percentage of GDP; Thailand and Haiti both have a high level of corruption and relatively low level of investment (Gantz, 1997). The IMF estimates that half of the $300 billion external debt of the world's 15 most heavily indebted countries is being held in private accounts transferred to tax havens (*World Press Review*, 1996). A survey conducted by the World Bank of 3,600 companies in 69 countries revealed that 40 percent of firms paid bribes. The figure in industrial countries was 15 percent, and in the former Soviet Union it increased to 60 percent (Omestad 1997). Likewise, the London-based European Bank for Reconstruction and Development (EBRD), which encourages investments in the formerly Communist East bloc, has called Eastern Europe's bribe-seeking a "major deterrent" to foreign investment (Chaddock, 1996).

Consequently, some observers recommended that the FCPA be repealed or revised to allow U.S. firms to engage in the same practices (Kaikati and Label, 1980). This recommendation is adamantly rejected by U.S. government officials who are encouraged by the emerging global ethics revolution. Over the past several years, several national governments have been toppled, a number of top government officials and corporate executives have been sent to jail, and hundreds of politicians have been pushed out of their offices for ethical misconduct. It is encouraging to witness the revival of interest in moral values. Rather than softening the FCPA, the U.S. should continue to press other nations to deal more honestly.

MULTILATERAL ARRANGEMENTS

When Congress enacted the FCPA in 1977, it intended to encourage other nations to join the U.S. in combating corporate bribery by enacting similar laws. It was originally believed that such cooperation was necessary because unilateral action by the U.S. to halt overseas bribery would presumably put American corporations doing business abroad at a competitive disadvantage in the international arena.

There has been substantial criticism of the FCPA because, since its inception, there has been little movement toward the U.S. position nor has there been an agreement on an international agreement. The U.S. government has long sought international agreements criminalizing bribery of foreign officials by all capital-exporting countries. These attempts can be traced to a series of discussions under United Nations auspices that broke down in 1981. More recently, the U.S. has called for criminalizing bribery and adopting tough standards on government procurement through multilateral organizations such as the Paris-based group of two dozen industrialized nations, the Organization for Economic Cooperation and Development (OECD), the World Trade Organization (WTO), and the Organization of American States (OAS).

OECD

The 1988 amendments to the FCPA authorized the President to negotiate an international agreement with the member countries of the OECD to curb bribing foreign officials. The 1988 amendments required the President to submit a report to Congress outlining the steps that the Executive Branch, along with Congress, should take to eliminate competitive disadvantages to U.S. business interests. Should these negotiations fail, the President should outline legislative and other steps to be taken in furtherance of the objective. Thus far, however, these efforts have brought little progress.

There are policies in some OECD countries that actually serve to encourage bribery. In most

OECD countries, excluding the U.S., Britain, and Canada, bribery payments to foreign officials have been tax deductible as long as the recipient is identified by name. Laws are most lax in Belgium, Luxembourg, and Greece, which have not even required the recipient's name. At the behest of the U.S., western nations have pledged to make their first concerted effort to put an end to bribery in international projects.

The U.S. has repeatedly asked OECD countries to enact antibribery legislations since at least 1978. After years of lobbying by at least three administrations, the United States has finally signed a landmark accord on December 17, 1997. The agreement, negotiated among members of the OECD plus Argentina, Brazil, Bulgaria, Chile, and the Slovak Republic, is a major breakthrough for the United States. The inclusion of the five non-OECD members is significant mainly because they are large exporters in their own right and partially because it reaffirms their intent in playing by the rules of the developed world.

The treaty's central provisions would, for the first time, force countries to prosecute companies for paying bribes to foreign government officials. However, the treaty has three main loopholes. First, one obstacle to the convention was finding an acceptable definition for "foreign public official." Consequently, the treaty does not fully ban bribes to officials of political parties, as opposed to holders of public office. A second loophole is that the treaty does not force countries to revoke the tax-deductibility of bribes, which many European countries permit. The third loophole revolves around the fact that the treaty does not call for penalizing the bribe-takers—that is, the public officials.

In spite of these three loopholes, the treaty still represents an important breakthrough. The treaty will go into effect after five of the OECD's ten largest members have ratified it or, at the earliest, in early 1999. While the OECD has no supranational power to ensure compliance with the treaty, member countries are to monitor themselves and one another.

WTO

Unlike the OECD, the World Trade Organization (WTO) has the power to enforce agreements. The WTO is being pressed to promote stronger standards regarding greater openness and due process in government purchasing decisions. The U.S. had proposed that a rule outlawing bribery on government contracts should be placed on the agenda of the ministerial meeting of the WTO that was held in Singapore in December 1996. Some members of the Association of Southeast Asian Nations (ASEAN) issued a statement denouncing the U.S. proposal. Malaysian officials characterized the U.S. proposal as a tool for Western protectionism. Indonesian Trade and Industry Minister Tunky Ariwibowo said, "We do not have common standards on issues like corruption . . . Any effort to relate them to trade will be detrimental to the functioning of the WTO in the future" (*Wall Street Journal*, May 6, 1996).

While some ASEAN countries denounced the U.S. proposal to place corporate bribery on the WTO agenda, national campaigns to curb corruption are gaining ground in other Asian countries. Popular disgust over corruption scandals helped to end the 38-year single-party rule of Japan's Liberal Democrats in 1993. South Korea is also attempting to flush public corruption out of its system. Two former presidents and several corporate executives face corruption charges connected with a political slush fund that may have reached $1 billion. Indeed, the attempts by South Korea and Japan to curb corruption suggest that bribery and corruption is, in fact not an Asian value.

ORGANIZATION
OF AMERICAN STATES

At the behest of the U.S., the nations of Latin America negotiated an anticorruption convention through the Organization of American States (OAS). The Inter-American Convention Against Corruption agreement was adopted at a conference in Caracas in March 1996. Twenty-two OAS member nations have signed the agreement, including the U.S. This unprecedented convention obligates all signatories to the agreement to adopt laws on bribing foreign officials. Although it is much too soon to assess the potential effectiveness of this regional agreement, it goes much further than any other international agreement in seeking not only to make bribery of foreign officials a crime in [the] home country, but in encouraging local governments to deal more effectively with this problem.

FUNDING ORGANIZATIONS

Pressure from the U.S. is also mounting on funding organizations, such as the International Monetary Fund (IMF) and the World Bank, to police loans more thoroughly and to take action against companies and countries offering and receiving bribes. The IMF and the World Bank have toughened efforts to combat corruption. The IMF has agreed to press for bribery reforms in borrowing countries and has insisted that funds may be withheld from countries that refuse to cooperate. The World Bank's President, James Wolfensohn, has promised that if corruption is found in projects for which the Bank provides financing, the project will be cancelled. The World Bank would also bar any firm that offers a bribe from Bank-financed contracts indefinitely.

The new get-tough policy of the IMF and the World Bank is illustrated in the case of Kenya. In 1977 the IMF and the World Bank suspended $292 million in loans to Kenya until the African country cleaned up its act by stopping bribery and corruption.

BILATERAL ARRANGEMENTS

While the U.S. is currently stepping up multilateral arrangements to fight against bribery in international business, it has warned that it could impose sanctions against countries that allow the prevalent practice to continue. Should multilateral efforts to address the problem fail, the U.S. might use section 301 of the 1974 Trade Act against countries where bribes are an accepted way of doing business or that failed to prevent domestic companies from offering bribes to win contracts. Section 301 allows the United States to impose sanctions on countries that it unilaterally finds guilty of unfair trading practices. The Clinton Administration is consulting with Congress to ensure that bribery and corruption are included under the range of "trade barriers" to which the statute may be applied.

While this may be a viable proposal, it will probably spark strong criticism abroad. Countries that become the target of Section 301 action almost certainly would accuse the U.S. of violating the spirit of the World Trade Organization (WTO) which bars the use of unilateral sanctions in a trade dispute. The U.S. undoubtedly would argue that, because bribery and corruption currently fall outside the jurisdiction of the arbiter of international trade rules, unilateral action represents the only viable policy response to the problem. At the same time, though, proving that bribery affected the outcome of a given business deal could be notoriously difficult for the U.S. Some observers note that the definition of bribery is often fuzzy at best. For example, in much of Asia lavish gift giving is an accepted and common business practice. Target countries might find it relatively easy to portray themselves as the innocent victim of strong-arm tactics by the U.S., thereby giving them an advantage in the important public relations campaign that inevitably accompanies a trade dispute. It is doubtful that the U.S. proposal of imposing big unilateral sanctions on offenders is sustainable. . . .

CONCLUSION

If the war on overseas bribery and corruption were measured by new regulations on the international scene, 1996 and 1997 are perceived as banner years. The biggest problem is that the U.S.-led efforts dealt with the supply side of graft. The United States government must now focus on the demand side where government officials seek and accept bribes. More specifically, the U.S. government must now aggressively urge

countries to reform their government procurement practices. Greater transparency in government procurement will significantly increase opportunities for U.S. firms in the global procurement market, which is estimated to be worth more than $3 trillion. The U.S. must aggressively nudge more WTO members to adopt more open and transparent rules. There is a WTO agreement covering government procurement, but only 25 countries have signed it. In the meantime, it is the local citizens, who grow bolder with their wealth and, subsequently, force governments to clean up their game, but that takes time. In the meantime, where bureaucrats in developing countries are paid a pittance and wield power over profitable markets, the window for corruption is wide open. ◆ ◆ ◆

◆ References

'The Antibribery Act Splits Executives', *Business Week* (September 19, 1983), p. 16.

Chaddock, Gail Russell: 1996, 'More Trade Brings Graft to Light—and to Trial', *Christian Science Monitor* (January 10), 1 and 7.

'Corruption: U.S. Firms Handicapped', *Intelligence Newsletter* (March 21, 1996), p. 7.

Fremantle, Adam and Sherman Katz: 1989, 'The Foreign Corrupt Practices Act Amendments of 1988', *International Lawyer* **23**(3) (Fall), 755–767.

Gantz, David A.: 1997, 'The Foreign Corrupt Practices Act: Professional and Ethical Challenges for Lawyers', *Arizona Journal of International and Comparative Law* **14**(10) (Winter), 97–116.

Graham, John L.: 1983, 'Foreign Corrupt Practices Act: A Manager's Guide', *Columbia Journal of World Business* (Fall), 89–94.

Greenberger, Robert S.: 1995, 'Foreigners Use Bribes to Beat U.S. Rivals in Many Deals, New Report Concludes', *Wall Street Journal* (November 12).

Hines, James R. Jr.: September 1996, *Forbidden Payment: Foreign Bribery and American Business After 1977* (National Bureau of Economic Research, Working Paper 5266, Cambridge, Massachusetts).

Kaikati, Jack G. and Wayne A. Label: 1980, 'American Bribery Legislation: An Obstacle to International Marketing', *Journal of Marketing* **44**(4) (Fall), 38–43.

Omestad, Thomas: 1997, 'The Industrial World Takes Aim at Official Corruption', *US. News and World Report* (December 22).

Pendergast, William F: 1995, 'Foreign Corrupt Practices Act: An Overview of Almost Twenty Years of Foreign Bribery Prosecutions', *International Quarterly* **7**(2) (April), 187–217.

Securities and Exchange Commission: 1976, *Report on Questionable and Illegal Corporate Payments and Practices*, 94th Congress, 2nd Session (Government Printing Office).

'Is Corruption an Asian Value?', *Wall Street Journal* (May 6, 1996), p. A14.

'Nations United in Sleaze', *World Press Review*, Vol. **43**(1) (January 1996), pp. 18–19.

Values in Tension
Ethics Away from Home

Thomas Donaldson

Donaldson has been a pioneer in promoting awareness of ethical issues in international business. Here he balances considerations between the home country values and those of the host, especially in those tricky cases where there is a competitive advantage in following the host's values. Donaldson asserts that a corporation needs to base its actions on three principles: respect for core human values, respect for local traditions, and the belief that context matters when deciding what is right and wrong.

The key is working out which values are not subject to negotiation. Ought we to allow African workers to unload barrels of toxic chemicals without protective gear, even if they agree to it, for example? Donaldson says that some home values will apply, but many have to be framed with local conditions in mind. Later in the article he states that we should use "moral imagination" when we generate standards in these cases. When reading the article, it is worthwhile revisiting arguments dealing with ethical relativism in general.

WHEN IS DIFFERENT JUST DIFFERENT, AND WHEN IS DIFFERENT WRONG?

When we leave home and cross our nation's boundaries, moral clarity often blurs. Without a backdrop [of] shared attitudes, and without familiar laws and judicial procedures that define standards of ethical conduct, certainty is elusive. Should a company invest in a foreign Country where civil and political rights are violated? Should a company go along with a host country's discriminatory employment practices? If companies in developed countries shift facilities to developing nations that lack strict environmental and health regulations; if those companies choose to fill management and other top-level positions in a host nation with people from the home country, whose standards should prevail?

Even the best-informed, best-intentioned executives must rethink their assumptions about business practice in foreign settings. What works in a company's home country can fail in a country with different standards of ethical conduct. Such difficulties are unavoidable for businesspeople who live and work abroad.

But how can managers resolve the problems? What are the principles that can help them work through the maze of cultural differences and establish codes of conduct for globally ethical business practice? How can companies answer the toughest question in global business ethics: What happens when a host country's ethical standards seem lower than the home country's?

COMPETING ANSWERS

One answer is as old as philosophical discourse. According to cultural relativism, no culture's ethics are better than any other's; therefore there are no international rights and wrongs. If the people of Indonesia tolerate the bribery of their public officials, so what? Their attitude is no better or worse than that of people in Denmark or Singapore who refuse to offer or accept bribes. Likewise, if Belgians fail to find insider trading morally repugnant, who cares? Not enforcing insider-trading laws is no more or less ethical than enforcing such laws.

The cultural relativist's creed—When in Rome, do as the Romans do—is tempting, especially when failing to do as the locals do means forfeiting business opportunities. The inadequacy of cultural relativism, however, becomes apparent when the practices in question are more damaging than petty bribery or insider trading.

In the late 1980s, some European tanneries and pharmaceutical companies were looking for cheap waste-dumping sites. They approached virtually every country on Africa's west coast from Morocco to the Congo.

Nigeria agreed to take highly toxic polychlorinated biphenyls. Unprotected local workers, wearing thongs and shorts, unloaded barrels of PCBs and placed them near a residential area. Neither the residents nor the workers knew that the barrels contained toxic waste.

We may denounce governments that permit such abuses, but many countries are unable to police transnational corporations adequately even if they want to. And in many countries, the combination of ineffective enforcement and inadequate regulations leads to behavior by unscrupulous companies that is clearly wrong. A few years ago, for example, a group of investors became interested in restoring the SS *United States*, once a luxurious ocean liner. Before the actual restoration could begin, the ship had to be stripped of its asbestos lining. A bid from a U.S. company, based on U.S. standards for asbestos removal, priced the job at more than $100 million. A company in the Ukranian city of Sevastopol offered to do the work for less than $2 million. In October 1993, the ship was towed to Sevastopol.

A cultural relativist would have no problem with that outcome, but I do. A country has the right to establish its own health and safety regulations, but in the case described above, the standards and the terms of the contract could not possibly have protected workers in Sevastopol from known health risks. Even if the contract met Ukranian standards, ethical businesspeople must object. Cultural relativism is morally blind. There are fundamental values that cross cultures, and companies must uphold them. . . .

At the other end of the spectrum from cultural relativism is ethical imperialism, which directs people to do everywhere exactly as they do at home. Again, an understandably appealing approach but one that is clearly inadequate. Consider the large U.S. computer-products company that in 1993 introduced a course on sexual harassment in its Saudi Arabian facility. Under the banner of global consistency, instructors used the same approach to train Saudi Arabian managers that they had used with U.S. managers: the participants were asked to discuss a case in which a manager makes sexually explicit remarks to a new female employee over drinks in a bar. The instructors failed to consider how the exercise would work in a culture with strict conventions governing relationships between men and women. As a result, the training sessions were ludicrous. They baffled and offended the Saudi participants, and the message to avoid coercion and sexual discrimination was lost.

The theory behind ethical imperialism is absolutism, which is based on three problematic principles. Absolutists believe that there is a single list of truths, that they can be expressed only with one set of concepts, and that they call for exactly the same behavior around the world.

The first claim clashes with many people's belief that different cultural traditions must be respected. In some cultures, loyalty to a community—family, organization, or society—is the foundation of all ethical behavior. The Japanese, for example, define business ethics in terms of loyalty to their companies, their business networks, and their nation. Americans place a higher value on liberty than on loyalty; the U.S. tradition of rights emphasizes equality, fairness, and individual freedom. It is hard to conclude that truth lies on one side or the other, but an absolutist would have us select just one.

The second problem with absolutism is the presumption that people must express moral truth using only one set of concepts. For instance, some absolutists insist that the language of basic rights provides the framework for any discussion of ethics. That means, though, that entire cultural traditions must be ignored. The notion of a right evolved with the rise of democracy in post-Renaissance Europe and the United States, but the term is not found in either Confucian or Buddhist traditions. We all learn ethics in the context of our particular cultures, and the power in the principles is deeply tied to the way in which they are expressed. Internationally accepted lists of moral principles, such as the United Nations' Universal Declaration of Human Rights, draw on many cultural and religious traditions. As philosopher Michael Walzer has noted, "There is no Esperanto of global ethics."

The third problem with absolutism is the belief in a global standard of ethical behavior. Context must shape ethical practice. Very low wages, for example, may be considered unethical in rich, advanced countries, but developing nations may be acting ethically if they encourage investment and improve living standards by accepting low wages. Likewise, when people are malnourished or starving, a government may be wise to use more fertilizer in order to improve crop yields, even though that means settling for relatively high levels of thermal water pollution.

When cultures have different standards of ethical behavior—and different ways of handling unethical behavior—a company that takes an absolutist approach may find itself making a disastrous mistake. When a manager at a large U.S. specialty-products company in China caught an employee stealing, she followed the company's practice and turned the employee over to the provincial authorities, who executed him. Managers cannot operate in another culture without being aware of that culture's attitudes toward ethics.

If companies can neither adopt a host country's ethics nor extend the home country's standards, what is the answer? Even the traditional litmus test—What would people think of your actions if they were written up on the front page of the newspaper?—is an unreliable guide, for there is no international consensus on standards of business conduct.

BALANCING THE EXTREMES: THREE GUIDING PRINCIPLES

Companies must help managers distinguish between practices that are merely different and those that are wrong. For relativists, nothing is sacred and nothing is wrong. For absolutists, many things that are different are wrong. Neither extreme illuminates the real world of business decision making. The answer lies somewhere in between.

When it comes to shaping ethical behavior, companies must be guided by three principles.

- ◆ Respect for core human values, which determine the absolute moral threshold for all business activities.
- ◆ Respect for local traditions.
- ◆ The belief that context matters when deciding what is right and what is wrong.

Consider those principles in action. In Japan, people doing business together often exchange gifts—sometimes expensive ones—in keeping with long-standing Japanese tradition. When U.S. and European companies started doing a lot of business in Japan, many Western businesspeople thought that the practice of gift giving might be wrong rather than simply different. To them, accepting a gift felt like accepting a bribe. As Western companies have become more familiar with Japanese traditions, however, most have come to tolerate the practice and to set different limits on gift giving in Japan than they do elsewhere.

Respecting differences is a crucial ethical practice. Research shows that management ethics differ among cultures; respecting those differences means recognizing that some cultures have obvious weaknesses—as well as hidden strengths. Managers in Hong Kong, for example, have a higher tolerance for some forms of bribery than their Western counterparts, but they have a much lower tolerance for the failure to acknowledge a subordinate's work. In some parts of the Far East, stealing credit from a subordinate is nearly an unpardonable sin.

People often equate respect for local traditions with cultural relativism. That is incorrect. Some practices are clearly wrong. Union Carbide's tragic experience in Bhopal, India, provides one example. The company's executives seriously underestimated how much on-site management involvement was needed at the Bhopal plant to compensate for the country's poor infrastructure and regulatory capabilities. In the aftermath of the disastrous gas leak, the lesson is clear: companies using sophisticated technology in a developing country must evaluate that country's ability to oversee its safe use. Since the incident at Bhopal, Union Carbide has become a leader in advising companies on using hazardous technologies safely in developing countries. . . .

DEFINING THE ETHICAL THRESHOLD: CORE VALUES

Few ethical questions are easy for managers to answer. But there are some hard truths that must guide managers' actions, a set of what I call core

WHAT DO THESE VALUES HAVE IN COMMON?	
Non-Western	**Western**
Kyosei (Japanese) Living and working together for the common good.	Individual liberty
Dharma (Hindu) The fulfillment of inherited duty.	Egalitarianism
Santutthi (Buddhist) The importance of limited desires.	Political participation
Zakat (Muslim) The duty to give alms to the Muslim poor.	Human rights

human values, which define minimum ethical standards for all companies.[1] The right to good health and the right to economic advancement and an improved standard of living are two core human values. Another is what Westerners call the Golden Rule, which is recognizable in every major religious and ethical tradition around the world. In Book 15 of his Analects, for instance, Confucius counsels people to maintain reciprocity, or not to do to others what they do not want done to themselves.

Although no single list would satisfy every scholar, I believe it is possible to articulate three core values that incorporate the work of scores of theologians and philosophers around the world. To be broadly relevant, these values must include elements found in both Western and non-Western cultural and religious traditions. Consider the examples of values in the insert "What Do These Values Have in Common?"

At first glance, the values expressed in the two lists seem quite different. Nonetheless, in the spirit of what philosopher John Rawls calls overlapping consensus, one can see that the seem-ingly divergent values converge at key points. Despite important differences between Western and non-Western cultural and religious traditions, both express shared attitudes about what it means to be human. First, individuals must not treat others simply as tools; in other words, they must recognize a person's value as a human being. Next, individuals and communities must treat people in ways that respect people's basic rights. Finally, members of a community must work together to support and improve the institutions on which the community depends. I call those three values respect for human dignity, respect for basic rights, and good citizenship.

Those values must be the starting point for all companies as they formulate and evaluate standards of ethical conduct at home and abroad. But they are only a starting point. Companies need much more specific guidelines, and the first step to developing those is to translate the core human values into core values for business. What does it mean, for example, for a company to respect human dignity? How can a company be a good citizen?

I believe that companies can respect human dignity by creating and sustaining a corporate culture in which employees, customers, and suppliers are treated not as means to an end but as people whose intrinsic value must be acknowledged, and by producing safe products and services in a safe workplace. Companies can respect basic rights by acting in ways that support and protect the individual rights of employees, customers, and surrounding communities, and by avoiding relationships that violate human beings' rights to health, education, safety, and an adequate standard of living. And companies can be good citizens by supporting essential social institutions, such as the economic system and the education system, and by working with host governments and other organizations to protect the environment.

The core values establish a moral compass for business practice. They can help companies identify practices that are acceptable and those that are intolerable—even if the practices are compatible with a host country's norms and laws. Dumping pollutants near people's homes and accepting inadequate standards for handling hazardous materials are two examples of actions that violate core values.

Similarly, if employing children prevents them from receiving a basic education, the practice is intolerable. Lying about product specifications in the act of selling may not affect human lives directly, but it too is intolerable because it violates the trust that is needed to sustain a corporate culture in which customers are respected.

Sometimes it is not a company's actions but those of a supplier or customer that pose problems. Take the case of the Tan family, a large supplier for Levi Strauss. The Tans were allegedly forcing 1,200 Chinese and Filipino women to work 74 hours per week in guarded compounds on the Mariana Islands. In 1992, after repeated warnings to the Tans, Levi Strauss broke off business relations with them.

CREATING AN ETHICAL CORPORATE CULTURE

The core values for business that I have enumerated can help companies begin to exercise ethical judgment and think about how to operate ethically in foreign cultures, but they are not specific enough to guide managers through actual ethical dilemmas. Levi Strauss relied on a written code of conduct when figuring out how to deal with the Tan family. The company's Global Sourcing and Operating Guidelines, formerly called the Business Partner Terms of Engagement, state that Levi Strauss will "seek to identify and utilize business partners who aspire as individuals and in the conduct of all their businesses to a set of ethical standards not incompatible with our own." Whenever intolerable business situations arise, managers should be guided by precise statements that spell out the behavior and operating practices that the company demands.

Ninety percent of all Fortune 500 companies have codes of conduct, and 70% have statements of vision and values. In Europe and the Far East, the percentages are lower but are increasing rapidly. Does that mean that most companies have what they need? Hardly. Even though most large U.S. companies have both statements of values and codes of conduct, many might be better off if they didn't. Too many companies don't do anything with the documents; they simply paste them on the wall to impress employees, customers, suppliers, and the public. As a result, the senior managers who drafted the statements lose credibility by proclaiming values and not living up to them. Companies such as Johnson & Johnson, Levi Strauss, Motorola, Texas Instruments, and Lockheed Martin, however, do a great deal to make the words meaningful. Johnson & Johnson, for example, has become well known for its Credo Challenge sessions, in which managers discuss ethics in the context of their current business problems and are invited to criticize the company's credo and make suggestions for changes. The participants' ideas are passed on to the company's senior managers. Lockheed Martin has created an innovative site on the World Wide Web and on its local network that gives employees, customers, and suppliers access to the company's ethical code and the chance to voice complaints.

Codes of conduct must provide clear direction about ethical behavior when the temptation to behave unethically is strongest. The pronouncement in a code of conduct that bribery is unacceptable is useless unless accompanied by guidelines for gift giving, payments to get goods through customs, and "requests" from intermediaries who are hired to ask for bribes.

Motorola's values are stated very simply as "How we will always act: [with] constant respect for people [and] uncompromising integrity." The company's code of conduct, however, is explicit about actual business practice. With respect to bribery, for example, the code states that the "funds and assets of Motorola shall not be used, directly or indirectly, for illegal payments of any kind." It is unambiguous about what sort of payment is illegal: "the payment of a bribe to a public official or the kickback of funds to an employee of a customer. . . ." The code goes on to prescribe specific procedures for handling commissions to intermediaries, issuing sales invoices, and disclosing confidential information in a sales transaction—all situations in which employees might have an opportunity to accept or offer bribes.

Codes of conduct must be explicit to be useful, but they must also leave room for a manager to use his or her judgment in situations requiring cultural sensitivity. Host-country employees shouldn't be forced to adopt all home-country values and renounce their own. Again, Motorola's code is exemplary. First, it gives clear direction: "Employees of Motorola will respect the laws, customs, and traditions of each country in which they operate, but will, at the same time, engage in no course of conduct which, even if legal, customary, and accepted in any such country, could be deemed to be in violation of the accepted business ethics of Motorola or the laws of the United States relating to business ethics." After laying down such absolutes, Motorola's code then makes clear when individual judgment will be necessary. For example, employees may sometimes accept certain kinds of small gifts "in rare circumstances, where the refusal to accept a gift" would injure Motorola's "legitimate business interests." Under certain circumstances, such gifts "may be accepted so long as the gift inures to the benefit of Motorola" and not "to the benefit of the Motorola employee."

Striking the appropriate balance between providing clear direction and leaving room for individual judgment makes crafting corporate values statements and ethics codes one of the hardest tasks that executives confront. The words are only a start. A company's leaders need to refer often to their organization's credo and code and must themselves be credible, committed, and consistent. If senior managers act as though ethics don't matter, the rest of the company's employees won't think they do, either.

CONFLICTS OF DEVELOPMENT AND CONFLICTS OF TRADITION

Managers living and working abroad who are not prepared to grapple with moral ambiguity and tension should pack their bags and come home. The view that all business practices can be categorized as either ethical or unethical is too simple. As Einstein is reported to have said, "Things should be as simple as possible—but no simpler." Many business practices that are considered unethical in one setting may be ethical in another. Such activities are neither black nor white but exist in what Thomas Dunfee and I have called moral free space.[2] In this gray zone, there are no tight prescriptions for a company's behavior. Managers must chart their own courses—as long as they do not violate core human values.

Consider the following example. Some successful Indian companies offer employees the opportunity for one of their children to gain a job with the company once the child has completed a certain level in school. The companies honor this commitment even when other applicants are more qualified than an employee's child. The perk is extremely valuable in a country where jobs are hard to find, and it reflects the Indian culture's belief that the West has gone too far in allowing economic opportunities to break up families. Not surprisingly, the perk is among the most cherished by employees, but in most Western countries, it would be branded unacceptable nepotism. In the United States, for example, the ethical principle of equal opportunity holds that jobs should go to the applicants with the best qualifications. If a U.S. company made such promises to its employees, it would violate regulations established by the Equal Employment Opportunity Commission. Given this difference in ethical attitudes, how should U.S. managers react to Indian nepotism? Should they condemn the Indian companies, refusing to accept them as partners or suppliers until they agree to clean up their act?

Despite the obvious tension between nepotism and principles of equal opportunity, I cannot condemn the practice for Indians. In a country, such as India, that emphasizes clan and family relationships and has catastrophic levels of unemployment, the practice must be viewed in moral free space. The decision to allow a special perk for employees and their children is not necessarily wrong—at least for members of that country.

How can managers discover the limits of moral free space? That is, how can they learn to distinguish a value in tension with their own from one that is intolerable? Helping managers develop good ethical judgment requires companies to be clear about their core values and codes of conduct. But even the most explicit set of guidelines cannot always provide answers. That is especially true in the thorniest ethical dilemmas, in which the host country's ethical standards not only are different but also seem lower than the home country's. Managers must recognize that when countries have different ethical standards, there are two types of conflict that commonly arise. Each type requires its own line of reasoning.

In the first type of conflict, which I call a conflict of relative development, ethical standards conflict because of the countries' different levels of economic development. As mentioned before, developing countries may accept wage rates that seem inhumane to more advanced countries in order to attract investment. As economic conditions in a developing country improve, the incidence of that sort of conflict usually decreases. The second type of conflict is a conflict of cultural tradition. For example, Saudi Arabia, unlike most other countries, does not allow women to serve as corporate managers. Instead, women may work in only a few professions, such as education and health care. The prohibition stems from strongly held religious and cultural beliefs; any increase in the country's level of economic development, which is already quite high, is not likely to change the rules.

To resolve a conflict of relative development, a manager must ask the following question: Would the practice be acceptable at home if my country were in a similar stage of economic development? Consider the difference between wage and safety standards in the United States and in Angola, where citizens accept lower standards on both counts. If a U.S. oil company is hiring Angolans to work on an offshore Angolan oil rig, can the company pay them lower wages than it pays U.S. workers in the Gulf of Mexico? Reasonable people have to answer yes if the alternative for Angola is the loss of both the foreign investment and the jobs.

Consider, too, differences in regulatory environments. In the 1980s, the government of India fought hard to be able to import Ciba-Geigy's Entero Vioform, a drug known to be enormously effective in fighting dysentery but one that had been banned in the United States because some users experienced side effects. Although dysentery was not a big problem in the United States, in India, poor public [sanitation] was contributing to epidemic levels of the disease. Was it unethical to make the drug available in India after it had been banned in the United States? On the contrary, rational people should consider it unethical not to do so. Apply our test: Would the United States, at an earlier stage of development,

have used this drug despite its side effects? The answer is clearly yes.

But there are many instances when the answer to similar questions is no. Sometimes a host country's standards are inadequate at any level of economic development. If a country's pollution standards are so low that working on an oil rig would considerably increase a person's risk of developing cancer, foreign oil companies must refuse to do business there. Likewise, if the dangerous side effects of a drug treatment outweigh its benefits, managers should not accept health standards that ignore the risks.

When relative economic conditions do not drive tensions, there is a more objective test for resolving ethical problems. Managers should deem a practice permissible only if they can answer no to both of the following questions: Is it possible to conduct business successfully in the host country without undertaking the practice? and Is the practice a violation of a core human value? Japanese gift giving is a perfect example of a conflict of cultural tradition. Most experienced businesspeople, Japanese and non-Japanese alike, would agree that doing business in Japan would be virtually impossible without adopting the practice. Does gift giving violate a core human value? I cannot identify one that it violates. As a result, gift giving may be permissible for foreign companies in Japan even if it conflicts with ethical attitudes at home. In fact, that conclusion is widely accepted, even by companies such as Texas Instruments and IBM, which are outspoken against bribery.

Does it follow that all nonmonetary gifts are acceptable or that bribes are generally acceptable in countries where they are common? Not at all. . . . What makes the routine practice of gift giving acceptable in Japan are the limits in its scope and intention. When gift giving moves outside those limits, it soon collides with core human values. For example, when Carl Kotchian, president of Lockheed in the 1970s, carried suitcases full of cash to Japanese politicians, he went beyond the norms established by Japanese tradition. That incident galvanized opinion in the United States Congress and helped lead to passage of the Foreign Corrupt Practices Act. Likewise, Roh Tae Woo went beyond the norms established by Korean cultural tradition when he accepted $635.4 million in bribes as president of the Republic of Korea between 1988 and 1993.

GUIDELINES FOR ETHICAL LEADERSHIP

Learning to spot intolerable practices and to exercise good judgment when ethical conflicts arise requires practice. Creating a company culture that rewards ethical behavior is essential. The following guidelines for developing a global ethical perspective among managers can help.

Treat corporate values and formal standards of conduct as absolutes. Whatever ethical standards a company chooses, it cannot waver on its principles either at home or abroad. Consider what has become part of company lore at Motorola. Around 1950, a senior executive was negotiating with officials of a South American government on a $10 million sale that would have increased the company's annual net profits by nearly 25%. As the negotiations neared completion, however, the executive walked away from the deal because the officials were "asking for $1 million for 'fees.'" CEO Robert Galvin not only supported the executive's decision but also made it clear that Motorola would neither accept the sale on any terms nor do business with those government officials again. Retold over the decades, this story demonstrating Galvin's resolve has helped cement a culture of ethics for thousands of employees at Motorola.

Design and implement conditions of engagement for suppliers and customers. Will your company do business with any customer or supplier? What if a customer or supplier uses child labor? What if it has strong links with organized crime? What if it pressures your company to break a host country's laws? Such issues are best not left for spur-of-the-moment decisions. Some companies have realized that. Sears, for instance, has developed a policy of not contracting production to companies that use prison labor or infringe on workers' rights to health and safety. And BankAmerica has specified as a condition for many of its loans to developing countries that environmental standards and human rights must be observed.

Allow foreign business units to help formulate ethical standards and interpret ethical issues. The French pharmaceutical company Rhone-Poulenc Rorer has allowed foreign subsidiaries to augment lists of corporate ethical principles with their own suggestions. Texas Instruments has paid special attention to issues of international business ethics by creating the Global Business Practices Council, which is made up of managers from countries in which the company operates. With the overarching intent to create a "global ethics strategy, locally deployed," the council's mandate is to provide ethics education and create local processes that will help managers in the company's foreign business units resolve ethical conflicts.

In host countries, support efforts to decrease institutional corruption. Individual managers will not be able to wipe out corruption in a host country, no matter how many bribes they turn down. When a host country's tax system, import and export procedures, and procurement practices favor unethical players, companies must take action.

Many companies have begun to participate in reforming host-country institutions. General Electric, for example, has taken a strong stand in India, using the media to make repeated condemnations of bribery in business and government. General Electric and others have found, however, that a single company usually cannot drive out entrenched corruption. Transparency International, an organization based in Germany, has been effective in helping coalitions of companies, government officials, and others work to reform bribery-ridden bureaucracies in Russia, Bangladesh, and elsewhere.

Exercise moral imagination. Using moral imagination means resolving tensions responsibly and creatively. Coca-Cola, for instance, has consistently turned down requests for bribes from Egyptian officials but has managed to gain political support and public trust by sponsoring a project to plant fruit trees. And take the example of Levi Strauss, which discovered in the early 1990s that two of its suppliers in Bangladesh were employing children under the age of 14—a practice that violated the company's principles but was tolerated in Bangladesh. Forcing the suppliers to fire the children would not have ensured that the chil-

dren received an education, and it would have caused serious hardship for the families depending on the children's wages. In a creative arrangement, the suppliers agreed to pay the children's regular wages while they attended school and to offer each child a job at age 14. Levi Strauss, in turn, agreed to pay the children's tuition and provide books and uniforms. That arrangement allowed Levi Strauss to uphold its principles and provide long-term benefits to its host country.

Many people think of values as soft; to some they are usually unspoken. A South Seas island society uses the word *mokita*, which means, "the truth that everybody knows but nobody speaks." However difficult they are to articulate, values affect how we all behave. In a global business environment, values in tension are the rule rather than the exception. Without a company's commitment, statements of values and codes of ethics end up as empty platitudes that provide managers with no foundation for behaving ethically. Employees need and deserve more, and responsible members of the global business community can set examples for others to follow. The dark consequences of incidents such as Union Carbide's disaster in Bhopal remind us how high the stakes can be. ◆ ◆ ◆

◆ **Notes**

1. In other writings, Thomas W. Dunfee and I have used the term *hypernorm* instead of core human value.
2. Thomas Donaldson and Thomas W. Dunfee, "Toward a Unified Conception of Business Ethics: Integrative Social Contracts Theory," *Academy of Management Review*, April 1994; and "Integrative Social Contracts Theory: A Communitarian Conception of Economic Ethics," *Economics and Philosophy*, spring 1995.

Ethical Dilemmas for Multinational Enterprise
A Philosophical Overview

Richard T. De George

American companies have great leverage and negotiating power when it comes to setting the terms of working in a host country in the Third World; essentially, they have the ability to set their own standards.

De George tries to disentangle some of the criticisms leveled at U.S. multinational corporations by presenting a set of claims and norms that allow us to distinguish immoral actions. The discussion brings into play a number of our earlier readings and frames some of the main issues in international and global business ethics.

First World multinational corporations (MNCs) are both the hope of the Third World and the scourge of the Third World. The working out of this paradox poses moral dilemmas for many MNCs. I shall focus on some of the moral dilemmas that many American MNCs face.

Third World countries frequently seek to attract American multinationals for the jobs they provide and for the technological transfers they promise. Yet when American MNCs locate in Third World countries, many Americans condemn them for exploiting the resources and workers of the Third World. While MNCs are a means for improving the standard of living of the underdeveloped countries, MNCs are blamed for the poverty and starvation such countries suffer. Although MNCs provide jobs in the Third World, many criticize them for transferring these jobs from the United States. American MNCs usually pay at least as high wages as local industries, yet critics blame them for paying the workers in underdeveloped countries less than they pay American workers for comparable work.

When American MNCs pay higher than local wages, local companies criticize them for skimming off all the best workers and for creating an internal brain-drain. Multinationals are presently the most effective vehicle available for the development of the Third World. At the same time, critics complain that the MNCs are destroying the local cultures and substituting for them the tinsel of American life and the worst aspects of its culture. American MNCs seek to protect the interests of their shareholders by locating in an environment in which their enterprise will be safe from destruction by revolutions and confiscation by socialist regimes. When they do so, critics complain that the MNCs thrive in countries with strong, often right-wing, governments.[1]

The dilemmas the American MNCs face arise from conflicting demands made from opposing, often ideologically based, points of view. Not all of the demands that lead to these dilemmas are equally justifiable, nor are they all morally mandatory. We can separate the MNCs that behave immorally and reprehensibly from those that do not by clarifying the true moral responsibility of MNCs in the Third World. To help do so, I shall state and briefly defend five theses.

Thesis 1: Many of the moral dilemmas MNCs face are false dilemmas which arise from equating United States standards with morally necessary standards.

Many American critics argue that American multinationals should live up to and implement the same standards abroad that they do in the United States and that United States mandated norms should be followed.[2] This broad claim confuses morally necessary ways of conducting a firm with United States government regulations. The FDA sets high standards that may be admirable. But they are not necessarily morally required. OSHA specifies a large number of rules which in general have as their aim the protection of the worker. However, these should not be equated with morally mandatory rules. United States wages are the highest in the world. These also should not be thought to be the morally necessary norms for the whole world or for United States firms abroad. Morally mandatory standards that no corporation—United States or other—should violate, and moral minima below which no firm can morally go, should not be confused either with standards appropriate to the United States or with standards set by the United States government. Some of the dilemmas of United States multinationals come from critics making such false equations.

This is true with respect to drugs and FDA standards, with respect to hazardous occupations and OSHA standards, with respect to pay, with respect to internalizing the costs of externalities, and with respect to foreign corrupt practices. By using United States standards as moral standards, critics pose false dilemmas for American MNCs. These false dilemmas in turn obfuscate the real moral responsibilities of MNCs.

Thesis 2: Despite differences among nations in culture and values, which should be respected, there are moral norms that can be applied to multinationals.

I shall suggest seven moral guidelines that apply in general to any multinational operating in Third World countries and that can be used in morally evaluating the actions of MNCs. MNCs that respect these moral norms would escape the legitimate criticisms contained in the dilemmas they are said to face.

1. *MNCs should do no intentional direct harm.* This injunction is clearly not peculiar to multinational corporations. Yet it is a basic norm that can be usefully applied in evaluating the conduct of MNCs. Any company that does produce intentional direct harm clearly violates a basic moral norm.

2. *MNCs should produce more good than bad for the host country.* This is an implementation of a general utilitarian principle. But this norm restricts the extent of that principle by the corollary that, in general, more good will be done by helping those in most need, rather than by helping those in less need at the expense of those in greater need. Thus the utilitarian analysis in this case does not consider that more harm than good might justifiably be done to the host country if the harm is offset by greater benefits to others in developed countries. MNCs will do more good only if they help the host country more than they harm it.

3. *MNCs should contribute by their activities to the host country's development.* If the presence of an MNC does not help the host country's development, the MNC can be correctly charged with exploitation, or using the host country for its own purposes at the expense of the host country.

4. *MNCs should respect the human rights of its employees.* MNCs should do so whether or not local companies respect those rights. This injunction will preclude gross exploitation of workers, set minimum standards for pay, and prescribe minimum standards for health and safety measures.

5. *MNCs should pay their fair share of taxes.* Transfer pricing has as its aim taking advantage of different tax laws in different countries. To the extent that it involves deception, it is itself immoral. To the extent that it is engaged in to avoid legitimate taxes, it exploits the host country, and the MNC does not bear its fair share of the burden of operating in that country.

6. *To the extent that local culture does not violate moral norms, MNCs should respect the local culture and work with it, not against it.* MNCs cannot help but produce some changes in the cultures in which they operate. Yet, rather than simply transferring American ways into other lands, they can consider changes in operating procedures, plant planning, and the like, which take into account local needs and customs.

7. *MNCs should cooperate with the local government in the development and enforcement of just background institutions.* Instead of fighting a tax system that aims at appropriate redistribution of incomes, instead of preventing the organization of labor, and instead of resisting attempts at improving the health and safety standards of the host country, MNCs should be supportive of such measures.

Thesis 3: Wholesale attacks on multinationals are most often overgeneralizations. Valid moral evaluations can be best made by using the above moral criteria for context-and-corporation-specific studies and analysis.

Broadside claims, such that all multinationals exploit underdeveloped countries or destroy their culture, are too vague to determine their accuracy. United States multinationals have in the past engaged—and some continue to engage—in immoral practices. A case by case study is the fairest way to make moral assessments. Yet we can distinguish five types of business operations that raise very different sorts of moral issues: (1) banks and financial institutions; (2) agricultural enterprises; (3) drug companies and hazardous industries; (4) extractive industries; and (5) other manufacturing and service industries.

If we were to apply our seven general criteria in each type of case, we would see some of the differences among them. Financial institutions do not generally employ many people. Their function is to provide loans for various types of development. . . . Financial institutions can help and have helped development tremendously. Yet the servicing of debts that many Third World countries face condemns them to impoverishment for the foreseeable future. The role of financial institutions in this situation is crucial and raises special and difficult moral problems, if not dilemmas.

Agricultural enterprises face other demands. If agricultural multinationals buy the best lands and use them for export crops while insufficient arable land is left for the local population to grow enough to feed itself, then MNCs do more harm than good to the host country—a violation of one of the norms I suggested above.

Drug companies and dangerous industries pose different and special problems. I have suggested that FDA standards are not morally mandatory standards. This should not be taken to mean that drug companies are bound only by local laws, for the local laws may require less than morality requires in the way of supplying adequate information and of not producing intentional, direct harm.[3] The same type of observation applies to hazardous industries. While an asbestos company will probably not be morally required to take all the measures mandated by OSHA regulations, it cannot morally leave its workers completely unprotected.[4]

Extractive industries, such as mining, which remove minerals from a country, are correctly open to the charge of exploitation unless they can show that they do more good than harm to the host country and that they do not benefit only either themselves or a repressive elite in the host country.

Other manufacturing industries vary greatly, but as a group they have come in for sustained charges of exploitation of workers and the undermining of the host country's culture. The above guidelines can serve as a means of sifting the valid from the invalid charges.

Thesis 4: On the international level and on the national level in many Third World countries the lack of adequate just background institutions makes the use of clear moral norms all the more necessary.

American multinational corporations operating in Germany and Japan, and German and Japanese multinational corporations operating in the United States, pose no special moral problems. Nor do the operations of Brazilian multinational corporations in the United States or Germany. Yet First World multinationals operating in Third World countries have come in for serious and sustained moral criticism. Why?

A major reason is that in the Third World the First World's MNCs operate without the types of constraints and in societies that do not have the same kinds of redistributive mechanisms as in the developed countries. There is no special difficulty in United States multinationals operating in other First World countries because in general these countries *do* have appropriate background institutions.[5]

More and more Third World countries are developing controls on multinationals that insure the companies do more good for the country than harm.[6] Authoritarian regimes that care more for their own wealth than for the good of their people pose difficult moral conditions under which to operate. In such instances, the guidelines above may prove helpful.

Just as in the nations of the developed, industrial world the labor movement serves as a counter to the dominance of big business, consumerism serves as a watchdog on practices harmful to the consumer, and big government serves as a restraint on each of the vested interest groups, so international structures are necessary to provide the proper background constraints on international corporations.

The existence of MNCs is a step forward in the unification of mankind and in the formation of a global community. They provide the economic base and substructure on which true international cooperation can be built. Because of their special position and the special opportunities they enjoy, they have a special responsibility to promote the [cooperation] that only they are able to accomplish in the present world.

Just background institutions would preclude any company's gaining a competitive advantage by engaging in immoral practices. This suggests that MNCs have more to gain than to lose by helping formulate voluntary, UN (such as the code governing infant formulae),[7] and similar codes governing the conduct of all multinationals. A case can also be made that they have the moral obligation to do so.

Thesis 5: The moral burden of MNCs does not exonerate local governments from responsibility for what happens in and to their country. Since responsibility is linked to ownership, governments that insist on part or majority ownership incur part or majority responsibility.

The attempts by many underdeveloped countries to limit multinationals have shown that at least some governments have come to see that they can use multinationals to their own advantage. This may be done by restricting entry to those companies that produce only for local consumption, or that bring desired technology transfers with them. Some countries demand majority control and restrict the export of money from the country. Nonetheless, many MNCs have found it profitable to engage in production under the terms specified by the host country.

What host countries cannot expect is that they can demand control without accepting correlative responsibility. In general, majority control implies majority responsibility. An American MNC, such as Union Carbide, which had majority ownership of its Indian Bhopal plant, should have had primary control of the plant. Union Carbide, Inc. can be held liable for the damage the Bhopal plant caused because Union Carbide, Inc. did have majority ownership.[8] If Union Carbide did not have effective control, it is not relieved of its responsibility. If it could not exercise the control that its responsibility demanded, it should have withdrawn or sold off part of its holdings in that plant. If India had had majority ownership, then it would have had primary responsibility for the safe operation of the plant.

This is compatible with maintaining that if a company builds a hazardous plant, it has an obligation to make sure that the plant is safe and that those who run it are properly trained to run it safely. MNCs cannot simply transfer dangerous technologies without consideration of the people who will run them, the local culture, and similar factors. Unless MNCs can be reasonably sure that the plants they build will be run safely, they cannot morally build them. To do so would be to will intentional, direct harm.

The theses and guidelines that I have proposed are not a panacea. But they suggest how moral norms can be brought to bear on the dilemmas American multinationals face and they suggest ways out of apparent or false dilemmas. If MNCs observed those norms, they could properly avoid the moral sting of their critics' charges, even if their critics continued to level charges against them. ◆ ◆ ◆

◆ Notes

1. The literature attacking American MNCs is extensive. Many of the charges mentioned in this paper are found in Richard J. Barnet and Ronald E. Muller, *Global Reach: The Power of the Multinational Corporations*, New York: Simon & Schuster, 1974, and in Pierre Jalee, *The Pillage of the Third World*, translated from the French by Mary Klopper, New York and London: Modern Reader Paperbacks, 1968.

2. The position I advocate does not entail moral relativism, as my third thesis shows. The point is that although moral norms apply uniformly across cultures, U.S. standards are not the same as moral standards, should themselves be morally evaluated, and are relative to American conditions, standard of living, interests, and history.

3. For a fuller discussion of multinational drug companies see Richard T. De George, *Business Ethics*, 2nd ed., New York: Macmillan, 1986, pp. 363–367.

4. For a more detailed analysis of the morality of exporting hazardous industries, see my *Business Ethics*, 367–372.

5. This position is consistent with that developed by John Rawls in his *A Theory of Justice*, Cambridge, Mass.: Harvard University Press, 1971, even though Rawls does not extend his analysis to the international realm. The thesis does not deny that United States, German, or Japanese policies on

trade restrictions, tariff levels, and the like can be morally evaluated.

6. See, for example, Theodore H. Moran, "Multinational Corporations: A Survey of Ten Years' Evidence," Georgetown School of Foreign Service, 1984.

7. For a general discussion of UN codes, see Wolfgang Fikentscher, "United Nations Codes of Conduct: New Paths in International Law," The *American Journal of Comparative Law*, 30 (1980), pp. 577–604.

8. The official Indian Government report on the Bhopal tragedy has not yet appeared. The Union Carbide report was partially reprinted in the *New York Times*, March 21, 1985, p. 48. The major *New York Times* reports appeared on December 9, 1984, January 28, 30, and 31, and February 3, 1985.

The Moral Responsibility of Multinational Corporations to Be Socially Responsible

Patricia H. Werhane

Milton Friedman made the point that business managers are trained and rewarded for maximizing profits; they are not trained to be social workers or urban planners. His view is that managers should not become involved in corporate social responsibility at all. Other theorists, in contrast, suggest that corporations ought to be proactive in their social obligations, particularly when operating abroad; for example, companies operating in South Africa during the apartheid era invoked the Sullivan principles that outlined conditions for proper constructive intervention.

Werhane wants to strike a balance between appropriate intervention and none at all. Are our standards actually better, or are we being imperialistic to impose them on other countries? She notes potential problems stemming from paternalism, threats to national sovereignty, and lack of expertise on the part of the corporation. She concludes we do not have to do business abroad, but if we do "we should be very cautious in ascribing social responsibility to multinational corporations when they are guests in another country."

There is a truism that multinational corporations should act like good corporate citizens in the host countries and cities in which they operate. The grounds for this truism and the extent of these obligations have been variously spelled out by a number of thinkers. These arguments include the idea that multinational corporations have a moral imperative to be socially responsible, which has sometimes been traced to a notion of a social contract.[1] The claim is that multinationals have at least implicit contracts to act in a morally decent manner in the countries and cities that allow them to do business. In return for the opportunity to exist and do business, corporations, like ordinary citizens, have obligations to contribute to the well-being of the community.

Alternatively, one can develop an argument that as guests in a host country, corporations have special duties to their host—not merely to behave appropriately within the customs or mores of the host country, but, as guests, to contribute positively to the social well-being of that society.

One could also appeal to a rights theory or a sense of justice. As members of the universal community of human beings, and organizations created by human beings, multinationals have responsibilities to respect basic rights wherever they operate, including obligations not to cause harm, obligations to respect freedoms, and obligations to act in a fair manner in business dealings with all stakeholders. Such a position appears in at least two guises: (1) that a multinational has positive obligations to the community, or (2) that a multinational has merely negative obligations not to violate more rights nor to create more harm than the status quo.

Finally, one could take up a Friedmanesque argument that the social responsibility of managers of multinationals is to increase the return on investment for their shareholders within the restraints of law and custom. So, while a multinational's responsibility is to operate within the law and customs of the host country, it has no further commitments to social responsibility. Indeed, it would be a violation of fiduciary duties to extend such responsibilities.

All of these elaborations of the moral responsibility of multinationals to be socially responsi-

ble, are interesting and important, and they have been developed by a number of theoreticians. This chapter, however, deals with a more specific problem. If we assume that multinationals have some responsibilities to the communities in which they do business, what is the extent and limits of those responsibilities?

To begin, let's briefly discuss and eliminate from consideration the Friedmanesque position. This view has been labeled "Friedmanesque" because it is a caricature of Milton Friedman's much more carefully argued theses; but it is one that is often attributed to him. This position, in the exaggerated manner in which I have stated it, is problematic. If the primary responsibility of business is defined in terms of its fiduciary corporate-shareholder relationship, this conclusion allows corporations to do business under morally reprehensible conditions if those conditions do not violate law or custom of the host country. So one would have been allowed to practice apartheid in South Africa, to discriminate against women in the workplace in Saudi Arabia, not to hire Palestinian PLO members in Israel, use dangerous pesticides, or market untested drugs in some Third World countries where such products are not illegal. Moreover, such a thesis does not take into account the consideration of customers, employees, or citizens of the host community as stakeholders, except when the well-being of those stakeholders directly affects the interests of the shareholders. So a multinational could pollute, export a country's natural resources, discriminate against some of its citizens, hire away its skilled laborers and professionals to work in the corporate home country, or produce or sell dangerous products, [with] impunity. This is not to argue that multinationals do this or that these activities are all always morally wrong. But each of these examples raises ethical issues which, if one takes a Friedmanesque position seriously, are not to be counted as important considerations in corporate decision making except as they affect fiduciary interests or violate law or custom.

A less offensive but restrained approach to the question of multinational social responsibilities emanates from a negative rights theory. In brief, if each of us has the right to be left alone and the right not to be interfered with, so too, nations have such rights. No institution, then, has a right to disturb that communal equilibrium or create harm to the citizens of that community. Therefore, as long as a company does not contribute to the further harm of a community (e.g., by adding to pollution, by creating more joblessness, interfering with local politics, not honoring contracts, or disobeying the law), and as long as that company does not contribute to further violations of human rights, a multinational would be fulfilling its social obligation to that host community.

Now there is nothing wrong with this point of view. But we tend to ask more of multinationals than that they merely mind their own business and do not create further harms. The question then becomes, what is the "more" we demand?

Let us look at the question of social responsibility from a more positive perspective. Let us consider the argument that corporations, like good citizens, have positive social responsibilities to the long-term viability and well-being of the community in which they operate, as well as ordinary moral obligations to other stakeholders (e.g., employees, customers, suppliers, and shareholders). It will turn out that while one is often worried that a Friedmanesque or a negative rights approach does not demand enough of multinational business, one must be equally cautious in spelling out the nature and extent of positive social responsibilities. For if one demands too much of business, and if a corporation accedes to our demands, a corporation could become overly paternalistic or politically embroiled in community affairs, an involvement that is neither desirable for the corporation nor the host community. In

the case of multinationals, it shall be argued, its responsibility as a "guest" in another community is more restricted than that of a corporate citizen in its home country.

To attempt to answer the question, "What is the extent of moral responsibility of a multinational corporation to be socially responsible?," let us look at a concrete example—the famous Sullivan Principles and their adoption by American multinationals operating in South Africa. The original principles made six demands: (1) integrate workplace, washrooms, and eating facilities; (2) provide equal and fair employment practices for all employees; (3) provide equal pay for equal or comparable work; (4) expand training programs for non-whites; (5) increase non-whites in supervisory and managerial positions; and (6) improve housing and education opportunities for employees outside the workplace. These principles sound like motherhood and apple pie. But the sixth principle demands that companies be proactive in improving the quality of life outside the workplace. Generalized, this is the requirement that corporations contribute to the viability and long-term well-being of the community in which they operate.

The sixth Sullivan Principle appears to be a fairly straightforward, although sometimes costly, demand, but it could be quite complex indeed. For if a corporation, particularly a multinational, becomes involved in the social and educational affairs of a host community, a number of difficulties might crop up. For instance, while housing and education may be crucial for employee advancement (particularly in South Africa where, until recently, there were restrictions on where non-whites could live and go to school), one must take care that the extension of corporate obligations does not lead to the paternalism of nineteenth-century America where some companies, such as Pullman, provided housing, education, and a whole way of life for its employees, leading to a form of paternalism that affected the freedoms of these employees. In the past, this paternalism has been replicated by some multinationals such as the East India Company. So one would want to restrict the extent of multinational corporate social responsibility such that paternalistic outcomes would not reoccur.

Second, a corporation could find itself politically involved. In the 1978–1979 amplification of these principles, Reverend Sullivan asked corporations to "support the elimination of all . . . laws" that were discriminatory or prevented the free movement of non-whites. This was a demand that corporations not merely break South African law within the confines of their workplaces, but to become involved in revolutionary proactive schemes to change those laws. The requirement not only asked more of corporations than they are capable of executing, but it also threatened the value of national political sovereignty. This is not in any way an argument in favor of apartheid or a proposal that a corporation should accommodate that abhorrent phenomenon. Nor is it an argument that national sovereignty is an absolute value. But, as Michael Walzer has reminded us, interfering with that sovereignty should be undertaken only as a last resort, because it might be interpreted as suggesting that intervention should be the first instead of the last resort.[2] If nations are morally required to respect the sovereignty of each other, one should always question whether it is the role of corporations to conduct such interferences. It gives to a multinational, at least partially and temporarily, the status of nationhood, a status which is, at best, questionable.

Obviously, most corporations are not experts at political interference. This is neither their aim nor expertise and not their responsibility. Such demands not only ask too much of business—if corporations begin to engage in local politics of a host community they are overstepping their bounds as multinational visitors. If successful, a multinational company might succeed in interfering with the political balance of that community. One need only to be reminded of ITT's interactions with the Chilean government in the 1970s to worry about this possibility.

But, one might protest, if there are obvious social ills or political evils in a country in which one is doing business, if these violate rights of citizens of that country, and if a multinational has the power and resources to make improvements in these malaises, is it not its responsibility to do so? I would argue that even if totalitarianism, apartheid, human rights violations, lack of democratic procedures, etc. are evils, one surely questions the interference of one nation with another except on very stringent moral grounds. There is a presumption for national political sovereignty unless circumstances are most abhorrent. Nations are independent states. Because states are made up of individuals who have autonomous moral standing, they too have such standing. They are collectives made up of individuals whose autonomy is defined both by international law and by moral principle. Except in the most inhumane circumstances, a nation's right to self-determination ordinarily overrides most arguments for intervention.[3] If a nation seldom has justifiable moral grounds for intervening with the autonomy of another nation, a multinational corporation's positive moral responsibilities to become engaged in politics is an even more questionable conclusion. The fact that some multinationals have enormous capital resources, sometimes greater than the community in which they are conducting business, should give further strength to the arguments defending the presumption of sovereignty. The revised Sullivan Principles, then, ask too much of business, and its demands are antithetical both to the role of business and to political sovereignty.

Third, while one can make a viable argument that corporations have social responsibilities to their home communities, one must take care in transferring those same sorts of obligations to multinational settings. One is tempted to use a model such as the Lilly Corporation which has been very proactive in improving job opportunities and education in the Indiana community in which it is headquartered. Its aim has been to create a stable community, which is to its and the community's benefit.[4] But Lilly is a citizen of that community. There is a fine line, not merely between honoring one's obligations to a community and paternalism, but also between operating and interfering in a community where one is a guest rather than a citizen. To illustrate, the Minneapolis-based H. B. Fuller company opened a glue manufacturing plant in Honduras, offering industrialization and a number of new jobs to that poor country. Unfortunately, the glue they manufactured became the "drug of choice" for street children who sniffed it and became addicted.[5] What is Fuller's social responsibility in this case? If Fuller stops manufacturing glue in Honduras, there is a loss of over a thousand jobs in a country with little industry and high unemployment. But if it engages in drug education and social reform in that country, it may overstep the bounds of being a "good guest," because these activities can entail interferences with the autonomy and politics of Honduras.

What, then, is the extent of the moral responsibility of multinationals to be socially responsible in a host community? How can we hold multinationals responsible for what they do without extending that requirement to duties that involve them in political and social activities in which they have no skills and which extend their power beyond that of corporate guest status in a host country? First, and most obviously, as a guest, a multinational has a social responsibility to obey the laws and respect the customs of the host country, except where exceptions are allowed and encouraged. The American corpora-

tions who practiced the Sullivan Principles within their company in South Africa are evidence of such an exception, because the South African government condoned the practice. Even so, a number of American companies did not have South African offices rather than either obey or disobey South African apartheid laws. Second, it is not the duty nor the privilege of multinationals to engage in political activities in another country or community where they are not citizens. The revised Sullivan Principles asked too much of corporations.

Third, if a corporation cannot uphold its own policies and code of ethics while operating in a foreign context, it should not engage in activities there. For example, if a corporation has an explicit affirmative action policy, it should think carefully before operating in Saudi Arabia.

Fourth, if what a company is engaged in, produces, or affects causes more harms to the citizens of a host country than the present status quo in that country, the multinational has a responsibility either to stop that activity or redress these harms. So H. B. Fuller, for example, must engage in some set of proactive activities that either prevents further uses of its glue as a drug or withdraw from Honduras. However, when those proactive activities involve interference with social or political life of a host country, one should only engage in such activities with utmost restraint.

How can one test whether a particular set of activities is required, desirable, or questionable as part of multinational social responsibility? One might ask the following types of questions:

1. Is this set of activities necessary? "Necessity" is often defined as: what is needed in order to do business in that community. But, in order to justify engaging in allegedly socially responsible activities in a host country a multinational must consider two other provisos: is the activity necessary to redress harms created

by the company and/or necessary because of the laws and expectations of that community.[6] With these provisos one should ask:

2. Can this activity be carried out without interfering with the political sovereignty or social fabric of the host country?

3. If this activity requires social change, can it be carried out without violence to the acceptable practices of that society? Or, more simply put, would such a set of activities be acceptable to dispassionate rational persons in that society, even when performed by "foreigners?"

4. Does this set of activities pass a "publicity" test? That is, can these activities be made public in the community in which they are to occur? Can they be made public internationally?

5. Does this set of activities coincide with, or not contradict, common sense moral principles by which the corporation operates in its home country?

6. Can such activities be conducted in cooperation with the host country or are there conflicts?

The sixth question is very important, because often one can engage in socially responsible activities (or avoid morally questionable ones) by making agreements with the host country. In the case of H. B. Fuller, Fuller now works with the Honduras government in drug education; it assists but does not take the lead in such activities. It also packages the glue in larger, more expensive, containers not readily affordable by children.

In conclusion, one must be unduly cautious in ascribing social responsibilities to multinationals, particularly when they are guests in another community. Proactivism should be restrained. When there appear to be social ills that need redress, social ills caused by, or within the purview of, the multinational in question, social activism should be tempered by quiet cooperation with host country agencies. Problems of paternalism, political and social interference, threats to national sovereignty, and lack of expertise are such that the moral responsibility of a multinational corporation may be simply not to interfere or even not to do business in a particular milieu. This conclusion may seem too harsh both to those corporations wishing to expand economically and to those companies that take proactive social responsibility as part of doing business, but it is required of morally responsible corporations in transnational business environments. ◆ ◆ ◆

◆ Notes

1. See, for example, Thomas Donaldson, *Corporations and Morality* (Englewood Cliffs, N.J.: Prentice-Hall, 1982). Donaldson uses the social contract argument to support the claim that corporations have moral responsibilities. He does not focus so much on the social obligations of such institutions.

2. See Michael Walzer, *Just and Unjust Wars* (New York: Basic Books, 1977), especially Chapters 4 and 6 for an expansion of this argument.

3. *Id.*

4. See "Eli Lilly Corporation," in Robert D. Hay, Edmund R. Gray, and Paul H. Smith, eds., *Business and Society* (Cincinnati: South-Western Publishing, 1976) 17–24.

5. See Norman Bowie and Stephanie Lenway, "H. B. Fuller in Honduras," in Thomas Donaldson and Patricia Werhane, eds., *Ethical Issues in Business*, 4th Ed. (Englewood Cliffs, N.J.: Simon and Schuster, 1993).

6. See Thomas Donaldson, *The Ethics of International Business* (New York: Oxford Univ. Press, 1989), especially Chapter Six.

13

THE ETHICS
OF GLOBALIZATION

Globalization means more than doing business internationally. It refers to the increasing economic integration around the world caused by the expansion of capitalism. Globalization has been fueled by technological development in communication and banking, combined with liberalization of trade policies. Consider a student who has to buy an expensive book. It would be commonplace today for her to use the Internet to search for the best price worldwide and then pay for it online using a credit card. Quite possibly, she could buy it from abroad and have it shipped to her address for less than it would cost her in the local bookstore; it may be free of import duties, and she would not have to pay local sales tax. The power of globalization transforms the world into one open and free market dominated by the internal logic of capitalism.

Some economists hail the move toward globalization as beneficial because it expands the free movement of goods, labor, and capital and because they link these conditions with a promotion of economic growth and a rise in the overall standard of living. For instance, if a manufacturing firm relocates its operations from Pittsburgh

to China, it may cause distress in Pittsburgh, but on a worldwide scale this may not be a bad thing: The U.S. economy is transforming to a more service-oriented one, and China is experiencing economic development. Advocates claim that production is more efficient, and quality goods are available to all at a reasonable price as a result. U.S. workers who are afraid of losing their jobs and who demand that tariffs be imposed on cheap imported goods are misguided, according to this view, because open markets are universally beneficial, and trade barriers and protectionism hinder them. The workers would be wise to recognize the direction of global development and retrain for the jobs of the future.

Globalization transcends national borders and standards. Trade groups such as the World Trade Organization (WTO) may impose penalties on members who do not comply with its rulings, although it has no democratic mandate in any traditional political sense. The influence of these supernational groups may also run counter to policies instituted by individual states. Thus, if the United States were to impose protective tariffs on Chinese steel imports as a result of successful lobbying by activists in politically powerful states, the new national policy could be overridden by previous commitments the United States has made to the WTO.

The Thomas Friedman reading contrasts the homogenizing effects of globalization and the human need to feel rooted in traditions and nation-states. He believes that we can achieve balance (his book has a picture of a devout Jew at the Wailing Wall in Jerusalem holding a cell phone to the stones so a relative in France can pray near them). However, he argues that achieving balance requires a conscious effort by producers and consumers and demands that we reassess what is important to achieve a good life. It may mean restraining some of the forces that drive globalization. He believes that although states inevitably are going to participate in the new economic world order, they still should recognize and celebrate their history and tradition. He feels that humans have a very elemental need to feel connected to places and a cultural identity.

Pietra Rivoli's article addresses some concerns about so-called sweatshops. These are labor-intensive enterprises that typically employ low-skill or unskilled workers for minimal wages. There is no question that by Western standards sweatshops exploit workers: Unionization is discouraged, there are often health and safety issues, they may use child or captive labor, and generally workers are employed for long hours in miserable conditions. Rivoli does not minimize these features, but she believes that we should view them in historical context. She contends that since the beginning of the Industrial Revolution there has been a continuous cycle of developing industry; an area begins with unskilled workers in an unpleasant environment, but later the workers become more skilled and demand higher wages and more rights. At this point, the unskilled industry moves on, and other, more economically developed businesses come in. She uses the example of the textile industry, which was once centered in northern England (and notorious for its awful treatment of workers); then it moved successively to New England, the southern states, Japan, Asia, and now China.

If Rivoli is correct, then globalization may indeed represent industrial evolution that, in the long run, benefits countries that host unskilled labor. Some opponents feel that rather than creating a series of progressing economies around the world, globalization results in a constant "race to the bottom," where an operation is only supported up to the point that businesses can find cheaper resources elsewhere. So, for example, a shoe manufacturer would take its contract to whichever country offered the best deal, leading to a reverse auction where subcontractors compete against one another to work for less. Instead of leaving behind a more developed economy where more skilled workers can command higher wages, the host country is left exploited and abandoned.

The apparently unstoppable tide of international free markets has mobilized a large number of groups to protest around the world. Peter Singer traces some of the positions of various actors promoting and objecting to globalization. Some are worried about threats to national sovereignty, others about threats to workers' rights. Another powerful voice against globalization comes from environmentalists.

The assumption behind neoliberal views of globalization is that it will lead to universal prosperity. Recall, though, a couple of the conditions that are embedded in capitalism: It is dedicated to growth and transformation of raw resources into marketable goods. The concern here is that global growth depends on ever-expanding consumption rather than sustainability. For example, currently, a typical person in India causes 50 times less impact on the environment every year than a person in the United States, because the Indian drives less, eats less processed food, and indulges in less climate control among other things. But if Indian consumption patterns matched those of the United States, they would impose a significant burden on the environment. To illustrate the point, in rough terms, there are 200 million vehicles on U.S. roads and 24 million in China. At present, China emits about a third of the amount of carbon dioxide as America, but it claims to be the world's largest producer of automobiles. The growing use of cars is likely to have a deleterious effect on the world's pollution levels, but globalization assumes that growth is good and need not be restricted by any mechanism other than the market. Many environmentalists fear that the earth will be irreparably harmed unless growth is regulated.

Singer sees at least one potential benefit from globalization: He believes that the emergence of trade organizations with economic leverage might lead to social improvements. He considers the case of AIDS treatment in South Africa, where a quarter of the population is presently HIV positive. The United States defended the practice of drug companies refusing to license generic versions of their products overseas, which would have reduced the cost per patient from about $10,000 to $350 a year. In the face of international pressure and a change in U.S. policy, the drug companies relented.

Admittedly, the emergence of super-national authorities such as the World Trade Organization may pose a challenge to national sovereignty. However, Singer contends that this may not always be a bad thing, as the drug company example shows. Singer believes that globalization has the potential for bringing about benefits within sovereign states, and he also feels that globalization could become useful in restraining rogue states or repressive regimes. International trade groups could, for instance, impose economic sanctions that would be much more effective in bringing about political change than those imposed by individual nations.

At this point it would be worth revisiting John Stuart Mill's claim that paternalism is hardly ever justified and that intervention can lead to harm as well as good. If we are going to hand authority to a body that controls nations, we have an ethical duty to design appropriate safeguards that ensure its power could not be misused.

The Lexus and the Olive Tree

Thomas L. Friedman

The Lexus and the Olive Tree is a reflection on the contradictions in a world with a global economy that is still immersed in centuries-old allegiances to national identity and pride. Friedman visits a Lexus factory in Japan that constructs cars primarily by using robots that can do the job more exactly than humans; it is an enterprise dedicated to "modernizing, streamlining, and privatizing . . . to thrive in the system of globalization." At the same time, he reads about continuing conflict in the Middle East. He uses an olive tree growing on the banks of the river Jordan to symbolize "everything that roots us" in this world. He feels we have a deep desire to assert our national identity that works against the modernizing forces of the global economy. He concludes that the future of globalization as a system depends on how well nations can balance the demands of the Lexus and the olive tree.

Once you recognize that globalization is the international system that has replaced the Cold War system, is this all you need to know to explain world affairs today? Not quite. Globalization is what is new. And if the world were made of just microchips and markets, you could probably rely on globalization to explain almost everything. But, alas, the world is made of microchips and markets and men and women, with all their peculiar habits, traditions, longings and unpredictable aspirations. So world affairs today can only be explained as the interaction between what is as new as an Internet Web site and what is as old as a gnarled olive tree on the banks of the river Jordan. I first started thinking about this while riding on a train in Japan in May 1992, eating a sushi box dinner and traveling at 180 miles per hour.

I was in Tokyo on a reporting assignment and had arranged to visit the Lexus luxury car factory outside Toyota City, south of Tokyo. It was one of the most memorable tours I've ever taken. At that time, the factory was producing 300 Lexus sedans each day, made by 66 human beings and 310 robots. From what I could tell, the human beings were there mostly for quality control. Only a few of them were actually screwing in bolts or soldering parts together. The robots were doing all the work. There were even robotic trucks that hauled materials around the floor and could sense when a human was in their path and would "beep, beep, beep" at them to move. I was fascinated watching the robot that applied the rubber seal that held in place the front windshield of each Lexus. The robot arm would neatly paint the hot molten rubber in a perfect rectangle around the window. But what I liked most was that when it finished its application there was always a tiny drop of rubber left hanging from the tip of the robot's finger—like the drop of toothpaste that might be left at the top of the tube after you've squeezed it onto your toothbrush. At the Lexus factory, though, this robot arm would swing around in a wide loop until the tip met a tiny, almost invisible metal wire that would perfectly slice off that last small drop of hot black rubber—leaving nothing left over. I kept staring at this process, thinking to myself how much planning, design and technology it must have taken to get that robot arm to do its job and then swing around each time, at the precise angle, so that this little thumbnail-size wire could snip off the last drop of hot rubber for the robot to start clean on the next window. I was impressed.

After touring the factory, I went back to Toyota City and boarded the bullet train for the ride back to Tokyo. The bullet train is aptly named, for it has both the look and feel of a speeding bullet. As I nibbled away on one of those sushi dinner boxes you can buy in any Japanese train station, I was reading that day's *International Herald Tribune*, and a story caught my eye on the top right corner of page 3. It was about the daily State Department briefing. State Department spokeswoman Margaret D. Tutwiler had given a controversial interpretation of a 1948 United Nations resolution, relating to the right of return for Palestinian refugees to Israel. I don't remember all the details, but whatever her interpretation was, it had clearly agitated both the Arabs and the Israelis and sparked a furor in the Middle East, which this story was reporting.

So there I was speeding along at 180 miles an hour on the most modern train in the world, reading this story about the oldest corner of the world. And the thought occurred to me that these Japanese, whose Lexus factory I had just visited and whose train I was riding, were building the greatest luxury car in the world with robots. And over here, on the top of page 3 of the

Herald Tribune, the people with whom I had lived for so many years in Beirut and Jerusalem, whom I knew so well, were still fighting over who owned which olive tree. It struck me then that the Lexus and the olive tree were actually pretty good symbols of this post–Cold War era: half the world seemed to be emerging from the Cold War intent on building a better Lexus, dedicated to modernizing, streamlining and privatizing their economies in order to thrive in the system of globalization. And half of the world—sometimes half the same country, sometimes half the same person—was still caught up in the fight over who owns which olive tree.

Olive trees are important. They represent everything that roots us, anchors us, identifies us and locates us in this world—whether it be belonging to a family, a community, a tribe, a nation, a religion or, most of all, a place called home. Olive trees are what give us the warmth of family, the joy of individuality, the intimacy of personal rituals, the depth of private relationships, as well as the confidence and security to reach out and encounter others. We fight so intensely at times over our olive trees because, at their best, they provide the feelings of self-esteem and belonging that are as essential for human survival as food in the belly. Indeed, one reason that the nation-state will never disappear, even if it does weaken, is because it is the ultimate olive tree—the ultimate expression of whom we belong to—linguistically, geographically and historically. You cannot be a complete person alone. You can be a rich person alone. You can be a smart person alone. But you cannot be a complete person alone. For that you must be part of, and rooted in, an olive grove.

This truth was once beautifully conveyed by Rabbi Harold S. Kushner in his interpretation of a scene from Gabriel García Márquez's classic novel *One Hundred Years of Solitude*:

Márquez tells of a village where people were afflicted with a strange plague of forgetfulness, a kind of contagious amnesia. Starting with the oldest inhabitants and working its way through the population, the plague causes people to forget the names of even the most common everyday objects. One young man, still unaffected, tries to limit the damage by putting labels on everything. "This is a table," "This is a window," "This is a cow; it has to be milked every morning." And at the entrance to the town, on the main road, he puts up two large signs. One reads "The name of our village is Macondo," and the larger one reads "God exists." The message I get from that story is that we can, and probably will, forget most of what we have learned in life—the math, the history, the chemical formulas, the address and phone number of the first house we lived in when we got married—and all that forgetting will do us no harm. But if we forget whom we belong to, and if we forget that there is a God, something profoundly human in us will be lost.

But while olive trees are essential to our very being, an attachment to one's olive trees, when taken to excess, can lead us into forging identities, bonds and communities based on the exclusion of others. And when these obsessions really run amok, as with the Nazis in Germany, or the murderous Aum Shinrikyo cult in Japan or the Serbs in Yugoslavia, they lead to the extermination of others.

Conflicts between Serbs and Muslims, Jews and Palestinians, Armenians and Azeris over who owns which olive tree are so venomous precisely because they are about who will be at home and anchored in a local world and who will not be. Their underlying logic is: I must control this olive tree, because if the other controls it, not only will I be economically and politically under his thumb, but my whole sense of home will be lost. I'll never be able to take my shoes off and relax. Few things are more enraging to people

than to have their identity or their sense of home stripped away. They will die for it, kill for it, sing for it, write poetry for it and novelize about it. Because without a sense of home and belonging, life becomes barren and rootless. And life as a tumbleweed is no life at all.

So then what does the Lexus represent? It represents an equally fundamental, age-old human drive—the drive for sustenance, improvement, prosperity and modernization—as it is played out in today's globalization system. The Lexus represents all the burgeoning global markets, financial institutions and computer technologies with which we pursue higher living standards today.

Of course, for millions of people in developing countries, the quest for material improvement still involves walking to a well, subsisting on a dollar a day, plowing a field barefoot behind an ox or gathering wood and carrying it on their heads for five miles. These people still upload for a living, not download. But for millions of others in developed countries, this quest for material betterment and modernization is increasingly conducted in Nike shoes, shopping in integrated markets and using the new network technologies. The point is that while different people have different access to the new markets and technologies that characterize the globalization system, and derive highly unequal benefits from them, this doesn't change the fact that these markets and technologies are the defining economic tools of the day and everyone is either directly or indirectly affected by them.

The Lexus versus the olive tree, though, is just a modern version of a very old story—indeed one of the oldest stories in recorded history—the story of why Cain slew Abel. The Hebrew Bible says in Genesis: "Cain said to his brother Abel; And when they were in the field, Cain rose up against his brother Abel and killed him. Then the Lord said to Cain, 'Where is your brother Abel?' And he said, 'I do not know. Am I my brother's keeper?' And the Lord said, 'What have you done? The voice of your brother's blood is crying to me from the ground.'"

If you read this paragraph closely you notice that the Hebrew Bible never tells us what Cain actually said to Abel. The sentence reads that "Cain said to his brother Abel," and then it just stops. We are not privy to the conversation. What happened in the conversation between them that got Cain so angry that he would actually kill his brother Abel? My theology teacher, Rabbi Tzvi Marx, taught me that the rabbinic sages in Genesis Rabbah, one of the fundamental rabbinic commentaries on the Bible, give three basic explanations of what was said. One is that the two brothers were arguing about a woman—Eve. After all, there was only one woman on earth at the time, their mother, and they were arguing over which brother would get to marry her. They were arguing over sexual fulfillment and procreation. Another interpretation posits that Cain and Abel had basically divided up the world between them. Cain had all the real estate—or as the Bible says, "Cain became a tiller of the soil"—and Abel had all the movables and livestock—"Abel became a keeper of sheep." And according to this interpretation, Cain told Abel to get his sheep off Cain's property and this triggered a fight over territory that eventually ended with Cain slaying Abel in the heat of the argument. They were fighting over economic development and material fulfillment. The third interpretation is that the two brothers had already neatly divided everything in the world between them, except one critical thing that was still up for grabs: Where would the Temple be built that would reflect their particular religious and cultural identity? Each wanted to control that Temple and have it reflect his identity. Each wanted that Temple in his olive grove. They were fighting over the issue of identity, and

which of them would be the keeper of their family's source of legitimacy. So, the rabbis noted, all the basic elements of human motivation are potentially there in one story: the need for sexual intimacy, the need for sustenance and the need for a sense of identity and community. I will leave matters of sex for somebody else. This book is about the other two.

That's why I like to say that information arbitrage provides the lenses we need to look into today's world, but lenses alone are not enough. We also need to know what we are looking at and for. And what we are looking at and for is how the age-old quests for material betterment and for individual and communal identity—which go all the way back to Genesis—play themselves out in today's dominant international system of globalization. This is the drama of the Lexus and the olive tree.

In the Cold War system, the most likely threat to your olive tree was from another olive tree. It was from your neighbor coming over, violently digging up your olive tree and planting his in its place. That threat has not been eliminated today, but, for the moment, it has been diminished in many parts of the world. The biggest threat today to your olive tree is likely to come from the Lexus—from all the anonymous, transnational, homogenizing, standardizing market forces and technologies that make up today's globalizing economic system. There are some things about this system that can make the Lexus so overpowering it can overrun and overwhelm every olive tree in sight—breaking down communities, steamrolling environments and crowding out traditions—and this can produce a real olive tree backlash. But there are other things about this system that empower even the smallest, weakest political community to actually use the new technologies and markets to preserve their olive trees, their culture and identity. Traveling the world in recent years, again and again I have come on this simultaneous wrestling match, tug-of-war, balancing act between the Lexus and the olive tree.

The Lexus and olive tree wrestling with each other in the new system of globalization was reflected in Norway's 1994 referendum about whether or not to join the European Union. That should have been a slam dunk for Norwegians. After all, Norway is in Europe. It is a rich, developed country and it has a significant amount of intra-European trade. Joining the EU made all the economic sense in the world for Norway in a world of increasing globalization. But the referendum failed, because too many Norwegians felt joining the EU would mean uprooting too much of their own Norwegian identity and way of life, which, thanks to Norwegian North Sea oil (sold into a global economy), the Norwegians could still afford to preserve—without EU membership. Many Norwegians looked at the EU and said to themselves, "Now let me get this straight. I am supposed to take my Norwegian identity and deposit it into a Euro-Cuisinart, where it will be turned into Euromush by Eurobureaucrats paid in Eurodollars at the Euro-Parliament in the Eurocapital covered by Eurojournalists? Hey, no, thanks. I'd rather be Sten from Norway. I'd rather cling to my own unique olive tree identity and be a little less efficient economically."

The olive tree backlashing against the Lexus is the August 1999 story from France, by *The Washington Post*'s Anne Swardson, about Philippe Folliot, the mayor of the southwestern French village of St. Pierre-de-Trivisy—population 610. Folliot and the St. Pierre-de-Trivisy town council slapped a 100-percent tax on bottles of Coca-Cola sold at the town's camp ground, in retaliation for a tariff that the United States had slapped on Roquefort cheese, which is produced only in the southwestern French region around St. Pierre-de-Trivisy. As he applied some Roquefort to a piece of crusty bread, Folliot told Swardson, "Roquefort is made from the milk of only one breed of sheep, it is made in only one place in France, and it is made in only one special way. It is the opposite of globalization. Coca-Cola you can buy anywhere in the world and it is exactly the same. [Coke] is a symbol of the American multinational that wants to uniformize taste all over the planet. That's what we are against."

The Lexus and the olive tree in a healthy balance was the story related to me by Glenn Prickett, a senior vice president at the environmental group Conservation International, about when he visited the Kayapo Indian village of Aukre, which is located in a remote corner of the Brazilian Amazon rain forest reached only by small-engine plane. "Touching down on the grass landing strip we were met by the entire village in traditional dress—and undress—and painted faces, with a smattering of American baseball caps bearing random logos," recalled Prickett. "I was there with Conservation International to inspect the progress of a biological research station we were running upriver with the Kayapo. The Kayapo have defended a large chunk of intact Amazon for centuries through sheer force. Now they are learning to protect it through alliances with international scientists, conservationists and socially conscious businesspeople. Their village has a little main street with a Conservation International store and a branch of the Body Shop, the ecoconscious soap makers. So after a two-day stay at the biological research station, we came back to the village to do a final bit of business. We had arranged for an open-air market of Kayapo culture, artifacts, baskets, war clubs, spears and bows and arrows to be set up. Then our group proceeded to buy all of it for very steep prices in U.S. dollars. We then went and sat in the men's hut in the center of this Kayapo village, which could have come out of prehistory. While sitting in this hut with the leading men of the village, I noticed that they were all watching a single TV, connected to a large satellite dish. The men were flipping the channels back and forth between a Brazilian soccer match and a business channel that carried the running price of gold on world markets. The Kayapo men wanted to be sure that they were charging the small miners, whom they let dig on the edges of their rain-forest property, the going international rate for whatever gold they found. They then used these profits earned on the world gold market to protect their own unique lifestyle in the middle of the Amazon rain forest."

The Lexus struggling with the olive tree was a scene I witnessed at NATO headquarters in Brussels. I was sitting on a couch in the lobby, waiting for an appointment. Nearby was a lady Russian journalist, speaking Russian into her cell phone. But what struck me most was the fact that she was walking in circles next to the Coke machine, underneath a television tuned to CNN that was broadcasting the surprise entry of Russian troops into Pristina, Kosovo—ahead of NATO forces. A Russian journalist, circling the Coke machine, under the CNN screen, speaking Russian into a cell phone, in NATO headquarters, while Kosovo burned—my mind couldn't contain all the contradictions. . . .

The olive tree exploiting the Lexus is the story that came to light in the summer of 1999 about Adolf Hitler's racist manifesto *Mein Kampf*, which is banned in Germany by the German government. You cannot sell it in any German bookstore, or publish it in Germany. But Germans found that they could order the book over the Internet from Amazon.com and it would come in the mail in a way that the German government was powerless to stop. Indeed, so many Germans ordered *Mein Kampf* from Amazon.com that in the summer of 1999 Hitler made Amazon.com's top-ten bestseller list for Germany. Amazon.com at first refused to stop shipping *Mein Kampf* to

Germany, insisting that the English translation was not covered by censorship, and that it was not going to get in the business of deciding what its customers were allowed to read. However, after this was publicized, Amazon.com was so bombarded with angry E-mails from all over the world that it stopped selling Hitler's works.

The olive tree trumping the Lexus, and then the Lexus then coming right back to trump the olive tree, was the nuclear-testing saga that unfolded in India in the late 1990s. In the spring of 1998 India's newly elected nationalist Bharatiya Janata Party (BJP) decided to defy the world and resume testing its nuclear weapons. Asserting India's right to test had been a key plank in the BJP's election campaign. I visited India shortly after the tests, where I talked to rich and poor, government and nongovernment types, villagers and city slickers. I kept waiting to meet the Indian who would say to me, "You know, these nuclear tests were really stupid. We didn't get any additional security out of them and they've really cost us with sanctions." I am sure that sentiment was there—but I couldn't find anyone to express it. Even those Indian politicians who denounced their nuclear tests as a cheap, jingoistic maneuver by India's new Hindu nationalist government would tell you that these tests were the only way for India to get what it wants most from the United States and China: R-E-S-P-E-C-T. I finally realized the depth of this sentiment when I went to see a saffron-robed Indian human rights campaigner, Swami Agnivesh. As the two of us sat cross-legged on the floor of his living room in his simple Delhi home, I thought, "Surely he will disavow this test." But no sooner did we start talking than he declared to me: "We are India, the second-largest country in the world! You can't just take us for granted. India doesn't feel threatened by Pakistan, but in the whole international game India is being marginalized by the China-U.S. axis." The next day I went out to

Dasna, a village north of New Delhi, where I randomly stopped shopkeepers to talk. Dasna is one of the poorest places I have ever seen. Nobody seemed to have shoes. Everyone seemed to be skin and bones. There were more water buffalo and bicycles than cars on the road. The air was heavy with the smell of cow dung used for energy. But they loved their government's nuclear sound-and-light show. "We are nine hundred million people. We will not die from these sanctions," pronounced Pramod Batra, the forty-two-year-old village doctor in Dasna. "This nuclear test was about self-respect, and self-respect is more important than roads, electricity and water. Anyway, what did we do? We exploded our bomb. It was like shooting a gun off into the air. We didn't hurt anybody."

But while India's olive tree impulse seemed to have prevailed over its needs for a Lexus, when this happens in today's globalization system there is always a hidden long-term price. While in New Delhi, I stayed at the Oberoi Hotel, where I swam laps in the pool at the end of each day to recover from the sweltering 100-degree heat. My first day there, while I was doing my breaststrokes, there was an Indian woman also swimming laps in the lane next to me. During a rest stop we started talking and she told me she ran the India office of Salomon Brothers–Smith Barney, the major American investment bank. I told her I was a columnist who had come over to write about the fallout from the Indian nuclear tests.

"Have you heard who's in town?" she asked me as we each trod water. "No," I said, shaking my head. "Who's in town?"

"Moody's," she said. Moody's Investors Service is the international credit-rating agency which rates economies, with grades of A, B and C, so that global investors know who is pursuing sound economics and who is not, and if your economy gets a lower rating it means you will have to pay higher interest rates for international loans. "Moody's has sent a team over to re-rate the Indian economy," she said.

"Have you heard anything about what they decided?"

No, I hadn't, I replied.

"You might want to check," she said, and swam away.

I did check. It turned out that the Moody's team had moved around New Delhi almost as quietly and secretly as India's nuclear scientists had prepared their bomb. I couldn't find out anything about their decisions, but the night I left India, I was listening to the evening news when the fourth item caught my ear. It said that in reaction to the Indian government's new bloated, directionless budget, and in the wake of the Indian nuclear tests and the U.S. sanctions imposed on India for blowing off some nukes, Moody's had downgraded India's economy from "investment grade," which meant it was safe for global investors, to "speculative grade," which meant it was risky. The Standard & Poor's rating agency also changed its outlook on the Indian economy from "stable" to "negative." This meant that any Indian company trying to borrow money from international markets would have to pay higher interest. And because India has a low savings rate, those foreign funds are crucial for a country that needs $500 billion in new infrastructure over the next decade in order to be competitive.

So yes, the olive tree had had its day in India. But when it pushes out like that in the system of globalization, there is always a price to pay. You can't escape the system. Sooner or later the Lexus always catches up with you. A year and a half after India's nuclear test, I picked up *The Wall Street Journal* (Oct. 7, 1999) to read the following headline: "India's BJP Is Shifting Priority to the Economy." The story noted that the BJP came to power some two years earlier "calling for India to assert its nuclear capability—a pledge it fulfilled two months later with a series of weapons tests that sparked global sanctions and stalled investment." Upon its reelection, though, Prime Minister Atal Bihari Vajpayee wasn't even waiting for the votes to be counted before signaling his new priority: economic reform. "The priority is to build a national consensus on the acceptance of global capital, market norms and whatever goes with it. You have to go out and compete for investments," Vajpayee told the *Indian Express* newspaper.

An example of the Lexus and olive tree forces in balance was the Gulf Air flight I took from Bahrain to London, on which the television monitor on my Business Class seat included a channel which, using a global positioning satellite (GPS) linked into the airplane's antenna, showed passengers exactly where the plane was in relation to the Muslim holy city of Mecca at all times. The screen displayed a diagram of the aircraft with a white dot that moved around the diagram as the plane changed directions. This enabled Muslim passengers, who are enjoined to pray five times a day facing toward Mecca, to always know which way to face inside the plane when they unrolled their prayer rugs. During the flight, I saw several passengers near me wedge into the galley to perform their prayer rituals, and thanks to the GPS system, they knew just which way to aim.

The Lexus ignoring the olive tree in the era of globalization was a computer part that a friend of mine sent me. On the back was written: "This part was made in Malaysia, Singapore, the Philippines, China, Mexico, Germany, the U.S., Thailand, Canada and Japan. It was made in so many different places that we cannot specify a country of origin."

The Lexus trumping the olive tree in the era of globalization was the small item that appeared in the August 11, 1997, edition of *Sports Illustrated.* It said: "The 38-year-old Welsh soccer club Llansantffraid has changed its name to 'Total Network Solutions' in exchange for $400,000 from a cellular phone company."

The Lexus and olive tree working together in the era of globalization was on display in a rather unusual *Washington Times* story of September 21, 1997, which reported that Russian counterintelligence officers were complaining about having to pay twice as much to recruit a CIA spy as a double agent than the other way around. An official of Russia's Federal Security Service (the successor to the KGB), speaking on condition of anonymity, told the Itar-Tass news agency that a Russian spy could be bought for a mere $1 million, while CIA operatives held out for $2 million to work for the other side.

At roughly the same time that this report appeared, Israel's *Yediot Aharonot* newspaper published what seemed to me to be the first-ever totally free-market intelligence scoop. *Yediot* editors went to Moscow and bought some Russian spy satellite photographs of new Scud missile bases in Syria. Then *Yediot* hired a private U.S. expert on satellite photos to analyze the pictures. Then *Yediot* published the whole package as a scoop about Syria's new missile threat, without ever having once quoted a government official. Who needs Deep Throat when you have deep pockets?

Finally, my favorite "Lexus trumps olive tree in the era of globalization" story is about Abu Jihad's son. I was attending the Middle East Economic Summit in Amman, Jordan, in 1995, and was having lunch by myself on the balcony of the Amman Marriott. Out of the blue, a young Arab man approached my table and asked, "Are you Tom Friedman?" I said yes.

"Mr. Friedman," the young man continued politely, "you knew my father."

"Who was your father?" I asked.

"My father was Abu Jihad."

Abu Jihad, whose real name was Khalil al-Wazir, was one of the Palestinians who, with Yasser Arafat, founded el-Fatah and later took over the Palestine Liberation Organization. Abu Jihad, meaning "father of struggle," was his nom de guerre, and he was the overall commander of Palestinian military operations in Lebanon and the West Bank in the days when I was the *New York Times* correspondent in Beirut. I got to know him in Beirut. Palestinians considered him a military hero; Israelis considered him one of the most dangerous Palestinian terrorists. An Israeli hit team assassinated Abu Jihad in his living room in Tunis on April 16, 1988, pumping a hundred bullets into his body.

"Yes, I knew your father very well—I once visited your home in Damascus," I told the young man. "What do you do?"

He handed me his business card. It read: "Jihad al-Wazir, Managing Director, World Trade Center, Gaza, Palestine."

I read that card and thought to myself, "That's amazing. From Jesse James to Michael Milken in one generation."

The challenge in this era of globalization—for countries and individuals—is to find a healthy balance between preserving a sense of identity, home and community and doing what it takes to survive within the globalization system. Any society that wants to thrive economically today must constantly be trying to build a better Lexus and driving it out into the world. But no one should have any illusions that merely participating in this global economy will make a society healthy. If that participation comes at the price of a country's identity, if individuals feel their olive tree roots crushed, or washed out, by this global system, those olive tree roots will rebel. They will rise up and strangle the process. Therefore the survival of globalization as a system will depend, in part, on how well all of us strike this balance. A country without healthy olive trees will never feel rooted or secure enough to open up fully to the world and reach out into it. But a country that is only olive trees, that is only roots, and has no Lexus, will never go, or grow, very far. Keeping the two in balance is a constant struggle.... ◆ ◆ ◆

Labor Standards
in the Global Economy
Issues for Investors

Pietra Rivoli

Claims about working conditions in the Third World tend to be inflammatory, and sometimes it is difficult for investors and other stakeholders to perceive what is really going on. Rivoli suggests that one way of understanding industries in developing countries is to use a historical lens; by looking at emerging industry in various parts of the world over the past 250 years, we see a pattern of low-wage manufacturing being contested by the protests of activists. She suggests this kind of struggle has led to social progress, higher wage industries, and migration of poor-paying industries to less developed areas of the world. Rivoli believes that discussions over sweatshops need not be so polarized when they are seen in the wider context of global industrial growth.

The time we are required to labor is altogether too long. It is more than our constitutions can bear. If anyone doubts it, let them come into our mills on a summer's day, at four or five o'clock and see the drooping, weary persons moving about . . . and many times have I had girls faint in the morning, in consequence of the air being so impure . . .[1]

Since the mid-1990s, global labor standards have emerged as a new and important area of concern for socially responsible investors. In particular, the proliferation of alleged "sweatshops" and exploitive labor practices, especially those related to the manufacturing and distribution systems of U.S. and European retailers, has attracted increasing attention from public pension funds, religious investors, mutual funds, educational institutions, and individuals. For example, preliminary data show that the number of shareholder resolutions on these topics in the 2001 proxy season is likely to be at least double the number seen in 2000 (IRRC, 2001). As recently as the mid-1990s, in contrast, this issue was receiving virtually no attention from SRI investors.

Concerns about abusive or exploitive labor practices are, of course, not limited to investors. Since the mid-1990s, and in particular since the 1999 World Trade Organization meetings in Seattle, a prime focus of the globalization "backlash" [has] been the alleged exploitive effects of rapidly liberalizing trade, especially in products utilizing a high degree of unskilled labor. According to the "backlash" arguments, the recent liberalization of trade has released competitive pressures that are sending unskilled workers into a downward spiral of low wages and poor working conditions. The main targets of the activists have been U.S. apparel and footwear firms, especially those with brand name recognition. GAP, Nike, Liz Claiborne, and The Limited have all been recent targets of anti-sweatshop protests by labor, consumer, and student groups. Fueling the flames, of course, has been a steady stream of stories from the factory floor.[2]

The manufacturing and distributions systems now employed by U.S. firms complicate the issue considerably. As recently as the early 1980s, most firms owned and operated the factories in which their apparel and toys were made. Today, however, virtually all "name brand" firms employ independent contractors in the manufacturing process. Typically, these subcontractors are locally owned and produce for a variety of retailers. As a result, while the U.S. firms certainly have influence over factory labor conditions through their bargaining power as purchasers, they do not directly control working conditions in the factories. Indeed, in the early 1990s, it was relatively common for U.S. firms to disavow responsibility for conditions in subcontractors' factories. By the late 1990s, however, pressure from consumers, activists, and shareholders had led to significant changes to U.S. firms' approaches to the controversy.

My objective in this paper is to elucidate some of the major "sweatshop" issues facing investors. In general, how may investors make sense of the complex moral, economic, and social issues surrounding the sweatshop debate? More specifically, how might investors evaluate

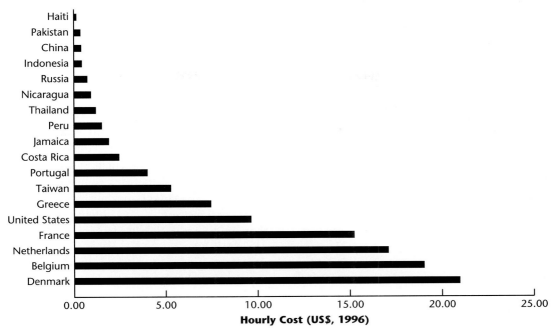

Figure 1 ◆ LABOR COSTS IN APPAREL PRODUCTION, 1996

Source: Werner International; Adapted from Dickerson, p. 30.

U.S. firms on this issue? Finally, how may investors contribute to fruitful discourse on this complex and important topic?

WHAT IS A SWEATSHOP?

The rallying cry to "stamp out sweatshops" is well-intentioned but less than helpful to investors and others who seek to understand the specific practices in factories around the world today. Investors must clarify the aspects of work life that they wish to document or change, identify the practices that they find acceptable or not acceptable, and communicate to corporations regarding the attributes of work life that should be measured and monitored.

For most investors involved with this issue, the fundamental matter of concern is the protection of human rights in the workplace. These rights may be civil, economic, political, or social. The extent to which workers are or are not accorded these rights may be assessed by a number of measurable criteria, including those discussed below.

Wages and Wage Practices

Perhaps the most defining attribute of a sweatshop is low wages. Figure 1 shows wages for apparel workers from a number of countries as of 1996. Figure 2 shows employment patterns in the textile and apparel industry. Consistent with economic theory, textile and apparel production has indeed between shifting rapidly to lower wage countries. In general, employment in high wage areas such as the U.S. and Europe has been falling compared to employment in low wage

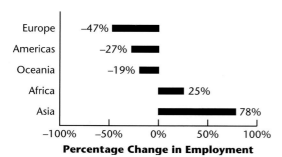

Figure 2 ◆ EMPLOYMENT CHANGES IN THE APPAREL INDUSTRY, 1990–1998

Source: ILO, "Labor Practices in the Footwear, Textiles and Clothing Industries", 2000.

countries in Latin America and Asia. Long run patterns of dislocation in these industries have followed the predictions of neoclassical trade theory, which suggests that countries with a relative abundance of low skill and unskilled labor will specialize in the production and export of goods using this factor intensively. In China, for example, the world's biggest clothing exporter, labor accounts for more than half of value added in the apparel industry (Yang and Zhong, 1998). Because of its labor intensity, production in the apparel industry is concentrated in low wage countries.

Of course, wage data alone are not sufficient to allow analyses of economic income. Perhaps the most important adjustment that is necessary is a correction for varying degrees of purchasing power across countries. The burgeoning research to develop a "living wage" methodology explicitly attempts to account for the purchasing power of wages across countries.[3] In addition, wage rates alone may not provide information about alternative economic benefits associated with employment, such as housing and meal subsidies, medical care, and so forth. Another confounding factor, particularly in the apparel industry, is the practice of "piece rate" compensation, which complicates attempts to standardize wage data.

Finally, in a number of countries, including the United States, apparel producers have often been found to be in violation of minimum wage laws (Ross, 1997). Some activists also point out that legally-mandated minimum wages, even when paid, may not be sufficient to sustain workers and their families. As a result, activists have argued for the implementation of a "living wage" or at a minimum, some attention by corporations to the issue of sustainable employment.

Many investors do not view compensation levels per se as an appropriate topic for investor activism, and the SEC has consistently disallowed shareholder resolutions addressing the level of wages (IRRC, 2001). Therefore, investors must draw the important distinction between wage *levels*, which some believe to be outside the purview of investor activists, and wage *practices*, which are an appropriate area of questioning for investors concerned with labor issues. Wage practices garnering recent attention include unexplained or arbitrary fines and deductions from workers' paychecks, the practice of "training wages" that do not meet minimum wage requirements, as well as significant delays in compensation.

Health and Safety

Standards of occupational health and safety, as well as the enforcement of those standards, are prime issues for many labor activists. Fire safety—or lack thereof—has become a common cause for concern in factories, particularly in Asia. In a number of cases, blocked fire exits have resulted in deaths and injuries.[4] Particularly in shoe and toy factories, exposure to toxic materials under conditions of poor ventilation also may constitute a threat to workers' health. Another issue relates to the availability of potable water. In factories with dormitory facilities, the safety and cleanliness of the living facilities have also been criticized by some observers. Various forms of mental abuse and humiliation have also been widely reported.[5] In general, problems lie not with occupational health and safety laws, but with their consistent enforcement.

Freedom of Association

With the very significant exception of China, most countries engaged in large scale apparel and toy production for the world market have legal protection for independent unions and union members. At the same time, however, very few workers in apparel and toy factories in developing countries are actually represented by independent unions. In practice, a variety of tactics suppress union activity in many countries. In addition to firing union activists, workers also report that union members and activists are discriminated against in other ways (ILO, 2000). In many cases, local governments are loathe to protect workers' rights to union activity because a compliant labor force is seen as a comparative advantage in attracting foreign investment.

Captive and Child Labor

In a number of countries, labor market transactions are entered into unwillingly and/or unknowingly, or under conditions wherein basic rights are violated. Debt bondage, an arrangement whereby workers are kept in servitude to pay off debts incurred, has been widely reported in Asia as well as in the U.S. (Kwong, 1997). The use of involuntary prison labor continues to be problematic (ILO, 2000). Arrangements governing migrant labor have also been called into question by human rights groups.[6] Finally, child labor has been widely reported in the textile and apparel industries, particularly in Pakistan, India, and Bangladesh (Hobbs et al., 1999). A related problem, particularly around holiday periods, has been the practice of "forced overtime" wherein employees are required to exceed legal hours of work limits to meet production quotas (Varley, 1998).

HOW COMMON?

How common are the types of "sweatshop" abuses discussed above? Unfortunately, there are few reliable data to help in addressing this question. First, most of the evidence surrounding the most egregious abuses is anecdotal and therefore does not allow for generalization to an entire industry or country. Certainly it should be noted that the more systematically gathered evidence, such as publicly available monitoring reports, have generally identified some areas requiring attention, but have not uncovered the types of "worst case" abuses often publicized by activists. Indeed, the worst case abuses are newsworthy often because they do represent departures from the norms.

It is also important to note that the U.S.-based apparel industry generates its fair share of "sweatshop" anecdotes. For example, in 1995, more than 70 Thai immigrants were found working in captivity for approximately 70 cents per hour in El Monte, California. In the New York garment district, evidence of debt bondage, physical threats, and below minimum wage work is widespread (Kwong, 1997). In any country, of course, it would unfair to tar an entire industry with the brush from these anecdotes. At the same time, investors seeking not to be associated with practices such as those described above, or those seeking to change such practices, should systematically evaluate firms, particularly in the more problematic apparel, toy, and footwear industries.

A FRAMEWORK FOR EVALUATING U.S. FIRMS

I suggest that investors with concerns over global labor standards should evaluate U.S. firms on four dimensions: (1) the code of conduct applicable to the firm's manufacturing operations as well as its contractors, (2) the dissemination of the code of conduct, (3) the disclosure mechanisms in place, and (4) the monitoring scheme employed. I discuss each of these in turn.

Codes of Conduct

Most U.S. firms have adopted codes of conduct governing their international business relationships. Firms in the industries most vulnerable to sweatshop charges, particularly apparel and toys, generally have adopted codes specific to their supplier relationships. Some codes represent collective efforts of firms through industry associations, some represent the work of human rights or religious groups, while some codes are company-specific.

Perhaps the most basic question for investors is, what code of conduct governs the firm's supplier relationships? A number of industry, religious, and human rights groups have compiled recommended codes of conduct in recent years. These groups include the American Apparel Manufacturers Association, the Fair Labor Association, and the Worker Rights Consortium. Other widely regarded codes include the Global Sullivan Principles, which are modeled on the Sullivan Principles proposed for business in South Africa during the 1980s, the Social Accountability 2000 code, as well as the Caux Principles.

In general, these codes have a high degree of overlap. For example, most of the codes have a prohibition on child labor, prohibit discrimination on the basis of race or sex, and require adherence to minimum health and safety standards. However, there are significant differences as well. Perhaps the most striking (and controversial) difference among the codes is the inclusion, in the case of the Worker Rights Consortium, of a requirement that employers pay a "living wage."

It is far more common for firms to adopt company specific codes. A study by the Investor Responsibility Research Center (IRRC) as well as a study sponsored by the ILO (Sajhau, 1997) found a high degree of variation in both the stringency and the content of supplier and manufacturer codes across firms.[7] For example, while the great majority of corporate codes had stated requirements related to worker health and safety, only a small number explicitly supported the workers' rights to organize collectively. Figure 3 shows the issues represented in 121 corporate codes of conduct studied by the IRRC. The study also showed that the specificity of the codes varied considerably, as did the strength of the language used.

It is important to note that the codes of conduct proposed by activists, and especially those adopted by firms, do not represent a set of radical demands. The great majority of the codes' requirements relate to matters already protected by the labor laws of most countries. The codes are also quite consonant with the provisions of the ILO's core labor standards. The primary case in which a code goes beyond legally mandated principles, or at least widely accepted principles, is the "living wage" clause included [in] the Worker Rights Consortium code.

Dissemination

The mere existence of a code of conduct, of course, is insufficient reassurance to those concerned with labor standards. In particular, investors should also assess how the codes of conduct are disseminated, and to whom. Of particular interest is whether workers or employees of subcontractors are aware of the provisions of the code. Both IRRC and the ILO found that few U.S. companies have written provisions for translating and posting codes of conduct.

Disclosure

The level and types of disclosure by firms have emerged as significant issues in student and shareholders campaigns. For example, should U.S. firms publicly disclose the names and addresses of all subcontracting factories? When fac-

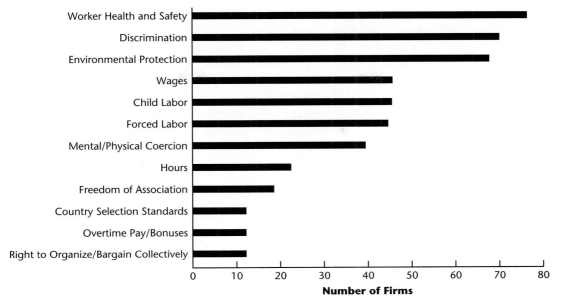

Figure 3 ◆ ISSUES COVERED IN COMPANY CODES OF CONDUCT

Source: Peter DeSimone, "Global Labor and Environmental Standards", IRRC Social Issues Service, February 29, 2000.

tories are monitored for compliance with codes of conduct, who should receive the results and in what forms? Many activists argue for maximum disclosure, believing that exposure is a powerful tool for changing firm behavior.[8] According to this view, the publicity associated with maximum disclosure serves as a powerful incentive for firms to adhere to high level standards. On the other hand, many firms are reluctant to share large amounts of raw data about internal operations with the general public. A key issue for investors is the attempt to balance the companies' legitimate needs for propriety with demands for disclosure. Investors should also be aware that more liberal disclosure requirements may lead to less in-depth monitoring. In other words, the wider the disclosure, the less forthcoming firms may be in the monitoring process.[9]

Another disclosure issue, indeed the issue most widely addressed by shareholder resolu-

tions, relates to the level and type of information that should be provided to the firm's shareholders. During the 2000 and 2001 proxy season, at least 60 resolutions calling for reports to shareholders on international labor issues were introduced at U.S. firms. The issues relating to the types of data or analyses such reports to investors should include, remain unresolved.

Monitoring and Enforcement

Who should monitor factories for compliance with corporate codes of conduct? The great majority of U.S. manufacturers monitor compliance with an internal audit system. Often, managers charged with responsibility for general issues of quality control are also given oversight responsibilities for labor standards issues. When subcontractors are employed, the codes may be a part of the contractual agreement between the supplier and the U.S. firm. This system, in effect, "outsources" the monitoring of the code to the subcontractor (DeSimone, 1999). Predictably, labor activists question the objectivity of these internal monitoring mechanisms.

An alternative approach to monitoring utilizes independent monitoring by non-profit, nongovernmental organizations (NGOs). Arguably, these "independent" monitors would come to the task with greater objectivity than company-sponsored monitors. However, a number of observers to these processes have noted that while the NGOs are not biased in favor of the firms, they come to the monitoring task with an unfair bias against the corporation. Both Rev. David Shilling, Director of the Interfaith Center on Corporate Responsibility, and Professor Prakash Sethi, an academic expert on the topic, have noted that the relationships between monitoring NGOs and corporations are confounded by adversarial and confrontational relationships which may impede rather than facilitate the gathering of high quality data (DeSimone, 1999).

A third alternative for U.S. firms is to turn to the for-profit monitoring services of consulting and audit firms. The clear leader in the industry is PriceWaterhouse Coopers (PWC). PWC believes that the extension to labor standards represents a natural extension of its significant presence in the financial and environmental audit business. Social and labor activists, however, again question the impartiality of a process which employs monitors with which firms have other business relationships.

In addition to questions regarding who should undertake the monitoring activities, there are a large number of unresolved issues surrounding the process and mechanisms of monitoring. One issue, for example, concerns the question of whether the visits by monitors should be surprise "unannounced" visits or those for which factory managers should prepare. A second issue relates to the extent to which sampling is or is not a valid method of drawing inferences. Related to this question is the issue of the frequency with which monitoring should take place. While it is clearly not possible for all factories to be visited in every year, is it sufficient, for example, for 10% of a supplier's factories to be visited? If so, how should the 10% be selected? A further issue is who should bear financial responsibility for monitoring costs. Some observers believe that if firms pay monitors directly, an inevitable conflict of interest will ensue. An alternative mechanism is for industry associations or non-profit organizations to pay independent monitors using proceeds from corporate dues or memberships.

THE SWEATSHOP DEBATE IN A BROADER CONTEXT

It is worthwhile for investors to address not only the operational issues relating to monitoring, codes of conduct, and so forth, but also to give thought to the sweatshop debate in a broader context. Brian Langille (1997) has very correctly noted the relatively low quality of the discourse related to global labor standards in which protagonists on different sides of the debate have repeatedly failed to engage one another. Labor activists on the one hand and "mainstream" economists on the other, have made relatively little progress in reconciling their views and prescriptions on this important issue. Investors, however, have a unique vantage point from which a reasoned middle ground can proceed. I suggest that the quality of the dialogue may be enhanced by examining the sweatshop issue in a broader historical context. At least some middle ground emerges from an examination of this historical context.

To many free trade economists, as well as others, the credibility of the labor standards movement, in particular the anti-sweatshop activism, is undermined by the identity of many of its protagonists. For example, much of the leadership and support for activism in the apparel industry has been from UNITE (Union of Needletrades, Industrial, and Textile Employees) and is believed by many to be thinly veiled protectionism rather than well-motivated concern for workers in developing countries. Relatedly, many observers note that developing country workers and their representatives are rarely well represented in discussions or governing boards of active organizations. While the validity of the arguments presented should not depend on the identity of their protagonists, many point out that the problems inherent in relying on U.S. labor unions for data and analyses on developing country labor issues should be apparent.

A far more serious and complex charge that has dogged the anti-sweatshop movement from the beginning is the "perversity thesis" that the movement risks leaving in worse straits the very people allegedly being helped by the movement.[10] This position is that, however objectionable certain labor conditions may be to U.S. observers, low-skill factory work represents the best alternative available to many citizens in developing countries. In general, particularly in the apparel and toy industries, the alternative available to these workers is rural poverty. However well-intentioned, attempts to help improve the lots of workers may reduce employment and, therefore, be detrimental to the working poor. The activists have long argued, correctly, that manufacturing of apparel and toys flows to low cost, low wage locations. If demand for unskilled labor is indeed price-elastic, as observers on both sides of the debate agree, then increasing wages to meet, for example, a "living wage" target, will reduce employment in these sectors.

Both sides agree that recent trends in liberalizing trade have facilitated a "race to the bottom" in low skill manufacturing industries. It is useful, however, to put this "race" in appropriate historical context. Today, Great Britain has virtually no position as an export-competitive producer of textiles and apparel. Yet, as recently as the late 1800s, Great Britain dominated world trade in these sectors. British dominance was lost, first to New England and then, in the early 1900s, to the southern United States. After World War I, the textile producers in the American south were challenged by Japanese producers. Japanese firms, by the 1960s, had been seriously challenged by the so-called Asian tigers. In each case, the dislocation was facilitated by an abundant and low wage labor force in the next location. Today, China is the world's largest exporter of apparel. Yet wage rates, particularly in eastern China, are increasing, and production is shifting to even lower-cost locations. Thus, the "race to the bottom," far from being a "90s" phenomenon, is, at a minimum, a 200 year old process. In addition, countries occupying a place at the bottom have, in virtually all cases, used low skill manufacturing as their entrée into the industrialized economy. In brief, without a race to the bottom, all of the world's textile factories would still be clustered around Manchester, England. In 1748 David Hume extolled the virtues of the race to the bottom:

> There seems to be a happy concurrence of causes in human affairs, which checks the growth of trade and riches, and hinders them from being confined entirely to one people . . . When one nation has gotten the start of another in trade, it is very difficult for the latter to regain the ground it has lost because of the superior industry and skill of the former. . . . But these advantages are compensated in some measure, by the low price of labor in every nation which has not had an extensive commerce . . . Manufacturers therefore gradually shift their places, leaving those countries and provinces which they have already enriched, and flying to others, whither they are allured by the cheapness of provisions and labor, till they have enriched those also, and are again banished by the same cause . . . (Hume, 1748)

Today's mainstream economists largely concur with the views expressed by Hume 250 years ago: The key point is that low wage manufacturing enriches rather than exploits workers; that the race to the bottom is to be facilitated rather than checked if the working poor are to helped.

At the same time, democratic processes have since the beginning served as traction in the race to the bottom. And, in virtually all cases, the impetus for these democratic processes has come from labor and social activists. For example, child labor laws, occupational safety regulations, minimum wage laws and maximum hours of work laws have arisen not organically through the competitive market mechanism but instead through the work of political activists attempting to check the effects of the competitive market mechanism. And as Albert Hirschman (and later Brian Langille) have eloquently pointed out, this progressive activism (as well as activism relating to a large number of other issues, from civil rights to political rights) has rather predictably been challenged by the pervasity thesis. In summary, both the competitive market "race to the bottom" in manufacturing, as well as the political reaction to the race by activists, are part of a very long historical process.

There is a middle ground to be found in the observation that both the "race" (resulting from the competitive market mechanism) and the reaction to the race (resulting from political activism) have over time also been very *effective* processes: the race has been effective in providing employment to the poorest, raising living standards and ameliorating poverty, while the reaction has been very effective in expanding our common conception of the inalienable rights of workers. For example, even the most progressive New England textile factory in the 1800s would today grossly violate most codes of conduct provisions as well as a large number of labor and occupa-

tional health and safety laws. In addition, the freedoms accorded the women mill workers in early New England industry were far more limited than those granted in even the most repressive regimes today. On virtually any dimension, today's textile and apparel factories in developing countries are better places to work than their historical counterparts in New England, the American south, Great Britain, Japan, and 1949 China.[11]

Many alternative labor arrangements, including indentured servitude, slavery, and child labor, have been defended at one point or another on the basis of the perversity thesis. However, during the past 150 years, labor and social activists have been markedly successful in gradually expanding our common conceptions of the basic rights of workers so that today such practices are far outside the legal and moral boundaries of society. As a result, arguments that such practices are economically efficient means of production, or arguments that the elimination of such practices would leave the affected group in worse straits, are of course not sufficient defenses given our conception of inalienable rights. Economic efficiency is but one of many criteria that a production system must satisfy, while the perversity thesis, if true, simply obligates us to design an effective system for dismantling the practice, not to continue the practice.

A middle ground emerges with the proposal that participants involved on both sides of the global labor standards debate should hope for history to continue to repeat itself: that manufacturing will continue to flow to low wage locations so that workers in the poorest countries may participate in the process of economic growth and industrialization, and that political activism will continue to provide the traction necessary for the race to the bottom to take place against a steadily expanding backdrop of rights and economic resources for all workers.　◆　◆　◆

◆ Notes

1. "R", *Voice of Industry*, March 26, 1847, quoted in Dickerson, 1999.
2. See Pamela Varley, ed., *The Sweatshop Quandary*, IRRC, 1998, especially Chapter 4, "Tales from Factory Floor."
3. See, for example, the methodology proposed in www.sweatshopwatch.org/swatch/ wages/formula.
4. Varley, p. 66–67.
5. Ibid., p. 68–69.
6. http://www.hrchina.org/reports/cleanup
7. See Varley (1998) for a summary of the results of both studies.
8. Maximum disclosure is clearly one of the organizing principles of the Worker Rights Consortium. See www.workersrights.org.
9. Ms. Heather White, the Director of Verite, a non-profit monitoring organization, has found that, in general, "the only way to get access to factories is to agree reports will not be released publicly" (Van Der Werf, 2001).
10. For a statement of this view, see material from the Academic Consortium on International Trade at www.spp.umich.edu/rsie/acit.
11. For descriptions of early factory life in the textile industry see Hareven and Langenbach (1978) for New England, Tsurumi (1990) for Japan. Hall et al. (1987) for the American South, Inglis (1971) for the United Kingdom, and Honig (1986) for China.

◆ References

Anderson, Kym: 1992, *New Silk Roads: East Asia and World Textile Markets* (Cambridge Press, New York).

DeSimone, Peter: 1999, Global Environmental and Labor Standards, Social Issues Background Report F (Investor Responsibility Research Center, Washington, DC).

Dickerson, Kitty G.: 1999, *Textiles and Apparel in the Global Economy* (Prentice Hall-Inc, Upper Saddle River, New Jersey).

Hall, Jacqueline Dowd: 1987, *Like a Family: The Making of a Southern Cotton Mill World* (Norton, New York).

Hareven, Tamara K. and Langenbach Randolph: 1978, *Amsokeag: Life and Work in an American Factory City* (University Press of New England, Hanover and London).

Hirschman, Albert O.: 1991, *The Rhetoric of Reaction* (Harvard, Cambridge).

Hobbs, Sandy, Jim McKechnie and Michael Lavalette: 1999, *Child Labor/A World History Companion* (ABC-CLIO, Santa Barbara).

Honig, Emily: 1986, *Sisters and Strangers: Women in the Shanghai Cotton Mills, 1919–1949* (Stanford, Stanford, CA).

Hume, David: 1748, *Essays Moral and Political*, ed. E. Rotwein, London, Nelson, 1955, 34–35.

Inglis, Brian: 1971, *Poverty and the Industrial Revolution* (Hodder and Stoughton, London).

International Labor Organization: 2000, Labour Practices in the Footwear, Leather, Textiles and Clothing Industries (International Labour Office, Geneva).

Investor Responsibility Research Center: 2001, *2001 Social Policy Proxy Season Guide* (IRRC, Washington, DC).

Kwong, Peter: 1997, *Forbidden Workers: Illegal Immigrants and American Labor* (New Press, New York).

Langille, Brian A.: 1997, 'Eight Ways to Think About International Labour Standards', *Journal of World Trade* **31**(4) (August 1997), 27–53.

Ross, Andrew (ed.): 1997, *No Sweat: Fashion, Free Trade, and the Rights of Garment Workers* (Verso, New York).

Sajhau, Jean-Paul: 1997, *Business Ethics in the Textile, Clothing and Footwear Industries* (International Labor Organization, Geneva).

Tsurumi, Patricia E.: 1990, *Factory Girls: Women in the Thread Mills of Meiji Japan* (Princeton, Princeton, NJ).

Van Der Werf, Martin: 2001, 'Anti-Sweatshop Groups Find it Difficult to Turn Campus Idealism Into Real Change', *Chronicle of Higher Education* (January 5, 2001).

Varley, Pamela (ed.): 1998, *The Sweatshop Quandary/Corporate Responsibility on the Global*

Frontier (Investor Responsibility Research Center, Washington, DC).

Yang, Yongzheng and Chuansui Zhong: 1998, 'China's Textile and Clothing Exports in a Changing World Economy', *The Developing Economies* **XXXVI**–1 (March), 2–23.

One World
One Economy

Peter Singer

The World Trade Organization (WTO) is an international body that has authority over international trade and standards, yet its representatives are not elected or accountable to the people the WTO affects. This has brought about an unusual alliance of opponents, from environmental groups to political conservatives.

In this selection, Singer examines the role of the WTO. It holds the promise of greater prosperity for all its members and yet has resulted in job loss in America and Europe. Singer describes worldwide opposition to the WTO and protests that have grown since Seattle in 1999; he also traces the development of the General Agreement on Tariffs and Trade (GATT). He assesses the trend toward globalization in terms of its likely effects on economic efficiency, the environment, and national sovereignty. He concludes that the WTO may have beneficial influence if it recommends that corporations shun trade with dictatorships and deal with only legitimate governments.

THE WORLD TRADE ORGANIZATION FRACAS

If there is one organization that critics of globalization point to as responsible for pushing the process onward—and in the wrong way—it is the World Trade Organization. Tony Clarke, director of the Ottawa-based Polaris Institute, expresses a now-widespread view when he describes the WTO as the mechanism for "accelerating and extending the transfer of peoples' sovereignty from nation states to global corporations."[1] We have become so familiar with protests against the development of a single global economy that it is already difficult to recall the mentality of the period before the December 1999 Seattle meeting of the WTO, when the very existence of that organization had barely penetrated the minds of most Americans. Before the dramatic events in Seattle, if the popular media mentioned the WTO at all it was in glowing terms of the economic benefits that were flowing from the expansion of world trade. Since, as the most prevalent metaphor of the time put it, "a rising tide lifts all boats," these benefits were bound to reach the poorest nations as well. Very few people had any idea that there was serious opposition to the WTO and its program of removing barriers to world trade. Television footage from Seattle of demonstrators dressed as sea turtles protesting against WTO decisions, anarchists in black tights throwing bricks at the commanding heights of global capitalism, and ordinary American unionists marching against cheap imports made by child labor awakened the American public to the existence of opposition to the WTO. When the protesters unexpectedly proved capable of disrupting the schedules of presidents and prime ministers, they immediately became front-page news. Their impact was reinforced when the new round of trade negotiations expected to begin in Seattle failed to get started. Even then, the initial response of media commentators was bewilderment, incomprehension, and ridicule. Thomas Friedman wrote an intemperate op-ed piece for the *New York Times* that began by asking: "Is there anything more ridiculous in the news today than the protests against the World Trade Organization in Seattle?" He went on to call the protestors "a Noah's ark of flat-earth advocates, protectionist trade unions and yuppies looking for their 1960's fix."[2] These "ridiculous" protestors succeeded in generating a whole new debate about the impact of world trade and the WTO.

Has any non-criminal organization ever been so vehemently condemned on such wide-ranging grounds by critics from so many different countries as the WTO? According to Victor Menotti, director of the Environment Program of the U.S.-based International Forum on Globalization, the regime of trade and investment fostered by the WTO has "unleashed global economic forces that systematically punish ecologically sound forestry while rewarding destructive practices that accelerate forest degradation."[3] From the standpoint of Compassion in World Farming, a leading British campaigner for farm animals, the WTO is "The Biggest Threat Facing Animal Welfare Today."[4] Martin Khor, the Malaysia-based leader of the Third World Network, claims that the WTO is "an instrument to govern the South."[5] Vandana Shiva, founder and president of India's Research Foundation for Science, Technology and Ecology and author of *Biopiracy: The Plunder of Nature and Knowledge*, writes that the rules of the WTO are "primarily rules of robbery, camouflaged by arithmetic and legalese," and global free trade in food and agriculture is "the biggest refugee creation program in the world." It is, not to put too fine a point on it, "leading to slavery."[6] All in all, many of these critics would agree with the summary judgment attributed to the Zapatistas, an organization of Mexican peasants, that the WTO is simply "the biggest enemy of mankind."[7]

A few weeks after the failure of the Seattle meeting, I found myself in Davos, Switzerland, as an invited speaker at the annual meeting of the World Economic Forum. Pre-Seattle attitudes—and a baffled incomprehension about the protests—were still evident. I heard politicians like President Ernesto Zedillo of Mexico, and corporate leaders like Lewis Campbell, chief executive of Textron, a corporation with a turnover of $10 billion a year, swiftly dismiss the protesters as falling into one of two groups: those who were well-intentioned in their concern to protect the environment or help the world's poorest people but were naïve and misled by their emotions; and those who, under the cynical guise of defending human rights and the environment, were seeking to protect their own well-paid jobs in inefficient industries by high tariff barriers that raise costs for domestic consumers and leave workers in less developed countries stuck in dire poverty.

There were dissenting voices at Davos—U.S. labor leader John Sweeney and Martin Khor spoke against the dominant view, but at first they found little resonance among the large international audience of corporate chieftains and heads of government departments of economics and finance. Then British Prime Minister Tony Blair and U.S. President Bill Clinton showed that they were quicker learners than most of the corporate chief executives present, saying that genuine issues had been raised and they needed serious consideration. Nevertheless there was no real discussion of what those issues might be or of how they might be resolved. It was as if everyone already knew that globalization was economically beneficial, and "good for the economy" was identical in meaning to "good all things considered." So the real question was how to brush off the vexing opposition and make faster headway toward the goal of a single world economy, free of all barriers to trade or investment between different states. The alternative was, in Zedillo's word, just "globaphobia."[8]

The International Forum on Globalization helped to organize the protests at Seattle and is one of the WTO's most prominent critics. In September 2000, to coincide with the Millennium Assembly of the United Nations, the IFG held a forum on "Globalization and the Role of the United Nations," in New York. It was a sharp contrast to the Davos meeting. For ten hours speaker after speaker blasted the WTO and global corporate power. No one supportive of the WTO had been invited to speak, and there was no opportunity to ask questions or discuss anything that had been said. Though the IFG advocates grassroots involvement in decision-making, the World Economic Forum allowed more audience participation and presented a greater diversity of viewpoints.

As the protests at meetings of the WTO, the World Bank and other international bodies continue—from Seattle to Washington, D.C., Prague, Melbourne, Quebec City, Gothenburg, Genoa, and New York—genuine open-minded exploration of the crucial and difficult issues arising from globalization is losing out to partisan polemics, long in rhetoric and thin in substance, with each side speaking only to its own supporters who already know who the saints and sinners are. Endlessly repeated rituals of street theater do not provide opportunities for the kind of discussion that is needed. Economics raises questions of value, and economists tend to be too focused on markets to give sufficient importance to values that are not dealt with well by the market. . . .

. . . The World Trade Organization was created by the "Uruguay Round" of talks held by member nations of the General Agreement on Tariffs and Trade, or GATT. It came into existence in January 1995, and by January 2002 had 144 member nations, accounting for more than 97 percent of world trade.[9] Although it seems as if the WTO is a new organization, it is essentially the successor to GATT, which has been around for fifty years. Its raison d'étre is also the same as that of GATT, namely the belief that free trade makes people better off, on average and in the long run. This belief is based on the usual rationale of the market, that if two people have different abilities to make products that they both desire, they will do better if they each work in the areas of production where they are most efficient (or least inefficient) relative to the other person, and then exchange, rather than if they both try to make the full range of products they want. This will be true, it is claimed, whether the people are neighbors or live on opposite sides of the world, as long as the transaction costs involved in making the exchange are less than the differences in their costs of production. Moreover this exchange should be particularly good for countries with low labor costs, because they should be able to produce goods more cheaply than countries with high labor costs. Hence we can expect the demand for labor in those countries to rise, and once the supply of labor begins to tighten, wages should rise too. Thus a free market should have the effect not only of making the world as a whole more prosperous, but more specifically, of assisting the poorest nations.

The agreement by which the WTO was set up gives it the power to enforce a set of rules and agreements relating to free trade that now total about 30,000 pages.[10] If one member nation believes that it is disadvantaged by actions taken by another member nation that are in breach of these rules, the first nation can make a complaint. If efforts to mediate the dispute fail, a dispute panel, consisting of experts in trade and law, is set up to hear it. These dispute panels are the most distinctive difference between the old GATT and the new WTO. In formal terms, the dispute panel does not decide the dispute but recommends a decision to the membership. In practice the decision of the dispute panel is invariably adopted. If the complaint is upheld and the member nation continues to act in breach of WTO rules, it can be subjected to severe penalties, including tariffs against its own goods. . . .

INTERFERENCE WITH NATIONAL SOVEREIGNTY

If the WTO does give precedence to commercial interests, is it reasonable to say that it does so only at the behest of its member states, which have the final decision on whether or not to go along with the WTO's rules? The standard response by WTO supporters to the claim that the organization overrides national sovereignty is that it is no more than the administrative framework for a set of agreements or treaties freely entered into by sovereign governments. Every member-nation of the WTO is a member because its government has decided to join, and has not subsequently decided to leave. Moreover decisions on matters other than the resolution of disputes are generally reached by consensus. Since the WTO is an expression of the decisions of sovereign governments, it is not something that can interfere with national sovereignty.

This account of the WTO as merely the administrator of a set of multilateral agreements may be true in formal terms, but it leaves out some important practical details. Once a government joins the WTO, it and its successors come under considerable pressure to remain a member. Export industries based on free trade develop, employing substantial numbers of people, and the threat that these industries will collapse if the nation withdraws from the treaties administered by the WTO becomes so potent that going one's own way becomes almost unthinkable. This is a form of Friedman's "Golden Straitjacket." In the WTO's eyes it is a good thing, because it means "good discipline" for governments, discourages "unwise" policies, and is good for business.[11] But it is not always true that what is good for business is good overall. A policy that the WTO considers "unwise" may have merits that do not count for much in its calculus of values.

While it is true that nations are free—at a price—to stay outside the WTO, or to leave it, when nations are members they can have their sovereignty significantly curtailed—and this is far from a trivial matter. The recent history of the availability of drugs for the treatment of AIDS in Africa indicates the crucial importance of getting these matters right. In South Africa alone, at the end of 2001, more than 4 million people—or 20 percent of the adult population—were infected with HIV, the virus that causes AIDS. In the rich nations, to have the virus is no longer a death sentence, because there are drugs that effectively, and as far as we know indefinitely, suppress the infection. But the drugs cost about $10,000 per person a year, far out of reach of almost all infected Africans. In this desperate situation, the South African government floated the idea of licensing manufacture of the drugs in South Africa, a procedure known as "compulsory licensing," and a recognized means of dealing with a health emergency. Local manufacture would mean that the drugs could be produced at a cost of about $350 a year. Even this sum is too much for many Africans, who live in countries in which the annual per capita spending on health care is about $10. But $350 a year is a realistic amount for some, especially South Africans.

When the South African government began to consider the possibility of licensing local drug manufacture, the United States responded with the threat of trade sanctions to defend the intellectual property rights of the drug manufacturers. After pressure from AIDS activists, the Clinton Administration dropped this threat. The world's major pharmaceutical corporations then went to court to stop South Africa from providing life-saving treatment for its people at a price that they could afford. In April 2001 public outrage led them to abandon their case and enter into arrangements to supply their products to African nations free or at greatly reduced prices. In October of the same year, amidst the bioterrorism panic that followed the discovery of anthrax in letters addressed to prominent Americans, the Canadian government announced that it would compulsorily license the manufacture of Cipro, the antibiotic most effective against anthrax. With some American politicians calling on the U.S. Government to follow Canada's lead, the U.S. Secretary for Health and Human Services instead persuaded Bayer, the pharmaceutical corporation that holds the patent for Cipro, to slash the drug's price. If they were not willing to do so, he made it clear, the United States would buy a cheaper generic version. Not surprisingly, since the U.S. Government was still trying to restrict the ways in which African countries could obtain generic anti-AIDS drugs, the pressure that the U.S. Government put on Bayer led to an immediate outcry that the Administration was using one standard for protecting Americans—only a handful of whom had been infected with anthrax—and another for African countries, with an estimated 25 million people infected with the AIDS virus.[12]

Though the anthrax outbreak was a tragedy for the unlucky few who were its victims, its timing could not have been better for millions of people needing cheaper drugs, because it came just before the November 2001 Doha WTO Ministerial meeting. The developed nations, embarrassed by the accusation of double standards, agreed to a declaration that the WTO Agreement on Trade-Related Aspects of Intellectual Property Rights (known as the TRIPS Agreement) "does not and should not prevent Members from taking measures to protect public health." The declaration added that each Member "has the right to determine what constitutes a national emergency or other circumstances of extreme urgency" and specifically included "HIV/AIDS, tuberculosis, malaria and other epidemics" as representing such a situation, in which compulsory licensing of necessary drugs is permissible.[13]

Despite this highly encouraging development, the issue shows how sharply trade agreements can intrude into the most vital decisions a government can face. Granted, South Africa, as a free and sovereign nation, did not have to take part in the original TRIPS agreement. But there may have been substantial economic costs in refusing to take part. If nations, once they join the WTO, can lose significant national sovereignty in important areas, and if they are under constant pressure to remain in the WTO, the view that the WTO is no threat to national sovereignty is simplistic.

If we conclude that a nation under pressure to remain a member of the WTO has diminished national sovereignty, that is not in itself grounds for condemning the WTO. The loss of national sovereignty might be a price worth paying for the benefits the WTO brings. The choice is either to enter the agreement or not, and presumably those governments that decide to enter the agreement judge it to be better to do so, both for their own generation and for future generations. Before we criticize the WTO for eroding national sovereignty, then, we should ask: Is there any alternative means by which nations and their citizens could gain these benefits?

Traditionally those on the left, now ranged in opposition to the WTO, have been internationalists, whereas conservatives have been nationalists, opposing any constraints on state sovereignty. It is because the WTO puts free trade above both environmental values and national sovereignty that opposition to the WTO brings together such strange allies, from left and right. The alliance would split if the WTO were to be reformed in a way that enabled it to protect workers' rights and the environment, since this would give it more, rather than fewer, of the powers of global governance. Thus it would satisfy some critics on the left, but it would further inflame the nationalists on the right. The WTO's critics on the left support the supremacy of national legislatures and defend their right to make laws to protect the environment because they believe that the legislators are at least answerable to the people. Global corporations are not, and the WTO, in the eyes of the left, makes it too easy for global corporations to do as they please. This suggests that the WTO could meet the criticisms from the left—if not those from the right—by claiming that it provides the possibility of democratic rule over the global corporations. Then just as in the philosophy of social contract theorists like Rousseau, people forming a political community give up some of their individual freedom in order to gain a voice in the running of the whole community, so nations entering the WTO would give up some of their national sovereignty in order to gain a voice in the running of the global economy. . . .

CAN [WE] DO BETTER?

In the *Communist Manifesto*, Karl Marx described the impact of the capitalist class in terms that might today be applied to the WTO:

> It has resolved personal worth into exchange value, and in place of the numberless indefeasible chartered freedoms, has set up that single, unconscionable freedom—Free Trade. . . . All fixed, fast-frozen relations, with their train of ancient and venerable prejudices and opinions are swept away, all new-formed ones become antiquated before they can ossify. All that is solid melts into air, all that is holy is profaned.[14]

Defenders of the WTO would reject loaded words like "unconscionable" but might otherwise accept this account of what they are seeking to achieve. That free trade is a goal of overriding importance is implicit in the decisions of the WTO dispute panels. They would also agree that a global free market will sweep away "ancient and venerable prejudices" and they would see this as a good thing, because such prejudices restrict the use of individual creativity that brings benefits both to the innovative producer and to the consumers who can choose to take advantage of it.

Whether we accept or reject the claim that economic globalization is a good thing, we can still ask if there are ways of making it work better, or at least less badly. Even those who accept the general argument for the economic benefits of a global free market should ask themselves how well a global free market can work in the absence of any global authority to set minimum standards on issues like child labor, worker safety, the right to form a union, and environmental and animal welfare protection.

According to standard economic models, if various assumptions hold—including the assumptions that people always act fully rationally and on the basis of perfect information—free trade within a single, well-governed nation can be expected to create a state of affairs that is "Pareto efficient"—in other words, a state of affairs where no one's welfare can be improved without reducing the welfare of at least one other person. This is because the government will have legislated so that the private costs of production are brought into line with their costs to society overall. A corporation that pollutes a river into which it discharges wastes will be made to clean it up and to compensate those who have been harmed. Thus the costs of keeping the environment clean become part of the costs of production—in economic jargon, they are "internalized"—and producers who try to save money by not cleaning up their wastes gain no economic advantages over their competitors. But when we consider global free trade in the absence of any global authority to regulate pollution, or any civil law that provides remedies to the victims of pollution, the situation is different. A national government may have little interest in forcing a producer to internalize damage done to the global environment, for example to the oceans or the atmosphere or to stocks of cetaceans, fish, or migrating birds. Even though all nations share the global environment, the "tragedy of the commons" rules here, and a nation may benefit more by allowing its fishing fleet to catch as much as it can than by restraining the fleet so that the fleets of other nations can catch more. Thus, judged strictly in economic terms, without global environmental protection there is no reason to expect free trade to be Pareto efficient, let alone to maximize overall welfare.

Even if we ignore goods that belong to no nation, and focus on the quality of life in each nation, since governments are imperfect, unconstrained globalization is likely to lead to economic inefficiencies. If a ruling elite does not care about the working classes, or about the people of a particular region of its territory, it may not take into account the cost to them of air or water pollution, or for that matter of being forced to work long hours for little pay. Countries governed by such elites can then out-compete countries that provide some minimal conditions for their workers and, as Herman Daly puts it, "more of world production shifts to countries that do the poorest job of counting costs—a sure recipe for reducing the efficiency of global production."[15] The result is that the nexus between human welfare and the growth of the global economy, incomplete at the best of times, will be further eroded.

Significantly, the desirability of uniform global environmental and labor standards is a point on which critics of the WTO from the poorer countries often differ with labor and environmental activists from the rich countries. The fear is that the rich countries will use high standards to keep out goods from the poor countries. Vandana Shiva claims "social clauses make bedfellows of Northern trade unions and their corporations to jointly police and undermine social movements in the South."[16] There is no doubt that this could happen, but what is the alternative? Various measures could be taken to give developing countries more time to adjust, but in the end, just as national laws and regulations were eventually seen as essential to prevent the inhuman harshness of nineteenth century laissez-faire capitalism in the industrialized nations, so instituting global standards is the only way to prevent an equally inhuman form of uncontrolled global capitalism. The WTO accepts this idea, at least in theory. At its 1996 Ministerial meeting in Singapore, the WTO ministers renewed an earlier commitment "to the observance of internationally recognized core labor standards" and affirmed its support for the International Labor Organization as the body to set these standards. In Doha in 2001 the ministers reaffirmed that declaration and noted the "work under way in the International Labor Organization (ILO) on the social dimension of globalization."[17] Unfortunately nothing concrete had happened in the five years between those statements.

The WTO has up to now been dominated by neoliberal economic thinking. With some signs that the WTO is willing to rethink this approach, it is possible to imagine a reformed WTO in which the overwhelming commitment to free trade is replaced by a commitment to more fundamental goals. The WTO could then become a tool for pursuing these objectives. There are even clauses in the GATT agreement that could become the basis for affirmative action in trade, designed to help the least developed nations. In article XXXVI (3) the contracting parties agree that there is a "need for positive efforts designed to ensure that less-developed contracting parties secure a share in the growth in international trade commensurate with the needs of their economic development."[18] Under the present WTO regime, such clauses have been nice-sounding words with no practical impact. Far from making positive efforts to help the less-developed nations, the rich nations, especially the United States and the European Union, have failed to do even their fair share of reducing their own trade barriers in those areas that would do most good for the less developed nations. As *The Economist*—usually an avid supporter of the WTO—has reported, "Rich countries cut their tariffs by less in the Uruguay Round than poor ones did. Since then they have found new ways to close their markets."[19] The *New York Times* has said that several protectionist measures in the richest countries "mock those countries' rhetorical support for free trade."[20] Rich countries impose tariffs on manufactured goods from poor countries that are, according to one study, four times as high as those they impose on imports from other rich countries.[21] The WTO itself has pointed out that the rich nations subsidize their agricultural producers at a rate of $1 billion a day, or more than six times the level of development aid they give to poor nations.[22]

As we have already noted, there were signs at the November 2001 WTO meeting that the criticisms of the WTO are having some effect. If the WTO begins to take seriously GATT articles like XXXVI (3), we could in time come to see the WTO as a platform from which a policy of laissez-faire in global trade could be replaced by a more democratically controlled system of regulation that promotes minimum standards for environmental protection, worker safety, union rights, and animal welfare. But if the WTO cannot respond to these influences, it would be best for its scope to be curtailed by a body willing to take on the challenges of setting global environmental and social standards and finding ways of making them stick.

TRADE, LEGITIMACY, AND DEMOCRACY

We tend to think of trade as something politically neutral. In trading with a country, governments do not think that they are taking an ethical stand. They often trade with countries while disapproving of their regimes. In extreme cases, this neutrality breaks down. Many corporations and some governments recognized that doing business with South Africa under apartheid raised serious moral questions. Normally, however, governments keep the question of whether they should trade with a country separate from the question of whether they approve of its government. The United States has attacked China for its human rights record while at the same time expanding its trade with China. But sometimes trading with a country implies an ethical judgment. Many trade deals are done with governments. This is especially likely to be the case when transnational corporations make arrangements with the governments of developing countries to explore for oil and minerals, to cut timber, to fish, or to build big hotels and develop tourist complexes. Nigeria, for example, gets more than $6 billion a year, or about a quarter of its Gross Domestic Product, from selling oil. When multinational corporations like Shell trade with governments like those that Nigeria has had for most of the past thirty years—that is, military dictatorships—they are implicitly accepting the government's right to sell the resources that lie within its borders. What gives a government the moral right to sell the resources of the country over which it rules?[23]

The same question can be asked about international borrowing privileges. Corrupt dictators are allowed to borrow money from foreign countries or international lending bodies, and if they should happen to be overthrown, then the next government is seen as obliged by the signature of its predecessor to repay the loan. Should it refuse to do so, it will be excluded from international financial institutions and suffer adverse consequences. No questions are asked by the lenders about whether this or that dictator is entitled to borrow in the name of his or her country. Effective control of a territory is seen as being enough to obviate any inquiry into how that person came by that degree of control.

Both the conventional moral view, and the view taken in international law, is that once a government is recognized as legitimate, that legitimacy automatically confers the right to trade in the country's resources. The plausibility of this answer rests in the assertion that the government that is doing the trading is "legitimate." That sounds like a term that expresses an ethical judgment about the right of the government to hold

power. If this were so, then the answer to the challenge to the government's right to trade in the country's resources would be: a government that satisfies certain ethical standards regarding its claim to rule has the right to trade in the resources of the country over which it rules. But in fact that is not what is usually meant by calling a government "legitimate." The standard view has long been that the recognition of a government as legitimate has nothing to do with how that government came to power, or for that matter with how it governs. "The Law of Nations prescribes no rules as regards the kind of head a State may have," wrote Lassa Oppenheim in his influential 1905 text on international law, and he added that every state is "naturally" free to adopt any constitution "according to its discretion."[24] The sole test is whether it is in effective control of the territory. More recently Roth has put it this way:

> In such a conception, the international system regards ruling apparatuses as self-sufficient sources of authority—or rather deems their authority to derive from their characteristic ability to secure the acquiescence of their populaces, by whatever means . . . a government is recognized simply because its existence is a fact of life.[25]

International bodies, including the United Nations and the World Trade Organization, use this concept of legitimacy when they accept governments as the representatives of member nations.

The dominance of this conception makes alternatives seem unrealistic. There is, however, an alternative view with strong ethical credentials. In November 1792, in the wake of the French National Convention's declaration of a republic, Thomas Jefferson, then U.S. Secretary of State, wrote to the representative of the United States in France: "It accords with our principles to acknowledge any government to be rightful which is formed by the will of the people, substantially declared."[26] Now it is true that we cannot assume, from this statement, that Jefferson also intended the converse: that a government that cannot show that it has been formed by the declared will of the people is not rightfully the government of the nation. There may well be other grounds on which a government could be considered legitimate, perhaps by ruling unopposed for a long period without employing repressive measures to stifle dissent. The Jeffersonian principle does seem to imply, however, that some governments would *not* be regarded as legitimate—for example, one that had seized power by force of arms, dismissed democratically elected rulers, and killed those who spoke out against this way of doing things.

The claim that there is a fundamental human right to take part in deciding who governs us provides one reason for denying the legitimacy of a government that cannot show that it represents the will of the people. We could reach the same conclusion by arguing, on consequentialist grounds, that democratic governments can be expected to have more concern for the people over whom they rule than governments that do not answer, at regular intervals, to an electorate. In international law, this view of legitimacy has been gathering support in recent years, although it could not yet be said to be the majority view. In support of it, its defenders can point to many international documents, beginning with the opening words of the United Nations Charter, "We the peoples." The signatories of the Charter apparently regarded themselves as representatives of, and deriving their authority from, the peoples they governed. Next comes the Universal Declaration of Human Rights, which in Article 21 (3) states:

> The will of the people shall be the basis of the authority of government; this will shall be expressed in periodic and genuine elections which shall be by universal and equal suffrage and shall be held by secret vote or by equivalent free voting procedures.

The Universal Declaration of Human rights is not a treaty with explicit legal force, but the International Covenant on Civil and Political Rights is. Its first article states:

> All peoples have the right of self-determination. By virtue of that right they freely determine their political status and freely pursue their economic, social and cultural development.

In the second article, the parties to the Covenant undertake to ensure that each individual in its territory has the rights it contains "without distinction of any kind, such as race, color, sex, language, religion, political or other opinion, national or social origin, property, birth or other status." The inclusion of "political or other opinion" is important here, since Article 25 reads:

> Every citizen shall have the right and the opportunity, without any of the distinctions mentioned in article 2 and without unreasonable restrictions: (a) To take part in the conduct of public affairs, directly or through freely chosen representatives; (b) To vote and to be elected at genuine periodic elections which shall be by universal and equal suffrage and shall be held by secret ballot, guaranteeing the free expression of the will of the electors.

If we were to take these statements seriously, we would have to develop an entirely new concept of legitimate government, with far-reaching implications not only for trade but also for issues like the use of military intervention for humanitarian purposes. . . . But how would we decide when a government is sufficiently democratic to be recognized as legitimate? During the counting and recounting of votes in the United States presidential election in November 2000, jokes circulated to the effect that the United Nations was about to send in a team of observers to ensure that the elections were fair and democratic. The jokes had a serious point to make . . . the use of the electoral college, rather than the popular vote, to elect the president of the United States gives greater value to the votes of people living in states with small populations than to those living in states with large populations, and hence fails the basic "one vote, one value" requirement of democracy, and the "equal suffrage" stipulation of Article 25 (b) of the Universal Declaration of Human Rights. Nevertheless, the evident imperfections of democracy in the United States are not of the kind that should lead us to withdraw recognition of the legitimacy of the U.S. government. A minimalist concept of democracy is needed, for otherwise there will be few legitimate governments left. It may be useful to distinguish between governments that, although not democratic, can claim a traditional, long-standing authority that enables them to rule with the apparent acquiescence of the population, and without severe restrictions on basic civil liberties, and other regimes that, having seized power by force, use repressive measures to maintain themselves in power. A traditional absolute monarchy might be an example of the first form of government; a military regime that has come to power through a successful coup, does not hold free elections, and kills or jails its opponents is an example of the second.

Even if we focus only on those governments that gain power by force and hold it through repression of opposition, accepting the democratic concept of sovereignty would make a huge difference to the way we conduct world affairs. With regard to trade issues, we can imagine that an internationally respected body would appoint a tribunal consisting of judges and experts to scrutinize the credentials of each government on a regular basis. If a government could not, over time, satisfy the tribunal that its legitimacy stemmed from the support of its people, it would not be accepted as having the right to sell its country's resources, any more than a robber who overpowers you and takes your watch would be

recognized as entitled to sell it. For a private citizen to buy that watch, knowing or reasonably suspecting it to be stolen, is to commit the crime of receiving stolen goods. Under a minimalist democratic concept of sovereignty, it would similarly be a crime under international law for anyone to receive goods stolen from a nation by those who have no claim to sovereignty other than the fact that they exercise superior force.

Far-reaching as they are, such suggestions are gaining increasing recognition. At the Summit of the Americas meeting held in Quebec City in April 2001, the leaders of 34 American nations agreed that "any unconstitutional alteration or interruption of the democratic order in a state of the hemisphere constitutes an insurmountable obstacle to the participation of that state's government in the Summit of the Americas process." This means that a country that ceases to be a democracy cannot take part in the continuing talks on the free trade pact that the Summit planned, nor receive support from major international institutions like the Inter-American Development Bank.[27] In other words, democracy takes precedence over free trade, and the perceived benefits of participation in the proposed free trade agreement provide an incentive for all the nations of the Americas to maintain democratic institutions.

Though most leaders present at the Summit of the Americas, including President George W. Bush, are strong defenders of free trade and of the WTO, there is a potential conflict between the vision implicit in their Quebec City agreement and that of the WTO. The leaders of the nations of the Americas envision a kind of club of democratic nations, who trade with each other, assist each other in various ways, and deny these benefits to undemocratic outsiders or to any democracies that fall into the hands of dictators. In contrast the rules of the WTO do not allow its member nations to refuse to trade with other members because they are not democratic. If the WTO should realize its vision of a global free trade zone, regional free trade agreements would become irrelevant, and there would be no way in which trade sanctions could encourage democracy.

In Europe the lure of entry into the European Union is already encouraging democracy and support for basic human rights. For the former communist nations of Central and Eastern Europe, membership in the European Union is an extremely desirable goal, one that is likely to bring with it stability and prosperity. The European Union is a free trade zone, but it is much more than that. It has criteria for admission that include a democratic form of government and basic human rights guarantees.[28] Implicitly, by refusing to accept nations that fail to meet these standards, the European Union puts democracy and human rights ahead of free trade. As a result, those Central and Eastern European nations that are plausible candidates for membership are gradually bringing their laws in line with the minimum standards required by the European Union.

It is not only in Europe and the Americas that there are moves to strengthen and encourage democracy. In Africa, there has been increasing acceptance of the monitoring of elections by international observers, and the Organization of African Unity has now monitored elections in 39 countries.[29] At the inaugural meeting of the Community of Democracies in Warsaw in June 2000, representatives of the governments of 106 countries signed the *Warsaw Declaration*, recognizing "the universality of democratic values," and agreeing to "collaborate on democracy-related issues in existing international and regional institutions, forming coalitions and caucuses to support resolutions and other international activities aimed at the promotion of democratic governance" in order to "create an external environment conducive

to democratic development."[30] Here too democracy is seen as a great value, to be promoted through international collaboration. A trade pact between democracies, like that proposed for the Americas, would be a powerful means of promoting the value of democracy. So too would be a blacklist of illegitimate governments with no color of entitlement to rule, and with whom there is therefore no ethical basis for doing business. Corporations that wished to be perceived, not as the receivers of stolen goods, but as respectable global citizens and as supporters of democracy, might then be deterred from entering into agreements with these governments. This result would deny dictators the resources they need for buying weapons, paying their supporters, and boosting their bank balances in Switzerland. Obtaining power by ways that do not confer legitimacy would become just a little less attractive, and the prospects of an illegitimate government staying in power would be slightly reduced. Though the reduced prospects of development might be seen as a cost incurred not only by the illegitimate government but also by the people of the country, such development is, at best, a mixed blessing, and is often very damaging to the local people. For example, Shell's use of oil rights under the regime of the former Nigerian dictator General Sani Abacha was highly detrimental to the Ogoni people who lived above the oil fields. It can also be argued that it was, on balance, bad for Nigeria as a whole. In a study of the impact of extractive industries on the poor, Michael Ross, a political scientist at the University of California, Los Angeles, found that the living standards and quality of life experienced by the general population in countries dependent on selling minerals and oil are much lower than one would expect them to be, given the countries' per capita income. Mineral dependence correlated strongly with high levels of poverty and with unusually high levels of corruption, authoritarian government, military spending, and civil war. Ross's findings are in accord with those of an earlier influential study of natural resources and economic growth by Jeffrey Sachs and Andrew Warner.[31]

Consistently with such studies, we may think it is no coincidence that Nigeria has over the last 30 years had a preponderance of military governments, one of the world's highest levels of corruption, and enormous revenue from the sale of oil. Control of such vast wealth is a constant temptation for generals and others who have the means to overthrow civilian governments and then divert some of the wealth into their own pockets. If overthrowing the government did not bring with it control of the oil revenues, the temptation to do so would be that much less.[32]

A refusal to accept a dictatorial government as entitled to sell off the resources of the country over which it rules is not the same as the imposition of a total trade boycott on that country. Such boycotts can be very harmful to individual citizens in the country boycotted. Renewable resources, like agricultural produce and manufactured goods, might still be traded under private agreements. But when a corporation or a nation accepts the right of dictators to sell their country's non-renewable natural resources, it is accepting the dictators' claims to legitimate authority over those resources. This is not a neutral act, but one that requires ethical justification. In the rare case in which the dictatorship's record indicates that the money will be used to benefit the entire nation, that justification may be available, despite the absence of democracy. When, however, corporations can see that the money they are paying for a country's natural resources will be used primarily to enrich its dictator and enable him or her to buy more arms to consolidate his or her rule, there is no ethical justification for dealing with the dictator. The old-growth forests, oil, and minerals should be left alone, awaiting a government that has legitimate authority to sell them. ◆ ◆ ◆

◆ Notes

1. Tony Clarke, *By What Authority? Unmasking and Challenging the Global Corporations' Assault on Democracy through the World Trade Organization*, International Forum on Globalization and the Polaris Institute, San Francisco and Ottawa, no date (1999), p. 14.

2. Thomas Friedman, "Senseless in Seattle," *New York Times*, 1 December 1999, p. A23.

3. Victor Menotti, *Free Trade, Free Logging: How the World Trade Organization Undermines Global Forest Conservation*, International Forum on Globalization, San Francisco, 1999, p. ii.

4. *Agscene*, Autumn 1999, p. 20.

5. Martin Khor, "How the South Is Getting a Raw Deal at the WTO," in Sarah Anderson, ed., *Views from the South: The Effects of Globalization and the WTO on Third World Countries*, International Forum on Globalization, San Francisco, n.d. (1999), p. 11.

6. Vandana Shiva, "War Against Nature and the People of the South," in Anderson, *Views from the South*, pp. 92, 93, 123.

7. Thomas Friedman, *The Lexus and the Olive Tree*, Anchor Books, New York, 2000, p. 190.

8. See World Economic Forum, *Summaries of the Annual Meeting 2000*, Geneva (2000) summary of session 56.

9. World Trade Organization website, www.wto.org, 1.1.2002.

10. "The WTO in Brief, Part 3: The WTO Agreements," available at www.wto.org/english/thewto_e/whatis_e/inbrief_e/inbr03_e.htm.

11. See www.wto.org/english/thewto_e/whatis_e/10ben_e/10b10_e.htm.

12. See, for example, the *New York Times* editorial "The Urgency of Cheaper Drugs," 31 October 2001, p. A14, and Nicolo Itano, "Double Standards," *Christian Science Monitor*, 9 November 2001.

13. World Trade Organization, "Declaration on the TRIPS Agreement and Public Health," 14 November 2001, WT/MIN(01)/DEC/2, paragraphs 4, 5; www-chil.wto-ministerial.org/english/thewto_e/minist_e/min01_e/mindecl_trips_e.htm.

14. Karl Marx, *Communist Manifesto*, Penguin, Harmondsworth, 1967, p. 82.

15. Herman E. Daly, "Globalization and Its Discontents," *Philosophy and Public Policy Quarterly*, 21, 2/3, 2001, p. 19.

16. Vandana Shiva, "Social Environment Clauses — A 'Political Diversion'," in *Third World Economics*, 118, 1996, pp. 8–9, as quoted in Michelle Swenarchuk, "The International Confederation of Free Trade Unions Labour Clause Proposal: A Legal and Political Critique," in Stephen McBride and John Wiseman, eds., *Globalization and Its Discontents*. St. Martin's Press, New York, 2000, p. 167.

17. For the Singapore declaration, see World Trade Organization, Ministerial Declaration, 13 December 1996, WT/MIN(96)/DEC, paragraph 4, www.wto.org/english/thewto_e/minist_e/min96_e/wtodec_e.htm. For Doha, see World Trade Organization, Ministerial Declaration, 14 November 2001, WT/MIN(01)/DEC/1, paragraph 8, www-chil.wto-ministerial.org/english/thewto_e/minist_e/min01_e/mindecl_e.htm.

18. The agreement is available at member.nifty.ne.jp/menu/wto/1947/1947e36.htm. This clause could provide the legal basis for Thomas Pogge's proposal, in "A Global Resources Dividend" in David Crocker and Toby Linden, eds., *Ethics of Consumption: The Good Life, Justice and Global Stewardship*, Rowman and Littlefield, Lanham, Md., 1997, that states be required to share with the world's poor a small part of the value of any resources they use or sell.

19. *Economist*, 25 September 1999, p. 89, citing J. Michael Finger and Philip Schuler, "Implementation of Uruguay Round Commitments: The Development Challenge," *World Bank Research Working Paper* 2215, econ.worldbank.org/docs/941.pdf. I owe this reference to Thomas Pogge, "Global Poverty: Explanation and Responsibility."

20. Joseph Kahn, "U.S. Sees Trade Talks as a Test of Leadership," *New York Times*, 9 November 2001, p. C6.

21. Thomas Hertel and Will Martin, "Would Developing Countries Gain from the Inclusion of Manufactures in the WTO Negotiations?," Working Paper 7, presented to the conference on WTO and the Millennium Round, Geneva, September 1999, http://ae761e.agecon.purdue.edu/gtap/resources/download/42.pdf.

22. World Trade Organization, "Background Paper: The WTO's 2-Year Strategy Comes to Fruition," January 2002, paragraph 17, available at www.wto.org/english/news_e/news_e.htm.

23. This issue was brought to my attention by Thomas Pogge, to whom the following discussion is indebted. See his "Achieving Democracy," *Ethics and International Affairs* 15:1, 2001, pp. 3–23, as well as his *World Poverty and Human Rights*, Blackwell, Cambridge, Mass., 2002, chapter 4.

24. Lassa Oppenheim, *International Law*, vol. I, London, Longmans, 1905, p. 403; cited by Gregory H. Fox, "The Right to Political Participation in International Law," in Cecelia Lynch and Michael Loriaux, eds., *Law and Moral Action in World Politics*, University of Minnesota Press, Minneapolis, 1999, p. 83.

25. Brad Roth, *Governmental Illegitimacy in International Law*, Clarendon Press, Oxford, 1999, pp. 162–163.

26. Thomas Jefferson to Gouverneur Morris, 7 November 1792, *Works*, fourth edition, vol. III, p. 489, cited in Roth, *Governmental Illegitimacy in International Law*, p. 321.

27. Anthony DePalma, "Talks Tie Trade in the Americas to Democracy," *New York Times*, 23 April 2001, p. A1.

28. Well, maybe not so basic — if the United States were to apply for admission to the European

Union, its application would be rejected because the European Union considers the death penalty to be a violation of human rights. The European Union's position on the death penalty was re-affirmed in Article 2(2) of the EU Charter on Fundamental Freedoms signed at Nice in December 2000.

29. Severine M. Rugumamu, "State Sovereignty and Intervention in Africa: Nurturing New Governance Norms," Discussion paper presented to the International Commission on Intervention and State Sovereignty, Maputo, 10 March 2001, http://web.gc.cuny.edu/icissresearch/maputu %20discussion%20paper%20nurturing%20new %20norms.htm#N_1_.

30. *Final Warsaw Declaration: Towards a Community of Democracies*, 27 June 2000, circulated by the United Nations Secretariat as General Assembly Doc. A/55/328; available at www.democracy conference.org/declaration.html.

31. Michael Ross, *Extractive Sectors and the Poor*, Oxfam America, Boston, 2001; available at www.eireview.org/eir/eirhome.nsf/(DocLibrary)/ 6F177A935572B21785256AE3005AD736/$FILE/ Oxfam_EI_Report.pdf; Jeffrey Sachs and Andrew Warner, "Natural Resource Abundance and Economic Growth," National Bureau of Economic Research Working Paper 5398, 1995; available at http://papers.nber.org/papers/W5398.

32. See Pogge, *World Poverty and Human Rights*, chapter 4.

14

BUSINESS AND THE ENVIRONMENT

We all share in the fate of the planet; the way we conduct business may significantly affect our quality of life—whether through increasing pollution or altering the climate. Therefore, we must consider our welfare in the widest possible perspective and, viewed in this light, there may well be a continuing tension between individual economic welfare and our collective good.

Imagine that your neighbor drives a recreational vehicle to and from work, a total distance of about a mile. He likes to run the engine for a while so that the vehicle reaches a pleasant temperature for the ride. It needs a tune-up and belches smoke along the way while it drips oil from a leak. Many people would say this is unconscionable because the distance would be easy to walk, and the environmental burdens from his personal choices impose a cost on us all. However, we generally do not feel the same resentment toward someone who chooses to fly to Las Vegas for a vacation—an action that all in all is likely to hurt the planet more, given the massive consumption of fuel and water used in traveling to and staying at an artificial city in the desert. We also tend not to question the purchase of furniture made of exotic wood or to ask what happens to the trash we create. The point is that environmental consciousness amounts to more than looking at a series of discrete decisions; instead, we might look at our overall relationship with the planet. Are its resources here to be sustained or to be used up?

The notion of sustenance means that we should not use more resources than we can replace; in effect, we should not leave future generations less resources than we take advantage of today. A wholehearted commitment to a sustainable economy may mean that we reduce consumption, actively recycle, and support research and development of alternative technologies. For example, worldwide consumption of oil at present levels means that we will deplete our known oil fields in 25 years, but if consumption goes up by 5 percent a year, we will deplete them 10 years earlier. Hence, there is an ecological imperative to cut down on use or develop other fuels.

Our choices also affect animal life. Human economic decisions have an impact on the habitat of wild animals, and we have developed industries around others—we eat them, do research on them, domesticate them as pets, and hunt them for sport. Americans spent $34 billion on their pets in 2004. It has also been estimated that the methane emissions from cattle account for roughly the same amount as the energy industry releases into the air every year (about 8 million tons), making agriculture a major factor in discussions of global warming.

In order to frame a discussion about business and the environment, we can look at three issues:

◆ What does the word *natural* mean in this context?
◆ How should we value the environment?
◆ Do nonhuman animals have rights?

NATURAL

The word *natural* has a number of meanings in English. It conjures up pictures of pristine mountain streams and fields of spring flowers. In advertising it is used to connote products that are healthy or unprocessed. The word is often contrasted to *synthetic*, which makes us think of something artificial or human-made.

However, for better or worse, human beings have affected the world. Human development, and the changes it has brought about, may be perfectly natural in the sense that it springs from the same evolutionary forces that have shaped the rest of the environment; thus, it is natural that humans use fire, and hence a forest fire started by humans is just as natural as one started by lightning. Following this line of reasoning, it is natural for humans to use antibiotics or wear eyeglasses, and the development of cars and concrete shopping malls is as natural as a tree growing in the woods.

This ambiguity means that we need to be careful in the way we use the term *natural*. We must recognize that we cannot defend a stand of old-growth trees solely on the basis that they have been there untouched for a long time; preserv-

ing nature because it is natural to do so amounts to a circular argument that is not evidently true to everyone. Our challenge is to construct arguments that are not founded merely on intuition or sentiment.

VALUATION

The readings in this chapter all ask in various ways how we put a value on the environment, adapting the adage "If it can't be measured, it can't be managed." In general, we should look at three elements in valuation: intrinsic and instrumental value, proxy value, and political decisions.

Intrinsic and Instrumental Value

Some literature in environmental philosophy distinguishes between so-called deep and shallow ecology. Deep ecologists believe that the environment has intrinsic value and should be held absolutely immune from economic arguments. How could we value the song of a wild bird or the view of a sunset, they ask. Shallow ecologists (who would rarely use that term to describe themselves) feel that there are ways to measure our preferences in economic terms, and they challenge their counterparts to provide non-economically based decision procedures. Take the case of the unspoiled Alaskan wilderness, for example. A deep ecologist might say that it has value in and of itself and should not be treated as a commodity that can be traded.

Intrinsic value is a difficult concept, though. A supporter would have to claim legitimacy for her position; for example, do mosquito-infested swamps have intrinsic value, and if so, who is the authority to assign it? Additionally, do all holders of intrinsic value have it equally? Are there any compromises that could be made (maybe allowing a pathway to be built through a wilderness area) or does intrinsic value absolutely preclude human intervention?

Proxy Values

In William Baxter's selection, he contends that humans are the only ones who can endow entities with value and that doing so provides a useful decision process. So, for example, the only value of a penguin is what we assign to it. He points out that we make trade-offs all the time, and if it comes to deciding whether we value the continued existence of penguins more than cheap oil, the market is a reliable way for the decision to be made. The proxy is not that we actually make the choice but that we ask how much people would be willing to pay if they had to decide. In much the same way, you could ask your friend to put a price on an injury by asking him to say if he broke his leg and won the lottery in the same week, how much would he have to win in order to consider it not such a bad week after all?

Even if we agree with Baxter's view, there are still some practical difficulties in realizing it. We would have to be able to poll all those affected and have them put a price on something to which they have not given a lot of consideration. The evidence is that people do not have uniform values when presented with this sort of question. If an issue is highlighted in the press and is more immediate, it is likely to command a higher price. Our assignment of value also changes depending on whether we perceive a change as a gain or a loss; in general, we want to be compensated more for a loss than we would pay for a gain. Psychologists tell us that the amount you would demand in compensation from a company that proposed polluting a pristine stream you owned is more than you would be willing to pay for it to be cleaned up if it were already fouled. This dynamic shows us that the way an act is framed matters, and we cannot assign a set value on environmental change.

Cost/benefit analyses depend on assigning the correct values. The environment represents a complicated web of interrelated systems, and it is possible that causing a species of plant to go extinct in the rain forest will deprive us of a potential cure for cancer or that we come to realize after the fact that penguins played a critical role in the worldwide food chain. A prudent approach would say that we should err on the side of conservation, given that we cannot replace extinct species and that we are working in the absence of complete information.

Nevertheless, Baxter argues that we ought to recognize that we typically make decisions based on our instrumental preferences. From an economist's point of view, the market will let us know how much pollution we accept as optimal in exchange for our other preferences.

Political Decisions

Mark Sagoff contends that we reduce a resource's value by putting a price on it, but at the same time he recognizes that we have to make decisions. In the reading he is visiting the Civil War battlefield at Gettysburg, which arguably would be more popular and profitable if it were turned into an educational theme park, run along the lines of Disneyworld. We could have animatronics in a "Hall of Generals" and restaurants replicating the era. Sagoff argues there is something special and precious in preserving the area. Baxter might claim that we simply present the alternatives to all those possibly affected by the decision and let the market decide. Sagoff's response is that proxy valuation fails to capture our values accurately, and there are some cases where we should ignore the market evidence in favor of a democratic political decision.

BUSINESS AND THE ENVIRONMENT

The business community has usually treated environmental concerns that are beyond legal compliance as negative externalities, or as unnecessary costs. A negative externality is a cost imposed on a third party, usually without their knowledge or consent. Thus, sulphur emissions from power plants in Pennsylvania mix with water vapor in the atmosphere, and because of the prevailing winds, they fall over Canada as mild sulphuric acid. This acid rain causes harm; for instance, it has destroyed a number of Canadian forests. However, the Canadians are not compensated by the power plants, and if they were, then the cost of electricity would increase. In effect, consumers in the northeastern United States are benefiting by the power company omitting the costs of environmental impact when it calculates the cost of electricity.

A recent movement advocates that companies take a wider view of their impact on society and the world. John Elkington suggests that companies engage in "triple bottom line accounting," which assesses the firm not only in traditional economic measures but in terms of its effect on society and the environment. A company that opens a plant in a community might have a beneficial effect on the local economy, enhance civic life, and hurt or improve the ecosystem. The printer manufacturer Canon, for example, posts the company expenditures for environmental conservation and management activities on its Web site, noting the qualitative and quantitative benefits that result. Volvo, the Swedish carmaker, has adopted environmentalism as a key part of its corporate mission and issues environmental accounting to its shareholders. This certainly seems a reasonable move; looking at the success of a firm by only assessing its profits fails to account for its wider impact. Environmental and social accounting provides a more realistic picture of the more expansive effects of the enterprise; it also gives companies a means of justifying expenses that were otherwise not funded or poorly tracked.

ANIMALS

There is a tension in environmental philosophy between those who place paramount value on the biosphere and those who are dedicated to animal welfare. Many of those animals, of course, have been deliberately bred by humans, would not exist in the wild, and put a considerable strain on the environment.

Following remarks made by Jeremy Bentham in the 18th century, many animal rights proponents believe the key factor in determining how animals should be treated is whether they are subject to undue suffering. Humans, they argue, should not inflict suffering if they do not have to, and they should relieve it, especially if the cost to us is minimal and it will make a significant difference to the animal's quality of life. So, for example, hens are often kept in small wire cages and have their beaks cut off to stop them pecking one another, a behavior confinement produces. Veal calves are often force-fed and restrained from moving around to keep their meat succulent.

Jerry Rifkin dramatically shows us that rearing cattle is big business. There are 1.5 billion cattle in the world, and over a quarter of farmed land is dedicated to cattle production. Beef is the main source of protein for most Americans, and the industry had a retail equivalent of $87 billion in trade in 2002. In America, four companies control 80 percent of the cattle production. To increase efficiency farmers routinely use pharmaceuticals to promote growth and minimize infection.

Here again the question is whether business has an independent duty of care. There are considerable economic incentives for corporations to become as efficient as they can, whether they are producing shoes, needles, or chicken nuggets. If customers are aware of factory farming conditions, they can make purchasing choices; this effect is reflected in the burgeoning market for organic and free-range foods. Eric Katz examines the arguments presented by animal liberationists. He notes there are two ways that business affects animals: by impacting their natural habitat and by how it treats what he calls "animal artifacts." His conclusion is that businesses have an active responsibility to minimize unnecessary suffering, but his reforms are relatively minor.

THE PLANETARY WAGER

The final reading comes from Edward Freedman and his colleagues. They review the various stances a business might take toward environmental responsibility, which they describe as various shades of green. A company might take a purely legal approach or only consider environmental action if there is some payoff involved. The deeper shades of green represent a less self-interested view.

Freedman and his colleagues pose a critical question about the fate of the earth. It is drawn from a wager by the philosopher Blaise Pascal in

the 1600s. They ask how seriously we should consider environmental issues such as global warming, given conflicting scientific information. We can put the possible responses in a two-by-two matrix: We ignore the alarms, or we take action on one axis; we assume the problem is genuine, or it is not on the other. If it turns out there is no problem after all, we would be fine if we ignored it and will have wasted some resources if we took action. Alternatively, if there is a problem, and we have addressed it, then we would be able to mitigate some of the effects. However, if it is, in fact, a genuine problem, and we chose to ignore it, the consequences could be monumental and decisive.

These authors conclude that given the gravity of making a mistake with these possible outcomes, the only rational choice is to risk business inefficiency and wasting resources by assuming environmental concerns to be both pressing and immediate. The consequences of making a bad decision about the welfare of the planet, they argue, may be profound—not only for business but for all life.

People or Penguins

The Case for Optimal Pollution

William F. Baxter

What is the value of a penguin? Would it make much difference to most people if they did not exist? Would we rather have healthier penguins or cheap gas?

It is hard for people—and corporations—to think of the environment in the abstract. Baxter proposes some basic assumptions when considering arguments about the environment. In many ways his views are reminiscent of Milton Friedman or Ayn Rand: Human welfare and individual choice are paramount virtues. Baxter is an economist, and in the terms used earlier in the text, he is a "market moralist," that is, he believes that people's values are reflected in their economic choices and that we should cut through the rhetoric to see where individuals actually spend their money. He states that we make trade-offs all the time—among them, human welfare (for example the convenience of driving in a car) and a clean environment. Furthermore, he asserts that the only values that matter are human values; penguins are valuable because we value them, and it is perfectly possible that we might decide that we value other things more. He believes environmental choices are not usually between a pristine environment and a polluted one, but they are rather about finding an optimal level of pollution—one where we have the cleanest planet we can in exchange for the maximum convenience we enjoy.

I start with the modest proposition that, in dealing with pollution, or indeed with any problem, it is helpful to know what one is attempting to accomplish. Agreement on how and whether to pursue a particular objective, such as pollution control, is not possible unless some more general objective has been identified and stated with reasonable precision. We talk loosely of having clean air and clean water, of preserving our wilderness areas, and so forth. But none of these is a sufficiently general objective: each is more accurately viewed as a means rather than as an end.

With regard to clean air, for example, one may ask, "how clean?" and "what does clean mean?" It is even reasonable to ask, "why have clean air?" Each of these questions is an implicit demand that a more general community goal be stated—a goal sufficiently general in its scope and enjoying sufficiently general assent among the community of actors that such "why" questions no longer seem admissible with respect to that goal.

If, for example, one states as a goal the proposition that "every person should be free to do whatever he wishes in contexts where his actions do not interfere with the interests of other human beings," the speaker is unlikely to be met with a response of "why." The goal may be criticized as uncertain in its implications or difficult to implement, but it is so basic a tenet of our civilization—it reflects a cultural value so broadly shared, at least in the abstract—that the question "why" is seen as impertinent or imponderable or both.

I do not mean to suggest that everyone would agree with the "spheres of freedom" objective just stated. Still less do I mean to suggest that a society could subscribe to four or five such general objectives that would be adequate in their coverage to serve as testing criteria by which all other disagreements might be measured. One difficulty in the attempt to construct such a list is that each new goal added will conflict, in certain applications, with each prior goal listed; and thus each goal serves as a limited qualification on prior goals.

Without any expectation of obtaining unanimous consent to them, let me set forth four goals that I generally use as ultimate testing criteria in attempting to frame solutions to problems of human organization. My position regarding pollution stems from these four criteria. If the criteria appeal to you and any part of what appears hereafter does not, our disagreement will have a helpful focus: which of us is correct, analytically, in supposing that his position on pollution would better serve these general goals. If the criteria do not seem acceptable to you, then it is to be expected that our more particular judgments will differ, and the task will then be yours to identify the basic set of criteria upon which your particular judgments rest.

My criteria are as follows:

1. The spheres of freedom criterion stated above.
2. Waste is a bad thing. The dominant feature of human existence is scarcity—our avail-able resources, our aggregate labors, and our skill in employing both have always been, and will continue for some time to be, inadequate to yield to every man all the tangible and intangible satisfactions he would like to have. Hence, none of those resources, or labors, or skills, should be wasted—that is, employed so as to yield less than they might yield in human satisfactions.
3. Every human being should be regarded as an end rather than as a means to be used for the betterment of another. Each should be afforded dignity and regarded as having an absolute claim to an evenhanded application of such rules as the community may adopt for its governance.
4. Both the incentive and the opportunity to improve his share of satisfactions should be preserved to every individual. Preservation of incentive is dictated by the "no-waste" criterion and enjoins against the continuous, totally egalitarian redistribution of satisfactions, or wealth; but subject to that constraint, everyone should receive, by continuous redistribution if necessary, some minimal share of aggregate wealth so as to avoid a level of privation from which the opportunity to improve his situation becomes illusory.

The relationship of these highly general goals to the more specific environmental issues at hand may not be readily apparent, and I am not yet ready to demonstrate their pervasive implications. But let me give one indication of their implications. Recently scientists have informed us that use of DDT in food production is causing damage to the penguin population. For the present purposes let us accept that assertion as an indisputable scientific fact. The scientific fact is often asserted as if the correct implication—that we must stop agricultural use of DDT—followed from the mere statement of the fact of penguin damage. But plainly it does not follow if my criteria are employed.

My criteria are oriented to people, not penguins. Damage to penguins, or sugar pines, or geological marvels is, without more, simply irrelevant. One must go further, by my criteria, and say: Penguins are important because people enjoy seeing them walk about rocks; and furthermore, the well-being of people would be less impaired by halting use of DDT than by giving up penguins. In short, my observations about environmental problems will be people-oriented, as are my criteria. I have no interest in preserving penguins for their own sake.

It may be said by way of objection to this position, that it is very selfish of people to act as if each person represented one unit of importance and nothing else was of any importance. It is undeniably selfish. Nevertheless I think it is the only tenable starting place for analysis for several reasons. First, no other position corresponds to the way most people really think and act—i.e., corresponds to reality.

Second, this attitude does not portend any massive destruction of nonhuman flora and fauna, for people depend on them in many obvious ways, and they will be preserved because and to the degree that humans do depend on them.

Third, what is good for humans is, in many respects, good for penguins and pine trees—clean air for example. So that humans are, in these respects, surrogates for plant and animal life.

Fourth, I do not know how we could administer any other system. Our decisions are either private or collective. Insofar as Mr. Jones is free to act privately, he may give such preferences as he wishes to other forms of life: he may feed birds in winter and do with less himself, and he may even decline to resist an advancing polar bear on the ground that the bear's appetite is more important than those portions of himself that the

bear may choose to eat. In short my basic premise does not rule out private altruism to competing life-forms. It does rule out, however, Mr. Jones' inclination to feed Mr. Smith to the bear, however hungry the bear, however despicable Mr. Smith.

Insofar as we act collectively on the other hand, only humans can be afforded an opportunity to participate in the collective decisions. Penguins cannot vote now and are unlikely subjects for the franchise—pine trees more unlikely still. Again each individual is free to cast his vote so as to benefit sugar pines if that is his inclination. But many of the more extreme assertions that one hears from some conservationists amount to tacit assertions that they are specially appointed representatives of sugar pines, and hence that their preferences should be weighted more heavily than the preferences of other humans who do not enjoy equal rapport with "nature." The simplistic assertion that agricultural use of DDT must stop at once because it is harmful to penguins is of that type.

Fifth, if polar bears or pine trees or penguins, like men, are to be regarded as ends rather than means, if they are to count in our calculus of social organization, someone must tell me how much each one counts, and someone must tell me how these life-forms are to be permitted to express their preferences, for I do not know either answer. If the answer is that certain people are to hold their proxies, then I want to know how those proxy-holders are to be selected: self-appointment does not seem workable to me.

Sixth, and by way of summary of all the foregoing, let me point out that the set of environmental issues under discussion—although they raise very complex technical questions of how to achieve any objective—ultimately raise a normative question: what *ought* we to do. Questions of *ought* are unique to the human mind and world—

they are meaningless as applied to a nonhuman situation.

I reject the proposition that we *ought* to respect the "balance of nature" or to "preserve the environment" unless the reason for doing so, express or implied, is the benefit of man.

I reject the idea that there is a "right" or "morally correct" state of nature to which we should return. The word "nature" has no normative connotation. Was it "right" or "wrong" for the earth's crust to heave in contortion and create mountains and seas? Was it "right" for the first amphibian to crawl up out of the primordial ooze? Was it "wrong" for plants to reproduce themselves and alter the atmospheric composition in favor of oxygen? For animals to alter the atmosphere in favor of carbon dioxide both by breathing oxygen and eating plants? No answers can be given to these questions because they are meaningless questions.

All this may seem obvious to the point of being tedious, but much of the present controversy over environment and pollution rests on tacit normative assumptions about just such nonnormative phenomena: that it is "wrong" to impair penguins with DDT, but not to slaughter cattle for prime rib roasts. That it is wrong to kill stands of sugar pines with industrial fumes, but not to cut sugar pines and build housing for the poor. Every man is entitled to his own preferred definition of Walden Pond, but there is no definition that has any moral superiority over another, except by reference to the selfish needs of the human race.

From the fact that there is no normative definition of the natural state, it follows that there is no normative definition of clean air or pure water—hence no definition of polluted air—or of pollution—except by reference to the needs of man. The "right" composition of the atmosphere is one which has some dust in it and some

lead in it and some hydrogen sulfide in it—just those amounts that attend a sensibly organized society thoughtfully and knowledgeably pursuing the greatest possible satisfaction for its human members.

The first and most fundamental step toward solution of our environmental problems is a clear recognition that our objective is not pure air or water but rather some optimal state of pollution. That step immediately suggests the question: How do we define and attain the level of pollution that will yield the maximum possible amount of human satisfaction?

Low levels of pollution contribute to human satisfaction but so do food and shelter and education and music. To attain ever lower levels of pollution, we must pay the cost of having less of these other things. I contrast that view of the cost of pollution control with the more popular statement that pollution control will "cost" very large numbers of dollars. The popular statement is true in some senses, false in others; sorting out the true and false senses is of some importance. The first step in that sorting process is to achieve a clear understanding of the difference between dollars and resources. Resources are the wealth of our nation; dollars are merely claim checks upon those resources. Resources are of vital importance; dollars are comparatively trivial.

Four categories of resources are sufficient for our purposes: At any given time a nation, or a planet if you prefer, has a stock of labor, of technological skill, of capital goods, and of natural resources (such as mineral deposits, timber, water, land, etc.). These resources can be used in various combinations to yield goods and services of all kinds—in some limited quantity. The quantity will be larger if they are combined efficiently, smaller if combined inefficiently. But in either event the resource stock is limited, the goods and services that they can be made to yield are limited; even the most efficient use of them will yield less than our population, in the aggregate, would like to have.

If one considers building a new dam, it is appropriate to say that it will be costly in the sense that it will require x hours of labor, y tons of steel and concrete, and z amount of capital goods. If these resources are devoted to the dam, then they cannot be used to build hospitals, fishing rods, schools, or electric can openers. That is the meaningful sense in which the dam is costly.

Quite apart from the very important question of how wisely we can combine our resources to produce goods and services, is the very different question of how they get distributed—who gets how many goods? Dollars constitute the claim checks which are distributed among people and which control their share of national output. Dollars are nearly valueless pieces of paper except to the extent that they do represent claim checks to some fraction of the output of goods and services. Viewed as claim checks, all the dollars outstanding during any period of time are worth, in the aggregate, the goods and services that are available to be claimed with them during that period—neither more nor less.

It is far easier to increase the supply of dollars than to increase the production of goods and services—printing dollars is easy. But printing more dollars doesn't help because each dollar then simply becomes a claim to fewer goods, i.e., becomes worth less.

The point is this: many people fall into error upon hearing the statement that the decision to build a dam, or to clean up a river, will cost $X million. It is regrettably easy to say: "It's only money. This is a wealthy country, and we have lots of money." But you cannot build a dam or clean a river with $X million—unless you also have a match, you can't even make a fire. One builds a dam or cleans a river by diverting labor and steel and trucks and factories from making one kind of goods to making another. The cost in dollars is merely a shorthand way of describing the extent of the diversion necessary. If we build a dam for $X million, then we must recognize that we will have $X million less housing and food and medical care and electric can openers as a result.

Similarly, the costs of controlling pollution are best expressed in terms of the other goods we will have to give up to do the job. This is not to say the job should not be done. Badly as we need more housing, more medical care, and more can openers, and more symphony orchestras, we could do with somewhat less of them, in my judgment at least, in exchange for somewhat cleaner air and rivers. But that is the nature of the trade-off, and analysis of the problem is advanced if that unpleasant reality is kept in mind. Once the trade-off relationship is clearly perceived, it is possible to state in a very general way what the optimal level of pollution is. I would state it as follows:

People enjoy watching penguins. They enjoy relatively clean air and smog-free vistas. Their health is improved by relatively clean water and air. Each of these benefits is a type of good or service. As a society we would be well advised to give up one washing machine if the resources that would have gone into that washing machine can yield greater human satisfaction when diverted into pollution control. We should give up one hospital if the resources thereby freed would yield more human satisfaction when devoted to elimination of noise in our cities. And so on, trade-off by trade-off, we should divert our productive capacities from the production of existing goods and services to the production of a cleaner, quieter, more pastoral nation up to—and no further than—the point at which we value more highly the next washing machine or hospital that we would have to do without than we value the next unit of environmental improvement that the diverted resources would create.

Now this proposition seems to me unassailable but so general and abstract as to be unhelpful—at least unadministerable in the form stated. It assumes we can measure in some way the incremental units of human satisfaction yielded by very different types of goods. The proposition must remain a pious abstraction until I can explain how this measurement process can occur. . . . But I insist that the proposition stated describes the result for which we should be striving—and again, that it is always useful to know what your target is even if your weapons are too crude to score a bull's eye. ◆ ◆ ◆

Cannibals with Forks
The Triple Bottom Line of 21st Century Business

John Elkington

Business success has traditionally been measured in terms of growth and profitability. At the same time it affects human relationships and the environment, and these factors have rarely been assessed. Hunting elephants for ivory may appall many Western animal lovers, but it should be judged in the context that it used to be a perfectly acceptable practice by the cultural group that now condemns it, and it may be hugely profitable. The priorities of those just trying to survive may require using any means to make money, and so regulation needs to be accompanied by social changes that provide alternative sources of revenue. It would be hard, for example, to demand that an impoverished group in an undeveloped country abide by the strictest standards of environmental welfare unless there are clear economic incentives to do so.

Elkington coined the term triple bottom line *as a way for businesses to measure their impact in three dimensions: economically, socially, and environmentally. He is concerned that we are reaching the planet's limits of sustainability; that is, further development is likely to harm both the environment and people. Elkington believes that talk about sustainability needs to take into account all three integrated dimensions.*

Elkington's point is that we cannot neatly separate environmental and social issues from business issues, and to realistically discuss the problems we face we need to be able to measure the impact of business on the overall gains or losses of global resources. He is not antibusiness, however, and thinks that corporations making wise choices and marshalling their resources may be the key to future sustainability.

Like the ancient Trojans dragging the vast wooden horse through a great gap torn in the walls of their long-besieged city, some of the world's best business brains spent the 1990s struggling to take on board the emerging sustainability agenda. Many of their colleagues warned that success would end in disaster, just as it had done for the Trojans. Sustainable development, they argued, was a treacherous concept; basically, communism in camouflage. By the middle of the last decade of the 20th century, however, their fevered brows were being soothed by the concept of "eco-efficiency," promoted by the World Business Council for Sustainable Development (WBCSD). And then, as some had feared, the trap was sprung.

Communism had nothing to do with it. But the sustainability agenda, long understood as an attempt to harmonize the traditional financial bottom line with emerging thinking about the environmental bottom line, turned out to be more complicated than some early business enthusiasts had imagined. Today we think in terms of a "triple bottom line," focusing on economic prosperity, environmental quality, and—the element which business had preferred to overlook—social justice.

None of this was new, of course. *Our Common Future*, the 1987 report of the World Commission on Environment and Development, had made it perfectly clear that equity issues, and particularly the concept of inter-generational equity, were at the very heart of the sustainability agenda.[1] But most of the hundreds of companies that limbered up for the 1992 Earth Summit by signing the Business Charter for Sustainable Development, devised by the International Chamber of Commerce (ICC), had little idea of the deeper logic of sustainable development. As far as they, and the thousands of companies which have signed up since, were concerned, the basic challenge was simply one of "greening," of making business more efficient and trimming costs.

When the *Harvard Business Review* turned its spotlight on to the sustainability agenda in 1997,

ten years after the publication of *Our Common Future*, it noted that, "Beyond greening lies an enormous challenge—and an enormous opportunity. The challenge is to develop a sustainable global economy: an economy that the planet is capable of supporting indefinitely."[2] This represents a profound challenge. Although some parts of the developed world may be beginning to turn the corner in terms of ecological recovery, the planet as a whole is still seen to be on an unsustainable course.

"Those who think that sustainability is only a matter of pollution control are missing the bigger picture," explained Stuart Hart, director of the Corporate Environmental Management Program at the University of Michigan:

> "Even if all the companies in the developed world were to achieve zero emissions by the year 2000, the earth would still be stressed beyond what biologists refer to as its carrying capacity. Increasingly, the scourges of the late twentieth century— depleted farmland, fisheries, and forests; choking urban pollution; poverty; infectious disease; and migration—are spilling over geopolitical borders. The simple fact is this: in meeting our needs, we are destroying the ability of future generations to meet theirs."

And these problems are not simply economic and environmental, either in their origins or nature. Instead, they raise social, ethical, and, above all, political issues. The roots of the crisis, Hart concluded, are "political and social issues that exceed the mandate and capabilities of any corporation." But here is the paradox: "At the same time, corporations are the only organizations with the resources, the technology, the global reach, and, ultimately, the motivation to achieve sustainability."

There is no question that some of these issues can have—indeed, already have had—a profound impact on the financial bottom line. Think of the companies and industries making or using such products as asbestos, mercury, PCBs, PVC, and

CFCs and it is clear that the long-term sustainability of major slices of any modern economy is already being called into question.

Worryingly, at least on current trends, things can only get worse. "It is easy to state the case in the negative," as Hart pointed out. "Faced with impoverished customers, degraded environments, failing political systems, and unraveling societies, it will be increasingly difficult for corporations to do business. But," he stressed:

> "the positive case is even more powerful. The more we learn about the challenges of sustainability, the clearer it is that we are poised at the threshold of an historic moment in which many of the world's industries may be transformed."

The level of change implied by the sustainability transition is extraordinary. As the World-watch Institute put it in a recent *State of the World* report:

> "We are only at the beginning of this restructuring. New industries are emerging to reestablish natural balances—based on technologies that can produce heat and light without putting carbon into the atmosphere; on metals made out of the scrap of past buildings and cars; on papers made out of what was once considered wastepaper. Some homes and offices are heated entirely by the sun or from electricity generated by the wind."[3]

But sustainable capitalism will need more than just environment-friendly technologies and, however important these may be, markets which actively promote dematerialization. We will also need to address radically new views of what is meant by social equity, environmental justice and business ethics. This will require a much better understanding not only of financial and physical forms of capital, but also of natural, human, and social capital.

Business leaders and executives wanting to grasp the full scale of the challenge confronting their corporations and markets will need to carry out a sustainability audit . . . against the emerging requirements and expectations driven by sustainability's triple bottom line. In the spirit of the management dictum that what you can't measure you are likely to find hard to manage, we should ask whether it is even possible to measure progress against the triple bottom line?

The answer is yes, but the metrics are still evolving in most areas—and need to evolve much further if they are to be considered in an integrated way. . . .

THE ECONOMIC BOTTOM LINE

Let's begin in the area where business should feel most at home. Given that we are using the "bottom line" metaphor, however, we need to understand exactly what it means in its traditional usage. A company's bottom line is the profit figure used as the earnings figure in the earnings-per-share statement, part of standard accounting practice. In trying to assess a company's conventional bottom line performance, accountants pull together, record and analyze a wide range of numerical data. This approach is often seen as a model for environmental and social accounting, but the challenge can be even tougher in these emerging areas of corporate accountability.[4]

Economic Capital

So how should a would-be sustainable corporation assess whether its business operations are economically sustainable? Obviously, a critical first step is to understand what is meant by economic capital. In the simplest terms, your capital is the total value of your assets minus your liabilities. In traditional economic theory, capital as a factor of production can come in two main forms: *physical capital* (including machinery and plant) and *financial capital*. But as we move into the knowledge economy, the concept is gradually being extended to include such concepts as *human capital*—a measure of the experience, skills, and other knowledge-based assets of the individuals who make up an organization. We will also consider the *intellectual capital* concepts adopted by companies like Skandia.

Among the questions business people need to ask in this area are the following. Are our costs competitive—and likely to remain so? Is the demand for our products and services sustainable? Is our rate of innovation likely to be competitive in the longer term? How can we ensure that human or intellectual capital does not migrate out of the organization? Are our profit margins sustainable?[5] Longer term, too, the concept of economic capital will need to absorb much wider concepts, such as *natural capital* and *social capital*, both of which are discussed below.

Accountability

In most countries, companies have an obligation to give an account of their financial performance. In the case of limited companies, directors are accountable to shareholders. This responsibility is partly discharged by the production and—in the case of public companies—publication of an annual report and accounts. An annual general meeting (AGM) theoretically provides shareholders with an opportunity to oversee the presentation of audited accounts, the appointment of directors and auditors, the fixing of their remuneration, and recommendations for the payment of dividends.

Typically, there has been little, if any, overlap between the areas covered by financial auditors in serving the interests of shareholders and the issues of interest to other stakeholders in terms of the environmental and social bottom lines. But one area where we see a growing degree of overlap between a company's economic and environmental performance is "eco-efficiency." At the same time, too, there are early signs that, as the sustainability agenda becomes a board-level issue, we will see growing overlaps with the whole corporate governance agenda.

Accounting

By the very nature of their work and training, most traditional accountants are short-sighted. Typically, the so-called accounting period is 12 months. Internal accounts are often prepared on a monthly or quarterly basis, with full results produced annually. Worldwide, however, the pressure to perform on a quarterly basis is intensifying as Anglo-Saxon approaches to stock management and investment banking spread.

In preparing their accounts, accountants are guided by a range of reasonably well-established concepts. These include the *ongoing concern concept* (with assets not stated at break-up value, unless there is evidence that the company is no longer viable), the *consistency concept* (which calls for accounts to be prepared on a consistent basis, allowing accurate comparisons between quarters of years), the *prudence concept* (accounts should be prepared on a conservative basis, recording income and profits only when they are achieved, and making provision for foreseeable losses) and *depreciation* (with the value of most assets progressively written off over time). . . .

We have tended to see the bottom line as the hardest of realities, representing the unappealable verdict of impartial markets.[6] But it is increasingly clear that such accounting concepts are man-made conventions that change over space and time. Bottom lines are the product of the institutions and societies in which they have evolved. And, because accounting inevitably involves compromises, the bottom line turns out to be influenced by subjective interpretations, quite apart from "creative" accounting. So, for example, when Rover was taken over by BMW and subjected to Germany's stricter valuation criteria, a 1995 "profit" of £91 million became a £158 million "loss."

A key concept in relation to all three dimensions of sustainability—but particularly relevant in relation to environmental and societal costs—

is that of "externalities." These economic, social, or environmental costs are not recorded in accounts. So, to take an economic example, the decision of a company to locate a high-technology plant in a relatively undeveloped region may have such effects as drawing technical talent away from local firms, or forcing up property prices locally beyond what local people can afford. We will look at examples of environmental and social externalities under the appropriate sections below.

Issues and Indicators
These are key tools of the trade. Among the items you would expect to see in a company's report and accounts would be a profit and loss account, balance sheet and statement of total recognized losses and gains. When it comes to wider economic sustainability, however, there is a surprising lack of generally acceptable indicators. Key considerations here might include the long-term sustainability of a company's costs, of the demand for its products or services, of its pricing and profit margins, of its innovation programs, and of its "business ecosystem.". . .

Reporting, Risk-Rating, and Benchmarking
Audits are designed to produce information for internal consumption, but there are growing demands for transparency. How far should a company be expected to go? Levels of reporting by companies vary widely, partly reflecting different accounting regimes, partly different opinions on what it is appropriate to report, and partly on the different needs of report users. The information generated by such reports, and available from other sources, is used by analysts in risk-rating. They are interested, for example, in working out the appropriate levels of share pricing, premiums for insurance policies, or security for loans. Even today, environmental and social risks are not high on the agenda for most companies, with the

result that very few annual reports yet contain a robust section on social and/or environmental performance.

Another use for the reported data is benchmarking, which involves comparisons of processes and products, both within an industry and outside it, to identify and then meet or exceed best practice. Most benchmarking exercises in this area, however, now involve in-depth, in-company research, rather than simply relying on published reports. And it would be rare indeed in today's world for a company to spend much time on other aspects of the triple bottom line, unless it happened to be operating in a highly sensitive industry like waste disposal or nuclear power.

ENVIRONMENTAL BOTTOM LINE
The social agenda for business probably has a longer history than the environmental agenda. Think of the early controversies around slavery, child labor, and working conditions. But, following a flurry of interest in social accounting and auditing in the 1970s, the environmental agenda has tended to attract greater attention. The result, paradoxically, is that many business people these days feel happier being challenged on environmental issues than on social issues. This fact has had a marked impact on the way the sustainability agenda is defined by business.

Natural Capital
How can a would-be sustainable corporation work out whether it is environmentally sustainable? Again, a critical first step is to understand what is meant by natural capital. The concept of natural wealth is both complex and still evolving. If you try to account for the natural capital embodied in a forest, for example, it is not simply a question of counting the trees and trying to put a price-tag on the lumber they represent. You have to account for the underlying natural wealth

which supports the forest ecosystem, producing— as just one stream of benefits—timber and other commercial products. Wider forest functions that need to be added into the equation include contributions to the regulation of water (in the atmosphere, water table, soils, and surface waters) and of greenhouse gases like carbon dioxide and methane.[7] And then there are all the flora and fauna, including commercial fisheries, whose health is linked to the health of the forest.

Natural capital can also be thought of as coming in two main forms: "critical natural capital" and renewable, replaceable, or substitutable natural capital. The first form embraces natural capital which is essential to the maintenance of life and ecosystem integrity; the second forms of natural capital which can be renewed (e.g. through breeding or relocation of sensitive ecosystems), repaired (e.g. environmental remediation or desert reclamation), or substituted or replaced (e.g. growing use of man-made substitutes, such as solar panels in place of limited fossil fuels).[8]

Among the questions business people will need to ask are the following. What forms of natural capital are affected by our current operations—and will they be affected by our planned activities? Are these forms of natural capital sustainable given these, and other, likely pressures? Is the overall level of stress properly understood and likely to be sustainable? Is the "balance of nature" or the "web of life" likely to be significantly affected?

The interesting thing about a company's ecological bottom line is that the carrying capacity of most ecosystems varies in relation to the number—and behavior—of the economic actors operating within them. As a result, these bottom lines will vary over time and space. The more efficient the actors, however, the more actors can be sustained. . . .

Accountability

In many countries, companies are held accountable by regulators for aspects of their environmental performance. In the USA, the Toxic Release Inventory (TRI) requires companies producing more than certain threshold limits of over 600 chemicals to report their emissions. Some countries, like the Netherlands, also back up their regulations with voluntary programs designed to push companies towards sectorally agreed targets.

Just as often, however, business is held to account by environmentalist and media campaigns, which may bear little relation to regulated or voluntarily agreed targets. And as companies begin to challenge their supply chains, a new dimension of pressure is being introduced. While planning this book, for example, I was invited by Volvo to help facilitate their first environmental conference for supplier companies. The company's top management told the 500-plus audience that Volvo had started off by focusing on safety, then added quality. Now, they said, environmental performance was increasingly in the spotlight—and suppliers would find environmental aspects being covered in Volvo's regular supplier audits. . . .

Accounting

The field of environmental accounting is relatively embryonic, but is generating a growing literature.[9] Among other things, it aims to: rebalance the treatment of environmental costs and benefits in conventional accounting practice; separately identify environmental related costs and revenues within the conventional accounting systems; devise new forms of valuation which encourage better management decisions and increased investment in environmental protection and improvement; develop new performance indicators to track progress; and experiment with ways in which sustainability considerations can be assessed and incorporated into mainstream accounting.[10]

As far as environmental externalities go, many companies have been forced to take on to their books impacts and effects which were once externalized. Take the case of T&N, which as Turner & Newall was once one of the world's largest asbestos producers. For years, the company argued that the risks involved in the use of asbestos were acceptable. Eventually, however, the tide turned, not only against Turner & Newall but against the entire asbestos industry. At the time of writing, T&N had already paid out over £350 million over ten years to meet asbestos claims—and was busily selling off corporate assets to fund a further £323 million provision.[11] And, in an attempt to draw a line under its asbestos legacy, the company had announced a £515 million charge against annual profits to meet future personal injury claims and insurance costs. It was not alone in experiencing such problems.

Issues and Indicators

The sheer number of potential issues, and hence the expanding range of possible environmental risks, is reflected in the potential indicators. These include financial indicators such as: trends in legal compliance; provisions for fines, insurance, and other legally related costs; and landscaping, remediation, decommissioning, and abandonment costs. But there is also a growing need to measure environmental impacts in terms of new metrics, including: the number of public complaints; the life-cycle impacts of products; energy, materials, and water usage at production sites; potentially polluting emissions; environmental hazards, and risks; waste generation; consumption of critical natural capital; and performance against best-practice standards set by leading customers and by green and ethical investment funds.

At the company level, the task is being made somewhat easier by the development and publication of international environmental management standards. Globally, there is ISO 14001, developed by the International Standards Organisation (ISO) in the wake of the 1992 Earth Summit.[12] In Europe, there is the Eco-Management and Audit Scheme (EMAS), which takes a step beyond ISO 14001 by requiring companies to produce an environmental statement for each registered site. Both of these schemes are voluntary, but the expectation is that market forces will drive them down through value chains in the same way as the Total Quality Management (TQM) approach has spread.

But we will also need to consider environmental sustainability at the ecosystem level, where corporate environmental management systems are going to be of little help. This is an area where national and international government agencies and research organizations will continue to play a critically important role. . . .

Reporting, Risk-Rating, and Benchmarking

The environmental reporting and benchmarking trends are enormously significant. . . . The first few corporate environmental reports (CERs), or environmental annual reports (EARs), were published in 1990—and their number has subsequently mushroomed to many hundreds. Most of these reports have been prepared on a voluntary basis, with the result that the indicators used and the presentation of performance data are highly diverse, complicating comparisons. Nor are most much help yet for those trying to assess the risks associated with the operations of given companies.

These problems are, however, slowly being addressed as reporting companies begin to relate their performance against such indicators as the amount of emissions or waste produced per unit of either volume or value of production. So, for example, an oil company might link its environmental performance to a barrel of oil produced, while a water utility might compare its performance against sector averages.

But few, if any, companies have willingly reported on their performance against the sorts of indicators found at the interface between the environmental and social bottom lines. These include the challenging issue of "environmental justice,". . . which in recent years has proved a painful thorn in the side of the US chemical industry.

SOCIAL BOTTOM LINE

Some in the sustainable development community insist that sustainability has nothing to do with social, ethical, or cultural issues. A sustainable world, they argue, could equally well be more equitable or less equitable than today's world. The real issues, they say, relate to resource efficiency. Like King Canute, they are trying to hold back the tide by sheer force of will, or prejudice. Their views may be a useful counterbalance to attempts to turn sustainability into a new form of communism, but in the end our progress against the social bottom line is going to be critically important in determining the success or failure of the sustainability transition. If we fail to address wider political, social and ethical issues, the backlash will inevitably undermine progress in the environmental area.

Social Capital

So, how should a would-be sustainable corporation think about social capital? In part, it comprises human capital, in the form of public health, skills and education. But it also must embrace wider measures of a society's health and wealth-creation potential. . . .

. . . [Francis] Fukuyama says that social capital is "a capability that arises from the prevalence of trust in a society or in certain parts of it."[13] It is a measure of "the ability of people to work together for common purposes in groups and organizations." This ability is likely to be critical to the sustainability transition. It can be developed (or eroded) at every level in a society, from the basic family unit to the major institutions of international government. It depends on the acquisition and maintenance of such virtues as loyalty, honesty and dependability.

The central benefits flow from a lowering of social friction. So, for example, Fukuyama notes that:

> "if people who have to work together in an enterprise trust one another because they are all operating according to a common set of ethical norms, doing business costs less. Such a society will be better able to innovate organizationally, since the high degree of trust will permit a wide variety of social relationships to emerge."

In the same way, the degree of trust between a corporation or industry and their external stakeholders is likely to be a key factor determining their long-term sustainability. Conversely, "widespread distrust in a society imposes a kind of tax on all forms of economic activity, a tax that high-trust societies do not have to pay.". . .

Among the questions business people will need to ask are the following. What are the crucial forms of social capital in terms of our ability to become a sustainable corporation? What are the underlying trends in terms of the creation, maintenance, or erosion of these forms of capital? What is the role of business in sustaining human capital and social capital? To what extent are such concepts as environmental justice and intra- and inter-generational equity likely to change the ways in which we define and measure social capital?

Accountability

Whatever its critics may choose to believe, business is part of society. Governments try to regulate and otherwise control the social impacts associated with industry and commerce, but history is full of examples where the agenda was created outside the intertwined worlds of government and business. Whether it was the crusade to end slavery or the various campaigns to end child labor in European and North American factories, business people have long found their freedom of action being increasingly constrained by emerging social movements.

As globalization gathers steam, the interface between the economic and social bottom lines becomes increasingly problematic. Consider the abortive attempt by Germany's Krupp Hoesch to take over its rival Thyssen. This represented an attempt to make the German steel industry more competitive in the face of intensifying international competition. But, faced with massed rallies by tens of thousands of Ruhr steelworkers concerned about the implications for their jobs and protesting about "casino capitalism" and calling for "people before profit," Krupp—and its partner banks, Deutsche, Dresdner, and Goldman Sachs—backed down.[14] The decision was widely hailed by German politicians as evidence that the country's social consensus economy works; that "social responsibility" had prevailed. But there are short-term definitions of responsibility and longer-term definitions. The two companies may achieve the necessary efficiencies without redundancies, but if globalization continues Germany may simply have postponed the day of reckoning. In doing so, it may be ensuring that the inevitable economic and social quakes are worse than they need to have been.

It is against this background that we see a new stirring of interest in such concepts as social accounting and auditing. The evolution of social auditing, in particular, has more or less paralleled that of environmentalism, but with wilder swings between its "boom" and "bust" periods. In the USA, the pioneers in the late 1960s and early 1970s included Ralph Nader and organizations like the Council on Economic Priorities. In the UK the charge was led by the late George Goyder with books like *The Responsible Company*[15] and, later, by the likes of the Consumers Association, Social Audit Ltd, and Counter Information Services.[16]

The idea was to expand the range of stakeholders involved in industry's deliberations. To begin with, the focus was on consumers and those directly affected by a company's products, but the new, more inclusive models of stakeholder capitalism have progressively drawn the boundaries so as to include an ever-widening range of stakeholders. The social statement produced by the Body Shop as part of its 1995 *Values Report* . . . , and verified by the New Economics Foundation (NEF), provides a striking illustration of the trend. . . .

This is the wave of the future, but this area, inevitably, will also prove to have its own ethical dilemmas. In summing up the conference, Simon Zadek of NEF, a devoted proponent of social auditing, noted:

> "At the turn of the century, the dominant management systems were the so-called Taylorian systems—ways of controlling our bodies to maximise efficiency, productivity, and profit. As we moved into the 60s and 70s, we began thinking about flexible management systems, which used the imagination and flexibility of people's minds to further increase productivity and business success. Today, we have social auditing."

"There is a real possibility," he warned, "that it might be used as a way of controlling people's hearts and souls."

Accounting

Social accounting aims to assess the impact of an organization or company on people both inside and outside. Issues often covered are community relations, product safety, training and education initiatives, sponsorship, charitable donations of money and time, and employment of disadvantaged groups. . . .

As far as social externalities are concerned, an example from Japan would be *karoshi*, the word for death caused by overwork. The case of Ichiro Oshima is not unusual. By the time he committed suicide, he had worked eighteen months with only half a day off. The advertising agency executive started work at 7AM each day, often returning home at two in the morning. What was unusual was that his parents decided to sue his employer.[17] A flurry of litigation in the country has been forcing Japanese corporations to introduce "no overtime" days, in an attempt to give employees time off to spend with their families. How can such social costs be captured? Clearly, social accounting is another area where a great deal of further work is needed.

Issues and Indicators

Among the issues for which performance indicators have been developed are animal testing, armaments or other military sales, community relations, employment of minorities, human rights, impacts on indigenous peoples, involvement in nuclear power, irresponsible marketing, land rights, oppressive regimes, political contributions, trade union relations, wages and working conditions, and women's rights. . . .

Reporting, Risk-Rating, and Benchmarking

How do we get from words to action? The Danish health care and enzymes company Novo Nordisk, whose environmental reporting has consistently won plaudits internationally, is one of the companies that has been thinking through how to tackle the social reporting agenda. These areas are even more complex and political than the environmental agenda. But such companies are beginning to see social auditing as potentially offering a vitally important way of managing complexity.

The problem, says Dr. Chris Tuppen, who led BT's charge in the area of environmental reporting, is that all of this is "rather like learning a new language." And when you are learning a new language, nothing slows things down as much as different teachers speaking different dialects and disagreeing publicly on how the new language is to be used—or what it means. Unfortunately, this is exactly what has been happening, although a degree of turmoil is to be expected in

any area undergoing rapid evolution. More positively, Professor Peter Pruzan of the Copenhagen Business School is fairly optimistic, noting that there is currently "a strong convergence in terminology, methodology and practice."

The financial community remains largely unconvinced of the value of all of this, however. "Environmental issues are bottom line sensitive," comments Tessa Tennant of the National Provident Institution (NPI), a major pensions provider. But, she adds:

> "the bottom line implications of social issues are not clear. It would be difficult to justify why a company should produce a social report, although information on the level of absenteeism and employee turnover rates would be very relevant."

That said, she acknowledges that:

> "we are interested in seeing what companies are producing. Social reporting by most companies is quite incoherent. There may be sections on community relations, and perhaps charitable giving, but getting comprehensive data on social issues is still very difficult."

The 134-page *Social Statement* which formed part of the Body Shop's 1995 *Values Report*, is the report to beat.[18] . . . But if there is one report that might be viewed from a 21st century perspective as the seed of an impending accounting revolution, it could well be *Vizualizing Intellectual Capital in Skandia*, a supplement to the Swedish financial services company's 1994 annual report.[19]

Skandia argues that a company's value consists of more than what is traditionally shown in the income statement and balance sheet. Hidden assets, which they see as including employees' competence, computer systems, work processes, trademarks, customer lists, and so on are increasingly important in determining the value of a company. Concluding that "our intellectual capital is at least as important as our financial capital in providing truly sustainable

NEW SUSTAINABILITY INDICATORS

A future growth industry will focus on the development of new sustainability indicators. As an example of ongoing work, the social indicator movement has been trying to work out ways of measuring wealth creation and individual well-being more accurately than when conventional measures like gross national product (GNP) are used.

Until very recently, economists and business people alike thought of "quality of life" and "standard of living" as identical. They are not. Indeed, the sustainability transition will require a shift from the post-1945 paradigm based on quantity objectives to a 21st century paradigm based increasingly on perceived quality of life.

National surveys in countries like Norway have shown a disturbing trend: perceived quality of life grew until some time in the late 1960s or early 1970s, but has been falling almost constantly since.

In the UK, too, the perceived quality of life deteriorated substantially between 1975 and 1990—according to the country's first index of "real" social wealth—even though money incomes had continued to rise. According to the New Economics Foundation (NEF), despite a 230% increase in GNP over the period and a near-doubling in consumer spending, the costs of commuting, pollution, policing, and cumulative environmental damage all rose significantly.

Emerging indicators include the Human Development Indicator (HDI) and the Index of Sustainable Economic Welfare (ISEW). The latter adjusts normal measures of welfare by subtracting, for example, the costs of unemployment, commuting, automobile accidents, and all forms of environmental pollution. Increasingly, companies will need to use such measures to assess their net contributions to society's real wealth.

---

earnings," Skandia provides some "out-of-the-box" ideas on how a company's brainpower might be valued. . . .

ACCOUNTING FOR THE TRIPLE BOTTOM LINE

It is clear that progress—or the lack of it—can be measured against a wide range of indicators associated with each of the three bottom lines of sustainability. But the next step will be to tackle this agenda in an integrated way. Key tools will be sustainability accounting, auditing, and reporting. In many respects these concepts are still "black boxes," more talked about in generalities than defined in precise terms, but there is now fascinating work under way in each of these areas.

Ultimately, as Professor Rob Gray and his colleagues put it, sustainability reporting "must consist of statements about the extent to which corporations are reducing (or increasing) the op-

tions available to future generations."[20] This is an extremely complex task, but one which will probably look much easier once we have worked our way through a decade or two of experimentation in sustainability accounting, auditing and reporting. A key area of activity in this respect will be "full cost pricing"—underpinned by new forms of full cost accounting. The idea of full cost pricing is that all the costs associated with a product or service should be internalized, and, as a result, reflected in its price. Even where no markets exist for the values being considered, the "shadow pricing" approach can provide at least some guidance on relative values.

Very often, we will be unable to say whether or not a particular company or industry is "sustainable," but we will become increasingly sophisticated in terms of our ability to assess whether or not it is moving in the right direction. The triple bottom line approach clearly complicates matters. It is one thing to suggest, as some do, that a sustainable corporation is one which "leaves the biosphere no worse off at the end of the accounting period than it was at the beginning," but when we include the social and ethical dimensions of sustainability the range of sustainability-related issues and impacts grows dramatically. This does not mean that we should not try to move in this direction, but simply that we should be very careful about over-hyping the likely early benefits or pace of progress.

Most medium-term progress, in fact, is likely to be made against the first and second bottom lines (economic and environmental), although the rate of progress in social accounting, audit-ing, and reporting suggests that at least a core set of indicators could be available and in use within a matter of years. Meanwhile, the concept of the "sustainable corporation" is still evolving. . . .

In the most general terms [a sustainable corporation] would not only conserve and use nature and natural resources for the benefit of present and future generations, but also respect a range of human rights—including the right to a clean, safe environment—in the process. And it would contribute to progress against a range of new human welfare indicators which are currently still in development. . . . ◆ ◆ ◆

◆ Notes

1. World Commission for Environment and Development, *Our Common Future*, Oxford University Press, 1987.
2. Stuart L. Hart, "Beyond Greening: Strategies for a sustainable world," *Harvard Business Review*, January–February 1997.
3. Hal Kane, "Shifting to sustainable industries," *State of the World 1996*, Worldwatch Institute.
4. Many of the definitions under the "Economic bottom line" section are based on the *Oxford Dictionary of Business*, Oxford University Press, 1996.
5. Daniel Blake Rubenstein, *Environment Accounting for the Sustainable Corporation: Strategies and techniques*, Quorum Books, 1994.
6. Simon Caulkin, "When black means red," *Observer*, 14 April 1996.
7. Daniel Blake Rubenstein, *op. cit.*
8. Jan Bebbington and Rob Gray, "Sustainable development and accounting: incentives and disincentives for the adoption of sustainability by transnational corporations," in *Environmental Accounting and Sustainable Development: The final report*, Limperg Institute, The Netherlands, 1996.
9. See, for example, Rob Gray, Jan Bebbington and Diane Walters, *Accounting for the Environment*, Paul Chapman Publishing Ltd, 1993; Daniel Blake Rubenstein, *Environmental Accounting for the Sustainable Corporation: Strategies and techniques*, Quorum Books, 1994; and Wouter van Dieren (editor), *Taking Nature Into Account: Towards a sustainable national income*, a report to the Club of Rome, Copernicus, 1995.
10. Rob Gray, Jan Bebbington and Diane Walters, *Accounting for the Environment*, Paul Chapman Publishing Ltd, 1993.
11. Tim Burt, "T&N raises £42m for asbestos costs," *Financial Times*, 15 April 1997.
12. Christopher Sheldon (editor), *ISO 14001 and Beyond: Environmental management systems in the real world*, Greenleaf Publishing, 1997.
13. Francis Fukuyama, *Trust: The social virtues and the creation of prosperity*, Hamish Hamilton, 1995.
14. Michael Woodhead, "A Pyrrhic victory for Germany," *Sunday Times*, 30 March 1997.
15. George Goyder, *The Responsible Company*, Basil Blackwell, Oxford, 1961.
16. Rob Gray *et al.*, *op. cit.*
17. Peter Hadfield, "Overwork death case jolts Japan," *Sunday Times*, 4 May 1997.
18. The Body Shop International, Social Statement as part of *The Values Report*, 1995.
19. Skandia, *Visualizing Intellectual Capital in Skandia*, supplement to 1994 annual report.
20. Skandia, Intellectual Capital Development, 1996 (booklet and CD).

At the Monument to General Meade
or *On the Difference Between Beliefs and Benefits*

Mark Sagoff

How much is the environment worth? One answer is that it is priceless and cannot be traded. This might be true, but it is a poor basis for framing social policy. If a new road through an old-growth forest would allow many more tourists to appreciate the trees or stimulate the economy of a nearby resort, the easiest mechanism to make assessments about feasibility is cost/benefit analysis. All things considered, if the benefits outweigh the costs, then we should proceed. We may decide that a pristine environment is worth a very large amount indeed, but the point is that in making policy decisions there is always a price tag attached.

These issues are very much on Sagoff's mind when he gives a seminar near the Gettysburg battlefield. The park service had proposed constructing a $40 million visitor center on the site, including a theater, upscale restaurant, food court, gift shops, and a bus terminal. Economists have typically valued a site by asking people in fairly sophisticated ways how much they would pay to have it preserved rather than developed and then projected these figures for all those who are likely to be affected. The students at Sagoff's seminar seem alarmed by the prospect of development but have few good arguments to mount against it. Sagoff concludes that we should acknowledge that not everything can be decided by economic analysis, and political decisions may need to be made on moral grounds.

When you visit Gettysburg National Military Park, you can take a tour that follows the course of the three-day battle. The route ends at the National Cemetery, where, four months after the fighting, Abraham Lincoln gave the 270-word speech that marked the emergence of the United States as one nation.[1] The tour will not cover all of the battlefield, however, because much of it lies outside the park. Various retail outlets and restaurants, including a Hardee's and a Howard Johnson's, stand where General Pickett, at two o'clock on a July afternoon in 1863, marched [thousands of] Confederate soldiers to their deaths. The Peach Orchard and Wheatfield, where General Longstreet attacked, is now the site of a Stuckey's family restaurant.[2] The Cavalry Heights Trailer Park graces fields where General George Custer turned back the final charge of the Confederate cavalry.[3] Over his restaurant, Colonel Sanders, purveyor of fried chicken, smiles with neon jowls upon the monument to George Meade, the victorious Union general.[4] Above this historic servicescape looms a 310-foot commercial observation tower many Civil War buffs consider to be "a wicked blight on the battlefield vista."[5]

One spring day, on my way to give a seminar on "economics and the environment" at Gettysburg College, I drove quickly past the battlefield where 23,000 Union and 28,000 Confederate soldiers fell in three days. I felt guilty speeding by the somber fields, but I had to teach at two o'clock. I checked my watch. I did not want to be late. How do you keep your appointments and still find time to pay homage to history?

My ruminations were soon relieved by a strip of tawdry motels, restaurants, amusement arcades, and gift shops touting plastic soldiers and "original bullets! $6.95 each." At the battlefield entrance, I caught sight of the famous golden arches of the battlefield McDonald's where, on a previous occasion, my then eight-year-old son enjoyed a Happy Meal combo called the "burger and cannon." Nearby, a sign for General Pickett's All-You-Can-Eat Buffet beckoned me to a restaurant that marks the spot where rifle and artillery fire had torn apart Pickett's underfed troops. If you have young children, you understand the deep and abiding significance of fast food and convenient restrooms in historic and scenic areas. You may ask yourself, though, how you can have comfort, convenience, and commerce and at the same time respect 'hallowed ground.'

I. ARE BATTLEFIELDS SCARCE RESOURCES?

I began the seminar at Gettysburg College by describing a Park Service plan, then under discussion, to build new facilities to absorb the tide of visitors—an increase of 400,000 to 1.7 million annually—that welled up in response to "Gettysburg," a 1993 movie based on Michael Shaara's blockbuster novel, *The Killer Angels*.[6] Working with a private developer, the Park Service proposed to construct a new $40 million visitor center, including a 500-seat family food court, a 450-seat theater, and a 150-seat "upscale casual" restaurant with "white tablecloth" service, gift shops, parking lots, and a bus terminal not far from the place where Lincoln delivered the Gettysburg Address.[7] Several senators, including Senate Majority Leader Trent Lott (R-Miss.), objected that the project "commercializes the very ground and principle we strive to preserve."[8]

It is one thing to commercialize the *ground*; it is another to commercialize the *principle* we strive

to preserve. Tour buses, fast food, and trinket shops, although they commercialize the ground, express a local entrepreneurial spirit consistent with the freedom, vitality, and mystery of the place. The soldiers probably would have liked such haunts as the National Wax Museum, the Colt Firearms Museum, and the Hall of Presidents. They certainly would have appreciated General Lee's Family Restaurant, which serves great hamburgers practically at the site of Lee's headquarters. Homespun businesses try to tell the story and perpetuate the glory of Gettysburg—and even when they succeed only absurdly, they do so with an innocence and ineptitude that does not intrude on the dignity and drama of the park.

In contrast, the upscale tourist mall envisioned by the initial Park Service plan seemed, at least to Senator Lott, to elevate commercialism into a principle for managing Gettysburg. Rather than stand by the principle of commercialism or consumer sovereignty, however, the Park Service scaled back its plan.[9] In its defense, the Service pointed out that Ziegler's Grove, where its Visitor Center and Cyclorama now stand, overlooks the main battle lines. The revised proposal, which received Interior Department approval in November 1999, calls for razing these facilities and for returning Ziegler's Grove to its 1863 appearance, in order, as one official said, "to honor the valor and sacrifices of those men who fought and died on that ground for their beliefs."[10]

Since the seminar took place in mid-afternoon—siesta time in civilized societies—I had to engage the students. I did so by proposing a thesis so outrageous and appalling that the students would attack me and it. I told the class that the value of any environment—or of any of its uses—depends on what people now and in the future are willing to pay for it. Accordingly, the Park Service should have stuck with its original plan or, even better, it should have auctioned the battlefield to the highest bidder, for example, to Disney Enterprises.[11]

I asked the students to bear with me long enough to consider my proposal in relation to the subject of the seminar, the theory of environmental economics. This theory defends consumer sovereignty as a principle for environmental policy. More specifically, this theory asserts that the goal of environmental policy is to maximize social welfare at least when equity issues—matters involving the distribution of benefits among individuals—are not pressing.[12] Welfare, in turn, is defined and measured by consumer willingness to pay ("WTP") for goods and services. According to this theory, environmental policy should allocate goods and services efficiently, that is, to those willing to pay the most for them and who, in that sense, will benefit from their enjoyment, possession, or use.

In the United States, unlike Europe, I explained, battlefields are scarce resources which, like any scarce environmental asset, should be allocated efficiently. To be sure, the Park Service tries to accommodate tourists. The problem, though, is that the Park Service does not exploit heritage values as efficiently as a competitive market would. At present, Gettysburg is woefully underutilized, or so I argued. Even Dollywood, Dolly Parton's theme park in rural east Tennessee, attracts more visitors every year.[13] The Park Service does not even try to allocate the resources efficiently. It pursues goals that are not economic but ethical; it seeks to educate the public and honor "the valor and sacrifices of those men who fought and died on that ground for their beliefs."[14]

A young lady in the class blurted out, "But that's what the Park Service should do." She acknowledged that the Park Service has to provide visitor services. It should do so, she said, only to the extent that it will not "detract from what they did here," to paraphrase President Lincoln.[15]

This young lady thought that the history of the place, rather than what people are willing to pay for alternative uses of it, determined its value. She understood the significance of "what they did here" in moral and historical, rather than in economic, terms. The value of hallowed ground or of any object with intrinsic value has nothing to do with market behavior or with WTP, she said.

I explicated her concern the following way. A private developer, I explained, might not realize in gate receipts at Gettysburg the WTP of those individuals, like herself, who wished to protect an area for ethical or aesthetic reasons. I promised to describe to the class the contingent valuation ("CV") method economists have developed to determine how much individuals are willing to pay for policies consistent with their disinterested moral beliefs.[16] Using this method, the Park Service could take her preference and therefore her welfare into account. It could then identify the policy that maximizes benefits over costs for all concerned, whether that concern is based on consumer desire or on ethical commitment.

This reply, I am afraid, did little more than taunt the student. In stating her opinion, she said, she implied nothing about her own well-being. She described what she thought society ought to do, not what would make her better off. The student did not see how scientific management, by measuring costs and benefits, served democracy. The Park Service, she added, had no responsibility, legal or moral, to maximize "satisfactions," including hers. Rather, it had an obligation to keep faith with those who died on that ground for their beliefs. No CV survey, no amount of WTP, she said, could add to or detract from the value of Gettysburg. No action we take could alter, though it may honor or dishonor, what the soldiers did there; no cost-benefit study, however scientific, could change our obligation to those who gave their lives that this nation might live. . . .

To prepare for the seminar, I had asked the students to read *Conservation Reconsidered*,[17] an essay economist John V. Krutilla published in 1967 in response to neoclassical economists, who studied the effects of technological advance on economic growth. . . .

III. MORAL COMMITMENT AS MARKET DEMAND

At about the time neoclassical economics removed resource scarcity as a cause for concern, citizens across the country swelled the rolls of organizations such as the Sierra Club, which sought to preserve pristine places, endangered species, wild rivers, and other natural objects. These environmentalists, Krutilla pointed out, contributed to organizations such as the World Wildlife Fund "in an effort to save exotic species in remote areas of the world which few subscribers to the Fund ever hope to see."[18] Krutilla noted that people "place a value on the mere existence" of resources, such as species, even though they do not intend to consume or own them, as they would ordinary resources.[19]

Krutilla argued that if people value natural objects because they are natural, then technological advance cannot provide substitutes for them.[20] Among the permanently scarce phenomena of nature, Krutilla cited familiar examples including "the Grand Canyon, a threatened species, or an entire ecosystem or biotic community essential to the survival of the threatened species."[21] On this basis, Krutilla and many colleagues reinvented environmental economics as a "new conservation"[22] that addresses the failure of markets to respond to the "existence" or "nonuse" value of natural objects people want to preserve but may not intend to experience, much less use or consume.

Krutilla was correct, of course, in observing that people often are willing to pay to preserve natural objects such as endangered species. Among them, for example, is Tom Finger, a Mennonite, who said, "we're eliminating God's creatures. All these nonhuman creatures . . . have a certain intrinsic worth because they are part of God's creation."[23] People who believe species have an intrinsic worth may be willing to pay to protect them. Does this suggest that endangered species are scarce resources? Do those who believe extinction is wrong suffer a loss, a kind of social cost, when species vanish? Does endangered species habitat have an economic value that market prices fail to reflect?

Krutilla thought so. He reasoned that those who wished to protect natural objects or environments find it difficult to communicate their WTP to those who own those resources. Given this practical difficulty, "the private resource owner would not be able to appropriate in gate receipts the entire social value of the resources when used in a manner compatible with preserving the natural state."[24] Accordingly, Krutilla proposed that the analysis . . . offered to justify the regulation of pollution might also serve to justify governmental action to protect species, wilderness, and other natural objects. He wrote, "private and social returns . . . are likely to diverge significantly."[25]

Krutilla's analysis suggests an argument to show that a private firm should manage Dollywood but not Gettysburg, even if the principle of consumer sovereignty applies equally to both. At Dollywood, the owners can capture in gate and table receipts total WTP for the goods and services the resort provides. Owners who respond to market signals supply just those goods and services the public most wants to buy. The managers of Dollywood, moreover, cover all the costs in labor, materials, etc., of their business. The prices they charge, then, will reflect the full social costs involved in producing what they sell.

At Gettysburg, it is different. Patriotic Americans, many of whom may never visit the area, may be willing to pay to restore the battlefield or to save it from commercial exploitation. Private, for-profit owners of Gettysburg would have no incentive to take this WTP into account, however, because they cannot capture it in gate and table receipts. The prices managers charge for attractions, then, will not reflect the full social costs of providing them—particularly the costs to patriotic Americans who would suffer if the battlefield is desecrated. Because price signals distort true WTP for preservation, the government, rather than a for-profit firm, should manage or at least regulate Gettysburg. Thus, a[n] . . . argument may provide an economic and, in that sense, scientific rationale for the belief that society should restore Gettysburg to its 1863 condition rather than sell the area to Disney Enterprises to run as a theme park.

This kind of economic argument may appeal to environmentalists because it opposes the privatization of places, such as Gettysburg, that possess intrinsic value. This argument seems especially appealing because it rejects privatization for economic reasons—the very sorts of reasons that might be thought to justify it. Since this . . . analysis leads to comfortable conclusions, environmentalists might embrace it. Why not agree with economic theory that the goal of social policy is to maximize net benefits with respect to all environmental assets, whether in places like Dollywood or in places like Gettysburg? After all, the cost-benefit analysis, once it factors in the WTP of environmentalists, surely will come out in favor of protecting the environment.

The problem is this: to buy into this argument, one must accept the idea that the same goal or principle—net benefits maximization—applies to both Dollywood and Gettysburg.[26] Critics of economic theory may contend, however, that the approach to valuation appropriate at Daydream Ridge in Dollywood is not appropriate at Cemetery Ridge in Gettysburg. At Daydream Ridge,

the goal is to satisfy consumer demand. At Cemetery Ridge, the goal is to pay homage to those who died that this nation might live.

To say that the nation has a duty to pay homage to those from whom it received the last full measure of devotion is to state a moral fact. You can find other moral facts stated, for example, in the Ten Commandments.[27] The imperative "Thou shalt not murder" should not be understood as a policy preference for which Moses and other like-minded reformers were willing to pay. Rather, like every statement of moral fact, it presents a hypothesis about what we stand for— what we maintain as true and expect others to believe—insofar as we identify ourselves as a moral and rational community.

Our Constitution puts certain questions, for example, religious belief, beyond the reach of democracy. Other moral questions, over military intervention in conflicts abroad, for example, invite reasoned deliberation in appropriate legislative councils. Environmental controversies, once the issues of resource scarcity are removed from the agenda, turn on the discovery and acceptance of moral and aesthetic judgments as facts. The belief that society should respect the sanctity of Cemetery Ridge states a moral fact so uncontroversial nobody would doubt it. This tells us nothing, however, about a scarcity of battlefields, an inelasticity of hallowed ground, market failure, or the divergence of social and private costs. It suggests only that the principle of consumer sovereignty that economists apply to evaluate management decisions at Dollywood do not apply at Gettysburg or, indeed, wherever the intrinsic value of an environment is at stake.[28]

IV. ARE BELIEFS BENEFITS?

By construing intrinsic or existence value as a kind of demand that market prices fail to reflect, Krutilla and other environmental economists envisioned a brilliant strategy to respond to the quandary in which neoclassical economic theory had placed them.[29] They kept their credentials as mainstream economists by accepting the neoclassical macroeconomic model with respect to resources the economy uses. Yet they also "greened" their science by attributing a general scarcity to "non-use" resources such as wilderness, species, scenic rivers, historical landmarks, and so on, that people believe society has a duty to preserve. Indeed, by applying the divergence-of-private-and-social-cost argument not just to pollution but also to every plant, animal, or place that anyone may care about for ethical or cultural reasons, economic theory performed a great service to environmentalists. Environmentalists now could represent their moral, religious, or cultural beliefs that WTP market prices failed to reflect.[30] At last, they could claim that economic science was on their side.[31]

By transforming moral or cultural judgments about the environment into preferences for which people are willing to pay, Krutilla and his colleagues in the early 1970s achieved a great deal. First, they created a complex research agenda centering on the measurement of benefits associated with non-use or existence value.[32] Since 1970, indeed, research in environmental economics, both theoretical and empirical, has been preoccupied with measuring the economic benefits people are supposed to enjoy as a result of environmental policies consistent with their moral and religious beliefs.[33]

Second, Krutilla and his colleagues created a division of labor between policy scientists and policy consumers.[34] As policy scientists, economists lay down the goals and principles of environmental policy—indeed of all social policy—on the basis of their own theory and without any political deliberation, consultation, or process.[35] Economists Edith Stokey and Richard Zeckhauser, for example, assert that "public policy should promote the welfare of society."[36] A. Myrick Freeman III explains, "The basic premises of welfare economics are that the purpose of economic activity is to increase the well-being of the individuals who make up the society."[37] In a widely used textbook, Eban Goodstein states, "Economic analysts are concerned with human welfare or well-being. From the economic perspective, the environment should be protected for the material benefit of humanity and not for strictly moral or ethical reasons."[38]

As policy consumers, citizens make judgments about what is good for them.[39] Economists reiterate that "each individual is the best judge of how well off he or she is in a given situation."[40] Henry Ford is reputed to have said that people could have automobiles "in any color so long as it's black."[41] From the standpoint of economic theory, individuals can make any social judgment they wish, as long as it concerns the extent to which policy outcomes harm or benefit them.[42]

Economists may offer a ceremonial bow in the direction of markets, but this is quickly followed by a story of market failure followed by a call for centralized management based on cost-benefit analysis.[43] Experts, i.e., economists themselves, must teach society how to allocate resources scientifically, since markets cannot cope with environmental public goods. In markets, individuals make choices and thus function as agents of change. In microeconomic theory, in contrast, individuals function not as agents but primarily as sites or locations where WTP may be found.

Third, as the methodology for benefits estimation developed, it typically assigned very high shadow prices to existence values, and this appealed to environmentalists. An endangered butterfly, for example, may be worth millions if every American is willing to pay a dime for its survival. Public interest groups, who associated economists with the enemy, now saw that economic science could be their friend.[44] Environmentalists, who might have complained that industry groups had "numbers," could now come up with numbers, too.[45] And since WTP adds up quickly when aggregated over all members of society, environmentalists could be sure that the numbers would come out "right."

V. IS EXISTENCE VALUE A KIND OF ECONOMIC VALUE?

To establish a connection between existence value and economic value, economists have to explain in what sense people benefit from the existence of goods they may neither experience nor use. To be sure, individuals are willing to pay to protect endangered species, rain forests, and other wonders of nature they may never expect to see. That they are willing to pay for them, however, does not show that they expect to benefit from them. Generally speaking, just because a person's preferences are all his own, it does not follow that the satisfaction of all or any of those preferences necessarily improves his welfare or well-being. The students in my class were quite willing to contribute to a fund to protect hallowed ground at Gettysburg. They did so, however, largely from a sense of moral obligation and not in any way or manner because they thought they would be better off personally if the battlefield were preserved. . . .

VI. CONTINGENT VALUATION

During the past thirty years, economists have worked hard to develop a method, known as contingent valuation ("CV"), to assess the "existence" or "non-use" values of natural phenomena.[46] The CV method, as one authority writes, "is based on asking an individual to state his or her willingness to pay to bring about an environmental improvement, such as improved visibility from lessened air pollution, the protection of an endangered

species, or the preservation of a wilderness area."[47] The authors of a textbook write that the CV method "asks people what they are willing to pay for an environmental benefit. . . ."[48] They see this method as "uniquely suited to address non-use values."[49]

Contrary to what this textbook asserts, the CV questionnaire never asks people what they are willing to pay for an environmental *benefit*. It asks respondents to state their WTP for a particular policy outcome, for example, the protection of a rare butterfly. Economists interpret the stated WTP for the environmental improvement as if it were WTP for a personal benefit the respondent expects it to afford her or him. Yet a person who believes that society ought to protect a species of butterfly may have no expectation at all that he or she will benefit as a result. Indeed, as Tom Tietenberg observes, people who do not expect to benefit in any way from an environmental good may still be committed to its preservation.[50] He notes that "people reveal strong support for environmental resources even when those resources provide no direct or even indirect benefit."[51]

Empirical research shows that responses to CV questionnaires reflect moral commitments rather than concerns about personal welfare. In one example, a careful study showed that ethical considerations dominate economic ones in responses to CV surveys.[52] "Our results provide an assessment of the frequency and seriousness of these considerations in our sample: they are frequent and they are significant determinants of WTP responses."[53] In another study, researchers found that existence value "is almost entirely driven by ethical considerations precisely because it is disinterested value."[54]. . .

As philosopher Ronald Dworkin points out, many of us recognize an obligation to places and objects that reflects a moral judgment about what society should do, not a subjective expectation about what may benefit us.[55] He writes that many of us seek to protect objects or events—which could include endangered species, for example—for reasons that have nothing to do with our well-being. Many of us "think we should admire and protect them because they are important in themselves, and not just if or because we or others want or enjoy them."[56] The idea of intrinsic worth depends on deeply held moral convictions and religious beliefs that underlie social policies for the environment, education, public health, and so on. Dworkin observes:

> Much of what we think about knowledge, experience, art, and nature, for example, presupposes that in different ways these are valuable in themselves and not just for their utility or for the pleasure or satisfaction they bring us. The idea of intrinsic value is commonplace, and it has a central place in our shared scheme of values and opinions.[57]

Beliefs are not benefits. If economists believe that society should allocate resources to maximize welfare, they do not necessarily think this because they will be better off as a result. They are not simply trying to increase demand for their services. Similarly, as the evidence cited above suggests, people who believe that society should protect endangered species, old-growth forests, and other places with intrinsic value do not necessarily think that this will improve their well-being.[58] A person who wants the Park Service to respect hallowed ground may consider that policy justified by the historical qualities of the battlefield and not by the welfare consequences for her. It is hard to understand, then, how CV measures the non-market benefits of environmental goods.[59] If responses to CV surveys are based on moral beliefs or commitments, there would seem to be no relevant benefits to measure. . . .

The idea that society should use WTP as the standard by which to judge the merit of policy pro-

posals defies common sense. We do not measure the worthiness of political candidates and their positions by totaling up the campaign contributions they attract. On the contrary, those candidates able to raise the most money appear to be the most beholden to special interests. A recent survey revealed that about "half of young adults believe that separation of races is acceptable. . . ."[60] That individuals are willing to pay to segregate schools by race or to exclude non-Christians from office, however, would not make those policies any better. It would only make those individuals worse.

Democracy relies on deliberative discourse in public to evaluate policy options. The point of political deliberation in a democracy is to separate, on the basis of argument and evidence, more reasonable from less reasonable policy proposals. The Park Service held public meetings (but did not commission CV studies) to reevaluate its plan for Gettysburg. It sought out the opinions of those who knew the history of the place. As a result, it located the new facility in an area where no soldier had fallen.[61] The outcome of political and moral deliberation depends less on the addition of individual utilities than on the force of the better argument about the public interest.[62] . . .

The students who attended the seminar cared about the environment. One student opined that society has an obligation to save old-growth forests, which he thought intrinsically valuable. Another mentioned pollution in the Grand Canyon. She said we have a responsibility to keep the area pristine no matter who benefits from it. Another argued that even if a species had no economic use, it is wrong to cause its extinction. Another student proposed that the government should promote prosperity and try to give everyone an opportunity to share in a booming economy. She understood the importance of macroeconomic goals but saw no reason to apply microeconomic theory to social policy. . . .

X. RETREAT FROM GETTYSBURG

After the seminar, I chose a route out of Gettysburg that avoided the battlefield and, with it, the ghosts of the past. But my path was full of portents of the future. At a 110-acre site southeast of the battleground, which had served as a staging area for Union troops, I saw equipment gathered to construct the massive mall the Park Service decided not to build. The developer, the Boyle Group of Malvern, Pennsylvania, according to its promotional literature, promises to erect an "authentic village" containing seventy outlet stores, an eighty-room country inn, and a large restaurant. According to the flyer, visitors to Gettysburg will find the village a refuge from the drudgery of touring the battlefield and learning its history. "History is about the only thing these millions of tourists take home," the promo states. "That's because there is no serious shopping in Gettysburg."[63]

Society can count on firms such as the Boyle Group to provide shopping as serious as anyone could want at Gettysburg and everywhere else. The nation does not have to elevate shopping and, with it, the allocation of goods and services to those willing to pay the most for them, to the status of legislation. Environmental laws state general moral principles or set overall goals that reflect choices we have made together. These principles and goals do not include the empty and futile redundancy of environmental economics—the rule that society should allocate resources to those willing to pay the most for them because they are willing to pay the most for those resources.

An agency, such as the Park Service, may engage in public deliberation to determine which rule to apply in the circumstances. The principle economists tout, net benefits maximization, is rarely if ever relevant or appropriate. At Gettysburg, the principle speaks for itself. "What gives meaning to the place is the land on which the battle was fought and the men who died there," as longtime Gettysburg preservationist Robert Moore has said. "Keeping the place the same holy place, that's what's important."[64] ◆ ◆ ◆

◆ Notes

1. ABRAHAM LINCOLN, THE GETTYSBURG ADDRESS (1863), *reprinted in* LINCOLN ON DEMOCRACY at 307 (Mario M. Cuomo & Harold Holzer eds., 1990).

2. *See* George Will, *A Conflict over Hallowed Ground*, NEW ORLEANS TIMES-PICAYUNE, June 11, 1998, at B7. For a brief description of the events, see Lisa Reuter, *Gettysburg: The World Did Long Remember*, COLUMBUS DISPATCH, Dec. 5, 1999, at 1G ("At the wheat field alone, 6000 men fell in 2½ hours. One soldier would later write, 'Men were falling like leaves in autumn; my teeth chatter now when I think of it.' So many bodies covered the field, remembered another, that a person could walk across it without touching the ground.").

3. *See* Rupert Cornwell, *Out of the West; Developers March on Killing Fields*, INDEPENDENT (London), Dec. 18, 1991, at 10 (43,000 deaths in total).

4. The Kentucky Fried Chicken restaurant has long occupied the area near the monument and by now may have its own authenticity. Kentucky nominally never left the Union.

5. Will, *supra* note 2, at B7.

6. *See* MICHAEL SHAARA, THE KILLER ANGELS: A NOVEL (1974). For details about the effect on the visitor load, see Will, *supra* note 2, at B7.

7. For a description of the Park Service plan and its history, see Edward T. Pound, *The Battle over Gettysburg*, USA TODAY, Sept. 26, 1997, at 4A.

8. Stephen Barr, *Hill General Retreats on Gettysburg Plan*, WASH. POST, Oct. 2, 1998, at A25. *See*

also Ben White, *Lawmaker Criticizes Plan for Gettysburg*, WASH. POST, Feb. 12, 1999, at A33.

9. *See* Brett Lieberman, *Park Service Unveils Revised Gettysburg Plan*, PLAINS DEALER (Cleveland), June 19, 1999, at 14A.

10. APCWS POSITION ON PROPOSED GETTYSBURG DEVELOPMENT PLAN (statement by Denis P. Galvin, Deputy Director, National Park Service, Feb. 24, 1998) (visited Mar. 26, 2000) <http://users.erols.com/va-udc/nps.html> [hereinafter PROPOSED DEVELOPMENT PLAN].

11. In fact, such a proposal is not as far-fetched as it sounds. *See* Heather Dewar, *Corporate Cash Eyed for Parks, Bill Puts Sponsorships at $10 Million Apiece*, DENVER POST, June 8, 1996, at A1; *Parks May Get "Official" Sponsors, Senate Measure Would Lure Corporate Bucks*, ST. LOUIS POST-DISPATCH, June 9, 1996, at 1A. This plan was much derided. *See, e.g.*, Joshua Reichert, *Commercializing Our National Parks a Bad Joke*, HOUSTON CHRON., Sept. 23, 1996, at 19.

12. From the perspective of welfare economics, a regulation is rational—it promotes the welfare of society—only if it confers on members of society benefits in excess of costs. Since the benefits and costs may well accrue to different individuals, welfare economists recognize two fundamental values in terms of which regulatory policy may be justified. The first is economic *efficiency*, which is to say, the extent to which total benefits of the policy exceed total costs. The second goal is *equity*, which is to say, the extent to which the distribution of costs and benefits is equitable or fair. For a presentation of this view, see generally ARTHUR M. OKUN, EQUALITY AND EFFICIENCY: THE BIG TRADEOFF (1975). He writes, "This concept of efficiency implies that more is better, insofar as the 'more' consists in items people want to buy." *Id.* at 2.

13. Dollywood attracts about 2 million patrons annually and is open only during the warmer months. *See Dollywood* (visited Mar. 26, 2000) <http://company.monster.com/dolly/>.

14. PROPOSED DEVELOPMENT PLAN, *supra* note 10.

15. *See* LINCOLN, *supra* note 1.

16. *See* discussion *infra* Part VI.

17. John V. Krutilla, *Conservation Reconsidered*, 57 AM. ECON. REV. 777 (1967).

18. *Id.*, at 781.

19. *Id.*

20. *See id.* at 783 (arguing that "while the supply of fabricated goods and commercial services may be capable of continuous expansion from a given resource base by reason of scientific discovery and mastery of technique, the supply of natural phenomena is virtually inelastic"). Krutilla had to show, however, that technology cannot provide substitutes for natural phenomena (such as the Grand Canyon) as it can for natural resources. Krutilla apparently infers from the inelasticity of the supply of natural phenomena that technology cannot offer substitutes for them. This is obviously a non sequitor. Technology can provide amusements—for example, IMAX® theater presentations of the Grand Canyon followed by a great party where one can meet celebrities—for which people may be willing to pay as much as to go to the Canyon itself. It is not clear, then, that inelasticities of supply bear on the question of whether technology can provide economic substitutes for intrinsically valuable objects of nature. Technology may provide goods and services for which people are willing to pay the same amount.

21. *Id.* at 778.

22. *Id.* at 783.

23. Carlyle Murphy, *A Spiritual Lens on the Environment; Increasingly, Caring for Creation Is Viewed as a Religious Mandate*, WASH. POST, Feb. 3, 1998, at A1.

24. Krutilla, *supra* note 17, at 779.

25. *Id.*

26. "Market-determined prices," some economists claim, "are the only reliable, legally significant measures of value. . . . [T]he value of a natural resource is the sum of the value of all of its associated marketable commodities, such as timber, minerals, animals, and recreational use fees." Daniel S. Levy & David Friedman, *The Revenge of the Redwoods? Reconsidering Property Rights and the Economic Allocation of Natural Resources*, 61 U. CHI. L. REV. 493, 500–01 (1994)

(discussing the possibility of WTP estimates for existence values).

27. *See Exodus* 20:3–17.

28. Gettysburg here serves as an example of any moral decision that confronts society. Economists have applied the WTP criterion to adjudicate the most important moral decisions that confront society. For example, economists have argued that the decision to wage war in Vietnam represented not a moral failure or political failure, but a market failure. The decision to carry on the war failed to reflect the WTP demonstrators revealed, for example, in the travel costs they paid to protest against it. *See generally* Charles J. Cicchetti et al., *On the Economics of Mass Demonstrations: A Case Study of the November 1969 March on Washington*, 61 AM. ECON. REV. 179 (1971).

Whatever the question, from segregation in housing to certain kinds of slavery, practices people oppose for moral reasons may also be characterized as objectionable for economic reasons, once the WTP of those opponents is factored into the cost-benefit analysis. *See generally* Duncan Kennedy, *Cost-Benefit Analysis of Entitlement Problems: A Critique*, 33 STAN. L. REV. 387 (1981).

Microeconomists sometimes seem to hold that WTP can adjudicate all questions of truth, beauty, and justice. The use of WTP or utility "to measure preferences can be applied quite generally," three economists explain. "Utility or preference exists for any activity in which choice is involved, although the choices may themselves involve truth, justice, or beauty, just as easily as the consumption of goods and services." JONATHAN A. LESSER ET AL., ENVIRONMENTAL ECONOMICS AND POLICY 42 (1997).

29. That is, the quandary involved in finding a subject matter for environmental economics to study when mainstream economics had determined that natural resources could be taken for granted.

30. The high-water mark of this approach to environmental evaluation may be found in Robert Costanza et al., *The Value of the World's Ecosystem Services and Natural Capital*, 387 NATURE 253 (1997) (estimating the economic benefits of the world's ecosystem services and natural capital at $33 trillion per year).

31. *See, e.g.*, Pete Morton, *The Economic Benefits of Wilderness: Theory and Practice*, 76 DENV. U. L. REV. 465, 465 (1999) ("While steadfastly acknowledging that the economic benefits of wilderness will never be fully quantified, without at least qualitatively describing and understanding these benefits, politicians and public land managers will continue to make policy decisions that shortchange wilderness in public land management decisions."). Some environmentalists question the use of contingent valuation largely for technical reasons. *See, e.g.*, KRISTIN M. JAKOBSSON & ANDREW K. DRAGUN, CONTINGENT VALUATION AND ENDANGERED SPECIES 78–82 (1996).

32. For examples of this research agenda, see VALUING NATURAL ASSETS: THE ECONOMICS OF NATURAL RESOURCE DAMAGE ASSESSMENTS (Raymond J. Kopp & V. Kerry Smith eds., 1993).

33. For a good review of the literature, see generally A. MYRICK FREEMAN III, THE BENEFITS OF ENVIRONMENTAL IMPROVEMENT: THEORY AND PRACTICE (1979).

34. *See* Krutilla, *supra* note 17, at 779 n.7 (describing environmentalists as having subjective reactions to, rather than objective opinions about, the loss of a species or the disfiguring of an environment).

35. For a general statement and defense of the position of welfare economics in environmental policy, see Daniel C. Esty, *Toward Optimal Environmental Governance*, 74 N.Y.U. L. REV. 1495 (1999). *See also* Louis Kaplow & Steven Shavell, *Property Rules Versus Liability Rules: An Economic Analysis*, 109 HARV. L. REV. 715, 725 (1996) (taking the cost-benefit balance to define ideal regulation).

36. EDITH STOKEY & RICHARD ZECKHAUSER, A PRIMER FOR POLICY ANALYSIS 277 (1978).

37. A. MYRICK FREEMAN III, THE MEASUREMENT OF ENVIRONMENTAL RESOURCE VALUES 6 (1993).

38. EBAN S. GOODSTEIN, ECONOMICS AND THE ENVIRONMENT 24 (2d ed. 1999).

39. Commentators generally refer to this idea as the principle of consumer sovereignty. For a general statement of how this principle fits within the

foundations of economic theory, see Martha Nussbaum, *Flawed Foundations: The Philosophical Critique of (a Particular Type of) Economics*, 64 U. CHI. L. REV. 1197, 1197–98 (1997).

40. FREEMAN, *supra* note 37, at 6.

41. For a discussion of Ford's beliefs, see ROLAND MARCHAND, ADVERTISING THE AMERICAN DREAM: MAKING WAY FOR MODERNITY, 1920–1940, at 118, 156–58 (1985).

42. Following social choice theory, economists apply the principle of consumer sovereignty to all views but their own—in other words, they regard everyone else as having wants rather than ideas. For the classic statement of this position, see Joseph Schumpeter, *On the Concept of Social Value*, 23 Q.J. ECON. 213, 214–17 (1909).

43. *See, e.g.,* Allen V. Kneese & Blair T. Bower, *Introduction, in* ENVIRONMENTAL QUALITY ANALYSIS: THEORY AND METHOD IN THE SOCIAL SCIENCES 3–4 (Allen V. Kneese & Blair T. Bower eds., 1972).

44. *See* Kennedy, *supra* note 28, at 401–21.

45. Critics of Krutilla's approach charged that it came primarily "from economists desperately eager to play a more significant role in environmental policy and environmental groups seeking to gain the support of conservatives." Fred L. Smith, Jr., *A Free-Market Environmental Program*, 11 CATO J. 457, 468 n.15 (1992).

46. For commentaries, see generally John F. Daum, *Some Legal and Regulatory Aspects of Contingent Valuation, in* CONTINGENT VALUATION: A CRITICAL ASSESSMENT [389 (J. A. Hausman ed., 1993)]; William H. Desvousges et al., *Measuring Natural Resource Damages with Contingent Valuation: Tests of Validity and Reliability, in* CONTINGENT VALUATION: A CRITICAL ASSESSMENT 91.

47. JAMES R. KAHN, THE ECONOMIC APPROACH TO ENVIRONMENTAL AND NATURAL RESOURCES 102 (2d ed. 1998).

48. LESSER ET AL., *supra* note 28, at 282.

49. *Id.*

50. TOM TIETENBERG, ENVIRONMENTAL ECONOMICS AND POLICY 62–63 (1994).

51. *Id.*

52. D. A. Schkade & J. W. Payne, *How People Respond to Contingent Valuation Questions: A Verbal Protocol Analysis of Willingness to Pay for an Environmental Regulation*, 26 J. ENVTL. ECON. & MGMT. 88, 89 (1994).

53. *Id.*

54. [E. B. Barbier et al., *Economic Value of Biodiversity, in* GLOBAL BIODIVERSITY ASSESSMENT 836 (V. H. Heywood ed., 1995).]

55. *See* RONALD DWORKIN, LIFE'S DOMINION: AN ARGUMENT ABOUT ABORTION, EUTHANASIA, AND INDIVIDUAL FREEDOM 69–77 (1993).

56. *Id.* at 71–72. *See also id.* at 75–77 (discussing the preservation of animal species).

57. *Id.* at 69–70.

58. Experiments show again and again that responses to CV questionnaires express what the individual believes to be good in general or good for society and not—as the CV methods seek to determine—what individuals believe is good for *them*. *See, e.g.,* Thomas H. Stevens et al., *Measuring the Existence Value of Wildlife: What Do CVM Estimates Really Show?*, 67 LAND ECON. 390 (1991); Thomas H. Stevens et al., *Measuring the Existence Value of Wildlife: Reply*, 69 LAND ECON. 309 (1993).

59. Some economists agree and write: "[I]t may be inappropriate to use the [contingent valuation methodology] as an input to [benefit cost analysis] studies, unless means can be found to extract information on consumer preferences from data predominantly generated by citizen judgments." [R. Blamey *et al., Respondents to Contingent Valuation Surveys: Consumers or Citizens?*, 39 Australian J. Agric. Econ. 285 (1995)].

60. J. Balz, *Separation of Races Found OK by Many Young People*, L.A. TIMES, Aug. 17, 1999, at A10.

61. *See* Elizabeth Stead Kaszubski, Letter to the Editor, *Park Plan Honors 'Hallowed Ground'*, USA TODAY, June 24, 1999, at 14A (describing the events that transpired at the spot where the Park Service proposed to build its new Visitors' Center).

62. *See generally* JÜRGEN HABERMAS, JUSTIFICATION AND APPLICATION: REMARKS ON DISCOURSE ETHICS (Ciaran Cronin trans., 1993).

63. Pound, *supra* note 7, at 4A.

64. *Id.* (quoting Robert Moore).

Sacrifice to Slaughter*

Jeremy Rifkin

The extract is taken from Rifkin's book Beyond Beef, *a polemic against the cattle industry. His provocative and admittedly biased claims are likely to stimulate some interesting reflection on where our food comes from, in light of the business pressures and small margins in the food industry.*

In the cattle industry, for example, yield is kept up through extensive use of pharmaceuticals—especially hormones and antibiotics. The conditions in which animals are kept are often dictated more by efficiency concerns than animal welfare. Furthermore, packing plants are one of the nation's most dangerous industries; workers use sharp cutting tools at high speed in an environment that is often slippery.

Consumers demand high-quality food at low prices, and the industry has responded. To what extent should we balance our concerns about animals with the demands of business?

Several millennia before the birth of Christ a powerful king emerged among the peoples of the Nile River. Narmer-Menes united Upper and Lower Egypt into a single kingdom, creating the first great empire in Western history. Although he is remembered by historians for his extraordinary military accomplishments, Narmer-Menes's spiritual achievements were no less significant. The new king introduced bull worship throughout his kingdom, creating the first universal religion.

According to legend, the bull god Apis was conceived by a special cow who had been impregnated by a ray of moonlight. The young bull god was elevated to the spiritual throne of the new Egyptian empire, and from this vaunted position he ruled over the heavens and the affairs of society.

The bull god represented great strength and virility and the masculine passion for war and subjugation—an appropriate symbol for the age of conquest. Narmer-Menes ruled over Egypt by the grace of the new bull god. The king, in turn, was worshiped by the people as a bull god, as were all of his successors in the great dynastic reigns of the Egyptian empire. The kings were called "mighty bulls" and "bulls of the heavens." A thousand years after the reign of Narmer-Menes, kings of the eighteenth and nineteenth dynasties were described in court chronicles as great bull gods who destroyed their enemies with their powerful hoofs and gored them with their sharp horns.

The great bull god Apis shared the heavens with the cow goddess Hathor. It was believed that Hathor gave birth to the sun itself. Hathor represented fertility and nurture, the fecundity of the cosmos. The sky was conceived as a giant cow whose legs extend to the four corners of the earth and who is held up by other gods. The queens of ancient Egypt were all viewed as cow goddesses and worshiped by the people.

Apis symbolized the vigor of youth and everlasting life and was embodied in a real-life bull kept in sanctuary and attended to by the priests.

*Original notes have been omitted.

At the end of the old year the Apis bull was slaughtered in an elaborate ritual; his flesh was consumed by the king in an effort to incorporate the animal's fierce strength, majestic power, and virility into his being so that he might enjoy immortality. The ritual slaughter of the Apis bull was a time for renewal, for resurrecting the personal and political fortunes of the kingdom. It marked the end of the old year and the beginning of the new.

The impending death of the Apis bull sent the priests to scour the realm for a successor. When a new bull was located, its owner was handsomely rewarded and the priests immediately placed the animal in seclusion. For forty days and nights the bull was kept hidden away. Naked women were paraded in front of the animal to incite the god and secure the fertility of both the women and land of Egypt. At the end of the period of seclusion the bull was transported to the holy city of Memphis in a sacred barge inside a golden cabin. Upon arrival, the Apis bull was enthroned in the great temple of Ptah, where he occupied a suite of special rooms equipped with elaborate sleeping quarters. The Apis bull was served special foods and given holy water from the sacred wells of Egypt. Cows were kept in adjoining rooms to serve as concubines.

On holy days the bull was adorned with religious garments and paraded before the people in extravagant processionals. The birthday of the Apis god was preceded by a week of joyous feasting.

The Apis god was imbued with great powers, among which was the ability to predict the future. The animal's every movement and even its demeanor were viewed as signs or omens. The privileged often paid to spend a night in the temple near the Apis bull so that their dreams could be interpreted with the help of the bull's gestures. It is said that the bellowing of the Apis bull foretold the invasion of Egypt by the armies of Augustus.

After the ritual slaughter and eating of the Apis bull its remains were mummified and buried in a special chamber entombed inside a grand sarcophagus weighing over fifty tons.

Humanity's relationship to cattle has radically changed since the days of Narmer-Menes. Today, the birth of calves begins with "teaser bulls," also called "sidewinders." These animals are used to identify cows in estrus (heat). A teaser bull has undergone a surgical operation that reroutes his penis so that it comes out through his side. The bull becomes aroused in the presence of cows in heat and attempts to mount the females. Because his erect penis is off to the side, he can't penetrate the cow's vagina, but he does leave a colored dye on her rump from a marker that's been hung around his chin. Ranchers use the marker to identify the cows in heat so they can be sequestered and artificially inseminated.

More recently, a new generation of estrus-synchronizing drugs has been developed and commercially marketed, allowing cattlemen to dispense with teaser bulls. The drugs are injected into all of the cows in a herd at the same time so that they will all come into heat simultaneously. The Upjohn Company touts the efficiency and predictability of its own estrus-synchronizing drug with the advertising slogan "You call the shots." By synchronizing the estrus cycles of an entire herd, commercial ranchers can plan ahead, picking the ideal time of the year for the calving season.

After birth, young male calves are castrated to make them more "docile" and to improve the quality of the beef. There are several methods of castration. In one procedure, the scrotum is grasped and stretched out tightly, a knife is stuck up through the scrotum and then used to cut open the sac, and each testicle is pulled out with the long cord attached. In another procedure, a device called an emasculator is used to crush the cord.

To ensure that the animals will not injure one another, they are dehorned with a chemical paste that burns out the roots of their horns. Some ranchers prefer to wait until the calves are older and then use an electronic dehorner with a cupped attachment that cauterizes the horn tissue. With older steers, saws are also used to cut off the horns and the roots, without the use of anesthetics.

Calves enjoy a short reprieve and are allowed to run with their mothers for six to eleven months on the open range before being transported to the giant mechanized feedlots where they are fattened up and readied for slaughter. There are some 42,000 feedlots in thirteen major cattle-feeding states. The 200 largest lots feed nearly half the cattle in the United States. The feedlot is generally a fenced-in area with a concrete feed trough along one side. In some of the larger feedlots, thousands of cattle are lined up side by side in cramped quarters.

In order to obtain the optimum weight gain in the minimum time, feedlot managers administer a panoply of pharmaceuticals to the cattle, including growth-stimulating hormones and feed additives. Anabolic steroids, in the form of small time-release pellets, are implanted in the animals' ears. The hormones slowly seep into the bloodstream, increasing hormone levels by two to five times. Cattle are given estradiol, testosterone, and progesterone. The hormones stimulate the cells to synthesize additional protein, adding muscle and fat tissue more rapidly. Anabolic steroids improve weight gain by 5 to 20 percent, feed efficiency by 5 to 12 percent, and lean meat growth by 15 to 25 percent. Over 95 percent of all feedlot-raised cattle in the United States are currently being administered growth-promoting hormones.

In the past, managers used to add massive doses of antibiotics to the cattle feed to promote growth and fight diseases that run rampant through the animals' cramped, contaminated pens and feedlots. In 1988, over 15 million pounds of antibiotics were used as feed additives for livestock in the United States. While the cattle industry claims that it has discontinued the widespread use of antibiotics in cattle feed, antibiotics are still being given to dairy cows, which make up nearly 15 percent of all beef consumed in the United States. Antibiotic residues often show up in the meat people consume, making the human population increasingly vulnerable to more virulent strains of disease-causing bacteria.

Castrated, drugged, and docile, cattle spend long hours at the feed troughs consuming corn, sorghum, other grains, and an array of exotic feeds. The feed is saturated with herbicides. Today 80 percent of all the herbicides used in the United States are sprayed on corn and soybeans, which are used primarily as feed for cattle and other livestock. When consumed by the animals, the pesticides accumulate in their bodies. The pesticides are then passed along to the consumer in the finished cuts of beef. Beef ranks second only to tomatoes as the food posing the greatest cancer risk due to pesticide contamination, according to the National Research Council of the National Academy of Sciences. Beef is the most dangerous food in herbicide contamination and ranks third in insecticide contamination. The NRC estimates that beef pesticide contamination represents about 11 percent of the total cancer risk from pesticides of all foods on the market today.

Some feedlots have begun research trials adding cardboard, newspaper, and sawdust to the feeding programs to reduce costs. Other factory farms scrape up the manure from chicken houses and pigpens, adding it directly to cattle feed. Cement dust may become a particularly attractive feed supplement in the future, according to the United States Department of Agriculture, because it produces a 30 percent faster weight gain than cattle on only regular feed. Food and Drug Administration (FDA) officials say that it's not uncommon for some feedlot operators to mix industrial sewage and oils into the feed to reduce costs and fatten animals more quickly.

At Kansas State University, scientists have experimented with plastic feed, small pellets containing 80 to 90 percent ethylene and 10 to 20 percent propylene, as an artificial form of cheap roughage to feed cattle. Researchers point to the extra savings of using the new plastic feed at slaughter time when upward of "20 pounds of the stuff from each cow's rumen can be recovered, melt[ed] down and recycle[d] into new pellets." The new plastic pellets are much cheaper than hay and can provide roughage requirements at a significant savings.

Every aspect of the steers' environment is closely monitored, controlled, and regulated on the feedlot to optimize weight gain. Even flies can be a source of annoyance, disturbing the cattle and keeping them from eating; cattle can lose up to half a pound a day fending off swarms of flies. Flies also spread diseases, including pinkeye and infectious bovine rhinotraceitis. Highly toxic insecticides are sprayed from high-pressure nozzles atop tractors that drive along access roads next to feedlots "fogging the pens and sometimes the animals inside with a cloud of poison." In the biggest feedlots, where 50,000 head or more are sequestered, managers sometimes turn to aerial spraying. Crop-dusting aircraft fly back and forth over cattle pens and spray feedlots with insecticides, drenching the facilities with toxic rain.

After being fattened to their "ideal" weight of 1,100 pounds, the mature steers are herded into giant truck trailers, where they are cramped together without room to move. Because the journey to the slaughterhouse is often a rough and brutal one, animals frequently fall and are trampled upon inside the trucks, suffering broken legs or pelvises. Unable to rise, these animals are known as "downers."

The cattle are transported for hours or days along interstate highways without rest or nourishment and frequently without water. At the end of their journey, intact animals are deposited in a holding pen at the giant slaughterhouse complex. Downers, however, must wait hours to be unloaded. Although downed animals are frequently in severe pain, they are rarely euthanized or anesthetized, as that would translate into a lost carcass and additional expenses. Often spread-eagled on the floor of the trailers, unable to stand or walk, these hapless animals are chained by their broken legs and dragged from the truck onto the loading ramp to await their turn for slaughter. Animals who die en route are thrown into a heap on the "dead pile."

Some of the more modern plants, like the Holcomb, Kansas, plant of Iowa Beef, take up fourteen acres or more. The steers enter the slaughterhouse single-file. Immediately upon entry they are stunned by a pneumatic gun. As each animal sinks to its knees a worker quickly hooks a chain onto a rear hoof, and the animal is mechanically hoisted from the platform and hung upside down over the slaughterhouse floor. Men in blood-soaked gowns, handling long knives, slit each steer's throat, thrusting the blade deep into the larynx for a second or two, then quickly withdrawing the knife, severing the jugular vein and carotid artery in the process. Blood spurts out over the workstation, splattering the workers and equipment. A journalist describes the scene:

> The kill floor looks like a red sea . . . warm blood bubbles and coagulates in an ankle deep pool. The smell sears the nostrils. Men stand in gore . . . each night the gooey mess is wiped away. . . .

The dead animal moves along the main disassembly line. At the next workstation the animal is skinned. The hide is cut open at the midline of the stomach and a skinning machine strips the animal of its hide, leaving the skin in one piece. The carcass is decapitated, the tongue is split and removed, and both head and tongue are impaled on hooks attached to the disassembly line chain. The carcass is then gutted. The liver, heart, intestines, and other organs are removed. After the viscera are removed, the body is hurried along to the next station, where the carcass is cut down the center of the backbone with motorized saws and the tail is pulled off the animal. The split carcass is hosed down with warm water, wrapped in cloth, and sent to a meat cooler for twenty-four hours. The next day workers use power saws to cut the carcass into recognizable cuts—steaks, chuck, ribs, brisket. The cuts are tossed onto conveyor belts, each manned by thirty to forty boners and trimmers, who cut off and box the final products. The neatly trimmed, vacuum-packed cuts of beef are then shipped off to supermarkets across the country, where they are displayed along brightly lit meat counters. ◆ ◆ ◆

Defending the Use of Animals by Business
Animal Liberation and Environmental Ethics

Eric Katz

When we think of the environment, we often think of the trees and plants. But business affects animals in a number of ways: Some are grown and harvested as food; some are used in scientific experiments; and some are displaced or destroyed by economic exploitation of the landscape. In contrast to those who think that animals have rights and deserve respect and protection on those grounds, Katz believes that business has only a limited obligation to animals; he explains why he feels that animal liberationists, in particular, are mistaken.

In recent years much attention has been focused on the proper treatment of animals by business. Among those who care about animals, two concerns seem paramount: that animals are being used for the wrong purposes and that animals are being mistreated or abused, whether or not the purposes are justifiable. Thus, arguments are made against the use of animals for fur, food, or experimentation in the cosmetic industry; additionally, arguments are made against the treatment of animals in laboratories, on factory farms, and in zoological parks. In part, the role of business in the misuse and mistreatment of animals has received attention as a spillover from the organized protests against the use of animals in scientific and medical research.[1] Also in part, business has been scrutinized because of environmental concerns; the annual Canadian baby seal hunt and, more recently, the Exxon oil spill in Alaska drew attention to the killing and abuse of wild animals. But more directly, business has come under increasing attack from those who advocate the general principle that animals deserve moral consideration, that animals have both legal and moral rights, that animals should be "liberated" from the oppression and domination of humanity.

The animal liberation movement descends from the animal welfare or humane movement of the late nineteenth and early twentieth centuries, but its purposes and tactics clearly differ. The goals of animal liberation go far beyond urging the benevolent care of pets and animals used for labor. Animal liberation seeks to end all unnecessary cruelty and suffering that humans perpetrate on animal life, especially the use of animals in scientific experimentation, in industrial product testing, and in food production. Animal liberation thus advocates vegetarianism and alternative methods of research and experimentation. Most animal liberationists use traditional tactics for effecting social change; lobbying, boycotts, and philosophical and political arguments. But some elements of the movement have resorted to acts of violence, coercion, and terrorism. In 1989 demonstrators at Saks Fifth Avenue in New York protested the sale of furs and harassed wearers of fur coats who passed by the store. One splinter group, the Animal Liberation Front, is considered a terrorist organization by the FBI. Recently national attention was focused on this group because of the alleged bombing attempt of a surgical supply company that practiced vivisection in the sales demonstrations of its surgical tools.[2]

And so business is faced with the task of defending its treatment of animals from the moral arguments and political tactics of the animal liberation movement. . . . I present a method—or at least, several arguments—that business can employ to blunt these attacks. I suggest that the adoption by business of a more conscious environmentalism can serve as a defense against the animal liberation movement. This strategy may seem paradoxical: how can business defend its use of animals by advocating the protection of the environment? But the paradox disappears once we see that animal liberation and environmentalism are incompatible practical moral doctrines.

Arguments in favor of the direct moral consideration of animals follow two major lines of thought.[3] First, it is argued that no morally relevant criterion can be applied to all human beings to differentiate them from nonhuman animals. Traditional criteria such as rationality, autonomy, or linguistic capability are not possessed by all humans. Other criteria, such as the possession of an immortal soul, are problematic at best. Thus, the animal liberationist argues that a moral preference for humans over animals, insofar as it is based on mere species membership, is an irrational prejudice analogous to racial or sexual bias. Animal liberationists often label such arguments "speciesist."[4] Like racism or sexism, speciesism is a groundless bias in favor of one's own kind.

This first argument is essentially negative. It demonstrates the absence of a significant difference between humans and other animals in the establishment of moral consideration. The second argument for the moral consideration of animals is positive. It claims that moral standing is derived from the ability to feel pleasure and pain or, as it is commonly termed in the literature, sentience. As Peter Singer writes, "If a being suffers there can be no moral justification for refusing to take that suffering into consideration. . . . If a being is not capable of suffering, or of experiencing enjoyment or happiness, there is nothing to be taken into account."[5] Any moral agent must consider the pain and pleasure that result from his or her actions. This is the minimum requirement of morality. Since most animals experience pain and pleasure, a moral agent must take these experiences into account. Animals must be given moral standing, moral consideration. The capacity to suffer, to undergo experiences of pain and pleasure, is the primary moral similarity between human and nonhuman animals. Sentience, then, is the nonarbitrary, nonspeciesist basis of moral value.

These two lines of argument are generally combined to form the strongest case for the moral consideration of animals. Yet the two arguments are actually quite different; they derive from totally different philosophical roots. The second argument, with its focus on pain and pleasure, is an outgrowth of classical Benthamite utilitarianism. It is a consequentialist doctrine, in which pain and pleasure are the only two determinants of moral value.[6] The first argument, with its focus on rights, uses a deontological model of thought. Within this model, the central problem in normative ethics becomes the search for a moral criterion that is not directly connected to the results of an action. The possession of rights is not determined by the consequences of action but by the inherent qualities of the possessor. The differing supports for the moral consideration of animals suggest the possibility of differing critical attacks. Each line of thought can be subjected to a unique criticism that weakens the case for animal liberation and points in the direction of a more comprehensive doctrine of environmentalism.

The utilitarian criterion of sentience is problematic for at least two reasons. First, how far down the scale of animal life can one safely assume the experience of pain and pleasure? Is the kind of experience required for animal suffering (and hence for the moral consideration of animals) limited to the so-called higher animals—mammals, birds, and so on? One author suggests that insects have the requisite nervous system for the possible experience of pain.[7] Insects then would be serious candidates for moral consider-

ation. Does this possibility suggest that the utilitarian basis of an animal liberation ethic can be pushed too far, offering a reductio ad absurdum of the position? Or does it place limits on the operational application of the concept of sentience, rendering only higher animals morally considerable? Both alternatives are problematic. The first case includes too many animals under the purview of moral consideration. The second presents a new, more subtle form of speciesism: only animals that resemble humans, who experience pain and pleasure in ways recognizable to us, gain entry into the moral kingdom.[8]

To a certain extent, this criticism is a theoretical quibble. Except for insects killed by pesticides, almost all animals used in business meet the minimum standards of sentient experience. Animals that are used in scientific research, that are hunted, or that are raised for food clearly do feel pain. Nevertheless, this mere theoretical criticism tends to demonstrate that the arguments in favor of the moral consideration of animals are not consistent. There are implications, weak points, and even holes in the arguments that are not addressed by advocates of animal liberation.

The second problem with the criterion of sentience is the contextual significance of pain. The utilitarian advocate of animal consideration contends that pain is an intrinsic evil, but the argument focuses on an abstract concept of pain separated from natural reality. In its concrete natural existence pain has an instrumental function in organisms: a warning of internal stress or external danger. Understood in context, pain is not an evil at all; it is an essential part of a successful organic life. An organism that does not feel pain cannot survive. It cannot reproduce itself, condemning its species to extinction. Once one adopts a more contextual environmental perspective, one can understand the role of pain in organic life. In the natural world pain serves a crucial positive function. But the hallmark of utilitarian animal liberation—the absolute, abstract denial of pain—ignores this context. It proscribes the infliction of any and all pain. Such a denial is both practically impossible and conceptually meaningless.[9]

The deontological concern for animal rights fares no better as a moral argument. The advocates of animal moral consideration claim that the denial of animal rights without a specific moral criterion shows a preference for human beings that is analogous to racism or sexism. The absence of a nonarbitrary moral criterion that distinguishes all humans from all nonhuman animals leaves no justifiable defense of preferential treatment for human beings. This animal rights argument rests on the claim that "marginal" cases of humanity—the severely retarded, the insane, comatose humans, newborns with severe birth defects, fetuses—are treated as normal or typical humans from the moral point of view. The crucial point is that even though marginal humans do not meet standards of moral consideration such as rationality or linguistic capability, they are given a full moral standing that is denied to animals—even when the animals are not inferior to the marginal humans. The moral consideration of marginal humans thus shows the speciesist bias in our treatment of animals.

This argument is empirically false. No observer of the contemporary world, or the history of humanity, could possibly believe that marginal humans are given full moral consideration. The cases obviously differ, but all in all, these humans are clearly deemed to have less moral value because of their reduced capacities. It is true, as animal rightists claim, that we do not eat retarded humans or babies. But we do perform scientific and medical experiments on marginal humans, and we generally find it easier to sacrifice their lives. The factual moral truth, however depressing as it might be, is that the hierarchy of moral value exemplified in the human treatment of an-

imals is echoed and repeated in the human treatment of other humans. The animal rightist claim about human speciesism is hollow, for it assumes the equal treatment of all humans, a treatment that is superior to all animals.[10] There is not an arbitrary speciesist preference for humans. There is the imperfect application of ambiguous criteria such as rationality, autonomy, and linguistic capability. These criteria are used, not altogether consistently, to determine the moral considerability of various classes of humans and nonhumans alike. A recognition of this picture of moral thinking softens the sharpest attack of the animal rights advocates.

Defenders of the use of animals by business and industry thus can raise several problems for questioning the moral consideration of animals. These criticisms are supplemented by the adoption of an "environmental ethic," that is, a direct concern for the moral consideration of nature and natural processes.

The term *environmental ethic* has been used extensively since the mid-1970s to denote a more benign relationship between humanity and the natural world. Within academic philosophy the term has developed in several overlapping, but often contradictory, directions.[11] This is not the proper place for a review of these various formulations. Instead I will merely suggest that the most useful environmental ethic for business to adopt as a countermeasure to animal liberation is ecological holism. This ethic uses the normal functioning of natural ecological systems as the baseline for human decisions that affect the environment. The primary and direct ethical focus is on the continuation of environments, natural ecological systems, not the lives or experiences of individual natural entities. As Aldo Leopold wrote over forty years ago, "A thing is right when it tends to preserve the integrity, stability, and beauty of the biotic community. It is wrong when it tends otherwise."[12] Consequently the way animals live in and through natural ecological systems would be the model for their treatment by humans. Business, or any other human institution, would look to the operations of natural ecological systems as a guide to the proper behavior regarding animals and other natural beings.[13]

As a countermeasure to animal liberation, ecological holism reinforces the proper role of pain in organic life. Since pain is as necessary as pleasure in a successful organic life, it cannot, and should not, be considered a moral evil. Pain, and even death, are crucial aspects in the operation of natural systems. Pain is a warning to individual natural organisms. It is an instrumental good for the preservation of individual life. The death of individuals in nature is a means for reusing and redirecting the energy in the system. In being eaten by a predator, an organism "donates" its energy to another individual in the system. Its corpse decays into basic organic elements, donating its energy to the rest of the system. From an ecological point of view, it is thus a mistake to consider pain and death as merely intrinsic evils that must be eliminated.

Indeed, advocates of animal liberation have trouble with the basic natural process of predation. A utilitarian concerned with the lessening of pain in the world would be forced to prevent predation in the wild. The advocate of animal rights would also, it seems, consider the rights of the prey to be violated in the act of predation.[14] But the prevention of predation seems an absurd position to advocate; if the moral consideration of animals implies the implementation of such a moral policy, then animals cannot be morally considerable.

An environmental perspective acknowledges predation as a basic fact of natural existence. Killing other animals for food serves the interests of the individual carnivore by sustaining its life. Predation serves the interests of the carnivore species by preserving its function or niche in the ecological system. In addition, the killing of prey, often the weakest members of the herd, helps preserve and strengthen the species that is preyed upon. In sum, there is no ecological reason to attempt an elimination of pain, killing, and death in the animal kingdom.

Here the advocate of animal moral considerability can offer a serious objection: the use and mistreatment of animals by humans is not normally an act of predation in the wild. Indeed, the few humans who need to hunt for a food supply may be permitted to do so.[15] However, most of the harm inflicted on animals by humanity takes place through factory farming, scientific experimentation, and industrial testing. So, the objection goes, the beneficial instrumental value of pain in the wild is an irrelevant consideration. The pain of animals in slaughterhouses or research laboratories serves no useful natural function.

The answer to this objection lies in a consciously radical environmentalism. From the perspective of ecological holism, the pain of animals in factory farms, slaughterhouses, and research laboratories is not natural pain. The animals suffering the pain are domesticated animals. They are themselves irrelevant to a comprehensive environmental ethic.

This radical environmentalism is based on the fact that most domesticated species of animals are essentially human artifacts. For thousands of years they have been bred for the development of traits important for human life and human use. Recent advances in the technology of agriculture and recombinant DNA research only make this fact clearer. Consider the injection of antibiotics into beef cattle or the genetically altered Harvard mice that are susceptible to forms of cancer.[16] Thus, the animals used by business and industry are human creations designed to fulfill a specific human need. They are artifacts, living artifacts to be sure, but they are no more natural than the wooden table I am using to write this chapter. To consider them the moral equals of wild animals—who, analogously to autonomous humans, pursue their own goals in a natural system—is a serious category mistake.[17]

Nevertheless, there are proper and improper ways to treat human artifacts. Humans may be required to grant direct moral consideration to some artifacts. Works of art seem to be a paradigm example.[18] So the defender of the business use of animals may be led to a kind of moral pluralism in which various kinds of natural and artificial entities, human and nonhuman organisms, natural individuals and collectives, are each determined to have differing amounts of moral value. Adopting a serious environmental ethic may involve remapping the entire landscape of our moral obligations, so that we take into account wild and domestic animals, marginal humans, plants, ecosystems, nonliving natural entities, species, and even future generations. This remapping is clearly a formidable task, but I believe that it will yield more moral truth than the overly easy utilitarian and rights-based arguments proposed by the advocates of animal liberation.[19]

One possible direction for the development of moral pluralism is an emphasis on the context of moral decision making. I criticized the utilitarian consideration of animal pain as being too abstract. The value or disvalue of pain can be understood only in the exact context of an organism's life. This contextual approach to ethical decision making should be generalized to include all practical moral thought. An emphasis on context is inseparable from moral pluralism. This ethical viewpoint implies that there is no one objective overall moral standard. Various criteria—such as sentience, rationality, life, beauty, integrity—are applicable in varying situations. In one situation it may be morally obligatory to treat a dog better than a human; at a different time or situation the human would come first. The point is that no moral decision can be made abstracted from the

context of real life. The concrete situation determines the proper moral outcome.

I conclude by returning to the defense of business in its use of animals for food, fur, and research. The argument presented here suggests that business can blunt the criticisms of the animal liberation movement if it adopts an ethic of ecological holism and moral pluralism. Business must stress that the primary value to be promoted in the human interaction with the animal kingdom is the natural fit with ecological processes.[20] Pain and death are not absolute or intrinsic evils. They serve important instrumental functions in the preservation of individuals, species, and systems. They need not be avoided at all costs. As long as animals are used in ways that respect their natural integrity or their natural functions in ecological systems, then they are being treated with the proper moral consideration. Human beings, as natural omnivores, are not acting directly against moral value when they raise and kill animals for food.[21] The human use of domestic animals falls outside the realm of environmental ethics; domestic animals are nothing more than living human artifacts. This conclusion does not deny that there are proper and improper ways of treating animals bred for human purposes; however, these moral constraints are not the absolutes proposed by animal liberationists. Consequently business should argue for a contextual approach to the human treatment of animals. Harms and benefits, value and disvalue, can be determined only in concrete situations. Before making a moral decision, the complex relationship between human and animal, society and nature, individual and species, must be understood.

I have consciously avoided presenting specific proposals. I recommend a general approach to applied ethics that eschews the determination of specific ethical commands abstracted from actual situations. Nevertheless, this defense of the use of animals by business and industry does not imply approbation of current practices. Many of the specific techniques of factory farming, to cite one example, cause pain and suffering that is unnecessary from even a perspective of ecological holism. Although I have argued that pain is not an absolute evil and that it is a mistake to consider it as an evil abstracted from a concrete situation, I am not suggesting that it is never an evil in specific contexts. It can be unnecessary. Humans can reform their practices so that they gain the benefits of using animals without mistreating them. Business and industry ought to modify existing technologies in the raising, harvesting, and slaughtering of animals, even as they defend themselves against the critical attacks of animal liberation.

A final impetus for reform would be the sincere adoption of environmentalist attitudes. An ethic of ecological holism would require major revisions in human activities regarding wildlife and the natural environment. Industry would be compelled to develop alternative technologies with low impact on natural evolutionary processes, such as solar power and organic pesticides. These reforms would affect the animal kingdom in positive ways, for reducing air and water pollution benefits all organic life. However, the reforms required by an attitude of environmentalism are miniscule compared to the reforms demanded by the animal liberation movement. That prudential reason alone should be enough to convince business to adopt an environmental ethic. ◆ ◆ ◆

◆ Notes

1. One medical researcher gave up fourteen years of research because of protests against animal use. See Sarah Lyall, "Pressed on Animal Rights, Researcher Gives Up Grant," *New York Times*, November 22, 1988, sec. 2, p. 1.

2. The antifur demonstration was reported in Carole Agus, "The Fur and the Fury," *Newsday*, February 21, 1989, pt. 2, pp. 16–18. For more on fur protests see James Hirsch, "Animal-Rights Groups Step Up Attacks on Furriers," *New York Times*, November 27, 1988, sec. 1, p. 50. In the last year, the *New York Times* has printed several articles on the "animal rights" movement—a sure sign of public acceptance of the merits of the debate. See Kirk Johnson, "Arrest Points Up Split in Animal-Rights Movement," *New York Times*, November 13, 1988, sec. 2, p. 40; Robert A. Hamilton, "Advocates of Animal Rights See Influence Grow in State," *New York Times*, November 27, 1988, sec. 23, p. 1; Katherine Bishop, "From Shop to Lab to Farm, Animal Rights Battle Is Felt," *New York Times*, January 14, 1989, sec. 1, p. 1; Barnaby J. Feder, "Research Labs Look Away from Laboratory Animals," *New York Times*, January

ary 29, 1989, sec. 4, p. 24. The Trutt bombing case was originally reported by Robert D. McFadden, "A Bombing Is Thwarted in Norwalk," *New York Times*, November 12, 1988, sec. 1, p. 29, and McFadden, "Norwalk Bomb Inquiry: Did Suspect Have Help?" *New York Times*, November 14, 1989, sec. 2, p. 3.

3. These two lines are represented by Tom Regan, *The Case for Animal Rights* (Berkeley: University of California Press, 1983), and Peter Singer, *Animal Liberation: A New Ethics for Our Treatment of Animals* (New York: Avon Books, 1977).

4. Singer attributes the term speciesism to Richard Ryder, author of *Victims of Science* (London: Davis-Poynter, 1975); see *Animal Liberation*, pp. 7, 25.

5. Singer, *Animal Liberation*, p. 8.

6. Hedonistic utilitarianism, the moral doctrine that judges human action by the resulting pleasure and pain, derives from Jeremy Bentham: "Nature has placed mankind under the governance of two sovereign masters, *pain* and *pleasure*." An *Introduction to the Principles of Morals and Legislation* (1789; rpt. *The Utilitarians*, Garden City,

N.Y.: Anchor, 1973), p. 17. Bentham extends the moral significance of pain and pleasure to the animal kingdom; in an oft-quoted passage, he writes: "The French have already discovered that the blackness of the skin is no reason why a human being should be abandoned without redress to the caprice of a tormentor. It may come one day to be recognized, that the number of the legs, the villosity of the skin, or the termination of the *os sacrum*, are reasons equally insufficient for abandoning a sensitive being to the same fate. What else is it that should trace the insuperable line? Is it the faculty of reason, or, perhaps, the faculty of discourse? But a full-grown horse or dog is beyond comparison a more rational, as well as a more conversable animal, than an infant of a day, or a week, or even a month, old. But suppose the case were otherwise, what would it avail? The question is not, Can they *reason?* nor, Can they *talk?* but, Can they *Suffer?*" *Utilitarians*, p. 381.

7. Jeffrey A. Lockwood, "Not to Harm a Fly: Our Ethical Obligations to Insects," *Between the Species* 4 (3) (1988): 204–211.

8. See John Rodman, "The Liberation of Nature?" *Inquiry* 20 (1977): 83–131, esp. 90–91.

9. One of the most important criticisms of the animal liberationist use of pain can be found in J. Baird Callicott, "Animal Liberation: A Triangular Affair," *Environmental Ethics* 2 (1980): 311–338, esp. 332–333. Another movement in ethics that emphasizes context is feminist ethics, although many feminists advocate vegetarianism and other nonharmful treatment of animals. I argue that a proper attention to context permits the use and eating of animals. For feminist ethics in general see Carol Gilligan, *In a Different Voice: Psychological Theory and Women's Development* (Cambridge: Harvard University Press, 1982). For a feminist perspective on environmental issues, see Jim Cheney, "Ecofeminism and Deep Ecology," *Environmental Ethics* 9 (1987): 115–145; for a feminist perspective on animals, see Cora Diamond, "Eating Meat and Eating People," *Philosophy* 53 (1978): 464–479.

10. Many animals are treated better than humans. I provide my pet dog, for example, with a better life than millions of humans in the world. His nutritional and medical needs are met to a higher level (I am guessing) than any individual in the entire homeless population of New York City or in the famine regions of the Third World. Since we do not normally condemn this "preferential" treatment of pet animals, we can see that we are not speciesists.

11. The large literature on environmental ethics cannot be cited here. Some of the best book-length treatments of the subject are Mark Sagoff, *The Economy of the Earth* (Cambridge: Cambridge University Press, 1988), Holmes Rolston III, *Environmental Ethics: Duties to and Values in the Natural World* (Philadelphia: Temple University Press, 1988), and Paul Taylor, *Respect for Nature: A Theory of Environmental Ethics* (Princeton: Princeton University Press, 1986). Two excellent anthologies are Donald Scherer and Thomas Attig, eds., *Ethics and the Environment* (Englewood Cliffs, N.J.: Prentice-Hall, 1983), and Donald VanDeVeer and Christine Pierce, eds., *People, Penguins and Plastic Trees: Basic Issues in Environmental Ethics* (Belmont, Calif.: Wadsworth, 1986). Current debates in the field appear in the journal *Environmental Ethics*, edited by Eugene Hargrove, Department of Philosophy, University of Georgia, Athens. I have published an annotated bibliography of recent titles in the field: "Environmental Ethics: A Select Annotated Bibliography, 1983–1987," *Research in Philosophy and Technology* 9 (1989): 251–285.

12. Also Leopold, *A Sand County Almanac* (1949; rpt., New York: Ballantine, 1970), p. 262.

13. Rolston, *Environmental Ethics*, pp. 45–125.

14. For more on predation, see Steve F. Sapontzis, "Predation," *Ethics and Animals* 5 (2) (June 1984): 27–38, and J. Baird Callicott's review of Tom Regan's *The Case for Animal Rights* in *Environmental Ethics* 7 (1985): 365–372.

15. So argues Peter Wenz, despite his concern for the moral consideration of animals. See his

Environmental Justice (Albany: SUNY Press, 1988), pp. 324–331.

16. The creation and patenting of the so-called Harvard mice is reported in "U.S. Plans to Issue First Patent on Animal Today," *New York Times*, April 12, 1988, sec. 1, p. 21, and Keith Schneider, "Harvard Gets a Mouse Patent, a World First," *New York Times*, April 13, 1988, sec. 1, p. 1.

17. See Callicott, "Animal Liberation," pp. 329–336, and Rodman, "Liberation of Nature?" pp. 93–118, for more on domestication and its significance for animal and environmental ethics.

18. For discussion, see Alan Tormey, "Aesthetic Rights," *Journal of Aesthetics and Art Criticism* 32 (1973): 163–170, and a reply by David Goldblatt, "Do Works of Art Have Rights?" *Journal of Aesthetics and Art Criticism* 35 (1976): 69–77.

19. The idea of a morally pluralistic system of ethical value is being discussed seriously in the literature. See Christopher Stone, *Earth and Other Ethics:*

The Case for Moral Pluralism (New York: Harper & Row, 1987); Wenz, *Environmental Justice*, esp. pp. 310–343; Callicott, "Animal Liberation and Environmental Ethics: Back Together Again," *Between the Species* 4 (3) (1988): 163–169; and my two articles, "Organism, Community and 'The Substitution Problem,'" *Environmental Ethics* 7 (1985): 241–256, and "Buffalo-killing and the Valuation of Species," in *Values and Moral Standing*, ed. L. W. Sumner (Bowling Green: Bowling Green State University Press, 1986), pp. 114–123.

20. See Rolston, *Environmental Ethics*.

21. But they may be acting indirectly against their interests and the overall health of the biosphere. Meat production is one of the most inefficient means of converting biomass to protein. There would be more food for the human population of the earth if we ceased meat production and shifted to a basic vegetarian diet.

Shades of Green
Business, Ethics, and the Environment

R. Edward Freeman, Jessica Pierce, and Richard Dodd

If we believe the environment is in jeopardy and we work to relieve the problems, then we may save the future for our children. If it is not in danger, then we have used some resources needlessly. But if there is a real risk and we do nothing, we will lose it all.

In this reading, the authors present five ways of thinking about the environment that they believe hinder us from tackling the real issues. They then pose the question: Do we risk everything by ignoring the possibility of danger, or do we take a more conservative approach by moderating our behavior? They give us four strategies (the various shades of green) that companies might adopt and finally present three pro-environmental mind-sets.

INTRODUCTION

Edgar Woolard, former chairman of E. I. du Pont de Nemours and Company, spoke at a conference of environmentalists, business students, and business academics about the difficulty of implementing strict new pollution standards. DuPont, long seen as a big polluter and a favorite target of environmentalists, had worked extremely hard to clean up its act and had recently announced a commitment to zero pollution. Woolard recalled a story about a plant that was not able to meet the new environmental standards. The plant engineers assured Woolard that there was no way the plant could be changed to meet the new standards, so Woolard suggested that the plant would have to be closed. Several weeks later the engineers reappeared with a solution. When Woolard asked them how much the solution would cost, they sheepishly replied that the new methods would actually save money.[1]

THE CHALLENGE OF BUSINESS LEADERSHIP TODAY

It is possible for business leaders to make money, do the right thing, and participate in saving the earth. It is possible, but it is not easy. . . .

. . . Instead of showing the myriad ways that business, ethics, and the environment conflict and lead to impossible choices, we are going to ask the question, How is it possible to put these ideas together?[2] In today's world, as well as the one we are creating for our children, all three are necessary. Our businesses must continue to create value for their financiers and other stakeholders. In an interconnected global economy we can no longer afford the ethical excesses that many see as characteristic of the last several decades. And, if we are to leave a livable world for our children and their children, we simply must pay attention to en-

vironmental matters. Yet most of the methods, concepts, ideas, theories, and techniques that we use in business do not pull business, ethics, and the environment together. From discounted cash flow to human resources planning, neither ethics nor the environment is central to the way we think about business.

Everyone shares the joke about the very idea of "business ethics" as an oxymoron—two words whose juxtaposition is contradictory. Much of business language is oriented toward seeing a conflict between business and ethics. We routinely juxtapose profits with ethics, as if making an ethical decision costs profits.[3] We sometimes qualify difficult choices that distribute harms and benefits to communities and employees as "business decisions," signaling that business and ethics are not thought to be compatible.[4]

The environment fares no better. It is seen as a necessary evil, a cost to be minimized, or a regulation with which to comply. We almost never think about the environment as central to the main metaphors of business, its strategic and people management systems, unless, of course, there is some regulation that constrains business strategy, a mess to be cleaned up, or a public issue that pits executives against environmentalists. Historically, businesspeople have not been encouraged to get involved with environmental concerns or have been discouraged from doing so. Our models and theories of business have traditionally been silent on the subject of the environment. However, the world of the next century will hear a great deal of noise.

More and more citizens see themselves as environmentalists. Governments are increasing their cooperative actions to address global environmental concerns such as global warming and biodiversity. Interest groups are beginning to propose solutions to problems that involve business decision making outside of and beyond government regulation.

What we desperately need are new ideas, concepts, and theories that allow us to think about business, ethics, and the environment in one full breath. We need to see these issues coming together rather than conflicting. Today's challenge to business leadership is sustaining profitability, doing the right thing, *and* being green. . . .

THE ENVIRONMENT: IT'S EVERYWHERE

Early in the morning of March 24, 1989, the supertanker EXXON *Valdez* ran aground on Bligh Reef in Prince William's Sound off the coast of Alaska. In the days following the accident every action or inaction by EXXON executives, government officials, and environmentalists was subjected to unprecedented public scrutiny.[5]

In addition to damaging the ecosystem, the Valdez spill symbolizes an important milestone in business history. The environment is an issue that has come to stay. It is not a fad, a passing fancy, or the issue of the day.

There is not a single aspect of our world today that can escape the scrutiny of environmental analysis. Pollution of air, water, and land, the production and disposal of hazardous wastes, solid waste disposal, chemical and nuclear spills and accidents, global warming and the greenhouse effect, ozone depletion, deforestation and desertification, biodiversity, and overpopulation are a few of the issues that today's executive needs to understand to be environmentally literate.

We are treated to daily doom and gloom press reports about the state of the earth. Scientists have "discovered" that global warming is or is not a problem, is or is not caused by solar storms, is or is not related to the emission of greenhouse gases, and so forth. We want to know the answer, the whole truth, "just the facts," about the environment, and we get disturbed by so many conflicting reports.

The truth is that there is no one truth about the environment. The truth is that we have not lived in a way that respects the environment and preserves it for our children's children.

BARRIERS TO A GREEN CONVERSATION

If we are going to explore how we can rethink business along an environmental dimension, and if the outcome of this conversation is to include many different ways of creating and sustaining value, then we must be on the lookout for barriers that will prevent us from engaging the tough issues. These barriers are produced by our inability to entertain new ideas: our mind-set. We have identified five mind-sets. They all say that our project—integrating business, ethics, and the environment into new modes of thinking—is impossible. . . .

The Regulatory Mind-Set

This mind-set sees the environment as a part of the business government relationship to be spelled out in terms of regulation or public policy. The regulatory mind-set says that the best way to take care of the environment is through the public policy process that produces laws and rules with which business must comply. It discounts the possibility and the wisdom of voluntary initiatives that stem from deeply held environmental values, or even the desire to respond to the environmental preferences. Although the recent history of concern with the environment has usually meant passing laws and their attendant regulations, the debate today goes far beyond a regulatory mind-set. Regulation lags behind the real world, and regulation inevitably entails unforeseen consequences. Our question for the regulatory mind-set is, Are you confident that government, as it currently works, will create a sustainable future for your children?

The Cost-Benefit Mind-Set

The cost-benefit mind-set is sometimes related to the regulatory mindset simply because many regulatory regimes use cost-benefit methods to determine "proper" regulations. The cost-benefit mind-set says that cleaning up the environment or making products and services more environmentally friendly has costs and benefits. And we should go only as far as the benefits outweigh the costs.

There are several problems with this view. The first is that if you focus on costs and benefits you will fail to use "innovation." The argument is similar to the quality approach. By focusing on the cost of quality, managers make wrong decisions. Instead by focusing on quality processes like six sigma quality, human innovation takes over and drives quality up and costs down. The cost-benefit mind-set says that there is a contradiction between "environmentally friendly" and costs. Many companies that adopt one or more of the shades of green that we recommend are making money and becoming more environmentally friendly. By focusing on costs and benefits, managers are inevitably led to ask the wrong questions.

The second problem with the cost-benefit mind-set is that it assumes one particular set of underlying values: economic ones. Many environmentalists, executives, and other thinkers have questioned the priority of our current ways of thinking about economics. All value is not economic value, and anyone who believes that is trying to get us to live in a certain way. Does the last gorilla have just an economic value? What about the beauty of the Grand Tetons? What about the future of our children? Human life is rich and complex and is not reducible solely to an economic calculation. It is degrading to all of us to think that we only value people and things in simple economic terms.

The Constraint Mind-Set

Many argue that the main purpose of business is to create and sustain economic value, and everything else from ethics to the environment to meaningful work is best viewed as a side constraint. The business of business is business. Anything else is to be viewed as not the main objective of business.

There is a nugget of truth here, as there is in each of these prevalent mind-sets. Economic value has been the main focus of business, and other kinds of value have been seen as constraining a kind of unfettered capitalism that is driven by the urge to win, succeed, and compete. However, a more thoughtful analysis of "economic value creation" shows that it is impossible to separate out "economic, political, social, personal" aspects of value. When the employees of Delta Airlines buy a jet for the company, when Johnson and Johnson recalls Tylenol, when Body Shop employees volunteer to help the homeless, when Mattel donates money to a riot-torn part of Los Angeles, all of these actions imply a company can be driven by economics and by ethics. We are not arguing that economics is unimportant but that reducing all human value creation–value sustaining activity to economic measures misses the mark. Business does more, as Adam Smith realized, and to reduce capitalism to a narrow view of economics endangers our free society.[6]

The Sustainable Development Mind-Set

It may seem strange to categorize what is supposed to be a way to save the earth with mind-sets that prevent environmental progress. Obviously not all discussions of sustainable development act as barriers, but one recent discussion simply misses the mark. The Brundtland Report, the basis of the 1992 Rio Earth Summit, called on governments to redefine economic activity to become sustainable. The problem with this view is that it calls on governments to play an intrusive role in the process of value creation, but if we have learned anything from the collapse of state socialism, governments and centralized approaches do not work very well. Ultimately, a worldwide regime of environmental cooperation could become a threat to democratic freedom, especially if combined with the other mind-sets. Decisions on the future of whole industries and companies could become a matter of government beliefs about what is sustainable.

Recall our view that there is no one truth about the environment. We believe that it is necessary to adopt a radically decentralized approach that focuses on shared values, and a conversation about those shared values. If such an approach is not viable, then we should see the heavy hand of the state as part and parcel of our failure to integrate business, ethics, and the environment.

The Greenwashing Mind-Set

The greenwashing mind-set pervades many discussions of the environment.[7] Characteristic of it is the view that business could never act on values other than profit maximization. Whenever we see a company engaged in something that seems to be good for the environment, we should be deeply skeptical. Truth be told, the company is probably trying to make money, avoid some future cost, or engage in other narrowly self-interested schemes. Many environmental programs at companies are, on this view, cleverly disguised attempts to be seen as green while really continuing in an environmentally destructive mode.

As we have presented these ideas to groups of people who are deeply committed to environmental values but have little real contact with the inner workings of business, there has been an assumption that "business is bad."[8] Now it is surely true that there are attempts to greenwash—

portray trivial changes to products, services, and processes in grand and glorious environmental terms. And we should always examine such claims carefully. However, the assumption that therefore all business attempts at environmental action are suspect simply does not follow.

We want to suggest that we be skeptical of all grand environmental claims, whether they be from business, government, environmental groups, or scientists. The arena is very uncertain and complex. However, the greenwash mind-set makes our task impossible, so we shall set it aside. Of course, businesses want to make money, but it doesn't follow that the environment must be left out of the equation, or that profit is the only value which counts. . . .

OUR CHILDREN'S FUTURE: A WAGER

The seventeenth-century French philosopher Blaise Pascal formulated an interesting argument supporting the rationality of belief in the Christian God. He suggested that if Christianity were essentially true, then someone who did not believe was destined for an eternity in hell. But if Christianity were essentially false, someone who lived according to Christian principles would lose little or nothing. This argument, entitled "Pascal's wager," has been the subject of much discussion and debate over the years.[9] We want to suggest that there is a "Pascal's wager on the environment" that goes like this.

Let's assume an optimistic scenario which implies that the gloomy forecasts are all wrong. Maybe there is enough room for landfills for generations to come. Global warming may be elusive. Many chemicals may well be harmless. The destruction of forests may be insignificant and well worth the benefits of development. Clean and healthful water may someday be plentiful.

And perhaps we can invent the technology we need to compensate for whatever damage we have actually done to the earth.

Are you willing to bet the future of your children on this optimistic scenario? If it is wrong or even partially wrong with respect to, say, "global warming," then there will be no inhabitable world left for our children. As in Pascal's wager, we are going to assume that it is reasonable to bet that there is in fact an environmental crisis. The consequences of being wrong are too great to bet otherwise.

Yet the great majority of responses to the environmental crisis have been at best ineffective. The main response mode has been to marshal the public policy process to legislate that the air and water be cleaner and to assign the costs of doing so to states, localities, and businesses. Twenty-plus years of environmental regulation in the United States has led to "environmental gridlock." There is disagreement and contention at several important levels.

First, as we stated earlier, there isn't any one truth about the state of the environment. Many (but not all) individual scientific "facts" are disputable. There is widespread disagreement about the scientific answers to environmental questions and even about how the questions should be stated.[10]

Second, even those who agree about the science of a particular issue still disagree about the appropriate public policy. Even if we agree that greenhouse gases lead to global warming, we may well disagree that limiting carbon dioxide emissions to 1998 levels will solve the problem.

Third, there is disagreement about underlying values. How should we live? By exploiting the earth's resources? By conserving the earth's resources? By living with nature? Should we be vegetarians to improve the ability of advanced societies to feed the hungry and use land efficiently? Should we recycle or should we consume green products or should we build an ethic of anticonsumption — of saving the earth rather than consuming it?

These three levels of disagreement lead to gridlock, especially in a public policy process that purports to base policy on facts rather than values. Overlay these three levels of disagreement on a litigious system of finding, blaming, and punishing polluters of the past and the result is a conversation about the environment that goes nowhere fast.[11]

We believe that this public policy process needs to change and that we need to have a better conversation about the environment and the role of governments. . . . But we are not willing to wait for these changes to take place. Instead we want to suggest another mode of response to the environmental crisis: business strategy. If we can come to see how business activity can take place, systematically, in environmentally friendly ways, then we can respond to the environmental crisis in lasting and effective ways.[12]

THE BASICS OF BUSINESS: WHAT YOU STAND FOR

At the thousands of McDonald's franchises around the world one thing is the same: QVC — quality, value, and cleanliness. McDonald's is built around realizing these values. This is why at any McDonald's anywhere you get good quality fast food, a clean restaurant, and a good comparative price. The very meaning of McDonald's encompasses these values, and everyone from CEO to fry cook has to understand their job in terms of these values.[13]

Strangely enough, a tiny company, only a fraction of the size of McDonald's works the same way. The company is called Johnsonville Sausage in Johnsonville and Sheboygan, Wisconsin. It is highly profitable, is growing fast, and works on values that differ from McDonald's. At

Johnsonville Sausage the operating philosophy is self-improvement. The company exists in order for the individuals in it to realize their goals and to continue to improve themselves. Values drive Johnsonville Sausage and many other businesses in today's fast-changing world.[14]

There is a revolution afoot in business—a revolution with "values" at its core. It was sparked by Tom Peters and Bob Waterman's best-selling *In Search of Excellence*, the rediscovery of Edward Demming's ideas on the productive workplace and the role of values and quality. Countless programs for individual and organizational change have been ignited by an increasingly competitive global marketplace; business today is turning to values.[15]

At one level this emphasis on values cuts against the traditions of business. It has always been assumed that business promotes only one primary value—profits. Both the academic research and the how-to advice books on business are full of ideas on how to become more profitable. And profits are the lifeblood of business. But surely the purpose of life is not just to breathe or keep our hearts beating. Humans are capable of more, of standing for principles, of caring for others, or creating value for ourselves and others. Even those few people who care only for themselves must avoid trampling on the rights and projects of others.

Organizations are no different. Profits are important, necessary—add any words you want—but there is more. Businesses can and often do stand for something more than profitability. Some, like IBM, stand for creating value for customers, employees, and shareholders. Others, like Merck, stand for the alleviation of human suffering. Still others, like Mesa Petroleum, may well stand for creating value for shareholders only; but even those companies must do so within the confines of the law and of public expectations that could be turned into law.

This concern for values can be summarized in the idea of enterprise strategy, or asking the question, What do you stand for? The typical strategy process in a company asks someone to think about the following questions: (1) What business are we in? (2) What is our competitive advantage in this business? (3) How can we sustain competitive advantage? (4) What product/market focus should we take? (5) What needs to change in order to be successful? Some of these questions go into every company's architecture of its portfolio of businesses. Even small businesses have to have some business plan, perhaps in the mind of the entrepreneur, which articulates how that small business creates, captures, and sustains value.

For this values revolution in business to be meaningful, a prior question must be considered, the question of enterprise strategy: What do you stand for? A business's answer to this question sets forth a statement of the core values of the organization and provides a context in which the strategy questions mentioned earlier can be answered.[16] For instance, if you stand for human dignity and some basic idea of human rights for all, then there are probably some markets that you will not serve, and some products and services that you will not provide. If you stand for quality, cleanliness, and value, then there are certain business opportunities that you will forego because you cannot produce the quality service, cannot produce it in a clean environment, or cannot provide it at a price that gives good value.

All of this may sound rather fanciful, but the basic point is that businesses have discovered that articulating some bedrock—some foundation, some basic values—has enormous benefits. The business becomes focused around these values. People, from executives to mail clerks, begin to believe in them or may be attracted to the firm because of these values. In short, business strategy makes more sense in the context of values.

Indeed the logic of values provides the very engine of business. Far from the inhibiting mind-sets that we mentioned earlier, the innovation mind-set is central to thinking creatively about business. Employees who believe in values are moved to innovate to realize those values. When the organization is committed to realizing the values, then the values become all-important. People will try anything if it helps them realize what's important to them. . . .

It is easy to see how thinking about the environment, and about ethics, is compatible with the values revolution. By clearly stating and understanding the core beliefs that an organization has or wants to adopt about ethical issues such as honesty, integrity, dignity of individuals, caring about others, and so on, policies that are straightforward and easily implementable can be designed. By clearly thinking through a position on the environment, whether it just complies with the law or tries to leave the earth in better condition, we can begin to marshal resources to realize these basic beliefs.

Executives can begin to meet the challenge of leadership that we articulated earlier—being profitable, doing the right thing, and helping to save the earth—by understanding and articulating an enterprise strategy, an answer to the question, What do we stand for? . . . For now it is enough to mention that lots of companies are doing this today, and it works. From huge DuPont to little Ben and Jerry's, from oil and chemical companies to retail boutiques, articulating what you stand for on the environment is step one to a greener world, one that we can pass along to our children.

SHADES OF GREEN

There are many strategies that businesses can adopt which are more friendly toward the environment, four primary "shades of green," each having its own logic and admitting many interpretations. Let's call these shades (1) light green, (2) market green, (3) stakeholder green, and (4) dark green. You can think of these shades as phases of development in a company's strategy, moving from light green to dark green, but keep in mind that each shade has its own logic and it isn't necessary to move from one shade to the next. Each shade offers its own way to create and sustain value, so that business, ethics, and the environment go together. . . .

Light green, or "legal green," is a shade with which most companies are familiar. Being light green involves complying with the following principle: *Create and sustain competitive advantage by ensuring that your company is in compliance with the law.* The logic of light green relies on the public policy process to drive its strategy. But it is a mistake to think that no competitive advantage is possible, since every company has to obey the law. That idea is mistaken on two counts.

First, as Michael Porter and his colleagues have argued, countries with strict environmental standards seem to gain an edge in global marketplaces—they become more efficient and have better technology.[17] Second, within an industry, companies can actively pursue public policies that fit with their special competitive advantage. By innovating with technology and know-how, a company gains an advantage over a competitor who cannot comply as efficiently. Light green thinking thus creates the possibility for competitive advantage.

Market green logic focuses on customers rather than on the public policy process. The following principle is at work: *Create and sustain competitive advantage by paying attention to the environmental preferences of customers.*

Market green strategies are based on "the greening of the customer," a fast-growing and controversial phenomenon. Today's customer-focused, market-driven company cannot afford to miss the fact that customers prefer environmentally friendly products—without added costs. Clearly, creating and sustaining competitive advantage is a matter of "better, cheaper, faster." Companies that can meet these environmental needs will be the winners. Customer perceptions about the company's "shade of green" are crucial, but, most importantly, the products and services have to perform.

Market green logic applies good, old-fashioned "smell the customer" thinking to the environment. Note that this may or may not be in conjunction with legal green. Market green logic roots competitive advantage in customer needs and the ability of the customer-driven company to deliver on these needs. There is nothing unusual except giving up the costly belief that environmentally friendly products always entail higher costs and competitive disadvantages. Notice that market green logic can apply in the industrial sector as well as the consumer sector and to services as well as products. . . .

Stakeholder green is a shade darker than market green. It applies market green logic to key stakeholder groups such as customers, suppliers, employees, communities, shareholders, and other financiers. There are many different ways to slice the stakeholder pie. Companies can seek to maximize the benefits of one group or they can seek to harmonize the interests of all groups. . . . Stakeholder green gets its color from responding to the needs of some or all stakeholder groups. It obeys the following principle: *Create and sustain competitive advantage by responding to the environmental preferences of stakeholders.*

Stakeholder green strategies are based on a more thoroughgoing adoption of environmental principles to all aspects of a company's operations. Many companies have adopted a version of stakeholder green by requiring suppliers to meet environmental requirements and by setting strict standards for the manufacturing process. Paying attention to recyclable material in consumer packaging, educating employees on environmental issues, participating in community efforts to clean up the environment, and appealing to investors who want to invest in green companies are all a part of stakeholder green. This shade does not require one or a focused set of actions but does require anticipating and responding to a whole set of issues in regard to the environment. As such it is more complicated than the lighter shades. The logic of stakeholder green is similar to the logic of quality processes. Unless quality processes permeate a company at all levels, they are doomed to fail. There are different levels of commitment to stakeholder green, just as there are different levels of commitment to quality, but any effective commitment must be pervasive.

Dark Green is a shade for which few companies strive. Being dark green commits a company to being a leader in making environmental principles a fundamental basis of doing business. Dark green suggests the following principle: *Create and sustain value in a way that sustains and cares for the earth.*

To most businesspeople this principle sounds idealistic or fanciful, which shows how much we have ignored the environment in our thinking about business. Indigenous peoples know that this principle must be obeyed because they live close to the land. We teach our children to care for their things and those things, such as our homes and land, that we share. It does not require a large leap of the imagination to expect that the same values are possible in business.

Dark green logic is not antibusiness, though many people believe it is. Humans create value for each other, and "business" is the name we have given to that process. Dark green logic says that we must respect and care for the earth in this process of value creation. . . .

There are more than four shades of green. Indeed, you can invent your own shade for your company. Look at these four as anchors that can define what is possible for your company. Dark green is not for everyone, and light green may well be universal. Dark green raises more questions than it answers, for it reminds us that the very idea of "living with the earth" or "treating the earth with respect" are difficult issues that bring forth deep philosophical questions.

We are not trying to define the optimal shade for everyone; our argument is that *variation is good.* Imagine a world in which there are thousands of enterprises trying to realize competitive advantage through environmental means. Undoubtably, many of these innovations will fail, but some will succeed, and many will lead to other, more important innovations. It is only through a large-scale process of many small innovations that real, lasting change can occur. Perhaps while such innovation is emerging, someone, somewhere, will invent a revolutionary "pollution machine" that will cure all of our environmental ills, or some official will "discover" the perfect set of regulations. All well and good if that happens, but we are suggesting a more modest and, we believe, more workable approach.

UNDERSTANDING ENVIRONMENTALISM

Ultimately how we run our companies reflects our commitment to how we want to live. Our values are lived through our behavior. Someone who espouses "green values" but does nothing to realize those values lives in bad faith or self-deception. "Bad faith" means that we say one thing and do another, and "self-deception" means that we are not honest with ourselves about what we truly believe and how we really want to live. Ethics, in life and in business, starts with an assumption of good faith and self-awareness, or at least an acknowledgment of the difficulties involved in being authentic to our true beliefs.

Nowhere do we see these issues more plainly than in environmentalism and environmental values. Talk is cheap, and its price is related to a shared history and culture of not living in a way that guarantees our children a future. We believe that there are many ways to live—indeed, many ways to live in an environmentally sustainable way—but we also know that our values have not always led us in any sustainable direction.

Environmentalism is one expression of the responsibility that we have to live ethically. Environmentalism and environmentalists come in many guises. If executives are to adopt shades of green, they must understand the value bases of environmentalists and environmentalism. In contrast to the mind-sets that prevent firms from becoming environmentally active, there are three mind-sets that motivate environmentalism and environmentalists. We are not identifying one of these as the correct one, but executives need to understand all three.

Environmentalists with a conservation mind-set tell us to conserve the earth's resources for the future. This view of environmentalism is a minimal response to our children's wager.

Environmentalists with a social justice mind-set tell us that there are many ways to improve the institutions that we have created. These environmentalists focus on those who have been mistreated by those institutions—women, minorities, and indigenous peoples—and traces a connection between their mistreatment and our view of the environment.

Environmentalists with a deep ecology mind-set ask us to view the earth as a living organism and to find a way to talk about the earth and its creatures in our human-centered moral discourse. We should live in a way that is sustainable and self-renewing rather than destructive of current resources.

Each of these three mind-sets challenges our ways of doing business. It is easiest to integrate conservation-minded environmentalists with the normal ways we think about business, but we shall argue that what is necessary to meet our children's future is a conversation that takes all three kinds of environmentalists into account. . . .

SUMMARY

We want to engage you in a conversation about how to think about business, ethics, and the environment together rather than separately. We are confident that the results of this conversation can make a difference—to us and to our children. If you are confident that your children have a safe and secure future, then you don't need to wrestle with the questions that this conversation raises and you don't need to examine your values and behavior to see if changes need to be made. But we do not share your confidence.

We do not have confidence that the future is secure, nor do we have confidence that our current institutions, as well-meaning as they may be, are doing all that is necessary. We are confident that if we can begin to think about business in environmentally sound ways, we can make real progress. We shall ask difficult questions and suggest some nontraditional answers. Our goal is to challenge you to formulate your own environmental principles and ultimately to formulate your own answer to our children's wager. ◆ ◆ ◆

◆ *Notes*

1. Woolard spoke at the Ariel Halperin Symposium at Dartmouth College in 1991.

2. We have no doubt that there can be and indeed are multiple conflicts. These conflicts are a result of the conceptual schemes we have brought to bear on these issues. Our argument is that we need a new conceptual scheme, one that considers the possibility that these ideas can fit together. Arguments about what may be possible are fundamentally different from arguments that assess and judge what has been and is the case. By focusing on the possibility of how these ideas might work together, we hope to escape some of the morass that usually encumbers more academic arguments in business.

3. For a review of the literature on business ethics, see Patricia H. Werhane and R. Edward Freeman, "Business Ethics: The State of the Art." *International Journal of Management Research*, 1, no. 1 (1999), pp. 1–16.

4. Of course, these "business decisions" are moral in nature. The idea that business and morality have nothing to do with each other is called the Separation Thesis. If business is thought to be amoral and separate from ethics, and if ethics is thought to have nothing to say about the underlying process of value creation in society, then we have a logical explanation for why "business ethics" often appears as a joke. The Separation Thesis has long outlived any usefulness it may have had. See R. Edward Freeman, "The Politics of Stakeholder Theory," *Business Ethics Quarterly* 4, no. 4 (1994); and "Stakeholder Capitalism," *Financial Times*, July 26, 1996.

5. For a brief statement of the facts of the Exxon *Valdez*, see Patricia Bennett and R. Edward Freeman, "The Exxon Valdez" UVA-E-0085 (Charlottesville, University of Virginia, Darden Case Bibliography, 1995). For more in-depth analysis that is not particularly sympathetic to Exxon, see Art Davidson, *In the Wake of the Exxon Valdez* (San Francisco: Sierra Club Books, 1990).

6. Adam Smith was primarily concerned about justice.

7. A perfect example of this mind-set is Sharon Beder, *Global Spin: The Corporate Assault on Environmentalism* (Devon, VT: Green Books, 1997).

8. For a more careful analysis of this idea, see R. Edward Freeman, "The Business Sucks Story," Darden School of Business Working Paper no. 96–15 (Charlottesville: University of Virginia, 1996).

9. Pascal's wager does not work in its original form because it is a tenet of both Christianity and liberalism that individuals can decide for themselves whether to mortgage their own future in eternity for a few temporal moments of pleasure during life on earth. Our children's wager doesn't suffer from the same logical defect because the point is that our children will not get to make those choices if we do not begin to live differently. We have used "children" in the sense of future generations that include but may not be limited to existing children. For an analysis of Pascal's wager, see the volume of essays edited by Jeff Jordan, *Gambling on God: Essays on Pascal's Wager* (Lanham, Md.: Rowman & Littlefield, 1997).

10. For a canonical form of this argument, see Norman Myers and Julian Simon, *Scarcity or Abundance? A Debate on the Environment* (New York: Norton, 1994).

11. Combine this argument with the trend in many countries toward the devolution of government, and an increasing disenchantment with government as the solution rather than market mechanisms. The level of gridlock increases exponentially.

12. Our approach is radical—at least for business theorists and environmentalists. Most writing about the environment suggests that business is evil, and most writing on business suggests that business is separate from the environment. We want to stake out some new territory.

13. For an analysis of McDonald's restaurant chain, and its environmental strategy, see Susan Svoboda and Stuart Hart, "McDonald's/EDF: Case Studies and Notes," National Pollution Prevention Center for Higher Education, Ann Arbor, MI: University of Michigan, 1995; for more general information on the history of the company, see John F. Love, *McDonald's: Behind the Arches* (New York: Bantam, 1995).

14. See Ralph Stayer, "How I Learned to Let My Workers Lead," *Harvard Business Review*, November-December 1990, pp. 66–83.

15. Note that this shift to values is not always in moral terms, even though Freeman and Gilbert argue that it should be. Many executives see these values as instrumental, leading to profits.

16. The "what do you stand for" question is also known as "enterprise strategy" and is traceable to Peter Drucker. See R. Edward Freeman, *Strategic Management: A Stakeholder Approach* (Boston: Pitman, 1984).

17. See Michael Porter, *On Strategy* (Boston: Harvard Business School Press, 1998).

CASES

The cases are included as a springboard for discussion and reflection about the concepts and approaches found in the readings. They are generally short and deliberately do not try to give the full story. This is because events have more than one possible narrative and are open to multiple perspectives; they cannot be tied to a single script. The cases are designed to encourage further research about the events and issues they represent.

The cases reflect the actions of real people in real events. They allow us to put ethical issues in a context and often show that there is not a simple right or wrong answer but more nuanced answers; thus, the cases represent problems where the only answers involve some kind of moral compromise. They also demonstrate that managers are frequently unprepared to face ethical issues.

It is not unusual in business to discover that a problem has developed in small steps over time, with the result that no one noticed it until it has become an unexpected crisis.

The emphasis in the cases is on the moral view rather than the legal view. Legal analyses often look to human error and to assess appropriate compensation. Although these issues should not be ignored, it is often useful to examine the conceptual framework that the actors used, to gauge the larger set of conditions behind an event, and to look at ways to prevent difficulties in the future.

Lastly, the job of a manager is to make decisions, often under conditions of uncertainty. The cases should act as a learning tool—prompting us to ask at what point and how forcefully value questions should be integrated into business decisions.

The Bhopal Disaster

Bhopal is a densely populated city in central India. In 1984 it had a population of 850,000 — comparable to the District of Columbia or Stockholm.

Union Carbide, a U.S. company, had a chemical plant in the city. One of its products was pesticide. Early on December 3, 1984, 40 tons of the highly toxic gas methyl isocyanate (MIC) was accidentally released into the air. Some of the safety equipment had been out of service for months, and other parts failed when water was allowed into the MIC holding tanks. The toxic cloud exposed up to a half million people. According to statistics from local officials, 2,000 died immediately, 6,000 died in the next few months, and between 150,000 and 600,000 people were injured. Union Carbide puts the figures at 3,800 dead and 2,720 disabled; they claim there are no residual effects from exposure.

There were no emergency plans in place at the time, and government officials maintain that they were kept in the dark about the deadly nature of the chemicals at the plant. Union Carbide, now a subsidiary of Dow Chemical, claims the release was the result of sabotage. They denied liability, although in 1989 they agreed to a settlement of $470 million to the survivors.

The magistrate at Bhopal demanded that Warren Anderson, the CEO of Union Carbide at the time of the tragedy, answer to a charge of culpable homicide. The U.S. government has not acceded to an extradition request by India.

By July 2004, $300 million remained unused in the compensation fund. There were demonstrations in the streets against both Union Carbide and local politicians, and the Indian Supreme Court ordered distribution of the money. Dow feels that the fund has satisfied any obligation it may have had.

The plant was taken over by the Indian subsidiary of Eveready batteries but then seized by the local government, who are now in the process of suing Eveready for decontamination costs. There are concerns that pollution from the accident will make the area unsafe for decades unless there are significant detoxification efforts.

Issues to Consider

1. What responsibility do you believe a company has for its operations overseas?
2. If the accident was due to local workers not operating at standards that Union Carbide would enforce in the United States, is the company excused from blame? Would your opinion change if it turned out that Union Carbide owned the majority share in the plant?
3. What duties does the firm have to the local population?
4. What duties does the firm have to the environment?
5. Should any compensation be paid to the victims? What moral reason supports your view? Who should pay it? The company? The government? Consumers?
6. What moral lapses do you believe led to the tragedy? Argue for your view, citing research that supports it.
7. Which set of figures would you use if you were to compensate victims? How would you determine the injuries were, in fact, connected to exposure to MIC?

Dow Corning and Breast Implants

Dow Corning was formed during the Second World War as an offshoot of Dow Chemical and the Corning glass firm to specialize in the production of plastics. One of its primary products was silicone, a synthetic polymer. In the early 1960s surgeons developed the silicone breast implant, and Dow was one of the first to manufacture them commercially. Implants accounted for about 1 percent of Dow Corning's overall business at the time.

For the next 20 years, there were a number of cases that linked silicone implants to subsequent health problems, including breast cancer, diseases of the immune system (in particular, lupus), and rheumatoid arthritis.

In 1990 Connie Chung reported on CBS about breast implants, claiming that they contained "an ooze of slimy gelatin that could be poisoning" women.[1] In December 1991 Mariann Hopkins was awarded $7.3 million in damages arising from pains, fatigue, and autoimmune disease as a result of silicone implants. In 1992 the federal government called for a moratorium on the sale of silicone implants, saying that the manufacturers could not prove they were safe. Facing more than 176,000 cases against it in a class action, Dow Corning and other manufacturers put aside a $4 billion settlement fund.

In May 1995, Dow Corning filed for Chapter 11 bankruptcy protection, and the class action settlement collapsed. Other manufacturers settled a number of claims out of court. In 1998 Dow Corning offered to settle with payments of more than $3 billion over the next decade.

The evidence against Dow Corning comprised medical testimony and internal company documents that cited concerns about potential leakage, toxicity, and quality control. In 1990 the American Food and Drug Administration demanded technical data from implant manufacturers. In 1991 they requested additional information and prompted the moratorium while it was being reviewed. Spurred by this action, the British department of health commissioned its own study. In their 1993 report, they concluded that silicone was essentially inert and posed no health hazard. The Canadians reported there was insufficient evidence that the reported diseases occurred more often in women with implants than in those without. The American Medical Association set up its own task force, which reported in 1993 that there was no scientific data that linked disease and gel implants. In France, a 1996 review again cleared the implants.[2] A 1996 book by Dr. Marcia Angell, editor of the *New England Journal of Science* at the time of the moratorium, suggested that the U.S. government had been influenced by politics and public opinion. She noted that although researchers could find no definitive link, as good scientists they were unwilling to testify that they could conclusively rule out the possibility that there had been any connection at all. Consequently, jurors faced with someone in distress and the possibility of a cause, however remote, had often sided with the suffering party.

Issues to Consider

1. Although the tobacco industry rarely denies the alleged association between smoking and disease, it tends to deny that there is any conclusive evidence that smoking causes disease. How

much evidence is sufficient to assign moral responsibility in cases of corporations making goods that could be harmful?

2. Jury members in Texas awarded $1.5 million against 3M Corporation in an implant case. One said afterward that they had agreed there was no way to prove one way or another about the sickness, yet they sympathized with the victim's suffering and felt she deserved compensation. The appeals judge threw out the verdict, saying among other things that the plaintiff's expert witness was unqualified to testify about the scientific data. Do you feel the jury could have been correct? What standard of science would be appropriate in a case like this?

3. In most surgical cases patients are asked to recognize that there are certain risks and that outcomes cannot be guaranteed. Who do you think should assume the risk in these cases? Does it make a difference if the operation is elective—say, prompted by concerns about body image—as opposed to, say, reconstruction after cancer surgery?

4. Dow Corning declared bankruptcy as a result of the case; jobs were lost and goods were taken off the market. Could there have been a better way to handle the issue of allegedly harmful products than adversarial court proceedings? What would you recommend, and what is the basis for your view?

5. Should these implants have been tested on animals? What sort of testing would you assume to be appropriate and over what time period? From your analysis, what sort of research did Dow Corning actually do?

6. Imagine that you were one of the plaintiffs in the class action suit who exhibited symptoms of pain and fatigue after receiving implants. You took a settlement of $12,000 from Dow Corning. Your symptoms persist, but the scientific and medical communities say they believe there is no direct link between the implants and your disorder. Should you give the money back to Dow Corning?

DuPont and Benlate

DuPont is the world's second largest chemical company, with sales of over $30 billion in 2000. In 2001 the company announced that it would cease making its fungicide Benlate. The news release read:

> In 1987 DuPont introduced a dry-flowable form (Benlate 50DF) that was recalled in 1989 and 1991 due to the presence of the herbicide atrazine in

some lots. The recalls generated hundreds of claims, and growers and their lawyers began blaming Benlate for a wide range of problems. DuPont initially paid many claims to maintain good customer relations. . . . When testing could not duplicate the claimed plant injuries, the company declined to pay any further claims. . . . In the following decade DuPont faced hundreds of Benlate lawsuits. DuPont won cases before some courts . . .

other trials resulted in losses, including some that reflected the runaway verdicts being rendered by the U.S. jury system in the 1990s. Ultimately, for business reasons, the company decided to stop selling Benlate worldwide.[3]

Benlate was first synthesized in 1959 and introduced as a fungicide in 1970. It had remarkable properties because, unlike other compounds that stayed on the outside of the plant and acted as a shield, Benlate was able to penetrate the plant and actually protect it from the inside. It helped turn canola into Canada's main cash crop and effectively defeated a number of fungal infections and molds. By 1979 it was DuPont's top-selling fungicide, with over $100 million in annual sales. In 1987 the DF variant was introduced. Two years later it was permanently recalled because it had been contaminated by exposure to other chemicals during production.[4]

DuPont was repeatedly sued. Growers reported that Benlate use had caused crop damage. An Ecuadorian shrimp farm was awarded $12 million because Benlate was linked to poisoning from run-off water of a nearby banana plantation. In 1996 a Florida court awarded damages to the parents of a child who was born blind. Human eyes develop early in pregnancy, and experts testified that exposure to Benlate during the fourth to ninth week of pregnancy could lead to anopthalmia—a condition where the eyes fail to develop. Subsequently, a number of class action suits were filed in the United States, Canada, and Britain, claiming birth defects due to exposure. DuPont's response was that it knew of "no credible science to support these claims and will continue to defend the product."[5]

The company's image was also tarnished when, in a series of cases from 1995 to 1998, it was fined for perjury and obstruction of justice. By July 2001, the company claimed that it had spent over $1 billion in Benlate-related litigation and settlements.

In 2003 the company settled with shareholders, who wanted compensation for lost share value, by paying out another $77 million. Investors claimed that the company had underestimated the liability caused by the compound and that it had caused losses by issuing false and misleading public statements.

Issues to Consider

1. Should we balance the benefits and harms of products on the market? What would be an appropriate way to do this?

2. Torts—harms—could be handled more efficiently if society just demanded compensation rather than assigning fault. Thus, for example, DuPont would pay out compensation based on affidavits of exposure according to a schedule of harms. (Worker's compensation operates in much this way.) Similarly, a firm making lawn mowers could design a foolproof model or a cheaper one that is more likely to result in injuries to users. Without the need to assign fault or blame, considerable savings would be achieved through avoiding litigation. The cost of compensation would be passed on to consumers, who would ultimately decide through their purchasing choices whether they prefer more expensive and safer goods or less expensive riskier ones. If there were to be a large number of fraudulent claims, then the market forces at work would lower the amount of compensation for an injury. Do you see any moral problems with this approach?

3. In a Canadian case, there was an unusual cluster of children born about the same time in the same area with underdeveloped or missing eyes. Lawyers claimed that the mothers had all

been exposed to microscopic amounts of Benlate, as it was being sprayed on a local orchard. What standard of proof do you think should apply in a case like this? If you were on the board of DuPont, would you assume any responsibility or fight the claim?

4. If you were on the board of DuPont, how would you respond if a Third World country wanted to buy up all the remaining stocks of Benlate at a discount, with assurances that the company would be completely immune from any potential liability?

5. An alleged letter from an attorney advising DuPont says, roughly, that it would be more beneficial for the company to state that it continues to research the issue than to admit fault or issue a denial: "It is a much better litigation position to state that we have looked, are looking, and will continue to look but have had no success, leaving the issue unresolved than it is to have to admit that we have isolated the mechanism for injury."[6] If you were a business executive aware of significant data suggesting your product had caused harm, how would you react to this advice?

6. From an environmental point of view, do you believe that chemical pesticides are useful? How do you measure the efficiencies of farming with fungicides against a more natural approach?

7. How would you compare the effects of fungicides with those of genetically modified organisms (GMOs)? Are there any significant moral issues associated with using GMOs?

Enron—from Pipelines to Pipedreams

We want to be proud of Enron and to know that it enjoys a reputation for fairness and honesty and that it is respected. Gaining such respect is one aim of our advertising and public relations activities, but no matter how effective they may be, Enron's reputation finally depends on its people, on you and me. Let's keep that reputation high.

Kenneth L. Lay, CEO Enron,
Enron Code of Ethics, July 2000

Enron was created through the merger of Inter-North Incorporated and Houston Natural Gas Corporation in 1985. At the time there was a frenzy of takeover deals. An investor might incur a lot of debt to capture a company. The company might defensively buy back its stock at a premium, or, after a takeover, the investor would

sell off its assets rather than allow it to continue in operation. One reaction by companies was to go into debt to become less attractive targets. In this case, InterNorth bought out Houston at top dollar and then found it had to service a huge debt. One of the new Enron's first moves was to raid worker retirement funds. In 1987 Enron survived a scandal when its New York bank discovered that executives were moving funds to accrue them in one revenue year rather than another. In a meeting of the audit committee, Kenneth Lay allegedly said, "I've decided we're not going to discharge the people involved in this, because the company needs those earnings."[7]

As the government deregulated the oil and gas industry starting in the mid-80s, Enron moved from being an energy supplier to an energy broker. In the early 1990s Jeff Skilling joined the company to run a subsidiary called the Gas Bank, which bought resources while they were still in the ground, pooled them, and then sold future interests to consumers. The contracts were essentially long term, which meant that under an aggressive accounting method (called mark-to-market), the revenues could be accounted for immediately although they would come in over time. This lowered the paper debt but also acted as an incentive to create ever more deals. In 1991 Andy Fastow came to Skilling's attention by creating partnerships that spread the risk and hid debt. These "special purpose vehicles" allowed Enron to borrow from the bank and pay producers for a stake in their current reserves. These partnerships were especially lucrative if the producers were paid in Enron stock rather than cash, a scheme that would work well as long as the stock held its value.

In the heady days of dot.com firms, ideas mattered as much as assets, and *Fortune* magazine picked Enron as one of its "most innovative companies in America" and in 2001 said that Enron was one of its "ten stocks to last a decade." Enron expanded its deal making from natural resources to areas as diverse as bandwidth and advertising.

The firm instituted a system called "rank and yank" where managers would rate employees on a 1 to 5 scale, and the bottom 20 percent routinely would be fired. At the same time, many executives were paid with stock options. Normally these can only be cashed in over time, but Enron instituted a rule where they could be sold very quickly if the stock went up significantly.[8] Both sanctions and incentives stressed quantifiable performance.

By 1999 Fastow had devised schemes where subsidiaries of Enron were entering into partnerships. Enron was shifting its debt onto these partnerships and counting the subsidiary's liability as an asset. It was as if they were using credit cards that were issued by a bank they already owned. The accountants (Arthur Andersen) and their law firm (Vinson & Elkins) maintain that they were unaware of the close ties of Enron and the partnerships or that the deals were backed mainly by Enron stock.

In 2001, Lay had stepped down, and Skilling was CEO of Enron. The company was the seventh largest in America. However, the technology bubble had burst, and analysts started asking more questions. On August 14, Skilling quit after 14 months in his position, citing personal reasons. Lay returned to the helm. An accounting vice president, Sherron Watkins, wrote an anonymous memo directly to Lay two days after Skilling's resignation outlining questions about some of the partnership schemes, saying "I am incredibly nervous that we will implode in a wave of accounting scandals." Later she arranged a meeting with Lay, who asked Enron's own lawyers to look into her concerns. They found no illegalities.

On December 2, 2001, Enron filed for Chapter 11 bankruptcy relief. In the preceding months, Skilling, Lay, and Watkins had all sold Enron stock. Watkins testified in Congress, countering some of Skilling's claims that he was not hiding debt but merely hedging the company from risk. She was named one of *Time* magazine's "Persons of the Year" for whistle-blowing, and subsequently she wrote a book on Enron. Lay resigned on January 23, 2002, and subsequently refused to testify to Congress, invoking his 5th Amendment rights. By that time Enron shares were trading at 67 cents, compared to $90.75 in August 2000. Andersen reported to Congress that it had destroyed most of its Enron-related documentation. Two months later, Andersen, one of the country's most prestigious accounting firms, was indicted on criminal charges. Shortly afterward, it surrendered its license to practice auditing, effectively ending its business.

The president appointed a Corporate Fraud Task Force in 2002 that oversaw work by the Justice Department. By July 2004, they had indicted all of Enron's top brass including Fastow, Skilling, and Lay on counts ranging from conspiracy, securities fraud, and bank fraud. Deputy Attorney General James Comey of the Justice Department said that the indictments served to restore confidence in the markets and showed that no one and no fraudulent scheme were beyond the reach of the rule of law.

Issues to Consider

1. Watkins has said that she did not do more—for instance, report her findings to the SEC—partly from fear of reprisals. She had found a memo from the Enron lawyers that stated that whistle-blowing was not protected by Texas statute. She also felt that she had done enough by bringing her concerns to Lay. "I did my best; I hoped they would do the right thing."[9] Did she do all that was morally required in this case, or should she have done more? How should we determine how much action is morally required? Should the consequences be taken into account?

2. Enron was often praised for its innovation in making deals, and some of the details were extremely complicated. How much oversight would have been appropriate? How much information should have been available to the ordinary investor?

3. Enron spent a lot of money lobbying and supporting political candidates. Lay had personal connections with the president and vice president. Should a company cultivate political relationships to promote its cause? What would distinguish persuasion and influence from manipulation?

4. Research Enron's dealings in India with the Dabhol power plant. The proposed plant apparently was not economically viable yet it won the support of both the Indian and U.S. governments. What would you say were the most important moral issues in the Dabhol case?

5. What conditions would allow a $60 billion fraud to be perpetrated by only a few top executives? Were those conditions in place at Enron, or do you believe there were others who were either tolerant or compliant with wrongdoing?

6. How should we account for nontangible assets such as good innovative ideas? If they are worth what the market is willing to pay, then Enron stock might have been worth what it traded for, even in the absence of assets or a positive balance sheet. Are we morally obliged to rein in market speculation or enforce investors to go through a great deal of financial information that they do not demand? Should society be paternalistic with markets or let them operate freely even if some investors might get hurt in the process?

7. Research the South Sea Bubble financial scandal of 1720 and determine which dynamics are similar to those in the Enron case and which are significantly different.

The *Exxon Valdez*

"We've fetched up hard aground. . . . We're leaking some oil, and we're going to be here for a while."
                    Captain Hazelwood to the Coast Guard

The *Exxon Valdez* was a single-hulled supertanker designed to carry crude oil. It was almost 1,000 feet long and 150 feet wide, displacing over 200,000 tons (*Titanic's* displacement, in contrast, was 52,000 tons). It had a crew of 21 and could carry 1.48 million barrels—nearly 60 million gallons—of oil.

On the night of March 24, 1989, it departed fully loaded from Prince William Sound in Alaska bound for California. Just after midnight, the ship ran onto the Bligh Reef. Several gashes in the hull resulted in the largest oil spill in American history; roughly 11 million gallons of crude oil emptied into the sound, eventually touching 1,000 miles of coastline.

There were some small icebergs in the sound that night, and Captain Hazelwood had received permission from the coastguard to use the northbound shipping lane to avoid them. He left orders that the *Valdez* should be steered back into the southbound lane once it had passed Busby Island, and then he went below to his cabin. The exact cause of the grounding has never been established. The third mate was in charge and may have given the order too late, or the helmsman may have been tardy in following the order. The steering mechanism may have been faulty, and there are allegations that the ship's radar was not switched on. Witnesses testified that the captain, a known alcoholic, had been drinking on shore before embarking, although his blood-alcohol level was not tested until the following day, and he was only charged with the negligent discharge of oil.

The area had a contingency plan for an oil spill. The seven oil companies using the port had formed an association known as Alyeska. It quickly became clear that the scale of the spill overwhelmed the available resources. The first couple of days had calm weather, but then the sound became very choppy, which further hampered cleanup efforts. At first, two ships with a floating boom tried to capture the oil, take it away from the *Valdez*, and burn it off, with limited success. Burning became impractical as the weather got worse. An attempt was made to skim off the floating oil. The heavy, sticky crude quickly clogged the machinery, and it was difficult to transfer the oil to storage containers. A third strategy was to use chemical dispersants. However, there were only 4,000 gallons in the port. This stock was used up when the sea was calm, but to be fully effective it needed to be mixed up by wave action.

The remoteness of the area—accessible only by air or sea—hampered efforts to rescue wildlife. Many animals died from direct contact with the oil, while others were starved of their food or had their habitats destroyed. Thousands of seabirds and sea otters died in the days following the spill, along with sea lions, orcas, and bald eagles. The spawning areas for salmon and herring were significantly affected.

Cleanup efforts continued until 1996, mostly funded by Exxon and its insurance carriers. Exxon claims the sound is now "healthy, robust, and thriving."[10] Various environmental groups contest Exxon's assessment, noting, for instance, that there are still no otters living in the inner tidal basin, and the commercial herring industry has been forced to close. Evidence is interpreted differently by both sides: Residual oil found under rocks, for example, is seen by Exxon as a good sign, because it shows that it has not migrated, whereas some biologists consider the oil to be more toxic in its concentrated form.[11] Exxon disputes some scientific findings on the basis that there is no stable point for comparison; they say, for instance, that some animal populations were in decline before the spill, and present low numbers may be due to generally warmer temperatures in the area.

In 1990, Congress passed the Oil Pollution Act, which required more stringent contingency planning and set up a fund for the cleanup of spills. It also banned the further use of any tanker that had spilled more than a million gallons, a measure targeted specifically at the *Valdez*.

Exxon paid $300 million in damages shortly after the spill, and $1 billion in settlements to the government, in addition to over $2 billion on the cleanup itself. A tort suit by local residents and businesses resulted in a punitive award of $5 billion against Exxon. Exxon considers the case to be one of opportunistic gouging, and the case has been tied up in appeals for the past 15 years.

Issues to Consider

1. One of the appeals courts wrote that although Exxon had entrusted its tanker to a known alcoholic who had resumed drinking in violation of its own policies, nevertheless, "as bad as the oil spill was, Exxon did not spill the oil on purpose and did not kill anyone." How would you gauge moral responsibility in terms of both the intent and the consequences?

2. One new regulation states that by 2015 all tankers have to be double-hulled to provide an extra barrier to prevent spills. This will impose an extra cost on the companies, which may be passed on to consumers. Do you believe that it should ultimately be up to customers to decide if they care more about cheap gas than Alaskan wildlife?

3. The official report from the State of Alaska says,
   The human and natural losses were immense—to fisheries, subsistence livelihoods, tourism, wildlife. The most important loss for many who will never visit Prince William Sound was the aesthetic sense that something sacred in the relatively unspoiled land and waters of Alaska had been defiled.

   Is there a way to quantify the aesthetic loss? How should a business make decisions that involve a pristine environment?

4. Who, if anyone, should pay compensation to those affected by the spill? Some candidates might include the third mate, the captain, Exxon, the State of Alaska, the federal government, and Exxon's customers. Where do you think the moral responsibility chiefly lies?

5. If the effects of the spill on wildlife disturbed you, would it be appropriate to boycott your local Exxon gas station? Is your local dealer tainted in any way by the events in Alaska?

6. Exxon merged with Mobil in 1999. It is now one of the world's most profitable companies ($21 billion in profits in 2004). Does that alter your view of its moral responsibilities in this case? Would your opinion change if the punitive damages had forced the company out of business?

7. Imagine that a company is extremely diligent in training its employees about environmental pollution. It conducts seminars, tests affected areas frequently, and every truck has a notice attached to the sun visor about the dangers of toxic spillage. But one employee is running late one day and empties a barrel of toxic sludge into a stream in the countryside. Who would you consider morally responsible for the spill and any subsequent cleanup?

The Ford Explorer and Firestone Tires

In June 2004 a California jury awarded Benetta Buell-Wilson $122.6 million in compensatory damages and $246 million in punitive damages against the Ford Motor Company. Two years earlier while driving her 1997 Ford Explorer she swerved when she saw debris in the road ahead. She lost control, and the vehicle rolled four times, leaving her paralyzed below the waist and in constant pain. She offered to take $100 million off the award if Ford would recall all Explorers made between 1990 and 2001 within 72 hours to fix known defects. Ford appealed the ruling, and a spokesperson said

> Although the offer makes a great sound bite, it doesn't change the facts: The Explorer meets or exceeds all federal safety standards. There is no defect with the Explorer . . . [it] is an outstanding vehicle with a solid safety record and we will continue to aggressively defend our products.[12]

The trial was the first loss after 11 acquittals for Ford in trials related to rollover accidents.

The reputation of the Explorer had been tarnished after a recall of Bridgestone/Firestone tires in 2000. At high speed, the treads of defective tires had been separating, often leading to rollover accidents. Ford blamed the tire manufacturer, saying there was nothing wrong with the design of the profitable SUV that made up 25 percent of its sales.[13]

Starting in 1997, Ford was getting reports of tread separations on particular tires, the ATX and ATX II, from Saudi Arabia and Venezuela. Bridgestone originally claimed that users in the desert tended to deflate their tires to get a better grip on the soft surface. Yet that would not account for the Venezuelan reports. They still argued that under-inflation by owners was the likely cause. Ford countered that there was failure rate of 241 per million for the ATX and fewer than 3 per million in comparable Goodyear tires made to the same specifications. An investigation showed that over half the defective tires came from Firestone's plant in Decatur, Illinois. In congressional testimony, Bridgestone's CEO, Masatoshi Ono, said that he accepted full and personal responsibility for recalling the tires but at the same time said that his company could not find a design defect, leading him to believe that the cause was poor maintenance. Ford's CEO, Jacques Nasser, claimed that his company was not aware of the defect "until we virtually pried the claims data from Firestone's hands and analyzed it."[14] Yet in Venezuela, Ford had been offering free exchanges for the tires since 1997. The tire recall cost Ford about $3 billion, roughly the same as the profit it had made in the previous year.

Nasser testified to Congress that the problem was with the tires and not the vehicle, because there had not been "one single tread separation problem" on Explorers fitted with Goodyear tires.[14] In October 2000 the *Washington Post* published an analysis that concluded that the Explorer was relatively more dangerous than other SUVs, whatever tire was fitted. It showed:

- Explorers with Goodyear tires had a higher rate of tire-related accidents than comparable SUVs.
- Explorers were four times more likely to have an accident caused by a tire blowout than other SUVs.
- The high fatality rate linked to Explorer tire accidents was directly tied to its tendency to roll over.
- Ford's investigation in Venezuela said that the problem was unique to the Explorer.[15]

Congressional testimony showed that Ford had been analyzing data for several years. When Ford Executive Vice President Gary Crigger was asked about a 2000 report, he responded that it was compiled only to assess the company's financial liability and was not shared with company engineers. Although Ford received "hundreds" of complaints about the tires, these were treated as anecdotal and turned over to Firestone, who warranteed the tires.

In July 2004 Ford announced that it would add anti-rollover technology to the Explorer and several other models beginning with the 2005 model year. The system senses tilt and automatically compensates by controlling the engine speed and applying the brakes.

Issues to Consider

1. Automobiles are inherently dangerous goods. At what point should a manufacturer be concerned that it has produced an unreasonably dangerous vehicle?

2. There are more than 5 million Ford Explorers on the road. If a design defect were to be discovered, what would be the morally responsible course of action for Ford? Does the cost of the action matter?

3. If Ford issued a recall, how affirmative would they have to be in encouraging owners to have their vehicles modified? Would it be sufficient, perhaps, to notify owners at their last registered address, or should they be pursued more aggressively, say, through a media blitz?

4. Should Ford be responsible for the problems of its subcontractors? If Firestone warranteed the tires, is Ford immune from moral liability? What would you do as CEO of Ford if you were convinced that there was a problem with the Firestone tires, but the manufacturer denied it?

5. Imagine that you are CEO of Ford. Your own engineers can reproduce the rollovers, but they tend to happen at faster speeds (over the regular speed limit) and when the vehicle is carrying weight high (for example, if there is a roof carrier). They also say there is a quick and easy fix: Put two bags full of sand in the luggage area. How much information would you release to the public? How would you weigh the issues of moral responsibility and legal liability?

6. How transparent should a company be? That is, should it make all company data and materials available to the public? Do you think greater transparency leads to more trust, by a sympathetic public, or to greater skepticism, by people who cannot be expected to fully understand the business?

The Ford Pinto

Thirty years after its production, the Ford Pinto is still remembered as a dangerous firetrap.

In the late 1960s the baby boom generation was starting to attend college. With increasing affluence in America, there was a demand for affordable transportation, and foreign carmakers had captured the market with models like the Volkswagen Beetle and Toyota Corolla. Ford needed a competitive vehicle, and Lee Iacocca authorized production of the Pinto. It was to be small and inexpensive—under 2,000 pounds and under $2,000. The production schedule had it in dealer's lots in the 1971 model year, which meant that it went from planning to production in under two years. At the time it was typical to make a prototype vehicle first and then gear up production. In this case Ford built the machines that created the shell of the vehicle at the same time as they were designing the first model. This concurrent development shortened production time but made it harder to make modifications.

The compact design called for a "saddle-bag" gas tank that straddled the rear axle. In tests, rear impacts over 30 mph sometimes caused the tank to rupture in such a way that it sprayed gas particles into the passenger compartment, somewhat like an aerosol. Canadian regulations demanded a greater safety factor, and models for export were modified with an extra buffer layer. However, the Pinto met all U.S. federal standards at the time it was made.

Ford actively campaigned against stricter safety standards throughout the production of the Pinto. The government at the time actively embraced cost/benefit analysis, and Ford's argument against further regulations hinged on the purported benefits. Under pressure, the National Highway Traffic Safety Administration came up with a figure that put a value of just over $200,000 on a human life. Using this figure, and projecting some 180 burn deaths a year, Ford argued that retrofitting the Pinto would be overly burdensome.

At one point, there were over 2 million Pintos on the road, so it is not surprising that it was involved in a number of crashes. However, data began to indicate that in some kinds of crashes, particularly rear-end and rollover, the Pinto was more likely than comparable vehicles to result in a fire. A dramatic article in *Mother Jones* drew on internal Ford memoranda to show that the company was aware of the safety issue and indicted the company for selling cars "in which it knew hundreds of people would needlessly burn to death." It also claimed that installing a barrier between the tank and the passenger compartment was an inexpensive fix (less than $20). In 1978, in an almost unprecedented case in Goshen, Indiana, the state charged the company itself with the criminal reckless homicide of three young women. The company was acquitted, largely because the judge confined the evidence to the particular facts—the car was stalled and rammed at high speed by a pickup truck—but Ford was faced with hundreds of lawsuits and a severely tarnished reputation.

Under government pressure, and just before new standards were enacted, Ford recalled 1.5 million Pintos in 1978. The model was discontinued in 1980.

Lee Iacocca said that his company did not deliberately make an unsafe vehicle, that the proportion of deadly accidents was not unusually high for the model, and that the controversy was essentially a legal and public relations issue.

Issues to Consider

1. Should a manufacturer go beyond government standards if it feels there may be a potential safety hazard with its product?
2. The Pinto was often driven by college students. If you were studying accident data, would that affect your analysis?
3. Once the safety issue became apparent, should Ford have recalled the vehicle and paid for the retrofit? Should they have invited owners to pay for the new barrier if they so chose? If only half the owners responded to the recall, what would the company's obligation be?

4. Iacocca is quoted as saying "Safety doesn't sell." However, he would say that he is referring to unnecessarily including safety equipment as standard instead of optional features. In previous models, he found that the public preferred a lower price to having more safety features incorporated in the base model. Should he have included them anyway?

5. Is there a difference for a consumer between being able to make a conscious decision about upgrading safety features (such as side airbags) and relying on the manufacturer to determine features such as the tensile strength of the gas tank?

6. Once the Pinto gained a poor reputation, they were often sold at a discount. Do private sellers have the same obligations as Ford if they sell a car they know may have design defects? Does the discount price absolve sellers from any responsibility for the product?

Genetically Modified Foods

Human attempts at altering the genetic makeup of foods and animals have a long history. Different plant strains have been selectively developed by cross-cultivation. In the past 50 years, plants have also been exposed to radiation and mutations with potentially beneficial characteristics singled out and encouraged. However, in the past 20 years technology has enabled scientists to isolate individual genetic switches that program particular traits. Using a process that is similar to "cut and paste" in word processing, scientists can now determine the effect of a particular gene sequence, splice it out of one organism, and insert it into another. The alterations may be described as input and output: Input traits give the plant better protections against insects, cold, salt, drought, or infections. Output traits involve the quality of the plant—for example, the amount of protein it yields.

Genetically modified organisms (GMOs) make up about 70 percent of American processed foods. They are chiefly used in corn and soybeans but have been integrated into many other foods. Half the cheese made in the United States is now produced with a GMO enzyme called chymosin.

GMOs hold the promise of drought-resistant crops, greater yields, lower use of fertilizers or additives, and greater resistance to disease. Why, then, are GMOs banned in much of Europe and labeled "Frankenfoods"?

There are a number of arguments for and against GMOs. Advocates claim,

◆ Hunger could be eradicated by developing crops that can grow in land that is currently unusable.
◆ Many diseases could be eradicated through fortifying crops—for example, enriching rice with vitamins.
◆ GMOs are safe and thoroughly tested.
◆ GMOs will reduce our reliance on fertilizers and irrigation.

Opponents say,

◆ GMOs tamper with the environment in ways we cannot know. A modified strain of wheat, for example, may not host a kind of insect that it currently does, and that may have effects throughout the biotic web.

- The long-term effects of GMOs are unknown.
- The science is not perfect. We may unleash changes that we cannot control on the natural world. Genetic splicing is still largely hit or miss, using large numbers of trial organisms.
- Regulation has not been perfect in the past; for example, DDT and thalidomide were approved by the government.
- The problem with world hunger is not supply but distribution. We presently grow enough food on the planet to feed everyone adequately, but it is unevenly shared.
- Modified (as opposed to organic) food is unnatural and unhealthy.
- GMOs will reduce natural biodiversity.

Two other issues are controversial. The first is that some are concerned that use of GMOs will concentrate power and control in the hands of a few large suppliers. Farming will become dependent on large corporate conglomerates such as Monsanto and Aventis.

These fears have been compounded by the development of so-called Terminator seed technologies. Usually a farmer can harvest seed to use for the next year's crop. Monsanto has been able to create a sterile form of soybeans, with the result that it is now the sole source of that strain. Other possibilities that are being investigated include sprays that turn the gene sequence back on to make the seed viable after treatment. Monsanto claims that these technologies will enable it to protect its intellectual property rights in its products. Critics warn that it will lead to farmers being at the mercy of big corporations, monopolies, and a grain monoculture. They also express concerns that the sterility factor may unwittingly affect worldwide crops.[16]

Another concern is that currently U.S. products do not have to be labeled to show that they contain GMOs. The Food and Drug Administration has rejected mandatory labeling in favor of guidelines to be drawn up by the food industry, partially because the FDA only has legal mandates over food additives, not modifications. In contrast, Europe has a wide range of regulations that require the information to be displayed, and often foodstuffs proudly proclaim the absence of GMOs.[17]

Other concerns about foods with GMOs are that they may cause allergies in humans, and failing to label them may put people at unnecessary risk.

Some consumer advocates believe the public would be more resistant to GMOs if it were aware of the extent of the practice. They feel that consumers are not being given full information about the food they eat. They also contend that many people would prefer natural foods, and GMO labeling would differentiate the market in much the same way that organic foods demand higher prices than those produced with pesticides.

The American public became more aware of the extent of GMOs in 2000 when Aventis, a French firm, suspended sales of its StarLink genetically modified corn seed. StarLink had been created by using a protein from soil that repelled certain insects with the protein Cry9C. The corn was approved for animal feed or the production of ethanol, but atypically it was not approved for human consumption because of a concern that it might be an allergen.

Somehow the modified corn got into Kraft taco shells. Possibly the pollen blew into nearby fields planted with regular corn, or it was mixed in with ordinary grain through human error somewhere along the supply chain. The tests that were available were generally only able detect the GMO in unprocessed food and notoriously had a number of false positives. Kraft immediately recalled the entire suspect product from the market.

The watchdog group Friends of the Earth sounded the alarm on the tainted taco shells. They contended that the case demonstrated the need for mandatory labeling and greater regulation of GMOs.

Issues to Consider

1. How much information is a firm required to disclose about its product? How would you distinguish between relevant and irrelevant information? Is nondisclosure in this case the same as lying?
2. What sort of testing might have been appropriate before GMOs were widely used? Should we test for potential long-term effects?
3. There is huge consumer resistance to GMOs in Europe. Is this a case where the consumer should be sovereign in determining what should be on the market?
4. In July 2002 Zimbabwe turned away a 10,000 ton shipment of grain sent by the United States as food aid because it could not be certified as free of genetic modifications, even though 6 million people there faced starvation. If a company wants to act in a socially responsible way, should it accommodate the preferences of those it offers to aid?
5. If you were in authority in a Third World country, what reasons would you use to decide whether to embrace or reject this technology in your agricultural sector?
6. How do you understand the term *natural*? Would any foodstuffs produced by the agricultural industry be natural by your standard?
7. From your reading and research, do you believe the benefits of GMOs outweigh the risks? What do you think are the main potential risks and benefits?

HealthSouth

HealthSouth is America's largest provider of outpatient surgery and rehabilitation services. It owns or operates over 1,800 facilities across the country and serves 70 percent of the rehabilitation market. It was founded in 1984 by Richard Scrushy, a former respiratory therapist who believed that efficient one-stop shopping could be applied to the health care industry.[18] From the time it went public in 1986, the Birmingham, Alabama, firm exceeded Wall Street expectations, a pattern that would continue for the next 15 years. In 1992 Scrushy aggressively began to acquire other clinics, and HealthSouth stock soared 31 percent annually between 1987 and 1997.

Scrushy cut a charismatic figure; the headquarters housed a museum dedicated to his achievements. He flew his own jet, mingled with celebrities, and sang with a band. For his third wedding in 1997 he chartered a plane to fly 150 guests to Jamaica. His workers knew him as King Richard.

His management style impressed many analysts. *Fortune* magazine described him in 1999 as executing his ideas brilliantly, and said he was

> a taskmaster and a micromanager . . . Scrushy honed his technique . . . centralizing every piece of data imaginable. Every Friday a stack of printouts detailing the performance of each facility

landed on his desk; when any one of them had a problem, Scrushy pounced . . . HealthSouth managed everything out of Birmingham: construction, purchasing, billing, even personnel. While this kind of top-down management may sound impossibly bureaucratic, Scrushy's troops made it work efficiently. Needed supplies and authorizations arrived within 30 days. Administrators who couldn't hit budget targets were fired. Says Scrushy "We can call 'em and tell 'em, 'Jump through hoops! Stand on your head!'"[19]

However, behind the scenes was a pattern of institutionalized fraud. By the third quarter of 2002, the $8 billion company had overstated its assets by $800 million. According to testimony, the fraud began shortly after the company went public when Scrushy wanted to impress Wall Street. If the results were not what he expected, Scrushy would allegedly tell his staff to "fix it." They would then convene in what came to be known as a "family meeting" to adjust the figures, a process they called "filling the gap." The internal accountants kept two sets of books—one with the true figures and one that was presented to the outside world.

HealthSouth was able to keep up the deception in a number of ingenious ways that systematically fooled outside auditors. One scheme involved what are known as contractual adjustments. Sometimes the government or insurer would not fully reimburse a facility for the amount charged to a patient. This amount would be subtracted from gross revenues. In typical double entry accounting, any loss of revenue has to be balanced by an increase in liabilities. HealthSouth simply failed to enter the liability amount. They also posted regular expenses as long-term capital expenditures and billed group therapies as single person sessions. They routinely inflated the value of their assets. The practices were pervasive but individually so small that they rarely met the threshold levels that would trigger review by an outside auditor. The inside accountants were careful to make sure the adjustments were uneven and dispersed around the country so they appeared realistic.[20]

Five HealthSouth accounting employees have been convicted of fraud. Four did not receive prison sentences, though. Their lawyers argued that they were obeying orders, subject to constant intimidation, and relatively low on the organizational chart. The judge declared at sentencing that although three held the rank of vice president "These four were essentially data entry clerks, regardless of their job titles."[21]

Scrushy was fired by the board on March 31, 2003. On November 4, 2003, Scrushy was indicted for securities fraud, money laundering, and other charges. He had maintained throughout that he was unaware of the illegal accounting practices. He was secretly recorded saying that he was worried about signing "fixed up" financials. As part of the Sarbanes-Oxley Act of 2002, an executive has to certify the company's financial reports. In August of that year, Scrushy signed that he had reviewed and endorsed HealthSouth's 2001 annual report and the second quarter report for 2002. He claimed on CBS's 60 *Minutes* program in October 2003 that he had signed because he trusted the five chief financial officers who prepared the figures. In June 2005, an Alabama jury cleared Scrushy of all charges, although the Securities and Exchange Commission is currently pursuing a civil case against him.

Issues to Consider

1. Is it fair to hold a CEO responsible for any and all actions of a company? Consider that Scrushy was not an accountant and that the outside auditors Ernst & Young did not detect the fraud. If he were not involved, should he still be held accountable?

2. Would it have been appropriate for employees to blow the whistle in this case? Was there imminent harm to people? What would be an appropriate motive for whistle-blowing, and how much proof do you believe the employee would have needed to be credible?

3. From your research and reading, what dynamics set the moral tone at HealthSouth? Do you feel that employees were influenced by the corporate culture?

4. There seems to have been a significant amount of wrongdoing at HealthSouth. A number of executives were involved in fraud, but there also appears to have been a great deal of complicity on the part of more rank-and-file workers. How would you assign moral culpability in a case like this?

5. Derek Parfit describes a case called the Harmless Torturers. He says in the bad old days, one torturer gave a jolt of 1,000 volts to a victim, but nowadays 1,000 operators each flip a switch carrying 1 volt. Any individual contribution to the overall effect is negligible, and therefore each one believes he has not personally done any significant harm. Would the same logic apply in the HealthSouth case? What, if anything, is wrong with the reasoning involved?

6. For a long time, HealthSouth posted profits, and Scrushy was a darling of Wall Street analysts. At what point, if any, should there have been greater regulatory oversight? Do you believe the outside auditors or the board should have acted more like bloodhounds than watchdogs?

The *Herald of Free Enterprise*

On March 6, 1987, the *Herald of Free Enterprise*, a ferry sailing from Zeebrugge, Belgium, to Dover, England, capsized in calm water 100 yards from shore, just minutes after setting out. One hundred ninety-three people died—many from injuries sustained when the ship rolled onto its side, while others succumbed to hypothermia in the English Channel.

The ferry had a "Ro/Ro" (Roll On/Roll Off) design: It was essentially a floating platform. Large doors at both bow and stern could be opened, which meant that the ferry did not have to maneuver as much in port, leading to faster turnaround times.

There were two direct causes of the disaster. Because of the configuration of the loading ramp at Zeebrugge, the ferry had to be lowered in the water by having ballast pumped in. Typically, the water would be pumped out prior to departure, but as the ferry was running late, the captain decided to do so after leaving port. Second, the bow doors were left open. Because the ferry was running low in the water, hundreds of tons of seawater flowed through the doors onto the car deck, causing immediate instability.

The assistant bosun was in charge of closing the doors but failed to hear the call for the crew to go to their stations on departure. The bosun noticed the doors were not closed but did not close them himself because that had never been one of his duties. The chief officer left the deck to go to the bridge after he thought he saw the assistant bosun coming to close the doors. The official inquiry stated,

> All concerned in management, from the members of the Board of Directors down to the junior superintendents, were guilty of fault in that all must be regarded as sharing responsibility for the failure of management. From top to bottom the body corporate was infected with the disease of sloppiness. . . . It is only necessary to quote one example of how the standard of management fell short. . . . It reveals a staggering complacency.[22]

The Crown Prosecution Service charged the owners, P&O European Ferries, with corporate manslaughter and charged seven individual employees with manslaughter in 1989. P&O had bought the ferry line only six weeks before the disaster. The case later collapsed.

There were also a number of alleged design flaws with the vessel. The captain could not see that the doors were closed from the bridge. The safety systems in place generally only detected problems, which meant that in the absence of any warning indicators, there was no affirmative duty to check that all was well.

Issues to Consider

1. Who was morally responsible for the ferry disaster? What factors lead you to this conclusion?
2. Consider that no single individual can be held accountable. Can the company itself be responsible?
3. Do you feel that the disaster was the result of a number of system failures or was it the human factor?
4. Messick and Bazerman in Chapter 3 use this case as an example. What point do they make, and do you agree?
5. What moral lessons do you believe can be learned from this tragedy?

H.B. Fuller and Substance Abuse in Latin America

The H.B. Fuller Company was founded in 1887 and is based in St. Paul, Minnesota. Its chief products are adhesives, sealants, and coatings. It has a global market that generated sales of over $1.25 billion in 2003. Its vision statement says,

> We are committed to the balanced interests of our customers, employees, shareholders, and communities. We will conduct business ethically and

profitably, and exercise leadership as a responsible corporate citizen.[23]

Fuller does business in Latin America, including Honduras, Guatemala, and Nicaragua. Honduras is one of the poorest countries in the Western hemisphere. Its main crops are coffee and bananas, both of which are subject to devastation due to volatile weather in the region. Over half the population is under 20 years old, and the unemployment rate is conservatively estimated at 30 percent. A series of loans has left the country with a crippling overseas debt. The population of 7 million is concentrated in the urban areas.

Aid organizations estimate the number of children living on the streets of Honduras to be from 3,000 to 20,000. The official government estimate is 8,000. About a third are estimated to be HIV positive. Many are known as Resistoleros because of their addiction to sniffing glue. Resistol is the brand name of an H.B. Fuller product. The glue contains a neurotoxin that suppresses hunger and gives the feeling of warmth and euphoria. It is highly addictive and inevitably leads to irreversible damage to the lungs, brain, and kidneys. In 1996 the government restricted distribution of Resistol except through licensed industrial vendors, but there is a rampant illegal trade. Dealers pay $35 for a gallon of glue, dilute it with paint thinner and bleach, and sell it to addicts who sniff it from babyfood jars or from soaked rags.

Fuller encountered significant bad press when their product was linked to the plight of the street children. A 1992 *Dateline* NBC documentary aired nationally, and Fuller was charged in a notorious wrongful death suit filed by the relatives of a Guatemalan child. A coalition targeted Fuller, claiming the company knew of the abuse for years but did nothing to stop it. Questions were regularly raised about sales of the product at shareholder meetings.

One response could have been to add a nasal irritant to the formula. Fuller questioned the effectiveness of the irritant, adding that it could also harm their own workers as well as legitimate users. They also pointed out that the abuse was only a symptom of the much deeper social ills. Fuller contributed to a range of welfare agencies and commissioned studies of the problem. It marketed a reformulated water-based product. Fuller announced that it would cease distribution of Resistol in Honduras and Guatemala in November 1999.

Critics charge that although the company did stop sales in Honduras and Guatemala, Resistol was still marketed widely in Latin America and is still easily available. Fuller responded that withdrawing from the market in those countries served as a test and showed that Fuller could not be blamed for the abuse because it continued even when Fuller restricted distribution.[24]

Issues to Consider

1. Is a company morally responsible for its products, even if they are misused?

2. Once Fuller was aware that street children were abusing its product, did the company have any duty to make it less harmful or more difficult to inhale?

3. Will Weissert, writing in *Newsday* (July 2000) says, "One of the victims in the battle against glue addiction has been . . . H.B. Fuller. Resistol, a Fuller brand, has become the term that street kids use to describe all glue." Is Fuller a victim in this case? Should it have foreseen some of the moral issues before they arose? Did Fuller do the right thing at the right time?

4. Some commentators have claimed that Fuller is at fault for saying that it would withdraw the product, then not fully doing so, while deflecting any responsibility by saying the issue is societal and out of company hands. From your research and reading, how valid is this charge?

5. Which standards should apply in this case—home ones from the United States or those of the host country? Are there any threshold or universal minimum standards that are relevant to this case?

6. A youth worker in the region said, "These children will tell you they have nothing to live for. . . . We are a world treating this cancer with an aspirin. They are children who have been born into the dying class. That is their fate and the world doesn't really care. That is why they go to sleep with a grip on the glue. To try to forget."[25] Do corporations have a social responsibility to not make things worse in countries where they operate? Do they have a duty to make things better? What kinds of action by Fuller would amount to unwarranted interference with the national sovereignty of Honduras?

Hooters Restaurant

Hooters restaurant chain has over 350 restaurants worldwide. According to the company promotional material, it has a "delightfully tacky . . . casual, beach-theme," which involves the "element of female sex appeal."[26] It acknowledges that *hooters* is a slang term for female breasts but feels that the use of an owl as its corporate logo is enough to "allow debate over the meaning's intent."

The waitstaff are Hooters Girls who wear orange shorts and a white tank top. The restaurant targets male customers between 25 and 54. Nevertheless, it offers a children's menu. The company unabashedly uses the sex appeal of its employees to attract clients. It claims that women have the right to use their appeal to earn a living in the same way fashion models do.

Hooters has been criticized on several grounds. Chief among them are the apparent promotion of sexual harassment and discrimination in employment practices. Sexual harassment may involve a so-called hostile environment. One definition says it

> can be created by anyone in the work environment, whether supervisors, other employees, or even customers or vendors. It consists of verbiage

of a sexual nature, unwelcome sexual materials, or even unwelcome physical contact as a regular part of the work environment. Cartoons or posters of a sexual nature, vulgar or lewd comments or jokes, or unwanted touching or fondling all fall into this category.[27]

Businesses routinely are not allowed to discriminate on the basis of gender unless there is a bona fide occupational qualification (BFOQ). The BFOQ allows employers to discriminate in their personnel decisions based on necessary traits for the job: firefighters have to be able to climb ladders, for example, and commercial pilots have to have good eyesight. Employers are not allowed to discriminate on factors such as gender alone, even if there is a strong correlation, say, between being male and having the upper body strength to lift boxes; employers still have to test on the ability (strength in this case) and not make assessments based on which class typically has that ability.

If the main job of the waitstaff at Hooters is taking food orders and delivering them to customers, they ought to hire on those abilities alone. The restaurant chain maintains that Hooters Girls are entertainers and therefore should be considered in the same category as the Rockettes or as actors playing female roles.

The Equal Employment Opportunity Commission investigated Hooters and accused it of gender discrimination. The charge was lampooned in the media and Congress as political correctness gone awry. The EEOC has not pursued the case, but it has not formally closed it.

Issues to Consider

1. Can people be sexually harassed if they are willingly participants in a sexually charged environment?
2. Would you feel differently if the case were about race or age instead of gender?
3. Imagine a restaurant chain that had a theme of tipsy leprechauns. It employs waitstaff who have an Irish brogue, and it makes fun of the Irish in general. The employees do not seem to mind (some of them are little people). Is such a restaurant morally acceptable?
4. Is it morally acceptable for the market to lead issues about discrimination? That is, should we legislate what is morally acceptable or allow the market to decide?
5. Hooters says that it promotes women's rights, because it allows women to make personal choices about their career—"be it a Supreme Court Justice or Hooters Girl." Some have objected to this characterization because they believe the image of women that Hooters promotes objectifies and devalues women in general. Which side do you find more persuasive and why?
6. If an employee of Hooters were subject to unwelcome touching by a client, to what extent is the restaurant morally responsible?
7. Do you believe there is a morally relevant distinction between waitstaff and entertainers? Explain your view.
8. Should an East Indian restaurant be required to hire waitstaff of European descent if they apply for the job and are familiar with the cuisine? Is promoting the restaurant's atmosphere a BFOQ in your opinion?

Johnson & Johnson and the Tylenol Poisonings

Tamper-evident packaging is now commonplace. However, in the early 1980s it was relatively easy to contaminate products without detection. In fall 1982, seven people in the Chicago area died suddenly after taking Extra-Strength Tylenol capsules. The murderer had pulled capsules apart, removed the Tylenol, and replaced it with about 100 milligrams of grayish potassium cyanide. The substitution was crudely done, but no one suspected it. In one case, a 12-year-old girl had been given the drug by her parents for a cold and died shortly afterward. Another victim was a woman who had just given birth to her fourth baby. In a particularly cruel twist, Adam Janus died after taking Tylenol for chest pain, and then his grieving brother and sister-in-law collapsed and died after using pills from the same bottle. The poisoned Tylenol bottles had been purchased at different times at different stores.

There was no evident motive for the killings. A man called James Lewis tried to extort money from Johnson & Johnson, but the police concluded that he was merely an opportunist who was unaware of any of the details of the crime. He was jailed for 13 years for the extortion but never charged with the murders.

As news of the poisonings spread, there was panic nationwide. McNeil Consumer Products, a subsidiary of Johnson & Johnson, made the pills. They quickly determined that the contamination could not have happened prior to shipment because of their strict quality control procedures and because the capsules came from two different plants.

Tylenol was Johnson & Johnson's most profitable product line. James E. Burke, the chairman of the board, and other executives decided almost immediately to pull the suspect lots from the shelves and warn the medical community. The larger issue was whether to issue a national recall. A few days later, Johnson & Johnson announced that they would recall and destroy all remaining Tylenol capsules. A Johnson & John-son executive quoted David Clare, the president of the company, as saying

> No management could ever have been prepared for a tragedy like this. . . . [we were advised] "Don't admit anything, kill the Tylenol brand, and avoid a product recall" . . . We turned to the credo for help. It was the Credo that prompted our decisions.[28]

The company has no mission statement but uses a credo developed in the 1940s by its long-time president, Robert Wood Johnson. It says that if the company serves customers and society well, then the stockholders will also be taken care of.

The company recalled over 30 million bottles of Tylenol, at a cost of over $100 million. They ran national television advertisements telling the public not to use the product. Johnson & John-son offered a $100,000 reward for information on the poisoner, but it has never been claimed and no one has ever been charged.

There were a number of copycat crimes in the following years involving such brands as Lipton Cup-A-Soup, Excedrin, and Sudafed. Another deadly Tylenol poisoning occurred in 1986. Improved packaging and greater public awareness have diminished the number of tamperings in the past 20 years.

Tylenol is again a national leader in over-the-counter analgesics and a highly profitable product line for Johnson & Johnson.

Issues to Consider

1. Although Johnson & Johnson took a massive short-term loss by its actions, it was cushioned by the relative wealth of the company. Should it have acted the same way if the survival of the firm were at stake?

2. James E. Burke reportedly said that he felt that there was no other decision he could have made. Do you agree? Could he, for example, have recalled Tylenol only in the Midwest? Was there a moral imperative to recall all Tylenol?

3. What was the moral minimum required of the company in this case? Would it favor some stakeholders more than others? How would you defend balancing the interests of some stakeholders more than others?

4. Imagine that a Third World country volunteers to take the recalled product. Its representatives make assurances that all the tablets will be visually inspected and random samples taken before distribution. Would that be appropriate in these circumstances? Would it have been a better solution than destroying all remaining Tylenol capsules?

5. Apparently Johnson & Johnson was not sued by any relatives of the victims. Would they have had a moral case if they had? Should the company have foreseen a risk and done something about it?

6. How well do you think a general credo works in guiding action? Would you prefer a typical mission statement or a clear set of policy outlines, for example? Do you see any way in which the Johnson & Johnson credo could be improved or modified?

Johnson Controls

Federal regulation in the workplace restricts employers in a number of ways, and sometimes there is a clash of values. Discrimination occurs when individuals are treated differently based on factors that have no bearing on their performance. Some practices were outlawed by Title VII of the Civil Rights Act of 1964, which protected people against discrimination based on race, religion, national origin, and sex. The number of protected classes has subsequently been expanded and now includes age, marital status, and disabilities. The Pregnancy Discrimination Act of 1978 states that a woman cannot be discriminated against on the basis of her pregnancy as long as she is still capable of doing her job.

Regulations are also set and enforced by the Occupational Safety and Health Administration (OSHA). One of its mandates is to provide guidelines for safe levels of exposure to a range of chemicals and other substances in the workplace. Johnson Controls faced a dilemma when it tried to enact safety measures aimed particularly at women. Pregnant workers could be at special risk, yet by moving to protect them, the company might be practicing sexual discrimination.

Johnson Controls is a national firm based in Milwaukee, Wisconsin, that makes a number of products, including automotive batteries. Heavy-duty batteries are produced using lead. Before 1964 Johnson Controls employed only men in the battery plant but then opened the plant to women. Management realized that exposure to lead involved in making batteries might be hazardous to pregnant women, and so in 1977 it warned them, saying,

> Protection of the health of the unborn child is the immediate and direct responsibility of the prospective parents. While the medical profession and the company can support them in the exercise of this responsibility, it cannot be assumed for them without simultaneously infringing their rights as persons. . . . Since not all women can

become mothers, wish to become mothers . . . it would appear to be illegal discrimination to treat all who are capable of pregnancy as though they will become pregnant.[29]

Women who chose to work with batteries were required to sign a form declaring that they were aware of the risks.

Things changed after eight pregnant women on the line tested for critically high levels of lead, according to OSHA recommendations. In 1982 Johnson altered its policy and began banning fertile women from exposure. The company felt this was in the women's best interest but also realized that it could possibly be the subject of a tortuous lawsuit.

The United Auto Workers sued the company for sexual discrimination on behalf of its members: One woman had been sterilized in order to keep her job; one woman had lost pay when transferred out of the area; and one man was not allowed to move to another position after declaring that he wanted to become a father. The company claimed it was a bona fide occupational qualification for a woman to be sterile—that is, that the nature of the job would permit Johnson to discriminate lawfully. This is the same kind of defense that allows a theater to hire only women for female roles.

The Supreme Court agreed with the union. It said that the company could not discriminate on the basis of sex and that the provisions of the Pregnancy Discrimination Act were silent about the welfare of the fetus: "The unconceived fetuses of respondent's female employees are neither customers nor third parties whose safety is essential to the business of battery manufacturing."[30] The judges said that the potential for lawsuits over harm to the children was minimized by clear warnings.

Issues to Consider

1. What do you think is the relationship between law and morality? Can there be legal actions that are immoral or illegal actions that are moral?

2. For the sake of argument, assume that the company was working in the best interests of the women and their fetuses by following OSHA guidelines. Should they have been allowed to discriminate against pregnant women? Against potentially pregnant women?

3. What options do you believe Johnson Controls had when it realized that lead exposure could be harmful to pregnant women? Could it, for instance, have transferred them all to other (safer) jobs that paid equally well?

4. How much research is appropriate in cases where workers are exposed to potentially harmful materials? For example, it was unclear whether there was a risk to the male reproductive system from lead exposure. Should that have been studied, and who would pay for the research? Would your answer apply to other substances such as the chemicals used in producing compact discs? At what point should we just accept risk as part of the job?

5. Of the eight women who prompted the change in policy, only one gave birth to a child with elevated lead levels in the blood, but the baby did not seem to suffer any ill effects from the exposure. The company materials that warned of the risk said it believed the lead levels were less harmful than smoking during pregnancy, but the evidence was inconclusive. Do these facts change your view of the case? If the case had involved a nuclear plant and the risk of deformity or ill health to future children was very low but devastating if it occurred (contrasted, say, to a relatively high chance of a mild effect), would you come to a different conclusion?

6. Is this really a case of "Let the worker beware"? As long as there are warning signs posted, should the individual decide for himself or herself? Would the lack of other job opportunities in the area affect your analysis? Would it be appropriate for the company to pay danger money to workers in this area, but then excuse itself from any future liability?

Love Canal

At the turn of the 20th century, the area near Niagara Falls in upstate New York seemed ideal for the development of industry. The vast potential of hydroelectric power promised cheap and plentiful electricity for commercial and private use. Large sums of money were raised by the Modeltown Development Corporation, led by the visionary William T. Love. One of their projects was to build a canal near the town of Niagara Falls. However, by 1910 the endeavor was bankrupt: An economic depression had forced many of the backers to pull out, and the development of alternating current meant that electricity could be sent across the country so that industry did not have to be located near the source of the power.

Canals are made by cutting an artificial river bed and lining it with impervious material, like clay. Although never formally used as a canal, the cut was a local swimming hole and recreational site. By the 1920s it had been drained and was being used as a dump for chemicals from nearby plants. The nearby Hooker Chemical Company allegedly dumped over 20,000 tons of assorted chemical material in the canal over the next 30 years. Once the site was filled, it was sealed by being covered with more clay and dirt. There are no records of exactly what materials went into the site.

In 1953, the local school board wanted to take over the area for development. Concerned about a forced sale through eminent domain, Hooker deeded the area to the city for $1. Hooker warned that the area was unsafe for development, including a statement saying, "the grantee assumes all risk and liability" and a condition that the city could not sue Hooker based on claims of death, injury, or damage to property due to the stored wastes.[31] The school board went ahead and built a school and sold other land to a private developer who built houses near the canal site. During construction, it was unusually rainy, and it is likely that the heavy equipment such as bulldozers broke through the cap over the canal, allowing water to penetrate the site and mix with material below ground.

By 1978, local residents had organized because of what they perceived as a high incidence of serious illness, miscarriages, and birth defects. They became increasingly active, to the point of briefly holding representatives from the Environmental Protection Agency (EPA) hostage. The EPA reported chromosome damage in some residents, and by 1980 the state and federal government relocated 949 families. Lawsuits flourished, and in 1988 Occidental Chemical, which had purchased Hooker, was ordered to pay for cleaning up the site. Occidental appealed and in turn sued its insurers for failing to pay settlement costs. Many dislocated residents have received market cost payments for their houses along with compensation ranging from $2,000 to $40,000.

In March 2004, the EPA took the site off the Superfund list, signaling a formal end to its cleanup efforts. New York State authorities refurbished a number of houses in the area, now called Black Creek Village, and sold them to new owners. Most of the chemicals remain buried at the site, and the dump itself is surrounded by an 8-foot fence.

Issues to Consider

1. Who is responsible for the cleanup of the Love Canal site? Explain what you understand by the term *responsible* in this context.
2. Should a company or institution be held morally liable for the actions of its ancestors? That is, should the school board or Occidental be held accountable for the actions of Hooker Chemical?
3. Assume that many of the chemicals were dumped at a time of national emergency, the Second World War, when keeping accurate records of waste disposal was less important than rapid production for the war effort. Do you think that fact would alter your analysis of moral responsibility?
4. All of Hooker's actions were legal at the time. Do you believe they should have taken any action beyond legal requirements? Now transfer the case to modern-day Nigeria. If chemical dumping and loose record-keeping is legal, should a petroleum company go beyond the local regulations?
5. From your own research and reading, did the government respond in a timely manner to the concerns of the local residents? What do you perceive to be the relationship of government to the corporation, or the school board in this case?
6. Did the waiver that Hooker issued have any moral force? Do you think that responsibility is diluted as it goes along the causal chain from Hooker to the housing developer? If you were assessing moral culpability, is one party more blameworthy than others?

Malden Mills

Lawrence, Massachusetts, is 25 miles north of Boston. In the mid-1800s it was one of several planned industrial sites that developed the local textile industry based on the waterpower derived from the nearby Merrimack River. By 1900 the town had a population of over 95,000 and mills that worked day and night.

In 1906, Henry Feuerstein founded Malden Mills in nearby Lowell and relocated it to Lawrence in 1956. It has traditionally been a closely held private firm. The company survived a number of boom and bust cycles and watched the exodus of other manufacturers to the American South and overseas.

In 1981 the firm developed Polar Tec, a lightweight versatile fleece fabric that has become synonymous with outdoor gear, and its future seemed secure. However, on a bitterly cold night in December 1995, a devastating fire burned most of the plant to the ground.

The CEO, Aaron Feuerstein, could have accepted an insurance settlement and closed the factory or moved operations overseas. Instead, he spent $15 million of his own money keeping all 3,000 employees on the payroll, with benefits, for three months while the factory was rebuilt. Feuerstein said,

> I have a responsibility to the worker. . . . I have an equal responsibility to the community. It would have been unconscionable to put 3,000 people on the streets and deliver a deathblow to the cities of Lawrence and Methuen. Maybe on paper our

company is worth less to Wall Street, but I can tell you it is worth more.[32]

While the factory was being rebuilt, the human resources division used federal and state funding to give many of the displaced workers additional training, especially on computers. Feuerstein was lionized in the press and given a number of national and international awards for his stance. The new plant is environmentally sensitive, and reportedly individual productivity increased significantly.

Nevertheless, Malden Mills again hit hard times. Faced with financial difficulties that stemmed largely from financing the debt for rebuilding, it filed Chapter 11 bankruptcy in November 2001.

In October 2003, the firm successfully emerged from Chapter 11. Aaron Feuerstein has been replaced as CEO, and there are six new directors on the board. Recent orders from the U.S. armed forces have given Malden Mills a significant boost.

Issues to Consider

1. A deontologist might say that we can never know the outcome of our actions, but we can make sure that we make a moral choice. A utilitarian might say that an act can only be judged by its outcome. Which theory might be best to judge Feuerstein's approach in this case? Is there another way at looking at his behavior that is more appropriate?

2. It is possible that someone could act badly, do the decent thing, or go beyond what morality requires. How would you describe Feuerstein's approach to helping his workers and the community when the factory burned?

3. Feuerstein has stated very plainly that his view of business behavior is guided by his religious principles. What relationship do you think there should be between someone's religious beliefs and how that person acts in the workplace?

4. Do you believe that Feuerstein was acting paternalistically to his workers? Do you think they should have been expected to deal with the consequences of the fire without his help?

5. Lawrence has been through a series of tough times. Do you believe the federal or state government should have helped the city maintain its industrial base, for instance, by subsidizing the plant during reconstruction?

6. The language of stakeholder analysis would apply to Feuerstein's actions in supporting his workers: He looked after the employees, their families, and the community. To how many

stakeholder groups should a manager be responsible? How can you balance their various, and sometimes conflicting, claims?

7. Feuerstein's behavior after the fire earned him acclaim and numerous awards. Do you feel that others in business should emulate his behavior?

McDonald's and the McLibel Case

The fast-food chain McDonald's spends considerable sums in advertising to persuade and inform potential consumers of the merits of their products. In 2004, McDonald's in the United Kingdom spent about $75 million on advertising, including almost $10 million on television commercials that are typically shown during children's peak viewing times.

The chain has come under some criticism. Some British legislators, for example, have suggested banning advertising aimed at children that promotes foods high in sugar, salt, and fat. McDonald's has vigorously defended its products and made significant efforts to silence its critics. Under British libel law, a defendant has to prove that what he or she has written is true, which means someone who writes disparagingly about corporations may face the prospect of a long and very costly legal battle. Corporations have often used the presumption of libel and heavy penalties to intimidate critics.

According to commentator John Vidal, McDonald's had sued a number of publications in England, including a national newspaper (*The Guardian*), *Today* magazine, a national television network (*Channel 4*), *Sunday Times Magazine*, and the satirical television show *Spitting Image*. One McDonald's target, the Youth Section of the

Vegetarian Society, stated that it published an apology "because there was not the money to fight the case."[33]

Helen Steel and Dave Morris were members of London Greenpeace who handed out a pamphlet entitled "What's Wrong with McDonald's?" to passersby on a London street. Because the leaflet was published material, in legal terms it constituted potential libel. The leaflet alleged,

- McDonald's is linked to rain forest destruction.
- McDonald's supply practices exploit Third World nations.
- Their packaging is wasteful.
- Their products are of poor nutritional quality.
- There are links between McDonald's foods and heart disease and cancer.
- McDonald's exploits children in their advertising.
- McDonald's is responsible for many cruel farming practices.
- The corporation is antipathetic to unions and pays low wages.

McDonald's operatives infiltrated the Greenpeace branch and, later, company lawyers served libel writs on five members. Three gave public apologies to avoid litigation. Steel and Morris went to court, representing themselves. This led to the longest libel trial in British history—almost three years. The judge finally supported half the claims: cruelty to animals, misleading advertising, and low wages.

The case acted as a rallying point for people opposed to large corporations and globalization and has generated considerable negative publicity for McDonald's in Europe. Early in 2005 the European Court of Human Rights held that Steel and Morris should have been given legal aid by the British government in their fight against the corporate giant and awarded them over $46,000 in damages.

Issues to Consider

1. From your research, do you believe that the claims made by Steel and Morris have any validity?
2. What corporate strategy did McDonald's adopt in this case? Would you have made the same choice? Defend your view.
3. Corporations make many claims about their products through advertising. Do their claims have to be factual? Do you see any moral problems with advertisements that stretch the truth or promote a false image?
4. What moral issues do you see at work in the case? Choose one (for example, truth-telling or justice in compensation) and say how the actions of the company and the defendants can be analyzed in those terms.
5. Who do you think were the main stakeholders in this case? What was the company's moral responsibility to each stakeholder group?
6. McDonald's operates in over 100 countries. The opening of new franchises has inspired civil unrest in places as diverse as Sweden and India. What do you believe provokes such a reaction?
7. Does a multinational company have a duty to be culturally sensitive when operating overseas? Should it have any responsibilities to the host community or country?

McDonald's and the Stella Liebeck Scalding

Stella Liebeck was an 81-year-old woman who lived in Albuquerque, New Mexico. She became famous in 1992 after she was burned by coffee that she had purchased at a McDonald's drive-through and subsequently successfully sued the company for damages.

Her case became synonymous with frivolous lawsuits that cost business millions. There are annual "Stella" awards posted on the Web. Many people feel that consumers ought to take responsibility for their own actions, especially as in Liebeck's case it appeared that she had placed the cup in her lap while driving.

As it turns out, she was not driving at the time. Her grandson was driving, and they had pulled over so she could add sugar and cream to her coffee. The product had a plastic lid that came off suddenly, and some coffee spilled and burned

Liebeck, causing her to jerk and tip over the cup. She was wearing woolen garments, which soaked up the hot liquid and retained the heat. Liebeck suffered third-degree burns around the groin, requiring eight days in the hospital and over two years of treatment.

McDonalds refused to settle for $20,000. At trial the jury awarded Liebeck $200,000 in compensatory damages but reduced it to $160,000 because they found her 20 percent at fault. Initially, the jury also recommended $2.7 million in punitive damages. This was reduced to three times the compensatory amount ($480,000) by the trial judge, making the total award $640,000. McDonald's seemed determined to appeal but then entered into secret negotiations that led to a confidential final settlement that is almost certainly less than the amount granted at trial.

Although the evidence showed that the statistical possibility of burns was very low (roughly 1 in 25 million), the jury was disturbed by what they perceived to be McDonald's uncaring attitude. The judge described the company's conduct as "reckless, callous, and willful." It emerged that there had been over 700 reported hot liquid spill incidents in the prior 10 years. McDonald's served its coffee at 180 degrees Fahrenheit, whereas the ordinary home brewer maintains a temperature at about 140 degrees. Burns are certain to occur at the higher temperature, and the damage to the skin is exponential as the liquid gets hotter, but the McDonald's expert nevertheless testified that the company had no intention of reducing it. The company said that it needed to be hot because it cooled as people drove home, whereas their own research indicated that the majority of consumers drank it straight away. The *Wall Street Journal* reported that one juror felt that McDonald's testimony that there were very few spills relative to the number of hot drinks sold sounded like the company was indifferent to the welfare of customers in general and Liebeck's suffering in particular.[34]

Issues to Consider

1. Should a company be responsible for any and all of the consequences of someone using its product or service (strict liability)?

2. Should the consumer be fully responsible for any and all consequences of using a product or service (*caveat emptor*—let the buyer beware)?

3. McDonald's testimony at the trial admitted that most people did not recognize that coffee served at their holding temperature (180 degrees) poses a significant safety hazard. Should the consumer be warned? What form should the warning take?

4. In cases where consumers may be hurt by a product (that is, virtually all goods), what sort of standard should the company adopt? Should it be paternalistic and protect every customer no matter how ignorant, foolish, or unfortunate? Or should it operate on a "reasonable person" standard?

5. In the United States producers need to list nutritional facts on prepared foods. This information includes serving size, calories, nutrients such as fat and cholesterol, vitamins and minerals, and daily values based on a moderate diet. Some raw foods and so-called dietary supplements are exempt from these regulations. Do you think the current requirements are valuable? Do they provide sufficient information for consumers? What would you add or subtract? Would warning labels ever be appropriate?

6. Research the facts of the case and then say how you would have reacted if you were on the jury. Be prepared to justify your decision.

Merck and River Blindness

Onchocerciasis, otherwise known as river blindness, is thought to affect about 20 million people around the world, chiefly in sub-Saharan Africa, especially Sudan, Ethiopia, and Senegal. Over 100 million are at risk of being afflicted.

River blindness is caused by a parasite carried by the common black fly that thrives near fast-flowing water. The bite of the fly may transmit worms into the human body. They spread and grow, reaching maturity in 15 years, and some females may be up to 2 feet in length. As they develop the victim may suffer severe itching, disfigurement, weakness, and muscle fatigue. It is not uncommon for an infected person to harbor several million worms. Adult worms eventually attack the human eyes, causing the blindness. The disease has caused social upheaval as people have abandoned large areas of fertile land near rivers to avoid it.

Merck is one of the world's top five pharmaceutical companies. Its history goes back to 1668 when Friedrich Jacob Merck ran an apothecary in Darmstadt, Germany. The U.S. branch was founded in 1891 when George Merck set up his company in New York as a chemical supplier. It began its pharmaceutical research before the Second World War.

In the early 1970s Dr. William Campbell was conducting veterinary research for Merck's animal health division. While examining soil samples for antiparasitic qualities, he came across one from a Japanese golf course that showed great promise. Merck then funded a research team to pursue the lead, and eventually they came up with a powerful drug family: avermectins. When Campbell tested the drug on horses, he found it effective against the same sort of worms that cause river blindness. He realized that it had the

potential to help people and won the support of P. Roy Vagelos, the chairman of Merck, to test it further. Initial trials appeared promising.

However, the people that would most benefit from the drug would probably be unable to pay for it, and there were significant issues about how it could be distributed to remote areas. Merck contacted the World Health Organization and other entities including the U.S. Agency for International Development and the Department of State, hoping to get support or sponsorship for distribution of the human form of the antiparasitic drug now known as Mectizan.

In 1987 Vagelos announced that Merck would donate Mectizan to all who needed it for as long as it took to eradicate the disease. He cited a speech by George W. Merck, the company president from 1925 to 1950, who said,

> Medicine is for the people. It is not for the profits. The profits follow, and if we have remembered that, they have never failed to appear. . . . How can we bring the best of medicine to each and every person? We cannot rest until the way has been found with our help to bring our finest achievements to everyone.[35]

The distribution would be in the hands of the Onchocerciasis Control Programme (OCP), which is a coalition of the World Health Organization, individual countries, donors, and over 40 nongovernmental organizations such as the Carter Center and Sight Savers International. In May 2003, Merck marked the donation of 250 million doses. An individual requires one dose a year, and Merck estimates the cost at $1.50 per person annually. It may take up to 15 years to effectively eliminate the worm from its human host.

Issues to Consider

1. Merck's mission statement says,

   The mission of Merck is to provide society with superior products and services, innovations, and solutions that improve the quality of life and satisfy customer needs—to provide employees with meaningful work and advancement opportunities and investors with a superior rate of return.

   Do you think Merck's actions were in accordance with its mission statement? For example, do you think that investors could earn more if the company did not make the donations?

2. Perhaps Mectizan has long-term unforeseen consequences when used on humans. Should the company be held strictly liable for any and all results of its products? Would your answer change if Merck had produced a drug that cured acne and sold it to U.S. customers who then reported adverse effects several years later? What are the morally significant differences?

3. Did Campbell have an affirmative duty to pursue his belief that the drug he was working on for animals might benefit humans? What should he have done if his immediate managers or the CEO had rebuffed his efforts?

4. The pricing of pharmaceuticals is somewhat controversial, partially because manufacturers say they have to charge a premium to cover their ongoing research and development efforts. Someone might claim that Merck is not absorbing the cost of donating Mectizan but is passing it on to consumers in the form of higher prices for drugs to which it has exclusive right. How would you react (as a member of the public or as an investor) to such a charge?

5. How would you go about making a cost/benefit decision on the donation of Mectizan if you were CEO of Merck? How would you value the welfare of people in sub-Saharan Africa? What other sort of reasoning might be appropriate? Once you had decided to help, is there any point at which you could halt donations in the future?

6. If the company could have prevented harm (river blindness) but failed to do so, would that be morally condemnable? How would that case differ from someone who could afford to give to charity but chooses to buy a soda or candy instead? Is there a morally significant difference between positive acts (commission) and failure to do anything (omission)?

NASA and the *Challenger* Shuttle Disaster

On January 28, 1986, the *Challenger* space shuttle, mission 51-L, exploded 74 seconds after launch, killing all seven crew members. Millions watched the disaster, including many children at school who were following astronaut Christa McAuliffe, a teacher selected to present a lesson from space. The launch had originally been scheduled for January 22 but had been postponed six times because of mechanical glitches and weather problems.

Investigators soon focused on an O-ring leak. The shuttle has two orange booster rockets that fire at launch and then fall away at altitude. They are constructed in sections, and the joints fit together somewhat like tent poles, where the top section narrows slightly, and the one below slides on top. The joint is sealed by two large rubber rings, some 40 feet in circumference and less than an inch thick. Once the fuel is ignited, hot gases produce tremendous pressure, and the sections tend to rock. The rings are designed to form a flexible seal that contains the pressure. Film of the launch showed a plume of smoke coming from one of the lower joints of the right booster in the first second of ignition. Within the first minute, a flame can be seen in the same area directed at the huge external fuel tank. The official report on the cause of the disaster blamed the O-ring failure coupled with unusual wind conditions that caused exaggerated strain on the booster joints.

The temperature at launch was 36 degrees Fahrenheit (2 Celsius). This had the effect of making the O-rings less flexible, and so they were unable to fill the gap between sections before hot gases created a type of blowby. Once blow-by occurred the gases then caused further erosion of the rings, compounding the problem.

Gradually it emerged that there had been considerable discussion on the eve of the launch about the possibility of an O-ring leak. Morton Thiokol manufactured the boosters, and some of their engineers had expressed concern that there was a correlation between temperature at launch and the amount of blow-by detected on recovered booster sections. One engineer in particular, Roger Boisjoly, was adamant that Thiokol issue a warning not to launch that morning. He had persuaded his colleagues that there was a significant risk. During an evening conference call, Thiokol initially recommended that the launch be postponed until the outside temperature reached 53 degrees. NASA managers then questioned their reasoning. Earlier that day the launch had been scrubbed for mechanical reasons, but the temperature at launch time was 40 degrees, and Thiokol had not objected. The launch manager at NASA, Roger Mulloy, pointed out there was no empirical data for their position: The O-ring manufacturer believed they would be effective until 25 degrees, given the enormous pressure wedging the sections together, although they had not tested them in lower temperatures. Additionally, the temperature had been below 53 degrees for 19 days in December and 14 in January, and Thiokol had never raised the issue before. There were no written launch criteria with reference to the temperature and O-rings, and Thiokol seemed to be adding them the night before the launch; moreover, the 53-degree limit was apparently not based on science but on the lowest launch temperature for a previous mission. In retrospect, NASA engineers said they would have been more receptive had Thiokol proposed a 30-degree cutoff.

Back at Thiokol, the engineers had a heated discussion offline. Although Boisjoly and his colleague Arnold Thompson were adamant, they conceded they did not have data that would prove there was a risk. Their boss, Jerald Mason, felt that the various positions had been sufficiently aired. He said, "Well, we have to make a management decision. We're just spinning our wheels."[36] The senior managers took a vote, and when one hesitated, Mason asked him to "take off his engineering hat and put on his management hat."[37] They unanimously voted to rescind the earlier decision and recommended launch. Boisjoly says he was stunned: "I left the room feeling badly defeated, but I felt I really did all I could to stop the launch."[38]

As the *Challenger* crew were strapped into their seats, Rockwell International managers told the mission management team that they were concerned that ice chunks on the support gantry would break loose at launch, with the risk that they would hit the orbiter or be aspirated into the solid rocket boosters. They said that they were dealing with the unknown and could not assure NASA that it was safe to fly. The mission management team assessed the information and then took a vote to continue with the launch.

The Rogers Commission on the accident noted that there was a culture at NASA that resulted in pressure to launch; the emphasis had switched from a need to prove the flight would be safe to one where the onus was on those who urged caution. The commission felt that safety concerns had not been given appropriate weight or adequately communicated to senior management.

Issues to Consider

1. Some decisions are team decisions: There is dissent, but then there is a vote, and the participants agree to abide by the group's decision and move forward. Do you believe that Boisjoly and Thompson should have accepted the decision of their colleagues?

2. If Boisjoly felt that it was certain that there would be a fatal incident if the launch proceeded (he is quoted as saying, "I was 100 percent certain it would happen"), did he have a moral duty to take further action? What sort of action could he have taken?

3. Whistle-blowers face a quandary: If they are listened to, then the problems they predict may never happen. Or, they could predict incorrectly (here, for example, the blowby may not have been an issue if it had been directed away from the fuel tank or the wind did not cause the joints to loosen abnormally). In both cases, they may speak up and then face reprisals. What are the moral imperatives for someone who has a suspicion that there may be a risk to health and safety but cannot prove it?

4. Managers make decisions. Some decisions may be made in conditions of uncertainty, and they may involve risk (however small) to human life. How should a manager value human life?

5. Would it make a difference to your view of the case if the crew had been informed of all the risks involved—that is, told of the potential ice debris and the O-ring concern? Should the launch decision have been left to the captain?

6. One of the early astronauts, Alan Shepard, is quoted as saying, "It's a very sobering feeling to be up in space and realize that one's safety factor was determined by the lowest bidder on a government contract."[39] How should business balance issues of safety and cost?

NASA and the *Columbia* Shuttle Disaster

Just after 9 A.M. on February 1, 2003, residents of central Texas heard a loud boom overhead. The space shuttle *Columbia* had broken up during its descent for landing at six times the speed of sound, about 38 miles above the earth, killing all seven crew members.

Columbia had been a test vehicle designed to save a lot of data, and when its flight recorder was recovered, engineers were able to reconstruct what had happened. It became apparent that the surface of the left wing had been compromised, allowing hot plasma into the wing when *Columbia* began to enter the atmosphere. The hot gases rushing in widened the hole to the point where the breach caused extensive structural failure and the disintegration of the shuttle.

The initial damage to the wing was caused on takeoff by foam insulation that ricocheted off the shuttle during launch. However, in the words of an internal NASA memo,

> Last year we dropped the torch through our complacency, our arrogance, self-assurance, sheer stupidity, and through continuing attempts to please everyone. . . . Seven of our friends paid the ultimate price for our failure.[40]

The board investigating the crash pointed to the NASA culture of rigid bureaucracy that demanded that engineers prove an issue to be dangerous before it would be examined, favored performance over safety, and stifled warnings.

One warning came from Don Nelson, a longtime NASA employee who had helped design the space shuttle and spent his final 11 years at NASA as a mission operations evaluator for proposed advanced transportation projects. According to reports, after being rebuffed by senior NASA management, he wrote directly to President George W. Bush notifying him of a number of dangerous problems.

> I became concerned about safety issues in NASA after *Challenger.* I think what happened is that very slowly over the years NASA's culture of safety became eroded. . . . But when I tried to raise my concerns with NASA's new administrator, I received two reprimands for not going through the proper channels, which discouraged other people from coming forward with their concerns. When it came to an argument between a middle-ranking

engineer and the astronauts and administration, guess who won.[41]

The possibility of insulation breaking loose and damaging the shuttle during launch had been considered early on in the program. NASA's hazard analysis, revised in February 2000, recommended continuous inspections and photographic surveillance up to and throughout the launch. Because there was no way of actually testing the effects on a shuttle without damaging it, the report labeled the "failure trends or anomalies that would compromise an External Tank Mission" an "Acceptable Risk."

However, during *Columbia's* launch, the pictures of the falling debris and the effects of its impact were blurry or taken at obscured angles. Rodney Rocha, the chief structural engineer at the Johnson Space Center in Houston, sent a series of e-mails to his bosses asking for assistance from the military to get better shots of the shuttle from a satellite in space. Less than 30 minutes later he got a reply refusing his request. A team of NASA managers had already met with senior representatives from Boeing, the shuttle manufacturer, and determined that the impact of the insulation did not raise any "safety of flight" concerns. Despite their emphatic conclusion, it turns out their assessment acknowledged they had no engineering data about the impact of insulation; the only tests they had ever run were in the 1970s when they had used foam chunks the size of golf balls. The insulation that hit the *Columbia* was 600 times larger and may have been coated in ice.

Shuttle managers never asked the Air Force to get pictures of the shuttle. Rocha subsequently said that he felt that he could not press his case without more evidence, yet he was stymied in his attempts to get additional information. The crash investigation team found that the block in passing on his request was not due to the content of his e-mails outlining his concerns but to the fact that they were not sent through the correct procedural channels. NASA officials disputed the finding, saying that the system was designed so that anyone who sounded an alarm would get immediate attention.

Nine days after the launch and a week before the shuttle was due to return, mission managers had held a meeting that Rocha attended. The chairwoman of the meeting said at the time that there were no safety of flight issues. Rocha did not speak up. He is quoted as saying

> I remember a pause, and her looking around the room, like, "It's OK to say something now" . . . But no one did. That made me feel very uncomfortable because I felt we should have said something. . . . I just couldn't do it. . . . I was too low down here in the organization, and she is way up here.[42]

Issues to Consider

1. How would you allocate moral responsibility for the *Columbia* crash? How would you balance group versus individual responsibility in this case?

2. To what extent do you believe there was a culture of groupthink at NASA?

3. In one of his e-mails, Rocha used boldface type and the words "Can we petition [beg] for outside agency assistance?"[43] when referring to use of highly sensitive military technology. Given his place in the institutional hierarchy, could we morally expect him to have done any more?

4. Nelson went outside normal reporting chains and wrote directly to the White House. He was reprimanded for doing so. How far should one follow protocol when life and property are at risk? Would you say the same if he had acted that way and yet the *Columbia* (and any subsequent missions) had been safe and successful?

5. Do you see any parallel ethical issues between the *Challenger* and the *Columbia* cases? Are there any that are significantly different?

6. Imagine that you are the mission controller for the shuttle program. There are thousands of engineering details—some apparently trivial and some clearly critical. You rely on expert opinion to make decisions. For the sake of argument, imagine that engineers are cautious by training and often write e-mails to you saying there is an issue, warning "There are good scenarios (acceptable and minimal damage) to horrible ones" [the quote is from Rocha's January 22 e-mail].[44] What is your moral responsibility when you receive an e-mail like that? Are you obligated to let the crew know every time you have a safety concern?

Nike

Phil Knight was a middle-distance runner at the University of Oregon under coach Bill Bowerman in the late 1950s. Knight went on to Stanford Business School and later started distributing Japanese-made running shoes in America, getting his start selling shoes from his car trunk.

In 1972 Knight teamed up with Bowerman to form Nike, the name of the Greek goddess of victory, using the now-famous swoosh logo, which they bought from a freelance designer for $35.

In December 1980, Nike went public and in 2003 reported revenues of over $10 billion. It has recently acquired the Converse brand and diversified into apparel, casual footwear and accessories, hockey equipment, and many other products. Its world headquarters are in Beaverton, Oregon. There are 13 domestic and four international Niketown retail operations that average over 30,000 square feet, and there are over 80 factory outlet stores.

From the beginning, Nike has used celebrity athletes to promote its products, and its advertising budget in 2002 ran over $900 million. The swoosh is one of the most recognized symbols in the world, as is the advertising phrase "Just Do It."

Despite the vast sales, Nike owns very few manufacturing facilities and describes itself as a marketing operation. Most of the shoes and apparel are contracted out to companies in the United States and abroad. The three main operations in America act as distribution centers.

Nike came in for criticism when reports surfaced about sweatshop working conditions in factories overseas. Employees were said to be overworked, underpaid, abused, and denied the right to organize. Nike's initial response was to say that it was not responsible for the actions of its subcontractors. Since a boycott movement in the 1990s, Nike has taken positive steps to raise the standards of employment used by its subcontractors—for example, by banning certain petroleum-based glues and inviting independent monitors to visit the facilities.

Nike is not the only brand whose products are made in the Third World. However, it has been targeted largely because of its vast profit margins and its position as an industry leader. Several watchdog groups claim that Nike has failed to live up to its commitments to improve factory conditions. Nike's 1997 code of conduct states,

> Nike, Inc. was founded on a handshake. Implicit in that act was the determination that we would build our business with all of our partners based on trust, teamwork, honesty and mutual respect. We expect all of our business partners to operate on the same principles. At the core of the NIKE corporate ethic is the belief that we are a company comprised of many different kinds of people, appreciating individual diversity, and dedicated to equal opportunity for each individual. NIKE designs, manufactures and markets products for sports and fitness consumers. At every step in that process, we are driven to do not only what is required, but what is expected of a leader. We expect our business partners to do the same.[45]

Issues to Consider

1. Is a firm responsible for the acts of its overseas subcontractors?
2. What is the responsibility of consumers in sweatshop cases? If purchasers demanded union-made labels in clothing and were prepared to pay more for them, wouldn't producers react accordingly? Couldn't Nike (and others) respond that their actions merely reflect consumer values?
3. Is there anything morally objectionable in Nike having a large advertising budget or paying celebrities huge fees for endorsements? What makes a celebrity worth what he or she is paid?
4. Allegedly doubling the wages of Nike's Indonesian workers from 10 cents an hour to 20 cents would cost the company $20 million, or less than 3 percent of its advertising budget. What reasons might the company give to favor such a change? What arguments might it give against it?

5. Do students generally know where their clothes are made and the conditions under which they are made? If not, do you think that Nike has been unfairly targeted?
6. What is meant by "sweatshops"? Why are they morally problematic for businesses? Why do you think Nike decided to say it would try to improve conditions for its overseas workers?

Shell Oil in Nigeria

Nigeria is a West African nation that gained independence from Britain in 1960. It is composed of more than 300 different ethnic groups, and there are long-standing religious and tribal tensions. Its economy has depended almost entirely on the export of petroleum products. The country has a history of corruption and mismanagement, and for most of its existence has had military rulers. About 60 percent of its 55 million inhabitants live below the poverty level. Transparency International, a global corporate watchdog group based in Berlin, puts Nigeria just one level above the bottom of its national corruptibility rating.

In November 1995, the military ruler of Nigeria, General Abacha, ordered 10 protesters from Ogoniland hanged. Among them was Ken Saro-Wiwa, an internationally recognized poet and writer who had been instrumental in organizing protests in his native region.

The prime target of the Ogoni protest was Shell Oil Company. Shell has reportedly extracted some $30 billion worth of oil from Ogoniland since 1958. Among the charges leveled by Saro-Wiwa were

◆ Land grabbing of the traditional lands by Shell, which deprived inhabitants of their livelihood and led to impoverishment

◆ Widespread pollution of water and land by oil spills
◆ Collusion of the oil companies with local security forces to suppress dissent

At the time, Shell dismissed the charges. Protests grew, and some became unruly. Saro-Wiwa was arrested by government officials. A vigorous worldwide campaign was mounted to save Saro-Wiwa. Many international observers felt that Shell had sufficient political leverage to ensure that he and his colleagues were not executed. Shell's official stance was that the issue was the concern of the domestic administration of Nigeria, whose sovereignty ought to be respected.

There has been a recent transfer of power to civilian rule, although there is continuing unrest in the oil-producing areas. The potentially prosperous country has defaulted on loans from the International Monetary Fund. Once a net exporter of agricultural products, it now needs to import food. Shell's public response has changed in the past several years. Its Web site now claims that their community development program in the region is based on the principles of sustainable development and best global practice.

Issues to Consider

1. Can a company remain indifferent to the political climate of a country that hosts its operations?
2. Should a company abide by home or host standards when doing business abroad? If the standards abroad are lower but more cost efficient, does the company have a prime duty to its overseas workers or to its shareholders? How should it balance the interests of the various stakeholders involved?
3. A company might make deals with the rulers of a country, but then find that the benefits are not being passed on to the communities themselves; money for environmental cleanup, for example, may not be used for that purpose. Does the company have any duty to make sure the political leaders are responsible or honest?
4. Does a company have a duty to make restitution for incidents in the past when it may have acted badly?
5. One possible corporate point of view is that companies are essentially neutral and amoral—that is, they fulfill consumer demand and respond to the market: They exhibit the values of their customers. In this vein, if consumers disapproved of what Shell was doing in Nigeria, they would boycott its products, and Shell would then react to regain market share. Do you think consumers are ultimately responsible for corporate behavior? How should we judge the balance between corporate and consumer responsibility?

Turkish Airlines DC-10 Crash

Turkish Airlines flight 981 took off from Orly Airport in Paris on March 3, 1974, with 346 passengers and crew. A few minutes after departure as the aircraft climbed to 11,000 feet, the rear cargo door gave way, resulting in an explosive decompression in the aircraft. Part of the floor collapsed, severing crucial control cables and hydraulics and leading to an unrecoverable crash of the airplane and loss of all aboard.

The initial reports blamed an Algerian-born baggage handler for failing to ensure the door was latched properly. He could not read the instructions for the door, which were printed in English and French.

McDonnell-Douglas had recently introduced the DC-10 as a jumbo aircraft for medium to long hauls. Its main rival was the Lockheed L-1011, which was introduced at about the same time, although the bankruptcy of Rolls-Royce, which made the L-1011 engines, delayed production and gave the DC-10 a competitive advantage.

The cargo door was designed by a subcontractor, Convair. Most doors are designed to open inward, so that increasing pressure from inside the cabin during flight creates a tight seal. The Convair door opened outward and so relied heavily on a secure latching mechanism because the pressure difference pushed against the seal at altitude.

In 1972 an American Airlines DC-10 cargo door opened during flight. Although that aircraft lost its rudder and some of its elevator controls, it was able to land safely. That accident report concluded

> The probable cause of this accident was the improper engagement of the latching mechanism for the aft bulk cargo door during preparation of the airplane for flight. The design characteristics of the door latching mechanism permitted the door to be apparently closed when, in fact, the latches were not fully engaged, and the latch lockpins were not in place.[46]

Jackson McGowen, the president of the division in charge of producing the DC-10, was aware of the likely harmful effect on sales of an "airworthiness directive" that would ground the aircraft until modifications were made. He persuaded the National Transportation Safety Board (NTSB) to instead recommend (but not require) that modifications be made to the doors at the time of their next routine inspection.

In June 1972, three inspectors at McDonnell-Douglas in Long Beach certified that the modifications had been made to the Turkish Airlines DC-10 before it was put into service, although no work had actually been done.

On the day of the crash, the airplane had flown from Ankara, Turkey, to Paris, and then was going on to London. The British airline was on strike, and so many passengers had been re-booked onto the Turkish flight. Delays meant that the flight was some three hours late in taking off. The baggage handler had forced the door shut, and it had not fully latched, although the indicator light in the cabin showed it closed. The flight engineer (crew) and ground engineer at Orly could have inspected the plane before departure but chose not to.

Issues to Consider

1. Who is to blame for the crash of flight 981?
2. Although McDonnell-Douglas did pay compensation to relatives of the crash, their initial reaction was that the door was safe if the operator had only followed the printed instructions, and therefore they were not to blame. What, if anything, is wrong with that view?
3. If you were a worker for McDonnell-Douglas at the time of the crash, would you feel implicated by the incident?
4. McDonnell-Douglas sold over 440 DC-10s whereas Lockheed discontinued production of the comparable L-1011 after selling 250. There was apparently an advantage in being first on the market. Sales concerns also played into the NTSB not issuing a directive that would have troubled potential buyers. If there are pressures to put a product into service quickly (say, by adapting a current design for a latch instead of redesigning it from scratch), how much testing is appropriate?
5. How would you value a human life? What sort of risk assessment is appropriate in business activity when a product may have lethal potential?

WorldCom

WorldCom has a solid base of bill-paying customers, strong fundamentals, a solid balance sheet, manageable leverage, and nearly $10 billion in available liquidity. Bankruptcy or a credit default is not a concern.
                    Bernie Ebbers, CEO WorldCom, 2002[47]

WorldCom started as an idea on a napkin and resulted in bankruptcy, the loss of 17,000 jobs, and $9 billion in fraud—roughly 15 times the amount in the Enron case.

Bernie Ebbers was born into a working-class family in Canada. He won a basketball scholarship to Mississippi College in Jackson. After graduation he took a job at the local high school as a basketball coach and speculated by buying real estate. WorldCom was born when he met with a group of investors in 1983. The government had recently ordered the breakup of the AT&T monopoly on telephone service, which led to opportunities for start-up telephone service providers. The company they formed was LDDS (Long-Distance Discount Services).[48]

Ebbers had a dynamic leadership style. He deliberately shunned business jargon and did not focus on details. He was quoted as saying, "The thing that has helped me personally is that I don't understand a lot of what goes on in this industry."[49] However, he had a vision of success through growth in the industry. By acquiring other companies, LDDS became the nation's fourth largest long-distance carrier by 1992. In 1994 it bought out IDB WorldCom and changed its name to reflect its new global capabilities. The Telecommunications Act of 1996 allowed the company to become the long-distance provider for GTE, Ameritech, and SBC mobile systems. Later that year, it acquired UUNET, the world's largest Internet service. In September 1997, the company announced that it would buy the CompuServe service from H&R Block in a stock deal worth $1.2 billion. The next month, WorldCom made an unsolicited takeover bid to buy MCI for $34.5 billion. Many of these deals were funded by payments in WorldCom stock. Ebbers purchased the largest private ranch in Canada and a yacht he named *Acquisition*.

By 1999 the telecom industry faced several difficult problems. There was an overall economic downturn. The networks had invested heavily in developing technology and new equipment on the assumption of ever-increasing demand. The demand had not materialized, leaving the industry with surplus capacity. In the competitive market, carriers slashed prices to attract customers but failed to make much profit. Several went bankrupt, including Global Crossing, Teligent, and McLeod USA. WorldCom posted significant profits at a time when the other industry giants—Sprint and AT&T—were struggling. WorldCom's future looked bright to analysts when it made a bid for Sprint in 1999 for $115 billion in the world's largest takeover deal. However, European and American regulators blocked the merger in the summer of 2000, and investors began to lose confidence in the company. In November 2000, Ebbers announced his first profit warning.

Cynthia Cooper worked as head of WorldCom's internal audit division. She had heard rumors of impropriety, but in March 2002 an executive, John Stupka, called to say that Chief Financial Officer Scott Sullivan had transferred $400 million out of a reserve fund he managed in order to boost WorldCom's reported income. The audit for the prior two years had been done by Arthur Andersen, and this raised additional questions because of Andersen's role in the Enron fiasco. Cooper started a quiet investigation with her team, often redoing the Andersen audit; they worked at night and secretly copied material. They found a number of questionable practices, including $2 billion that was posted as capital expenditures instead of operating costs. A cost has to be deducted immediately, whereas expenditures can be spread over many years. By reassigning the costs, the company converted a loss of over $600 million into a $2.4 billion profit in 2001. The team also found $500 million had been expensed for new computer equipment but no record of the hardware. They eventually uncovered another $2 billion in other unaccounted expenses.

Events unfolded quickly after Cooper took her findings to both Andersen and Sullivan. Sullivan assured her that all was well, but she was not convinced. He requested that she delay her audit, but she refused. She presented the evidence to the firm's controller, David Myers. Myers admitted that WorldCom's books did not conform to generally accepted accounting prin-

ciples. Shortly after, on June 20, Cooper and Sullivan both faced an audit committee meeting of WorldCom's board of directors. The board asked for Sullivan's resignation, but he refused and was fired. On June 25, WorldCom formally announced that it had inflated profits by almost $4 billion in the previous five quarters. Stock trading was suspended on June 26, and WorldCom filed for bankruptcy on July 21. The company currently operates under the name MCI.

In August 2002, Sullivan was charged with securities fraud. Ebbers's hands-off style and refusal to use e-mail has made him a difficult target for prosecutors. In 2004, Sullivan pleaded guilty and testified against Ebbers. During his trial, Ebbers claimed that he was unaware of the details of the financial picture or any fraudulent activity. He said he relied on his subordinates who systematically misled him. However, in March 2005, a jury found Ebbers guilty of fraud, conspiracy, and filing false documents. Ebbers was sentenced to 25 years in prison and also faces fines and possible civil suits.

Issues to Consider

1. Many regulators and industry analysts took WorldCom's numbers to be accurate, especially because of its stellar past performance. How much transparency and oversight should we demand in the market?

2. Would you describe Cooper as a whistle-blower? She is not a certified accountant and was told by the company CFO and a partner at Andersen that there was no impropriety. Would it have been morally acceptable for her to drop her investigation at that point?

3. Cooper was named one of *Time* magazine's "Persons of the Year" for her role in exposing the fraud. Should we encourage similar behavior by corporate employees? Why do you think that a whistle-blower is often regarded as a snitch rather than a savior?

4. Ebbers often stated that he did not deal with the technical aspects of his job. How hands-on should a leader be? What are the moral implications of the kind of leadership involved in major corporations, including WorldCom?

5. From your reading and research, do you believe that the fraud—at least $9 billion—was the result of a few bad apples or were more people involved? What was the moral responsibility of individuals within the company who suspected something was not right but chose not to investigate or voice their suspicions?

6. Who do you think was hurt by the collapse of WorldCom? Suggest whether the doctrine of *caveat emptor*—let the buyer beware—should apply in this case.

CASE NOTES

1. A. Gianturco, "Breasts, the Media, and Boobs: The Implant Hysteria," *John Hopkins Newsletter*, Oct. 14, 1999.

2. "Silicone Gel Breast Implants," report of the Independent Review Group, Cambridge, UK (July 1998) (government-sponsored report published by Jill Roberts Associates).

3. http://heritage.dupont.com/floater/fl_benlate/floater.shtml, Oct. 22, 2004.

4. "Obituary for the Fungicide Benlate," *Pest Quarterly* 19, no. 3 (2002).

5. J. Greenwald "Court Reinstates Benlate Award," *Business Insurance*, July 11, 2003.

6. Taken from the partisan at http://www.angelfire.com/mi/microphthalmia/ywarlab.html.

7. J. Barnes, "How a Titan Came Undone," *U.S. News & World Report*, March 18, 2002.

8. A. Wheat, "System Failure," *Multinational Monitor*, Jan. 1, 2002.

9. N. Hala, "If Capitalists Were Angels," *Internal Auditor*, April 1, 2003.

10. http://www2.exxonmobil.com/corporate/Newsroom/NewsReleases/Corp_NR_Condition.asp.

11. "Look Back at *Exxon-Valdez*," CBS Evening News, March 24, 2004.

12. S. Hettena, "Ford Ordered to Pay Nearly $369 Million to Woman Paralyzed in Explorer Rollover," Associated Press Worldstream, June 3, 2004.

13. "Ford Chairman William Clay Ford Jr. to Take Spotlight in Tire/SUV Controversy," PR Newswire, Sept. 10, 2000.

14. "Explorer More Likely to Roll Regardless of Tire Type," *Consumer Affairs*, October 9, 2000.

15. D. Keating and C. Mayer, "Explorer Has Higher Rate of Tire Accidents," *Washington Post*, October 9, 2000, p. A01.

16. D. Whipple, "Seeds of Controversy," *Futurist*, Oct. 1999.

17. "Analysis: What's in Your Food?" *Talk of the Nation Science Friday* (NPR), Oct. 20, 2000.

18. P. Elkind, "Vulgarians at the Gate," *Fortune*, June 21, 1999.

19. Ibid.

20. "Feds Detail Role of Accounting Entries in Scandal at HealthSouth," *Accounting Department Management Report*, March 1, 2004.

21. Ibid.

22. http://business2.unisa.edu.au/cobar/corpresp/case_studies/study3.htm.

23. http://www.hbfuller.com/About_Us. 2004.

24. "Minnesota Company Continues Glue Sales in Latin America," *Weekend Edition*, NPR, Aug. 23, 1993.

25. P. McEnroe, "Latin America Glue Abuse Haunts H.B. Fuller," Minneapolis Star Tribune, April 21, 1996.

26. http://www.hooters.com/company/about_hooters/.

27. http://www.fwlaw.com/sexharas.html.

28. In L. G. Foster, *Robert Wood Johnson—The Gentleman Rebel* (State College, PA: Lillian Press, 1999).

29. http://biotech.law.lsu.edu/cases/EEOC/johnson_controls.htm.

30. http://caselaw.lp.findlaw.com/scripts/usscft.pl?CiWebhitsFile=/us/499/187.html&CiRestriction=%22472%20U.S.%20400%22.

31. http://civil.engr.siu.edu/301I_Ray/he_love.htm.

32. http://www.aish.com/societyWork/work/Aaron_Feuerstein_Bankrupt_and__Wealthy.asp.

33. http://www.mcspotlight.org/case/trial/verdict/legalint.html.

34. Material drawn from the *Wall Street Journal*, www.stellaawards.com, and the American Trial Lawyers Association.

35. 1950 address, Medical College of Virginia, cited at www.merck.com/about.

36. http://onlineethics.org/moral/boisjoly/RB1-6.html.

37. Ibid.

38. http://history.nasa.gov/rogersrep/v1ch5.htm.

39. http://www.cyberslayer.co.uk/jokes/joke0873.html.

40. http://www.jamesoberg.com/01282004_shr.html.

41. http://observer.guardian.co.uk/international/story/0,6903,887236,00.html.

42. http://sgp1.paddington.ninemsn.com.au/sunday/cover_stories/article_1325.asp.

43. Ibid.

44. Ibid.

45. www.ipielle.emr.it/mqsr/docs/esperienze/codici/NIKE%20NEW%20CODE%20OF%20CONDUCT.pdf.

46. http://aviation-safety.net/database/1972/720612-0.htm.

47. S. Mehta, "WorldCom's Bad Trip," *Fortune*, March 4, 2002.

48. T. Padgett, "The Rise and Fall of Bernie Ebbers," *Time*, May 13, 2002.

49. Ibid.

CREDITS

CHAPTER 1

Rogene Buchholz, "Elements of the Market System" from *Business Ethics: The Pragmatic Path Beyond Principles to Process*. Copyright © 1997 by Rogene Buchholz. Reprinted with the permission of Prentice-Hall, Inc., Upper Saddle River, NJ.

Ayn Rand, "What Is Capitalism?" from *Capitalism: The Unknown Ideal*. Copyright © 1966 by Ayn Rand. Reprinted with the permission of Dutton Signet, a division of Penguin Group (USA) Inc.

John Rawls, "An Egalitarian Theory of Justice" from *A Theory of Justice*. Copyright © 1971, 1999 by John Rawls. Reprinted with the permission of The Belknap Press of Harvard University Press.

Carl Cohen, "Socialist Democracy" from *Four Systems*. Copyright © 1982 by Random House, Inc. Reprinted with the permission of Random House, Inc.

Trudy Govier, "The Right to Eat and the Duty to Work" from *Philosophy of the Social Sciences* 5, no. 2 (1975). Copyright © 1975 by Sage Publications, Inc. Reprinted with the permission of Sage Publications, Inc.

Peter Ulrich and Ulrich Thielemann, "How Do Managers Think About Market Economies and Morality? Empirical Enquiries into Business-Ethical Thinking Patterns" from *Journal of Business Ethics* 12 (1993). Copyright © 1993 by Kluwer Academic Publishers. Reprinted with the permission of the authors and Springer Science and Business Media.

CHAPTER 2

Manuel Velasquez, Claire Andre, Thomas Shanks, S.J., and Michael J. Meyer, "Thinking Ethically: A Framework for Moral Decision Making" from *Issues in Ethics* 7, no. 1 (Winter 1996). Reprinted with the permission of The Markkula Center for Applied Ethics at Santa Clara University.

Donelson R. Forsyth, "Judging the Morality of Business Practices: The Influences of Personal Moral Philosophies" from *Journal of Business Ethics* 11, no. 5 (May 1992). Copyright © 1992 by Kluwer Academic Publishers. Reprinted with the permission of the author and Springer Science and Business Media.

Immanuel Kant, "The Ethics of Duty" from *Grounding for the Metaphysics of Morals*, translated by James W. Ellington. Copyright © 1981, 1993 by Hackett Publishing Company, Inc. Reprinted with the permission of Hackett Publishing Company, Inc. All rights reserved.

Aristotle, "Ethics as Virtues" from *The Ethics of Aristotle*, edited by J.A.K. Thomson. Copyright 1953 by J.A.K. Thomson. Reprinted with the permission of George Allen & Unwin, Ltd.

Daryl Koehn, "A Role for Virtue Ethics in the Analysis of Business Practice" from *Business Ethics Quarterly* 5, no. 3 (July 1995). Copyright © 1995 by Philosophy Documentation Center. Reprinted with the permission of *Business Ethics Quarterly*.

CHAPTER 3

CHAPTER 4

CHAPTER 5

Kevin Gibson, "Role Morality and Professional Morality" from *Journal of Applied Philosophy* 20, no. 1 (2003). Copyright © 2000 by Blackwell Publishers, Ltd. Reprinted with the permission of Blackwell Publishers, Ltd.

Lee Iacocca, "My View on the Pinto Affair" from *Iacocca: An Autobiography*. Copyright © 1984 by Lee Iacocca. Reprinted with the permission of Bantam Books, a division of Random House, Inc.

CHAPTER 6

Richard Nielsen, "Changing Unethical Organizational Behavior" from *Academy of Management Executive* 3, no. 2 (May 1989). Copyright © 1989 by the Academy of Management. Reprinted with the permission of the Academy of Management via the Copyright Clearance Center.

Michael Davis, "Some Paradoxes of Whistleblowing" (with cuts) from *Business and Professional Ethics* 15, no. 1 (1996). Reprinted with the permission of the author.

Richard Lacayo and Amanda Ripley, "Whistleblowers: Persons of the Year 2002" from *Time* (December 22, 2002). Copyright © 2002 by Time, Inc. Reprinted with the permission of *Time*.

Leonard Baynes, "Just Pucker and Blow? An Analysis of Corporate Whistleblowers, the Duty of Care, the Duty of Loyalty, and the Sarbanes-Oxley Act" from *St. John's Law Review* 76, no. 4 (2002). Copyright © 2002 by St. John's University Law Review Association. Reprinted with the permission of *St. John's Law Review*.

CHAPTER 7

Patrick Murphy, "Creating Ethical Corporate Structures" from *Sloan Management Review* 30, no. 2 (Winter 1989). Copyright © 1989 by Massachusetts Institute of Technology. Reprinted with permission.

Dove Izraeli and Mark S. Schwartz, "What Can We Learn from the U.S. Federal Sentencing Guidelines for Organizational Ethics?" from *Journal of Business Ethics* 17, no. 9/10 (July 1998). Copyright © 1998 by Kluwer Academic Publishers. Reprinted with the permission of Springer Science and Business Media.

Roger Leeds, "Breach of Trust: Leadership in a Market Economy" from *Harvard International Review* 25, no. 3 (2003). Copyright © 2003 by Harvard International Review. Reprinted with the permission of the author and Harvard International Review.

CHAPTER 8

Lynn Sharp Paine, "Work and Family: Should Parents Feel Guilty?" from *Public Affairs Quarterly* 5, no. 1 (January 1991). Copyright © 1991 by Philosophy Documentation Center. Reprinted with the permission of *Public Affairs Quarterly*.

Ian Maitland, "Rights in the Workplace: A Nozickian Argument" from *Journal of Business Ethics* 8, no. 12 (December 1989). Copyright © 1989 by Kluwer Academic Publishers. Reprinted with the permission of the author and Springer Science and Business Media.

Myrtle Bell, Mary E. McLaughlin, and Jennifer M. Sequeria, "Discrimination, Harassment, and the Glass Ceiling: Women Executives as Change Agents" from *Journal of Business Ethics* 37, no. 1 (April 2002). Copyright © 2002 by Kluwer Academic Publishers. Reprinted with the permission of Springer Science and Business Media.

D. W. Haslett, "Workplace Discrimination, Good Cause, and Color Blindness" from *Journal of Value Inquiry* 36, no. 1 (2002). Copyright © 2002 by Kluwer Academic Publishers. Reprinted with the permission of the author and Springer Science and Business Media.

Meg A. Bond and Jean L. Pyle, "Diversity Dilemmas at Work" from *Journal of Management Inquiry* 7, no. 3 (September 1998). Copyright © 1998 by Sage Publications, Inc. Reprinted with the permission of Sage Publications, Inc..

Michael Cranford, "Drug Testing and the Right to Privacy: Arguing the Ethics of Workplace Drug Testing" from *Journal of Business Ethics* 17, no. 16 (December 1998). Copyright © 1998 by Kluwer Academic Publishers. Reprinted with the permission of Springer Science and Business Media.

CHAPTER 9

Claudia Mills and Douglas MacLean, "Risk Analysis and the Value of Life" from *Values and Public Policy*,

CHAPTER 10

CHAPTER 11

CHAPTER 12